The Canadian Charter of Rights and Freedoms
Second Edition

Edited by

Gérald-A. Beaudoin & Ed Ratushny

Contributions by

M. Bastarache
G.-A. Beaudoin
C.F. Beckton
P. Blache
W. Black
F. Chevrette
I. Cotler
P. Garant
D. Gibson
S. Gibson
P.W. Hogg

W.R. Lederman
J.E. Magnet
A. Morel
K. Norman
W. Pentney
E. Ratushny
D. Sanders
L. Smith
R. Tassé
A. Tremblay

THE
CANADIAN CHARTER
OF
RIGHTS AND FREEDOMS

Second Edition

Edited by

The Honourable Gérald-A. Beaudoin, O.C., Q.C.
B.A., M.A., LL.L., LL.D. (Hon.), D.E.S.D., F.R.S.C.

and

Ed Ratushny, Q.C.
B.A., LL.B., LL.M. (London), LL.M. (Mich.), S.J.D.

CARSWELL
Toronto • Calgary • Vancouver
1989

Canadian Cataloguing in Publication Data

Main entry under title:

The Canadian Charter of Rights and Freedoms

2nd ed.
First ed. (1982) edited by Walter A. Tarnopolsky
and Gérald-A. Beaudoin.
Issued also in French under title: Charte canadienne
des droits et libertés.
Bibliography: p.
Includes index.
ISBN 0-459-32781-X (bound) ISBN 0-459-32771-2 (pbk.)

1. Canada. Canadian Charter of Rights and Freedoms.
2. Civil rights — Canada.   3. Canada — Constitutional
law — Amendments.   4. Civil rights — Canada — Cases.
5. Canada — Constitutional law — Cases.   I. Beaudoin,
Gérald A., 1929-   II. Ratushny, Ed, 1942-

KE4381.5.Z85C36 1989   342.71′085   C89-093936-5

Since the texts were not submitted or translated at the same time, the effective date to which the case law has been analyzed, varies with each chapter.

Preface

The first editions of both the *Canadian Charter of Rights and Freedoms* and *Charte canadienne des droits et libertés* were released on December 2, 1982, only a few months after the Charter itself came into force. This bilingual collection of articles by fifteen authors under the editorship of Professors Beaudoin and Tarnopolsky was the first work of its kind. Both versions have been cited and quoted from frequently by our courts at every level, including the Supreme Court of Canada.

This second edition has expanded to twenty authors from all parts of Canada. Moreover, the vacuum of case law and corresponding speculation, which formed the context for the first edition, have been replaced by the fifty Charter decisions rendered by the Supreme Court of Canada, as well as a torrent of Charter decisions flowing from the other courts. Indeed, in October 1985, at a colloquium on the Supreme Court of Canada held in Ottawa, Chief Justice Dickson described the Charter as posing the greatest challenge in the entire history of the Court.

In this second edition we have followed the basic plan of the first. All the original authors were invited to participate and most were able to do so. A few were prevented by their office or other circumstances from doing so, namely, Mr. Justice Walter Tarnopolsky, now of the Ontario Court of Appeal, Mr. Justice Kenneth Lysyk, now of the Supreme Court of British Columbia, Mr. Herbert Marx, now Solicitor General of Quebec and Professor Katherine Swinton of the University of Toronto Law School.

We would like to take this occasion to pay a personal tribute to Walter

Tarnopolsky who was a colleague and close friend as a professor at the Ottawa Law School and Director of the Human Rights Centre, a role in which both of us have succeeded him. His contribution to the understanding of human rights in Canada has been enormous as a teacher and author and continues to be made in his judicial writing.

We have been fortunate in attracting additional authors of impeccable credentials and great insight into Charter issues. They are Professors Michel Bastarache, William Black, William Lederman, Joseph Magnet, Ken Norman, William Pentney, Douglas Sanders, Lynn Smith and Mr. Roger Tassé. New chapters have been introduced on multiculturalism (section 27) by Professor Magnet and minority language educational rights (section 23) by Professor Bastarache.

We are grateful to all of the authors for their enthusiasm, fine work and patience with the editors.

Each author has written in his or her language of choice. Each article has been completely translated into the other official language. We are also grateful to the translators, whose names appear later, for their labours in striving not to lose nuances of style and meaning in the translations.

Eight texts were written in French: those of M. Bastarache, G.-A. Beaudoin, P. Blache, F. Chevrette, P. Garant, A. Morel, R. Tassé and A. Tremblay. Eleven were written in English: those of C. Beckton, W. Black and L. Smith, I. Cotler, D. Gibson, P. Hogg, W. Lederman, L. Magnet, K. Norman, W. Pentney, E. Ratushny and D. Sanders.

The Minister of Justice of Canada has been generous in subsidizing the translation of this work to a very great extent.

We also wish to thank our research assistants whose names appear later, and particularly Pierre Thibault and Maryse Jutras.

Dated at Ottawa, September 1988.

Ed Ratushny
Gérald-A. Beaudoin
Co-Editors

Contributors

Michel Bastarache. B.A.; LL.L.; LL.B.; D.E.S. Dean, École de Droit de l'Université de Moncton (1980-1983); Association Dean, Faculty of Law (Common Law Section), University of Ottawa (1983). Member of the Bars of Ontario, Alberta and New Brunswick. Co-author and editor of *Language Rights in Canada* (1987). On leave from the University of Ottawa, Mr. Bastarache is presently practising law with Lang, Michener, Lash, Johnston in Ottawa.

Gérald-A. Beaudoin. Professor, Faculty of Law (Civil Law Section), University of Ottawa, (since 1969). Civil Law Dean (1969-1979). Advisory Counsel, Justice Department (1956-1965); Assistant Parliamentary Counsel of the House of Commons (1965-1969); Queen's Counsel (1969). Member of the Pepin-Robarts Commission (1977-1979). Officer of the Order of Canada (1980). Fellow of the Royal Society of Canada (1977), of the Académie canadienne-française (1983), and of the International Academy of Comparative Law (1984). Research lecturer, University of Ottawa (1982). Director of the Human Rights Research and Education Centre, University of Ottawa (1986-1988). Author of *Le partage des pouvoirs* (1983) 3rd ed., and *Essais sur la Constitution* (1979). Editor of *La Cour suprême du Canada / The Supreme Court of Canada* (Yvon Blais, 1986); *Charter Cases 1986-87 / Causes invoquant la Charte 1986-87* (Yvon Blais, 1987); *Your Clients and the Charter / Vos clients et la Charte* (Yvon Blais, 1988). Co-editor of *Charte canadienne des droits et libertés* (Wilson-Lafleur, 1982); *Canadian Charter of Rights and Freedoms* (Carswell, 1982); *Perspectives canadiennes et européennes des droits de la personne* (Yvon Blais, 1986). Co-author of *Mécanismes pour une nouvelle Constitution* (1981); *Les quotidiens et la loi* (1981). Author of many articles in Canadian and foreign juridical reviews. Prix Marcel-Vincent (A.C.F.A.S., 1987); Vice-

President, International Commission of Jurists (1987); Vice-President, I.D.E.F. (1973). Mr. Beaudoin was appointed to the Senate of Canada on September 26, 1988.

Clare F. Beckton. B.A. (Saskatchewan) (1971); LL.B. (Saskatchewan) (1974); LL.M. Programme (University of Illinois) (1975). Equality Rights Co-ordinator, Department of Justice, Ottawa, (since 1984). Professor on leave from Dalhousie (since 1984); Associate Professor and Assistant Professor at Dalhousie (since 1975). Member, Nova Scotia Barristers' Society. Teaching subjects: Human Rights, Constitutional Law, Administrative Law, Public Law, Evidence. Publications: *The Media and the Law in Canada* (Carswell, 1982); *Constitutions of the World: Canada* (Oceana Publications) (contributor); "Freedom of Expression — Access to the Courts" (1983), 61 Can. Bar Rev. 101; "Freedom of Expression under the Charter" in Tarnopolsky & Beaudoin, eds., *Canadian Charter of Rights and Freedoms*, (Carswell, 1982); "The Impact on Women of Entrenchment of Property Rights" (1985), 9 Dalhousie L.J. 288; Co-author of *The Courts and the Charter / Les tribunaux et la Charte* (U. of T. Press, 1985). Member of the Royal Commission on the Economic Union and Development Prospects for Canada (1984-1985).

Pierre Blache. B.A. (Montreal) (1959); LL.L. (Montreal) (1962); LL.D. (Montreal) (1975). University of Sherbrooke: Professor (since 1974); Associate Professor (1970-1974); Assistant Professor (1965-1970). Member of Quebec Bar. Teaching subjects: Constitutional Law, Civil Liberties, Administrative Law. Publications: "La décision institutionnelle" (with Suzanne Comtois) (1985-86), 16 R.D.U.S. 645; "Affirmative Action: To Equality through Inequalities" in Weiler & Elliot, *Litigating the Values of a Nation* (Carswell, 1986); "The Mobility Rights" in Tarnopolsky & Beaudoin, eds., *Canadian Charter of Rights and Freedoms* (Carswell, 1982); "Les libertés de circulation des personnes sous la Charte canadienne des droits et libertés" in Turp & Beaudoin, eds., *Perspectives canadiennes et européennes des droits de la personne* (Yvon Blais, 1986).

William Black. B.A. (Stanford) (1962); LL.B. (Harvard) (1965). University of British Columbia: Associate Professor (since 1975); Assistant Professor (1970-1975). Tutorial Assistant, University of East Africa (1967-1969). Member of California Bar (1966). Teaching subjects: Civil Liberties, Torts, Legal Process. Co-author of "Section 15. Equality Rights under the Charter: Meaning, Institutional Constraints and a Possible Test" (with L. Smith), in *Your Clients and the Charter / Vos clients et la Charte*, G.-A. Beaudoin, ed., (Yvon Blais, 1988).

François Chevrette. B.A. (1961); LL.B. (1964); D.E.S. (Paris) (1968). University of Montreal: Professor, Faculty of Law (since 1968); Dean, Faculty of Law (1984-1988). Member of Quebec Bar (1966). Specialized fields: Constitutional Law, Fundamental Freedoms. Publications: Co-author of *Droit constitutionnel* (1982); Author of "Protection Upon Arrest or Detention and Against Retroactive Penal Law" in Tarnopolsky & Beaudoin, eds., *Canadian Charter of Rights and Freedoms* (Carswell, 1982); "Contrôler le pouvoir fédéral de dépenser: un gain ou un piège?" in *L'adhésion du Quebec à l'Accord du Lac Meech* (Thémis, 1988). Consultant for many ministries and governmental (federal and provincial) agencies. Closely associated with the Public Law Research Centre of the Faculty of Law, University of Montreal.

Irwin Cotler. Professor, McGill University; Visiting Professor, Harvard Law School (1983-84). Member of Quebec Bar. Teaching subjects: Constitutional Law, Human Rights Law, International Law, Poverty Law. Publications: *The Sharansky Case*; "Freedoms of Assembly, Association, Conscience and Religion" in Tarnopolsky & Beaudoin, eds., *Canadian Charter of Rights and Freedoms*, (Carswell, 1982); Co-editor of *Law and Poverty in Canada*. First New Member of Killam Lectureship (1978) for his contribution to human rights. Legal Adviser to many Soviet dissidents, including Anatoly Sharansky and political prisoners in Argentina and South Africa. Special Legal Adviser, Civil Liberties, to the MacDonald Commission of Inquiry into the R.C.M.P. Member of the Board of Directors of the Canadian Human Rights Foundation and the International Commission of Jurists (Canadian Section).

Patrice Garant. LL.L. (Laval) (1962); L. ès L. (Laval) (1967); Docteur en droit (Paris) (1966). Professor, Laval University (since 1966). Member of Quebec Bar. Teaching subjects: Administrative Law, Constitutional Law, Public Finance Law, Public Service Law, Education Law. Publications: *Droit administratif*, 2nd ed. (Yvon Blais, 1985); *La Fonction publique canadienne et québécoise* (Presses de l'Université Laval, 1973); *Droit et Législation scolaire* (McGraw Hill, 1971); "Fundamental Freedoms and Natural Justice" in Tarnopolsky & Beaudoin, eds., *Canadian Charter of Rights and Freedoms*, (Carswell, 1982); *Précis de droit des administrations publiques* (Yvon Blais, 1987).

Dale Gibson. B.A. (Manitoba) (1954); LL.B. (Manitoba) (1958); LL.M. (Harvard) (1959). University of Manitoba: Professor (since 1968); Associate Professor (1964-68); Assistant Professor (1959-64). Member of the Manitoba Law Reform Commission (1971-79). Editor of the Manitoba Law Journal (1963-66). Member of Manitoba Bar (1959). Teaching subjects:

Constitution Law, Torts, Legal Process. Publications: *Substantial Justice — Law and Lawyers in Manitoba 1670-1970* (with Lee Gibson) (1972); "Enforcement of the Canadian Charter of Rights and Freedoms", in Tarnopolsky & Beaudoin, eds., *Canadian Charter of Rights and Freedoms*, (Carswell, 1982); *Attorney for the Frontier: Enos Stutsman* (with Lee Gibson and Cameron Harvey) (1983); Editor and Contributor (with Janet Baldwin) of *Law in a Cynical Society: Law and Public Opinion in the 1980s* (1985); *The Law of the Charter: General Principles* (Carswell, 1986).

Peter W. Hogg. LL.B. (New Zealand) (1962); LL.M. (Harvard) (1963); Ph.D. (Monash) (1970); Professor, Osgoode Hall Law School, York University (since 1970). Monash University: Reader (1969-70); Senior Lecturer, (1966-69). Lecturer, Victoria University of Wellington (1964-65). Member of the Bars of New Zealand (1962); Victoria, Australia (1968); Ontario (1973). Appointed Queen's Counsel, Ontario, 1981. Teaching subjects: Constitutional Law, Trusts, Tax. Publications: *Liability of the Crown* (1971); "A Comparison of the Canadian Charter of Rights and Freedoms with the Canadian Bill of Rights", in Tarnopolsky & Beaudoin, eds., *Canadian Charter of Rights and Freedoms* (Carswell, 1982); *Constitutional Law of Canada*, 2nd ed. (1985); *Meech Lake Constitutional Accord Annotated* (Carswell, 1988). Consultant in many cases before the Supreme Court of Canada.

William R. Lederman. B.A. (1937); LL.B. (Saskatchewan) (1940); B.C.L. (Oxford) (1948); LL.D. (Saskatchewan) (1967), (Victoria) (1976), (Dalhousie) (1978), (York) (1979), (Montreal) (1986). Professor, Queen's University. Vinerian Scholar (Oxford) (1948). Assistant Professor, Saskatchewan (1945-46, 1948-49); Sir James Dunn Professor of Law, Dalhousie (1949-58); Dean, Queen's University (1958-68). Member of the Bars of Saskatchewan (1946); Nova Scotia (1954); Ontario (1961). Visiting Professor: McGill University (1959-61, 1968); York (1964-65); Centre of Research in Public Law, University of Montreal (1974-75); University of Victoria (1981-82). Teaching subjects: Constitutional Law, Conflict of Laws, Jurisprudence. Publications: *The Courts and The Canadian Constitution* (1964); *Canadian Constitutional Law, Cases, Notes and Materials* (with J.D. Whyte) (1977); *Continuing Canadian Constitutional Dilemmas, Essays on the Constitutional History, Public Law and Federal System of Canada* (1981).

Joseph E. Magnet. B.A. (Long Island) (1968); Ph.D. (McGill University) (1973); LL.B. (McGill University) (1976); LL.M. (University of Ottawa, Civil Law) (1978) University of Ottawa (Common Law Section): Professor, (since 1985); Associate Professor (1980-85); Assistant Professor (1977-

80). Teaching subjects: Constitutional Law, Administrative Law, Property. Publications: *Constitutional Law of Canada*, 2nd ed. (1985); *Withholding Treatment from Defective Newborn Children* (1985). Legal Adviser in constitutional law to federal and provincial governments and territories. Legal Adviser to both English and French language minorities, religious associations and aboriginal people, including representation before the Supreme Court of Canada. Law Clerk to Rt. Hon. Brian Dickson, now Chief Justice of the Supreme Court of Canada (1976-77).

André Morel. LL.L. (Montreal) (1953); M.A. (Law; Montreal) (1954); D.E.S. (Paris), LL.D. (Paris) (1957). Professor, Faculty of Law, University of Montreal (since 1969). Member of Quebec Bar. Visiting Professor, Faculty of Law, Laval University (1959-67). Associate Professor, Faculty of Law and Economic Science, Montpellier (1967-69). Teaching subjects: Legal History, Civil Liberties. Publications: "La reconnaissance du Québec comme société distincte dans le respect de la Charte" in *L'adhésion du Québec à l'Accord du Lac Meech* (Thémis, 1988); "Certain Guarantees of Criminal Procedure" in Tarnopolsky & Beaudoin, eds., *Canadian Charter of Rights and Freedoms*, (Carswell, 1982). Member of the Quebec Human Rights Commission, 1981-88.

Ken Norman. B.A., LL.B. (Saskatchewan); B.C.L. (Oxon). Professor, University of Saskatchewan (since 1975). Legal Adviser to the Saskatchewan Ombudsman, the Saskatoon Legal Assistance Clinic and the Canadian Indian Claims Commission. Chief Commissioner, Saskatchewan Human Rights Commission (1978-83). Teaching subjects: Legal Theory, Labour Law, Human Rights and Administrative Law. Publications: Many articles regarding Labour Law, Administrative Law, Human Rights Law and Public Administration. Contributor to Mahoney & Martin, eds., *Equality and Judicial Neutrality* (Carswell, 1987); Gérald-A. Beaudoin, ed., *Your Clients and the Charter / Vos clients et la Charte* (Yvon Blais, 1988).

William Pentney. B.A. (Queen's University) (1979); LL.B. (1982); LL.M. (Ottawa) (1986). University of Ottawa: Faculty of Law (Common Law Section): Assistant Professor (1983); Associate Professor (1988). Teaching subjects: Contracts, Remedies, Human Rights (Anti-Discrimination) Law, Civil Liberties, Constitutional Law. Publications: "Lovelace v. Canada: A Case Comment" (1982), 5 *Can. L. Aid Bulletin* 259; *Discrimination and the Law in Canada* (rev'd ed.) (1985); *Human Rights and Freedoms in Canada: cases, notes and materials* (with M. Berlin) (1987). Associate Director, Human Rights Research and Education Centre, University of Ottawa (1986-88); Acting-Director of the Centre (since October 1988).

Ed Ratushny. B.A. (1964); LL.B. (Saskatchewan) (1965); LL.M. (London) (1968); LL.M. (1972); S.J.D. (Michigan) (1979). Member of the Bars of Saskatchewan (1966); Ontario (1972). Appointed Queen's Counsel (Canada) (1985). Director of Human Rights Research and Education Centre, University of Ottawa (1983-86). Professor, University of Ottawa (Common Law) (since 1976); Associate Professor, Windsor Law School (1970-76). Special Adviser to Minister of Justice of Canada, Ottawa (1973-76). Consultant, Ontario Law Reform Commission (1972-73); Consultant, Canada Law Reform Commission (1977-79). Counsel, Cohen Board of Inquiry (Environmental Contaminents) (1980). Member, Ministerial Task Force on Immigration (1980). Special Advisor, Refugee Status Advisory Committee (1982). Chief Counsel, Robinson Inquiry into Illegal Migration in Canada (1983); Special Counsel, Minister of Transport of Canada (1983). Chairman, Boards of Inquiry under Ontario Human Rights Code. Teaching subjects: Administrative Law, Evidence, Criminal Procedure, Constitutional Law, Human Rights, Civil Liberties. Publications: *Self-Incrimination in the Canadian Criminal Process* (1979); "The Role of the Accused in the Criminal Process", in Tarnopolsky & Beaudoin, eds., *Canadian Charter of Rights and Freedoms* (Carswell, 1982); *A New Refugee-Determination Process for Canada* (1984); *Air Accessibility Standards for Disabled and Elderly Person* (1984); many articles in legal reviews.

Douglas E. Sanders. B.A. (1960); LL.B. (Alberta) (1961); LL.M. (California, Berkeley) (1963). Professor, Faculty of Law, University of British Columbia (since 1977); Associate Professor, Faculty of Law, University of Windsor, (1969-72). Member of the Bars of Alberta (1962); British Columbia (1964); Ontario (1972); Northwest Territories (1973). Teaching subjects: Constitutional Law, Contracts, International Law, Native Law. Publications: *Digest of Canada Indian Case Law* (with Paul Taylor), in *A Canadian Indian Bibliography* (Abler, Sanders, Weaver, 1974); *Family Law and Native People* (Law Reform Commission of Canada, 1975); *Legal Aspects of Economic Development on Indian Reserve Lands* (Department of Indian Affairs, 1976).

C. Lynn Smith. B.A. (Hons.) (1967); LL.B. (University of British Columbia) (1973). Associate Professor, University of British Columbia (since 1981). Private practice of law (1974-81). Member of the British Columbia Bar (1974). Teaching subjects: Civil Litigation, Evidence, Real Property, Equality Rights. Publications: "Charter Equality Rights: Some General Issues and Specific Applications in British Columbia to Elections, Juries and Illegitimacy" (1984), 19 *U.B.C.L. Rev.* 351-406; "Contempt of Court through Breach of an Anticipated Court Order: Baxter Laboratories of Canada Ltd. v. Cutlet (Canada) Ltd." (1985), 1 *Intellectual Property Journal*

205-323; Co-author of "Section 15 Equality Rights under the Charter: Meaning, Institutional Constraints and a Possible Test" (with W. Black), in Gérald-A. Beaudoin, ed., *Your Clients and the Charter / Vos clients et la Charte,* (Yvon Blais, 1988); Co-editor of *Righting the Balance: Canada's New Equality Rights* (Canadian Human Rights Reporter, 1986).

Roger Tassé. B.A. (1952); LL.L. (1955); D.E.S.D. (1958). Deputy Minister and Deputy Attorney General of Canada (1977-1985). Deputy Solicitor of Canada (1972-77). Officer of the Order of Canada (1981). Appointed Queen's Counsel (Canada) (1971). President, Bankruptcy Committee (1970). President, Young Delinquents Committee (1975). Member of Lang, Michener, Lash, Johnston, and Noël, Décary, Aubry et Associés (until September 1988). Executive Vice-President (Legal Affairs and Environment), Bell Canada (October 1988).

André Tremblay. B.A. (1959); LL.L. (Laval) (1962); D.E.S.D. (Public Law) (1964); LL.D. (Ottawa) (1966). Professor, University of Montreal. Vice-Dean (Research and Graduate Studies) (1982-86). Director of Public Law Research Centre (1972-76). President of the Canadian Association of Law Teachers (1974-75). Director, Graduate Studies, Ottawa (1968-70). Teaching subjects: Constitutional Law, Municipal Law, Natural Resources Law. Publications: *Les compétences législatives au Canada* (1967); *Les institutions municipales du Québec* (1969); *Précis de droit municipal* (1973); *Précis de droit constitutionnel* (1982); "The Language Rights", in Tarnopolsky & Beaudoin, eds., *Canadian Charter of Rights and Freedoms,* (Carswell, 1982).

French and English translations for this work were made by Traductions Devinat & Associés.

Translators and revisors: Alain-François Bisson
                            Fred Bobeaz
                            Pierre Devinat
                            Richard Goreham
                            André Jodouin
                            John Manwaring
                            John Marsh
                            Guy Mirabeau
                            Hugues Sirgent
                            Ruth Sullivan

Word processing: Micheline Cloutier
                            Monique Giffault

The Human Rights Research and Education Centre, University of Ottawa, a non-profit organization, seeks to advance human rights through education and research.

Human Rights Research and Education Centre
University of Ottawa
57 Louis-Pasteur
Ottawa K1N 6N5
(613) 564-3492

Table of Contents

Table of Cases

1

A Comparison of the Canadian Charter of Rights and Freedoms with the Canadian Bill of Rights

Peter W. Hogg

1. INTRODUCTION

The purpose of this chapter is to compare the *Canadian Charter of Rights and Freedoms*[1] with the *Canadian Bill of Rights*.[2]

2. BOTH INSTRUMENTS IN FORCE

(a) Preservation of Bill

The *Canadian Charter of Rights and Freedoms* became part of the Constitution of Canada by virtue of the enactment of the *Canada Act 1982*[3] by the Parliament of the United Kingdom. The *Canada Act* includes as a schedule the *Constitution Act, 1982*, Part I of which (sections 1 to 34) consists of the *Canadian Charter of Rights and Freedoms*. The *Constitution Act, 1982* includes as a schedule a table of all the statutes amended or repealed by the Act. That table does not refer to the *Canadian Bill of Rights*. It is clear therefore that the *Constitution Act, 1982* does not expressly repeal the *Canadian Bill of Rights*.[4] However, it is necessary to consider the extent to which the terms of the Charter may have the effect of impliedly repealing all or part of the Bill.[5]

(b) *Constitution Act, 1982*, Section 52(1)

Section 52(1) of the *Constitution Act, 1982* asserts that "the Constitution of Canada [which includes the Charter] is the supreme law of Canada, and any law that is inconsistent with the provisions of the Constitution is, to the extent of the inconsistency, of no force or effect". The question is, when is a law "inconsistent" with the provisions of the Charter? In particular, can the provisions of the *Canadian Bill of Rights* survive the enactment of the Charter, or have they been wholly supplanted by the Charter?

---

1 Part I of the *Constitution Act, 1982* [en. by the *Canada Act 1982* (U.K.), 1982, c. 11, Sched. B].
2 S.C. 1960, c. 44. The major study of the *Canadian Bill of Rights* is W.S. Tarnopolsky, *The Canadian Bill of Rights*, 2nd rev. ed. (Toronto: McClelland & Stewart, 1975) (hereinafter referred to as Tarnopolsky).
3 *Supra*, note 1.
4 Nor does the table list the provincial bills of rights, namely, the *Alberta Bill of Rights*, S.A. 1972, c. 1 (R.S.A. 1980, c. A-16); the Quebec *Charter of Human Rights and Freedoms*, S.Q. 1975, c. 6 (R.S.Q. 1977, c. C-12); the *Saskatchewan Bill of Rights Act*, S.S. 1947, c. 35 (R.S.S. 1978, c. S-9); repealed and replaced by the *Saskatchewan Human Rights Code*, S.S. 1979, c. 5-24.1.
5 Essentially the same issues arise for the provincial bills of rights as well.

(c) Charter, Section 26

Section 26 of the Charter gives some guidance to answering this question. Section 26 provides:

> The guarantee in this Charter of certain rights and freedoms shall not be construed as denying the existence of any other rights or freedoms that exist in Canada.

This provision makes clear that the Charter is not to be regarded as impliedly repealing the *Canadian Bill of Rights* or provincial bills of rights[6] or other constitutional[7] or statutory[8] provisions protecting "other rights or freedoms". To the extent that rights or freedoms other than those guaranteed by the new Charter are guaranteed by the *Canadian Bill of Rights*, those other rights or freedoms remain in force. In other words, a person would be entitled to invoke the provisions of the *Canadian Bill of Rights* where they are more favourable to him than the Charter, as they are with respect to several matters.[9]

(d) Duplication

Most of the provisions of the *Canadian Bill of Rights* have been reproduced in similar or broader language in the Charter. Do these provisions of the Bill, which have essentially been duplicated by the Charter, remain in force, or are they rendered nugatory by the Charter? Duplicative provisions are not expressly preserved by section 26 of the Charter because section 26 preserves "*other* rights or freedoms". Still, duplicative provisions of the Bill will not be overriden by the Charter unless they can be said to be "inconsistent" with the provisions of the Charter.

In the context of conflict between federal and provincial laws, it is now settled that duplication does not amount to an inconsistency which would cause the federal paramountcy doctrine to render the duplicative provincial statute inoperative.[10] But, in my opinion, a concept of inconsistency which is appropriate for resolving federal-provincial conflict should not be transferred to the context of competing civil libertarian guarantees. In the federal-provincial context, a very narrow definition of

---

6 *Supra*, note 4.

7 *E.g.*, the rights guaranteed by ss. 93 and 133 of the *Constitution Act, 1867* (U.K.), 30 & 31 Vict., c. 3, as well as equivalent provisions in the *Manitoba Act*, S.C. 1870, c. 3, the *Alberta Act*, S.C. 1905, c. 3, the *Saskatchewan Act*, S.C. 1905, c. 42 and the *British North America Act, 1949* (U.K.), 12-13 George VI, c. 22 (Terms of Union of Newfoundland). See also ss. 21 and 29 of the Charter.

8 *E.g.*, the rights guaranteed by provincial human rights codes.

9 *Infra*, p. 14.

10 *Multiple Access Ltd. v. McCutcheon*, [1982] 2 S.C.R. 161.

inconsistency can be justified on the ground that the narrow definition will have the effect of protecting provincial law-making autonomy from the centralizing force of federal legislation. No comparable consideration is relevant in the context of competing constitutional and statutory instruments, each pursuing essentially the same purposes. On the contrary, there seems to be no point at all in the same civil liberty being guaranteed by two instruments. I therefore take the view that those provisions of the *Canadian Bill of Rights* which purport to guarantee rights or freedoms which will be guaranteed by the new Charter are rendered "of no force and effect" by the enactment of the new Charter.

(e) Conflict

There does not seem to be any instance of actual conflict between the two instruments, which is not surprising since their purposes are so similar.

3. ENTRENCHMENT

(a) Charter's Constitutional Status

The Charter is part of the Constitution, so it can be repealed or amended only by the process of constitutional amendment. This is explicit in section 52(3) of the *Constitution Act, 1982*, which provides that: "Amendments to the Constitution of Canada shall be made only in accordance with the authority contained in the Constitution of Canada". The Constitution of Canada is defined in section 52(2) as including "this Act" and, of course, Part I of "this Act" is the Charter. The effect of this is that the Charter may be amended only in accordance with the general procedure established by section 38(1), which requires resolutions of the federal Parliament and the legislatures of at least two-thirds of all the provinces having a total of at least 50 percent of the population of all the provinces. Since the Charter cannot be amended by ordinary legislative action, it is therefore "entrenched".

(b) Bill's Statutory Status

The *Canadian Bill of Rights*, by contrast, never became part of entrenched constitutional provisions. It was enacted by the federal Parliament in 1960, and can be repealed or amended in the same way as it was enacted, that is, by another ordinary federal statute. Indeed, in 1985, the Bill was amended by an ordinary federal statute.[11]

---

11 *Statute Law (Canadian Charter of Rights and Freedoms) Amendment Act*, S.C. 1985, c. 26, s. 105 (amending s. 3 regarding pre-enactment scrutiny of bills and regulations).

4. OVERRIDING EFFECT

(a) *Constitution Act, 1982*, Section 52(1)

We have already noticed section 52(1) of the *Constitution Act, 1982*, which provides that any law which is inconsistent with the provisions of the Constitution of Canada (which includes the Charter) "is, to the extent of the inconsistency, of no force or effect". The Charter is thus expressly given overriding force over laws which conflict with its provisions.

(b) *Drybones* Case

The *Canadian Bill of Rights* does not state clearly what its effect is to be on federal laws that conflict with its provisions. It is not clear from its terms whether the Bill was to be merely a canon of interpretation for doubtful or equivocal language in federal statutes, or whether it was supposed to have overriding force over inconsistent federal statutes. The latter alternative would raise the constitutional question whether the Parliament of Canada could bind itself in this way by enactment of a simple statute. In *R. v. Drybones*,[12] the Supreme Court of Canada held that the Bill rendered inoperative a provision of the *Indian Act*,[13] which the court regarded as being in conflict with the Bill's guarantee of "equality before the law". This decision established that the Bill purported to have overriding force over inconsistent federal statutes. However, since the *Indian Act* was prior in time to the *Canadian Bill of Rights* and thus liable to repeal or modification by the later statute, *Drybones* did not settle the question whether the Bill could be effective over statutes enacted after 1960. However, there are *dicta* to the effect that the Bill is equally effective over later statutes,[14] and in one case three of six judges so decided.[15]

5. APPLICATION TO BOTH LEVELS OF GOVERNMENT

(a) Charter, Section 32(1)

A major difference between the Charter and the Bill is that the Charter

---

12 [1970] S.C.R. 282.

13 R.S.C. 1952, c. 149.

14 *Curr v. R.*, [1972] S.C.R. 889 at 893; *A.G. Canada v. Lavell*, [1974] S.C.R. 1349 at 1388; *Miller v. R.*, [1977] 2 S.C.R. 680 at 686.

15 *Singh v. Min. of Employment & Immigration*, [1985] 1 S.C.R. 177; discussed later in this chapter in text accompanying note 44, *infra*. Since the *Canadian Bill of Rights* is an ordinary statute, it is not easy to reconcile this result with the doctrine of parliamentary sovereignty: for discussion, see Tarnopolsky, *supra*, note 2 at 141-143; P.W. Hogg, *Constitutional Law of Canada*, 2nd ed. (Toronto: Carswell, 1985) at 643-644 (hereinafter referred to as Hogg).

is binding on both levels of government, whereas the Bill is binding only on the federal level. However, each instrument uses a different drafting technique to define its scope of operation, and the technique used in the Charter leaves some uncertainty on issues which are clear in the Bill.

The Charter's operative provision is section 32(1), which provides:

> This Charter applies
> (a) to the Parliament and government of Canada in respect of all matters within the authority of Parliament including all matters relating to the Yukon Territory and Northwest Territories; and
> (b) to the legislature and government of each province in respect of all matters within the authority of the legislature of each province.

The application of the Charter to both levels of government is thus clear in principle. However, it is not perfectly clear whether the Charter applies to private action as well as to governmental action and, if only the latter, what is encompassed within governmental action. These issues are taken up in a later chapter of this book.[16]

(b) Bill, Sections 2, 5(2)

The *Canadian Bill of Rights* does not purport to apply to provincial legislatures or governments, and since it is only a federal statute, it could not in any case have been given much effect over provincial laws or practices.[17] However, within this important limitation, the application of the Bill is, in my view, more clearly defined than is the application of the Charter. Section 2 of the Bill, which is the operative provision, applies to "every law of Canada". Section 5(2) then defines "law of Canada" in these terms:

> The expression "law of Canada" in Part I means an Act of the Parliament of Canada enacted before or after the coming into force of this Act, any order, rule or regulation thereunder, and any law in force in Canada or in any part of Canada at the commencement of this Act that is subject to be repealed, abolished or altered by the Parliament of Canada.

Under this definition, it is perfectly clear that private activity is excluded. The references to "an Act of the Parliament of Canada" and "any order, rule or regulation thereunder" make reasonably clear that all action taken

---

16 See R. Tassé, Chapter 3 "Application of the Canadian Charter of Rights and Freedoms", *infra*.

17 It is conceivable that a bill of rights confined to civil liberties within federal jurisdiction (*e.g.*, speech, religion) could be enacted by the federal Parliament as an ordinary statute and, through the doctrine of paramountcy, could have a nullifying effect on provincial laws. But the definition of "laws of Canada" in the *Canadian Bill of Rights* (see following text) makes clear that the *Canadian Bill of Rights* does not purport to go that far.

under statutory authority is included.[18] The reference to any law "that is subject to be repealed, abolished or altered by the Parliament of Canada" makes clear that the common law (and not just that part of the common law defining the prerogative powers of government), as well as pre-Confederation law, is also included.[19]

6. LIMITATION CLAUSE

(a) Charter, Section 1

The Charter, by section 1, provides as follows:

> The *Canadian Charter of Rights and Freedoms* guarantees the rights and freedoms set out in it subject only to such reasonable limits prescribed by law as can be demonstrably justified in a free and democratic society.

This limitation clause follows the pattern of the *International Covenant on Civil and Political Rights*, which has been adhered to by Canada (1976) and many other countries, and the *European Convention on Human Rights*, which has been adhered to by the United Kingdom and other countries of Western Europe. These instruments qualify the declared rights with limitation clauses similar to section 1 of the Charter.

Section 1 of the Charter enables Parliament or a legislature to enact a law which has the effect of limiting one of the guaranteed rights or freedoms, provided that the law is "reasonable" and can be "demonstrably justified in a free and democratic society". Unlike the override clause (discussed next), the limitation clause is too vague to be employed with confidence by Parliament or a legislature by itself. Only a judicial decision would settle conclusively the question whether a particular law transgressed the Charter or was saved by the limitation clause. The meaning and effect of the limitation clause is the topic of a later chapter of this book.[20]

(b) Bill's Implicit Limitations

The *Canadian Bill of Rights* contains no limitation clause comparable to section 1 of the Charter. Most of the freedoms, and in particular the guarantees of "equality before the law" (section 1(b)), "freedom of religion" (section 1(c)), "freedom of speech" (section 1(d)), "freedom of assembly and association" (section 1(e)) and "freedom of the press" (section 1(f)), are expressed in unqualified terms. This follows the pattern

---

18 *Brownridge v. R.*, [1972] S.C.R. 926.

19 Hogg, *supra*, note 15 at 639.

20 See W.R. Lederman, Chapter 4 "Assessing Competing Values in the Definition of Charter of Rights and Freedoms", *infra*.

of the *American Bill of Rights* which also lacks an explicit limitation clause. But the courts have not interpreted the guarantees of the *Canadian Bill of Rights* and the *American Bill of Rights* as absolutes; they have recognized the necessity to limit them in pursuit of other widely shared values. Thus a guarantee of "equality before the law" or "equal protection of the laws" must be qualified to accommodate laws which treat special groups in a special way for legitimate reasons,[21] and a guarantee of "freedom of speech" must be qualified to accommodate laws against sedition, obscenity, fraud, official secrecy, defamation, deceptive advertising and the like.[22] The position without a limitation clause is therefore not very different from the position with a limitation clause.[23] However, an explicit limitation clause does instruct the courts, albeit vaguely, as to the standards to be employed in determining whether a law transgresses a guaranteed civil liberty. In the absence of a limitation clause, the courts have to invent the applicable standards, a task that Canadian courts, in interpreting the *Canadian Bill of Rights*, did not perform very successfully.[24]

(c) "Frozen Concepts" Theory

One part of the *Canadian Bill of Rights* which was occasionally construed as a limitation on the various guaranteed civil liberties was the recitation in section 1 that the rights and freedoms declared in the Bill "have existed and shall continue to exist". This phrase led to the theory which Professor Tarnopolsky has aptly stigmatized as the "frozen concepts" theory, under which only rights in existence in 1960 (when the Bill was enacted) were guaranteed, and those rights were circumscribed by the state of the law in 1960. On this theory, any feature of our law which was in existence in 1960 (for example, capital punishment) could not be held to be contrary to the Bill; only post-1960 deprivations of civil liberties were within the scope of the Bill.[25] This theory, which would have robbed the Bill of much of its force, was never consistently applied, and is contradicted by the decision in *R. v. Drybones*[26] because the discriminatory provision struck out of the *Indian Act*[27] in that case had been in the *Indian Act* long before 1960. Still, the "frozen concepts" theory kept appearing

---

21 See W. Black & L. Smith, Chapter 14 "Equality Rights", *infra.*

22 See C.F. Beckton, Chapter 6 "Freedom of Expression", *infra.*

23 See R. Tassé, Chapter 3 "Application of the Canadian Charter of Rights and Freedoms", *infra.*

24 Hogg, *supra*, note 15 at 787-794.

25 W.S. Tarnopolsky, in "The Constitution and the Future of Canada", [1978] *Special Lectures L.S.U.C.* 161 at 181-191, gives an excellent critique of the theory.

26 *Supra*, note 12.

27 *Supra*, note 13.

from time to time as a ground of decision in other cases,[28] and has never been squarely laid to rest.

The Charter scrupulously avoids references to existing or continuing rights which could form the basis of a "frozen concepts" theory,[29] and the Supreme Court of Canada has explicitly held that the scope of the Charter is not limited by the state of civil liberties in Canada in 1982.[30]

7. OVERRIDE POWER

(a) Charter, Section 33

The Charter, by section 33, expressly permits the federal Parliament or a provincial legislature to exempt a statute from compliance with certain provisions of the Charter. Section 33(1) provides:

> Parliament or the legislature of a Province may expressly declare in an Act of Parliament or of the legislature, as the case may be, that the Act or a provision thereof shall operate notwithstanding a provision included in section 2 or sections 7 to 15 of this Charter.

Section 33(2) goes on to provide that:

> An Act or a provision of an Act in respect of which a declaration made under this section is in effect shall have such operation as it would have but for the provision of this Charter referred to in the declaration.

In other words, if the declaration is used in an Act, the Act operates free from the invalidating effect of the provision of the Charter referred to in the declaration.

Section 33 has come to be described as an "override power". It overrides the Charter only in the sense of exempting the Act containing the declaration from the provisions of the Charter referred to in the declaration. The existence of this power means that a government which wishes to enact a limit to a guaranteed right or freedom (or which wishes to preclude any legal question of whether or not a particular statute is a "reasonable" limit which "can be demonstrably justified in a free and democratic society") has the power to do so. The override power of section 33 is analyzed elsewhere in this book,[31] but for present purposes it should be noticed that the exercise of the power is subject to two restrictions that have no counterparts in the

---

28 *Robertson v. R.*, [1963] S.C.R. 651; *R. v. Burnshine*, [1975] S.C.R. 693; *Miller v. R.*, *supra*, note 14.

29 S. 35 of the *Constitution Act, 1982* (which is not part of the Charter) refers to the "existing" aboriginal and treaty rights of the aboriginal peoples of Canada, and the word "existing" could have a limiting effect on that particular provision.

30 *R. v. Big M Drug Mart*, [1985] 1 S.C.R. 295 at 343-344.

31 See R. Tassé, Chapter 3 "Application of the Canadian Charter of Rights and Freedoms", *infra*.

Canadian Bill of Rights. First, the power applies only to certain rights, namely, those guaranteed by sections 2 and 7 to 15. The "democratic rights" of sections 3 to 5, the "mobility rights" of section 6, the "language rights" of sections 16 to 22 and the "minority language educational rights" of section 23 are among the provisions which cannot be overriden. As well, in order to be effective under section 33(2), the express declaration must refer specifically to the provision of the Charter which is to be overriden; presumably more than one or even all of sections 2 and 7 to 15 could be referred to. But an express declaration which did not specify any particular provisions of the Charter would not be effective.

The second restriction on the override power is temporal. Section 33(3) provides:

> A declaration made under subsection (1) shall cease to have effect five years after it comes into force or on such earlier date as may be specified in the declaration.

This "sunset clause" makes the declaration expire automatically after five years. Section 33(4) permits the declaration to be re-enacted. But the necessity of re-enactment every five years will force periodic reconsideration of each exercise of the override power, at intervals which (in some jurisdictions at least) will often yield a change of government. This reinforces the already powerful political safeguards against an ill-considered use of the power.

(b) Bill, Section 2

The *Canadian Bill of Rights* also provides an override power. The Bill, by section 2, applies "unless it is expressly declared by an Act of the Parliament of Canada that it shall operate notwithstanding the *Canadian Bill of Rights*". This provision, which seems to be an indigenous Canadian invention, undoubtedly provided the model for section 33 of the Charter. But the override power in the Bill differs from that in the Charter in that the Bill power may be used to override all of the guarantees in the Bill, not just certain of them, and there is no need to be specific as to the particular guarantees which are being overridden. What is contemplated by section 2 of the Bill is the exclusion of all of its provisions. Nor does the Bill stipulate any time limit on the duration of the declaration or any requirement of periodic re-enactment. In these respects, the override power in the Bill is a less refined instrument than that in the Charter. The override power in the Bill has been used only once.[32]

---

32 The power was used in the *Public Order (Temporary Measures) Act*, S.C. 1970-71-72, c. 2, s. 12 (expired April 30, 1971), which is the statute that superseded the *War Measures Act, infra*, note 33, after the October crisis of 1970 in Quebec.

8. EMERGENCY MEASURES

The *War Measures Act*,[33] enacted by the federal Parliament in 1914 under the emergency branch of the peace, order and good government power, comes into force whenever the federal government proclaims that "war, invasion or insurrection, real or apprehended, exists". The Act then confers upon the federal government the power to make regulations on almost any conceivable subject, including censorship, arrest, detention and deportation. The Act has been proclaimed in force on three occasions: during the first world war, during the second world war, and during the October Crisis in Quebec in 1970; and on each occasion, the regulations made under the Act imposed severe restrictions on civil liberties which would not have been tolerable in normal times.

The *Canadian Bill of Rights*, by section 6, made two changes in the *War Measures Act*: it required that the proclamation bringing the Act into effect be laid before Parliament, and it made provision for debate in Parliament and revocation by Parliament of the proclamation. It then went on to provide that anything done under the *War Measures Act* was to be deemed not to be an infringement of the Bill. The *War Measures Act* was thus exempted from compliance with the Bill.

The *Charter* makes no mention of the *War Measures Act*, and the Charter grants only one exemption from its provisions in circumstances of emergency. The one exemption is section 4(2), which permits the House of Commons or a provincial legislative assembly to be continued beyond five years "in time of real or apprehended war, invasion or insurrection". Apart from this exception, the Charter gives no indication of whether and to what extent civil liberties can be impaired in time of emergency. It will be for the courts to decide whether the *War Measures Act*, or any other statute apparently curtailing a guaranteed civil liberty in time of emergency, comes within the qualifying clause of section 1, namely, "subject only to such reasonable limits prescribed by law as can be demonstrably justified in a free and democratic society." Of course, this issue could be finessed, and the emergency measure exempted from sections 2 and 7 to 15 of the Charter, by explicit use of the override power of section 33.

9. JUDICIAL ENFORCEMENT

(a) *Constitution Act, 1982*, Section 52(1)

The overriding effect of the Charter, rendering inconsistent statutes

---

33 See now R.S.C. 1970, c. W-2 [R.S.C. 1985, c. W-2].

"of no force or effect",[34] is an important enforcement measure, because it means that any court or tribunal has the power (and the duty) to disregard any statute which the court or tribunal finds to be inconsistent with the Charter. No special authority is needed for this mode of enforcement: it follows inexorably from the fact that the inconsistent law is of no force or effect. Thus, the provisions of the Charter may be relevant and applicable, and therefore enforceable, in any proceeding before any court or tribunal in which one side relies on a statute and the other side claims that the statute is a nullity because it is contrary to the Charter.

(b) Charter, Section 24

In addition to the remedial effect of the nullification of a law that violates the Charter, section 24 of the Charter specifically authorizes a remedy for a Charter violation. Section 24(1) authorizes "anyone whose rights and freedoms, as guaranteed by this Charter, have been infringed or denied" to "apply to a court of competent jurisdiction to obtain such remedy as the court considers appropriate and just in the circumstances". This provision implies two things. First, it implies that anyone who makes a plausible claim that one of his rights or freedoms has been infringed has the standing which is requisite to the initiation of a lawsuit. Second, it implies that anyone who establishes the infringement or denial of one of his rights or freedoms has, by that fact alone, made out a cause of action entitling him to an "appropriate and just" remedy. Section 24 is analyzed in a later chapter of this book.[35]

(c) Bill's Enforcement

The *Canadian Bill of Rights* contains no enforcement clause similar to section 24 of the Charter, and the Supreme Court of Canada has not shown any propensity to fashion new remedies for violations of the Bill.

The Supreme Court of Canada was much criticized for its decision in *Hogan v. R.*,[36] where it held that evidence obtained in violation of the *Canadian Bill of Rights* was nonetheless admissible if relevant. The court thus withheld the only obvious remedy for the breach of the Bill. In the new Charter, this issue is specifically addressed by section 24(2), which provides that evidence obtained in violation of the Charter "shall be

---

34 *Constitution Act, 1982*, s. 52(1), discussed *supra*, under "4.(a) Constitution Act, 1982, Section 52(1)".

35 See D. Gibson & S. Gibson, Chapter 19 "Enforcement of the Canadian Charter of Rights and Freedoms", *infra*.

36 [1975] 2 S.C.R. 574.

excluded if it is established that, having regard to all the circumstances, the admission of it in the proceedings would bring the administration of justice into disrepute". This provision is analyzed in a later chapter of this book.[37]

10. SCRUTINY BY MINISTER OF JUSTICE

The *Canadian Bill of Rights* contains an interesting noncurial enforcement clause. Section 3 of the Bill requires the (federal) Minister of Justice to scrutinize all proposed statutes and regulations in order to ascertain whether any provision is inconsistent with the Bill, and it requires that "he shall report any such inconsistency to the House of Commons at the first convenient opportunity". As Professor Peter Russell has noted, it is a weakness of this provision that it "entrusts the government itself with the responsibility of testing its own proposals against the Bill of Rights".[38] While only one report of inconsistency has ever been made, the contemplated scrutiny does take place within the Department of Justice, and legislative proposals are sometimes modified before they achieve their final form.[39]

The *Charter of Rights* contains no obligation of pre-enactment scrutiny like section 3 of the *Canadian Bill of Rights*. However, in 1985, the federal Parliament added a new section to the *Department of Justice Act*,[40] requiring the Minister of Justice to scrutinize all proposed federal statutes and regulations in order to ascertain whether any provision is inconsistent with the Charter, and requiring the Minister to report any such inconsistency to the House of Commons.[41] As the result of this amendment, the pre-enactment scrutiny by the Minister of Justice of proposed statutes and regulations must encompass compliance with the Charter as well as the Bill.[42]

---

37 See Gibson & Gibson, Chapter 19, *infra*.

38 P.H. Russell, "Democratic Approach to Civil Liberties" (1969), 19 *U.T.L.J.* 109 at 125.

39 *Report to the House of Commons by the Minister of Justice Pursuant to Section 3 of the Canadian Bill of Rights*, March 27, 1975. This was a report submitted by the then Minister of Justice, O.E. Lang, concerning a bill passed by the Senate: Bill S-10, *An Act to amend the Feeds Act*, passed March 6, 1975 (S.C. 1974-75-76, c. 94). On the modification of proposals before they achieve their final form, see Tarnopolsky, *supra*, note 2, at 125-128.

40 R.S.C. 1970, c. J-2 [R.S.C. 1985, c. J-2].

41 S. 4.1, added by *Statute Law (Canadian Charter of Rights and Freedoms) Amendment Act*, *supra*, note 11, s. 106 [R.S.C. 1985, c. 31 (1st Supp.), s. 93].

42 The scrutiny obligations imposed by s. 3 of the *Canadian Bill of Rights* and s. 4.1 of the *Department of Justice Act*, *supra*, note 40, are duplicated with respect to regulations by s. 3(2)(c) of the *Statutory Instruments Act*, S.C. 1970-71-72, c. 38 [R.S.C. 1985, c. S-22].

11. CONTENTS

(a) Introduction

As noted earlier, most of the provisions of the *Canadian Bill of Rights* have been reproduced in similar or broader language by the Charter. There are only three provisions of the Bill that are omitted from the Charter.

(b) Exile

First, there is a prohibition in section 2(a) of the Bill against the arbitrary "exile" of any person. The Charter contains no reference to exile. However, the Charter's "mobility rights" include in section 6(1) the right of "every citizen . . . to enter, remain in and leave Canada". This provision would appear to preclude the exile of a citizen. Section 6(1) of the Charter does not apply to non-citizens, but the banishment of a non-citizen would not normally be described as exile: exile carries the connotation of banishment from one's native land.

(c) Fair Hearing

Second, section 2(e) of the Bill provides that no law of Canada shall:

> deprive a person of the right to a fair hearing in accordance with the principles of fundamental justice for the determination of his rights and obligations.

The Charter contains no general right to a fair hearing for the determination of a person's rights and obligations. Section 7 of the Charter provides that "life, liberty and security of the person" may not be taken away "except in accordance with the principles of fundamental justice". But, as will be emphasized shortly, section 7 probably has no application where only economic interests are at stake. The other legal rights guaranteed in sections 8 to 14 of the Charter are often addressed to some aspect of a fair hearing, but most of them are applicable only to criminal trials. A civil proceeding before a court or administrative tribunal is not subject to the requirement of a "fair hearing" or of the application of "fundamental justice". This is a gap in the Charter, and is therefore an area where the continued existence of the Bill is important: an adjudication authorized by federal law of a person's rights and obligations will continue to be subject to the requirement of "a fair hearing in accordance with the principles of fundamental justice".[43]

---

43 Of the provincial bills of rights, *supra*, note 4, only the Quebec *Charter of Human Rights and Freedoms*, by s. 23, includes the right of a fair hearing for the determination of rights and obligations.

The significance of section 2(e) in the post-Charter world has been underlined by two cases. In *Singh v. Minister of Employment & Immigration*,[44] a person who had been denied refugee status without a proper hearing attacked the procedures established by the *Immigration Act*[45] to determine this issue. The main ground of attack was based on section 7 of the Charter, but this raised the difficult question of whether the threat of death, torture or imprisonment by a foreign government could count in Canada as a deprivation of life, liberty or security of the person. In the Supreme Court of Canada, Wilson J., with the concurrence of Dickson C.J. and Lamer J., held that such a threat could amount to a deprivation of security of the person, and she upheld the attack based on section 7. Beetz J., with the concurrence of Estey and McIntyre JJ., avoided the issue of whether section 7 protected against deprivations by foreign governments of life, liberty or security of the person. In his view, it was at least clear that the decision respecting an applicant's refugee status was a determination of the applicant's "rights and obligations" under section 2(e) of the *Canadian Bill of Rights*. He accordingly upheld the attack based on section 2(e). In the end, the six-judge bench agreed on the outcome, but three of the judges had recourse to the wider right of section 2(e) of the *Canadian Bill of Rights*.

In *MacBain v. Lederman*,[46] a person who had been the subject of a complaint to the Canadian Human Rights Commission challenged the tribunal that had been appointed to inquire into the complaint; he argued that the tribunal was biased because its members were selected by the Commission. No attack could be mounted against the tribunal under section 7 (or any other provision) of the Charter: the tribunal's powers were strictly of a civil nature, having no possible effect on life, liberty or security of the person. However, the Federal Court of Appeal held that the tribunal did possess the power to determine "obligations" within the meaning of section 2(e) of the *Canadian Bill of Rights*. The court held that the apprehension of bias flowing from the statutory provisions for appointment of the tribunal was a breach of the principles of fundamental justice, and that section 2(e) rendered those provisions inoperative. Thus, the *Canadian Bill of Rights* provided a remedy that the Charter could not provide.

(d) Protection of Property

The third legal right which is included in the *Canadian Bill of Rights* but omitted from the Charter is a "due process" protection of property.

---

44 *Supra*, note 15.
45 S.C. 1976-77, c. 52.
46 (1985), 22 D.L.R. (4th) 119 (F.C.C.A.).

Section 7 of the Charter provides as follows:

> Everyone has the right to life, liberty, and security of the person and the right not to be deprived thereof except in accordance with the principles of fundamental justice.

Contrast this provision with section 1(a) of the *Canadian Bill of Rights*:

> ... the right of the individual to life, liberty, security of the person *and enjoyment of property*, and the right not to be deprived thereof except by due process of law; [emphasis added]

In the Charter provision, the reference to "enjoyment of property" has been omitted, and the requirement of "due process of law" has been replaced by a requirement of "the principles of fundamental justice". What, if anything, is the difference between "due process of law" and "the principles of fundamental justice" only the course of litigation will tell.[47] But the omission of property rights from the list of protected rights is certainly significant. Aside from any guarantee in the Bill or the Charter, there is no requirement of Canadian constitutional law that a compulsory taking of property be effected by a fair procedure or that it be accompanied by fair compensation to the owner.[48] Section 1(a) of the *Canadian Bill of Rights* undoubtedly imposes a requirement of a fair procedure, and may also impose a requirement of fair compensation. The "due process" clause in the Fourteenth Amendment of the United States Constitution, which protects "life, liberty, or property", has been held to impose a requirement of fair compensation for property expropriated.[49] It is possible that Canadian courts would give the similar language of section 1(a) a similar interpretation. The Charter by contrast provides no guarantee of even a fair procedure, let alone compensation, for the expropriation of property. This is another area where the continued existence of the *Canadian Bill of Rights* is important. It provides protection for property owners whose property is to be taken or otherwise injuriously affected under the authority of federal law.[50]

---

47 For discussion of these phrases, see P. Garant, Chapter 10 "Fundamental Freedoms and Fundamental Justice", *infra*.

48 Hogg, *supra*, note 15 at 577-579.

49 *Chicago, Burlington & Quincy Rd. Co. v. Chicago*, 166 U.S. 226 (1897). Congress is subject to the same requirement, but it is explicit in the Fifth Amendment, which provides, *inter alia*, "nor shall private property be taken for public use without just compensation".

50 The provincial bills of rights, *supra*, note 4, include some rights with respect to property. The *Alberta Bill of Rights* protects the "enjoyment of property" by a "due process" clause. The Quebec *Charter of Human Rights and Freedoms* gives some protection to "the peaceful enjoyment and free disposition of his property" (s. 6) and to deprivation of "rights" (*droits*) (s. 24), but not in terms as strong as a "due process" clause.

12. JUDICIAL INTERPRETATION

The Supreme Court of Canada was much criticized for its "timid" approach to the *Canadian Bill of Rights*. In the 22 years that elapsed between the Bill's enactment in 1960 and the Charter's adoption in 1982, the *Drybones* case[51] was the only one in which the Supreme Court of Canada held a statute to be inoperative for breach of the Bill.[52] However, it is only fair to note that none of the cases which came up to the Supreme Court of Canada exhibited a shocking violation of a civil liberty. Moreover, the restrained attitude of the court is consistent with the long Anglo-Canadian legal tradition of parliamentary sovereignty.

The Supreme Court of Canada's attitude to the Charter has been entirely different. As explained in a later chapter of this book,[53] the court has articulated and implemented a generous interpretation of Charter rights leading inevitably to active judicial review, involving frequent holdings of invalidity. The reason for the change in attitude is not difficult to ascertain. The adoption of the Charter was preceded by a prolonged and public debate which created a public expectation that a significant change in the Canadian Constitution occurred with the adoption of the Charter. The judges could not easily ignore the deliberate and open decision to enhance their powers *vis-à-vis* the eleven elected governments.

The changed attitude of the Supreme Court of Canada to the protection of guaranteed civil liberties is dramatically illustrated by those Charter cases in which there was a prior *Canadian Bill of Rights* case which had decided the same point. In *R. v. Big M Drug Mart*,[54] the Supreme Court of Canada had to decide whether the federal *Lord's Day Act*,[55] which prohibited commercial activity on Sundays, offended the Charter right to "freedom of conscience and religion" (section 2(a)). The court had earlier decided in *Robertson v. R.*[56] that the *Lord's Day Act* did not offend the right to "freedom of religion" in section 1(c) of the *Canadian Bill of Rights*. In *Big M*, the court reached the opposite result, holding the Act to be invalid for breach of section 2(a) of the Charter. The court overruled *Robertson*,

---

51 *Supra*, note 12.
52 The *Drybones* case was followed in *R. v. Hayden* (1983), 3 D.L.R. (4th) 361 (Man. C.A.), leave to appeal to S.C.C. refused (1983), 3 D.L.R. (4th) 361n (S.C.C.), in which the *Indian Act* offence of being drunk on a reserve was held to be inoperative (*Drybones* had concerned the off-reserve offence). Since 1982, two more applications of the Bill must be noted: *Singh v. Min. of Employment & Immigration, supra*, note 15, described in text accompanying note 44, *supra*; *MacBain v. Lederman, supra*, note 46 and accompanying text.
53 See W.F. Pentney, Chapter 2 "Interpreting the Charter: General Principles", *infra*.
54 *Supra*, note 30.
55 R.S.C. 1970, c. L-13.
56 *Supra*, note 28.

giving as its reason the acceptance in that case of the "frozen concepts" theory of interpretation.[57] Dickson C.J. for the majority said that, unlike the *Canadian Bill of Rights*, the Charter did not merely recognize rights in existence at its inception, and "the meaning of the concept of freedom of conscience and religion is not to be determined solely by the degree to which that right was enjoyed by Canadians prior to the proclamation of the Charter".[58]

In *R. v. Therens*,[59] the Supreme Court of Canada had to decide whether a police demand for a breath sample from a motorist suspected of impaired driving was a "detention" within section 10 of the Charter so as to give rise to a right to counsel. The court had earlier decided in *Chromiak v. R.*[60] that there was no detention in this situation, so that the motorist had no right to counsel under the similar language of section 2(c) of the *Canadian Bill of Rights*. In *Therens*, the court reached the opposite result, holding that there was a detention and therefore a right to counsel. The court overruled *Chromiak*. Le Dain J., whose opinion on this issue was unanimously accepted (he dissented in the result), gave two reasons for the overruling. His first reason was based on the constitutional status of the Charter. He pointed out that:

> [O]n the whole. with some notable exceptions, the courts have felt some uncertainty or ambivalence in the application of the *Canadian Bill of Rights* because it did not reflect a clear constitutional mandate to make judicial decisions having the effect of limiting or qualifying the traditional sovereignty of Parliament.[61]

The Charter, on the other hand, "because of its constitutional character", must be regarded as "a new affirmation of rights and freedoms and of judicial power and responsibility in relation to their protection".[62] Le Dain J.'s second reason for giving a broader interpretation to Charter rights was the existence in the Charter of section 1. Since section 1 provided a means of limiting Charter rights, the rights themselves could safely be given a broad interpretation. Under the *Canadian Bill of Rights*, however, the absence of any limitation clause meant that "the meaning and application given to the word 'detained' in *Chromiak* was the only means by which reasonable limits could be placed on the right to counsel".[63] For these

---

57 The "frozen concepts" theory of interpretation is discussed in the text accompanying note 25, *supra*.

58 *R. v. Big M Drug Mart, supra*, note 30 at 343-344.

59 [1985] 1 S.C.R. 613.

60 [1980] 1 S.C.R. 471.

61 *R. v. Therens, supra*, note 59 at 639.

62 *Ibid*. at 638.

63 *Ibid*. at 639.

two reasons, his lordship concluded that the language carried over from the *Canadian Bill of Rights* to the Charter bore a different, wider meaning in its new context.

In *R. v. Oakes*,[64] the Supreme Court of Canada had to decide whether a "reverse onus" clause in the *Narcotic Control Act*[65] violated the right "to be presumed innocent until proven guilty" in section 11(d) of the Charter. The reverse onus clause provided that proof of possession of an illegal drug raised a presumption that the possession was for the purpose of trafficking; the onus of disproving the purpose of trafficking was thus placed on the accused. The *Canadian Bill of Rights*, in section 2(f), contained a similar presumption of innocence. The language of the *Canadian Bill of Rights* had been interpreted in two earlier decisions of the Supreme Court of Canada as permitting a reverse onus clause where there was a "rational connection" between the proved fact (here, possession) and the presumed fact (here, the trafficking purpose).[66] The court in *Oakes* overruled these decisions, holding that any provision that cast a burden of proof on the accused was a violation of section 11(d) of the Charter. Dickson C.J., for the majority of the court, relied upon all three reasons given in *Big M*[67] and *Therens*:[68] the constitutional status of the Charter, the "frozen concepts" interpretation of the Bill, and the existence of section 1 of the Charter.[69] However, he particularly relied upon the last point. He acknowledged that the "rational connection" test was an appropriate qualification to the right to be presumed innocent under the *Canadian Bill of Rights*, because the *Canadian Bill of Rights* contained no equivalent of section 1. However, under the Charter, "the appropriate stage for invoking the rational connection test [was] under s. 1".[70] In the result, the court struck down the challenged reverse onus clause.

These cases[71] make it abundantly clear that there is no presumption that language carried over from the *Canadian Bill of Rights* to the Charter bears the same meaning in its new context. On the contrary, the court's activist insistence on a generous interpretation of Charter rights makes it likely to reject the cautious, restrictive interpretations of the language of the *Canadian Bill of Rights*. In other words, decisions rendered under

---

64 [1986] 1 S.C.R. 103.

65 R.S.C. 1970, c. N-1.

66 *R. v. Appleby*, [1972] S.C.R. 303; *R. v. Shelley*, [1981] 2 S.C.R. 196.

67 *Supra*, note 30.

68 *Supra*, note 59.

69 *R. v. Oakes, supra*, note 64 at 124-125.

70 *Ibid.* at 134.

71 See also *Singh v. Min. of Employment & Immigration, supra*, note 15 at 209, *per* Wilson J.; *Reference re s. 94(2) of the Motor Vehicle Act (B.C.)*, [1985] 2 S.C.R. 486 at 509-512, *per* Lamer J.

the *Canadian Bill of Rights* are of little precedential value in determining the meaning of the Charter.

13. CONCLUSIONS

The foregoing review demonstrates that the Charter affords stronger protection of the rights and freedoms that it guarantees than the *Canadian Bill of Rights*. The chief differences between the Charter and the Bill are as follows:

(1) The Charter is entrenched in the Constitution; the Bill is a statute.

(2) The Charter expressly overrides inconsistent statutes; the Bill does not, although judicial interpretation has probably given it this effect.

(3) The Charter applies to both levels of government; the Bill applies only to the federal level.

(4) The Charter expressly subjects its guaranteed rights and freedoms to "such reasonable limits prescribed by law as can be demonstrably justified in a free and democratic society"; the Bill contains no similar limitation clause, but similar limits would be implied by the courts.

(5) The Charter and the Bill can each be rendered inapplicable by insertion in the statute of a "notwithstanding" clause; but the Charter's override power is more restricted than the Bill's.

(6) The Charter makes no exception for the *War Measures Act*; the Bill does.

(7) The Charter makes explicit provision for its curial enforcement; the Bill does not.

(8) The Charter does not provide for pre-enactment ministerial scrutiny of statutes and regulations, although this is now provided for by statute; the Bill itself provides for pre-enactment ministerial scrutiny of statutes and regulations.

(9) The Charter guarantees a number of rights and freedoms that are not guaranteed by the Bill, namely, voting and other democratic rights, mobility rights, more rights for criminal defendants, and language rights, including minority language education rights. The Charter does not, however, require a fair hearing for the determination of rights and obligations; nor does the Charter protect property rights with a "due process" clause; the Bill does both those things.

(10) The Charter has been given an expansive interpretation by the courts; the Bill was given a restrictive interpretation.

2

Interpreting the Charter: General Principles

William F. Pentney

1. Introduction
2. Constitutions are Different
3. Presumptions
4. Internal Aids
5. External Aids
6. Conclusion

1. INTRODUCTION

The skills needed to interpret the *Canadian Charter of Rights and Freedoms* have been expressed in a variety of metaphors: apparently one must be a poet,[1] bartender,[2] singer,[3] historian[4] and political diplo-

---

1 A.W. MacKay, "Interpreting the Charter of Rights: Law, Politics and Poetry", in G.-A. Beaudoin, ed., *Charter Cases 1986-87* (Cowansville, Que.: Yvon Blais, 1987) at 347 (Proceedings of Canadian Bar Association Conference).

2 D. Gibson, "Accentuating the Positive and Eliminating the Negative: Remedies for Inequality Under the Canadian Charter", in L. Smith *et al.*, eds., *Righting the Balance: Canada's New Equality Rights* (Saskatoon: Canadian Human Rights Reporter, 1986) (hereinafter Smith, *Righting the Balance*) at 311.

3 D. Gibson, "Protection of Minority Rights Under the Canadian Charter of Rights and Freedoms: Can Politicians and Judges Sing Harmony?" in N. Nevitte & A. Kornberg, eds., *Minorities and the Canadian State* (Oakville: Mosaic Press, 1985) at 31.

4 See the decision of Dickson J. in *R. v. Big M Drug Mart*, [1985] 1 S.C.R. 295.

mat[5] in order to do justice to Charter interpretation. The scope of this article will appear to be quite limited to anyone who accepts that such a diversity of talents are needed for this task — it will focus on the more usual interpretive devices available for legal argument and analysis.

In order to describe the interpretive principles which have evolved thus far, I will follow the general organization adopted by the author of the article on this topic in the first edition of this book.[6] Basically this requires an analysis of the appropriate attitude or approach to Charter interpretation, and a review of the technical interpretive aids that can be utilized. The first part of this calls for extra-legal skills and knowledge; the latter does not.

2. CONSTITUTIONS ARE DIFFERENT

(a) A Purposive Approach

The statement "constitutions are different" expresses a truism that has been reflected for more than a century in cases concerning the division of powers in the *Constitution Act, 1867*,[7] and it has informed Charter analysis in a dramatic way as well. The precise implications of the statement that the Charter is different from other laws because it is part of Canada's basic constitutional document are not yet fully clear. What is evident from the cases is that this will affect virtually all aspects of Charter analysis, including the definition of the scope and content of the substantive rights, and the determination of reasonable limits under section 1.

Perhaps the clearest expression of this doctrine in any Canadian constitutional case is the following statement of Dickson J. (as he then was) in *Hunter v. Southam Inc.*:

> The task of expounding a constitution is crucially different from that of construing a statute. A statute defines present rights and obligations. It is easily enacted and as easily repealed. A constitution, by contrast, is drafted with an eye to the future. Its function is to provide a continuing framework for the legitimate exercise of governmental power and, when joined by a *Bill* or a *Charter of Rights*, for the unremitting protection of individual rights and liberties. Once enacted, its provisions cannot easily be repealed or amended. It must, therefore, be capable of growth and development over time to meet new social, political and historical realities often unimagined by its framers.

---

5 D. Gibson, *The Law of the Charter: General Principles* (Toronto: Carswell, 1986) at 47 (hereinafter Gibson, *The Law of the Charter*).

6 D. Gibson, Chapter 2 "Interpretation of the Canadian Charter of Rights and Freedoms: Some General Considerations", in W.S. Tarnopolsky & G.-A. Beaudoin, eds., *The Canadian Charter of Rights and Freedoms* (Toronto: Carswell, 1982) at 25.

7 1867 (U.K.), 30 & 31 Vict., c. 3.

The judiciary is the guardian of the constitution and must, in interpreting its provisions, bear these considerations in mind. Professor Paul Freund expressed this idea aptly when he admonished the American courts "not to read the provisions of the Constitution like a last will and testament lest it become one".[8]

This description of the importance of the legal status of the Charter has already become a guiding principle of interpretation.

In *Hunter v. Southam*,[9] Dickson J. identified the elements of a "purposive" approach and he applied this to the Charter as a whole, as well as to the specific right relied on in the case. In relation to the Charter as a purposive document, he said:

> Its purpose is to guarantee and to protect, within the limits of reason, the enjoyment of the rights and freedoms it enshrines. It is intended to constrain governmental action inconsistent with those rights and freedoms; it is not in itself an authorization for governmental action.[10]

A more common and equally important application of the purposive approach to Charter interpretation is in the definition of the scope and content of a substantive right or freedom. In *Hunter v. Southam*, Dickson J. stated that it "is first necessary to specify the purpose underlying s. 8: in other words, to delineate the nature of the interests it is meant to protect".[11]

In order to understand the nature of this purposive analysis, it is necessary to recall that the Supreme Court has sanctioned a two-stage process of analysis for the application of the Charter in a specific case: at the first stage one must define the right or freedom involved in the case, and determine whether it has been infringed or abrogated; at the second stage one must determine whether the "limit" on the right or freedom meets the section 1 standard.[12] Although the purposive approach can be employed at both stages of analysis,[13] this chapter will focus upon the first stage, in which the scope and content of the right is determined.

The actual technique involved in applying the purposive approach has been elaborated upon by Dickson J. in *R. v. Big M Drug Mart*.

---

8 [1984] 2 S.C.R. 145 at 155; see also *L.S.U.C. v. Skapinker*, [1984] 1 S.C.R. 357 at 366.

9 *Ibid.*

10 *Ibid.* at 156.

11 *Ibid.* at 157.

12 See, *e.g.*, *R. v. Oakes*, [1986] 1 S.C.R. 103 at 134, where Dickson C.J.C. states: "To my mind it is highly desirable to keep s. 1 and s. 11(*d*) analytically distinct". See also P.W. Hogg, *Constitutional Law of Canada*, 2nd ed. (Toronto: Carswell, 1985), and *Que. Assn. of Protestant School Bds. v. A.G. Quebec*, [1984] 2 S.C.R. 66.

13 See, *e.g.*, *R. v. Oakes, ibid.*; *Black v. Law Soc. of Alta.*, [1986] 3 W.W.R. 590 (Alta. C.A.), leave to appeal to S.C.C. granted (1986), 69 N.R. 319n (S.C.C.).

> In my view this analysis is to be undertaken, and the purpose of the right or freedom in question is to be sought by reference to the character and the larger objects of the *Charter* itself, to the language chosen to articulate the specific right or freedom, to the historical origins of the concepts enshrined, and where applicable, to the meaning and purpose of the other specific rights and freedoms with which it is associated within the text of the *Charter*.[14]

The "character and larger objects of the Charter" were described by Dickson J. in the passage from *Hunter v. Southam* quoted earlier.[15] In another case, Mr. Justice Estey stated that the enactment of the Charter, as part of the *Constitution Act, 1982*, added a "new dimension" to constitutional interpretation; it provided "a new yardstick of reconciliation between the individual and the community and their respective rights, a dimension which, like the balance of the Constitution, remains to be interpreted and applied by the Court".[16]

An obvious starting point for any interpretation of writing are the words themselves. The Charter, as a constitutional guarantee of rights, is replete with "vague but meaningful generalities". This is not the result of a drafting error or lack of vision; indeed it is required by the very character and purpose of the enterprise. While the interpretation of the Charter must involve more than merely parsing over the words, and though the boundaries of interpretive creativity may shift depending upon the requirements of the situation, at some point the words actually employed to articulate the specific right or freedom must be respected. If a literal reading of the provision "defeats the nature and purpose of the section and furthermore leads to absurdity" and the words used are not absolutely intractable, then the interpretation which gives effect to the underlying values enshrined in the right or freedom should be chosen, even if it requires a departure from the literal reading.[17] Otherwise the words chosen must be adhered to; in the words of Mr. Justice Lamer: "We must, as a general rule, be loath to exchange the terms actually used with terms so obviously avoided."[18]

The purposive approach also requires an examination of "the historical origins of the concepts enshrined". This has been done in countless cases involving Charter claims, and eventually it may be expected to produce an accepted "orthodoxy" as to the antecedents of the rights or freedoms enshrined in the document. The dangers inherent in this use of history are obvious to anyone familiar with the "frozen concepts" approach that

---

14 *Supra*, note 4 at 344.
15 *Supra*, note 8.
16 *L.S.U.C. v. Skapinker, supra*, note 8 at 366.
17 *Dubois v. R.*, [1985] 2 S.C.R. 350 at 363.
18 *Reference re s. 94(2) of the Motor Vehicle Act (B.C.)*, [1985] 2 S.C.R. 486 at 503.

developed in cases involving the *Canadian Bill of Rights*.[19] Clearly this reference to "historical origins" was not intended to freeze the scope or content of the rights or freedoms, nor was it intended to sanctify the limits that were previously placed upon them. Its purpose is clarified by a close examination of the phrase, and by examining what judges have actually done.

The first point to note is that what is called for is an examination of the historical *origins* of the *concepts*. The purpose of the inquiry is to glean from the historical context the values underlying a right or freedom, and from that to "pour content" into it, in order to determine its meaning or scope. This does not require an analysis merely of specific enactments or judgments which are pertinent to a right or freedom; instead a purposive approach requires that the origins of a right or freedom in Canadian, British or (more broadly) western legal traditions be examined in order to provide an understanding of the *concept* embodied in the right or freedom. This is history writ large, and it may require an analysis of legal history and doctrinal antecedents, as well as an examination of broader social or political history.[20] This description amply demonstrates that this reference to "historical origins" is not intended to re-introduce the sterility of interpretation created by a "frozen concepts" approach; rather it seeks to draw inspiration and guidance from our legal tradition in order to place the rights and freedoms guaranteed by the Charter in their proper context. As in so many other areas of Canadian law, many of these concepts derive considerable legitimacy from their antiquity.

In some cases, the content of a particular right or freedom may be determined with reference to the other rights or freedoms with which it is associated in the Charter. This is distinct from the use of the special interpretive sections in the Charter (sections 25-29) as aids, because these sections are not "associated with" any particular provision: they can apply, in appropriate factual circumstances, to any Charter right or freedom.[21] Instead, this approach requires that the Charter be viewed as a whole, so that the scope or content of a particular right or freedom is consonant with, and in part derived from, similar guarantees, which will usually be

---

19 See W.S. Tarnopolsky, "A New Bill of Rights in Light of the Interpretation of the Present One by the Supreme Court of Canada", [1978] *L.S.U.C. Special Lectures* 161.

20 See D.M. Paciocco, *Charter Principles and Proof in Criminal Cases* (Toronto: Carswell, 1987), c. 2. This gives rise to another danger — one that many lawyers are familiar with: just as political scientists and other "social scientists" are apt to do bad legal analysis, so it seems that lawyers and judges are apt to do bad historical analysis.

21 These interpretation provisions are discussed more fully below.

found under the same heading in the Charter.[22] Several decisions provide examples of this aspect of a purposive approach.

In *Dubois v. R.*,[23] the court interpreted the words "any other proceedings" in section 13 with reference to the due process guarantees in section 11(c) and (d). The accused in the case was convicted of second degree murder at his original trial, but the conviction was overturned on appeal. At the second trial, the Crown sought to introduce his testimony from the earlier trial, but an objection was raised based on section 13. Mr. Justice Lamer interpreted the specific protection against self-incrimination in section 13 in light of two "closely related rights": the right of non-compellability (section 11(c)) and the presumption of innocence (section 11(d)).[24] He found that the concept of a "case to meet" is a common underlying feature of all three provisions, and therefore he ruled that the purpose of section 13 would be defeated if it did not apply to the introduction of previous testimony at a second trial. The other provisions are relevant according to Lamer J., because "[o]ur constitutional Charter must be construed as a system where 'Every component contributes to the meaning as a whole, and the whole gives meaning to its parts'".[25]

A similar approach to the interpretation of section 7 was employed by Lamer J. in *Reference Re Section 94(2) of the Motor Vehicle Act (B.C.)*,[26] in which he interpreted sections 8 to 14 as specific illustrations of the more general concepts expressed in section 7. According to this decision, sections 8 to 14 "address specific deprivations of the 'right' to life, liberty and security of the person in breach of the principles of fundamental justice . . . [and these provisions are] designed to protect, in a specific manner and setting, the right to life, liberty and security of the person set forth in s. 7".[27] This description of the relationship between the legal rights provisions is in accordance with the legislative history,[28] although this is not referred to by Mr. Justice Lamer. Instead, he grounds his analysis in the "purposive" approach established by the decisions previously discussed: he describes it as "textual and contextual analyses".[29]

---

22 See *Reference re Education Act (Ont.) and Minority Language Rights* (1984), 10 D.L.R. (4th) 491 at 528 (Ont. C.A.), where s. 23 (language) was interpreted in light of s. 15 (equality).

23 *Supra*, note 17.

24 *Ibid.* at 356.

25 *Ibid.* at 365, quoting P.A. Côté, *The Interpretation of Legislation in Canada* (Cowansville, P.Q.: Yvon Blais, 1984) at 236.

26 *Supra*, note 18.

27 *Ibid.* at 502.

28 R. Elliot, "Interpreting the Charter — Use of the Earlier Versions as an Aid", [1982] *U.B.C.L. Rev.* (Charter ed.) at 11.

29 *Supra*, note 18 at 512.

In her concurring judgment, Wilson J. discounts the relevance of sections 8 to 14 for the interpretation of the phrase "principles of fundamental justice" in section 7, but she goes on to state that she "find[s] them very helpful as illustrating facets of the right to life, liberty and security of the person."[30] From this judgment and others,[31] it is evident that the court is unanimously of the view that each Charter provision is to be interpreted in the context of other (associated) sections. Although views diverge about which precise provisions are relevant, and about the actual interpretive guidance which they provide, the general principle is well accepted.

This discussion of the "purposive" approach has focussed on the technical aspects of how it is done, but the real significance of this doctrine can only be understood by reference to its broader implications. Since the enactment of the Charter, there has been no doubt that its interpretation poses a unique challenge: the nature of the document, the way in which its provisions are framed, the nature of the issues raised pursuant to it and the public interest in the decisions have combined to create a new challenge for Canadian lawyers, judges and others. There are many ways to describe the type of judgment called for in Charter interpretation; Professor Gibson has labelled it "judicial statesmanship", and he describes it in the following way:

> By "statesmanship" is meant an appreciation by the court of the effect each of its constitutional interpretations will have on the way life is lived in Canada, and a conscious attempt to favour those interpretations most likely to have beneficial impact. An understanding of the priorities Canadians have historically assigned to various social, political and economic values is imperative, but so is a willingness to abandon traditional solutions that have ceased to serve long-term needs. The task is political, in the best sense, but not partisan; each judge properly takes cognizance of the priority assigned to particular societal values by his or her political philosophy (they cannot realistically avoid doing so), but not of the tactical or strategic interests of political parties.[32]

The purposive approach requires a distillation of the underlying values that a specific right or freedom is meant to protect, and an analysis of principles drawn from our legal system, or from our broader historical tradition, which reflect these values in order to ensure that the purpose for the right or freedom is advanced by the interpretation adopted. All of this must be done with a sense of the "political" (or social, moral,

---

30 *Ibid.* at 530.

31 See also *R. v. Therens*, [1985] 1 S.C.R. 613; *Société des Acadiens du Nouveau-Brunswick Inc.* v. *Assn. of Parents for Fairness in Education, Grand Falls Dist. 50 Branch*, [1986] 1 S.C.R. 549.

32 Gibson, *The Law of the Charter, supra*, note 5 at 47.

economic, etc.) implications of the decision, and it must incorporate the forward-looking view which is appropriate for constitutional adjudication. For obvious reasons, there is no easy way to describe this task.

(b) The Stages of Analysis

As mentioned earlier, the Supreme Court has sanctioned a two-stage approach to Charter analysis: at stage one the scope and content of the right or freedom is defined, and at stage two the section 1 standards concerning reasonable limits are applied. This distinction was most emphatically stated in *R. v. Oakes*,[33] where Dickson C.J.C. stated, in relation to the presumption of innocence guarantee in section 11(d):

> At the Court of Appeal level in the present case, Martin J.A. sought to combine the analysis of s. 11(*d*) and s. 1 to overcome the limitations of the *Canadian Bill of Rights* jurisprudence. To my mind, it is highly desirable to keep s. 1 and s. 11(*d*) analytically distinct. Separating the analysis into two components is consistent with the approach this Court has taken to the Charter to date . . .[34]

In several other cases the Supreme Court has applied this two-stage analysis, and it is submitted that this is the only method of giving proper effect to section 1 of the Charter. It also offers a means by which a uniquely Canadian jurisprudence of rights can be created.

Some Charter provisions are stated in absolute terms, such as section 2(a), (b) and (d), and these lend themselves to the two-stage analysis just described. Other provisions contain internal limitations, such as section 2(c) (peaceful assembly), section 8 (unreasonable search or seizure), section 9 (arbitrarily detained or imprisoned). These sections do not easily fit into this two-stage approach, because the provision itself contemplates some limitation or qualification on the scope of the right. For the provisions that are stated in absolute terms, however, it is submitted that this two-stage analysis is a vital ingredient in properly applying a purposive approach.

An excellent illustration of the danger of departing from this approach is the decision of the Ontario Court of Appeal in *R. v. Zundel*,[35] in which the prohibition of publishing false news was alleged to violate the freedom of expression guaranteed in section 2(b), a guarantee which is expressed in absolute terms. After examining the various rationales that support free expression, such as the promotion of democracy, the enhancement of our ability to achieve truth and the promotion of self-fulfillment, the court stated:

---

33 *Supra*, note 12.
34 *Ibid.* at 134.
35 (1987), 31 C.C.C. (3d) 97 (Ont. C.A.), leave to appeal to S.C.C. refused (1987), 23 O.A.C. 317n (S.C.C.).

The nub of the offence in s. 177 is the wilful publication of assertions of a fact or facts which are false to the knowledge of the person who publishes them, and which cause or are likely to cause injury or mischief to a public interest. It is difficult to see how much conduct would fall within any of the previously expressed *rationales* for guaranteeing freedom of expression. Spreading falsehoods knowingly is the antithesis of seeking truth through the free exchange of ideas. It would appear to have no social or moral value which would merit constitutional protection. Nor would it aid the working of parliamentary democracy or further self-fulfilment. In our opinion an offence falling within the ambit of s. 177 lies within the permissibly regulated area which is not constitutionally protected. It does not come within the residue which comprises freedom of expression guaranteed by s. 2(*b*) of the Charter.[36]

It is submitted that this analysis does not properly apply the two-stage approach to this case. It is difficult to understand how a law which prohibits certain oral or written statements of opinion or fact does not *prima facie* contravene the freedom of expression guarantee in section 2(b). Without entering too deeply into the area, which is the subject of another chapter, it is submitted that this judgment improperly intermingled the two stages of analysis. Although the analysis of the values underlying freedom of expression is enlightening, its application to the facts is not compelling because the court adopts a restrictive, content-based approach to sanction prior restraint of expressive activity without adequately defining the scope of freedom of expression.

The advantage of the two-stage approach is that the different concerns and factors which are, or ought to be, relevant to the two stages of the case are kept separate and distinct. One can pour content into the ample words of the substantive guarantees, and thus give effect to the presumed intention of the drafters, without fearing that this will protect the right or freedom in an absolute or inflexible way, because at the second stage of analysis the issue of "reasonable limits" will be addressed. At that stage of analysis, the reasons for limiting or restricting the right or freedom thus defined must then be articulated. In this respect, the Charter is unique, and this advantage must be utilized, in appropriate cases, if the purposive approach is to be meaningful.

(c) Individual and Collective Rights

The *Charter of Rights* contains both individual and collective rights guarantees.[37] Among the host of difficulties posed by this dichotomy, one basic question stands out: is the purposive approach applicable to both

---

36 *Ibid.* at 123.
37 *E.g.*, ss. 2, 7-15, 23, 25, 27.

types of rights or is it only appropriate for cases involving individual rights? As a matter of logic and principle, there is no basis for distinguishing between the interpretive approaches which are appropriate for these categories of rights. However, in *Société des Acadiens du Nouveau-Brunswick Inc. v. Association of Parents for Fairness in Education*,[38] Mr. Justice Beetz[39] introduced the possibility of a different approach to the interpretation of different categories of rights.

In this case the court was asked to determine whether the language-right guarantee in section 19(2), which provides that either English or French may be used in any court in New Brunswick, included a right to be heard by a judge who is bilingual. Mr. Justice Beetz stated that this language right (which he equated with the guarantee contained in section 133 of the *Constitution Act, 1867*) was not to be confused with the broader and more fundamental right of any party to a proceeding to be understood by the court and to understand what is going on in the court. This broader right, as an aspect of the right to a fair hearing, "belongs to the category of rights which in the *Charter* are designated as legal rights . . . ",[40] and according to Beetz J., although both legal rights and language rights "belong to the category of fundamental rights", they are "conceptually distinct".[41] The essence of this conceptual distinction, and its implications, are explained in the following passage:

> Unlike language rights which are based on political compromise, legal rights tend to be seminal in nature because they are rooted in principle. Some of them, such as the one expressed in s. 7 of the *Charter*, are so broad as to call for frequent judicial determination.
>
> Language rights, on the other hand, although some of them have been enlarged and incorporated into the *Charter*, remain nonetheless founded on political compromise.
>
> This essential difference between the two types of rights dictates a distinct judicial approach with respect to each. More particularly, the courts should pause before they decide to act as instruments of change with respect to language rights. This is not to say that language rights provisions are cast in stone and should remain immune altogether from judicial interpretation. But, in my opinion, the courts should approach them with more restraint than they would in construing legal rights.[42]

Language rights are collective rights, according to the prevailing view

---

38 *Supra*, note 31.

39 Estey, Chouinard, Lamer and Le Dain JJ. concurring (Dickson C.J.C. and Wilson J. wrote dissenting opinions).

40 *Société des Acadiens, supra*, note 31 at 577.

41 *Ibid.* at 578.

42 *Ibid.* at 578.

in Canada.[43] Although Beetz J. does not use this label in the foregoing passage, he does explicitly distinguish between legal rights which are undoubtedly individual rights, and language rights, which are not "seminal in nature" or "rooted in principle", but rather are "based on political compromise". Either Beetz J. intends to categorize the Charter's guarantees according to the heading under which they are found,[44] or he intends to draw a broader distinction between individual and collective rights. If the latter approach finds favour in the courts, it is submitted that a significant and uniquely Canadian aspect of the Constitution will be undermined. This is neither necessary nor desirable; collective rights guarantees should be interpreted and enforced as vigorously and expansively as individual rights, at least at the first stage of inquiry when their scope and content is determined. The purposive approach is one means of achieving such an interpretation, and it is submitted that this judgment does not offer a persuasive analysis in support of the conclusion that different interpretive approaches are required.

The key point of distinction between language rights and legal rights mentioned in the judgment is that legal rights are "seminal" and "rooted in principle", while language rights are "based on political compromise". It is submitted that this is an inadequate reason to differentiate between these categories because language rights are, in the Canadian constitutional tradition, at least as "seminal" as legal rights. Indeed, specific language-rights provisions, as a fundamental part of the original Confederation bargain, were explicitly enshrined in the Constitution long before individual legal rights attained that status.[45]

Similarly, although it may be factually correct to state that the specific language-rights provisions contained in the Charter were the product of political compromise, that is also true of the legal rights, equality rights and other provisions.[46] More fundamentally, it is unclear why the bargaining process which preceded the enactment of any provision in the Constitution should affect its subsequent interpretation by the courts. Surely the drafters knew that, whatever the result of their work, the words would be interpreted and applied by the courts.

It is also difficult to understand why language rights, even if they were the subject of political debate and compromise during the enactment

---

43 P. Carignan, "De la notion de droit collectif et de son application en matière scolaire au Québec" (1984), 18 *R.J.T.* 1; J.E. Magnet, "The Charter's Official Languages Provisions: The Implications of Entrenched Bilingualism" (1982), 4 *Sup. Ct. L. Rev.* 163.

44 The use of headings is discussed below.

45 *Constitution Act, 1867, supra,* note 7, s. 133.

46 *E.g., Constitution Act, 1982,* s. 6, concerning mobility rights, and ss. 25 and 35, concerning aboriginal peoples' rights.

process, are therefore less "rooted in principle" than legal rights or any other rights. One would think that the simple fact that they were included in the Charter would overcome any doubts as to their juridical or philosophical foundations, and there is certainly no *a priori* reason to distinguish between these categories of rights as a matter of legal philosophy.

If this reasoning is to be the foundation for a basic shift in interpretive approach, it will introduce a radically new element into Charter analysis, which may be expected to affect virtually all aspects of the document, since a careful examination of the legislative history of the Charter will reveal that most of it is the product of some "political compromise". This approach to Charter interpretation should be rejected, it is respectfully submitted, because it introduces an unnecessary and unwarranted distinction between categories of rights — a distinction which has neither textual nor logical support, and which has the potential to significantly reduce the scope and effectiveness of many fundamental guarantees in the Charter.[47]

An early indication that the distinction suggested by Beetz J. will not undermine the effectiveness of collective rights guarantees is contained in the decision of Madam Justice Wilson in *Reference re Bill 30 An Act to amend the Education Act (Ontario)*.[48] After quoting the pertinent parts of the judgment of Beetz J. in the *Société des Acadiens* case, she continued:

> While due regard must be paid not to give a provision which reflects a political compromise too wide an interpretation, it must still be one to the Court to breathe life into a compromise that is clearly expressed.[49]

In this judgment, Wilson J. applied a purposive approach to the interpretation of section 93 of the *Constitution Act, 1867*, which is a collective rights guarantee, and it thus appears that the court, though mindful of the cautionary words of Beetz J., does not regard them as foreclosing this approach.

(d) Purpose or Effect?

Canadian courts have considered both the purpose or intent of legislation and its effect in constitutional cases concerning division of powers and related matters, although the practice has not been entirely

---

47 See the text accompanying note 46, *supra*.
48 [1987] 1 S.C.R. 1148.
49 *Ibid.* at 1176.

uniform.[50] In non-constitutional cases, courts have traditionally referred to the intention or purpose of the legislature when interpreting a statute, but this approach has been criticized for many years.[51] For Charter interpretation, the relevance of both the purpose and the effect of legislation is now firmly established; only the proper order of analysis remains somewhat unsettled.

The first Supreme Court of Canada decision to address the issue was *R. v. Big M Drug Mart*,[52] and the court was unanimously of the view that both purpose and effect of legislation were relevant to the determination of conformity with the Charter. Writing for the majority, Mr. Justice Dickson stated:

> In my view, both purpose and effect are relevant in determining constitutionality; either an unconstitutional purpose or an unconstitutional effect can invalidate legislation. All legislation is animated by an object the legislature intends to achieve. This object is realized through the impact produced by the operation and application of the legislation. Purpose and effect respectively, in the sense of the legislation's object and its ultimate impact, are clearly linked, if not indivisible. Intended and actual effects have often been looked to for guidance in assessing the legislation's object and thus, its validity.
>
> Moreover, consideration of the object of legislation is vital if rights are to be fully protected. The assessment by the courts of legislative purpose focuses scrutiny upon the aims and objectives of the legislature and ensures they are consonant with the guarantees enshrined in the *Charter*. The declaration that certain objects lie outside the legislature's power checks governmental action at the first stage of unconstitutional conduct. Further, it will provide more ready and more vigorous protection of constitutional rights by obviating the individual litigant's need to prove effects violative of *Charter* rights. It will also allow courts to dispose of cases where the object is clearly improper, without inquiring into the legislation's actual impact.[53]

In a concurring decision, Wilson J. agreed with the majority that both purpose and effect are relevant in constitutional adjudication, but she distinguished between division-of-power cases and *Charter* cases. In the opinion of Wilson J., the determination of *vires* in division-of-powers cases should commence with an analysis of legislative purpose, while Charter analysis should begin with an analysis of the effects of the impugned statute.[54] The advantages of such an approach, according to Madam Justice

---

50 Gibson, *The Law of the Charter, supra,* note 5 at 52; W.W. Black, "Intent or Effects: Section 15 of the Charter of Rights and Freedoms", in J.M. Weiler & R.M. Elliot, eds., *Litigating the Values of a Nation: The Canadian Charter of Rights and Freedoms* (Toronto: Carswell, 1986) at 120.

51 For an early trenchant critique, see J.A. Corry, "The Use of Legislative History in the Interpretation of Statutes" (1954), 32 *Can. Bar. Rev.* 624.

52 *Supra*, note 4.

53 *Ibid.* at 331-332.

54 *Ibid.* at 360-362.

Wilson, are that it maintains the distinction between these two categories of "constitutional" cases and that, in respect of Charter cases, it places a less heavy evidentiary burden on the plaintiff. Wilson J. acknowledges the relevance of legislative purpose for the second stage of Charter analysis, in which the section 1 standards are applied.

The actual decision in *R. v. Big M Drug Mart*[55] illustrates the continued relevance of legislative purpose, because the court declared the *Lord's Day Act*[56] invalid because its original purpose, to enforce the Christian Sabbath, was contrary to the guarantee of freedom of conscience and religion in section 2(a) of the Charter. The subsequent decision on Sunday closing laws, *Edwards Books & Art Ltd. v. R.*[57] demonstrates that, although legislation (here the Ontario *Retail Business Holiday Act*)[58] was enacted with a valid purpose (a uniform day of rest), it may still be found to violate a Charter right or freedom if its effect is improper. In this case the legislation was ultimately upheld under section 1, and it should be noted that both the purpose and effect of the law was considered at the second stage of analysis as well. For our analysis, this decision is important as an indication that the discussion of this issue in *R. v. Big M Drug Mart*[59] is the prevailing law.

At a practical and a theoretical level, the reasoning of Wilson J. that supports an effects-oriented approach to Charter analysis is compelling. It places a lower burden on the plaintiff, which is surely appropriate in a Charter case, and it requires the court to focus on the actual impact of the law rather than the admittedly fictional purpose or intent of the legislature. On the other hand, the majority view, that one should examine legislative purpose first and only consider the law's effects if that purpose is found to be valid (in terms of both division of powers and Charter standards), does not diminish the effectiveness of the Charter nor does it impose an impossible burden on the plaintiff. Professor Gibson is probably correct when he states that the "differences between [these two] approaches appear to be minimal".[60] The real importance of these cases is that they allow courts to measure *all* relevant aspects of government action against the standards enunciated in the Charter, and thereby ensure the fullest protection of the rights and freedoms of individuals and groups.

---

55 *Supra*, note 4.
56 R.S.C. 1970, c. L-13.
57 [1986] 2 S.C.R. 713.
58 R.S.O. 1980, c. 453.
59 *Supra*, note 4.
60 Gibson, *The Law of the Charter, supra*, note 5 at 55.

3. PRESUMPTIONS

Prior to the enactment of the Charter, various presumptions were employed as aids in the interpretation of statutes and constitutional documents.[61] These presumptions will not be analyzed in detail here, because it is submitted that most of them simply are not relevant or useful for Charter interpretation. A few presumptions do seem to be relevant because they only apply to constitutional adjudication, or their content is directly on point. Although there is generally no harm in relying on these presumptions as aids in the interpretation of the Charter, it is submitted that most will add little or nothing to the "purposive" approach outlined earlier, and indeed these simple guides seem to be a barren source of inspiration in comparison with that approach. For example, although the presumption that ambiguities should be resolved in favour of the liberty of the subject may buttress a particular interpretation of a Charter provision, it is not as rich a source of guidance as the purposive approach by which the values which underlie that provision can be distilled and protected.

One potentially restrictive presumption which should be discussed because it is often alluded to in Charter cases is the presumption of constitutionality, which has heretofore been employed in division of power cases.[62] This presumption has been employed in pre-Charter cases to place the onus on the party alleging an infringement of the Constitution, and to guide the interpretation of impugned legislation. In division of powers cases, this presumption is a useful and sensible starting point for analysis, although a review of the cases and literature indicates that it is not uniformly applied or accepted.[63] The "onus" aspect of the presumption is applicable to Charter analysis. The case law demonstrates that the initial burden of proving on a balance of probabilities that a Charter right or freedom has been violated lies upon the party making that assertion.[64] This result could easily have been reached without reference to the presumption, based on the structure of the Charter itself, but there is no danger in relying on the presumption for this analysis.

A broader and potentially more damaging application of the presumption is referred to by Professor Hogg:

> It seems . . . that the lack of democratic accountability, coupled with the

---

61 E.A. Driedger, *Construction of Statutes*, 2nd ed. (Toronto: Butterworths, 1983); Côté, *supra*, note 25.

62 J.E. Magnet, "The Presumption of Constitutionality" (1980), 18 *Osgoode Hall L.J.* 87; Hogg, *supra*, note 12.

63 See, for a summary of the various opinions on this point, R.M. McLeod *et al.*, *The Canadian Charter of Rights: Prosecution and Defence of Criminal and Other Statutory Offences* (Toronto: Carswell, looseleaf) at 2-188.

64 See *R. v. Oakes, supra*, note 12; *R. v. Big M Drug Mart, supra*, note 4.

limitations inherent in the adversarial judicial process, dictates that the appropriate posture for the courts in constitutional cases is one of restraint: the legislative decision should always receive the benefit of a reasonable doubt, and should be overriden only where its invalidity is clear. There should be, in other words, a presumption of constitutionality. In this way a proper respect is paid to the legislators, and the danger of covert (albeit unconscious) imposition of judicial policy preferences is minimized.[65]

This use of the doctrine is inappropriate in Charter cases as a general guide to analysis, and it is unfortunate because of its tendency to undermine the legitimacy of vigorous judicial enforcement of these entrenched guarantees. Perhaps it is appropriate to approach certain aspects of Charter analysis with an attitude of restraint and deference to legislatures. For example, in devising a remedy for a violation, a judge should be reluctant to rewrite provisions in legislation or otherwise replace the legislature. However, as a general principle, to be applied at the first stage of analysis, it is submitted that this use of the presumption of constitutionality is unacceptable.

Earlier in this article the "political" aspects of Charter interpretation were described. Further discussion of this theme is beyond the scope of this article. The "political" aspect of the presumption of constitutionality is an alluring means of escape from the challenges posed by the Charter; one can seek refuge from expansive and troubling interpretations of particular rights or freedoms by relying on this attitude of restraint which supposedly arises from the separation of powers between the legislative, executive and judicial branches.

The enactment of the Charter forever altered the relationship between the judiciary and the other branches of government, and the political aspects of the presumption of constitutionality harkens back to a time before the Charter when Canadian judges were mainly concerned with disputes between federal and provincial governments. In the context of the Charter, which guarantees certain rights and freedoms and prescribes the only acceptable means by which these may be limited (section 1) or overridden (section 33), the courts are called upon to protect these guarantees against legislative or executive infringement. In this process, the previous attitude of restraint towards legislatures should generally be replaced by a neutral point of view which favours the rights and liberties of individuals and groups as much as it respects the acts of the state. Only in this way can the Charter's guarantees be interpreted in an appropriate manner. This branch of the presumption of constitutionality developed when the Canadian political structure was founded on two fundamental pillars: democracy and parliamentary supremacy. To this has been added a third,

---

65 Hogg, *supra*, note 12 at 99-100.

equally vital, pillar: the *Charter of Rights and Freedoms*.[66] The phraseology employed in the Charter and the *Constitution Act, 1982*, especially sections 1 and 24(1) of the former, and section 52 of the latter, provides no support for the use of the presumption to dictate for the courts a posture of restraint. Indeed, these provisions combine with the stature and context of the document to dictate an interpretation and application of the Charter which favours the rights of individuals and groups. As a guiding principle, the presumption of constitutionality is not appropriate for Charter interpretation; it has been replaced by the purposive approach, at least at the first stage of analysis when the scope and content of the right or freedom is defined.

4. INTERNAL AIDS

(a) French and English Versions

Section 57 of the *Constitution Act, 1982* states that "the English and French versions of this Act are equally authoritative". This provision embodies a rule of long standing in Canadian law,[67] and it provides a unique internal aid in the interpretation of certain Charter provisions. Most sections of the Charter are identical in both versions, and although the secondary definition of a word in one or the other language may illuminate the meaning or scope of the section, resort to the other official version will usually not prove helpful. Some provisions are not identical, however, and reference to the other language offers a means of clarifying and defining the scope of these sections.[68] In this respect one must, to some extent, rely on section 57 to validate the interpretation which is ultimately arrived at, since that section gives equal authority to both versions of the Charter. At the same time it must be admitted that this provision poses an interpretive challenge, since a choice of meaning based on the words expressed in *one* language will obviously reduce or expand the words used in the other language. To this extent, both versions are *not* authoritative and the strict terms of section 57 are therefore not respected. As a practical matter, this result cannot be avoided when the two versions are not identical and strict reliance on section 57 would deprive courts of a useful and valid source of guidance for interpretation.

One can utilize section 57 to support the argument that variations

---

66 See R.I. Cheffins & P.A. Johnson, *The Revised Canadian Constitution: Politics as Law* (Toronto: McGraw-Hill Ryerson, 1986); K.G. Banting & R. Simeon, eds., *And No One Cherred: Federalism, Democracy & the Constitution Act* (Toronto: Methuen, 1983).

67 R. Beaupré, *Interpreting Bilingual Legislation*, 2nd ed. (Toronto: Carswell, 1986).

68 A. Gautron, "French/English Discrepancies in the Canadian Charter of Rights and Freedoms" (1982), 12 *Man. L.J.* 220.

in the two texts should always be resolved by giving effect to the meaning which is common to both versions. This would always be the narrower of the two meanings: the "lowest common denominator". This is an accepted means of construing bilingual statutes in Canada,[69] and it has been referred to in Charter cases as well.[70]

Another reading of section 57 supports the argument that "[f]or both versions to be *equally* authoritative, the goal of such interpretation for the courts must be a reconciliation of the differences into a common understanding of the Charter".[71] This approach presumptively favours neither the broader nor the narrower version of the text. Instead it seeks to give effect to whichever one better reflects the intention and purpose of the provision. This use of the French and English versions of the Charter (which is the proper one, it is submitted) extends the purposive approach in an appropriate way. It offers the best means of using the two official texts as interpretive aids, while avoiding an inflexible, *a priori* rule which may needlessly diminish the scope of a provision in the Charter.

This approach was adopted by Lamer J. in *Collins v. R.*,[72] in which the most notorious discrepancy between the French and English texts was addressed. The case involved an argument that evidence obtained pursuant to an unreasonable search should be excluded under section 24(2). The English text requires exclusion of improperly obtained evidence if it is established that its admission "*would* bring the administration of justice into disrepute" (emphasis added). The French version provides for exclusion if admission "*est susceptible* de déconsidérer l'administration de la justice" (emphasis added). The key word in the French text is generally translated as "could" rather than "would", and this is the meaning given to the word in Mr. Justice Lamer's decision. In reaching this conclusion, he explicitly adopted a purposive approach:

> As one of the purposes of s. 24(2) is to protect the right to a fair trial, I would favour the interpretation of s. 24(2) which better protects that right, the less onerous French text.[73]

Although the adoption of this definition on its face appears to depart from the clear words of the English text, it is submitted that this is an inevitable, and indeed desirable, consequence of the equal validity of the English and French versions. A purposive approach is a more suitable means of discovering the appropriate definition of the words, and it is far more

---

69 See Beaupré, *supra*, note 67; Côté, *supra*, note 25.

70 See *R. v. MacIntyre* (1982), 69 C.C.C. (2d) 162 at 165 (Alta. Q.B.).

71 McLeod *et al.*, *supra*, note 63 at 2-66.

72 [1987] 1 S.C.R. 265; see also *Reference re Education Act (Ont.) and Minority Language Rights*, *supra*, note 22.

73 *Collins v. R.*, *ibid.* at 287.

consistent with the general approach to constitutional interpretation than is the alternative, which resembles the mechanical application of an *a priori* rule.

The equal validity of the French and English texts of the Charter presents a unique interpretive opportunity; in the words of the leading Canadian authority on the interpretation of bilingual statutes:

> With a bilingual literal context, one has the luxury of an additional authentic benchmark by which to appreciate the real intention of the constitutional legislator.[74]

When the other constitutional texts are enacted in bilingual form,[75] the challenges discussed here will be faced in all aspects of this branch of the law. A purposive approach is a flexible and intelligent method of utilizing both versions of the Constitution as an interpretive aid, which can be applied both to the Charter and other parts of the Constitution.

(b) Interpretation Sections (Sections 25-29)

The Charter contains several explicit interpretation sections which can be resorted to as aids in the construction of any of the substantive guarantees. These sections are interpretive guides rather than independently enforceable guarantees,[76] but their importance is not therefore diminished because they add a unique Canadian dimension to Charter interpretation. In order to apply these sections properly, one must situate them within the structure of the Charter and then examine the precise terms of each section.

The structure of the Charter supports the analysis of these provisions as interpretive guides, and it lends credence to the view that they are intended to operate in a basically similar way within Charter analysis. These sections are grouped under a single heading (General),[77] which is separate from the substantive guarantees. All these sections apply with reference to other rights or freedoms; they do not stand alone either as merely symbolic statements[78] or as independently enforceable guarantees.

The interpretive provisions in the Charter do not share identical wording, and they obviously pertain to different rights and interests. Despite this, it is submitted that sections 25, 26, 27 and 29 are intended to operate

---

74 See Beaupré, *supra*, note 67 at 207.

75 As required by s. 55 of the *Constitution Act, 1982*. A draft translation was submitted to the Minister of Justice on November 18, 1986.

76 *Boudreau v. Lynch* (1984), 16 D.L.R. (4th) 610 (N.S.C.A.).

77 The use of headings as interpretive aids is discussed below.

78 Although these provisions are undoubtedly of symbolic importance, they are of substantive value as well.

in a similar fashion in the Charter. It is submitted that section 28 falls within this classification as well, although its unique wording may lead to a separate manner of application. As well, section 27 provides a more "active" or substantive protection than the other sections, in that it provides for both the "protection" and the "enhancement" of the interests it protects.[79] Section 21 is another interpretive provision, but by its very terms it applies only with respect to sections 16 to 20.

These interpretive provisions operate, it is submitted, as a prism. The scope, content and operation of the rights and freedoms guaranteed by the Charter will differ depending on whether the factual circumstances trigger an interpretive section. If, for example, an equality rights claim involves a treaty right respecting an Indian, the section 25 interpretive "prism" will operate so as to alter the scope or content of the section 15 equality right. Without section 25, the equality claim could be resolved by applying the principles which ordinarily affect such cases.[80] Different principles must apply once section 25 comes into play, for otherwise the section would be meaningless.

The "prism" effect of each interpretive provision will depend on the particular phraseology employed. Section 25 states that, in giving effect to the rights and freedoms contained in the Charter, a court must construe these guarantees "so as not to abrogate or derogate from" the rights of the aboriginal peoples of Canada. Of the other interpretive provisions, only sections 21 and 29 employ the words "abrogate" and "derogate". Section 26 provides only that Charter guarantees do not "deny the existence of" other rights or freedoms, and this wording was also contained in an earlier version of section 25 (September 1980). Section 27 requires an interpretation of the Charter which is "consistent with the preservation and enhancement of the multicultural heritage of Canadians".

An examination of the case law indicates that the view of the function of the interpretive provisions presented here has been accepted and applied by the courts. The meaning and scope of the substantive guarantees contained in other Charter sections have changed when the "prism" effect of the interpretive provisions has been triggered.

The freedom of religion guarantee in section 2(a) of the Charter provides a useful example of this trend. In *R. v. Videoflicks Ltd.*,[81] several retailers challenged the validity of the "day of rest" provision of the Ontario

---

79 See, for a more complete discussion of s. 27, J.E. Magnet, Chapter 18 "Multiculturalism and Collective Rights", *infra*.

80 See, *e.g.*, M. Gold, "A Principled Approach to Equality Rights: A Preliminary Inquiry" (1982), 4 *Sup. Ct. L. Rev.* 131; and see W. Black & L. Smith, Chapter 14 "Equality Rights", *infra*.

81 (1984), 48 O.R. (2d) 395 (C.A.), rev'd in part (*sub nom. Edwards Books & Art Ltd. v. R.*), *supra*, note 57.

Retail Business Holiday Act[82] as a violation of section 2(a) of the Charter. In support of the conclusion that the guarantee of freedom of religion extends to the effects of a law upon the practice of one's religion, and that a law which had the effect of making the practice of one's religion more difficult or costly infringes that freedom, Tarnopolsky J.A. referred to section 27:

> Finally, I draw support for my conclusions, both as to the meaning of freedom of religion under the Charter and as to the distinction between that freedom and its interpretation under the United States *Bill of Rights* from a provision which has no counterpart in the American Constitution, namely s. 27 of the Charter. . . .
> It is not for the courts to express their opinion concerning the justification for this constitutional entrenchment of a policy of pluralistic cultural preservation and enhancement. Nor should the courts avoid giving it any significance. It is merely our duty to try to define how the Charter "shall be interpreted" in light of this provision. . . .
> It is thus the clear purpose of s. 27 that, where applicable, any right or freedom in the Charter shall be interpreted in light of this section.[83]

Similarly, in *R. v. Big M Drug Mart*,[84] Dickson C.J.C. referred to section 27 in support of the conclusion that the prohibition of Sunday commerce in the *Lord's Day Act*[85] violated section 2(a) of the Charter. In his judgment, Chief Justice Dickson stated that "to accept that Parliament retains the right to compel universal observance of the day of rest preferred by one religion is not consistent with the preservation and enhancement of the multicultural heritage of Canadians."[86]

In both these decisions, judges have departed from previous Canadian and American interpretations of the phrase "freedom of religion", partly in order to give effect to the command in section 27 to interpret the Charter so as to preserve and enhance the multicultural heritage of Canadians. The same result *might* have been reached in both cases without the interpretive guidance of section 27, but the provision guided the analysis and buttressed the conclusion.

A similar application of section 27 occurred in the *Ontario Education Act Reference*,[87] in which the guarantee in section 23 of minority language educational facilities was interpreted to mean that the linguistic minorities were entitled to manage and control their schools, in part because this

---

82 *Supra*, note 58.

83 *Supra*, note 81 at 426-427.

84 *Supra*, note 4. See also *R. v. Keegstra* (1984), 19 C.C.C. (3d) 254 (Alta. Q.B.).

85 *Supra*, note 56.

86 *Supra*, note 4 at 337-338; see, to the same effect, *R. v. W.H. Smith*, [1983] 5 W.W.R. 235 (Alta. Prov. Ct.).

87 *Supra*, note 22.

was the only means of harmonizing sections 23 and 27. In the words of the Court of Appeal:

> In the light of s. 27, s. 23(3)(*b*) should be interpreted to mean that minority language children must receive their instruction in facilities in which the educational environment will be that of the linguistic minority. Only then can the facilities reasonably be said to reflect the minority culture and appertain to the minority.[88]

Guidance on this matter also arises out of the issue of the preservation of denominational school privileges in section 29 of the Charter. In the *Ontario Education Act Reference*,[89] the Ontario Court of Appeal considered, *inter alia*, whether the scope and operation of the guarantee respecting minority language education rights in section 23 of the Charter was modified by section 29.[90] The court concluded that, as the terms of section 23 draw no distinction between denominational and non-denominational education, and since the rights protected by section 29 are those contained in section 93 of the *Constitution Act, 1867*, namely the rights and privileges of denominational schools, which do not include linguistic rights, therefore there was no need to modify section 23. The analysis of the court in this judgment is a clear indication of acceptance of the "prism" effect of these provisions. In the particular circumstances of the case, the interpretive provision did not affect the substantive guarantee, but the process of analysis reveals that it might have done so. After an analysis of the scope of section 93 as determined by prior case law, the court stated:

> Before the advent of the Charter, the province's power over education was plenary; with respect to the separate schools, its power was limited only to the extent provided in s. 93. Manifestly, s. 23 of the Charter imposes a further limitation, applicable to both public and denominational education, on the province's power to legislate in relation to education. Now, the constitutional right to minority language education created by s. 23 must be given effect — save only in so far as the exercise of that right conflicts with the denominational rights protected by s. 93 of the *Constitution Act, 1867* and reinforced by s. 29 of the Charter.[91]

Section 29 played an even more important role in the resolution of the issue of whether the extension of separate school funding violated other constitutional guarantees, in *Reference re an Act to amend the Education Act (Ontario)*.[92] The majority judgment[93] concluded that this was not a

---

88 *Ibid.* at 529.

89 *Ibid.*

90 *Ibid.* at 533 *et seq.*

91 *Ibid.* at 539.

92 (1986), 53 O.R. (2d) 513 (C.A.), aff'd (*sub nom. Reference re Bill 30, An Act to amend the Education Act*), *supra*, note 48].

93 Zuber, Cory and Tarnopolsky JJ.A.

constitutional violation, and this conclusion is supported mainly by a detailed analysis of the terms and prior versions of section 29. In this case, section 29 served to shield a bill dealing with denominational education, which was passed under the provincial authority in respect of education, from the Charter guarantees of freedom of religion (section 2(a)) and equality (section 15). The dissenting judgment[94] applied section 29 in the same fashion, but came to an opposite conclusion in the particular circumstances of the case.

These cases provide guidance on the operation of the interpretive provisions in a Charter case. These sections operate as a shield, to preserve existing rights guaranteed by or under the Constitution (or other law, in the case of section 26)[95] from diminution or obliteration by other Charter rights. Alternatively, these provisions act as a prism, which alters the content or scope of a right guaranteed by the Charter. In either situation, these sections have the effect of altering the operation of Charter rights in order to reflect unique Canadian historical, cultural and social realities.

The two functions of the interpretive provisions which have been referred to derive from their different purposes and phraseology. One unifying feature of these sections is their embodiment of Canadian values and traditions. Denominational school rights, multiculturalism, other existing rights and aboriginal rights are all a reflection of the unique fabric of Canadian society. In this respect, these provisions (along with sections 16 to 23, 24 and 33) are vital elements in the creation and maintenance of a Canadian jurisprudence of rights and freedoms.

Another unifying feature of these interpretive guides is their mandatory nature. All these sections except sections 28 and 29 employ the word "shall", and sections 28 and 29 are, by their terms, imperative. None of these sections is subject to legislative override by section 33 of the Charter. A final common aspect of these provisions is that they all apply to the determination of the scope or operation of substantive Charter guarantees and do not stand alone as independently enforceable rights protections. One could not apply pursuant to section 24 for a remedy for the simple violation of one of these provisions.

The last matter which requires clarification is *when* these provisions are to be applied in a Charter case. Obviously these sections will only be triggered in a case involving a Charter right. The real question to be determined is whether these guides will apply when the substantive Charter right is defined, or whether they will come into operation when the

---

94 Howland C.J.O. and Robins J.A.
95 *E.g.*, the *Canadian Bill of Rights*; see *Singh v. Min. of Employment & Immigration*, [1985] 1 S.C.R. 177, *per* Beetz J.

limitations clause (section 1) is applied.[96] This may seem to be a picayune detail, hardly worthy of analysis. Upon reflection, however, it becomes clear that this is a vital threshold question which will affect the presentation of a case, the content and structure of analysis and, inevitably, the outcome of certain decisions. It is submitted that sections 25, 26, 27, 28 and 29 apply to the definition stage of a Charter case, rather than to the limitations analysis.

There are two main arguments which can be advanced in support of this assertion: one based on the existing case law and one based on the logic and structure of the Charter itself. From the Charter case law discussed previously in this chapter, it is evident that the interpretive provisions have been applied at the first stage of analysis, when the definition and scope of the substantive rights are discussed. Thus, freedom of religion and minority language education rights have been shaped and moulded by the interpretive provisions into a uniquely Canadian structure.

The other relevant aspect of existing case law on the Charter are the decisions which indicate that section 1 analysis will only be triggered if the law or practice being challenged is properly described as a "limit".[97] As Professor Hogg points out: "The Supreme Court of Canada has decided that not every Charter infringement is a 'limit', and any infringement that is more severe than a limit cannot be justified under s. 1".[98] Thus some Charter cases will be analyzed and decided entirely without reference to section 1. In light of the mandatory direction in the interpretive provisions and their vital function of "Canadianizing" the rights and freedoms contained in the Charter, it would be anomalous indeed if a decision impinging on the interests sought to be protected by these sections was made without reference to them.

The other argument in favour of applying these interpretive guides at the "definitional" stage of a Charter case flows directly from the last argument advanced with respect to the decided cases, and is based on the logic and structure of the Charter itself. The purpose of the interpretive provisions has been described earlier as a "prism"; the framers of the Charter were aware of the potential impact of the guarantee of certain rights and freedoms upon other rights, values and interests which had gained recognition in Canada. The interpretive sections were added in order to minimize the adverse consequences of superimposing the Charter guarantees onto this existing structure.

---

96 This analytical structure for cases is accepted in many cases: see the discussion *supra*; and see *Re Germany and Rauca* (1983), 41 O.R. (2d) 225 (C.A.).

97 See especially *Que. Assn. of Protestant School Boards v. A.G. Quebec, supra*, note 12; *R. v. Big M Drug Mart, supra*, note 4.

98 Hogg, *supra*, note 12 at 682.

The limitations clause, on the other hand, was included out of an abundance of caution, so that courts, legislators and others would have a fixed standard against which limits on rights and freedoms could be measured. The terms of section 1 indicate the touchstones for this analysis: "reasonableness", "prescribed by law", and a "free and democratic society".[99] The leading case on section 1 contains an elaborate discussion of the various tests to be employed in analyzing whether a limitation on a Charter right is acceptable, which is preceded by the following statement:

> A second contextual element of interpretation of s. 1 is provided by the words "free and democratic society." Inclusion of these words as the final standard of justification for limits on rights and freedoms refers the Court to the very purpose for which the *Charter* was originally entrenched in the Constitution: Canadian society is to be free and democratic. The Court must be guided by the values and principles essential to a free and democratic society . . .
>
> The rights and freedoms guaranteed by the *Charter* are not, however, absolute. It may become necessary to limit rights and freedoms in circumstances where their exercise would be inimical to the realization of collective goals of fundamental importance.[100]

This statement, like the wording of section 1, emphasizes that the process of determining whether a limit on a Charter right is justified involves a balancing of the interests of individuals and groups, as reflected and embodied in the substantive Charter guarantees, and those of society as a whole. The limitations analysis called for in section 1 takes as its starting point the definition of the substantive right or freedom which is involved: that determination is the first stage of analysis. For example, if a law restricting commercial advertising is challenged as a violation of section 2(b), the first stage of analysis would involve the determination of whether "commercial speech" such as advertising is protected by section 2(b).[101] Only once the scope of the right itself is defined and a violation of the right as defined is found, may the court move to the second stage of analysis, which involves the question whether the restriction is a demonstrably justified limit in a free and democratic society (section 1).[102] Given this analytical structure, the argument in favour of triggering the interpretive provisions in the definitional stage of a Charter case proceeds along the following lines. If section 1 limitations analysis takes

---

99 The other important aspect of s. 1, which concerns onus of proof, is not relevant to this discussion. See Hogg, *ibid.* at 678-682.

100 *R. v. Oakes, supra*, note 12 at 136, *per* Dickson C.J.C.

101 See, on this point, *Re Klein and L.S.U.C.* (1985), 50 O.R. (2d) 118 (Div. Ct.); S. Braun, "Should Commercial Speech Be Accorded Prima Facie Constitutional Recognition. Under the Canadian Charter of Rights and Freedoms?" (1986), 18 *Ottawa L. Rev.* 37.

102 S. 1 states that only limits which satisfy its stringent standards will be acceptable.

as its starting point the substantive right *as defined in stage one*, and if the purpose of the interpretive provisions is to act as a prism, altering the prevailing scope and meaning of one of the substantive rights where appropriate, it follows that these provisions have no role to play in section 1 analysis. The "prism" must already have been applied before section 1 can operate, because it is the limit on the substantive right *as modified by* the interpretive prism which must be evaluated by reference to section 1.

The second-stage limitations analysis involves a balancing of interests, and it is submitted that it would be inappropriate to invoke the interpretive provisions in this process, for it is precisely in order to ensure that these particular rights and interests are not obliterated by the Charter guarantees or general social interests that these special provisions were inserted. Multiculturalism and aboriginal treaty and other rights, for example, are not to be factored into a Charter case only when the general social interests are balanced against the particular interest embodied in the Charter right. Instead, these overriding constitutionally protected values should be utilized, in an appropriate case, to modify the usual definition or under-standing of a Charter right so that it does not diminish, abrogate or infringe the values reflected in sections 25, 26, 27, 28 and 29. Any other approach would not adequately reflect the logical structure of the Charter, and it would raise the possibility that these mandatory directives would not be accorded an appropriate role or sufficient weight in the analysis of a particular case.

If the interpretive sections are applied at the second stage of analysis, it is antecedently likely that they would not be effective, because the interests they seek to protect would be intermingled with the other social interests in the balancing equation. The values reflected in these sections must be accorded the importance that their status as part of the Constitution requires. Otherwise there would have been no point in specifically including them in this way.

The logical structure of the Charter supports the argument advanced here in quite another way. The interpretive provisions are designed, as their wording indicates, to preserve certain pre-existing or overarching values and interests. They can accomplish this either by modifying the definition of the substantive guarantees, or by rendering otherwise valid "limits" on rights unacceptable when viewed in the light of the interpretive guides.

The latter option is plausible in view of the directive in these sections that the Charter be "construed" and "interpreted" in a particular way. The problem with it is that the provisions and section 1 do not refer to each other, and section 1 itself does not allow other limits to be placed on these rights. Furthermore, it is difficult to interpret these sections as applying to the limits on rights, rather than to the substantive guarantees. For example, a law which provides that the punishment for certain crimes may include termination of the privilege of possessing a firearm does not ordinarily impinge upon the guarantee against "cruel and unusual treatment or punishment" in section 12, as that right is usually understood. When that law is applied to a native person who relies on hunting or sustenance, however, the Charter right is triggered, *not* because a limit on a right in the particular situation has become unacceptable because of section 25, but rather because the right itself takes on new meaning when it is viewed through the prism of section 25.[103] These interpretive guides do not alter the section 1 tests directly; instead, they modify the meaning or scope of the substantive rights guaranteed by the Charter, and these "new" rights may then be subject to section 1 analysis.

In summary, it is submitted that the interpretive provisions in the Charter are to be applied at the first stage of analysis in a Charter case when the scope and meaning of the substantive right is defined. These interpretive guides function as a prism, which alter the traditional meaning attributed to Charter rights and freedoms so that the latter do not diminish or obliterate the former. This can be accomplished by adding a new dimension to the usual meaning of a right or freedom or by limiting the scope of a Charter right. The interpretive provisions will function properly, in the context of the Charter as a whole, only if they are applied in this fashion.

The terminology employed in these sections is concise and easily understood. Of these provisions, only sections 25, 28 and 29 will be analyzed in detail.[104] Sections 25 and 29 are essentially preservative; they are designed to shield pre-existing collective values from alteration by the guarantees of individual rights or freedoms in the Charter.

The terminology employed in sections 25 and 29 is similar to that contained in section 2 of the *Canadian Bill of Rights*, which requires the courts to construe and apply federal laws so as not to "abrogate, abridge or infringe" the rights or freedoms recognized and declared in the Bill. Like the *Bill of Rights* provision, these sections are mandatory. Unfortunately, as experience with the *Bill of Rights* demonstrates, this clear directive is not, of itself, a guarantee that the section will achieve its assigned purpose.

Dictionary definitions of the words used are a useful point of departure in the interpretation of section 25, in the absence of authoritative relevant

---

103 See *R. v. Tobac* (1985), 20 C.C.C. (3d) 49 (N.W.T.C.A.); *R. v. Weyallon*, [1985] 4 C.N.L.R. 184 (N.W.T.C.A.), leave to appeal refused (1985), 17 C.R.R. 101n (S.C.C.).

104 S. 27 is discussed in J.E. Magnet, Chapter 18 "Multiculturalism and Collective Rights", *infra*.

precedent. The *Oxford Illustrated Dictionary*[105] defines "abrogate" as "repeal, cancel", and "derogate" as "detract, make improper or injurious abatement". That dictionary defines "derogation" as "lessening or impairment of law, position, dignity . . . deterioration, debasement".[106] From this, one can conclude that sections 25 and 29 are intended to prevent a diminution, impairment or infringement of the rights they refer to. They will trigger even if there is no absolute denial of these rights.

Section 28. Section 28 states:

> Notwithstanding anything in this Charter, the rights and freedoms referred to in it are guaranteed equally to male and female persons.

Although it is accurate to describe this section as an interpretive provision, and although it shares many of the characteristics of the other sections previously discussed, section 28 merits separate attention because of its unique symbolic and substantive character. This section has been the subject of close scrutiny and some debate in academia,[107] and several judges have commented upon it as well.[108] The section has been dismissed as "a queer provision [which] . . . means and accomplishes nothing",[109] while others have hailed it as the essential "substantive" guarantee of gender equality.[110]

Section 28 was undoubtedly inspired by the dismal judicial and legal record of protection for women's rights in Canada.[111] The general guarantee of gender equality in section 15 was viewed as insufficient, given the failure of the similar clause in the *Canadian Bill of Rights*. In order to comprehend the symbolic importance of section 28, one must view it in this context. The substantive importance of this provision, though it cannot be abstracted completely from this context, must also be forward-looking and consistent with the larger objects of the Charter.

---

105 2nd ed. (London: Oxford University Press, 1975) at 3, 227.

106 *Ibid.* at 227-228.

107 See the articles listed in notes 109-111, *infra*.

108 *R. v. Red Hot Video Ltd.* (1984), 38 C.R. (3d) 275 (B.C. Co. Ct.), aff'd (1985), 45 C.R. (3d) 36 (B.C.C.A.), leave to appeal to S.C.C. refused (1985), 46 C.R. (3d) XXVn (S.C.C.); *Boudreau v. Lynch, supra,* note 76.

109 E.A. Driedger, "The Canadian Charter of Rights and Freedoms" (1982), 14 *Ottawa L. Rev.* 373 at 373.

110 C.A. MacKinnon, "Making Sex Equality Real", in Smith, *Righting the Balance, supra,* note 2, p. 37.

111 K.J. de Jong, "Sexual Equality: Interpreting Section 28", in A.F. Bayefsky & M. Eberts, eds., *Equality Rights and the Canadian Charter of Rights and Freedoms* (Toronto: Carswell, 1985) at 493; P. Kome, *The Taking of Twenty-Eight: Women Challenge the Constitution* (Toronto: The Women's Press, 1983).

With respect to most Charter-protected rights and freedoms, section 28 will cause little interpretive difficulty. It may be employed to affirm that women and men are equally entitled to security from unreasonable searches (section 8), or access to counsel upon arrest or detention (section 10), but this result could be achieved without reference to section 28, and resort to it would add little to the analysis. When will the section be important as a unique aid in the interpretation of the Charter? Experience to date indicates that the section will be most important in relation to sections 1, 15 and 33. The extent to which section 28 accomplishes its general purpose, which I submit is the protection and promotion of gender equality as a fundamental overarching constitutional value, will be determined by the manner in which it is treated in relation to these sections.

Section 28 will add little to the interpretation of most Charter provisions in most circumstances simply because issues of gender inequality will not be directly confronted in these cases. Section 15, however, is a crucible in which the inequalities in our society will be tested, and thus section 28 will inform our understanding of this provision in important ways. One view of section 28 is that it merely affirms, in a forceful way, the equality guarantee in section 15. On this reading it may be explained as adding to the guarantee in section 15 that men and women are equal in the eyes of the law, the exclamation "and we really mean it!" This would result in a higher status for gender equality under section 15 than is accorded other grounds of discrimination, and presumably this would enable section 28 to achieve its purpose, by making section 15 a more meaningful and effective equality guarantee. It is submitted that this is the minimum role that may be accorded to section 28. If it is not effective to ensure that gender equality is given the strongest possible protection under section 15, then it will be a superfluous provision, and its insertion in the Charter will have been a cruel sham.

A more difficult issue is the relationship between section 28 and sections 1 and 33. The opening phrase of section 28 states that it applies "notwithstanding anything in this Charter". Several authors have referred to these words in support of the argument that section 28 cannot be subject to limitations pursuant to section 1, or overridden pursuant to section 33.[112] The legislative history of section 28 supports this analysis in respect of section 33, because during the course of the political negotiations that preceded its enactment, a specific reference to section 33 that would have subjected section 28 to the "notwithstanding" clause was inserted and later withdrawn after a storm of protest.[113] This history, combined with the fact

---

112 de Jong, *ibid.*; Gold, *supra*, note 80; W.S. Tarnopolsky, "The Equality Rights", in Tarnopolsky & Beaudoin, *supra*, note 6, p. 395.

113 de Jong, *ibid.* at 510-511; Gibson, *The Law of the Charter, supra*, note 5, at 70.

that section 33 authorizes a temporary abrogation or denial of Charter guarantees rather than a mere limitation or qualification on their enjoyment, lends credence to the view that section 28 is not superseded by section 33.[114]

An opposing argument could be advanced, based on the idea that the reference in section 28 to "the rights and freedoms guaranteed by the Charter" indicates that these rights are to be enjoyed equally only to the extent that they are capable of enjoyment from time to time. Certain of these rights (sections 2 and 7 to 15) are subject to legislative override, and are therefore "guaranteed" in a permanently precarious fashion, and that is what section 28 refers to. On this view, section 28 would be subject to section 33, despite the attempt during its drafting to overcome that possibility. The opening phrase would thus be important only with reference to section 1.

What would the practical effect be if section 28 is made subject to section 33? Since section 28 is only an interpretive provision, section 33 could not be invoked to suspend its operation directly. Instead, section 33 would be utilized to override another Charter provision (*e.g.*, section 15), and section 28 would then have no role to play as an interpretive tool in respect of the right as overridden in the particular circumstances. If section 28 is not subject to section 33, presumably it could be applied to aid in the interpretation of the right or freedom, but in order for this to be meaningful it would have to suspend or prevent the override in respect of gender equality. The text of section 33 appears to admit of no such limitation,[115] but as the arguments examined earlier indicate, the matter is not yet settled.

An equally difficult and more frequently encountered problem concerns the relationship between section 28 and section 1. Section 1 subjects all the substantive guarantees in the Charter to "such reasonable limits, prescribed by law as can be demonstrably justified in a free and democratic society". Section 28, on the other hand, seeks to impose an absolute guarantee of gender equality in respect of the enjoyment of Charter rights or freedoms. These two sections clash, and again the resolution of this matter requires a determination of whether the reference in section 28 to "the rights and freedoms referred to in [the Charter]" means the rights and freedoms *as qualified by* section 1, or the rights and freedoms *per se*. As a practical matter, the question is whether section 28 requires a departure from the Canadian tradition, which in other respects the Charter

---

114 *Boudreau v. Lynch, supra*, note 76.
115 See, on the interpretation of s. 33, *Alliance des Professeurs de Montréal v. A.G. Quebec* (1985), 21 D.L.R. (4th) 354 (Que. C.A.), leave to appeal to S.C.C. granted (1985), 21 D.L.R. (4th) 354n (S.C.C.).

maintains, of hedging rights protections about with limitations, qualifications and exceptions.[116]

Once again the structure of the Charter, and the function of section 28 as an interpretive provision, provide guidance. If section 28 is applied to the interpretation of a right or freedom in the manner outlined earlier in this article, it will apply at the first stage of Charter analysis when the scope and content of the right or freedom is determined.[117] The section 1 standards will then be applied, in an appropriate case, to the right or freedom *as defined* at stage one. To this extent section 28 may be said to be subject to section 1, but this hardly deprives it of any meaning or importance.

An alternate view of this relationship is that the reference to the opening phrase of section 28 ("notwithstanding anything else in this Charter"), and the reference to rights and freedoms *"referred to"*, lead to the conclusion that section 28 imposes an absolute limit on the limits which are permissible under section 1. This argument would interpret section 28 as a non-derogation clause in relation to section 1. This would be compatible with a well-understood international approach, by which some restrictions on rights or freedoms are never allowed, because they violate fundamental values of human dignity.[118] Section 28 would be interpreted as a bar on certain forms of limitations, namely those which deny, by intent or effect, the equal enjoyment of rights or freedoms guaranteed by the Charter. Once again, although section 28 may be said to be subject to section 1 in some respects, in that it does not totally prevent the operation of the limitations clause, the section still meets its fundamental objective of ensuring that rights and freedoms are guaranteed equally to women and men. This view of section 28 does not enforce an absolute, inflexible equality which prohibits all limits and restrictions; rather it seeks to ensure that limits on rights or freedoms apply to both men and women. Given the history of discrimination (and paternalism) in Canada, and the frequent failure of the law to prevent or remedy it, this is a worthwhile and meaningful objective for this section, which is consistent with its background and current form.

---

116 This has been noted by the judiciary. See *Blainey v. Ont. Hockey Assn.* (1985), 52 O.R. (2d) 225 at 236-237 (H.C.), rev'd (1986), 54 O.R. (2d) 513 (C.A.), leave to appeal to S.C.C. refused (1986), 58 O.R. (2d) 274 (headnote) (S.C.C.).

117 See discussion *supra*, at pp. 28-29; *accord* de Jong, *supra*, note 111 at 524.

118 This is reflected in various international documents, including the *Universal Declaration of Human Rights*, the *International Covenant on Civil and Political Rights* and the *European Convention on Human Rights*.

(c) Preamble, Headings, Marginal Notes

The usefulness of the preamble, headings and marginal notes for the interpretation of the Charter is quite limited. None of these things can control or contradict the plain words of the statute, but they may occasionally help to clarify ambiguities.

A heading was used as an interpretive aid by the Supreme Court of Canada in its first Charter decision, *Law Society of Upper Canada v. Skapinker.*[119] The issue in the case was whether section 6(2)(b) of the Charter, which guarantees to all citizens and permanent residents the right "to pursue the gaining of a livelihood in any province" was contravened by the *Ontario Law Society Act,*[120] which requires that a person be a citizen or British subject in order to practise law in the province. The words of section 6(2)(b) are, on their face, capable of supporting an interpretation of the provision as a general right to work if qualified. The Supreme Court opted for a more restricted interpretation, in part because the words appear in a section which is otherwise devoted to mobility rights. This reading was also supported by reference to the heading under which section 6 appears: "Mobility Rights". Mr. Justice Estey explained the usefulness of headings as interpretive aids in the following way:

> The *Charter,* from its first introduction into the constitutional process, included many headings including the heading now in question. "Mobility Rights" precedes but a single section with only four subparagraphs. . . . It may have been intended by the various adopting authorities that such a document would be required to be read and interpreted by the populace generally, and not just by those engaged in the law. It may be that headings were adapted to make for easy reference to a very important document consisting of thirty-four separate provisions, most of which are of independent significance. It can be safely concluded that the *Charter of Rights* will be read by more members of the Canadian community than any other part of the *Constitution Acts, 1867 to 1982.* It is clear that these headings were systematically and deliberately included as an integral part of the *Charter* for whatever purpose. At the very minimum, the court must take them into consideration when engaged in the process of discerning the meaning and application of the provisions of the *Charter.* The extent of the influence of a heading in this process will depend upon many factors, including (but the list is not intended to be all-embracing) the degree of difficulty by reason of ambiguity or obscurity in construing the section; the length and complexity of the provision; the apparent homogeneity of the provision appearing under the heading; the use of generic terminology in the heading; the presence or absence of a system of headings which appear to segregate the component elements of the *Charter;* and the relationship of the terminology employed in the heading to the substance of the headlined provision. Heterogeneous rights will be less likely shepherded by a heading than a homogeneous group of rights.

---

119 *Supra*, note 8.
120 R.S.O. 1980, c. 233, s. 28.

At a minimum the heading must be examined and some attempt made to discern the intent of the makers of the document from the language of the heading. It is at best one step in the constitutional interpretation process. It is difficult to foresee a situation where the heading will be of controlling importance. It is, on the other hand, almost as difficult to contemplate a situation where the heading could be cursorily rejected although, in some situations, such as, in the case of "Legal Rights", which in the *Charter* is at the head of eight disparate sections, the heading will likely be seen as being only an announcement of the obvious.[121]

As Estey J. notes in his judgment, some of the headings relate to such disparate sections (such as "Legal Rights") that they will provide little guidance. Other headings, such as "Equality Rights", have been utilized to support particular interpretations of substantive provisions,[122] but as Estey J. correctly states, use of these headings is "at best one step in the constitutional interpretation process".[123]

Marginal notes are also available as interpretive aids, but are of limited assistance in most circumstances. A potentially more useful source of guidance is the preamble to the Charter.[124] The preamble declares:

Whereas Canada is founded upon principles that recognize the supremacy of God and the rule of law.

Preambles have often been utilized as interpretive aids in constitutional and non-constitutional adjudication.[125] The usefulness of *this* preamble as an interpretive aid for *this* document is difficult to determine.[126] The reference to the "supremacy of God" surely cannot be used to restrict the ambit of the guarantee of "freedom of conscience and religion" in section 2(a),[127] and it is difficult to imagine another use for it as an interpretive guide.[128] The reference to the "rule of law" may be of greater use as an interpretive aid, though examples are not readily apparent.[129]

As Professor Gibson points out, the sparse preamble to the Charter

---

121 *L.S.U.C. v. Skapinker, supra,* note 8 at 376-377.

122 de Jong, *supra,* note 111; L. Smith, "A New Paradigm for Equality Rights", in Smith, *Righting the Balance, supra,* note 2, p. 353.

123 *L.S.U.C. v. Skapinker, supra,* note 8 at 377.

124 For an analysis of the Preamble of the *Constitution Act, 1982,* see McLeod *et al., supra,* note 63 at 2-100.6 *et seq.*

125 See Driedger, *supra,* note 61; Côté, *supra,* note 25.

126 See Gibson, *The Law of the Charter, supra,* note 5 at 64-67, for a discussion of this subject.

127 Gibson, *ibid.* at 66; Hogg, *Constitutional Law of Canada, supra,* note 12. The preamble can be used to clarify ambiguous provisions, but surely it cannot be effective to restrict or control an explicit Charter guarantee of "freedom of conscience".

128 See *R. v. H.H. Marshall Ltd.,* Nfld. Prov. Ct., for an unusual application of the preamble.

129 Gibson, *The Law of the Charter, supra,* note 5 at 66-67, referring to *Reference re Manitoba Language Rights,* [1985] 1 S.C.R. 721.

stands "in stark contrast to the eloquent and often lengthy statements of purpose and principle with which national and international human rights documents are customarily prefaced".[130] It is submitted that the preamble should be resorted to sparingly: it was added late in the drafting process; it is sparse and apparently largely symbolic, and its reference to "God" appears to contradict the explicit words of two sections in the Charter.[131]

5. EXTERNAL AIDS

The purposive approach to Charter interpretation imposes unique obligations on Canadian judges and others to draw upon external aids for inspiration and guidance. Although there was a clear trend in recent constitutional cases to relax the former exclusionary rule concerning extrinsic evidence,[132] reliance on such evidence may be expected to become the rule rather than the exception in Charter cases. This increased reliance on extrinsic data is laudable in that it should lead to more informed and accurate interpretations, which are also more likely to suit the current and future situation, but it also has a cost. With the advent of this approach to Charter interpretation, lawyers, judges and others may be swamped with information, or may be urged to adopt willy-nilly the interpretations of other courts concerning other documents. There is a real danger that this greater reliance on external aids will not ultimately improve Charter interpretation, but rather will make it a tedious exercise in futility, which in turn may be expected to lead to decreased reliance on this sort of information.

Considerable guidance is now available from the courts on the admissibility and use of external aids in Charter interpretation, and these decisions indicate that the courts are determined to make intelligent use of these sources.

(a) Canadian Sources

A key aspect of the purposive approach is the context in which the right or freedom operates, and an obvious starting point in the examination of this context is the immediate national legal and social surroundings. Canadian courts have been remarkably open to the introduction of all sorts of data about the right or freedom, the historical context of the

---

130 Gibson, *ibid.* at 65.
131 Ss. 2(a) and 27.
132 See McLeod *et al.*, *supra*, note 63 at 2-112; Gibson, *The Law of the Charter*, *supra*, note 5 at 73-77.

impugned law, and current social circumstances.[133] For obvious reasons, one cannot catalogue in advance all the relevant sources, but one can confidently predict that this will test the ingenuity and research skills of all who interpret the Charter. Several Canadian sources should be considered, however, because of their significant and continuing relevance in the area.

(i) *Legislative history*

Courts have been asked to adopt interpretations of the Charter which are supported by reference to earlier versions of the document, to the Minutes of the Proceedings of the Special Joint Committee of the Senate and House of Commons on the Constitution, and to Parliamentary speeches about the Charter. Although all this material is admissible in these cases, and though it may be very useful in some cases, courts have shown an understandable and, it is submitted, proper reluctance to give any of it too much weight.

The arguments and authorities in favour of using the earlier versions of the Charter as an aid in interpreting the Charter have been set out, along with the relevant texts, in an article by Professor Robin Elliot,[134] and this will not be repeated here. With respect to the Minutes of the Proceedings of the Special Joint Committee, the decision of Lamer J. in *Reference re Section 94(2) of Motor Vehicle Act (B.C.)*[135] is enlightening and persuasive. In that case, the court was urged to accept the testimony of Mr. Barry Strayer, then Deputy Minister of Justice, concerning the scope of section 7. The court ultimately adopted a contrary interpretation of the section, and the comments of Lamer J. about reliance on these minutes as an interpretive aid are so detailed and persuasive that they must be quoted at length:

> . . . If speeches and declarations by prominent figures are inherently unreliable (*Reference re Upper Churchill Water Rights Revision Act*) and "speeches made in the legislature at the time of enactment of the measure are inadmissible as having little evidential weight" (. . . Re Residential Tenancies Act 1979 . . .), the Minutes of the Proceedings of the Special Joint Committee, though admissible, and granted somewhat more weight than speeches, should not be given too much weight. The inherent unreliability of such statements and speeches is not altered by the mere fact that they pertain to the *Charter* rather than a statute.
>
> Moreover, the simple fact remains that the *Charter* is not the product

---

133 See, *e.g.*, *R. v. Seo* (1986), 54 O.R. (2d) 293 (C.A.); *Edwards Books & Art Ltd. v. R.*, *supra*, note 57; McLeod *et al.*, *ibid.* at 2-112 *et seq.*

134 *Supra*, note 28.

135 *Supra*, note 18.

of a few individual public servants, however distinguished, but of a multiplicity of individuals who played major roles in the negotiating, drafting and adoption of the *Charter*. How can one say with any confidence that within this enormous multiplicity of actors, without forgetting the role of the provinces, the comments of a few federal civil servants can in any way be determinative?

. . .

Another danger with casting the interpretation of s. 7 in terms of the comments made by those heard at the Special Joint Committee Proceedings is that, in so doing, the rights, freedoms and values embodied in the *Charter* in effect become frozen in time to the moment of adoption with little or no possibility of growth, development and adjustment to changing societal needs. Obviously, in the present case, given the proximity in time of the *Charter* debates, such a problem is relatively minor, even though it must be noted that even at this early stage in the life of the *Charter*, a host of issues and questions have been raised which were largely unforeseen at the time of such proceedings. If the newly planted "living tree" which is the *Charter* is to have the possibility of growth and adjustment over time, care must be taken to ensure that historical materials, such as the Minutes of Proceedings and Evidence of Special Joint Committee, do not stunt its growth".[136]

The dangers of relying too much on these Minutes are amply demonstrated by the following passage from *Reference re Public Service Employee Relations Act (Alberta)*:

Ministerial comments to the joint parliamentary committee reviewing the original resolution proposed to the Canadian Parliament by the government of Canada are said to support the extended meaning [of s. 2(*f*)]. Ironically, the Attorney General offers a competing quotation from another minister. This trial by quotation serves to illustrate the futility of trying to step around the traditional rule that individual members of Parliament express personal and not parliamentary intent. This is specially true in the case of the Charter. While I do not intend to denigrate the contribution of that committee to the creation of the Charter, it was not the framer of the Charter. The tortured path to law of the Canadian Charter is unique in political history.[137]

These decisions reveal a healthy scepticism towards these Minutes as an interpretive aid, and one can add little to their reasoning. It is submitted that the Minutes should be treated as an occasionally useful, but never conclusive or governing, interpretive aid. The opinions offered to the Committee about the meaning of various provisions of the proposed bill should be accepted or rejected on their individual merits, and not treated with undue respect because they emanate from Parliament.

---

136 *Ibid.* at 508-509.
137 [1985] 2 W.W.R. 289 at 303 (Alta. C.A.), *per* Kerans J.A., aff'd *infra*, note 153.

(ii) *Canadian Bill of Rights decisions*

One significant advantage of the adoption of a purposive approach to Charter interpretation was that it offered a means of departing from the rigid and narrow interpretations that prevailed in respect of the *Canadian Bill of Rights*.[138] Canadian judges, particularly those at the Supreme Court of Canada, have taken advantage of this opportunity in several decisions, so that it is now fair to state that the *Bill of Rights* jurisprudence will not be controlling, and indeed may be given only minimal weight.

The *Bill of Rights* decisions are a relevant and often cited source of interpretive guidance for several reasons: they are Canadian, recent and they deal with similar or identical language in a document which is a written guarantee of rights. In a Charter case these precedents can be distinguished on the basis of the different language, structure and status in law of the two documents. The *Bill of Rights* simply "recognized and declared" that certain rights "have existed and ... shall continue to exist", while the Charter "guarantees" the enumerated rights. The phraseology employed in several of the sections, though similar, can provide a basis for departing from the *Bill of Rights* interpretation. Even where identical words have been employed in the two documents, the interpretation adopted under the *Bill of Rights* may be departed from.

Several different reasons for this somewhat startling willingness to reject *Bill of Rights* precedents have been articulated by the Supreme Court. In *R. v. Big M Drug Mart*,[139] Dickson J. rejected the definition of freedom of religion under the *Bill of Rights* because of the imperative language of the Charter. He also referred to the constitutional status of the Charter in contrast to the legal status of the Bill as a federal statute.[140]

Another basis for distinguishing between the two documents is structural, because the Bill lacks an equivalent of section 1, and therefore the clear separation between the definition and limitation stages of analysis under the Charter is not found in *Bill of Rights* cases.

These reasons for departing from *Bill of Rights* precedents, though valid and important, do not address the broader issue of whether the general approach to interpretation that prevailed in the *Bill of Rights* cases should continue under the Charter. At the time the Charter was enacted, this was

---

138 The critical commentaries on the Bill are legion. See W.S. Tarnopolsky, *The Canadian Bill of Rights*, 2nd rev. ed. (Toronto: Macmillan, 1975). On the relevance of this body of law for Charter interpretation, see B. Hovius, "The Legacy of the Supreme Court of Canada's Approach to the Canadian Bill of Rights: Prospects for the Charter" (1982), 28 *McGill L.J.* 31.

139 *Supra*, note 4.

140 *Ibid.* at 341-344.

a vexing question. Today it is clear that the Charter interpretation involves a purposive approach which is markedly different from the restrictive and cautious attitude that characterized the *Bill of Rights* jurisprudence. This point is made by Wilson J., in the *Singh* case:

> It seems to me . . . that the recent adoption of the *Charter* by Parliament and nine of the ten provinces as part of the Canadian constitutional framework has sent a clear message to the courts that the restrictive attitude which at times characterized their approach to the *Canadian Bill of Rights* ought to be re-examined.[141]

Mr. Justice Le Dain used similar language in *R. v. Therens*[142] to explain his rejection of the definition of "detention" under the *Bill of Rights*, in the interpretation of the same word in section 10:

> In considering the relationship of a decision under the *Canadian Bill of Rights* to an issue arising under the *Charter*, a court cannot, in my respectful opinion, avoid bearing in mind an evident fact of Canadian judicial history, which must be squarely and frankly faced: that on the whole, with some notable exceptions, the courts have felt some uncertainty or ambivalence in the application of the *Canadian Bill of Rights* because it did not reflect a clear constitutional mandate to make judicial decisions having the effect of limiting or qualifying the traditional sovereignty of Parliament.[143]

This judgment contains a comprehensive analysis of the linguistic, structural and philosophical bases for distinguishing between the Bill and the Charter, and it leads one to conclude that, although *Bill of Rights* precedents will continue to be relevant and important sources of guidance for the interpretation of the Charter, they will not be viewed as binding or authoritative.[144]

(b) American Sources

American authorities are being relied on extensively, perhaps more than in any other area of our law, in Charter interpretation, both judicial and academic. Certain provisions of the Charter parallel or match sections of the U.S. *Bill of Rights*, and in this area of Canadian life, as in so many others, the American experience is important. Some authors and judges have rightly pointed out that American precedents deal with a different document, address different social problems and are part of a unique legal and political structure, and therefore should not be incorporated blindly

---

141 *Singh v. Min. of Manpower & Immigration, supra*, note 95 at 209.
142 *Supra*, note 31.
143 *Ibid.* at 638-639.
144 See also *R. v. Oakes, supra*, note 12.

or completely into Canadian law.[145] Mr. Justice Dickson has stated that "American decisions can be transplanted to the Canadian context only with the greatest caution".[146] One can easily accept the validity of these concerns; the more difficult problem is to know exactly how to deal with this rich body of law. No one urges a return to the approach under the *Bill of Rights*, which was marked by an almost complete rejection of American precedents.[147] Instead a principled basis for considering these sources is required, and this approach must, in addition to the usual concerns about language and structure, take account of the different social, political and legal contexts that informed the interpretation of the two documents.

A basic and vitally important point of distinction between the American *Bill of Rights* and the Charter is structural: for example, the Bill lacks an "express limitations" clause and thus many U.S. decisions are influenced by the intermingling of the definition and limitation stages of analysis.[148] Many of these precedents will not be especially helpful in the interpretation of the Charter because of the difficulty in determining the actual influence of this structural difference on the reasoning and outcome of the case which is relied upon.

There are several other structural or textual differences between the two documents: the U.S. Bill lacks an equivalent of sections 24(2), 33, 27 and 28. Where any of these specific provisions are relevant in a particular analysis, the relevance of American authorities is diminished.

An equally difficult challenge is to place American precedents in their proper social, political, economic and philosophical contexts, in order to evaluate whether the Canadian context is sufficiently different to warrant discounting the U.S. decision. Each case must be considered on its merits, and there is no easy way to summarize this task. Professor Cameron has outlined a "purposive" approach to the consideration of American precedents, which is summarized in the following passage:

> Certain lines of inquiry should be pursued whenever American doctrine is being considered. A review of structural, textual and contextual differences

---

145 See particularly J. Cameron, "The Motor Vehicle Reference and the Relevance of American Doctrine in Charter Adjudication" in R.J. Sharpe, ed., *Charter Litigation* (Toronto: Butterworths, 1987) at 69.

146 *Hunter v. Southam Inc.*, *supra*, note 8 at 161.

147 See, *e.g.*, *Miller v. R.*, [1977] 2 S.C.R. 680; *A.G. Canada v. Lavell*, [1974] S.C.R. 1349. Professor W.S. Tarnopolsky (as he then was) identified the "Canadians have nothing useful to learn from Americans" principle in those cases: "The Historical and Constitutional Context of the Proposed Canadian Charter of Rights and Freedoms" (1981), 44 *Law & Contemporary Problems* 169 at 181-182.

148 See *Reference re s. 94(2) of the Motor Vehicle Act (B.C.)*, *supra*, note 18 at 498. Many of the American fundamental freedoms and equality cases reflect this mingling of definition and limitations analysis.

between the Canadian and American instruments is the first step to take in any such case. A consideration of the evolution of doctrine would be next. The third step involves assessment of the rationales for the doctrine under consideration. Reflection on the practical and institutional consequences of adopting American-style doctrinal solutions is the fourth and final step in the analysis.[149]

This is obviously a difficult and complex task — one which may cause some to conclude that the reward is simply not worth the effort. It is submitted that this conclusion is as incorrect now as it was when the similar approach under the *Canadian Bill of Rights* developed. American experience under their *Bill of Rights* is a sophisticated, complex and highly useful source of guidance for the interpretation of the Charter, but it must be dealt with carefully, if we are to create the uniquely Canadian solutions that the Charter demands and the public rightly expects.

(c) International Sources

Charter interpretation should be informed by the burgeoning international human rights materials, but this gives rise to two separate problems — access and interpretation. The problem of how one gains access to this material is quite real, but discussion of it is beyond the scope of this article.[150] Instead, the evaluation of the relevance of these materials for Charter interpretation will be discussed.

There is no question that the drafters of the Charter, and those who have since interpreted it, were and are aware of the international human rights standards. In some instances, Charter provisions parallel or match these standards. This is a large body of material which can be drawn upon to inform and enrich Charter interpretation, but, like the American cases, it must be dealt with intelligently and with due attention to the important structural, textual and "political" contexts that inform each.

Although many decisions refer to international standards in the interpretation of particular provisions, relatively few discuss how these

---

149 Cameron, "The Motor Vehicle Reference", *supra*, note 145 at 90.

150 The decisions of the United Nations bodies are not generally distributed, and many are extremely difficult to obtain. The *Canadian Human Rights Yearbook* (Toronto: Carswell) reprints the opinions of the U.N. Human Rights Committee in cases arising in Canada. An annotated compendium of the decisions of the Committee in respect of each article of the *Covenant on Civil and Political Rights* was also published in that journal: A. de Zayas, J. Moller & T. Opsahl, "Application by the Human Rights Committee of the International Covenant on Civil and Political Rights Under the Optional Protocol" (1986), 3 *Can. Hum. Rts. Y.B.* 101. Access to the materials in respect of the *European Convention on Human Rights* remains a more haphazard matter.

materials should be used.[151] Mr. Justice Linden addressed this issue in relation to the most relevant source — the *International Covenant on Civil and Political Rights*:

> On May 19, 1976, Canada acceded to the United Nations International Covenant on Civil and Political Rights. . . . [N]o Canadian legislation has been passed which expressly implements the Covenant. . . .
> The Covenant may, however, be used to assist a court to interpret ambiguous provisions of a domestic statute, . . . provided that the domestic statute does not contain express provisions contrary to or inconsistent with the Covenant. . . . This rule of construction is based on the presumption the Parliament does not intend to act in violation of Canada's international obligations.[152]

Although he did not rely on the Covenant in the particular circumstances of the case, his judgment clearly states the prevailing view.

The most comprehensive statement of the importance of international materials for Charter interpretation was made by Dickson C.J.C. in his dissenting judgment in *Reference re Public Service Employee Relations Act (Alberta)*:

> International law provides a fertile source of insight into the nature and scope of the freedom of association or workers. Since the close of the Second World War, the protection of the fundamental rights and freedoms of groups and individuals has become a matter of international concern. A body of treaties (or conventions) and customary norms now constitutes an international law of human rights under which the nations of the world have undertaken to adhere to the standards and principles necessary for ensuring freedom, dignity and social justice for their citizens. The *Charter* conforms to the spirit of this contemporary international human rights movement, and it incorporates many of the policies and prescriptions of the various international documents pertaining to human rights. The various sources of international human rights law — declarations, covenants, conventions, judicial and quasi-judicial decisions of international tribunals, customary norms — must, in my opinion, be relevant and persuasive sources for interpretation of the *Charter*'s provisions.

---

151 The Supreme Court of Canada has referred to international standards in the following cases: *Reference re s. 94(2) of the Motor Vehicle Act (B.C.)*, *supra*, note 18; *R. v. Oakes*, *supra*, note 12; *R. v. Jones*, [1986] 2 S.C.R. 284; *R. v. Mills*, [1986] 1 S.C.R. 863. There are many excellent articles on this subject; only a few will be listed here: M. Cohen & A.F. Bayefsky, "The Canadian Charter of Rights and Freedoms and Public International Law" (1983), 61 *Can. Bar Rev.* 265; J. Claydon, "International Human Rights Law and the Interpretation of the Canadian Charter of Rights and Freedoms" (1982), 4 *Sup. Ct. L. Rev.* 287: W.S. Tarnopolsky, "A Comparison Between the Canadian Charter of Rights and Freedoms and the International Covenant on Civil and Political Rights"(1983), 8 *Queen's L.J.* 211; M.A. Hayward, "International Law and the Interpretation of the Canadian Charter of Rights and Freedoms: Uses and Justifications" (1985), 23 *U.W.O.L. Rev.* 9; J. Humphrey, "The Canadian Charter of Rights and Freedoms and International Law" (1986), 50 *Sask. L. Rev.* 13.

152 *Re Mitchell and R.* (1983), 42 O.R. (2d) 481 at 492.

In particular, the similarity between the policies and provisions of the *Charter* and those of international human rights documents attaches considerable relevance to interpretations of those documents by adjudicative bodies, in much the same way that decisions of the United States courts under the Bill of Rights, or decisions of the courts of other jurisdictions are relevant and may be persuasive. The relevance of these documents in *Charter* interpretation extends beyond the standards developed by adjudicative bodies under the documents to the documents themselves. As the Canadian judiciary approaches the often general and open textured language of the *Charter*, "the more detailed textual provisions of the treaties may aid in supplying content to such imprecise concepts as the right to life, freedom of association, and even the right to counsel". J. Claydon, "International Human Rights Law and the Interpretation of the Canadian Charter of Rights and Freedoms" (1982), 4 *Supreme Court L.R.* 287, at p. 293.

Furthermore, Canada is a party to a number of international human rights Conventions which contain provisions similar or identical to those in the *Charter*. Canada has thus obliged itself internationally to ensure within its borders the protection of certain fundamental rights and freedoms which are also contained in the *Charter*. The general principles of constitutional interpretation require that these international obligations be a relevant and persuasive factor in *Charter* interpretation.[153]

6. CONCLUSION

Charter interpretation now appears to be as much an art as a science; it is as much a mystical as a technical exercise. The general words of the document, which derive from its unique status as an entrenched catalogue of rights, are capable of many meanings. Charter cases often touch raw nerve endings in our society. Difficult social, moral and political questions are now debated in courts as questions of "rights", and the resolution of these disputes draws judges more directly than before into the swirl of controversy. These judges are forced to articulate values about these issues more openly than was previously the case. None of this should lead to despair, nor should the purposive approach be abandoned as a unwieldy project. If the Charter is to be the enduring guarantee of rights and freedoms for Canadians that it was intended by its drafters to be, these challenges must be met.

The interpretation of the Charter should not be left to lawyers and judges, although both professions will undoubtedly continue to dominate the field. The Charter's meaning can and should be examined by people from other disciplines and backgrounds, whose unique expertise may shed new light on its contents. Lawyers and judges must expand their horizons to draw upon these resources, and to reach out to international comparative materials. The purposive approach requires this, and the reward for the

---

153 [1987] 1 S.C.R. 313 at 348-349.

effort will be a richer and more intelligent body of uniquely Canadian law.

The Charter must be interpreted in a dynamic and forward-looking manner. This is true, even though not that much has changed in Canadian society since 1982. Pollsters and politicians would point to shifts in the political "mood" or changed views on a particular issue, but of course it was precisely against these sorts of "transient majorities" that the Charter was designed to protect.

What is required is an interpretation of the Charter that preserves its *capacity* to change either with respect to the scope or content of a right or freedom, or with respect to reasonable limits under section 1.[154] This flexibility is required in order to ensure that the Charter continues to be meaningful in response to, and as a catalyst of, long-term social and legal evolution.

The requirement that the Charter be interpreted so as to preserve its capacity for change must be balanced against the need for certainty. The tensions inherent in this interpretive exercise are neatly summarized by Mr. Justice McIntyre in the following passage:

> It follows that while a liberal and not overly legalistic approach should be taken to constitutional interpretation, the *Charter* should not be regarded as an empty vessel to be filled with whatever meaning we might wish from time to time. The interpretation of the *Charter*, as of all constitutional documents, is constrained by the language, structure and history of the constitutional text, by constitutional tradition, and by the history, traditions and underlying philosophies of our society.[155]

Finally, one must acknowledge that the Charter is still in its infancy. Many years will be required before we have adequately plumbed the depths of its meaning. The enactment of the Charter was hailed as a milestone, a noble achievement that would profoundly alter Canadian life, and make ours a more just and equal society. A purposive interpretation of the Charter offers a useful and necessary way to turn that promise into a reality.

---

154 See the comments of Estey J. in *L.S.U.C. v. Skapinker, supra,* note 8 at 366: "The fine and constant adjustment process of these constitutional provisions is left by a tradition of necessity to the judicial branch. Flexibility must be balanced with certainty. The future must, to the extent forseeably possible, be accommodated in the present. The *Charter* is designed and adopted to guide and serve the Canadian community for a long time. Narrow and technical interpretation, if not modulated by a sense of the unknowns of the future, can stunt the growth of the law and hence the community it serves."

155 *Reference re Public Service Employee Relations Act (Alta.), supra,* note 153 at 394.

3

Application of the Canadian Charter of Rights and Freedoms*
(*Sections 30-33 and 52*)

Roger Tassé

1. The *Canadian Charter of Rights and Freedoms* and the Territories (Section 30)
2. The Charter Does Not Extend Legislative Powers (Section 31)
3. Who is Bound by the *Canadian Charter of Rights and Freedoms*? (Section 32)
4. Override Clauses (Section 33)
5. The Supremacy of the *Canadian Charter of Rights and Freedoms* (Section 52)

1. THE CANADIAN CHARTER OF RIGHTS AND FREEDOMS AND THE TERRITORIES (SECTION 30)

Section 30 of the Charter provides that a reference "to a province or to the legislative assembly or legislature of a province shall be deemed to include a reference to the Yukon Territory and the Northwest Territories, or to the appropriate legislative authority thereof". As Professor Katherine Swinton noted in the first edition of this book, this section presents few

---

* Translated from French.

difficulties.[1] It establishes that, for the purposes of the Charter, the Territories and their legislative bodies are to be treated as if they were provinces. Thus the competent legislative authorities of the Territories are obliged to respect the Charter in the same way as the provincial legislatures are.

It is arguable that, even in the absence of such a provision, the legislative powers of the Territories would be subject to the Charter. Because those powers have been conferred by Parliament, in exercising them a Territorial council is obliged to respect the Charter to the same extent as Parliament. The body which receives a delegated power to legislate cannot escape the constraints to which the delegating authority is subject.

This section, nevertheless, has the advantage of removing any ambiguity that might have resulted from section 32 of the Charter. It is arguable that the legislative councils of the Territories, made up as they are of elected representatives, constitute entities distinct from Parliament and the government of Canada and that, in consequence, the Charter does not bind them. This argument could not be accepted, given the provisions of section 30.

Even if one concedes that the legislative authorities of the Territories are subject to the Charter, however, an ambiguity could still persist. Do the provisions which deal with the provinces as geographical entities also apply to the Territories? Section 6, guaranteeing the right to mobility, and section 23, guaranteeing the right to minority language instruction, are examples.[2] One could argue, with some reason, that Charter provisions such as these, which deal with the provinces as geographical entities, do not apply to the Territories because the Territories lack provincial status. The answer, of course, could be that the Territories enjoy a quasi-provincial status and, by way of analogy therefore, these provisions should apply.

Again, section 30 removes all ambiguity. When section 6(2) of the Charter guarantees to every Canadian citizen the right to move to and take up residence in any province and to pursue the gaining of a livelihood in any province, one must add the words "or any Territory". The same reasoning applies to the right to minority language instruction, which is defined in terms of the parents' province of residence. Here again, as

---

1 W.S. Tarnopolsky & G.-A. Beaudoin, eds., *Canadian Charter of Rights and Freedoms* (Toronto: Carswell, 1982) at 41.

2 See also ss. 3 and 4 of the Charter which deal with democratic rights and the maximum duration of provincial legislatures. S. 30 assures the application of these provisions to the legislative councils of the Territories. The Territories could also, in my view, invoke s.16(3) of the Charter, which provides that Parliament and the provincial legislatures (and therefore the legislative councils of the Territories as well) are entitled "to advance the equality of status or use of English and French".

provided in section 30, the word "province" includes the Territories.

What is the position, however, respecting section 32 and, in particular, section 32(1)(b), which provides that the Charter applies "to the legislature and government of each province in respect of all matters within the authority of the legislature of each province"? The word "government" does not appear in section 30, which speaks only of provinces and their legislatures or legislative assemblies. This might suggest at first glance that the part of section 32(1)(b) which refers to the "government" of the provinces would not be applicable to the "governments" of the Territories, that is, to the executive and administrative branches of the Territories, because section 30 makes no reference to provincial governments. Such a result would certainly be surprising and could be avoided if the word "province" in section 30 were taken to refer to the provinces, not only as geographical entities, but also as governments. However, the word "province" is not used in the Charter to refer to provincial governments.

There is perhaps another way of approaching this question. One could argue that section 30 applies only to those provisions of the Charter which precede it, namely sections 1 to 29. In these sections, which entrench the rights and freedoms guaranteed by the Charter, only the words "province", "legislative assembly" and "legislature" appear. Since the words "provincial government" are not used in these sections, there is no reason to include them in section 30.

On this approach, section 30 would not apply to section 32. Section 32 in a sense is positioned outside the main body of the Charter in that it stipulates that the rights and freedoms guaranteed by the sections which precede it apply to the Canadian state in its entirety at both federal and provincial levels. In contrast to the *Canadian Bill of Rights*, which applies only within areas of federal jurisdiction, section 32 makes it clear that all the sovereign powers of the state, federal as well as provincial, are subject to the Charter. In this context it would have been inappropriate to refer specifically to the Territories, for they are not endowed with any of the sovereign powers of the state. For the same reason, it would be inappropriate and unnecessary to extend the application of section 30 to the provisions of section 32. In this respect, it is significant in my view that section 30 precedes rather than follows section 32.

We may now return to the question posed above: does the Charter apply to the governments, that is, to the administrative and executive branches, of the Territories? One important observation must be made. Because the Territories are not endowed with sovereign powers, their executive and administrative authority is not derived from the Constitution, but is delegated by the federal government. On this basis one may argue that the exercise of the executive and administrative powers conferred on the Territories is subject to the Charter by virtue of section 32(1)(a), which makes the Charter applicable to "the Parliament and government of Canada in respect of all matters within the authority of Parliament including all matters relating to the Yukon Territory and Northwest Territories". On this approach the Territories would be bound by the Charter to the same extent as the Parliament and Government of Canada for all purposes, whether legislative, executive or administrative.[3]

2. THE CHARTER DOES NOT EXTEND LEGISLATIVE POWERS (SECTION 31)

Section 31 provides that "[n]othing in this Charter extends the legislative powers of any body or authority".

As will be seen when section 32 is examined, the Charter limits and constrains the legislative authority of Parliament and the provincial legislatures, but it cannot be invoked to enlarge their powers. Thus Parliament could not rely on the Charter to enact laws outside of its area of legislative competence with a view to remedying a presumed oversight on the part of provincial authorities. In the first edition of this book, Professor Swinton described the differences which exist in this respect between the Canadian Charter and the American *Bill of Rights*. In the United States, Congress has the power to enact legislation to implement the guarantees of the Thirteenth amendment (guarantee against slavery), the Fourteenth amendment (the right to due process of law) and the Fifteenth amendment (equal protection of the laws) of the American *Bill of Rights* in opposition to any state legislation which impairs these guarantees.[4] The Canadian Parliament, on the other hand, could not rely on the Charter to claim that it possessed legislative authority outside its normal jurisdiction in order to ensure that provincial Charter obligations are fulfilled.

By virtue of section 52 of the *Constitution Act, 1982*, the task of ensuring compliance with the Charter is vested exclusively in the courts. Under this section, laws that are inconsistent with the provisions of the Charter will be declared by a competent court to be of no force or effect.[5]

3. WHO IS BOUND BY THE CANADIAN CHARTER OF RIGHTS AND FREEDOMS? (SECTION 32)

It is relatively simple to determine who are the beneficiaries of the rights and freedoms guaranteed by the Charter. It is much harder to

---

3 See the discussion concerning the Territories and s. 32 under "3. (b) Legislative Power", *infra* at p. 70.

4 Tarnopolsky & Beaudoin, *supra*, note 1 at 42 *et seq.*

5 See *infra*, 5. The Supremacy of the *Canadian Charter of Rights and Freedoms*.

determine who is obliged to respect them.

The Charter obviously limits the state's freedom of action by requiring it to respect the values that the Charter guarantees. The difficulty lies in determining how the state is to be defined for the purpose of applying the Charter. Are all the activities of the state included — legislative, executive and judicial? The obligation to respect the Charter is clearly imposed on Parliament and the provincial legislatures, which together exercise the legislative power of the Canadian state. However, what of the persons and bodies which exercise regulatory powers delegated by either Parliament or the legislatures? Are they bound by the Charter? It is equally clear that the government, insofar as it exercises the executive power of the state, is bound. But how is government to be defined for this purpose? Does it include Crown corporations, corporations acting as Crown agents, corporations that are regulated by the government, corporations that receive financial assistance from the government? What of local government bodies such as municipalities and school boards? What of universities, community colleges and hospitals? Are these bodies part of the government and are they subject as such to the Charter? Finally, to what extent are the courts, insofar as they exercise the judicial power of the state, themselves bound to respect the Charter?

Clearly, these questions would be superfluous if everyone — not only the state — was bound by the Charter. Some have so argued.[6] However, in a recent judgment, the Supreme Court of Canada has unequivocally rejected the theory of the general application of the Charter to private law relations,[7] with the result that one of the most complex questions posed by the Charter consist in determining and defining who is bound by it. These are the questions that shall be addressed in this section.

(a) The Charter Limits the State's Freedom of Action

The provisions of section 32 of the *Canadian Charter of Rights and*

---

6 Among the authors who argue that the Charter binds individuals as much as the state, see the following: D. Gibson, "The Charter of Rights and the Private Sector" (1982), 12 *Man. L.J.* 213; "Distinguishing the Governors from the Governed: The Meaning of 'Government' under Section 32(1) of the Charter" (1983), 13 *Man. L.J.* 505; *The Law of the Charter: General Principles* (Toronto: Carswell, 1986) (hereinafter Gibson, *The Law of the Charter*). D. Lluelles & P. Trudel, "L'application de la Charte canadienne des droits et libertés aux rapports de droit privé" (1984), 18 *R.J.T.* 219; M. Manning, *Rights, Freedoms and the Courts, A Practical Analysis of the Constitution Act, 1982* (Toronto: Emond-Montgomery, 1983); Y. De Montigny, "Section 32 and Equality Rights", in A.F. Bayefsky and M. Eberts, eds., *Equality Rights and the Canadian Charter of Rights and Freedoms* (Toronto: Carswell, 1985); B. Slattery, "Charter of Rights and Freedoms — Does it Bind Private Persons?" (1985), 63 *Can. Bar Rev.* 148.

7 *R.W.D.S.U., Local 580 v. Dolphin Delivery Ltd.*, [1986] 2 S.C.R. 573.

Freedoms leave no doubt respecting its application to the state. The section reads as follows.

Application of Charter
> 32.(1)   This Charter applies
> (*a*) to the Parliament and government of Canada in respect of all matters within the authority of Parliament including all matters relating to the Yukon Territory and Northwest Territories; and
> (*b*) to the legislature and government of each province in respect of all matters within the authority of the legislature of each province.[8]

One should note that, contrary to the *Canadian Bill of Rights* of 1960 which applies only to matters within federal jurisdiction,[9] it is the Canadian state in its entirety, provincial as well as federal, that is subject to the *Canadian Charter of Rights and Freedoms*. Section 32(1)(a) establishes this unequivocally.

(b) Legislative Power: Parliament and the Provincial Legislatures

The obligation to respect the Charter applies to the totality of legislative authority exercisable by the Canadian state, for Parliament and the provincial legislatures which in their respective domains enjoy complete legislative sovereignty are equally bound. Parliament is defined in section 17 of the *Constitution Act, 1867* as consisting of the Queen (represented in Canada by the Governor General), an Upper House called the Senate, and the House of Commons. It is on Parliament so defined that the Constitution of 1867 conferred the exercise of federal legislative authority. The exercise of provincial legislative authority is entrusted to the provincial legislatures, each consisting of a Lieutenant Governor and a legislative assembly.[10]

---

8 Part I of the *Constitution Act, 1982,* [en. by the *Canada Act 1982* (U.K.), 1982, c. 11, Sched. B] (referred to hereinafter as "the Charter"). S. 32(2) provides that s. 15, guaranteeing the right to equality, was not to come into force until three years after the proclamation of the Charter. This subsection is spent, as s. 15 came into force April 17, 1985.

9 S.C. 1960, c. 44.

10 See, *e.g.*, with respect to Ontario and Quebec, ss. 69 and 71 of the *Constitution Act, 1867* (U.K.), 30 & 31 Vict., c. 3, as amended. In this respect, it is to be noted that the amendment of the Constitution is authorized by proclamations adopted by the provincial legislative assemblies and not the provincial legislatures. The Lieutenant Governors therefore do not participate in the formal process of amending the Constitution. Similarly, the Governor General of Canada, although he or she proclaims the amendments authorized by the two federal Houses and the required number of legislative assemblies, does not, strictly speaking, participate in the adoption of resolutions amending the Constitution. This, of course, contrasts with his or her role in the enactment of ordinary federal laws.

Section 52 of the *Constitution Act, 1982* explicitly affirms that any law that is inconsistent with the provisions of the Charter is of no force or effect.[11] It is evident that the term "law" refers *inter alia* to statutes enacted by Parliament and the provincial legislatures. Sections 32 and 52 read together lead clearly to the conclusion that the framers intended federal and provincial legislation to be subject to the Charter.

(i) *The Senate and the House of Commons and Charter compliance*

It is clear that Parliament and the provincial legislatures are bound by the Charter in exercising their respective legislative powers. However, what is the position when the Senate and the House of Commons act alone? Although the Senate and the House of Commons are fundamental components of Parliament and play an essential role in the process of enacting federal statutes, strictly speaking, they do not constitute Parliament. Does it follow that inquiries or disciplinary proceedings undertaken by the House of Commons, for example, are not subject to the Charter? Could this reasoning apply to the administrative apparatus of the Senate and the House of Commons? Are those who administer this apparatus, including the speakers of the Senate and the House, bound by the Charter in their dealings with support staff? Can any person who has dealings with this apparatus insist on compliance with the Charter?

There can be no doubt that legislation enacted by Parliament respecting the Senate and the House of Commons as well as their personnel is subject to the Charter. Every legislative act of Parliament is subject to the Charter, pursuant to sections 32(1) and 52(1). This includes, for example, the *Senate and House of Commons Act*[12] and the recent federal legislation extending the right of collective bargaining to some of the staff of the two Houses.[13] These legislative initiatives are subject to judicial review under section 52 of the *Constitution Act, 1982* in order to ensure compliance with the provisions of the Charter. Moreover, any person who relies on this legislation to justify his actions is subject to the same power of review. Policies for hiring, promotion and the granting of contracts must equally comply with the Charter.

The supremacy of the Charter over the Senate and the House of Commons is much greater than this, however. In my view, it extends to every action taken by the Senate and the House of Commons, by virtue

---

11 S. 52(1) reads as follows: "The Constitution of Canada is the supreme law of Canada, and any law that is inconsistent with the provisions of the Constitution is, to the extent of the inconsistency, of no force or effect."

12 R.S.C. 1970, c. S-8 [*Parliament of Canada Act*, R.S.C. 1985, c. P-1]

13 *Parliamentary Employment and Staff Relations Act*, S.C. 1986, c. 41.

of their traditional rights and privileges, which affects individual rights. Thus it would apply, for example, to the penal sanctions which may be imposed on a person found guilty of contempt of Parliament. The Charter applies to Parliament in the exercise of its legislative power. It would be incongruous if the Houses of Parliament could ignore the Charter in circumstances where their non-legislative actions violate fundamental values protected by the Charter.[14]

(ii) *Subordinate legislation*

While it is clear that legislation enacted by Parliament and the legislatures must comply with the Charter, what of subordinate legislation? Whether it be the Cabinet, a minister, a civil servant, a commission or an administrative tribunal, in delegating to others their power to legislate, Parliament and the legislatures must respect the provisions of the Charter. The law that confers legislative authority on a body must itself respect the Charter. Section 52(1) of the *Constitution Act, 1982* is conclusive on this point. However, it is not enough in my view that the enabling legislation in no way violates the Charter. The receiving authority must also respect the Charter in the exercise of the legislative powers conferred on it by Parliament or the legislature. The subordinate authority to which legislative powers are delegated must be subject to the same obligations and constraints as the enabling authority. If it were otherwise, Parliament and the legislatures could avoid their constitutional obligations simply by confiding to others the authority to exercise their powers. This means that all regulation-making authority conferred on Cabinet, individual ministers, civil servants, commissions or administrative tribunals must be exercised so as to comply with the Charter. It means still more, however. Not only must the regulations themselves comply with the Charter, but actions taken under the authority of those regulations must also comply.[15] Moreover, it is not necessary that the person who exercises this legislative authority or acts pursuant to it be, properly speaking, part of the government. If the person purports to act on the basis of a law or a regulation, his action is subject to the Charter. This applies most notably to individuals who

---

14 See H. Street, *Freedom, the Individual and the Law*, 4th ed. (1977), especially Chapter 6 "Freedom of expression: contempt of court and contempt of Parliament", where the author gives a number of examples of abuses committed by the two Houses of the British Parliament over the course of history, *e.g.*, imprisoning journalists without giving them the opportunity to be heard, etc. See also the decision of Chief Justice Glube of the Supreme Court of Nova Scotia, in *Maclean v. A.G. Nova Scotia* (1987), 76 N.S.R. (2d) 296 (T.D.) where the court raised but did not resolve the question of the application of the Charter to the traditional rights and powers of the legislative assembly.

15 P.W. Hogg, *Constitutional Law of Canada*, 2nd ed. (Toronto: Carswell, 1985) at 671.

make arrests pursuant to powers conferred by the *Criminal Code*.

There has been a tremendous increase in subordinate legislation over the course of the past 25 years. Government by way of regulation is much more commonplace today than is government by conventional legislation. In the federal domain, one can no longer count the statutes which confer on Cabinet or a minister or a commission or administrative tribunal the power to enact regulations and thus exercise by way of delegation the legislative authority of Parliament. The situation is much the same at the provincial level. The enabling legislation, and equally the subordinate legislation and all actions taken pursuant to it, must respect the rights and freedoms guaranteed by the Charter. Otherwise they may be declared inoperative or unconstitutional by the courts under section 52(1) of the Charter.

This is the case, for example, with the professional associations on which the state confers the task of regulating the professions and controlling professional conduct. Provincial legislatures have delegated regulation-making authority to these bodies. By virtue of the legislation creating and governing them, they exercise a subordinate legislative power. In exercising this power, they are obliged to respect the rights and freedoms guaranteed by the Charter. This has already been established in connection with the legal profession. In *Re Klein and Law Society of Upper Canada*,[16] Callaghan J. wrote as follows:

> In promulgating rules relating to legal advertising or relations between the press and bar, the Law Society is performing a regulatory function on behalf of the "Legislature and government" of Ontario within the meaning of s. 32 of the Charter . . . In my view, the fact that the Rules and commentaries in the code of professional conduct have not been adopted as regulations under the *Law Society Act* does not prevent them from falling within the ambit of the Charter . . . In enforcing the prohibitions against fee advertising and commenting to the press through the discipline process, the Law Society effectively makes these prohibitions part of the law of Ontario and subject to the constitutional restraint of the Charter.

The same conclusion would be reached respecting any person or body on which Parliament or a provincial legislature conferred the authority to exercise part of its legislative power.

(iii) *The Territories*

What is the position of Canada's Territories? Do these principles apply

---

16 (1985), 13 C.R.R. 120 at 153-154 (Ont. Div. Ct.); see also *Black v. Law Soc. of Alberta* (1986), 20 C.R.R. 117 (Alta. C.A.), leave to appeal to S.C.C. granted (1986), 22 C.R.R. 192n (S.C.C.).

to the Territories, whose status is not protected by the Canadian Constitution and whose existence depends entirely on the Canadian Parliament?

There can be no doubt that the constitutive legislation for the Yukon and Northwest Territories which provides for their good government and confers upon them the delegated legislative authority necessary for this purpose is subject to the provisions of the Charter. Section 32(1)(a) is explicit on this point. It states that the Charter applies to Parliament and to the government of Canada in respect of all matters within the authority of Parliament, "including all matters relating to the Yukon Territory and Northwest Territories". Given that the Territories exercise, by way of delegation from Parliament, powers which in the rest of Canada are conferred on the provinces by the Constitution, this specific reference in section 32 is no doubt designed to eliminate any possible ambiguity as to the application of the Charter to federal legislation relating to the Territories, especially in matters which are within provincial jurisdiction.[17]

In exercising the legislative powers conferred on them by Parliament, the territorial authorities are, in my view, and for the reasons already explained, bound by the Charter. This means that any legislation enacted by the legislative council of a Territory must comply with the provisions of the Charter and so must any administrative action taken by territorial authorities pursuant to either the federal enabling legislation or the territorial law.

In the *St-Jean* case,[18] the Supreme Court of the Yukon had to determine whether section 133 of the *Constitution Act, 1867* applies to the legislative council of the Yukon. The issue, more precisely, was whether the laws or ordinances of the Territory are Acts of Parliament within the meaning of section 133 and whether, in consequence, they should be printed and published in both official languages. The scope of the words "Acts of the Parliament" had earlier been considered by the Supreme Court of Canada in the *Blaikie* cases.[19] That court gave the words a scope much broader than their ordinary meaning would at first glance suggest, thereby extending the application of section 133 to the vast areas of federal and provincial

---

17 Mr. Justice Myer of the Supreme Court of the Yukon Territory expressed a different opinion in *Re St-Jean and R.* (September 26, 1986): "The purpose of mentioning the Yukon Territory, expressly in s. 32(1)(a), seems to me to be simply to ensure that those Charter protections, which apply in all of the provinces of Canada in matters relating to federal as compared with provincial matters, will also apply in the Yukon Territory in those areas not delegated to the Commissioner in Council by s. 16 of the *Yukon Act* and therefore not covered by s. 30 and s. 32(1)(b) of the Charter." (p. 18)

18 *Re St-Jean and R.*, ibid.

19 *Blaikie v. A.G. Quebec (No 1)* (1979), 101 D.L.R. (3d) 394 (S.C.C.) (hereinafter referred to as "*Blaikie (No. 1)*") and *A.G. Quebec v. Blaikie (No. 2)*, [1981] 1 S.C.R. 312 (hereinafter referred to as "*Blaikie (No 2)*").

governmental regulation. For both legal and historical reasons, however, the court refused to apply the words to municipal bylaws. On similar grounds, the Yukon Supreme Court refused to find that ordinances of the legislative council of the Territory constitute "Acts of the Parliament" within the meaning of section 133 of the *Constitution Act, 1867.*

In my view, neither the *St-Jean* case[20] nor the *Blaikie* cases[21] apply to section 32(1) of the Charter. The issue in these cases is the meaning of the words "Acts of the Parliament" in section 133. These words do not appear in section 32(1) of the Charter, and there is no valid reason why the ordinances of the legislative councils of the Territories should not be subject to the Charter. Quite apart from the principle that the subordinate authority to which legislative power is delegated is subject in exercising this power to the same constraints as the delegating authority, this result follows clearly from section 30 of the Charter. This reasoning applies as well, in my view, to the exercise of the executive powers of the Territories.[22]

However, it remains to be determined whether the legislative and executive agencies of the Territories are institutions of Parliament and the government of Canada for the purpose of section 16(1) of the Charter. This would give the French and English languages equality of status and equal rights and privileges as to their use in the legislative councils and in the institutions of the governments of the Territories.

The reference to the institutions of Parliament in the expression "institutions of the Parliament and government of Canada" creates difficulties because it is ambiguous. It could be construed as a reference either to the institutions *created* by Parliament or to the institutions which *constitute* Parliament. If the first meaning were adopted, the expression would include all bodies created by Parliament. It would extend to every public entity brought into existence by an Act of Parliament; this would include the Territories and any courts created by Parliament.

If the expression were understood to refer to those institutions which, strictly speaking, constitute Parliament, then it would include only the Senate and the House of Commons, their respective committees, the various administrative structures of Parliament properly defined and the institutions directly connected with Parliament, such as the Auditor General, the Commissioner of Official Languages, the Chief Electoral Officer and the like. On this approach, the legislative councils of the Territories would not be institutions of Parliament within the meaning of section 16(1), even

---

20 *Re St-Jean and R., supra,* note 17.

21 *Blaikie (No. 1)* and *Blaikie (No. 2), supra,* note 19.

22 See *infra*, 1. The *Canadian Charter of Rights and Freedoms* and the Territories".

though they are creatures of Parliament.[23] In the *St-Jean* case,[24] the Court concluded that neither the legislative council nor the executive government of the Yukon Territory constituted an "institution of the Parliament or government of Canada" within the meaning of section 16(1) of the *Constitution Act, 1982.*

(iv) *Municipalities*

Like the Territories of the North, municipalities in Canada do not have a status protected by the Constitution. Their existence and their powers depend entirely on the legislative authority of the provinces.

Although the municipalities are not expressly mentioned in section 32 of the Charter where the position of the provinces is addressed, it is clear in my view that the constitutive laws relating to municipalities are subject to the provisions of the Charter. This follows from the fact that, under sections 32(1) and 52(1), all provincial legislation must comply with the Charter. In my view, the Supreme Court judgments in the *Blaikie* cases[25] could not be relied on to support the proposition that the Charter does not apply to municipalities. Section 32 does not limit the application of the Charter to "Acts of the Parliament" (section 133 of the *Constitution Act, 1867*). It ensues that the Charter provisions apply to the legislature itself.

It follows that the municipalities must comply with the Charter in exercising the legislative powers delegated to them as is the case with any body exercising delegated legislative authority. This means that municipal bylaws which do not respect the Charter are subject to review by the courts and may be declared inoperative and of no effect under section 52.[26] The fact that section 30 of the Charter expressly makes this point in connection with the Territories does not in my view prevent it from implicitly applying to municipalities. The Territories are in a special position in that they are physically situate outside the borders of any province and they exercise a legislative authority delegated by Parliament over matters within provincial jurisdiction. It was necessary to remove any ambiguity that could arise as a result of the quasi-provincial character of their legislative powers. This problem does not arise in the case of

---

23 As to the concept of "institutions of Parliament and the Government of Canada", see the definition proposed by the Minister of Justice in Bill C-72, *An Act respecting the Status and Use of the Official Languages of Canada*, 2d Sess., 33d Parl., 1987.

24 *Re St-Jean and R., supra*, note 17.

25 *Blaikie (No. 1)* and *Blaikie (No. 2), supra*, note 19.

26 See, *inter alia, Re McCutcheon and Toronto* (1983), 41 O.R. (2d) 652 at 662 (H.C.); *Hardie v. Summerland (District)* (1985), 22 C.R.R. 204 (B.C. S.C.).

municipalities and, with respect to them therefore, there was no ambiguity to remove.[27]

(v) *Conclusion*

While it is clear that Parliament and the provincial legislatures are obliged to respect the rights and freedoms guaranteed by the Charter in enacting legislation, this is equally true of all persons and all bodies, private or public, to whom a power to legislate has been delegated. The legislative councils of the Territories, municipalities, the Cabinet, ministers, indeed all who receive the power to legislate from Parliament or the legislatures, are bound by the Charter. As well, the action of any person who acts pursuant to a legislative provision is reviewable under the Charter.

(c) Executive Power: The Government of Canada and the Provincial Governments

Under this heading, two main questions will be examined: first, the meaning of the term "government" in the context of section 32 of the Charter and, second, the types of governmental activities to which the Charter applies.

(i) *The concept of government*

Section 32 makes the Charter applicable not only to Parliament and the provincial legislatures, but also to the government of Canada and the governments of the provinces. This means that the Charter applies not just to the legislative activity of the state, but equally to its activities of an administrative or executive nature. What is meant by the word "government" in this context?

Section 9 of the *Constitution Act, 1867* expressly vests executive power in the Queen by stating that "the Executive Government and authority of and over Canada is hereby declared to continue and be vested in the Queen". Section 12 of the *Constitution Act, 1867* establishes the office of the Governor General. The Governor General governs Canada in the name of the Queen by exercising the executive powers that are vested in the Queen in respect of Canada. These powers are exercised by the Governor General alone or with the consent of the Privy Council for Canada. At

---

27 S. 30 reads as follows: "A reference in this Charter to a province or to the legislative assembly or legislature of a province shall be deemed to include a reference to the Yukon Territory and the Northwest Territories, or to the appropriate legislative authority thereof, as the case may be."

the provincial level, the office of Lieutenant Governor is provided for in section 58. The Lieutenant Governor of each province represents the Crown as head of the province.

The functions of the Queen's representatives are today largely symbolic, their real powers having been considerably diminished over time. In practice, the executive power of the state in a narrow sense is exercised at the federal level by a committee of the Privy Council — the Cabinet or Council of Ministers — and at the provincial level, in Quebec for example, by the Executive Council. Technically, however, the executive power of the Canadian state remains vested in the Crown.

The Crown, acting through the Queen's federal or provincial representatives, each within their respective jurisdictions, possesses all the attributes of a legal person. The Crown has the capacity to own, acquire and dispose of property and to sue in law. The Crown may provide services, run businesses and administer programs. The Queen possesses all the powers which are granted her under the Constitution as well as certain special prerogatives and immunities which are not available to her subjects.[28]

In a broader sense, executive power includes the administration of the affairs of the state. The concepts of legislative and executive power are not watertight, and the legislative authority sometimes confers a power to legislate on a body exercising what is essentially an executive function. This is what happens each time Parliament delegates to the Cabinet the power to make regulations. The making of regulations by Cabinet is a legislative rather than an executive function. On the other hand, the administrative structures of the state — the government departments and agencies which carry on the work of consultation, decision making, regulation, administrative and commercial management — are in principle part of the executive branch of the state, even if in a narrow sense they are not part of the executive power.

It appears, then, that a preliminary question must be resolved in the context of section 32 of the Charter. It is clear that the word "government" includes the federal and provincial Crown. It also includes, in my view, all persons and bodies which in fact exercise the executive power of the federal state as opposed to the legislative power that is assigned to the Parliament of Canada. In other words, at the federal level, "government" refers to bodies which exercise an executive or administrative function. On this approach, the expression "government of Canada" in the context of section 32 does not embrace the government of Canada in the broadest, most general sense of the federal state with its legislative, executive and

---

28 On this question, see R. Dussault & L. Borgeat, *Administrative Law: A Treatise*, 2d ed. (Toronto: Carswell, 1985), Vol. 1, at 51-56, and Hogg, *supra*, note 15 at 216-217.

judicial components; the reference rather is to the executive and administrative branches of the state.[29] Even on this approach, however, the meaning of the word "government" remains in doubt.

A. *Departments, boards, secretariats, commissions, etc.* At the federal level, the expression "government of Canada" refers, we have seen, to the Crown in whom is vested responsibility for the good government of Canada. It also refers to all those who act in the name of the Sovereign or who exercise in her name or as her representative the executive power of the federal state. This includes the Cabinet, the Prime Minister and his ministers, civil servants, and representatives or agents of the government of Canada when exercising the powers of the Sovereign or acting in the name of the Crown. The various departments, offices, and administrative bodies established under the statutes of the Canadian Parliament are also included in the term.[30]

This should include bodies established by federal statute to carry out regulatory or supervisory tasks. Examples include the Canadian Transport Commission, which exercises regulatory and supervisory functions in the field of national transportation; the National Energy Board, which plays an important role in the management of energy resources; the Canadian Radio and Television Commission which exercises authority in the field of communications and broadcasting; and the National Parole Board, which assists in the administration of certain sentences imposed by the courts. These bodies exercise a governmental function and are, in my view, obliged to respect the rights and freedoms guaranteed by the Charter in all their actions. The National Energy Board, for example, is bound by the Charter to the same extent as the Department of Energy Mines and Resources. In this respect, the Board and the Department owe the same duty to comply.

Having established this, however, there remains the task of determining in each specific case what right or freedom guaranteed by the Charter has been infringed. In the case of licences issued by the Canadian Radio and Television Commission, for example, the issue might be freedom of expression as guaranteed by section 2 of the Charter. In proceedings before

---

29 See *Dolphin Delivery Inc.*, *supra*, note 7 at 598. Even if there is no equivalent of s. 9 of the *Constitution Act, 1867* respecting the provinces, the expression "government of each province" must include the provincial authority which is commonly referred to formally as "Her Majesty the Queen in right of the province" or "the provincial Crown".

30 On the subject of the Cabinet, see Dickson C.J. in *Operation Dismantle Inc. v. R.*, [1985] 1 S.C.R. 441 at 455, to the effect that the decisions of Cabinet are subject to review by the courts in order to ensure compliance with the Charter and that the executive government in general is bound to act in accordance with the dictates of the Charter.

the National Parole Board, on the other hand, the legal rights set out in the Charter are likely to figure prominently.[31]

B. *Crown corporations.* What is the position of Crown corporations? The Canadian Broadcasting Corporation is an agent of the Crown. Is it obliged as such to comply with the Charter? Air Canada and Petro Canada are both Crown corporations, but they are not declared to be Crown agents in their enabling legislation. Must they comply with the Charter? The answer depends on whether they are thought to come within the meaning of the words "government of Canada" in section 32 of the Charter.

Traditionally, Crown corporations that are Crown agents are thought to exercise their powers and manage their affairs in the name of the Crown and, on this basis, are entitled to claim Crown privileges and immunities; Crown corporations which are not Crown agents, lacking the basis for such a claim, are excluded.

To determine whether Parliament has expressly made a corporation an agent of the Crown, it will often be enough to consult the incorporating Act. If the corporation is a Crown agent, it must comply with the Charter. However, even if the incorporating legislation is silent on this point, the corporation may yet be a Crown agent by virtue of the common law. Over the years the courts have developed rules to determine whether particular public enterprises are entitled to the benefit of Crown privileges and immunities in areas such as, *inter alia,* immunity from prosecution and civil liability, immunity from taxation and the non-application of statutes, to name a few.

In essence, determining whether a corporation is an agent of the Crown at common law depends on the nature and scope of the control that the Crown or its representative exercises over the corporation. The greater the ministerial control, the greater the likelihood that the corporation will be regarded as a Crown agent. As Professor Hogg points out, it is not enough for the minister to exercise *de facto* control over the corporation; his control must be *de jure.* The courts will focus on the degree of control conferred on the minister by the legislation rather than the degree of control that the minister exercises in fact. The power to appoint the officers of the corporation or the members of the board of directors or even to appropriate public funds to the corporation is not in itself enough to warrant the conclusion that the corporation is an agent of the Crown. Conversely, the presence of the minister at the head of the corporation will suffice

---

31 See *Evans v. R.* (1986), 30 C.C.C. (3d) 1 (Ont. H.C.), aff'd (1986), 30 C.C.C. (3d) 313 (Ont. C.A.).

to justify the conclusion that the corporation is a Crown agent.[32]

Corporations which by virtue of these common law principles are found to be Crown corporations would also be bound by the Charter. The control exercised by the government over such corporations would be enough to bring them within the scope of the governmental apparatus to which the Charter applies. However, Crown corporations which are not Crown agents would not be subject to the Charter. Their autonomy and freedom of action would preclude their being included in the concept of "government" embodied in section 32 of the Charter.

This approach, based on a literal interpretation of the words "government of Canada", leads to surprising results. On this approach, the C.B.C. as agent of the Crown would be subject to the Charter, while the private broadcasting corporations with which it competes would not. The C.B.C. would be obliged to respect the fundamental freedom of expression guaranteed by section 2, while its competitors would not.

This problem has been explored by Professors Swinton and Gibson who suggest a number of possible solutions. Professor Swinton, for example, recommends adopting the notion of "governmental function". On this approach, Crown agents would not automatically be bound by the Charter. Whether a Crown agent or not, whether private or not, an entity would be bound by the Charter only if it exercised a "governmental function".[33]

However, what meaning can be given to the notion of "governmental function"? Professor Gibson was quick to point out the difficulties of defining such a concept.[34] There are no clear and generally accepted criteria for determining when a function is properly judged to be governmental. National defence, the conduct of foreign affairs and the regulation of air transport are doubtless governmental functions. However, the line soon becomes blurred. With the advent of modern messenger services, can one say that mail delivery is strictly speaking a governmental function? It would be easy to turn over the delivery of airline passenger service to the private

---

32 See in particular the Supreme Court of Canada's judgment in *Fidelity Ins. Co. of Can. v. Cronkhite Supply Ltd.*, [1979] 2 S.C.R. 27, and generally Hogg, *supra*, note 15 at 217. See also the important legislation enacted by Parliament in 1984 (S.C. 1984, c. 31) on Crown corporations in the form of amendments to the *Financial Administration Act*, R.S.C. 1970, c. F-10 [R.S.C. 1985, c. F-11]. Under s. 99 [s. 89] of the *Financial Administration Act*, as amended by c. 31, the Governor in Council may give directions to a Crown corporation that is wholly owned by Her Majesty, where he or she believes that it is in the public interest to do so. In my view, such directions as well as any actions taken by the corporation pursuant to such directions would have to comply with the Charter.

33 K. Swinton, Chapter 2 "Application of the Canadian Charter of Rights and Freedoms", in Tarnopolsky & Beaudoin, *supra*, note 1 at 72-73.

34 Gibson, *The Law of the Charter, supra*, note 6 at 100 *et seq.*

sector. Could one seriously suggest that Air Canada, once privatized, would exercise a governmental function?

What of broadcasting? Do the private sector networks which operate in this area exercise a governmental function? Do the C.B.C., Radio-Québec or TV Ontario exercise a governmental function? Do we consider the sale of alcoholic beverages, which in our country traditionally has been handled by public authorities, to be a governmental function? Would it cease being a governmental function if it were handed over to private enterprise? Just asking these questions illustrates the difficulty of defining what constitutes a governmental function. Professor Gibson explores several ways to define the notion of "governmental function" before concluding that there is none which is really satisfactory. Indeed, this is one of the reasons which lead him to recommend the application of the Charter to the whole of the private sector.

If the traditional ways of interpreting the expression "government of Canada" lead to incongruous results, it is open to the courts, in my view, to adopt a purposive interpretation of section 32. On this approach, the concept of government would be clarified by analyzing the framers' purpose in entrenching a particular right or freedom in the Constitution. To determine whether a private entity is bound to respect a given right or freedom protected by the Charter, one would examine the character of its activities, the role that these activities play in the maintenance and growth of a free and democratic society based on respect for the person, tolerance and the principle of equality without discrimination and, finally, how seriously the action complained of interferes with the protected value.

Using this analysis, the court's response to a violation of the freedom of expression guaranteed by section 2 of the Charter would depend on the gravity of the entity's interference with the values protected by freedom of expression. For example, any interference with the freedom of political expression that jeopardized the proper functioning and quality of our democratic system would contravene the Charter whether the interfering entity was a Crown corporation or a private broadcaster. Given the key role played by broadcasting corporations in securing the goals of freedom and tolerance enshrined in the *Charter*, it is essential that they be required to respect these fundamental freedoms whenever their actions would place them seriously in jeopardy.

This approach to the question of the Charter's application rejects a literal interpretation of section 32 based on criteria established for other purposes in order to focus attention on the fundamental objectives sought by the Charter. In the *Blaikie* cases,[35] the Supreme Court of Canada adopted a purposive approach similar to the one suggested here in its construction

---

35 *Supra*, note 19.

of the words "Acts ... of the Legislature" in section 133 of the *Constitution Act, 1867*. In the *Dolphin Delivery* case,[36] however, the court appears to have slammed the door on this approach to section 32 of the Charter. The method adopted by the court in this judgment has more in common with the traditional approach to statutory construction and leaves little room for a purposive interpretation of section 32.[37]

C. *Corporations whose activities are regulated by the government.* What is the position of commercial corporations whose activities are regulated by a governmental agency such as the Canadian Radio and Television Commission (C.R.T.C.)? Can one conclude from the fact that a corporation's activities are regulated by the government that the corporation itself is obliged to comply with the Charter?

As pointed out above, any regulations established by the C.R.T.C. respecting broadcasting entities subject to its jurisdiction as well as any individual decisions made by the C.R.T.C. pursuant to federal legislation or its own regulations must comply with the Charter. In my view, the Commission is equally bound with respect to the licences it issues and the conditions it attaches thereto.

Moreover, in keeping with the judgment of the Supreme Court in the *Dolphin Delivery* case,[38] the Charter might well be invoked in a dispute with a private corporation whose activities are regulated by the government if the corporation sought to rely on governmental authority (whether legislative or otherwise) to justify its actions. For example, a corporation might seek to rely on federal legislation to justify its policy of compulsory retirement for employees reaching a certain age. However, in such a case the Charter could be invoked, not because the corporation engages in activities which are regulated by the government or one of its agencies, but because it has relied on governmental authority to which the Charter applies. To this extent only may the Charter be invoked against corporations regulated by the government.[39]

D. *Commercial corporations generally.* On the approach taken so far, the mere fact that a corporation owes its existence to governmental authority would not suffice to make it subject to the Charter. Corporations created by the state pursuant to general or specific legislation are not *ipso*

---

36 *Supra*, note 7.
37 *Ibid.*
38 *Ibid.*
39 See *Madisso v. Bell Canada* (1985), 22 C.R.R. 162 (Ont. H.C.), aff'd (February 25, 1987) CA 629/85 (Ont. C.A.), where the court held that the fact that an enterprise was regulated by the C.R.T.C. did not suffice to make the Charter applicable to it.

facto Crown corporations. They are creations of the state, but they do not form part of the machinery of government. To conclude otherwise would effectively extend the application of the *Charter* to a considerable portion of the private sector. This was the conclusion reached by the Court of Queen's Bench of Saskatchewan in a case involving the Appraisal Institute of Canada, a voluntary association incorporated under a statute of the Parliament of Canada and possessing no statutory powers. Wright J. held as follows:

> If a body exercises a statutory power — that is authority expressly granted by a legislative body — it *may* be brought within the scope of the Charter as it represents a kind of governmental power. Conversely, if the body scrutinized is a private and voluntary association or corporation created pursuant to a general or public law of the Legislature, it cannot and should not be categorized as governmental in nature even if its activities affect important interests of its members.[40]

Equally, the fact that a corporation receives financial assistance from the government would not suffice to make it part of the government and thus subject to the *Charter of Rights.*

E. *Municipalities.* Municipalities raise an interesting question. We have seen that municipalities must comply with the Charter in exercising the legislative powers which are delegated to them by provincial legislatures. In other words, municipal bylaws are subject to the Charter. Furthermore, it is clear that any municipal action taken pursuant to its bylaws or its enabling legislation is also subject to the Charter. However, what of actions that depend on neither bylaw nor legislation? A municipality might, for example, introduce internal directives which impose severe restraints on its employees' freedom of expression. Its policy for granting municipal contracts might violate rights or freedoms guaranteed by the Charter. The question, in short, is whether the Charter applies not only to the regulatory or legislative acts of municipalities, but to their executive and adminis-trative acts as well.

Section 32 provides that the Charter applies to the legislative and executive institutions of the state, both federal and provincial. At first glance, on a narrow interpretation of this section, one might conclude that municipalities do not form part of the provincial government and that the Charter therefore does not reach them, at least in the exercise of their executive and administrative functions. This, however, would give too

---

40 *Chyz v. Appraisal Institute of Can.* (1984), 13 C.R.R. 3 at 12 (Sask. Q.B.), rev'd (1985), 44 Sask. R. 165 (Sask. C.A.). See also *Peg-Win Real Estate Ltd. v. Winnipeg Real Estate Bd.* (1985), 19 D.L.R. (4th) 438 (Man. Q.B.), aff'd (1986), 27 D.L.R. (4th) 767 (Man. C.A.). See also Gibson, *The Law of the Charter, supra,* note 6 at 105.

narrow a scope to section 32. In Canada, municipalities play a significant role in the lives of their citizens. The functions they exercise within their territories are governmental in character and they are derived, moreover, from provincial authority which is itself subject to the Charter. In my view, it would be incongruous for a governmental agency like a municipality to be exempt from the Charter when the provincial governmental authority from which it derives its powers is bound.[41]

F. *Universities and community colleges.* The question whether the Charter applies to universities has been raised in a number of judgments. To date, the courts have held that the Charter does not apply. In each case, the issue was whether the nature and extent of the control which the provincial government exercises over the university are sufficient to warrant the conclusion that the university is effectively part of government.

The judgment of Gray J. of the High Court of Ontario, in *Re McKinney and Board of Governors of the University of Guelph*,[42] is particularly interesting on this point. The court conducted an exhaustive study of the legal framework in which Ontario universities have developed, the role played by the government in university affairs at the level of financing, tuition fees and the like, and the status of Ontario universities in today's society generally and in their relations with the provincial government in particular. It arrived at the conclusion that the Charter does not bind Ontario universities. In the words of Mr. Justice Gray:

> I have had regard to the nature of universities, the extent to which they are created and regulated by statute, the nature of the relationship between the universities and the elected or executive branches of government, and the nature of the function or role which universities play in public life of the province. In my view, the "governmental function", "governmental control", "State action" or "nexus" which links the essentially private universities with the province is insufficient to invoke s. 32(1)(*b*) of the Charter.
>
> In arriving at this conclusion I am cognizant of the need for a cautious, case-by-case approach to the applicability of the Charter. Because of the extent of government involvement in funding the private sector, there is a risk of extending governmental action by way of the Charter instead of honouring the Charter's purpose of constraining government action. In this regard, the following passage of Dickson J. in *Hunter et al. v. Southam Inc.* . . . [1984] 2 S.C.R. 145 at p. 156 (quoted by Dubin J.A. in *Blainey* [(1986), 54 O.R. (2d) 513] at p. 521 . . . is important:

---

41 Although certain cases have held that the Charter binds municipalities in the exercise of legislative authority (see *supra*, note 16), I am not aware of any decisions concerning the executive or administrative power of municipalities in the sense intended here.

42 (1986), 57 O.R. (2d) 1 (H.C.), aff'd (1987), 63 O.R. (2d) 1 (C.A.), leave to appeal to S.C.C. granted April 21, 1988 (S.C.C.). See also *Bancroft v. Univ. of Toronto* (1986), 24 D.L.R. (4th) 620 (Ont. H.C.).

I begin with the obvious. The *Canadian Charter of Rights and Freedoms* is a purposive document. Its purpose is to guarantee and to protect, within the limits of reason, the enjoyment of the rights and freedoms it enshrines. It is intended to constrain governmental action inconsistent with those rights and freedoms; it is not in itself an authorization for governmental action.[43]

The same court, speaking this time through Mr. Justice White, arrived at a different conclusion respecting Ontario's community colleges.[44] This conclusion was based on a provision of the *Ministry of Colleges and Universities Act of Ontario* (section. 5(2)) which authorizes the creation of the Board of Regents, whose task it is to assist the minister responsible for colleges and universities. The Board is an agent of the Crown and for this reason, according to White J., is subject to the Charter. The judgment of White J. in the *Lavigne* case[45] is distinguished by Gray J. in the *McKinney* case[46] on the grounds that the minister exercises much greater authority over colleges than he does over universities. The approach adopted by the court in these two judgments does not differ significantly from the approach to Crown corporations discussed above.[47]

G. *School boards, hospitals, etc.* The same question arises in connection with school boards, hospitals and community health centres. These agencies will be obliged to comply with the Charter only if it is possible to demonstrate that the nature and extent of the control which the government exercises over them warrant the conclusion that they are part of the machinery of government. The result in particular cases will vary depending on the governing legislation which itself will vary from province to province.[48]

---

43 *Re McKinney, ibid.* at 21-22.
44 *Re Lavigne and O.P.S.E.U.* (1986), 55 O.R. (2d) 449 (H.C.), additional reasons (1987), 60 O.R. (2d) 486 (H.C.).
45 *Re McKinney, supra,* note 42.
46 *Re Lavigne, supra,* note 44.
47 *Supra,* pp. 80-83.
48 See *Stoffman v. Vancouver General Hosp.* (1986), 30 D.L.R. (4th) 700 (B.C.S.C.), aff'd (1987), 21 B.C.L.R. (2d) 165 (C.A.), leave to appeal to S.C.C., granted [1988] 4 W.W.R. lxxii (note) (S.C.C.) which held that the Charter applies not only to hospital regulations but also to the manner in which the regulations are applied. With respect to school boards, see *Ont. English Catholic Teachers Assn. v. Essex Co. Roman Catholic Separate School Bd.* (1987), 58 O.R. (2d) 545 at 561 (Ont. Div. Ct.), where the court decided that "a school board is created under a comprehensive statute dealing with education and has a clearly defined role within the scheme of the statute, and . . . in consequence . . . the actions of a board may properly be said to be, for the purposes of the Charter, the actions of the 'legislature' or 'government' of Ontario".

H. *Professional associations.* On the basis of this criterion, one would doubtless conclude that the bodies responsible for regulating the professions are too independent of provincial government to justify the conclusion that, according to section 32, they must comply with the Charter in hiring staff, for example, or setting a policy for the granting of service contracts. This proposition is perfectly consistent with the conclusion reached above that these bodies are bound by the Charter when they exercise their regulatory powers or when they act pursuant to provincial laws or subordinate legislation.[49]

(ii) *Government acts and activities that are subject to the Charter*

The application of the Charter to the activities of government and of agencies judged to form part of the government within the meaning of section 32 is sweeping. This at least is the implication of the Supreme Court of Canada's judgment in the *Operation Dismantle* case.[50] In the course of his reasons for judgment in this case, Chief Justice Dickson stated that "cabinet decisions . . . are . . . reviewable in the courts and subject to judicial scrutiny for compatibility with the Constitution".[51] "I have no doubt," he added, "that the executive branch of the Canadian government is duty bound to act in accordance with the dictates of the *Charter*".[52] Wilson J. as well expressed disagreement with the argument by the Attorney General of Canada that, with respect to government action, the Charter only applies to the exercise of powers directly conferred by statute.[53]

It thus appears that all the acts and activities of the government and of the agencies that form part of the government for the purpose of section 32 are subject to the rights and freedoms guaranteed by the Charter. This would include, for example, government policies on hiring, the granting of contracts, government appointments, the issue of passports, etc. The Charter applies to all the administrative decisions of government even if these decisions are not taken pursuant to a statute or to subordinate legislation and do not represent the exercise of a statutory power. Decisions which have legislative authorization are doubly bound. It follows that the judgment of the Supreme Court of Canada in the *Martineau* case,[54] which held that a decision of the Prison Disciplinary Committee was not reviewable because it was administrative in nature, would not apply in

---

49 See *Re Klein and L.S.U.C., supra,* note 16.
50 *Supra,* note 30.
51 *Ibid.* at 455.
52 *Ibid.* at 455.
53 *Ibid.* at 463.
54 *Martineau v. Matsqui Institution Inmate Disciplinary Bd. (No. 1),* [1978] 1 S.C.R. 118.

the context of section 32. In his reasons for judgment in *Martineau*,[55] Pigeon J. noted that the Commissioner of Penitentiaries had acted, not in the capacity of a lawmaker, but as an administrator. In my view, every act of the Commissioner is subject to the Charter regardless of the capacity in which he performs it.

For these reasons, as decided by the Supreme Court of Canada in the *Operation Dismantle* case,[56] the exercise of the royal prerogative is subject to the provisions of the Charter. Similarly, one must suppose that the Attorneys General of Canada, both federal and provincial, are bound by the Charter in exercising the powers enjoyed by them under the royal prerogative as well as the *Criminal Code*. In each instance, however, it is still essential to determine whether the particular provisions of the Charter apply in the circumstances of the particular case.[57]

Section 32 provides that the Charter applies to the "government of Canada in respect of all matters within the authority of Parliament". The matters in question, since we are speaking here of the federal Parliament, are those set out primarily in section 91 of the *Constitution Act, 1867*. It is well established in Canada that executive powers are divided between the federal government and the provinces on the same basis as legislative competence, so that legislative jurisdiction over a particular matter implies executive authority as well.[58]

(iii) *Section 1 of the Charter and executive acts*

Under section 1 of the Charter, only a law may restrict the rights and freedoms guaranteed by the Charter and only within such limits as are reasonable and justifiable in a free and democratic society. The issue at stake in applying the Charter will often be whether a given law — usually a legislative provision, but possibly a common law rule — which restricts a right or freedom guaranteed by the Charter meets the requirements of section 1.[59]

---

55 *Ibid.* at 129. Moreover, in my opinion, a directive of the Commissioner would not constitute a "law" in the sense of s. 1 of the Charter.

56 *Supra*, note 30.

57 See, *inter alia*, *Campbell v. A.G. Ontario* (1987), 58 O.R. (2d) 209 (H.C.), aff'd (1987), 60 O.R. (2d) 617 (C.A.), leave to appeal to S.C.C. refused (1987), 60 O.R. (2d) 618n (S.C.C.); *Re Balderstone and R.* (1983), 4 D.L.R. (4th) 162 (Man. C.A.), leave to appeal to S.C.C. refused (1983), 4 D.L.R. (4th) 162n (S.C.C.); *Chartrand v. Quebec (Min. of Justice)* (1986), 55 C.R. (3d) 97 (Que. S.C.), rev'd (1987), 59 C.R. (3d) 388 (Que. C.A.).

58 Hogg, *supra*, note 15 at 255.

59 Respecting the meaning of "law" in the context of s. 1 of the Charter, see Gibson, *The Law of the Charter, supra*, note 6 at 152 *et seq.*

What happens, however, when the challenged act is not legislative but executive or administrative in character? Can the executive branch restrict rights and freedoms guaranteed by the Charter without relying on a "law", as that term is used in section 1?

Law can only be made by the legislature or by the courts, in the case of the common law. Strictly speaking, governments possess no legislative authority apart from what is delegated to them by the legislature. Given this, what is the position of restrictions imposed by a government on Charter rights or freedoms without reliance on a statutory authority conferred by a legislature or at the least on a common law rule? In the context of service contracts or real estate transactions, for example, would it be possible for the government to avoid its Charter obligations with the consent of the person whose rights or freedoms were affected? The suggestion is incongruous in my view. In practice, a defendant who seeks to rely on section 1 of the Charter has a heavy burden to discharge.[60] It would be improper if the executive branch were able to exempt itself from Charter obligations more easily than the legislative branch. Where the government seeks to restrict guaranteed rights or freedoms, it should be obliged in every case to do so pursuant to "law" as that term is understood in section 1 of the Charter.

To recognize the validity of a contractual provision that restricted Charter rights or freedoms, even if consented to by those affected, would raise some serious problems. Would the consent of those affected be enough, regardless of the nature of the Charter violation and the circumstances in which it occurred? In all likelihood, the courts would at least insist on the right to review the reasonableness of such a provision. What criteria would they use for this purpose? Would they look for guidance to the terms of section 1, thus in effect substituting the will of the parties for the "law" which section 1 requires?[61]

It is true that the Quebec Court of Appeal, in a case decided under the *Canadian Bill of Rights*, recognized the validity of a restriction on the freedom of association contained in an employment contract to which the employee had consented. The restriction consisted of an undertaking by the employee of the company which operated in northern Canada not to associate with Eskimos. The Court of Appeal refused to declare the restriction contrary to the provisions relating to freedom of association

---

60 *R. v. Oakes*, [1986] 1 S.C.R. 103.

61 See the remarks of Gibson on this point, in *The Law of the Charter, supra,* note 6 at 168, as well as Mr. Justice Anderson in *Re Bhindi and B.C. Projectionists* (1985), 24 C.R.R. 302 at 312-314 (B.C.C.A.), leave to appeal to S.C.C. refused [1986] 6 W.W.R. lxv (note) (S.C.C.).

in the *Canadian Bill of Rights*.[62]

It is not clear that the result would be the same under the *Canadian Charter of Rights and Freedoms*. The Charter is endowed with a section which precisely sets out the conditions under which restrictions may be imposed on the rights and freedoms it guarantees. In light of this, it would be bad legal policy to allow the parties to a contract, simply by their consent, to impose restrictions on those rights and freedoms. The danger here is significant to the extent that the government is in a position to impose its own will on the parties it deals with. If the government believes that a restriction of some sort is justified, it should obtain the appropriate authority under a law that meets the requirements of section 1. This way of proceeding has the advantage of conforming to both letter and the spirit of the Charter.

It is relevant in this context to recall that the Supreme Court of Canada, in *Ontario Human Rights Commission v. Etobicoke*,[63] held that the parties to a collective agreement could not agree to exclude the provisions of the *Ontario Human Rights Code* relating to the age of mandatory retirement. This conclusion would be still more compelling in the context of the Charter, which is a fundamental part of our Constitution.[64]

While the Supreme Court of Canada has recognized on several occasions that it is lawful for an accused to waive certain of the procedural legal rights guaranteed by the Charter in sections 7 to 14, the court has not explained the legal basis of such waivers.[65] It is not clear, in my view, that these cases are applicable to the other rights and freedoms guaranteed by the Charter.

(d) Judicial Power: The Courts

Does the Charter bind only the legislative and executive branches of the state or does it also bind the courts? The combination of the words

---

62 *Whitfield v. Cdn. Marconi Co.*, [1968] Q.B. 92 (C.A.), aff'd (1968), 68 D.L.R. (2d) 766n (S.C.C.), application for rehearing dismissed [1968] S.C.R. 960 (S.C.C.). It is to be noted that the employment contract was between an individual and a private enterprise which was itself bound by a contract with the federal government. Rather than explaining what led it to conclude that there was no violation of the *Canadian Bill of Rights*, the court was content to demonstrate that the clause in question did not contravene public order and good morals.

63 [1982] 1 S.C.R. 202 at 213-214.

64 See also Gibson, *The Law of the Charter, supra*, note 6 at 163-168.

65 See, *inter alia, R. v. Clarkson*, [1986] 1 S.C.R. 383, which examines the conditions under which an accused will have waived the right to counsel guaranteed by s. 10(b) of the Charter. The principles asserted in that case would no doubt apply to any waiver of a guaranteed procedural right, but not to other guaranteed rights or freedoms entrenched in the Charter. See also Gibson, *The Law of the Charter, supra*, note 6 at 163 *et seq.*

"Parliament" — repository of the legislative power — and "government" — repository of the executive power — suggests that the courts are to be excluded. However, as Professor Hogg has shown, certain provisions of the Charter are necessarily binding on the courts.[66] Take, for example, the right of an accused to be tried within a reasonable time as guaranteed in section 11(b). The obligation on the part of the courts to respect this right was confirmed by the Supreme Court of Canada in *R. v. Rahey*.[67] The same reasoning would prevail with respect to section 11(i), which guarantees to every accused the right, "if found guilty of the offence and if the punishment for the offence has been varied between the time of commission and the time of sentencing, to the benefit of the lesser punishment". This provision clearly binds the court that imposes sentence. Yet another example may be found in section 14, conferring the right to an interpreter in certain circumstances. This provision obviously imposes a duty on the court to ensure that adequate translation services are provided where required. To this extent one may fairly say that the *Canadian Charter of Rights and Freedoms*, or at least some of its provisions, are binding on the courts.

(i) *Are the courts part of government?*

Is it possible to extend the reasoning further and to argue that the courts are included in the word "government" as used in section 32? To include them would have important consequences. As Professor Hogg points out, such a conclusion would lead to the imposition of Charter constraints on certain private activities which would otherwise be exempt. Under this theory, the courts would be obliged to deny redress to a party in private litigation whenever the remedy sought entailed violation of a Charter right or freedom, even in cases where neither Parliament nor the government was in any way involved. In such circumstances, action by the court would itself constitute a form of governmental action and so subject to the dictates of the Charter.[68]

This approach was rejected by the Supreme Court of Canada in the *Dolphin Delivery* case.[69] *Dolphin Delivery* was concerned with a common law rule according to which secondary picketing is considered tortious and may be enjoined on the ground that it induces a breach of contract. The issue in the case was whether this rule constituted a form of governmental intervention, as a legislative provision would have done, so

---

66 Hogg, *supra*, note 15 at 672.
67 [1987] 1 S.C.R. 588.
68 Hogg, *supra*, note 15 at 672 *et seq*.; Lluelles & Trudel, *supra*, note 6.
69 *Supra*, note 7.

as to attract the application of the Charter. The Supreme Court of Canada held that it did not. In its view, a court order could not be regarded as a form of governmental intervention. It appears, then, that judgments rendered by the courts do not constitute the sort of governmental action to which the Charter applies.

McIntyre J., speaking for five of the seven judges who heard the appeal in *Dolphin Delivery*, noted that:

> [W]here the word "government" is used in s. 32 it refers not to government in its generic sense — meaning the whole of the governmental apparatus of the state — but to a branch of government. The word "government", following as it does the words "Parliament" and "Legislature", must then, it would seem, refer to the executive or administrative branch of government. This is the sense in which one generally speaks of the Government of Canada or of a province. I am of the opinion that the word "government" is used in s. 32 of the *Charter* in the sense of the executive government of Canada and the Provinces.[70]

Even if the courts in a larger sense constitute one of the three basic branches of the government, their decisions cannot be considered a form of governmental action within the meaning of section 32.

McIntyre J. later goes on to note that:

> [A]ction by the executive or administrative branches of government will generally depend upon legislation, that is, statutory authority. Such action may also depend, however, on the common law, as in the case of the prerogative . . . The action will . . . be unconstitutional to the extent that it relies for authority or justification on a rule of the common law which constitutes or creates an infringement of a *Charter* right or freedom.[71]

He concludes that the Charter "will apply to the common law . . . only in so far as the common law is the basis of some governmental action which, it is alleged, infringes a guaranteed right or freedom."[72] In this sense the Charter can be said to apply to the common law as much in private litigation as in public litigation. The remarks of Mr. Justice McIntyre are well illustrated in my view by the *Operation Dismantle* case,[73] where the governmental action complained of was an exercise of the royal prerogative.

In refusing to treat court orders as a type of governmental intervention, McIntyre J. relies on a practical policy argument: "To regard a court order as an element of governmental intervention necessary to invoke the *Charter* would, it seems to me, widen the scope of *Charter* application to virtually

---

70 *Ibid.* at 598.
71 *Ibid.* at 599.
72 *Ibid.* at 599.
73 *Supra*, note 30.

all private litigation".[74] The implications of this observation are somewhat qualified, however, when McIntyre J. goes on to assert that "the judiciary ought to apply and develop the principles of the common law in a manner consistent with the fundamental values enshrined in the Constitution".[75] In this sense, the Charter is far from irrelevant in private litigation involving the principles of the common law.

In other words, although the Charter in principle does not reach or constrain the common law in the context of private litigation, the courts are nonetheless urged to bring the common law into line with the fundamental values of the Charter. If the Charter applied to the common law in private litigation, these actions would all be in effect "constitutionalized". However, if the Charter merely requires the introduction of Charter values into the common law, such litigation retains its private law character. The difference is significant, at least in terms of procedure and remedies. In terms of substantive outcomes, the difference may be insignificant. It remains to be seen how the courts, including the Supreme Court of Canada, will respond to Mr. Justice McIntyre's invitation.

In any case, this passage from the judgment of the court is not without ambiguity. It says in effect that, in an action between private parties, although the Charter does not apply to the common law directly, it should apply indirectly. However, Mr. Justice McIntyre is silent as to the means by which the Charter is to influence the common law. Is the influence to be general or quasi-philosophical in character so that by a process of osmosis the Charter's fundamental values will come, almost imperceptibly, to reshape the principles of the common law? Or is the influence to operate more concretely, the courts treating the Charter as a fundamental basis on which to examine and if necessary modify the common law? Mr. Justice McIntyre does not say how this transformation of the common law is to occur. Only future events will clarify the ambiguity apparent in this passage of *Dolphin Delivery*.[76]

At first glance it would appear that the private law of Quebec, because it has been codified, is subject to the provisions of the Charter in a way that the common law, having been formulated by the courts, is not. This would create a significant disparity between the impact of the Charter on the private law of Quebec and its effect on the common law. It is possible that the Supreme Court of Canada, sensitive to this disparity, sought a way to diminish it in the *Dolphin Delivery* case.[77]

---

74 *Dolphin Delivery Inc.*, *supra*, note 7 at 600.

75 *Ibid.* at 603.

76 *Ibid.*

77 See Mr. Justice Anderson in *Bhindi*, *supra*, note 61 at 314.

(ii) *Does the Charter affect the Civil Code of Quebec differently than the common law?*

It is easy to see that private law concepts such as fault and public order, concepts known equally to the *Civil Code of Quebec* and the common law, will be influenced by the fundamental values of the Charter and will in this way become important mechanisms through which the Charter will affect private law relationships.

Article 831 of the *Civil Code of Quebec*, which guarantees freedom of testamentary capacity, may be used to illustrate the range of questions that arise in this respect as a result of the *Dolphin Delivery* case.[78] This article of the Code guarantees to every person of sound mind and legal capacity the absolute freedom to dispose of his property by will subject only to provisions or conditions that are contrary to public policy and good morals.

A legislative provision that guarantees absolute testamentary freedom, without more, might well come into conflict with the Charter if, for example, it permitted a testator to force his beneficiary to choose between accepting a bequest and relinquishing a Charter freedom. Consider a clause in a will which obliged the beneficiary to convert to a particular religion, for example, in order to receive a bequest. Such a clause would be contrary to section 2 of the Charter, which guarantees freedom of conscience and religion. It is highly doubtful that the courts would find a law guaranteeing absolute testamentary freedom without qualification of any sort to be in compliance with the Charter. A legislative provision to this effect would, in my view, constitute governmental action of the sort to which the provisions of the Charter apply. However, according to *Dolphin Delivery*,[79] a common law rule guaranteeing the same testamentary freedom would not serve as a basis on which to grant a remedy under the Charter.

In fact, however, article 831 of the *Civil Code* does not guarantee absolute testamentary freedom, for the testator may not make dispositions or impose conditions that are contrary to public order or morality. These legislative qualifications are, in my view, sufficient to ensure that article 831 complies with the Charter. Concepts like public order are malleable; they may be shaped and influenced by Charter values. To the extent that freedom of religion, for example, as guaranteed by section 2, is recognized as an integral aspect of the concept of public order, article 831 will be brought into line with the Charter. If freedom of religion is protected by the civil law itself through the use of the concept of public order, any incompatibility with the Charter disappears.

---

78 *Supra*, note 7.
79 *Ibid.*

On this approach, a clause in a will that interfered with the freedom of religion of a particular legatee would be contrary to public order and therefore null. The nullity would result from the application of the civil law concept of public order as shaped by Charter values, rather than the direct application of constitutional law. This distinction is important, for the clause on this approach would raise a private law rather than a constitutional law question, with all that this entails in terms of procedure and remedies.

In discussing this issue, Professors Lluelles and Trudel have observed that the Charter:

> . . . is capable of leading to modifications at the heart of many of the more fundamental institutions of Quebec civil law . . . The content of open-ended concepts that make up civil law, such as public order and fault, would henceforth not be defined in a way to interfere with the Constitution. On the contrary, the Constitution, because of its superordinate nature, henceforth imposes a framework within which will be defined the content of the open-ended concepts essential for the application of the principles of civil law [translation].[80]

Of course, the open-ended concepts referred to by Professors Lluelles and Trudel are certainly not alien to the common law. While the common law concepts of public policy, fault and negligence reflect their particular evolution, they are not fundamentally different from the concepts of public order and fault found in the civil law. They too may be influenced by the Charter.[81]

While it may be fair to say that concepts such as public order and fault must be shaped by the values enshrined in the Constitution, must

---

80 *Supra*, note 6, at 251-252.
81 See Gibson, *The Law of the Charter, supra*, note 6 at 99. See also Mr. Justice Anderson (dissenting) in *Bhindi, supra*, note 61 at 313-314, where in my opinion he clearly illustrates how the *Charter* could influence the common law and especially the notion of public order: "As to freedom of contract, it is my view that while this cherished right falls within the purview of s. 26 of the *Charter*, it is not an unfettered freedom. The courts have long held that certain contracts are void or unenforceable as being contrary to public policy. For example, at common law collective agreements and 'closed shop' provisions were void and unenforceable in the courts as being in restraint of trade. It may also be that, even if the *Charter* does not apply directly to the private sector, the principles of the common law may be reshaped in the light of the *Charter* and freedom of contract will be further restricted having regard to the extent and seriousness of the alleged breach of 'Charter' rights: see, for example, the judgment of Dickson C.J.C. in *Fraser*, [[1985] 2 S.C.R. 455] at p. 468 where he held that mere criticism of the government would not constitute 'just cause' for dismissal. Would a contract of employment providing that any criticism of the private employer would constitute 'just cause' for dismissal be upheld at common law or would the common law be revised in order to protect the right of freedom of expression? The judgment of Dickson C.J.C. in *Fraser* would seem to require, even in the absence of the *Charter*,

one regard these values as absolute? Are they not subject to any qualification? It is well established that generally speaking the rights and freedoms guaranteed by the Charter are not absolute. Under section 1, they may be constrained by law within limits that are reasonable and can be demonstrably justified in a free and democratic society. The requirements of this section are rigorous, as the Supreme Court of Canada makes clear in its judgment in the *Oakes* case.[82] The question that arises, in light of the relationship between Charter values and concepts such as public order and fault, is whether the rights and freedoms guaranteed by the Charter are absolute in character such that they may not be attenuated by the parties to a contract. This question is not without significance. If the legislator can restrict Charter rights and freedoms only by enacting a law which meets the requirements of section 1, what is the position of parties to a contract? Can they by mutual consent agree to restrict these rights or freedoms without thereby offending against public order and morality?

These are difficult questions. As noted above, where the government is one of the contracting parties, it appears that it may not, even with the consent of the other party, agree to conditions which restrict rights or freedoms guaranteed by the Charter unless it acts pursuant to a law which meets the requirements of section 1.[83] Where both are private parties, given the assumption that the Charter does not apply directly to private relations, the problem is somewhat different. The Charter influences private law by influencing the content of its open-ended concepts, by helping to define the meaning of concepts like public order. A contractual clause that restricted freedom of association or expression as guaranteed by section 2 of the Charter might well be declared invalid as being contrary to public order. For this purpose, however, do we mean freedom of association or expression as defined in section 2 alone or as defined in section 2 and section 1 together? Can these freedoms be made subject to restrictions agreed to by the parties and, if so, under what conditions would the courts recognize the validity of such restrictions?

---

that such a clause in a contract of employment could not stand. Lastly, in respect of freedom of contract, it seems to me that no reasonable objection could be taken to reshaping the common law so that all contracts, private or otherwise, would be made subject to the provisions of the *Charter*, including s. 1. Thus, all *Charter* rights would, in the field of contract law, be subject to such reasonable contractual limits as could be demonstrably justified in a free and democratic society."

82 *Supra*, note 60.
83 See *supra*, p. 79 *et seq.*

(e) Does the Charter Apply to Private Law Relations?

Perceiving a certain ambiguity in the language of section 32 of the Charter, many commentators have advocated its application to private law relations. Their arguments have relied primarily on considerations of expediency.[84] However, almost unanimously, the courts have rejected this thesis[85] and the Supreme Court of Canada's judgment in the *Dolphin Delivery* case[86] dealt the final blow to the proposition that the Charter binds everyone, not only the state. Had the court found the Charter to be binding on everyone, a number of the questions examined above concerning the legislative, executive and judicial activities of the state would have become academic. If the Charter applies to everyone, there is no need to define the scope of the government. In the event, however, these questions will inevitably engage the attention of litigants and courts over the course of years to come.

One misunderstanding must be avoided, however. *Dolphin Delivery* does not completely exclude the application of the Charter to private law relations. Mr. Justice McIntyre recognizes the application of the Charter to such relations "[w]here such exercise of, or reliance upon, governmental action is present and where one private party invokes or relies upon it to produce an infringement of the *Charter* rights of another".[87]

This principle is extremely important and Mr. Justice McIntyre refers to the judgment of the Ontario Court of Appeal in *Re Blainey and Ontario Hockey Association* to illustrate its application.[88] In that case, proceedings were commenced against a hockey association on behalf of a twelve-year-old girl who was refused permission to play hockey on a boys' team sponsored by the Association. The litigation raised two important questions: first, the application of the Charter to the relationship between the Association and the girl; second, the validity of the provisions of the Ontario *Human Rights Code* relied on by the Ontario Human Rights Commission, which made the Code inapplicable "where membership in an athletic organization or participation in an athletic activity is restricted to persons of the same sex" (section 19(2)).

The Ontario Court of Appeal held that the Charter did not apply to private law relationships and that, accordingly, the Association was not

---

84 See *supra*, note 6.
85 See, *inter alia*, *Re Blainey and Ont. Hockey Ass.* (1986), 54 O.R. (2d) 513 (Ont. C.A.), leave to appeal to S.C.C. refused (1986), 58 O.R. (2d) 274 (headnote) (S.C.C.); *Re Bhindi and B.C. Projectionists, supra*, note 61; *Baldwin v. B.C.G.E.U.* (1987), 25 C.R.R. 312 (B.C.S.C.). See also *supra*, notes 39, 40 and 42.
86 *Supra*, note 7.
87 *Ibid.* at 603.
88 *Supra*, note 85.

bound by it in its relations with the girl. The court went on to find that section 19(2) of the *Human Rights Code* was in conflict with the Charter and therefore of no force or effect. In commenting on this judgment, Mr. Justice McIntyre wrote:

> In the *Blainey* case, a law suit between private parties, the *Charter* was applied because one of the parties acted on the authority of a statute, i.e., s. 19(2) of the Ontario *Human Rights Code* which infringed the *Charter* rights of another. *Blainey* then affords an illustration of the manner in which *Charter* rights of private individuals may be enforced and protected by the courts, that is, by measuring legislation — government action — against the *Charter*.[89]

Mr. Justice McIntyre refuses "to define with narrow precision that element of governmental intervention which will suffice to permit reliance on the Charter by private litigants in private litigation".[90] He relies on Professor Hogg to illustrate situations where the Charter would apply:

> [T]he Charter would apply to a private person exercising the power of arrest which is granted to "any one" by the Criminal Code, and to a private railway company exercising the power to make by-laws (and impose penalties for their breach) that is granted to a "railway company" by the Railway Act; all action taken in exercise of a statutory power is covered by the Charter by virtue of the references to "Parliament" and "legislature" in s. 32. The Charter would also apply to the action of a commercial corporation that was an agent of the Crown, by virtue of the reference to "government" in s. 32.[91]

It is a little surprising that Mr. Justice McIntyre chose the *Blainey* case[92] for his example. Since section 15 of the Charter guarantees the right of equality before the law and section 19(2) of the *Human Rights Code* was clearly in conflict with this right, it was not necessary to invoke the principle of governmental action as Mr. Justice McIntyre did. The essential requirement of section 15 is that neither the content of a law nor its application interferes with the guaranteed right of equality. Thus, there can be no recourse to section 15 unless there exists a legislative provision, and this of necessity presupposes an element of governmental intervention.[93]

What is the position, however, in respect of other provisions of the Charter which are not based on the principle of equality under the "law". According to *Dolphin Delivery*,[94] a private party to private litigation may rely on the Charter to reject a claim if it is based on some form of

---

89 *Dolphin Delivery Ltd., supra*, note 7 at 602.

90 *Ibid.* at 602.

91 *Ibid.* at 602.

92 *Ibid.*

93 For an illustration of such a situation, see *Ont. English Catholic Teachers Assn. v. Essex Co. Roman Catholic Separate School Bd., supra*, note 48.

94 *Supra*, note 7.

governmental intervention, for example, a legislative provision restricting one of the freedoms guaranteed by section 2. In such circumstances, the Charter would apply even in the context of private litigation between private parties.

It is not clear that every instance of governmental intervention will suffice to permit reliance on the Charter by private parties in private litigation. As noted above, Mr. Justice McIntyre refused to define with narrow precision that element of governmental intervention. The examples he cites to illustrate his point do not pose any difficulties. However, a judgment rendered by the British Columbia Court of Appeal in June 1986,[95] before *Dolphin Delivery*,[96] which was handed down in December of that year, will serve to illustrate the difficulties that do arise in attempting to define the element of governmental intervention needed to justify the application of the Charter.

Two projectionists (Jim Bhindi and Edward London) were refused membership in a union that was bound by a collective agreement containing a closed shop clause. Such clauses are permitted under the *Labour Code* of British Columbia. The inability to obtain membership in the union seriously affected the employment prospects of the two projectionists. Their challenge to the closed-shop clause was rejected by the court of first instance and also by the Court of Appeal of British Columbia.[97]

The central question for the court was the following: did the enactment by the provincial legislature of a provision in the *Labour Code* permitting the inclusion of a closed-shop clause in collective agreements constitute a governmental intervention sufficient for the purposes of section 32 of the Charter? Chief Justice Nemetz, speaking for the majority of a five-judge bench, concluded that the permissive provision of the *Labour Code* did not constitute a governmental intervention of the sort contemplated by section 32. The Chief Justice seemed to attach importance to the fact that the appellants were not attacking the legislation itself, but were claiming only that the closed-shop provision constituted a governmental action sufficient to bring the Charter into play. The Chief Justice concluded as follows:

> In my opinion the government's enactment of the *Labour Code* with a provision allowing the closed shop does not transform the closed shop provision into governmental action. The collective agreement before us was not mandated by the Legislature. It was entered into by two parties to a contract. Its contents do not reflect government policy. The *Labour Code* establishes the procedure

---

95 *Re Bhindi and B.C. Projectionists, supra*, note 61.
96 *Supra*, note 7.
97 See *Bhindi, supra*, note 61, for the decision of the Court of Appeal, aff'g (1985), 20 D.L.R. (4th) 386 (B.C.S.C.) (the decision of the trial court).

whereby private parties may conclude an enforceable collective agreement but clearly it does not require the parties to reach such an agreement or to include in it a closed shop provision.[98]

Mr. Justice Anderson, one of two judges in the minority, wrote a vigorous dissent in which he arrived at the opposite conclusion:

In my opinion, the inclusion of the "closed shop" provision in the collective agreement was carried out pursuant to a "governmental" power and, hence, is subject to the provisions of the *Charter*. I say so for three basic reasons:

(1) All powers relating to collective bargaining are statutory in nature and foreign to the common law and thus are powers bestowed by government.
(2) In particular, the discretionary power granted to trade unions and employers to include a "closed shop" provision in a collective agreement is a statutory power conferred by government overriding the common law which held such provisions to be voided and unenforceable.
(3) The exercise of a statutory power is "governmental" in nature whether it is exercised by the government or by persons or corporations on whom the government has conferred such a power.[99]

The fifth judge based his dissent on the following grounds:

It does not matter, in my opinion, that s. 9 is permissive rather than mandatory. Section 32 of the *Charter* does not suggest any distinction to be drawn between statutory provisions that permit and those that compel.[100]

The majority, in my opinion, placed too much importance on the fact that the legislative provision permitting the inclusion of the closed-shop clause in collective agreements had not been challenged. This resulted in the emphasis being placed on the agreement itself rather than the legislation. On this point, the argument of Mr. Justice Anderson is compelling. Having regard to the position of the common law before the enactment of the permissive provision by the legislature, how could one conclude that there was no governmental intervention subjecting the clause of the collective agreement to the Charter? Finally, it is difficult to see how a legislative provision could be insulated from the provisions of the Charter simply because it is permissive. In this respect, it is not without interest to note that the illustrations drawn by Mr. Justice McIntyre from the work of Professor Hogg were all exercises of powers which by their very nature are permissive .

To claim that the Charter applies to such facts does not necessarily mean that the closed-shop clause and the legislation authorizing it will be declared of no force and effect as being contrary to the Charter. That

---

98 *Ibid.* at 311 (C.A.).
99 *Ibid.* at 314-315.
100 *Ibid.* at 329, *per* Hutcheon J.A.

is a distinct question involving a number of considerations, including the application of section 1 of the Charter.

(f) Conclusion

While the Supreme Court of Canada's judgment in *Dolphin Delivery*[101] clearly establishes that not everyone is bound by the Charter — that the state alone is bound — numerous uncertainties remain to be resolved. There are a number of significant gray areas which will have to be clarified, particularly concerning the scope of the concept of "government". The answers to these questions will be determinative of the impact of the Charter in the life of Canadians.

The court's judgment in the *Dolphin Delivery* case[102] gives some indication of what the future will hold. The fundamental idea of "state intervention" will be the focus of attention both of litigants and the courts, for such intervention is needed to trigger the application of the Charter. It must be recognized, however, that to raise in the abstract the question of the Charter's application to private law relations is somewhat misleading. In concrete cases, the question always arises in the context of specific Charter provisions. If the question arises specifically in connection with the fundamental freedoms guaranteed by section 2, there are few other sections of the Charter which apply so readily to private law matters. Of course, there is section 15 which guarantees the right of equality. However, this right can be asserted only in relation to some law, involving either the content of a legislative provision or its administration. Since a law of necessity represents an intervention by the legislative branch, just as its administration involves the executive or administrative branch, a claimant who relies on section 15 must always point to some intervention by the state consisting in the exercise of either its legislative or executive power. It is impossible for a private party in private litigation to succeed under section 15 without invoking in one way or another the intervention of the state.

The point to be made is that the application of the Charter to private law relations will almost always occur in the context of the fundamental freedoms guaranteed by section 2. These freedoms are significant enough. However, the answer to the question whether section 2 applies to private law relations in the absence of state intervention is less dramatic in its impact than the answer to the question, posed in the abstract, whether the Charter as a whole applies to private relations.

---

101 *Supra*, note 7.
102 *Ibid.*

4. OVERRIDE CLAUSES (SECTION 33)

As we have seen,[103] the *Canadian Charter of Rights and Freedoms* limits the supremacy of Parliament and the provincial legislatures in the exercise of the powers conferred on them by the Canadian Constitution. It follows that any subordinate legislation authorized by these legislatures must also respect the rights and freedoms guaranteed by the Charter. Legislation which fails to comply with the Charter is of no force or effect.

This does not mean that Charter rights and freedoms are absolute. Section 1 of the Charter stipulates that the rights and freedoms set out in it are "subject only to such reasonable limits prescribed by law as can be demonstrably justified in a free and democratic society". It is obviously up to the courts, and ultimately the Supreme Court of Canada, to determine whether limits established by Parliament or the provincial legislatures are in accordance with the requirements of section 1. Thus, even in the context of this section, the exercise of legislative authority is subject to judicial review. However, the ultimate supremacy of Parliament and the legislatures is ensured by means of the override clauses which are provided for in section 33 with respect to certain rights and freedoms. Section 33 provides:

33. (1) Parliament or the legislature of a province may expressly declare in an Act of Parliament or of the legislature, as the case may be, that the Act or a provision thereof shall operate notwithstanding a provision included in section 2 or sections 7 to 15 of this Charter.

(2) An Act or a provision of an Act in respect of which a declaration made under this section is in effect shall have such operation as it would have but for the provision of this Charter referred to in the declaration.

(3) A declaration made under subsection (1) shall cease to have effect five years after it comes into force or on such earlier date as may be specified in the declaration.

(4) Parliament or a legislature of a province may re-enact a declaration made under subsection (1).

(5) Subsection (3) applies in respect of a re-enactment made under subsection (4).

(a) The Historical Significance of Section 33

Section 33 was introduced into the Charter by Prime Minister Trudeau on November 5, 1981 in an effort to win the support of certain recalcitrant provinces for his proposed constitutional resolution.[104] One of the chief

---

103 "3. Who Is Bound by the *Canadian Charter of Rights and Freedoms*?", *supra*.

104 Ontario and New Brunswick from the beginning supported the federal government in its efforts to repatriate the Constitution. Quebec did not endorse the November 1981 agreement and did not consent to be part of the Canadian constitutional family until signing the *Meech Lake Accord*, as amended by the first ministers' meeting held in the Langevin Building at Ottawa on June 2 and 3, 1987.

objections raised by these provinces concerned the powers that the Charter would confer on the courts at the expense of the principle of parliamentary supremacy. By guaranteeing to the elected representatives of the people the ultimate power to impose their will concerning a number of the matters governed by the Charter, the November 1981 agreement assured that the last word would belong to the legislatures rather than the courts. This was a major concession to the traditional British principle of parliamentary supremacy. By permitting Parliament and the provincial legislatures to override certain of the rights and freedoms guaranteed by the Charter, section 33 confirms in principle — at least to a degree — the supremacy of the legislative branch over the judiciary.[105]

(b) The Rights and Freedoms Which May be Affected

Not all Charter rights and freedoms may be overridden by section 33. Override clauses may be enacted by Parliament and the provincial legislatures only with respect to the rights and freedoms guaranteed by sections 2 (fundamental freedoms), sections 7 to 14 (legal rights) and section 15 (equality rights). Democratic rights (sections 3 to 5), mobility rights (section 6), the provisions relating to the official languages of Canada (sections 16 to 22), minority language educational rights (section 23) and the guarantee of rights equally to both sexes (section 28) may not be the subject of an override clause under section 33 and may not be infringed by Parliament or the provincial legislatures in the exercise of their legislative powers.

(c) The Authority to Enact an Override Clause

Section 33 explicitly confers on Parliament and the provincial legislatures the power to enact laws notwithstanding certain provisions of the Charter. It appears that only Parliament itself or the provincial legislatures acting within their respective jurisdictions may exercise this power. Clearly subordinate bodies such as the Cabinet, governmental agencies and municipalities are not empowered to enact override clauses. Only Parliament and provincial legislatures possess the power to enact laws within their respective jurisdictions and it would be incongruous to give the words "Act of Parliament" in section 33 the broad sense given

---

105 On the genesis of s. 33, see J.G. Matkin, "The Negotiation of the Charter of Rights: The Provincial Perspective", in J.M Weiler & R.M. Elliot, eds., *Litigating the Values of a Nation: The Canadian Charter of Rights and Freedoms* (Toronto: Carswell, 1986) at 27. See also Gibson, *The Law of the Charter, supra*, note 6 at 124 *et seq.*

these words by the Supreme Court of Canada in the *Blaikie* cases.[106] In the context of section 33, the words "Act of Parliament" cannot extend to "regulation" or any other form of subordinate legislation passed by a subordinate body. To conclude otherwise would trivialize the Charter and could lead to the introduction of override clauses without consideration by either Parliament or a provincial legislature. Such a result would clearly be contrary to the intention of the framers in adopting section 33.[107]

What, however, is the position respecting the legislative councils of the Territories? Are they empowered to enact provisions in derogation of Charter rights and freedoms? On the basis of the principles discussed above, one would conclude that the legislative councils of the Territories are not empowered to act under section 33. These principles suggest that Parliament alone may enact override clauses, even in respect of matters concerning the Territories which ordinarily fall within provincial jurisdiction.

In my view, section 30 of the Charter which provides that "a reference . . . to a province or to the legislative assembly or legislature of a province shall be deemed to include a reference to the Yukon Territory and the Northwest Territories, or to the appropriate legislative authority thereof" does nothing to alter this conclusion. As I have argued above, in examining the position of the Territories in relation to the Charter,[108] section 30 was not intended to apply to the provisions of section 32 nor to the provisions of section 33. In my view, sections 32 and 33 both apply only to authorities which enjoy complete sovereignty within their respective spheres of power. This excludes subordinate bodies.

(d) The Requirements for Applying Section 33

The enactment of an override clause must comply with three important requirements set out in section 33. First, the intention to derogate from the Charter must be expressly declared. The fact that a statute is manifestly contrary to a provision of the Charter will not be a sufficient basis on which to conclude that the legislature intended to override it. For this purpose, clearly, presumed intent is not good enough. Second, the intention to override must be made a part of the legislation which the legislator wishes to exclude from the application of the Charter. Thus, a declaration made by a minister in the House of Commons or elsewhere, designed to prevent the application of the Charter to a particular piece of legislation,

---

106 See *supra*, note 19.

107 On this question, see Gibson, *The Law of the Charter, supra*, note 6 at 127, 128.

108 See "1. The *Canadian Charter of Rights and Freedoms* and the Territories", *supra*, at p. 65.

would have no effect. Finally, the declaration that the legislation shall operate notwithstanding the Charter must clearly indicate which provision of the Charter the legislator wishes to avoid. It is not sufficient for the legislation to assert that the Charter has no application without stipulating the particular provisions which do not apply.

Each of these requirements, of course, is designed to ensure that the legislative decision to enact an override clause is taken with full knowledge of the facts, thereby encouraging public discussion of the issues raised by the use of such a clause. A comparison with the override provisions of the *Canadian Bill of Rights*,[109] moreover, clearly indicates the determination of the framers to restrict legislatures wishing to derogate from the provisions of the Charter by imposing strict requirements. It is up to the courts, in my view, to determine whether the use that the legislators have made of this exceptional power to derogate from the provisions of the Charter is in conformity with the strict requirements laid down in section 33.

In *Alliance des professeurs de Montréal v. A.G. Quebec*,[110] the Court of Appeal of Quebec had to decide the validity of the *Act respecting the Constitution Act, 1982*,[111] which excepted all the laws of the province from the provisions of section 2 and 7 to 15 of the Charter. The court concluded that the provincial law providing for a general derogation was invalid, thus reversing the judgment of Chief Justice Deschênes in the court below.[112] The Chief Justice had held that it was permissible for the legislature to enact a general law provided each statute to which the override clause applied was effectively made subject to it. The Court of Appeal held that the provincial law was invalid because the legislature had failed to indicate the provisions of the Charter that were to be overriden.[113] Furthermore, in the view of Mr. Justice Jacques, the words "shall operate notwithstanding a provision" which appear in section 33 have no purpose unless they refer to a provision of the Charter that is specifically set out in the derogating statute.[114] It is not enough, in his view, that the derogating statute simply mention the numbers of the sections it intends to override.[115]

---

109 S. 2 of the *Canadian Bill of Rights, supra,* note 9, reads in part: "Every law of Canada shall, unless it is expressly declared by an Act of the Parliament of Canada that it shall operate notwithstanding the *Canadian Bill of Rights,* be so construed and applied. . . ."

110 (1985), 18 C.R.R. 195 (Que. C.A.), leave to appeal to S.C.C. granted (1985), 18 C.R.R. 195n (S.C.C.).

111 S.Q. 1982, c. 21. This Act, enacted June 23, 1982, was not re-enacted by the Quebec legislature and thus ceased to be in force five years after it came into force.

112 [1985] C.S. 1272 (Que. S.C.).

113 *Supra,* note 110 at 201.

114 *Ibid.* at 201.

115 *Ibid.* at 202.

One hopes that the courts will be strict when called on to verify compliance with the formal requirements of section 33. As noted by Mr. Justice Mayrand in the *Alliance des professeurs* case:

> Respect for this formal requirement [specifying the provisions in respect of which the override power is to be exercised] is all the more important because the override power recognized in s. 33 of the *Charter* is not subject to any substantial rules. In exercising this power, the Parliament of Canada and the provincial Legislature regain in the areas mentioned the sovereignty they had prior to the enactment of the *Charter* . . . At most, the courts can be called upon to verify whether the override power has been exercised in accordance with the requirements of s. 33 [translation].[116]

(e) An Override Clause is Valid for a Maximum of Five Years

The legislature may stipulate how long the override clause it enacts is to remain in force up to a maximum of five years. By following the same procedure, however, the clause may be re-enacted for successive periods of five years. This temporal limitation on the validity of override clauses shows the framers' determination to ensure that citizens are not deprived of their constitutional rights and freedoms without valid reasons to be established after a serious and clear-sighted examination of the stakes. It is worth noting in this connection that with a maximum life span of five years it will normally be possible to re-enact an override clause only after the election of a new government.

(f) The Effect of the Override Clause

An override clause has the effect of suspending the application of the Charter for the period of time specified therein to a maximum of five years. During this period, no legal remedy is available under the Charter. As soon as the clause ceases to have effect, the Charter resumes its previous operation and once again applies.

(g) Section 1 and Section 33

A number of scholars have wondered whether the requirements of section 1 apply to the exercise of the override power under section 33. If so, Parliament and the provincial legislatures could enact an override clause only if it imposed "such reasonable limits . . . as can be demonstrably justified in a free and democratic society". This would introduce significant prerequisites for the use of the override power and would confer on the

---

116 *Ibid.* at 207.

courts a jurisdiction to review not only the formal requirements to which the power is subject but also the substantive conditions set out in section 1.[117]

However, this is a difficult conclusion to accept. Once enacted in accordance with section 33, an override clause effectively suspends the rights and freedoms to which it applies. It is difficult to see how section 1 could continue to apply to a right or a freedom thus suspended. It is interesting to note in this respect that section 33(2) provides that the derogating legislation has the effect it would otherwise have but for the provision of the Charter referred to in the override clause. This assures the supremacy of the legislature despite the contrary provisions of the Charter and at the same time withdraws from the courts their power to review legislation to ensure compliance with the Charter.

Section 1 applies to the Acts of legislatures and limits the rights and freedoms guaranteed by the Charter. However, override clauses enacted under section 33 have the effect of suspending or temporarily shelving these rights and freedoms. Once such a clause is enacted, there is no point in going through the section 1 exercise to determine whether a given limitation on rights or freedoms is justified.[118]

(h) Use of Section 33

Only the provinces of Quebec and Saskatchewan have enacted override clauses. As noted above,[119] in June 1982, Quebec enacted a law of general application which incorporated an override clause into each of its existing statutes. This general law was declared invalid by Quebec's Court of Appeal. An appeal from this judgment has been taken to the Supreme Court of Canada, but it has not yet rendered its decision. At this point, the question has become somewhat academic, as Quebec did not re-enact the 1982 law and it ceased to have effect in 1987. Particular override clauses enacted by the Quebec legislature after June 1982 remain in force. However, they too cease to have effect five years from their enactment unless re-enacted by the legislature.

Since the December 1985 election of the Liberal Party to power in

---

117 See B. Slattery, "Canadian Charter of Rights and Freedoms — Override Clauses Under Section 33 — Whether Subject to Judicial Review Under Section 1" (1983), 61 *Can. Bar Rev.* 391, and D.J. Arbess, "Limitations on Legislation Override Under the Canadian Charter of Rights and Freedoms: A Matter of Balancing Values" (1983), 21 *Osgoode Hall L.J.* 113, which argued that s. 1 applies to s. 33.

118 See Gibson, *The Law of the Charter, supra,* note 6 at 130, 131; and Hogg, *supra,* note 15 at 690, 691, who also suggests that override clauses enacted pursuant to s. 33 are not subject to the requirements of s. 1 of the Charter.

119 See *supra,* note 111 and accompanying text.

Quebec, the legislature has enacted an override clause on three occasions. In each case the right overridden was the right to equality guaranteed by section 15.[120] Saskatchewan has enacted an override clause on one occasion only.[121]

5. THE SUPREMACY OF THE CANADIAN CHARTER OF RIGHTS AND FREEDOMS (SECTION 52)

From the very beginning, the *Constitution Act, 1867* has served as the supreme standard for Canadian legislation, both federal and provincial. Shortly after the creation of Canada in 1867, first the Privy Council and later the Supreme Court of Canada exercised the right to review Canadian legislation to ensure its conformity to this Act. As an Imperial statute, the Act of 1867 had supremacy over the statutes enacted by Canadian legislatures by virtue of the *Colonial Laws Validity Act*.[122] It provided that colonial legislation that was inconsistent with an Imperial statute applicable to the colony was invalid.[123]

The doctrine of the supremacy of the Constitution over laws enacted by Canadian legislatures still exists, but now finds its basis in section 52(1) of the *Constitution Act, 1982* which formally declares that: "The Constitution of Canada is the supreme law of Canada, and any law that is inconsistent with the provisions of the Constitution is, to the extent of the inconsistency, of no force or effect." Although this provision does not expressly confer on the courts the responsibility of ensuring that Canadian laws comply with the Constitution, this responsibility is implicit in the section.[124] Section 52(2) expressly declares that the Constitution of Canada includes the *Constitution Act, 1982*, of which the *Canadian Charter of Rights and Freedoms* constitutes Part 1. Such constitutional recognition was never accorded to the *Canadian Bill of Rights*, enacted by Parliament in 1960,[125] which may explain the timid attitude adopted by the courts, particularly the Supreme Court of Canada, in dealing with the problems of interpre-

---

120 *An Act to amend the Act to promote the development of agricultural operations*, S.Q. 1986, c. 54, s. 16: *Act to again amend the Education Act and the Act respecting the Conseil supérieur de l'éducation Act to amend the Act respecting the Ministère de l'Education*, S.Q. 1986, c. 101, ss. 10, 11, and 12; and *Act to amend various legislation respecting the Pension Plans of the Public and Parapublic Sectors*, S.Q. 1987, c. 47, s. 157.

121 *The SGEU Dispute Settlement Act*, S.S. 1984-85-86, c. 111.

122 1865 (U.K.), 28 & 29 V̇ict., c. 63.

123 On the question of judicial review of statutes in Canada, see Hogg, *supra*, note 15, at 93 *et seq.* and B.L. Strayer, *The Canadian Constitution and the Courts*, 2nd ed. (Toronto: Butterworth, 1983), c. 1.

124 Strayer, *ibid.* at 33.

125 *Supra*, note 9.

tation raised by the Bill in the years following its enactment.

Of course, the Charter is not without its own problems of interpretation. However, the Supreme Court of Canada has already, on a number of occasions, emphasized the fundamentally different character of the Charter and approached it with all the respect due such an important document. In its very first judgment concerning the Charter, the court, speaking through Mr. Justice Estey, indicated how it conceived its new responsibilities under the Charter:

> We are here engaged in a new task, the interpretation and application of the *Canadian Charter of Rights and Freedoms*. . . . This is not a statute or even a statute of the extraordinary nature of the *Canadian Bill of Rights*. . . . The *Canadian Bill of Rights* is, of course, in form, the same as any other statute of Parliament. It was designed and adopted to perform a more fundamental role than ordinary statutes in this country. It is, however, not a part of the Constitution of the country. It stands, perhaps, somewhere between a statute and a constitutional instrument . . .
>
> There are some simple but important considerations which guide a Court in construing the *Charter*, and which are more sharply focussed and discernable than in the case of the federal *Bill of Rights*. The *Charter* comes from neither level of the legislative branches of government but from the Constitution itself. It is part of the fabric of Canadian law. Indeed, it "is the supreme law of Canada": *Constitution Act, 1982*, s. 52. It cannot be readily amended. The fine and constant adjustment process of these constitutional provisions is left by a tradition of necessity to the judicial branch. Flexibility must be balanced with certainty. The future must, to the extent forseeably possible, be accommodated in the present. The *Charter* is designed and adopted to guide and serve the Canadian community for a long time. Narrow and technical interpretation, if not modulated by a sense of the unknowns of the future, can stunt the growth of the law and hence the community it serves. All this has long been with us in the process of developing the institutions of government under the *B.N.A. Act, 1867* (now the *Constitution Act, 1867*). With the *Constitution Act, 1982* comes a new dimension, a new yardstick of reconciliation between the individual and the community and their respective rights, a dimension which, like the balance of the Constitution, needs to be interpreted and applied by the Court.[126]

In the second Charter decision to come before the court, Mr. Justice Dickson (as he then was) was equally eloquent:

> The task of expounding a constitution is crucially different from that of construing a statute. A statute defines present rights and obligations. It is easily enacted and as easily repealed. A constitution, by contrast, is drafted with an eye to the future. Its function is to provide a continuing framework for the legitimate exercise of governmental power and, when joined by a *Bill* or a *Charter of Rights*, for the unremitting protection of individual rights and liberties. Once enacted, its provisions cannot easily be repealed or amended. It must, therefore, be capable of growth and development over time to meet

---

126 *L.S.U.C. v. Skapinker*, [1984] 1 S.C.R. 357 at 365-367.

new social, political and historical realities often unimagined by its framers. The judiciary is the guardian of the constitution and must, in interpreting its provisions, bear these considerations in mind.[127]

The power of judicial review has been considerably enlarged with the adoption of the *Constitution Act, 1982* and, more particularly, the *Canadian Charter of Rights and Freedoms.* As indicated by Mr. Justice Lamer in *Reference re Section 94(2) of the Motor Vehicle Act (B.C.),*[128] this is not a responsibility which the courts have attributed to themselves; it is a responsibility conferred on them by the framers when they took the historical decision to entrench the Charter in the Canadian Constitution.

Section 52 is central to the Charter. It is one of the fundamental tools for implementing the Charter's principles and values; the other is section 24. In the pages which follow, my task will be to delineate first the scope and then the significance of section 52, leaving to others an examination of the other forms of redress provided for in section 24.

(a) Persons Who May Invoke Section 52

As Mr. Justice Dickson (as he then was) explains in *R. v. Big M Drug Mart Ltd.,*[129] section 24(1) of the Charter is not the only recourse available in the face of an unconstitutional law: "Where, as here, the challenge is based on the unconstitutionality of the legislation, recourse to s. 24 is unnecessary and *the particular effect on the challenging party is irrelevant*" [emphasis added].[130] After alluding to section 52, Mr. Justice Dickson goes on to note that:

> The undoubted corollary to be drawn . . . is that no one can be convicted of an offence under an unconstitutional law. . . .
>   Any accused, whether corporate or individual, may defend a criminal charge by arguing that the law under which the charge is brought is constitutionally invalid.[131]

The respondent in the *Big M* case, a commercial corporation, argued that the statute under which it was charged was inconsistent with section 2(a) of the Charter and was therefore without force or effect under section 52. Whether a corporation is capable of enjoying the freedom of religion guaranteed by this section was immaterial for the purpose of invoking section 52. The key issue was whether the statute in question impaired that freedom. In the words of Mr. Justice Dickson, "[i]t is the nature of

---

127 *Hunter v. Southam Inc.,* [1984] 2 S.C.R. 145 at 155.
128 [1985] 2 S.C.R. 486 at 497.
129 [1985] 1 S.C.R. 295 at 313.
130 *Ibid.*
131 *Ibid.* at 313, 314.

the law, not the status of the accused, that is in issue".[132]

The point made here is an important one. An accused does not have to show that he or she personally benefits from a Charter right or freedom in order to successfully challenge a law. If the accused can show that the provision on which the charges are based does not conform to the principles and values entrenched in the Charter, he or she is entitled to an acquittal.

(b) The Meaning of the Word "Law"

Section 52(1) stipulates that "any law that is inconsistent with the provisions of the Constitution is . . . of no force or effect". What is to be understood by the word "law" in this context?

The essential feature of law is the establishment of a coercive norm. The law binds, on pain of an appropriate sanction, those who are subject to it. Thus defined, law obviously includes legislation and, according to the Supreme Court of Canada in the *Dolphin Delivery* case,[133] it also includes the rules of the common law. In the opinion of Mr. Justice McIntyre, there could be no doubt that the Charter applies to the common law:

> To adopt a construction of s. 52(1) which would exclude from *Charter* application the whole body of the common law which in great part governs the rights and obligations of the individuals in society, would be wholly unrealistic and contrary to the clear language employed in s. 52(1) of the Act.[134]

In *Operation Dismantle Inc. v. R.*, [135] Chief Justice Dickson expressed the view that the word "law" in section 52 is not confined to statutes, regulations and the common law, and could well extend to "all acts taken pursuant to powers granted by law".[136] In the same case, Madame Justice Wilson said she was ready to assume, without however deciding, that the decision of the Canadian government to conclude an agreement with the American government to test cruise missiles was covered by the expression "law" in section 52.[137]

The status of regulations is particularly interesting in light of the Supreme Court of Canada's judgments in the *Blaikie* cases.[138] The issue

---

132 *Ibid.* at 314.
133 *Supra*, note 7.
134 *Ibid.* at 593. Mr. Justice McIntyre considerably restricted the scope of this statement when he later stated that the *Charter* "will apply to the common law . . . only in so far as the common law is the basis of some governmental action which, it is alleged, infringes a guaranteed right or freedom" (p. 599).
135 *Supra*, note 30.
136 *Ibid.* at 459.
137 *Ibid.*
138 *Supra*, note 19.

in *Blaikie* was whether section 133 of the *Constitution Act, 1867*, which provides that "the Acts of the Parliament of Canada and of the Legislature of Quebec shall be printed and published in both those languages [French and English]", applies to regulations and in particular to the bylaws of municipalities and school boards. After noting the degree of integration between the provincial executive power and the legislature, the court expressed the following view:

> Legislative powers so delegated by the Legislature to a constitutional body which is part of itself must be viewed as an extension of the legislative power of the Legislature and the enactments of the Government under such delegation must clearly be considered enactments of the Legislature for the purposes of s. 133 of the *B.N.A. Act*.[139]

This led the court to conclude that section 133 applies "to regulations enacted by the Government of Quebec, a minister or a group of ministers and to regulations of the civil administration and of semi-public agencies ... which, to come into force, are subject to the approval of that Government, a minister or a group of ministers".[140] Measures passed by the executive branch are thus assimilated to measures enacted by the legislature for the purpose of section 133. Regulations which do not require the assistance of the executive branch to breathe life into them are not assimilated to measures enacted by the legislature for the purpose of this section and are not considered Acts of the legislature. This would include, for example, regulations made by agencies without the assistance of the executive branch in the exercise of delegated legislative authority. Such regulations would not be subject to section 133.

This judgment, in my opinion, does not apply to section 52. The language of section 52 is different. Section 133 refers to "the Acts of the Parliament of Canada and of the Legislature of Quebec". This language would normally refer to the legislation enacted by Parliament or a provincial legislature. The reason given by the court for including governmental regulations was that "[t]he requirements of s. 133 of the *B.N.A. Act* would be truncated ... should this section be construed so as not to govern such regulations".[141] Section 52, on the other hand, employs the much broader term "law". There is no valid reason, in my view, to limit the word "law" to regulations which were brought by the court in the *Blaikie* cases within the purview of section 133.[142] The word "law" as used in section 52 should extend to all delegated legislation, including rules or directives of internal management.

---

139 *Blaikie (No. 2)*, *ibid.* at 320.
140 *Ibid.* at 333.
141 *Ibid.* at 321.
142 *Ibid.*

In the same judgment the Supreme Court of Canada concluded, on historical and also legal grounds, that the bylaws of municipalities and school boards are not subject to the provisions of section 133. In my view, for the reasons discussed above, this ruling should not apply to section 52 and the bylaws made by municipalities and school boards should be regarded as "law" within the meaning of the section.[143]

Finally, although the word "law' in section 52 should be given a broad meaning to enable the courts to exercise effective control over the legislative actions of the state so as to ensure compliance with the Charter, its meaning in section 1 should be carefully circumscribed. As Professor Gibson has suggested, the purpose of section 1 is to permit the limitation of Charter rights and freedoms in exceptional circumstances only. The strict requirements set out in the section would be undermined if too liberal a meaning were attached to the word "law" in this context.[144]

(c) The Application of the Charter to Other Provisions of the Constitution

The Canadian Charter of Rights and Freedoms is part of the Constitution of Canada (section 52(2)). The question arises whether the provisions of the Charter apply to the other provisions of the Constitution. For example, section 99 of the *Constitution Act, 1867*, as amended by the *Constitution Act, 1960*, establishes 75 years as the retirement age for Superior Court judges. Is this section subject to section 15 of the Charter which guarantees equality before the law without discrimination based on age?

In the *Reference re an Act to amend the Education Act (Ontario)*,[145] the Supreme Court of Canada had to decide whether the Charter applied to Bill 30. Its purpose was to implement a policy of full funding for Catholic separate schools at the secondary school level in Ontario. Several of the counsel who appeared before the court conceded that Bill 30 was discriminatory and violated sections 2 and 15 of the Charter. However, the court took the view that the Charter is not applicable to section 93 of the *Constitution Act, 1867* which, while conferring jurisdiction over matters of education on the provinces, at the same time protects the rights of the Protestant and Roman Catholic minorities. Mr. Justice Estey is clear on this point:

> The role of the *Charter* is not envisaged in our jurisprudence as providing for the automatic repeal of any provisions of the Constitution of Canada which

---

143 See Gibson, *The Law of the Charter, supra*, note 6 at 153.
144 See *ibid.* at 96 *et seq.*
145 [1987] 1 S.C.R. 1148.

includes all of the documents enumerated in s. 52 of the *Constitution Act, 1982*. Action taken under the *Constitution Act, 1867* is of course subject to *Charter* review. That is a far different thing from saying that a specific power to legislate as existing prior to April 1982 has been entirely removed by the simple advent of the *Charter*. It is one thing to supervise and on a proper occasion curtail the exercise of a power to legislate: it is quite another thing to say that entire power to legislate has been removed from the Constitution by the introduction of this judicial power of supervision. The power to establish or add to a system of Roman Catholic separate schools found in s. 93(3) expressly contemplates that the province may legislate with respect to a religiously-based school system funded from the public treasury . . . [T]he Charter . . . cannot be interpreted as rendering unconstitutional distinctions that are expressly permitted by the *Constitution Act, 1867*.[146]

As the majority in the Ontario Court of Appeal noted, "[t]hose educational rights, granted specifically to the Protestants in Quebec and the Roman Catholics in Ontario, make it impossible to treat all Canadians equally".[147]

However, it is only the essentially Catholic or Protestant character of the schools that will be protected by section 93 of the *Constitution Act, 1867* as well as section 29 of the Charter. The provisions of the Charter, in particular freedom of conscience and religion as guaranteed by section 2(a) and the equality rights protected by section 15, are inapplicable to the separate schools only to the extent that they impair the Catholic or Protestant character of these schools.[148]

(d) The Consequences of Conflict Between a Statute and the Charter

The supremacy of the Constitution of Canada gives rise to draconian consequences: inconsistent laws are of no force or effect (section 52(1)). As guardians of the Constitution, the courts must declare unconstitutional those laws enacted by Parliament or the legislatures which exceed their respective areas of legislative competence. With the advent of the Charter, the courts have been given the additional responsibilities of ensuring that the legislative provisions enacted by the federal and provincial governments comply with the Charter and of declaring inoperative those provisions which violate protected rights and freedoms.

---

146 *Ibid.* at 1206. It is not without interest to note that the Constitution of a province is subject to the provisions of the Charter. On this point, see *Maclean v. A.G. Nova Scotia, supra*, note 14; *Dixon v. A.G. British Columbia* (1986), 31 D.L.R. (4th) 546 (B.C.S.C.).

147 (1986), 53 O.R. (2d) 513 at 575 (C.A.), aff'd *supra*, note 145.

148 *Ibid.* at 576. According to this approach, a Roman Catholic school board would have the right to dismiss Catholic teachers who marry civilly but would not have the right to refuse to hire women.

(i) *Reading down*

Where a law is subject to more than one interpretation, the courts can avoid declaring it inconsistent with the Charter and thus of no force or effect by choosing an interpretation that is consistent with the Charter. Mr. Justice Beetz, in *A.G. Manitoba v. Metropolitan Stores Ltd.*,[149] explains this principle as follows:

> This rule of construction is well known and generally accepted and applied under the provisions of the Constitution relating to the distribution of powers between Parliament and the provincial legislatures. It is this rule which has led to the "reading down" of certain statutes drafted in terms sufficiently broad to reach objects not within the competence of the enacting legislature: *McKay v. The Queen*, [1965] S.C.R. 798. In the *Southam* case, [[1984] 2 S.C.R. 145], a *Charter* case, it was held at p. 169 that it "should not fall to the courts to fill in the details that will render legislative lacunae constitutional". But that was a question of "reading in", not "reading down". The extent to which this rule of construction otherwise applies, if at all, in the field of the *Charter* is a matter of controversy.[150]

Where a statute can fairly receive more than one interpretation, it makes sense for the courts to prefer a construction which does not violate the Charter and to avoid constructions which do. This technique permits the statute to successfully survive judicial review, while at the same time assuring its conformity with the Charter.

This approach has its limitations, however. Since what is involved is merely a rule of interpretation, it could not be used to justify a construction that contradicts the language of the statute. For example, one could not rely on the rule to substitute the word "may" for the word "shall" in a legislative provision. The limitations of this approach are discussed by Chief Justice Dickson in the following passage from the *Hunter* case:[151]

> In the present case, the overt inconsistency with s. 8, manifested by the lack of a neutral and detached arbiter renders the appellants' submissions on reading in appropriate standards for issuing a warrant purely academic. Even if this were not the case, however, I would be disinclined to give effect to these submissions. While the courts are guardians of the Constitution and of individuals' rights under it, it is the legislature's responsibility to enact legislation that embodies appropriate safeguards to comply with the Constitution's requirements. It should not fall to the courts to fill in the details that will render legislative lacunae constitutional. Without appropriate safeguards legislation authorizing search and seizure is inconsistent with s. 8 of

---

149 [1987] 1 S.C.R. 110.

150 *Ibid.* at 125. In *McKay v. R.*, [1965] S.C.R. 798, the Supreme Court of Canada held that, on its true construction, a municipal bylaw prohibiting signs on private property did not apply to federal election advertising which, as a federal legislative matter, is reserved exclusively to Parliament.

151 *Hunter v. Southam Inc., supra*, note 127.

the *Charter*. As I have said, any law inconsistent with the provisions of the Constitution is, to the extent of the inconsistency, of no force or effect. I would hold subss. 10(1) and 10(3) of the *Combines Investigation Act* to be inconsistent with the *Charter* and of no force and effect, as much for their failure to specify an appropriate standard for the issuance of warrants as for their designation of an improper arbiter to issue them.[152]

As Professor Gibson points out, the problem raised in *Hunter* was complex, namely the creation and implementation of procedures for obtaining search warrants which comply with the Charter. These procedures could take a number of different forms and it would hardly be appropriate for the courts to choose among them. A choice of this sort should be made by members of the legislature.[153]

(ii) *Reading in*

The question whether the courts can avoid declaring a law inconsistent with the provisions of the Charter by reading in words or provisions which are not there has already been raised. The Court of Appeal of Nova Scotia was forced to address this question in a challenge to the constitutionality of section 5(4) of the *Family Benefits Act*,[154] which provided benefits for unemployed single mothers, but not for single fathers in similar circumstances. The issue was whether this provision was consistent with the right to equality guaranteed by section 15. The Court of Appeal, like the court below, refused to construe the word "mother" as signifying "parent". Both courts held that the provision was contrary to sections 15 and 28 of the Charter and could not be justified under section 1 or section 15(2). The provision was consequently of no force or effect.[155]

This result is hardly surprising. To hold otherwise would effectively substitute the court for the legislature and, in this particular case, would extend benefits to a category of persons which the legislature very clearly wished to exclude. The practical consequences of a decision such as this are obviously enormous. Once the provision is declared invalid, mothers in needy circumstances are deprived of benefits that the legislature intended them to have. To avoid such consequences, the courts could, in appropriate circumstances, suspend the effect of their decision for a period of time in order to give members of the legislature an opportunity to consider their options and amend the faulty legislation if desired.

The judgment of the Manitoba Court of Queen's Bench in the *Badger*

---

152 *Ibid.* at 168-169.

153 Gibson, *The Law of the Charter, supra*, note 6 at 188.

154 S.N.S. 1977, c. 8.

155 *A.G. Nova Scotia v. Phillips* (1986), 26 C.R.R. 332 (N.S. C.A.), aff'g (1986), 26 C.R.R. 109 (*sub nom. Phillips v. Lynch; A.G. Nova Scotia (Intervenor)*) (N.S.T.D.).

case[156] is of particular interest on this point. The case arose when inmates of the Stony Mountain Federal Penitentiary challenged the validity of section 31(d) of the *Elections Act* of Manitoba,[157] which deprived persons sentenced to prison of the right to vote in provincial elections.The inmates argued that this provision was contrary to section 3 of the Charter, which guarantees the right to vote to every Canadian citizen. At trial, Mr. Justice Scollin held that the provision was contrary to section 3 of the Charter and could not be justified under section 1. The provision was therefore found to be of no force or effect within the meaning of section 52. However, and this is the interesting point, Mr. Justice Scollin refused to accede to the inmates' request to have their names inscribed on the list of electors eligible to vote. He held that it would not be just and appropriate to make such an order under section 24(1) of the Charter only days before the election, given the difficulty of exercising appeal rights in a timely fashion.[158]

Inspired by this reasoning, a court might well decide to suspend the effect of its judgment for a period of time in order to give to the authorities concerned an opportunity to amend legislation found to be inconsistent with the Charter and consequently of no force or effect. This manner of proceeding would doubtless have been inappropriate in *Hunter v. Southam Inc.*,[159] where the litigants' rights were directly impaired by the challenged legislation, but in *Phillips*,[160] the circumstances were different. In this type of situation, it would be open to the court, in my view, to give the legislature time to amend the offending legislation. In this way, needy mothers would not be deprived of their allowance while the government and legislature decide whether the benefit of such allowances should be extended to others.

There is perhaps an exception to the principle that courts are not entitled to rewrite legislation that is inconsistent with the Charter. This is illustrated in *R. v. Hamilton*,[161] a judgment of the Ontario Court of Appeal. The issue before the court was whether sections 234(2) and 236(2) of the *Criminal Code* apply in Ontario. These subsections provide that a court may, under certain conditions, grant a discharge to an accused found guilty of impaired driving, on condition that he or she submits to curative treatment relating to his or her consumption of alcohol or drugs. These

---

156 *Badger v. A.G. Manitoba* (1986), 21 C.R.R. 277 (Man. Q.B.), aff'd (*sub nom. Lukes v. Chief Electoral Officer; Badger v. Chief Electoral Officer*), (1986), 21 C.R.R. 379 (Man. C.A.).

157 R.S.M. 1980, c. 67 (C.C.S.M., c. E30).

158 *Supra*, note 156.

159 *Supra*, note 127.

160 *Supra*, note 155.

161 (1987), 57 O.R. (2d) 412 (C.A.), leave to appeal to S.C.C. (1987), 59 O.R. (2d) 399n (S.C.C.).

sections of the *Criminal Code* are to come into force in each province only on proclamation, which normally takes place after consultation with the Attorney General of the province. In Ontario, the Attorney General opposed the proclamation of these sections. The accused accordingly based his challenge on section 15 of the Charter, which guarantees the right to the equal protection and equal benefit of the law. Mr. Justice Dubin, speaking for the court, wrote as follows:

> I do not read s. 15 of the Charter as requiring each province to enact the same laws within its own provincial jurisdiction. That would be destructive of the federal system and a denial of federalism. However, we are dealing here with the criminal law which, as has been noted, is within the exclusive jurisdiction of the Parliament of Canada. As a matter of legislative power only, Parliament does have the right to give its criminal or other enactments special application whether in terms of locality or otherwise, but, by the enactment of s. 15 of the Charter, laws enacted by the Parliament of Canada are now subject to challenge if the law or the effect of the law denies equality before or under the law, or denies the right to the equal protection or the equal benefit of the law on a discriminatory basis. That is not to say that in every case where special application is given to the criminal law a successful challenge can be mounted on the basis that it constitutes a denial of equality before the law.[162]

Mr. Justice Dubin went on to assert that "[t]he equal application of the criminal law, once enacted, cannot depend upon the acquiescence of the provincial Attorneys-General".[163] In the event, the court concluded that the accused's right to equality before the law had been violated contrary to section 15 and the situation could not be saved through the application of section 1.

The relevant sections of the *Criminal Code* were to come into force in Ontario only on a proclamation specifically declaring them to be in force in that province. Curiously enough, the provisions relating to this proclamation were not challenged by the accused. Given this, what was the appropriate remedy in the circumstances? Mr. Justice Dubin answered this question as follows:

> No attack having been made on the constitutionality of the *Criminal Code* provisions under consideration, it is for an individual to show that his rights or freedoms as guaranteed by the Charter have been infringed or denied. Only such an individual is entitled to a remedy. Where the evidence discloses that the individual is within the class of persons contemplated as one eligible for the court's consideration for a discharge, the appropriate remedy is to provide such an individual with the same right that individuals have in like circumstances in other parts of Canada.[164]

---

162 *Ibid.* at 431.
163 *Ibid.* at 436.
164 *Ibid.* at 438.

Although it does not do so expressly, it appears to me that the court here has indirectly but effectively amended the legislation which it judged to be in conflict with the right to equality. The *Criminal Code* provided that the relevant sections were to come into force in a province only after a proclamation to that effect was issued. To recognize that the accused in this case had a right to the benefit of these sections in the same way as the citizens of other provinces required the court, in my view, to ignore the provisions of the Code which provided for the proclamation of these sections on a province-by-province basis.

It must be noted that, in this particular case, the facilities and personnel necessary to administer the relevant sections of the Code were available in Ontario. The sections were not proclaimed there essentially because of philosophical differences concerning the appropriateness of the measures they contained. The Attorney General of Ontario took the view that a minimum prison sentence would have a more beneficial impact than the sections of the Code providing for curative treatment.

It appears that only an absence of facilities and personnel would have justified the Attorney General's refusal in this case to agree to a proclamation. This implies that the sections should have been proclaimed in force in the province as soon as it was evident that the necessary facilities and personnel were available. However, the court did not expressly declare that the proclamation should have been made. It simply dealt with the accused in the same manner as if the proclamation had been made.

A similar question came before the Saskatchewan Court of Queen's Bench in *Tremblay v. R.*[165] The accused Tremblay had asked that his trial be conducted in French, arguing, among other things, that section 462.1 of the *Criminal Code* gave him that right, even though the government had neglected to proclaim it into force in that province. This, he argued, violated his right to equality guaranteed by section 15. Mr. Justice Halvorson was of the opinion that the facilities and personnel required for the conduct of a criminal trial were available in the province, and consequently there was no valid reason for the failure to proclaim this section into force. The judge then addressed the following issue:

> What relief is available to the accused? Can s. 462.1 be ruled in effect in Saskatchewan? Should the ruling merely be that Parliament must now proclaim the enactment?
>
> Section 52 of the *Constitution Act, 1982* provides that "The Constitution of Canada is the supreme law of Canada, and any law that is inconsistent with the provisions of the Constitution is, to the extent of the inconsistency, of no force or effect".
>
> As I see it, s. 6 is inconsistent with s. 15 of the Constitution in that the

---

165 (1985), 17 C.R.R. 309 (Sask. Q.B.).

delay provisions of s. 6 improperly discriminate against the accused in contravention of his right under s. 15 to the equal benefit of the law, by depriving him of a right granted to others under s. 462.1 to a criminal trial in French. To the extent of this inconsistency, s. 6 is of no force or effect. That is, the provisions of s. 6 are of no force or effect to the extent they preclude an accused from applying under s. 462.1 to be tried on an indictable offence in the Court of Queen's Bench for Saskatchewan in the official language of Canada, that is the language of the accused.[166]

On this basis, the court held that the accused had the right, as claimed, to a trial in French. This brings us to discussion of the interpretive technique called partial invalidation.

(iii) *Partial invalidation*

Professor P.-A. Côté explains that this technique "consists in distinguishing those applications of a law which are contrary to the Charter from those which are not in order to arrive at a declaration of invalidity that is limited to the unconstitutional applications of the challenged law" [translation].[167] This approach has been used on several occasions by the courts.

It was used, for example, by the Ontario Court of Appeal in *R. v. Rao*,[168] in dealing with a challenge to the validity of section 10(1)(a) of the *Narcotic Control Act*.[169] This section authorizes a search without warrant of any place other than a dwelling-house by a peace officer who has reasonable grounds to believe that there is a narcotic in that place. Mr. Justice Martin expressed the following opinion:

> I have, for the reasons which I have set forth, concluded that the search of an office without a warrant where the obtaining of a warrant is not impracticable, is unreasonable and, to that extent, s. 10(1)(*a*) is of no force or effect. On the other hand, the search of an office without a warrant in circumstances where it is not practicable to obtain a warrant may be entirely reasonable. Further, a warrantless search of vehicles, vessels or aircraft, which may move quickly away, may be reasonable where there are reasonable grounds for believing that such contains a narcotic.
>
> Section 10(1)(*a*) does not, on its face, necessarily clash with s. 8 of the Charter although in some circumstances a warrantless search authorized by that subsection may, in fact, infringe the constitutional requirement of reasonableness secured by s. 8 of the Charter, depending upon the circum-

---

166 *Ibid.* at 319-320.
167 "La préséance de la Charte canadienne des droits et libertés" (1984), 18 *R.J.T.* 105 at 127.
168 (1984), 46 O.R. (2d) 80 (C.A.).
169 R.S.C. 1970, c. N-1.

stances surrounding the particular search. The statute is inoperative to the extent that it authorizes an unreasonable search.[170]

Somewhat later, after referring to the decision in *Oakes*,[171] he adds:

> The Court in that case held that it was not entitled to rewrite the provisions of s. 8 of the Act or to apply it on a case-by-case basis, depending upon whether the facts of a given case made the presumption created by the section reasonable. The presumption created by the section was on its face unreasonable and hence could not survive when measured against the Charter's guarantee of the presumption of innocence. In my view, the warrantless search powers conferred by s.10(1)(*a*) of the *Narcotic Control Act* are not on their face necessarily unreasonable and do not necessarily collide with the Charter, although warrantless searches authorized by s. 10(1)(*a*) may in some circumstances, come into collision with the Charter's protection against unreasonable searches and seizures. It is not like the reverse onus contained in s. 10 of the *Narcotic Control Act*, which on its face collided with the presumption of innocence secured by s. 8 of the Charter. The right to be presumed innocent prescribed by s. 11(*d*) of the Charter is a concept of fixed meaning (even if there is not universal agreement as to that meaning), whereas whether a particular search and seizure, under statutory authority, meets the standard of reasonableness may depend upon the circumstances surrounding that search and seizure. Accordingly, I do not consider that s. 10(1)(*a*) is unconstitutional, but hold that it is inoperative to the extent that it is inconsistent with s. 8 of the Charter. In my opinion, s. 10(1)(*a*) is inoperative to the extent that it authorizes the search of a person's office without a warrant, in the absence of circumstances which make the obtaining of a warrant impracticable; beyond that it is unnecessary to go in the present case. In that respect, my views differ somewhat from those of the trial judge.[172]

As Mr. Justice Martin notes, in such circumstances the law is inoperative only to the extent that it authorizes an unreasonable search, and the declaration of invalidity is therefore restricted to this application. It is the law in this particular application that is declared inoperative. In other contexts, it continues to apply.

Another illustration of this principle of interpretation can be found in the Ontario Court of Appeal's judgment in the *Videoflicks* case.[173] In this case, the *Retail Business Holidays Act*,[174] which prohibits businesses generally from opening on Sundays, was challenged and the issue was whether the statute infringed section 2(a) of the Charter, which guarantees freedom of religion. The court concluded that the legislation was valid because it was not aimed at protecting the religious character of Sundays

---

170 *R. v. Rao, supra*, note 168 at 109.

171 *Supra*, note 60.

172 *R. v. Rao, supra*, note 168 at 109-110.

173 *R. v. Videoflicks Ltd.* (1984), 14 D.L.R. (4th) 10 (Ont. C.A.), rev'd in part (*sub nom. Edwards Books & Art Ltd. v. R.*) [1986] 2 S.C.R. 713.

174 R.S.O. 1980, c. 453.

and was therefore not a law concerning religion. However, as Mr. Justice Tarnopolsky noted, a law may be valid in the sense that its intent and purpose come within the jurisdiction of the legislature that enacted it, but at the same time it may have effects that are contrary to provisions of the Charter. For Mr. Justice Tarnopolsky, this was a crucial point. Laws that violate the Charter on their face are relatively rare. Thus, to limit the reach of the Charter to the substance of the laws would greatly diminish its impact. The judge made the point in the following way:

> [I]n my view the interpretation of the Charter necessarily requires an assessment of the "effect" of impugned legislation. Intent and purpose will undoubtedly still have relevance. For the most part, however, in determining the appropriate balance between government action on the one hand and individual rights as set out in the Charter on the other, it will be the determination of the "effect" or "effects" of impugned legislation that is most important. While a law may have a legitimate purpose, its actual operation may result in the infringement of rights and freedoms guaranteed by the Charter. In the absence of legislative resort to s. 33 of the Charter, it will be rare indeed that legislation will have the direct and open purpose of taking away Charter rights or limiting Charter freedoms. An adverse impact, however, can occur as a result of the operation and enforcement of legislation or even because of its intended scope. To ignore the "effect" of the Act in issue before this Court would be to ignore reality and to concede the rights of the individual or a minority to the interests of the majority, even if these interests appear legitimate as far as the majority are concerned.[175]

This led the court to hold, among other things, that the legislation prohibiting the opening of businesses on Sunday could not apply to the businesses of Orthodox Jews who, because of their sincere religious belief, did not open for business on Saturdays.

On this approach, the statute is valid but inoperative to the extent that its effects (that is, its actual application) are incompatible with the freedom of religion guaranteed by the Charter. The application of this principle may explain the decisions in the *Hamilton*[176] and *Tremblay* cases as well.[177]

(iv) *Severance*

Canadian Newspapers Co. v. A.G. Canada[178] is a good illustration of another technique available to the court when faced with a conflict between the Charter and a statutory provision. Section 442(3) [since amended] of the *Criminal Code* provided as follows:

---

175 *R. v. Videoflicks, supra,* note 173 at 31, *per* Mr. Justice Tarnopolsky.
176 *Supra,* note 161.
177 *Supra,* note 165.
178 (1985), 14 C.R.R. 276 (Ont. C.A.).

Where an accused is charged with an offence mentioned in section 264.4, the presiding judge, magistrate or justice may, or if application is made by the complainant or prosecutor, shall, make an order directing that the identity of the complainant and any information that could disclose the identity of the complainant shall not be published in any newspaper or broadcast.

In the *Canadian Newspaper* case, the Court of Appeal of Ontario held that this subsection, insofar as it requires a non-publication order to be made when requested by the complainant or the prosecutor without the exercise of any discretion on the part of the judge, is inconsistent with the freedom of the press guaranteed by section 2(b) of the Charter. Chief Justice Howland explained the use of severance in the following way:

> Under s. 52(1) of the *Constitution Act, 1982* s.442(3) of the Code is, to the extent that it requires the making of a mandatory order, inconsistent with the *Charter* and of no force and effect. This does not result in s. 442(3) being declared invalid in its entirety. The offending portion of s. 442(3) can be severed. The test to be applied as to severability is set forth in *A.-G. Alta. v. A.-G. Can.*, [1947] A.C. 503, where Viscount Simon in delivering the judgment of the Judicial Committee of the Privy Council stated at p. 518:
>
> "The real question is whether what remains is so inextricably bound up with the part declared invalid that what remains cannot independently survive or, as it has sometimes been put, whether on a fair review of the whole matter it can be assumed that the legislature would have enacted what survives without enacting the part that is ultra vires at all".
>
> Here, if the offending clause is deleted, the remainder of the subsection, which simply gives the presiding judge a discretion to make the order, can stand. The valid portion of the subsection is not inextricably bound up with the invalid portion. Parliament clearly intended that the presiding judge should have the discretionary power to make a prohibitory order quite apart from having the obligation to make such an order if requested by the complainant or the prosecutor to do so. Accordingly the offending portions of s. 442(3) can be severed: see Barry L. Strayer, *The Canadian Constitution and the Courts*, 2nd ed. (1983), at pp. 262-264.[179]

(v) *The invalidating or suspensive effect of the Charter*

In an intriguing article, Professor Pierre-André Côté has examined the question whether conflict with the Charter has the effect of invalidating the conflicting law or of merely overriding it.[180] To adopt the model of invalidity founded initially on the provisions of the *Colonial Laws Validity*

---

179 *Ibid.* at 301
180 *Supra*, note 167.

Act,[181] would lead to the conclusion that the Charter establishes jurisdictional limits on the legislative competence of Parliament and the provincial legislatures. However, as Professor Côté reminds us, "the declaration of total invalidity is not the sole method of ensuring the supremacy of the Charter: the framers may have been content to give to the Charter a paramount effect" [translation].[182] The author then puts the following question. "Is it possible that our law now recognizes two distinct sanctions for the unconstitutionality of laws, namely inoperability for the laws that are contrary to the Charter and invalidity for the others?" [translation][183]

Professor Côté discusses five sources on which the courts might rely in attempting to determine what consequences the framers intended to flow from a conflict between legislation and the Charter: the language of the Charter, its legislative history, the presumption against implicit amendment of the law, the type of Charter-law conflict and the authorities. He ultimately concludes that the question is an open one and we must look to the Supreme Court of Canada for a definitive answer.[184]

This question is not without practical importance, for as Professor Côté remarks:

> If a law which conflicts with the *Charter* is deemed to be *ultra vires*, it could not become effective again unless it were re-enacted following either an amendment of the *Charter* or an amendment of the law itself which either brought the law into line with the *Charter* or provided for it to operate notwithstanding the relevant provision(s) of the *Charter*. If, on the other hand, a law which conflicts with the *Charter* is considered to be merely inoperative, it could resume operation once the obstacle to its application is removed [translation].[185]

This question has received little attention in the cases decided to date. Most courts speak in terms of the supremacy of the Charter without explicitly addressing the question of invalidity.[186] However, in *Re Ontario Film & Video Appreciation Society and Ontario Board of Censors*,[187] the Ontario Court of Appeal, having affirmed the decision of the court below

---

181 *Supra*, note 122. This statute provides that any colonial law repugnant to the provisions of an Imperial law applicable to the colony "shall, to the Extent of such Repugnancy, but not otherwise, be and remain absolutely void and inoperative" (s. 2).

182 *Supra*, note 167 at 108.

183 *Ibid.* at 110.

184 *Ibid.* at 119.

185 *Ibid.* at 119.

186 See, *inter alia, Hunter, supra*, note 127; *Big M Drug Mart, supra*, note 129; *Reference re S. 94(2) of the Motor Vehicle Act (B.C.), supra*, note 128; *R. v. Oakes, supra*, note 60.

187 (1984), 7 C.R.R. 129 (Ont. C.A.), leave to appeal to S.C.C. granted (1984), 3 O.A.C. 318 (S.C.C.).

that certain provisions of the Ontario scheme for censoring films were incompatible with freedom of expression as guaranteed in section 2(b) of the Charter, declared that it was willing to go further. As Mr. Justice MacKinnon, Associate Chief Justice of Ontario, wrote:

> We would go further than the Divisional Court on this issue. In our view, s. 3(2)(*a*), rather than being of "no force or effect", is *ultra vires* as it stands. The subsection allows for the complete denial or prohibition of the freedom of expression in this particular area and sets no limits on the Board of Censors. It clearly sets no limit, reasonable or otherwise, on which an argument can be mounted that it falls within the saving words of s. 1 of the Charter — — "subject only to such reasonable limits prescribed by law".[188]

The Chief Justice did not explain the reasons which led him to conclude that the legislation was not only inoperative but also *ultra vires* and therefore invalid. It appears, however, that in making these remarks he was seeking to repudiate the conclusion reached by the Divisional Court below:

> This does not mean that the censorship scheme set out in the *Theatre Act* is invalid. Clearly the classification scheme by itself does not offend the Charter. Nor do we find that ss. 3, 35 and 38 are invalid but the problem is that standing alone they cannot be used to censor or prohibit the exhibition of films because they are so general, and because the detailed criteria employed in the process are not prescribed by law. These sections, insofar as they purport to prohibit or to allow censorship of films, may be said to be "of no force or effect", but they may be rendered operable by the passage of regulations pursuant to the legislative authority or by the enactment of statutory amendments, imposing reasonable limits and standards.[189]

By expressing itself as it did and by characterizing the law as "*ultra vires*", the Court of Appeal apparently sought to repudiate the possibility that the law could again begin to operate following the adoption of regulations or an amendment of the law eliminating its incompatibility with the Charter.

As Professor Côté suggests, the question whether the Charter has an invalidating or merely a suspensive effect remains unanswered.

---

188 *Ibid.* at 131.
189 *Re Ont. Film & Video Appreciation Soc. and Ont. Bd. of Censors* (1983), 5 C.R.R. 373 at 383 (Ont. Div. Ct.), aff'd *supra*, note 187.

4

Assessing Competing Values in the Definition of Charter Rights and Freedoms

(*The Interpretative Process and Charter Section 1*)

William R. Lederman

Professor Frank R. Scott:

I saw that every legal change involves a choice of values, a selection of objectives, and in this sense I was greatly attracted to the concept of law as social engineering being then advanced by the great American jurist, Roscoe Pound. Changing a constitution confronts a society with the most important choices, for in the constitution will be found the philosophical principles and rules which largely determine the relations of the individual and of cultural groups to one another and to the state. If human rights and harmonious relations between cultures are forms of the beautiful, then the state is a work of art that is never finished. Law thus takes its place, in its theory and practice, among man's highest and most creative activities.

F.R. Scott, *Essays on the Constitution* (Toronto: University of Toronto Press, 1977), p. ix.

Mr. Justice Ivan C. Rand:

That law is reason . . . is as applicable to statutes as to the unwritten law.

Johnson v. Attorney General of Alberta, [1954] S.C.R. 127 at 138.

1. GENERAL AND INTRODUCTORY CONSIDERATIONS

The *Canadian Charter of Rights and Freedoms*[1] guarantees the rights and freedoms set out in it subject only to such reasonable limits prescribed by law as can be demonstrably justified in a free and democratic society.

(Section 1)

The Constitution of Canada is the supreme law of Canada, and any law that is inconsistent with the provisions of the Constitution is, to the extent of the inconsistency, of no force or effect.

(Section 52(1))

The Constitution of Canada includes the [Charter].

(Section 52(2)(a))

(a) Understanding the significance of section 1 of the Charter requires a full analysis of the total process of interpretation whereby the applicability or non-applicability of the Charter to certain particular societal situations is determined. In effect, the terms of section 1 apply as if those very words of guarantee and reasonable limits were repeated in every subsequent Charter section conferring rights or freedoms, even those with their own internal qualifying words (for example, section 8 — "unreasonable search or seizure").

(b) I use the words "applicable" or "non-applicable" to include all the elements that enter into, or may enter into, the total interpretative process. The final decision that a Charter standard is *applicable* is indeed a complex one, involving different stages — certain tests that must all be satisfied cumulatively in their proper order to reach the positive result. On the other hand, the final decision that a Charter standard alleged to be applicable is not applicable results from a failure to meet *any one* of the above tests, whether early or late (or even last) in the series. Also, we shall see that the usual meaning of the words in which a given Charter standard is expressed (*prima facie* meanings) may only be a starting point for reasoning and may in the end have to be qualified.

---

1 Part I of the *Constitution Act, 1982* [en. by the *Canada Act 1982* (U.K.), 1982, c. 11, Sched. B], proclaimed in force April 17, 1982.

(c) From this point on, my plan for this chapter is to state my position on certain controversial issues boldly and succinctly in this introductory part, in order to clear the way for an intensive effort in part 2 to explain the heart of the process of Charter interpretation. Then I shall come back to the controversial issues I have raised in part 1 and defend, in detail and in depth, the positions I have taken.

(d) In the first place, the total legal system (including the Charter) is not all-pervasive throughout the whole of societal relations and arrangements. There are, in these latter respects, important extra-legal areas. In other words, the total legal system is selective and partial in its direct impact on the whole of society. The Charter itself is part of the total legal system and, as superior constitutional law within the system, provides standards with which certain other parts of that system should comply. The Charter standards are laws about laws, and as such are not potentially applicable beyond the total legal system. Moreover, neither is the Charter all-pervasive *within* the total legal system. Even here, Charter applicability is partial and highly selective. Many, if not most ordinary statutes, for example, are simply beyond the reach of Charter standards. In other words, taken collectively, the definitions of all the Charter rights and freedoms are not relevant to everything in all the books of statutes and regulations.

(e) Here we have an important difference from that older branch of superior Canadian constitutional law, the federal division of legislative powers of 1867 between the Parliament of Canada and the legislatures of the provinces, which is also law about laws. It is a principle of the latter system that all legislative powers *are* distributed.[2] In other words, the categories of legislative subjects in the *Constitution Act, 1867*, are relevant, one way or another, to everything in the statute books of Canada or the provinces. This is far from true of the impact of the *Canadian Charter of Rights and Freedoms*.

(f) In any event, if I am right, we are at this point left with one initial and firm negative test of possible Charter applicability: the Charter does not apply at all to extra-legal societal relations. Some jurists have a broader view of the reach of law in relation to society than I do. They conceive of the legal system as reaching potentially to the whole of societal activity. They would deny the existence of areas of extra-legal societal relations and, accordingly, the negative threshold test of potential Charter applicability that I have just given. Professor Dale Gibson, for example, says:

> It is axiomatic under our legal system that whatever is not prohibited is permitted. This axiom can be viewed as one feature of the "rule of law"

---

2 *A.G. Ontario v. A.G. Canada* (Reference Appeal), [1912] A.C. 571 (P.C.).

principle, which the preamble to the Charter explicitly recognizes. By that principle, every aspect of life falls within the purview of law, in the sense that everything one does is either prohibited or permitted by law. That the law permits what it does not clearly proscribe is one of the most fundamental bulwarks of our freedom."[3]

In contrast to this, there are jurists who, in another respect, would be much narrower than Dale Gibson is or than I would be about the nature and extent of the ordinary laws that are potentially subject to the Charter. These experts take the view that the Charter applies only to public law relationships, not to private law relationships. In other words, given that each legal relationship requires at least two parties, they say that the Charter is not potentially applicable at all unless one of those parties represents the government in some significant official form, though the other party — usually the complaining party appealing to the Charter — may be a private person. If these jurists are correct, then we have here another threshold test for potential Charter applicability which is capable in and of itself of yielding a conclusive negative result to start with. If the legal relationship in question is a private one (that is, between two private persons), they say, the Charter is not even potentially applicable and there can be no appeal to its provisions. On this view, the possibility of Charter applicability depends, as a first step in the reasoning, on finding the government to be in some appropriate sense an actor or participant in the legal relationship in question. Professor Katherine Swinton is one of the principal protagonists of this opinion concerning Charter interpretation.[4]

This "state action" doctrine, so-called, has been a source of controversy and confusion for over 100 years in the United States Supreme Court respecting certain *Bill of Rights* clauses of the American Constitution, and the uncertainty in the United States continues. Nevertheless, we seem determined to import both the controversy and the confusion to Canada for interpretation of the Canadian Charter. This is unfortunate for the integrity of that process of interpretation as a process reliant on consistent reasoning. The recent Supreme Court of Canada decision in the *Dolphin Delivery* case[5] apparently accepted the "state action" doctrine for Canada. Nevertheless, after close study of the judgments in that case, I respectfully doubt that they have succeeded in settling the controversy or clearing away the confusion. I do think the "governmental action" doctrine is wrong *as*

---

3 D. Gibson, *The Law of the Charter: General Principles* (Toronto: Carswell, 1986) at 100.
4 K. Swinton, Chapter 3 "Application of the Canadian Charter of Rights and Freedoms", in W.S. Tarnopolsky & G.-A. Beaudoin, eds., *Canadian Charter of Rights and Freedoms* (Toronto: Carswell, 1982), p. 41.
5 *R.W.D.S.U., Local 580 v. Dolphin Delivery Ltd.*, [1986] 2 S.C.R. 573.

a threshold test, which it purports to be when it says "no governmental action, no Charter applicability". The appropriate legislative body is always present, that is, always involved, in a statute which it has passed or respecting specific common law which it could replace with a statute. Consequently, a Charter complainant should never be stopped initially because there is said to be "no governmental action" involved. Nevertheless, if a Charter complainant makes out a *prima facie* case and the later stage of applying Charter section 1 is reached, *then* the nature or extent of the inevitable governmental involvement may be a critical factor in determining whether the challenged ordinary statute is or is not a reasonable limit prescribed by law. As we shall see in part 2 of this chapter, in the former event the government succeeds and in the latter event the complainant succeeds. We shall return to this later in connection with the balancing of competing values.

To sum up my position at this point: I accept the threshold test concerning what I call "extra-legal societal activity" (which Professor Gibson excludes), and I reject the threshold test that Professor Swinton accepts concerning "state" or "governmental" action, for reasons just given. My objection to Professor Gibson's view that the law blankets all societal relations because it permits what it does not forbid should be further explained. The general condition of societal peace and order that results from the observance of the basic crimes and torts against violence and disorder creates many peaceful options and opportunities in the total of societal activities for individuals and voluntary groups. Concerning some societal activities, this general background of peace and order is the *only* respect in which the law touches the situation. There are no further directive laws setting limits on the peaceful choices the persons or voluntary groups involved may make. But, concerning other societal activities, there are, beyond the general background of peace and order, further specific directive laws placing limits on peaceful choices or alternatives. In the former case, the peaceful choices are made entirely on extra-legal considerations, giving rise to extra-legal societal relations that are beyond the reach of the Charter. But, in the latter case, the legal system does more than simply keep the peace in the background; further and specific ordinary laws come into the foreground and control, at times in great detail, how or even whether persons may pursue the peaceful alternatives they wish to pursue. The societal relations resulting from action are now legal relations as well, and, as such, may be within reach of one of the Charter standards.

These distinctions involve the difference between "freedoms" and "rights". Some Charter provisions specify freedoms and others specify rights. In an earlier essay on the Charter, I explained the significance of this as follows:

The *Charter* speaks of both *rights* and *freedoms*, and there is a jurisprudential difference between these concepts. Speaking first of the nature of the freedoms (specified in *Charter* section 2), one must realize that the total legal system is quite partial in its direct and specific coverage of *all* aspects of community life, individual or collective. There are not laws about everything, and life would be quite intolerable if there were. Some laws there must be, but too much law is worse than too little. A "free and democratic society" leaves its people with many areas of option and opportunity that are free of legal prescriptions either positive or negative. The quality of life in such a society depends in great measure on the assurance that these extra-legal areas are large and important. The principal function of the *Charter* freedoms of religion, expression, assembly and association is to safeguard the essential boundaries of such areas of option and opportunity by prohibiting unwarranted legal intrusions into them. So the law does have pertinence here, but the relevance is indirect and residual.

Freedom of expression affords a good example. The potential range and depth of natural and original freedom of expression is as broad and varied as the capacity of the human mind to conceive things to be expressed. The law intervenes only marginally with a few specific negative limits on what may be expressed. Obscene words are forbidden, in aid of minimum standards of public decency. Defamatory words (libel and slander) are forbidden in order to protect personal reputations from false and damaging disparagement. Treasonable or seditious words are prohibited because they promote the overthrow of basic institutions of the democratic state by force, and so on.

In other words, the direct relevance of law to the positive definition of freedom of expression is residual only. What is not forbidden is permitted, and only a few specific forms of expression are legally prohibited. Moreover, *Charter* section 1 requires that these few prohibitions must be "reasonable limits prescribed by law that are demonstrably justified in a free and democratic society". Whether they have this character can always be reviewed in the courts. The few specific *permissible* legal prohibitions on what may be expressed mark the boundary at which positive freedom of expression starts, and this latter is a broad and extra-legal area. So, the direct impact of the *Charter* guarantee of freedom of expression is, through *Charter* section 1, to determine only which legal prohibitions on expression are justifiable as exceptions to freedom. The same reasoning applies to the other freedoms specified in *Charter* section 2. As we shall see later, there may be some occasional positive implementation of freedom of speech or religion by specific laws, but these instances are few, and do not constitute the whole positive essence of these freedoms. Generally speaking, if I wish to express political opinions I can do so, but I must make my own opportunities and take my own chances on whether an audience can be attracted. No public official or other citizen has any legal duty to see to these things for me. Contrast with this *Charter* section 3 which says that every citizen of Canada has the right to vote and hold elective office. The positive definition of this right in meaningful detail is in the election laws themselves, which establish voters lists, polling stations and elaborate administrations staffed by public officials with the legal duty to see that eligible citizens wishing to vote have the opportunity to do so. There are sanctions if the public officials do not do their duty. So, when one speaks of a *right* under the *Charter*, one is usually contemplating a complex of relevant laws that specifically define, implement and vindicate the right, and without which there would be no right. The rights of accused persons to a fair trial, or of young people to minority language education are also of this character, as indeed are many other guarantees of the *Charter.*

As a matter of main emphasis, these theoretical distinctions between rights and freedoms are valid and helpful in understanding the operation in real life of our specially entrenched *Charter.* Nevertheless, there are no pure states in law or politics, so the distinctions do get blurred at times. For example, effective freedom of speech in a modern day political campaign depends in part on some positive and very specific laws giving political parties the right to fair allotments on time on radio and television.[6]

The foregoing reasoning, among other things, expresses my view that there are many peaceful societal relations that are extra-legal in the sense just explained and illustrated; that is, to them, no specific ordinary laws are precisely or directly relevant. But the Charter standards, as respectively defined, and Charter section 1 contemplate only societal relations and activities concerning which such precisely relevant ordinary laws do obtain and, even then, by no means all of them. Therefore, the *absence* of such ordinary laws gives us a quick threshold test to the effect that the Charter is *not* applicable.

Obviously, I must return later to these issues concerning governmental action and the nature of extra-legal societal relations and activities in relation to the Charter standards.[6a] But first, let us suppose that the possibility of Charter applicability has not been foreclosed at the start either by findings of no governmental action (if you believe in that test), or by

---

6 W.R. Lederman, "Democratic Parliaments, Independent Courts, and The Canadian Charter of Rights and Freedoms" (1985), 11 *Queen's L.J.* 1 at 5–7 (first published in J.C. Courtney, ed., *The Canadian House of Commons: Essays in Honour of Norman Ward*) (University of Calgary Press, 1985).

6a The content of the extra-legal segment of societal relations may be listed as follows. One of its components is related to the freedoms of religion, expression, assembly and association in Charter s. 2. Ordinary specific laws negatively relevant to these subjects are constitutionally prohibited unless they embody reasonable limits under Charter s. 1. Very few specific laws so qualify. The same may be said of everyone's right to "liberty" under Charter s. 7 (whether liberty is broadly or narrowly construed). Respecting these areas of societal relations, specific laws are absent because they are constituionally forbidden to intrude. In addition, there are other areas where there could be specific legal regulations that would be unrelated to any Charter freedoms, but in fact there are none simply because no competent legislative body has seen fit to enact any. In the whole extra-legal segment of societal relations thus delineated, people have options and opportunities that respond to non-legal influences and not legal ones. It is a large and important area. I do not say it is paradise; parts of it may be rough and nasty. Nevertheless, its existence is of some service to autonomy and privacy, which are among the public values of a "free and democratic society". If the foregoing were the limit of what Professor Swinton and others mean by "no government action", I could agree with them. But obviously this is not their limit.

the fact that the societal relations concerned are extra-legal. There is no quick one-shot negative solution to the problem of whether a particular Charter provision applies. We are through the gates into the Charter ball park, so to speak. Now what are the rules of the game? How does a complainant appealing to the Charter become a winner? This brings us to part 2 of this analysis.

2. THE POSITIVE PROCESS OF FINDING CHARTER STANDARDS APPLICABLE

Critical to the process of interpretation from this point on is further development of the root idea of relevance whereby certain Charter provisions are linked positively or negatively to certain ordinary laws. We shall now use the concept of relevance in a much more precise sense than we used it for the two negative general threshold tests for the complete initial exclusion of Charter applicability, just explained in part 1 of this chapter.

Let us recall now something else that was said in part 1. The definitions of the Charter standards, taken collectively, are not relevant to everything that is in the ordinary law, that is, the contents of the books of statutes and regulations and the common law. The relevance of Charter standards is controlled by their respective definitions, and collectively they do not reach everywhere among specific ordinary laws. Some ordinary laws are beyond the reach of *any* Charter provision. They are simply irrelevant to anything in the Charter. Notice now that, to determine which is which, we are assessing relevance or irrelevance precisely on a one-to-one basis between a given Charter standard and a specific ordinary law. (The contrast between this and the threshold tests is obvious.) At this stage, if the linkage of specific relevance is not found (and there is much irrelevance), the particular ordinary law in question is beyond the reach of the Charter and the complainant fails. But, if the linkage of relevance is found, there are still further steps in the reasoning that the complainant must successfully take if he is to succeed.

Before explaining this full process in general terms, it would be helpful to do so in the form of a particular example. In the *Rauca* case in the Ontario Court of Appeal in 1983,[7] Rauca, by then a Canadian citizen, was alleged to have committed multiple crimes of murder of prisoners in German-occupied territory in 1943, when he was a member of the German armed forces. The West German government wished to extradite him from Canada to West Germany in accordance with the *Extradition*

---

7 *Re Germany and Rauca* (1983), 41 O.R. (2d) 225 (Ont. C.A.).

Act[8] of the Parliament of Canada, which implemented an Extradition Treaty with the West Germans. But Rauca invoked section 6(1) of the Canadian Charter, claiming that, as a Canadian citizen, he had an unqualified right to remain in Canada, even if a *prima facie* case of guilt were made out against him in a Canadian court, and even though the *Extradition Act* said he may then be arrested, handed over to the West German police and compulsorily removed by them to West Germany for trial. The *Extradition Act* is relevant here in two senses. It is relevant to the facts of Rauca's situation on the one hand, and on the other hand is also *prima facie* relevant in the negative sense to Charter section 6. At this point, Charter section 1 enters the picture for the first time. It provides in effect that the *prima facie* definition of Charter section 6 is subject to reasonable limitations prescribed by law which are demonstrably justified in a free and democratic society. In saying this, Charter section 1 in effect tells us that the negative relevance of the *Extradition Act* to Charter section 6 is relevance to a *prima facie* definition of Charter section 6, and that this *prima facie* definition may be reduced by an exception in favour of the *Extradition Act*. Both Charter section 6 and the *Extradition Act* embody and implement public interests and values, which must now be identified, compared, and their relative importance determined. The *Extradition Act* implements the public value of suppressing and punishing serious crimes regardless of international boundaries, whereas Charter section 6 implements the public value of protecting citizens from exile as an oppressive instrument of their own government's policy. The court considered the relative importance of these competing values, and decided that the suppression and punishment of serious crimes regardless of international boundaries was the more important value. Accordingly, by judicial decision, the final legal definition of Charter section 6 was reduced from the *prima facie* definition by an exception for the *Extradition Act*, which thus continues in force. Note that this reduction was not by virtue of logic; rather it occurred because of a determination of comparative values, as just explained. This process of weighing competing values and choosing the more important one is the heart of Charter interpretation.

Consequently Rauca was extradited, and the same fate now awaits others in essentially similar circumstances in the future. As a matter of precedent, the reduced definition of Charter section 6 is now the final definition in law. There is no going back unless and until a higher court overrules the Ontario Court of Appeal, which is not likely. If a person in Rauca's position now attempts to invoke Charter section 6(1), he would be told that he has no cause of action. This is the normal, centuries-old operation of the doctrine of judicial precedent, now harnessed to shaping

---

8 R.S.C. 1970, c. E-21 [now R.S.C. 1985, c. E-23].

and refining the definitions of Charter standards.

To speak now in more general terms, we must appreciate that both ordinary laws and Charter standards are value-laden. They all express and seek to implement values approved in our society. But we must also realize, as I have stated in an earlier essay, that

> [M]any of the accepted values and goals of our society, each attractive in itself if looked at in isolation, are nevertheless inconsistent with one another, at least to a degree, when taken together. So far as these values and goals are embodied in the laws, those laws must frequently determine priorities and devise compromises to give conflicting values properly limited operation. Section 1 of the *Charter* in effect warns us that the accepted values and goals of a free and democratic society are not just those explicitly declared in the *Charter.* The full range of values and goals of such a society is broader than the latter, so that, constitutionally and legally, these other values and goals may well come into play by virtue of section 1 of the *Charter.* This is without prejudice to the truth that the values which *are* declared explicitly in the *Charter* as having special constitutional status are certainly among the more important ones. Though they are not absolute, whenever logically relevant they must be taken into account by parliamentary bodies framing statutes, and by courts framing judgments on existing or proposed laws. This should mean a clear gain for the people in the quality of the rule of law.[9]

Remember though that the Charter provisions collectively are not relevant to everything in the statute books or the common law. Accordingly, there are some statutory provisions, for example, that indeed are value-laden, but are simply irrelevant to any Charter provision. There is much irrelevance between the ordinary body of specific laws and the Charter. Here is one reason why, so to speak, the Charter does not open floodgates that expose virtually all ordinary laws to hostile judicial review. Proper attention to the concept of relevance will shut the floodgates and allow only a controlled flow of water through the sluices.

It is clear by now that the concept of relevance is a key to the meaning and functioning of the *Canadian Charter of Rights and Freedoms.* But what then is relevance? The Oxford Dictionary tells us that "relevant" means "bearing upon, connected with, pertinent to, the matter in hand". Professor J.B. Thayer of Harvard states that:

> The law furnishes no test of relevancy. For this it tacitly refers to logic and general experience, assuming that the principles of reasoning are known to its judges and ministers, just as a vast multitude of other things are assumed as already sufficiently known to them.[10]

Professor Ronald Delisle, in his treatise on evidence, enlarges on this as follows:

---

9 *Supra*, note 6 at 24–25.
10 J.B. Thayer, *Preliminary Treatise on Evidence at the Common Law* (1898) at 264.

Thayer later explained that by "logic" he was not referring to the deductive logic of the syllogism, but the inductive logic of knowledge or science. He noted that his book used " . . . the word relevancy merely as importing a logical relation, that is to say, a relation determined by the reasoning faculty. . . . The law has no orders for the reasoning faculty, any more than the perceiving faculty — for the eyes and ears".[11]

Notice that Professor Thayer says the determination of relevance rests on personal appreciation of *common* principles of reasoning which are a blend of logic and general experience. This is so whether judges are declaring what the law is because they are responsible for applying it, or whether government ministers or members of Parliament are framing new laws, or whether citizens are reading the laws for themselves (with or without the aid of lawyers) to determine whether they are subject to them. Thus, when Professor Thayer speaks of logic, reason and general experience, he is not thinking of highly specialized or technical senses of these terms, but rather of the common understanding that most people have of them. Moreover, in the common understanding of relevance in legal reasoning, there is an element of directness in the bearing upon, connecting with or pertinence to the matter in hand. Quite remote, very tenuous or highly speculative bearings, connections or pertinences do not count as foundations for relevance in the law. In *Operation Dismantle Inc. v. R.*,[12] the Cruise Missile case, both the Federal Court of Appeal and the Supreme Court of Canada held that the complainants had no cause of action. In giving reasons, Chief Justice Dickson in the Supreme Court of Canada was, I submit, endorsing the concept of relevance (and irrelevance) just explained when he said:

> My concerns in the present case focus on the impossibility of the Court finding, on the basis of evidence, the connection, alleged by the appellants, between the duty of the government to act in accordance with the *Charter of Rights and Freedoms* and the violation of their rights under s. 7. As stated above, I do not believe the alleged violation — namely the increased threat of nuclear war — could ever be sufficiently linked as a factual matter to the acknowledged duty of the government to respect s. 7 of the *Charter.*[13]

Section 7 of the Charter says: "Everyone has the right to life, liberty and security of the person and the right not to be deprived thereof except in accordance with the principles of fundamental justice".

Having established what I mean by relevance, let us continue in general terms systematically to set out the steps in the process of Charter interpretation, given that the complainant has passed the threshold tests

---

11 R.J. Delisle, *Evidence: Principles and Problems* (Toronto: Carswell, 1984), at 5.

12 [1985] 1 S.C.R. 441, aff'g (1983), 3 D.L.R. (4th) 193 (F.C.A.).

13 *Ibid.* at 459 (S.C.R.).

(if any) explained in part 1 of this chapter. We will continue to assume that our complainant is pursuing his Charter right in court, as this facilitates exposition of the process and affords a model for the reasoning that anyone attempting to interpret the Charter should follow.

As stated, the concept of relevance to a given Charter standard is vital to the process, but relevance to that standard is controlled by the definition of the standard. Thanks to the terms of Charter section 1, there are two levels of definition of a Charter right or freedom, and therefore two levels of relevance to it. Section 1 says that the rights and freedoms set out in the Charter are subject to reasonable limits prescribed by law that can be demonstrably justified in a free and democratic society.

The courts have said that a Charter complainant alleging breach of a given Charter right by an ordinary law has to show a *prima facie* case of breach. If he succeeds, the respondent, often a government, then has the burden of making the case that, nevertheless, the ordinary law complained of is a reasonable limit in our free and democratic society on the Charter right. As we saw in the *Rauca* example,[14] if the respondent succeeds in this, the complainant loses, in spite of having made out a *prima facie* case. So there is initial or *prima facie* definition of a Charter provision (and relevance thereto of the challenged ordinary law). But then the possibility of the challenged law being a reasonable limit arises. If this is established, the result is a reduction of the *prima facie* definition of the Charter provision so as to exclude from relevance thereto the challenged law, in the very case and, as a matter of precedent, in essentially similar cases in the future. In other words, the final definition is reduced from the *prima facie* definition, and the ordinary law that was relevant to the *prima facie* definition is irrelevant to the reduced definition. The reduced or limited definition becomes the *prima facie* definition of the Charter provision for future cases.

We are now in a position to explain in general terms the whole range of steps or tests that may be involved in Charter interpretation (given that any threshold test has been passed). First I will give a brief outline of these tests in order, and then attempt to explain them in detail.

3. DEFINITION OF A CHARTER PROVISION FOR PURPOSES OF THE COMPLAINANT'S ALLEGATION OF BREACH

There are five different situations in relation to the initial or *prima facie* definition of the Charter provision.

1. The ordinary law complained of is irrelevant to the initial or *prima*

---

14 *Supra*, note 7.

facie definition of any Charter provision. Result: The ordinary law stands, and so do the definitions of Charter provisions. They go their separate ways. This should not be confused with the extra-legal area of societal relations described in part 1 of this chapter. We are speaking here of conduct that *is* regulated with meaningful precision and particularity by an ordinary law, but this law is simply not relevant to any Charter standard. Example: The *Financial Administration Act*[15] of the Parliament of Canada specifies which Crown corporations are subject to the Auditor General and which are not. There is no relevance between this and any Charter provision. The parliamentary statute is the last word legally and constitutionally. This is because the Charter provisions are *not* relevant to all ordinary laws, as explained earlier.

2. The ordinary law complained of is *positively relevant* to (harmonious with) the initial or *prima facie* definition of one of the Charter provisions. The ordinary law is facilitative in some way of the Charter provision concerned; it is not conflicting. Result: The ordinary law stands and so does the *prima facie* definition of the Charter right. Example: *Criminal Code* provisions[16] forbidding an outsider to disrupt a regular religious service are supportive of freedom of religion (Charter section 2(a)); they do not contradict or limit it.

3. The ordinary law complained of is *negatively relevant* to the initial Charter definition of one of the Charter provisions, because it is inconsistent (in conflict) with the Charter right or freedom as thus defined. Charter section 1 tells us that if, nevertheless, the limiting effect of the ordinary law is *reasonable* in our free and democratic society, the ordinary law prevails in spite of the conflict, and the initial or *prima facie* definition of the Charter right is reduced accordingly, for the instant case and for the future as a precedent for essentially similar ordinary laws. Example: the *Extradition Act*[17] of the Parliament of Canada is a reasonable limit on the citizen's rights to remain in Canada[18] (Charter section 6(1)).

4. The ordinary law complained of is negatively relevant (as in 3 above) to the Charter standard invoked, but is *unreasonably* limiting in relation to the initial or *prima facie* definition of the Charter standard. Result: The ordinary law is null and void and the initial or *prima facie* definition of the Charter provision in question is confirmed as final for the instant case, and for the future as a precedent for essentially similar ordinary

15 R.S.C. 1970, c. F-10 [R.S.C. 1985, c. F-11].
16 R.S.C. 1970, c. C-34, s. 172(2) [R.S.C. 1985, c. C-46].
17 *Supra*, note 8 [R.S.C. 1985, c. E-23].
18 See the *Rauca* case, *supra*, note 7.

laws. Example: the *Theatres Act* of Ontario[19] gave the Ontario Censor Board a plenary discretion to prohibit the public display of films in the province, but specified no guidelines for the exercise of the discretion. This was found to be an unreasonable limitation on freedom of expression[20] (Charter section 2(b)).

5. The ordinary law complained of is negatively relevant to the Charter standard invoked in the sense that it completely denies the *prima facie* definition of that Charter standard. Result: The ordinary law is null and void and the *prima facie* definition of the Charter standard prevails as a final matter. Example: Bill 101 (the *Charter of the French Language*), an ordinary statute of Quebec, completely denied certain English-speaking parents resident in Quebec the right to send their children to the established English school system of Quebec, in spite of the grant of that right to those parents by Charter section 23. When there is such denial, the ordinary law in question cannot be saved as a "reasonable" limit under Charter section 1.[21] It is said that Charter section 1 is simply not applicable. Question: When does "limitation" end and "denial" start? Probably 5 is just the obvious and extreme case of unreasonable limits in 4 above.

In the series of tests just listed, given common sense relevance in the first place, whether such relevance is positive or negative enables us to identify harmony or conflict between the two types of normative (that is, value-laden) propositions being compared — ordinary laws and specially entrenched Charter standards. But now there is no further aid from the linkages of relevance. We are left with the conflicts of values revealed at stages 3, 4 or 5 above. What the authoritative decision-maker (legislator or judge) must now do is to refer such conflicts to the hierarchical system of the accepted values of our free and democratic society, whereby some values are assessed (located in the hierarchy) as more important than others in circumstances where it is necessary to put one value ahead of the other. In the example of the *Rauca* case given earlier,[22] the international suppression of crime by extradition under the ordinary *Extradition Act*[23] was deemed more important than the citizen's Charter right to remain in his own country. Rauca was extradited.

Let us look again at the words of Charter section 1:

---

19 R.S.O. 1980, c. 498.

20 *Re Ont. Film & Video Appreciation Soc. and Ont. Bd. of Censors* (1983), 41 O.R. (2d) 583 (Ont. Div. Ct.), aff'd (1984), 45 O.R. (2d) 80 (C.A.), leave to appeal to S.C.C. granted (1984), 3 O.A.C. 318 (S.C.C.).

21 *Quebec Assn. of Protestant School Bds. v. A.G. Quebec*, [1984] 2 S.C.R. 66.

22 *Supra*, note 7.

23 *Supra*, note 8.

The *Canadian Charter of Rights and Freedoms* guarantees the rights and freedoms set out in it subject only to such reasonable limits prescribed by law as can be demonstrably justified in a free and democratic society.

I claim that, in the four (or five) steps outlined above, we see what these words may require. We see the framework of what is necessarily a complex process of decision-making that may and often will have to be pursued through all its stages before a final decision, one way or the other, can be reached. We need now to review these stages one more time to consider problems arising at one stage or the other that have not yet been mentioned or, at least, which have not yet been fully explained.

First, we look again at the complainant's task of making out a *prima facie* case of Charter violation if he wishes to have a full trial on the merits.[24] We mean by this that he must persuade the court that there is credible negative relevance between the ordinary law of which he complains and the initial definition of the Charter provision he is invoking. I say negative relevance because, as we have seen, nothing changes if the relevance is purely positive — if the ordinary law is clearly facilitative of the Charter provision. Why then have stage 2 at all in the process? It is there to complete the analytical picture, and because in any event in some situations positive and negative relevance may not be readily distinguishable. The ordinary law in question may be a complex statutory system having both positive and negative elements in it, each credibly relevant to the Charter provision invoked. Problems of severance could then arise. Or if severance were not feasible, the statutory scheme may be beneficial in its main thrust with the limiting elements merely incidental, so that, *in that context*, one could say that the limiting incidentals lose their negative character, being a part of the larger positive scheme. The converse situation might also arise. Some of these problems were present in the recent Supreme Court of Canada case concerning the Ontario *Retail Business Holidays Act*.[25]

One further point needs to be made on the complainant's *prima facie* case. His task here is to show believable common sense negative relevance between the ordinary law complained of and the initial definition of the Charter right invoked. Frequently this will be easy or obvious. However, this task should not be confused with the much heavier burden that falls on the respondent who invokes the reasonable limits clause of Charter section 1 at a later stage in the process, given that trial on the merits has proceeded. This burden is "proof" of the reasonable character of the limitation by a preponderance of probabilities. As we have already seen, this latter task goes beyond consideration of simple relevance.

---

24 See *Re Ont. Film Soc. and Censor Bd.*, *supra*, note 20.
25 *R. v. Edwards Books & Art Ltd.*, [1986] 2 S.C.R. 713, referring to the *Retail Business Holidays Act*, R.S.O. 1980, c. 453.

I continue now with other problems of the Charter interpretative process that need more attention. What remains to be done can be summed up as follows. How do we arrive at the initial or *prima facie* definition of a Charter right or freedom? Some of these definitions have in them express qualifying words. What is the relation of these qualifiers to the application of the "reasonable limits prescribed by law" specified in Charter section 1? What indeed does "prescribed by law" imply about the nature of the ordinary rules of statute law or common law or of the Quebec *Civil Code* that are capable, given relevance, of triggering a problem of Charter application in the first place? Further, when we find negative relevance and move on to comparison of the inconsistent societal values involved, it is all very well to say that the decision-makers (whether legislators or judges) must assign priorities to these values, but how do they make that assessment? In this connection, we need to take a further look at "governmental action" *as a threshold test*. Finally, I will attempt some conclusions about the range and importance of the influence of the Charter, arising from this overview of its operation.

As we have seen in the four (or five) interpretative stages given earlier, the start of the interpretative process is with the initial definitions of Charter rights or freedoms, which I have also been calling *prima facie* definitions. With any given Charter right or freedom, there are always some definitional limitations *to start with*. How do we determine what they are, definition by definition?

The initial Charter definitions run at many different levels of generality, from the quite specific or particular to the very general or abstract. By this means, the Charter sets out certain of the more important rights and freedoms of our free and democratic society, though by no means all of them. But no Charter rights or freedoms are absolute. There are always qualifications of some kind, implicit or explicit, limiting the reach of the *initial* definitions, even those that are more or most abstract.

First, let us review the Charter sections as to their respective degrees of particularity or generality. The freedoms of section 2 are very brief and general indeed — conscience, religion, thought, belief, opinion, expression (including the press and other media of communication), peaceful assembly and association. The same can be said of section 7, the "right to life, liberty and security of the person and the right not to be deprived thereof except in accordance with the principles of fundamental justice"; and of section 15 which speaks of the right to equality before and under the law and to the equal protection and equal benefit of the law. Charter sections 2 and 7 pertain to "everyone" and Charter section 15 pertains to "every individual". The remaining Charter rights as expressed are much less abstract. One moves through increasingly lower levels of abstraction to definitional terms that are rather specific and particular, and thus are heavily qualified both as to content and often as to the persons to whom they apply. Consider the Charter sections expressing democratic rights, mobility rights, legal rights (other than section 7), official language rights and minority language education rights; and the reservations in favour of historic denominational education rights and aboriginal rights. All of them, while still briefly expressed, are at decidedly lower levels of abstraction than are Charter sections 2, 7 and 15.

But, regardless of the level of generality involved, the initial definitions of Charter standards, even the more abstract ones, are not new with the Charter of 1982. Take, for example, Charter sections 7 to 14, section 7 being quite abstract and sections 8 to 14 being much less so. Sections 8 to 14 sum up important elements of systematic fairness in the administration of criminal justice, with even more generalized implications, as section 7 puts it, for "life, liberty and security of the person".[26] They have behind them generations and indeed centuries of particular law-making in the legal and constitutional history of England, Canada and the United States. Over a long historical period to the present time, we have had the accumulation of a very large body of specific laws of criminal procedure and of specific crimes themselves. This has been an ever-developing body of laws because over the years judges, by judicial precedents, and legislators, by statutes, have added to, refined and changed these specifics as the needs and attitudes of society changed.

Moreover, in these processes of change and development, the judges and legislators concerned historically and currently engaged in the balancing of competing interests and values as part of the ordinary interpretative or legislative processes, long before the Charter was put in place. Thereby they shaped the ordinary laws to implement what they determined to be socially desirable results according to the standards of the time and place. In their authoritative legal reasoning in pre-Charter days, judges and legislators did not only deal in particulars of laws, though this was and is always necessary; they also dealt in the more general implications of the particulars, because this too is essential if one is to identify and compare the competing societal interests and values implicit in the particulars. As I expressed in an essay in 1979:

> [G]eneral principles mean little unless developed on a massive scale in meaningful detail; and yet they also show that we need to appreciate the general implications of what it is we are doing in detail. Particular detailed rules cannot be properly understood, or kept in their respective places as part of a reasonable and just system, unless we pursue the general implications of particulars as far as the mind can reach. In other words, general principles and their detailed implications are all necessary parts of the total constitutional

26 *Reference re s. 94(2) of the Motor Vehicle Act (B.C.)*, [1985] 2 S.C.R. 486.

and legal system. They are complementary one to the other, so that there is necessarily constant interaction between them in living legal processes.[27]

So, in our pre-Charter days when all depended on law-making powers at the ordinary level of parliamentary statutes and judicial precedents, some of the general or abstract principles involved found expression in the statutes themselves and in the reasons of judges.[28] In addition they found informal expression to some extent in the general reasoning of jurisprudential scholars. A further example will illustrate this. By virtue of the judge-made law of contract, two parties were empowered to make law for themselves in the terms of an agreement that consisted of the exchange of reciprocal promises. Then, if need be, the courts would enforce the terms to which the parties had agreed. But not always. Certain types of agreements did not turn into enforceable law for the parties because they had immoral or improper purposes in the eyes of the law. They were, as the courts put it, "contrary to public policy". And the judges added: "The categories of public policy are never closed". Also, the courts could declare a contract to be void where the agreement had been extracted from one party by oppressive means. Finally, the legislatures took a hand and enacted unconscionable transactions relief statutes which gave judges certain specific powers to reform the terms of oppressive loan contracts.[29] In this example, one can see the general public value of personal autonomy for individuals (freedom of contract) being assessed against other and conflicting general public values. The resulting compromises, putting some limits on individual autonomy, were settled and particularized in terms of the ordinary law as indicated, by virtue of the ordinary legislative power, whether the latter consisted of judges making the common law by precedents or legislatures enacting statutes. In modern times, the parliamentary statute has been the usual manifestation of the ordinary legislative power.

The constitutional Charter of 1982 assumes the prior and continued functioning of the ordinary parliamentary legislative process in all respects, resulting in laws of meaningful particularity for the persons contemplated by their terms. In that case, what is new with the Charter? What is new is this: the Charter sets up a system for subsequent review by the courts of some of the results or products of the ordinary legislative process, but

---

27 W.R. Lederman, "The Canadian Constitution and the Protection of Human Rights", in R. St.J. Macdonald & J.P. Humphrey, eds., *The Practice of Freedom* (Toronto: Butterworths, 1979) at 409-410.

28 In this respect, remember especially ordinary statutory bills of rights like the Diefenbaker *Bill of Rights*, S.C. 1960, c. 44 and corresponding provincial statutes like the *Ontario Human Rights Code*, R.S.O. 1980, c. 340.

29 See, *e.g.*, *Unconscionable Transactions Relief Act*, R.S.O. 1980, c. 514.

not all of them. This is a power to *re-assess* the compromises of conflicting societal values and interests embodied in certain of the ordinary laws passed by the legislature. How does the Charter give the courts this power? It selects some of the more important rights and freedoms established in our society, it expresses them in general terms, and then guarantees those rights and freedoms a constitutional status superior to ordinary laws. Accordingly, the declared rights and freedoms become standards with which ordinary laws must comply. The Charter provisions are laws about laws, and not just the generalized and informal speculations of jurisprudential scholars. In the cases where the Charter makes judicial review for compliance with Charter standards appropriate, and such review is unfavourable, then the ordinary law in question is declared null and void by the court. This leaves the parliamentary body concerned with the task of filling the void with new statutory provisions that do comply with Charter standards as defined by the judges. Such new legislation can only be provided by the parliamentary body concerned. This is the combined effect of Charter section 1 and the "supremacy of the Constitution" clause which is section 52 of the *Constitution Act, 1982.* The authority of the superior courts to interpret and uphold the specially entrenched clauses of the Constitution is not explicitly stated in section 52, but such authority is a basic implied fundamental of the Canadian Constitution and of the rule of law itself.[30]

It is true that a Charter right or freedom could be amended by the appropriate extraordinary amending process in Part V of the *Constitution Act, 1982,* but this would be politically very difficult and unlikely. It is also true that, by a carefully specific use of the "notwithstanding clause" of the Charter (section 33), a provincial legislature or the federal Parliament may, by ordinary statute, exclude the operation of section 2 or any one of sections 7 to 15 of the Charter, but not any other Charter sections. When invoked, section 33 restores the pre-Charter situation for the particular ordinary law at issue, but politically, this is also very unlikely. Therefore, saving these two unlikely eventualities, we are very much in the hands of the superior court judges for Charter interpretation and enforcement.

We are now in a position to give some answers to the question: how do the judges arrive at the initial or *prima facie* definitions of the respective Charter rights and freedoms? They are generalizations distilled from the specifics of our legal and constitutional history reaching to the present time. Chief Justice Dickson demonstrates this in *R. v. Big M Drug Mart*

---

30 See W.R. Lederman, "Amendment and Patriation" (1981), *19 Alta. L. Rev.* 372; and "Constitutional Amending Procedures: 1867–1982" (1984), 32 Am. J. Comp. L. 339 at 357–358. See also *Reference re Manitoba Language Rights,* [1985] 1 S.C.R. 721.

Ltd.[31] when he defines freedom of religion, and Mr. Justice Blair does the same in *R. v. Bryant*[32] for the meaning of the right to trial by jury. Anyone who knows Canadian history does not need to be told where the Charter sections on official languages or minority language education rights come from. But, while the historical component is strong, history alone does not account for all the features of these definitions. Being more or less abstract general postulates, they have some capacity to reach with relevance to new and different ordinary laws as these develop at the particular level in the future at the hands of parliamentary bodies to meet the needs of a changing society.[33]

But man is not omniscient, so no Charter standards are perfectly general or complete. Even the most apparently abstract ones have significant original and internal limits. We have just had a striking example of this with respect to "freedom of association" in Charter section 2(d). On April 9, 1987, the Supreme Court of Canada gave its decisions in three critical labour relations cases.[34] The panel consisted of six judges, and the basic issue in all three cases was the definition of "freedom of association" for Charter purposes. Did it or did it not include for a trade union the right to collective bargaining and the right to strike? The trade unions involved were complaining of ordinary statutes that limited or denied these two rights.

Justices Beetz, Le Dain, McIntyre and La Forest held that the Charter guarantee of freedom of association, as superior constitutional law, did not include for a trade union either the right to collective bargaining or the right to strike. Chief Justice Dickson and Madam Justice Wilson held

---

31 [1985] 1 S.C.R. 295.

32 (1984), 15 D.L.R. (4th) 66 (Ont. C.A.).

33 At this point I enter a caveat. I am definitely not claiming that, for *Charter* interpretation, we are really back with the "frozen concepts" notion that was typical of judicial interpretations of the general rights and freedoms in the Diefenbaker *Bill of Rights* of 1960. The tendency then was to make general expressions in that document the prisoners of the particulars in the pre-existing and current ordinary laws. Such general concepts, it was thought, could reach no further than to embrace such particulars. But the Charter is superior constitutional law, and the Supreme Court of Canada has made it clear that the general Charter concepts deserve purposive and liberal definitions, flexible or "living tree" interpretations, so that they have the capacity to reach beyond historical or current legal particulars to embrace relevant new legal relations in the future as they emerge from the needs of our dynamic society. As Mr. Justice Lamer put it, Charter section 7 includes and goes beyond the particulars of Charter sections 8 to 14. It went beyond them in *Reference re s. 94(2) of the Motor Vehicle Act (B.C.)*, *supra*, note 26, by extracting the further implication that mandatory imprisonment and absolute liability could not be combined in any particular criminal statute.

34 *Reference re Public Service Employee Relations Act (Alta.)*, [1987] 1 S.C.R. 313; *P.S.A.C. v. Canada*, [1987] 1 S.C.R. 424; *R.W.D.S.U. v. Saskatchewan*, [1987] 1 S.C.R. 460.

that "freedom of association" did include these two rights. The majority agreed with the following words of Mr. Justice Le Dain:

> In considering the meaning that must be given to freedom of association in s. 2(*d*) of the *Charter* it is essential to keep in mind that this concept must be applied to a wide range of associations or organizations of a political, religious, social or economic nature, with a wide variety of objects, as well as activity by which the objects may be pursued. It is in this larger perspective, and not simply with regard to the perceived requirements of a trade union, however important they may be, that one must consider the implications of extending a constitutional guarantee, under the concept of freedom of association, to the right to engage in particular activity on the ground that the activity is essential to give an association meaningful existence.
>
> In considering whether it is reasonable to ascribe such a sweeping intention to the *Charter* I reject the premise that without such additional constitutional protection the guarantee of freedom of association would be a meaningless and empty one. Freedom of association is particularly important for the exercise of other fundamental freedoms, such as freedom of expression and freedom of conscience and religion. These afford a wide scope for protected activity in association. Moreover, the freedom to work for the establishment of an association, to belong to an association, to maintain it, and to participate in its lawful activity without penalty or reprisal is not to be taken for granted. That is indicated by its express recognition and protection in labour relations legislation. It is a freedom that has been suppressed in varying degrees from time to time by totalitarian regimes.
>
> What is in issue here is not the importance of freedom of association in this sense, which is the one I ascribe to s. 2(*d*) of the *Charter*, but whether particular activity of an association in pursuit of its objects is to be constitutionally protected or left to be regulated by legislative policy. The rights for which constitutional protection is sought — the modern rights to bargain collectively and to strike, involving correlative duties or obligations resting on an employer — are not fundamental rights or freedoms. They are the creation of legislation, involving a balance of competing interests in a field which has been recognized by the courts as requiring a specialized expertise. It is surprising that in an area in which this Court has affirmed a principle of judicial restraint in the review of administrative action we should be considering the substitution of our judgment for that of the Legislature by constitutionalizing in general and abstract terms rights which the Legislature has found it necessary to define and qualify in various ways according to the particular field of labour relations involved. The resulting necessity of applying s. 1 of the *Charter* to a review of particular legislation in this field demonstrates in my respectful opinion the extent to which the Court becomes involved in a review of legislative policy for which it is really not fitted.[35]

Mr. Justice Le Dain wrote cogently, but only briefly, and speaking for Justices Beetz and La Forest as well as himself, he said that they all agreed with Mr. Justice McIntyre who gives a thorough and penetrating

---

35 *Reference re Public Service Employee Relations Act, supra*, note 34, at 390-392.

analysis of the meaning to be given to freedom of association in section 2(d) of the Charter:

> [W]hile a liberal and not overly legalistic approach should be taken to constitutional interpretation, the *Charter* should not be regarded as an empty vessel to be filled with whatever meaning we might wish from time to time. The interpretation of the *Charter*, as of all constitutional documents, is constrained by the language, structure and history of the constitutional text, by constitutional tradition, and by the history, traditions, and underlying philosophies of our society.[36]

At a later point, Mr. Justice McIntyre, defending the exclusion of the right to strike from the Charter definition of "freedom of association", points out that if it were included, a judicial Charter section 1 inquiry into the challenged ordinary laws would follow in many cases. He said (referring to the dissenting judgments):

> This has occurred in the case at bar. The section 1 inquiry involves *the reconsideration by a court of the balance struck by the Legislature in the development of labour policy*. The Court is called upon to determine, as a matter of constitutional law, which government services are essential and whether the alternative of arbitration is adequate compensation for the loss of a right to strike. . . . This is a legislative function into which the courts should not intrude. It has been said that the courts, because of the *Charter*, will have to enter the legislative sphere. Where rights are specifically guaranteed in the *Charter*, this may on occasion be true. But where no specific right is found in the *Charter* and the only support for its constitutional guarantee is an implication, the courts should refrain from intrusion into the field of legislation. That is the function of the freely-elected Legislatures and Parliament.[37]

For present purposes (an overview of the total process of Charter interpretation), these recent labour relations cases and the majority reasons given illustrate some vital points. Recall the five stages of Charter interpretation given earlier. The exclusion of the right to bargain collectively and to strike from the *initial definition* of the Charter's right to freedom of association means that the legal regulation of these rights (granting them, limiting them or denying them) is left to ordinary statutes and to the balancing of competing interests that they embody. These statutory provisions being irrelevant to the Charter, with respect to them the legislative supremacy of our parliamentary bodies is still conclusive. In general, there are many statutory provisions on many subjects in the statute books that are irrelevant to Charter standards. Such irrelevance is determined at stage one of my five-stage process of Charter interpretation given earlier. Obviously, the foregoing consequences of irrelevance are

---

36 *Ibid.* at 394.
37 *Ibid.* at 419–420 [emphasis added].

very important for the balance of powers and functions between our courts on the one hand and our parliamentary bodies, federal and provincial, on the other. Notice though that final authoritative definition of the scope of Charter rights and freedoms is in the hands of the superior court judges. They have the last word in this respect, so they fix the boundary line between legislative and judicial supremacy that we have just been examining.

This initial definitional problem is at its most critical respecting the most abstractly expressed Charter rights and freedoms. In addition to Charter section 2 (the freedoms), we have seen that this includes as well section 7 (life, liberty and security of the person) and section 15 (equality rights). There is neither time nor space for detailed discussion of these sections here, but there are probabilities of implied limitation on their initial definitions that may be briefly noted. Concerning the initial definition of section 7, the implications of the more specific sections 8 to 14 that follow may have a considerable restricting effect. Also, concerning section 15, this clause does not speak simply of "equality", it speaks of "without discrimination" and of "the amelioration of conditions of disadvantaged individuals or groups". These words should be read together. As I would read them, "equality" is synonymous with "without discrimination", and discrimination does not mean just any differentiation whatever between individuals or groups made by the ordinary laws. It means rather only those differentiations or distinctions that are truly obnoxious or harmful.[38] This restrictive approach to original definition is aided by the words about "*disadvantaged* individuals or groups" in the affirmative action part of the equality clause (section 15(2)). Insofar as there are restrictive elements in the initial definition of the equality clause, the complainant attempting to invoke the clause must satisfy them, or the ordinary law of which he complains is irrelevant to the Charter, with the same consequences as just described for falling outside the original restraints of the freedom of association clause. To continue with equality, the key to the overall application of the Charter's equality clause is the contrast between harmful distinctions made by ordinary laws between persons or groups, and differences that are either beneficial or at least neutral.[39] When the Charter says "let there be no discrimination", it is prohibiting the former differences and not the latter, and, so far as the Charter is concerned, the elements of definition that establish or deny a protected equality may occur cumulatively in two places — first, in the initial or *prima facie* definition of the equality clause, and second, in my stages (3) and (4) of the interpretative process (relevance and inconsistency), assuming the com-

---

38 See reasoning of McLachlin J.A. in *Re Andrews and Law Soc. of B.C.* (1986), 27 D.L.R. (4th) 600 (B.C. C.A.).

39 *Ibid.*

plainant made out his *prima facie* case.

But why should the process of finding a particular Charter violation be so complex? The answer seems to be that the Charter review process is no less complex than the society, the legal system and the Constitution out of which the Charter provisions themselves arise and to which they relate back. Not only does the Charter review process reflect our law and Constitution historically and currently, but also, by the review it mandates, the Charter has a vital influence in shaping our legal and constitutional systems now and in the future. But, as far as it goes, it is a *review process* — an umpiring process. Where applicable, the Charter mandates a *second* and critical look at something that has always been done before at least once, usually these days by one of our parliamentary legislative bodies. For example, in passing the *Extradition Act*,[40] Parliament had already weighed the conflicting public values of the suppression of crime across international boundaries versus the citizen's right to remain in his own country and had given the former values priority. In the *Rauca* case,[41] the courts took a second look at the public values in conflict and agreed with Parliament about the priority.

If we remember this "second-look" characteristic of the Charter process, it is easier to deal with the problem posed by explicit qualifying words, which of course enter into and are part of the initial definition of the Charter rights, where they occur. Examples are "*unreasonable* search or seizure" (section 8), "*cruel* and *unusual* punishment" (section 12), and "except in accordance with *principles of fundamental justice*" (section 7). The dilemma may be stated as follows. A complainant makes out his *prima facie* case of "unreasonable search and seizure", and so proceeds to a judicial review, the essence of which at the next stage is to determine whether the challenged ordinary law concerned was or was not a *reasonable* limit prescribed by law on Charter section 8. But why is there now anything left for judicial review so far as the reasonable character of the challenged law is concerned? There may well be something left for review because the assessment of reasonableness by virtue of Charter section 1 is potentially more careful and comprehensive than the one the court engaged in when it recognized the complainant's *prima facie* case on the basis of the initial Charter definition of section 8, and allowed him to proceed. The sense of what is "reasonable" may change between the initial or *prima facie* definition and the Charter section 1 assessment. If it does, as we have seen, the latter prevails and the initial meaning of Charter section 8 is modified accordingly, retroactively for the instant case and prospectively for all essentially similar future cases.

---

40 *Supra*, note 8.
41 *Supra*, note 7.

Professor Dale Gibson approves this solution. He points out the versatility and flexibility of the concept of what is reasonable. Gibson says:

> There is nothing absurd about applying the standard of reasonableness at two different stages of the adjudicative process. The victim first explains why it is unreasonable in normal circumstances to treat citizens as he or she has been treated. Those responsible for the treatment in question are then called upon to show, if they can, that there are special circumstances which justify (or render "reasonable") a law authorizing the treatment in that situation.[42]

Moreover, there is a difference, as we have seen, in the respective procedural burdens of complainant and respondent. The former has only to show believable negative relevance to the initial Charter definition concerned, whereas the latter must attempt to justify the challenged law, as a reasonable limit on that Charter provision, by a preponderance of probabilities. This last task is clearly the more exacting of the two, and from the point of view of the judge, it concerns the central dilemma of Charter interpretation.

So we move on to this central dilemma. In my earlier explanation of Charter interpretation, stages 3 and 4 described the situations where the ordinary law complained of was negatively relevant to (in conflict with) the initial definition of the Charter right invoked, but was either a reasonable limit (stage 3) or an unreasonable limit (stage 4) to that Charter right, by virtue of the standards of our free and democratic society. I have given examples of these alternatives and shown what the legal and constitutional results are. But I have not yet asked the question: *how* does a judge decide whether the ordinary law before him is a reasonable or unreasonable limit on the Charter right invoked? I attempt to answer this question now.

What can the judge properly expect of counsel for the respondent? As we have seen, counsel should "prove" by a reasonable preponderance of probabilities on the evidence (the normal burden of proof for civil court cases) that the ordinary law complained of is a reasonable limit within the terms of Charter section 1. However, this type of determination is different to a significant degree from an ordinary civil case in contract or in tort. To some extent it is dependent on establishing facts, but the point inevitably comes where two conflicting public values have been identified — the public value embodied in and given particular expression by the ordinary law complained of, versus the public value embodied in and directly expressed by the Charter right or freedom invoked. Both public values have status as accepted values in our free and democratic society.

---

42 *Supra*, note 3 at 138.

Nevertheless, the specific law complained of must be either confirmed or struck down. So, *for that purpose and to that extent*, the judge must give one value priority over the other, with the consequences specified in step 3 or step 4 of my stages of Charter interpretation. So the judge must ask himself: in this context, which of these accepted and competing societal values is the more important? The answer solves his problem and yields a solution. But the answer is not determined by mere facts in any ordinary sense of the word "fact". It is in the end a personal ethical preference which has complex roots.

This can be illustrated from a famous American case decided by the appeal division of the Supreme Court of California in 1964, *The People v. Woody*.[43] Peyote is a narcotic drug, though a relatively mild one and not dangerous if not taken in excess. Its moderate use plays a central role in ceremonies and practices of an Indian religious group, the Native American Church, long established in several American states. The use of peyote by the adherents is analogous to the use of bread and wine by Christians in communion ceremonies. Yet peyote was a forbidden narcotic under the criminal law of California, and participants in one of the religious ceremonies were arrested. The accused successfully invoked the First Amendment of the United States Constitution, which, among other things, guarantees that no law should prohibit the free exercise of religion. Mr. Justice Tobriner for the court said:

> We have weighed the competing values represented in this case on the symbolic scale of constitutionality. On the one side we have placed the weight of freedom of religion as protected by the First Amendment; on the other, the weight of the state's "compelling interest". Since the use of peyote incorporates the essence of the religious expression, the first weight is heavy. Yet the use of peyote presents only slight danger to the state and to the enforcement of its laws; the second weight is relatively light. The scale tips in favor of the constitutional protection.
>
> We know that some will urge that it is more important to subserve the rigorous enforcement of the narcotic laws than to carve out of them an exception for a few believers in a strange faith. They will say that the exception may produce problems of enforcement and that the dictate of the state must overcome the beliefs of a minority of Indians. But the problems of enforcement here do not inherently differ from those of other situations which call for the detection of fraud. On the other hand, the right to free religious expression embodies a precious heritage of our history. In a mass society, which presses at every point toward conformity, the protection of a self-expression, however unique, of the individual and the group becomes ever more important. The varying currents of the subcultures that flow into the mainstream of our national life give it depth and beauty. We preserve a greater value than an ancient tradition when we protect the rights of the Indians who honestly

---

43 (1964) 394 P. (2d) 813 (Cal. S.C. *en banc*).

practiced an old religion in using peyote one night at a meeting in a desert hogan near Needles, California.
    The judgment is reversed.[44]

The California court ordered that the ordinary criminal law of California should in effect have an exception inserted in it exempting this or any essentially similar religious ceremonial use of peyote. There are differences between the United States *Bill of Rights* and the *Canadian Charter of Rights and Freedoms* but concerning the need to compare the relative importance of competing public values as explained, they reach the same dilemma and solve it in the same way.

    Moreover, the words of the California court reveal one thing that played an important role in solving his dilemma. The decision-maker must be careful to appreciate and to express in equivalent generalized terms the conflicting and competing values and interests involved. Narcotic addiction is a great evil and the state has a "compelling interest" in suppressing it. However, the court did not allow counsel for the state to trivialize the Indian religious use of peyote as the aberration of "a few believers in a strange faith". The court generalized the practice as part of religious freedom, a "precious heritage" of our history. *Then* the judges weighed the competing values, and their scales showed that the weight on the side of religious freedom was the heavier. In our much used example of the *Rauca* case,[45] the public values in conflict were well appreciated and expressed — the citizen's Charter right to remain in the country versus the need to suppress serious crimes across international boundaries as expressed in the ordinary statute, the *Extradition Act*.[46] The Ontario judges came down on the side of the *Extradition Act* as serving the greater value in this context. Neither one of the competing values should be trivialized; if one is, this just signals that the decision-maker has already made up his mind for unstated reasons against the value or interest that has been trivialized. If this does not happen and the competing values are generalized to the extent each deserves, even that may not make the choice between them obvious or easy, though at least it does bring a wise choice closer.

    Given that the competing public values have been identified and expressed in equally general terms, then what? Chief Justice Dickson has delineated the further questions that now need or may need to be answered in order to assess the relative weights of these values in the circumstances, questions which guide in detail the balancing of considerations of comparative importance. The Chief Justice said:

---

44 *Ibid.*
45 *Supra*, note 7.
46 *Supra*, note 8.

Two requirements must be satisfied to establish that a limit is reasonable and demonstrably justified in a free and democratic society. First, the legislative objective which the limitation is designed to promote must be of sufficient importance to warrant overriding a constitutional right. It must bear on a "pressing and substantial concern". Second, the means chosen to attain those objectives must be proportional or appropriate to the ends. The proportionality requirement, in turn, normally has three aspects: the limiting measures must be carefully designed, or rationally connected, to the objective; they must impair the right as little as possible; and their effects must not so severely trench on individual or group rights that the legislative objective, albeit important, is nevertheless outweighed by the abridgment of rights. The Court stated that the nature of the proportionality test would vary depending on the circumstances. Both in articulating the standard of proof and in describing the criteria comprising the proportionality requirement the Court has been careful to avoid rigid and inflexible standards.[47]

Note that this is a checklist of questions for guidance, not a cumulative list, every question of which must be answered one way or the other in every case. The two main questions must be addressed of course, but not necessarily the proportionality subquestions. In many cases the subquestions will turn out to overlap one another or the main "second" question itself. Frequently, the main second question can be answered directly to the effect that, in its particular terms, the challenged ordinary law is *one* reasonable means of serving the general objective concerned, though there may be other equally reasonable alternative drafts of particular laws that would address the same objective and implement it. Frequently, there will be more than one right way.

Chief Justice Dickson's checklist of questions is quoted from the *Edwards Books* case[48] with respect to the Ontario *Retail Business Holidays Act*.[49] His first and earlier version was given in *R. v. Oakes*,[50] where his list of questions was so stated as to give the impression that, under an exacting burden of "proof", all questions had to be answered favourably to the challenged ordinary law, if that law was to prevail over the Charter right invoked. In the *Edwards Books* case ten months later, he seems to have considerably relaxed what he was saying in *Oakes*.

In between these two cases came the Supreme Court of Canada judgment in *R. v. Jones*.[51] In this case, the complainant was challenging the Alberta *School Act*[52] as an infringement of his religious freedom. He was the pastor of a fundamentalist church who educated his own children

---

47 *R. v. Edwards Books & Art Ltd.*, *supra*, note 25 at 768–769.
48 *Ibid.*
49 *Supra*, note 25.
50 [1986] 1 S.C.R. 103.
51 [1986] 2 S.C.R. 284.
52 R.S.A. 1980, c. S-3.

and others at a private school he held in the basement of his church. The Alberta *School Act* permitted such private religious schools, but put those conducting them under a duty to apply for approval to the Department of Education, which approval depended upon expert inspection and certification that the children were being effectively educated. Mr. Jones asserted that he was, according to his religion, responsible only to God and that to seek the approval of the government department was a breach of his freedom of religion under Charter section 2(a).

Mr. Justice La Forest, with the concurrence of Chief Justice Dickson and Mr. Justice Lamer, found that there was a breach of freedom of religion, since the definition of religious beliefs was necessarily so highly subjective. Nevertheless, he found the Alberta *School Act* requirements for official inspection and approval to be reasonable limits under Charter section 1. Mr. Justice La Forest pointed out that the Chief Justice had said in *Hunter v. Southam Inc.*[53] that the onus of establishing that a limitation of a Charter right is justified is on the person relying on the limitation, but had also said later in *R. v. Oakes*[54] that this was only where evidence is required in order to prove the constitutive elements in a section 1 inquiry. Then Mr. Justice La Forest continued:

> I do not think such evidence is required here. A court must be taken to have a general knowledge of our history and values and to know at least the broad design and workings of our society. We are not concerned [here] with particular facts.
> No proof is required to show the importance of education in our society or its significance to government. The legitimate, indeed compelling interest of the state in the education of the young is known and understood by all informed citizens. Nor is evidence necessary to establish the difficulty of administering a general provincial educational scheme if the onus lies on the educational authorities to enforce compliance. The obvious way to administer it is by requiring those who seek exemptions from the general scheme to make application for the purpose. Such a requirement constitutes a reasonable limit on a parent's religious convictions concerning the upbringing of his or her children.[55]

However, the *Edwards Books* case[56] concerning the Ontario *Retail Business Holidays Act*[57] was as complex as the *Jones* case was simple. Here, Chief Justice Dickson and Mr. Justice La Forest parted company on the tests for finding reasonable limits under Charter section 1. In the *Edwards Books* case, the Ontario statute provided for compulsory closing of most

---

53 [1984] 2 S.C.R. 145.

54 *Supra*, note 50.

55 *R. v. Jones, supra*, note 51, at 299–300.

56 *Supra*, note 25.

57 *Supra*, note 49.

retail businesses on every Sunday and a few other special days in the year. The purpose was the secular one of providing a *common* pause day to promote rest, recreation and family life. The court found that the legislative scheme pursued a compelling and substantial public purpose, but that in so doing, it did place a special burden on retailers who closed their stores on Saturdays for religious reasons. The Act did contain a severely limited exemption from Sunday closing for small stores operated by Saturday religious observers. In Chief Justice Dickson's opinion, without some such exemptions, the whole secular Sunday closing scheme might fail as a trespass on the religious freedom of Saturday observing retailers. He thought this exemption did indeed save the Act under Charter section 1.

Mr. Justice La Forest disputed this. He said:

> I have had the advantage of reading the judgment of the Chief Justice and while I agree with his disposition of the case and with most of his supporting reasons, we have significant differences of views regarding the Sabbatarian exemption that impel me to write a separate judgment.[58]

Mr. Justice La Forest then made it clear that he considered the Ontario Act to be valid as a reasonable limit on freedom of religion without any exemptions for Sabbatarian retailers or indeed for retailers whose holy day of religious observance was one of the days Monday to Friday. Then he continued:

> [H]aving accepted the importance of the legislative objective, one must in the present context recognize that if the legislative goal is to be achieved, it will inevitably be achieved to the detriment of some. Moreover, attempts to protect the rights of one group will also inevitably impose burdens on the rights of other groups. There is no perfect scenario in which the rights of all can be equally protected.
>
> In seeking to achieve a goal that is demonstrably justified in a free and democratic society, therefore, a legislature must be given reasonable room to manoeuvre to meet these conflicting pressures. Of course what is reasonable will vary with the context . . . That being so, it seems to me that the choice of having or not having an exemption for those who observe a day other than Sunday must remain, in essence, a legislative choice. . . . They are choices a court is not in a position to make.[59]

My sympathies here are with Mr. Justice La Forest's views as to the necessary confines within which a court should operate in performing its review function respecting ordinary statutes and their impact on Charter rights and freedoms. Nevertheless, there is still more to be said about how to provide the judges, or how they provide themselves, with the data for such decisions. This is far from being just a routine procedural matter

---

58 *Edwards Books & Art, supra*, note 25, at 792.
59 *Ibid.* at 795–796.

about which counsel have certain burdens of "proof". In *R. v. Bryant*,[60] Mr. Justice Houlden of the Ontario Court of Appeal spoke of the *"burden of justification"*. He said:

> The burden of justification under s. 1 of the Charter has been met in a variety of ways. The following are some of the more common ones: an examination of the *rationale* and purpose of the legislation; comparable legislation in other free and democratic societies, including judicial interpretation of such legislation; international conventions and agreements on the same or similar subject-matter; judicial decisions of other Canadian courts on the same legislation; the calling of oral evidence, and the argument of counsel.[61]

The *burden of justification* is the appropriate phrase, and for elaboration on how to meet it, I refer to an excellent paper given by John I. Laskin in 1983, entitled "Evidentiary Considerations Under the Canadian Charter of Rights and Freedoms".[62] Mr. Laskin says:

> Helpful in this context is the very useful distinction drawn by Professor Kenneth Davis (in "An approach to Problems of Evidence in the Administrative Process" 5 *Harvard Law Review*, 1942, 364) between adjudicative facts and legislative facts. Adjudicative facts are facts about the immediate parties to the litigation — who did what, where, when, how and with what motive or intent; legislative facts are those which help the tribunal to determine the content of law and policy. They are facts of a general nature concerning not the immediate parties to the dispute but rather the political, economic and social context of legislation.

As Mr. Laskin further points out, "adjudicative facts will still remain important in Charter cases. There will have to be proof in the ordinary way of particular facts giving rise to a Charter issue". But the Charter review function in relation to the specific ordinary law pertinent for the complainant calls for evidence of legislative facts and indeed beyond that for some personal decisions by judges on the relative importance of competing and conflicting public values. Also, there are questions about the respective institutional capabilities, questions as to what courts as compared to legislatures can and should do about conflicts of societal values. In this connection, Mr. Laskin draws attention to judicial notice, formally tendered evidence by expert witnesses and the Brandeis Brief. Notorious and undisputed legislative facts may be judicially noticed, and other legislative facts may be testified to formally by expert witnesses. The Brandeis Brief is an informal document giving legislative facts only

---

60 *Supra*, note 32.

61 *Ibid.* at 88.

62 This paper was originally presented at a program entitled "The Charter: The Civil Context" sponsored by the Law Society of Upper Canada, February 26, 1983 (Xerox version).

some of which would be entitled to judicial notice. Other legislative facts are included and affirmed at length in the Brandeis Brief. Typically, the Brandeis Brief is part of the factum of one of the parties, and there may be rival Brandeis Briefs in a single case. This is an acceptable way of introducing relevant statistical and other social science evidence. However, what weight it is to have, if any, is a matter for the court.

In the *Edwards Books* case,[63] it was clear that there was in effect a major Brandeis Brief in the picture. In 1970, after a year of intensive investigation and study, the Ontario Law Reform Commission brought in a major "Report on Sunday Observance Legislation in Ontario", running to 470 pages.[64] The Report and its proposals shaped the Ontario *Retail Business Holidays Act*,[65] and was much quoted in the Ontario legislature when the Act was being passed. During 1969–70, the Commission, consisting of two full-time and three part-time members, organized an extensive research program by experts, conducted surveys of public opinion, invited submissions from the public, held public hearings in five Ontario cities, and gathered comparative jurisprudential data from other countries. They deliberated on the results of all this and made proposals for secular pause-day legislation relying on Sunday as the day, with a few additions. In their proposals, they took positions on the conflicts of societal values involved.

It is striking that, some years later, the Ontario Court of Appeal and the Supreme Court of Canada, in performing their review functions under the Charter, turned to the above Report, quoted from it often and relied on it frequently. They concluded that the Ontario *Retail Business Holidays Act* did not offend the *Charter of Rights and Freedoms*. One wonders what the Legislative Assembly of Ontario and later the appeal courts would have done without the 1970 Report of the Law Reform Commission. In any event, we see here once again and very clearly that the judicial function of review under the Charter is precisely that — a *review*, a *second* look at the balancing of competing public interests and values arrived at first by the parliamentary body concerned and expressed by it in the terms of the specific statutory provisions now to be measured against the appropriate Charter standard.

Perhaps we may now reach these conclusions. Evidence of legislative facts along with expert opinion on their normative implications may lead the judges often enough to definition of the public societal values in conflict and to appreciation of which of them is the more important in the particular

---

63 *Supra*, note 25.
64 *Report on Sunday Observance Legislation*, Ontario Law Reform Commission Department of Justice (Ontario), 1970.
65 *Supra*, note 25.

circumstances. In some instances there will be an ascertainable community consensus on value propositions of great importance. But in other instances there will be disagreement and conflict on public values between large and powerful groups of citizens. Then compromises (reasonable limits) that keep the peace, but please no one, may be the best that can be done. Paradoxically, the fact that everyone is displeased to some extent in such a situation may be the sign that the best compromise available for the time being has been found. There is a third group of instances where community normative standards and priorities are elusive or non-existent. There is not a "public opinion" about everything. In these circumstances, the judge should resort to his or her own system of values, on the assumption that he or she is typical of fellow citizens. After all the evidence and argument is in, the personal element of responsibility remains.[66] One may generalize what Mr. Justice La Forest said in the *Jones* case: "A court must be taken to have a general knowledge of our history and values and to know at least the broad design and workings of our society."[67]

What now remains to be said can be discussed in connection with the two subjects considered in part 1 of this chapter to which I promised to return: the threshold tests of extra-legal societal relations and governmental action. Respecting the first, we have seen that the whole legal and constitutional system ranges through different levels of generality from the very general to the quite specific. But, so far as judicial review of compliance with Charter standards is concerned, the starting point is always at the particular level, the retail level so to speak, at which the laws by their terms are intended to be and are ready for application to persons in the circumstances those laws specify.

Laws *of this type* do not blanket the whole of societal relations by any means, and hence my threshold test of the extra-legal segment of societal relations, where no ordinary specific laws give directions one way or the other. But the terms of Charter section 1 are such that only such specific and ordinary laws have the possibility of triggering judicial Charter review — and then only if negatively relevant to the Charter provision invoked by the complainant. Only quite specific ordinary laws can be negatively relevant to the Charter standard invoked and yet capable also of being a reasonable or an unreasonable exception to that standard. It is true that some specific ordinary laws might be specific only as to prohibition orders on exhibition of films in the discretion of a censor board, for example, but give no reasons or guidelines for when prohibitions would issue. This would violate

---

66 In this connection, see my analysis of this responsibility in a 1958 essay entitled "The Common Law System in Canada", now reprinted as Chapter 2 in W.R. Lederman, *Continuing Canadian Constitutional Dilemmas* (Toronto: Butterworths, 1981), pp. 38–42.

67 *Supra*, note 51 at 299.

freedom of expression and has no chance of being found a reasonable exception under Charter section 1, but my point about specificity remains. The judicial decisions on which I rely here are: *The Sunday Times Case*, of the European Court of Human Rights;[68] the *Ontario Film Society and Censor Board* case, of the Ontario Divisional Court;[69] and *Re Luscher and Deputy M.N.R. (Customs & Excise)*, of the Federal Court of Appeal.[70]

There is a corollary of this requirement for specificity in the challenged ordinary law. If that law is negatively relevant to a Charter provision and is a reasonable limit on it, the scope of that decision as a precedent reducing the definition of the Charter right is limited to the particular ordinary law in question or specific laws essentially similar. In the recent case of *Re McTavish and Director, Child Welfare Act*,[71] a child of Jehovah's Witness parents was made a temporary ward of the Child Welfare Society as authorized by the *Child Welfare Act*[72] so that a blood transfusion necessary to save its life could be given, the parents having refused to authorize this for genuine religious reasons. The parents complained of the pertinent provisions of the *Child Welfare Act* as a breach of their religious freedom under Charter section 2(a), but the *Child Welfare Act* provision was upheld as a reasonable limit on freedom of religion. The judge pointed out that, though the *Child Welfare Act* did *prima facie* breach the parents' freedom of religion, it was also in harmony with and facilitative of the child's right to life under Charter section 7. This conflict of general values was triggered by the very specific terms of the wardship provision of the *Child Welfare Act*. As a Charter precedent, its impact is likewise limited. These are rare circumstances. Nearly all the time, the duty of parents to see to necessary medical care for a child will be fully harmonious with their religion and with the child's right to life. So, in our overview of the Charter, we should not exaggerate the extent to which accepted public general societal values are in conflict. The conflicts, when they do occur, tend to show up at the quite particular levels of the legal system, as illustrated, and their precedential effect is likewise limited.

Finally, a further word is needed about the alleged governmental action threshold test referred to in part 1 of this chapter. Its effect was that, unless the alleged Charter breach is a complaint about governmental action of some kind, no provision of the Charter is even possibly applicable and the complainant loses his case then and there for that reason. This expresses

---

68 (1979), 2 E.H.R.R. 245.
69 *Supra*, note 20.
70 (1985), 17 D.L.R. (4th) 503 (F.C.A.).
71 (1986), 32 D.L.R. (4th) 394 (Alta. Q.B.), appeal quashed (*sub nom Re S.E.M.*) (1988), 88 A.R. 346 (C.A.).
72 S.A. 1984, c. C-8.1.

the pure American doctrine which some jurists and judges say we should adopt in Canada. Obviously, if there is such a threshold test, everything depends on what the court characterizes as "state" or "governmental" action. In over 100 years of judicial interpretation, the United States Supreme Court has found many varieties and manifestations of "state" action and has not to this day succeeded in spelling out coherent guidelines for separating the "governmental" from the "non-governmental" for purposes of the applicability of their *Bill of Rights* to ordinary laws.

Some things are obviously state action, such as the procedural and substantive laws of the criminal justice system. Most of the Canadian judicial Charter decisions since 1982 have been in this area. But, with the coming into force of Charter section 15 (the equality clause) in 1985, the picture is changing. Is the civil law of so-called "private" legal relations entirely beyond the reach of the Charter because of some sort of a direct governmental action requirement? The answer is surely "no". Some private legal relations are logically relevant to Charter standards and are therefore subject to detailed Charter review; other private relations are not relevant and are *for that reason* beyond the reach of Charter review. Some Canadian judges in some of their cases make rhetorical gestures of respect to the American doctrine, but then proceed to ignore its true implications by proceeding in those same cases to a detailed review of the challenged ordinary law under the reasonable limits part of Charter section 1. It is a good thing that they do thus recognize that the Canadian Charter review process is different from the American.[73]

But why then has this governmental action test had such a long run in the United States, so that now it threatens to enter the Canadian scene? I suggest this is because of a very proper concern in both countries for the public values of autonomy and privacy in our free and democratic societies. But in Canada I see these as public societal values entitled to be weighed in the balance when reasonable limits on Charter standards are being assessed under Charter section 1.

This is a large topic, and I can only set out the reasons for my position briefly and generally.[74]

---

73 See, *e.g.*, *Re Blainey and Ont. Hockey Assn.* (1986), 54 O.R. (2d) 513 (Ont. C.A.), leave to appeal to S.C.C. refused (1986), 10 C.P.R. (3d) 450n (S.C.C.); *Re McKinney and Univ. of Guelph Bd. of Governors* (1986), 32 D.L.R. (4th) 65 (Ont. H.C.), aff'd (1987), 46 D.L.R. (4th) 193 (Ont. C.A.), leave to appeal to S.C.C. granted April 21, 1988 (S.C.C.). In both cases, in spite of lip service to a finding of "no governmental action", full-fledged review of "reasonable limits" under Charter section 1 took place, and was decisive in favour of the complainant in *Blainey* and against the complainant in *McKinney*.

74 My understanding of autonomy as a public value owes much to discussions I had with Mr. John G. Mendes, LL.M. (Queen's), 1986. I supervised his graduate thesis on Equality and the Charter.

1. In every instance where there is ordinary statute law or common law in force, the state is *always* present. The statute is the standard way a parliamentary body (federal or provincial) takes action. And wherever there is a statute (or common law that could be altered by statute), there is a public policy, purpose or interest of some kind being served by it.

2. To be more precise, the modern law of contract facilitates public purposes. Freedom of contract is an autonomy concept, which means that, within wide limits, private parties or voluntary groups may make detailed laws for themselves in the terms of contracts to which they agree. Once agreed, the terms are indeed law for the parties and may be enforced in court. The power to make law by contract is a power given to all legal persons, including private persons, by the law, but it is not now and never has been an unlimited power. There have always been public policy limitations on the extent of the power to contract which constrained the purposes for which it could be used. The judges spoke of "contracts contrary to public policy", and legislatures enacted statutes like the *Unconscionable Transactions Relief Act*.[75] These restraints gave priority over autonomy of the parties to other and conflicting public values. *Some of these categories of restraint now have Charter status*; for example, the non-discrimination provisions of Charter section 15. To the extent that there are no such restraints, freedom of contract flourishes and serves the public value of autonomy for private individuals and groups, that is to say, *non-official* individuals and groups. Indeed, it may be said that in some cases the autonomy value has support within the Charter itself from the section 7 reference to liberty and security of the person and the section 2 reference to freedom of association.

3. Consequently, my position is this. Under the two-step Canadian system of Charter interpretation mandated by Charter section 1 (*prima facie* relevance tested and perhaps reduced by possibly reasonable exceptions), the autonomy value as a public value can be openly identified and defended in detail against other and conflicting public values. Autonomy will not always win in a Charter "reasonable limits" contest, but it has historically had important victories before the Charter and will continue to have a proper share of victories under the Charter. Given our Charter section 1, the American "governmental action" test is simply superfluous in Canada. We have no need for endless refinements and fictions concerning what is or what is not "governmental action". I respectfully submit that judicial statements in the

---

75 *Supra*, note 29.

Supreme Court of Canada apparently approving the American test in the *Dolphin Delivery* case[76] ought to be reconsidered by the court.

4. CONCLUSIONS

I mentioned early in this chapter the fear that the Charter would prove to be all-pervasive and thus applicable to just about everybody and everything. The Charter is important, but I hope I have demonstrated that it is far from all-pervasive.

Consider where the Charter is *not* applicable if my analysis is correct.

1. It is not applicable to extra-legal societal relations as I have defined them.
2. Many, if not most, statutes are simply irrelevant to any Charter standards in the first place, since the latter are not relevant to everything in the statute books.
3. Statutes positively relevant to Charter standards are harmonious or facilitative respecting those standards, and hence continue unchanged.
4. Statutes negatively relevant to Charter standards, and thus inconsistent with such standards, nevertheless continue in effect if they are judicially found to be reasonably limiting. Only if a statute is found to be unreasonably limiting of a Charter standard, or an outright denial thereof, is the statute judicially declared null and void.

So the primary law-making initiative is definitely with the parliamentary bodies. Judicial review by virtue of the Charter is highly selective and is a *second* look at a balancing of values and interests that has already been done at least once before by the legislature enacting the statute concerned. But selective though it is, Charter scrutiny has a salutary effect where applicable, on the original legislative balancing of values and interests. I conclude as I did in a previous essay:

> The total process of government under the rule of law needs umpires and referees, just as do the teams in athletic contests. No analogy is perfect, but perhaps this one helps in a rough sort of way to explain what is happening. The judges are in the position of umpires or referees, while the parliamentarians have to field the teams, and plan and initiate the action. The referees cannot *play* the game themselves, but you cannot have the game without them. Thanks to the *Charter*, now the referees have new powers to enforce compliance with the better standards of a free and democratic society. Moreover, both referees and players must now pay better attention to the general purposes and objects of the game.[77]

---

76 *Supra*, note 5.
77 Lederman, "Democratic Parliaments, Independent Courts, and the Charter", *supra*, note 6.

5

Freedom of Conscience and Religion
(Section 2(a))*

Irwin Cotler

* This text was previously published in *Your Clients and the Charter/Vos clients et la Charte*, Gérald-A. Beaudoin (ed.) (Cowansville: Yvon Blais Inc., 1988) at 101. It is reproduced here with the authorization of Yvon Blais Inc. and the Canadian Bar Association.

1. INTRODUCTION

According to a recent judgment of the Supreme Court of Canada, the "fundamental" character of religious and conscientious freedom within the scheme of Charter[1] rights and freedoms reflects "the centrality . . . of individual conscience . . . both to basic beliefs about human worth and dignity and to a free and democratic political system."[2] The present analysis of that central and fundamental freedom will be organized around six principal themes: first, some essential "givens" about the freedom in Canadian law, including reference to its historical wellspring; second, religious freedom under the *Constitution Act, 1867*[3] (formerly the *British North America Act*), wherein denominational rights have enjoyed entrenched status under section 93, now affirmed in section 29 of the Charter; third, the definition of "conscience" and "religion" for human rights legislation; fourth, the continuing relevance of the "historical double override" to section 2(a) of the Charter; fifth, the scope of freedom of conscience and religion in Canadian law, with particular reference to comparative features of American First Amendment jurisprudence; and finally, the international law dimension to section 2(a), especially in light of pertinent norms of the *International Covenant on Civil and Political Rights*.[4] A list of concluding observations provides an "overview" of the prevailing status of conscientious and religious freedom under the Charter regime.

2. ESSENTIAL "GIVENS" ABOUT FREEDOM OF RELIGION IN CANADIAN LAW: THE HISTORICAL AND JURIDICAL CONTEXT

It would be useful to commence this discussion with four basic propositions concerning the legal and constitutional basis of religious freedom in pre-Charter law.

First, as with the other fundamental freedoms, there is no express protection for freedom of religion under the *Constitution Act, 1867*. Unlike the other freedoms, however, freedom of religion has received a limited protected status respecting denominational schools in section 93 of the Act.

---

1 *Canadian Charter of Rights and Freedoms*, Part I of the *Constitution Act, 1982* [en. by the *Canada Act* 1982 (U.K.), 1982, c. 11, Sched. B.].

2 *R. v. Big M Drug Mart Ltd.*, [1985] 1 S.C.R. 295 at 346 (*per* Dickson C.J.C.).

3 1867 (U.K.), 30 & 31 Vict., c. 3.

4 *Infra*, note 130.

Second, the absence of such express constitutional protection in Canada contrasted sharply with the situation in the United States, where the "free exercise of religion" has enjoyed entrenched protection as a First Amendment freedom. Moreover, the *American Bill of Rights* sought to guard against the entanglement of Church and State by providing that "Congress shall make no law respecting an establishment of religion".

Third, our primary constitutional document, the *Constitution Act, 1867*, not only omitted any safeguard over the establishment of religion (or "establishment clause"), but on the contrary, even afforded in section 93 a measure of protection to certain denominations. Establishment provisions are not unknown in Canadian constitutional history, and some statutory expressions, be they pre-Confederation law in the matter of denominational rights recognized in section 93 or as otherwise protecting certain denominations, remain part of the received law. While space does not permit a review of the history of "established churches" that accompanied the colonies into Confederation, some examples might be instructive in evincing the historical context from which the "establishment" idiom in our law has developed.

The Roman Catholic Church was the established church in New France and, although probably legally disestablished from the time of the British conquest in 1759 until the *Quebec Act of 1774*, it remained in a privileged position after Confederation in 1867.[5] Indeed,

> For two hundred years, from 1759 to 1959, the Catholic Church had stood guardian to the French-speaking population in Quebec. The Church spoke not only for the next world, it was intensely concerned with this one . . . The Church in Quebec was a monolithic presence, and its influence extended into every aspect of Quebec life, including politics.[6]

Similarly, the Church of England was the established church in New Brunswick, Nova Scotia and Prince Edward Island at least until the second half of the nineteenth century.[7] While probably not disestablished in strict legal terms, this, as Schmeiser points out, has limited practical significance. Equally, the Church of England was the privileged if not the established church in Upper Canada from 1791 until the *Freedom of Worship Act of 1851*,[8] and has continued to exercise an influence in the life of Ontario.[9] By the time of Confederation, the *1851 Freedom of Worship Act*, enacted

---

5 See D.A. Schmeiser, *Civil Liberties in Canada* (London: Oxford University Press, 1964) at 60-64.

6 T. Berger, *Fragile Freedoms: Human Rights and Dissent in Canada* (Toronto: Clarke Irwin, 1981) at 163.

7 Schmeiser, *supra*, note 5 at 67-70.

8 1850-51 (Upper Can.), 14 & 15 Vict., c. 175.

9 Schmeiser, *supra*, note 5 at 64-67.

by the Legislature of Upper Canada and therefore applicable to Quebec and Ontario, had provided for religious toleration:

> That the free exercise and enjoyment of Religous Profession and Worship, without discrimination or preference, so as the same be not made an excuse for acts of licentiousness, or a justification of practices inconsistent with the peace and safety of the Province is by the constitution and laws of this province, allowed to all Her Majesty's subjects within the same.[10]

Likewise, in the Maritime provinces, the Church of England was deemed judicially by 1887 to be in the same legal position as other churches:

> The Church of England, in places where there is no Church established by law, is in the same situation with any other religious body — in no better, but in no worse position.[11]

As a fourth and final proposition, since the *Constitution Act, 1867* specifically allocated no legislative jurisdiction with regard to "religion" either to the provincial legislatures, on the one hand, or to Parliament, on the other, the courts have traditionally had to characterize laws touching religion as matters falling respectively within section 92 or section 91 of the Act. Laws in relation to religion, it would seem, generally concern matters comprised in the "criminal law" class of subject under the jurisdiction of Parliament.

3. FREEDOM OF RELIGION UNDER THE CONSTITUTION ACT, 1867

On the second reading of the *British North America Bill* in the Imperial Parliament on February 19, 1867, Lord Carnarvon, who was sponsoring the measure, spoke as follows with reference to section 93:

> This clause has been framed after long and anxious controversy, in which all parties have been represented, and on conditions to which all have given their consent . . . but I am bound to add as the expression of my own opinion that the terms of the arrangement appear to me to be both equitable and judicious.[12]

Nevertheless, Lord Carnarvon's optimism notwithstanding, no other provision of the Act of 1867 has engendered so much bitterness and, in

---

10 *Supra*, note 8.

11 Schmeiser suggests that although this statement is probably correct in practice since no later statutes disestablished the Church of England in the three maritime provinces, the latter might yet possess an established church in strict legal theory. See note 5, *supra* at 69-70.

12 W.P.M. Kennedy, ed., *Statutes, Treaties and Documents of the Canadian Constitution 1713-1929*, 2nd ed. (Toronto: Oxford University Press, 1930) at 182.

the process, so much litigation. As Deschênes C.J. put it in one of the most comprehensive pre-Charter judgments in a section 93 case: "La bataille s'est transportée des Plaines d'Abraham à l'Assemblée nationale et, de là, au Palais de justice."[13]

Under that section, it is the provincial legislatures that "may exclusively make laws in relation to Education." But in the only express protection anywhere in the *Constitution Act, 1867,* for "fundamental freedoms" — albeit limited to denominational rights — provincial jurisdiction was made subject to a number of protective provisions, the first of which reads:

> Nothing in any such law shall prejudicially affect any Right or Privilege with respect to Denominational Schools which any Class of Persons have by law in a Province at the Union.[14]

This protection afforded denominational school has been deemed "a fundamental part of the Confederation compromise",[15] enjoying further entrenchment in section 29 of the Charter. Indeed, the specific protection of rights "at the Union" in section 93(1) finds absolute immunity from any challenge respecting Charter provisions of equality or religious freedom, under the terms of section 29:

> Nothing in this Charter abrogates or derogates from any rights or privileges guaranteed by or under the Constitution of Canada in respect of denominational, separate or dissentient schools.[16]

Does this entrenched protection extend to rights or privileges in *post-Confederation* provincial legislation, as contemplated in section 93(3) of the Act of 1867? In the principal judgment to date of the Supreme Court of Canada on the scope of section 93,[17] it was held that, while provincial legislatures can repeal or amend such post-1867 denominational enactments, the "plenary power" of the legislature to do so remains "guaranteed".[18] Accordingly, the Charter cannot constrain provincial discretion in legislating in furtherance of certain historical denominational rights or privileges, no matter how discriminatory such educational policy is in the modern context.

What then, are these rights or privileges sought to be protected? The

---

13 *Bureau Métropolitan des Écoles Protestantes de Montréal v. Ministre de l'Éducation du Québec,* [1976] C.S. 430 (Que. S.C.).

14 *Constitution Act, 1867,* s. 93(1).

15 *Reference re Bill 30, An Act to amend the Education Act,* [1987] 1 S.C.R. 1148 at 1197-1198 (*per* Wilson J.).

16 *Constitution Act, 1982,* s. 29.

17 *Reference re Bill 30, supra,* note 15.

18 *Ibid., per* Wilson J.

following findings, stemming from the case law respecting section 93,[19] and constituting the baseline from which challenges engaging section 29 will proceed, should be noted:

1. No provincial law may "prejudicially affect" means that the impugned legislation must cause injury; it is insufficient for it merely to "affect" those rights. Conversely, the rights need not have been extinguished in order to prove injury: they may exist yet be prejudicially affected.

2. The "Right or Privilege" in section 93 is not any right or privilege of an educational character but one "with respect to Denominational Schools", in other words, denominational rights or privileges. This has been one of the most contentious issues before the courts, as some have argued that "denominational" qualifies the school but not the rights or privileges, the latter referring to any rights or privileges of an educational character in denominational schools.

3. "Denominational Schools" are those that "were permanently and by law denominational", not schools that happened to be denominational for a time due to section 93 not having been enforced initially.

4. The words "any class of persons" to whom the right or privilege is reserved refer to "a class of persons determined according to religious belief and not according to race or language."[20]

5. The rights or privileges reserved in section 93(1) must have existed and been protected by law at Confederation. It does not suffice that they existed as a matter of "natural" or "acquired" rights. There is no immunity from government interference for natural or acquired rights, a finding concurred in by the European Court of Human Rights, and quoted with approval in the judgment of Deschênes J., in the *Bureau Métropolitan* case.[21]

6. As for the Catholic minorities in New Brunswick and Ontario and the Protestant and Jewish minority in Quebec, it is necessary to make proof of rights and privileges acquired or maintained by tolerance or sufferance. In this connection, one might witness a renewed interest in pre-Confederation law respecting denominational rights, as demonstrated in recent archival work regarding the *1832 Act of Lower Canada* granting "equal rights and privileges" to "persons professing the Jewish religion".[22]

---

19 *Bureau Métropolitan, supra*, note 13 (where Deschênes C.J. reviews relevant case law), and *Reference re Bill 30, supra*, note 15.

20 *Ottawa R.C. Sep. School Trustees v. Mackell*, [1917] A.C. 62 (P.C.).

21 *Supra*, note 13.

22 *An Act to declare persons professing the Jewish Religion entitled to all the rights and privileges of the other subjects of His Majesty in this Province*, 1832 (Lower Can.), 1 Will. 4, c. 57.

7. Relatedly, with specific reference to Catholic separate schools in Ontario, the Supreme Court of Canada has upheld legislation extending full public funding thereto at the secondary level on the grounds, *inter alia*, that this restores pre-Confederation rights enjoyed by that minority in the province.[23]

8. Where a provincial legislature grants new denominational rights or privileges pursuant to its plenary power in section 93 and subsection 93(3), these remain immune from the application of the Charter, though not from subsequent provincial amendment or repeal. Thus, while section 93(1) has no application to British Columbia, Nova Scotia and Prince Edward Island, where no laws respecting denominational rights or privileges existed upon entry into Confederation, the respective legislatures could grant new — albeit unguaranteed — rights or privileges to the denominations recognized in section 93, free from Charter scrutiny.

9. The provisions of section 93 were applied, in somewhat modified form, to the provinces of Alberta, Manitoba and Saskatchewan in the Acts constituting them. However, when in 1890 the legislature of Manitoba abolished the denominational school system and French-language guarantees in the *Manitoba Act* equivalent respectively to sections 93 and 133 of the *Constitution Act, 1867*, neither the courts,[24] nor the Governor General in Council, to whom the right of appeal is provided under section 93(3), reversed that action.[25] The 1979 decision in the *Forest* case,[26] now incorporated in section 21 of the Charter, has partially redeemed the historical injury in the matter of language rights, but the prejudice concerning denominational rights awaits redress.

10. Newfoundland adopted a different version of section 93 in its *Terms of Union* incorporated in the *Constitution Act, 1949*, and applied it in different circumstances. Recognition of rights was provided not just for two school systems, but rather for the following denominations: Roman Catholic, Church of England, United Church of Canada, Salvation Army, Presbyterian, Congregational, Seventh Day Adventist and Pentecostal Assemblies. Apart from this, there is thought to have been no other provision respecting denominational schools in any provincial law in Canada that recognizes any other Christian, or indeed any other religious, faith.[27]

---

23 *Reference re Bill 30, supra*, note 15, *per* Wilson J.

24 *Winnipeg v. Barrett*, [1892] A.C. 445 (P.C.).

25 For a discussion of "denominational education", see Schmeiser, *supra*, note 5, especially pp. 139-185.

26 *A.G. Man. v. Forest*, [1979] 2 S.C.R. 1032.

27 *Cf.* the recent surfacing of the pre-Confederation *1832 Act of Lower Canada, supra*, note 22, with whatever legal fallout that may ensue.

In light of the foregoing, the ambivalence of section 93 in protecting historic denominational rights, while detracting from the "establishment principle", appears to have been compounded by section 29 of the Charter. Ironically, the Supreme Court of Canada expressed doubts over the need for section 29 in entrenching the protection of section 93, while acknowledging that "it sits uncomfortably with the concept of equality embodied in the *Charter*".[28] Yet, it was open to the court in the *Education Act Reference*[29] to confine its upholding of the provincial legislation granting full funding to Catholic secondary schools solely on the ground that pre-Confederation law recognized the appropriate right, rather than on the additional basis of provincial "plenary power" to enact further discriminatory legislation at its discretion despite the Charter.

Such an approach would also have accorded with the court's previous holding as to the First Amendment parallels of religious freedom under section 2(a) of the Charter.[30] In the United States, governmental assistance to denominational ("parochial") schools has been stringently scrutinized under the "establishment" principle, with the courts barring even oblique state subsidies since 1971.[31] Although concern has recently been voiced within and outside the courts over unduly disadvantaging religion in the name of the establishment principle,[32] no radical reversal of the traditional notion of church-state is in sight.

In the final analysis, critical as the "constitutional compact" in respect of (primarily) Catholic and Protestant rights was upon Canadian Confederation, should it be allowed to resist the demands of equity flowing from the contemporary multicultural fabric, enshrined in section 27 of the Charter?

4. THE DEFINITION OF "RELIGION" AND "CONSCIENCE" FOR PURPOSES OF HUMAN RIGHTS LEGISLATION

Although it remains disconcerting that the legislative protection of religion in this country is unaccompanied by a formal definition of "religion" (or of cognate terms such as "creed" or "conscience"), the Supreme Court of Canada finally appears to have poured some content into the phrase "religion or conscience" in section 2(a) of the Charter. In addressing the "purpose" of that section in *Edwards Books & Art Ltd.*

---

28 *Reference re Bill 30, supra,* note 15 at 1197 (*per* Wilson J).

29 See "Financing the schools" (editorial), *Globe and Mail,* June 26, 1987, p. A6.

30 *Edwards Books & Art Ltd. v. R.,* [1986] 2 S.C.R. 713.

31 *Lemon v. Kurtzman,* 403 U.S. 602 (1971).

32 See M. Stern, "Freedom of Religion in the U.S.A.", in *Patterns of Prejudice,* Vol. 21:1 (London: World Jewish Congress, Spring 1987), p. 15, especially at 24.

v. R.,[33] Dickson C.J. stated for the majority that the provision proscribed interference "with profoundly personal beliefs that govern one's perception of oneself, humankind, nature, and in some cases, a higher or different order of being. Those beliefs, in turn, govern one's conduct and practices."[34]

It is intriguing that having thus far been embroiled in satisfying the demands of the historic "double override", whereunder the courts sought to define the scope of the enumerated heads in relation to which "religion" would be assigned rather than religion itself, the proferred description in *Edwards Books & Art* is distinguished foremost by its breadth. Clearly, it encompasses not only the beliefs of the major organized religions of east and west, but a myriad of quasi and non-religious, even purely private, sets of beliefs and practices. In this regard, it echoes the open-ended approach adopted by a California court over a century ago:

> The word "religion", in its primary sense . . . imports, as applied to moral questions, only a recognition of a conscious duty to obey restraining principles of conduct. In such sense we suppose there is no one who will admit that he is without religion.[35]

However, Anglo-American case law does not reveal a consistent acknowledgement of such a broad conception of religion outside the sphere of traditional major religions, and sometimes not even within a narrow sphere. In *Borchert v. City of Ranger, Texas*,[36] for instance, the term was held as denoting "conformity in faith and life to the precepts inculcated in the Bible, respecting conduct of life and duty toward God and man; the Christian faith and practice."[37] An earlier decision by a Pennsylvanian court, though God-specific, was somewhat wider:

> "Religion" is squaring human life with superhuman life . . . belief in a superhuman power and an adjustment of human activities to the requirements of that power, such adjustment as may enable the individual believer to exist more happily . . . The term "religion" has reference to one's views of his relations to his Creator, and to the obligations they impose of reverence for his being and character, and of obedience to his will.[38]

A more recent judgment of the United Kingdom Court of Appeal in *R. v. Registrar General; Ex parte Segerdal*[39] was equally insistent upon a deity-centered conception of religion, when confronted with the question of "religious worship". For Lord Denning M.R., this latter phrase meant

33 *Supra*, note 30.
34 *Ibid.* at 759.
35 *Re Hinckley's Estate*, 58 Cal. 457 at 512 (1881).
36 42 F. Supp. 577 (1941).
37 *Ibid.* at 580.
38 *Minersville School Dist. v. Gobitis*, 108 F. 2d 683 at 685 (1939).
39 [1970] 2 Q.B. 697 (C.A.).

"reverence or veneration of God or of a Supreme Being", subject to such exceptions as Buddhist practice wherein a deity was not involved.[40] No rationalization was offered by the court for the general rule or the exception.

The more expansive Canadian approach is facilitated, axiomatically, by the inclusive *"conscience* and religion" in section 2(a) of the Charter. As an Alberta court observed in *R. v. .H. Smith,*[41] the addition of "conscience"

> is intended to provide scope for including as protected certain codes or systems of belief which are as fundamentally important and vital to their adherents as are more "orthodox" religions but which do not include the concept of a theistic centre among the cardinal principles of belief.[42]

Indeed, there is a virtual subsumation of "religion" under "conscience" in the particular context of section 2(a), given the more encompassing connotations of the latter. The Supreme Court of Canada has perceived behind the section the "notion of the centrality of individual conscience and the inappropriateness of governmental intervention to compel or to constrain its manifestation".[43] This harmonizes with the court's holding that freedom of conscience and religion includes the freedom to manifest religious non-belief, as well as the freedom to refuse to participate in religious practice.[44] It is likewise consistent with the Charter provision favouring "the preservation and enhancement of the multicultural heritage of Canadians" (section 27), which transcends the sphere of traditional theistic beliefs.

One consequence of the preceding conceptual distinction between the affirmative right to manifest one's belief (or non-belief) and the negative right to abstain from conformity with others' beliefs, is to engender a Canadian parallel to the First Amendment "free exercise" and "establishment" clauses in the American constitutional law. In the United States the growing diversity of religious and quasi-religious beliefs and practices has demanded an increasingly permissive definition of "religion" for purposes of the "free exercise" clause, beyond the hitherto theistic focus of the courts. Concurrently, a more restrictive definition is called for under the "establishment" clause, lest all "humane government" programs be deemed constitutionally suspect. This tension between the two clauses may well be played out in Canada, following the inevitable bifurcation between affirmative and negative freedoms under section 2(a).

As early as 1944, American courts decided that where "free exercise"

---

40 *Ibid.* at 707.

41 (1983), 25 Alta. L.R. (2d) 238 (Prov. Ct.).

42 *Ibid.* at 258.

43 *Big M Drug Mart, supra,* note 2 at 361 (*per* Dickson C.J.C.).

44 *Ibid.* at 346, as summarized in *Edwards Books & Art, supra,* note 30 at 758.

claims were at issue, the validity of the tenets or requirements of a particular religious belief or practice should be subordinated to the question of the sincerity of the claimant's views.[45] Subsequently, in *Fowler v. Rhode Island*,[46] the U.S. Supreme Court held that "it is no business of courts to say what is a religious practice or activity for one group is not religion under the protection of the First Amendment".[47] More recently, in a holding not unrelated to the interpretation that might be put on the "supremacy of God" invocation in the preamble of the Canadian Charter, the U.S. Supreme Court decided that a declaration of belief in God as a condition of becoming a notary public was unconstitutional, for it placed the state "on the side of one particular sort of believers".[48]

In a similar vein, where a military exemption was conditional upon a belief "in relation to a Supreme Being", the court in *United States v. Seeger*[49] interpreted belief to mean any sincere belief occupying "a place in the life of its possessor parallel to that filled by the orthodox belief in God of one who clearly qualifies for the exemption".[50] The propinquity of this conception of religion to the Canadian rulings in the *Edwards Books & Art*[51] and *W.H. Smith*[52] cases is evident. It is not surprising, therefore, that in this country as well as in the United States, the question of *bona fide* belief continues to take precedence over the question of validity of the particular moral tenets or perceptions invoked.

While deploring the "indignity" of a judicial inquiry into the sincerity of a claimant's beliefs — an exercise that "should be avoided whenever reasonably possible" — the Supreme Court of Canada has reconciled itself to the frequent necessity of so doing.[53] That such a practice "is all the worse when it is demanded only of members of a non-majoritarian faith"[54] has not escaped the court's recognition.

A further gloss upon the foregoing, and not confined to non-majoritarian faiths, would result from the application of *dicta* in a recent British Columbia Tax Court judgment as to the "basis" of religious or moral beliefs protected under section 2(a).[55] The claimant, a Quaker, had

---

45 *U.S. v. Ballard*, 322 U.S. 78 (1944).
46 345 U.S. 67 (1953).
47 *Ibid.* at 70. See also *Fulwood v. Clemmer*, 206 F. Supp. 370 at 373 (1962) (merits or fallacies of a religion not within the court's purview).
48 *Torcaso v. Watkins*, 367 U.S. 488 at 490 (1961).
49 380 U.S. 163 (1965).
50 *Ibid.* at 166.
51 *Supra*, note 30.
52 *Supra*, note 41.
53 *Edwards Books & Art*, *supra*, note 30 at 780-781.
54 *Ibid.* at 779.
55 *Prior v. M.N.R.*, [1987] 1 C.T.C. 2076 (T.C.C.).

withheld a portion of her taxes corresponding to the percentage devoted by the Canadian government to military purposes, to which she took conscientious objection. Tremblay T.C.J. found that the limits placed on the claimant's freedom by the tax system were justifiable under section 1 of the Charter, then reverted to the observation that an offence against freedom must, in the first place, have an "objective basis".[56] Without apparently doubting the sincerity of the claimant's beliefs, the court appeared to be challenging their "validity", at least in terms of the "subjective" interpretation thereof under Christian religious principles. This would seem irreconcilable with the import of Chief Justice Dickson's definition of "conscience and religion" in the *Edwards Books & Art* case,[57] as well as with standard practice in Canadian-American case law noted above. It is to be hoped that such inquiries, over and above those into *bona fide* belief, do not become the *quid pro quo* for a liberal conception of "conscience and religion" under the Charter.

5. FREEDOM OF RELIGION AND THE "DOUBLE OVERRIDE" — RELEVANCE UNDER THE CHARTER

Although the *Constitution Act, 1867*, lacked an express protection of religious freedom beyond the references to denominational schools in section 93, a modicum of statutory protection avails under assorted post-World War II enactments. These include the *Saskatchewan Bill of Rights Act, 1947*, section 3[58] (now the Saskatchewan *Human Rights Code*, section 4), the Alberta *Bill of Rights*, section 1(c),[59] the Quebec *Charter of Human Rights and Freedoms*, section 3,[60] and the *Canadian Bill of Rights, 1960*, section 1(c).[61] In addition, the *1851 Freedom of Worship Act*[62] referred to earlier continues to apply in the provinces of Ontario and Quebec, by virtue of section 129 of the *Constitution Act, 1867*.

Nevertheless, the dominant motif for the determination and disposition of religious — and other "fundamental" — freedoms remained the "double override", *viz.* the interaction of parliamentary sovereignty with the division

---

56 *Ibid.* at 2091-2092. The court felt that "[i]f the basis of an infringement is purely subjective, a scrupulous person would have more right pursuant to paragraph 2(*a*) of the Charter than another citizen". But surely that prospect is endemic to assertions of religious or conscientious freedom under the Charter.

57 *Supra*, note 30.

58 S.S. 1947, c. 35, which became R.S.S. 1978, c. S-9 [now repealed]. See now the *Saskatchewan Human Rights Code*, S.S. 1979, c. S-24.1

59 S.A. 1972, c. 1, now R.S.A. 1980, c. A-16.

60 S.Q. 1975, c. 6, now R.S.Q. 1977, c. C-12.

61 S.C. 1960, c. 44.

62 *Supra*, note 8

of powers. In the absence of a specific assignment of "religion" to either federal or provincial jurisdiction under sections 91 and 92 of the *Constitution Act, 1867*, laws touching religion had to be characterized in terms of the existing heads of power under those sections. Legal federalism, then, was the organizing frame of reference for freedom of religion.

Typically, the first order of judicial inquiry entailed characterizing the matter according to its "pith and substance". Failing a characterization, *ab initio*, as a matter of religious freedom, the case could be disposed of under a number of alternative heads of power, federal or provincial. Thus, in a 1969 decision involving the validity of Alberta legislation regulating communal property, the Supreme Court of Canada upheld the statute notwithstanding its negative effect upon the Hutterite sect, for whom such land-holding is a fundamental tenet of faith.[63] Maitland J. characterized the matter for the court as follows:

> The Act is not directed at Hutterite belief or worship, or at the profession of such belief. It is directed at the practice of holding large areas of Alberta land as communal property, whether such practice stems from religious belief or not.[64]

Accordingly, the religious freedom of the claimants was not deemed as engaged at all.

The second order of judicial review, pursuant to characterization, was the appropriate assignment of the matter. Among the leading contenders for the assignment of "religion" would be the federal criminal law power, provincial power over property and civil rights, and increasingly, as *A.G. Canada v. Dupond*[65] illustrated, provincial power over matters of a local and private nature. Since the courts have construed the criminal power broadly — any act prohibited with penal consequence being criminal, and any law thus prohibiting with a penalty being criminal law[66] — religious matters have tended to be encompassed therein. Thus interpreted, criminal law has long been reserved for the exclusive legislative jurisdiction of Parliament,[67] allowing federal legislation to affect property or contractual rights otherwise within provincial jurisdiction.

However, Parliament could not invade provincial jurisdiction by seeking to enact "colourable legislation" under its criminal law power[68]

---

63 *Walter v. A.G. Alta.; Fletcher v. A.G. Alta.* (1969), 3 D.L.R. (3d) 1 (S.C.C.).

64 *Ibid.* at 8.

65 [1978] 2 S.C.R. 770.

66 *Proprietary Articles Trade Assn. v. A.G. Can.; Re Combines Investigation Act, and s. 498 Criminal Code,* [1931] A.C. 310 (P.C.).

67 *A.G. Ontario v. Hamilton Street Ry.,* [1903] A.C. 524 (P.C.).

68 *In Re Board of Commerce Act, 1919 and Combines and Fair Practices Act, 1919,* [1922] 1 A.C. 191 (P.C.). The test applied in such instances is whether the legislation is aimed

— any more than the provinces could legislate on essentially religious matters under the guise of their property, contractual or other heads of power.[69]

In the only decision of the Supreme Court of Canada respecting religious freedom under the *1960 Bill of Rights, Robertson v. R.,*[70] the *Lord's Day Act*[71] was considered to be secular in its effect, and therefore out of federal jurisdiction. While affirming that "religion" was essentially within the jurisdiction of Parliament, the case obfuscated matters somewhat in not appraising the *purpose* of the Act, which an earlier court had deemed to be religious and therefore a federal criminal law matter.[72]

Finally, pre-Charter jurisprudence evinces a degree of judicial cognizance of the "fundamental" character of religious freedom, reminiscent of the *dicta* by Justice Rand in *Switzman v. Elbling,*[73] apropos the status of freedom of speech in Canadian constitutional law. Whether or not reflective of an implied *Bill of Rights* protecting religious freedom, these judicial statements are suggestive at least of the potential status that might be accorded such fundamental freedoms under an entrenched Charter:

On Freedom of Religion:

> From 1760 . . . to the present . . . religious freedom has . . . been recognized as a principle of fundamental character; and although we have nothing in the nature of an established church, that the untrammelled affirmations of religious belief and its propagation, personal or institutional, remain as of the greatest constitutional significance throughout the Dominion is unquestionable.[74]

On Freedom of Speech and Religion:

> [F]reedom of speech, religion and the inviolability of the person, are original

---

at some evil, injurious or undesirable effect upon the public, such as laws relating to public peace, order, security, health or morality: *Reference re s. 5(a) of the Dairy Industry Act (Margarine Case),* [1949] S.C.R. 1, affirmed (*sub nom. Cdn. Federation of Agriculture v. A.G. Quebec*) [1951] A.C. 179 (P.C.).

69 *Saumur v. Quebec (City),* [1953] 2 S.C.R. 299; *Henry Birks & Sons (Montreal) Ltd.* v. *Montreal,* [1955] S.C.R. 799.

70 [1963] S.C.R. 651.

71 R.S.C. 1952, c. 171.

72 *Henry Birks, supra,* note 69.

73 [1957] S.C.R. 285 at 306-307: "[Freedom of discussion] is the political expression of the primary condition of social life, thought and its communication by language. Liberty in this is little less vital to man's mind and spirit than breathing is to his physical existence. As such an inherence in the individual it is embodied in his status of citizenship." See also observations in, *inter alia, Re Alberta Statutes,* [1938] S.C.R. 100, appeal dismissed [1939] A.C. 117 (P.C.); *A.G. Ont. v. Winner,* [1954] A.C. 541 (P.C.); *Roncarelli v. Duplessis,* [1959] S.C.R. 121; and *Henry Birks, supra,* note 69.

74 *Saumur v. Quebec (City), supra,* note 69 at 327.

freedoms which are at once the necessary attributes and modes of self-expression of human beings and the primary conditions of their community life within a legal order.[75]

On Prior Restraint:

> Their [original freedoms] significant relation to our law lies in this, that under its principles to which there are only minor exceptions, there is no prior or antecedent restraint placed upon them: the penalties, civil or criminal, attach to results which their exercise may bring about, and apply as consequential incidents.[76]

And again:

> [G]overnment resting ultimately on public opinion reached by discussion and the interplay of ideas. If that discussion is placed under license, its basic condition is destroyed: the government, as licensor, becomes disjoined from the citizenry.[77]

Lest it be thought that questions concerning the "double override" and the fundamental nature of certain freedoms belong only to pre-Charter jurisprudence, the discussion that follows will illustrate otherwise. Primarily, the traditional two-step review process, involving the characterization and assignment of legislative matters within the division of powers analysis, remains integral to judicial review under the Charter. Second, the new "double override" under sections 1 and 33 of the Charter imports a reappraisal of the status of religious and other "fundamental" freedoms amidst competing considerations of public morality, safety and the like. The remainder of this section will address the first of these issues, while the next section will examine some of the limits applicable to freedom of conscience and religion under the Charter.

The clearest demonstration of the continuing relevance of the "historic double override" is provided by the Supreme Court of Canada's judgment in *R. v. Big M Drug Mart,*[78] where the process of determining constitutional validity under the Charter was delineated.

Faced with a challenge to the constitutionality of the *Lord's Day Act*[79] as a violation of religious freedom under section 2(a), the majority of the court took as the initial question the validity of purpose of the legislation, in terms of the heads of power under sections 91 and 92 of the *Constitution Act, 1867.* The court maintained that where the purpose was violative of

---

75 *Ibid.* at 329. See also remarks by Casey J. in *Chabot v. School Commrs. of Lamorandière* (1957), 12 D.L.R. (2d) 796 at 807 (Que. C.A.).

76 *Ibid.*

77 *Ibid.* at 330.

78 *Supra*, note 2.

79 *Supra*, note 71.

the Charter, it would invalidate the legislation irrespective of its actual effects. This, indeed, was the verdict on the *Lord's Day Act*, pre-empting what would otherwise have been the next step: an evaluation of the effects in light of the Charter, including a possible override under section 1. It should be observed that this purposive focus of the court was not exclusively for determining the *vires* of the impugned legislation, but also its constitutionality as a whole.

In essence, the Supreme Court indicated its willingness to import the hazards of the "historic double override" within the initial step of characterizing the issue, albeit allowing for the countervailing effect of invalidation as to purpose under the Charter.[80] If the matter at bar were characterized as not engaging "conscience or religion", but rather an alternative head of power under sections 91 and 92, the court would effectively obviate further scrutiny as to the effects of the legislation upon religious or conscientious freedom. Moreover, where the "purpose" of the legislation relative to the division of power and the Charter is found to be valid and acceptable, does this not render it more probable that a justificatory override under section 1 will be found to apply, the incidence of impermissible effects notwithstanding?

It was over the significance of the "analytic approach" adopted by the majority of the court that Wilson J. dissented in *Big M Drug Mart*.[81] Decrying the "analytic focus on purpose" typical of "pre-Charter division of powers cases", Justice Wilson opined that "the constitutional entrenchment of civil liberties in the . . . *Charter* . . . necessarily changes this analytic approach the courts must adopt in such cases."[82] Useful guidance in this regard was felt to be provided by the United States Supreme Court in *Griggs v. Duke Power Co.*[83] where Burger C.J. took as the starting point "the *consequences* of (discriminatory) employment practices, not simply the motivation" (Wilson J.'s emphasis).

Although subsequent analysis under section 1 may require examining the purpose of the legislation, according to Justice Wilson this could be the appropriate starting point:

> [The Charter] asks not whether the legislature has acted for a purpose that is within the scope of the authority of that tier of government, but rather whether in so acting it has had the effect of violating an entrenched individual right. It is, in other words, first and foremost an effects-oriented document.[84]

One result of this approach, as Justice Wilson noted, would be with

---

80 *Supra*, note 2.
81 *Ibid.* at 358-359.
82 *Ibid.*
83 401 U.S. 424 at 432 (1970).
84 *Supra*, note 2 at 360.

regard to the weight of the evidentiary burden: "Once the plaintiff can point to an actual or potential impingement on a protected right, it will not matter that the underlying legislative purpose is subject to conjecture."[85]

In the Supreme Court of Canada's next consideration of Sunday-closing legislation, this time the Ontario *Retail Business Holidays Act* in *Edwards Books & Art Ltd. v. R.*,[86] the application of the two analytical processes above led to very different judicial determinations. The majority first found the statute to be secular in purpose and *intra vires* the provincial legislature, then inquired into its effects *vis-à-vis* the Charter. The Act was deemed violative of section 2(a), but upheld as a reasonable limitation on that freedom under section 1.

The separate opinions of Beetz and McIntyre JJ. bear out the apprehensions adverted to earlier as to the hazards of characterizing "purpose" *ab initio*: the legislation was considered not to engage religious freedom because of its secular purpose, and simply upheld as *intra vires* the Ontario legislature.

Justice Wilson's "effects-oriented" approach led her to find the Act discriminatory under section 2(a) — though within the jurisdiction of the provincial legislature — with insufficiently compelling evidence to sustain an override under section 1. It would seem that, consistent with her observation in the *Big M Drug Mart* case,[87] the effects-first analysis placed a heavier burden of proof on reliance upon the section 1 override, a burden Wilson J. found not to have been discharged.

It is noteworthy that at the Appeal Court level in *Edwards Books & Art*,[88] Tarnopolsky J.A., for the majority, echoed the earlier sentiments of Justice Wilson as to the primacy of effects under the Charter:

> The interpretation of the *Charter* necessarily requires an assessment of the "effect" of impugned legislation. Intent and purpose will undoubtedly still have relevance. For the most part, however, in determining the appropriate balance between government action . . . and individual rights . . . it will be the determination of the "effect" or "effects" of impugned legislation that is most important.[89]

Interestingly enough, the Supreme Court of Canada's unanimous judgment in *Ontario Human Rights Commission and O'Malley v. Simpsons-Sears Ltd.*[90] apparently offers support to Justice Wilson's approach in *Big*

---

85 *Ibid.* at 361.
86 *Supra*, note 30.
87 *Supra*, note 2.
88 *R. v. Videoflicks* (1984), 48 O.R. (2d) 395 (C.A.), reversed in part (*sub nom. Edwards Books & Art Ltd. v. R.*) *supra*, note 30.
89 *Ibid.* at 415.
90 [1985] 2 S.C.R. 536.

M Drug Mart and Edwards Books & Art. In finding indirect — or "adverse effect" — discrimination to be included within the scope of protection under the Charter, the court in *O'Malley* held it sufficient for the complainant to establish a *prima facie* case of discrimination, in order to shift the onus of proving "reasonable accommodation" upon the respondent. This suggests a differential standard for "private" discrimination — one that is "effects-oriented" — as against the "purpose-oriented" approach towards legislative discrimination. No rationale has yet been advanced by the court for such a distinction.

A cautionary note from U.S. jurisprudence is apposite at this juncture, with reference to the "purpose" test preferred by the majority of the Supreme Court of Canada in *Big M Drug Mart* and *Edwards Books & Art.* In its 1971 decision in *Lemon v. Kurtzman,*[91] the U.S. Supreme Court propounded a three-pronged test of constitutional validity for "establishment" challenges. The courts would invalidate legislation where its purpose was religious, where its primary effect was to advance religion, or where excessive governmental entanglement in religious affairs was entailed.

However, that seemingly fastidious test was to metamorphose a decade later into something very different. In *Lynch v. Donelly,*[92] the court held that *any* secular purpose could save legislation that was primarily intended to advance religion, a dilution more recently affirmed in *Wallace v. Jaffree.*[93] Indeed, O'Connor J., in the latter case, advocated a "deferential" attitude to "state intent", a posture that would surely weaken both the "establishment" and "free exercise" clauses in the face of majoritarian encroachment on minority rights.[94]

A corresponding evolution of the purpose-test by the Supreme Court of Canada is not inconceivable, with everything that is implied for "colourable" legislation purporting to serve secular ends. Once again, the effects-oriented analysis favoured by Justice Wilson seems preferable, inherently resistant as it is to "colourable purpose". This preference is only accentuated in light of the pre-Charter record of judicial treatment of civil liberties cases, including those involving religious freedom.

---

91   *Supra*, note 31. Affirmed strictly in *Ctee. for Pub. Education v. Nyquist*, 413 U.S. 756 (1973).

92   465 U.S. 668 (1984).

93   105 S. Ct. 2479 (1985).

94   See R.G. Teitel, "The Supreme Court's 1984-1985 Church-State Decisions: Judicial Paths of Least Resistance", *Harvard Civil Rights — Civil Liberties Review*, Vol. 21:2 (Summer, 1986), p. 651, especially at 672-673. See also Stern, *supra*, note 32 at 18.

6. THE MEANING AND SCOPE OF FREEDOM OF RELIGION IN CANADIAN CONSTITUTIONAL LAW

Religious freedom in Canadian pre-Charter case law, as already indicated, was defined in scope and substance within the framework of legal federalism. Although section 1(c) of the *Canadian Bill of Rights* granted express protection to the "freedom of religion", this was construed by the Supreme Court of Canada in *Robertson v. R.*[95] as reflecting only existing "rights and freedoms" as of 1960. In determining the scope of religious freedom under this "frozen concepts" perspective, however, Ritchie J., for the majority, invoked expansive statements from two earlier decisions of the court, *Chaput v. Romain*[96] and *Saumur v. Quebec (City).*[97] The first of these eschewed, in general terms, any established religion in Canada, while asserting the full and free exercise thereof as a matter of conscience.[98] *Saumur* provided a classic summation of the status of religious freedom in Canada, *per* Rand J.:

> From 1760, therefore, to the present moment religious freedom has, in our legal system, been recognized as a principle of fundamental character; and although we have nothing in the nature of an established church, that the untrammeled affirmations of religious belief and its propagation, personal or institutional, remain as of the greatest constitutional significance throughout the Dominion is unquestionable.[99]

In conjunction with Ritchie J.'s endorsement of a United States Supreme Court judgment[100] as being "directly applicable" to freedom of religion in Canadian law, the latter might have been thought to parallel First Amendment jurisprudence. Indeed, the court could also have adverted in this regard to the Australian Constitution, section 116 of which provides:

> The Commonwealth shall not make any law for establishing any religion, or for imposing any religious observance, or for prohibiting the free exercise of any religion, and no religious test shall be required as a qualification for any office or public trust under the Commonwealth.[101]

---

95 *Supra*, note 70.

96 [1955] S.C.R. 834.

97 *Supra*, note 69.

98 *Supra*, note 96 at 840 (*per* Taschereau J.).

99 *Supra*, note 69 at 327.

100 *West Virginia State Bd. of Education v. Barnett*, 319 U.S. 624 at 653 (1943) (*per* Frankfurter J., dissenting).

101 Satham C.J. in the Australian case of *Adelaide Co. of Jehovah's Witnesses v. The Commonwealth* (1943), 67 C.L.R. 116 at 124 stated: "[I]t should not be forgotten that such a provision . . . is not required for the protection of the religion of a majority. The religion of the majority of people can look after itself. Section 116 is required to protect the religion (or absence of religion) of minorities, and in particular of unpopular minorities."

Fundamentally, however, the protection of religious freedom in United States as well as Australian law incorporates a guarantee not only against the abridgement of free exercise but also against the official establishment of religion. In Canada, quite clearly, the separation of Church and State has never constituted articulate governmental or legislative policy. On the contrary, section 93 of the *Constitution Act, 1867,* evinces an institutionalized accommodation of majoritarian religions, whereas the preamble to the Charter refers explicitly to the Supreme Deity. Moreover, the very fact that *Robertson*[102] upheld the *Lord's Day Act,* enacted for the purpose of safeguarding the sanctity of Sunday in furtherance of Christian tenets, suggests the prevalence only of a guarantee of free exercise, without one against establishment.

Upon the advent of the Charter protection of religious as well as conscientious freedom, Canadian law lacked any definition of the operative terms, and offered limited guidance as to the scope of this "fundamental" freedom. If, according to the Supreme Court of Canada's holding in *Robertson* the scope of religious freedom was akin to First Amendment theory in the United States, how was this to be reconciled with the aforementioned establishment practices in this country? And given the express "double override" under sections 1 and 33 of the Charter, where would the courts search for a rationale of limitations on the protection of section 2(a)?

A series of expansive delineations of the scope of freedom of religion and conscience under the Charter has been forthcoming from Canadian courts, beginning with the Ontario Court of Appeal's 1984 judgment in *R. v. Videoflicks.*[103] Disposing of the "frozen concepts" perspective in *Robertson* apropos the protection of the *Canadian Bill of Rights,* Tarnopolsky observed for the majority:

> Freedom of religion goes beyond the ability to hold certain beliefs without coercion and restraint and entails more than the ability to profess those beliefs openly . . . [I]t also includes the right to observe the essential practices demanded by the tenets of one's religion and, in determining what those essential practices are in any given case, the analysis must proceed not from the majority's perspective of the concept of religion but in terms of the role that the practices and beliefs assume in the religion of the individual or group concerned.[104]

If *Videoflicks* emphasized the "free exercise" dimension in affirmatively manifesting the freedom of conscience or religion, the Supreme

---

102 *Supra,* note 70.
103 *Supra,* note 88.
104 *Ibid.* at 420.

Court of Canada's ruling in *Big M Drug Mart*[105] highlighted the "negative" freedom to abstain from religious conformity. At minimum, according to Dickson J. for the majority, religious and conscientious freedom meant that "government may not coerce individuals to affirm a specific religious belief or to manifest a specific religious practice for a sectarian purpose".[106]

These "affirmative" and "negative" aspects were reiterated by the Chief Justice in *Edwards Books & Art Ltd.*,[107] where he referred to them as "the freedom from conformity to religious dogma" and "the freedom to manifest one's own religious beliefs".[108] As indicated earlier, this bifurcation of section 2(a) corresponds somewhat to the First Amendment clauses concerning respectively "establishment" and "free exercise" of religion.[109] Accordingly, as in the United States, Canadian courts have applied a different standard of constitutionality to each aspect of the freedom.

With regard to free exercise, the Supreme Court of Canada in *Edwards Books & Art Ltd.* envisaged a wide-ranging application of the Charter to alleged violations of section 2(a), whether "direct or indirect, intentional or unintentional, foreseeable or unforeseeable".[110] However, the court hastened to add a *de minimis* qualification: "trivial or insubstantial" burdens on religious freedom were outside the ambit of the section.

As for the "establishment-type" (negative) freedom, the operative criterion, according to the court in *Edwards Books & Art Ltd.*, was legislative *purpose*:

> [L]egislation with a secular inspiration does not abridge the freedom from conformity to religious dogma merely because statutory provisions coincide with the tenets of a religion.[111]

In *Big M Drug Mart*,[112] therefore, the *Lord's Day Act* was struck down on account of its sectarian purpose, whereas the "secular" Ontario *Retail Business Holidays Act* survived the challenge in *Edwards Books & Art Ltd.*

How do these two sets of standards compare with those applied to their First Amendment counterpart clauses? In "free exercise" cases, the U.S. courts have long applied the "compelling state interest" requirement

---

105 *Supra*, note 2.
106 *Ibid.* at 347.
107 *Supra*, note 30.
108 *Ibid.* at 760.
109 *Cf.* Dickson C.J.C.'s remark in *Big M Drug Mart, supra*, note 2 at 341, that "applicability of the *Charter* guarantee of freedom of conscience and religion does not depend on the presence or absence of an 'anti-establishment principle' ".
110 *Supra*, note 30 at 759.
111 *Ibid.* at 761.
112 *Supra*, note 2.

to burdens on religious freedom,[113] typified by the Supreme Court's holding in *People v. Woody*,[114] where a ban on the drug peyote was struck down on the grounds that state concern for the harm done by an hallucinogenic was insufficiently compelling *vis-à-vis* the centrality of peyote to the beliefs of the Native American Church.

For "establishment" challenges, as noted earlier, the complex purpose-test in *Lemon*[115] has developed into a "secular-purpose" requirement, whereby otherwise religiously motivated legislation or practice will be upheld if a single secular purpose exists.[116]

In pre-Charter Canadian case law, the courts appeared readier to override individual religious freedom for assorted "reasons of state" on an *ad hoc* basis: in the absence of constitutional entrenchment, the former was often seen as less "compelling" than the latter. Nor did the absence of a clear "establishment" principle make for a robust treatment of the "negative" element of religious freedom. Thus, in *R. v. Harrold*,[117] the British Columbia Court of Appeal upheld the conviction of a member of the Hare Krishna sect under a Vancouver anti-noise bylaw, and in *Ruman v. Lethbridge School Board Trustees*,[118] an Alberta statute mandating patriotic exercises was held to be unexceptionable for Jehovah's Witnesses.

Under the Charter, the courts appear to be actively advancing the inclusive approach to alleged violations of "affirmative" religious freedom, while being more tentative in "negative" freedom cases. In *O'Malley*,[119] for example, otherwise neutral employment practices were held account-able for indirect — "adverse effect" — discrimination towards a Seventh Day Adventist who was unable to work on Saturdays for religious reasons. The Supreme Court of Canada demanded "reasonable accommodation" of such religious needs, with the onus of demonstrating such accommo-dation resting on the respondent.

With respect to the purpose-test applied in *Big M Drug Mart*[120] and *Edwards Books & Art Ltd.*,[121] negative freedom exercises, the drawbacks of the Supreme Court of Canada's approach were noted earlier. It might be added that absent an express anti-establishment principle in Canadian

---

113 *Sherbert v. Verner*, 374 U.S. 398 (1963); *Wisconsin v. Yoder*, 406 U.S. 205 (1972).
114 40 Cal. Rptr. 69 (1964).
115 *Supra*, note 91.
116 *Supra*, notes 92-94.
117 [1971] 3 W.W.R. 365 (B.C.C.A.), leave to appeal to S.C.C. refused 3 C.C.C. (2d) 387n.
118 [1943] 3 W.W.R. 340 (Alta. S.C.). *Cf. Donald v. Hamilton Bd. of Education*, [1945] O.R. 518 (C.A.) (Jehovah's Witnesses excused from requirement to salute the flag and recite the national anthem, because contrary to their religious beliefs).
119 *Supra*, note 90. *Cf. Bhinder v. C.N.R.*, [1985] 2 S.C.R. 561.
120 *Supra*, note 2.
121 *Supra*, note 30.

law, an emphasis upon the effects of the impugned legislation or practice might seem all the more warranted.

Any consideration of the scope of religious or conscientious freedom must ultimately address the question of limits pertaining thereto. In American jurisprudence, such limits are invoked implicitly through doctrines or "compelling interest", "secular purpose" and the like, with no express limitations articulated in the Constitution. The Canadian Charter, on the other hand, provides for explicit overrides under sections 1 and 33, the first of which indicates the conceptual parameters of entrenched protection:

> The *Canadian Charter of Rights and Freedoms* guarantees the rights and freedoms set out in it subject only to such reasonable limits prescribed by law as can be demonstrably justified in a free and democratic society.

In *R. v. Oakes*,[122] the Supreme Court of Canada expounded upon the nature of the limits implied by section 1, to be subject to evidence on a preponderance of probabilities. The first essential criterion related to the need for "societal concerns which are pressing and substantial" in order to override a protected right or freedom — to the exclusion of "trivial objectives or those discordant with the principles of a free and democratic society".[123] Second, a tripartite "proportionality test" applies to the means used in advancing those concerns: the measures must be "fair and not arbitrary", they "should impair the right in question as little as possible", and they should be proportional in effect to the importance of the objectives.[124]

Clearly, the preceding bears a striking resemblance to the First Amendment "compelling state interest" doctrine enunciated in *Sherbert v. Verner*,[125] whereunder the U.S. Supreme Court accorded religious freedom an especially "preferred" status in the constitutional order. Indeed, this kinship of constitutional preference for fundamental freedoms was averred by the Supreme Court of Canada itself in *Big M Drug Mart*,[126] in an eloquent passage by Dickson J.:

> What unites freedoms in the American First Amendment, s. 2(a) of the *Charter* and in the provisions of other human rights documents in which they are associated is the notion of the centrality of individual conscience and the inappropriateness of governmental intervention to compel or constrain its manifestation . . . It is because of the centrality of the rights associated with freedom of individual conscience both to basic beliefs about human worth

---

122 [1986] 1 S.C.R. 103.
123 *Ibid.* at 105 (headnote).
124 *Ibid.* at 106 (headnote).
125 *Supra*, note 113. See also *Adelaide Co. of Jehovah's Witnesses, supra*, note 101.
126 *Supra*, note 2.

and dignity and to a free and democratic political system that American jurisprudence has emphasized the primacy or "firstness" of the First Amendment. It is this same centrality that in my view underlies their designation in the *Canadian Charter of Rights and Freedoms* as "fundamental".[127]

Yet, the extrapolation of the American notion of "preferred rights" to Canadian constitutional law would involve a number of serious obstacles. In particular, the "establishment" principle in the First Amendment has an analogous, but not precise, counterpart in the "negative" freedom protected by section 2(a), rendering the latter provision inherently less extensive, and curtailing the relative scope of the "preference" it can enjoy. As well, section 33 of the Charter seemingly permits an "inarticulate" override, capable of eluding any substantive scrutiny by the courts. This limitation to the "preferred" status of religious freedom has yet to be tested.

In the passage quoted above from the Supreme Court of Canada's judgment in *Big M Drug Mart*, the Chief Justice recognized the common ground not only between section 2(a) and the American First Amendment, but also "other human rights documents". In fact, the very text of section 1, as of other provisions in the Charter, draws upon the language of international human rights norms which Canada has affirmed. This dimension to the scope and the limits of freedom of conscience and religion is the subject of the next section.

This discussion of religious freedom in Canadian law would be remiss without a reference to pertinent protections in the *Criminal Code*,[128] particularly in respect of the free exercise of religion.

Section 172 of the *Criminal Code* renders it an offence to obstruct a minister officiating at a religious meeting, or to wilfully disturb or interrupt "an assemblage of persons met for religious worship or for a moral, social or benevolent purpose". The importance of this section was illustrated in the Quebec case of *Chaput v. Romain*.[129] Three members of the provincial police, acting upon superior orders, entered the house of the plaintiff-appellant where a religious service of the Witnesses of Jehovah was being conducted. It was admitted that the meeting was orderly, but the police officers seized a bible and other religious literature and ordered those present to disperse. There was no warrant for entry or seizure, no charges were laid against the appellant or any of the participants, and none of the objects seized was returned to its owner. The plaintiff brought action for damages and for the value of the articles seized. The Supreme Court of Canada held unanimously that the police officers had acted

---

127 *Ibid.* at 346.
128 R.S.C. 1970, c. C-34. What follows is based substantially on W.S. Tarnopolsky, *The Canadian Bill of Rights*, 2nd ed. rev. (Toronto: Macmillan, 1975) at 179.
129 *Supra*, note 96.

illegally. Three of the justices decided that the conduct of the police was clearly violative of the *Criminal Code*, while the other five agreed on that and additional grounds for illegality. The Jehovah's Witness was therefore entitled to succeed in his action for damages under the *Quebec Civil Code*. The ninth judge concurred as to the wrongdoing, without referring specifically to the *Criminal Code*. In effect, then, the Supreme Court gave unanimous protection to the appellant's freedom of religious worship.

7. FREEDOM OF CONSCIENCE AND RELIGION IN INTERNATIONAL LAW

The relevance of the *International Covenant on Civil and Political Rights*[130] — ratified by Canada in 1976 — to the section 2(a) protection of religious and conscientious freedom was attested to by the Ontario Court of Appeal in *R. v. Videoflicks*.[131] Specifically, article 18 of the Covenant is inclusive and elaborate in its proclamation of this fundamental norm:

1. Everyone shall have the right to freedom of thought, conscience and religion. This right shall include freedom to have or to adopt a religion or belief of his choice, and freedom, either individually or in community with others and in public or private, to manifest his religion or belief in worship, observance, practice and teaching.

2. No one shall be subject to coercion which would impair his freedom to have or to adopt a religion or belief of his choice.

3. Freedom to manifest one's religion or beliefs may be subject only to such limitations as are prescribed by law and are necessary to protect public safety, order, health, or morals or the fundamental rights and freedoms of others.

4. The States Parties to the present Covenant undertake to have respect for the liberty of parents and, when applicable, legal guardians to ensure the religious and moral education of their children in conformity with their own convictions.

With particular regard to section 2(a), the court in *Videoflicks* interpreted article 18 as mandating a multifaceted right to observe and express religious beliefs — "beyond the ability to hold certain beliefs without coercion and restraint".[132] The court might likewise have adverted to the *1981 U.N. Declaration on the Elimination of All Forms of Intolerance*

---

130 Adopted December 16, 1966, entered into force March 23, 1976, G.A. Res. 2200 (XXI), 21 U.N. GAOR, Supp. (No. 16) 52, U.N. Doc.A/6316 (1966).

131 *Supra*, note 88.

132 *Ibid.* at 420.

and of Discrimination based on Religion or Belief,[133] of which Canada was a principal sponsor. In the spirit of article 18 of the Covenant, the Declaration details state obligations to prevent discrimination and permit the free exercise of religion.

The provision in article 18(3) of the Covenant as to the limits attending the norm echoes section 1 of the Charter, and is coterminous with the Supreme Court of Canada's holding in *Big M Drug Mart*[134] that "freedom" under the Charter is "subject to such limitations as are necessary to protect public safety, order, health, or morals or the fundamental rights and freedoms of others".

In that connection, the Covenant provides in article 4 that no derogation whatsoever is permissible, even during "public emergency", from the scope of the obligations outlined in, *inter alia*, article 18. Guidance as to the limitations contained in article 18(3), and the implications of the non-derogability provision in article 4, is offered by the deliberations of a distinguished panel of international jurists in 1984, at which Canada was represented by John Humphrey.[135] The panel adopted the "Siracusa Principles" (on the Limitation and Derogation Provisions of the Covenant),[136] which confirm the "preferred status" of religious and conscientious (among other fundamental) freedoms in the normative order of international human rights.

A further reference to the *Covenant on Civil and Political Rights* was made by the Ontario Appeal Court in *Videoflicks*,[137] as to the mutual reinforcement of section 2(a) and the multiculturalism provision in section 27 of the Charter. The court read article 27 of the Covenant — which recognizes the right of cultural, ethnic and religious minorities to collectively exercise their cultural, religious and linguistic rights — as giving sustenance to a wide interpretation of the preceding "interactive" right in the Charter.[138]

It is appropriate that Canadian courts, and not least the Supreme Court, should draw upon this country's international human rights commitments as interpretive guides to the scope of fundamental freedoms under the Charter, in light of the normative antecedents they have provided in the

---

133 Adopted November 25, 1981, G.A. Res.55 (XXXVI), 36 GAOR, Supp. (No.51), UN Doc.A/RES/36/55 (1981). See generally on freedom of religion in international law and under the European Convention on Human Rights, H. Hannum, *Materials on International Human Rights and U.S. Constitutional Law* (Washington, D.C.: Procedural Aspects of International Law Institute) at 91-93.

134 *Supra*, note 2 at 337.

135 See International Commission of Jurists (ICJ), *Review*, No. 36 (June 1986), 47 at 55-56.

136 *Ibid.* at 47-55.

137 *Supra*, note 88.

138 *Ibid.* at 427-428.

framing of the Charter. That those antecedents reflect the according of "preferred status" to freedom of conscience and religion by the international community should, in this context, bode well for Canadian jurisprudence.

8. SOME CONCLUDING PROPOSITIONS ON FREEDOM OF CONSCIENCE AND RELIGION UNDER THE CHARTER

(1) The historical "double override" may no longer be overriding, but it will not simply wither away; indeed, it still remains as a baseline test or first order of judicial review, and therefore an important part of the lawyer's arsenal. As well, the dialectic of legal federalism might, according to the case law, provide a protection for religious freedom. One caveat, of course, is that legal federalism is a double-edged sword, and the process of characterization may even pre-empt consideration of freedom of conscience or religion as a fundamental freedom. Accordingly, constitutional battles can be expected to engage both a power process and a rights theory.

(2) A jurisprudence of preferred rights or First Amendment theory appears to be emergent, though in a particularly Canadian mold given the absence of an explicit "establishment" principle in the Charter. Such a jurisprudence is prospectively supported by an invocation of the normative sources of pertinent Charter provisions in international law, wherein limits to the freedom of conscience and religion are to be narrowly construed.

(3) As a corollary, the parameters of the override under section 1 have been tightly defined, in respect of both justificatory objectives and the means usable in their furtherance. However, the actual operation of these criteria may or may not warrant comparison with the "compelling state interest" doctrine in the United States. A principal concern in this regard is the brooding presence of the inarticulate override under section 33, which could emerge as more "compelling" in effect than the "fundamental" freedoms of section 2.

(4) The straitjacket of the "frozen concepts" perspective on religious freedom in pre-Charter jurisprudence has been decisively laid to rest. In its place, and facilitated by the inclusion of "conscience" in section 2(a), an expansive definition encompassing the "affirmative" right to manifest one's belief or non-belief, as well as the "negative" right to abstain from conformity with the beliefs of others, has been adopted by the courts.

(5) If the preceding is suggestive of the dual-clause protection under the First Amendment, it is less clear how far the respective tests of constitutionality under each clause in the United States will parallel those adopted in Canada. The evolution of the purpose-test attending the "establishment" clause in the United States into a "secular purpose" one

simpliciter, invites cautious emulation at best. Yet, the Supreme Court of Canada has embraced in "negative" freedom cases an analytical approach approximating the American, rather than an effects-oriented one less susceptible to colourable legislation or practice. In "free exercise" cases, it remains to be seen whether the Supreme Court of Canada's broad interpretation of affirmative freedom will be constrained by it.

(6) Since governmental assistance to denominational schools under section 29 of the Charter and section 3 of the *Constitution Act, 1867*, constitutes a departure from the "establishment" principle and eludes the validity tests above, the permissive interpretation accorded this exception by the courts underscores the countervailing force of collective rights within the scheme of the Charter. As such, religious freedom in this country diverges from corresponding First Amendment protections, notwithstanding *dicta* to the contrary by the Supreme Court of Canada.

(7) While the need to develop an indigenous jurisprudence under the Charter, one that reflects the peculiarities of Canadian history, culture and contemporary society, cannot be gainsaid, neither can the importance of drawing upon relevant constitutional experience in the United States and elsewhere, and upon the international human rights regime to which Canada is legally committed. As recognized by the Supreme Court of Canada, these disparate sources are united by a perception of conscientious and religious freedom as central to individual liberty, and as warranting the most stringent safeguards against official encroachment "compelling state interests" as in the United States.

(8) Statutory protections, in both the *Criminal Code* and the human rights codes, provide important safeguards for freedom of conscience and religion, sometimes in an indirect fashion. Furthermore, the provisions respecting those freedoms under, *inter alia*, the *European Convention on Human Rights*, the *International Covenant on Civil and Political Rights* and the *U.N. Declaration on Religious Intolerance*, constitute vital normative referents for the interpretation, if not protection, of conscientious and religious freedom in Canada.

(9) The recent signing of the constitutional accord with Quebec at Meech Lake raises a novel question as to whether recognizing that province as "a distinct society" will constrain the scope of fundamental freedoms under the Charter in respect of Quebec legislation or practice.[139] In this respect, the purpose-oriented approach to constitutional validity favoured by the majority in the Supreme Court of Canada might be rendered all the more vulnerable to colourable action by the provincial legislature, which

---

139 See, *e.g.*, W. Marsden, "Experts ask what a 'distinct society' can do to your rights"; and R. Orr and M. Goldbloom, "Two cheers only for the first ministers" ("Dialogue"), *Gazette* (Montreal), June 23, 1987, p. 33.

an effects-first analysis would perhaps better penetrate.

(10) Finally, inasmuch as effective lawyering is often a *sine qua non* for good judging, the willingness of counsel to develop innovative approaches that are sensitive to Canada's new constitutional regime as well as its multicultural fabric may well be critical to both. It will be necessary, in this regard, to develop the capacity to marshall arguments from Charter-relevant sources elsewhere, including the jurisprudential and normative ones referred to earlier. Effective lawyering and the Charter may yet revolutionize one another to the benefit of fundamental rights and freedoms.

6

Freedom of Expression
(*Section 2(b)*)

Clare Beckton

1. INTRODUCTION

While it might be tempting to state that the *Canadian Charter of Rights and Freedoms* has heralded a new era of freedom of expression, reality would belie such a statement. In the Supreme Court of Canada, McIntyre J. made this explicit when he stated in *Dolphin Delivery*[1] that

> "[f]reedom of expression is not, however, a creature of the *Charter*. It is one of the fundamental concepts that has formed the basis for the historical development of the political, social and educational institutions of western society.

There is no doubt, however, that the Charter had added a new dimension to freedom of expression issues. The purpose of this chapter is to examine how the courts have interpreted the guarantees in section 2(b) of the Charter in the five years since it came into force.

Although, prior to 1982, freedom of expression was not an "entrenched" right, it was deeply embedded in the fabric of Canadian society particularly as it related to the realm of political ideas. In the 1938 *Alberta Press Reference*,[2] the Supreme Court had made it clear that freedom of expression was necessary for maintenance of our "democratic society". The court focussed upon the right of individuals to be informed about the activities of their governments and stressed the need to have this information be available from sources other than the government.

In the last pre-Charter decision of the Supreme Court relating to freedom of expression, the court reiterated the view that freedom of speech is "a deep-rooted value in our democratic system of government".[3] In all of the cases prior to the entrenchment of the Charter, the courts had been quick to note that freedom of expression, "while fundamental", is not an absolute value. These statements made it clear that, in Canada, there would be no need for a debate such as ensued in the United States as to whether freedom of expression was an absolute value.[4] In *Fraser*,[5] the court re-affirmed that "[a]ll important values must be qualified, and balanced against, other important, and often competing, values". Needless to say, when *Fraser* was decided, the courts had the benefit of knowing that the Charter contained a clause which made it explicit that all of the rights and freedoms guaranteed were subject to reasonable limits.

Therefore, both in pre-Charter and post-Charter decisions, the courts have recognized the fundamental nature of freedom of expression while still making it clear that limitations would be permissible when other vital interests were affected.

---

1 *R.W.D.S.U. Local 580 v. Dolphin Delivery Ltd.*, [1986] 2 S.C.R. 573 at 583.
2 *Reference re Alberta Legislation*, [1938] S.C.R. 100.
3 *Fraser v. P.S.S.R.B.*, [1985] 2 S.C.R. 455 at 462.
4 See, *e.g.*, the dissenting judgments of Justices Black, Douglas and Warren in *Konisberg v. State Bar of California*, 366. U.S. 36 (1961).
5 *Supra*, note 3 at 463.

Since the Charter came into force in 1982, there have been a large number of challenges premised upon the guarantee of freedom of expression in section 2(b). These challenges have dealt with diverse questions ranging from bans on publication of evidence taken at a preliminary hearing to obscenity and censorship laws, hate propoganda, a requirement that all signs be in one language and to restrictions on lawyer advertising. The Supreme Court of Canada has only recently considered the question of freedom of expression under section 2(b) in *Dolphin Delivery*[6] (mentioned in the opening paragraph). However, there was no requirement in that case for the court to make any difficult decisions respecting the ambit of the protections in section 2(b).

In most of the cases to date under the Charter, the courts have been grappling with drawing the line between justifiable and unacceptable limitations upon freedom of expression or trying to decide if the expression in question is within the ambit of the protection offered by section 2(b) guarantees. To make these determinations, the courts have either tried to assess the significance of other rights or freedoms when considering whether freedom of expression has been unduly infringed by legislation or governmental action or have made decisions adopting a "purposive" approach to exclude some forms of expression from the section 2(b) protection.

Has the Charter substantially changed the Canadian position on freedom of expression? Traditionally in Canada the courts have not given pre-eminence in fact to freedom of expression. While recognizing its significance to the maintenance of a democratic system, the courts have never hesitated to uphold laws relating to defamation, obscenity and the conduct of a fair trial, which impose limitations upon freedom of expression. In fact, in many of the pre-Charter cases, no mention was made of freedom of expression when the courts were faced with these issues. Instead the courts focussed, for example in cases relating to obscenity, upon whether the material in question was obscene according to the *Criminal Code* definition and prevailing community standards.[7] It seemed to be generally accepted by the courts that areas of expression, such as defamation and obscenity, were clearly justifiably limited by legislation or the common law.

Furthermore, prior to the Charter, Canadian jurisprudence was remarkably sparse on the issue of freedom of expression. In fact, very

---

6 *Supra*, note 1.

7 See, *e.g.*, *Brodie v. R.*, [1962] S.C.R. 681, where the court was called upon to determine whether D.H. Lawrence's *Lady Chatterly's Lover* was obscene. They concentrated on the definition of obscenity and the prevailing community standards rather than upon freedom of expression and the limitation that was being imposed upon it.

little attention had been paid by academics and commentators to the theoretical underpinnings of freedom of expression and the values it served. That is not surprising, however, given that there was no constitutionally entrenched provision, which also meant that there was no real impetus for the courts to attempt to articulate a theory of freedom of expression or to balance interests. Since the entrenchment of the Charter, however, the courts have been confronted with the need to balance the right to freedom of expression with other fundamental values in Canadian society. They have been struggling with the balance and with the problems presented by difficult areas such as hate propaganda and commercial expression. In some of these earlier cases, the courts have looked to American jurisprudence for guidance.

In the United States, the literature is replete with writing expounding the philosophy which justifies the primacy of the right of free expression in a democratic society. There are also innumerable decisions where the American courts have struggled with questions concerning limitations sought to be imposed on freedom of speech as guaranteed in the First Amendment, and with ascertaining the values served by freedom of speech which have an impact on where the balance is drawn.

That is not to say, however, that there was or is any consensus amongst the writers or the courts as to the values served by freedom of expression. But there seems to be a consensus in the United States that freedom of speech is one of the most fundamental guarantees in the Constitution. This is reflected in many decisions which place freedom of expression above other values and where the courts have demanded an overriding interest before accepting the validity of a limitation.

It is important for the Canadian courts, now that the Charter is entrenched, to develop a theory which will enable them to determine in any given case whether the speech in question is protected by the guarantees in section 2. Once that is determined, then an assessment can be made as to whether the value served by the limitation outweighs the value of freedom of expression in the given circumstances. It is submitted that unless the values served by freedom of expression are clearly articulated, it will be difficult to assess correctly whether other interests should be protected by imposing limits upon freedom of expression, and the courts will risk encountering the same problems as those experienced in the United States.

This is so because, when a challenge is made that a law infringes upon the guarantees in section 2(b), the first step is to determine whether the matter in question constitutes expression for the purpose of section 2(b). In some cases there will be a fine line between expression and conduct. For example, can it be said that when a prostitute attempts to solicit customers on the street, this constitutes expression? If it is expression, is it expression that is worthy of protection? To answer that question the courts must have some sense of the values served by freedom of expression. If, for example, Meiklejohn's argument that the primary value served by freedom of expression is the guarantee of and enhancement of the democratic process, then soliciting may not be considered worthy of protection since it does not contribute to a discussion of the merits or demerits of government activities.[8] Meiklejohn's theory was later extended to philosophical or literary expression, but only if these forms of expression contribute to the furtherance of the democratic government. If his theory was utilized, many forms of expression not related to the democratic process would not be considered worthy of protection. In fact, it seems that the Supreme Court of the United States followed this approach for a period of time particularly during the 1940s and 1950s. This approach allowed the courts to summarily exclude obscenity, commercial speech and defamation from the protection of the First Amendment guarantees of free speech. In *Roth v. United States*,[9] the court affirmed their earlier position, stating that "implicit in the history of the First Amendment is the rejection of obscenity as utterly without redeeming social importance". This rejection of entire categories of speech created confusion and forced the courts to draw arbitrary boundaries when dealing with, for example, literary works which contained obscene portions. Furthermore, this approach tends to ignore broader values that may be served by freedom of expression that relate to the individual and his or her personal growth.

Professor Emerson, on the other hand, rejected the Meiklejohn narrow thesis in favour of an approach which states that freedom of expression is not only valuable for its political functions but as an end in itself. He believed that freedom of expression is essential to the dignity of all individuals.[10] As a consequence of this approach, categories of speech would not be automatically excluded from protection since within those categories some speech may be an important part of individual growth and dignity. The Supreme Court of the United States appeared to move somewhat toward the Emerson theory in the 1960s by rejecting their earlier

---

8 See the debate, *e.g.*, between Meiklejohn, *Free Speech and its Relation to Self-Government (1948)* and T.I. Emerson, *The System of Freedom of Expression* (New York: Random House, 1970), and those who support their views.

9 354 U.S. 476 (1957), affirming the position taken by the court in *Chaplinsky v. New Hampshire*, 315 U.S. 568 (1942). Similarly in *Valentine v. Chrestinsen*, 316 U.S. 52 at 54 (1942), the court stated in relation to commercial speech: This court has unequivocally held that the streets are proper places for the exercise of the freedom of communicating information and dissemination of opinion and that though the states and municipalities may appropriately regulate the privilege in the public interest, they may not unduly burden or proscribe its employment in these public thoroughfares. We are equally clear that the Constitution imposes no such restraint on government as respects purely commercial advertising.

10 See Emerson, *supra*, note 8.

positions taken with respect to defamation and commercial speech and to a certain extent obscenity. In *New York Times Co. v. Sullivan*,[11] the court required the states to safeguard freedom of speech and freedom of the press in their defamation laws, while a series of cases also moved the courts toward offering protection for commercial speech albeit somewhat less than for other forms of speech.[12] The court moved in 1973 in *Miller v. California*[13] to a broad community standards test for obscenity which somewhat mitigated the broad enclusionary approach taken in *Roth*.[14] But in *New York v. Ferber*,[15] Mr. Justice White again adopted the statements of the court in *Chaplinsky v. New Hampshire*[16] that "[t]here are certain well-defined and narrowly limited classes of speech, the prevention and punishment of which have never been thought to raise any constitutional problem. These include the lewd and obscence".[17]

Professor Tribe, in his treatise on constitutional law, indicates that the Supreme Court has, over the years, attributed three distinct purposes to the freedom of speech guarantees in the First Amendment. These are:

> (1) to ensure that the democratic system of government established by the Constitution remains intact and operates as it should;
> (2) to assist in the advancement of knowledge and the discovery of truth;
> (3) to ensure that each individual member of society is free to develop his or her own "intellect, interests, taste, and personality".[18]

It would seem that these statements taken together encompass the broad range of human endeavours where freedom of expression is significant and seem to identify the leading values served by freedom of expression. It is submitted that the courts in Canada could use these three statements as guidelines for evolving a uniform theory of freedom of expression against which any limitations could be tested. If the courts were to adopt these values, there would be no need to exclude entire categories of speech, but rather instead they would measure the other interests in question protected by the limitation against the value of the expression in question and the impact of the limitation upon expression.

In some of the most recent decisions of the Canadian courts on difficult

---

11 376 U.S. 254 (1964).
12 See *Pittsburg Press Co. v. Pittsburg Comm. on Human Relations*, 413 U.S. 376 (1973); *Bigelow v. Virginia*, 421 U.S. 809 (1975); and *Virginia State Bd. of Pharmacy v. Virginia Citizens Consumer Council*, 425 U.S. 748 (1976).
13 413 U.S. 15 (1973).
14 *Supra*, note 9.
15 73 L.Ed. 2d 1113 (1982).
16 *Supra*, note 9.
17 *Supra*, note 15, at 1120-1121.
18 L.H. Tribe, *American Constitutional Law* (Mineola, N.Y.: Foundation Press, 1978) at 576-579.

issues relating to freedom of expression, the courts have taken an approach which seems to suggest that limitations on speech should be ascertained pursuant to section 2(b) rather than under section 1. These cases appear to be taking a very narrow approach to the values served by freedom of expression. In fact, these decisions have given a very narrow definition to the guarantee of freedom of expression in section 2(b). In *R. v. Zundel*,[19] the Ontario Court of Appeal was asked to determine if section 177 of the *Criminal Code*,[20] which prohibits wilful publication of false statements, tales or news, infringed the guarantees in section 2(b) of the Charter. Initially the court determined that freedom of expression was not an absolute unqualified value and that it could be limited by powerful competing values, a fact that seems to have been generally accepted in Canada. Then the court went on to say, however, that a distinction must be drawn between rights and freedoms. The court stated that:

> A "freedom" . . . is defined by determining first the area which is regulated. The freedom is then what exists in the unregulated area — a sphere of activity within which all acts are permissible. It is a residual area in which all acts are free of specific legal regulation and the individual is free to choose.[21]

This was an approach which the court indicated was similar to that adopted by the British Columbia Court of Appeal in *Re Cromer and British Columbia Teachers' Federation*.[22] In *Cromer*, the court concluded that the freedom of expression described in section 2(b) was not absolute but rather "the residue within the periphery created by recognition of civil rights in persons who may be injured by the exercise of absolute freedom of expression".[23] The court took the position that the balancing should occur within section 2(b). This approach is very similar to that adopted by the same court in *Andrews v. Law Society of British Columbia*,[24] where the court was considering a challenge pursuant to the equality guarantees in section 15 of the Charter.

After that comparison, the court in *Zundel*[25] concluded that section 177 of the *Criminal Code* was not an infringement of section 2(b) because it falls within the permissibly regulated area. The court went on to say that:

> It is difficult to see how such conduct would fall within any of the previously

---

19 (1987), 58 O.R. (2d) 129 (C.A.), leave to appeal to S.C.C. refused (1987), 61 O.R. (2d) 588n (S.C.C.).

20 R.S.C. 1970, c. C-34.

21 *Supra*, note 19 at 150.

22 (1986), 29 D.L.R. (4th) 641 (B.C. C.A.).

23 *Ibid.* at 657.

24 [1986] 4 W.W.R. 242 (B.C. C.A.).

25 *Supra*, note 19.

expressed *rationales* for guaranteeing freedom of expression. Spreading falsehoods knowingly is the antithesis of seeking truth through the free exchange of ideas. It would appear to have no social or moral value which would merit constitutional protection.[26]

Finally, the court concluded that section 177 did not come within the residue which constitutes freedom of expression protected by section 2(b).

Similarly, in *Cromer*,[27] the court concluded that the *Code of ethics* of the British Columbia Teachers Federation overrode the right of Mrs. Cromer to state her views about another teacher at a meeting of the parents' Advisory Committee.

The approach adopted by these courts presents grave difficulties. While one can understand the concern of the court in *Zundel* about the kind of information that he was disseminating, the effect of the judgment would have serious consequences for protection of freedom of expression since it accepts that there are broad categories where limitations can be placed on freedom of expression without having to balance the interests involved. This approach also seems to suggest that areas limited in the past would be difficult to challenge.

Another factor which suggests that the approach in *Cromer* and *Zundel* may not be the most appropriate is its similarity to the leading approaches taken with respect to section 15 as outlined in *Andrews*.[28] However, section 15 of the Charter contains a strong limiting word, "discrimination", which suggests that some limits must be drawn to ensure that not every distinction constitutes an infringement of section 15. That approach seems clearly acceptable since all legislation contains distinctions and section 15 is primarily aimed at distinctions which involve stereotyping, prejudice and historical disadvantage. Section 2(b), however, contains no such limiting words. Rather it merely guarantees freedom of expression, the press and other media of communication. Certainly, section 2(b) has its limits in that it would not likely go beyond speech or expression to encompass conduct. There will also be gray areas where a line must be drawn between speech and conduct, since that line is not always clear. But there are no words in section 2(b) which suggest that any further limiting or balancing should occur at that stage. It is equally clear that section 1 was established to define the test that is to be used in any given case when assessing the validity of a limitation — an approach adopted early in the history of the Charter by the Ontario Court of Appeal in *R. v. Southam*.[29]

Given the division between the guarantee in section 2(b) and the

---

26 *Ibid.* at 155.
27 *Supra*, note 22.
28 *Supra*, note 24.
29 (1983), 6 C.R.R. 1 (Ont. C.A.).

limitation clause in section 1, there is an argument that American court cases are not strong precedent when determining the approach to be followed. The First Amendment to the United States Constitution contains no limiting words, nor is there any limitations clause elsewhere in the Constitution. As a consequence, the United States courts may have initially felt compelled to exclude entire categories of speech from the First Amendment protection. Later, as it became clear that the courts considered freedom of speech had limitations, they seemed willing to retreat from that position to engage in more of a balancing approach. The history of the development of free speech in the United States offers an example of the pitfalls in adopting the approach suggested by the courts in *Cromer*[30] and *Zundel.*[31] That is not to say, however, that American jurisprudence will not be valuable when it is necessary to balance the values which are in conflict, since many of the issues have already been dealt with by the United States courts.

The problem in *Zundel* and *Cromer* may also stem from the criteria adopted by the Supreme Court of Canada in *R. v. Oakes*[32] to demonstrate that a limitation is a reasonable limit within section 1 of the Charter. Since there was a very heavy onus of justification placed by the court on those who seek to impose a limitation on Charter rights, the courts, when faced with hate propaganda, may not feel confident to use section 1 to find that the law is justifiable. If this is indeed the case, it may lead the courts down the same road followed in the United States, a path that is not appropriate or desirable in Canada. It remains to be seen whether the Supreme Court will continue to use this stringent approach when they are faced with cases such as *Zundel.*

The remainder of this chapter will examine some of the key cases on freedom of expression since the entrenchment of the Charter in 1982. The purpose of this examination will be to show which direction the courts are taking with respect to some of the key areas where freedom of expression conflicts with other fundamental values.

2. COMMERCIAL SPEECH

Commercial speech is one area where the courts have experienced difficulties in deciding whether it should be within the ambit encompassed by section 2(b) of the Charter.

Commercial speech basically is speech of any kind that advertises a product or service for profit or for some business purpose. For example,

---

30 *Supra*, note 22.

31 *Supra*, note 19.

32 [1986] 1 S.C.R. 103.

television advertising aimed at children or adults would be considered to be commercial speech. In the United States, for a number of years, commercial speech was excluded from the protection of the First Amendment.[33] The courts had essentially taken the position that commercial speech was not deserving of protection, basically on the assumption that it did not serve any important values which were worthy of protection. It was not an easy exemption to deal with, however, since the courts had to struggle with trying to ascertain what actually constituted commercial speech.[34]

By the 1970s, the American courts began to display some unease about making such a stark distinction between commercial and non-commercial speech. In 1975, in *Bigelow v. Virginia*,[35] which involved a prosecution for placing an advertisement promoting legal abortion services in New York, the court indicated that *Valentine*[36] did not support any sweeping proposition that advertising is unprotected *per se*. The following year, in *Virginia State Bd. of Pharmacy v. Virginia Citizens Consumer Counsel*,[37] the Supreme Court declared unconstitutional a ban on the advertising of prescription drug prices. While the court in this case made it clear that the First Amendment protection extended to even pure commercial speech, it emphasized that the courts need not be so vigilant in protecting commercial speech as they must be in protecting other speech. It appeared that the courts considered the value served by commercial speech was not as high as other forms of speech.

To date, the Canadian courts seem to be caught up in the problems that were faced by the American courts in this area. Some courts have held that commercial speech is not protected under section 2(b).[38] Callaghan J. and Eberle J., concurring in *Klein*,[39] indicated that commercial speech flowed from the realm of economic activity while political speech flowed from politics and government. In a democratic society, the economic realm must be subordinate to the political realm. Justice Callaghan examined the United States courts' struggle with the concept of commercial

33 See *Valentine, supra*, note 9.
34 See *e.g.*, *Camarano v. United States*, 358 U.S. 498 (1959) (the profit motive should make no difference); *Murdoch v. Pennsylvania*, 319 U.S. 105 (1943) (holding unconstitutional a tax on the sale of religious material where the main object was to preach and publicize the doctrines).
35 *Supra*, note 12.
36 *Supra*, note 9.
37 *Supra*, note 12.
38 See *Re Klein and L.S.U.C.; Re Dvorak and L.S.U.C.* (1985), 16 D.L.R. (4th) 489 (Ont. Div. Ct.) (currently before the Ontario Court of Appeal); *R. v. Prof. Technology of Can. Ltd.* (1986), 7 C.R.D. 525; *Grier v. Alta. Optometric Assn.* [1985] 5 W.W.R. 436, (Alta. Q.B.), rev'd [1987] 5 W.W.R. 539 (Alta. C.A.).
39 *Ibid.*

speech as it related to the First Amendment. He looked in particular at recent decisions where the courts had indicated that it was not deserving of the same degree of protection as other rights. He maintained that the position of the United States courts in recent cases, where a lesser degree of protection has been given to commercial speech, would have a tendency to water down the right to be protected by section 2(b). In conclusion, he emphasized that:

> Commercial speech contributes nothing to democratic government because it says nothing about how people are governed or how they should govern themselves. It does not relate to government policies or matters of public concern essential to a democratic process.[40]

In emphasizing this latter point, Callaghan J. seems clearly to be adopting the early Meiklejohn approach to the value served by freedom of expression. His suggestion that since it serves little value it should be protected, presents problems with respect to the creation of a uniform theory. Although it is clear that the United States courts have experienced problems in this regard, again it may be related to their lack of a limitation clause. But in the context of the Charter, there is an opportunity to balance the interests and rights in section 1. If in fact commercial speech serves few values, it should be possible to justify any limitations placed upon it where another important right is at stake.

On the other hand, the Quebec Court of Appeal has taken the opposite view in the recent case of *Irwin Toy Ltd. v. Procureur Général du Québec*.[41] The Quebec government had passed laws aimed at prohibiting certain forms of advertising directed at children. The court held that section 2(b) protects all forms of expression including commercial expression. In this case the court indicated that the freedom encompasses the right of viewers to receive the message as well as the right of the disseminator to impart the message. As such, it was not just the freedom of expression of the company in question that was being affected. The court then went on to say that economic choices of Canadians are as important as artistic and cultural choices. In order for choices to be informed, it is necessary to have commercial advertising.

This position echoed the dissent by Henry J. in *Klein*,[42] where he had taken the position that in a free market economy, freedom of communication in economic affairs is no less important to the proper functioning of society than freedom of political communication. It is essential in such an economy for producers and distributors to pass on the best possible

---

40 *Ibid.* at 539.
41 [1986] R.J.Q. 2441 (Que. C.A.), leave to appeal to S.C.C. granted (1986), 32 D.L.R. (4th) 641n (S.C.C.).
42 *Supra*, note 38.

information to their users who want to choose the best combination of price, quality and volume.

The position taken by Henry J. and the court in *Irwin Toy* seems a more realistic assessment of the needs and concerns of our modern society. While no one can dispute the essential need to have full information and communications about our government's activities, there is a real concern about product information. Individuals are not truly free to choose a lifestyle if they are not aware of all of the options. Advertising serves the function of making individuals fully aware of the range of products and services that are available to them and therefore does have value. While it may be easier to limit the dissemination of commercial speech because there are more significant rights, that does not mean it has to be excluded as a category. Rather, the Quebec court's approach of balancing the interests under section 1 seems more appropriate than not recognizing it as protected speech. Now the Supreme Court has been called upon to determine the direction to be taken in Canada with respect to commercial expression.

3. THE JUDICIARY AND THE PRESS

Many of the cases under section 2(b) of the Charter have related to the court process dealing with issues such as laws which impose restrictions on access to juvenile trials to publication bans on evidence given at a preliminary hearing. In all these cases the courts have struggled to balance the need for a fair trial and respect for the judicial system with the need to protect freedom of expression and freedom of the press. It can be said that, in general, the Canadian courts have continued to defer to the fair trial interests in most cases rather than extending the interest in free expression. That is not to say, however, that this approach results in abrogation of the right to freedom of expression or the press. Rather, the courts have made it clear that they will balance the interests carefully and will only tolerate limitations on freedom of expression where the necessity can be demonstrated. In general, the courts tend to be more restrictive when they think that an accused's right to a fair trial may be affected by allowing publication or access in a given set of circumstances.

In sharp contrast, the United States courts have tended to defer more to free speech in this area, refusing to protect the judiciary from criticism[43]

---

43 See, *e.g.*, *Pennekamp v. Florida*, 328 U.S. 331 (1946), where the editor and publisher of the *Miami Herald* had been charged under Florida law with contempt. The published editorials at issue intimated bias on the part of the courts towards those who were charged with crimes. The court weighed free speech against the danger to the orderly and fair administration of justice and concluded that the danger to free speech, if the contempt citation was upheld, was greater than the danger to the judicial system created by the publication of the editorials.

and holding that pre-trial gag orders are an unacceptable restraint on freedom of speech.[44] In essence, the American judicial philosophy appears to be that protecting the court from criticism is not an interest which should be placed above free speech. While the United States courts have considered prejudicing a fair trial to be a strong interest worthy of protection, alternate methods of protection have been considered to be superior to abridging free speech in order to accomplish this goal. Contempt laws in Canada and Great Britain have indicated in the past that the judicial interest will be protected even at the expense of restricting free expression. In general, as indicated, the courts in the initial Charter cases seemed to have been following more closely the British and past Canadian approaches than moving toward the United States approach.

4. ACCESS TO THE COURTS

One area where the Canadian courts have stressed the freedom of expression value is in access to the courts. The leading, and one of the earliest cases in this regard, was *Hunter, Director of Investigation & Research, Combines Investigation Branch v. Southam Inc.*[45] In this case, the action was initiated, not by a juvenile alleging that his or her freedom of expression or his or her right to a fair trial was being infringed, but rather by Southam Press. Southam argued that section 12(1) of the *Juvenile Delinquents Act*,[46] which required that all trials of children shall take place *in camera*, was an unjustifiable infringement on section 2(b) of the Charter. In its judgment, the Alberta Court of Appeal reaffirmed the principle that "openness of the courts to the public is one of the hallmarks of a democratic society". This principle had been upheld by the Supreme Court, just before the Charter came into force, in *MacIntyre v. A.G. Nova Scotia.*[47]

In that case, MacIntyre, a television journalist, had applied for an order requiring a justice of the peace to make available to him for inspection search warrants and information in his possession. The Supreme Court upheld the right of access by the journalist to executed search warrants. In arriving at this conclusion, the court emphasized the necessity to take into consideration the need for the privacy of individuals, protection of the administration of justice, including the need to maintain the search warrant as an effective aid in the investigation of crime, and a strong public

---

44 *Nebraska Press Assn. v. Stuart*, 427 U.S. 539 (1976), where the majority determined that gag orders may be appropriate in some cases but they would be very exceptional cases.

45 [1984] 2 S.C.R. 145, aff'g (*sub nom. Southam Inc. v. Dir. of Investigation & Research*) [1983] 3 W.W.R. 385 (Alta. C.A.).

46 R.S.C. 1970, c J-3 [repealed 1980-81-82-83. c. 110. s. 80].

47 (1982), 65 C.C.C. (2d) 129 (S.C.C.).

policy in favour of "openness" in respect of judicial acts.

The court concluded that what was required was maximum account-ability and accessibility but not to the extent of harming the innocent or of impairing the efficiency of the search warrant as a weapon. In drawing the balance, the court concluded that the effective administration of justice would be frustrated if individuals were permitted to be present when the warrants were issued. Therefore, the exclusion of the public from the proceedings attending the actual issuance of the warrant was justified, but once it had been executed access was the overriding interest in most situations.

The court in *Southam*, using *MacIntyre* as a basis, held that while free access to the courts is not specifically enumerated under the heading of fundamental freedom, given the history of access, it is an implicit and integral part of the protection given to freedom of expression. Once the court determined that section 12(1) of the *Juvenile Delinquents Act prima facie* infringed the guarantees in section 2(b) of the Charter, they went on to assess whether this limitation was justifiable in a free and democratic society. The court looked to the jurisprudence of other countries to assist them in this regard. Although the court agreed that section 12(1) served the important value of protection of juveniles, there was no justification for an absolute ban. No doubt the court was influenced by the knowledge that the new *Young Offenders Act*[48]contained a section making access to the court discretionary depending on the particular needs in a specific case.

5. PROTECTION OF IDENTITY

Once the newspapers had successfully challenged the constitutionality of section 12(1) of the *Juvenile Delinquents Act*,[49] they began to turn their attention to the *Young Offenders Act*.[50] While the *Juvenile Delinquents Act* had contained a requirement that all juvenile hearings be held *in camera*, the *Young Offenders Act*, in section 38(1), prohibits the publication of the names of juveniles or any information which would result in their identification, and section 39(1)(a) provides guidelines by which a youth court judge must decide whether to exclude any person from the court. This permits an assessment in each case of whether it is necessary to exclude persons to ensure protection of young offenders, witnesses or victims. A representative of Southam Press was excluded from a hearing of a juvenile and subsequently challenged the constitutionality of sections 38(1) and

---

48   S.C. 1980-81-82-83, c. 110 [R.S.C. 1985, c. Y-1].

49   *Supra*, note 46.

50   *Supra*, note 48.

39(1).[51] It was readily conceded that sections 38(1) and 39(1) did impose a limitation upon freedom of expression. The court weighed the restriction on freedom of expression against the value to society and to involved youths of protecting young persons involved in youth proceedings from the damaging effects of publicity. In essence, the court concluded that section 38(1) only barred publication of names and any information which might lead to identification, leaving the press free to publish everything else. As such it was not an unreasonable restriction on freedom of expression.

Second, the court reasoned that since section 39(1) was also not an absolute ban, but left room for assessment in individual cases, this was not an unreasonable limitation given the value it protects. Therefore, in major cases to date the courts have refused to permit the press freedom to freely publish information concerning juvenile trials. It is interesting to note that Parliament, when examining the proposed *Young Offenders Act*, had considered the question of freedom of expression raised by the provisions which provided for restricted access. As a consequence, this may have influenced the courts to support the line drawn by Parliament between protection of the individual youth and the resultant benefit to society and the need to preserve freedom of expression. This was also consistent with the statements made by the Ontario Court of Appeal in *Southam* when striking down section 12(1) of the *Juvenile Delinquents Act*.

While the courts have been willing to protect youths from the glare of publicity, they have been more reluctant to do so when dealing with adult offenders or witnesses. In *R. v. Robinson*,[52] Justice Boland refused to grant an order prohibiting publication of the name of an accused person charged with murder. The accused had argued that publication of his name would infringe his right to be presumed innocent and to have a fair trial as guaranteed by section 11(d) of the Charter. Justice Boland indicated that section 11(d) was to ensure the presumption of innocence operated at the trial and was not there to ensure an accused remained anonymous. According to Madam Justice Boland, numerous procedures exist to ensure a fair trial, thereby making it unnecessary to withhold names. In fact, Justice Boland emphasized that absence of secrecy is the essential quality of a criminal process in a democracy since secrecy can result in abuse. In stressing that prior restraint should be reserved for extraordinary circumstances, Justice Boland seemed to be following somewhat the American approach in that regard.

However, in *R. v. McArthur*[53] at the trial of an accused on a charge

---

51 *Southam Inc. v. R.*, (1984) 12 C.R.R. 212 (Ont. H.C.), aff'd (1986), 20 C.R.R. 7 (Ont. C.A.), leave to appeal to S.C.C. refused (1986), 20 C.R.R. 7n (S.C.C.).

52 (1983), 5 C.R.R. 25 (Ont. H.C.).

53 (1984), 10 C.R.R. 220 (Ont. H.C.).

of first degree murder, the Crown sought an order prohibiting or restricting publication of the names and identity of certain Crown witnesses who were inmates of the federal or provincial systems. The Crown alleged that the physical safety of such persons would be jeopardized if their identity was disclosed. The court reasoned that, while the foundational rule is that trial proceedings are to be conducted in public, there is a fundamental interest in ensuring that evidence which might assist in the administration of justice is available to the court. Fear of interference with the witnesses or external threats could preclude access by the courts to essential information in any given case. A refusal to order disclosure of names in these instances will not affect the fairness of the trial. This case was not a departure from the past, but simply built on the common law where the courts have permitted public informers and police informers to be protected in the interests of ensuring the feasibility of the administration of justice.[54]

Similarly, in *Hirt v. College of Physicians & Surgeons of British Columbia*[55] where the issue was disciplinary proceedings against a doctor, the British Columbia Court of Appeal ruled that the names and identities of complainants who gave evidence before an *in camera* inquiry committee could be kept secret when these proceedings were published. The court, in deciding the ban was acceptable, reasoned that this was only a partial ban on publication and the infringement of freedom of expression was minor compared to the interest in having persons such as the complainant come forward to ensure abuse of confidence by a doctor can be dealt with.

The guarantee of freedom of expression has been successfully used to limit the ambit of reforms that were made in the *Criminal Code* relating to the disclosure of the identity of a victim in a sexual assault case. In *Canadian Newspapers Co. v. A.G. Canada*,[56] the appellant challenged an order made at the trial of a person accused of committing a sexual offence pursuant to section 442(3) of the *Criminal Code*, prohibiting the publication of the name of the complainant or information that would disclose her identity. While the court was aware that the rationale for this provision was to encourage women to report sexual offences without the fear of being identified and stigmatized in the press, they held that the provision was an unnecessary limitation on freedom of expression. It was held to be such because an order would be made upon the application of the

---

54 See, for public informers, *D. v. National Soc. for Prevention of Cruelty to Children*, [1977] 1 All E.R. (H.L.) and for policy informers see *Solicitor-General Canada v. Royal Comm. of Inquiry into Confidentiality of Health Records in Ont.*, [1982] 2 S.C.R. 494.

55 (1985), 17 D.L.R. (4th) 472 (B.C. C.A.).

56 (1985), 49 O.R. (2d) 557 (C.A.), rev'd [1988] 2 S.C.R. 122.

complainant or her counsel without consideration of whether such an order is necessary in the particular case to achieve the objective of section 442(3). The court concluded that a judge could reasonably make an order providing for a prohibition against publication, so all that was necessary was to sever the portion of the statute requiring an order when requested, and thus merely leave the decision to the discretion of the judge in each case. This case undoubtedly caused some consternation for women's groups who saw the *Criminal Code* provision as a major step forward in the fight for equality and protection of women, because even though there is still an opportunity for an order to be made, it places a greater onus on the complainant who would presumably have to show some possible harm. Here again was a clear example of a case where two vitally important rights were at issue, but the courts were only prepared to permit limitation on freedom of expression which did not go beyond what was necessary to protect the vital interest at stake. Thus the court reinforced the position taken in the juvenile cases that an assessment must be made in every case to determine whether there is a need for a ban and not merely use a blanket prohibition. In this case the judges seemed sympathetic to both the values at stake and tried to draw the line where both values would be limited the least.

6. CONTEMPT — SCANDALIZING THE COURT

Another area affecting freedom of expression and the courts that is now under attack is the contempt offence of scandalizing the court. This is an offence that is not often used. It involves any accusation of bias, perverted justice or improper motives on the part of the court or the judge in the discharge of a judicial duty.[57] In this instance a case has arisen against Toronto lawyer Harry Kopyto who made comments criticizing the decision of a judge in another case, suggesting that the judge was biased in favour of police officers. Mr. Kopyto is challenging the constitutionality of this offence on the basis that it restricts freedom of expression unduly and is therefore in conflict with section 2(b) of the Charter. No other group is offered the same degree of protection as the judiciary; others are merely offered the protection of the defamation laws. The concern underlying this offence seems to be for fair trials and ensuring respect for the judiciary, since there seems to be concern that judges have no way to protect themselves when they are personally attacked and that permitting such comments would create disrespect for the judiciary. Also, there is an underlying concern that it would be unseemly to permit judges to take defamation actions to protect their own reputations.

---

57 *R. v. Murphy; Ex parte A.G. New Brunswick*, [1969] 4 C.C.C.; 147 (N.B. C.A.); *Re Borowski* (1971), 3 C.C.C. (2d) 402 (Man. Q.B.).

In the United States the argument that danger of disrespect for the judiciary justifies curtailment of free speech has been dismissed:

> The assumption that respect for the judiciary can be won by shielding judges from published criticism wrongly appraises the character of American public opinion. For it is a prized American privilege to speak one's mind, although not always with perfect good taste, on all public opinions. An enforced silence, however limited, solely in the name of preserving the dignity of the bench, would probably engender resentment, suspicion and contempt much more than it would enhance respect.[58]

While the Canadian balance has traditionally been drawn in favour of protecting the interests of the judiciary, it is necessary for the courts to re-examine this balance in view of the Charter. The question which must be asked is whether permitting an infringement on freedom of expression to protect the judiciary is the least restrictive means of accomplishing that result, particularly since the offence is common law and is very broad in its application. The lack of criteria for ascertaining when one is in breach of the law is somewhat analogous to those in the *Ontario Censor Board* case.[59] Second, there is some real question whether imposing limitations on the ability to criticize the judiciary actually results in respect for the judiciary or more likely, as the American courts have suggested, cases such as Mr. Kopyto's may result in diminished respect for the judiciary, since it may be perceived that they are above criticism. In assessing the impact on freedom of expression, it may be that the current offence is too broad a limitation. It may be necessary to re-examine the ambit of the offence to see if it is the least restrictive alternative for protecting the sanctity of the judicial process. It would seem doubtful that at the present time this offence could meet the strict standard of justification required by *Oakes*.[60]

7. BANS ON THE PUBLICATION OF EVIDENCE

The courts have also had occasion to consider other aspects of the trial process where orders have been made to prohibit the publication of evidence, generally for a temporary period of time. In *Re Global Communications Ltd. and California*,[61] the Ontario Court of Appeal upheld an order made at a bail hearing for Catherine Smith, who was seeking to avoid extradition to the United States, where she was accused of murdering

---

58 *Bridges v. California*, 314 U.S. 252 at 270 (1941).
59 *Re Ont. Film & Video Appreciation Soc. and Ont. Bd. of Censors* (1984), 7 C.R.R. 129 (Ont. C.A.).
60 *Supra*, note 32.
61 (1984), 7 C.R.R. 22 (Ont. C.A.).

John Belushi. The order made was to prohibit publication of any evidence taken at the bail hearing until she was discharged or her hearing in California was concluded. The plaintiff alleged that section 457.2(1) of the *Criminal Code* which permitted such an order, was an arbitrary infringement on the right of freedom of expression. This provision again required an order to be made upon application, irrespective of the evidence presented. The court noted that it was indeed true that such an order would not be permitted in the United States, but then went on to make the important point that the United States has other procedures, such as more searching examination of jurors and sequestration of juries, which minimizes the impact of advance publicity. In Canada, however, these measures are not as stringent. Fundamentally though, each country aims to ensure that an accused is given a fair trial despite the differences in the approach taken to achieve this result. In deciding that the order should stand, the court emphasized that proceedings were still open to the public and that the ban, unlike some of the other cases, was only temporary. In balancing the interest, the court indicated that this evidence may cause severe prejudice to an accused person who is attempting to obtain a fair trial. The court seemed to ignore the fact that it was a mandatory order and seemed to be particularly influenced by the fact that it was temporary and that access to the court was still open. There are some difficulties, however, in rationalizing this with *Southam*,[62] where the court was concerned that judges were left with no discretion to assess the particular degree of prejudice in each case. While a temporary ban may be less restrictive, no demonstration was made that it was necessary to impose a ban in every case where an application is made to ensure a fair trial. It would appear to be more consistent with the guarantee in section 2(b) if a determination was to be made in each individual case similar to the position taken is cases such as *Southam*.

　　Similarly, in *R. v. Banville*,[63] a New Brunswick Court of Queen's Bench upheld the validity of section 467(1) of the *Criminal Code* which again permitted an order, upon application, banning evidence introduced at the preliminary inquiry until the conclusion of the case. While the court expressed some concern about the mandatory nature of these orders, it did say that the order was temporary, that the hearing was open and that, if any interest were to be given paramountcy, it must be the right to a fair trial.

　　However, in *R. v. Sophonow*,[64] the Court of Appeal refused to grant an order restricting the publication of extra-judicial commentary concern-

---

62 *Supra*, note 45.

63 (1983), 5 C.R.R. 142 (N.B. Q.B.).

64 (1983), 34 C.R. (3d) 287 (Man. C.A.), aff'd (1984), 11 C.R.R. 183 (S.C.C.).

ing Sophonow's guilt or innocence pending his appeal. While the court criticized the media for the excess in their stories, they refused to make a blanket order on the basis that such an order would be equivalent to censorship. In that case, the court was, no doubt, affected by the fact that the appeal court should not be influenced by the stories and that the commentary did not relate to portions of a trial that were in progress.

In general though, the courts to date have taken a fairly balanced approach to section 2(b) as it relates to court proceedings. They have made it clear that openness is an essential aspect of any trial, but they have been prepared to protect interests such as protection of juveniles and the fair trial of an accused. On the whole, the courts have not followed the United States' approach in this area of giving deference to freedom of speech and finding alternative ways to ensure a fair trial. In fact, in some cases the courts have emphasized their desire to create a uniquely Canadian approach which is more in keeping with Canadian tradition and values. There is no question, however, that in this area the courts have engaged in a balancing process rather than making any effort to restrict the ambit of the freedom guaranteed in section 2(b).

8. PRIVACY

Similarly, the courts have been willing to recognize privacy interests, although only where the protection is necessary. In *Canadian Newspapers Co. v. A.G. Canada*,[65] a challenge was made to section 443.2(1), a new provision of the *Criminal Code*. This provision prohibited publication of any information in certain search warrants that related to the location of the place to be searched or the identity of persons in the place, without having the consent of every person mentioned, unless a charge had been laid in respect of any offence in relation to which the warrant was issued. The court indicated that, while privacy was important, as mentioned in *MacIntyre*,[66] freedom of expression was a very important value which should not be readily infringed upon. In conclusion, the court stated that, while the objective was valid, the means chosen were unduly restrictive of freedom of expression, and therefore, the provision offends the Charter. It is interesting to speculate, as a consequence of this decision and *MacIntyre*, on what might be considered a privacy interest which would override freedom of expression or a fair trial when it relates to the trial process.

In *Re R. and Several Unnamed Persons*,[67] the court refused to prohibit

---

65 *Supra*, note 56.
66 *Supra*, note 47.
67 (1983), 44 O.R. (2d) 81 (H.C.).

publication of the names of some men charged with gross indecency despite the effect this might have upon their private lives. The court stressed that openness in the context of criminal trials is considered necessary to protect the integrity of the process. Obviously, the court was not prepared to see this as a privacy interest merely because the nature of the offence in question would result in strong societal condemnation.

9. HATE PROPAGANDA

The hate propaganda provisions of the *Criminal Code* and those relating to the spread of false information raise difficult freedom of expression issues. The Special Committee on Hate Propaganda in Canada, which was chaired by Maxwell Cohen, pointed out the need for such provisions.[68] After referring to the atrocities committed in Italy and Germany where false propaganda had spread hatred, the Committee went on to say that "[b]oth experience and the changing circumstances of the age require us to look with great care at abuses of freedom of expression".[69]

Since the Charter came into force, the courts have been faced with several instances of individuals who were allegedly promoting hatred or spreading false information about the holocaust. The first case was that of an Alberta school teacher, James Keegstra, who was charged under section 281.2(2) of the *Criminal Code* with wilfully promoting hatred against an identifiable group.[70] Keegstra challenged section 281.2 of the *Criminal Code* on the basis that it was an unjustifiable infringement of section 2(b) of the Charter. The court approached this question by first examining whether there had been an infringement of section 2(b). The court stated that freedom of expression relates to the willingness of society to tolerate criticism of its fundamental values and institutions, but that section 281.2(2) of the Code is not a proscription against freedom to criticize national institutions, but rather deals with a social value which is to protect groups of individuals from being the victims of wilful promotion of hatred. The court went on to point out that the Charter and the *Canadian Bill of Rights* were premised upon respect for moral and spiritual values and the dignity and worth of the human person. To be certain, while these are general statements of principle, section 15 of the Charter embodies many of these by guaranteeing a right of equality. In the end, Quigley J. concluded that section 281.2(2) cannot be considered as an infringement upon freedom of expression but rather as a safeguard which promotes it:

---

68 *Report of the Special Committee on Hate Propaganda in Canada*, 1966.
69 *Ibid.*
70 *R. v. Keegstra* (1984), 19 C.C.C (3d) 254 (Alta. Q.B.).

> The protection afforded by the proscription tends to banish the apprehension which might otherwise inhibit certain segments of our society from freely expressing themselves upon the whole spectrum of topics whether social, economic, scientific, political, religious or spiritual in nature. The unfettered right to express divergent opinions on these topics is the kind of freedom of expression the Charter protects.[71]

These comments by Quigley J. make it difficult to rationalize the judge's conclusion since the topics he mentioned are the very subject of Mr. Keegstra's comments. It appears that, according to Quigley J., discourse will be expression provided the content of the religious, political, etc., commentary is acceptable. As discussed earlier, the United States courts have made distinctions with respect to the content of expression which has created problems and resulted in artificial distinctions being made. It is difficult to comprehend how Keegstra's statements could not be characterized as expression. Clearly, the judge is correct in pointing out that freedom of expression is limited and that section 15 giving a right to equality must be balanced against the right to freedom of expression in section 2. It would seem more appropriate to engage in this balancing, however, in section 1 after acknowledging that Keegstra's expression is covered within section 2(b). Section 1 provides the mechanism for ensuring that the dignity and worth of individuals is considered when assessing the validity of any limitation placed upon a right. Under section 1, the court could weigh the objective of protecting groups from hatred against the need to protect freedom of expression. This latter approach, as discussed earlier in this chapter, would permit the courts to take a uniform approach to freedom of expression. It would also be a recognition that freedom of expression is important beyond its relationship to the functioning of democratic institutions.

Similarly, in *R. v. Zundel*,[72] the court chose to exclude Zundel's writings and comments from the application of the guarantee in section 2(b). Zundel was charged with publishing a tale that he knew to be false. The court, however, looked at the past history of freedom of expression and determined that the word freedom was only intended to encompass the area "free from regulation".

Both these cases illustrate the difficulty experienced by the courts when they are confronted with unpleasant forms of expression. While the majority of Canadians would, no doubt, find the speeches and writings of Zundel and Keegstra to be unacceptable or reprehensible, it is equally clear that majority views are not what should be used to determine the ambit of the freedom of expression guarantees in section 2. If minority views are

---

71 *Ibid.* at 268.
72 *Supra*, note 19.

to be meaningful, speech should only be limited where an overriding value is at stake and this should be done through the mechanisms provided by section 1 of the Charter. The courts have an opportunity to avoid the trap of trying to exclude unpopular or unpleasant speech from the ambit of section 2. If hate propaganda provisions are justifiable, it should be because they recognize other overriding objectives and are not restrictive beyond what is necessary to protect those interests, not because hate propaganda does not constitute speech.

10. OBSCENITY

The question of pornography or obscenity has long been of concern to Canadians. In recent years however, there has been an increasingly strong reaction against pornography by feminist groups and others concerned about the effects pornography may have on how men view women and children.[73] At the same time, not all feminists have urged that freedom of expression should be restricted in order to ban obscene material.[74] Increasing incidences of sexual assault against women and children has reopened this debate and sent parliamentarians scrambling to find new ways to deal with pornography in Canada.

The Fraser Committee report to the government was a hard look at the issue in Canada and the feelings of Canadians toward this subject.[75] The Fraser Committee concluded that there were two kinds of harm flowing from pornography. These were the offence done to the public, who were involuntarily subject to it, and a broader social harm which undermines the right to equality in section 15 of the Charter. At the same time in the United States, the courts and governments were also trying to find new ways to deal with the subject. In fact, the Attorney General's Commission on Pornography in the United States recently supported a national attack on pornography, concluding that there had been a dramatic increase in pornographic material in that country and harm could result from exposure to this material.[76]

The *Criminal Code* has contained a prohibition against the sale and

---

73 See, *e.g.*, L. Lederer, ed., *Take Back the Night: Women on Pornography* (New York: Bantam Books, 1980); Colloquium, "Violent Pornography: Degradation of Women versus Right of Free Speech" (1978), 8 *N.Y.U. Rev. Law & Soc. Change* 181.

74 See V. Burstyn, ed., *Women Against Censorship* (Douglas & McIntyre, 1985). This book is a collection written by a number of Canadian feminists who argue that, while violent pornography is indeed harmful and pornography degrades women, censorship is not the solution and in fact can also work against feminist forms of expression.

75 *Report of the Special Committee on Pornography and Prostitution*, Canada, 1985.

76 Attorney General's Commission on Pornography, U.S. Dept. of Justice, *Final Report* (1986).

distribution of obscene material for a number of years. In 1959, the Code was amended to include a definition of obscenity to assist Canadians to know when they might be in contravention of the law.[77] The new definition, however, proved to be anything but a simplified method of ascertaining whether material is obscene. For example, to determine if a book or piece of art is obscene, the section requires that one of the dominant characteristics must be the undue exploitation of sex. This will depend upon the author's purpose, the literary or artistic merit of the work and whether the work offends against community standards.[78] The test of community standards is a very difficult one since it will vary from region to region.[79] In all the cases involving the *Criminal Code*, the primary focus was an attempt to ascertain whether the material in question was obscene. In the majority of the cases, no concern was expressed for the freedom of expression issue, although Justice Freedman, in *Dominion News*,[80] did raise some concerns when he emphasized that in borderline cases tolerance was to be preferred to proscription, because suppression of a publication that is not clearly obscene may have repercussions and implications beyond what is immediately visible by inhibiting creative impulses and endeavours which ought to be encouraged in a free society.

However, since the Charter came into force in 1982, the courts have been forced to grapple with not only trying to find whether material is obscene, but also with assessing the impact of obscenity laws on the guarantees of freedom of expression in section 2(b). This is a difficult task because obscenity, like abortion, is a very emotional topic with very strong views expressed by the opposing parties in the debate. There are those who argue that the publication or dissemination of obscene material should only be limited when it can be shown that other interests clearly override.[81] Others indicated that obscene publications or statements are not a form of expression and are therefore not worthy of protection under section 2(b).[82] Little assistance can be gleaned from the American courts since they are still struggling with this issue. As mentioned earlier in *Roth*

---

77 S. 159(8) [163(8)] of the Code states: "For the purposes of this Act, any publication a dominant characteristic of which is the undue exploitation of sex, or of sex and any one or more of the following subjects, namely, crime, horror, cruelty and violence, shall be deemed to be obscene."

78 See *Brodie v. R.*, [1962] S.C.R. 681; *Dechow v. R.* (1977), 35 C.C.C. (2d) 22 (S.C.C.).

79 *R. v. Dom. News & Gifts Ltd.*, [1963] 2 C.C.C. 103 (Man. C.A.), rev'd [1964] S.C.R. 251. The dissent of Freedman J.A. was upheld by the Supreme Court of Canada.

80 *Ibid.* at 117.

81 See, *e.g.*, Burstyn, *supra*, note 74.

82 See, *e.g.* K. Lahey, "The Charter and Pornography; Toward A Restricted Theory of Constitutionally Protected Expression" in J.M. Weiler and R.M. Elliot, *Litigating the Values of a Nation: The Canadian Charter of Rights and Freedoms* (Toronto: Carswell, 1986), p. 265.

v. United States,[83] the United States Supreme Court held that obscenity was not worthy of protection under the First Amendment. While in *Miller v. California*[84] the Supreme Court articulated a definition of obscenity that was similar to that in Canada, the court did not specify any clear approach to obscenity and the First Amendment.

Some of the earlier cases under the Charter dealt with censorship laws. In *Re Ontario Film & Video Appreciation Society and Ontario Board of Censors*,[85] the challenge was to sections 3(2)(a), 35 and 38 of the Ontario *Theatres Act*.[86] This Act granted the Ontario Board of Censors power to "censor any film" and "subject to the regulations, to approve, prohibit or regulate the exhibition of any film in Ontario". All films had to be submitted to the Board and no film could be shown unless it was approved by the Board. The court was quick to quash the decision of the Board relating to the film "Amerika". According to the court, there was no need to strike down the provisions of the *Theatres Act*, but merely to state that they could not be used to censor films because, in the absence of criteria, they are too broad. In expressing concern about the impact on freedom of expression the court made it clear that the freedom of expression of the viewer as well as the exhibitor was at stake when censorship laws were used. Again the court made it explicit that all forms of expression, whether "oral, written, pictorial, sculpture, music, dance or film" are equally protected by the Charter. Therefore, there was no question that the section 2(b) protections encompassed the exhibition of films. The court used the "prescribed by law" limitation in section 1 to ascertain that the lack of criteria made it impossible for the government to justify the actions of the censor board.

Similarly in *Re Luscher and Deputy M.N.R. Customs and Excise*,[87] the court was faced by a challenge to a statutory prohibition of the importation of obscene materials. Section 14 of the *Customs Tariff*[88] prohibits the importation of:

> Books, printed paper, drawings, paintings, prints, photographs or representations of any kind of a treasonable or seditious, or of an immoral or indecent character.

In this case, the court seemed to accept that the material aimed at was a form of expression encompassed by section 2(b) because they immediately proceeded to focus on the question whether it was a reasonable

---

83 *Supra*, note 9.
84 *Supra*, note 13.
85 (1983), 5 C.R.R. 373 (Ont. Div. Ct.), aff'd *supra*, note 59.
86 R.S.O. 1980, c. 498.
87 (1985), 15 C.R.R. 167 (F.C.A.).
88 R.S.C. 1970, c. C-41.

limit. The court determined that the words "immoral" or "indecent" were much too broad to meet the requirement of "prescribed by law", since in their present form they could exclude all kinds of speech because they were not defined. Second, the court went on to say that those words *were* highly subjective and emotional in their content. As a consequence, this provision cannot be supported as a reasonable limit. In making their determination, the court was quick to point out that section 2(b) is designed to protect thought, expression and depiction, not acts or deeds. This is an important fact because it is essential in determining acceptable limits; there will be much greater tolerance of thought and expression than action. Finally, in *Information Retailers Association of Metropolitan Toronto*,[89] the question related to a bylaw which regulated the sale of adult books and magazines. The bylaw defined an "adult book or magazine" as one which: (1) portrays or depicts by means of photographs, drawings or otherwise, female breasts, any person's pubic perineal and perianal areas and buttocks and (2) appeals to, or is designed to appeal to erotic or sexual appetites or inclinations. The bylaw required a licence and required these books to be displayed in a special way. The court determined that, while freedom of expression is important, sometimes another value such as protection of children permits of reasonable limitations. In this case, while the court agreed with the principle, they held that the bylaw was overly broad and would discourage the display of books that might be borderline. Thus, the bylaw would have to be redrafted to be more specific. Both of these cases demonstrate the need for precision when imposing limitations on rights. This can create problems for legislators who must struggle to find language that is precise enough but which still captures the values to be protected.

Yet when a serious challenge was made to section 159(8) of the *Criminal Code*, even though the courts had indicated that laws must not be vague, they held that section 159(8) test did not infringe this requirement.[90] The British Columbia Court of Appeal, in *Red Hot Video*,[91] seemed to accept that obscenity was a form of speech and went on to assess whether section 159(8) was an infringement of section 1 of the Charter.

The court held that there was nothing vague about the community standards test even though community standards may vary. Anderson J. said it was clear that depictions of violent sex or sex involving children

---

89 *Information Retailers Assn. of Metro. Toronto Inc. v. Metro. Toronto*; *Cdn. Periodical Publishers Assn. v. Metro Toronto* (1985), 22 D.L.R. (4th) 161 (Ont. C.A.) (on appeal to S.C.C.).

90 *R. v. Red Hot Video Ltd.* (1985), 18 C.C.C. (3d) 1 (B.C. C.A.), leave to appeal to S.C.C. refused (1985), 46 C.R. (3d) xxv (note) (S.C.C.).

91 *Ibid.*

results in substantial harm to the community and is justifiably prohibited. This decision raises the question of why the *Customs Tariff*[92] provision was judged to be too vague when another provision also containing a broad definition is not considered to be too vague. One reassuring feature of this and some of the other cases relating to obscenity is that the courts in general have accepted obscenity as a form of speech and have sought to test the validity pursuant to section 1 rather than excluding it from the ambit of protection under section 1. For example, in *R. v. Wagner*,[93] the court determined that the limit imposed by section 159 of the *Criminal Code* was a reasonable limit within the meaning of section 1 of the Charter. The court emphasized that the contemporary Canadian community is not prepared to tolerate sexually violent pornography involving the overt infliction of pain and the overt use of force or the threat of either, nor will it tolerate sexually explicit pornography that is degrading. This is reflected in the community standards test evolved pursuant to section 159 of the *Criminal Code*. While the courts seem to be prepared to strike down broad discretion if there appears to be some general criteria, the courts have accepted these as reasonable for the purposes of section 1. It might be noted that many of these cases were decided before *Oakes*[94] articulated stringent criteria for meeting the requirements of section 1.

If the Supreme Court continues to adhere to its position in *Oakes*, it is conceivable that the courts may move to exclude obscenity from the ambit of section 2(b) in the same manner as hate propaganda was excluded in *Zundel*.[95] This would be very unfortunate since the present approach to the obscenity provisions is consistent with a uniform theory of freedom of expression.

11. OTHER AREAS

The courts have also been asked to make important decisions relating to freedom of expression in areas concerning airports, language of commercial activities, activities of public servants, election activities and labour matters such as in *Dolphin Delivery*.[96]

---

92 *Supra*, note 88.
93 (1985), 43 C.R. (3d) 318 (Alta. Q.B.), aff'd. (1986), 50 C.R. (3d) 175 (Alta. C.A.), leave to appeal to S.C.C. refused (1986), 50 C.R. (3d) 175n (S.C.C.). See also *R. v. Ramsingh* (1984), 14 C.C.C. (3d) 230 (Man. Q.B.).
94 *Supra*, note 32.
95 *Supra*, note 19.
96 *Supra*, note 1.

12. ELECTION EXPENSES

In an early decision entitled *National Citizens' Coalition Inc. v. Attorney General Canada*,[97] the plaintiffs brought an action for a declaration that section 72 of the *Canada Elections Act*,[98] which prohibited the printing, distribution and posting of any election literature unless it bore the name and authorization of a registered political party or candidate, and section 70.1(1) which prohibited anyone other than registered parties or candidates from incurring election expenses, conflicted with section 2(b) of the Charter. The court held that the sections in question, on their face, imposed a limitation on the actions of anyone other than registered parties or candidates. Freedom of expression, according to the court, is a significant value and is of particular importance at election times. While the justification offered was that this was necessary to ensure a level of equality amongst all participants in federal elections, the court refused to accept this as sufficient to override freedom of expression. It appeared that there was not sufficient evidence to support the need for such a provision which imposed limitations upon freedom of expression that pertained to elections — a fundamental matter in a democracy.

13. LANGUAGE OF COMMERCIAL ACTIVITY

In *Procureur Général du Québec v. Chaussure Brown's Inc.*,[99] a challenge was made to the provisions of Bill 101,[100] which requires that all signs, placards, etc. and commercial advertising be exclusively in French in the province of Quebec. A challenge was made on the basis that this provision was an infringement of the freedom of expression guarantees in both section 2(b) of the *Canadian Charter of Rights and Freedoms* and those in the Quebec *Charter of Human Rights and Freedoms*.[101] On January 2, 1985, the Quebec Superior Court had struck down the provisions on the basis that they were an infringement of the guarantees in the Quebec Charter. The Quebec Court of Appeal however, concluded that the provisions of Bill 101 infringed both the Quebec and Canadian Charters. In making this determination Justice Bisson, who gave the lead judgment, concluded that freedom of expression, as guaranteed by the Charters, includes the freedom to use the language of a person's choice. Similarly, following *Irwi Toy*,[102] he held that commercial expression was encompassed

---

97 (1984), 14 C.R.R. 61 (Alta. Q.B.).
98 R.S.C. 1970, c. 14 (1st Supp.).
99 [1987] R.J.Q. 80 (Que. C.A.), aff'd December 15, 1988 (S.C.C.).
100 *Charter of the French Language*, R.S.Q. 1977, c. C-11.
101 R.S.Q. 1977, c. C-12.
102 *Supra*, note 41.

within the section 2(b) protection. Finally, the court concluded that, although the Quebec government's objective of protecting the French language in Quebec was valid, the means chosen to achieve this was not proportional. In other words, allowing only signs in French was unduly restrictive of the right of freedom of expression and certainly not the only means to achieve the objective. The Supreme Court of Canada has been asked to consider an appeal in this decision.

14. FREEDOM OF EXPRESSION IN AIRPORTS

In March 1984, members of the Comité pour la république du Canada went to the airport at Dorval in Montreal to "discuss with the public the aims and objectives of the Comité", etc. The plaintiffs were asked to leave the airport because they were engaging in political propaganda. The plaintiffs sought a declaration that the defendant (Her Majesty The Queen), had not observed their fundamental freedom of expression and that the areas of the Montreal airport open to the public constitute a public forum for the exercise of fundamental freedoms. They succeeded at the trial level and this was appealed to the Federal Court of Appeal. There were three separate judgments in the Court of Appeal.[103] Mr. Justice Hugessen held that removal of the plaintiffs was a clear breach of freedom of expression since its sole purpose was to prevent dissemination by the plaintiffs of their political ideas. He held that there was no justification for telling the committee members to leave, but he was not prepared to hold that airports were a public forum. Justice MacGuigan held that the purpose and effect of the Department of Transport's policy on activities in airports was contrary to the Charter. He also held that, while the Department may have legitimate objectives relating to passage of individuals in airports, the means chosen here to achieve this were not proportional to the objective.

Justice Pratte, on the other hand, characterized the question in terms of use of property. He held that, since the airport was owned by the government, they had a right to restrict its use to certain purposes. He quoted from the Chief Justice's comments in *New Brunswick Broadcasting Co. v. CRTC*,[104] to the effect that the freedom guaranteed under section 2(b) of the Charter does not include the right to use someone else's property. As a consequence, he held that the committee was using the airport in a manner which was not intended and therefore they could not argue that their freedom of expression was infringed. This is a difficult argument,

---

103 *Ctee. for the Commonwealth of Can. v. Canada*, [1987] 2 F.C. 68 (F.C.C.A.), leave to appeal to S.C.C. granted (1987), 81 N.R. 86n (S.C.C.).

104 [1984] 2 F.C. 410 at 426 (F.C.A.), leave to appeal to S.C.C. granted (1984), 20 C.R.R. 28n (S.C.C.).

since it could lead to a very narrow interpretation of section 2(b) if issues are characterized as a property interest instead of a freedom of expression issue. Undoubtedly, this issue will ultimately be determined by the Supreme Court. It will be interesting, however, to see if the courts adopt a "public place" doctrine which limits governments' abilities to permissibly restrict the free exercise of expressive activities in areas such as streets and sidewalks and airports. This approach has been adopted by the United States Supreme Court with respect to places such as streets and sidewalks,[105] although they have not yet made a determination with respect to airports.

15. PUBLIC SERVANTS

The question of the political activities of public servants has given rise to a number of challenges. One particular case of note is *Fraser v. Attorney General Nova Scotia.*[106] In that case Fraser, a civil servant, sought a declaration that three sections, sections 34(2), 34(3) and 35(c) of the *Nova Scotia Civil Service Act,*[107] were an infringement of his rights under the Charter, including the right to freedom of expression. These provisions would have prevented him from joining a political party, attending meetings, associating with members, contributing financially or running for office. The court concluded that section 34(2), which prohibited civil servants from doing partisan work in connection with elections, was an unjustifiable limitation of freedom of expression. The court accepted, as in *Fraser v. Public Service Staff Relations Board,*[108] that political neutrality in the public service necessitates the placing of some restraints on partisan political activity. However, the provisions in Nova Scotia were much more restrictive than those in the federal Act.[109]

The issue of restrictions upon political activities of public servants is a difficult one and the subject of much debate; it is certain that this issue will continue to be litigated in the years to come.

16. CONCLUSION

It is apparent from a survey of cases since the Charter that the freedom

---

105 *United States v. Grace,* 103 S.Ct. 1702 (1982). See, on airports, *Jews for Jesus Inc. v. Bd. of Airport Commrs. of Los Angeles,* 783 F. 20 791 (1986, 9th circ.).

106 (1986), 74 N.S.R. (2d) 91 (T.D.). See also *Osborne v. Canada Treasury Bd.*), [1986] 3 F.C. 206 (F.C.T.D.), rev'd in part (July 15, 1988) Doc. No. A-542-86, A-543-86, A-556-86, (F.C.A.).

107 S.N.S. 1980, c. 3.

108 *Supra,* note 3.

109 *Public Service Staff Relations Act,* R.S.C. 1970, c. P-35, s. 91(1).

of expression guarantee raises many complex and difficult issues. A number of these issues will be before the Supreme Court of Canada in the coming months.

Certainly, from the cases to date it is clear that the courts have not developed a uniform theory of freedom of expression. They appear to be very willing to protect expression that relates to the process of government or to ensuring that judicial proceedings are open to the public to ensure abuses do not occur. These forms of expression have also traditionally been protected in Canada. As a consequence, decisions in these areas tend to be reasonably consistent with past jurisprudence and are also consistent with a theory of demanding that the limitations on freedom of expression be assessed pursuant to section 1 of the Charter.

On the other hand, challenges have occurred and will, no doubt, continue to occur in relation to areas such as hate propaganda, commercial expression and obscenity. Some of the decisions, as pointed out earlier, give cause for concern that the courts may be headed in a direction followed by the United States courts, of excluding entire categories of expression from the protection of section 2(b).

It will be necessary for the Supreme Court to give direction in these areas, because there is still an opportunity to develop a uniform theory of expression and to avoid the pitfalls experienced by the United States courts. In that context it may be necessary for the courts to deviate somewhat from the stringent criteria adopted in *Oakes*[110] to determine if a limitation is reasonable to ensure that section 1 is the mechanism for ensuring that the limitation is valid.

---

110 *Supra*, note 32.

7

Freedom of Peaceful Assembly and Freedom of Association
(*Section 2(c) and (d)*)

Ken Norman

1. FREEDOM OF PEACEFUL ASSEMBLY

> [T]he basic problem is one of compromise between public order and convenience on the one hand and individual liberty on the other. Throughout the analysis of this problem, however, there is assumed as a general proposition that a broad right of peaceable assembly is a vital element in the maintenance of the democratic process.[1]

Standing in sharp contrast are the following holdings of the majority of the Supreme Court of Canada in *Dupond*:

> Demonstrations are not a form of speech but of collective action. They

---

1 M.G. Abernathy, *The Right of Assembly and Association*, 2nd ed. (U. of S. Carolina Press, 1981) at 4.

are of the nature of a display of force rather than of that of an appeal to reason; their inarticulateness prevents them from becoming part of language and from reaching the level of discourse.

. . .The right to hold public meetings on a highway or is a park in unknown to English law. Far from being the object of a right, the holding of a public meeting on a street or in a park may constitute a trespass against the urban authority in whom the ownership of the street is vested even though no one is obstructed and no injury is done; it may also amount to a nuisance.

. . .

Being unknown to English law, the right to hold public meetings on the public domain of a city did not become part of the Canadian Constitution under the preamble of the *British North America Act, 1867.*[2]

Dupond has been the subject of a good deal of criticism, both before and after the proclamation of the new fundamental freedom of peaceful assembly.[3] Berger's conclusion, authored two years before the *Canadian Charter of Rights and Freedoms*, applies *a fortiorari* in the effort to make some Canadian sense of section 2(c):

The Supreme Court in the 1980s will be forced to grapple with the ramifications of its judgment in *Dupond* in any consideration of the true nature of Canadian democracy.[4]

The court has yet to come to grips with section 2(c). Some indication of what it might say, however, can be derived from its *Dolphin Delivery* judgment.[5] McIntyre J. speaking for the court, except for Beetz J. on this point, expressed the opinion that there is always some element of expression in picketing. In other words, contrary to *Dupond*, demonstrations do indeed reach the level of constitutionally protected discourse.

The union is making a statement to the general public that it is involved in a dispute, that it is seeking to impose its will on the object of the picketing,

---

2 *A.G. Can. v. Dupond,* [1978] 2 S.C.R. 770 at 797-798, *per* Beetz J. for the majority.
3 K. Swinton, "Comments" (1979), 57 *Can. Bar Rev.* 326; C.F. Beckton, "A.G. for Canada v. Claire Dupond: The Right to Assemble in Canada?" (1979), 5 *Dalhousie L.J.* 169; T.R. Berger, "The Supreme Court and Fundamental Freedoms: The Renunciation of the Legacy of Mr. Justice Rand"(1980), 1 *Supreme Court L. Rev.* 460; I. Cotler, "Freedom of Assembly, Association, Conscience and Religion", in the first edition of W.S. Tarnopolsky & G.A. Beaudoin, *Canadian Charter of Rights and Freedoms: Commentary* (Toronto: Carswell, 1982), c. 6; E. Vogt, "Dupond Reconsidered: Or the "Search for the Constitution and the Truth of Things Generally", [1982] *U.B.C. L. Rev.(Charter ed.)* 141; R. Stoykewych, "Street Legal: Constitutional Protection of Public Demonstration in Canada"(1985), 43 *U. T. Fac. L. Rev.* 43; and D. Holland, "Freedom of Expression in Public Places, A Constitutional Comparison" (L.L.M. thesis, University of Toronto, 1985) [unpublished] at 195 *et seq.*
4 Berger, *ibid.* at 467.
5 *R.W.D.S.U., Local 580 v. Dolphin Delivery Ltd.,* [1986] 2 S.C.R. 573.

and that it solicits the assistance of the public in honouring the picket line. Action on the part of the picketers will, of course, always accompany the expression, but not every action on the part of the picketers will be such as to alter the nature of the whole transaction and remove it from *Charter* protection for freedom of expression.[6]

That *Dolphin Delivery* was treated as an expression case does not detract from its importance to section 2(c). As MacGuigan has pointed out, freedom of assembly is best regarded as an aspect of freedom of expression.[7] What seems to follow from McIntyre J.'s *dictum* is that a distinct Canadian course may well be set on the matter of picketing as a constitutionally protected activity. The distinction between "speech" and "conduct" which has emerged in recent years in American doctrine was argued in *Dolphin Delivery*[8] but is implicitly rejected by the court.

(a) American Doctrine Respecting Picketing

The Supreme Court of the United States came down strongly in support of picketing as a constitutionally protected activity in *Thornhill.*[9] An Alabama statute which banned all forms of labour picketing, under which Thornhill was convicted, did not pass muster with the court. Mr. Justice Murphy linked picketing to a basic tenet of democracy in these words:

> Free discussion concerning the conditions in industry and the causes of labour disputes appears to us indispensable to the effective and intelligent use of the processes of popular government to shape the destiny of modern industrial society. The issues raised by regulations, such as are challenged here, infringing upon the right of employees effectively to inform the public of the facts of a labour dispute, are part of this larger problem.[10]

This sweeping assertion that picketing was a form of protected speech was weakened by two doctrines fashioned over the years since *Thornhill.* First, at least in labour disputes, picketing which combines speech with action has been held to be without constitutional protection.[11] Second, if the picketers have an "unlawful objective", the picket line may well run afoul of statutory prohibitions which will withstand judicial review under

---

6 *Ibid.* at 588.

7 M. R. MacGuigan, "Hate Control and Freedom of Assembly" (1966), 31 *Sask. Bar Rev.* 232.

8 *Supra*, note 5 at 587.

9 *Thornhill v. Alabama*, 310 U.S. 88 (1940).

10 *Ibid.* at 102.

11 *N.L.R.B. B. v. Fruit & Vegetable Packers & Warehousemen*, 377 U.S. 58 (1964); *Bakery & Pastry Drivers v. Wohl*, 315 U.S. 769 (1942). That this "speech-plus-conduct" doctrine seems not to apply outside the field of labour disputes is demonstrated in *U.S. v. O'Brien*, 391 U.S. 367 (1968).

the American *Bill of Rights*.[12] This narrowing of *Thornhill* has been criticized as bordering on a retreat,[13] but it does reveal the Supreme Court of the United States to be engaged in a delicate balancing process.[14]

(b) American Right of Assembly Doctrine Generally

Mr. Justice Powell's concurring opinion in *Spock*[15] outlines the settled framework of analysis engaged in by the Supreme Court of the United States in right of assembly cases. Like other First Amendment rights, right of assembly is not absolute but may be circumscribed when necessary to further a sufficiently strong public interest.

> But our decisions properly emphasize that any significant restriction of First Amendment freedoms carries a heavy burden of justification.[16]

In striking the balance, the court has often divided, as it did in *Spock*, but it usually does so by asking itself the question "whether the manner of expression is basically incompatible with the normal activity of a particular place at a particular time."[17] In *Spock*, the majority of the court found that Dr. Benjamin Spock and his colleagues in The People's Party and Socialist Workers' Party enjoyed no generalized constitutional right to make political speeches or distribute leaflets on the Fort Dix military reserve.

The vigorous political activism, fueled first by the civil rights movement and then by opposition to the war in Vietnam, involved the Supreme Court of the United States in several opportunities to think again about the doctrine in *Cox*,[18] which permits a local authority to require that a licence or permit be obtained before holding a parade. In *Shut-*

---

12 *N.L.R.B. v. Retail Store Employees Union*, 447 U.S. 607 (1980). The Supreme Court refused to protect a consumer picket line because it threatened a third party business with ruin.

13 J. Etelson, "Picketing and Freedom of Speech: Comes the Evolution" (1976), 10 *John Marshall Jo. of Prac. & Proc.* 1.

14 As what must now stand simply as pre-Charter historical footnote, the majority of the Supreme Court of Canada flatly rejected an invitation to engage in such an exercise in *Harrison v. Carswell*, [1976] 2 S.C.R. 200 at 218-219, *per* Dickson J.

15 *Greer v. Spock*, 96 S. Ct. 1211 (1976).

16 *Ibid.* at 1220.

17 *Grayned v. City of Rockford*, 408 U.S. 104 at 116 (1972).

18 *Cox v. New Hampshire*, 312 U.S. 569 (1941). For criticism of the *Cox* doctrine which allows a local authority to impose a tax or fee for a parade licence or permit, see D. Goldberger, "A Reconsideration of Cox v. New Hampshire: Can Demonstrators Be Required to Pay the Costs of Using America's Public Forums?" (1983), 62 *Texas L. Rev.* 403.

tlesworth,[19] a parade ordinance which left a Police Commissioner with the authority to arbitrarily deny a permit was struck down. In *Gregory*,[20] a Chicago ordinance which prohibited such things as collecting in crowds to the annoyance or disturbance of other persons did not pass muster. In *Jeanette Rankin Brigade*,[21] a coalition of women against the war in Vietnam who wanted to march on Capitol Hill successfully challenged a statute which prohibited all assemblies aimed at publicizing a party, organization or movement.

The high-water mark of this doctrine is generally regarded to be the *Skokie* decision of the Illinois Supreme Court.[22] The proposed parade of Nazis through Jewish neighbourhoods containing many survivors of the holocaust was initially enjoined on the ground of the "fighting words" doctrine. But the court quashed the injunction, ruling that even the anticipation of a hostile audience would not justify a prior restraint of the proposed parade. Ordinances passed by the village of Skokie designed to curb the proposed street activities of the Nazis were eventually struck down by the Seventh Circuit Court of Appeals.[23] Abernathy sums up the developing doctrine concerning the right of assembly in these words:

> With the exception of assemblies in private shopping centres, the protections afforded by the decisions of the Court to the right of assembly in the past two decades have at least remained firm and, in some instances, have been broadened. Demonstrations and picketing are increasingly, being used as tools of interest groups to attempt to influence public opinion and, ultimately, public policy.
>
> The decisions of the United States Supreme Court have come down strongly on the side of protection to such assemblies as long as the purposes and conduct are lawful and the times and places are not inappropriate for such gatherings. . . . [G]overnmental restrictions, to be upheld, must be shown to accomplish justifiable ends with the least feasible impediment to the exercise of that right.[24]

(c) Criminal and Quasi-Criminal Prohibitions

Unlawful assemblies and riots are proscribed in sections 64 to 69

---

19 *Shuttlesworth v. Birmingham*, 394 U.S. 147 (1969).

20 *Gregory v. Chicago*, 394 U.S. 111 (1969).

21 *Jeanette Rankin Brigade v. Chief of Capitol Police*, 342 F. Supp. 575 (1972).

22 *Village of Skokie v. National Socialist Party of America*, 373 N.E. 21 (Ill. App. Ct., 1977).

23 *Collin v. Smith*, 578 F.2d 1197 (1978). The Supreme Court refused leave to appeal in *Smith v. Collin*, 439 U.S. 916 (1978). The court had clearly made the point in *Brown v. Louisiana*, 383 U.S. 131 (S.C. 1966) that the mere threat or likelihood of violence from onlookers put a burden on the police to control the crowd. It did not serve as a warrant to curtail the proposed parade. See "Note: Free Speech and the Hostile Audience" (1951), 26 *N.Y.U.L. Rev.* 489.

24 *Supra*, note 1 at 266.

[63-68], 745 [810] and 746 [811] of the *Criminal Code*.[25] Section 64 is
of particular interest because it requires the Crown to prove that someone
was fearful, on reasonable grounds, rather than prove the fact of a
tumultuous disturbance of the peace.[26]

> 64. (1) An unlawful assembly is an assembly of three or more persons who,
> with intent to carry out any common purpose, assemble in such a manner
> or so conduct themselves when they are assembled as to cause persons in
> the neighbourhood of the assembly to fear, on reasonable grounds, that they
> (a) will disturb the peace tumultuously . . .

Stoykewych has argued that what emerged as doctrine under section 64
[63] and its predecessor, is a sort of "heckler's veto"[27] which, fifty years
ago, was established in a line of successful prosecutions of assemblies of
unemployed workers.[28] If the Supreme Court of Canada adopts a test which
at all resembles that of the American Supreme Court, this section will
not stand.[29] In addition, the *Criminal Code* creates an offence of causing
a public disturbance in section 171 [175]. As well, the offence of obstructing
a police officer in the execution of his duty of keeping the peace or in
anticipation of a breach of the peace, created by section 118 [129], has
obvious implications for any sort of robust public assembly.

Quasi-criminal municipal bylaws and ordinances frequently have
something to say about public assemblies. They range from the outright
ban of *Dupond*,[30] where the City of Montreal passed an ordinance
prohibiting "the holding of any assembly, parade or gathering on the public
domain of the City of Montreal for a time-period of 30 days" to an "anti-
noise" bylaw of the City of Vancouver in *Harrold*,[31] which prohibited any
objectionable noise "either in or on a public or private place or premises
in such a manner as to disturb the quiet, peace, rest or enjoyment of the
neighbourhood, or of persons in the vicinity, or the comfort or convenience
of the public". Neither Claire Dupond nor Mr. Harrold and his colleagues
in the International Society for Krishna Consciousness (Canada) Ltd. were
successful in their attempts to attack these restrictive regulations. Similarly,
a challenge to a Toronto bylaw banning meetings in certain parks held
without permission as to time and place being first obtained from a
Commissioner of Parks, received short shrift from McRuer C.J.H.C. in

---

25 R.S.C. 1970, c. C-34 [R.S.C. 1985, c. C-46].

26 Cotler, *supra*, note 3 at 144.

27 *Supra*, note 3 at 55-56.

28 *Ibid.* at 78.

29 See *Skokie, supra*, note 22.

30 *Supra*, note 2 at 784.

31 *R. v. Harrold*, [1971] 3 W.W.R. 365 at 366 (B.C.C.A.), leave to appeal to S.C.C. refused
3 C.C.C. (2d) 387n (S.C.C.).

Campbell.[32] In *Saumur*,[33] a Quebec City bylaw requiring that printed materials could only be distributed on the streets with the prior written permission of the Chief of Police, barely withstood scrutiny by a badly split Supreme Court. However, Saumur's conviction was quashed. All of this would simply astonish an American constitutional scholar.

Only one municipal restriction on assembly has failed to survive judicial scrutiny. In *Storgoff*,[34] a bylaw prohibiting a certain class of Doukhobors from entering the Municipality of Kent was struck down, on a division of powers analysis by the Supreme Court of British Columbia. But the judgment offers no support at all for freedom of assembly. It simply turns on the characterization of the bylaw as criminal in nature and thus within the competence of the federal Parliament and not the Municipality of Kent.

(d) Litigation Under Section 2(c)

There are only seven reported cases on the freedom of peaceful assembly. And, only two of these are at the appellate level. Three of the four cases which saw section 2(c) successfully relied upon are authored by Provincial and County Court judges. In *Butler*,[35] a federal inmate learned from the Trial Division of the Federal Court that section 2(c) was powerless to prevent his being transferred to another prison for reasons of security. Butler, who was an active member of a group seeking to practise aboriginal religious ceremonies, was said to possess no assembly rights such as to trump the institutional need to preserve discipline and security. In *Pitts Atlantic Construction*,[36] the Newfoundland Court of Appeal upheld a statute prohibiting secondary picketing by a labour union. The court found that freedom of assembly was not infringed because primary picketing was not prohibited. Thus, the impugned statute was characterized as simply regulating rather than prohibiting picketing by specifying the place and time when it could be lawfully undertaken. The British Columbia Court of Appeal approved an injunction preventing pickets from locating at the doors of court houses in the province in the *British Columbia Government Employees' Union* case.[37] Although the matter was not even argued, the

---

32 *R. v. Campbell* (1962), 35 D.L.R. (2d) 480. (Ont. H.C.), aff'd (1963), 38 D.L.R. (2d) 579 (Ont.C.A.).

33 *Saumur v. Quebec (City)*, [1953] 2 S.C.R. 299.

34 *Kent Dist. v. Storgoff* (1962), 38 D.L.R. (2d) 362 (B.C.S.C.).

35 *Butler v. R.* (1983), 5 C.C.C. (3d) 356 (F.C.T.D.).

36 *Re United Assn. of Journeymen & Apprentices of Plumbing Industry of U.S. and Canada, Loc. 740 and Pitts Atlantic Construction Ltd.* (1984), 7 D.L.R. (4th) 609 (Nfld. C.A.).

37 *B.C.G.E.U. v. A.G. British Columbia* (1985), 20 D.L.R. (4th) 399 (B.C.C.A.), aff'd [1988] 12 S.C.R. 214.

court ruled that it was prepared to assume that the injunction infringed the picketers' assembly and expression rights. It then easily justified such an incursion under section 1 in the name of "the public's unfettered right to access to the courts of justice".[38]

In *Fraser*,[39] the Supreme Court of Nova Scotia found provisions of the *Civil Service Act*,[40] which prohibited civil servants from assembling at "members only" partisan political meetings, to infringe section 2(c). In *Collins*,[41] an accused charged with obstruction during the course of a demonstration against the Cruise missile, at Litton Systems, successfully attacked a bail condition which required him to not attend at or near Litton Systems, in part, on the ground that the government had not shown anything other than a speculative reason for his freedom of assembly to be so curtailed. In *Fields*,[42] an accused was convicted of wilfully damaging a vehicle which had attempted to cross a picket line. He was placed on nine months' probation with a condition that he take no part in any strike of a firm other than one at which he was employed. Salhany Co. Ct. J. found this sweeping restriction to infringe Fields' freedom of peaceful assembly. Finally, in *Skead*,[43] the accused were denied a permit to march through Calgary in their "Long Walk in Total Objection to the Canadian Constitution". They marched anyway in an orderly and peaceful fashion and still found themselves charged with obstruction. The court acquitted them, in part, on the footing that the behaviour of the police amounted to an infringement of the accused's rights of expression and assembly.

(e) "Peaceful Assembly" in Other Human Rights Instruments

It is a matter of some interest that the language of assembly rights changed between 1960 and 1982. In the *Canadian Bill of Rights*, section 1(e) spoke of "freedom of assembly and association" in one breath. In the Charter, they are split apart into two separate subsections because that is the way they are treated in the *International Covenant on Civil and Political Rights*.[44] By the same token, "assembly" is modified by the word "peaceful".

---

38 *Ibid.* at 406. See *Cox v. Louisiana*, 379 U.S. 536 at 559 (U.S.S.C., 1965) for discussion of the question of how highly the state's legitimate interest in keeping the court houses free of picketers might be put. It is a good question whether the issue is as simple as physical access or whether it has more to do with saving the judiciary from "mob" pressures.

39 *Fraser v. A.G. Nova Scotia* (1986), 24 C.R.R. 193 (N.S.T.D.).

40 S.N.S. 1980, c. 3.

41 *Collins v. R.* (1982), 4 C.R.R. 78 (Ont. Co. Ct.).

42 *Fields v. R.* (1984), 42 C.R. (3d) 398 (Ont. Co. Ct.).

43 *R. v. Skead*, [1984] 4 C.N.L.R. 108 (Alta Prov. Ct.)

44 See *infra*, note 55.

Article 20 of the *Universal Declaration of Human Rights*,[45] Article 18 of the *International Covenant on Civil and Political Rights*[46] and Article 11 of the *European Convention on Human Rights*[47] all refer to "peaceful assembly".

2. FREEDOM OF ASSOCIATION

> The most natural privilege of man, next to the right of acting for himself, is that of combining his exertions with those of his fellow creatures and of acting in common with them. The right of association therefore appears to me almost as inalienable in its nature as the right of personal liberty. No legislator can attack it without impairing the foundations of society.[48]

Although de Tocqueville was speaking in universals, Lindsay has argued that the belief in both England and America in the primary importance of free association, stemming as it does from religious dissenters, especially the Puritan congregations, goes to the very heart of our conception of democracy:

> It makes a profound difference to the temper of English and American democratic thought that it started with the non-political and voluntary democratic organizations, regarding them as the true type of democracy and the state as only imperfectly imitating them; regarding therefore the state's use of force as its inherent defect and not as its glory. That attitude which abides persistently in English and American democracy is part of its inheritance from the Puritans of the Left.[49]

Prior to the entrenchment of the Charter, however, there is little to be found in Canadian law and legal literature on the subject of freedom of association.[50] Some statutory protection of association linked with peaceable assembly existed, beginning with the *Saskatchewan Bill of Rights*

---

45 Adopted and proclaimed by the General Assembly of the United Nations resolution 217 A (III) of December 10, 1948.
46 Adopted and opened for signature, ratification and accession by the General Assembly of the United Nations resolution 2200 A (XXI) of December 16, 1966; in force March 23, 1976.
47 Signed by the Council of Europe on November 4, 1950; in force September 3, 1953.
48 A. de Tocqueville, *Democracy in America*, ed. by P. Bradley (New York: 1945) at 196.
49 A.D. Lindsay, *The Modern Democratic State* (London: Oxford U. Press, 1943) at 121.
50 D.A. Schmeiser, in *Civil Liberties in Canada* (London: Oxford U. Press, 1964) at 221-222, spends less than two pages on the topic, and asserts that freedom of association is inseparably connected with freedom of speech and of the press and will stand or fall with them. W.S. Tarnopolsky, in *The Canadian Bill of Rights*, 2nd rev'd ed. (Toronto: Macmillan, 1975) at 201-209, devotes a few more paragraphs to the matter. And this is after seventeen years of experience under the *Bill of Rights*. This discussion includes treatment of freedom of assembly.

in 1947.[51] However, there are practically no cases. Only twice did Supreme Court judges deal with the question. Rand J. found freedom of association to be part of an implied bill of rights in *Smith & Rhuland*[52] and Abbott J. founded a dissent on the matter in the *Oil, Chemical & Atomic Workers* case.[53]

It is, thus, particularly worth noting that the framers of the Charter saw fit to have freedom of association stand alone. However, this conclusion was not reached until the third draft of the Charter.[54] This version was submitted to the Special Parliamentary Committee on the Constitution by the Minister of Justice on January 12, 1981, following weeks of hearings by that Committee, and was justified on the footing that assembly and association were expressed separately in the *International Covenant on Civil and Political Rights.*[55]

Cavalluzzo makes much of both of these points, arguing that the American doctrine of freedom of association, being derivative of other First Amendment freedoms, ought to be seen to be less robust and that Canada's international commitments, especially under the *International Labour Organization's 87th Convention, Concerning Freedom of Association and Protection of the Right to Organize*, ratified by Canada in 1972, might be looked to in developing a strong doctrine of freedom of association.[56]

---

51 *Saskatchewan Bill of Rights Act*, S.S. 1947, c. 35, s. 5. This was followed in 1960 by s. 1(e) of the *Canadian Bill of Rights*, S.C. 1960, c. 44, guaranteeing assembly and association, and the Quebec *Charter of Human Rights and Freedoms*, S.Q. 1975, c. 6, s. 3 protecting peaceable assembly and association along with other fundamental freedoms.

52 *Smith & Rhuland Ltd. v. R.*, [1953] 2 S.C.R. 95.

53 *Oil, Chemical & Atomic Wks. Int. Union v. Imperial Oil Ltd.*, [1963] S.C.R. 584. It is possible to read Martland J.'s judgment, for the majority, as endorsing a civil right of association in voluntary organizations. However, he finds trade unions to be legal entities not governed by the same principles as those which would apply to voluntary associations.

54 The first two drafts contained s.2(c) which provided for "freedom of peaceful assembly and of association".

55 R. Elliot, "Interpreting The Charter — Use of The Earlier Versions As An Aid", [1982] *U.B.C. L. Rev.* (Charter ed.) 11 at 25, where the government's Explanatory Note states that "Paragraph (c) would be divided into two paragraphs to make it clear that the freedoms contained therein are separate freedoms and need not exist in conjunction. These freedoms are expressed separately in the International Covenant on Civil and Political Rights".

56 P.J.J. Cavalluzzo, "Freedom of Association and the Right to Bargain Collectively", in J.M. Weiler & R.M. Elliot, eds. *Litigating the Values of a Nation: The Canadian Charter of Rights and Freedoms* (Toronto: Carswell, 1986) 189 at 197 and 195. For a discussion of the theoretical basis for Cavalluzzo's second point, see A. Brudner, "The Domestic Enforcement of International Covenants on Human Rights: A Theoretical Framework" (1985), 35 *U.T.L.J.* 219.

MacNeil rejects both of these points.[57] In *Re Lavigne and Ontario Public Service Employees Union*,[58] White J. of the Ontario High Court of Justice relies upon the Charter's independent and explicit right to freedom of association to give him a basis for concluding that when a governmental agent requires a person to make monetary contributions to a union, it thereby infringes upon his freedom of association. White J. was of the opinion that such a conclusion would not follow from the American doctrine of derivative freedom of association.[59]

What might be made of this "constitutional record" as an aid to interpreting the phrase "freedom of association" is an open question, in light of *Reference re Section 94(2) of the Motor Vehicle Act (B.C.)*.[60] Lamer J., for the majority of the court, left no doubt about the admissibility of the Minutes of the Proceedings and Evidence of the Special Joint Committee on the Constitution. He did, however, display a good deal of doubt about the weight to be given to matters such as speeches given and statements made to the Special Joint Committee, given their inherent unreliability.[61] However, an explanatory note, such as was provided by the government with regard to its proposal to have freedom of association stand alone, might well be given more weight, since it is less encumbered by the factor of inherent unreliability than are speeches and statements by particular witnesses before the Special Joint Committee.

The best guidance from the Supreme Court on the matter of how to interpret any given fundamental freedom or right in the Charter is given by Chief Justice Dickson in the *Big M* case:[62]

> In *Hunter v. Southam Inc.*, [1984] 2 S.C.R. 145, this Court expressed the view that the proper approach to the definition of the rights and freedoms guaranteed by the *Charter* was a purposive one. The meaning of a right or freedom guaranteed by the *Charter* was to be ascertained by an analysis of

---

57 M. MacNeil, "Recent Developments in Canadian Law: Labour Law" (1986), 18 *Ottawa L. Rev.* 83 at 92. On both points, MacNeil cites *Reference re Public Service Employee Relations Act* (1984), 85 C.L.L.C. 12, 149 (Alta. C.A..). On the second point, he argues that international covenants are not helpful in interpreting freedom of association because there is a lack of consensus on its meaning and because Canada's international obligations do not force the courts to give terms contained in those obligations a generous interpretation. Additional support for this latter contention is to be found in *N.A.P.E. v. Newfoundland* (1985), 85 C.L.L.C. 12,079 at 12,090 (Nfld. T.D.); and *Public Service Alliance v. R.*, [1984] 1 F.C. 562 at 582-586 (T.D.).

58 (1986), 55 O.R. (2d) 449 (Ont. H.C.), additional reasons (1987), 60 O.R. (2d) 486 (Ont. H.C.).

59 *Ibid.* at 508 (55 O.R.).

60 [1985] 2 S.C.R. 486.

61 *Ibid.* at 553-554.

62 *R. v. Big M Drug Mart Ltd.*, [1985] 1 S.C.R. 295.

the *purpose* of such a guarantee; it was to be understood, in other words, in the light of the interests it was meant to protect.

In my view this analysis is to be undertaken, and the purpose of the right or freedom in question is to be sought by reference to the character and the larger objects of the *Charter* itself, to the language chosen to articulate the specific right or freedom to the historical origins of the concepts enshrined, and where applicable, to the meaning and purpose of the other specific rights and freedoms with which it is associated within the text of the *Charter*. The interpretation should, be as the judgment in *Southam* emphasizes, a generous rather than a legalistic one, aimed at fulfilling the purpose of the guarantee and securing for individuals the full benefit of the *Charter's* protection.[63]

(a) Collective Bargaining

No Canadian institution is more in question, in the aftermath of the Charter's proclamation, than that of collective bargaining. Litigation in this area, before both courts and labour boards, has produced more decisions on freedom of association and its limitations than have all other areas of dispute about freedom of association put together.[64] In light of this recent history, it is particularly strange that organized labour did not put forward any significant effort to influence the framers of the Charter. Weiler explains that the Canadian Labour Congress (C.L.C.) decided that its priority at the time, in the fall of 1980, was to concentrate its energies on the issue of unemployment. Thus, only a short written submission from the C.L.C. was received by the Special Committee, together with a somewhat longer brief from the British Columbia Federation of Labour.[65] The C.L.C.'s decision largely to opt out of the framing process is criticized by Weiler as being "monumentally wrong", given the marked successes of many other special interest groups before the Special Committee.[66] Supporters of collective bargaining can take some comfort from the Acting Minister of Justice's assurance directed to the Special Committee that collective bargaining was included by necessary implication within the reach of freedom of association.[67]

---

63 *Ibid.* at 344.
64 By the end of 1986, some 29 cases had addressed freedom of association and collective bargaining, as opposed to only 19 non-collective bargaining freedom of association cases arising out of such diverse institutions as prisons, law societies, families, bawdy houses, political parties, marketing and licensing boards, landed immigrant status and citizenship status.
65 J.M. Weiler, "The Regulation of Strikes and Picketing Under the Charter", in Weiler & Elliot, *supra*, note 56, p. 211 at 213.
66 *Ibid.*
67 Minutes of Proceedings and Evidence of the Special Joint Committee of the Senate and of the House of Commons on the Constitution of Canada, Issue No. 43, at 69-70,

But this has not served to stem the tide of litigation. Two major areas have occupied the courts to date. The first has to do with whether freedom of association brings with it not only the right to form and join trade unions, but also the right of union members to act in concert and withdraw their services, in furtherance of a union's collective bargaining goals. The second entails the other side of the coin. Does freedom of association necessarily carry with it the obverse right to be free from association in the same way that freedom of religion must be taken to protect the atheist?

(i) The right to strike

The first reported decision on freedom of association and collective bargaining was *Broadway Manor*.[68] Three applications for judicial review were brought before the Divisional Court in Ontario with regard to the *Inflation Restraint Act, 1982*.[69] This statute extended the life of the terms and conditions of collective agreements covering public sector employees for up to two years, and suspended the right of some of the affected public servants to strike during that period of time and removed the right which other public servants had to refer compensation issues to arbitration. Two of the applications had to do with whether a result of this statute was to extend collective agreements themselves or just to extend their terms and conditions. The Ontario Labour Relations Board took the former position; the Ontario Education Relations Commission took the latter. The third application was launched by the Ontario Public Service Employees Union directly attacking the law on the footing that it ran afoul of section 2(d) of the Charter in putting limits both on the right to bargain and the right to strike.

All three members of the Divisional Court gave a large and liberal reading to freedom of association. Galligan J. ruled that freedom of association included freedom to engage in conduct reasonably consonant with the lawful objects of an association. What this meant for trade unions was freedom to form and join unions, to bargain and to strike.[70] O'Leary

---

Testimony of Hon. Robert Kaplan: "Our position on the suggestion that there be specific reference to freedom to organize and bargain collectively is that it is already covered in the freedom of association that is provided in the *Declaration* or *Charter*, and that by singling out association for bargaining, one might tend to diminish all the other forms of association which are contemplated — church associations; association of fraternal organizations or community organizations." Both Cavalluzzo, *supra*, note 56 at 207, and MacNeil, *supra*, note 57 at 87, cite this important statement.

68 *Re S.E.I.U., Loc. 204 and Broadway Manor Nursing Home* (1983), 4 D.L.R. (4th) 231 (Ont. Div. Ct.), rev'd in part *infra*, note 74.

69 S.O. 1982, c. 55.

70 *Broadway Manor, supra*, note 68 at 248.

J. stated that the right to organize and to bargain collectively would be made virtually meaningless if the right to strike were taken away. Thus, freedom of association must be read as including the right to strike.[71] Smith J. pointed out that the lawful objects of a union embraced the well-being, economic and otherwise, of its members. It followed from this that section 2(d) of the Charter protected the freedom to organize, to bargain collectively, and as a necessary corollary, to strike.[72]

The upshot of the decision, for the purposes of this discussion, was that the *Inflation Restraint Act* was found to be offensive to section 2(d) of the Charter to the extent that it stopped workers from opting for a new union and from bargaining on non-monetary issues during the freeze period of the statute. The Ontario Court of Appeal was presented with an opportunity to consider freedom of association, but declined. It agreed with the Education Relations Commission that the statute had the effect only of extending terms and conditions of employment, rather than the collective agreements themselves. Given this interpretation of the challenged statute, the freedom of association issue became moot. As well, the direct Charter challenge was dismissed for jurisdictional reasons, given the absence of an exercise of statutory power as required under the *Judicial Review Procedure Act*.[73] No comment was made, one way or the other, on the Divisional Court's liberal interpretations of freedom of association.[74]

The next opportunity for an appellate court to treat the subject of freedom of association came in the *Public Service Alliance* case.[75] The case came before the Federal Court as a direct Charter challenge to the federal wage restraint program embodied in the *Public Sector Compensation Restraint Act*.[76] This statute operated in much the same way as the Ontario *Inflation Restraint Act*, extending the life of collective agreements for two or more years and suspending the right to strike for the same period of time. The Federal Court of Appeal had before it a judgment of Reed J. rejecting the proposition that freedom of association carried with it the right to strike.[77] It did not disagree. In a brief judgment, freedom of association was determined by the Court of Appeal to address only the threshold question of access to an association. It did not speak to either the objects of an association or to the means employed by an association

---

71 *Ibid.* at 284.

72 *Ibid.* at 302.

73 R.S.O. 1980, c. 224.

74 *Re S.E.I.U., Loc. 204 and Broadway Manor Nursing Home* (1984), 13 D.L.R. (4th) 220 (Ont. C.A.), leave to appeal to S.C.C. refused (1985), 8 O.A.C. 320 (S.C.C.).

75 *P.S.A.C. v. Canada* (1984), 11 D.L.R. (4th) 387 (F.C.C.A.), aff'd [1987] 1 S.C.R. 424.

76 S.C. 1980-81-82, c. 122.

77 *P.S.A.C. v. Canada* (1984), 11 D.L.R. (4th) 337 (F.C.T.D.) aff'd *supra*, note 75.

to achieve its objects.[78] As authority for this assertion, the decision of the Judicial Committee of the Privy Council in *Collymore*[79] was cited. Freedom of association, as guaranteed under the Constitution of Trinidad and Tobago, was there held to encompass only the freedom to enter into consensual arrangements to promote the common interest objects of the association. Thus, a statute which suspended the right to bargain collectively and to strike did not offend freedom of association.

Within a few months, the Alberta Court of Appeal handed down a judgment to much the same effect.[80] Seven questions were referred to the court by the Government of Alberta as to whether the imposition of compulsory arbitration in the stead of the right to strike and lockout offended the Charter. Kerans J.A., for the majority, was persuaded that there was less merit in looking to Canada's international obligations, in the *International Covenant on Civil and Political Rights* or in *Convention 87 of the I.L.O.*, than in looking to the experience of other Commonwealth countries with entrenched freedom of association. Just because Canada has agreed in a treaty to protect the right to strike did not carry with it the requirement that the Charter be read as entrenching that right. He relied on *Collymore*[81] together with constitutional decisions from India and Jamaica in support of the conclusion that freedom of association does not protect the right to strike.[82] The contention that freedom of association protected associational actions, subject to section 1 of the Charter, was rejected. On the facts at hand, in the absence of evidence that the substitution of compulsory arbitration for the right to strike somehow undermined the vitality of the trade union movement, nothing could be made of the proposed group right of union members to strike as an exercise of section 2(d) rights. In a philosophical concluding note, Kerans J.A. discussed the western idea of political liberty and opined that the right to strike was, at best, a "weak" right, as Dworkin would say. It did not rank with cherished fundamental moral rights such as free speech. It was a common law liberty which may be exercised, so long as legislation does not curtail it.[83]

---

78 *Supra*, note 75 at 392, *per* Mahoney J.

79 *Collymore v. A.G. Trinidad and Tobago*, [1969] 2 All E.R. 1207 (P.C.).

80 *Reference re Public Service Employee Relations Act (Alta.)* (1985), 16 D.L.R. (4th) 359 (Alta. C.A.), aff'd *infra*, note 111.

81 *Supra*, note 79.

82 *Supra*, note 80 at 373. See *All India Bank Employees Assn. v. Nat. Industrial Tribunal* (1962), 49 A.I.R. (S.C.) 171; *Banton v. Alcoa Minerals of Jamaica, Inc.* (1971), 17 W.I.R. 275 (W. Indies).

83 *Ibid.* at 377. It is far from certain that Dworkin would agree with the point made by Kerans J.A.. Dworkin's example of a "weak" right was the right to drive both ways on Fifty-seventh Street. No moral argument is available against a governmental decision

Belzil J.A., dissenting in part, in support of answering even more of the referenced questions in the government's favour, expressed the view that fundamental freedoms were about individual rights. Freedom for a group can thus amount to no more than the freedom of any given member of the group. Freedom of association means that two or more individuals may, in concert, do that which they are free to do individually "provided they do not harm others".[84] Because the strike and the lockout have to do with intentionally causing economic harm, neither action can be said to be protected by the Charter.

The Saskatchewan Court of Appeal entered the debate about section 2(d) in the *Dairy Workers* case.[85] What was in question was a back-to-work law entitled the *Dairy Workers (Maintenance of Operations) Act*[86] enacted in the face of threatened strikes and lockouts at two large dairy companies operating some twelve dairies in Saskatchewan. The Act declared the expired collective bargaining agreement to continue to be in force, and suspended the right to strike in favour of a compulsory arbitration mechanism. The court found the Act to be constitutionally impermissible, so far as section 2(d) of the Charter was concerned. Bayda C.J.S. advanced an argument from first principles. Freedom of association cannot just be taken to mean that a person is free to be in an association, it must extend to one's freedom to act in such a grouping. "For a human being, to be is to act."[87]

Based upon two leading American articles,[88] the Chief Justice concluded that: "Where an act is capable of being performed by a person alone or in association, then only if a person acting alone is forbidden

---

to turn that particular street into a one-way street. This example is hardly equivalent to the common law right to strike. See R. Dworkin, *A Matter of Principle* (Cambridge: Harvard University Press, 1986) at 198, where Dworkin grounds his theory of fundamental rights, rights as trumps, in the egalitarian goal of protecting equal concern and respect. On this basis, the right to strike might well pass muster with Dworkin as a "strong" right.

84 *Ibid.* at 388. This smacks very much of the American focus on individualism. See T.I. Emerson, "Freedom of Association and Freedom of Expression" (1964), 74 *Yale L.J.* 1 at 4, where the point is boldly made that "the individual is the ultimate concern of the social order". Cavalluzzo questions the applicability of this singular assertion in Canada, where our history and political culture reflects no similar preoccupation with the individual. As a second argument, Cavalluzzo places some stock in the framers' decision to set freedom of association up as a free-standing provision of the Charter. See *supra*, note 56 at 202.

85 *Re R.W.D.S.U. and Saskatchewan* (1985), 19 D.L.R. (4th) 609 (Sask. C.A.), rev'd *infra*, note 111.

86 S.S. 1983-84, c. D-1.1.

87 *Supra*, note 85 at 615.

88 R. Raggi, "An Independent Right to Freedom of Association" (1977), 12 *Harv. Civil Rights-Civil Liberties L. Rev.* 15; Emerson, *supra*, note 84.

to perform the act, is the person acting in association forbidden."[89] But, where an action can only be taken in association, section 2(d) protects it only where there is no intention to cause harm to some other or others. And, in sharp contradistinction to Belzil J.A. in the *Alberta Reference* case,[90] it was concluded that the act of engaging in a strike does not carry with it the intention to cause harm. Rather, "often the aim of a strike is more to rectify an injustice than it is to use economic power to gain positive advantages over another group".[91] The mental element behind a strike is to force an employer to agree to terms and conditions of employment. It is not normally to inflict harm.[92]

Cameron J.A., in a concurring opinion, authored a judgment along *Broadway Manor*[93] lines, although he made a distinction between ends and means. While section 2(d) did not necessarily protect all of an association's objects, it did protect some of the means employed in pursuit thereof. The right to strike is among those protected means, for without it there would be little if anything left of collective bargaining. Cameron J.A. found assistance in reaching this broad interpretation of section 2(d) by looking to Canada's international obligations and by noting that the presence of section 1 and section 33 encouraged the judiciary to read rights and freedoms liberally. Brownridge J.A. dissented, taking the point made in *Collymore*.[94]

(b) International Commitments

Given that the *International Covenant on Civil and Political Rights* is the genesis of the free-standing status of freedom of association in the Charter, it is surprising that international law on the right to strike has received such short shrift in the foregoing analyses of Canadian appellate courts.[95] In the literature to date, Cavalluzzo must keep company with himself in the argument that Canada's international commitments in this regard ought to be taken seriously.[96] Most recently, Canada was party to the *Final Act of the Conference on Security and Cooperation in Europe* (the Madrid Conference), signed on March 15, 1983. It states, in part:

---

89 *Supra*, note 85 at 619.

90 *Supra*, note 80.

91 *Supra*, note 85 at 621.

92 Support for this interpretation as to the paramount objective in a strike not being the "intention to cause harm" may now be found in the majority judgment of McIntyre J. in *Dolphin Delivery, supra* note 5.

93 *Supra*, note 68.

94 *Supra*, note 79.

95 *Supra*, note 55. Cameron J.A.'s judgment in *Dairy Workers, supra*, note 85, is an exception.

96 *Supra*, note 56 at 194-197.

The participating States will ensure the right of workers freely to establish and join trade unions, the right of trade unions freely to exercise their activities and other rights as laid down in relevant international instruments. They note that these rights will be exercised in compliance with the law of the State and in conformity with the State's obligations under international law.[97]

In 1976, Canada ratified and acceded to the two great Covenants flowing from the *Universal Declaration of Human Rights.* Article 22 of the *International Covenant on Civil and Political Rights* provides:

1. Everyone shall have the right to freedom of association with others, including the right to form and join trade unions for the protection of his interests.

2. No restrictions may be placed on the exercise of this right other than those which are prescribed by law and which are necessary in a democratic society in the interests of national security or public safety, public order (*order public*), the protection of public health or morals or the protection of the rights and freedoms of others. This article shall not prevent the imposition of lawful restrictions on members of the armed forces and of the police in their exercise of this rights.

3. Nothing in this article shall authorize States Parties to the International Labour Organisation Convention of 1948 concerning Freedom of Association and Protection of the Right to Organize [hereinafter referred to as *I.L.O. Convention No. 87*] to take legislative measures which would prejudice, or to apply the law in such a manner as to prejudice the guarantees provided for in that Convention.[98]

Article 8 of the *International Covenant on Economic, Social and Cultural Rights* states:

1. The States Parties to the present Covenant undertake to ensure:

(a) The right of everyone to form trade unions and join the trade union of his choice, subject only to the rules of the organization concerned, for the promotion and protection of his economic and social interests. No restrictions may be placed on the exercise of this right other than those prescribed by law and which are necessary in a democratic society in the interests of national security or public order or for the protection of the rights and freedoms of others;

(b) The right of trade unions to establish national federations or confederations and the right of the latter to form or join international trade-union organizations;

(c) The right of trade unions to function freely subject to no limitations

---

97 *Ibid.* at 195.
98 Adopted and opened for signature, ratification and accession by the General Assembly of the United Nations resolution 2200 A (XXI) of December 16, 1966; in force March 23, 1976.

other than those prescribed by law and which are necessary in a democratic society in the interests of national security or public order or for the protection of the rights and freedoms of others;

(d) *The right to strike, provided that it is exercised in conformity with the laws of the particular country.* [Emphasis added][99]

The implication of Articles 3, 8 and 10 of *I.L.O. Convention No. 87*, ratified by Canada in 1972, has repeatedly been said to prevent States Parties from banning the right to strike, at wholesale. These articles provide:

Article 3

1. Workers' and employers' organisations shall have the right to draw up their constitutions and rules, to elect their representatives in full freedom to organise their administration and activities and to formulate their programmes.

2. The public authorities shall refrain from any interference which would restrict this right or impede the lawful exercise thereof.

Article 8

1. In exercising the rights provided for in this Convention workers and employers and their respective organisations, like other persons or organised collectivities, shall respect the law of the land.
2. The law of the land shall not be such as to impair, nor shall it be so applied as to impair, the guarantees provided for in this Convention.

Article 10

In this Convention the term "organisation" means any organisation of workers or of employers for furthering and defending the interests of workers or of employers.[100]

Four separate I.L.O. bodies have interpreted these provisions so as to imply a right to strike. They are: A Commission of Inquiry into Greece, the Committee of Experts, the Fact-Finding and Conciliation Committee and the Freedom of Association Committee. Bendel has forcefully argued that these interpretations ought to be deferred to by Canadian courts.[101]

---

99 Adopted and opened for signature, ratification and accession by United Nations General Assembly resolution 2200 A (XXI) of December 16, 1966; in force January 3, 1976.
100 Adopted on July 9, 1948 by the General Conference of the International Labour Organization at its thirty-first session.
101 M. Bendel, "The International Protection of Trade Union Rights: A Canadian Case Study" (1981), 13 *Ottawa L.R.* 169, where the judgment of the Alberta Court of Queen's Bench in *Re A.U.P.E. and Alberta* (1980), 120 D.L.R. (3d) 590, aff'd 130 D.L.R. (3d) 191, leave to S.C.C. refused 130 D.L.R. (3d) 191 (S.C.C.). is criticized for ignoring Convention No. 87.

246 Canadian Charter of Rights and Freedoms

This argument from deference is very much bolstered by the view taken of domestic human rights legislation by the Supreme Court of Canada. Beginning with *Heerspink*[102] and culminating in *Craton*,[103] human rights laws have been placed on a sort of quasi-constitutional pedestal above all other legislation. In *Craton*, McIntyre J., said, for the Court:

> Human rights legislation is of a special nature and declares public policy regarding matters of general concern. [It] is not constitutional in nature in the sense that it may not be altered, amended, or repealed by the Legislature. It is, however, of such nature that it may not be altered, amended, or repealed, nor may exceptions be created to its provisions, save by clear legislative pronouncement. To adopt and apply any theory of implied repeal by later statutory enactment to legislation of this kind would be to rob it of its special nature and give scant protection to the rights it proclaims.[104]

Brudner makes an argument, which would apply fully to an international human rights treaty, such as *I.L.O. Convention No. 87*, in the following language:

> [I]nternational covenants on human rights may lay claim to the same deference that is accorded statutes as authoritative sources for the elaboration of common-law principles. Indeed, if statutes deserve this respect because the legislature reflects most authentically the moral consciousness of a nation, how much more worthy of regard are international human rights norms, which, denuded even of national particularity, express the purest moral insight of an epoch?[105]

In further support of the right to strike, Bendel has contended that:

> [A] good arguable case can be made for the existence of a rule of customary law, binding on Canada, to the effect that the right to strike is to be enjoyed by all workers except those in genuinely essential services.[106]

Canada's official position on the matter of the right to collective bargaining and the right to strike based upon international commitments can be seen in two statements. First, at the time of ratification of Convention No. 87, in 1972, the Preamble to Part V of the *Canada Labour Code*[107] was enacted with these two provisos:

> And Whereas Canadian workers, trade unions and employers recognize and support freedom of association and free collective bargaining as the bases of effective industrial relations for the determination of good working conditions and sound labour-management relations;

---

102 *Ins. Corp. B.C. v. Heerspink*, [1982] 2 S.C.R. 145.
103 *Winnipeg School Div. No. 1 v. Craton*, [1985] 2 S.C.R. 150.
104 *Ibid.*, at 156.
105 A. Brudner, *supra*, note 56 at 243.
106 *Supra*, note 101 at 191.
107 S.C. 1972, c. 18.

And Whereas the Government of Canada has ratified Convention No. 87 of the International Labour Organization concerning Freedom of Association and Protection of the Right to Organize and has assumed international reporting responsibilities in this regard.

Although Canada has yet to ratify *Convention No. 98 concerning the Right to Organize and to Bargain Collectively,*[108] due to certain provinces continuing to exclude professionals and farm workers from collective bargaining, the Government of Canada has stated that "there is substantial compliance in Canada with the basic provisions of the Convention".[109]

Whether the Supreme Court of Canada will place its feet upon these two assertions endorsing Canada's international commitments to the I.L.O. so as to "expand rights to embrace ideals that have motivated member nations of the I.L.O. for 75 years"[110] or stand with Alberta courts, no longer remains to be seen. On April 9, 1987, the Supreme Court delivered its judgments in the *Alberta Reference, Dairy Workers* and *Public Service Alliance* cases.[111] Two of the six participating judges stand firmly on Canada's international human rights commitments in the field of labour. Chief Justice Dickson, writing for himself and Wilson J., found that international law provides "a fertile source of insight into the nature and scope of the freedom of association of workers".[112] He said that it is a "clear consensus amongst the I.L.O. adjudicative bodies that Convention No. 87 goes beyond merely protecting the formation of labour unions and provides protection of their essential activities — that is of collective bargaining and the freedom to strike".[113] He went so far as to declare that there ought to be a presumption that the Charter provides protection at least as great as that afforded by similar provisions in international human rights documents which Canada has ratified.[114]

The rest of this panel of the Supreme Court said nothing at all on the subject. The plurality opinion authored by Le Dain J., concurred in

---

108 Adopted July 1, 1949, by the General Conference of the International Labour Organization at its thirty-second session.

109 Labour Canada, *Canada and the International Labour Code* (1978) at 7.

110 J.E. Dorsey, "International Labour Conventions and the I.L.O.: Application in British Columbia" (1985), 43 *Advocate* 619 at 625.

111 *Reference re Public Service Employee Relations Act* (Alta.), [1987] 1 S.C.R. 313; *R.W.D.S.U. v. Saskatchewan*, [1987] 1 S.C.R. 460; *P.S.A.C. v. Canada*, [1987] 1 S.C.R. 424. From the point of view of the definition of freedom of association, the *Alberta Reference* opinions are the vital ones. In the other two cases, the discussion proceeds on the footing of the meaning given to s. 2(d) in *Alberta Reference*. Dickson C.J.C. and Wilson J. discuss s. 1 at some length in their dissenting opinions in *Dairy Workers* and *Public Service Alliance* cases. S. 1 does not arise in the plurality opinions.

112 *Alberta Reference, ibid.* at 348.

113 *Ibid.* at 359.

114 *Ibid.* at 349.

by Beetz and La Forest JJ., takes only a few lines beyond two pages in order to assert the conclusion that collective bargaining and the right to strike are not constitutionally justiciable as embraced by the fundamental freedom of association. McIntyre J. reached the same conclusion after discussing the meaning to be given to section 2(d) at some length. But although he began his judgment by advising that he had read Dickson C.J.C.'s reasons, no mention was made of Canada's international human rights commitments in the field.

As for the reading given to section 2(d) by McIntyre J., one is left with a narrow American gloss on the *status quo ante* of the Charter. Freedom of association first amounts to the right to join with others in lawful common pursuits and to establish and maintain organizations directed at such ends. "This is essentially the freedom of association enjoyed prior to the adoption of the Charter."[115] Second, the American "derivative right of association" is included. This guarantees the collective exercise of individual constitutional rights and incidentally entitles an individual in concert with others to do that which he or she may lawfully do alone.[116]

In the course of reaching this articulation of the meaning to be given to section 2(d), McIntyre J. accepted the American proposition that "it is the individual who is the ultimate concern of the social order. His interests and rights are paramount".[117] It follows from this that freedom of

---

115 *Ibid.* at 407. To this extent we are left with something quite like the "frozen concepts" doctrine developed by the Supreme Court with regard to the *Canadian Bill of Rights.* Dickson C.J.C., at 338, distinguished the *Collymore (supra,* note 79), judgment of the Privy Council on the footing that the Constitution of Trinidad and Tobago is like the *Canadian Bill of Rights* and thus properly subject to a "frozen rights" analysis such as provided by the judgment in that case. But as for the Charter, the Chief Justice insists that it "ushers in a new era in the protection of fundamental freedoms. We need not ground protection for freedom of association in pre-existing freedoms".

116 *Ibid.*

117 *Ibid.* at 398, quoting from Emerson, *supra,* note 84 at 4. As was the case with regard to McIntyre J.'s apparent wilful blindness concerning Dickson C.J.C.'s lengthy reliance on Canada's international human rights commitments in this field, there is no reference to the Chief Justice's two grounds for distinguishing the United States *Bill of Rights* from the Charter. At 345, Dickson C.J.C. pointed out that freedom of association "is not explicitly protected in the United States Constitution, as it is in the *Charter.* Instead, it has been implied by the judiciary as a necessary derivative of the First Amendment's protection of freedom of speech, 'the right of the people to peaceably assemble,' and freedom to petition". Second, the American Constitution contains no provision like s. 1. What has resulted is that for the American Supreme Court "the balancing of the protection of rights and freedoms with the larger interests of the community, therefore, must be done in the context of defining the right or freedom itself. . . . Accordingly, one would expect a more limited approach to the delineation of the freedom itself."

association cannot be regarded as any sort of group right.[118] As Chief Justice Dickson saw it, the narrowness of "constitutive/derivative" definition of freedom of association is shown by a marriage example:

> While the constitutive approach might find a possible violation of s. 2(d) in a legislative enactment which prohibited marriage for certain classes of people, it would hold inoffensive an enactment which precluded the same people from engaging in the activities integral to a marriage, such as cohabiting and raising children together. If freedom of association only protects the joining together of persons for common purposes, but not the pursuit of the very activities for which the association was formed, then the freedom is indeed legalistic, ungenerous, indeed vapid.[119]

McIntyre J. offered three interpretive justifications, bolstered by a "social policy" argument for his narrow definition. First, he turned to the Parliamentary record and noted that, although a resolution was put before the Special Joint Committee of the Senate and of the House of Commons on the Constitution for the inclusion of a right to bargain collectively, no such proposal was advanced with regard to the right to strike. "This affords strong support for the proposition that the inclusion of the right to strike was not intended."[120] Second, he looked to the inclusion of the right to strike in the constitutions of France, Italy and Japan for the

---

118 *Ibid.* at 397. What then follows is a remarkable statement about the primary thrust of the Charter. "While some provisions in the Constitution involve groups, such as s. 93 of the *Constitution Act, 1867* protecting denominational schools, and s. 25 of the *Charter* referring to existing aboriginal rights, the remaining rights and freedoms are individual rights; they are not concerned with the group as distinct from its members" (at 397). It is noteworthy that no mention is made of s. 23 or of s. 27 or of the explicit reference to disadvantaged groups in s. 15(2). Moreover, the literature in the field is not mentioned. See N. MacCormick, "Nations and Nationalism" in C. MacLean, ed., *The Crown and The Thistle: the Nature of Nationhood* (Edinburgh: Scottish Academic Press, 1979); C. Bay, "From Contract to Community: Thoughts on Liberalism and Postindustrial Society", in F.R. Dallmayr, ed., *From Contract to Community: Political Theory at the Crossroads* (New York: Marcel Debber Inc., 1978); V. Van Dyke, "Human Rights and the Rights of Groups" (1974) 18 *Am. J. Pol. Sc.* 725; V. Van Dyke, "Justice as Fairness: For Groups?" (1975), 69 *Am. Pol. Sc. Rev.* 607; V. VanDyke, "The Individual, The State, and Ethnic Communities in Political Theory" (1977), 29 *World Politics* 21; V. Van Dyke, "Collective Entities and Moral Rights: Problems in Liberal-Democratic Thought" (1982), 44 *J. Politics* 21; F. Svensson, "Liberal Democracy and Group Rights: The Legacy of Individualism and its Impact on American Indian Tribes" (1979), 37 *Pol. Studies* 421; K.D. McRae, "The Plural Society and the Western Political Tradition" (1979), 12 *Can. Jour. Pol. Sc.* 675; S. Lynd, "Communal Rights" (1984), 62 *Texas L. Rev.* 1417

119 *Ibid.* at 362-363.

120 *Ibid.*, at 413. Why such an "intention of the framers" argument counts for much in light of the Supreme Court's decision in *Reference re S. 94(2) of the Motor Vehicle Act (B.C.), supra,* note 60, is something of a puzzle. Lamer J., for the court, said that it would be erroneous to give such materials anything but minimal weight.

conclusion that the framers must have known of these clauses and must be taken to have deliberately omitted the right to strike from the Charter.[121] Third, McIntyre J. noted that the legislative right to strike is of relatively recent vintage in Canada such as to warrant the conclusion that:

> It cannot be said that it has become so much a part of our social and historical traditions that it has acquired the status of an immutable, fundamental right, firmly embedded in our traditions, our political and social philosophy.[122]

Finally, one is offered the supporting "social policy" argument that the court ought not to, in effect, put its thumb on labour's side of the dynamic balance of collective bargaining by constitutionalizing the right to strike, subject only to section 1, and at the same time trespass upon the territory of the legislative branch and that of specialized tribunals dedicated to the resolution of labour disputes.[123]

(c) Freedom from Unions

Does it necessarily follow that the guarantee of freedom of association must carry with it the right to be free from association in the same way that freedom of religion protects the atheist? Gall has so argued.[124] He begins with the libertarian proposition that freedom for the individual is at the heart of the Charter.[125] Freedom means choice. This means not only that freedom from association is a corollary of section 2(d), but that it must be seen to carry no less importance. So runs the self-regarding argument. As a bolster for his argument, Gall points out that both the Irish and the German constitutional protection of associational rights have been interpreted so as to include the right not to associate.[126] Fichaud adds the Indian Constitution to the list.[127]

The first test case on this question saw White J. adopt such a theory

---

121 *Ibid.*

122 *Ibid.* 413.

123 *Ibid.* 413 *et seq.*

124 P.A. Gall, "Freedom of Association and Trade Unions: A Double-Edged Constitutional Sword", in Weiler & Elliot, *supra*, note 56, p. 245.

125 For McIntyre J.'s endorsement of this debatable point in the recent *Alberta Reference* case, *supra*, note 80, see text accompanying note 117, *supra.*

126 *Supra*, note 124 at 250.

127 J. Fichaud, "Analysis of the Charter and its Application to Labour Law" (1984), 8 *Dalhousie L. J.* 402 at 415. But the majority of the European Court of Human Rights avoided commenting specifically on the right not to associate in *Young, James & Webster* (1981), 3 E.H.R.R. 20. The upshot of the decision was that the plaintiffs were protected from losing their jobs for refusing to join a union under a newly-bargained closed shop agreement, but this result was not justified on the footing that they possessed the "freedom from" association.

of fundamental freedoms. In *Lavigne*,[128] the question before the court was whether a compulsory union dues check-off clause between a governmental agency and a union, sanctioned by statute, was constitutionally impermissible under section 2(d), to the extent that such dues were applied by the union to social rather than bilateral collective bargaining issues.[129] Along the way to answering this question in the affirmative, White J. purchased the American literature and case law at wholesale.

The starting point of his analysis is Emerson's contention that the individual must be regarded as the ultimate concern of the social order.[130] It follows from this that the value in freedom of association lies not in any sort of collective enhancement of equality for employees, but in "increased opportunities for self-realization".[131] And, "[f]orced association can restrict the free flow of ideas and thus distort the market place."[132] Although Francis Lavigne was not forced to join a union, he was compelled to pay dues, as a sort of fair taxation device commonly utilized in such "agency shop" situations. White J. found that this forced mixing of Lavigne's money with that of union members in funds which were directed to other-regarding social purposes of the union amounted to a violation of his section 2(d) right to be free from forced association. This conclusion follows the position taken by the Supreme Court of the United States in *Abood*.[133]

Like *Lavigne*, *Abood* involved an agency shop agreement which had a union dues check-off clause requiring a teacher who was not a member of the union to pay full dues, so as not to be the recipient of a "free ride" on the backs of his co-workers who were union members. The Supreme Court found no constitutional barrier under the First Amendment to an agency shop clause so long as the forced dues were directed by the union exclusively to cover the costs of collective bargaining, contract administration and grievance adjustment. But, to the extent that the union spent the dues "for the support of ideological causes not germane to its duties as collective bargaining agent" the First Amendment was violated. In *Ellis*,[134] the Supreme Court provided a test for drawing the line between *Abood's* so-called "collective bargaining" and "ideological" purposes.

---

128 *Re Lavigne and O.P.S.E.U. supra*, note 58.
129 *Ibid.* S. 53(1) of the *Colleges Collective Bargaining Act*, R.S.O. 1980, c. 74, stated: "The parties to an agreement may provide for the payment by the employees of dues or contributions to the employee organization." On the facts before White J., the parties had so provided.
130 See text accompanying note 117, *supra*, quoting Emerson, *supra*, note 84.
131 *Ibid.* at 494.
132 *Ibid.* at 495.
133 *Abood v. Detroit Bd. of Education*, 97 S. Ct. 1782 (1977).
134 *Ellis v. Railway Clerks*, 104 S. Ct. 1883 (1984).

Finally, the court authored its decision in *Chicago Teachers Union*,[135] which added a "due process" requirement to the *Ellis* criteria. White J. simply approved the *Abood* line of cases as being entirely applicable in Canada.

An argument by Cantor that this line of cases is "essentially askew" was taken into account by White J.[136] Cantor starts with the proposition that unions are voluntary service organizations, as are state bar associations or certain educational institutions. He finds it to be incoherent for the Supreme Court to have found forced fees with regard to the latter two organizations to be constitutionally permissible, but to have found otherwise with regard to unions. Cantor reminds his readers that *Abood* is founded on *Barnette*,[137] which established the principle that government could not force an unwilling person to identify with a particular political orthodoxy. There, Barnette, a Jehovah's Witness who refused to salute the flag and recite the pledge of allegiance, found a friend in the Supreme Court. Cantor's argument is that the *Barnette* principle was wrongly applied in *Abood*, where the union makes contributions to certain social purposes out of anonymous funds with no forced public identification of the dissenting Abood with the causes in question. White J. was not moved. He simply rejected Cantor's premise. Unions are not voluntary organizations in the same way that bar associations are. Bar associations exist to regulate the practice of law, to maintain high professional standards and to protect the public interest.[138] Unions in Canada, on the other hand, have a strong tradition of political activism behind them and are presently linked to the New Democratic Party. "The word 'union' in the labour context is practically synonymous with a certain ideological and indeed political perspective."[139]

Set against *Lavigne* and Gall's argument are two points. First, it is far from clear that the Supreme Court of Canada will take Emerson's thesis and ground freedom of association exclusively in libertarian, self-regarding political theory, with its necessary implication of rollbacks in the power of certain unions. Dickson C.J.C.'s majority decision in *Edwards Books*[140] opens the door to another conclusion. Albeit in the context of a section 1 discussion in a section 2(a) Charter challenge, Dickson C.J.C.

---

135 *Chicago Teachers Union v. Hudson* 106 S. Ct. 106 (1986).

136 N. Cantor, "Forced Payments to Service Institutions and Constitutional Interests in Ideological Non-Association" (1984), 36 *Rutgers L.R.* 3.

137 *West Virginia State Bd. of Education v. Barnette*, 319 U.S. 624 (1943).

138 *Lavigne, supra*, note 58 at 507.

139 *Ibid.* at 508. It is noteworthy that White J. accepted Cantor's argument in the context of the freedom of expression claim finding, accordingly, that the forced dues check-off when used anonymously for social issues did not offend Lavigne's freedom from forced expression.

140 *R. v. Edwards Books & Art Ld.*, [1986] 2 S.C.R. 713.

made a particular point of reminding his readers that the impugned Ontario *Retail Business Holidays Act*[141] had as its object a common weekly day of rest for retail employees who "do not constitute a powerful group in society."[142] He then offered the following advice to the judiciary of Canada:

> In interpreting and applying the *Charter*, I believe that the courts must be cautious to ensure that it does not simply become an instrument of better situated individuals to roll back legislation which has as its object the improvement of the condition of less advantaged persons.[143]

As it would not be difficult to obtain agreement as to the proposition that statutory union security provisions, such as forced dues check-off, exist in order to make unions effective collective bargaining agents, with the sole objective of improving the working conditions of less advantaged persons, Gall's strong negative corollary may not fall on fertile soil in the Supreme Court of Canada.

A second line of argument, in opposition to the freedom from unions contention, is available even on the American individualistic premise. Abernathy has suggested that the right of association can be said to be entitled to a much higher degree of protection than its negative corollary because it is a necessary vehicle for influencing public policy in a democratic society.[144] This draws on Meiklejohn's contention that "public" speech ought to receive more constitutional protection than "private" speech, given that the former clearly serves essential democratic values. Under the *American Bill of Rights*, what this would amount to would be a First Amendment position for the right of association, with strict scrutiny of all legislative limitations. The right not to associate would then find itself interpreted as a Fourteenth Amendment "liberty' interest subject to legislation which would have only to withstand judicial scrutiny on a much less strict balancing test.[145]

Footings for such an argument can be found in Chief Justice Dickson's judgment in *Oakes*,[146] where it is plainly stated that there was one purpose and one purpose only in entrenching the Charter as the supreme law of Canada — that was to ensure that Canada is to be free and democratic. He then provided his vision of such a society, in these words:

> *The Court must be guided by the values and principles essential to a free and democratic society which I believe embody,* to name but a few, respect for the inherent dignity of the human person, commitment to social justice and

---

141 R.S.O. 1980, c. 453.
142 *Ibid.* at 778.
143 *Ibid.* at 779.
144 Abernathy, *supra*, note 1 at 298.
145 A. Meiklejohn, *Free Speech and Its Relation to Self-Government* (New York: Harper, 1948).
146 *R. v. Oakes*, [1986] 1 S.C.R. 103.

equality, accommodation of a wide variety of beliefs, respect for cultural and group identity, and *faith in social and political institutions which enhance the participation of individuals and groups in society.* [Emphasis added][147]

The long-established rights to form and join trade unions, to bargain collectively and to strike can all be said to flow from the Chief Justice's highlighted tenet of Canadian society, with its reference to groups as well as to individuals. The negative corollary seems to stand on a less secure foundation as a necessary vehicle for influencing the continuing debate as to how best to enable Canadian democracy to flourish.

Freedom of association arguments have been advanced in order to attack most of the institutional structures of statutory collective bargaining. Not surprisingly, these points have not been taken by labour relations boards.[148] Nor have they found any favour with reviewing courts.[149]

(d) Other Statutory Restrictions

The breadth of common law conspiracy is made clear by the progressively expansive definitions provided a century ago by Willes J. and Fitzgerald J.:

A conspiracy consists not merely in the intention of two or more, but in the agreement of two or more to do an unlawful act, or to do a lawful act by

---

147 *Ibid.* at 136.
148 See *Powell River Dist. v. Malaspina Mun. Management Assn.* (1985), 11 C.L.R.B.R. (N.S.) 129 (B.C.L.R.B.); *Ratcliffe & Sons Const. Co. v. C.J.A., 27 Locs.* (1984), 8 C.L.R.B.R. (N.S.) 343 (B.C.L.R.B.); *Union of Bank Employees, Loc. 2104 v. C.I.B.C.* (1985), 85 C.L.L.C. 16,021 (Can. L.R.B.); *T. Eaton Co. v. R.W.D.S.U.* (1985), 10 C.L.R.B.R. (N.S.) 289 (Ont. L.R.B.), varied on reconsideration [1985] O.L.R.B. Rep. 1683 (Ont. L.R.B.) aff'd (1987), 62 O.R. (2d) 337 (Ont. Div. Ct.); *Brick & Brew Holdings Ltd. v. H.R.E.U., Loc. 40* (1983), 4 C.L.R.B.R. (N.S.) 129 (B.C.L.R.B.); *C.P.R. v. Cdn. Telecommunications Union* (1984) 8 C.L.R.B.R. (N.S) 378 (Can. L.R.B.); *Mun. Technicians Assn. of Thunder Bay v. Thunder Bay* (1984), 84 C.L.L.C. 16,046 (Ont.L.R.B.); and *Edmund Northcott & Group of K-Mart Employees & Teamsters* (1983), 6 C.L.R.B.R. (N.S.) 19 (Ont.L.R.B.).
149 *Re Assn. of Clerical Office & Technical Workers of Nordair Ltd. and Can. Labour Relations Bd.* (1985), 18 C.R.R. 130 (F.C.C.A.); *C.I.B.C. v. Rifou*, [1986] 3 F.C. 486 (C.A.); *United Headwear, Optical & Allied Workers Union of Can. v. Biltmore/Stetson (Can.) Inc.* (1983), 43 O.R. (2d) 243 (C.A.); *Chung v. A.C.T.W.U. — Toronto Joint Bd.*; *Re Ports Int. Ltd. v. Ont. Labour Relations Bd.* (1986), 27 D.L.R. (4th) 247 (Ont. Div. Ct.); *Re Prime and Man. Labour Bd.* (1983), 3 D.L.R. (4th) 74 (Man. Q.B.), rev'd (1984), 8 D.L.R. (4th) 641 (Man. C.A.); *Pruden Building Ltd. v. Const. & Gen. Workers Union* (1984), 13 D.L.R. (4th) 584 (Alta. Q.B.); *S.G.E.U. v. Saskatchewan* (1984), 14 D.L.R. (4th) 245 (Sask. Q.B.); *Halifax Police Officers' & N.C.O.'s Assn. v. Halifax* (1984), 64 N.S.R. (2d) 368 (T.D.); *I.B.E.W. Electrical Power Systems Const. Council of Ont. v. Ont. Hydro* (1986), 12 O.A.C. 155 (Ont. Div. Ct.); *Re Bhindi and B.C. Projectionists* [1986] 5 W.W.R. 303 (B.C.C.A.) (Anderson and Hutcheon JJ.A. dissenting), leave to appeal to S.C.C. refused [1986] 6 W.W.R. 1xv (note) (S.C.C.).

unlawful means. So long as such a design rests in intention only, it is not indictable. When two agree to carry it into effect, the very plot is an act in itself . . . punishable if for a criminal object or for the use of criminal means.[150]

Conspiracy has been aptly described as divisible under three heads — i.e., where the end to be attained is in itself a crime; where the object is lawful, but the means to be restored to are unlawful; and where the object is to do injury to a third party or to a class, though if the wrong were effected by a single individual it would be a wrong but not a crime.[151]

Related statutory conspiracy provisions are seditious conspiracy, in section 60(3) [59(3)] of the *Criminal Code* and treasonable conspiracy, in section 46(2)(c), (e) and (4). Then there are the peculiar provisions of section 424 [466] dealing with conspiracy in restraint of trade:

(1) A conspiracy in restraint of trade is an agreement between two or more persons to do or to procure to be done any unlawful act in restraint of trade.

(2) The purposes of a trade union are not, by reason only that they are in restraint of trade, unlawful within the meaning of subsection (1).

Just why this offence remains under the *Criminal Code* is something of a mystery given the penal provisions of the *Competition Act*.[152]

32.(1) [45.1] Every one who conspires, combines, agrees or arranges with another person

(a) to limit unduly the facilities for transporting, producing, manufacturing, supplying, storing or dealing in any product,

(b) to prevent, limit or lessen, unduly, the manufacture or production of a product, or to enhance unreasonably the price thereof,

(c) to prevent, or lessen, unduly, competition in the production, manufacture, purchase, barter, sale, storage, rental, transportation or supply of a product, or in the price of insurance upon persons or property, or

(d) to otherwise restrain or injure competition unduly,

is guilty of an indictable offence and is liable to imprisonment for five years or to a fine of one million dollars or to both.

(1.1) For greater certainty, in establishing that a conspiracy, combination, agreement or arrangement is in violation of subsection (1), it shall not be necessary to prove that the conspiracy, combination, agreement or arrangement, if carried into effect, would or would be likely to eliminate, completely or virtually, competition in the market to which it relates or that it was the

---

150 *Mulcahy v. R.* (1868), L.R. 3 H.L. 306 at 317.

151 *R. v. Parnell* (1881), 14 Cox C.C. 508 at 513 (Q.B.).

152 R.S.C. 1970, c. C-23 [am. 1974-75-76, c. 76, s. 14; 1986, c. 26, s. 30] [R.S.C. 1985, c. C-34].

object of any or all of the parties thereto to eliminate, completely or virtually, competition in that market.

Section 4(1) provides for an exemption for combinations of employees with respect to activities "for their own reasonable protection". But it is far from settled just what the courts may make of this exception, which is based upon the exemption in section 424(2) [466(2)] of the *Criminal Code*. With regard to the latter provision, the Supreme Court of Canada in *Stern*[153] found the expulsion of a union member for failing to comply with a boycott of a third party to be unlawful. Fauteux J. said:

> The criminal law has been amended to grant immunity to trade unions from prosecution for agreements in restraint of trade. This is qualified immunity which flows from a policy designed to promote legitimate endeavours of the working classes. It does not follow that this special immunity will operate in cases of combinations absolutely foreign to such endeavours and of which the end or the means are unlawful.[154]

In the *Electrical Contractors* case,[155] several electrical contractors were found guilty of a conspiracy to suppress competition. What is particularly interesting is that the union was a very significant partner in the impugned scheme. The union, in effect, policed the system by refusing to send its members to work for any contractor who was not a member of the conspiring association of employers. Yet, the union was not charged. Adams points out that there is a similar ambiguity in the combines law of the United States:

> While historically American courts have also given broad scope to the immunity afforded to trade unions, the recent case of *Connell Construction v. Plumbers & Steamfitters, Local 100* striking down a construction industry subcontracting clause extending beyond a particular job site demonstrates that the exemption in that country is by no means clear.[156]

In *Jabour*,[157] the Supreme Court of Canada determined that section 32 of the *Combines Investigation Act*[158] did not apply to the Benchers of the Law Society of British Columbia in the exercise of their discretionary power to discipline a member for advertising in violation of their rules. This "division of powers" judgment effectively exempts from section 32 a professional body's capacity to define professional misconduct as it sees fit despite the court's acknowledgment that amendments to section 32

---

153 *S.I.U. v. Stern*, [1961] S.C.R. 682.

154 *Ibid.*, at 688.

155 *R. v. Electrical Contractors Ass. of Ont.*, [1961] O.R. 265 (C.A.).

156 G.W. Adams, *Canadian Labour Law* (Toronto: Canada Law Book Inc. 1985) at 861.

157 *A.G. Canada v. Law Society of B.C.; Jabour v. A.G. Canada*, [1982] 2 S.C.R. 307.

158 R.S.C. 1970, c. C-23; see now the *Competition Act, supra*, note 152.

proclaimed in 1975 were aimed at expanding the ambit of the section to include professions.[159]

The *Criminal Code* speaks to the matter of several other economic offences which may be committed by a combination of persons. Section 380 [422] creates an indictable offence punishable by imprisonment for up to five years for wilfully breaking a contract, alone or in combination with others which puts life or "valuable" property at risk. There is a saving provision protecting union activity which reads:

(2) No person wilfully breaks a contract within the meaning of subsection (1) by reason only that

(a) being the employee of an employer, he stops work as a result of the failure of his employer and himself to agree upon any matter relating to his employment, or,

(b) being a member of an organization of employees formed for the purpose of regulating relations between employers and employees, he stops work as a result of the failure of the employer and a bargaining agent acting on behalf of the organization to agree upon any matter relating to the employment of members of the organization,

if, before the stoppage of work occurs, all steps provided by law with respect to the settlement of industrial disputes are taken and any provision for the final settlement of differences, without stoppage of work, contained in or by law deemed to be contained in a collective agreement is complied with and effect given thereto.

Section 381 [423] includes in its definition of the crime of intimidation "watching and besetting" which, on its fact, might well prevent all forms of picketing activity by unions or consumers or citizens. However, it allows for an exception so long as the person is watching and besetting "for the purpose only of obtaining or communicating information". Further protection for the freedom of workers to associate in trade unions can be found in section 382 [425] which makes it a summary conviction offence for an employer to discriminate against an employee on the ground that he is a member of a union. Finally, there are the saving provisions of section 425 [467] which prevent a person from being convicted of conspiracy by reason only that he refuses to work with a certain person or for a certain employer or acts in support of his union. As Tarnopolsky has pointed out, these saving provisions of the *Criminal Code* were summarized by Locke J. in the *Zambri* decision in these terms:

The objections to the legality of strikes on the ground that they are unlawful conspiracies or in restraint of trade which might formerly be made the subject

---

159 *Jabour, supra*, note 157 at 346, *per* Estey J.

of criminal charges have long since disappeared by reason of the provisions of the *Criminal Code.*[160]

Several regulatory restrictions on association have passed judicial muster since the proclamation of the Charter. Only two have not. In *Reyes,*[161] the statutory grant of discretionary power to the Governor in Council to refuse to grant citizenship in a case where public order or security was at risk was found to be constitutionally permissible, so far as section 2(d) was concerned. In *Horbas,*[162] section 4(3) of the *Immigration Regulations,*[163] which is aimed at preventing contrived marriages for the purposes of immigration, was found by the Trial Division of the Federal Court not to infringe on freedom of association. In *Downes,*[164] the deportation of a parent who faced leaving his children behind in Canada was found not against section 2(d) of the Charter. In the opinion of McNair J. of the Federal Court Trial Division, freedom of association did not include the parent/child relationship. In *McLean,*[165] the Supreme Court of British Columbia found that section 195.1(1)(c) of the *Criminal Code,* creating the offence of communicating in a public place for the purpose of prostitution, did not offend anyone's freedom of association. In *Re S.,*[166] it was held that the apprehension of a child in need of protection under a child welfare statute was justified under section 1 even if such an act was violative of the child's freedom of association. In *Clearview Dairy Farm Inc.,*[167] a milk board's requirement that a producer not sell his milk privately

---

160 W.S. Tarnopolsky, *The Canadian Bill of Rights,* 2nd ed. rev. (Toronto: Macmillan, 1975) at 209. This assertion by Locke J. is from *C.P.R. v. Zambri,* [1962] S.C.R. 609 at 621.

161 *Reyes v. A.G. Canada* (1983), 149 D.L.R. (3d) 748 (F.C.T.D.).

162 *Horbas v. Min. of Employment & Immigration of Can.* (1985), 22 D.L.R. (4th) 600 (F.C.T.D.). In *Re Gray and Min. of Manpower & Immigration,* May 6, 1985 (F.C.T.D.), Denault J. a similar decision was handed down stating that freedom of association does not embrace freedom to marry.

163 S.O.R. 78/172.

164 *Downes v. Min. of Employment & Immigration of Can.* (1986), 4 F.T.R. 215 (F.C.T.D.). In *Re Gittens and R.* (1982), 137 D.L.R. (3d) 687 (F.C.T.D.), a deportation order was found to infringe s. 2(d) but was saved by s. 1.

165 *R. v. McLean; R. v. Tremayne* (1986), 2 B.C.L.R. (2d) 232 (S.C.).

166 *Re S. and Min. of Social Services,* [1983] 21 A.C.W.S. (2d) 219 (Sask. Q.B., Halvorson J.). For a similar decision, see *Re Shingoose and Min. of Social Services* (1983), 149 D.L.R. (3d) 400 (Sask. Q.B.), leave to appeal granted (1983), 4 D.L.R. (4th) 765 (Sask. C.A.) where the court found that even if s. 2(d) extended to the parent/child relationship, s. 1 saved the child apprehension section. See also *P.M.W. v. Dir. of Child Welfare* (1985), 40 Alta. L.R. (2d) 31, 313 (Alta. Q.B.), for the ruling that an adoption order which had the effect of severing the relationship between a child and a grandmother was not offensive to s. 2(d).

167 *Milk Bd. v. Clearview Dairy Farm Inc.* (1986), 69 B.C.L.R. 220 (B.C.S.C.), aff'd 12 B.C.L.R. (2d) 116 (B.C.C.A.), leave to appeal to S.C.C. refused [1987] 4 W.W.R. 1xvi (note) (S.C.C.).

was found not to infringe upon the producer's freedom of association. Similarly, in *Rio Hotel Ltd.*,[168] a liquor licence which prevented its holder from providing striptease entertainment survived judicial scrutiny under section 2(d). Prison restrictions on visiting rights for remand inmates were found not to infringe section 2(d) in *Re Maltby*.[169] The transfer of a federal inmate from one prison to another was said not to infringe section 2(d) in *Butler*.[170] Finally, according to the Youth Court of British Columbia in *R. v. G.*,[171] the criminal prohibition against keeping a common bawdy house was salvageable under section 1.

The two judgments which found in favour of the restricted individual are remarkable due to the size and long-standing traditions of the impugned restrictive institutions. In *Fraser*,[172] several provisions of the Nova Scotia *Civil Service Act*[173] were found to offend freedom of association. Civil servants were prevented by these sections from working for a political party or contributing money thereto, at a provincial level. Exceptions were allowed in the arena of municipal politics. The government's section 1 justification fell on barren ground because the court was satisfied that less restrictive means were available than the prohibitory measures set forth by the statute. In *Black*,[174] the walls which the Law Society of Alberta had erected to prevent non-residents from practising in partnership with Albertan firms were brought down by the Alberta Court of Appeal because they violated section 2(d). The court rejected the argument that freedom of association must be read as addressing those associations which are formed in order to express or advance some other fundamental freedom listed in section 2 of the Charter. The preambulatory reference to the Rule of Law, coupled with the free-standing status of section 2(d), led the court to conclude that it could properly look to Canadian "socio-ethical convictions". From this analysis, the court concluded that "association to gain a livelihood" was a freedom so fundamental as not to require formal expression in section 2. The Law Society's section 1 argument foundered for the same reason as was given in *Fraser*.

---

168 *Rio Hotel Ltd. v. Liquor Licensing Bd.* (1986), 69 N.B.R. (2d) 20 (N.B.C.A.), aff'd [1987] 2 S.C.R. 59.
169 *Maltby v. A.G. Saskatchewan* (1982), 143 D.L.R. (3d) 649 (Sask. Q.B.), aff'd (1984), 10 D.L.R. (4th) 745 (Sask. C.A.).
170 *Butler v. R.*, *supra*, note 35.
171 *R. v. G.* (1985), 17 C.R.R. 334 (B.C. Youth Ct.).
172 *Fraser v. A.G. Nova Scotia*, *supra*, note 39. A different decision was reached in *Osborne v. Canada (Treasury Bd.)*, [1986] 3 F.C. 206 (T.D.), rev'd in part (July 15, 1988), Doc. No. A-542-86, A-543-86, A-556-86 (Fed. C.A.), where statutory restrictions on the political activities of federal public servants were upheld.
173 *Supra*, note 40.
174 *Black v. Law Soc. of Alta.* (1986), 27 D.L.R. (4th) 527 (Alta. C.A.), leave to appeal to S.C.C. granted (1986), 22 C.R.R. 192n (S.C.C.).

(e) Tribe's Taxonomy of Impermissible Restrictions

Because there is still so little available from the Supreme Court to build upon by way of how to think about freedom of association and its limits, it is of some assistance to have available a means of classifying the various sorts of ways in which the state might attempt to intervene restrictively. The most helpful analysis available is the set of models offered by Tribe, as modified by Cotler.[175]

(i) *Model 1: Where the government seeks to define an organization or association as illegal and/or to punish the fact of membership or affiliation in such group or association.*

The Supreme Court of the United States has developed a twofold test for such a limitation. The group must be shown to have engaged in lawless conduct or in incitement to lawless conduct such as to itself amount to a "clear and present danger" of harm that more speech could not avoid. Second, no individual may be punished for being affiliated with such a group unless the first requirement of lawless conduct on the part of the group is made out and it is then shown that the individual affiliated with it both with knowledge of its lawless conduct and with the specific intention of furthering the group's lawless aims through such affiliation.[176] Nothing resembling these tests has emerged in Canada. Though, as Cotler has reminded us, instances of Canadian governmental invocation of Model 1 can be easily cited. The enactment of section 98 of the *Criminal Code*[177] following the Winnipeg General Strike of 1919 and the invocation of the *War Measures Act*[178] in 1970 are discussed at some length.[179]

(ii) *Model 2: Where the government makes no attempt to label the association as unlawful; but nonetheless interferes significantly either (a) with its internal organization or structure or (b) with an activity integral to the association in the sense that the association's protected purposes would be seriously prejudiced if the activity were disallowed.*

Under American constitutional doctrine, this amounts to a corollary of the tests for Model 1 intervention with the burden on the state to demonstrate a "compelling state interest" that could not be met by any "less intrusive means".

---

175 L. Tribe, *American Constitutional Law* (Mineola, N.Y.: Foundation Press, 1978), at 700-712; Tarnopolsky & Beaudoin, *supra*, note 3, c. 6 by I. Cotler, at 165-185.
176 Tribe, *ibid.* at 704.
177 R.S.C. 1927, c. 36.
178 R.S.C. 1970, c. W-2.
179 Cotler, *supra*, note 3 at 166-169.

(iii) *Model 3: Where the government singles out an association, or persons affiliated with that association, for discriminatory treatment on racial, religious or political grounds.*

Under this model, the state does not attempt to brand the association, as such, but rather aims at persons who have affiliated with it. Although, *Switzman*[180] was treated as a "speech" case, Cotler suggests that it had associational elements in it, such as to make it an example of:

> [W]hat Model 3 envisages, and *Switzman* illustrates, is not the branding of an organization, such as the Communist Party as unlawful, or interference with the internal structure or activity of an otherwise protected association, denying certification to an organization because its leader is a Communist. Rather, what you had here is the prohibition of an act (propagation of Communism), on discriminatory grounds (political belief), and the punishment ,of anyone "associated" with the act (the occupant of premises used for the propagation of Communism.)[181]

(iv) *Model 4: Where associational ties are made the basis for a denial of a government benefit, e.g., where government makes non-membership in disfavoured associations a condition of various opportunities, or conditions such opportunities on oaths of disaffiliation with such associations.*

The Supreme Court of the United States has a doctrine reaching back to Reconstruction, in the aftermath of the Civil War, which sees restrictions on this model struck down because they are unrelated to occupational qualification. The trick is to be able to make a sufficient connection between political association or ideas and occupation. In *Pickering*,[182] the court said that a teacher could not be dismissed for criticizing the Board of Education because, on a balancing test, the speech interests of the public employee weighed against the disruptive effect of the employee's criticism on the governmental authority's capacity to provide its mandated services, were of more significance. But in *National Association of Letter Carriers*,[183] a law which restricted federal employees from taking an active part in political campaigns or organizations was upheld. And, in *Myers*,[184] the *Pickering* doctrine was narrowed in favour of the state by reducing its burden of proof of disruption of public services due to the criticism of an employee, especially in cases where the employee is commenting on a matter of

---

180 *Switzman v. Elbling*, [1957] S.C.R. 285.
181 Cotler *supra*, note 3 at 172.
182 *Pickering v. Bd. of Education*, 391 U.S. 563 (1968). A similar line of reasoning was followed by Rand J. in *Smith & Rhuland, supra*, note 52 at 98-99.
183 *U.S. Civil Service Comm. v. Nat. Assn. of Letter Carriers*, 413 U.S. 548 (1973).
184 *Connick v. Myers*, 103 S. Ct. 1684.

personal interest rather than of public concern.

In the past decade, the Supreme Court of the United States has developed a doctrine which speaks to the practice of political patronage. In the *Burns* decision,[185] the court held that patronage dismissals infringed upon First Amendment rights of association and belief, but exempted employees in confidential policy positions. In *Branti*,[186] the court tightened up the test in favour of First Amendment rights by imposing a burden on the state of demonstrating that a certain political party affiliation is a requirement for a particular public office to be effectively discharged.

The most cited Canadian example of judicial review condemning a government which moved to deny a certain benefit to a person on the footing of this association with a disfavoured organization is the *Roncarelli* case.[187] However, no clear doctrine has been developed, as the checkered history of the cases in this area demonstrate.[188]

(v) *Model 5: Where a government inquires of an organization who its members are, or of an individual what organizations he or she has joined.*

As Tribe has pointed out, American case law in this area has been anything but constant:

> Early cases, never quite repudiated, upheld state power to ascertain the membership of the Ku Klux Klan and the Communist Party. Later cases, now clearly representing settled law, refused to permit suspicion of connection with the Communist Party to justify compelled disclosure of the membership of the NAACP. In a parallel vein, early cases upheld contempt convictions for refusing to answer legislative questions about past or present Communist Party membership, while later cases held such questions impermissible at least when the membership was other than extremely recent.[189]

In *Buckley*,[190] the Supreme Court dealt with the issue of compelled disclosure of political contributions, siding very strongly with the individual's First Amendment rights. It ruled that the state may only compel such disclosure if it can demonstrate that its demand is the very least restrictive means available to serve the compelling state interest in an open political process.

---

185 *Elrod v. Burns*, 427 U.S. 347 (1976).
186 *Branti v. Finkel*, 445 U.S. 507 (1980).
187 *Roncarelli v. Duplessis*, [1959] S.C.R. 121.
188 See *Smith & Rhuland Ltd.*, *supra*, note 52; *Martin v. Law Soc. of B.C.*, [1950] 3 D.L.R. 173 (B.C.C.A.); *Co-op Ctee. on Japanese Canadians v. A.G. Canada*, [1947] A.C. 87 (P.C.); and Cotler's discussion, *supra*, note 175 and note 3 at 177-182.
189 Tribe, *supra*, note 175 at 708.
190 *Buckley v. Valeo*, 424 U.S. 1 (1976).

In *National Citizens' Coalition Inc.*,[191] Medhurst J., of the Alberta Court of Queen's Bench, found himself faced with a similar situation and adopted the same line as *Buckley*, although the case was presented and determined as an expression rather than an association case. The court found two provisions of the *Canada Election Act*,[192] which forbade anyone other than a registered political party or candidate from incurring election expenses during a campaign to be contrary to section 2(b) of the Charter. The argument from equality of the government, that without such a restriction an unfair advantage would go to those third parties who have large amounts of money at their disposal, was rejected. The testimony of an American constitutional expert to the effect that *Buckley* was distinguishable on the ground that Canada might be said to be more fundamentally committed to ensuring that its electoral system "equalizes the ability of all citizens to participate in elections by limiting campaign expenditures"[193] than was the United States, was not taken up by Medhurst J.

3. CONCLUSION

By far the most crucial question to be answered by our Supreme Court under section 2(d) is whether Canada's political culture, including our international human rights commitments, is sufficiently different from that of the United States as to warrant a departure from American constitutional individualist doctrines on freedom of association. It is a matter of more than passing interest that the National Citizens' Coalition has, thus far, succeeded in getting two superior court judges to answer this question in the negative.[194] Thus, we end where Tribe begins with his comment that criticism of the freedom of association doctrines fashioned by the Supreme Court of the United States, as being "insufficiently sensitive to the social dimension of humanity and the communal dimension of society", is well founded.[195]

---

191 *Nat. Citizens' Coalition Inc./Coalition Nationale des Citoyens Inc. v. A.G. Canada* (1985), 11 D.L.R. (4th) 481 (Alta. Q.B.).

192 R.S.C. 1970, c. 14 (1st Supp.).

193 *Nat. Citizens' Coalition, supra*, note 191 at 494.

194 The issue was directly put to Medhurst J. in the *Nat. Citizens'; Coalition* case and, although not as clearly presented to White J. in *Lavigne, supra*, note 58, he fully endorsed the American preoccupation with the individual's right to association and imported it into Canada. The *Lavigne* challenge is supported by the National Citizens' Coalition who have launched a national fund-raising campaign.

195 Tribe, *supra*, note 175 at 700.

For association in its communal sense — activity understandable only as it exists in the context of group experience, as in a family or a commune, for example — has thus far been of no real concern in first amendment doctrine. Likewise, ardent believers in the richness and diversity of a pluralist society . . . will find little comfort in the freedom of association as it has evolved under the umbrella of the first amendment.[196]

---

196 *Ibid.*, at 701.

8

Democratic Rights*
(*Sections 3, 4 and 5*)

Gérald-A. Beaudoin

1. Introduction
2. The Right to Vote, Representation and the Right to be Qualified for Membership (Section 3)
3. Maximum Duration of Legislative Assemblies (Section 4)
4. The Annual Sitting of Legislative Bodies (Section 5)
5. General Conclusion

> The government of a democracy brings the notion of political rights to the level of the humblest citizens.
>
> Alexis de Tocqueville, *Democracy in America.*

1. INTRODUCTION

Democracy is a political system wherein the will of the people is sovereign. The people may exercise power in more than one way: directly, as in the city-states of ancient Greece, or indirectly, by choosing their representatives and leaders.

---

* Translated from French.

The concept of representative democracy developed over a period of several centuries. The ideas and writings of Locke, Montesquieu, Rousseau and Payne and many others promoted its advent in our western societies.

The recognition of modern democratic rights began in the nineteenth century.

The right to choose the government, the right to seek public office, the right to vote periodically, freely and in secret and the right for those elected to sit regularly are the bases of democratic rights.

Canada lives under a system of parliamentary democracy.

Sections 3, 4 and 5 of the *Canadian Charter of Rights and Freedoms*, proclaimed in force on April 17, 1982, deal with democratic rights. They read as follows:

> 3. Every citizen of Canada has a right to vote in an election of members in the House of Commons or of a legislative assembly and to be qualified for membership therein.
> 4.(1) No House of Commons and no legislative assembly shall continue for longer than five years from the date fixed for the return of the writs at the general election of its members.
> (2) In time of real or apprehended war, invasion or insurrection, a House of Commons may be continued by Parliament and a legislative assembly may be continued by the legislature beyond five years if such continuation is not opposed by the votes of more than one-third of the members of the House of Commons or the legislative assembly, as the case may be.
> 5. There shall be a sitting of Parliament and of each legislature at least once every twelve months.

While the right to vote and the right to be qualified for membership are not to be found in the *Constitution Act, 1867*, the principle of the yearly session is stated in section 20; this section was replaced by section 5 of the Charter of 1982. The right to elect a government periodically is mentioned in section 50 of the *Constitution Act, 1867*; it is completed by section 4 of the Charter dealing with continuation of Parliament in circumstances of emergency. Section 4 partly replaces section 91.1 (repealed in 1982) which had been added in 1949 to the *Constitution Act, 1867*. The *Canadian Charter of Rights and Freedoms* affirms the right of every Canadian citizen, without discrimination, to vote in federal and provincial elections. The Charter is part of our Constitution.

Although very important areas under the *Canadian Charter of Rights and Freedoms* are subject to the "notwithstanding clause" of section 33, this is not the case with regard to democratic rights. The only possible override of sections 3, 4 and 5 is by way of formal constitutional amendment.

Section 1 of the Charter contains a limitation clause which applies to the whole of the Charter and which reads as follows:

1. The *Canadian Charter of Rights and Freedoms* guarantees the rights and freedoms set out in it subject only to such reasonable limits prescribed by law as can be demonstrably justified in a free and democratic society.

Exceptions to the principles stated in sections 3, 4 and 5 of the Charter must be examined in the light of this provision.

R. v. Oakes[1] was the first decision defining the scope of the limitations authorized by section 1. Chapter 4 of this book deals with section 1. It is enough to say, for the moment, that the purpose of a law that restricts a right or a freedom must be important and that the means chosen to achieve it must be proportionate to the purpose. As we shall see, this test is very demanding.

This chapter will be divided into three main parts:

1. The right to vote, representation, and the right to be qualified for membership in the federal and provincial elections.
2. The maximum duration of legislative bodies.
3. The annual sitting of legislative bodies.

2. THE RIGHT TO VOTE, REPRESENTATION AND THE RIGHT TO BE QUALIFIED FOR MEMBERSHIP (Section 3)

This analysis will be divided into three sections: (a) the right to vote; (b) the matter of representation; (c) the right to be qualified for membership.

(a) The Right to Vote

(i) *Introduction*

The right to vote is a victory that was won after a lengthy battle. It does not yet exist in all countries. It has been the subject of international agreements, charters and conventions.

Article 25 of the *International Covenant on Civil and Political Rights*[2] provides as follows:

> Every citizen shall have the right and the opportunity, without any of the distinctions mentioned in article 2 and without unreasonable restrictions:
> (a) To take part in the conduct of public affairs, directly or through freely chosen representatives;
> (b) To vote and to be elected at genuine periodic elections which shall

---

1 [1986] 1 S.C.R. 103.

2 In *The International Bill of Human Rights*, Minister of Supply and Services Canada, 1980. The *International Covenant on Civil and Political Rights* became operative on March 23, 1976.

be by universal and equal suffrage and shall be held by secret ballot, guaranteeing the free expression of the will of the electors;

(c) To have access, on general terms of equality, to public service in his country.

This covenant was ratified by Canada on May 19, 1976 and came into force in our country on August 19, 1976. On December 10, 1976, the ten provinces had given their consent at a federal-provincial conference of ministers responsible for the recognition of human rights.

(ii) *Importance*

The right to vote is of paramount importance. After the right to life and liberty, it is one of the most fundamental rights. As Chief Justice James McRuer observed:

> In any truly democratic country, the right or power to vote should be included as a political right. In fact, it is the keystone in the arch of the modern system of political rights in this country.[3]

The right to vote constitutes the very basis of democratic political systems. Mr. Justice Black of the United States Supreme Court, in the case of *Wesberry v. Sanders*,[4] wrote: "Other rights, even the most basic, are illusory if the right to vote is undermined". In the case of *Reynolds v. Sims*,[5] the United States Supreme Court observed that "the right to exercise the franchise in a free and unimpaired manner is preservative of other basic civil and political rights".

(iii) *Pre-Charter guarantees*

The provincial legislatures were empowered by section 92.1 of the *Constitution Act, 1867*, to legislate in the area of electoral law. Parliament was empowered to legislate in the area of federal electoral law by sections 18 and 91.1 as well as by its residual power. The powers previously set forth in sections 91.1 and 92.1 (repealed) can now be found in sections 44 and 45 of the *Constitution Act, 1982*. In Canada, certain statutory charters of rights and freedoms guarantee the right to vote;[6] moreover,

3 J. McRuer, *Royal Commission: Inquiry into Civil Rights*, Vol. 4, Report no. 2 (Toronto: Queen's Printer, 1969) at 1561.

4 376 U.S. 1 at 17 (1964).

5 377 U.S. 533 at 562 (1964).

6 See, *e.g.*, s. 22 of the Quebec *Charter of Human Rights and Freedoms*, R.S.Q. 1977, c. C-12, which provides that: "Every person legally capable and qualified has the right to be a candidate and to vote at an election". See also s. 8 of the *Saskatchewan Human Rights Code*, S.S. 1979, c. S-24.1. As P. Boyer states in *Political Rights: The Legal*

federal and provincial electoral Acts provide for this right. Certain sections of the *Constitution Act, 1867* (such as sections 41, 50 and 51) refer to it. The right to vote was also part of our constitutional conventions, yet the principle of universal suffrage was not expressly entrenched in our written Constitution. Charters which are merely statutory are subject to explicit legislative derogation. Consequently, the legislator could grant or withdraw the right to vote at will.

In the *Homma*[7] decision, a British Columbia statute which disenfranchised the Chinese, Japanese and Indians was declared *intra vires* by the judicial committee of the Privy Council; it was held to be a valid exercise of section 92.1 of the *Constitution Act, 1867*, which enabled the province to modify its Constitution.

In the *Winner* case,[8] Justice Rand referred to the *Homma* case[9] and observed that not all British subjects benefit from the same political privileges; Chief Justice Laskin made reference to this in the *Morgan* case.[10]

The right to vote was extended progressively. Its history constitutes a veritable odyssey. At the outset, it was tied to property rights, and was not secret. Women's suffrage is recent, dating back to the First World War at the federal level and to the Second World War in Quebec. Suffrage has become truly universal only quite recently.[11] Even though it has become part of our mores, it was not protected by any direct constitutional guarantee.

Framework of Elections in Canada (Toronto: Butterworths, 1981) at 124, even though the right to vote is not "enshrined" in the Constitution, it has been protected just as effectively by the courts. A number of cases are quoted to support this: *Re North Perth; Hessin v. Lloyd* (1891), 21 O.R. 538 (C.A.); *Re Brockville and Elizabethtown* (1871), 32 U.C.Q.B. 132 (C.A.); *Re Provincial Elections Act* (1903), 10 B.C.R. 114 (C.A.); *Lancaster v. Shaw* (1906), 12 O.L.R. 66; *Cawley v. Branchflower* (1884), 1 B.C.R. (Pt. 2) 35; *R. v. Knox* (1912), 1 D.L.R. 843; *Crawford v. St. John* (1898), 34 N.B.R. 560 (C.A.).

7 *Cunningham v. Tomey Homma*, [1903] A.C. 151 (P.C.).

8 *Winner v. S.M.T. (Eastern) Ltd.*, [1951] S.C.R. 887 at 919, var'd [1954] A.C. 541 (*sub nom. A.G. Ont. v. Winner*) (P.C.).

9 *Cunningham, supra*, note 7.

10 *Morgan v. A.G. Prince Edward Island*, [1976] 2 S.C.R. 349.

11 *Dominion Elections Act*, S.C. 1919-20, c. 46, s. 29(1); *An Act granting to women the right to vote and to be eligible as candidates*, S.Q. 1940, c. 7. See T. Casgrain, *Une femme chez les hommes* (Montréal: Editions du jour, 1971). In France, J.P. Cot and P. Gabont in *Citoyens et Candidats* (Paris: Laffont, 1977), write at 15: "Each citizen has an equal voice in political elections, since 1848 for men, 1945 for women" [translation]. In the United States, women have had the right to vote since 1919-20, as we will see further on. At the federal level, the unrestricted and unqualified right to vote was acquired by the Indians and Doukhobors in 1960. See Boyer, *supra*, note 6, at 134.

(iv) *Constitutional guarantees since April 17, 1982*

Section 3 of the Charter now confers on the right to vote the status of an explicit constitutional norm and compels its recognition by Parliament and the legislatures.

In principle, the coming into force of the Charter gives every Canadian citizen the right to vote. The federal Parliament has jurisdiction over citizenship. This can no longer be doubted following the *Winner*[12] and *Morgan*[13] cases. This power is based on section 91.25 of the *Constitution Act, 1867* and also on the federal residual power.[14] Section 3 entrenches the right to vote and the right to be qualified for membership in federal and provincial legislative assemblies. (Yukon and the Northwest Territories are considered provinces for this purpose, according to section 30 of the Charter).

Section 3 makes no reference either to the municipal or the school board level. The right to vote at these levels enjoys the same protection as that which existed before April 17, 1982. At the municipal level, the right to vote is protected by statutes; the same is true with regard to school boards, unless the right to vote were to be considered by the courts as part of the denominational rights guaranteed under section 93. The answer to this question involves a study of section 93 and not a study of the Charter.[15]

(v) *Comparative law*

The American Constitution of 1787 refers in section 2 of article 1 to the election of the members of the House of Representatives every two years by the "People of the several States". The Seventeenth Amendment provides for two senators for each state, elected by the people of those states for a term of six years.

A number of other constitutional amendments relate to the right to vote:

> XV. The right of citizens of the United States to vote shall not be denied or abridged by the United States or by any State on account of race, colour or previous condition of servitude.

---

12 *Supra*, note 8.
13 *Supra*, note 10.
14 The first *Citizenship Act* came into force January 1, 1947 and a second one followed in 1977. See G.-A. Beaudoin, *Le partage des pouvoirs*, 3rd ed. (Ottawa: Editions de l'Université d'Ottawa, 1983) at 433-438.
15 See Beaudoin, *ibid.*, c. VIII.

XIX. The right of citizens of the United States to vote shall not be denied or abridged by the United States or by any State on account of sex.

XXIV. The right of citizens of the United States to vote in any primary or other election for President or Vice-President for electors for President or Vice-President, or for Senators or Representatives in Congress, shall not be denied or abridged by the Untied States or any State by reason of failure to pay any poll tax or other tax.

XXVI. The right of citizens of the United States who are eighteen years of age or older, to vote shall not be denied or abridged by the United States or any State on account of age.[16]

In the United States, the Constitution and state laws provide for the existence and the exercise of the right to vote. Once recognized in the constitution of a state, the right to vote can no longer be abridged. According to the federal Constitution, the states may not discriminate in this area and must respect "due process of law". The legislator must respect the principle of "equal and free voting".

The American Constitution confers powers on the states to impose certain limitations on the right to vote relating, for example, to nationality, residence or criminal record.

In France, article 3 of the Constitution states that:

Suffrage may be direct or indirect under the conditions stipulated by the Constitution. It shall always be universal, equal and secret. All French citizens of both sexes who have reached their majority and who enjoy civil and political rights may vote under the conditions to be determined by law.[17] [Translation]

Conditions relating to the right to vote or to qualifications for elective office are largely similar in our democracies, although certain constitutions may be more explicit than others. A number of countries have established the voting age at eighteen years.

The *Canadian Charter of Rights and Freedoms* mentions neither the voting age nor secret balloting. This is a constitutional lacuna which calls for legislative or judicial intervention. It appears inconceivable that in our modern democracies an election could proceed otherwise than by secret ballot. At the federal level, secret ballots have been the rule since 1875.

---

16 Fifteenth Amendment, 1869-70; Nineteenth Amendment, 1919-20; Twenty-fourth Amendment, 1962-64; and Twenty-sixth Amendment, 1971.

17 Constitution of the Fifth French Republic, October 4, 1958. The translation is from A.P. Blaustein and G.H. Flanz, *Constitutions of the Countries of the World*, Vol. V (New York: Oceana Publications Inc., 1974) at 4 of the Constitution annex.

(vi) *Present legislative electoral provisions*

Section 14 of the *Canada Elections Act*[18] establishes the basic principle that every man and woman who has attained the age of eighteen years and is a Canadian citizen has a right to vote. Sections 16 and 17 add the criterion of ordinary residence.

According to section 16(1) of the *Canada Elections Act*:

[E]very person who is qualified as an elector is entitled to have his name included in the list of electors for the polling division in which he is ordinarily resident on the enumeration date for the election and to vote at the polling station established therein.

The voting age was set at eighteen at the federal level in 1970.[19]

The age set by the *Canada Elections Act* appears reasonable. This is the age of majority in almost all the provinces. The provinces, under section 92.13 of the *Constitution Act, 1867*, have the authority to enact legislation establishing the age of majority. The federal Act could simply incorporate by reference the age of majority set by the provinces or set an age of its own.

Only one province, British Columbia, sets the voting age in provincial elections at nineteen years of age. This is also the case in the Northwest Territories.[20] At the federal level and in all the other provinces, the voting age is set at eighteen.

Is this disparity reconcilable with sections 3 and 15 of the Charter? It will be up to the courts to decide in the light of the criteria established by the *Oakes* decision.[21] Such a disparity would appear to be of marginal importance.

Sections 44, 45(8), (9) and (10) and 69(b) of the *Canada Elections Act*[22] guarantee the secrecy of the vote.

Not every person who is qualified to vote is entitled to exercise that right.

---

18 R.S.C. 1970, c. 14 (1st Supp.) [R.S.C. 1985, c. E-2].

19 S.C. 1969-70, c. 49, s. 14(1).

20 For the required voting age in the ten provinces, see the following legislative provisions: British Columbia, R.S.B.C. 1979, c. 103, s. 2(1)(a); Alberta, R.S.A. 1980, c. E-2, s. 1 (f.1)(ii); Saskatchewan, R.S.S. 1978, c. E-6, s. 28(2)(b); Manitoba, R.S.M. 1970, c. E30, s. 17(1)(b); Ontario, S.O. 1984, c. 54, s. 15(1)(a); Quebec, R.S.Q. 1977, c. E-3,2, s. 54; New Brunswick, R.S.N.B. 1973, c. E-3, s. 43(1)(a); Nova Scotia, R.S.N.S. 1967, c. 83, s. 25(1)(a); Prince Edward Island, R.S.P.E.I. 1974, c. E-1, s. 20(a); Newfoundland, R.S.N. 1970, c. 106, s. 3(a)[1971, c. 69, s.2; 1974, c. 80, s. 3]. The voting age of 18 is the same in all provinces except British Columbia, where it is 19 years. In the Northwest Territories, it is 19 years of age: R.S.N.W.T. 1974, c. A-1, s. 2(1).

21 *Supra*, note 1.

22 *Supra*, note 18.

(vii) *Persons disqualified from voting*

The following persons are not qualified to vote according to the terms of section 14(4) of the *Canada Elections Act*:

(a) the Chief Electoral Officer;

(b) the Assistant Chief Electoral Officer;

(c) the returning officer for each electoral district during his term of office, except when there is an equality of votes on the recount, as provided in this Act;

(d) every judge appointed by the Governor in Council [with the exception of a judge of the Citizenship Court];

(e) every person undergoing punishment as an inmate in any penal institution for the commission of any offence;

(f) every person who is restrained of his liberty of movement or deprived of the management of his property by reason of mental disease; and

(g) every person who is disqualified from voting under any law relating to the disqualification of electors for corrupt or illegal practices.[23]

With the adoption of the Charter, the right to vote became a "constitutional right", which is affirmed in absolute terms in section 3. One may accordingly wonder whether any exceptions can exist. These exceptions will have to be examined in the light of the criteria stated in the limitation clause of section 1, as interpreted by the *Oakes* decision,[24] in order to determine whether they will be acceptable in a free and democratic society. If they are found not to be so, the court will set them aside as contravening section 3 of the Charter, which henceforth constitutes part of the fundamental law of the country.

We believe that very few exceptions to the right to vote can be justified under the criteria formulated in the *Oakes* decision.[25]

In this context, the question of the negation rather than the limitation of the right to vote and the right to qualify for electoral office is raised. Section 1 of the Charter speaks of limitations and not of outright denial. The case law on this point has been somewhat unclear. Since 1984 however, the Supreme Court appears to recognize that the limitation of a right can, in certain cases, amount to a denial of such right. This appears to be the better opinion. It was affirmed, however, only by way of *obiter* in the *Quebec Association of Protestant School Boards* decision (the *Bill 101* case).[26]

---

23 These exceptions can be found in the provincial electoral acts *mutatis mutandis*. *E.g.*, in Quebec, the Director General of Elections. With respect to the judges of the Citizenship Court, see the *Citizenship Act*, S.C. 1974-75-76, c. 108, s. 42.

24 *Supra*, note 1.

25 *Ibid.*

26 *A.G. Quebec v. Que. Assn. of Protestant School Bds*, [1984] 2 S.C.R. 66.

(viii) *Analysis of each exception*

A. *The Chief Electoral Officer and his assistant.* The Chief Electoral Officer is a senior civil servant answerable to the legislative and not the executive branch of government.[27] Appointed by resolution of the House of Commons, he has the rank of a Deputy Minister and receives the salary of a Federal Court judge; he may only be removed by the Governor General on an address of both federal legislative Houses. He has executive powers and plays a most important role in Canadian democracy, particularly in setting up and operating the electoral process. He must, by definition, be impartial and enjoy the most absolute trust of all the political parties in the House of Commons. According to a tradition which has been incorporated in the *Canada Elections Act*, he is disqualified from voting.

In our opinion, the Supreme Court could accept such a limitation to section 3 of the *Canadian Charter of Rights and Freedoms*. This exception meets the criteria contained in the limitation clause of section 1. This is a matter of evaluation, of course. In the United Kingdom, the Clerk of the Crown in Chancery does not vote. Neither does the Director General of Elections in Quebec.[28]

Since the *Canada Elections Act* allows the Chief Electoral Officer to delegate important powers to his assistant,[29] it follows that whatever is appropriate for the former must also apply to the latter; it is reasonable that these two officers be above the fray. As Lord Hewart C.J. pointed out in the case of *R. v. Sussex Justices*:

> [A] long line of cases shows that it is not merely of some importance but is of fundamental importance that justice not only be done, but should manifestly and undoubtedly be seen to be done.[30]

This judicial principle would apply, by analogy, to the electoral process.

B. *The Returning Officer.* This person, in fact, benefits from a conditional voting right that may be exercised only when a recount results in a tie.

---

27 As Chief Justice Duff stated in the case of *Temple v. Bulmer,* [1943] S.C.R. 265 at 267, the Chief Electoral Officer at the provincial level (and this applies to the federal level) is an "officer under the control of the Legislative Assembly and answerable to the Legislative Assembly". The office was created in 1920. This senior civil servant replaced the Clerk of the Crown in Chancery. This office also exists in the United Kingdom: see *Erskine May's Treatise on the Law, Privileges, Proceedings and Usage of Parliament,* Sir Barnett Cocks, ed., 17th ed. (London: Butterworths, 1964) at 181-182, 186-187.

28 *Election Act,* R.S.Q. 1977, c. E-3.2, s. 55.

29 *Canada Elections Act, supra,* note 18.

30 [1924] 1 K.B. 256 at 259.

It is difficult to understand why this officer is disqualified from voting, especially since he is granted the right to vote in the case of a tie. Why then take away his right to a secret vote since, in the rare cases where he is called upon to cast it, his vote becomes publicly known? However, the annual reports of 1984 and 1985[31] of the Chief Electoral Officer of Canada do not recommend that the Returning Officer be granted the right to vote.

C. *Judges appointed by the Governor General.* Citizenship Court judges have the right to vote.[32] The exception we are considering refers to judges presiding over the courts mentioned in section 96 of the *Constitution Act, 1867* (including, of course, courts of appeal) as well as courts established by federal statute, according to the terms of section 101 of the *Constitution Act, 1867*, such as the Supreme Court of Canada and the Federal Court.

Provincially appointed judges are not listed in the exceptions in the *Canada Elections Act.* There appears to be nothing to prevent them from voting at the federal level. However, judges appointed by the Governor General cannot vote in federal elections. Such has been the tradition, based, it seems, on the theory of the separation of powers and on the principle of judicial independence. The independence of the judiciary is a fundamental principle recognized, in part, by section 99 of the *Constitution Act, 1867*, by a long tradition and by judicial decisions.[33] Once the *Meech Lake Accords* are ratified, the principle of judicial independence will be clearly, explicitly and totally affirmed.

The independence of the judiciary was enshrined in England by, *inter alia*, the *Act of Settlement* of 1701. For more than 250 years, as Lord Denning observed,[34] the judiciary in the United Kingdom has been totally separated from the legislative and executive branches of government.

Must we conclude from these principles that judges should not vote?

31 J.-M. Hamel, *Statutory Report of the Chief Electoral Officer of Canada,* 1984 (Ottawa: Supply and Services, 1985) (SEI-5/1985, ISBN 0-662-53354-2); *Report of the Chief Electoral Officer of Canada on Proposed Legislative Changes, 1985* (Ottawa: Supply and Services, 1985) (SEI-5/1985, ISBN 0-662-53998-2).

32 Citizenship Court judges have been granted the right to vote: *Citizenship Act, supra* note 23, s. 42.

33 Lord A. Denning, *The Spirit of the British Constitution* (1951), 29 *Can. Bar Rev.* 1180; B.L. Strayer, *Judicial Review of Legislation in Canada* (Toronto: U. of T. Press, 1968); W.R. Lederman, *"The Independence of the Judiciary"* (1956), 34 *Can. Bar Rev.* 769 and 1139; J. Deschênes, *Masters in Their House* (Montreal, Judicial Council of Canada 1981); P.S. Millar & C. Baar, *Judicial Administration in Canada* (Montreal: McGill-Queen's University Press, 1981); B.L. Strayer, *The Canadian Constitution and the Courts,* 3rd ed. (Toronto: Butterworth, 1988).

34 *Ibid.,* at 1182.

We believe on the contrary that they should, and that the exception is not justified.

In *Judges v. A.G. Saskatchewan*,[35] the Judicial Committee of the Privy Council declared that judges' salaries were not protected by some higher principle that would make inoperative an act levying a tax on the remuneration of judges; neither their independence nor any other judicial attribute would be affected by such a tax.

Just as judges are subject to tax laws of general application without their judicial independence being affected, so could they exercise the right to vote, in our view, without deleterious effect on their independence.

Let us remember that in France, in the United Kingdom and in the United States, the judges vote. Judges in Quebec and in Ontario are entitled to vote in provincial elections.

In its June 1986 *White Paper on the Reform of the Elections Act*,[36] the Canadian government recommends permitting judges to exercise the right to vote.

Bill C-79, tabled June 30, 1987, gives effect to the Mulroney government's intention of granting the right to vote to judges appointed by the federal executive. This, in our view, is justified.

Parliament and the provincial legislatures have given the judges jurisdiction over contested elections. Should such a case occur in a district where a judge had voted, it could be heard by a judge from another district.

D. *Inmates.* Prison inmates have the right to vote in Newfoundland, Ontario, Manitoba, Saskatchewan, Alberta, British Columbia, the Yukon and the Northwest Territories. In Quebec, prison inmates have the right to vote and they exercise that right in those institutions when a provincial general election is called; inmates in penitentiaries in Quebec also have the right to vote and can effectively exercise this right under an agreement between the Quebec Chief Electoral Officer and the director of a federal or provincial penal institution.[37] At the federal level and in provincial

---

35 (1937), 53 T.L.R. 464 at 466 (P.C.). See R.A. Olmsted, *Decisions of the Judicial Committee of the Privy Council relating to the British North American Act 1867 and the Canadian Constitution*, Vol. III (Ottawa: Queen's Printer, 1954) at 174.

36 *White Paper on Election Law Reform*, June 1986, at 2. In *Muldoon*, the Federal Court per Walsh J. on November 3, 1988, ruled that s. 14(4)(d) of the *Canada Elections Act*, which deprived judges appointed by the Governor General of the right to vote, is invalid. The judges were thus allowed to vote in the federal elections of 1988.

37 In the case of *Forget v. Kaplan* (1981), 2 C.H.R.R. D/441-443 (F.C.T.D.), inmates in a penitentiary requested that the Federal Court (Trial Division) prevent the Solicitor-General from interfering when penitentiary inmates vote in the Quebec provincial election. It was decided by Mr. Justice Louis Marceau that this was not a case involving

elections in Prince Edward Island, Nova Scotia and New Brunswick, inmates of either provincial or federal institutions do not have voting rights. This exception to the right to vote is found in many countries. The loss of the right is no doubt considered traditionally as an additional punishment to the loss of freedom. Other justifications have also been advanced, such as considerations of security: the possibility of escape, of violence, etc.

It has also been argued that prisoners do not have access to candidates. This is not quite as valid now that candidates appear on television and speak on the radio; moreover, prisoners read newspapers. A number of people among the general public no longer bother to attend political meetings or to participate in them. Inmates of our penal institutions could have access to information to the point of being able to cast an enlightened vote.

Is it reasonable in a free and democratic society to deprive prisoners of their voting rights? Are the reasons which justify depriving prisoners of their freedom applicable to voting rights? We believe that the courts should recognize the right of prisoners to vote; the exception, in our view, is contrary to the principle of section 3 of the *Canadian Charter of Rights and Freedoms* and cannot be justified under section 1 of the Charter.

Except for the *Badger* decision,[38] the courts, on the whole, have limited the recognition of voting rights to persons on probation.

In *Reynolds v. A.G. British Columbia,*[39] the British Columbia Court of Appeal, in a majority decision, confirmed a decision of the provincial Supreme Court to the effect that persons on probation should have the right to vote. In that case, Reynolds, who was on probation, wished both to vote and to run as a candidate in the provincial election. The trial court ruled against him because of section 3(1)(b) of the British Columbia *Election Act*[40] which deprives both inmates and persons on probation of the right to vote. Moreover, persons who are not entitled to vote cannot run for office.

The Court of Appeal was of the view that the denial of the right to vote in the case of a person on probation could not be justified under section 1 of the Charter. Chief Justice Nemetz expressed the opinion that the right to vote in a free and democratic society as an essential step towards an individual's complete rehabilitation.

---

the right to vote but rather the impact of imprisonment on the exercise of such a right. The court rejected the petition for the reason that the Quebec *Election Act* cannot prescribe the manner in which federal authorities should organize the penal system.

38 *Badger v. A.G. Manitoba* (1986), 30 D.L.R. (4th) 108 (Man. Q.B.), aff'd (1986), 32 D.L.R. (4th) 310 (Man. C.A.).

39 (1982), 143 D.L.R. (3d) 365 (B.C.S.C.), aff'd (1984), 11 D.L.R. (4th) 380 (B.C.C.A.), leave to appeal to S.C.C. granted (1984), 11 D.L.R. (4th) 380n (S.C.C.).

40 R.S.B.C. 1979, c. 103.

The court did, however, state that to deprive an inmate in a penal institution of the exercise of the right to vote constituted a justifiable limit under section 1 of the Charter.[41]

In *Maltby v. A.G. Saskatchewan*,[42] the Saskatchewan Court of Appeal held that a provision of that province's electoral Act, which did not provide for any mechanism enabling persons in custody while awaiting trial to exercise their right to vote, contravened section 3 of the Charter and could not be justified under section 1. Such mechanisms exist for inmates of hospitals and sanatoria.

In *Re Jolivet and Barker and R.*,[43] two inmates challenged the validity of section 14(4)(e) of the *Canada Elections Act*.[44] This section deprives penitentiary inmates of the exercise of voting rights. Mr. Justice Taylor held that voting rights could be restricted; the requirements of order and discipline prevent the exercise by the inmate of an enlightened democratic choice; the negation of the right to vote may be justified in this case. Restrictive conditions entailed by imprisonment result in the impossibility for inmates to exercise their rights in a judicious manner. We believe that in today's electronic age, with the media increasingly present, this argument is not very convincing.

In *Gould v. A.G. Canada*,[45] the Supreme Court of Canada confirmed a decision of the Federal Court of Appeal which had refused to grant an injunction enabling an inmate to vote in the federal election of September 4, 1984. Justice Mahoney of the Federal Court of Appeal, writing for the majority, observed that the purpose of an interlocutory injunction was to maintain the *status quo* or to re-establish a former situation and not to grant the plaintiff the remedy he requested in his action.

Justice Thurlow, in a dissenting opinion, observed:

> When it is necessary, the Court, as it seems to me, must be prepared to be innovative in devising procedures and means, not heretofore employed, to enforce rights guaranteed by the Charter.[46]

In the *Badger* case,[47] Mr. Justice Scollin of the Manitoba Court of Queen's Bench held that section 31(d) of the *Manitoba Elections Act*,[48] which prohibited any person who was serving a sentence in a prison or place of detention for the commission of an offence from voting at a

---

41 *Supra*, note 39.

42 (1984), 10 D.L.R. (4th) 745 (Sask. C.A.).

43 (1983), 7 C.C.C. (3d) 431 (B.C.S.C.).

44 *Supra*, note 18.

45 [1984] 2 S.C.R. 124.

46 *Gould v. A.G. Canada*, [1984] F.C. 1133 at 1138 (C.A.), aff'd *supra*, note 45.

47 *Supra*, note 38.

48 *Manitoba Elections Act*, C.C.S.M.), c. E30.

provincial election, contravened section 3 of the Charter and did not constitute a reasonable limit under section 1. This absolute unqualified prohibition does not conform to the criterion of proportionality set out in the *Oakes* decision.[49] In our view, the *Badger* decision is a step in the right direction.

In the *Lukes* case,[50] the Manitoba Court of Queen's Bench confirmed the trial court's judgment and rejected the appellants' request for an order.[51] In this case, the appellants, who were inmates in a federal penal institution, requested an order against the Chief Electoral Officer of Manitoba enjoining him to establish directives which would have enabled them to exercise their right to vote. Because of time limitations (the elections were to be held on the following day) and certain required details which were lacking, the court refused to grant the order. Would it have done so if the election had not been held at such a close date? Possibly so, judging by the reasons advanced for the refusal to grant the order.[52]

E. *Persons whose liberty of movement is restrained or who are deprived of the management of their property by reason of mental disease.* It is possible for chronically ill persons in our system to exercise their right to vote in hospitals, since polling stations are provided for that purpose.

It is also possible for a sick person undergoing regular treatments to vote at an advance poll or by proxy. In this respect, the *Canada Elections Act*[53] would appear to meet the criteria stated in sections 1 and 3 of the Charter.

In principle, the mental patient does not vote. Insofar as the exercise of the right to vote is concerned, criteria used to gauge mental illness appear to be somewhat nebulous. The question has received some attention. We agree with the remarks made by the Honourable Mr. Justice James McRuer:

> The confinement to a hospital or the restraint on liberty because of illness are not the proper tests to apply to the right to vote. The test should be the extent of mental illness, which would be subject to certification or the order of the court in proper cases.[54]

Professor Viateur Bergeron in his book on persons suffering from mental disease states that only those patients who are in custodial treatment, who

---

49 *Supra*, note 1.
50 *R. v. Lukes* (1986), 39 Man. R. (2d) 107 (Q.B.). Decision handed down concurrently with *Badger, supra*, note 38.
51 *Ibid.*
52 *Ibid.* at 112.
53 *Supra*, note 18.
54 McRuer, *supra*, note 3, at 1520, 1596. The quote is taken from p. 1520.

are under the jurisdiction of the public trustee or who have been declared legally incompetent should be deprived of the right to vote.[55]

In its June 1986 *White Paper on Election Law Reform*,[56] the federal government recommends that section 14(4)(f) of the *Canada Elections Act* be amended to enable Canadians suffering from mental disease to be enumerated and to vote. However, in order to prevent difficulties, the government believes that (1) no polling station should be established in mental hospitals; (2) that persons suffering from mental disease and confined to psychiatric hospitals should vote in person and should not be entitled to vote by proxy; and (3) that persons suffering from mental disease who have the right to vote should vote in the riding where the institution in which they reside is situated, as is the case for residents of hospitals for the chronically ill under the provisions of the present law.

The Mulroney government in Bill C-79, tabled June 30, 1987 has indicated its willingness to grant the mentally handicapped an unlimited right to vote.

F. *Persons deprived of their right to vote as a result of corrupt or illegal practices.* This provision constitutes both a punishment of the guilty person and a protection for society. The punishment is for a limited time. Until recently it seemed to be an acceptable restriction in a free and democratic society. However, Chief Justice Glube of Nova Scotia held differently in the *Maclean* decision.[57] This decision is analyzed below under "(C) The Right to be Qualified for Membership".

G. *Other cases.* Certain other persons cannot vote. First among these is the Sovereign. The Queen, in law, is Queen of Canada; however, she is not a Canadian citizen and consequently does not vote.

But what of the Crown's representative? The Governor General and the Lieutenant Governors should continue, in practice, not to exercise their right to vote. The choice of a Prime Minister by the Crown's representative is almost always automatic; however, in those rare cases where there is an impasse, the Crown's representative may be called upon to choose and

---

55 V. Bergeron, *L'attribution d'une protection légale aux malades mentaux* (Montréal: Éditions Blais, 1981) at 87, 193 *et seq.*

56 *Supra*, note 36. On October 17, 1988, in *Cdn. Disability Rights Council v. Canada*, Madam Justice Reed of the Federal Court, *in banco*, declared invalid s. 14(4)(f) of the *Canada Elections Act*, which deprives persons suffering from mental disease of their right to vote.

57 *Maclean v. A.G. Nova Scotia* (1987), 76 N.S.R. (2d) 296 (T.D.).

to invite one person rather than another to form a cabinet. Nowhere, however, does the act limit their right to vote and this, in our view, is quite surprising.

Section 15 of the *Canada Elections Act*, which deprived certain persons working for pay during elections of the right to vote, was repealed in 1983.[58] This provision, in our view, was incompatible with the principle affirmed in section 3 of the *Charter.*

(ix) *Voting*

The entrenchment of the right to vote leads us to examine voting abroad, compulsory voting, proxy voting, advance polling, voting by mail and protest votes.

A. *Voting abroad.* Members of the armed forces,[59] public servants[60] and their dependents[61] are entitled to vote abroad, as provided by the *Canada Elections Act.*[62] We fail to see why, within acceptable limits, it should not be possible to ensure to other Canadians the right to vote abroad.

In its June 1986 *White Paper on Election Law Reform,*[63] the federal government expressed the view that voting abroad by public servants and their dependents in Canadian embassies and military bases has proven itself as a method which enables a reasonable degree of control over the identity of voters. It recommends that this procedure be followed in the future for public servants and their dependents and that other Canadians abroad have the choice between voting in a Canadian diplomatic mission or military base or voting by correspondence. I subscribe to this opinion.

Bill C-79, presented for first reading on June 30, 1987 provides that all Canadian citizens residing abroad may vote in a general election. Voting will be by correspondence.

B. *Compulsory voting.* Does the entrenchment of the vote imply compulsory voting? Such is the case in Australia, where, unlike in Canada, voting is compulsory at the federal level as well as at the state level.

One can think of several good reasons to implement such a system; however, compulsory voting is not a necessary implication of entrenchment.

---

58 S.C. 1980-81-82-83, c. 164, s. 5.

59 See *Canada Elections Act, supra*, note 18, s. 17(7) and Sched. II.

60 *Ibid.*

61 *Ibid.*, Sched. II.

62 *Ibid.*, s. 17(7) and Sched. II.

63 *Supra*, note 36 at 8.

If the right to vote exists, why would it not be possible for certain reasons also to have the right not to exercise it or to register a protest vote on the ballot? I do not believe that section 3 of the *Canadian Charter of Rights and Freedoms* requires that voting become compulsory.

C. *Voting by proxy.* According to section 46 of the *Canada Elections Act*,[64] students, sick persons, mariners, fishermen and prospectors may all vote by proxy. The basic principle is that anyone unable to get to a polling station on election day may vote by proxy. In general, students vote at the place where they ordinarily reside; students away from home on account of their studies may vote by proxy. Single students who have left their parents' home must vote in the riding where they normally reside.

Persons held while awaiting trial, those that are absent and people on holiday may not vote by proxy. The government recommends, in its *White Paper*[65] that persons who are detained before trial should be allowed to vote by proxy.

Our prisoners of war, in certain cases, may vote by proxy as provided by Schedule IV of the *Canada Elections Act*.[66] This possibility is also extended to handicapped persons.

The federal government in its *White Paper*[67] also recommends an extension of proxy voting.

In his annual report of 1985,[68] Mr. Jean-Marc Hamel properly subscribes to the recommendations of the Standing Committee on Privileges and Elections to the effect that proxy voting should be extended to all persons who are entitled to vote.

If the right to vote is granted to Canadians living abroad, *a fortiori* should it be provided that Canadians in Canada who are temporarily absent from their domicile be entitled to vote? Bill C-79 is to this effect.

The Court of Appeal of British Columbia dealt with the issue of proxy voting in *Hoogbruin v. A.G. British Columbia*.[69] Hoogbruin and Raffa, two British Columbia students, were pursuing a course of studies in Ontario. Their names appeared on the list of electors. However, the law of their province did not provide for the exercise of the right to vote for persons absent on the day of the election. The two students were entitled only to vote in advance or to present themselves at the polling station on election day. As their course was not scheduled to end until after election day,

---

64 *Supra*, note 18.
65 *Supra*, note 36 at 30.
66 *Supra*, note 18, Sched. IV: Canadian Prisoners of War Voting Rules.
67 *Supra*, note 36 at 29.
68 *Supra*, note 31 at 7. (1985 Report).
69 (1986), 70 B.C.L.R. 1 (C.A.).

neither of these options would have enabled the students to exercise their right to vote.

Chief Justice Nemetz, writing for the Court of Appeal, invalidated section 2(1) of the *Elections Act*[70] on the grounds that the provision contained no procedure giving effect to the right to vote. It is not enough to provide for a right to vote. This right to vote must be efficacious, otherwise it is deprived of all substance.

D. *Advance Polling.* It is likely that on election day more than one voter will be away from his ordinary residence. This is the reason for advance polling as provided by the *Canada Elections Act.*[71]

Basically, those who cannot vote on election day may do so in advance. People going on holidays, for example, may take advantage of this; otherwise, the fact that they are away from their place of residence on election day will entail a loss of their voting right. Handicapped persons may also vote in advance.

Bill C-79 provides that any person absent on election day be entitled to vote in advance.

E. *Voting by mail.* Section 3 of the *Canadian Charter of Rights and Freedoms* should normally encourage the legislator to favour this form of voting for those unable to attend at the polls, although appropriate measures should be taken to avoid possible fraud. We suggest that this manner of exercising the right to vote be added to our electoral laws.

F. *Protest votes.* Protest votes are a matter of some interest. The Chief Electoral Officer, in his 1985 report,[72] recommends an amendment to accommodate this possibility. The voter should therefore be entitled to cast a protest vote "effected by means of a mark on a specific section of the ballot itself". This suggestion appears compatible with our democratic concerns.

(x) *Conclusion*

The right to vote is entrenced in the Constitution. This means that exceptions to this right must be drafted with great care in order that the courts, through the constitutional review process, be able to evaluate if

---

70 R.S.B.C. 1979, c. 103.

71 *Supra*, note 18, ss. 91 *et seq.*

72 Hamel, *supra*, note 31, at 6 (1985 Report).

it is reasonable in a free and democratic society to deprive certain categories of individuals of the right to vote. These limitations can only be very rare.

The different exceptions presently recognized by the federal and provincial election acts will tend to become less numerous.

The exercise of the right to vote is implicitly protected. The citizen must benefit from a reasonable time period in order to vote. Moreover, the citizen is entitled to exercise his vote in an enlightened fashion, which presupposes a certain right to information.

In any event, courts will recognize the *locus standi* of any elector because the right to vote is the basis of our system of parliamentary democracy; any citizen may raise the question of voting rights before the courts. The *Thorson*,[73] *McNeil*[74] and *Borowski*[75] decisions are pertinent in this respect. The *Canadian Charter of Rights and Freedoms* itself provides for a remedy in section 24.

A. *The issue of residence.* It is reasonable for the right to vote to imply certain criteria of residence.

The courts have dealt with the issue of residence requirements. In the *Storey v. Zazelenchuk* decision,[76] the Saskatchewan Court of Queen's Bench unanimously held that the requirement of a six-month period of residence was reasonable under the terms of section 1 of the Charter.

In *Reference re Yukon Election Residency Requirements*,[77] the British Columbia Court of Appeal unanimously recognized that a twelve-month period of residence was a reasonable requirement. The court wrote: "Residency is implied . . . in order to reflect the geographic distribution of political units within our Canadian federal system."[78] The concern with establishing a minimal residence requirement is a legitimate objective of the government: (1) such a requirement protects the integrity of the electoral process; (2) it enables the voters to be well-informed on the election issues; and (3) it ensures that the voter has a sufficient interest in his riding.

Residence requirements of twelve months exist in Quebec, the Yukon and the Northwest Territories; in the other nine provinces, six months are required. At the federal level there are no residence requirements.

---

73 *Thorson v. A.G. Canada*, [1975] 1 S.C.R. 138.
74 *N.S. Bd. of Censors v. McNeil*, [1976] 2 S.C.R. 265.
75 *Min. of Justice (Canada) v. Borowski*, (1982), 24 C.R. (3d) 352 (S.C.C.).
76 (1984), 36 Sask. R. 103 (C.A.) In *Arnold v. A.G. Ontario* (1987), 61 O.R. (2d) 481, the High Court of Justice of Ontario came to the conclusion that s. 15(1)(c) of the *Elections Act*, S.O. 1984, c. 54, which imposes a six-month Ontario residency requirement for voters in provincial elections contravenes s. 3 of the Charter, but is a reasonable limit under s. 1.
77 (1986), 27 D.L.R. (4th) 146 (B.C.C.A.).
78 *Ibid.* at 148.

B. *Exercise of the right to vote.* A reasonable period of time to vote must be provided to electors on polling day. According to our laws, an employer must grant his employees a period of time for voting without loss of salary. At the federal level, a period of four hours has been prescribed by the legislation since 1969-1970.

In *R. v. Falconer Marine Industries Ltd.*,[79] a British Columbia County Court judge held that the legislative provision did not entitle the employee to take two hours off (at that time it was two hours) for voting. In that case the employer had allowed his employees to quit work at 4:00 p.m. instead of the ususal 4:30 p.m. time and paid them for a full day. Thus, the employer had complied with the Act.

Mr. Patrick Boyer writes that if an employee is entitled to a four-hour period for voting, his employer is not obliged to grant him that period in the middle of the day. If the polls close at 7:00 p.m., and the work day is over at 5:00 p.m., the employer must permit his employees to leave at 3:00 p.m., in order to leave them a consecutive four-hour period of time to vote.[80]

C. *Enumeration of electors.* The enumeration of electors is carried out at the federal level for each election. The *Canada Elections Act* provides for such a procedure. No permanent lists are set up except in British Columbia. Quebec and Alberta have implemented a system of annual lists. Are permanent lists implied by section 3 of the *Canadian Charter of Rights and Freedoms*? This would not seem to be a necessary implication. However, the obligation to constantly improve our lists remains.

In its June 1986 *White Paper on Election Law Reform* the federal government recommended that the present system of enumeration be continued.

D. *Electoral spending.* The Quebec Superior Court held, in *Roberge v. P.G. Québec*[81] and *Boucher v. C.E.Q.*,[82] that freedom of expression did not imply the freedom to incur expenses in order to express oneself. The issue was raised by section 3 of the *Charter of Human Rights and Freedoms* of Quebec. The court held that Quebec legislation regulating spending during a referendum or an election did not violate section 3 of the Quebec Charter.

---

79 [1946] 1 D.L.R. 687 (B.C. Co. Ct.).

80 Boyer J.P., *Political Rights: The Legal Framework of Elections in Canada* (Toronto: Butterworth, 1981) at 123.

81 Confirmed by the Quebec Court of Appeal at [1987] R.D.J. 461.

82 *Boucher v. C.E.Q.* [1982] C.S.P. 1003 (Que.).

In *Re Mackay and Manitoba*,[83] the Manitoba Appeal Court was faced with the issue of whether a provision of the *Elections Finances Act*[84] of that province contravened freedom of thought protected by section 2 of the *Canadian Charter of Rights and Freedoms*. That provision guaranteed the refunding by the state of certain electoral expenses of a minority group. The majority of the court held that voters were free to think as they thought fit. Mr. Justice Twaddle quoted Chief Justice Dickson in *Big M. Drug Mart*:[85] "[N]o one is to be forced to act in a way contrary to his beliefs or his conscience."[86] Mr. Justice Twaddle stated: "No citizen, by payment of tax or otherwise, is required to contribute to or support a political cause."[87] On February 28, 1986, the Supreme Court of Canada granted leave to appeal.

In the United States, the Supreme Court, in *Buckley v. Valeo*,[88] declared that statutory limits to individual political contributions were valid but limits to electoral spending were invalid, as contravening freedom of expression.

In *National Citizens' Coalition Inc.*,[89] Mr. Justice Medhurst of the Alberta Court of Queen's Bench held that sections 70.1(1) and 72 of the *Canada Elections Act*[90] were incompatible with section 2(b) of the Charter (freedom of expression). The issue was whether those sections which reserve to registered parties the right to election expenses in favour of a candidate or against a candidate contravened freedom of expression. The trial judge had answered the question affirmatively. He added that such a limit could not be justified under section 1. Apprehension of harm is insufficient to justify a limit to freedom of expression. The harm must be present and real. The right to vote is closely related to freedom of opinion, of thought, freedom of the press and freedom of expression.

Mr. Justice Whyte, in the *Lavigne* decision,[91] held that the use by a union of its member's union fees for political purposes, against the will of the members, contravenes the individual's freedom of expression under section 2(b) of the Charter and cannot be justified in a free and democratic

---

83 (1985), 24 D.L.R. (4th) 587 (Man. C.A.), leave to appeal to S.C.C. granted 24 D.L.R. (4th) 587n (S.C.C.).

84 S.M. 1982-83-84, c. 45.

85 *R. v. Big Drug Mart Ltd.*, [1985] 1 S.C.R. 295 at 337.

86 *Re Mackay and Manitoba, supra*, note 83 at 594.

87 *Ibid.* at 595.

88 *Buckley v. Valeo*, 424 U.S. 1 (1976).

89 *Nat. Citizens' Coalition Inc./Coalition Nationale des Citoyens Inc. v. A.G. Canada* (1984), 11 D.L.R. (4d) 481 (Alta. Q.B.) The decision was not appealed.

90 *Supra*, note 18.

91 *Re Lavigne and O.P.S.E.U.* (1986), 29 D.L.R. (4th) 321 (Ont. H.C.), additional reasons (1987), 41 D.L.R. (4th) 86 (Ont. H.C.).

society. This decision was appealed.

In *Oil, Chemical & Atomic Workers International Union v. Imperial Oil Ltd.*,[92] a decision which preceded the Charter, the Supreme Court of Canada confirmed the validity of a British Columbia statute preventing trade unions from contributing financially to the election funds of political parties with moneys deducted from employees' salaries. It was decided that this was a valid exercise of provincial legislative authority over "property and civil rights". There was no unjustifiable encroachment on freedom of expression.[93]

There are numerous decisions where the Supreme Court of Canada emphasized the importance of freedom of expression in a parliamentary democracy such as ours: *Reference re Alberta Legislation*,[94] *Boucher v. R.*,[95] *Switzman v. Elbling*[96] and, since the advent of the Charter, *Dolphin Delivery*.[97] As Mr. Justice McIntyre observed in the latter case, freedom of expression was a constitutional right even before the advent of the *Canadian Charter of Rights and Freedoms*, a right which the Supreme Court had more or less entrenched.

He writes:

> Freedom of expression is not, however, a creature of the *Charter*. It is one of the fundamental concepts that has formed the basis for the historical development of the political, social and educational institutions of western society. Representative democracy, as we know it today, which is in great part the product of free expression and discussion of varying ideas, depends upon its maintenance and protection.[98]

(b) Representation in the Legislative Bodies

Our society enjoys a system of representative democracy. The people elect representatives to the legislative assemblies. This is a basic democratic right.

This concept raises three questions that will be considered consecutively:

  (i) representation by population;
  (ii) the "one person, one vote" principle;
  (iii) the question of proportional representation.

---

92 *Oil, Chemical & Atomic Workers Int. Union v. Imperial Oil Ltd.*, [1963] S.C.R. 584.
93 Beaudoin, *supra*, note 14 at 143.
94 [1938] S.C.R. 100, appeal dismissed [1939] A.C. 117 (P.C.).
95 [1951] S.C.R. 265.
96 [1957] S.C.R. 285.
97 *R.W.D.S.U., Loc. 580 v. Dolphin Delivery Ltd.*, [1986] 2 S.C.R. 573.
98 *Ibid.* at 583.

(i) *Representation by population*

This concept is closely related to the right to vote. The principle of representation by population saw the light under the Union Government of 1840 to 1867. It is expressly enshrined in the Constitution by section 51 of the *Constitution Act, 1867*. It followed soon after the establishment of responsible government, which holds that a government must have the confidence of the members of the House in order to remain in power. The principle of responsible government is one of our constitutional conventions.[99] As the Supreme Court explained it in 1981 in its advisory opinion in *Re Resolution to Amend the Constitution*[100] those conventions are indeed part of our Constitution even though courts will not, in principle, enforce them if infringements occur.

Representative government goes much further back than Confederation. It was established in Nova Scotia in 1758, in Prince Edward Island in 1773, in New Brunswick in 1784, in Upper and Lower Canada in 1791, in Newfoundland in 1832, in British Columbia in 1856, in Manitoba in 1870 and in the Territories in 1888.[101]

The readjustment of representation in the House of Commons after each decennial census is provided for by section 51 of the *Constitution Act, 1867*. Section 52 of the same Act further states that the number of members in the House of Commons may be increased "provided the proportionate Representation of the Provinces prescribed by this Act is not thereby disturbed".

Section 42(1)(a) of the *Constitution Act, 1982* provides that "the principle of proportionate representation of the provinces in the House of Commons", shall be amended by way of the general procedure for amending the Constitution (section 38), which requires the concurrence of the federal government and of seven provinces comprising at least 50 per cent of the total population.

Section 51A of the *Constitution Act of 1867* states: "Notwithstanding anything in this Act, a province shall always be entitled to a number of members in the House of Commons not less than the number of senators representing such province".

In the new amending formula, section 41(b) of the *Constitution Act, 1982* requires the concurrence of the eleven legislatures to amend

---

99 *Constitutional Decisions, September 28, 1981* (Ottawa: Canadian Government Publishing Centre, 1981) at 86, 87, 88. "Ministers must continuously have the confidence of the elected branch of the legislature, individually and collectively" (at 87).
100 [1981] 1 S.C.R. 753.
101 W.F. Dawson & R.M. Dawson, *Democratic Government in Canada*, 4th ed. (Toronto: University of Toronto Press, 1971), at 6, note 1.

(b) the right of a province to a number of members in the House of Commons not less than the number of Senators by which the province is entitled to be represented at the time this Part comes into force.

Can the federal Parliament amend section 51 of the *Constitution Act, 1867* by virtue of the powers it has retained under the terms of section 44 of the *Constitution Act, 1982*, to amend the Constitution of Canada?

Under section 91.1 (repealed in 1982) the federal Parliament amended section 51 in 1952[102] and in 1974,[103] readjusting the representation in the House of Commons, and has raised to two the number of members from the Northwest Territories in the House.[104] Section 51 was further amended in 1986.[105] In *Reference re Legislative Authority of Parliament of Canada to alter or replace Senate*,[106] the expression "Constitution of Canada" in section 91.1 of the *Constitution Act, 1867* was held to mean only the internal federal Constitution. Under section 44 of the *Constitution Act, 1982*, the federal Parliament may amend the Constitution of Canada in relation to the executive government of Canada or the Senate and House of Commons subject, however, to sections 41 and 42.

In *Campbell v. A.G. Canada*,[107] the issue of the federal power to amend section 51 without the concurrence of the provinces was raised before the Supreme Court of British Columbia.

Chief Justice Allan McEachern concluded that electoral redistribution which reduces from five to four the number of ridings in Vancouver does not offend the principle of representation according to population which is affirmed in the Constitution. It was not necessary, in his view, that such representation be mathematically perfect. Representation is based principally but not exclusively on population.

The Court of Appeal confirmed the judgment of first instance and the Supreme Court of Canada refused the leave to appeal on May 30, 1988.

The next section of this part deals with the impact of sections 3 and 15 of the Charter on disparities authorized by the electoral legislation as to the number of voters in different ridings. We will then consider the question of proportional representation.[108]

---

102 S.C. 1952, c. 15 (repealed).

103 S.C. 1974-75-76, c. 13.

104 S.C. 1974-75-76, c. 28.

105 S.C. 1986, c. 8.

106 [1980] 1 S.C.R. 54.

107 [1988] 2 W.W.R. 650 (B.C.S.C.), aff'd [1988] 4 W.W.R. 441, leave to appeal to S.C.C. refused (1988), 27 B.C.L.R. (2d) XXXV (note) (S.C.C.).

108 Task Force on Canadian Unity (Pepin-Roberts Report), *A Future Together, Observations and Recommendations* (Ottawa: Supply & Services, 1979) at 105-106.

(ii) *One person, one vote*

The "one person, one vote" theory has been extensively implemented in the United States. In Canada, Mr. Justice McRuer dealt with it:

> No doubt "one-man, one-vote" is the essential basis of the democratic process in this country. But the right to vote is extremely difficult to define in constitutional terms . . . The point is that it is most difficult to define in constitutional terms how the simple democratic principle of "one-man, one-vote" should be expressed.[109]

Let us now turn to three famous American cases dealing with the principle.

The case of *Baker v. Carr*[110] established the principle that courts could decide whether the criteria of county representation were adequate. The Supreme Court declared that the standard of measurement had to be just, acceptable and reasonable.

In the case of *Gray v. Sanders*,[111] the plaintiff alleged that the use of the "county unit system" which resulted in disproportionate vote weighing, violated the "equal protection" and "due process" clauses of the Fourteenth Amendment.

The court stated that the "equal protection" clause required that each voter's ballot have the same weight as that of any other voter.

Mr. Justice W.O. Douglas, for the court, drew attention to the following:

(1) Once a class of voters is chosen and their qualifications specified, there is no constitutional way by which equality of voting power may be evaded;
(2) The equal protection clause of the Fourteenth Amendment is violated by the use, in tabulating the votes in statewide elections, of a county unit system which results in disproportionate vote weighing;
(3) Nor does it present the question, inherent in the bicameral form of our Federal Government, whether a state may have one house chosen without regard to population;
(4) States can within limits specify the qualifications of voters in both state and federal elections; the Constitution indeed makes voters' qualifications rest on state law even in federal elections;
(5) The conception of political equality from the Declaration of Independence to Lincoln's Gettysburg Address, to the Fifteenth, Seventeenth and

---

109 McRuer, *supra*, note 3 at 1596.
110 369 U.S. 186 (1962); 7 L. Ed. (2d) 663.
111 372 U.S. 368 (1963); 9 L. Ed. (2d) 821. The Fourteenth Amendment reads in part:
> (1) [N]or shall any State deprive any person of life, liberty, or property without due process of law; nor deny to any person within its jurisdiction the equal protection of the laws.
> (2) Representatives shall be apportioned among the several States according to their respective numbers, counting the whole number of persons in each State, excluding Indians not taxed.

Nineteenth Amendments can mean only one thing — one person, one vote;

(6) Once the geographical unit for which a representative is to be chosen is designated, all who participate in the election are to have an equal vote, whatever their race, whatever their sex, whatever their occupation, whatever their income, and wherever their home may be in that geographical unit.[112]

It was in the third case, *Reynolds v. Sims*,[113] that the United States Supreme Court stated the famous principle "One man, one vote", which today would be more appropriately restated as "One person, one vote".

Is the system in force in our country today in harmony with sections 1, 3 and 15 of the *Canadian Charter of Rights and Freedoms*?

Before the advent of the Charter, Professor Yves Caron[114] analyzed the situation in 1967, at a time when the important American cases were having major impact. Disparities in Canada are far greater than in the United States. We have the urban, semi-urban and rural district systems. Canada is a very large country whose population is relatively small. These two factors make it extremely difficult to attain equality in the ridings. To these factors one must add, among other things, what Professor Caron called "geographic accidents"[115] such as mountain ranges and isolated areas.

I doubt that our system, in its present form, could successfully meet the test of section 1 of the *Canadian Charter of Rights and Freedoms*. The courts will force the legislative bodies to reduce the discrepancies which presently exist with respect to representation. In our view, these disparities between ridings are much too pronounced. The degree of disparity which is acceptable will doubtless emerge through successive cases.

(iii) *The question of proportional representation*

In Canada, as in the United Kingdom and in the United States, voters choose one member only on a single ballot. It is a system of direct election by simple majority on a single ballot. France, on the other hand, has adopted the two ballot uninominal majority system. In many democracies, proportional representation has been adopted. One could discuss at length the merits and disadvantages of the respective systems, and the debate is far from ended. In Canada, it is practically possible for a member to be elected by less than 35 per cent of the votes cast in a riding. Such a member would have been elected even against the will of a clear majority.

---

112 *Gray, supra,* note 111 at notes 17 and 19, and at pp. 828-831 (9 L.Ed.).
113 377 U.S. 533 (1964).
114 *"Un homme, un vote?"* (1967), 2 *R.J.T.* 209.
115 *Ibid.* at 227.

Can this fact be reconciled with the terms of section 3 of the Charter? We must point out that even though the United States Supreme Court enforced the "one person, one vote" principle, it did not declare that proportional representation had to be introduced. In Australia, at the Senate level, there exists a system of "preferential voting" which combines many advantages of both systems. We do not believe that sections 3 and 15 force us to introduce proportional voting in Canada.

(c) The Right to be Qualified for Membership

Section 3 of the Charter stipulates that every citizen of Canada has a right to be qualified for membership in federal and provincial legislative bodies. Exceptions to this principle must be considered in the light of section 1 of the Charter.

According to section 20 of the *Canada Elections Act*,[116] it is necessary to be qualified as an elector in order to be a candidate at an election. Section 20 refers to section 14, which deals with the qualifications of electors. It is not necessary to reside in the riding where one chooses to be a candidate.

However, according to section 21, the following persons are disqualified from membership:

(a) those deprived of their right to vote for having committed any corrupt or illegal practice at an election;
(b) members of a provincial legislature;
(c) members of a royal commission or permanent or temporary Crown employees;
(d) every person disqualified from voting by subsection 14(4) of the *Canada Elections Act*;
(e) sheriffs, clerks of the peace and Crown attorneys;
(f) members of the armed forces, unless on active duty at war.

Various reasons (differing in each case) may understandably justify preventing judges, the Chief Electoral Officer, his assistant, prisoners and mental patients from being candidates.

Members of a provincial legislature and those from the Council of the Yukon or the Northwest Territories cannot be elected to the House of Commons. The double mandate existing at the beginning of Confederation, which was later abolished, was fundamentally contrary to the federal principle itself.

The same person cannot represent two orders of government which constitutionally exercise exclusive legislative and executive powers and

---

116 *Supra*, note 18.

between which, according to case law,[117] the interdelegation of legislative powers is not possible. This is a normal exception. Section 21(2) of Bill C-79 would permit a member to run in an election in the other level of government, providing that such member, on being elected to the other body, resigned his or her former seat. This provision is constitutionally acceptable.

A Senator cannot be a member of the House of Commons, according to section 39 of the *Constitution Act, 1867*. It is obvious that Senators should not run for election to the House of Commons. These two federal legislative houses are mutually exclusive.

Public servants who wish to run for election may obtain leave.[118] In my view, this provision meets the terms of section 3 of the Charter.

In *Fraser v. A.G. Nova Scotia*,[119] Mr. Justice Grant of the Nova Scotia Supreme Court held that sections 34(3) and 35(c) of the Nova Scotia *Civil Service Act*,[120] which *inter alia* prohibited public servants from partisan activity in federal or provincial elections and did not provide for the time of leave for election purposes, infringed the right to be qualified for membership recognized by section 3 of the Charter and were not justified under section 1 of the Charter. The sections of the Act in Justice Grant's view also contravened freedom of expression, freedom of peaceful assembly, freedom of association and equality rights and were also not justifiable under section 1. With respect, we must express our disagreement with this decision.

---

117 See the famous case on interparliamentary delegation, *A.G. Nova Scotia v. A.G. Canada*, [1951] S.C.R. 31. If Parliament cannot delegate powers to provincial legislatures, it may delegate powers to courts. As Chief Justice Deschênes pointed out in the case of *Bélanger v. Commission de révision du comté de Sauvé*, [1973] C.S. 814 at 820-821 (Que. S.C.),"for as long as one can remember in the British parliamentary system, Parliament has jealously kept for itself the control of its internal procedure and of its electoral mechanism" [translation]; to that effect, he quotes the case of *Théberge v. Landry* (1876), 2 A.C. 102. The principle stated in this last case was followed in the case of *Valin v. Langlois* (1879), 3 S.C.R. 1, leave to appeal refused (1879-80), 5 A.C. 115. Parliament has subsequently delegated powers to judges and courts. The latter do not, however, have any powers other than those delegated to them. House powers have been interpreted generously as may be seen in the cases of *Temple v. Bulmer*, [1943] S.C.R. 265; *R. v. Clark*, [1943] 3 D.L.R. 684, leave to appeal refused [1944] S.C.R. 69; *Sideleau v. Davidson*, [1942] S.C.R. 318; *Re Temiscouata (Can.)*; *Plourde v. Gauvreau* (1912), 47 S.C.R. 211. In the United States, s. 5 of art. 1 of the Constitution provides that each House may decide issues relating to the validity of elections, the membership of the House: see *Powell v. McCormack*, 395 U.S. 486 (1969); 23 L. Ed. 2d 491.

118 See s. 21(2)(g). The civil servant who wishes to be a candidate may request leave without pay.

119 (1986), 30 D.L.R. (4th) 340 (N.S.T.D.).

120 S.N.S. 1980, c. 3.

However, in *Public Service Employees Union of Ontario*,[121] the Supreme Court of Canada in 1987 dealt with the issues raised on the basis of the division of powers, and the Charter issues involved were not decided, the facts having arisen before the coming into force of the Charter; nonetheless, opinions were divided on the appropriateness for the court to express its view on these issues (4-3). In this case, one of the issues was that of the validity of an Ontario statute which obliged public servants in Ontario who wished to run in federal elections to first obtain leave without pay and which prohibited public servants from participating in federal election campaigns.

Basing itself on section 92(4) of the *Constitution Act, 1867* and on former paragraph 1 of section 92 of that Act, the court recognized the validity of the Ontario statute, in our view, quite properly.

In that case, the Supreme Court cited the *Fraser* decision[122] which enumerated some parameters to the right of a public servant to criticize the government which employs him or her.

If the issue raised in *Public Service Employees Union of Ontario*[123] arose under the Charter, the restriction, in our opinion, would appear justified under section 1.

Concerning the exclusion of sheriffs and Crown attorneys, the June 1986 *White Paper on Electoral Law Reform*[124] recommends (and, in our view, properly so) that sheriffs, clerks of the peace and Crown attorneys be entitled to run for election at the House of Commons. Bill C-79, June 30, 1987, would entitle them to seek election. They would no longer appear in the list of exceptions.

It seems reasonable that members of royal commissions should be prohibited from seeking election to the House during their term of office. They are accountable to the executive branch which results in a natural incompatibility. It appears reasonable under section 1 of the Charter to compel them to resign if they wish to run for public office.

The right to vote and the right to be qualified for membership are different in nature. The exceptions may overlap partly but not entirely. In our opinion, for instance, a judge should be allowed to vote but should not be eligible as a candidate in federal or provincial elections.

---

121 *O.P.S.E.U. v. A.G. Ontario*, [1987] 2 S.C.R. 2.

122 *Fraser v. P.S.S.R.B.*, [1985] 2 S.C.R. 455.

123 *Supra*, note 121. In July 1988, in *Millar*, s. 32(1)(a) of the *Public Service Employment Act*, which limits the right of federal civil servants (with some exceptions) to participate in political compaigns, was declared of no force and effect by the Federal Court of Appeal. This limitation was held to be contrary to freedom of expression and freedom of association, as guaranteed by s. 2 of the Charter.

124 *Supra*, note 36.

Let us say a few words about the famous *MacLean* case.[125]

Billy Joe Maclean, a member of the legislative assembly of Nova Scotia, was found guilty of having filed fraudulent expense claims to the amount of $22,000. He was sentenced to a fine of $6,000 and ordered to reimburse the sum of $2,000. Because of his refusal to resign as a member, he was expelled from the House by a special Act entitled *An Act Respecting Reasonable Limits for Membership in the House of Assembly*[126] This Act prohibited, moreover, all persons convicted of an offence punishable by more than five years of imprisonment from being candidates in provincial elections for a period of five years.

Mr. Maclean decided to run as an independent candidate in the by-election resulting from his expulsion. He challenged the validity of the Act. Chief Justice Constance Glube held that the legislature had the power to expel a member for a fraudulent act. However, in her view, the legislature could not, because of section 3 of the Charter, stop Mr. Maclean from running in an election for a period of five years; the choice was a matter for the electorate. Mr. Maclean was re-elected on February 24, 1987 as an independent candidate.

The decision in the *Maclean* case is based on tenable arguments.

(d) Conclusion

In concluding this part, we would like to point out that the right to vote and the right to be qualified for membership are in many ways related to more than one important fundamental freedom, such as freedom of opinion, freedom of expression, freedom of association and freedom of the press.

3. MAXIMUM DURATION OF LEGISLATIVE ASSEMBLIES (Section 4)

The limits set by section 4 of the *Constitution Act, 1982* is five years for both the House of Commons and the provincial legislative assemblies, except in time of real or apprehended war, invasion or insurrection.

(a) Duration of the House of Commons

(i) *General principle*

Section 50 of the *Constitution Act, 1867* provides that the House of Commons shall continue for five years from the day of the return of the

---

125 *Maclean v. A.G. Nova Scotia, supra,* note 57.
126 S.N.S. 1986, c. 104.

writs, unless it is dissolved at an earlier date by the Governor General (as warranted by our principle of responsible government). We are thus given the opportunity by the Constitution itself to elect our government periodically.

On the average, legislatures customarily last four years; this is mandated by tradition, but they may be shorter or longer. The federal House of Commons rarely lasts the five-year limit; certain legislatures are shorter and may last only a few months.

In most cases, the term comes to an end when the Prime Minister feels that the time is right to request a dissolution of the House by the Crown's representative. According to convention, the Governor General, except in very rare cases, will follow the advice of the Prime Minister.[127] One of these rare cases would be where a minority government formed after a general election failed to win a vote of confidence at the beginning of the session immediately following the election. The Governor General could then refuse to dissolve the House and could invite the leader of the opposition to form a government.

Some legislatures are ended earlier following a vote of non-confidence. This has occurred many times in our parliamentary history. This was the case in 1979, 1974 and 1963, to state some recent examples. The principle of responsible government is deeply rooted in our constitutional conventions.[128]

The right to periodic elections results partly from our constitutional law and partly from our constitutional conventions.

Chief Justice McRuer emphasized the importance of periodic elections in these terms:

> As the constitutional authorities cited earlier have pointed out, periodic elections and the parliamentary process of law-making are appeals to reason — to the rational nature of man. The highest recognition of the equality and final worth of human individuals in the realm of politics and law is the right of each to vote on the basis of universal adult suffrage, in periodic and free elections, where the constituencies are so arranged by population that one man's vote is substantially as great in influence as another's.[129]

(ii) *Exceptions*

Section 4(2) of the *Constitution Act, 1982* reads as follows:

---

127 Task Force on Canadian Unity (Pepin-Robarts Report), *Coming to Terms, the Words of the Debate* (Ottawa: Supply & Services, 1979) at 36, "Governor General".

128 *Supra*, note 99 at 87.

129 McRuer, *supra*, note 3 at 1590.

(2)   In time of real or apprehended war, invasion or insurrection, a House of Commons may be continued by Parliament and a legislative assembly may be continued by the legislature beyond five years if such continuation is not opposed by the votes of more than one-third of the members of the House of Commons or the legislative assembly, as the case may be.

Prior to patriation, section 91.1 of the *Constitution Act, 1867* (repealed) provided an exception to the five-year duration of Parliament. In time of real or apprehended war, invasion or insurrection, Parliament could be continued as long as such continuation was not opposed by the votes of more than one-third of the members of the House of Commons.[130] Section 4(2) of the Charter has reproduced this provision, which now also applies to the provinces. As we all know, a constitutional amendment adopted by the Parliament of Westminster was required in 1916 to continue for one year the Parliament that had been elected in 1911.[131]

The five-year limit is a democratic right. The Supreme Court could be called upon to intervene, should there be abuses relating to emergency continuations. The Supreme Court could also be called upon to deal with an emergency situation with respect to the division of powers between both levels of government.

The emergency situation defined in section 4 of the Charter is not the same as the emergency power recognized by the case law in time of war[132] and in time of peace.[133] As far as Parliament itself is concerned, an emergency situation may give rise merely to a continuation of the life of the legislature. At the constitutional level, it allows the central Parliament to encroach on provincial legislative jurisdiction[134] under the theory of emergency powers.

The Crown itself may also ensure respect for the Constitution.[135]

---

130 The House of Commons presently consists of 282 members. The continuation of the legislature beyond five years in time of real or apprehended war, invasion or insurrection must not be opposed by more than 94 members. Otherwise, a simple majority is sufficient for the working of the House. The number will be raised to 295 when the House is dissolved, providing the dissolution comes after July 13, 1988. In such an event the figure 94 should be 99. S. 91.1 is repealed by Sched. I of the *Constitution Act, 1982*.

131 *British North America Act, 1916* (6 & 7 Geo. V), c. 19, repealed (17 & 18 Geo. V), c. 42.

132 *Fort Frances Pulp & Power Co. v. Man. Free Press Co.* [1923] A.C. 695 (P.C.).

133 *Reference re Anti-Inflation Act*, [1976] 2 S.C.R. 373.

134 *Ibid.* at 463, where the emergency power is defined by Mr. Justice Beetz as giving to Parliament "concurrent and paramount jurisdiction over matters which would normally fall within exclusive provincial jurisdiction".

135 *Supra*, note 99, at 89: "[A]t law, the Government is in office by the pleasure of the Crown although by convention it is there by the will of the people".

(b) The Electoral Mandate of Provincial Members

Section 85 of the *Constitution Act, 1867* provides that the Ontario and Quebec legislatures shall continue for four years, unless the assembly is dissolved earlier by the Lieutenant Governor of the province. However, following constitutional amendments based on section 92.1 dealing with the provincial power of amendment, the maximum duration of the legislature in Ontario and Quebec has been extended to five years.[136]

In Manitoba, the substance of section 50 of the *Constitution Act, 1867* is restated in section 19 of this province's constitutive statute. The electoral mandate is four years; however, the Manitoba legislature has extended the term to five years.[137]

In the other provinces, the rule is based either on the constitutive statute of those provinces, or on constitutional provisions, or on simple statutes.[138]

Before patriation, a provincial legislature, on the basis of section 92.1 (now repealed) of the *Constitution Act, 1867* was able to extend its normal life beyond five years.

The *Canadian Charter of Rights and Freedoms* puts both the federal and the provincial legislatures on an equal footing for the duration as well as for the continuation of the legislature in cases of emergency. To be valid in case of emergency, the continuation shall not be opposed by more than one-third of the assembly.

4. THE ANNUAL SITTING OF LEGISLATIVE BODIES (Section 5)

Section 20 of the *Constitution Act, 1867* states:

> There shall be a Session of the Parliament of Canada once at least in every Year, so that Twelve Months shall not intervene between the last Sitting in the Parliament in one Session and its first sitting in the next Session.

Section 86 of the *Constitution Act, 1867* restates the content of section 20 and applies it to Quebec and Ontario. This is also the case with respect to section 20 of the *Manitoba Act, 1870.*

Prior to patriation, section 91.1 of the *Constitution Act, 1867* precluded Parliament from amending section 20 (and section 50), but provincial legislatures were not subject to an explicit restriction.

Sections 20 and 86 of the *Constitution Act, 1867* differ from section

---

136 See *Legislative Assembly Act*, R.S.O. 1980, c. 235, s. 3; *National Assembly Act*, R.S.Q. 1977, c. A-23.1 c. 62, s. 6.

137 See *Legislative Assembly Act*, R.S.M. 1970, c. L 110, s. 5(1).

138 Section 8 of the *Saskatchewan Human Rights Code supra*, note 6, provides that "every qualified voter resident in Saskatchewan shall possess the right to require that no Legislative Assembly shall continue for a period in excess of five years".

5 of the *Constitution Act, 1982*. Section 20 provides for a session of Parliament at least once in every year, while section 5 of the Charter provides for a sitting at least once every twelve months. The same principle applies to both Parliament and the legislatures.

Let us first say that the new formulation is much more in keeping with what has really been happening for a number of years: a session often lasts more than a year and one resorts to adjournment rather than prorogation, no doubt in order to allow Parliamentary committees to sit while the debates in the House are adjourned. Second, we wish to point out that section 20 of the *Constitution Act, 1867* has been repealed by the *Constitution Act, 1982*.

According to section 20, no more than twelve months could elapse between two sessions. This provision was adopted at a time when sessions were much shorter than is the case today. Henceforth, sessions may be longer or shorter, but no more than eleven months and thirty days may elapse between two sittings.

A session may be quite short. Thus, in 1940, Prime Minister Mackenzie King arranged to hold a one-day session.[139]

In Canada, we have not experienced "government by decree" over lengthy periods. The Governor in Council and the Lieutenant Governor in Council may avail themselves of their regulatory powers; the Houses nevertheless sit regularly, even in time of emergency. It is rather unlikely that legislative Houses in Canada will be "suspended" for lengthy periods. However, it is wiser to anticipate such a possibility.

Finally, we would like to add that our constitutional conventions are very prominent in the proceedings of Parliament and are part of our Canadian Constitution. They complete the three sections of the Charter which deal with democratic rights.

What would happen if a Prime Minister chose not to hold a sitting in a given year? A court, if the matter were referred to it, could declare the necessity of such a sitting but could not, by way of injunction, order that it be held. The ultimate recourse in such a case would then be in the hands of the Governor General, who would have the power to dismiss the Prime Minister and call upon someone else to form a government. Such a situation has never occurred.

5. GENERAL CONCLUSION

Of all the rights entrenched in the *Canadian Charter of Rights and Freedoms*, the democratic rights are probably those upon which the consensus between the various governments in Canada has been the easiest

---

139 6th Sess., 18th Parl., January 25, 1940.

to achieve. Quebec did not oppose this part of the Charter in November 1981, quite the contrary. It is thus not surprising that the "notwithstanding" clause has no application to this part of the Charter and that no government, in November 1981, insisted that the override clause be available with respect to these sections.

Our Constitution of 1867 describes our parliamentary system and contains some sections which, to a certain extent, guarantee democratic rights. With the years, the democratic principle became rooted in our statutes and in the conventions of the Constitution.

In *Re Resolution to Amend the Constitution*,[140] the Supreme Court deeply and fully considered our constitutional conventions and ruled that several aspects of our parliamentary regime and democratic system were protected by conventions: resignation of a government, choice of a prime minister, dissolution of Parliament, etc. The court stated that "at law, the government is in office by the pleasure of the Crown although by convention it is there by the will of the people".[141]

We seem to forget sometimes, because it is so natural for us to vote, that the right to vote periodically, the right to take part in the conduct of public affairs and the right to maintain in power a government or to terminate it are the fruits of a lengthy struggle. We forget how recently universal suffrage was established.

It is fortunate that our fundamental law at last entrenches, for every Canadian citizen, the right to vote and the right to be qualified for membership in the legislative bodies. Certain categories of persons who presently are not entitled to vote should acquire this right. It is imperative also to improve the rules dealing with alternate voting methods, such as advanced voting, voting by mail, by proxy and voting abroad. Bill C-79, tabled in 1987, is a step in the right direction.

In our view, the discrepancies between electoral districts are still too extreme. We must not forget that the *International Covenant on Civil and Political Rights*, which has been ratified by Canada, requires equality of suffrage.

In recent years, the two levels of government have started to legislate on the financing of elections, the aim being to create a better and fairer system. We should continue on that path. The entrenchment of the right to vote and the right to become a member of legislative Houses cannot but help us. The Charter has a normative value but it must also have an educational value, both for our legislators and for all citizens.

It should be underlined that the limitation clause contained in section 1 of the *Canadian Charter of Rights and Freedoms* and which provides

---

140 *Supra*, note 100.
141 *Supra*, note 99, at 89.

for the limitation of rights within reasonable limits is based on the criterion of a free and democratic society. Once again, reference is made to democratic values.

Our Constitution is very specific on the duration of legislative bodies. Such a degree of precision is most desirable.

It is fortunate that section 5 of the Charter more clearly establishes the principle that a government cannot govern for a long period, without the concurrence of the elected chamber, and without having to answer to the people.

Although our conventions and statutes already guarantee the secret ballot, we would have preferred that this be explicitly stated in the Charter.

Sections 3, 4 and 5 of the Charter are part of the Constitution of Canada and under the terms of section 52 of the *Constitution Act, 1982,* may be amended only by the amendment procedure provided in Part V of the Act.

Our democratic rights are often taken for granted, and we forget how easy it is for the legislature to turn back the clock at will. Our history mentions several examples of this, in peace and in war.[142] Sections 3, 4 and 5 of the Charter which, *prima facie*, attract little attention, and which are taken for granted, add much to our electoral system and to our parliamentary regime. We hope that the legislators derive from sections 3, 4 and 5 of the Charter the necessary inspiration to perfect our democratic system, and that the courts of justice find in those sections an additional and fruitful base for the construction of statutes to attain that end.

---

142 See Boyer, *supra*, note 6 at 134.

9

Mobility Rights*
(*Section 6*)

Pierre Blache**

1. Introduction
2. The General Effect of Section 6 of the Canadian Charter of Rights and
   Freedoms
3. The Impact of Section 6 of the Canadian Charter of Rights and Freedoms on
   Federal Powers

1. INTRODUCTION

Section 6 of the *Canadian Charter of Rights and Freedoms* deals with
the rights and freedoms[1] of Canadian citizens and permanent residents

---

* Translated from French. This chapter includes a section devoted exclusively to the impact
  of the Charter on federal legislative powers because its main purpose is to study its impact
  on those powers. However, the first and main part will help the reader who is interested
  in the issue to understand the impact of section 6 on provincial powers as well.

** This chapter was revised during the summer of 1986 with the valuable assistance of
  Ms. Marie-Josée Hogue, a graduate of the Faculty of Law of the Université de Sherbrooke.

 1 The terms "right" and "freedom" are sometimes used theoretically as contrasting terms,
   the former conferring a right to the payment of benefits, whereas the latter only creates
   a zone of autonomy with which the state must not interfere. See C.A. Colliard, *Libertés*

of Canada relating to mobility and the gaining of a livelihood.[2] Section 32 makes it clear that the Charter applies to Parliament and the government of Canada and to the provincial legislatures and governments within their respective jurisdictions. The effect is to diminish the powers of the legislatures and governments of Canada to the extent required by these rights and freedoms. It is also possible that governments and legislatures will find themselves obliged to take positive steps to give effect to these rights.

In the first part of this chapter, the general effect of section 6 will be discussed. The right to mobility and the rights to move, take up residence and gain a livelihood will each be treated separately. The impact of the qualifications on these rights that flow from both section 1 and section 6(3) will also be considered.

In the second part of this chapter, the effect of section 6 on legislative powers within federal jurisdiction will be analyzed. The legislative powers which are most likely to be affected by the Charter will be identified. The limits to which they are already subject by either the *Canadian Bill of Rights*[3] or international law will also be described.

2. THE GENERAL EFFECT OF SECTION 6 OF THE *CANADIAN CHARTER OF RIGHTS AND FREEDOMS*

Three preliminary remarks are necessary. First, in focussing on the general effect of section 6, we will set aside the question of constitutional jurisdiction in order to examine what the rights enshrined in section 6 prohibit or require. Second, while the limitations imposed by section 6 will be the main focus, for that is the section's most far-reaching effect, the issue of whether this section requires the adoption of legislation will also be discussed. Finally, it is important to understand that, at this stage, the effort is simply to identify prohibited or required forms of regulation. Because a specific legislative initiative can come within both federal and provincial jurisdictions under the "double aspect" doctrine, the conclusion that an initiative is prohibited or required under section 6 does not necessarily affect a single jurisdiction, either federal or provincial. Thus, in the second part of this chapter, the argument will not be that the effect

---

publiques, 5th ed. (Paris: Dalloz, 1975), at 18-25. It is submitted that the use of these terms in the French version of s. 6 is not based on this distinction. The term "freedom" is not used in the English version and appears in the French version only in the title and the marginal notes.

2 Only Canadian citizens have the right to enter, remain in and leave Canada, whereas both permanent residents and citizens of Canada have the right to move and take up residence in any province and earn a livelihood.

3 S.C. 1960, c. 44.

of section 6 is limited solely to federal legislative initiatives. The objective will be simply to identify which federal powers are likely to be affected by the prohibitions and requirements discussed in the first part of the chapter. Let us begin by looking at just what prohibitions or requirements are imposed on legislatures by the right to mobility and the right to move and gain a livelihood.

(a) Section 6 and the Mobility of Citizens

(i) *The purpose of the prohibitions or requirements imposed on the legislature by section 6(1)*

Section 6(1) states that: "Every citizen has the right to enter, remain in and leave Canada." Is this a freedom in the technical sense which creates only a duty on the part of the state not to interfere? Or does it impose on the state a duty to go to the assistance of any citizen in trouble who is detained in a foreign jurisdiction against his or her will or prevented from leaving by some other form of problem? If the subsection did create such a positive duty, it would be difficult to argue that it did not also create a duty to help citizens leave the country. The radical consequences that would flow from an interpretation which creates a duty of state assistance suggest, in my view, that section 6(1) merely creates a freedom or a zone of individual autonomy.

This freedom is granted to Canadian citizens only, but it is granted to all Canadian citizens. It seems obvious that discrimination in relation to mobility rights among categories of citizens, such as those born in Canada and those who are naturalized, is forbidden.

One must consider as well whether this subsection leaves unfettered the power to define who is a Canadian citizen. There are two reasons for believing that the definition of Canadian citizenship, which obviously entails discrimination amongst individuals in Canada on the basis of their citizenship, will be subject to judicial review. First, giving unfettered control of this definition to the legislature would effectively permit the legislature to define a part of the constitutional norm enshrined in section 6(1). In effect, the legislature, which is subject to the Charter, would be able to define its own jurisdiction.[4] This is logically inadmissible. The courts have recognized this problem and confirmed the principle that the legislature cannot define its own jurisdiction. The courts, for example, have denied the power of the legislature to enact rules governing the *situs* of property,

---

4 See, *e.g.*, *A.G., Quebec v. Que. Assn. of Protestant School Bds.*, [1984] 2 S.C.R. 66, at 86, where the court stated: "[A] legislature cannot by an ordinary statute validly set aside the means so chosen by the framers and affect this classification. Still less can it remake the classification and redefine the classes."

persons or transactions for the purpose of applying the territorial limits to which their power of taxation is subject under section 92(2) of the *Constitution Act, 1867.* In lieu of the legislative solution, the courts have relied on the rules of the British law of conflicts.[5]

Second, section 15 of the Charter, the equality provision, states that: "Every individual is equal before and under the law." This section effectively restricts the power of the federal Parliament to legislate on matters pertaining to citizenship, naturalization and foreigners regardless of the type of rule enacted in exercising this power, including rules defining Canadian citizenship. Thus, the reasoning of Mr. Justice Ritchie in *A.G. Canada v. Lavell*[6] cannot apply here. He was able to conclude that the power of Parliament to define the term "Indian" was not limited by the equality requirements of the *Canadian Bill of Rights* because, in his view, the *Bill of Rights* could not affect the division of powers set out in the *Constitution Act, 1867.* We are no longer dealing with a law such as the *Canadian Bill of Rights.* Section 6 of the Charter is part of the Constitution. It thus has the legal force required to restrict the content of legislation enacted pursuant to a jurisdiction to legislate in relation to particular matters, including legislation that defines Canadian citizenship, which is an essential first step in any attempt to legislate in relation to citizenship. Undoubtedly, the courts will allow Parliament considerable discretion under section 1 in enacting such legislation.

In light of these observations, it is submitted that the courts will want to approach the problem of defining Canadian citizenship from two perspectives. First, they will want to consider the legal conception of the framers respecting the criteria for citizenship which prevailed when the Charter was first adopted. For this purpose, consideration should doubtless be given to both Canadian and British law having regard to the process followed.[7] This could easily lead to the introduction into Canadian law of the minimal definition of the concept of citizenship recognized in international law and, in particular, the rules found in international conventions of which Canada is a signatory nation. Second, the egalitarian

---

5 *R. v. National Trust Co.*, [1933] S.C.R. 670. See also G. Laforest, *The Allocation of Taxing Power under the Canadian Constitution* (Canadian Tax Foundation, 1967), at 94-121.

6 [1974] S.C.R. 1349. The learned judge concluded that the *Canadian Bill of Rights* could not limit the power of the federal government to define the meaning of the term "Indian" given it by s. 91 of the *Constitution Act, 1867* because the defining of the term was essential to the exercise of its constitutional jurisdiction under that section.

7 Professor Hogg does not share this view. He argues that it is unlikely that the courts would develop their own definition of "citizen". In his view, they would rely on the definition adopted by Parliament in the *Citizenship Act*, S.C. 1974-75-76, c. 108. See P.W. Hogg, *Constitutional Law of Canada*, 2nd ed. (Toronto: Carswell, 1985).

requirements of the Charter as set out in sections 1, 15 and 28 will also be applied.[8]

The use of the term "Canadian citizen" raises the issue of its application to legal entities such as corporations. Strictly speaking, under existing Canadian law the concept of citizenship does not embrace entities of this sort.[9] Insofar as the definition of citizenship under the Charter is based on criteria independent of the powers of the legislatures, the state of Canadian law at the time of the adoption of the Charter could serve as the basis for a narrow definition of citizenship which would be restricted to natural persons. Moreover, legal entities cannot exercise the rights enshrined in section 6 because these rights appear to deal solely with physical movement.[10] Finally, the similarities between section 6 of the Charter and Article 12 of the *International Covenant on Civil and Political Rights* also suggest that section 6 confers rights on individuals only.

Section 6(1) gives every citizen the right to remain in Canada. The English version uses the word "remain" which shows clearly that it is a right not to be expelled from the country. Thus, this section does not in itself give a citizen the right to live anywhere in the country that he or she wishes.[11] It would not, for example, prevent a legislature from assigning citizens to habitation zones within Canada assuming the legislation was otherwise valid.

The same subsection creates the right to enter and leave the country. The right to enter, like the right to remain, does not create the right to take up residence in a particular part of the country. As long as entry into the country is permitted, the right has been respected. Some have argued that the right to leave the country includes a right to a passport.[12] According to this view, the government is currently in violation of section 6 because its legislation, by giving an unfettered discretion to bureaucrats in the handling of requests for passports, permits them to refuse to issue one. Moreover, they argue, this discretion cannot be justified under section 1 because this section requires that the restriction on any Charter right be prescribed by law.

As in the case of the rights to enter and remain in the country, the right to leave does not include a right to go anywhere one pleases outside

---

8 See J.B. Laskin, "Mobility Rights Under the Charter" (1982), 4 *Supreme Ct. L. Rev.* 89 at 89-90.

9 See S. Slosar, "La citoyenneté canadienne et ses effets juridiques" (1979), 10 *R.D.U.S.* 157 at 176.

10 See Laskin, *supra*, note 8 at 90-91.

11 S. 6(2) deals with this issue.

12 See Laskin, *supra*, note 8 at 90-91 and A.J. Arkelian, "Freedom of Movement of Persons Between States and Entitlement to Passports" (1984-85), 49 *Sask. L. Rev.* 15, especially at 23 *et seq.*

the country. Thus, it appears that the competent authorities still have the power, unless taken away by some other source, to limit the countries to which a Canadian citizen can travel. Finally, it should be noted that section 6 restricts the power of the legislature to prohibit entry and exit from the country. It does not prevent the legislature from enacting legislation creating administrative procedures which must be followed in order to exercise the right of entry or exit.

It is worth noting that the Charter does not create a right in Canadian citizens to live outside the country. The symmetry evident in the rights of entry and exit is not found here and the right to remain in the country is not balanced by the right to remain without.[13] This seems justified when one considers the importance of the territorial connection in the definition of citizenship. For example, existing legislation provides for the automatic loss of Canadian citizenship for all citizens born outside the country after February 15, 1977 unless they follow certain procedures providing for its retention.[14]

The purpose of section 6(1) can thus be described as follows. It guarantees certain freedoms to "every citizen of Canada". The definition of "citizen of Canada" is subject to judicial review. The right to move freely is guaranteed, without discrimination, to all citizens, but there is a strong possibility that legal entities such as corporations are not Canadian citizens for the purposes of section 6. The right to remain in Canada, like the right to enter, does not on the basis of section 6(1) alone confer a right to take up residence anywhere in the country. The right to leave does not include the right to travel to any destination chosen by the traveller. Administrative or non-prohibitory regulations are permitted. Although citizens do not have the right to remain indefinitely outside the country, the right to leave must necessarily include the right to reside outside the country for reasonable periods of time.

(ii) *The relationship between section 6(1) and section 1*

The rights conferred by section 6(1) are subject to such limits as are permissible under section 1 which states that they are: "subject only to such reasonable limits prescribed by law as can be demonstrably justified in a free and democratic society". This section raises some difficult questions of interpretation. At one extreme, it could be interpreted as constituting a virtual ratification of all existing law. One could argue that, since Canadian society has long been free and democratic, those limits

---

13 It is not possible to infer a right to remain indefinitely outside the country from the mere right to leave.
14 See Slosar, *supra*, note 9, at 180.

which were part of Canadian law prior to the Charter must be justified. However, this extreme interpretation is inconsistent with the language of section 1 which introduces an additional criterion of reasonableness that, in general, did not apply to sovereign legislative bodies prior to the adoption of the Charter.[15] Thus, it will not be possible to escape the control of the section by arguing that the challenged legislation simply reproduces restrictions that are found in previous laws.

What sort of restrictions can survive the test under section 1? In the first place, any such restrictions will have to meet the formal requirement that they are "prescribed by law" or, as expressed in the French version, founded on a "règle de droit". This formulation refers first of all to formally enacted provisions of the legislature and to provisions which derive their authority from an express or implied delegation of legislative power.[16] It also includes the common law as developed by the courts. However, rules established pursuant to the exercise of a judicial discretion may not be prescribed by law as required by section 1. If so, the courts would not be able to use their discretion to create restrictions on mobility rights.

It is impossible, given the very general nature of these principles, to provide an exhaustive account of the restrictions permissible under section 1, but some examples may be helpful. Undoubtedly quarantine for health reasons would be permissible under section 1. Rules allowing for extradition would be acceptable in the context of the right to remain in Canada.[17] Similarly, regulations prohibiting accused persons and witnesses from leaving the country would, in the great majority of cases, be considered reasonably justified in a free and democratic society. The difficulty, of course, lies in determining exactly what restrictions on the right of mobility are reasonable. In my view, the extremely loose test applied in the United States under the doctrine of reasonableness is not applicable here.[18] Section 1 includes the additional requirement that the restrictions "be demonstrably

---

15 One will recall that Canadian courts introduced the criterion of reasonableness in applying the requirement of equality before the law under the *Canadian Bill of Rights*: see *Mackay v. R.*, [1980] 2 S.C.R. 370; *R. v. Burnshine*, [1975] 1 S.C.R. 693.

16 Thus, if one can rely on the dissenting opinion of Mr. Justice Pigeon in *Martineau v. Matsqui Institution Inmate Disciplinary Bd. (No. 1)*, [1978] 1 S.C.R. 118, any restriction introduced in the form of a simple directive issued by an administrative authority without authorization would not be prescribed by law for the purposes of s. 1.

17 The case law supports this view: see *Re Germany and Rauca* (1983), 145 D.L.R. (3d) 638 (Ont. C.A.); *Re Decter and United States* (1983), 5 C.C.C. (3d) 364 (N.S. T.D.), aff'd (1983), 5 C.C.C. (3d) 364 at 380 (N.S. C.A.); *Cotroni v. Centre de prevention de Montréal* (1986), 53 C.R. (3d) 339 (Que. C.A.), leave to appeal to S.C.C. granted (1986), 53 C.R. (3d) 339n (S.C.C.).

18 The test merely requires that the regulations have a rational relationship with some legitimate state objective. If they do, they avoid judicial scrutiny. See J. Tussman & J. Tenbroek, "The Equal Protection of the Laws" (1948-49), 37 *Cal. L. Rev.* 341.

justified in a free and democratic society".[19] This requirement suggests that, in order to justify its restriction, the legislature must satisfy the intermediate test formulated by the American courts which requires proof that the challenged legislation is of substantial utility in the achievement of an important goal.[20] Because this issue is dealt with elsewhere in works on equality, it will not be discussed here save to say that the interpretation offered here is not inconsistent with the language of section 1.

Only those restrictions which meet the following criteria can be justified under section 1:

1. the restriction must be prescribed by law;
2. it must promote important state objectives; and
3. it must be proportional to the ends sought.[21]

---

19 The Supreme Court of Canada made it clear in *L.S.U.C. v. Skapinker*, [1984] 1 S.C.R. 357, that it expects lawyers to prepare briefs which provide adequate information for the purposes of argument concerning the application of s. 1. In so doing, it indicated its intention to make the burden of proof imposed on the state more onerous than that generally applied by the American courts. Mr. Justice Jones shared this view when he stated that "[t]he onus, as pointed out in *Skapinker*, is on the Crown to show that the limit is 'demonstrably justified'. That onus cannot be lightly discharged in view of the fact that the regulation is a direct affront to s. 6(2) of the Charter"; and, further on, that "[i]t has not been demonstrated that the legitimate provincial aims cannot be obtained by both licensing and bonding which were the principal measures in the Act.": *Basile v. A.G. Nova Scotia* (1984), 62 N.S.R. 410 at 415 (N.S. C.A.). However, Mr. Justice Dea in *Black v. Law Soc. of Alta.* (1984), 33 Alta. L.R. (2d) (Q.B.), rev'd [1986] 3 W.W.R. 590 (Alta. C.A.) leave to appeal to S.C.C. granted (1986), 22 C.R.R. 192n (S.C.C.), stressed that the restriction does not have to be "demonstrably necessary" but only "demonstrably justified". This distinction followed his statement at 247 that: "[T]he court should exercise a high degree of caution before substituting its opinion for that of the legislature."
      Since these decisions, the Supreme Court of Canada has rendered its decision in *R. v. Oakes*, [1986] 1 S.C.R. 103, in which it outlined the principles that it will use to determine whether s. 1 applies. The court stated that only important state objectives can justify infringing fundamental rights and freedoms. Such infringements must be kept to a minimum. The burden of proof is on the government and is quite onerous. Thus, we can expect the courts to be at least as demanding as the American courts when the latter apply the intermediate test and possibly even the strict scrutiny test which is used by American courts only in special circumstances.

20 D. Proulx, "Egalité et discrimination dans la Charte des droits et libertés de la personne, Etude comparative" (1980), 10 *R.D.U.S.* 381 at 439-441. See also Jacquier, *infra*, note 25.

21 In *Cotroni, supra*, note 17, the Quebec Court of Appeal held that a regulation allowing extradition to a foreign country for prosecution for a crime when the acts upon which the accusation is based occurred in Canada and, if proven, constitute a crime in this country, is not a restriction on the right to remain in Canada which meets the criteria outlined in s. 1. In the opinion of the court, extradition in these circumstances did not constitute a means "reasonably and proportionately related to the end sought" [translation]. The ends sought — punishment of criminal acts and fulfillment of Canada's international obligations — did not clearly require extradition on the facts before the

(b) Section 6 and the Rights to Move and Gain a Livelihood

As with mobility rights, here also it is important to deal separately with two questions: the purpose of the right and the qualifications to which it is subject. However, one must note that the qualifications here do not derive exclusively from section 1 as was the case for the right of mobility. Sections 6(3) and 6(4) introduce distinct grounds for justifying restrictions on the rights to move and gain a livelihood, the scope of which must be understood. We may begin by looking at the purpose of section 6(2).

(i) *The purpose of the prohibitions or requirements imposed on the legislature by section 6(2)*

The first task is to determine whether this subsection merely requires the state to refrain from interference or whether its requirements are more onerous. It is submitted that this section does more than simply prohibit restrictions on access to, taking up residence in or working in any province, although it does not of itself mandate particular legislative initiatives. Section 6(3)(b) implies more than a simple prohibition against interference. It provides that the rights conferred in section 6(2) are subject to "any laws providing for reasonable residency requirements as a qualification for the receipt of publicly provided social services". The right to social services is not inherent in the rights of access to, taking up residence in and working in any province. However, if such social services are offered by the government out of the public purse and eligibility is determined by rules which have an impact on the rights created in section 6(2), the residency requirements must be reasonable. Thus section 6(2) does more than simply forbid infringement of the rights created therein.

However, section 6(3)(b) does not impose any obligation on the state to offer social services. Its purpose is to ensure that any criteria of eligibility for social services based on residency are reasonable. It only applies where such services are offered to residents. The effect of section 6(2) is thus to prohibit the state not only from directly interfering with the rights set out therein but also from enacting eligibility criteria based on residency which unreasonably infringed those rights. Obviously, any residency requirements which do not affect these rights are not subject to scrutiny under section 6.[22]

---

court. The ends "could be achieved through means other than those" [translation] being used in this case. Canada could prosecute for the crimes in its own jurisdiction. This is an interesting illustration of the rigour of the requirements of s. 1 as described by the Supreme Court of Canada in *Oakes, supra*, note 19.

22 For a differing point of view see D.A. Schmeiser, & K.J. Young, "Mobility Rights in Canada" (1983), 13 *Man. L.J.* 615.

The preceding comments relate solely to the right to take up residence in a province or to reside and work in the same province. Is it possible to argue that the right to have access to and to work in a province other than the province in which one resides imposes an obligation to legislate on the state? The answer appears to be "no". Section 6(3)(a), which applies to the entire range of rights embodied in section 6(2), merely prohibits discrimination on the basis of present or previous province of residence. Thus, it does not require legislative action but merely limits the power to enact legislation which has an impact on these rights.

Section 6(2) gives rights to Canadian citizens and to "every person who has the status of a permanent resident of Canada". The problem of defining the classes of persons on whom these rights are conferred has been dealt with above.[23] The views expressed there apply as much to defining the class of "permanent resident" and as they do to defining "citizen" for the purpose of section 6(2).[24]

Does section 6(2) protect the rights of legal entities such as corporations as well as those of individuals? In my view, the subsection confers a right to take up residence on individuals alone.[25] For one thing, the classes designated in the subsection — citizens and permanent residents — include only individuals under existing Canadian law.[26] Moreover, the character of the rights conferred as formulated in the subsection mandates this interpretation. The right to "gagner sa vie" or "to pursue the gaining of a livelihood" only makes sense if the holder of the right is an individual.

Does the right to take up residence apply to self-employed persons as well as employees? The answer is obviously "yes". The language of the section does not restrict its application to those earning their living in any particular fashion.

Paragraphs (a) and (b) of section 6(2) raise difficult questions of interpretation. There are two significant differences in the wording of the English and French texts concerning the right to move. The English text confers a right "to move to . . . any province" whereas the French text refers to the right to "se déplacer dans tout le pays". Thus, the one is only concerned with access to the interior of Canadian territorial divisions whereas the other gives a general right to move anywhere in the country.

---

23 See *supra*, pp. 304-305.

24 However, Mr. Justice Arnup held that the definition of "permanent resident" found in the *Immigration Act, 1976*, S.C. 1976-77, c. 52, applied to s. 6: see the Ontario Court of Appeal decision in the case of *Re Skapinker* (1983), 145 D.L.R. (3d) 502 at 514, rev'd *supra*, note 19 (*sub nom. Skapinker v. L.S.U.C.*).

25 See also Hogg, *supra*, note 7 at 668; Laskin, *supra*, note 8 at 90; Schmeiser & Young, *supra*, note 22 at 627; C. Jacquier, "La liberté de circulation des étudiants au Canada: une liberté garantie et quasi-absolue" (1985), 16 *R.G.D.* 511 at 532.

26 See *supra*, pp. 306-307.

Moreover, the English version confers the right only with respect to the provinces whereas the right set out in the French version relates to the entire country. According to the English text, the right conferred is merely a right of access to any province so that an individual could not complain of restrictions on his or her freedom of movement within a province, which is the only territorial unit to which the right applies. In contrast, the French text is doubly generous. It confers not simply a right of access to the territorial division but a general right of movement within the division, and this right applies throughout the whole of Canada.

In my opinion, section 6(2)(a) does not on its true construction create a general right of movement, as suggested by the French text, but only the right to take up residence in any province.[27] There are several grounds for this conclusion. First, the linking of the right to move with the right to take up residence suggests that the exercise of the right to move must be for a certain purpose. Second, the fact that the rights to move and to take up residence are presented together in the same paragraph suggests an intention to create a single right or to subject the right to move to the right to take up residence. If these were autonomous rights, they would have been set out in separate paragraphs. The structure of the French text as well as the heading and the marginal notes also justify this interpretation. The heading in French mentions two rights, "la liberté de circulation et d'établissement". According to the marginal note, the "liberté de circu-lation" is the concern of section 6(1). Logically then, one would expect section 6(2) to deal solely with the "liberté d'établissement". This is confirmed by the marginal note.

The Supreme Court of Canada appears to have adopted the same approach in *L.S.U.C. v. Skapinker*,[28] when it refused to interpret section 6(2)(b) as conferring a right to work independently of any sort of interprovincial mobility. In addition, the court refused to accept the argument that section 6(2)(a) creates more than one right and it limited that right by defining it in terms of the purpose of interprovincial movement, namely the taking up of residence. Mr. Justice Estey wrote:

> The two rights (in para. (*a*) and para. (*b*)) both relate to movement into another province, either for the taking up of residence, or to work without establishing residence.[29]

It is not yet decided whether the right to take up residence applies to the whole of Canada as such or only to the provinces. In my opinion, the

---

27 See, *contra*, E.S. Binavince, "The Impact of the Mobility Rights: The Canadian Economic Union — A Boom or a Bust?" (1982), 14 *Ottawa L. Rev.* 340 at 361.

28 *Supra*, note 19.

29 *Ibid.* at 382-383.

answer is clear given the formulation of the right to take up residence, which in both the English and French versions is limited to the provinces alone.

Assuming that the right of access to a province is tied to the right to take up residence therein under section 6(2)(a), the next step is to define this right. Is it a right to take up residence anywhere in any province or is it simply a right to take up residence in any province? In my view, the paragraph confers the more limited right to establish a residence in the province of one's choice. The expressions "in any province" and "dans toute province" suggest that the objective was to protect the choice of province rather than the choice of location within the province. Even if the words "in" and "dans" could be used to justify the more liberal definition of the right, the fact that they are related to the right to take up residence rather than reside supports the more restrictive interpretation. The expression "to take up residence" has a connotation of stability which the verb "to reside" lacks. This suggestion of stability is more consistent with a relationship to the province in general rather than the different regions and places within the province.

The general context in which this right is found also supports this interpretation. Section 6(3)(a) speaks of the "province of present or previous residence" and section 6(4) contrasts the national average with the situation in the province, its purpose being to exempt discrimination based on residence in the province rather than in a particular region therein. Thus, in my view, the right to take up residence described in section 6(2) is limited to the right to take up residence within the borders of any Canadian province.

What is the right "to pursue the gaining of a livelihood in any province" or "de gagner leur vie dans toute province"? The Supreme Court of Canada made it clear in *L.S.U.C. v. Skapinker*[30] that an individual does not have to reside in the province where he or she works. One important issue is whether this section creates a right to work. The answer is that it does not. The provision appears in the part of the Charter relating to mobility rights. Moreover, the wording of section 6(2)(b) is perfectly consistent with the heading of this part, for it deals with the place where individuals may gain their livelihood and it confers the right to do so "in any province". Its sole purpose is to abolish obstacles to interprovincial mobility and it would be inappropriate to read into the paragraph a right to work which would necessitate the abolition of many other types of obstacles.[31] It is also important to note that this provision only protects the right to "gain

---

30 *Ibid.*
31 The Supreme Court of Canada adopted this interpretation in *L.S.U.C. v. Skapinker, ibid.*

a livelihood". Thus, it does not protect the right to acquire property.[32]

What, then, does section 6(2)(b) protect? Does it merely preclude a province from denying Canadian citizens and permanent residents access to all employment in the province? Or is the province precluded from denying Canadian citizens and permanent residents access to any employment? There is a line of Canadian cases which, although not recent, sheds some light on this question.[33] In these cases, provincial laws which denied foreigners access to certain types of employment were struck down on the grounds that they effectively denied access to the labour market in general. The factors which led to this result may assist in the effort to understand the scope of section 6(2)(b). In *Cunningham v. Tomey Homma*,[34] the Privy Council summarized the ratio of its decision in *Union Colliery Co. v. Bryden*[35] in the following words:

> This Board . . . came to the conclusion that the regulations there impeached were not really aimed at the regulation of coal mines at all, but were in truth devised to deprive the Chinese, naturalized or not, of the ordinary rights of the inhabitants of British Columbia and, in effect, to prohibit their continued residence in that province, since it prohibited their earning their living in that province.

In this passage, the refusal to allow individuals to work in the province is treated as the equivalent of refusing to allow them to reside in that province. If this perspective is adopted, one must conclude that section 6(2)(b) does not simply prohibit the exclusion of individuals from the labour market in general, for section 6(2)(a) already prohibits interference with the right to take up residence. Section 6(2)(b) must provide additional protection. It thus seems reasonable to conclude that section 6(2)(b) prevents the legislature from denying any Canadian citizen or permanent resident access to any type of employment whatsoever, not simply employment in general, for the prohibition against denying access to employment in general is implicit in the right to take up residence.[36] It

---

32 See, *contra*, Binavince, *supra*, note 27; Schmeiser & Young, *supra*, note 22 at 625 and 636. For a similar view, see Laskin, *supra*, note 8 at 97. It is worth noting that the provision does not cast any doubt on the decision reached in *Morgan v. A.G. Prince Edward Island*, [1976] 2 S.C.R. 349.

33 *Union Colliery Co. v. Bryden, infra*, note 35, which was interpreted in *Cunningham v. Tomey Homma, infra*, note 34 at 157, and *Brooks-Bidlake & Whittall Ltd. v. A.G., B.C.*, [1923] A.C. 450 at 457 (P.C.).

34 [1903] A.C. 151 at 157 (P.C.)

35 [1899] A.C. 580 (P.C.).

36 Mr. Justice Dea in *Black v. Law Soc. of Alta.*, *supra*, note 19, reached the same conclusion although for different reasons, since he stated at 239: "A broad and liberal interpretation of s. 6(2)(*b*) does not permit of a construction which would hold that so long as the plaintiffs may pursue the gaining of their livelihood in 'some way' that no infringement occurs."

appears likely that this view will prevail. In fact, in the *Skapinker* case,[37] no one even suggested that the Canadian citizenship requirement was compatible with section 6(2)(b) on the grounds that it did not prevent those affected from working in any of the many other types of employment available in the province.

The purpose of section 6(2) can be summarized in the following terms. It creates a freedom and also imposes certain legislative requirements by prohibiting certain forms of discrimination identified in section 6(3). Only individuals benefit from this protection, but it applies to the self-employed as well as employees. The right enshrined in section 6(2)(a) allows any individual who is a Canadian citizen or permanent resident to take up residence in the province of his or her choice but does not permit the individual to determine where in that province he or she will reside. The right set out in section 6(2)(b) is merely a right to gain a livelihood in any province, which is not the same as a right to gain a livelihood. Interprovincial mobility is the only issue here. The effect of this right is that the legislature may not exclude Canadian citizens or permanent residents from the exercise of any trade or profession in the province.

(ii) *The relationship of sections 6(3) and 6(4) and section 1 to section 6(2).*

The rights created by section 6 are first of all subject to section 1, as discussed above.[38] There is no need to re-examine the general effect of section 1, but its application to section 6(2) will be noted. These rights are also subject to the restrictions permitted under section 6(3), namely:

(a) any laws or practices of general application in force in a province other than those that discriminate among persons primarily on the basis of province of present or previous residence; and

(b) any laws providing for reasonable residency requirements as a qualification for the receipt of publicly provided social services.

Finally, they are subject to section 6(4) which permits measures intended to promote the amelioration of disadvantaged individuals in provinces with high rates of unemployment.

Before discussing the exact character of the restrictions allowed under

---

See also *Mia v. Medical Services Comm. of B.C.* (1985), 61 B.C.L.R. 273 at 296 (S.C.), in which Mr. Justice McEachern stated: "This is because the language of Charter, s. 6(2)(*b*), ' . . . to pursue the gaining of a livelihood . . .', can only mean the right to practise on a viable economic basis." In this case, the challenged regulation did not prohibit doctors newly resident in the province from working, but rather it denied them a billing number which would have enabled them to be paid directly by the provincial government.

37 *Supra*, note 19.

38 See *supra*, pp. 6-9.

sections 6(3), 6(4) and 1, it is necessary to address two broad difficulties that are raised by section 6(3) and section 6(4). The resolution of these difficulties will determine what burden of proof must be met when seeking a remedy under section 6.

The wording of section 6(3)(a) raises two important issues of interpretation. The first is whether the exemption created by this paragraph is relative, that is, applicable only on proof of a violation of section 6(2), or absolute in the sense that it applies regardless of proof of such a violation.[39] If the first interpretation is adopted, the exemption to the protection provided by section 6(2) is limited to measures which apparently violate that subsection. If the second interpretation is adopted, the exemption must be extended to any measure that comes within the terms of the paragraph. The effect of this interpretation would be to prohibit any measure which violates section 6(3)(a) regardless of its relationship to interprovincial mobility.

In my view, the role of section 6(3) is to define the kinds of legislation and practices which may validly restrict the rights granted by section 6(2). Thus, only measures which affect mobility rights need satisfy the requirements of section 6(3). This interpretation is supported by both the French and English versions, which introduce paragraphs (a) and (b) as limitations on the rights set out in section 6(2).

The interpretation offered here is also supported by the reasoning of the Supreme Court of Canada in the *Skapinker* case.[40] The court there sought to determine whether the challenged regulations were contrary to section 6(2) and did not even address the question whether they satisfied the requirements of section 6(3). By taking this approach, the court showed that section 6(3) applies only where it has first been established that a contested measure violates section 6(2). The Nova Scotia Court of Appeal adopted the same approach in *Basile v. A.G. Nova Scotia.*[41]

The second difficulty encountered in interpreting section 6(3)(a) concerns the nature of the restrictions it permits. The question that inevitably arises is whether these restrictions help define the rights which constitute mobility rights or rather are limitations imposed *a posteriori* on the mobility rights set out in section 6(2). This issue is very important because the chosen interpretation will determine what is meant by a "violation" of these rights. If section 6(3) is regarded as an integral part of the definition of mobility rights, it would follow that a law or practice permitted under this section is not a violation of protected rights and

---

39 Professor Hogg appears to prefer the second interpretation of this section: P.W. Hogg, *Canada Act 1982 Annotated* (Toronto: Carswell, 1982) at 25.

40 *Supra*, note 19.

41 *Supra*, note 19.

therefore section 1 would not apply. If, on the other hand, the second interpretation is preferred, section 1 would probably be applicable whether or not the measures in question were permissible under section 6(3).

It is submitted that section 6(3) contributes to the declaration of mobility rights and acts as an internal limitation on the definition of these rights. The wording of section 1 supports this interpretation. It applies to limitations on the rights which are "set out" in the Charter, that is to limitations which do not form an essential part of that setting out itself. The language of section 1 militates against the creation of external limitations or restrictions elsewhere in the Charter, for it indicates that the only restrictions or limitations of that type which are allowed are those described in that section.

In addition, the interdependence of sections 6(3) and 6(2) suggests that these two subsections should be read together. It is worth considering the following passage from the decision of the Supreme Court of Canada in *Reference re British Columbia Motor Vehicle Act*[42] in which the court had to interpret the final words of section 7 of the Charter. Section 7 states:

> Everyone has the right to life, liberty and security of the person and the right not to be deprived thereof except in accordance with the principles of fundamental justice.

Mr. Justice Lamer, for the majority, wrote the following:

> The principles of fundamental justice, on the other hand, are not a protected interest, but rather a qualifier of the right not to be deprived of life, liberty and security of the person.

He later wrote:

> As a qualifier, the phrase serves to establish the parameters of the interests but it cannot be interpreted so narrowly as to frustrate or stultify them.[43]

The position adopted by the court respecting section 7 is similar to the one presented here concerning the nature of the limitations introduced in section 6(3).

In any case, in my view, it is difficult if not impossible to interpret section 6(3) as constituting an *a posteriori* limit which must be justified

---

42 [1985] 2 S.C.R. 486.

43 *Ibid.* at 501. The position taken by Madam Justice Wilson is different from the approach taken in this article. She wrote at p. 523 that: "I do not view the latter part of the section as a qualification on the right to life, liberty and security of the person in the sense that it limits or qualifies the right or defines its parameters." She clearly refused to interpret the last part of s. 7 as part of the definition of the rights created in that section. Thus, she concluded that it is still possible to apply s. 1 even where there is no violation of the last part of the section.

under section 1, for section 6(3) makes the rights described in section 6(2) subject to "any laws and practices of general application in force in a province". Section 1, on the other hand, requires that any restriction on the rights and freedoms set out in the Charter be prescribed by law. A practice is obviously not a law. We would do well to avoid an interpretation of section 6(3) which renders part of it otiose or possibly even unconstitutional.[44]

What is the character of the limitations introduced in section 6(4)? In the first place, unlike section 6(3), this subsection must be interpreted as applying to all laws, programs or activities which serve the indicated purpose regardless of whether they have an impact on mobility rights. The subsection states that sections 6(2) and (3) "do not preclude" and "n'ont pas pour objet d'interdire" the measures which it describes so that it is perfectly clear that the rights enshrined in those subsections have nothing to do with these measures. In addition, there is no obvious relation between mobility rights and the kinds of measures described in section 6(4); an external territory is prohibited.

For similar reasons, it seems obvious that section 6(4) creates an external limitation on mobility rights. Nonetheless, it is not possible to use section 1 to challenge government action which falls within the ambit of section 6(4). The subsection creates an absolute immunity and such action would therefore not constitute a violation of mobility rights.

The power to restrict rights and freedoms under section 1 is thus quite distinct from the authority conferred on the legislatures by sections 6(3) and (4). Under these subsections the legislatures may narrow the scope of mobility rights or avoid them altogether, whereas under section 1 they are given a power to limit them. Section 1 does not apply unless it is first established that a mobility right has been violated either by the imposition of a limitation which is not authorized by a law or practice of general application or by the imposition of a limitation pursuant to a law or practice which discriminates among persons primarily on the basis of province of present or past residence. It is possible to invoke section 1 in the case of the latter type of violation because paragraph 6(3)(a) does not exclude the possibility that measures which are not protected therein can be upheld under other sections of the Charter.[45]

We are now in a position to consider the exact scope of each of the restrictions included in sections 6(3) and 6(4). Section 1 will not be

---

44 See also Schmeiser & Young. *supra*, note 22 at 647.
45 See *Basile v. A.G. Nova Scotia, supra*, note 19; *Re Decter and United States, supra*, note 17; *Black v. Law Soc. of Alta., supra*, note 19. In these cases, the courts agreed that it would be possible to justify a limit on the rights in s. 6 under s. 1.

reconsidered here, for it has been discussed previously in this chapter[46] and is dealt with elsewhere in this volume.

A. *Laws and practices of general application which do not discriminate on the basis of province of residence.* It is clear from the language of section (6)(3)(a) that there are four conditions which must be satisfied by the measure considered here. The measure must be a law or a practice. It must be of general application. It must be in force in a province. It must not discriminate among persons primarily on the basis of province of present or past residence.

It is submitted that the term "law" includes regulations adopted pursuant to enabling legislation.[47] This interpretation can be reconciled with the position of Mr. Justice Deschênes in *Malartic Hygrade Gold Mines (Québec) Ltd. v. Quebec.*[48] Relying on the decision of the Supreme Court of Canada in *A.G. Québec v. Blaikie*[49] concerning section 133 of the *Constitution Act, 1867,* Deschênes J. held that the scope of the term "law" was limited to regulations subject to government approval. However, in the context of a provision which extends to "laws and practices", this interpretation is unconvincing in my view. Moreover, section 6 is included in a charter of rights and freedoms which must be interpreted liberally.[50] Finally, the fact that the term "laws" is used in the English version also supports this interpretation. The term "practices" most likely refers to various administrative practices.

The second condition requires that the laws and practices be of general application. This expression was interpreted in the case of *Kruger v. R.*[51] which dealt with the *Indian Act.*[52] Mr. Justice Dickson (as he then was) identified two criteria which can be used to determine whether a law is of general application. First, the law must apply generally throughout the whole territory. If it does, then the second step is to consider the purpose of the legislation and its effects. The legislation must not be in relation to a class of citizens so as to impair the status or capacity of the particular group.[53]

---

46 See *supra*, pp. 308-310.

47 See *Black v. Law Soc. of Alta.*, *supra*, note 19, in which the judge held that a regulation was a law of general application without discussing the type of regulation or the formalities of its adoption.

48 [1982] C.S. 1146 at 1153, 1154 (Que. S.C.).

49 [1981] 1 S.C.R. 312 at 333.

50 See D. Gibson, "Interpretation of the Canadian Charter of Rights and Freedoms: Some General Considerations", in W.S. Tarnopolsky and G.A. Beaudoin , eds. *The Canadian Charter of Rights and Freedoms: Commentary* (Toronto: Carswell, 1982), 25 at 29-48.

51 [1978] 1 S.C.R. 104.

52 R.S.C. 1970, c. I-6.

53 It is this two-pronged test that has led certain authors to disagree with some decisions interpreting s. 6 of the Charter. See, *e.g.*, M. Jackman, "Interprovincial Mobility Rights Under the Charter" (1984-85), 2 *U.T. Fac. L. Rev.* 16 at 31-33.

In my view, Professor Schmeiser is correct when he argues that this second criterion cannot constitute the sole test under the Charter.[54] It was used in the *Kruger* case[55] in order to determine at what point a provincial law of general application became legislation in relation to Indians and thereby encroached on the exclusive federal jurisdiction to legislate in respect of Indians. One interesting approach would be to treat as laws and practices of general application those which are not directed at non-residents as such.[56] This approach would allow for the interpretation of this paragraph as prohibiting laws and practices which *de facto* or indirectly discriminate on the basis of province of residence.[57]

The third condition requires that the measure be in force in the province. A measure which is in force in a province can be of either federal or provincial origin.[58] However, it is not clear whether a measure adopted by local or regional authorities and applying only to part of the provincial territory would satisfy this condition. It is submitted that, contrary to the situation in the *Kruger* case,[59] the expression "of general application" employed in section 6 does not necessarily mean of application to the whole provincial territory. Here the expression is linked directly to the words "in force in a province", which clearly indicate the scope of territorial application. This can be the province or a part of the province.

The last requirement is that the measures must not discriminate primarily on the basis of province of present or previous residence. In order to understand this requirement, we must discuss three dimensions of the concept of discrimination: intention, impact and discriminatory language.

It is obvious that a text which discriminates on its face is a prohibited form of discrimination under section 6(3)(a). The Court of Appeal of Nova Scotia stated this position very clearly in a case concerning a regulation which required, as a condition of eligibility for a permit as an itinerant seller, that the applicant be a permanent resident of the province.[60] The court accordingly overruled the decision of the trial judge who had held that the regulation was not discriminatory because it was intended to protect

---

54 Schmeiser & Young, *supra*, note 22.
55 *Supra*, note 51.
56 Laskin, *supra*, note 8 at 100.
57 See *Basile v. A.G. Nova Scotia, supra*, note 19 at 414, where the Nova Scotia Court of Appeal stated: "While the *Act* is a law of general application in the Province, with respect Regulation 7 is not a law of general application within the meaning of s. 6(3)(a) of the *Charter*. Regulation 7 is directed at one specific group, namely, non-residents."
58 The Federal Court of Appeal shares this opinion: *Demaere v. Canada* (1984), 52 N.R. 288. See, as well, Jacquier, *supra*, note 25 at 538.
59 *Supra*, note 51.
60 *Basile v. A.G. Nova Scotia, supra*, note 19.

consumers rather than to discriminate on the basis of provincial residence.[61] It is submitted that the Court of Appeal was correct in deciding that a text which discriminates on its face is discriminatory regardless of the intention of the legislator.

We must also consider whether a measure which is neither discriminatory on its face nor intended to be discriminatory can constitute discrimination for the purpose of section 6 solely because it has discriminatory consequences. Two recent Supreme Court of Canada decisions in which the court dealt with similar provisions suggest that the answer to this question is "yes".[62] The majority of judges clearly stated that the intention to create a distinction is not a deciding factor in interpretation of human rights legislation intended to eliminate discrimination.

If the courts adopt the same approach in interpreting section 6, three forms of discrimination will be prohibited: discrimination on the face of the text, intentional discrimination and discrimination that is systemic or results from the law's detrimental effect.[63]

B. *Laws providing for reasonable residency requirements as a qualification for the receipt of publicly provided social services.*   Here again, for the reasons outlined above, the term "laws" would include regulations adopted under enabling legislation. To come within the ambit of section 6(3)(b), the social services must first of all be found to be inherent in interprovincial mobility rights. This point is explained above.[64] The test of reasonableness used in applying this provision will probably be very similar to that used in applying section 1. This point will be discussed briefly below. In my view, the residence referred to in section 6(3)(b) could be provincial or even municipal. However, it is in the context of interprovincial mobility that these residency requirements will be analyzed. They would not apply to intraprovincial mobility or establishing residence in different areas within a province because, as previously explained, the exemption only relates to the rights found in section 6(2).

---

61 *Basile v. A.G. Nova Scotia* (1983), 148 D.L.R. (3d) 382 at 384 (N.S. T.D.), rev'd *supra*, note 19.

62 *Ont. Human Rights Comm. v. Simpson-Sears Ltd.*, [1985] 2 S.C.R. 536; *Bhinder v. C.N.R.*, [1985] 2 S.C.R. 561.

63 Mr. Justice McEachern adopted this interpretation of s. 6 in *Mia v. Medical Services Comm. of B.C.*, *supra*, note 36, where he stated at 299-300: "This exception to s. 6(3) does not deal with purpose or intention but rather with the fact or result of discrimination. If the law or practice — even if it is one of general application — has the result or effect of discriminating against the petitioner primarily on the basis of previous residence, then it cannot override a Charter right arising under s. 6(2)."

64 See *supra*, p. 16.

C. *Measures intended to ameliorate the conditions of the disadvantaged in provinces with high rates of unemployment.* Section 6(4) was introduced into the Charter by the constitutional agreement of November 5, 1981; it was not part of the original version of this section.[65] The measures permitted by this subsection can be adopted by all levels of government subject to the Charter with the jurisdiction to introduce them.

Although inspired by a desire to protect provincial labour forces, this subsection protects measures having other objectives as well. It applies to any measure that seeks "the amelioration . . . of conditions of individuals . . . who are socially or economically disadvantaged". It will be necessary to formulate criteria for the identification of those individuals who are socially or economically disadvantaged. It is submitted that the status of individuals should be determined through intraprovincial comparison between ordinary conditions in the province and the conditions of the targeted group.

It will also be necessary to determine whether a law, program or activity has as its object the amelioration of the conditions of such individuals. There is a real risk that the interpretation of the section eventually adopted will not provide the protection for discriminatory employment policies that many hoped would result from its inclusion. The failure of such a policy to have as its object the amelioration of the conditions of a specific category of individuals may well result in the refusal to apply section 6(4).

Finally, the measures covered by section 6(4) must have as their object the amelioration of conditions of individuals "in" the province. Therefore, it follows that they must apply only to certain categories of individuals in the province; those designed to improve the condition of all provincial residents are excluded.

3. THE IMPACT OF SECTION 6 OF THE *CANADIAN CHARTER OF RIGHTS AND FREEDOMS* ON FEDERAL POWERS

Having explored the ambit of section 6 of the Charter and noted the nature of the restrictions it imposes on Canadian legislatures, we are now in a position to examine in more detail the impact of this section on the powers of the federal Parliament. This turns on the extent to which the restrictions identified above are applicable to matters of federal jurisdiction. It is thus necessary to begin by specifying what is entailed by the right of mobility and the rights to move and gain a livelihood. It will then be

---

65 For a historical analysis of mobility rights under the Charter, see Schmeiser and Young, *supra*, note 22, at 624-626.

possible to identify the federal heads of power that are affected and the consequences for each of the rights in question.

(a) Federal Powers Relating to the Mobility of Citizens

(i) *The mobility of citizens*

At the beginning of this chapter, it was shown that section 6(1) of the Charter has three major effects. First, it limits the power of the federal government to define the meaning of citizenship.[66] Second, it eliminates the power to discriminate between different classes of Canadian citizens in respect of mobility. Finally, it circumscribes the right of mobility itself by singling out three components that we underlined the limit: the right to enter and the right to remain in Canada, and the right to leave.

(ii) *Federal powers relating to the mobility of citizens*

The first federal power affected is obviously federal jurisdiction over citizenship. It is clear that citizenship is indeed a federal matter. The only issue is where it should be slotted among the federal heads of power. While section 91(25) of the *Constitution Act, 1867* is often invoked, others point to the residual power of the federal Parliament.[67] It is generally accepted that the essence of this jurisdiction is the power to define the criteria of eligibility for citizenship and the circumstances in which it can be withdrawn.[68] Thus, the first aspect of the mobility of citizens directly affects this jurisdiction.

Federal jurisdiction over quarantine is affected by the prohibition on preventing citizens from entering or leaving Canada.[69] Jurisdiction over criminal law in a broad sense is affected by each of the three components of mobility identified in section 6(1). The power to impose criminal sanctions and to enact legislation relating to criminal procedure includes the power to order deportation or to prohibit entry into, or exit from, the country. Similarly, federal jurisdiction over national defence would doubtless authorize the enactment of measures which might violate section 6(1) mobility rights. The general power as well, at least to the extent that it grants emergency powers, could serve as the jurisdictional basis for measures of the same type.[70]

---

66 See *supra*, pp. 2-4.
67 See Slosar, *supra*, note 9 at 168-169.
68 *Ibid.* See also *Cunningham v. Tomey Homma, supra*, note 34 at 156-157.
69 *Constitution Act, 1867*, s. 91(11).
70 *Cooperative Committee on Japanese Canadians v. A.G. Canada*, [1947] A.C. 87.

(iii) *Other restrictions on federal powers*

While the federal Parliament under the *Constitution Act, 1867* is granted several powers which were affected by the coming into force of section 6(1) of the Charter, it is important to note that even before the Charter, Parliament did not enjoy an unqualified freedom in the exercise of these powers. There are other important sources of limitation.

International law plays an important role here. Thus, article 12(2) of the *International Covenant on Civil and Political Rights* states that:

> Everyone shall be free to leave any country, including his own.

This freedom includes two of the three components included in the mobility rights of citizens under the Charter: the right to remain in Canada and the right to leave. The third component is dealt with by article 12(4) of the Covenant in the following terms:

> No one shall be arbitrarily deprived of the right to enter his own country

Article 12(1) of the Covenant is also directly concerned with mobility rights. It reads:

> Everyone lawfully within the territory of a State shall, within that territory, have the right to liberty of movement and freedom to choose his residence.

The Covenant here grants a right to circulate freely throughout the entire country, something which, it is submitted, is not granted by either section 6(1) or 6(2) of the Charter. In this respect the Covenant imposes greater limitations on Parliament than does the Charter. Given that Canada has signed the Optional Protocol which permits the citizens of signatory states to take complaints to the Human Rights Committee of the United Nations, it is not easy to dismiss these provisions as mere declaratory texts. They constitute important limitations on the federal powers described above.

The *Canadian Bill of Rights*[71] includes in section 2(a) a provision which directly relates to the rights to enter and to remain in Canada. This paragraph states that no law shall be construed or applied so as to "authorize or effect the arbitrary . . . exile of any person". In addition, section 1(a) establishes the right to liberty which cannot be infringed by any Canadian law. Of course, it is possible for Parliament under section 2 to effectively immunize its laws against the application of the Bill, but to do so carries real political risks which give substance to the limitations imposed by the Bill on federal powers.

It would be wrong to conclude, however, that the adoption of section 6(1) of the Charter did not substantially change the law relating to the

---

71 *Supra*, note 3.

mobility of citizens. Although the federal government had previously consented to certain limitations on its powers, these were modest at best. In the first place, the limits imposed by the *Canadian Bill of Rights* are subject to the will of Parliament which can preclude its application provided the intention to do so is clearly expressed. This possibility does not exist under section 6 of the Charter because the power to derogate by express declaration conferred by section 33 does not apply to this section. Similarly, the sanctions available under the *International Covenant on Civil and Political Rights* leave a great deal to be desired. Thus, although it would be incorrect to say that section 6(1) represents a radical evolution of the law, its introduction did have an important impact on the jurisdiction of the federal Parliament.

(b) Federal Powers Relating to the Rights to Move and Gain a Livelihood

(i) *The rights to move and gain a livelihood*

The analysis of section 6(2) carried out above[72] showed that three types of regulation are affected by this provision. First, the power to define the status of Canadian citizens and permanent residents is subject to restriction. Second, the power of Parliament to discriminate in relation to the three rights enshrined in section 6(2) is limited. Thus, Parliament may not enact a law which discriminates between individuals on the basis of province of present or previous residence, except insofar as it relates to access to publicly provided social services. Any such law would be subject to judicial censure if the discrimination related to one of these rights and could not be justified under section 1. Finally, in the one area where the Charter allows distinctions based primarily on the province of present or previous residency — access to publicly provided social services — Parliament must establish reasonable residency requirements.

Apart from these limitations, the regime established by sections 6(2) and 6(3) permits the enactment of any laws of general application as expressly spelled out in section 6(3)(a). The rights created by these subsections thus boil down to an obligation on the federal Parliament when legislating on matters affecting the right to move to, to take up residence in or to pursue the gaining of a livelihood in any province not to discriminate among citizens and permanent residents on the basis of their present or previous residence unless justified under section 1 and to impose only reasonable residency requirements as a qualification for the receipt of publicly provided social services.

---

72 See *supra*, pp. 3-13.

(ii) *Federal powers relating to the rights to move and gain a livelihood*

The following discussion will be divided into three parts. The first will cover the right to enter and take up residence in any province. The second will analyze the right to gain a livelihood in any province. The final section will discuss the right to social services.

The federal Parliament has exclusive jurisdiction to prohibit access to a province or the establishment of residence in a province. This view is based on the opinion expressed by the Supreme Court of Canada and the Judicial Committee of the Privy Council in *Union Colliery Co. v. Bryden*[73] The issue in this case was whether a provincial law prohibiting Chinese persons from working in the mines of British Columbia was constitutional. The Judicial Committee of the Privy Council held that it was not. In its opinion, the law was directed solely at foreigners and naturalized citizens and therefore was a law in relation to "Naturalization and Aliens". The Committee expressed its view as follows:

> [B]y virtue of section 91, sub-s. 25, the legislature of the Dominion is invested with exclusive authority in all matters which directly concern the rights, privileges, and disabilities of the class of Chinamen who are resident of the provinces of Canada.[74]

This proposition describes the very broad jurisdiction of the federal government in matters relating to naturalization and aliens. However, this jurisdiction is more limited when applied to Canadian citizens because it applies solely to those who have been naturalized.[75]

This holding was clarified in two respects in the subsequent decision of the Judicial Committee in *Cunningham v. Tomey Homma*.[76] The provincial statute scrutinized in this case denied citizens of Japanese descent, whether naturalized or Canadian born, the right to vote in provincial elections. The Judicial Committee first adopted a more restrictive interpretation of the jurisdiction over naturalization and aliens:

> The truth is that the language of that section does not purport to deal with the consequences of either alienage or naturalization. It undoubtedly reserves these subjects for the exclusive jurisdiction of the Dominion — that is to say, it is for the Dominion to determine what shall constitute either the one or the other, but the question as to what consequences shall follow from either is not touched. The right of protection and the obligations of allegiance are

---

73 *Supra*, note 35.

74 *Ibid.* at 587.

75 In the same case, the Judicial Committee expressed the following opinion on the jurisdiction over Canadians who acquired citizenship by birth: "It can hardly have been intended to give the Dominion Parliament the exclusive right to legislate for the latter class of persons resident in Canada."

76 *Supra*, note 34.

necessarily involved in the nationality conferred by naturalization; but the privileges attached to it, where these depend upon residence, are quite independent of nationality.[77]

This amounts to a qualification of the position adopted in the *Bryden* case,[78] for Parliament's jurisdiction is no longer defined as including the consequences of naturalization and the rights and privileges of the naturalized citizens, subjects which the Judicial Committee had *prima facie* included. It now embraces merely the definition of the status of citizen. In addition, the proposition as formulated extends the principle to all citizens since the legislation in question also applied to native-born Canadians.

The Judicial Committee next proceeded to reinterpret its decision in the *Bryden* case.[79] In its opinion, the conclusion in that case was based on the fact that the law was characterized as legislation which sought to prohibit Chinese persons from residing in British Columbia.[80] According to the Privy Council, the right to vote is merely a privilege and as such is not beyond provincial jurisdiction, in contrast to the right of residency which is an inherent part of the right of protection attaching to nationality.

In *Morgan v. A.G. Prince Edward Island*,[81] the issue was the validity of provincial legislation which discriminated between residents and non-residents in restricting the right to acquire land in the province. After locating federal jurisdiction over citizenship in section 91(25) or in the general power of the federal government[82] and making it clear that he was dealing with citizens and foreigners alike,[83] Chief Justice Laskin adopted respect for the right of access and the establishment of residence as the test of validity in upholding the provincial law.[84]

It is thus fair to conclude that under our Constitution only the federal Parliament has jurisdiction to prohibit access to and the establishment of residence in a province. It follows that the federal Parliament is the only legislature affected by the provisions of the Charter which grant the right to move to and take up residence in any province to all citizens and persons having the status of permanent resident.

The position is quite different, however, with respect to the right to pursue the gaining of a livelihood without discrimination based on present or previous residence. As noted above, this is a right to do any kind of work whatsoever. In this area, the provincial jurisdiction is of much greater

---

77 *Ibid.* at 156-157.
78 *Supra*, note 35.
79 *Ibid.*
80 *Cunningham, supra*, note 34 at 157.
81 *Supra*, note 32.
82 *Ibid.* at 351-352.
83 *Ibid.* at 355.
84 *Ibid.* at 357, 359.

importance,[85] for the regulation of labour and services is a matter of property and civil rights in the province. In a line of important cases that affirmed the right of the provinces to legislate in respect of working conditions and unemployment insurance, the courts also recognized that the provinces have jurisdiction to regulate the trades and professions.[86] This provincial power is limited to some extent by the federal jurisdiction over interprovincial and international works and undertakings. Similarly, the regulation of services is for the most part within provincial jurisdiction over property and civil rights. Federal jurisdiction in this area is limited to the works and undertakings mentioned above, federal companies whose status and essential powers cannot be impaired, banks, and interprovincial and international commerce. Although in principle Parliament's jurisdiction over interprovincial and international commerce could serve as a basis for extensive federal regulation of services, in practice it does not give Parliament much of a role to play.

The provision of social services appears to be a matter within the federal spending power. By imposing requirements for the receipt of social services, the federal government is able to intervene in this area which for the most part is within the exclusive jurisdiction of the provinces under the division of legislative powers. From this perspective, it can be said that the Charter restricts the spending power of the central government by requiring it to impose only reasonable residency requirements.

In conclusion, it appears that section 6(2) of the Charter has an important impact on federal jurisdiction to legislate concerning the right to move to and take up residence in any province. However, the provisions which deal with the gaining of a livelihood and access to social services have less impact because Parliament has a very limited jurisdiction over these matters.

(iii) *Other restrictions on federal powers*

Examination of the restrictions which, apart from the Charter limit Parliament's power to deal with matters involving the rights to move and to gain a livelihood should begin with article 12(1) of the *International Covenant on Political and Civil Rights*. It reads:

---

85 See I. Bernier, "Le concept d'union économique dans la Constitution canadienne: de l'intégration commerciale à l'intégration des facteurs de production" (1979), 20 *C. de D.* 177 at 210-213.

86 *Re Imrie and Institute of Chartered Accountants of Ont.*, [1972] 3 O.R. 275; *Buzunis v. Walker*, [1972] 4 W.W.R. 337 (Man. C.A.); *Re Dickenson and Law Soc. of Alta.* (1978), 84 D.L.R. (3d) 189 (Alta. T.D.).

> Everyone lawfully within the territory of a State shall, within that territory, have the right to liberty of movement and freedom to choose his residence.

This provision creates the right to move about freely within a country. Since such a right of free movement is not in fact conferred by section 6 of the Charter, the effect of the *International Covenant on Civil and Political Rights* is first of all to give an additional right of freedom of movement within Canada. Thus, prior to the adoption of the Charter, federal powers were already restricted by international law.[87]

The second right created by article 12 is conferred on every person who is legally within the territory of any state and amounts to a complete freedom to take up residence in any part of the country. It is clear that this right to choose one's place of residence cannot be assimilated to the right to establish a provincial residence within the meaning of the Charter. One establishes residence in a province by locating there with the intention of remaining there for an extended period, longer than a year.[88] Because article 12 grants the right to choose a residence to "everyone lawfully within the territory of a state", the intention was probably not to confer a right to take up permanent residence. In my view, then, the term "residence" as used in article 12 has a different meaning than in section 6 of the Charter and refers merely to the right to reside temporarily in the locality of one's choice.

If this conclusion is correct, it affects the right to take up residence found in section 6 of the Charter for it implies that residence can be established anywhere on Canadian soil whether or not within a province. As shown above, section 6 only grants the right to establish a territorial connection with a province. The Covenant goes farther and grants the "freedom to choose . . . residence" in any part of the country. It follows that article 12 of the Covenant further restricts federal jurisdiction respecting both the choice of a temporary residence and the establishment of more permanent residence within a province.

It will suffice here to recall that the *Canadian Bill of Rights* imposes minimal restrictions on the federal power to legislate on matters relating to residence. Undoubtedly, the right to equality limits the ability of the federal government to adopt discriminatory legislation. However, the application of the principle of reasonableness, as interpreted by Canadian courts in the past,[89] would suggest there is little cause to hope or to fear that the right to equality will constitute a serious impediment to the exercise of federal powers.

---

87 See *supra*, p. 19.
88 See *supra*, p. 11.
89 See *R. v. Burnshine, supra*, note 15.

10

Fundamental Rights and Fundamental Justice*
(Section 7)

*Patrice Garant***

1. Introduction
2. The Affirmation of the Rights to Life, Liberty and Security of the Person
3. The Protection of the Rights to Life, Liberty and Security of the Person

1. INTRODUCTION

Section 7 of the *Canadian Charter of Rights and Freedoms*[1] raises difficulties of two kinds. On the one hand, it entrenches three fundamental rights — the rights to life, liberty and security of the person. On the other hand, section 7 provides for the protection of these rights from interference by public authorities, by requiring that they act in accordance with "principles of fundamental justice".

In the first part of this chapter we will be concerned with the meaning

---

* Translated from French.
** With the contributions of Isabelle Hudon and Sylvain Lepage, research assistants.
1 Part I of the *Constitution Act, 1982* [en. by the (U.K.), 1982, c. 11, Sched. B].

of the affirmation of these three fundamental rights. In the second part we will study fundamental justice and the relationship between this requirement and the fundamental rights protected by the Charter. This study is difficult in that it requires us to synthesize, in a few pages, three of the most difficult texts in the domain of fundamental liberties. Moreover, while it was not difficult before 1982 to describe the state of existing law with regard to the principles of fundamental justice, it was significantly less easy to articulate the protection of these rights in the procedural context — a context that seems to fluctuate or be seriously imprecise. With the advent of the Charter, controversy has gradually emerged respecting the scope of the expression "principles of fundamental justice" in the context of the Charter. The Supreme Court of Canada has finally had occasion to rule on this and in so doing has given the expression an extremely broad scope.

2. THE AFFIRMATION OF THE RIGHTS TO LIFE, LIBERTY AND SECURITY OF THE PERSON

(a) Scope of Section 7 — *Ratione Personae*

It is appropriate to begin this study of the constitutive elements of section 7 of the Charter with a careful examination of the word "everyone" in order to determine the categories of protected persons. Additionally, we will examine from what source the infringement must originate in order to entitle one to protection.

(i) *The word "everyone" and corporations*

The issue of whether the expression "everyone" includes corporations arose immediately upon the introduction of the Charter. The courts have been almost unanimous in holding that this expression is broad enough to include corporations.[2] Some argued against this extension by noting that some Charter rights cannot be claimed by a corporation. However, it was quickly decided that the expression "everyone" includes corporations and must be so interpreted whenever the rights claimed are capable of applying to corporations.

---

2 See, *inter alia*, *Re Balderstone and R.* (1983), 2 C.C.C. (3d) 37 (Man. Q.B.), aff'd (1983), 8 C.C.C. (3d) 532 (Man. C.A.), leave to appeal to S.C.C. refused 8 C.C.C. (3d) 532n (S.C.C.); *Re Seaway Trust Co. and Ontario* (1983), 143 D.L.R. (3d) 623 (Ont. Div. Ct.); *Re R.L. Crain Inc. and Couture* (1984), 6 D.L.R. (4th) 478 (Sask. Q.B.); *Southam Inc. v. Hunter* (1982), 136 D.L.R. (3d) 133 (Alta. Q.B.), aff'd (1982), 42 A.R. 108 (Alta. C.A.); *Gershaman Produce Co. v. Motor Transport Bd.* (1984), 14 D.L.R. (4th) 722 (Man. Q.B.), rev'd (1985), 22 D.L.R. (4th) 520 (Man. C.A.).

This proposition is supported by the *Southam* case[3] which concerned section 8 of the Charter. This section protects against unreasonable searches and seizures, a protection which is easily applicable to corporations. Given that the expression "everyone" used in section 7 is identical to that used in section 8, it could hardly be given a different meaning.

(ii) *The word "everyone" and citizenship*

One must deal with the question whether it is possible to restrict the application of section 7 to Canadian citizens. Contrary to other provisions of the Charter which guarantee certain rights only to Canadian citizens, section 7 does not contain any such limitation. The Supreme Court of Canada, speaking through Madam Justice Wilson, has held that "everyone" refers to any person whose life, liberty or security is infringed, provided that the person is present in Canada:

> Counsel for the Minister concedes that "everyone" is sufficiently broad to include the appellants in its compass and I am prepared to accept that the term includes every human being who is physically present in Canada and by virtue of such presence amenable to Canadian law.[4]

One may ask what would happen if a Canadian, while visiting abroad, suffered an infringement of a right protected by section 7 through the application of a Canadian law. Could this person rely on the Charter, or are we to take Madam Justice Wilson literally when she says that "the term includes every human being who is physically present in Canada and by virtue of such presence amenable to Canadian law"? It appears that Madam Justice Wilson is here speaking only of the situation of the non-citizen. As for Canadian citizens, wherever they may be found and to the extent they are subject to Canadian laws, they are covered by the Charter. The language of Madam Justice Wilson raises another problem, however, when she states that "everyone" encompasses all "human beings". It will suffice at this point to simply allude to the controversy concerning the potential person or the foetus; the matter will be examined more fully below.[5]

(iii) *The source of the infringement*

For the Charter to apply, must the infringement complained of be exclusively and directly the result of an action by a Canadian authority?

---

3 *Hunter v. Southam Inc.*, [1984] 2 S.C.R. 145.

4 *Singh v. Min. of Employment & Immigration*, [1985] 1 S.C.R. 177 at 202.

5 "2 (d)(i) The right to life", *infra.*

For example, in the case of the Sikhs, the issue was whether section 7 applied to a deportation order where the infringement was liable to result more from the state to which the person was to be deported than from Canadian authorities. Mr. Justice Pratte of the Federal Court of Appeal declared that:

> The decision of the Board did not have the effect of depriving the applicant of his right to life, liberty and the security of the person. If the applicant is deprived of any of those rights after his return to his country, that will be as a result of the acts of the authorities or of other persons of that country, not as a direct result of the decision of the Board. In our view, the deprivation of rights referred to in section 7 refers to a deprivation of rights by Canadian authorities applying Canadian law.[6]

Madam Justice Wilson, however, considered that the decision of the Board to return the appellants to their own country where they would possibly be victims of corporal punishment constituted a violation of section 7, since it was made by a Canadian authority applying Canadian laws. Thus, where a decision by a Canadian authority exposes a person to an infringement of life, liberty or security, this will suffice to make section 7 applicable to that authority.

The infringement must result from the application of a Canadian law and not from the application of a foreign law. Furthermore, section 7 may not be invoked by a person who refuses to testify before a Canadian court by relying on a law of the Bahamas.[7] On the other hand, it applies in extradition matters, but only to Canadian authorities.[8]

(b) Life, Liberty and Security: Distinct or Interchangeable Concepts

Given the obvious connections among interferences with life, liberty and security of the person in many circumstances, one must consider whether the framers of the Charter envisaged the protection of a single reality or single right having different facets but complementing each other most of the time.

This theory was advanced by Mr. Justice Marceau of the Federal Court of Appeal in the *Operation Dismantle* case.[9] According to Mr. Justice

---

6 *Singh v. Min. of Employment & Immigration*, [1983] 2 F.C. 347 at 349.

7 *Spencer v. R.*, [1985] 2 S.C.R. 278.

8 *Canada v. Schmidt* [1987] 1 S.C.R. 500; *Argentina (Republic) v. Mellino*, [1987] 1 S.C.R. 536.

9 *Canada v. Operation Dismantle Inc.*, [1983] 1 F.C. 745 (C.A.), aff'd (*sub nom. Operation Dismantle v. R.* [1985] 1 S.C.R. 441. This is also the view of the Court of Appeal of Saskatchewan ("bound in one structure with a mutual and reciprocal influence on each other"): *Beare v. R.*, [1987] 4 W.W.R. 309 at 317, rev'd (December 1, 1988), Doc. No. 20384 (S.C.C.).

Marceau, the legislator did not create three distinct rights in section 7 but really one single right which may only be interfered with by respecting the principles of fundamental justice. Such a view of section 7 can only find support through a narrow interpretation of its terms.

The opinion of Mr. Justice Marceau was the subject of some criticism in the *Singh* case, a recent decision of the Supreme Court of Canada.[10] Strictly speaking, the "one right" theory was not categorically rejected. However, it was strongly tempered by a refusal to envisage the three concepts globally and by an attempt rather to specify the meaning of each of the three elements. Madam Justice Wilson thought that independent meaning must be given to these three rights.[11] This has since been confirmed by the court in the judgment by Lamer J. in *Re Section 94(2) of the Motor Reference Vehicle Act (B.C.)*,[12] and by Chief Justice Dickson in the *Morgentaler* case.[13]

While the debate has not yet been definitively resolved, in our view the theory of three rights gives a much better perspective of the rights guaranteed, namely the right to life, the right to liberty and the right to security of the person.

(c) Positive or Negative Rights?

A number of authors have raised the question of whether the Charter envisages a negative or a positive protection for the rights it confers.[14] According to the theory of negative rights, the objective is the absence of all coercion *vis-à-vis* the person. Under the other theory, the objective is the imposition of positive obligations on the state with a view to protecting and, indeed, even promoting these rights.

The courts have addressed this question but have not as yet given a sufficiently precise answer so as to enable an overall conclusion in favour of one theory or the other. Moreover, one has the impression that the answer may vary according to which of the three rights is in issue. This point will be developed below.

---

10 *Supra*, note 4.

11 *Ibid.* at 204.

12 [1985] 2 S.C.R. 486 at 500.

13 *R. v. Morgentaler*, [1988] 1 S.C.R. 30 at 45.

14 The problem is very well treated in an article by T.J. Christian, "Section 7 of the Charter of Rights and Freedoms: Constraints on State Action" (1984), 22 *Alta. L. Rev.* 222 at 227, 228; see also the article by T. Lee, "Section 7 of the Charter: An Overview" (1985), 43 *U.T. Fac. L. Rev.* 1 at 8, where the author argues in favour of the theory of positive rights relying on the affirmative style of the first part of s. 7.

(d) The Object of the Rights

(i) *The right to life*

What is life, this precious thing that Western civilization has traditionally surrounded with the greatest of respect. Is there a judicial definition of this concept? What are the criteria that allow us to determine the beginning of life, and to determine death? These are the difficult questions that we must briefly attempt to answer.

A. *The beginning of life.* We do not propose to give an account of the range of opinions on this question, but to review them briefly without distinguishing those whose foundation is theological, philosophical or legal. Keyserlingk summarizes opinion with regard to that which he calls the attributes which constitute personhood:

> But at least there is a certain consistency in agreement (among those who feel person is relevant) in the questions asked, and in the conviction or intuition that the central question has to do with personhood, and that the attributes which constitute it are the actual or potential capacity for functions variously referred to as self-awareness, consciousness, rationality, self-consciousness, freedom, communication, etc.
>
> These attributes often overlap and some argue that just one or another of them is sufficient. Some insist that at the moment of conception all these functions are potentially present genetically, and that [therefore] potential persons are in fact persons, with all the rights of persons. Others disagree and maintain that a foetus only moves from potential person without rights to actual persons with rights when the anchor of moral prerogatives and rights becomes present in the foetus biological constitution. That anchor or "fundamentum" (it is argued) is the constitutive potential for self-awareness, the applicable criterion of which is the presence of a nervous system complete in its basic cellular structure, though not necessarily yet fully developed as in adults. In this view and according to this criterion a foetus would become a person possibly at four months and certainly by seven months.[15]

He concludes in these terms:

> In my view this latter position is more compelling than the previous which identifies actual personhood with potential personhood based on genetics. But my real point here is only that both of these views, and the others, tend to consider as normative of personhood (and rights) similar stable attributes of foetal life. The attributes are in fact similar in substance to the ones I and others propose as normative at other stages in life when faced with treatment decisions, namely a minimal capacity (at least potentially) to experience and to relate.[16]

---

15 Law Reform Commission of Canada, *Sanctity of Life or Quality of Life* (study paper) by E.W. Keyserlingk (1979) at 95.

16 *Ibid.*

From a strictly legal point of view, the Supreme Court of the United States, in the celebrated 1973 case of *Roe v. Wade*,[17] refused to resolve the difficult question of the moment when human life begins, deciding only that from the moment of viability, the state has an interest in protecting this potential life. Judge Blackman of the United States Supreme Court thus introduced a new concept, that of "potential life".

The theory of potential life has been rejected in an interesting case that came before the courts of Saskatchewan.[18] In this matter it was argued that section 251(4) of the *Criminal Code* dealing with abortion was contrary to section 7 of the Charter since it infringed the right to life.

After reviewing the Canadian legislation, Mr. Justice Matheson declared that the foetus has never been recognized as a human being. The judge maintained that, if the framers had intended to include the foetus within the term "everyone", they would have indicated this intention more clearly. Accordingly, it was a matter for Parliament and not the court to determine the advisability of extending to the foetus the protections accorded to human persons. The judge thus concluded that a foetus is not included in the term "everyone". For its part, the Court of Appeal considered that the term "everyone" must have the same meaning throughout sections 7 to 14 and this can only include human beings as defined in the *Criminal Code*:

> 206.(1) A child becomes a human being within the meaning of this Act when it has completely proceeded, in a living state, from the body of its mother
> . . . .

Civil law considers the foetus "an unborn child" who has certain rights without having legal personality. According to Michèle Rivet, who gives a good summary of Québec law on the subject: "we may thus define the unborn child by reference to a negative: he is not a human being and he does not possess legal personality."[19] (translation)

Article 18 of the *Civil Code* provides that "every human being possesses juridical personality"; section 1 of the Québec *Charter of Human Rights and Freedoms*[19a] is to the same effect. Neither the *Civil Code* nor the Quebec

---

17 410 U.S. 113 (1973).

18 *Borowski v. A.G. Canada* (1984), 4 D.L.R. (4th) 112 (Sask. Q.B.), aff'd [1987] 4 W.W.R. 385 (Sask. C.A.), leave to appeal to S.C.C. granted [1987] 5 W.W.R. lxiii (note) (S.C.C., referring to the *Criminal Code*, R.S.C. 1970, c. C.-34.

19 M. Rivet, "La situation juridique de l'enfant non encore né au Canada: Canada, droit civil" (13è Colloque international de droit comparé) (Editions de l'Université d'Ottawa, 1975) 73 at 75. See also by the same author, "Le droit à la vie ou 'l'hominisation' du XXIe siècle: l'éthique et le droit répondent à la science", in D. Turp & G.-A. Beaudoin, eds., *Perspectives canadiennes et européennes des droits de la personne*, (Cowansville: Yvon Blais, 1986) 445.

19a R.S.Q., c. C-12.

legislature has indicated precisely when legal personality begins; the cases indicate that it is with birth: "a child yet to be born is certainly not a person and the principles of civil law concerning death do not apply."[20] (translation)

In 1933 the Supreme Court of Canada, in a classic fashion, recognized by a majority "the separate existence of an unborn child", but had recourse to a legal fiction to explain why the unborn child could be considered as "another" for the purposes of article 1053 of the *Civil Code*.[21]

Civil law recognizes certain patrimonial rights in the unborn child, the viable foetus; consideration is also taken of the status of the unborn child for certain particular legal ends, such as establishment of legitimacy.[22] However, civil law does not recognize the principle that foetal life is human life that merits protection by the recognition of the right to life.

At common law the situation is essentially the same.[23] With regard to whether or not the foetus enjoys legal personality, there are two tendencies: one confers legal personality on the foetus, but the other, which is predominant, refuses to go to that length.[24] Mr. Keyserlingk, in a study published by the Law Reform Commission of Canada, summarizes the common law position as follows:

> But this does not mean an unborn child has no rights in law. Though not considered a "legal person" in the full sense before birth, it is noteworthy that courts in many jurisdictions, including Canada, allow the recovery of damages for injuries caused to them before birth. It may not be entirely logical especially since no right to the logically prior "right to life" of an unborn child is recognized, but whether "formally" considered a person or not, a number of cases, statutes and articles suggest that the injured foetus is at least to this extent treated as if a person.[25]

As the law, whether criminal or civil, refuses to grant legal personality, and thus human personality, to the foetus, it is to related disciplines that we must turn to determine the question. Here we discover that the question of the beginning of life is liable to be posed in the same terms as that of the end of human life. We will return to this issue below in considering the views of biologists, philosophers and theologians with regard to the notion of "human person".

Certain authors, on the basis of an affirmation that at a certain stage

---

20 *Langlois v. Meunier*, [1973] C.S. 301 at 305 (Qué. S.C.).
21 *Montreal Tramways CO. v. Léveillé*, [1933] S.C.R. 456 at 463.
22 M. Rivêt, "La situation juridique . . .", *supra*, note 19, at 73: R. Kouri, "Réflexions sur le statut juridique du foetus" (1980-81), 15 *R.J.T.* 193.
23 K. Weiler & K. Catton, "The Unborn Child in Canadian Law" (1976), 14 *Osgoode Hall LJ.* 643.
24 *Ibid.*, at 655.
25 Keyserlingk, *supra*, note 15, at 94.

of its development the foetus becomes a "potential person", conclude that for this reason the law should recognize in the foetus a right to life. The courts have already recognized the right of the foetus to "non-negligent treatment", and this presupposes the recognition of a right to life.[26] Kluge states that there is a flagrant contradiction in the state of the law:

> The right to life and the right to non-negligent treatment are just such rights. The latter presupposes the former, since the right to a certain sort of treatment cannot attach to an individual unless that individual has a right to live. Therefore, if a foetus has the right to non-negligent treatment, it will also have the right to life.[27]

Professor Kouri is of the view that it would be logical to recognize a right to life and to inviolability in favour of the foetus:

> We believe that the infant once conceived is invested with the qualities of a subject of law, subject to a condition subsequent if it is not born living or viable [translation].[28]

According to this author, in the event that the condition is realized, the right of the foetus disappear retroactively, in such a fashion that the academic question as to whether or not the "infant once conceived is a person" need not be asked.[29]

As the Charter uses the term "everyone" (*chacun*) to designate the person entitled to the right and not the expression "all persons" (*toute personne*), perhaps the intention of the legislators was to move away from the traditional concept of "human person" and to turn towards the notion of potential person so that the "viable foetus" would be protected by section 7.

It will be up to the Supreme Court of Canada to rule either in favour of the traditional interpretation of "human person" or in favour of a different solution. Relying on the use of the term "everyone", will the court extend the protection of section 7 to potential persons, that is, to the "viable foetus"? It is our view that the court will adopt as cautious an attitude as that of the lower courts because of the difficulty in reconciling the right to life of this so-called "potential" person with the right of the pregnant woman to freely dispose of that part of herself that is, in certain respects, the foetus.

---

26 E.H.W. Kluge, "The Right to Life of Potential Persons" (1976-77), 3 *Dalhousie L.J.* 837. Rivet claims that "the right to life contained in the Charter extends as much to the right to give life as to the right to have access to life "[translation]: see "La situation juridique . . .", *supra*, note 19 at 476.

27 *Ibid.*, at 846-847.

28 Kouri, *supra*, note 22 at 197.

29 *Ibid.*

B. *The end of life.*   When does life, this reality that the law protects against any invasion, cease? It is recognized that the definition of death is not a purely bio-medical problem; it is a complex problem having legal, moral and social aspects. The Law Reform Commission of Canada has performed important work on this subject, to which it is essential to refer. The differences between the definition of death included in the proposed reforms of the Law Reform Commission and the definition in current law will be noted.

The Law Reform Commission.   The Law Reform Commission has proposed a text to be incorporated in the *Interpretation Act*,[30] which may serve as a useful guide. In Working Paper No. 23[31] and its Report to Parliament No. 15, the Commission recommends:

> (2) That Parliament adopt the following amendment to the *Interpretation Act*, R.S.C. 1970, c. I-23.
> Section 28A — Criteria of death.
> For all purposes within the jurisdiction of the Parliament of Canada
>
> (1) a person is dead when an irreversible cessation of all that person's brain functions has occurred.
> (2) the irreversible cessation of brain functions can be determined by the prolonged absence of spontaneous circulatory and respiratory functions.
> (3) when the determination of the prolonged absence of spontaneous circulatory and respiratory functions is made impossible by the use of artificial means of support, the irreversible cessation of brain functions can be determined by any means recognized by the ordinary standards of current medical practice.[32]

It is hoped that Parliament approves the recommendation of the Law Reform Commission, which is based on serious inter-disciplinary research and reflection.

Current Law.   Only the province of Manitoba has adopted a legislative definition of death, based on irreversible cessation of cerebral function.[33]

With regard to the case law, no Canadian court has directly pronounced on the legal criteria for death. Most of the cases refer to the classic

---

30 R.S.C. 1970, c. I-23. [R.S.C. 1985, c. I-21].

31 Law Reform Commission of Canada, *The Criteria for the Determination of Death* (Working Paper No. 23) (Ottawa: 1979) at 58-59.

32 Law Reform Commission of Canada, *The Criteria for the Determination of Death* (Report No. 15) (Ottawa: 1981) at 24-25.

33 *Vital Statistics Act*, R.S.M. 1970, c. V-60, s. 2.1 [am. 1975, c. 51, enacted following the Report of the Law Reform Commission of Manitoba entitled *Report on Statutory Definition of Death* (Winnipeg: 1974).

criteria of cardiac and respiratory arrest. However, two decisions, including one in 1976 from the Manitoba Court of Appeal, appear to recognize criteria of a neurological type.[34]

Now that the Charter is in effect, it will be necessary to opt between the following solutions with regard to the beginning of life and the concept of "everyone' referred to in section 7. From one point of view, "everyone" may include the viable foetus. The only possible point of departure for such a position is the theory of "potential personhood", recognized for certain purposes by civil law, or at least implicit in certain rules of civil law. Criminal law is to a contrary effect, and brings no reinforcement to such a position. On the other hand "everyone" may refer only to male or female persons at the moment of birth. This solution is based on the statements found in the civil cases that refuse to recognize complete legal personality in a child not yet born; it is not a human person even if by a legal fiction it has certain rights. This solution is consistent with the criminal law and the previously cited *Borowski* case.[35]

With regard to the definition of death, we hope that the recommendation of the Law Reform Commission of Canada contained in Report No. 15, will receive an attentive ear from Parliament and thus finally clarifies Canadian law on this subject.

(ii) *The right to "liberty" of the person*

The liberty of the person envisaged by section 7 must be distinguished from those liberties enumerated in section 2, which is also concerned with the person, but from its moral, spiritual or psychological aspect.

Certainly in a general sense, one can conceive that the term "liberty" has a value with regard to all the rights and freedoms recognized by the Charter. However, the structure of the Charter requires us to give the concept a residual and restrictive sense in considering section 7. Contrary to the *Canadian Bill of Rights*,[35a] which recognizes the right to liberty in section 1 in a broad and introductory way, section 7 of the Charter is concerned with the right to liberty following other provisions which grant rights of a moral order, like the fundamental freedoms (section 2), democratic rights (sections 3 to section 5), and mobility rights (section 6). The "liberty" envisaged by section 7 is found in a section devoted to "legal rights" and it precedes sections 8 to 14, which deals with various

---

34 *R. v. Kitching*, [1976] 6 W.W.R. 697 (Man. C.A.), leave to appeal to S.C.C. dismissed at 32 C.C.C. (2d) 159n (S.C.C.); *R. v. Page* (unreported) cited in *Report on Statutory Definition of Death, supra*, note 33.

35 *Supra*, note 18.

35a S.C. 1960, c. 44.

aspects of liberty of the person, and notably, though not exclusively, with physical liberty.

This concept of "liberty", however, has given rise to numerous debates in the case law. The issue is whether this right includes only physical liberty or all forms of liberty. There are two conflicting views on this subject. The first favours a narrow interpretation which seeks to limit section 7 protection to interferences with physical liberty such as detention or search.[36] However, it is difficult to reconcile this approach with sections 8 to 14 which explicitly provide protections against this kind of interference. Why would the framers have included a section that adds nothing to the rights explicitly protected by sections 8 to 14?

Logically then, we must turn to a solution similar to that adopted by American courts, that extends the sphere of protection to the domain of personal privacy.[37] In fact, simply reading the language of the provision would lead one to believe that what the legislature wished to protect is the physical integrity of the person and all that is closely connected therewith. However, the American precedent cannot be slavishly followed for the respective provisions differ. While the Canadian version speaks of "liberty and security of the person", the American text, in addition to explicitly including the right to property, does not specifically employ the phrase "of the person" and this lends itself to a broader interpretation. The American provision reads as follows: " . . . not be deprived of life, liberty, or property, without due process of law".

Despite a reluctance on the part of most Canadian courts to give the word "liberty" a broader meaning than physical liberty,[38] there are some cases which move in the other direction and prefer the broader

---

36 *Pannu v. Min. of Employment & Immigration*, [1983] 1 F.C. 204 (T.D.) (detention under the *Immigration Act; Lussa v. Health Science Center* (1984), 5 C.H..R.R. D/2203 (Man. Q.B.) (detention in a psychiatric center); *Canada v. Schmidt, supra*, note 8 (extradition. Issues relating to parole of inmates concern their liberty: *Latham v. Solicitor General of Canada*, [1984] 2 F.C. 734 (T.D.); *Bryntwick v. National Parole Bd.* [1987] 2 F.C. 184 (T.D.); *Litwack v.National Parole Bd.*, [1986] 3 F.C. 532 (T.D.) (imposing unduly restrictive conditions on parole found to be contrary to s. 7). The threat of potential imprisonment affects liberty: *Grande Prairie (City) v. Wytrykush* (1987), 78 A.R. 175 (Alta. Prov. Ct.). However, the threat of fine only does not go to liberty: *Kindersley (Town) v. Boisvert*, [1986] 6 W.W.R. 636 (Sask. Q.B.); the transfer of a prisoner does not affect his liberty: *Pilon v. Yeomans*, [1984] 2 F.C. 932 (T.D.); *Horbas v. Min. of Employment & Immigration of Canada*, [1985] 2 F.C. 359 (T.D.) (freedom to choose a spouse anywhere in the world is not included).

37 *Belloti v. Baird*, 444 U.S. 821 (1979) (right to an abortion for a woman despite the opposition of those around her); *Griswold v. Connecticut*, 381 U.S. 479 (1965) (right to use oral contraceptives; "the private life of a couple is a protected zone").

38 See *supra*, note 36.

American sense. In *Re Rowland and R.*,[39] the right not to be deprived of
a driver's licence was considered to fall within section 7:

> I am not persuaded that the right to liberty guaranteed by s. 7 should
> be limited to matters of physical restraint of the person. In both the
> International Covenant on Civil and Political Rights and the European
> Convention on Human Rights, the right to "liberty and security of person"
> is stated in a context which clearly restricts the meaning of those words to
> the area of arrest and detention. In contrast, s. 7 stands alone, unless it can
> be said to be qualified by ss. 8 to 14, inclusive. In my opinion, there is nothing
> in the latter sections, read together with s. 7, which indicates that the rights
> protected therein are definitive or descriptive of the right to liberty. I do not
> intend to venture an opinion as to what restraints or classes of restraints on
> individual activity might amount to an interference with the right to liberty
> guaranteed by s. 7. I am of the view, however, that the right of an individual
> to use the public highways is a right which comes within the concept of
> the right to liberty guaranteed by the Charter. It follows that a deprivation
> of that right through suspension of an individual's operator's licence must
> be in accordance with the principles of fundamental justice.[40]

This innovative and interesting theory, which nevertheless preserves
a physical connotation in that the deprivation of a driver's licence hampers
the person in his freedom of movement, was adopted by the British
Columbia Court of Appeal in the *Robson* case.[41] More recently, the Alberta
Court of Appeal rejected this point of view and held that the right to
freedom of movement did not include the freedom to select the means
of transportation.[42]

In the *Morgentaler* case,[43] the courts in Ontario decided that the right
to privacy which, for example, permits a woman to obtain an abortion,
is not protected by section 7. Before extending the protection of section
7 to a right, the court must determine that the liberty relied on is considered
to be fundamental in Canada. This would be true, for example, of the

---

39 (1984), 10 D.L.R. (4th) 724 (Alta. Q.B.); see also *Ginther v. Sask.* Government Insurance,
   [1987] 5 W.W.R. 350 (Sask. Q.B.).
40 *Rowland, ibid.*, at 733.
41 *R. v. Robson* (1984), 11 D.L.R. (4th) 727 (B.C.S.C.), aff'd (1985), 19 D.L.R. (4th) 112
   (B.C.C.A.). S. 214(2) of the *Motor Vehicle Act* was held to be contrary to s. 7 because
   it permitted a police officer to suspend a driver's licence for a period of 24 hours where
   an individual was suspected of having consumed alcohol. The provision restricted the
   right to liberty of an individual (freedom of movement) without respecting the principles
   of fundamental justice.
42 *R. v. Neale*, [1986] 5 W.W.R. 577 (Alta. C.A.), leave to appeal to S.C.C. refused [1987]
   1 W.W.R. lxviii(note) (S.C.C.). The court expressly declined to follow the American
   case *Meyer v. Nebraska*, 262 U.S. 396 (1923); *Léger v. Montréal*, [1986] D.L.Q. 391
   (Que. C.A.) (s. 7 does not create the right to drive without a seat belt).
43 *R. v. Morgentaler* (1984), 12 D.L.R. (4th) 502 (Ont. H.C.), aff'd on this point by (1984),
   14 D.L.R. (4th) 184 (Ont. C.A.).

right to marry or have children, as was recognized by the Supreme Court in *E. v. Eve*.[44] This could be true of the right of parents to educate their children as they see fit, as was suggested by the Supreme Court in the *Jones* decision.[45]

In the *Morgentaler* case,[46] Madam Justice Wilson enlarged the concept of liberty of the person by introducing a new dimension, namely the right to dignity: the right of an individual to "a degree of autonomy in making decisions of fundamental personal importance", the right to "a degree of personal autonomy over important decisions intimately affecting their private lives".[47] Referring to American case law, the learned justice ruled that this liberty includes the right to marry and to procreate, the right to attend private schools, etc.

This approach is appealing. As underlined by Tanya Lee, constitutional interpretation must evolve and should not always look to a tradition which often is outmoded and discriminatory:

> If constitutional interpretation is to be constantly evolving it cannot be unduly fettered to the past. Second, the traditions of a society are not necessarily admirable. Thus, for example, a tradition of Canadian society may be that of treating women as second-class citizens. Finally, if traditions represent the majority view of past generations, it is open to the same objections that consensus was. The views of the majority should not be the basis on which minority rights are protected. The anomaly of using the traditions approach becomes apparent when the constitutional challenge is to the provisions of a statute and the answer to that challenge is that the statute has existed for a long period of time. The *Charter* was not implemented merely to prevent the incursion of recent statutes into rights.[48]

We must press for a new interpretation and a broad reading of the terms employed in a constitutional document such as the Charter. As T.J. Christian[49] observes, a broad interpretation of the concept of "liberty" is necessary to protect the many aspects of the right to liberty which are not expressly enumerated in the other sections of the Charter.

However, this concept of liberty does not cover rights that are economic in character, such as the right to practise a profession;[50] the right to enlist

---

44 [1986] 2 S.C.R. 388.

45 *R. v. Jones*, [1986] 2 S.C.R. 284.

46 However, Wilson J. was the only judge to base his or her decision to legalize abortion on liberty (reasons at 163-172).

47 *Ibid.*

48 Lee, *supra*, note 14 at 5.

49 Christian, *supra*, note 14 at 231.

50 *Stoffman v. Vancouver General Hosp.* (1986), 30 D.L.R. (4th) 700 at 717 (B.C.S.C.); aff'd [1988] 2 W.W.R. 708 (B.C.C.A.), leave to appeal to S.C.C. granted [1988] 4 W.W.R. lxxii(note) (S.C.C.) *Beltz v. Law Society of B.C.* (1987), 31 D.L.R. (4th) 685 (B.C.S.C.).

in the armed forces;[51] the right to engage in commerce or business;[52] the right to offer professional services;[53] any form of the right to work or of economic rights;[54] and, of course, the right to property.[55] Equally, this concept of liberty does not extend to the right to access to the courts, notably the right to take proceedings against the Crown.[56]

While section 7 envisages the protection of a general right to liberty, the weight of the case law is against a concept extending to the totality of human activities.[57]

(iii) *The right to security of the person*

A. *The notion of "security of the person".* The Law Reform Commission defines "security" thus:

Security of the person means not only protection of one's physical integrity, but the provision of necessaries for its support.[58]

This notion of security corresponds to the World Health Organization's definition of health as "a state of complete physical, mental, and social

---

51 *R. v. Sylvestre* (1987), [1986] 3 F.C. 51 (C.A.). Similarly for the public service: *Forgie v. P.S.S.R.B.* (1987), C.R.D. 400 (F.C.A.).

52 *Parkdale Hotel Ltd. v. A.G. Canada*, [1986] 2 F.C. 514 (T.D.); *Edwards Books & Art Ltd. v. R.*, [1986] 2 S.C.R. 713; *R.V.P. Enterprises Ltd v. Min. of Consumer & Corporate Affairs (B.C.)* (1987), 37 D.L.R. (4th) 148 (B.C.S.C.), aff'd (*Sub nom. R.V.P. Enterprises Ltd. v. A.G. British Columbia* [1988] 4 W.W.R. 726 (B.C.C.A.); *R. v. Myrrmidon Inc.*, [1987] 6 W.W.R. 204 (Man. Q.B.), aff'd [1988] 5 W.W.R. 385 (Man. C.A.); *Groupe des Eleveurs de Volailles de l'est de l'Ont. v. Cdn. Chicken Marketing Agency*, [1985] 1 F.C. 280 (T.D.); *Reference re Criminal Code, ss. 193 & 195.1(1)(c)*, [1987] 6 W.W.R. 289 (Man. C.A.) (including the business of prostitution). *Contra, Ass. des Détaillants en Alimentation du Qué. v. Ferme Carnaval*, [1986] R.J.Q. 2513 at 2530 (Qué. S.C.).

53 *Re Wilson and Medical Service Comm. of B.C.* (1987), 36 D.L.R. (4th) 31 (B.C.S.C.).

54 *Byrt v. Saskatchewan*, [1987] 2 W.W.R. 475 (Sask. Q.B.).

55 *Zutphen Bros. Const. v. Bywidag System* (1987), 35 D.L.R. (4th) 433 (N.S.C.A.); *Mirhadizadeh v. R. (Ont.)* (1987), 33 D.L.R. (4th) 314 (Ont. H.C.); *Smith, Kline and French Laboratories v. A.G. Can.*, [1986] 1 F.C. 274.

56 *Id.* Also: *Budge v. W.C.R.*, [1987] 6 W.W.R. 217 (Alta. Q.B.); see O.H. Jack, "Suing the Crown and the Application of the Charter" (1986-87), 7 *Advocates Quarterly* 227-336.

57 *R. v. Neale, supra*, note 42 at 583 (" . . . is not to embrace the full range of human conduct"). *Contra, Dion v. P.G. Canada*, [1986] R.J.Q. 2196 at 2201 (Que. S.C.), According to this judge, liberty "encompasses the right of a citizen, if only occasionally, to make use of certain hallucinogenic substances and the right to refuse to provide a sample of urine" [translation]; position held by the Supreme Court of British Columbia in *R. v. Speicher* (1983), 150 D.L.R. (3d) 167. See also Lee, *supra*, note 14.

58 Law Reform Commission of Canada, *Medical Treatment and the Criminal Law* (Working Paper No. 26) (Ottawa: Supply and Services, 1980) at 7.

well-being". The right to security understood in this sense is defined by article 25 of the *Universal Declaration of Human Rights, 1948*:

> Every one has the right to a standard of living adequate for the health and well-being of himself and of his family, including food, clothing, housing and medical care and necessary social services, the right to security in the event of unemployment, sickness, disability, widowhood, old age, or other lack of livelihood in circumstances beyond his control.

If one accepts this concept of security of the person one concludes, as the Law Reform Commission did, that "[t]hose general terms of wide public use have ethical, social and political implications and their reach extends to every element of human happiness".[59] However, to accept such a proposition would effectively commit us to accepting the previously discussed theory of positive rights.

The term "security", as found in the *Canadian Bill of Rights* of 1960, has not been interpreted by the courts. Of course, since 1982 there have been many attempts to delineate the scope of this concept.[60]

In many of the cases decided to date, it was the protection of physical security of the person which was in issue. In this context, the Supreme Court of Canada has held that section 7 is designed to protect not only against all forms of corporal punishment or physical suffering, but also against the threat of such punishment or suffering.[61]

The problem of extending the concept of security to protection of property or private property has also arisen. One will recall that the idea of protecting the right to property, along the lines of the American Constitution, was expressly rejected during the debates surrounding the adoption of the Charter.[62] Despite this, some attempts have been made to introduce a very broad interpretation of security which would lead to the same result, namely the protection of the free enjoyment of property. These efforts have not succeeded.

In fact, when the New Brunswick Court of Queen's Bench accepted this extended interpretation, thereby giving the term "security" a certain

---

59 *Ibid.*

60 Many scholars have attempted to determine just how far the notion of security can go: see P.W. Augustine, "Protection of the Right to Property under the Canadian Charter of Rights and Freedoms" (1986), 18 *Ottawa L.R.* 66 *et seq.*; G.J. Brandt, "Canadian Charter of Rights and Freedoms — Right to Property as an Extension of Personal Security — Status of Undeclared Rights" (1983), 61 *Can. Bar. Rev.* 398, on the right to property; and C.P. Stevenson, "A New Perspective on Environmental Rights After the Charter" (1983), 21 *Osgoode Hall L.J.* 390, where the possibility of including the right to the protection of the environment in the right to security was considered.

61 *Singh, supra*, note 4 at 207.

62 See the views of the then Minister of Justice, Jean Chretien in the Debates of the Special Joint Committee of the Senate and the House of Commons (Vol. 45 at 10-11).

economic connotation,[63] the Court of Appeal rejected its analysis and excluded the right to property from section 7. Mr. Justice La Forest, sitting then in the Court of Appeal, wrote as follows:

> The courts should not, for example, place themselves in the position of frustrating regulatory schemes or measures obviously intended to reallocate rights and resources simply because they affect vested rights . . .
>
> It is probably to avoid difficulties of this kind that the security of property was not expressly protected by the *Canadian Charter of Rights and Freedoms.*[64]

This interpretation was recently reaffirmed, by way of *obiter* remark, in a case before the Federal Court of Appeal. The court wrote the following:

> We should not leave this application without expressing the view that by no stretch of the imagination can the refusal of the Minister of Energy, Mines and Resources to make a discretionary grant based on hardship to Regal Petroleum Limited be said to constitute an infringement of the latter's right to life, liberty and security of the person guaranteed by section 7 of the *Canadian Charter of Rights and Freedoms.*[65]

One notes the strong reluctance of judges to bring economic protection within the purview of the words used in section 7, namely "security of the person". This attitude is expressed both in *obiter* and in the reasons for judgment. The result has been followed in a wide variety of cases where attempts were made to invoke section 7 in challenging statutes or regulations affecting the right to property[66] or economic interests connected to the exercise of the right to property.[67]

Attempts have been made to relate the idea of security to measures taken by penitentiary authorities affecting the situation of inmates, especially those concerning the transfer of inmates between institutions. In one 1983 case, the Trial Division of the Federal Court held that the transfer of an inmate with a heart condition to a maximum security unit where it would be more difficult to obtain access to adequate medical services

---

63 *New Brunswick v. Fisherman's Wharf Ltd.* (1982), 135 D.L.R. (3d) 307 (N.B.Q.B.), aff'd (*sub nom. New Brunswick v. Estabrooks Pontiac Buick Ltd.; New Brunswick v. Fisherman's Wharf Ltd.*) *infra,* note 64.

64 *New Brunswick v. Estabrooks Pontiac Buick Ltd.; New Brunswick v. Fisherman's Wharfs Ltd.* (1982), 144 D.L.R. (3d) 21 at 31 (N.B.C.A.).

65 *Regal Petroleum Ltd. v. Min. of Energy,* Mines & Resources (1985), 63 N.R. 135 at 136 (F.C.A.).

66 *Axler v. R.*(May 31, 1982) No T-2631-82 (F.C.); *Re W.C.B.N.S. and Coastal Rentals, Sales & Service* (1983), 12 D.L.R. (4th) 564 (N.S.T.D.); *Becker v. Alberta* (1983), 148 D.L.R. (3d) 539 (Alta. C.A.); *R. v. Yellowquill* (1984), 12 W.C.B. 9 (Man. Q.B.).

67 *Gershman Produce Co. v. Motor Transport Bd., supra,* note 2; *Re Appotive and Ottawa* (1984), 16 O.M.B.R. 316 (Ont. H.C.).

constituted an infringement of his right to security.[68] The Court of Appeal reversed this decision, reasoning that "there was nothing in the evidence on the basis of which it could be said that the respondent's transfer jeopardized the security of his person".[69] However, the court did not rule on the relation between the difficulty of access to medical services and the security of the person. In another case, the Federal Court held that the transfer of inmates from a medium security institution to a maximum security institution did not constitute a violation of the Charter and that there was no duty on the administrative authority responsible for the transfer to grant a hearing.[70]

The common law has traditionally maintained that a person's reputation is one of the most precious rights which the law must secure. As Blackstone wrote:

> The security of his reputation or good name from the arts of detraction and slander, are rights to which every man is entitled, by reason and natural justice; since without these it is impossible to have the perfect enjoyment of any other advantage or right.[71]

If the protection of reputation were to be linked to the idea of security, one can imagine the considerable impact this would have on the large number of administrative or disciplinary decisions affecting the integrity of the reputations of those being administered. This possibility has been considered by the courts which have not seen fit to give a clear or affirmative answer. The balance of opinion appears to reject the idea of extending section 7 protection to the right to a secure reputation. In a case before the Federal Court, Trial Division, Mr. Justice Collier, in *obiter*, said:

> In any event I am not persuaded the right "to life, liberty and security of the person" includes interference with one's good name, reputation or integrity.[72]

In a case involving the publication of the name of an individual accused of gross indecency, along with a statement of the accusations made against him and information on the proceedings, the court held that the right to preserve a person's good reputation within the community was not

---

68 *Collin v. Lussier*, [1983] 1 F.C. 2187 (T.D.), rev'd *infra*, note 69; to the same effect, see *R. v. Chester* (1984), 5 Admin. L.R. 111 (Ont. H.C.).

69 *Lussier v. Collin*, [1985] 1 F.C. 124 at 125 (C.A.); to the same effect, see *Pilon v. Yeomans, supra*, note 36.

70 *Pilon, ibid.* at 941.

71 W. Blackstone, *Commentaries on the Laws of England* (U. of Chicago Press: 1979) 117 at 125.

72 *MacBain v. Cdn. Human Rights Comm.*, [1984] 1 F.C. 696 at 710 (T.D.), rev'd [1985] 1 F.C. 856 (*sub nom. MacBain v. Lederman*) (C.A.).

necessarily included in section 7 when set against the freedom of the press.[73] In any case, it is always possible to avoid the question, at least in part, by applying the test in section 1. It is almost inevitable that these kinds of interferences with reputation will pass the test of section 1 as they will often result from administrative decisions and their publication in newspapers at the time of the proceedings. It will thus be difficult to find much protection for reputation in section 7 of the Charter.

Prior to the *Morgentaler* decision on January 28, 1988,[74] the chief tendency of the courts when faced with the concept of security was to restrict it to what is encompassed by the physical and mental integrity of the person in a broad sense.[75] However, in certain cases the court was prepared to extend the concept to whatever concerns human dignity. This could include a right to reputation, personal autonomy and privacy. Thus in the *Crain and Couture* case, one reads:

> Furthermore, the phrase "security of the person" includes a right to personal dignity and a right to an area of privacy or individual sovereignty into which the State must not make arbitrary or unjustified intrusions. These considerations also underlie the privilege against the self-incrimination.[76]

In another 1984 case, the concept of security is once again extended to cover the private life or the autonomy of the individual.[77] In that case, the complainant was slightly wounded in the head as a result of an accident. At the hospital, without obtaining the consent of the patient, the attending physician took a blood sample which was not required for treatment. The physician gave the sample to the police and it showed a blood alcohol content in excess of the limit provided for in section 236 of the *Criminal Code*. The judge noted that both at the time of the accident and at the hospital, neither the police officer nor the physician had reason to believe that the individual was impaired. He accordingly felt bound to exclude this evidence, it having been obtained in violation of the individual's right to privacy and autonomy.

The Court of Appeal of British Columbia, however, did not consider the fact that a ten-year-old girl was obliged to undergo a hysterectomy to be an infringement of the right to security in the sense of personal

---

73 *Re R. and Several Unnamed Persons* (1983), 4 D.L.R. (4th) 310 (Ont. H.C.).

74 *Supra*, note 13.

75 *R. v. Videoflicks* (1984), 14 D.L.R. (4th) 10 at 48 (Ont. C.A.), rev'd in part (*sub nom. Edwards Books & Art Ltd.* v. *R.*) *supra*, note 52; *Re Kahlon*, [1985] 2 F.C. 124 (T.D.), rev'd [1986] 3 F.C. 386 (C.A.) (normal disquiet and anxiety attributable to a separation).

76 *Re R.L. Crain and Couture*, *supra*, note 2 at 502; *S.S.* v. *Director of Child & Family Services*, [1987] 5 W.W.R. 309 (Man. Q.B.).

77 *R. v. Dyment* (1984), 9 D.L.R. (4th) 614 (P.E.I.S.C.), leave to appeal to S.C.C. granted (1986), 26 D.L.R. (4th) 399n (S.C.C.).

autonomy.[78] In that case, a mentally handicapped ten-year-old girl reacted fearfully to the sight of blood. To avoid multiple crises which would arise with the onset of menstruation, her parents decided that she should have a hysterectomy. The official guardian objected, claiming that the right to security provided for in section 7 gave the young girl the right to decide for herself whether or not to have children. The court did not accept this argument and agreed with the parents on the ground that the hysterectomy was in the best interest of the child.

There is an aspect of security of the person that might be called psychological security, that is, protection against anxiety or stress. In a case decided before the High Court of Ontario, a young girl, following a multiple rape, laid charges and testified at the preliminary hearing of some of the accused. However, she refused to testify at the hearing of another accused because prior to the hearing she had received telephone calls which, even though no words were spoken, she took to be threatening. In refusing to testify, she invoked her right to security. The High Court held that for there to be an infringement of rights,

> [i]t is necessary for there to be some serious and substantial interference with them. It is not enough, in my view, to cause only upset, worry and anxiety, for these fleeting feelings may be present, to a greater or lesser extent, in a great many situations. . . .
>
> I am unable to hold that the security of the person of this particular applicant had been interfered with by the State in requiring her to testify at the preliminary hearing in this case. Although it is clearly a stressful situation for her to testify, and it would certainly be to her emotional detriment, the evidence is not strong enough for me to conclude that her security of the person would be interfered with. Anxiety and stress, as real and as unpleasant as they may be, are not enough to qualify as infringements of the security of the person.[79]

This case does not completely shut the door to protection for psychological security; all depends on the seriousness of the interference in the circumstances of the case. More recently, however, the Court of Appeal of Saskatchewan refused to consider employment discrimination as an infringement of psychological security.[80]

---

78 *K. v. Public Trustee* (1985), 63 B.C.L.R. 145 (C.A.), application for leave to appeal dismissed [1985] 4 W.W.R. 757 (S.C.C.).

79 *R. v. X* (1983), 3 D.L.R. (4th) 253 at 256, 257 (Ont. H.C.).

80 *Re Kodellas and Sask. Human Rights Comm.* (1987), 34 D.L.R. (4th) 30 (Sask. Q.B.), motion to extend deadline to appeal [1987] 3 W.W.R. 558 (anxiety caused by the Human Rights Commission's attitude in response to a complaint of sexual discrimination and assault was found to be an infringement of security); *Pasqua Hospital v. Harmatiuk*, [1987] 5 W.W.R. 98 at 114 (Sask. C.A.); *West End Construction Ltd. v. Ministry of Labour (Ontario)* (1987), 33 D.L.R. (4th) 285 (Ont. Div. Ct.) (awarding exemplary damages for discrimination) Prohibiting an action in damages for injury caused by

The January 28, 1988 decision in the *Morgentaler* case[81] finally affirmed a concept of security extending to the psychological as much as to the physical dimension. The five judges in the majority ruled that all "serious psychological tension caused by the State" is an interference with security.[82] They referred to the following passage from the dissenting opinion of Mr. Justice Lamer in the *Mills* case:

> [S]ecurity of the person is not restricted to physical integrity; rather, it encompasses protection against "overlong subjection to the vexations and vicissitudes of a pending criminal accusation" . . . These include stigmatization of the accused, loss of privacy, stress and anxiety resulting from a multitude of factors, including possible disruption of family, social life and work, legal costs, uncertainty as to the outcome and sanction.[83]

This extension of the concept of security to all forms of psychological trauma caused by state action is extremely dangerous, in our view, unless strictly confined to the field of criminal law. Even then, it exposes courts to the duty of carefully sifting through the provisions of the *Criminal Code*, all of which are likely to be a source of tension and anguish. This could be the case of the power constraining the state in fiscal matters, in matters of economic regulation, etc.

Another aspect of the notion of security which is closely connected to the theory of positive rights is what we commonly refer to as social security, particularly the right to social assistance benefits. This theory of positive rights, which would oblige the government to furnish social assistance benefits, has been argued on a number of occasions without receiving acceptance by Canadian judges. In a case before the Manitoba Court of Appeal, the question was whether social assistance benefits could be cut without contravening section 7 of the Charter. An affirmative reply was given to the question as asked.[84] The theory of positive rights has also been rejected in a case relating to the financial protection of elderly persons.[85]

---

accident in the workplace is not an infringement of security: *Re Terzian and W.C.B.* (1983), 148 D.L.R. (3d) 380 (Ont. Div. Ct.); *Martin v. Iliffe* (1984), 7 D.L.R. 94th) 755 (Man. Q.B.) (excluding trial by jury in civil matter). *Contra*, see *Dion v. P.G. Canada, supra*, note 57 at 2202 (Qué. S.C.) (prohibition against taking hallucinogenic substances would be infringement of the right of a prisoner to seek well-being, the right and perhaps even the pleasure of becoming moderately intoxicated!).

81 *Supra*, note 13.

82 *Ibid.* (Dickson C.J.C., at 45; Beetz J. at 80; Wilson J. at 161).

83 *R. v. Mills*, [1986] 1 S.C.R. 863 at 919, cited in *Morgentaler, ibid.*, by Dickson C.J.C. at 55 and Wilson J. at 173.

84 *Elliott v. Dir. of Social Services* (1982), 17 Man. R. (2d) 350 (C.A.).

85 *Manitoba Society of Seniors Inc. v. Greater Winnipeg Gas Co.* (1982), 18 Man. R. (2d) 440 (C.A.).

To arrive at a coherent interpretation of the Charter, one in keeping with its underlying philosophy, we believe it is necessary clearly to distinguish between approaches based on the theory of negative rights and those based on the theory of positive rights. It seems contrary to the spirit of a liberal type Charter such as ours to argue that it may oblige the state to take positive measures aimed at favouring the promotion of particular rights. The rights to life, liberty and security are not creatures of the Charter; it merely enshrines them by providing protection against certain infringements. On the one hand, there is nothing in the second half of section 7 nor in section 1 to suggest that the framers envisaged the imposition of positive obligations on the state. On the other hand, the Charter did not abolish the sovereignty of Parliament nor the democratic process which is normally used to establish such positive measures directed at procuring peace, order and security in society. This is not the proper role of the judicial power.

Moreover, even assuming that the Charter embodies a theory of negative rights alone, prudence is still required in moving from the concept of physical security to the domain of psychological or economic security. In doing so, one enters a sphere which is imprecise, uncertain and full of subjective factors which accord poorly with the imperatives of even such an inexact science as the law. Countless standards, provisions and measures which affect the security of individual citizens are established by public authorities. Would it be necessary to see in each case an interference with or a threat to the security of the individual or corporation?

We believe that it is necessary to accept a fairly broad concept of the notion of security, one encompassing a state of physical, mental and social well-being. Nevertheless, it is necessary to distinguish the ideal proposed to the state as the political authority from the much more limited task imposed on the state as judicial authority. While the political branch may attempt to embrace all aspects of human well-being, it is not for the judicial branch to play this role, even in a secondary way.

(e) The Nature of Protected Interference

In the context of section 7, interference with the three fundamental rights set out therein must come from a public authority, for in the tradition of our public law, the principles of fundamental justice apply above all to the public administration. In what ways, then, might the authorities engage in such interference?

(i) *Infringement of the right to life*

A. *Interruption of pregnancy.*   Given the present state of our law, the interruption of pregnancy or abortion does not constitute an interference with human life, as the foetus or child is not regarded as a human person.

That is the effect of the *Borowski* case,[86] at least until the Supreme Court of Canada renders its judgment.

In criminal law, homicide, which constitutes the ultimate interference with life, is possible only with regard to an infant who is born viable, as provided in section 206 [223] of the *Criminal Code*. Section 221 [238] stipulates that the fact of causing death during the act of birth of a child who has not become a human being constitutes a crime, but not a murder. In addition, the section does not apply to a person who, in good faith, acts to preserve the life of the mother (therapeutic abortion).

Similarly, under section 226 [242] of the Code, it is a crime but not a murder for a pregnant woman about to give birth to fail to obtain necessary assistance. Finally, section 251 [287] makes it a crime to procure or seek to procure a miscarriage, unless the miscarriage fits the definition of a therapeutic abortion. However, as a result of the Supreme Court's decision in the *Morgentaler* case,[87] this is no longer the law. In all of these provisions, the legislature has obviously taken the view that these interferences with life amount to the extinction of a being that has not "become a human being", to use the expression of section 221 [238] even though the interference occurs during the act of birth.

Section 251 [287] of the *Criminal Code*, authorizing therapeutic abortion, cannot be considered as legalizing an interference with the right to life, for legally the foetus is not a person. Section 251 [287] of the Code was challenged in cases prior to the Charter using the *Bill of Rights*. In 1976, in the *Morgentaler* case, the Supreme Court of Canada ruled that Parliament had the constitutional authority needed to enact section 251.[88] Subsequently, the Ontario Court of Appeal, in the *Dehler* case,[89] held that the therapeutic abortion permitted by section 251 could not constitute a murder since it did not contravene section 1 of the *Bill of Rights* concerning the right to life. Therapeutic abortion does not interfere with the life of a person because the foetus is legally not yet recognized as a person.

It remains to be seen whether the analysis found in the case law to date regarding the legal status of the foetus will resist pressures coming as much from medical science as from those with moral concerns. The debate is far from over.

B. *Interruption of treatment and euthanasia.*   Does the "right to life" recognized by section 7 imply that the human person whose life is menaced

---

86 *Borowski v. A.G. Canada, supra*, note 18.
87 *Supra*, note 13.
88 *Morgentaler v. R.*, [1976] 1 S.C.R. 616.
89 *Dehler v. Ottawa Civic Hospital* (1979), 25 O.R. 92d) 748 (Ont. H.C.), aff'd (1980), 29 O.R. (2d) 677 (C.A.).

by illness or accident has a right to require adequate treatment from public authorities or that all possible treatment should be used? If so, at what point would the interruption of treatment not be considered a violation of this right?

The right of access to medical care, which is part of the right to security of the person, must be considered in the context of the right to life when one is in a terminal phase. Interruption or refusal of treatment can thus become an interference with life if there is still hope that life would otherwise continue. If a clear definition of death could be arrived at, as we have seen, this difficulty would be largely resolved.

In addition, it is important here to distinguish between what we normally call "ordinary" care and treatment and "extraordinary" care and treatment in terminal illnesses.[90] With regard to that ordinary care and treatment necessary to the patient's survival, our law already recognizes an obligation imposed on public establishments and doctors. Section 43 of the Québec *Public Health Protection Act*[91] requires that:

> An establishment or a physician shall see that care or treatment is provided to every person in danger of death; if the person is a minor, the consent of the person having paternal authority shall not be required.

If the theory of positive rights were to be adopted, section 7 of the Charter could be considered as enshrining the right to this treatment and care.

What about extraordinary treatment? One should point out, first of all, that the concept of extraordinary treatment is difficult to define. The Law Reform Commission of Canada has made it the subject of several important studies.

Does the automatic termination of treatment in the terminal phase give rise to difficulties under section 7 of the Charter? Professor Dickens summarizes the state of the law as follows:

> Regarding extraordinary care, however, the patient and the patient's family cannot insist that it be given, since allocation of the perhaps scarce and costly resource is discretionary. The decision is governed by factors such as clinical assessment of individual prognosis, and the needs of other patients in the hospital and prospective patients in the community. Further, where extraordinary means are initiated, they remain discretionary on the part of those bound by a legal duty of care. They may thereafter be withdrawn at will and without consent, unless the patient's prognosis has changed with the effect of making those medical means ordinary in the circumstances of the patient.

---

90 On these questions see the following: B.M. Dickens, "The Right to Natural Death" (1981), 26 *McGill L.J.* 847 at 856; A.J. Fama, "Classification of Critically Ill Patients: A Legal Examination" (1980), 24 *St-Louis University L.J.* 514; *Dehler, supra*, note 89.
91 R.S.Q., c. P-35.

Discretion on use of extraordinary means is mutual, however, and such means cannot be applied over the patient's refusal.[92]

Can one rely on section 7 of the Charter to claim, as has been attempted in the United States,[93] that the refusal to provide extraordinary treatment or the withdrawal of such treatment by medical authorities, constitutes a decision that has to be taken in conformity with fundamental justice, that is, pursuant to an adequate procedure? It is in these terms that the problem will most likely arise in our view.

If the person is incapable of manifesting his or her will and has never made known his or her intentions, both law and practice opt for life:

> The proposed system of rules should never depart from the principle that in the absence of reasons to the contrary the patient would prefer life to death, even when unable to express that preference[94]

However, this presumption weakens when the patient is in a terminal phase, for where the result is certain and its course irreversible, one is less hesitant in withdrawing extraordinary care. Maintaining such care would amount to imposing cruel and unusual treatment. In such cases, the right to a dignified death is therefore implicitly recognized.[95] In positing a right to a dignified death, one raises the delicate question of euthanasia. The problem is posed in these terms:

> If a person has a right to a dignified death, and the suffering or the type of illness which affects the person impedes him or her from the exercise of this right, should it be considered a crime to give aid or assistance to this person? Logically, one must admit that the right to death authorizes the non-aggressive intervention of a third part to aid the victim who may not, given his or her condition, achieve his or her choice. Humanitarian reasons favour this solution, but the risks of abuse are great [translation][96]

The Law Reform Commission of Canada has, moreover, refused to recommend the decriminalization of euthanasia and murder by compassion. It is not in favour of the recognition of active euthanasia in any of its forms and has recommended that the current prohibitions of the *Criminal*

---

92 Dickens, *supra*, note 90 at 862.

93 "Due Process in the Allocation of Scarce Life-Saving Resources" (1975), 84 *Yale L.J.* 1734.

94 Law Reform Commission of Canada, "Euthanasia, Assisting Suicide and Interrupting Treatment" (Report No. 20) (Ottawa: Supply and Services, 1983) at 11.

95 M. Ouellette, "La Charte canadienne et certains problèmes de bioéthique" (1984), 18 *R.J.T.* 271 at 273.

96 *Ibid.* at 279. See also F. Carnerie, "Euthanasia and Self-Determination (1987), 32 *McGill L.J.* 299; J.L. Baudouin, "La liberté du patient devant le traitement et la mort in D. Turp & G. Beaudoin, eds., *Perspectives canadiennes et europcennes des droits de la personne*, Yvon Blais, ed., Cowansville, 1986, at 505.

Code concerning homicide be maintained, as well as those relating to murder by compassion.[97] These refer to active euthanasia, which demands positive conduct, rather than passive euthanasia, which consists in the failure to provide extraordinary care or its interruption in order to permit a dignified death, conduct which may be justified even under the Charter.

The right to refuse treatment. The criminal law preserves the fundamental principle of the common law which recognizes the right to refuse treatment, except where expressly forbidden by legislation. The case law confirms this right of refusal.[98] Civil law cases take the same approach, provided the patient is an adult with legal capacity.[99]

The question whether or not it is necessary to respect a refusal of treatment which is considered to be unreasonable or irrational is controversial; certain cases have recognized such a right.[100] On the other hand, it seems that American case law is to the effect that the right to refuse treatment does not apply to justify a choice which the majority would consider irrational.[101]

In *A.G. Canada v. Notre-Dame Hospital*,[102] the issue was whether a person may withhold consent to a medical act capable of saving his or her life. The Superior Court of Québec dismissed the application, maintaining that respect for life is paramount over respect for free will and that the right to refuse treatment must not prevail where the choice is one the majority would consider irrational.

This debate presupposes the distinction between "ordinary" and "extraordinary" care and treatment in terminal illness.[103]

There are two situations which appear to be equally complex: first, that of the adult who is completely unable to express his consent and, second, that of the minor.

In the case where the adult patient is completely incapable of consenting, the doctrine of implied consent authorizes medical personnel to administer treatment, even if extraordinary. Dickens summarizes the law in the following manner:

The law presumes the patient's wish to survive in life and optimal health.

---

97 *Supra*, note 94 at 78.

98 *R. v. Burns*, [1965] 4 C.C.C. 298 (Ont. H.C.); *Laporte v. Laganière* (1972), 18 C.R.N.S. 357 (Qué. Q.B.).

99 See the cases cited in Working Paper No. 26, *supra*, note 58 at 146, note 375.

100 *Ibid.* at 144, note 356.

101 I. Kennedy, "The Legal Effect of Requests by Terminally Ill and Aged Not to Receive Further Treatment from Doctors", [1976] *Crim. L. Rev.* 217.

102 (1984), 8 C.R.R. 382 (Qué. S.C.).

103 See *supra*, note 90.

The law may go further, however, and permit treatment to save life over the protest of the would-be suicide; it has been seen that such a patient's mental balance will be questioned, and any error in management will be legally justifiable if it favours life and preservation of the patient's future options.[104]

This doctrine has been adopted by several provinces as the basis of hospital regulations in which it is stipulated that, if the patient is not able to consent to surgical intervention and is in danger of death, the surgeon may nonetheless proceed.[105]

With regard to minors, consent is normally granted by the parents or guardians, but certain legislation dispenses with the necessity of obtaining such authorization. Section 7 protects the right to life of the minor whose parents would deny medical treatment.[106]

The moment the right to refuse medical care can legitimately be exercised by other persons on behalf of the patient, the problem of procedure arises. It is to procedure that recent legislation on natural death has turned its attention, inspired by a California statute enacted in 1977. A comparable act was proposed in Ontario in March 1977.[107] This kind of legislation, dealing with the right to a natural death, is not contrary to section 7 of the Charter.

C. *The death penalty.* Death by hanging constituted, in Canadian criminal law, a legal form of interruption of life. However, the *Criminal Law Amendment Act (No.2)*[108] abolished the death penalty, so that there is no longer any reason to consider the procedural requirements imposed on such a penalty in criminal law. However, the death penalty still applies for two crimes contemplated by the *National Defence Act*:[109] the crime of spying on behalf of an enemy and that of mutiny with violence committed by a person subject to the code of military discipline. It is thus still relevant to ask whether the death penalty constitutes a violation of the right to life capable of contravening section 7 of the Charter.

The interpretation of section 2(a) of the *Canadian Bill of Rights* by the majority of the Supreme Court of Canada in the *Miller* case was to the effect that:

---

104 Dickens, *supra*, note 90 at 851.
105 *Ibid.* at 852.
106 *Re McTavish and Director, Child Welfare Act* (1986), 32 D.L.R. (4th) 394 (Alta. Q.B.), appeal quashed (*sub nom. Re S.E.M.* (1988), 88 A.R. 346 (C.A.); *Re R.K.* (1987), 79 A.R. 140 (Alta. Fam. Ct.); *Re S.D.*; *Russell v. Supt. of Family & Child Service*, [1983] 3 W.W.R. 618 (B.C.S.C.).
107 Dickens, *supra*, note 90 at 873.
108 S.C. 1974-75-76, c. 105.
109 R.S.C. 1970, c. N-4, ss. 68,69 [R.S.C. 1985, c. N-5, ss. 78,79].

it cannot be that Parliament intended to create anew the absolute right not to be deprived of life under any circumstances.[110]

This interpretation cannot be applied to the Charter. If Parliament re-establishes the death penalty, it would do so in the face of a right enshrined in section 7 of the Charter and any such legislation would thus be subject to the test imposed by section 1 thereof. However, the arguments raised by the appellant in the *Miller* case[111] would have to be studied by the court, which would have to take account of the evolution in social and moral ideas, and of progress in the discipline of criminology and in related disciplines.

(ii) *Infringement of the right to liberty*

Apart from the infringements expressly listed in sections 8 to 10 of the Charter, measures aimed at restricting the free disposition of one's body or one's physical person, including the prohibition against suicide, are also infringements on liberty. Measures aimed at requiring medical or prophylactic treatment are infringements on liberty as well.

The civil law recognizes a principle of corporeal autonomy implying the right to dispose of one's own body, the right to refuse medical care and treatment, the right to therapeutic sexual sterilization or contraceptive sterilization and the right to consent to medical or scientific experimentation.[112] These rights are subject, however, to various limits imposed in the public interest. Notable examples include the obligatory treatment of alcoholism or drug addiction (*Criminal Code* section 239(5) [255(5)]) and obligatory psychiatric evaluation (*Criminal Code* sections 465, 543, 608.2, 738(5),(6)) [537, 615, 681, 803(5), (6)]. One may also refer to the obligatory committal provided for by provincial laws dealing with protection of the mentally ill.[113] At the federal level, section 19 [22] of the *Penitentiary Act*[114] stipulates that the Minister may enter into agreements with the government of a province for the confinement in a psychiatric hospital or other appropriate institution of detained persons having been declared to suffer from mental illness or other mental disability. Other

---

110 *Miller v. R.*, [1977] 2 S.C.R. 680 at 704.

111 *Ibid.*

112 On these questions see R. Kouri & M. Ouellette-Lauzon, "Corps humain et liberté individuelle" (1975), 6 *R.D.U.S.* 85; F. Héleine "Dogme de l'intangibilité du corps humain et ses atteintes normalisées dans le droit des obligations du Québec contemporain" (1976), 36 *R. du B.* 2.

113 *Mental Patients Protection Act*, R.S.Q., c. P-41.

114 R.S.C. 1970, c. P-6 [R.S.C. 1985, c P-5].

examples are found in legislation dealing with venereal disease[115] and in the various measures that may be taken under the *Public Health Protection Act*,[116] the *Occupational Health and Safety Act*,[117] etc.

The repeal in 1972 of the criminal law prohibition against suicide[118] reinforces the idea of the free disposition of one's own person. However, section 14 of the *Criminal Code* still prohibits a person from consenting "to have death inflicted on him". This section contemplates primarily euthanasia, duels and suicide pacts. These prohibitions constitute the limits on the freedom enshrined in section 7. With regard to suicide, it is conceivable that the public interest could require regulation of the circumstances in which it may be carried out. Such legislation might prohibit public immolation, certain forms of hunger strikes, etc. This type of regulation would, in our opinion, meet the requirements of section 1 of the Charter.

We have seen above that the concept of liberty cannot be limited to physical liberty. Many fetters to liberty are contained in our statutes and regulations. Numerous infringements on the right to liberty, as that term is understood here, are provided for in laws that impose a duty on public authorities to introduce particular measures. In cases where the administration has an obligation to act, the principles of fundamental justice have no application.

(iii) *Infringement of the right to security of the person*

Security of the person is a concept so large that the possibilities of its infringement are numerous. Certainly, the state or appropriate public authority has as one of its essential obligations that of procuring the maximum security for its citizens. Nonetheless, certain measures, even though taken in the interests of the general public, constitute infringement of the right of security of the person.

We will attempt briefly to illustrate what could constitute such an infringement, and to distinguish infringement of physical integrity from infringement of physical, mental and social well-being. One will recall that section 7 of the Charter may apply to the free disposition of one's body by a capable, consenting adult as well as the treatment or surgical intervention which a person can insist upon receiving; it applies above all to any infringement by an external authority.

---

115 *Public Health Act*, R.S.Q., c. P-35, which presently covers this subject, as the *Venereal Diseases Act*, R.S.Q. 1964, c. 168, was repealed in 1972.

116 *Ibid.*

117 R.S.Q., c. S-2.1.

118 S. 225 of the *Criminal Code*, R.S.C. 1970, c. C-34, repealed S.C. 1972, c. 13, s. 16.

A. *Interference with physical integrity.* Interference with physical integrity raises important moral and legal problems. We shall deal with three sorts: medical or surgical treatment, experimentation on humans and sterilization.

Medical treatment. In certain cases, treatment is made obligatory by legislation; in such cases it constitutes an infringement of liberty. Even though imposed for the purposes of improving the security or well-being of all persons, it nonetheless may constitute a risk to this very same security. When a surgical treatment capable of saving life is imposed by law or regulation, the right to security may be infringed by this very same act. In fact, whether it occurs following consent or not, medical treatment which entails a risk for physical integrity constitutes an act which infringes the security of the person.

Experimentation on humans. Both therapeutic and pure experimentation have recently been the object of intense reappraisal.[119] Certain forms of experimentation, whether therapeutic or purely scientific, impose a risk of serious harm to the integrity of the person. Any regulation or legislation of these scientific or medical activities must conform to the requirements of the Charter.

In this matter, as in the case of ordinary medical treatment, the rule of consent is fundamental, but this rule involves complex arrangements in the case of minors or the mentally ill; this question has been thoroughly discussed in recent writings.[120] Under the Charter, it is necessary that any legislation or regulation concerning these matters conform to sections 1 and 7.

Sterilization. Imposed sterilization constitutes an infringement of one's physical integrity.[121] Normally one distinguishes three types of sterilization: therapeutic, eugenic and contraceptive.[122] Whether we are concerned with sterilization of competent or incompetent normal persons or of persons suffering from mental illness, it seems evident that sterilization constitutes an infringement of the right to physical integrity conferred by section 7 of the Charter. However, the issue merits special attention in

---

119 J.L. Baudouin, "L'expérimentation sur les humains: un conflit de valeurs" (1981), 26 *McGill L.J.* 809 at 819-831.

120 See W.F. Bowker "Minors and Mental Incompetents: Consent to Experimentation, Gifts of Tissue and Sterilization" (1980), 26 *McGill L.J.* 951; Baudouin, *supra*, note 119.

121 See J.L. Baudouin, "Corps humain et actes juridiques" (1976), 6 *R.D.U.S.* 387.

122 Kouri & Ouellette-Lauzon, *supra*, note 112.

the case of persons who are mentally ill, because the sterilization of such persons cannot be voluntary. The case law indicates that such sterilization must be expressly authorized by legislation or by a superior court exercising its *parens patriae* jurisdiction.[123] It requires as well as a procedural framework which conforms to the principles of fundamental justice.

A recent case, decided in 1985,[124] is a good illustration of the problem. It concerned a mentally handicapped ten-year-old girl who experienced intense fear at the sight of blood. To spare her the recurring crises which would arise with the onset of menstruation, her parents decided to have her undergo a hysterectomy. The official guardian [*ministère public*] objected. Relying on the right to security under section 7, he argued that the young girl had the right to decide for herself whether or not she wanted children. The court did not accept this argument and held in favour of the parents on the grounds that the hysterectomy was in the best interest of the child.

This case, far from giving a definitive solution to the problems of sterilization for the mentally handicapped, shows us rather that when the delicate question of sterilization of a person afflicted with such a handicap arises, it is necessary to look at all aspects of the problem before making a decision: degree of the handicap, reactions to various situations, etc. Each case must be decided on its own facts, but always bearing in mind the requirements of section 7, since sterilization, whether justified or not, is in every case a significant interference with bodily integrity affecting the right to security protected by section 7.

Non-consensual sterilization was legalized in Alberta from 1928 to 1971 by virtue of the *Alberta Sterilization Act*.[125] During this period, of 4,725 cases submitted for consideration, 2,822 sterilizations were authorized. A Commission composed of four persons, two doctors and two members of the public, was charged with the administration of the legislation. The legislation detailed five categories of persons upon whom sterilization could be imposed[126] and established two criteria for sterilization: danger of the transmission of incapacity or mental deficiency to offspring, and the risk of mental injury for the individual or his offspring. Where the Commission was of the view that a psychotic person was capable

---

123 *Re Eve* (1981), 115 D.L.R. (3d) 283 and 320 (P.E.I. C.A.), rev'd (*sub nom. E. v. Eve*) *supra*, note 44. On these questions, see the working paper prepared for the *Colloque sur la stérilisation des déficients mentaux*: Barreau du Québec (Montreal: November 13-14, 1981). See also B. Starkman, "Sterilization of the Mentally Retarded Adult: The Eve Case" (1981), 26 *McGill L.J.* 931.

124 *K. v. Public Trustee*, *supra*, note 78.

125 S.A. 1928, c. 37, repealed S.A. 1972, c. 87.

126 Law Reform Commission of Canada, *Sterilization and the Mentally Handicapped* (Working Paper No. 24) (Ottawa: 1979).

of giving a valid consent, his consent was required; if the patient was incapable, the husband, wife, parent, guardian or Minister of Health could consent on his behalf. In the case of a person who was mentally deficient, no consent was required. Personal consent of the individual was required for the three other categories. As revealed by the Blair Report in 1968, the Alberta legislation raised many difficulties in its application. In 1972, the legislation was repealed.

In British Columbia, legislation on eugenic sterilization was in effect from 1933 to 1973.[127] A tripartite Commission, composed of a judge, a psychiatrist and a social worker, administered the legislation. Sterilization was authorized by the Commission wherever procreation seemed likely to result in children who, for hereditary reasons, would have had a tendency to serious mental illness or serious intellectual deficiency. The legislation required the consent of the individual if he was capable of giving it; if not, consent of the spouse, parent, guardian, or Secretary of the Province was necessary.

Numerous difficulties caused the legislatures of these two provinces to abandon eugenic sterilization. The arguments most frequently raised against such legislation included the weakness of the eugenic rationale, the gravity of the socio-political consequences, psychological damage often suffered and finally difficulty in reconciling coercive sterilization and the fundamental rights of human beings. These difficulties have been summarized by the federal Law Reform Commission as follows:

> In summary, widespread sterilization of mentally handicapped persons has been opposed on the grounds that it discriminates against certain classes and races because the criteria for determining mental retardation and mental illness differentiate between classes and races; that it is difficult to determine equitably who should be sterilized because of the imperfections of intelligence tests and the lack of knowledge concerning the role of cultural deprivation in individual and familial deprivation; that there is doubt that anyone is qualified to make decisions about who should be sterilized; that sterilization will be used punitively; that sterilization is immoral and that individual rights and dignity have priority, in any case, over the societal benefits that would be derived from such a policy. There is also concern that the need for social services is being translated as a need for a sterilization program.[128]

> The federal Law Reform Commission recommended the retention of four categories of sterilization:

> (a) *Voluntary therapeutic sterilization:* this would be any procedure carried out for the purpose of ameliorating, remedying, or lessening the effect of disease, illness, disability, or disorder of the genito-urinary system, and with the fully-informed consent of the patient.

---

127 See the *Sexual Sterilization Act*, R.S.B.C. 1960, c. 353, s.5(1).
128 *Supra*, note 126 at 60.

(b) *Emergency therapeutic sterilization*: this would be the same procedure as in (a) (above) carried out in the medical emergency and where the patient or next-of-kin is unable to give consent.

(c) *Voluntary non-therapeutic sterilization*: this would be a safe and effective procedure resulting in sterilization when there is no disease, illness, disability, or disorder requiring treatment but the surgery is performed, with the fully-informed consent of the patient, for:

(i) the control of menstruation for hygienic purposes;

(ii) the prevention of pregnancy in a female; and

(iii) the prevention of ability to impregnate by a male.

(d) *Involuntary non-therapeutic sterilization*: this classification would be for the same procedures as in (c) (above) but where the person is not competent to give consent.[129]

B. *Infringement of the right to physical, mental and social well-being.* If we define the term "security of the person" in the broad sense that we have done, there are numerous ways in which public authorities may interfere with the right to physical, mental and social well-being of any person or group. For example, the granting of a construction permit for a factory which will pollute, or the authorization to market or to transport a dangerous product, or the authorization to construct or to demolish a public building in certain areas. Of course, it will not be easy to demonstrate that a given decision in fact constitutes an infringement of the right to security.

This point was confirmed in the *Operation Dismantle* case[130] which concerned the government's decision to permit American cruise missile tests in Canada. It was argued that this decision could possibly threaten the physical, mental and social well-being of the population. The Supreme Court asserted that the nexus between the governmental decision and the infringement of the right must be clear:

> It is apparent, however, that the violation of s. 7 alleged turns upon an actual increase in the risk of nuclear war, resulting from the federal cabinet's decision to permit the testing of the cruise missile. Thus, to succeed at trial, the appellants would have to demonstrate, *inter alia*, that the testing of the cruise missile would cause an increase in the risk of nuclear war. It is precisely this link between the cabinet decision to permit the testing of the cruise and the increased risk of nuclear war which, in my opinion, they cannot establish.[131]

---

129 *Ibid.* at 123-124.
130 *Operation Dismantle Inc. v. R.*, [1985] 1 S.C.R. 441.
131 *Ibid.* at 451.

Finally, one must deal with the question whether the Charter protects against all infringement or only against serious infringement. A decision of the High Court of Ontario in 1984[132] opted clearly for the second alternative. In order for there to be a violation of the right to security, it held, the infringement must be serious and substantial.[133]

This restrictive view was confirmed by the Supreme Court of Canada, which leads one to suppose that this is the approach to follow. In *Operation Dismantle*,[134] Madam Justice Wilson required a serious and substantial infringement but above all a real infringement, as we have seen. Though not excluding threats from the purview of section 7, she suggested that the mere possibility of an increase in danger to life would not constitute a violation of the right to security contained in section 7 of the Charter.

Chief Justice Dickson arrived at virtually the same conclusion. He ruled that:

> the causal link between the actions of the Canadian government and, the alleged violation of appellants rights under the *Charter* is simply too uncertain, speculative and hypothetical to sustain a cause of action.[135]

This restrictive conception of what counts as infringement of a right should serve as a valuable guide in the useful and coherent application of the Charter, thereby permitting the elimination of futile and abusive claims before the courts.

3. THE PROTECTION OF THE RIGHTS TO LIFE, LIBERTY AND SECURITY OF THE PERSON

The startling originality of section 7 lies in it relating the infringement of these rights to the principles of fundamental justice. This section is one of several which are grouped together under the heading "legal rights", suggesting that the framers envisaged a specific legal protection rather than a simple unqualified recognition of these three rights. Indeed, in *Operation Dismantle*,[136] the Supreme Court of Canada appeared to take the view that the first part of section 7 does not have an independent existence.

It follows that one cannot, in dealing with a law or a measure which affects the right to life, liberty or security, proceed directly to section 1 of the Charter with a view to determining whether it represents a limitation that is reasonable. Nor can one seek a remedy from a court of competent

---

132 *R. v. X, supra*, note 79.
133 *Ibid.* at 256-257.
134 *Supra*, note 130 at 489-491.
135 *Ibid.* at 447.
136 *Ibid.*

jurisdiction under section 24 in disregard of the second part of section 7.

Thus, section 7 does not forbid infringements of the three enshrined rights; rather, it forbids doing so without respecting the principles of fundamental justice.

For all practical purposes, then, section 7 creates the right to fundamental justice where there is an infringement of the right to life, liberty or security. It is this right to fundamental justice which may not be limited save in conformity with the requirements of section 1.[137] When one is faced with an alleged violation of section 7, a three-step process must be followed. First of all, determine whether there has been an infringement of one of the three rights. If so, secondly, determine whether the right to fundamental justice has been violated. If so, thirdly, determine whether this violation is justified under section 1.[138]

Section 7 should be understood as having a content independent of the sections which follow it (sections 8-15) under the heading "legal rights".[139] However, this does not prevent a claimant from invoking section 7 along with one or more of the following sections, as frequently happens in practice.

Before studying this new constitutional concept of "fundamental justice", it will be useful to look briefly at the case law interpreting the 1960 *Canadian Bill of Rights*, which contains a concept that is significantly broader and more vague, namely "due process of law". The change in perspective should be noted as we look first at the scope of the protection afforded by the 1960 provision as construed by the courts.

(a) The Meaning and Scope of the "Due Process of Law" Clause

The "due process of law" clause included in the *Canadian Bill of Rights* was borrowed from the Fourteenth Amendment of the American Constitution, but the judicial interpretation that the clause has received in Canada was more directly inspired by the British tradition of the "rule of law".[140]

This clause, invoked in the United States in thousands of cases, has been given a substantive and procedural content by the American courts. The clause served to formulate a concept of protection of individual rights

---

137 *Singh, supra,* note 4 at 220-221, *per* Wilson J.
138 Very well illustrated by the Saskatchewan Court of Appeal in *Beare v. R., supra,* note 9 at 321; *Pasqua Hospital v. Harmatiuk, supra,* note 80 at 113. It is also the approach adopted by the Supreme Court in *Morgentaler, supra,* note 13.
139 *Re R.L. Crain Inc. and Couture, supra,* note 2.
140 On the entire question, see W.S. Tarnopolsky, *The Canadian Bill of Rights,* 2nd rev. ed. (Toronto: McClelland & Stewart, 1975) at 222 *et seq.*

inspired by the philosophy of "*laisser-faire*" in the face of socio-economic intervention by the state. This tendency was abandoned by the Supreme Court of the United States in the late 1930s.

With regard to its procedural content, the clause has had considerable effect, particularly since 1960. It has served to support the constellation of rights recognized by the Constitution. It guarantees, in a general fashion, the entitlement of all citizens to equitable treatment, whenever their rights are affected. Thus, the clause has served to protect the citizen against unreasonable search and seizure[141] and from cruel and unusual punishment;[142] it prevents an individual from being forced to testify against oneself;[143] it confers on the accused the right to cross-examine witnesses[144] and to be represented by counsel;[145] it even obliges the state in some circumstances to supply an accused with legal assistance so that a defence can be made.[146] The clause has served to protect the accused against involuntary confession and to ensure that he has legal representation from the moment that he is considered to be a suspect. It requires that an accused is informed of the right to legal representation and has a speedy trial.[147] The clause ensures that there are procedures in place to secure the obligatory presence of witnesses.[148] The clause has preserved the right to trial by jury[149] and has protected the accused against double jeopardy.[150]

Canadian case law has not given the "due process of law" clause in section 1 of the *Canadian Bill of Rights* the same breadth. Rather, there has been a tendency to interpret the clause as meaning "according to law", that is, conforming to the provisions of existing law or legislation.

In the first two cases in which the clause was considered, *Louis Yuet Sun v. R.*[151] and *Rebrin v. Bird*,[152] the Supreme Court was content to determine whether or not deportation orders were taken in conformity with the procedural requirements of the *Immigration Act*.[153] The persons affected by the orders, the court held, had not been deprived of their liberty otherwise than by regular application of law.

---

141 *Mapp v. Ohio*, 367 U.S. 643 (1961).

142 *Robinson v. California*, 370 U.S. 660 (1962).

143 *Malloy v. Hogan*, 378 U.S. 1 (1964); *Murphy v. Waterfront Comm.*, 378 U.S. 52 (1964).

144 *Pointer v. Texas*, 380 U.S. 400 (1965).

145 *Betts v. Brady*, 316 U.S. 455 (1942); *Bute v. Illinois*, 333 U.S. 640 (1948).

146 *Gideon v. Wainwright*, 372 U.S. 335 (1963); *Miranda v. Arizona*, 384 U.S. 436 (1966); *Escobedo v. Illinois*, 378 U.S. 478 (1964).

147 *Klopper v. North Carolina*, 386 U.S. 213 (1967).

148 *Washington v. Texas*, 385 U.S. 817 (1966).

149 *Duncan v. Louisiana*, 391 U.S. 145 (1968).

150 *Benton v. Maryland*, 395 U.S. 784 (1969).

151 [1961] S.C.R. 70.

152 [1961] S.C.R. 376.

153 R.S.C. 1952, c. 325.

In the decade from 1960 to 1970, Canadian courts manifested a good deal of reticence in establishing a precise content to the "due process" clause.[154] On March 30, 1972, in *Lowry v. R.*,[155] the Supreme Court of Canada linked the clause to section 2(e) of the *Bill of Rights*, relating to the right to an impartial hearing according to the principles of fundamental justice, in interpreting section 613(4)(b)(ii) of the *Criminal Code*. Section 613(4)(b)(ii) [686(4)(b)(ii)] confers a power on the Court of Appeal to make a finding of guilt and impose an appropriate sentence where the accused was acquitted as a result of an error of law. Then the *Curr* decision[156] was rendered.

In the *Curr* case,[157] May 1, 1972, the Supreme Court of Canada decided that sections 223 and 224A(3) (now section 241(2) [258(2)]) of the *Criminal Code* are compatible with sections 1(a) and (b) and 2(d), (e) and (f) of the *Bill of Rights*. These sections of the *Criminal Code* provide that the refusal or default of an accused to submit to a breathalyzer test may not be admitted in evidence against him. A majority of the court (five judges) concurred with the judgment of Mr. Justice Laskin, confirming the Court of Appeal of Ontario, and held that the provisions of the *Criminal Code* were not incompatible with the *Bill of Rights*. With respect to the "due process of law" clause, Mr. Justice Laskin was of the view that the clause could impose procedural requirements beyond those imposed by section 2 of the *Bill of Rights*, though he admitted that he could not imagine what they could be:

> The phrase "due process of law" has its context in the words of s. 1(a) that precede it. In the present case, the connection stressed was with "the right of the individual to . . . security of the person". It is obvious that to read "due process of law" as meaning simply that there must be some legal authority to qualify or impair security of the person would be to see it as declaratory only. On this view, it should not matter whether the legal authority is found in enacted law or in unenacted or decisional law.
>
> . . .
>
> I am unable to appreciate what more can be read into s. 1(a) from a procedural standpoint than is already comprehended by s. 2(e) ("a fair hearing in accordance with the principles of fundamental justice") and by s. 2(f) ("a fair and public hearing by an independent and impartial tribunal").[158]

Moreover, Mr. Justice Laskin, without directly ruling on the issue of

---

154 See Tarnopolsky, *supra*, note 140, at 229.
155 [1974] S.C.R. 195.
156 *Curr v. R.*, [1972] S.C.R. 889.
157 *Ibid.*
158 *Ibid* at 897-898.

whether to review the substance of the legislation, left the door open to that possibility in the following passage:

> Assuming that "except by due process of law" provides a means of controlling substantive federal legislation — a point that did not directly arise in *Regina v. Drybones* — compelling reasons ought to be advanced to justify the Court in this case to employ a statutory (as contrasted with a constitutional) jurisdiction to deny operative effect to a substantive measure duly enacted by a Parliament constitutionally competent to do so, and exercising its powers in accordance with the tenets of responsible government, which underlie the discharge of legislative authority under the *British North America Act*. Those reasons must relate to objective and manageable standards by which a Court should be guided if scope is to be found in s. 1(*a*) due process to silence otherwise competent federal legislation. Neither reasons nor underlying standards were offered here. For myself, I am not prepared in this case to surmise what they might be.[159]

The former Chief Justice of the Supreme Court again opened this door in 1976 when he indicated in the *Morgentaler* case:

> I am not, however, prepared to say, in this early period of the elaboration of the impact of the *Canadian Bill of Rights* upon federal legislation, that the prescriptions of s. 1(*a*) must be rigidly confined to procedural matters. There is often an interaction of means and ends, and it may be that there can be a proper invocation of due process of law in respect of federal legislation as improperly abridging a person's right to life, liberty, and security and enjoyment of property. Such a reservation is not, however, called for in the present case.[160]

The Supreme Court was called upon to interpret this phrase once more in *Miller v. R.*[161] Two accused were condemned to death for the murder of a police officer, in accordance with sections 214(2) and 218(1) of the *Criminal Code*.[162] They argued that the *Criminal Code* sections were incompatible with the "due process" clause. Mr. Justice Ritchie, speaking for the majority, defined the phrase as follows:

> The declaration of the right of the individual not to be deprived of life which is contained in s. 1(*a*) is clearly qualified by the words "except by due process of law", which appear to me to contemplate a process whereby an individual *may* be deprived of life. At the time when the *Bill of Rights* was enacted there did not exist and had never existed in Canada the right not to be deprived of life in the case of an individual who had been convicted of "murder punishable by death" by the duly recorded verdict of a properly instructed jury and, in my view, the "existing right" guaranteed by s. 1(*a*) can only

---

159 *Ibid.* at 899-900.
160 *Morgentaler v. R.*, [1976] 1 S.C.R. 616 at 633.
161 [1977] 2 S.C.R. 680.
162 The death penalty provisions were later repealed by the *Criminal Law Amendment Act (No. 2)*, S.C. 1974-75-76, c. 105.

relate to individuals who have not undergone the process of such a trial and conviction.[163]

Mr. Justice Laskin, speaking for himself and two of his colleagues, said the following:

> I take the same view here as I expressed in the majority judgment of this court in *Curr v. Queen* at p. 896, that it is s. 2 of the *Canadian Bill of Rights* which gives force to s. 1 and hence, especially since the prescriptions of s. 2 are stated to be effective "in particular", I would not diminish their import by reference to what is more generally prescribed in s. 1.[164]

Following the judgment in *Curr*,[165] the provincial courts and the Federal Court were called upon to interpret and apply the phrase, but these courts adopted almost unanimously the view that "due process of law meant no more than the law existing or in force".[166]

According to the opinion of Mr. Justice Laskin, to give the due process clause a scope going beyond the strictly procedural, one would require convincing reasons or an authority granted by the Constitution itself and not an ordinary statute such as the *Bill of Rights*.

The history of the interpretation of the due process clause probably convinced the framers of the Charter to abandon that phrase and to substitute a reference to the principles of fundamental justice. We shall attempt to define the nature and scope of this concept as it is presently understood.

(b) The Meaning and Scope of the "Principles of Fundamental Justice" Clause

(i) *Under traditional public law*

These principles, arising from the common law, consist of a body of rules which are termed "rules of natural justice". In their modern formulation, they originated in England in the 17th century and underwent significant development beginning around the middle of the 19th century.

The terms "fundamental justice", "natural justice" or even "British justice" have always been considered as synonymous. They signify an

---

163 *Miller, supra*, note 161 at 704.
164 *Ibid.* at 686-687.
165 *Supra*, note 156.
166 D. Mullan, "Human Rights and Administrative Fairness", in R. St. J. MacDonald and J.P. Humphrey, eds., *The Practice of Freedom* (Toronto: Butterworth, 1979) 111 at 126: citing *National Capital Comm. v. Lapointe* (1972), 29 D.L.R. (3d) 376 at 379 (F.C.T.D.); see also Tarnopolsky, *supra*, note 140, at 234-235.

attachment to fundamental values of the legal system known as the common law.[167]

These rules have almost always been considered rules of procedure applicable to inferior jurisdictions and, by extension, to administrative authorities charged with determining the rights of persons affected. However, the notion of procedure has been conceived of in a sufficiently broad fashion so as to include even rules concerning the status, conduct and even attitudes.

The principles of natural justice have always had, as their central objective, the protection of the individual against public authority exercising judicial or quasi-judicial power. This includes courts of civil or criminal jurisdiction, as well as administrative authorities having a power of decision which must be exercised in a quasi-judicial manner. Certain private authorities called "domestic tribunals" had these principles applied to them in certain circumstances. In addition, "the duty to act fairly" has been imposed on authorities applying administrative processes leading to a determination of rights or interests. Scholars have called this development "the new natural justice".[168]

Case law from the Supreme Court of Canada, notably the decisions

---

167 See De Smith's *Judicial Review of Administrative Action*, 4th ed., J.M. Evans, ed. (London: Stevens, 1980) at 156-277; P. Garant, *Droit Administratif*, 2nd ed.(Montreal: Yvon Blais, 1985) ch. 15-16; M. Loughlin, "Procedural Fairness: A Study of the Crisis in Administrative Law Theory" (1978), 28 *U.T.L.J.* 215; D. Mullan, "Fairness: the New Natural Justice?" (1975), 25 *U.T.L.J.* 281; D. Mullan, "Martineau and Butters v. Matsqui Institution Inmate Disciplinary Board: Its Potential Impact on the Jurisdiction of the Trial Division of the Federal Court" (1978), 24 *McGill L.J.* 92; N. Brown & M. Bouchard, "Le contrôle judicaire en droit britannique: justice naturelle ou 'fairness'?" (1977), 18 *C. de D.* 155; J.H. Grey, "The Duty to Act Fairly After Nicholson" (1980), 25 *McGill L.J.* 598; R.A. Macdonald, "Judicial Review and Procedural Fairness in Administrative Law" (1980), 25 *McGill L.J.* 520 and (1981) 26 *McGill L.J.* 1; R. Carter, "Fair Play Comes to Canada" (1979), 44 *Sask. L. Rev.* 349; D.P. Jones, "Administrative Fairness in Alberta" (1980), 18 *Alta. L. Rev.* 351; M. Rankin & M. Horne, "Procedural Fairness . . ." (1979-80), 14 *U.B.C.L. Rev.* 205; G. Pépin, "Pouvoir de surveillance de la Cour supérieure — Justice naturelle" (1979), 39 *R. du B.* 121. See also D.H. Clark, "Natural Justice: Substance and Shadow", [1975] *Pub. L.* 27; J.M. Evans, "Some Limits to the Scope of Natural Justice" (1973), 36 *Mod. L. Rev.* 439; Lord Morris of Borth-y-Gest, "Natural Justice" (1973), 26 *Current Legal Prob.* 1; C.P. Seepersad, "Fairness and Audi Alteram Partem", [1975] *Pub. L.* 242; G.D.S. Taylor, "Fairness and Natural Justice — Distinct Concepts or Mere Semantics?" (1977), 3 *Monash L. Rev.* 191; G.D.S. Taylor, "Natural Justice — The Modern Synthesis" (1975), 1 *Monash L. Rev.* 258; G.D.S. Taylor, "The Unsystematic Approach to Natural Justice" (1973), 5 N.Z.U.L. Rev. 373; P. Wallington, "Natural Justice and Delegated Legislation" (1974), 33 *Cambridge L.J.* 26.
168 See Mullan, "Fairness: the New Natural Justice?", *ibid.*; P. Garant et al., "L'équité procedurale et la révolution tranquille du droit administratif" (1986), 16 *R.D.U.S.* 495.

in *Nicholson*[169] and *Martineau*,[170] clearly delineate the distinction between traditional natural justice and the new natural justice. This distinction is in some respects captured by Parliament in section 28 of the *Federal Court Act*.[170a] The consequences of this distinction on the content of the rules is significantly less clear, as we shall see.

Section 7 of the Charter is designed to impose a certain procedural structure upon decisions that may constitute an infringement of the three rights enshrined therein. That constitutes, without doubt, minimal protection. To discover the scope of this protection one can consult the standard works on administrative law, which provide analysis and synthesis of the requirements of traditional natural or fundamental justice that are applicable to the exercise of quasi-judicial functions, and the requirements which flow from the new natural justice that are applicable to purely administrative functions.

Without doubt, the advent of the Charter has reinforced judicial control of procedural unfairness in the broadest sense of the term.[171] One noteworthy development has been the very diverse range of application of the new natural justice. By way of illustration, we will examine several situations where the courts have upset administrative decisions for not respecting procedural fairness in the context of section 7 of the Charter.

The High Court of Ontario[172] has held that the decision to transfer an inmate must be made according to procedural fairness. This means that the decision must be preceded by a sufficiently detailed notice so that the inmate can make representations in a timely fashion. The same court held that there was a requirement for the Parole Board to grant an in-person hearing when considering the revocation of parole. This was so regardless of the fact that no such requirement existed under either federal or provincial legislation or the common law. The court explained as follows:

> Considering that the rights protected by s. 7 are the most important of all those enumerated in the Charter, that deprivation of those rights has the most severe consequences upon an individual, and that the Charter establishes a

---

169 *Nicholson v. Haldimand-Norfolk Regional Bd. of Police Commrs.*, [1979] 1 S.C.R. 311.
170 *Martineau v. Matsqui Institution Inmate Disciplinary Bd. (No. 1)*, [1978] 1 S.C.R. 118 and *(No. 2)*, [1980] 1 S.C.R. 602.
170a R.S.C. 1970, c. 10 (2nd Supp.) [R.S.C. 1985, c. F-7].
171 See *R. v. Young* (1984), 13 C.C.C. (3d) 1 (Ont. C.A.). See also Lee, *supra* note 14 at 12, where she claims that the field of procedural protection is very extensive. See also *Staples v. National Parole Bd.*, [1985] 2 F.C. 438 (T.D.); *Law v. Solicitor General of Canada* [1985] 1 F.C. 62 (C.A.); A.W. MacKay, "Fairness after the Charter: A Rose by Any Other Name?" (1985), 10 *Queen's LJ.* 263; F. O'Connor, "The Impact of the Canadian Charter of Rights and Freedoms on Parole in Canada" (1985), 10 *Queen's LJ.* 336.
172 *R. v. Chester*, *supra*, note 68.

constitutionally mandated enclave for protection of rights, into which government intrudes at its peril, I am of the view that the applicant could not be
lawfully deprived of his liberty without being given the opportunity for an
in-person hearing before his parole was revoked.[173]

The courts have gone so far as to affirm that the exclusion of the
inmate during even part of the hearing amounts to a refusal to hear him
and so does not conform to the requirements of fundamental justice.[174]

In another case, it was held that revoking an inmate's participation
in a program of non-escorted leave without giving the inmate an
opportunity to be heard is contrary to section 7. The Federal Court took
the view that the liberty in question, even though considerably more limited
than the liberty at stake in parole, was nevertheless of the same character.[175]
On the other hand, a probation order prohibiting an accused from residing
near the place where the offences had been committed was not considered
contrary to section 7.[176] Similarly, where a condition not to consume alcohol
was, without notice, added to a parole order originally granted without
conditions, it was held valid. Since parole is a privilege, adding a condition
does not terminate it and therefore does not infringe the protected
liberty.[177]

The issue of the right to be represented by counsel before administrative bodies has been frequently debated in the context of section 7
of the Charter. The Federal Court had been quite conservative, however.
In the *Howard* case, Mr. Justice Thurlow made the following remarks:

> I am of the opinion that the enactment of section 7 has not created any absolute
> right to counsel in all such proceedings. It is undoubtedly of the greatest
> importance to a person whose life, liberty or security of the person are at
> stake to have the opportunity to present his case as fully and adequately as
> possible. The advantages of having the assistance of counsel for that purpose
> are not in doubt. But what is required is an opportunity to present the case
> adequately and I do not think it can be affirmed that in no case can such
> an opportunity be afforded without also as part of it affording the right to
> representation by counsel at the hearing.
>
> Once that position is reached it appears to me that whether or not the
> person has a right to representation by counsel will depend on the circum-
> stances of the particular case, its nature, its gravity, its complexity, the capacity

---

173 *R. v. Cadeddu; R. v. Nunery* (1982), 40 O.R. (2d) 128 at 139 also *Re Martens and A.G.
British Columbia* (1983), 7 C.R.R. 354 (B.C.S.C.): *Re Lowe and R.* (1983), 5 C.C.C.
(3d) 535 (B.C.S.C.); *Latham v. Solicitor General of Canada, supra,* note 36; *Hewitt v.
National Parole Bd.,* [1984] 2 F.C. 357 (T.D.); *Re Conroy and R., infra,* note 177.

174 See *Re Martens, ibid.,* and *Re Lowe, ibid.*

175 *Cadieux v. Director of Mountain Institution* (1984), 13 C.C.C. (3d) 330 (F.C.T.D.).

176 *Saila v. R.* [1984] N.W.T.R. 176 (N..W.T.S.C.).

177 *Re Conroy and R.* (1983), 149 D.L.R. (3d) 610 (Ont. H.C.).

of the inmate himself to understand the case and present his defence. The list is not exhaustive.[178]

In the *Latham* case, Mr. Justice Strayer maintained that:

> . . . the guarantee in section 7 of the Charter requires that a parolee should have every reasonable opportunity to be represented by counsel at a revocation hearing. The importance of the outcome to him, at least in a case like the present, means that a fair procedure requires that he should have counsel if he so wishes and if he can find counsel willing to serve. Sufficient time should be assured to him to make all reasonable efforts to achieve this.[179]

It appears that with the adoption of the Charter and section 7, procedural requirements may well be more stringent than ever before. Given the fundamental character of the rights protected, it is natural that any interference with them must conform to stringent standards.

In purely administrative matters, as well as in strictly quasi-judicial matters, the influence of section 7 of the Charter has been equally felt. The *Singh* case, dealing with deportation, is a notable example.[180] In this case, the Supreme Court of Canada, sitting with a six-judge bench, heard an appeal in which the appellants Sikhs claimed refugee status within the meaning of the United Nations Convention relating to the status of refugees. The Minister of Employment and Immigration, on the advice of the Refugee Status Advisory Committee, had rejected the appellants' claim and they were not able to obtain a review of their claim by the Immigration Appeal Board. The Federal Court of Appeal then dismissed the application to review and set aside that was finally brought by the applicants. The issue before the Supreme Court was whether the procedure relating to the claim for refugee status provided for in the *Immigration Act, 1976*[181] conformed to the Charter. The Court ultimately ordered the matter referred to the Immigration Appeal Board so that the Board could hold a formal hearing on the merits in conformity with the principles of fundamental justice enshrined in section 7 of the Charter.

Madam Justice Wilson, along with Chief Justice Dickson and Mr. Justice Lamer, felt that "the present situation raised the constitutional protection furnished by the *Charter*" and consequently based her decision on it even though the *Canadian Bill of Rights* clearly remained applicable by virtue of section 26 of the Charter.

The decision process leading to the determination of refugee status can be understood as being made up of three steps. The first two are purely

---

178 *Howard v. Stony Mountain Institution*, [1984] 2 F.C. 642 at 662-663 (C.A.), appeal quashed [1987] 2 S.C.R. 687.

179 *Latham v. Solicitor General of Canada, supra*, note 36 at 749.

180 *Singh, supra*, note 4 at 215-216.

181 S.C. 1976-77, c. 52.

administrative while the third is a quasi-judicial or judicial procedure. The claim for refugee status is received by the Minister of Immigration and gives rise to an inquiry. Should a refusal be contemplated, with the consequence of a possible deportation order or notice to depart in the country, a senior immigration officer must hold an examination under oath. The transcript is sent to the Refugee Status Advisory Committee which then advises the Minister. It is the Minister who makes the decision. These stages have a simple administrative character, but the procedure followed must nevertheless conform to the principle of procedural fairness.

Madam Justice Wilson undertook to determine the content of this procedural fairness by recalling the general rules of administrative law. Varying according to the circumstances and economy of the law in question, this duty of procedural fairness requires the administration at least to permit the appellants to make their case other than through their submissions or interviews alone. The court came to the same conclusion with respect to the Refugee Status Advisory Committee since this body, even though not clothed with a power of decision, does not make available the policies and the information used in assessing the claim. The overall process thus proceeds in what amounts to a vacuum, very much contrary to the requirements of procedural fairness. The decision of the Minister may be appealed to the Immigration Appeal Board, an autonomous quasi-judicial body, by way of an application for a redetermination. By virtue of section 71 of the Act, the Board is only obliged to hold a hearing where "it is of the opinion that there are reasonable grounds to believe that a claim could be established". Thus, the Act expressly authorizes the Board not to hold a hearing. However, the issue is whether this option is compatible with section 7 of the Charter. Prior to the Charter, it was recognized that the legislator could expressly relax or even exclude the principles of fundamental natural justice.

In order for the applicants to demonstrate to the Board that the Minister has acted in error, they must at least be made aware of the reasons for the decision of the Minister. Once this is conceded, it follows that this "highly adversarial" procedure must give the applicants access to their files so that they might prepare their case.[182]

Fundamental justice was violated both by the Minister and the Committee in this case because they did not permit the applicants access to all the files which concerned them. However, the more serious error was that, by refusing a hearing, the Immigration Appeal Board impeded the applicants from obtaining justice. However, Madam Justice Wilson qualified the requirement to hold a formal hearing stating:

---

182 *Singh, supra*, note 4 at 214-216.

My greatest concern about the procedural scheme envisaged . . . is not, therefore, with the absence of an oral hearing in and of itself, but with the inadequacy of the opportunity the scheme provides for a refugee claimant to state his case and know the case he has to meet.[183]

These cases help to advance administrative law. We are witnessing the development of this branch of the law due to the constitutionalization of certain of its elements; the consequence is the raising of standards and the tightening up of procedural requirements.

(ii) *The case law prior to the 1985 Supreme Court decision*

The question that arose after 1982 was whether the framers of section 7, even though they used existing legal terms, envisaged giving them a different significance or scope.

Until the beginning of 1985, the majority of judges who pronounced on the meaning of the expression "fundamental justice" considered that the expression ought to have a procedural content.[184] On this point, the Supreme Court of Canada decision in *Curr v. R.*[185] was cited as an authority to be used in the interpretation of section 7. It appears that in referring to the Supreme Court decision in *Duke v. R.*, the Ontario Court of Appeal adopted the same view when it said:

The concepts of "fundamental justice" and "fair hearing" relevant here are the same whether considered under ss. 7 and 11(*d*) of the Charter, under s. 2(*e*) and (*f*) of the *Bill of Rights*, or under the common law. In so far as this case is concerned, while the Charter accords recognition to the well-established rights asserted by the appellant, it effects no change in the law respecting those rights. Sections 7 and 11(*d*) cannot be construed to operate so as to reverse the decision reached in the like circumstances of *Duke* that non-production of evidence of this kind does not infringe the right to a fair trial in accordance with fundamental justice.

This is not to suggest that "the principles of fundamental justice" now recognized by the Charter of Rights and Freedoms are immutable. "Fundamental justice", like "natural justice" or "fair play", is a compendious expression intended to guarantee the basic right of citizens in a free and democratic society to a fair procedure. The principles or standards of fairness

---

183 *Ibid.* at 214.
184 See *R. v. Holman* (1982), 16 M.V.R. 225 (B.C. Prov. Ct.), aff'd (1982), 17 M.V.R. 306 (B.C.S.C.); *Re Jamieson and R.* (1982), 70 C.C.C. (2d) 430 (Que. S.C.); *R. v. Anson*, [1982] 5 W.W.R. 280 (B.C. Co. Ct.), aff'd [1983] 2 W.W.R. 654 (B.C.S.C.), aff'd [1983] 3 W.W.R. 366 (B.C.C.A.); *R. v. D.A.C.* (1983), 9 W.C.B. 201 (Man. Prov. Ct.); *R. v. Carrière* (January 3, 1983) Bélanger J. (Ont. Prov. Ct.); *R. v. Gustavson* (1982), 143 D.L.R. (3d) 491 (B.C.S.C.); *Re R. and Mason* (1983), 1 D.L.R. (4th) 712 (Ont. H.C.); *R. v. MacIntyre* (1982), 69 C.C.C. (2d) 162 (Alta. Q.B.); *R. v. Duff*, [1982] B.C.D. Crim. Conv. 5445-02.
185 *Supra*, note 156.

essential to the attainment of fundamental justice are in no sense static, and will continue as they have in the past to evolve and develop in response to society's changing perception of what is arbitrary, unfair or unjust.[187]

In a more recent case, the Court of Appeal of Manitoba adopted the same point of view:

> With respect, it is my opinion that the learned provincial court judge was in error in reviewing the substantive justification for deprivation of liberty. My reading leads me to the conclusion that the phrase "principles of fundamental justice" in the context of s. 7 of the Charter as a whole does not go beyond the requirement of fair procedure and was not intended to cover substantive requirements as to the policy of the law in question. To hold otherwise would require all legislative enactments creating offences to be submitted to the test of whether they offend the principles of fundamental justice. In other words, the policy of the law as determined by the Legislature would be measured against judicial policy of what offends fundamental justice. In terms of procedural fairness, that is an acceptable area for judicial review but it should not, in my view, be extended to consider the substance of the offence created.[188]

Mr. Justice Strayer of the Federal Court, who had already expressed the same opinion in 1981 in his capacity as Associate Deputy Minister when appearing before the Special Joint Committee of the Senate and the House of Commons on the Constitution, adopted the same approach in 1985:

> Further, I have held elsewhere and remain of the view that there are no substantive rights guaranteed by section 7. Rather, its purpose is to provide procedural protection with respect to the manner of denial of those rights.[189]

Moreover, this was the view of the Court of Appeal in *R. v. Swain*[190] when it considered the decision-making procedures of section 542[614] of the *Criminal Code*.

What, then, do we mean by "procedure" as opposed to substantive law and what is the specific scope of the protection provided by section

---

187 *Re Potma and R.* (1983), 41 O.R. (2d) 43 at 52 (C.A.), leave to appeal to S.C.C. refused (1983), 41 O.R. (2d) 43n (S.C.C.).

188 R. v. Hayden (1983) 3 D.L.R. (4th) 361 at 363 (Man. C.A.), leave to appeal to S.C.C. refused (1983), 3 D.L.R. (4th) 361n (S.C.C.).

189 *Eleveurs de volailles v. Cdn. Chicken Marketing Agency, supra,* note 52, at 323. See also *Latham v. Solicitor General of Canada, supra,* note 36; *Re Jamieson and R., supra,* note 184; *Re Mason and R., supra,* note 184; *P.S.A.C. v. Canada,* [1984] 2 F.C. 889 (C.A.) aff'd [1987] 1 S.C.R. 424; *Re Potma and R., supra,* note 187; *R. v. Chester, supra,* note 68; *Canada (Eve Studio) v. Winnipeg* (1984), 28 Man. R. (2d) 211 (Man. Q.B.), aff'd (1985), 31 Man. R. (3d) 9 (Man. C.A.), leave to appeal to S.C.C. refused (1985), 58 N.R. 160 (S.C.C.).

190 (1986), 53 O.R. (2d) 609 (C.A.). See the Annotation of A. Manson, (1986), 50 C.R. (3d) 101.

7? In a criminal matter, it is necessary to consider as "procedure" everything that concerns the means or manner in which evidence is obtained. Thus, it includes a remand to trial on consent by counsel for the accused;[191] it includes section 507(b) [577(b)] of the *Criminal Code*,[192] which concerns the preferring of an indictment after an accused has been discharged at a preliminary hearing.[193] The Manitoba Court of Queen's Bench maintained in *Balderstone*[194] that the decision of the Attorney General was not a quasi-judicial one. It was a purely discretionary power which did not have to be exercised in a "judicial manner". Consequently, the indictment could not be quashed on the grounds that the accused had not been heard or consulted by the Attorney General.

Generally speaking, the courts have tended to treat legislative provisions relating to evidence, especially in respect to criminal proceedings, as questions of procedure. Thus, in *R. v. Gallant*,[195] it was decided that section 7 would be infringed should the Crown be allowed to enter into evidence prior convictions for robberies committed by the accused in a trial for possession of stolen property. In *R. v. Kehayes*,[196] the court decided, in proceedings under section 4(2) of the *Narcotic Control Act*,[197] that section 8 of that Act, which created a presumption against a person in possession of a narcotic, did not relieve the Crown from its duty to make a complete case before the accused produced his defence. However, this did not mean that a reversal of the burden of proof, as is the case under section 457(5.1) [515(6)] of the *Criminal Code*, is contrary to section 7 of the Charter.[198] Similarly, section 8 of the *Narcotic Control Act*[199], which shifted the burden of the proof, was not, in itself, contrary to section 7 of the Charter.[200]

The Superior Court of Québec has given a very wide meaning to the concept of procedure. It is to cover the totality of the "judicial process".

---

191 *R. v. Brittain* (Sask., Q.B.) (June 2, 1982) Estey J.

192 See, *e.g.,Re Balderstone and R. supra*, note 2; *R. v. Stolar* (1983), 20 Man. R. (2d) 132 (C.A.); leave to appeal to S.C.C. refused (1983), 21 Man. R. (2d) 240 (S.C.C.); *R. v. Musitano* (1982), 39 O.R. (2d) 732 (H.C.), aff'd (1982), 39 O.R. (2d) 732 at 733 (C.A.); *R. v. Provençal* (March 15, 1983) Montreal No. 500-01-001-585-83 (Qué. S.C.).

193 See, in particular, *Balderstone, supra*, note 2, and *Provençal, supra*, note 192.

194 *Supra*, note 2.

195 (1982), 38 O.R. (2d) 788 (Prov. Ct.).

196 (1982), 54 N.S.R. (2d) 587 (Co. Ct.).

197 R.S.C. 1970, c. N-1.

198 See *R. v. Franforth*, [1982] B.C.D. Crim. Conv. 5160-01.

199 *Supra*, note 197.

200 This proposition was established in many cases. See *R. v. Anson, supra*, note 184; *R. v. Cranston* (1983), 55 N.S.R. (2d) 376 (T.D.), leave to appeal to C.A. refused (1983), 60 N.S.R. (2d) 269 (C.A.); *R. v. Clarke & Norwood*, [1982] B.C.D. Crim. Conv. 5455-04 (B.C. S.C.).

Since fundamental justice requires that this process be clothed with the greatest integrity and impartiality, in *R. v. Vermette*[201] it considered that section 7 of the Charter was violated because of the intemperate and abusive words spoken by the Prime Minister of Quebec in the House and extensively reported in the media. The behaviour of the Prime Minister was considered to be an unprecedented attack on the judicial system. At issue was the trial of members of the Royal Canadian Mounted Police accused of a break-in and theft of Parti Québécois membership lists.

On the other hand, some procedural matters, such as entering a stay of prosecution by the Crown because the principal witnesses were not available, have been found not to constitute violations of the right to a full and complete defence.[202]

An unwarranted delay in the execution of an arrest warrant without any explanation on the part of the Crown has been considered a violation of section 7.[203] Similarly, it was held that sections 7 and 9 of the Charter were violated when an accused was detained for a 40-hour period before being brought before a justice.[204] It appears that any "abuse of process" may be remedied by the court on the basis of section 7 of the Charter.[205]

(iii) *The case law subsequent to the 1985 Supreme Court decision*

The Court of Appeal of British Columbia in its judgment in *Reference re Section 94(2) of the Motor Vehicle Act (B.C.)*[206] held that:

> With these considerations in mind the meaning to be given to the phrase "principles of fundamental justice" is that it is not restricted to matters of procedure but extends to substantive law and that the courts are therefore called upon, in construing the provisions of s. 7 of the Charter, to have regard to the content of legislation.[207]

This approach will be followed. After 1985, one finds a number of judgments of superior courts that are along the same lines.[208] There are

---

201 (1982), 30 C.R. (3d) 129 (Qué. S.C.), aff'd (1984), 45 C.R. (3d) 341 (Qué. C.A.).
202 *R. v. Marquez* (July 22, 1982) No. 5875/81 (Man. Co. Ct.).
203 *R. v. Belton* (1982), 29 C.R. (3d) 59 (Man. Proc. Ct.), rev'd (1983), 31 C.R. (3d) 223 (Man. C.A.), leave to appeal to S.C.C. refused (1983), 20 Man. R. (2d) 179 (S.C.C.).
204 *R. v. Sybrandy* (January 19, 1983) Sherwood J. (Ont. Prov. Ct.).
205 See *Re R. and Bruneau* (1982), 2 C.R.R. 223 (B.C. S.C.), where a *mandamus* was granted to require the judge to rule on the question whether there had been an abuse of process.
206 (1983), 147 D.L.R. (3d) 539 (B.C. C.A.), aff'd *infra*, note 210.
207 *Ibid.* at 763. See also *R. v. Stevens* (1983), 3 C.C.C. (3d) 198 (Ont. C.A.), aff'd [1988] 1 S.C.R. 1153.
208 *Re R.L. Crain Inc. and Couture*, *supra*, note 2, at 507 (Mr. Justice Scheibel held: "The phrase 'principles of fundamental justice' should not be interpreted as limiting the courts to a review of procedural matters"); *R. v. Watch* (1983), 10 C.C.C. (3d) 521

certain scholars who have likewise adopted this point of view.[209]

This issue came before the Supreme Court on an appeal from the previously cited decision of the Court of Appeal of British Columbia. Section 94(1) of the *Motor Vehicle Act*[210] of that province provided for minimum periods of imprisonment for a person convicted of driving on a public highway without a valid driver's licence or while that person's driver's licence was suspended. Section 94(2) went on to stipulate that this offence was one of absolute liability in that there could be a conviction whether or not the accused knew that his licence was suspended. The issue before the court was to determine if an absolute liability offence for which a mandatory term of imprisonment was the punishment violated the fundamental right guaranteed by section 7 of the Charter.

In a unanimous judgment, the court held that section 94(2) was incompatible with section 7. To arrive at this conclusion, the court examined the meaning of the expression "fundamental justice". It went on to hold that this expression did not have an exclusively procedural content but also had a substantive content.

Mr. Justice Lamer, with the concurrence of five other judges, wrote the principal judgment. Madam Justice Wilson, providing reasons of her own, arrived at the same conclusion though by a slightly different approach.

To determine the scope of this expression, Mr. Justice Lamer examined the general objectives of the Charter. He then proceeded to a detailed study of the legislative text, its structure and organization, as well as its context. According to Mr. Justice Lamer, "fundamental justice" constitutes neither a right nor a protected interest, but a qualification of the right not to be deprived of one's life, liberty or security of the person. This expression has a particular function, namely to establish the parameters of the right. Furthermore, he considered that sections 8 to 14, being specific infringements of the right to life, liberty and security, may aid in its interpretation. They are, according to him, examples of cases where there is an infringement of the right to life, to liberty and to security of the

---

(B.C. S.C.); *R. v. Robson, supra*, note 41; *Howard v. Stony Mountain Institution, supra*, note 178; *Lasalle v. Disciplinary Tribunals of Leclerc Institute* (1983), 5 Admin. L.R. 23 (F.C. T.D.); *R. v. Westfair Foods Ltd.*, [1985] 3 W.W.R. 423 (Sask. Q.B.); *R. v. Campagna* (1982), 141 D.L.R. (3d) 484 (B.C. Prov. Ct.).

209 D.P. Jones, "Natural Justice and Fairness in the Administrative Process" (1983), 43 *R. du B.* 456; J.D. Whyte, "Fundamental Justice: The Scope and Application of Section 7 of the Charter" (1983), 13 *Man. L.J.* 455 at 461-462; T.J. Christian, "Section 7 of the Charter of Rights and Freedoms: Constraints on State Action" (1984), 22 *Alta. L. Rev.* 222 at 239; T. Cumming, "Fundamental Justice in the Charter" (1986), 11 *Queen's L.J.* 134; Mackay, *supra*, note 171; L. Tremblay, "Section 7 of the Charter: Substantive Due Process?" (1984), 18 *U.B.C.L.R.* 201.

210 R.S.B.C. 1979, c. 288.

person in ways which do not conform to the principles of fundamental justice. It flows from this analysis that the expression "fundamental justice" in section 7 is a broader concept than that of "natural justice" and that the choice of determining its parameters has been left to the courts.

Mr. Justice Lamer refused to accept the evidence and testimony presented by the drafters of section 7 before the Special Joint Committee on the Constitution as a conclusive element in the interpretation of the expression in question. In this evidence and testimony, the concept of "fundamental justice" was equated with "natural justice". Equally, he refused to apply the case law relating to section 2(e) of the *Canadian Bill of Rights* where the expression "fundamental justice" appears. According to these cases, the expression has an exclusively procedural connotation. In the *Bill of Rights*, the expression is associated with the "right to a fair hearing" which it qualifies, whereas in section 7 of the Charter, the expression is associated with a much more fundamental right.

The final argument which led him to think that "fundamental justice" is not equivalent to "natural justice" was based on the attitude of the legislators. They could easily have used the expression "natural justice", which is now well understood, but they chose not to do so. Mr. Justice Lamer concluded that "we must, as a general rule, be loath to exchange the terms actually used with terms so obviously avoided".[210a]

Mr. Justice Lamer also discussed the issue of absolute liability in the context of the criminal law. According to him, this kind of liability does not in itself violate section 7. It is the combination of imprisonment and absolute liability which violates the section.

Madam Justice Wilson rehearsed the same argument as Mr. Justice Lamer. The legislator, being fully familiar with the concept of "natural justice", chose not to use it and chose instead to use different words to express a different concept. She interpreted section 7 of the Charter very broadly. According to her, this section must not be limited to procedural injustice. She stated:

> It has been argued very forcefully that s. 7 is concerned only with procedural injustice but I have difficulty with that proposition. There is absolutely nothing in the section to support such a limited construction.[211]

In her view, section 7 was meant to cover substantive injustices as well: "[I]t is hard to see why one's life and liberty should be protected against procedural injustice and not against substantive injustice.[212] She justified her view with reference to the preamble of the Charter where the rule

---

210a *Reference re Section 94(2) of the Motor Vehicle Act (B.C.)*, [1985] 2 S.C.R. 486 at 503.
211 *Ibid.* at 530-531.
212 *Ibid.* at 531.

of law is recognized as one of the foundations of our society and to section 1 which sets out the guarantee in general terms.

The effect of this case is to introduce a new concept into our legal system, namely "fundamental justice", a concept which is highly imprecise. This was recognized by Mr. Justice Lamer himself:

> Consequently, those words cannot be given any exhaustive content or simple enumerative definition, but will take on concrete meaning as the courts address alleged violations of s. 7.[213]

Along with others, we are somewhat concerned as to the eventual outcome of such a concept. As expressed by Professor Duplé:

> What legal criteria will the courts be able to rely on to declare that the ends sought to be achieved by the legislator are not compatible with the principles of fundamental justice? Because to admit that there is a substantive component to the principles of fundamental justice is to grant the courts the power to review the legitimacy of the legislative goal. [translation][214]

Later on, in examining the relationship between section 1 and section 7 of the Charter, she notes that:

> [I]f a law may contravene section 7 and nevertheless be constitutional because it passes the test of section 1, it necessarily follows that the criteria for constitutionality applicable under section 7 are different from those applicable under section 1. [translation][215]

Most certainly the Supreme Court took advantage of this case to end a conflict over the interpretation of one of the most important provisions of the Charter, even though it could have resolved the case before it in less dramatic fashion by focusing on the essential issue. The heart of the problem was that the legislation in question absolutely excluded any defence. A statute creating an absolute liability offence in principle violates section 7 to the extent that a sentence of imprisonment is possible.[216] As Professor Duplé notes, this is very much a mixed problem, partly substantive and partly procedural.[217] However, the Court of Appeal of Manitoba[218] in a similar case arrived at the same result on the narrow ground that

---

213 *Ibid.* at 513.

214 N. Duplé, "L'article 7 de la Charte canadienne des droits et libertés et les principes de justice fondamentale" (1984), 25 *C. de D.* 94, at 124. See also P.J. Monahan & A. Petter, "Developments in Constitutional Law" (1987), 9 *Supreme Court L.R.* 72-102.

215 Duplé, *ibid.*

216 Lamer J., in *Reference re s. 94(2) of the Motor Vehicle Act (B.C.), supra,* note 210. See also *R. v. Metro News Ltd.* (1986), 32 D.L.R. (4th) 321 (Ont. C.A.), leave to appeal to S.C.C. refused (1986), 32 D.L.R. (4th) 321n (S.C.C.) (s. 159(b) of the *Criminal Code* contrary to s. 7 of the Charter).

217 Duplé, *supra,* note 214 at 122-123.

218 *R. v. Hayden, supra,* note 188.

a conviction without a trial, that is, without an adequate proceeding, violated the right to a full and complete defence, a requirement of fundamental justice.

The fallout from the *Reference Motor Vehicle Act* case[219] has not been long in coming. The courts have held that the *Identification of Criminals Act*[220] is contrary to fundamental justice to the extent that it applies to individuals charged, but not convicted, with indictable offences.[221] A minimum sentence of seven years' imprisonment for importing a narcotic is also contrary to fundamental justice.[222] Fundamental justice also includes the principle that a person should not be punished unless he has personally committed a fault.[223] However, fundamental justice is not violated when a person is convicted of several offences arising out of one act.[224]

On the other hand, a number of recent cases have raised procedural and evidentiary issues and, in nearly every case, the court reached the conclusion that no violation of natural justice had occurred.[225]

It is clear that where the constitutional challenge does not relate to procedural or evidentiary matters, the judge is being asked to rule on the very substance of the law, its merits and its wisdom, thereby usurping the role normally reserved for the legislator.

If one turns from criminal law to administrative law, the implications

---

219 *Supra.*, note 210.

220 R.S.C. 1970, c. I-1 [R.S.C. 1985, c. I-1].

221 *Beare v. R.*, *supra*, note 9.

222 *R. v. Smith*, [1987] 1 S.C.R. 1045; *R. v. Cancoil Thermal Corp.* (1986), 23 C.R.R. 257 (Ont. C.A.) (an absolute liability offence is contrary to s. 7); *R. v. Church of Scientology* (1987), 30 C.R.R. 238 (Ont. C.A.), leave to appeal to S.C.C. refused (1987), 23 O.A.C. 320n (S.C.C.) (an offence that entails detention for a specific period does not violate the Charter).

223 *Ginther v. Sask. Government Insurance,supra*, note 39.

224 *Krug v. R.*, [1985] 2 S.C.R. 255.

225 *R. v. LeGallant* (1986), 33 D.L.R. (4th) 444 (Ont. C.A.) (exclusion of proof of *mens rea* in cases of sexual assault on minors under 14 (s. 246.1 of the *Criminal Code*)); *Albright v. R.*, [1987] 6 W.W.R. 577 (S.C.C.) (admissibility of hearsay at sentencing); *Thompson Newspapers Ltd. v. Director of Investigation & Research (Can.)* (1986), 34 D.L.R. (4th) 413 (Ont. C.A.), leave to appeal to S.C.C. granted (1987), 23 O.A.C. 318n (S.C.C.) The right to know the reason for judgment is not protected by fundamental justice: *R. v. Baumet* (1986), 50 Sask. R. 210 (Sask. C.A.); *R. v. Hill* (1987), 57 Sask. R. 234 (Q.B.); *R. v. Benoit* (1987), 29 C.R.R. 100 (Nfld. C.A.); *R. v. Grant* (1986), 63 Nfld. & P.E.I.R. 153 (P.E.I. S.C.); *R. v. Jarvis* (1986), 76 N.S.R. (2d) 268 (C.A.), leave to appeal to S.C.C. refused, (1987), 78 N.S.R. (2d) 360n (S.C.C.); *R. v. B.E.S.T. Plating Shoppe Ltd.* (1987), 21 O.A.C. 62 (C.A.); *R. v. Seaboyer* (1987), 20 O.A.C. 345 (C.A.) leave to appeal to S.C.C. granted (*sub nom. Re Seaboyer and R.*) (1988), 39 C.C.C. (3d) vi (note) (S.C.C.) (validity of ss. 246.6 and 346.7 of the *Criminal Code*); *R. v. Bourget* (1987), 54 Sask. R. 178 (C.A.); *R. v. Felipa* (1986), 24 C.R.R. 40 (Ont. C.A.); *R. v. Robillard* (1986), 23 C.R.R. 364 (Ont. C.A.); *R. v. Shupe*, [1987] 5 W.W.R. 656 (Alta. Q.B.).

of Mr. Justice Lamer's observations are cause for a certain amount of dismay. To permit judges to review not simply the fairness of the administrative or quasi-judicial procedure, but the substantive merits of a regulation or a decision so as to determine whether it is just or reasonable, is this not to initiate judicial review of the expediency of administrative action? Herein lies a dilemma. How are we to live with such an interpretation of a Charter that is meant to ensure the rule of law, not the rule of judicial wisdom.[226]

Up to this point, the administrative law matters brought before the courts have mainly been concerned with procedural issues, such as the right to examine or cross-examine witnesses.[227] In another case, the issue was whether the failure of a human rights commission to investigate a complaint of sexual discrimination in a timely fashion was contrary to fundamental justice.[228] Finally, in two other cases, the issues raised were the right to a hearing[229] and the right to be represented by counsel,[230] neither of which were held to be absolute rights.

The *Morgentaler (No. 2)* case was in the end dealt with by the majority of the Supreme Court of Canada as an administrative law case.[231] The majority found that the procedure provided by section 251 of the *Criminal Code* for obtaining a therapeutic abortion did not conform to fundamental justice for several reasons, which varied according to the judges: difficult access, cumbersome procedure, inadequate composition, lengthy delays, lack of precise criteria, *etc.* It becomes evident that the judges deliberately mixed together the design of the procedure itself with its implementation, which then led them to rule on the human and financial resources provided by the administration or the legislator.

(c) The Relationship between section 7 and section 1 of the Charter

Section 1 of the Charter guarantees that the rights and freedoms that

---

226 The Federal Court held that certain conditions of a parole order were too restrictive: *Litwack v. National Parole Bd.*, *supra*, note 36.

227 *Re Davenport*, [1987] 1 W.W.R. 666 (B.C. C.A.), leave to appeal to S.C.C. refused [1987] 2 W.W.R. lxx (note) (S.C.C.); *Re College of Physicians & Surgeons of Ont. and K.* (1987), 36 D.L.R. (4th) 707 (Ont. C.A.).

228 *Re Kodellas and Sask. Human Rights Comm.*, *supra*, note 80; *Argentina v. Mellino*, *supra*, note 8 (delay found not unreasonable in an extradition matter); *Re Robinson and College of Physicians & Surgeons (B.C.)* (1987), 32 D.L.R. (4th) 589 (B.C. S.C.) (delay found not abusive).

229 *Dempsey v. R.*, [1987] 1 F.C. 528; *McDonald v. N.P.B.*, [1986] 3 F.C. 157; *Tonato v. M.E.I.*, [1985] 1 F.C. 927; *Kindler v. F. MacDonald*, [1985] 1 F.C. 676.

230 *Mitchell v. Crozier*, [1986] 1 F.C. 255 (T.D.); *Howard v. Stony Mountain Institution*, *supra*, note 178.

231 *Supra*, note 13.

are set out in the Charter are subject only to such limits as can be demonstrably justified. Does this apply equally to the rights set out in section 7?

As we have seen, recent case law, notably the decisions of the Supreme Court, is to the effect that a person wishing to rely on section 7 has the initial burden of demonstrating that there has been a denial of his life, liberty or security of the person and that this denial is not in accordance with the principles of fundamental justice. It is at that point that section 1 may come into play and permit the government to demonstrate that the denial results from a reasonable law, one which is acceptable in a free and democratic society. To be valid the law must pass the tests of constitutional permissibility established by section 1.

The *Singh* case[232] is a good illustration of this type of situation. The Supreme Court held, in the first place, that the challenged measure — the order of deportation — infringed the security of the applicant. Next, the court found that the procedure followed, as well as the provisions of the Act which prescribed that procedure, were in conflict with the requirements of fundamental justice. Finally, the court rejected the arguments presented by the government to the effect that the procedure was reasonable and acceptable in a free and democratic society.

This three-stage approach has been adopted by the courts in numerous cases,[233] even though in some cases the section 1 test was applied without being actually necessary. The test was applied in the event there had been a violation of fundamental justice.[234]

Some have argued that section 1 may have a bearing on section 7 even where there is no violation of fundamental justice. According to Professor Bender, the enumeration of the three rights in the first part of section 7 calls for, in and of itself, "substantive limits" that the government should justify with reference to the section 1 test.[235] This would mean that a denial of liberty, for example, which might be affected in accordance with the principles of fundamental justice, could nevertheless be declared unreasonable and not justifiable in a free and democratic society.

---

232 See *Singh supra*, note 4, and *Operation Dismantle,supra*, note 130; also *Beare v. R.*, *supra*, note 9 at 321; *Pasqua Hospital v. Harmatiuk*, *supra*, note 80 at 113; *R. v. Metro News Ltd, supra*, note 216 at 333.

233 In addition to *Operation Dismantle, supra*, note 130 and *Singh, supra*, note 4, see *Cadieux v. Dir. of the Mountain Institution, supra*, note 175; *R. v. F.*, [1987] 7 W.W.R. 481 (B.C. C.A.) (s. 146.1 of the *Criminal Code* found justifiable under s. 1); *R. v. Grant* (1986), 31 D.L.R. (4th) (B.C. S.C.).

234 *Re U.S.A. and Smith* (1984), 10 C.C.C. (3d) 540 (Ont. C.A.).

235 P. Bender, "Canadian Charter and U.S. Bill of Rights" (1983), 28 *McGill L.J.* 810. See also H. Brun, "Quelques notes sur les articles 1, 2, 7 et 15 de la Charte . . . (1982), 23 *C. de D.* 781.

This approach has certain merit insofar as it protects the right to life, liberty and security against any restriction that would not pass the test of section 1, irrespective of any reference to fundamental justice. However, it makes the construction of section 7 difficult to explain, especially the French version.

At the least, one can say that the leading case law, and most notably the case law of the Supreme Court of Canada, has not adopted this latter approach.[236] Enlarging the concept of "fundamental justice" in order to give it a substantive connotation, as was done by the Supreme Court in its 1985 decision,[237] is vulnerable to the extent that it forces the fundamental justice clause to fulfill pretty much the same function as section 1 of the Charter. Would one not say that what is fundamentally just is that which is reasonable and demonstrably justified in a free and democratic society?

We would prefer the Supreme Court to use section 7 more to strengthen the procedural framework within which policies are implemented rather than calling into question the policies themselves.[238] There would then be no overlap with section 1. We would see a strengthening and a reaffirmation of traditional natural justice derived from the common law, as envisaged by some scholars[239] and a number of judges,[240] including certain judges of the majority in the *Morgentaler* case.[241]

---

236 In *Morgentaler, supra*, note 231, Wilson J. seemed to be of this opinion but it must be noted that she considered that there was an infringement of s. 2 of the Charter (Freedom of Conscience) as well.

237 *Reference re S. 94(2) of the Motor Vehicle Act (B.C.), supra*, note 210.

238 A.J. Petter, "The Politics of the Charter" (1986), 8 *Supreme Court L.R.* 473-505.

239 D. Mullan, "Administrative Law and the Charter", in *Développements récents en droit administratif* (Montreal: Yvon Blais, 1987).

240 Notably McGuigan J. in *Howard v. Stony Mountain Institution, supra*, note 178, and the authorities cited by him.

241 Beetz and Dickson JJ. with the support of Estey and Lamer JJ.

11

Protection Upon Arrest or Detention and Against Retroactive Penal Law*
(*Sections 8, 9, 10(c), 11(e), (g), and (i)*)

François Chevrette

1. PROTECTION AGAINST UNREASONABLE SEARCH AND SEIZURE

Section 8 provides:

Everyone has the right to be secure against unreasonable search and seizure.

A preliminary observation must be made concerning this provision, which has no equivalent in the *Canadian Bill of Rights*. As initially drafted,

---

* Translated from the French.

section 8 of the proposed Charter guaranteed "the right not to be subjected to search or seizure except on grounds, and in accordance with procedures, established by law". In other words, a search and seizure conforming to the law was automatically in conformity with the Charter. This is no longer the case, and it is now possible for a search or seizure conforming to the law to be unreasonable and therefore contrary to the Charter.[1]

A provision of the sort contained in section 8 is difficult to interpret. For verification of this point, one need only look to judicial construction of the Fourth Amendment of the Constitution of the United States, which offers similar protection, though one drafted in more precise terms.[2] In order to appreciate the impact of section 8 on existing law and practice, we will first investigate the scope of the concepts of search and seizure. In other words, we will attempt to determine the type of conduct to which the guarantee of the section is theoretically applicable, ignoring for the moment the reasonable or unreasonable character of such conduct. Take, for example, electronic surveillance or the use of a lie detector: are such activities searches within the meaning of the section? Is the concept of search limited to acts by which evidence is obtained for use in criminal proceedings or does it embrace the procurement of evidence for civil cases as well (for example, evidence for a divorce)? Does it extend to security checks (on prisoners, or airline passengers) or to administrative inspections (for example, customs)? As these questions show, some attempts must be made to elucidate the theoretical scope of section 8.

Our second task will be to determine what is meant by unreasonable as opposed to reasonable conduct. This task is a difficult one, for it is up to the courts to decide what is unreasonable in terms of each particular situation. For our purposes, we shall be content to examine first the general and fundamental principles in this area and second a certain number of particular rules or practices, for example, searches without warrant, administrative inspections, tax inquiries, border searches, searches of prisoners and vehicle inspections.

Once it is decided that a law or practice contravenes section 8, and that, if it is a law, it cannot be saved by section 1, the problem of sanctions arises and it is with this problem that the conclusion of our study shall deal.

---

1 For one example among many, see the important case of *Hunter v. Southam Inc.*, [1984] 2 S.C.R. 145, which will be referred to below.
2 The Fourth Amendment reads as follows: "The right of the people to be secure in their persons, houses, papers, and effects, against unreasonable searches and seizures, shall not be violated, and no warrants shall issue, but upon probable cause, supported by oath or affirmation, and particularly describing the place to be searched, and the persons or things to be seized."

(a) Definition and Scope of Concepts

It is clear that the protection against search afforded by section 8 is both a protection of the person and a protection of his private environment. The word "search" refers indiscriminately to both searches of the person and searches of a place[3] and it is rendered in French by the words "*les fouilles, les perquisitions*". The word "*fouilles*" has the same double sense as "search". But the fact that "*fouilles*" is followed by the word "perquisitions", which refers to searches in a place, indicates all the more clearly that the basic protection of the section applies not only to the latter but to searches of the person as well. On this point, there appears to be no room for doubt.[4]

To search a person is to inspect his clothing, the receptacles he is carrying with him, or his body for the purpose of discovering some object. It is obvious that this includes inspection of the various orifices of the human body. To administer an emetic or an enema, to pump out a stomach or to perform surgery for the purpose of retrieving an object from a person's body, are all uncontestably acts to which section 8 is directed. It has been held that performing an operation for the purpose of removing a bullet from the shoulder of an accused is not a search in the sense of section 443 [487] of the *Criminal Code* and that a warrant authorizing such a search could not be legally issued, since the human body is not a "building, receptacle or place".[5] But the court in this case was construing a provision of the *Criminal Code* and not section 8 of the Charter. If this section covers the inspection of a person's clothing, *a fortiori* it covers surgery on a person to recover an incriminating object from his body.

A more difficult question is whether the notion of search is limited to seeking out objects that are distinct from the person or whether, on the contrary, it includes the taking of physical specimens capable of serving as evidence in a trial — a blood sample, for example, or a spinal tap. In common parlance, perhaps, the taking of a physical specimen is not thought of as a search. But in our view, it would be difficult and artificial at best, for constitutional purposes, to maintain a distinction between things distinct from the person and things forming part of the person, especially as the means by which the latter are obtained often constitute a more

---

3 D.M. Walker, *The Oxford Companion to Law* (Oxford: Clarendon Press, 1980) at 1122; R.S. Vasante, ed., *The Canadian Law Dictionary* (Toronto: Law and Business Publications (Canada) Inc. 1980) under the word "search".

4 *Southam Inc. v. Hunter*, (1982) 68 C.C.C. (2d) 356 at 360-361 (Alta Q.B.), aff'd (1982), 42 A.R. 108 (C.A.), where it was held that section 8 guarantees also applied to legal entities (p. 364). The decision was reversed on other grounds *Southam v. Hunter* (1983), 3 C.C.C. (3d) 497 (Alta. C.A.), aff'd [1984] 2 S.C.R. 145.

5 *Re Laporte and R.* (1972), 29 D.L.R. (3d) 651 (Qué. Q.B.).

serious violation of the person than the means used to obtain the former. If the purpose of section 8 is to protect the person against certain methods of obtaining evidence, such a distinction obviously makes little sense.[6]

But another problem arises and it is doubtless one of the most important posed by the construction of section 8. In effect, one can argue that in standard legal terminology, as much as in ordinary speech, the notion of search or *fouille* and *perquisition* refers to the process of obtaining "tangible things".[7] It is for this reason that the courts have decided that a search warrant cannot authorize the electronic monitoring of conversations.[8] One might possibly consider a physical specimen a "thing", but admissions, confessions or ordinary conversations are clearly not "things", no more than are certain types of physical data (measurements, fingerprints), certain bodily reactions (responses to a lie detector) or certain indicators of identity (voice prints, police line-ups, writing samples). At first glance, then, the language of section 8 appears to suggest that the guarantee it contains applies only to the procurement of "tangible things'. Furthermore, were one to extend this guarantee to every type of evidence, it could effectively amount to establishing a general principle of non-self-incrimination, whereas matters relating to self-incrimination are dealt with, in a narrow and precise fashion, by two specific provisions of the Charter: section 11(c), the right of an accused not to be a witness against himself, and section 13, the right of a witness not to have incriminating evidence used against him in subsequent proceedings.

Before looking further into this subject, we should point out that a similar difficulty arises not only in relation to searches of the person but in relation to searches of a place as well. Traditionally searching a place suggests the idea of an 'intrusion" into the place in order to find a "tangible thing". On this view, the installation of a recording device at the residence of a person without his knowledge for the purpose of recording his conversations would not be conduct within the ambit of section 8, because the object sought is not a tangible thing. The section would be even less

---

6 In *R. v. Pohoretsky*, [1987] 1 S.C.R. 945 at 949, Mr. Justice Lamer, referring to a blood sample taken from an unconscious person for purposes of evidence, stated: " ... I consider this unreasonable search to be a very serious one. First, a violation of the sanctity of a person's body is much more serious than that of his office or even of his home." It is obvious that the taking of a blood sample, a spinal tap and other similar procedures fall within the scope of section 8. As to whether they are reasonable or not, see below.

7 Reference to any dictionary will confirm this. As an illustration, *The Canadian Law Dictionary, supra*, note 3, under the word "search" mentions an examination with a view to the discovery of "contraband or illicit or stolen property or of some evidence of guilt" and states that the purpose of a "search" is "procuring things that will in some degree afford evidence of the commission of an alleged crime".

8 *Re Bell Telephone Co. of Can.* (1947), 89 C.C.C. 196 (Ont. H.C.).

likely to apply where the apparatus is installed on an outside wall of the residence, for then there would be no intrusion. This element would probably be considered absent as well if the eavesdropper secretly planted his device after being invited into the residence by its occupant. And since mere looking and listening also do not constitute searches in the traditional sense of the term, the police would be able to spy into the home of a person from a distance, record his voice and photograph him, all without running afoul of section 8!

One sees, then, to what absurdities a purely literal construction of section 8 can lead. For this reason it is fortunate that Canadian courts refused to become embroiled, as the American courts at one time did,[9] in a morass of distinctions of the sort just considered, which in fact have no relevance to the construction of a constitutional provision dating from 1982. One must not forget that a constitutional provision affording protections to the individual cannot be construed in the same manner as an ordinary provision of criminal law, especially when the latter grants special powers, of search in particular, to public officials. One must also not forget that construction of the expression "unreasonable search or seizure" does not depend entirely on dictionary definitions and the language of existing federal laws. This expression is a classic one, appearing as it does in the Fourth Amendment of the American Constitution. The point here is not to suggest that interpretation of section 8 must follow interpretation of the Fourth Amendment, especially given the differences in their formulation. But the borrowing is evident and indicates that the aim of section 8 is indeed to protect, specifically in the matter of obtaining evidence, the privacy of the individual and his environment. From this point of view, electronic surveillance, to take only one example, is not excluded from the ambit of protection afforded by section 8, subject to the question whether such an activity is inherently unreasonable or may, in some circumstances or some forms, be reasonable.[10]

To put things in the form of a generalization, one may say then that

---

9 For a general survey, see in particular the excellent analysis of A.G. Amsterdam, "Perspectives on the Fourth Amendment" (1973-74), 58 *Minn. L. Rev.* 349.

10 Certain witnesses before the Special Joint Committee of the Senate and the House of Commons on the Constitution of Canada clearly suggested that s. 8 could apply to the interception of telephone communications. See *Minutes of the Proceedings and Evidence of the Special Joint Committee of the Senate and of the House of Commons on the Constitution of Canada*, Issue No. 46, at 104. The case law has recognized that this investigative technique falls under the scope of s. 8: see *R. v. Finlay* (1985), 23 C.C.C. (3d) 48 (Ont. C.A.), leave to appeal to S.C.C. refused (1986), 54 O.R. (2d) 509n (headnote) (S.C.C.); *R. v. Atwal* (1987), 36 C.C.C. (3d) 161 (F.C.C.A.). The same applies to surveillance using a hidden video camera: See *R. v. Wong* (1987), 34 C.C.C. (3d) 51 (Ont. C.A.); *R. v. Lofthouse* (1986), 27 C.C.C. (3d) 553 (Ont. Dist. Ct.).

section 8, insofar as it is concerned with searches, is designed to protect the individual against those methods of investigation that violate the privacy of the person. Nothing in the wording of the section limits its scope to the procurement of evidence for criminal proceedings, so that in principle it applies equally to security checks (on prisoners or airline passengers) and to customs inspections, for example.[11] On the other hand, the section does not entrench in the Constitution a general right to privacy; the individual is secured against modes of investigation only.[12] For this reason it appears doubtful that section 8 could be relied on to prevent the establishment of data banks containing personal information on individuals, nor could it be used, as it is in the United States, to invalidate laws that criminalize purely private conduct.[13]

It must be noted, however, with respect to the foregoing restrictions, that Mr. Justice Dickson (as he then was) in the important case of *Hunter v. Southam Inc.*,[14] analyzed below, gave section 8 a remarkably wide scope, stating:

> Like the Supreme Court of the United States, I would be wary of foreclosing the possibility that the right to be secure against unreasonable search and seizure might protect interests beyond the right of privacy, but for purposes of the present appeal I am satisfied that its protections go at least that far.[15]

Moreover, like every other provision of the Charter, by virtue of section 32, section 8 applies only to acts of the state — "state action".[16] It follows that it could not apply, for example, to the conduct of a private investigator hired by a husband to gather evidence of his wife's adultery for proceedings in divorce. There is little likelihood in our view that Canadian courts would follow the reasoning of the American Supreme Court, based on the guarantee of equal protection of the law, and conclude that the act of a court in receiving such evidence of adultery is itself a form of "state action".[17] However, Canadian courts may respond differently to criminal as opposed to civil matters, and one could argue that where an ordinary citizen or a private security officer obtains by unreasonable means evidence that is to be used in a criminal prosecution, he is by virtue of this fact

---

11 On these applications of s. 8, see below.

12 See *Minutes of the Special Joint Committee, supra*, note 10 at 67 and 69, where the Minister of Justice, Mr. Chrètien, indicated that s. 8 is intended to provide a specific protection of the right to privacy.

13 See in particular *Griswold v. Connecticut*, 381 U.S. 479 (1965), where the court struck down a law prohibiting the use of contraceptives, and *Roe v. Wade*, 410 U.S. 113 (1973), which authorized abortion under certain conditions.

14 [1984] 2 S.C.R. 145.

15 *Ibid.* at 159.

16 See *R.W.D.S.U., Local 580 v. Dolphin Delivery Ltd.*, [1986] 2 S.C.R. 573.

17 See *Shelley v. Kraemer*, 334 U.S. 1 (1948).

acting in the name of the state and that his actions fall within the scope of section 8.[18]

If one accepts a functional construction of section 8 in place of a purely literal one, as the courts have already begun to do, and if the section is seen to offer protection specifically against methods of investigation that violate a person's right to privacy — methods that may or may not be unreasonable, a matter to which we shall return — it seems clear that the use of a device such as the lie detector is covered by this section, simply because it permits an investigator to capture and attach meaning to physical reactions that would otherwise remain imperceptible. Conversely, voice prints, writing samples, police line-ups, fingerprints and other data of this sort wholly escape the ambit of the section[19] and are more properly subsumed under the concept of self-incrimination. As already noted, the Charter does not contain a guarantee of a general character respecting self-incrimination.

The sanctity of the home is a well-established principle in our law, and it was reaffirmed in 1981 by the Supreme Court.[20] Equal importance is attached to the privacy of the mails. There is no doubt that inspection of a person's domicile or his correspondence are acts covered by section 8. But at what point does the protected zone of privacy surrounding a person begin and where does it end? What of a person's office or car, his room at a hotel, a secondary residence or outbuilding, a safety deposit box, a telephone booth, a discreet restaurant where one dines *tête-à-tête*: are these places within the zone? Does it extend to the apartment of a friend where personal articles, left by a visitor, are seized and carried off by the police after forcing their way into the apartment? In such a case, has the privacy of the host alone been violated, but not that of the visitor, so that the former but not the latter has grounds for complaints? There is American case law on all these questions and it is so copious and complex that one prominent scholar felt free to conclude that "the Fourth Amendment cases are a mess".[21] On this point one should notice that, unlike section 8, the Fourth Amendment specifies that the objects to be secured from "unreasonable searches and seizures" are the "persons, houses, papers

---

18 On this point, compare *R. v. Lerke* (1986), 24 C.C.C. (3d) 129 (Alta. C.A.) with *R. v. Breckles* (February 7, 1984) (Ont. Co. Ct.) and *Cat Productions Ltd. v. Macedo* (1985), 5 C.P.R. (3d) 71 (F.C.T.D.).

19 This conclusion regarding fingerprints is confirmed by the case law: *R. v. McGregor* (1983), 3 C.C.C. (3d) 200 (Ont. H.C.); *Re M.H. and R. (No. 2)* (1984), 14 C.C.C. (3d) 210 (Alta. Q.B.), additional reasons aff'd (1985), 17 C.C.C. (3d) 443 (Alta. Q.B.), 21 C.C.C. (3d) 384 (Alta. C.A.), leave to appeal to S.C.C. granted 21 C.C.C. (3d) 384n (S.C.C.).

20 *Colet v. R.*, [1981] 1 S.C.R. 2.

21 R.B. Dworkin, "Fact Style Adjudication and the Fourth Amendment: The Limits of Lawyering" (1973), 48 *Ind. L.J.* 329, quoted by Amsterdam, *supra*, note 9 at 349.

and effects [of the people]."

Starting with this language, American courts undertook to fix the boundaries of the constitutionally protected zone of privacy, using every imaginable refinement, until the Supreme Court finally came to the conclusion, in a celebrated judgment of 1967, that 'the Fourth Amendment protects people, not places", and that "[w]hat a person knowingly exposes to the public, even in his own home or office, is not a subject of Fourth Amendment protection", whereas "what he seeks to preserve as private, even in an area accessible to the public, may be constitutionally protected".[22] It was also stated that the citizen's privacy protected by the Fourth Amendment is the "privacy upon which he justifiably relied"[23] and there must be a "reasonable expectation of privacy".[24]

It is fortunate that Canadian case law, and in particular the case of *Hunter v. Southam Inc.*,[25] appears disposed to adopt this flexible test, warranted, moreover, by the terms of section 8 granting to "everyone" a right to be secure against unreasonable search and seizure. It is not only at home, after all, that one may feel a sense of privacy.

This interpretation of section 8 that we have just suggested puts the emphasis not on the nature, tangible or intangible, of the evidence sought, nor on the necessity of an intrusion into a well-defined geographic zone of privacy, but rather on the issue of whether the means by which evidence was procured or its use violates the privacy of the individual or what can reasonably be considered a private situation.[26] If this approach is correct, and taking into account the fact that section 8 must, in our view as explained above, apply to conduct such as electronic surveillance and the interception of private and spontaneous conversations, may one not argue that the

---

22 *Katz v. United States*, 389 U.S. 347 at 351-352 (1967). In that case, the court decided that the monitoring of conversations taking place in a telephone booth was a "search" within the meaning of the Fourth Amendment.

23 *Ibid.* at 353.

24 *Ibid.* at 360.

25 *Supra*, note 1. Justice Dickson states: "There is, further, nothing in the language of the section to restrict it to the protection of property or to associate it with the law of trespass. It guarantees a broad and general right to be secure from unreasonable search and seizure" (at 158).

26 This subjective criterion derived from the *Katz* case, *supra*, note 22, is somewhat dangerous, as the state or the society may diminish the citizens' expectation of privacy. Mr. Justice Dickson, in the *Hunter* decision, *supra*, note 1 at 159, dealing with the right of the public "to be let alone by their people" appeared to recognize an objective dimension to the right. On this question, see K. Murray, "The 'Reasonable Expectation of Privacy Test' and the scope of Protection Against Unreasonable Search and Seizure Under Section 8 of the Charter of Rights and Freedoms" (1986), 18 *Ottawa L. Rev.* 25; M. Rosenberg, "Unreasonable Search and Seizure: *Hunter v. Southam Inc.*" (1985), 19 *U.B.C.L. Rev.* 271 at 276-283.

section applies as well to certain "elicited" conversations, for example, confidences made by persons under arrest to policemen representing themselves as priests, doctors or fellow prisoners?[27] Even though it would be quite logical and probably desirable to extend section 8 to such situations, it is doubtful that the courts will be willing to go this far. They may reason that a person must bear the risks involved in making friends or trusting to confidants[28] and that such a means of procuring evidence is not unreasonable. They may also reason, perhaps, that recording the conversation of two persons at the home of one of them is more nearly a "search" than a policeman misrepresenting himself to a person in a particular guise in order to elicit confidences! It remains true, however, that if the courts adopt a functional interpretation of section 8, they will find it difficult to exclude its application to cases of this sort.

We are all familiar with the controversy in the case law on the question whether the rule of privileged communication between a lawyer and his client is merely rule of evidence applicable at trial or in addition constitutes grounds for quashing a search warrant.[29] It is clear that section 8 will serve to reinforce the latter position, already preferred in the case law, so that the fact that a search is conducted at the office of a lawyer for the purpose of procuring evidence against his client will be grounds for concluding that the search is an unreasonable one.[30] But one may also ask whether section 8 is directed only to the case where public authorities, normally the police, go themselves to collect the evidence, or whether it would apply as well to a judicial order obliging an individual to produce evidence that would be unreasonable for the police to go get themselves.

---

27 The reference here is to the well-known case law in which the courts have held that such declarations are admissible in evidence at trial: See *e.g.*, *Rothman v. R.*, [1981] 1 S.C.R. 640.

28 See R. v. Sanelli (1987), 61 O.R. (2d) 385 (C.A.), where the provision of the *Criminal Code* dealing with interception of communications when one of the speakers, in this case a policeman, consented to such interception was held valid. It was observed in that decision that, by the mere fact of speaking to someone, there was an acceptance of the risk that the conversation would be repeated. See also *R. v. Mancuso* (1987), 1 W.C.B. (2d) 300 (Que. S.C.).

29 See, in particular, J. Schnoor, "Privilege — Solicitor and Client — Whether Applicable to Powers of Search and Seizure" (1976-77), 7 *Man. L.J.* 341.

30 In *Descôteaux v. Mierwinski*, [1982] 1 S.C.R. 860, Mr. Justice Lamer, although obviously not referring to s. 8 (the case having arisen prior to the coming in force of the section), held that a search in a lawyer's office must respect stringent conditions and that a search warrant may be quashed for reasons of confidentiality. It may be argued that violation of these conditions, which have been incorporated into s. 444.1 of the *Criminal Code* by s. 72 of the *Criminal Law Amendment Act of 1985*, S.C. 1985, c. 19 would amount to a violation of s. 8 of the Charter. See *Nightingale Galleries Ltd. v. Director of Theatres Branch* (1984), 15 C.C.C. (3d) 398 at 410 (Ont. Co. Ct.) where, in the analysis of the scope of s. 8, the court refers to the *Descôteaux* decision.

In other words, might a subpoena *duces tecum* in some circumstances be considered a search, as it apparently was once held in the United States?[31] Or suppose that section 4(3) of the *Canada Evidence Act*[32] were amended so that a person could be compelled to disclose a communication made to him by his spouse during their marriage. Could one argue that compelling a disclosure in such circumstances is a form of search that is potentially unreasonable? To answer "no" to these questions could mean that what section 8 forbids to be done directly, by means of a search, may be done indirectly, through an obligation to disclose. However, it is not clear that the courts will be willing to give such an extended application to the section, especially if they favour a literal interpretation, since an obligation to testify or to produce evidence before a court is obviously not a search.[33]

Some remarks must now be made on the concept of "seizure". By virtue of this term, section 8 effectively protects not only the person but also his property,[34] by forbidding that it be taken from him, whether permanently or temporarily, in an unreasonable fashion. It appears to us that contrary to what the American courts have decided, [35] on the basis of a different constitutional text, the seizure referred to in section 8 does not include seizure of persons, that is, does not include arrest or detention. For protection in this area, one must look to section 9, which grants the right "not to be arbitrarily detained or imprisoned".[36]

A further issue to be dealt with is whether the protection against unreasonable seizure is a general guarantee of the "enjoyment of property", such as one finds in section 1(a) of the *Canadian Bill of Rights*, covering every method of confiscating property including expropriation, or whether it is a more limited guarantee affording security against confiscations only

---

31 See Amsterdam, *supra*, note 9 at 364-365.

32 R.S.C. 1970, c. E-10, s. 44(3) [R.S.C. 1985, c. C-5, s. 4(3)] provides that no person is compellable to disclose a communication made to him by his spouse during their marriage.

33 To date, case law tended to raise the question whether an order to produce documents was a seizure under the terms of s. 8 and to answer negatively: see *Re Ziegler and Hunter* (1983), 8 D.L.R. (4th) 648 (F.C.C.A.), Marceau J. dissenting on the point; *Thomson Newspapers Ltd. v. Director of Investigation & Research* (1986), 30 C.C.C. (3d) 145 (Ont. C.A.), leave to appeal to S.C.C. granted (1987), 23 O.A.C. 318n (S.C.C.); *Gershman Produce Co. v. Transport Bd.* (1984), 22 D.L.R. (4th) 520 (Man. C.A.). *Contra*, see *Re Alta. Human Rights Comm. and Alta. Blue Cross Plan* (1983), 1 D.L.R. (4th) 301 (Alta. C.A.); *Bishop v. College of Physicians & Surgeons of B.C.* (1985), 22 D.L.R. (4th) 185 (B.C.S.C.), aff'd on different grounds (1986), 26 D.L.R. (4th) 15 (B.C.C.A.).

34 The *Minutes of the Special Joint Committee*, *supra*, note 10 at 104, indicate clearly that s. 8 applies to persons and to property.

35 See Amsterdam, *supra*, note 9 at 357.

36 As authority for the statement that s. 8 does not deal with arrest of persons, see *R. v. Parton* (1983), 9 C.C.C. (3d) 295 (Alta. Q.B.). *Contra*: see *Re T. and Catholic Children's Aid Society of Metro. Toronto* (1984), 46 O.R. (2d) 347 (Ont. Prov. Ct.).

within the framework of an investigation or criminal conviction. In our view, the second interpretation is clearly to be preferred. If the framers had wished to introduce into the Charter a general guarantee of the enjoyment of property, it would probably have been written into section 7, not section 8, and the draftsmen would have avoided using a word with such narrow connotations, so closely tied to the idea of judicial process, as the word "seizure". The meaning of the word "seizure" must be construed in relation to the rest of section 8. Thus, it does not apply to expropriations,[37] taxes,[38] attachment for debt[39] or the detention of goods until payment of customs dues.[40] To claim, however, that detention of goods can never amount to a seizure[41] is, in our view, incorrect. To detain articles in the framework of an investigative process, either administrative or criminal, would clearly appear to constitute a seizure under the terms of section 8.[42]

We conclude this analysis of the theoretical scope of the concepts of search and seizure by suggesting that these terms should receive a liberal interpretation. The present tendency of the case law with respect to orders to produce documents or subpoenas *duces tecum* is thus to be regretted. Even if the court held that the matter constituted a search or a seizure, it would still retain a vast discretion to hold that the search or seizure was not unreasonable — a question we shall now examine — or to save the statute by invoking section 1 of the Charter or to refuse to exclude under section 24(2) the evidence obtained in violation of section 8.

(b) Conduct That is Unreasonable and Conduct That is Not

An unreasonable or abusive practice — the French equivalent of "unreasonable" is *abusive* — is obviously not easy to define. For this purpose, all sorts of factors might be taken into account, for example,

---

37 *Becker v. Alberta* (1983), 148 D.L.R. (3d) 539 (Alta. C.A.).

38 *Vanguard Coatings & Chemicals Ltd. v. M.N.R.*, [1986] 2 C.T.C. 431 (F.C.T.D.).

39 *Re W.C.B., N.S. and Coastal Rentals, Sales & Service Ltd.* (1983), 12 D.L.R. (4th) 564 (N.S.T.D.).

40 *Montreal Lithographing Ltd. v. Dep. M.N.R. (Customs and Excise)* (1983), 8 C.R.R. 299 (F.C.T.D.), additional reasons at [1984] 2 F.C. 22 at 24.

41 *Jim Pattison Industries Ltd. v. R.; Mediacom Industries Ltd. v. R.* (1984), 3 C.P.R. (3d) 9 (F.C.T.D.).

42 *Re Church of Scientology and R. (No. 6); Re Walsh and R.* (1985), 21 C.C.C. (3d) 147 (Ont. H.C.), aff'd (1987), 31 C.C.C. (3d) 449 (Ont. C.A.). See also *Bertram S. Miller Ltd. v. R.* (1986), 28 C.C.C. (3d) 263 (F.C.A.), leave to appeal refused (1986), 75 N.R. 158n (S.C.C.). In *Nightingale Galleries Ltd. v. Director of Theatres Branch, supra,* note 30 at 405, our interpretation of the concept of seizure, which applies to a confiscation of articles in the course of an investigative process, even if this confiscation occurs without any violation of privacy, is expressly adopted.

the nature and importance of the crime involved, the manner in which
an operation is carried out, its repetition, the presence of reasonable grounds
for believing that one will find what is sought, the nature of the place
to be searched and of the objects that one hopes to discover.

Before examining questions of this nature, however, an issue of
principle must be determined: does section 8 require a warrant or a prior
authorization or does it merely set out a requirement of "reasonableness",
of which the warrant would constitute one possible criterion, albeit an
important one?

(i) *Prior authorization and "reasonableness"*

As section 8 does not specifically refer to warrants, it could have
been argued that the existence of a warrant was only one possible criterion
for determining the reasonableness of a search or of a seizure.[43] However,
the Supreme Court of Canada, in the case of *Hunter v. Southam Inc.*, [44]
seems to have gone beyond this position, conceding an even greater
importance to warrants. The case dealt with the compatibility with section
8 of a search which had been authorized under the *Combines Investigation
Act*.[44a] Writing for the Court, Mr. Justice Dickson (as he then was), stated
that:

> That purpose [of section 8] is, as I have said, to protect individuals from
> unjustified state intrusions upon their privacy. That purpose requires a means
> of *preventing* unjustified searches before they happen, not simply of deter-
> mining, after the fact, whether they ought to have occurred in the first place.
> This, in my view, can only be accomplished by a system of *prior authorization*,
> not one of subsequent validation.[45]

He adds further:

> "I recognize that it may not be reasonable in every instance to insist on prior
> authorization in order to validate governmental intrusions upon individuals'
> expectations of privacy. Nevertheless, where it is feasible to obtain prior
> authorization, I would hold that such authorization is a precondition for a
> valid search and seizure . . . and would require the party seeking to justify
> a warrantless search to rebut this presumption of unreasonableness".[46]

---

43 See the very thorough notes of Mr. Justice Martin in *R. v. Rao* (1984), 12 C.C.C. (3d)
    97 (Ont. C.A.).
44 *Supra*, note 1.
44a R.S.C. 1970, c. C-23.
45 *Ibid*, at 160.
46 *Ibid.*, at 161.

This prior authorization, moreover, must be obtained from a "neutral and impartial" person, "capable of acting judicially"[47] and on the basis of "reasonable and probable grounds, established upon oath, to believe that an offence has been committed and that there is evidence to be found at the place of the search . . . [such reasonable and probable grounds constituting] the minimum standard, consistent with s. 8 of the *Charter*, for authorizing search and seizure."[48]

These requirements are substantially those prescribed by what could be termed the law of the land concerning searches, that are set out in sections 443 [487] *et seq.* of the *Criminal Code.* As a result of their being accorded constitutional status, any statute or action which violates these rules becomes unreasonable under the terms of section 8. This will be the case when a judge, without further inquiry, merely subscribes to allegations which are presented to him,[49] when the ground alleged are insufficient[50] or when the offence or the section sought are not specified.[51]

The *Hunter* case having declared the standards it set out to be minimum requirements, the question arises as to whether any breach of legal rules in the obtaining or the execution of the warrant automatically entails a violation of section 8. The answer would appear to be "no". A technical

---

47 *Ibid.*, at 162.
48 *Ibid.*, at 168. There is reason to believe that the new procedure of telephone warrants satisfied these requirements. On the *Hunter* case, see D.F. Dawson, "Unreasonable Search and Seizure: A Comment on the Supreme Court of Canada Judgment in *Hunter v. Southam Inc.*" (1985), 27 *C.L.Q.* 450; N. Finkelstein, "Constitution Law - Search and Seizure After Southam" (1985), 63 *Can. Bar Rev.* 178; Rosenberg, *supra*, note 26; R.S. Russel & D.R. O'Connor, "Search and Seizure Powers in the Aftermath of Southam" (1985), 2 *Business and Law* 68; K.E. Thomson, "Limiting the Search and Seizure Powers of Combines Investigators: the Southam Decision and its Aftermath" (1985), 10 *Can. Bus. LJ.* 55. For an overview of s. 8, written at the time of its adoption, see M.R. Dambrot, "Section 8 of the Canadian Charter of Rights and Freedoms" (1982), 26 C.R. (3d) 97.
49 *R. v. Moran* (1987), 36 C.C.C. (3d) 225 (Ont. C.A.); *Re Trudeau and R.* (1982), 1 C.C.C. (3d) 342 (Qué. S.C.); *Re Vella and R.* (1984), 14 C.C.C. (3d) 513 (Ont. H.C.) (with respect to s. 181 of the *Criminal Code*).)
50 *R. v. Dombrowski* (1985), 18 C.C.C. (3d) 164 (Sask. C.A.); *R. v. Rowbotham* (1984), 13 W.C.B. 105 (Ont. H.C.).
51 *R. v. Dombrowski, ibid; R. v. Guiller* (1985), 14 W.C.B. 258 (Ont. Dist. Ct.); *Re Gillis and R.* (1982), 1 C.C.C. (3d) 545 (Qué. S.C.); *R. v. Caron* (1982), 3 C.R.R. 275 (Ont. Dist. Ct.); *Re Trudeau and R., supra*, note 49. On the total process of the issue of a search warrant, see *P.G. Québec v. Mathieu,* [1986] R.J.Q. 790 (Qué. C.A.).

breach[52] or one that is removed and indirect[53] would not have this effect. However, necessary recourse to force or execution of the warrant after its expiry would constitute a violation.[54] Nonetheless, as stated by Mr. Justice Martin of the Ontario Court of Appeal, "generally speaking, conformity to law would seem to be an essential component of reasonableness."[55] It is to be noted that the powers granted by the legislature in this area are to be strictly construed. Thus, the Supreme Court has held that an ordinary warrant to seize firearms does not authorize the police to conduct a search of a person's domicile and that the latter could lawfully resist.[56]

In light of the *Hunter v. Southam* criteria, summarized above, what is the situation with respect to electronic surveillance and the opening of mail? In the absence of all regulation, and even if such practices in no way amounted to an offence under any law, they would constitute unreasonable conduct clearly contrary to section 8, so directly do such practices violate the privacy of the individual. But as clear as this appears to us, it seems equally clear that the exceptional procedure for the interception of private communications written into the *Criminal Code* some years ago satisfies the demands of "reasonability" under section 8. It is not our purpose to describe this procedure in detail,[57] but among the factors warranting this conclusion one may point to the fact that the procedure is ordinarily commenced with an application by the Solicitor General or the Attorney General for judicial authorization, it is limited in terms of duration and type of offence and it is conceived of as a measure

---

52 *R. v. Christiansen* (1983), 6 C.C.C. (3d) 448 (N.S. C.A.) (on the absence of any mention of the policeman's name); *R. v. Cameron* (1984), 16 C.C.C. (3d) 240 (B.C. C.A.) (on the absence of narcotics at the place indicated at the time of the issue of a warrant); *R. v. Harris & Lighthouse Video Centres Ltd.* (1987), 35 C.C.C. (3d) 1 (Ont. C.A.); leave to appeal to S.C.C. refused (1987), 38 C.C.C. (3d) vi (Note) (S.C.C.);*R. v. Capson* (1985), 13 W.C.B. 272 (B.C. Co. Ct.) (on the absence of a signature). On errors in the address: *R. v. Kevany* (1982), 1 C.C.C. (3d) 157 (B.C. C.A.). On the possibility for the police officer named in the warrant to have assistance: *R. v. Fekete* (1985), 17 C.C.C. (3d) 188 (Ont. C.A.).

53 *R. v. Haley* (1986), 27 C.C.C. (3d) 454 (Ont. C.A.).

54 *Re McGregor and R.* (1985), 23 C.C.C. (3d) 266 (Man. Q.B.); compare with *R. v. Rowbotham, supra*, note 50, where the violence was held to be justified. On the expiry of the warrant: *R. v. Moran, supra*, note 49.

55 *R. v. Noble* (1984), 16 C.C.C. (3d) 146 at 173 (Ont. C.A.).

56 *Colet v. R., supra*, note 20. The case was decided before the Charter.

57 See in particular the detailed analysis of D.A. Bellemare, *L'écoute électronique au Canada* (Montréal: Yvon Blais, 1981), which analyses Part IV.I [V] of the *Criminal Code*. See also N. MacDonald, "Electronic Surveillance in Crime Detention: An Analysis of Canadian Wiretapping Law" (1986-87), 10 *Dalhousie L.J.* 3-141.

of last resort.[58] The same principle probably applies to opening mail: such conduct may be reasonable, provided it is done in accordance with a procedure of the sort just considered and incorporating as extensive safeguards.

As we have seen, the *Hunter v. Southam* case raised prior authorization, "where it is feasible to obtain [it]", to the rank of a constitutional standard and has imposed on the party seeking to make use of a warrantless search the onus of establishing that such search was not unreasonable. In this perspective, let us now study warrantless searches and seizures.

(ii) *Warrantless searches and seizures*

Let us begin with the writ of assistance, which has historically been authorized under four federal Acts.[59] The writ is a general warrant which the Court is obliged to issue without any obligation on the part of the applicant to allege facts of any sort, that need not be tied to the suspected commission of a particular offence, that remains in force for an indefinite period and that can be used to carry out an unlimited number of operations. It is clear that such a procedure, which may, moreover, be used to enter a private residence at any time, is incompatible with section 8 of the Charter.[60]

Personal searches are authorized by Canadian law on arrested persons as an incident of the arrest, and there is no reason to believe that section 8 will make this illegal. If necessary, the person arrested may be ordered to strip,[61] but rectal or vaginal searches[62] or the administration of a emetic[63] should only occur in a case of extreme necessity and under medical control.

---

58 See, to this effect, *R. v. Finlay, supra*, note 10. It will become unreasonable if legislative and constitutional requirements are not complied with at the time when it is used. See *R. v. Whitley; R. v. Hunter* (1987), 34 C.C.C. (3d) 529 (Ont. H.C.), leave to appeal to S.C.C. refused (1987), 34 C.C.C. (3d) 529n (S.C.C.); *R. v. Arviv* (1987), 37 C.C.C. (3d) 369 (Ont. H.C.).

59 This procedure was dealt with at length in the corresponding chapter of the first edition of this book (p. 303-305). The sections of the *Narcotic Control Act*, R.S.C. 1970, c. N-1 [R.S.C. 1985, c. N-1] the *Food and Drugs Act*, R.S.C. 1970, c. F-27 [R.S.C. 1985, c. F-27], the *Customs Act*, R.S.C. 1970, c. C-40 [repealed; see now S.C. 1986, c.1] and the *Excise Act*, R.S.C. 1970, c. E-12 [R.S.C. 1985, c. E-14], providing for writs of assistance, were repealed by ss. 190, 191, 196 and 200 of the *Criminal Law Amendment Act, 1985*, S.C. 1985, c. 19.

60 See to this effect, *R. v. Noble, supra*, note 55. The writs were presumed in violation of s. 8, in the absence of any evidence to the contrary by the Crown, in *R. v. Sieben*, [1987] 1 S.C.R. 295 and *R. v. Hamill*, [1987] 1 S.C.R. 301.

61 *R. v. Morrison* (1987), 35 C.C.C. (3d) 437 (Ont. C.A.).

62 *R. v. McCready* (1982), 9 W.C.B. 109 (B.C. Prov. Ct.).

63 *R. v. Meikle* (April 29, 1983) (Ont. Co. Ct.).

When justified, the taking of a sample of hair from the arrested person is not an unreasonable requirement.[64] Search as an incident to arrest, which may occur after the arrest[65] or a short time before,[66] may encompass also the immediate environment of the arrested person — not his entire house but, for instance, his hotel room.[67] A citizen may make an arrest, although it is doubtful whether he may search the person he has arrested to find evidence of an offence.[68]

A number of statutes provide for searches without warrant, and often grant exceptional powers with respect to personal searches. Thus, section 99 [101] of the *Criminal Code* permits a peace officer who has reasonable grounds to believe that an offence relating to a weapon has been committed to search without warrant any person, vehicle or place other than a dwelling-house and to seize anything related to the offence. Once seized, these things are disposed of in conformity with sections 446 [490] and 446.1 [491]. In the case of illegal possession of firearms, section 100 [102] also authorizes seizure without a warrant and stipulates special rules for the restoration or forfeiture of seized arms. Like section 99 [101], section 101 [103] permits a peace officer to search, in this case anywhere, and to seize any weapon or other dangerous thing in order to protect the safety of the possessor or other persons. He may do so without a warrant when it would be impracticable to first apply to a provincial court judge. Property seized under this section is brought before a provincial court judge to whom the officer must justify his search. Section 101 [103] also regulates the terms of restoration, sale and orders prohibiting possession, all of which are subject to judicial control.

The *Narcotic Control Act*[69] also permits a peace officer on reasonable grounds to enter and search, without a warrant, at any time in any place other than a dwelling-house, to search any person found in the place and to seize anything related to an offence, including a vehicle or other conveyance. The *Food and Drugs Act*[70] grants powers of the same kind, although the powers of seizure are limited to drugs or things that may be evidence of an offence. These two Acts establish a procedure under which a person may apply to a provincial court judge for a restoration order and, in the event of a conviction, provide for the automatic forfeiture of the prohibited product, any money used for the purchase of a prohibited

---

64 *R. v. Alderton* (1985), 17 C.C.C. (3d) 204 (Ont. C.A.).
65 *R. v. Miller* (1987), 62 O.R. (2d) 97 (C.A.).
66 *R. v. Debot* (1986), 30 C.C.C. (3d) 207 (Ont. C.A.).
67 Compare *R. v. Rex* (1983), 8 C.R.R. 170 (B.C. Co. Ct.) with *R. v. Wong, supra*, note 10.
68 *R. v. Lerke, supra*, note 18.
69 *Supra*, note 59, ss. 10 [10] and 11 [17].
70 *Supra*, note 59, s. 37 [ss. 24, 25, 26, 27, 42-44].

product and, in the case of a narcotic, any apparatus used in the commission of the offence. The forfeiture under the *Narcotic Control Act* of a conveyance belonging to a third party may appear unreasonable; however, in addition to the fact that such a forfeiture is not automatic and may occur only at the request of the Crown, the Act provides a procedure by which an innocent third party may oppose the forfeiture and these measures appear to safeguard the property rights of the latter in a satisfactory manner. Finally, we may note that under the *Customs Act*[71] an officer may, if there are reasonable grounds, search any vessel or vehicle, search any person found therein and seize anything so discovered. The *Excise Act*,[72] for its part, gives any officer the right to enter at any time, even by force, any building or place used to carry out a trade or a business subject to excise, other than a dwelling-house, in order to make an inspection.

Are these different procedures to search without warrant, often accompanied by a right to search the person, unreasonable? In the perspective of the criteria of the *Hunter* case, section 101 [103] of the *Criminal Code* would appear to conform with section 8 because section 101 [103] is justified on the grounds of physical safety and it grants the power to search only when it is impracticable to first apply to a provincial court judge. Somewhat akin to administrative inspections, the searches authorized under the provisions, summarized above, of the *Customs Act* and the *Excise Act*, as we shall see, might also be reconcilable. As for warrantless searches for the purpose of discovering drugs, narcotic and weapons, though limited to places other than dwelling-houses, they clearly create difficulties in connection with section 8.[73] The latter section charges the Crown, once it is proved that a warrantless search has taken place, with the onus of establishing that the search was reasonable.[74] Case law will probably adopt an approach based on the weighing of all the circumstances rather than a rule of systematic invalidation of all powers of search and seizure without warrant. In any event, section 8 should at least serve to require the reversal of certain judicial decisions and certain applications by the police of the relevant provisions of the *Food and Drugs*

---

71 *Supra*, note 59, ss. 133 and 143.

72 *Supra*, note 59, ss. 70 [72] and 71 [73].

73 *R. v. Rao, supra*, note 43, where it was held, in the case of narcotics, that the power could only be exercised in an urgent situation where it was impossible to obtain a warrant, in the search of a vehicle and in a search incident to an arrest. See also *R. v. Singh* (1983), 8 C.C.C. (3d) 38 (Ont. C.A.), where it was held that s. 99 was correctly applied. See also *R. v. Rowbotham, supra*, note 50, where s. 10(1)(c) of the *Narcotic Control Act* was held not to operate to the extent that it authorized the seizure of articles other than narcotics.

74 Stated in the *Hunter* decision, *supra*, note 1 at 161 and restated in *Collins v. R.*, [1987] 1 S.C.R. 265 at 278.

Act and the *Narcotic Control Act.* For example, it has been held that the words "any place" in section 10(1) [ss.10 and 11] of the *Narcotic Control Act,* indicating where a peace officer may conduct a search, including a search of persons, includes a highway or a street.[75] This construction, to the extent it allows policement to search pedestrians in the street, for the purpose of discovering drugs on them, on the basis probably of their physical appearance, authorizes searches that are clearly unreasonable; such a power appears directly contrary to the guarantee of section 8. Similarly, repeated searches of a particular place, such as a tavern or discotheque, even though each search appears proper when examined separately, may in some cases amount to harassment, so harmful to the reputation of the establishment in question that one could fairly call this practice unreasonable.

It is apparent that not only the express provisions of the law, but also, and perhaps even especially, their application and the practices flowing from them, can be attacked by virtue of section 8. In this area particularly considerable finesse will be required. Where a practice or course of conduct on which statute law is silent has been judged reasonable and proper by the courts and in conformity with the common law, it may be difficult for them to now declare that the practice or conduct is unreasonable, thereby acknowledging the unreasonableness of a judge-made law. Take, for example, the case of *Eccles v. Bourque,*[76] where the Supreme Court decided that policemen, with reasonable grounds to believe that a person who may be arrested is at the apartment of a friend, have the right to enter that apartment even by force, after seeking admission in the usual way. It may be difficult to judge this case of warrantless search, so to speak, unreasonable under section 8, even though one would wish that the rules governing the search of "things" would apply equally to the search of "persons", save in the context of a "fresh pursuit" where no warrant would be required.[77]

In summary then, it might be said that of all the provisions examined above, those creating the most serious difficulties are the provisions of

---

75 *R. v. Hamilton* (1978), 7 B.C.L.R. 146 (B.C. Co. Ct.); *R. v. Morrison* (1983), 6 C.C.C. (3d) 256 (B.C. Co. Ct.), aff'd (1984), 15 C.C.C. (3d) 415 (B.C. C.A.); *R. v. Marceau* (1987), 2 W.C.B. (2d) 165 (B.C. Co. Ct.). In the two latter cases, s. 8 did not prevent the Court from adopting this interpretation. See *contra R. v. Tyrell* (1982), 8 W.C.B. 476 (Ont. Prov. Ct.); *R. v. Stevens* (1983), 7 C.C.C. (3d) 260 (N.S. C.A.).

76 [1975] 2 S.C.R. 739.

77 In support of this view, see the case comment on *Eccles* by J. Manley, "Criminal Law: Powers of Police to Search Private House for Wanted Person" (1975), 7 *Ottawa L. Rev.* 649. See also the analysis of W.F. Foster and J.E. Magnet, "The Law of Forcible Entry" (1977), 15 *Alta. L. Rev.* 271.

the *Narcotic Control Act* and *Food and Drugs Act,* which authorize warrantless searches and searches of persons outside a dwelling-house.

By way of conclusion, we should say a few words on certain police practices. We have up to this point especially emphasized the fact that the purpose of section 8 is to protect the privacy of the individual. This is obviously not the only purpose of the section and to privacy must be added in particular the security of the person and his property. There is no need to demonstrate at length that an officer who, in the course of searching a dwelling-house, offers gratuitous violence to the occupant and ransacks his possessions, is guilty of unreasonable conduct. We have also pointed out above that repeated searches of a place can be unreasonable. But it is perhaps chiefly searches of the person that give rise to difficulties here. As we have seen, one may search a person who has been arrested — one may even unclothe him if necessary — and one may also conduct a search of persons under the authority of certain statutes, such as the *Narcotic Control Act.* But the taking without warrant of a blood sample on an unconscious or unconsenting person is clearly an unreasonable search,[78] while the taking of fingerprints or a sample of breath, legally done, are not.[79]

Before the adoption of the Charter, it had been held that a policeman could use force to inspect the mouth of an individual suspected of possessing narcotics,[80] or could squeeze his throat to prevent him from swallowing.[81] It was also held that a policeman can subject a person whom he has arrested to a rectal search conducted by a doctor where there are reasonable grounds to believe that he has hidden capsules of heroin in his anus.[82] However, as indicated above, the Superior Court of Québec prohibited the issue of a search warrant authorizing recovery of a bullet from the shoulder of an accused, while refusing to pass judgment on the question whether minor

---

78 *R. v. Pohoretsky, supra,* note 6; *R. v. DeCoste* (1983), 60 N.S.R. (2d) 170 (T.D.); *R. v. Dyment* (1986), 25 C.C.C. (3d) 120 (P.E.I. C.A.); aff'd (December 8, 1988) (S.C.C.); see *contra: R. v. Myers* (1984), 14 C.C.C. (3d) 82 (P.E.I. C.A.). The seizure, under warrant, of a blood sample already taken for medical purposes was, however, held not to violate s. 8. See *R. v. Carter* (1982), 2 C.C.C. (3d) 412 (Ont. C.A.). In *R. v. L.A.R.* (1985), 18 C.C.C. (3d) 104 (Man. C.A.), rev'd (*sub nom. R. v. Pohoretsky*), *supra,* note 6, the seizure of a sample of urine was also held to be valid. The procedure of taking a blood sample under a warrant in the case of impaired driving (240 [256] of the *Criminal Code*) is probably compatible with s. 8: see *R. v. Mara* (1985), 42 M.V.R. 171 (B.C. Co. Ct.). Nor does the taking of a blood sample in a civil paternity suit offend s. 8: see *Re N and D* (1985), 13 C.R.R. 26 (Ont. Fam. Ct.).

79 See *supra,* note 19. On breath samples, see *R. v. Holman* (1982), 28 C.R. (3d) 378 (B.C. Prov. Ct.).

80 *R. v. Brezack* (1949), 96 C.C.C. 97 (Ont. C.A.).

81 *Scott v. R.* (1975), 24 C.C.C. (2d) 261 (F.C.C.A.).

82 *Reynen v. Antonenko* (1975), 20 C.C.C. (2d) 342 (Alta T.D.).

interventions such as taking a blood sample or an X-ray are permissible under the general law of searches.[83]

What is the situation since the coming into force of section 8? Squeezing the throat of an individual is not necessarily an unreasonable practice when there are serious grounds to believe that narcotics will be found.[84] Nor is the search, in the proper context, of persons wishing to attend a public event such as a concert or an inquiry.[85] However, there is good reason to believe that any procedure involving a risk, however small, to the health or physical integrity of the person, as would be the case in nearly every type of surgical operation, would be judged unreasonable. Less dangerous procedures such as enemas, intubations, rectal or vaginal searches should be possible only under medical supervision and on reasonable grounds. The criterion of health is certainly not the only criterion for assessing the unreasonableness of searches; it is likely that the dignity of the person will count for something as well.

As one of the cases reminds us, "legislation authorizing a warrantless seizure which directly infringes upon a guaranteed freedom provided by the Charter must be subjected to a more rigorous test of reasonableness than other such seizures."[86] Applicable to legislation, this observation is even more pertinent with respect to certain practices which are not clearly authorized by statute.

The requirement set out in the *Hunter* decision,[87] according to which a warrant, when obtainable, is a prior condition to the validity of a search or seizure, has been criticized by one commentator as being both too liberal — some searches are unjustifiable without a warrant even when the latter is unobtainable — and too narrow because certain warrantless searches are not unreasonable, there being no "significant privacy interest at stake".[88] This would be the case with regard to searches carried out with the consent of the person or owner of the premises being searched and with regard to the seizure of articles in plain view.

---

83 *Re Laporte and R. supra*, note 5.

84 *R. v. Collins, supra*, note 74. On this point, see also *R. v. Cohen* (1983), 5 C.C.C. (3d) 156 (B.C. C.A.); *R. v. Maclean* (1982), 9 W.C.B. 109 (B.C. Prov. Ct.).

85 *R. v. Heisler* (1984), 11 C.C.C. (3d) 475 (Alta C.A.); *R. v. Roy* (1985), 25 C.C.C. (3d) 473 (Ont. H.C.); *Re McKeown and Law Society of Upper Can.* (1986), 18 O.A.C. 19 (Ont. Div. Ct.).

86 *Nightingale Galleries Ltd. v. Director of Theatres Branch, supra*, note 30 at 409. The case dealt with the seizure without warrant of films and film equipment, which was held unreasonable.

87 *Supra*, note 1.

88 Rosenberg, *supra*, note 26 at 284.

(iii) *Search with consent and seizure of articles in plain view*

Privacy of the person and privacy of the personal environment are not the only values protected by section 8.[89] However, when these values are in issue, it is accepted that the claimant of the right must have had a reasonable expectation of privacy. It is also accepted that this requirement is both subjective — the person must believe that the situation is one of privacy — and objective. The latter aspect means that persons, no matter how deprived and lacking any expectation to privacy, must nonetheless be protected while, on the other hand, those whose subjective expectations are unreasonable or irrational must not be. This requires striking a most delicate balance.

In this light, it was held that a person freely opening his door to the police, even when the latter are acting without a warrant, loses the benefit of section 8. Once the police have entered, they are entitled to seize illegal articles or material evidence which is in plain view.[90] The consent must be real, which is not the case when police officers stop a person on the street, even when there is no resistance, and tell that person that they are authorized under law to search him.[91] It has been held that, although there must be no violence, the prosecution was not required to establish that the individual was aware of his right to refuse to be searched.[92] A group of individuals indulging in gaming in a hotel room rented by one of the group does not have any expectation of privacy with respect to a hidden video camera.[93] An individual in a toilet booth obviously has such an expectation.[94] The absence of an expectation of privacy and the risk inherent in speaking to someone were invoked as grounds to validate a provision of the *Criminal Code* which authorizes the interception of telephone communications when one of the speakers consents.[95] It is to be observed that consent is not the only justification for these rules. Articles in plain view may be seized after a forced entry has been legally authorized even if the authorization did not,

---

89 See, *e.g.*, *Nightingale Galleries Ltd. v. Director of Theatres Branch, supra*, note 30.

90 *R. v. Wirth* (1982), 9 W.C.B. 74 (Sask. Prov. Ct.); *R. v. Longtin* (1983), 5 C.C.C. (3d) 12 (Ont. C.A.); *R. v. Sheppard* (1984), 11 C.C.C. (3d) 276 (Nfld. C.A.); *Laforest v. Paradis*, [1987] R.J.Q. 364 (Qué. S.C.). With respect to the seizure of articles abandoned or disposed of as waste, see *R. v. Taylor* (January 26, 1984) (B.C. S.C.).

91 *R. v. Gaudet* (1987), 29 C.R.R. 288 (P.E.I. S.C.).

92 *R. v. Good* (1983), 11 W.C.B. 228 (B.C. Co. Ct.).

93 *R. v. Wong, supra*, note 10. See, however, *Asencios v. R.*, [1987] R.J.Q. 540 (Qué. C.A.).

94 *R. v. Lofthouse, supra*, note 10; see, however, the curious case of *R. v. O'Flaherty* (1986), 35 C.C.C. (3d) 33 (Nfld. C.A.).

95 *R. v. Sanelli, supra*, note 28.

at the outset, include any such right to seize.[96]

Canadian law dealing with the concept of consent and with seizure of articles in plain view is in its first stages of development and requires a considerably greater degree of articulation.

(iv) *Administrative searches and seizures*

That such a concept exists is obvious by comparison between the inspection for reasons of health and hygiene of premises where food products are found and searches in the context of an investigation of a murder. Obviously, the objectives are not the same. In administrative matters — even acknowledging the difficulty of defining such a category — the expectation of privacy is low, random sampling is more relevant than searching on the basis of reasonable and probable grounds and seizures or confiscations for long periods of time can cause much inconvenience. The necessity thus exists to develop original constitutional standards in this area and to adopt a slightly different interpretation of section 8.[97] Any retreat from the standards, analyzed above, established by the *Hunter* decision would require a justification conforming to the requirements of that case.

A number of appeal courts have validated warrantless inspections — often stating that they did not occur in homes — as well as forced production of documents in areas such as control of fisheries,[98] discrimination in

---

96 *Re R. and Shea* (1982), 1 C.C.C. (3d) 316 (Ont. H.C.); *R. v. Rowbotham, supra,* note 50.

97 See, in particular, A.D. Reid & A.H. Young, "Administrative Search and Seizure under the Charter" (1985), 10 *Queen's L.J.* 392; Y. Ouellette, "La Charte canadienne et les tribunaux administratifs" (1984), 18 *R.J.T.* 295; A.J. Roman, "The Possible Impact of the Canadian Charter of Rights and Freedoms on Administrative Law" (1985), 26 *C. de D.* 339. Concerning the establishment of different criteria and the lowering of requirements when national security, in particular, is at stake, see *R. v. Harris & Lighthouse Video Centres Ltd., supra,* note 52. Developing original standards is a much better solution than stating, against all evidence, that the procedure is not covered by s. 8. As an example, see *Re Cole and F.W. Woolworth Co.* (1985), 22 D.L.R. (4th) 609 (Sask. Q.B.), where it was stated that a search, under the authority of the *Saskatchewan Human Right Code,* did not fall within the scope of s. 8!

98 *Re Milton and R.* (1986), 32 C.C.C. (3d) 159 (B.C. C.A.). See also *R. v. Burton* (1983), 7 C.C.C. (3d) 87 (Nfld. C.A.); *R. v. Sewid* (1986), 1 W.C.B. (2d) 319 (B.C. Co. Ct.); *R. v. Gibson* (February 2, 1984) (B.C. Co. Ct.) (where it was held that boats and fishing equipment had been unreasonably seized). In *R. v. Legacy* (1984), 17 C.C.C. (3d) 352 (N.B. Q.B.), an administrative inspection was held unreasonable in the case of residences.

employment,[99] game protection laws,[100] work standards,[101] pesticides,[102] zoning control[103] and racing.[104] The practice was however held to be unreasonable in the case of a physician's files.[105]

Inspections without warrant were also authorized in the area of mail services,[106] in houses where fires had occurred,[107] and in licensed drinking establishments.[108] Compulsory disclosure of information for statistical purposes was held not unreasonable,[109] nor were searches and seizures related to immigration.[110] However, standards relating to commercial practices were considered penal rather than administrative in nature, hence a warrant was necessary in order to enter premises and consult documents.[111]

---

99 *Re Alta. Human Rights Comm. and Alta. Blue Cross Plan, supra,* note 33, where interesting criteria are articulated.

100 *R. v. Sheppard, supra,* note 90, where was considered that a warrant was necessary to enter residences.

101 *Re Belgoma Transportation Ltd. and Director of Employment Standards* (1985), 51 O.R. (2d) 509 (Ont. C.A.), where it was observed that the Act made the possession of a warrant a condition to enter residences. The case emphasizes the distinction between a search in administrative matters and one in criminal matters. See also *R. v. Quesnel* (1985), 24 C.C.C. (3d) 78 (Ont. C.A.), leave to appeal to S.C.C. refused (1986), 55 O.R. (2d) 543n (S.C.C.), concerning farm products, where search and inspection is distinguished.

102 *Bertram S. Miller Ltd. v. R., supra,* note 42.

103 *R. v. Bichel* (1986), 29 C.C.C. (3d) 438 (B.C. C.A.); but see *Re Yorkville North Development Ltd. and North York (City)* (1986), 57 O.R. (2d) 172 (Ont. Dist. Ct.), appeal quashed at (1988), 64 O.R. (2d) 225 (C.A.).

104 *Re Ozubko and Man. Horse Racing Comm.* (1986), 33 D.L.R. (4th) 714 (Man. C.A.), leave to appeal to S.C.C. refused (1987), 50 Man. R. (2d) 79n (S.C.C.).

105 *Bishop v. College of Physicians & Surgeons of B.C., supra,* note 33; *Re Reich and College of Physicians & Surgeons of Alta. (No. 2)* (1984), 8 D.L.R. (4th) 696 (Alta. Q.B.); *Charbonneau v. College of Physicians & Surgeons of Ont.* (1985), 22 D.L.R. (4th) 303 (Ont. H.C.).

106 *C.U.P.W., Calgary Loc. 710 v. Can. Post Corp.* (1987), 40 D.L.R. (4th) 67 (Alta. Q.B.).

107 *R. v. Desmarais,* December 20, 1983 (Man. Prov. Ct.); *R. v. Mehdi* (1984), 65 N.S.R. (2d) 389 (N.S. Co. Ct.).

108 *R. v. Fourteen Twenty-Five Management Ltd.* (1984), 10 C.R.R. 181 (Sask. Prov. Ct.). But see *R. v. Hartmann* (1985), 20 C.R.R. 313 (Sask. Prov. Ct.) rev'd (1987), 65 Sask. R. 255 (Q.B.); and *R. v. Kaizer* (1985), 70 N.S.R. (2d) 125 (N.S. Prov. Ct.), where reasonable grounds were emphasized.

109 *R. v. Holman* (1983), 28 Alta L.R. (2d) 35 (Prov. Ct.).

110 *Nunes v. Min. of Employment & Immigration (Can.),* [1986] 3 F.C. 112 (C.A.). Concerning the seizure of devices under the *Weights and Measures Act,* see *R. v. Halpert* (1984), 15 C.C.C. (3d) 292 (Ont. Co. Ct.).

111 *Re Ont. Chrysler (1977) Ltd. v. Rush* (1987), 59 O.R. (2d) 725 (Ont. H.C.). The *Hunter* decision, *supra,* note 1, also considered combines law as criminal in nature.

What is the situation as regards tax laws? If, according to the suggestion of two writers,[112] administrative searches are related to the idea of inspection and commerce, and the search under ordinary law is related to the concept of an investigation in the private domain, tax laws, applicable to all taxpayers, are closer to the second concept than to the first. Slight departures from the requirements of the ordinary law might be necessary, and the statement that "because of the extent and complexity of business affairs, made possible by modern technology and merchandising methods, it is impossible to define with exact precision the documents sought in cases involving fraud or tax evasion"[113] seems quite possible. But it appears difficult to consider reasonable the powers of the minister, in the enforcement of a tax statute, to require from any person the production of any thing.[114] Also, the power of the minister, when it appears in the course of an audit that an offence might have been committed, to enter any premises and seize any article which might serve as evidence of any offence in the statute[115] is questionable under section 8. Similar powers were held unreasonable on the grounds that the search could relate to any offence in the statute even though there were only reasonable grounds to believe in the commission of a specific offence,[116] and on wider grounds, because the decision was not taken by an independent arbiter.[117] Other decisions in the area of tax have held that detention of goods or property until tax had been paid did not contravene section 8[118] and that the detention of

---

112 Reid & Young, *supra*, note 97 at 427.

113 *Print Three Inc. v. R.* (1985), 51 O.R. (2d) 321 at 326 (C.A.), leave to appeal to S.C.C. refused (1985), 53 O.R. (2d) 319 (headnote) (S.C.C.).

114 This was the effect of s. 231(3) of the *Income Tax Act*, S.C. 1970-71-72, c. 63, which was held to be of no effect in *R. v. McKinlay Transport Ltd. and C.T. Transport Inc.*, [1986] C.T.C. 29 (Ont. Prov. Ct.), rev'd (1987), 32 C.C.C. (3d) 1 (H.C.), aff'd 40 C.C.C. (3d) 94 (Ont. C.A.), leave to appeal to S.C.C. granted (1988), 64 O.R. (2d) ix (note) (S.C.C.); *R. v. Marcoux*, [1985] 2 C.T.C. 254 (Alta. Prov. Ct.) and *R. v. Oldfield*, [1986] 1 C.T.C. 321 (B.C. Prov. Ct.), aff'd [1987] 3 W.W.R. 671 (B.C.C.A.), leave to appeal to S.C.C. refused [1987] 4 W.W.R. lxvii (note) S.C.C.). Section 231(3), s. 231(1)(d) and s. 231(4), mentioned in notes 115 and 116, *infra*, were amended by section 121 of the *Income Tax Act*, S.C. 1986, c. 6.

115 S. 231(1)(d) of the *Income Tax Act*, *supra*, note 114, was held to be valid in *Re New Garden Restaurant & Tavern Ltd. and M.N.R.* (1983), 1 D.L.R. (4th) 256 (Ont. H.C.), and was held to be of no effect in *R. v. Dzagic*, [1985] 1 C.T.C. 346 (Ont. H.C.), rev'd on other grounds [1986] 2 C.T.C. 288, aff'd [1988] 1 S.C.R. 669 (*sub nom. R. v. James*).

116 *M.N.R. v. Kruger Inc.* (1984), 13 D.L.R. (4th) 706 (F.C.C.A.), invalidating s. 231(4) of the *Income Tax Act*, *supra*, note 114.

117 *Print Three Inc. v. R.*, *supra*, note 113.

118 *Re McLeod and M.N.R.* (1983), 146 D.L.R. (3d) 561 (F.C.T.D.); *Canada v. Central Tobacco Mfg. (1980) Ltd.* (1985), 85 D.T.C. 5300 (F.C.T.D.). See also note 40, *supra*.

books or documents for a maximum period of 120 days was not unreasonable.[119]

(v) Vehicles, customs, prisons and other specific areas

Expectation of privacy is not as high in a vehicle as in a residence, to the point where, according to the Supreme Court, there is none at all and a person required by law to submit to a driver's licence or insurance card check does not benefit from the protection of section 8.[120] That is not to say that any warrantless search of a vehicle is allowed. Such a search must be authorized by statute, be based on reasonable and probable grounds of belief that products such as alcohol, tobacco, or narcotics will be found[121] and it was even argued that such a search can only take place in a context where it is not possible to obtain a warrant.[122] If an illegal article other than that which is the object of the search is in plain view, it can be seized.[123] It is clear that the search of a vehicle may be rendered unreasonable by the circumstances in which it occurs.[124] This was held not to be the case, however, when a vehicle was searched because of its presence in an area known to be frequented by drug traffickers or because of its strange comings and goings.[125] But the detention of a vehicle to ensure statutory compliance, without any possibility of establishing that the statute had not been

---

119 *M.N.R. v. Russell* (1984), 28 Man. R. (2d) 294 (Co. Ct.). See also *Thyssen Canada Ltd. v. R.*, [1984] 2 F.C. 27 (T.D.), rev'd 87 D.T.C. 5038 (F.C.C.A.), leave to appeal to S.C.C. refused (1987), 79 N.R. 400n (S.C.C.), which, surprisingly, states that the photocopy of documents in the course of a tax audit does not constitute a seizure. On the application of s. 8 in tax law, see H. Brun, "Le recouvrement de l'impôt et les droits de la personne" (1983), 24 *C. de D.* 457; G. Corn, "Illegal Search and Seizure and Application of Charter of Rights and Freedoms" (1986), *Can. Curr. Tax. J.* 123; A. St. Jean, "La jurisprudence et les pouvoirs de perquisition et de saisie des ministres du Revenu", [1985] 7 *R.P.F.S.* 139.

120 "In my opinion the demand by the police officer, pursuant to the above legislative provisions, that the appellant surrender his driver's licence and insurance card for inspection did not constitute a search within the meaning of s. 8 because it did not constitute an intrusion on a reasonable expectation of privacy." Justice Le Dain in *R. v. Hufsky*, [1988] 1 S.C.R. 621 at 638. See also *R. v. Doohan*, (1984), 28 M.V.R. 109 (Ont. P.C.).

121 *R. v. Annett* (1984), 17 C.C.C. (3d) 332 (Ont. C.A.) leave to appeal to S.C.C. refused (1985), 17 C.C.C. (3d) 332n (S.C.C.).

122 *R. v. Belliveau* (1986), 30 C.C.C. (3d) 163 (N.B.C.A.); *R. v. Debot* (1986), 30 C.C.C. (3d) 207 (Ont. C.A.).

123 *R. v. Annett, supra,* note 121; *R. v. Blackstock* (1983), 32 C.R. (3d) 91 (Sask. Prov. Ct.). In *R. v. Hebb* (1985), 17 C.C.C. (3d) 545 (N.S.C.A.), it was held that merely looking inside a vehicle did not constitute a search.

124 *R. v. Guberman* (1985), 23 C.C.C. (3d) 406 (Man. C.A.).

125 *R. v. Tulk* August 19, 1982 (N.S. Prov. Ct.); *R. v. Esau* (1983), 4 C.C.C. (3d) 530 (Man. C.A.).

breached, was held to be an unreasonable seizure.[126]

The expectation of privacy is quite limited also with respect to customs checks, to the point where a search carried out without any alleged grounds was held to be valid.[127] In another case, the *Hunter* criteria were applied strictly.[128] It seems clear that section 8 must, in these cases, be given a varied interpretation.[129] A search based only on physical appearance is unreasonable,[130] one based on grounds of suspicion — and not on grounds of belief — is possibly not unreasonable.[131] A justified search or one that is carried out with consent, which is often the case, does not create any problem,[132] nor does a search resulting from a person's incapacity to make an oral statement.[133] The discovery of narcotics in baggage justifies the search of the body of the owner of the baggage,[134] and it can be stated that the search of a package[135] is less problematic than that of persons.

The expectation of privacy is also diminished in prison. Such an expectation, however, must not be considered as nonexistent. The judgment of the Supreme Court in *Solosky v. R.*[136] quite probably passes, so to speak, the test of section 8. In that case, the court held that the mail of a detainee, including correspondence between himself and his lawyer, could be opened on the instructions of the institution in certain cases and for certain purposes. On the other hand, a systematic opening and reading of the mail of every detainee would not pass the test.[137] To this day, the case law appears to have been very sensitive to security requirements in prisons. Strip searches of prison visitors were authorized, provided there were reasonable grounds to believe that they were carrying contraband;[138] so

---

126 *Re. Rock Island Express Ltd. and P.U.C. Bd. (Nfld.)* (1986), 27 D.L.R. (4th) 89 (Nfld. T.D.).

127 *R. v. Jordan* (1984), 11 C.C.C. (3d) 565 (B.C.C.A.).

128 *R. v. Jagodic* (1985), 19 C.C.C. (3d) 305 (N.S.T.D.), However, all was held to be valid because of the impossibility of obtaining a warrant. This was affirmed by *R. v. Jagodic* (1986), 73 N.S.R. (2d) 342 (C.A.).

129 See F.C. O'Donell, "The Thin Blue Line: Customs Searches and the Charter of Rights" (1984), 16 *Ottawa L. Rev.* 467.

130 *R. v. Corinthian* (1983), 10 W.C.B. 9 (Ont. Prov. Ct.).

131 *R. v. Simmons* (1984), 11 C.C.C. (3d) 193 (Ont. C.A.).

132 *R. v. Gladstone* (1983), 10 W.C.B. 412 (B.C. Co. Ct.).

133 *R. v. Arroyo* (1983), 6 C.R.R. 115 (Ont. Co. Ct.).

134 *R. v. Thompson* (1984), 11 W.C.B. 410 (Ont. Co. Ct.), which refers to a common law power to search vested in the government by virtue of its control over its own borders.

135 *Schindler v. Dep. M.N.R. (Customs & Excise)* (1984), 12 C.R.R. 270 (F.C.C.A.).

136 [1980] 1 S.C.R. 821.

137 See *Henry v. R.*, [1987] 3 F.C. 429 (T.D.), (1987), which gave a narrow interpretation of the concept of privileged mail between a lawyer and an inmate.

138 *R. v. Greenwood* (1986), 16 W.C.B. 226 (B.C. Co. Ct.).

were those of inmates after they had had visitors.[139] Preventive (but not punitive) anal inspection of inmates, even without a requirement of reasonable grounds to believe in the presence of prohibited articles, was also held acceptable.[140] Also held acceptable without warrant and without specific grounds was the routine and general strip search of inmates, by persons of the same sex, provided that such searches were subject to norms concerning circumstances in which they could be conducted in order to avoid any abuses of discretion. Individual searches require grounds and authorization by a superior officer.[141]

Finally, it must be noted that school is also a place where expectations of privacy are diminished. Pupils are subject to the authority of the teachers who may, when there are grounds to do so, carry out limited searches.[142]

Once a law or a practice is found to be in violation of section 8, what judicial sanctions may follow? Under section 52 of the *Constitution Act, 1982*, a judge may declare the offending law inoperative and, under section 24(1), may grant an appropriate remedy. It is not our purpose to analyze these two provisions here. We rather wish to draw attention to the fact that section 8, of all the sections in the Charter, is the one inherently most likely to give rise to the application of section 24(2), stipulating the exclusion of evidence whose admissibility "would bring the administration of justice into disrepute". When section 8 is violated, the evidence has not simply been "obtained in a manner that infringe[s]" the section, but has been obtained by virtue of the very infringement itself. There is no necessary connection between, for instance, an act of arbitrary detention (section 9) or a violation of the right to retain and instruct counsel (section 10(b)) and the procurement of certain evidence. There is such a connection between the procurement of evidence and a violation of section 8. It is obviously not accidental that the American rule excluding illegally obtained evidence was first developed with reference to the Fourth Amendment.[143]

---

139 *Re Maltby and A.G. Saskatchewan* (1982), 2 C.C.C. (3d) 153 (Sask. Q.B.), aff'd (1984), 13 C.C.C. (3d) 308 (Sask. C.A.).

140 *Re Soenen and Thomas* (1983), 8 C.C.C. (3d) 224 (Alta. Q.B.).

141 *Weatherall v. A.G. Canada* (1987), 59 C.R. (3d) 247 (F.C.T.D.) rev'd in part (*sub nom. Weatherall v. Canada*) (1988), 65 C.R. (3d) 27 (F.C.C.A..).

142 *R. v. J.M.G.* (1986), 29 C.C.C. (3d) 455 (Ont. C.A.), leave to appeal to S.C.C. refused (1987), 59 O.R. (2d) 286n (S.C.C.) in which a school principal, in the belief that drugs were concealed, ordered a student's shoes and stockings to be removed. See A.W. MacKay, "Students as Second Class Citizens under the Charter" (1987), 54 C.R. (3d) 390.

143 See the comparative study by L.R. Katz, "Reflections on Search and Seizure and Illegally Seized Evidence in Canada and the United States" (1980), 3 *Can.-U.S. L.J.* 103. See also P.J. Connelly, "The Fourth Amendment and Section 8 of the Canadian Charter

Nor is it merely accidental that the provisions of the *Criminal Code* regulating electronic surveillance (section 178.16(2) [189(2)]) include important rules stipulating the inadmissibility of directly and indirectly obtained evidence where its "admission . . . would bring the administration of justice into disrepute", a test echoed in section 24(2) of the Charter.

The fact that evidence obtained in violation of section 8 is very often pre-existent — as opposed, for example, to a confession — and that the police, had they acted legally, could have made the use of it, should have no bearing on the issue. This should be an aggravating rather than a mitigating circumstance.

Given this close connection, one may well ask whether evidence obtained by means of conduct that is unreasonable within the meaning of section 8 is not in many cases evidence whose admission "would bring the administration of justice into disrepute". This standard, like the standard of unreasonableness, is difficult to define and we shall not attempt to do so. But what is still more difficult is to distinguish the one standard from the other. If it is abusive or unreasonable to search out a particular item of evidence, so that the search itself contravenes the supreme law of the land, it should not be easy to demonstrate that the use of this evidence in a trial does not bring the administration of justice into disrepute.

The relation between sections 1 and 8 of the Charter raises a similar problem. Can an unreasonable search under the terms of section 8 become reasonable in terms of section 1? Possibly so.[144] However, a varied interpretation of section 8 would, in our view, be preferable to a uniform interpretation, which would make it necessary to resort frequently to section 1.

2. PROTECTION AGAINST ARBITRARY DETENTION OR IMPRISONMENT

Section 9 provides:

Everyone has the right not to be arbitrarily detained or imprisoned.

This provision already appears in a slightly different form in section 2(a) of the *Canadian Bill of Rights*, which prohibits "the arbitrary detention, imprisonment or exile of any person", and one may notice that article

---

of Rights and Freedoms: What Has Been Done? What is to Be Done?" (1984-85), 27 *C.L.Q.* 182; G. Corn, "Legality of Search and Seizure and Application of the Charter of Rights and Freedoms as to Admissibility of Illegally Obtained Evidence", (1985), 1 *Can. Curr. Tax J.* 75.

144 See the opposed opinion of Mr. Justice Marceau, dissenting on other grounds, in *M.N.R. v. Kruger Inc., supra*, note 116 at 723.

9(1) of the *International Covenant on Civil and Political Rights* also provides that "No one shall be subjected to arbitrary arrest or detention." It appears that the protection against exile, mentioned in the *Bill of Rights* but not in the Charter, is guaranteed by section 6(1) of the Charter, which grants to all citizens the right to remain in Canada.

Section 9 of the Charter gives rise to two questions: First, what scope should be given to the concepts of detention and imprisonment? And second, how should the word "arbitrarily" be defined?

(a) The Concepts of Detention and Imprisonment

It is obvious that sections 9 and 10 must be read together. The former defines, so to speak, the conditions on which a detention is permitted or prohibited and the latter guarantees certain rights to a person who has been detained. Section 9 refers to detention or imprisonment, while section 10 refers to arrest or detention. These variations in wording do not have much significance. Imprisonment is merely one form of detention, the latter term being broader in scope and obviously including deprivation of liberty in a place other than a prison. Arrest likewise is simply a form of detention, although not all detainees have necessarily been arrested.[145] The truly relevant question in all this is: What is the exact scope of the concept of detention?

In *Chromiak v. R.*,[146] the Supreme Court tied the notion of detention found in section 2(c)(ii) of the *Canadian Bill of Rights*, dealing with the right to counsel, to the notion of detention found in section 2(c)(iii), dealing with the right to *habeas corpus* (the equivalent to section 10(c) of the Charter). The court concluded that before there can be a detention "some form of compulsory restraint" is necessary, and a person required merely to submit to a "sobriety" test has not been detained. This narrow construction is open to criticism to the extent that it may have the effect of depriving a person, who is not arrested, but who cooperates with police authorities because he wants to or believes himself obliged to, of the benefit of important guarantees. The court was thus perfectly justified in rejecting it in *R. v. Therens*.[147] In that case, the court decided that a person required to submit to a breathalyzer test was a person under detention within the meaning of section 10(b) of the Charter (right to counsel), even if the deprivation of liberty was very brief and if the constraint exercised by the police authority was of a moral or psychological, rather than a physical,

---

145 *R. v. MacDonald* (1974), 22 C.C.C. (2d) 350 at 356 (N.S.C.A.). It is here suggested that an arrest is a detention but detention is not necessarily an arrest.

146 [1980] 1 S.C.R. 471 at 478.

147 [1985] 1 S.C.R. 613.

nature. More recently, in *R. v. Hufsky*,[148] the court also decided that this broad definition of detention was applicable, not only to section 10, but also to section 9 of the Charter, with the result that a motorist who is asked to stop at the roadside by a police officer is a person detained within the meaning of section 9.

We therefore see that the concept of detention in section 9 of the Charter is not limited to deprivations of liberty which might give rise to a writ of *habeas corpus*. Rather, one can argue that the section is aimed at all deprivations of liberty ordered by a public authority, no matter how brief. It was thus wrongly decided that an order to appear for fingerprinting,[149] or a request to provide identification,[150] did not amount to detentions. Even a truck driver required to have his vehicle weighed on a roadside scale would be detained within the meaning of section 9 of the Charter.[151]

However a deprivation of liberty giving rise to *habeas corpus* is, *a fortiori*, a detention within the meaning of section 9. It follows that the latter, like the former, is not restricted to the domain of criminal or penal process, but includes every form of confinement ordered by public authorities, for example, for medical reasons or for the purpose of deportation within the framework of immigration legislation.[152]

(b) The Arbitrary Character of the Detention

An arbitrary detention can ensue from conduct; it can also result from the law itself.[153] In the first case, section 24 of the Charter will permit the court to grant the victim an appropriate remedy. In the second case, the court, under section 52, can invalidate the offensive law itself. One cannot presume that, simply because the power to detain is authorized by law, the detention in question is not arbitrary. A detention is arbitrary

---

148 *Supra*, note 120.
149 *Re Jamieson and R.* (1982), 70 C.C.C. (2d) 430 (Qué. S.C.); *R. v. McGregor, supra,* note 19; *Re M.H. and R. (No. 2), supra*, note 19.
150 *Re L.M.L.* (1985), 66 A.R. 132 (Alta. Youth Ct.).
151 *R. v. Gray,* (1987), 35 C.C.C. (3d) 178 (P.E.I. Prov. Ct.), aff'd (1987), 39 C.C.C. (3d) 463 (P.E.I. S.C.).
152 With respect to the arrested or detained person's right to *habeas corpus* (s. 10(c) of the Charter), see below.
153 See, *e.g. Re Mitchell and R.* (1983), 6 C.C.C. (3d) 193 (Ont. H.C.); *R. v. Konechny* (1983), 10 C.C.C. (3d) 233 (B.C.C.A.), leave to appeal to S.C.C. refused (1984), 25 M.V.R. 132 (S.C.C.). Note that the question whether s. 9 permits the law itself to be challenged, rather than simply its application, was left open by the Supreme Court in *R. v. Lyons,* [1987] 2 S.C.R. 309 at 346.

if it is discretionary, lacking in standards, capricious or despotic.[154] A law authorizing a detention of this sort would therefore violate section 9. The *Hufsky* case[155] provides an example of a provincial law granting a police officer the power to stop motorists on a random basis and carry out roadside tests, a law which, because it contained no criteria for the selection of motorists, was deemed to be contrary to section 9, although it was saved by the limitation provision of section 1.

This was also the view taken by Parliament when, in response to the October crisis of 1970, it enacted the *Public Order (Temporary Measures) Act, 1970*,[156] which authorized the arrest without warrant and the prolonged detention of persons suspected of belonging to *Le Front de Libération du Québec*. Section 12 provided that the Act was to operate notwithstanding section 2(a) of the *Canadian Bill of Rights*. This provision shows that Parliament thought it possible that the courts would find the Act contrary to the section.

Is every illegal detention necessarily an arbitrary detention within the meaning of section 9? Probably not.[157] Certain illegalities may in fact stem from pure technicalities having no relation to the discretionary or despotic character of the detention.

Analysis of the case law rendered to date under section 9 of the Charter reveals that the section has been invoked, sometimes to challenge the reasons for detention, sometimes the manner in which it has been decided on and sometimes its character and duration.

With respect to reasons for detention, it has been held that the fact of being a dangerous offender (Part XXI [XXIV] of the *Criminal Code*) justified indeterminate detention, so long as the concept of dangerous offender was precisely and narrowly defined.[158] Nor were detentions following the revocation of parole,[159] or the cancellation of earned

---

154 *R. v. Ladouceur* (1987), 35 C.C.C. (3d) 240 at 251-252 (Ont. C.A.). leave to appeal to S.C.C. granted (1988), 38 C.C.C. (3d) vi (note) (S.C.C.). See also *Levitz v. Ryan* (1972), 29 D.L.R. (3d) 519 at 526 (Ont. C.A.), with respect to s. 2(a) of the *Canadian Bill of Rights*. On the meaning of the term *arbitrary*, see in particular M. Manning, *Rights, Freedoms and the Courts: A Practical Analysis of the Constitution Act, 1982* (Toronto: Emond-Montgomery, 1983) 322-334.

155 *Supra*, note 120.

156 S.C. 1970-71-72, c. 2.

157 See in this regard *R. v. Duguay* (1985), 18 C.C.C. (3d) 289 (Ont. C.A.).

158 *R. v. Lyons, supra*, note 153. See also *R. v. Simon (No. 1)* (1982), 68 C.C.C. (2d) 86 (N.W.T.S.C.); *R. v. Langevin* (1984), 8 D.L.R. (4th) 485 (Ont. C.A.). Note that the continued detention of a person after the repeal of the legislation upon which the detention was based was not deemed to be arbitrary on that basis alone. See *R. v. Milne*, [1987] 2 S.C.R. 512, but note however the dissent by Justice Estey; *Re Mitchell and R., supra*, note 153.

159 *Belliveau v. R.*, (1984), 13 C.C.C. (3d) 138 (F.C.T.D.).

remission after the commission of an offence,[160] or a refusal to release on the grounds that the inmate was likely to commit an offence,[161] deemed to be arbitrary. Similarly, an overnight detention of a drunk person charged with impaired driving, in order to avoid a repetition of the offence, was found not to be arbitrary.[162] However, the overnight detention of a person arrested for prostitution,[163] the overnight detention of a person arrested for impaired driving who cooperated with the police and whose car had been towed away,[164] and the arrest of a person without reasonable grounds in order to have him assist in an investigation,[165] were held to be arbitrary.

The guarantee against arbitrary detention has also been invoked to challenge the procedures which result in a detention being ordered. The more a decision-making process involves standards, the less it is likely to be found arbitrary. However, so far, the courts have not tended to find arbitrary *per se* (in the absence of specific arbitrary decisions) the discretionary powers of the lieutenant governor of a province with regard to the detention of persons found not guilty by reason of insanity (section [614] 542 of the *Criminal Code*),[166] or those of the Attorney General to declare that a person is a dangerous offender[167] or to opt for a direct indictment (section 507 [577] of the *Criminal Code*)[168] or to opt for a mode of proceeding which will lead automatically to a prison term if there is a conviction.[169] The medical and judicial controls surrounding the committal of mental health patients under Manitoba law were found to

---

160 *Maxie v. National Parole Bd.* (1985), 47 C.R. (3d) 22 (F.C.T.D.), aff'd [1987] 1 F.C. 617 (C.A.).

161 *Evans v. R.* (1986), 30 C.C.C. (3d) 313 (Ont. C.A.).

162 *R. v. Remlinger* (1983), 23 M.V.R. 294 (Sask. Prov. Ct.); *R. v. McIntosh* (1984), 29 M.V.R. 50 (B.C.C.A.).

163 *R. v. Pithart* (1987), 34 C.C.C. (3d) 150 (B.C. Co. Ct.).

164 *R. v. Christiensen*, (1987) 2 W.C.B. (2d) 400 (B.C. Co. Ct.).

165 *R. v. Duguay, supra,* note 157. In *R. v. Sunila* (1986), 28 D.L.R. (4th) 450 (N.S.C.A.), the arrest of the crew of a boat being made legally, and in conformity with the rules on international law, was held not to infringe on their rights under s. 9.

166 *R. v. Swain* (1986), 24 C.C.C. (3d) 385 (Ont. C.A.).

167 *R. v. Lyons, supra,* note 153, where it was suggested instead that an absence of prosecutorial discretion could render the law arbitrary (at 348-349); *R. v. N.* (1987), 22 B.C.L.R. (2d) 45 (C.A.), leave to appeal to S.C.C. refused (1988), 27 B.C.L.R. (2d) xxxv (note) (S.C.C.).

168 *R. v. Andrew*, [1986] 6 W.W.R. 323 (B.C.S.C.); *R. v. Ertel* (1987), 35 C.C.C. (3d) 398 (Ont. C.A.), leave to appeal to S.C.C. refused (1987), 30 C.R.R. 209n (S.C.C.). It is to be noted in that case that this power which the Attorney General possesses does not automatically bring about a detention.

169 *Darbishire v. R.* (1983), 83 D.T.C. 5164 (Ont. Co. Ct.), aff'd (1983), 11 W.C.B. 5 (Ont. C.A.).

be sufficient to meet the demands of section 9.[170] The fact that in certain serious cases an accused is obliged to demonstrate that his detention is unjustified and that he should be released, was not deemed to violate section 9, since the detention was not a whim of the court, but rather the result of procedures specified under section 457 [515] of the *Criminal Code*.[171]

Finally, section 9 of the Charter has been used to assess the nature and duration of a detention. Given the rigid time limits within which an accused must be brought before a justice under section 454 [503] of the *Criminal Code*, it is not surprising that the cases have found an arbitrary detention where these limits were not met.[172] But section 9 has also been invoked in an attempt to establish, albeit unsuccessfully, that the minimum seven-year sentence for importation of narcotics,[173] the minimum ten-year sentence for murder,[174] and the minimum seven-day sentence for knowingly driving with a suspended licence,[175] all constituted arbitrary detention or imprisonment.

One can draw a number of observations from this case law.[176] In the majority of cases, the protection against arbitrary detention is not the only protection invoked; it is supplemented by appeal to other, at times more pertinent, guarantees. If, for example, a disparity is alleged between the reasons for a detention and its character, its duration or its material conditions, section 12 of the Charter respecting cruel and unusual treatment or punishment will be as relevant as section 9, if not more so. If the issue is rather the manner in which the detention has been decided upon, the principles of fundamental justice (section 7 of the Charter) will be invoked.[177] Does this mean, in effect, that section 9 has merely an accessory character and that in order for a detention to be arbitrary, within the

---

170 *Re Thwaites and Health Sciences Centre* (1986), 33 D.L.R. (4th) 549 (Man. Q.B.), rev'd (1987), 48 D.L.R. (4th) 338 (Man. C.A.).

171 *R. v. Frankforth* (1982), 70 C.C.C. (2d) 448 (B.C. Co. Ct.).

172 *R. v. M* (1982), 70 C.C.C. (2d) 123 (Ont. Fam. Ct.), where s. 454 of the *Criminal Code* was found applicable to a young offender; *R. v. Sybrandy* (1983), 9 W.C.B. 328 (Ont. Prov. Ct.); *R. v. Erickson* (1984), 11 W.C.B. 344 (B.C. Co. Ct.); *Re Marshall and R.* (1984), 13 C.C.C. (3d) 73 (Ont. H.C.); *R. v. Reeves* (1985), 70 N.S.R. (2d) 165 (Prov. Ct.).

173 *R. v. Newall (No. 4)* (1982), 70 C.C.C. (2d) 10 (B.C.S.C.). A penalty like this one was held contrary to s. 12 of the Charter in *R. v. Smith*, [1987] 1 S.C.R. 1045.

174 *R. v. Mitchell* (1987), 39 C.C.C. (3d) 141 (N.S.C.A.).

175 *R. v. Konechny, supra*, note 153.

176 The case law under s. 2(a) of the *Canadian Bill of Rights* is analyzed in the corresponding version of this study (Chapter 10) in the first edition of this book.

177 See *R. v. Lyons, supra*, note 153, at 346, where Justice La Forest comments that the argument based on s. 9 is simply a repetition of those based on ss. 7 and 12. To a somewhat similar effect, see also the comments in Justice Estey's otherwise dissenting opinion in *R. v. Milne, supra*, note 158 at 532.

meaning of this section, it must contravene the law or some other provision of the Charter? We do not think so. Even though section 9 is likely to be invoked often in conjunction with one or more of the other guarantees, it is capable of operating in an autonomous fashion. A few examples will suffice to demonstrate this claim.

Let us suppose that Parliament were to enact during a time of peace a statute inspired by the secret Order in Council of October 6, 1945,[178] which would permit the Minister of Justice to interrogate and detain "in such place and under such conditions as he might from time to time determine", all persons who, in his opinion, are likely to communicate information to a foreign power or to act in a manner prejudicial to public safety. The guarantee of section 9 would be the most appropriate ground on which to challenge such a measure. It is not so much the treatment or punishment that is at issue here, or procedural guarantees of justice (supposing that these must be respected in exercising a power of this sort), as the discretion itself and its unreasonable character.

Let us next consider the less extreme case of a deportation order against an immigrant convicted of a criminal offence. The Minister decides to suspend its execution and leave the immigrant at liberty under surveillance for a given period. Long after this period has expired, during which time the behaviour of the immigrant has been irreproachable, he is arrested and the Minister now decides to execute the order. Without referring to the *Canadian Bill of Rights*, the Supreme Court has held that to execute such an order in this fashion, at any time whatsoever, is arbitrary and that the law does not permit it.[179] Here again it is section 9 that furnishes the most relevant argument, ultimately against the legislation itself. To permit the possibility of detention to float in an indefinite and discretionary fashion — which is not what happens in the case of revocation of parole — is clearly a measure that contravenes section 9 and one might well argue that the victim of such a decision could challenge it by invoking section 9, even though he is at liberty and only under the threat of a possible detention. Unlike the right to *habeas corpus* under section 10(c), which we shall see can probably be exercised only by a person who is actually detained, the protection against arbitrary detention implies, in our view, the possibility of challenging a decision that merely opens the door to detention. It follows that section 9 has a broader scope than section 10(c) and the latter is simply a procedural form of the former.

---

178 P.C. 6444. See on this subject F. Chevrette & H. Marx, *Droit constitutionnel* (Montréal: Université de Montréal, 1982) at 33-34.

179 *Violi v. Superintendent of Immigration*, [1965] S.C.R. 232 at 241. This example is analyzed by W.S. Tarnopolsky, *The Canadian Bill of Rights*, 2nd rev. ed. (Toronto: Macmillan, 1975) at 235-236.

It is also possible that by reason of the general terms in which section 9 is formulated, it serves to complete certain other guarantees of the Charter. For example, section 11(b) ensures to every accused the right to be tried within a reasonable time. If this provision were narrowly construed, so as to benefit persons charged with an offence but not detainees against whom no charge has been laid, one could argue that a prolonged detention in the context of criminal proceedings is arbitrary, where the detainee is not charged and tried within a reasonable time. Is there any need to add, finally, that in conjunction with section 24 of the Charter section 9 may, if violated, entitle a person to such remedies as damages or the inadmissibility of evidence? The release or discharge of a detainee will be analyzed in the course of examination of section 10(c).

Let us conclude by saying that, even if it is not easy to do, it is profoundly desirable, for coherence in the law, to delimit as clearly as possible the scope of section 9, particularly in relation to sections 7 and 12 of the Charter.[180]

3. THE RIGHT TO HABEAS CORPUS

Section 10(c) provides:

> Everyone has the right on arrest or detention
>
> . . .
>
> (c) to have the validity of the detention determined by way of *habeas corpus* and to be released if the detention is not lawful.

Section 2(c)(iii) of the *Canadian Bill of Rights* already prohibits depriving "a person who has been arrested or detained . . . of the remedy by way of *habeas corpus* for the determination of the validity of his detention and for his release if the detention is not lawful", and article 9(4) of the *International Covenant on Civil and Political Rights* provides:

> Anyone who is deprived of his liberty by arrest or detention shall be entitled to take proceedings before a court, in order that that court may decide without delay on the lawfulness of his detention and order his release if the detention is not lawful.

Of the various provisions in the Charter, section 10(c) is somewhat peculiar in that it entrenches a guarantee of a procedural character that is already well developed in our law. It is obviously not our purpose here to offer a detailed analysis of this celebrated, important and complex remedy. We shall be content to examine a number of specific problems

---

180 See *e.g.*, the overlaps described in the cases cited *supra*, note 177.

which may be classified into two categories. The first deals with the conditions on which the remedy is available — in other words, what is an illegal detention and who may complain of one? The second relates to the scope of judicial review and attendant procedural requirements. However before proceeding to this analysis, a preliminary observation must be made concerning the basic character of section 10(c).

One may formulate the problem in the following way. Given that this section refers to a procedure that is well defined in both federal legislation and that of the various provinces, is its effect to freeze existing law, and to prevent any legislative body from amending that law, either substantially or with respect to particular details (for example, limiting the right of appeal in the matter of *habeas corpus*)? If a legislature at some point decided to broaden the range of application of this remedy, would it be prevented from later restricting it and reintroducing traditional limits? And would this restrictive effect on the legislature be accompanied by an inverse effect on the courts, which might deem certain procedural modes of supervising the legality of detentions insufficiently efficacious and require something more? Since the right to *habeas corpus* varies significantly among the various Canadian jurisdictions, to the point where one commentator has fervently wished for a greater standardization,[181] could section 10(c) permit the courts to effect such a standardization gradually, in the way the Supreme Court of the United States has done in the case of several procedural guarantees in criminal law?

As we shall see, certain of these difficulties are real ones, although on the whole their extent should not be exaggerated. For what is entrenched by section 10(c) is judicial control of the legality of detentions and not existing procedures in all their current detail, even though in certain respects existing procedures will inevitably determine the scope of the guarantee of the section. To illustrate this basic point, one may suggest a parallel between section 10(c) and the principle of judicial review of constitutionality. The legislature may regulate judicial review, for example, by requiring that notice be given to the Attorney General of all constitutional challenges, but it cannot entirely abrogate it or render it ineffectual.[182] It is a limit of the same sort that section 10(c) imposes on Canadian legislatures.

In any event, it appears certain that the authority of the courts under section 10(c) of the Charter is sufficient to allow them to improve traditional

---

181 D.A. Cameron Harvey, *The Law of Habeas Corpus in Canada* (Toronto: Butterworths, 1974) at 174. On *habeas corpus*, see also in particular R.J. Sharpe, *The Law of Habeas Corpus* (Oxford: Clarendon Press, 1976). In the notes which follow, these authors will be cited as Harvey and Sharpe. On the need for uniformity in matters of *habeas corpus*, see also V.M. Del Buono, "Bail in Light of the Charter of Rights", in *Criminal Procedure in Canada*, by the same author (Montreal: Wilson & Lafleur/Sorej, 1983) at 215.

182 Chevrette & Marx, *supra*, note 178 at 189.

habeas corpus procedures so as to make them more effective. This clearly is one effect of the important decision in *R. v. Miller*,[183] which will be examined below.

(a) Circumstances Warranting Application of the Right

Let us first review the conditions which must be met for this section to apply.

As pointed out in our analysis of section 9, it is clear that the notion of detention includes not only restriction of the freedom to come and go within the framework of criminal or penal proceedings, but also confinement for reasons of health,[184] for example, or commitment of an alien whom one wants to deport. The *habeas corpus* guaranteed in section 10(c) is as much civil in character as criminal. But does it include the civil *habeas corpus* traditionally available in cases where the detention is not the work of the public authorities, for example, the unlawful detention of a child by a parent or a stranger? We believe that it does, even though as a rule, the Charter, in our view, applies only to acts of public authorities, notably on account of section 32. In the first place, this recourse is traditionally available in such cases and one can argue further that the object of section 10(c) is to impose a duty on public authorities to ensure the liberty of the individual and to make available to everyone judicial supervision of his detention. The act of the public authorities would thus reside in this duty, and not just the duty of the state to refrain from illegally detaining persons, so that the fact that a detention was effected by a private individual would not exclude it from the ambit of this section.

Where a person is released on bail or paroled, or benefits from a suspended sentence or a probation order, is he under detention within the meaning of section 10(c)? We saw in examining section 9 that the courts gave quite a narrow construction to the concept of detention in the *Canadian Bill of Rights*. However, this interpretation has been broadened under the Charter.[185] Similarly, the traditional case law surrounding *habeas corpus*, which only allows for its application in cases where a person is

---

183 [1985] 2 S.C.R. 613 at 625. In delivering judgment, Mr. Justice Le Dain relied on s. 10(c) of the Charter to justify a relaxation of procedural rules, upon which I will elaborate below.

184 *Reference re the Mental Health Act* (1984), 5 D.L.R. (4th) 577 (P.E.I. C.A.). It was emphasized in this decision that, in addition to any remedies provided for under the *Mental Health Act*, review by way of *habeas corpus* was still available by virtue of s. 10(c).

185 *R. v. Therens, supra,* note 147.

deprived of his freedom in the narrow sense,[186] may give way to a broader interpretation under the Charter.[187] One commentator has suggested that the requirement of a complete deprivation of liberty be relaxed, pointing out that a person on parole or subject to probation order is legally detained and that a person at liberty on bail must, curiously enough, arrange to be reincarcerated, to the extent such a thing is possible, before he can apply for a writ of *habeas corpus*.[188] In the case of children, the concept of detention has never been given such a narrow meaning; rather, it has been viewed as including situations where a child is under the care and control of another, not just situations involving the deprivation of his freedom of movement. Finally, the proposition that the illegal revocation of a person's parole can give rise to an application for *habeas corpus* as a means of rectifying the situation does not appear open to serious dispute.[189]

An examination of the type of deprivation of liberty which can give rise to a *habeas corpus* application also raises the issue of the type of remedy which would be appropriate. Should the remedy consist of an unqualified release from detention, or does it also warrant that measures be taken to control particularly harsh conditions of detention in a penitentiary and to reintegrate a prisoner into the general prison population? In this regard, one commentator has written:

> While the courts have been reluctant to act in the past, it is submitted that the fact that a prisoner cannot be released altogether should be no reason to refuse relief on *habeas corpus*. If, for example, a prisoner is improperly put in solitary confinement . . . there seems to be no reason why he should not be able to use *habeas corpus* to be freed from that restraint. The situation may be seen as a "prison within a prison" and the applicant is simply released from the inner prison while being kept within the confines of the outer one. In child custody cases, *habeas corpus* has been used to transfer rather than release from custody, and the same principle could be applied. From there, it might be possible to develop a more sophisticated approach which would allow anyone confined to contest the legality of the conditions of his

---

186 *R. v. Cameron* (1897), 1 .C.C.C. 169 (Qué. S.C.) and *De Bernonville v. Langlais*, [1951] C.S. 277 (Qué. S.C.), two decisions where a person out on parole was able to benefit from review by way of *habeas corpus*. These decisions were disapproved of in *Masella v. Langlais*, [1955] S.C.R. 263 at 272-276.

187 In *R. v. Miller, supra*, note 183 at 638, 639, Mr. Justice Le Dain cited, without approval or disapproval, certain American decisions where access to review by way of *habeas corpus* was allowed for a person on parole and for a person who had not yet started to serve his sentence.

188 Harvey, *supra*, note 181 at 174. See also the very thorough analysis of Sharpe, *supra*, note 181 at 158-170. These authors rightfully point out that the requirement of a detention in the strict and narrow sense is debatable and anachronistic.

189 *R. v. Cadeddu; R. v. Nunery* (1982), 4 C.C.C. (3d) 97 (Ont. H.C.), abated (1983), 4 C.C.C. (3d) 112 (Ont. C.A.).

confinement even where he does not complain of some added physical restraint.[190]

With good reason, the Supreme Court has adopted this view in *R. v. Miller*.[191] Mr. Justice Le Dain, giving judgment for the court, presented a thorough analysis of the question and concluded:

> Confinement in a special handling unit, or in administrative segregation . . . is a form of detention that is distinct and separate from that imposed on the general inmate population. It involves a significant reduction in the residual liberty of the inmate. It is in fact a new detention of the inmate, purporting to rest on its own foundation of legal authority. It is that particular form of detention or deprivation of liberty which is the object of the challenge by *habeas corpus*. It is release from that form of detention that is sought. For the reasons indicated above, I can see no sound reason in principle, having to do with the nature and role of *habeas corpus*, why *habeas corpus* should not be available for that purpose. I do not say that *habeas corpus* should lie to challenge any and all conditions of confinement in a penitentiary or prison, including the loss of any privilege enjoyed by the general inmate population. But it should lie in my opinion to challenge to validity of a distinct form of confinement or detention in which the actual physical constraint or deprivation of liberty, as distinct from the mere loss of certain privileges, is more restrictive or severe than the normal one in an institution.[192]

This conclusion is well founded; for if one can use *habeas corpus* in cases involving a transfer between places of detention, such transfer being required in order to satisfy legal requirements as to the place where a sentence is to be served,[193] one would have difficulty denying recourse to *habeas corpus* in cases where the conditions of detention rendered the detention illegal. At bottom, it is the traditional request on a *habeas corpus* application that a person be released immediately from detention, and that he regain complete freedom. However, to require such a remedy in all cases would preclude a prisoner from challenging the validity of a second sentence where he has not yet finished serving the first sentence, even if his eligibility for parole were affected. In addition, such a requirement would deny him the possibility of challenging one of two sentences being served concurrently. Even if strictly speaking there is no right to parole, a blanket denial of *habeas corpus* in the first example would be unjust. The same is also true in the second example of concurrent sentences, for a prisoner challenging the second sentence would be denied access to *habeas corpus* simply because he had not yet finished serving the first,

---

190 Sharpe, *supra*, note 181, at 148-149.

191 *Supra*, note 183.

192 *Ibid.* at 641.

193 Amongst others, see *Bell v. Director of Springhill Medium Security Institution* (1977), 34 C.C.C. (2d) 303 (N.S.C.A.); *Re Hass and R.* (1978), 40 C.C.C. (2d) 202 (Ont. H.C.).

yet he could not challenge the first because he had not finished serving the second.[194]

Who may apply for a writ of *habeas corpus?* The answer is the detainee himself; the language of section 10(c) is perhaps clearer on this point than that of the *Canadian Bill of Rights*. However, in matters of capacity and standing, the law of *habeas corpus* has long been extremely flexible. Neither age nor mental capacity are obstacles preventing a detainee from seeking a writ, and proceedings may also be initiated at the instance of a third party where the detainee is physically or mentally unable to act for himself.[195] Is it the case that this important aspect of *habeas corpus* has been excluded from section 10(c) and that the section only entrenches the right of the detainee alone to initiate proceedings? We do not think so. The spirit of the guarantee and the practical considerations to which we have just alluded lead rather to the conclusion that the right recognized by section 10(c) is the right of all detainees to have the legality of their detention determined by way of *habeas corpus* and a purely literal construction of the words "everyone has the right . . . to have the validity of the detention determined", must be rejected.

The case law is divided on whether a conscript has the right to *habeas corpus*,[196] and it seems to deny this right to aliens coming from an enemy country and prisoners of war.[197] Invoking the Royal Prerogative, the courts have held that a detention ordered by the Governor General may not be challenged by way of *habeas corpus*,[198] and the same conclusion was reached in a case where the Lieutenant Governor, acting under the authority of the *Criminal Code*, ordered the detention of a person who was mentally ill.[199] These holdings appear doubtful, especially now that the right to *habeas corpus* has been entrenched. In the first place, some cases seem to confuse the difficulty of issuing a writ of *habeas corpus* with the impossibility of finding a detention unlawful on account of the highly discretionary character of the norms under which it was ordered.[200] Next, by virtue of section 2(a) of the *Canadian Bill of Rights* and section 9 of the Charter, a power to detain, even one exercised by the Lieutenant Governor, is subject to control if it is arbitrary.[201] In addition, one may

---

194 With good reason, the Québec Court of Appeal refused to adopt this reasoning in *Gagnon v. R.*, [1971] C.A. 454 (Qué. C.A.).

195 Harvey, *supra*, note 181 at 76; Sharpe, *supra*, note 181 at 213-214.

196 Harvey, *ibid.* at 23, and Sharpe, *ibid.* at 166-167.

197 Harvey, *ibid.* at 13, and Sharpe, *ibid.* at 112-114.

198 *Brouillette v. Fatt* (1926), 64 Que. S.C. 222.

199 Harvey, *supra*, note 181 at 24, and Sharpe, *supra*, note 181 at 156.

200 This is the conclusion reached by Sharpe, *ibid.* at 112-114 respecting prisoners of war.

201 This possibility was recognized in *Re Brooks* (1961), 38 W.W.R. 51 (Alta. S.C.), and *Ex Parte Kleinys* (1965), 49 D.L.R. (2d) 225 (B.C.S.C.), two cases of *habeas corpus*

question the validity of arguments based on immunity or the prerogative to the extent that section 32 of the Charter renders its provisions, including section 10(c), applicable to both federal and provincial governments.[202] Finally, section 10 clearly states that it is everyone who has a right to *habeas corpus*. This right may be suspended by recourse to section 33 and, possibly limited by the effect of section 1, but subject to these two reservations, and if there is a genuine detention, one must conclude that every detainee has the right.

(b) Scope of Right and Review Procedures

Some of the procedural issues to be broached here are of crucial importance because of their relationship to the scope of judicial review available by way of *habeas corpus*.

Could one abolish *habeas corpus* as it relates to specific matters and replace it by a different procedure which provides for equivalent or even broader judicial review? It seems that this has already been done in the area of bail or judicial interim release, which traditionally was dealt with by way of *habeas corpus*. Today the decision of a justice of the peace can be reviewed by a judge of a superior court (*Criminal Code*, section 457.5[520]) or, in the case of Quebec, by three judges of the Sessions of the Peace or the Provincial Court. In the case of certain serious offences, only a judge of a superior court may order release and his decision is subject to review by a court of appeal (*Criminal Code*, section 457.7(2.2)[522(4)]). Although now repealed, section 459.1 of the *Criminal Code* expressly excluded proceedings in *habeas corpus* respecting "interim release" or "for the purpose of reviewing or varying any decision . . . relating to interim release or detention".

It was decided in certain cases where section 10(c) was at issue that section 459.1 of the *Criminal Code* could not have the effect of denying recourse to proceedings in *habeas corpus*. Thus it was determined, in *Re Jack and R.*,[203] that proceedings in *habeas corpus* were available where a prisoner's detention had not been reviewed within a certain required

---

where the detention was found to be lawful. See also *Ex parte Tirey* (1971), 21 D.L.R. (3d) 475 (Alta. T.D.), where it was held that the discretion of an immigration officer had not been exercised arbitrarily and *habeas corpus* was refused.

202 With respect to government decisions being subject to the Charter, see *Operation Dismantle v. R.*, [1985] 1 S.C.R. 441.

203 (1982), 1 C.C.C. (3d) 193 (Nfld. T.D.).

time period,[204] despite the provisions of section 459.1. In *Re Kot and R.*,[205] section 459.1 was found to be inoperative, thus making it possible to challenge the legality of the arrest by way of proceedings in *habeas corpus*. Much like other privative clauses, section 459.1 proved ineffective where the illegality in question was equivalent to an excess of jurisdiction, even where another remedy was available.[206] The constitutional entrenchment of *habeas corpus* clears the way for courts to declare inoperative any legislative provision which denies access to proceedings in *habeas corpus*, or to interpret ambiguous legislative provisions[207] in such a way as to preserve the right set out in section 10(c) of the Charter.

Section 10(c) prohibits the abolition of *habeas corpus* and may also prohibit its replacement by some other procedure, unless this can be justified as a reasonable limit under section 1. At the same, we do not think it is beyond the power of an otherwise competent legislature[208] to establish or exclude appeals from the decision of the judge of first instance or to allow or prohibit successive applications. Such provisions merely regulate the manner in which the guaranteed right is to be exercised, much like rules governing territorial jurisdiction assuming always that the purpose of the provisions is not to systematically thwart recourse to the remedy. One might expect, however, that the section guarantees access to a superior court.

---

204 On this point, the decision in *Ex parte Mitchell* (1975), 23 C.C.C. (2d) 473 (B.C.C.A.), where s. 2(c)(iii) of the *Canadian Bill of Rights* had been invoked, is very similar. Still on the same point as to whether s.459.1 was inoperative in light of the *Bill of Rights*, see *Ex parte Clarke (No.1): Ex parte White* (1978), 41 C.C.C. (2d) 511 (Nfld. T.D.); *Amyotte v. A.G. Quebec*, [1980] C.S. 429 (Qué. S.C.) where s. 459.1 was not interpreted as denying recourse to *habeas corpus* if parole were revoked without having heard the parties (*Criminal Code*, s. 457.8(2)[523(2)]).

205 (1983), 10 C.C.C. (3d) 297 (Ont. H.C.), quashed (1984), 11 C.C.C. (3d) 96 (Ont. C.A.).

206 It is often said that review by way of *habeas corpus* is only available in the absence of a right to appeal or other adequate remedy: Harvey, *supra*, note 181 at 13. To say the least, this proposition invites a number of qualifications: Sharpe, *supra*, note 181 at 57.

207 See *R. v. Cadeddu, supra*, note 189, and *Reference re Procedures and the Mental Health Act, supra*, note 184, where two provincial statutes were interpreted as not denying *habeas corpus*. One commentator takes the position, however, that the abrogation of *habeas corpus* accompanied by replacement procedures which provide a means of review of equal effectiveness would constitute a reasonable limit to s. 10(c). On the other hand, a total abrogation would have no effect and would not preclude a review of the legality of a detention. See P. Béliveau, "Le contrôle judicaire en droit pénal canadien" (1983), 61 *Can. Bar Rev.* 735 at 786. This is a logical and acceptable solution. A detailed analysis of *habeas corpus* is found at pp. 783-796.

208 Important rules exist in constitutional law regarding the respective jurisdiction of the federal Parliament and the provinces in the area of *habeas corpus*, but it is not my intent to review this question here.

There remains the important and difficult question of the scope of the judicial control that is entrenched in the Charter by virtue of section 10(c).

It is well known that determining whether a detention is legal at the time of return of the writ is the sole purpose of *habeas corpus*. To take a definition of the Supreme Court, it involves inquiry "into the jurisdiction of the Court by which process the subject is held in custody and into the validity of the process upon its face".[209] The proceeding thus has nothing to do with an appeal where an accused could allege that he was detained on the basis of insufficient evidence, nor does it permit a challenge to the legality of steps taken prior to detention, for example, arrest.[210] On this point some fairly subtle distinctions may have to be made. On a *habeas corpus* application, every irregularity that potentially affects the legality of a detention, even past ones, can logically be invoked. Thus, it has been held that a vaguely framed indictment warranted release where the detainee did not know what he was accused of or how to make his defence. Conversely, it was held possible to correct a warrant for arrest which failed to recite that it was issued on the basis of a deportation order, where this order was in fact a valid one: this irregularity did not affect the legality of the detention.[211]

Although it was often said that review by way of *habeas corpus* was confined to determining if the warrant of detention was lawful on its face, more recent case law emphasizes the distinction between substantive questions and questions related to jurisdiction. Where the legality of the detention is affected by these latter questions, review by way of *habeas corpus* is the proper procedure.[212]

In this regard, it is interesting to consider the impact of several other guarantees of the Charter on that of section 10(c). It is incontestable that a person who is arbitrarily detained (section 9), who is not informed promptly of the reasons for his detention (section 10(a)), or who is not allowed to retain and instruct counsel without delay or is not informed of this right (section 10(b)), is a person whose detention is unlawful. Similarly, violation of the guarantees of sections 11 to 14 renders detention unlawful, either directly (sections 11(a), (b), (e) and 12) or indirectly, by invalidating the proceedings leading to this detention by invalidating the punishment (section 11(i)). Certainly many of the guarantees mentioned above are such that they could be invoked by means of proceedings other

---

209 *Goldhar v. R.*, [1960] S.C.R. 431 at 439.

210 Harvey, *supra*, note 181 at 125; Sharpe, *supra*, note 181 at 175.

211 Compare *Recorder's Court of Quebec v. DuFour*, [1947] Que. K.B. 331 (Qué. C.A.) with *Ex parte Fong Goey Jow*, [1948] S.C.R. 37.

212 *R. v. Miller, supra*, note 183.

than *habeas corpus*. But where the conditions of application of this writ are all present, no one would claim that a detainee who has not been promptly informed of the reasons for his detention, who has been denied prompt recourse to the assistance of a lawyer or who, charged with an offence, is not tried within a reasonable time, does not have a right to *habeas corpus*, because the illegality could soon be cured by recourse to some other remedy. For it is in the delay itself that the illegality resides and the illegality makes release obligatory, however unsatisfactory this sanction may appear given the possibility of re-arrest and the reluctance of the courts to quash an indictment because of delay in acting on it. Once again, however, it is important to remember that there must be an illegality which goes to jurisdiction. One should also not jump to the conclusion that a certain judicial discretion, which was traditionally exercised in *habeas corpus* proceedings to determine the remedy to apply to an illegal detention,[213] has now been removed by section 10(c).

As we have seen, review by way of *habeas corpus* goes beyond a simple facial review of the warrant of detention. Consequently, the scope of admissible evidence with respect to an illegal detention must also be expanded.

We are familiar with the Canadian practice of applying for *habeas corpus* with *certiorari* in aid, in order to bring the entire record before the court and to permit the filing of affidavit evidence. It is also well known that in a much-disputed judgment, four judges of the Supreme Court — — Mr. Justice Ritchie and three of his colleagues — expressed the view that a provincial court has no jurisdiction to issue *certiorari* in aid against a federal body. This was so because section 18 of the *Federal Court Act*[213a] gives jurisdiction in the matter of *certiorari* against federal bodies to the Federal Court. Mr. Justice Ritchie thus assimilated ordinary *certiorari* and *certiorari* in aid of *habeas corpus* and refused to allow the appellant to submit evidence showing that he had been arrested and detained without being informed of the reasons therefor, in violation of section 2(c)(i) of the *Canadian Bill of Rights*, for, in his view, the court on a *habeas corpus* may not look behind the facts disclosed on the face of the warrants filed with the return of the writ.[214] In his dissenting opinion, Chief Justice Laskin, with the support of Dickson J., referred to section 2(c)(iii) of the *Bill of Rights* and added that "if necessary, I would read it as embracing *certiorari* in aid to make the remedy an effective one and not simply an exhibit in a show-case".[215]

---

213 Béliveau, *supra*, note 207 at 791–792.
213a R.S.C. 1970, c. 10 (2nd Supp.) [R.S.C. 1985, c. F-7].
214 *Mitchell v. R.*. [1976] 2 S.C.R. 570 at 595.
215 *Ibid.* at 578.

In *R. v. Miller*,[216] the Supreme Court has, fortunately, unanimously endorsed and adopted the opinion of the late Chief Justice Laskin, relying also on section 10(c) of the Charter to support its decision.[217] As a result, the Supreme Court has allowed provincial superior courts to issue *habeas corpus* with *certiori* in aid with a view to determining if the detention imposed by a federal body is valid. The court also ruled that a court reviewing an application for *habeas corpus* can receive affidavits or other extrinsic evidence for the purpose of determining if there has been an excess of jurisdiction, subject to "the conclusive character of the records of courts of superior or general common law jurisdiction".[218]

It is satisfying to see how section 10(c) has contributed to ensuring that substance has won over mere form, and that we have not ended with a situation of the tail wagging the dog.

4. RELEASE ON BAIL

Section 11(e) provides:

> Any person charged with an offence has the right

> . . .

> (e) not to be denied reasonable bail without just cause.

This provision is found in nearly identical language in section 2(f) of the *Canadian Bill of Rights* which prohibits depriving "a person charged with a criminal offence . . . of the right to reasonable bail without just cause". Article 9(3) of the *International Covenant on Civil and Political Rights* provides:

> It shall not be the general rule that persons awaiting trial shall be detained in custody, but release may be subject to guarantees to appear for trial, at any other stage of the judicial proceedings, and, should occasion arise, for execution of the judgment.

We shall first turn to examine the compatibility with section 11(e) of legislative provisions followed by an examination of the compatibility of the use a judge may make of them.

In light of the liberalization in 1971 of the law governing bail,[219] and even though this reform was tempered to a degree in 1976,[220] one can probably say of section 11(e) of the Charter what one scholar, writing

---

216 *Supra*, note 183.
217 *Ibid.* at 625.
218 *Ibid.* at 633.
219 *Bail Reform Act*, S.C. 1970-71-72, c. 37.
220 *Criminal Law Amendment Act, 1975*, S.C. 1974-75-76, c. 93.

in 1975, said of the part of section 2(f) of the *Bill of Rights* respecting bail: "[I]t is unlikely that there will be much reliance upon 'the right to reasonable bail' ".[221] In themselves, the sections of the *Criminal Code* governing what is now called judicial interim release (sections 457-459.1[515-526]) scarcely appear likely to come into conflict with section 11(e). They affirm the principle of release before trial and it is up to the prosecutor to convince the judge that incarceration is necessary and that none of the intermediary solutions (undertaking with conditions, recognizance to pay a sum of money with or without sureties, deposit of a sum of money) is appropriate.

Of course the burden of proof is reversed in certain circumstances (*Criminal Code* section 457(5.1)[515(6)], and, with respect to very serious offences, the right to judicial interim release has been abolished, leaving the issue within the discretionary power of a judge (section 457.7[522]). But it would be difficult to maintain that such restrictions on interim release are without just cause, especially in light of the very reasonable criteria which must be met, as set out in section 457(7)[515(10)], to justify continued detention.[222] The possibility of adjourning bail proceedings for a maximum of three days (section 457.1[516]) is certainly not excessive. As for reversing the burden of proof where the accused is not ordinarily resident in Canada (section 457(5.1)[515.6]), and the possibility of requiring a deposit from an accused who does not reside in the province or within one hundred miles of the place where he is in custody (section 457(2)[515(2)]), it is possible that these measures could encounter difficulties in connection with the principle of equality before the law. On the other hand, they do not seem either unjust or unreasonable if one takes into account the principal rationale for detaining an accused, namely to ensure his presence before the court. To this, one should add that every order respecting interim release is not only subject to review but may also be modified by the trial court (section 457.8(2)[523]): this means that the question of bail is not one that need be decided only once and for all.[223]

The guarantee of section 11(e) is certainly not without value. Take,

---

221 Tarnopolsky, *supra*, note 179 at 277.
222 On the validity of a s. 457(5.1) [515.6] see *R. v. Lundrigan* (1982), 67 C.C.C. (2d) 37 (Man. Prov. Ct.), aff'd (1982), 1 C.C.C. (3d) 350 (Man. Co. Ct.); *Ibrahim v. A.G. Canada*, (1982), 1 C.R.R. 244 (Que. S.C.); *R. v. Frankforth*, *supra*, note 171; *R. v. Colosino* (1982), 8 W.C.B. 263 (Ont. Prov. Ct.) On the validity of s. 457.7[522], see *R. v. Bray* (1983), 2 C.C.C. (3d) 325 (Ont. C.A.); *R. v. Dubois (No. 2)* (1983), 8 C.C.C. (3d) 344 (Qué. S.C.); *contra*: *R. v. Pugsley* (1982), 2 C.C.C. (3d) 266 (N.S.C.A.).
223 See *R. v. Lee* (1982), 69 C.C.C. (2d) 190 (B.C.S.C.), where it was suggested that there existed a remedy amounting to a modification of the order based directly on s. 24 of the Charter, in cases where remedies available under the *Criminal Code* had been exhausted.

for example, the *Public Order (Temporary Measures) Act, 1970,*[224] enacted by Parliament in response to the October crisis of 1970. Under this statute an accused could be detained in custody for a prolonged period on the mere filing of a certificate by the Attorney General. Such a provision is clearly contrary to section 11(e). However, section 12 of this statute stipulated that it was to apply notwithstanding the guarantee respecting bail in the *Bill of Rights.* If that guarantee has not been used to render any federal enactment inoperative, it has nonetheless proved useful as a principle of statutory construction. Thus, invoking section 2(f) of the *Bill of Rights,* one court held that it had the power to grant bail to a person detained under the *Extradition Act,* even though the Act was silent on this matter,[225] and, in another case where the court arrived at the same conclusion, the judge clearly stated that the right to bail secured under the *Bill of Rights* benefits persons charged with an offence in a foreign country as much as it does those charged in Canada.[226]

It should also be noted that, by virtue of section 11(e), the right to bail has been found to apply to the area of extradition,[227] as well as to matters within the realm of military justice,[228] despite the silence in this regard of the relevant legislative texts. With respect to military justice, the Supreme Court of British Columbia has also ruled that the concept "accused", within the meaning of section 11(e), includes a person who has been found guilty and has appealed the verdict.

Given that section 6 of the Charter guarantees mobility rights to every citizen of Canada, the possibility that a judge could restrict the freedom of movement of an accused out on interim release raises a difficulty, one that can only be solved by reference to the reasonable limits formula of section 1 of the Charter. One can also wonder whether the prohibition on questioning and cross-examining the accused, during hearings related to judicial interim release, about the offence of which he has been accused (section 457.3 *Cr. Code*), is not contrary to the right of a full and complete defence,[229] even though this prohibition is favorable to the accused in many cases.

Not only can section 11(e) be invoked to challenge or interpret a legislative provision, it can also be used to challenge the manner in which procedures operate or to challenge an actual order regarding a specific accused. Detention without just cause or unreasonable bail conditions thus

---

224 *Supra,* note 156.
225 *Re Di Stefano* (1976), 30 C.C.C. (2d) 310 (N.W.T.S.C.).
226 *Meier v. United States (No. 2)* (1978), 45 C.C.C. (2d) 455 at 457 (B.C.S.C.).
227 *Re Global Communications Ltd. and A.G. Canada* (1984), 10 C.C.C. (3d) 97 (Ont. C.A.).
228 *Re Hinds and R.* (1983), 4 C.C.C. (3d) 322 (B.C.S.C.).
229 *R. v. Millar* (1983), 7 C.C.C. (3d) 286 (Qué. S.C.), where it was decided that this prohibition was contrary to s. 7 of the Charter.

most often emerge out of the actual treatment in specific cases. It has been decided that a hearing on the issue of interim release should be conducted expeditiously, which means that there should be a relaxation of the rules of evidence for the purposes of such a hearing.[230] In addition, our courts have ruled that it is essential that an accused be in a position to understand completely all of the proceedings.[231] The imposition of conditions on interim release which are clearly impossible to fulfill could easily constitute unreasonable bail.[232]

Let us conclude with some remarks about procedural matters. Supposing that the legislature itself contravenes section 11(e), it is clear in our view that any detention ordered by a judge under the offending provision would amount to an excess of jurisdiction and the accused could proceed by way of *habeas corpus* even if the now repealed section 459.1 of the *Criminal Code* were still in effect.[233] But supposing a detained person simply alleges that his detention has been ordered without just cause or that the bail fixed in his case is excessive, would he be obliged to rely exclusively on the provisions for review in the matter of interim release set out in the *Criminal Code*? Probably so.[234] It is doubtful that every violation of the Charter, simply on account of its constitutional character, constitutes an excess of jurisdiction. An analysis of this question, however, could not be made without a simultaneous examination of section 24 of the Charter and would take us well beyond the framework of this study.

5. THE RIGHT NOT TO BE FOUND GUILTY UNDER RETROACTIVE PENAL LAW

Section 11(g) provides:

> Any person charged with an offence has the right
>
> . . .
>
> (g) not to be found guilty on account of any act or omission unless, at the time of the act or omission, it constituted an offence under Canadian or international law or was criminal according to the general principles of law recognized by the community of nations.

This provision, in combination with paragraph (i) of the same section, asserts the well-known principle *nullum crimen, nulla poena sine lege*. The application of this principle to punishments is analyzed later on, in

---

230 *R. v. Kevork* (1984), 12 C.C.C. (3d) 339 (Ont. S.C.).
231 *Re R. and Brooks* (1982), 1 C.C.C. (3d) 506 (Ont. H.C.).
232 *Fraser v. R.* (1982), 38 O.R. (2d) 172 (Ont. Dist. Ct.).
233 See my review of s. 10(c) of the Charter.
234 However, see the decision *R. v. Lee, supra*, note 223.

connection with the study of paragraph (i). The subject to be considered here is the non-retrospective character of laws which create an offence.

It is well established that, until the proclamation of section 11(g), the non-retrospective nature of an offence in Canadian law was only a rule of interpretation. The legislature could thus derogate from this rule, provided it did so clearly.[235] One can find at least one example of a retroactive penal law in the past, which was, moreover, found by the courts to be valid.[236] By virtue of section 11(g) of the Charter, this principle of construction is now entrenched in the Constitution.

Paragraph (g) presents three problems of interpretation. The first concerns the notion of an offence. The second concerns what is meant by the existence or non-existence of an offence. The third arises out of the reference made to international law and the general principles recognized by the community of nations.

(a) The Notion of an Offence

A person may not, according to the terms of subsection (g), be convicted of an offence that was not an offence at the time he performed or failed to perform the relevant act. It is clear that this provision does not simply prohibit the creation of entirely new offences out of past acts; it also prohibits the application to past acts of changes to one or more elements of an existing offence.[237] Suppose, for example, that an existing offence consists of the acquisition of a certain type of drug with intention to traffic, and that acquisition for a non-commercial purpose is not prohibited: if the intentional element of this offence were later repealed, the new offence of simple acquisition of drugs could not be imputed to a person who acquired drugs for purely non-commercial purposes before the law was changed. It is clear that the notion of an offence must be analyzed with reference to its various constitutive elements. If an aggravating element is added or a mitigating element withdrawn, the new provision may not be applied to acts or omissions that have already taken place.

It is important to notice, however, that nothing in paragraph (g) guarantees an accused the right to benefit from an amending provision,

---

235 See *Gagnon v. R.*, [1971] C.A. 454 (Qué.) and the authorities cited at 462.

236 *R. v. Madden* (1866), 10 L.C. Jur. 342 (L.C.Q.B.). In this case the court upheld a statute of the Province of Canada which sought to suppress an influx of Fenians (29-30 Vict., c. 3).

237 "The presumption against retrospection applies in general to legislation of a penal character, and to be presumed that a statute creating a new offence, or *extending an existing one*, is not intended to render criminal an act which was innocent when it was committed": *Halsbury's Laws of England*, 3rd ed., 1961, Vol. 36 at 425 [emphasis added].

enacted after his contravention, that reduces the offence either by removing an aggravating element or adding a mitigating one. Such a right exists with respect to punishments (section 11(i) of the Charter) but not with respect to offences. On this point the existing rule has been preserved: the applicable law is the law existing at the time the offence was committed and prosecutions are not affected by the repeal or amendment of this law.[238] However, paragraph (g) would not prevent the legislature from expressly extending the benefit of its repeal of an offence to a person who committed the relevant act prior to the repeal. Would it prevent the legislature from making a reduced offence applicable to him on the ground that this offence did not exist when the act was committed? Probably not. To add to the offence of possession of drugs the element of intention referred to above is to mitigate the offence by requiring an additional constituent element. So long as the mere possession of a drug is an offence, persons in possession of the drug for the purpose of trafficking are guilty of the offence.

If the offence were subsequently amended, becoming possession for the purpose of trafficking, paragraph (g) would not prevent the application of the new provision to such persons, provided that paragraph (i) is observed and such persons are not made liable to a more severe punishment than that stipulated in the original provision.

The preceding observations in all probability apply to defences as well as to elements that are strictly speaking constitutive of an offence, for in truth defences are properly characterized as substantive law and a provision that takes away a defence to a charge affects the very nature of the offence in question.[239] It is not difficult to grasp that if an offence initially consists in the possession of explosives without reasonable excuse and under a new enactment the possibility of pleading reasonable excuse is withdrawn, a new offence is effectively created.[240]

The case of legislation relating to evidence and procedure is more complex. Under currently existing principles of statutory construction, it appears established that newly enacted legislation concerned with purely

---

238 S. 35[43] of the *Interpretation Act*, R.S.C. 1970, c. I-23 [R.S.C. 1985, c. I-21] provides that the repeal of an enactment that creates an offence has no effect on offences already committed (para. (d)) nor on the prosecution of such offences (para. (e)). By virtue of this section, a case like *R. v. Maltais*, [1970] C.A. 596 (Que.), where the accused was allowed to benefit from an amendment enacted after he committed the offence, appears to be wrongly decided.

239 "This statute does not alter the character of the offence or *take away any defence* . . . It is a mere matter of procedure and . . . it is therefore retrospective": *R v. Chandra Dharma*, [1905] 2 K.B. 335 at 339 (C.R.R.) [emphasis added].

240 See, however, *R. v. Kumps*, [1931] 3 D.L.R. 767 (Man. C.A.), where reasonable excuse was considered a matter of evidence and procedure. See also *R. v. Cdn. International Paper* (1974), 20 C.C.C. (2d) 557 (Ont. C.A.).

procedural matters applies to proceedings pending before the courts. The rationale is that legislation of this sort deals with the discovery of facts and the judicial enforcement of rights, rather than with the rights themselves, and it is logical for such activities to be governed by the law in existence when the activities take place. Thus, in one case an amendment that came into force after the offence was committed, and which changed certain rules on corroboration in a manner prejudicial to the accused, was held to apply to him;[241] the same result was reached respecting an amendment that reversed the burden of proof to the detriment of an accused,[242] and an amendment that gave probative value to documents found in the possession of a person accused of commercial conspiracy.[243]

There are, however, certain exceptions to this rule. If the activity to be governed relates neither to the conduct of trial nor to the evaluation of evidence presented at trial, but rather to the methods of procuring evidence during the pre-judicial phase, the applicable law is the law in force at the time the evidence is obtained. Thus, the results of a breathalyzer test do not lose their probative value because a subsequently enacted provision introduces more exacting standards for administering the test.[244] Similarly, were a new provision to relax these standards, one could argue that the admissibility of prior test results would continue to be governed by the previous law. Legal presumptions should constitute another exception to the practice of giving retrospective effect to procedural legislation. A provision that creates a legal presumption of guilt, upon proof that certain acts were performed by an accused, should not apply to acts performed prior to its commencement, for unlike a provision that merely governs the proceedings or the assessment of evidence, a provision of this sort might have governed the behaviour of the accused if, of course, it had been in existence when he performed the acts in question.[245]

---

241 *Re Wicks and Armstrong*, [1928] 2 D.L.R. 210 (Ont. C.A.) and *R. v. Firkins* (1977), 80 D.L.R. (3d) 63 (B.C.C.A.); leave to appeal to S.C.C. refused (1977), 37 C.C.C. (2d) 227n (B.C.C.A.); but see *R. v. Turner* (1976), 31 C.C.C. (2d) 170 (N.W.T.S.C.). On the immediate effect of procedural law, see *Halsbury, supra*, note 237 at 426-427 and *Wigmore on Evidence*, 3rd ed. (Boston: Little, Brown & Co., 1940) Vol. 1 at 209.

242 *R. v. Bingley*, [1929] 1 D.L.R. 777 (N.S.C.A.); but see *R. v. McGlone* (1976), 32 C.C.C. (2d) 233 (Alta. Dist. Ct.).

243 *Howard Smith Paper Mills Ltd. v. R.*, [1957] S.C.R. 403.

244 *R. v. Ali*, [1980] 1 S.C.R. 221. Regarding electronic surveillance, see *R. v. Demeter* (1975), 19 C.C.C. 321 (Ont. H.C.). Regarding the non-applicability, subject to certain qualifications, of s. 11(g) to rules of procedure, see Manning, *supra*, note 154 at 422, where the author refers to American law. Pp.418-424 of this book deal with s. 11(g).

245 See *Bingeman v. McLaughlin* (1977), 77 D.L.R. (3d) 25 (S.C.C.). Although the legal presumption in this case was civil in character, the reasoning is transposable to penal matters. The opposite conclusion was reached in *Gagnon v. R.*, *supra*, note 235, but

One will have noticed that the various principles discussed above are principles of statutory construction. It remains to be seen whether the effect of the language of section 11(g) is to entrench these principles in the Constitution. The question, more precisely, is whether the concept of an offence in this section includes merely the constitutive elements of an offence, or extends as well to defences, to facts giving rise to presumptions, and to the rules of evidence and procedure. For the reasons already stated, we believe that the concept does extend to defences. However, we do not see how it could be extended to embrace questions of evidence and procedure, subject to what follows respecting legal presumptions.

In our view, the concept of an offence does include acts that give rise to presumptions. On this point, one could argue that an act which triggers a presumption is distinct from the offence, that it is merely a form of evidence and that consequently it may occur prior to the law creating the offence without any violation of section 11(g).

It is possible that this is the position the courts will adopt.[246] But this position is quite formalistic, for an act that gives rise to a presumption of guilt effectively amounts to a constitutive element of the offence. As noted above, an accused would have been able to modify his behaviour appropriately if he had known that the act contemplated was going to later create a presumption against him. From this perspective, one can see that the retrospective application of a presumption violates the spirit of section 11(g).

This does not mean that no act performed prior to the creation of an offence can be taken into consideration in determining whether an accused is guilty. Proving similar facts, for example, is not the same as applying a legal presumption, and nothing in section 11(g) prevents consideration of relevant similar acts performed by an accused prior to the commencement of the offence. In somewhat analogous fashion, the conviction of a person for theft would be admissible evidence in the subsequent trial of that person for repeated theft, even though this conviction occurred before the offence of repeated theft was created, for one could hardly argue that the person would have refrained from committing the first theft had he known an offence of repeated theft existed. The retrospective application of a legal presumption is of a different order and is more likely to infringe section 11(g).

---

in that case the retrospective character of the presumption was clearly indicated by the language of the statute, so that in the absence of any constitutional restriction, the court had no choice but to apply the law according to its terms.

246 In *Gagnon v. R., ibid.* at 464, Mr. Justice Brossard observed that acts performed by the accused prior to October 16, 1970, created merely a rebuttable presumption of their membership in the *Front de libération du Québec* on or after that date. "It is necessary that the crime have been committed on or after October 16th [translation]" he wrote.

Determining the time of an offence can pose certain difficulties in the case of so-called continuing offences, such as possession or forcible confinement. According to the general principles of construction, if an offence is created while the relevant acts are on-going, the new enactment has an immediate application and so applies to acts already begun.[247] To be sure, it may be difficult to determine whether an offence is a continuing one. This question might arise, for example, in the case of a refusal to obey a judicial or administrative order to rehire an employee.[248] But subject to this question, the detailed examination of which is beyond the scope of this study, the time of commission of an offence would probably be determined for the purposes of section 11(g) with reference to the general principles of statutory construction. It is always possible that a case will arise in which a law adopted during an on-going course of action is so clearly aimed at particular individuals, and is so pointedly repressive of their conduct, that one could conclude that the legislature had attempted to render a judgment rather than pass a law.[249] But that, strictly speaking, is another question.

By virtue of section 6 of the *Interpretation Act*,[250] an enactment that by its terms is to come into force on a particular day "shall be construed as coming into force on the expiration of the previous day", and an enactment that is silent on the matter "shall be construed as coming into force . . . on the expiration of the day immediately before the day" the enactment was enacted. These provisions are intended less to render enactments retrospective than to provide a convenient method for determining precisely when acts and regulations come into force. It is nonetheless true that if an individual contravenes an enactment creating an offence on the very day the enactment commences, but at a time prior to formal assent, section 11(g) ought to prohibit his conviction. We should also notice that section 11(2) of the *Statutory Instruments Act*[251] provides that, subject to certain exceptions, no person may be convicted for having contravened a regulation that was not published at the time of the offence. This protection goes beyond that provided by section 11(g) of the Charter, which refers to the existence of the offence and not to publication of the enactment establishing it.

Certain features of the budget pose a difficult problem in connection with section 11(g). In Canada, the secrecy of the budget is a well-established

---

247 *R. v. Levine* (1926), 46 C.C.C. 342 (Man. C.A.), on the possession of alcohol.

248 *Cdn. Marconi Co. v. Cour des Sessions de la Paix*, [1945] Qué. K.B. 472 (C.A.).

249 This hypothetical case is reminiscent of *Liyanage v. R.* [1966] 1 All E.R. 650 (P.C.), where the impugned statute, in addition to being strongly individualized, was also clearly retroactive.

250 *Supra*, note 238.

251 S.C. 1970-71-72, c. 38.

practice and many budgetary measures, enacted into law in some cases long after the day on which the budget was introduced, are given retroactive application to that day. The reasons for this are readily understood, especially in the case of a sales or excise tax: foreknowledge of an increase or decrease in the rate of tax could stimulate or retard purchases, thereby causing inimical economic consequences and distorting expected revenues. One should note that in England, at the beginning of this century, the practice of collecting taxes before the enactment of the statute establishing them, on the sole authority of a Parliamentary resolution, was held to be illegal and this necessitated the adoption of a statutory provision, still on the books, giving the force of law to this class of resolutions.[252]

For our purposes, the question that arises is whether a person who refuses to pay or withholds a tax, for example, or who takes advantage of a certain fiscal manoeuver, and who thereby contravenes a law that has not yet been adopted, has done something or failed to do something that "at the time of the act or omission . . . constituted an offence under Canadian . . . law".

It is important to realize that, unlike the Constitution of the United States, section 11(g) of the Canadian Charter in no way prohibits retroactive taxation, for example the imposition of tax on income that was already earned or on a transaction or gift that was already completed before the adoption of the statute imposing the tax. Even in the United States, the clause prohibiting "*ex post facto*" laws (article 1, section 9 of the Constitution) was held at an early date to apply to penal matters only.[253] Fiscal legislation was excluded because levying a tax is not a measure "in punishment of a crime".[254] It is rather the "due process" clause of the Fifth Amendment that hinders retroactive taxation, but only to a very limited degree.[255] Thus, American courts readily uphold the retroactive taxation of income on the grounds that the taxpayer would not have refused the income had he known it was going to be taxed. The retroactive taxation of a gift is more difficult to justify and a tax of this type was held

---

252 *Bowles v. Bank of England*, [1913] 1 Ch. 57. This decision necessitated the adoption of the *Provisional Collection of Taxes Act*, 1913 (3-4 Geo. 5), c. 3. On this point, see E.C.S. Wade & G.G. Phillips, *Constitutional and Administrative Law*, 9th ed., by A.W. Bradley (New York: Longman Group, 1977), at 191-192. In relation to Canada, see especially R.J. Bertrand, A. Desjardins & R. Hurtubise, *Les mécanismes de législation, d'administration et d'interprétation de la fiscalité fédérale* (1967), at 39-45 and 55 *et seq.*

253 *Calder v. Bull*, 3 U.S. (3 Dall.) 386 (1798).

254 *Bankers' Trust Co. v. Blodgett*, 260 U.S. 647 (1923).

255 See in particular F.A. Ballard, "Retroactive Federal Taxation" (1934-35), 48 *Harv. L. Rev.* 592; C.B. Hochman, "The Supreme Court and the Constitutionality of Retroactive Legislation" (1959-60), 73 *Harv. L. Rev.* 692 at 706-711.

unconstitutional to the extent that it applied to a gift made while the taxing measure was still before Congress, just prior to its final passage and approval by the President. The taxpayer, wrote the Supreme Court, "cannot foresee and ought not be required to guess the outcome of pending measures".[256]

This type of limitation does not exist in Canada and the government can legally introduce a retroactive tax and can legally exact its payment. But can the government prosecute a person for contravening a fiscal provision if the contravention occurred before the provision was enacted into law? No one could claim that fiscal offences are not covered by section 11(g). Therefore, unless it seems that the offence is of a continuing nature, begun before the enactment of the new provision and continuing at its commencement, the government is facing a serious problem.[257] One method of solving it would be to distinguish between provisions that impose the tax and provisions dealing with offences and penal sanctions. On this approach section 11(g) would prohibit the legislature from retroactively making an offence of acts such as swearing a false or misleading declaration, omitting to deduct certain sums at the source, evading the payment of tax, or failing to give notice of the disposition of certain property, while section 11(i) would prohibit the imposition of a penalty more severe than the one provided for at the time of the offence. On the other hand, section 11(g) would not prohibit the legislature from retroactively establishing such matters as the tax to be paid, the value of deductions, and the kinds of property whose disposition must be disclosed. However, this is a fragile distinction, and it may be that in order to prosecute a person for contravening fiscal legislation that was not in force when the contravention occurred, section 1 of the Charter should be relied upon, except if the legislation expressly stipulates that it is to apply to such contraventions "notwithstanding" section 11(g), all of which must conform to section 33.

(b) The Existence and Non-Existence of an Offence

A double question arises here. On the one hand, does the notion of a new offence, as defined above, refer only to a legislative creation, or does it include a jurisprudential creation? On the other hand, does the

---

256 *Untermyer v. Anderson*, 276 U.S. 440 at 445-446 (1928).

257 See *Beauchamp v. Outremont (City)*, [1970] C.A. 286 (Qué.). The headnote in this case is as follows: "It is recognized that municipal by-laws may not be retroactive, but an annual tax, being indivisible, is not an instance of a retroactive by-law where it is imposed for the current year." The issue here was not a penal offence, but the imposition of tax by municipal bylaw.

idea of a non-existent offence include the case of an imprecise or poorly defined infraction, so that section 11(g) can be said not only to prohibit retroactive offences, but also to guarantee clarity in penal law?

With respect to the first question, we have every reason to conclude that a shift in the case law which amounts to the creation of a new offence should not be applied to acts committed before the shift.[258] Take, for example, a judgment from a superior court which effectively expands the scope of what constitutes obscene material. Subject to the difficulty of whether section 11(g) applies, analyzed above, the fact that the expansion arises from the case law should not mean, in and of itself, that section 11(g) does not apply. Article 7 of the *European Convention on Human Rights*, similar to section 11(g) of the Charter, is interpreted as prohibiting not only retroactive legislation, but also every form of expanded application of penal law.[259] The application of a jurisprudentially expanded definition of obscene material to acts committed prior to the new interpretation would amount to what the *European Convention* prohibits under its present interpretation. Of course, this issue only arises when one is faced with a clear shift in the case law.

In line with the above logic, one should also conclude that an imprecise or poorly defined offence amounts to an offence which is non-existent within the meaning of section 11(g). Such an interpretation has been given to article 7 of the *European Convention*, although one must be clear that the mere fact that an offence requires judicial interpretation does not mean that the offence is imprecise and constitutionally inoperative.[260]

(c) International Law

In its initial draft, the Charter made no reference to international law in connection with the non-retrospective application of penal legislation (see section 11(e)). At the suggestion of the Canadian Jewish Congress, this version was modified so that a person could claim the right not to be found guilty of an offence only if his act or omission was not at the

---

258 See *Marks v. U.S.*, 430 U.S. 188 (1977).

259 With respect to the principle of non-retroactivity under the *European Convention*, one author writes: "The principle has a dual application, affecting on the one hand the legislature, on the other hand the criminal courts. In the first place, it prohibits retrospective penal legislation. Secondly, it precludes the courts from extending the scope of the criminal law by interpretation" F.G. Jacobs, *The European Convention of Human Rights* (Oxford: Clarendon Press, 1975) at 20.

260 Manning, *supra*, note 154 at 420. In *Skoke-Graham v. R.*, [1985] 1 S.C.R. 106, the appellants contended that s. 172(3) of the *Criminal Code*, which makes it an offence to disturb religious ceremonies, was contrary to s. 11(g) and that the offence was not one recognized in law. The court did not examine this argument.

relevant time "an offence under Canadian or international law". In January 1981, again in response to the representations of the Canadian Jewish community, a further requirement was added: the act or omission must not have been "criminal according to the general principles of law recognized by the community of nations". This final amendment was clearly inspired by article 15(2) of the *International Covenant on Civil and Political Rights*, for the formulation of the two provisions is nearly identical.

What is an offence under international law and in what way, if any, does the notion of an act that is "criminal according to the general principles of law recognized by the community of nations" add to the notion of an offence under international law?

"An offence at international law is an illicit act of a guilty person which, being harmful to human interrelationships in the international community, is prohibited and punished by international law".[261] Genocide, war crimes and crimes against peace or humanity come readily to mind. It is clear that the existence of an offence under international law can be established not only on the basis of the primary sources of this law — custom and treaty — but also on the basis of secondary sources and in particular the general principles of law, those "principles of a higher order which, being inherent in the legal conscience of man, are generally recognized by civilized nations in their respective municipal laws".[262] Given that the "general principles of law recognized by civilized nations" are, in the words of article 38(c) of the *Statute of the International Court of Justice*, among the sources of law that the court is required to apply, the notion of an offence under international law clearly includes violations of these general principles. However if, following the example of article 15(2) of the *Covenant on Civil and Political Rights* and article 7(2) of the *European Convention on Human Rights*, section 11(g) of the Charter refers to these principles in specific fashion, the purpose is to indicate as clearly as possible that the constitutional protection against the retrospective application of penal law may not be relied on to preclude convictions such as those obtained against Nazi criminals in the aftermath of the last world war.[263]

---

261 S. Plawski, *Étude des principes fondamentaux du droit international pénal* [L.G.D.J.] (Paris: 1972) at 74-75.

262 S. Glaser, *Introduction à l' étude du droit international pénal* (Paris: 1954) at 44. The author demonstrates that the notion of an offence under international law includes violations of generally recognized principles of law.

263 One should note that the European Commission of Human Rights has held that by virtue of art. 7(2) of the Convention, a journalist could be deprived of his right to practise his profession by way of punishment after the war for acts of collaboration committed by him during the war: see A.H. Robertson, *Human Rights in Europe*, 2nd

As pointed out during the debates of the Joint Committee leading up to the proclamation of the Charter,[264] section 11(g) does not exclude the necessity for an empowering statutory provision before Canada can prosecute war criminals. Its effect is simply to remove any constitutional impediment to the enactment of the necessary provision, provided that the act or omission in question was at the relevant time prohibited by the municipal law of Canada, by international law or by generally recognized principles of law. One may thus conclude that, even if an act were legal under Canadian municipal law, a person committing that act could be prosecuted if the act were contrary to international law, and *vice versa*. This being established, there is still work to be done. The harmonization of municipal and international law remains a desirable goal, and some thought should perhaps be given to revising section 15 of the *Criminal Code*.[265]

6. THE RIGHT TO THE BENEFIT OF THE LESSER PUNISHMENT

Section 11(i) provides:

> Any person charged with an offence has the right
>
> . . .
>
> (i)   if found guilty of the offence and if the punishment for the offence has

---

ed. (Manchester University Press, 1977) at 85. This author reports that at the time of ratifying the Convention, Germany made a reservation respecting this article on the grounds that it was contrary to art. 103(2) of the German *Basic Law* respecting the non-retroactivity of penal law.

264   *Minutes of the Joint Committee on the Constitution, supra,* note 10, Vol. 47 at 59.

265   See H. Fischer, "The Human Rights Covenants and Canadian Law" (1977), 15 *Can. Yr. Bk. Int. L.* 42 at 79-80. In the author's view, this section is contrary to the spirit of art. 15 of the *International Covenant on Civil and Political Rights.* Art. 15 of the Covenant reads as follows:

1.   No one shall be held guilty of any criminal offence on account of any act or omission which did not constitute a criminal offence, under national or international law, at the time when it was committed. Nor shall a heavier penalty be imposed than the one that was applicable at the time when the criminal offence was committed. If, subsequent to the commission of the offence, provision is made by law for the imposition of the lighter penalty, the offender shall benefit thereby.

2.   Nothing in this article shall prejudice the trial and punishment of any person for any act or omission which, at the time when it was committed, was criminal according to the general principles of law recognized by the community of nations.

Section 15 of the *Criminal Code* provides: "No person shall be convicted of an offence in respect of an act or omission in obedience to the laws for the time being made and enforced by persons in *de facto* possession of the sovereign power in and over the place where the act or omission occurs."

been varied between the time of commission and the time of sentencing, to the benefit of the lesser punishment.

One cannot say that this provision is entirely new in Canadian law. Section 36(e)[44(e)] of the *Interpretation Act* already provides that the law applicable in the matter of punishment is the law existing at the time the punishment is imposed, whenever this law provides a less severe penalty than the one provided for at the time the offence was committed.[266] In cases where the punishment has been increased between the commission of the offence and the imposition of the sentence, the general principle of construction, that penal laws do not operate retrospectively, dictates that the applicable punishment is the one provided at the time the offence was committed.[267] Prior to the enactment of the Charter, the legislature could disregard this principle, as it could disregard section 36(e) of the *Interpretation Act*, and require the application of the more severe penalty existing at the time of sentencing, provided it did so in clear language.[268] Thus, the effect of section 11(i) of the Charter is to raise to the rank of constitutional law two principles that were formerly ordinary principles of interpretation: section 36(e) of the *Interpretation Act*, and the presumption against the retrospective application of a greater punishment.

We may begin by noting that a person charged with an offence has a right to the benefit of the lesser punishment only if the law is changed before he receives his sentence, and not while he is serving it.[269] This is a point on which the wording of section 11(i) is very clear and contrasts, for example, with article 15 of the *International Covenant on Civil and*

---

266 *Supra*, note 238. This section reads as follows: "Where an enactment, in this section called the "former enactment", is repealed and another enactment, in this section called the "new enactment", is substituted therefor, when any punishment, penalty or forfeiture is reduced or mitigated by the new enactment, the punishment, penalty or forfeiture if imposed or adjudged after the repeal shall be reduced or mitigated accordingly." This section is applied in *R. v. Dawdy* (1973), 12 C.C.C. (2d) 477 (Ont. C.A.), where the maximum penalty for theft had been reduced from ten years to two years between the offence and the trial. The appellant, first sentenced to three years' imprisonment, received a reduced sentence of a year and a half. S. 746 of the *Criminal Code*, S.C. 1953-54, c. 51, a section not consolidated in 1970, also asserted the rule of the lesser punishment. For an example of a provision that violates this rule, see *An Act to amend the Criminal Code* (Capital Murder), S.C. 1960-61, c. 44, s. 17.

267 "The presumption against retrospection applies in general to legislation of a penal character, and a statute increasing the penalties for existing offences is not intended to apply in relation to offences committed before its commencement": *Halsbury, supra*, note 237 at 425.

268 See, *e.g.*, the English cases *D.P.P. v. Lamb*, [1941] 2 K.B. 89; *Buckman v. Button*, [1943], K.B. 405 (D.C.); *R. v. Olivier*, [1944] K.B. 68 (C.C.A.).

269 *Re Mitchell and R., supra*, note 153; *Compeau v. National Parole Bd. (Can)* [1987] 3 F.C. 682 (T.D.); *R. v. Gamble* (1986), 17 W.C.B. 188 (Ont. H.C.), aff'd (April 30, 1987) Doc. No. C.A. 832/86 (Ont. C.A.), rev'd (December 8, 1988) Doc. No. 20433 (S.C.C.).

Political Rights which simply states: "If, subsequent to the commission of the offence, provision is made by law for the imposition of a lighter penalty, the offender shall benefit thereby." The greater precision of section 11(i) is of a kind which robs it of much of its impact, in that it is principally while a sentence is being served that changes in the existing scheme of penalties are likely to occur.

The first question arising in connection with this section is — what is a "punishment"? Corporal punishment, imprisonment, confinement in a reformatory, fines, forfeitures, certain civil or political disabilities, the suspension of a sentence accompanied by a probation order: these are clearly forms of punishment. One may question whether the notion of punishment also embraces the loss of certain rights — the right to operate a vehicle, for example, or the right to engage in a particular activity or profession. Such rights may be lost automatically upon conviction for an offence or they may be withdrawn after a conviction by an administrative body — a professional corporation, for example. However, the answer to this question appears to be "no". Since the whole of section 11 applies only criminal or quasi-criminal procedures, matters involving administrative law and procedures are not affected by it, although section 7 would apply.[270]

One should be careful not to confuse a change in the sentence with a change in the definition of the offence. Thus, an accused could not invoke section 11(i) as a way of enjoying the lesser punishment attached to a new and different offence, even if the new offence is very similar to the one he faces.[271] Having said this, section 11(i) should be applicable to the situation of a person charged with an offence which has been abolished between the time of commission and sentencing, but not replaced. In such circumstances the accused should not be convicted, for the disappearance of the offence causes the punishment to disappear as well, meaning that the lesser punishment is no punishment at all. Even if the rule against non-retroactive offences in section 11(g) does not guarantee that an accused will not be convicted of an offence which is non-existent at the time of sentencing, section 11(i) should complement it and give rise to such a result.

One should also not confuse a change in sentence with a change in the jurisdiction of a court. An accused could not use section 11(i) to require

---

270 Regarding the fact that the suspension of a licence to drive is not punishment within the meaning of s. 11(i), see *R. v. Pellerin; R. v. Lauzon* (1982), 17 M.V.R. 203 (Qué. C.S.P.); *Lebel v. R.* (1982), 30 C.R. (3d) 285 (Qué. S.C.). *Contra: R. v. Michaud* (1982), 17 M.V.R. 210 (Qué. S.C.).

271 *R. v. Tremblay* (1983), 34 C.R. (3d) 183 (Qué. S.C.); *R. v. L.G.T.* (1986), 1 W.C.B. (2d) 163 (B.C. Co.Ct.).

that he be tried by a court recently created, rather than by the court before which he was arraigned, even if the new court were empowered to impose a lesser sentence than could be imposed by the original one. In any event, this is the direction taken by the case law on this point.[272]

Section 11(i) was intended to deal with situations where changes in sentence occur as a result of changes to the law. One could not therefore contend that a fine which increased as a function of delays in payment is covered by this provision, for the increase flows from delay in payment, not from a modification of the legislation.[273] What happens though if the change in sentence arises as a result of a Supreme Court judgment, rendered in another matter, but between the commission of an offence and the moment of sentencing; for example, a judgment determining that a minimum sentence was invalid? In analyzing the scope of section 11(g), we concluded that a new offence could be either created by legislation or arise as a result of judicial interpretation of an existing offence. In somewhat the same way, one could contend that the lesser punishment under section 11(i) includes, in addition to legislatively modified punishment, a sentence which the courts have softened, by way of interpretation, between the commission of an offence and the moment of sentencing.

Finally, it appears quite evident that the manner in which a sentence is experienced and administered is covered by the right not to be subject to cruel and unusual punishment found in section 12 and not included in matters covered by section 11(i). The latter is limited to what is handed down to an accused by a judge, pursuant to the law and following the conclusion of his trial.

Is it possible to isolate specific criteria on the basis of which one punishment may be judged more or less severe than another? Such a judgment is easy when it only includes comparing two different terms of imprisonment. But in many cases this assessment must be purely qualitative and subjective, and without going so far as to claim that it would be left to the accused to decide, one may urge that a judge ought to pay special attention to the representations of an accused. When the right to trial by jury was being discussed (section 11(f) of the Charter), it was suggested that corporal punishment is a more severe penalty than the loss of liberty. This analysis is obviously relevant to the interpretation of section 11(i). From a subjective point of view, imprisonment may not

---

272 *R. v. L.* (1985), 10 O.A.C. 308 (Ont. C.A.); *Re M. and R.* (1985), 21 C.C.C. (3d) 330 (C.A.), leave to appeal to S.C.C. refused Ont. (1985), 52 O.R. 688n (S.C.C.); *Re Jones and R.* (1985), 20 C.C.C. (3d) 91 (B.C.S.C.).

273 *Re McCutcheon and Toronto* (1983), 147 D.L.R. (3d) 193 (Ont. H.C.). This case also decided that voluntary payment of a fine out of court does not constitute punishment within the meaning of s. 11(i), because of its non-coercive nature.

in every case be perceived as a more severe penalty than a fine. But objectively speaking, it is, and doubtless it is this interpretation that will prevail in the construction of paragraph (i). As between imprisonment for a certain period and being sent to a reformatory or rehabilitation centre for a longer period, which is the more severe punishment? It is probably the former, for the latter is not in principle strictly punitive, and the character of a sentence is no less important than its duration in assessing the severity of a punishment.[274]

Another possibility is the amendment of maximum or minimum penalties. A law that increases either or both or that introduces a minimum penalty for an offence where no minimum was formerly stipulated obviously increases the severity of the punishment, just as a law decreasing such penalties or introducing a maximum for the first time renders the punishment less severe. Were a law to both increase the minimum and decrease the maximum penalty for a particular offence, or *vice versa*, the best solution would be for the judges to fix the punishment in terms of the penalty that is in each case, maximum and minimum, the less severe.[275] This is what section 11(i) of the Charter requires in according an accused the right to the benefit of the lesser punishment, which must include both the maximum and the minimum of the punishment.

Finally, we should call attention to certain difficulties that may arise in determining the time that an offence is committed. These difficulties have been analyzed in connection with the non-retrospective application of penal law (section 11(g) of the Charter) and the remarks made there are equally relevant here.

As for the time of sentencing, which often follows the time of judgment, the question here is what punishment a court of appeal ought to impose in cases where the legislature has reduced the penalty in the interim between the initial sentencing and the rendering of judgment on an appeal against the sentence. As a general rule, of course, an appeal court applies the same law as the court of first instance. However, there are exceptions. Procedural laws, for example, are generally given immediate application

---

274 In *R. v. Burnshine*, [1975] 1 S.C.R. 693, the court took this into account in reaching the conclusion that a certain provision did not violate the principle of equality before the law as found in the *Canadian Bill of Rights*, even though it authorized the confinement of a juvenile in a reformatory for a longer period than the maximum term prescribed under the general law for the offence he had committed.

275 P. Roubier, *Le droit transitoire* (Paris: Dalloz & Sirey, 1960) at 499 *et seq.*. One should take into account the fact that this is a work on French law and is not in the least concerned with constitutional law, but rather with ordinary principles of construction.

to actions pending before the courts.[276] Of course, no one would claim that a provision that imposes a penalty is a procedural law. But it too is a type of law whose application should be immediate, inasmuch as the imposition of a sentence is the example, *par excellence*, of a judicial act that does not simply declare a state of law, but is constitutive of that state. If one accepts that the purpose of section 11(i) is to ensure that an accused is punished in accordance with the norms existing at the time his punishment is being studied and decided, whenever these norms are less severe than those previously existing, it is plausible to maintain that the time in question is the last occasion on which such study is undertaken. That, moreover, is the conclusion of certain commentators.[277] The language of paragraph (i), it is true, is not explicit on this point. It refers to the time of sentencing rather than the time when the sentence is made final, whereas paragraph (b) of the section uses the expressions "finally acquitted" and "finally found guilty". In our opinion, this is not conclusive. To hold that the time of sentencing is the time when the sentence is definitively established is in keeping with the spirit of paragraph (i), which derogates from the principle of non-retroactivity in cases where a law posterior to the offence reduces the penalty, and it also accords with the fact that the court which hears the appeal against sentence is to consider the fitness and not simply the legality of the sentence, and has as much discretion in this regard as the court whose sentence is appealed.

We can finally ask if paragraph 11(i) offers only the choice between two penalties — the one at the time of the infraction and the one at the time of the sentence — or whether it creates a third one which exists between those two moments. We think that the latter is preferable. In effect, it appears from a careful reading of this section that neither the time of the information nor that of the offence determines the applicable penalties. Rather, they determine the period within which the less severe punishment should be identified.[278]

---

276 *Maxwell on the Interpretation of Statutes*, 12th ed. by P. St. J. Langan (London: Sweet & Maxwell, 1969) at 222 *et seq.* The principle of the immediate application of procedural law is complex. It is investigated more extensively in the study on the non-retrospectivity of penal law (s. 11(g) of the Charter).

277 Roubier, *supra*, note 275 at 506.

278 In *R. v. Gamble*, supra, note 269, the court seems to reject that solution, but the infraction, the hearing and the appeal were happened before the coming into force of the Charter. The Supreme Court of Canada has reversed that judgement on the footing of section 7 instead of paragraph 11(1) of the Charter.

Note: The author wants to thank Mr. Jean Ledair, former student of the Faculty of Law of the Université de Montréal, for the ueful work he did as research assistant on the above study.

12

The Role of the Accused in the Criminal Process

(Sections 10(a), (b), 11(a), (c), (d) and 13)

Ed Ratushny

1. INTRODUCTION

This chapter will deal with the cluster of provisions in the *Canadian Charter of Rights and Freedoms* that relate to the role which a suspect or an accused, respectively, may be required to play in the investigation of a criminal offence or the adjudication of guilt in relation to such an offence. The provisions to be examined are:

Section 10:

Everyone has the right on arrest or detention

(a) to be informed promptly of the reasons therefor;
(b) to retain and instruct counsel without delay and to be informed of that right.

Section 11:

Any person charged with an offence has the right
(a) to be informed without reasonable delay of the specific offence;
(c) not to be compelled to be a witness in proceedings against that person in respect of the offence;
(d) to be presumed innocent until proven guilty according to law in a fair and public hearing by an independent and impartial tribunal.

Section 13:

A witness who testifies in any proceedings has the right not to have any incriminating evidence so given used to incriminate that witness in any other proceedings, except in a prosecution for perjury or for the giving of contradictory evidence.

While the other "legal rights" in the Charter also define the relationship of an individual to the criminal process, they do not as directly establish the extent to which the suspect or accused may be required to participate in the investigation or proof of an offence which he is alleged to have committed.[1]

It is impossible to deal, even superficially, with all the judicial developments in relation to these provisions of the Charter since the first edition of this book. This article, therefore, does not purport to be comprehensive. Rather, it is selective in canvassing some of the key judicial developments since the Charter has come into force.

The concept of a "privilege against self-incrimination" is usually the focal point of any discussion of the role that an individual may be required to play in the proof of his guilt. A suspect or an accused is said to have the "right to remain silent". It is said that the state should not be permitted to force an accused to establish the case against himself out of his own mouth. In Latin, the idea has been expressed as *nemo tenetur seipsum accusare* or *nemo tenetur seipsum prodere*. Although the phrase "protection against self-incrimination" is contained in the *Canadian Bill of Rights*,[2] it does not appear in the Charter. Why?

The explanation is to be found in a series of Canadian cases decided in the decade following the passage of our *Bill of Rights*. Early in that period, the thesis was advanced that there was no such thing as a general

---

1 S. 9 of the Charter may also be significant in relation to this general issue although it has wider implications. Since it is analyzed in another chapter, it is considered only peripherally below.

2 S.C. 1960, c. 44, s. 2(d), reprinted in R.S.C. 1970, App. III [R.S.C. 1985, App. III].

right or privilege against self-incrimination in Canada.[3] It was argued that the concept amounted to no more than a descriptive phrase for two specific rules: the non-compellability of an accused at his criminal trial and the privilege of a witness not to have his testimony used against himself in future proceedings.

In *Marcoux v. R.*,[4] Mr. Justice Dickson, delivering the judgment of the Supreme Court of Canada, pointed out that the concept was "often incorrectly advanced in favour of a much broader proposition"[5] than the two rules referred to above. Subsequently, the Ontario Court of Appeal stated bluntly that "there does not exist in this country a general privilege against self-incrimination".[6]

This general subject area has been analyzed by the author in considerable detail in *Self-Incrimination in the Canadian Criminal Process.*[7] The following discussion draws freely from that earlier study. In general, it is submitted that the absence of the "self-incrimination" phraseology from the formulation of rights in the Charter is a laudable development. It encourages attention to be focussed upon the specific procedural protections to which an accused is entitled without the distractions of emotive political battles of the past.[8]

What procedural protection, then, does the *Canadian Charter of Rights and Freedoms* provide to the suspect or accused in relation to the role which he must play in the investigation or adjudication of his criminal guilt or non-guilt? Three distinct situations must be considered:

1. the investigatory stage which, essentially, involves the relationship of the suspect or accused person to the police;
2. the trial stage which, basically, involves the compellability of an accused to testify at his own trial; and

---

3 E. Ratushny, "Is there a Right Against Self-Incrimination in Canada?" (1973), 19 *McGill L.J.* 1. See also E. Ratushny, "Self-Incrimination: Nailing the Coffin Shut" (1978), 20 *C.L.Q.* 312.

4 (1975), 29 C.R.N.S. 211 (S.C.C.). See also *Di Iorio v. Montreal Jail Warden*, [1978] 1 S.C.R. 152.

5 *Ibid.* at 214.

6 *R. v. Sweeney (No. 2)* (1977), 35 C.C.C. (2d) 245 at 250 (Ont. C.A.), *per* Zuber J.A., delivering the judgment of the court (Arnup and Blair JJ.A.). See also *Stickney v. Trusz* (1973), 25 C.R.N.S. 257 (Ont. H.C.), aff'd (1974), 28 C.R.N.S. 125 (Ont. Div. Ct.), aff'd (1974), 28 C.R.N.S. 125 at 126 (Ont. C.A.), leave to appeal to S.C.C. refused (1974), 28 C.R.N.S. 125 at 127n (S.C.C.); *Royal American Shows Inc. v. Laycraft*, [1978] 2 W.W.R. 169 at 193-94, (Alta. T.D.) *per* Miller J.

7 E. Ratushny, *Self Incrimination in the Canadian Criminal Process* (Toronto: Carswell, 1979).

8 *Ibid.* at 159-174. See also the Haines-Maloney debate in "Future of the Law of Evidence — The Right to Remain Silent — Two Views", in *Studies in Canadian Evidence*, R. Salhany & R. Carter eds. (Toronto: Butterworths, 1972) at 322.

3. the status of a suspect or accused *qua* witness at some other proceeding (i.e., other than his own criminal trial) where his testimony might provide potential evidence against him at his own, subsequent, criminal trial.

Each of these will be discussed in turn.

2. THE INVESTIGATORY STAGE

Police interrogation of suspects, including persons who have been arrested for a specific offence, has been a significant feature of our criminal process for many years. It is an area in which police powers have remained largely unregulated. Nowhere have our legislators defined the limits of police authority to interrogate citizens. Nor have they articulated the rights or obligations of an individual in the face of such questioning. The law has been left to the courts to develop on an *ad hoc* basis, largely in relation to the admissibility of evidence gathered as a result of police interrogation. It may be useful to begin by summarizing briefly the existing state of the law and practice in this area.

There are only two ways in which a person may be lawfully taken to the police station and questioned. The first is when the police have sufficient grounds for an arrest and take the suspect into custody for the purpose of charging and/or bringing the suspect before the courts. The second is when a person simply agrees to attend at the police station or elsewhere and to submit to questioning. In both situations, the individual is entitled to remain silent. There is no legal requirement to respond to police questioning.

Many citizens, quite properly, feel a moral obligation to cooperate with the police by answering questions in relation to the investigation of offences. Such a citizen might also be willing to attend at the police station to examine photographs or witness an identification line-up. However, where the citizen is personally implicated in the commission of the offence under investigation, he will usually be well-advised to take the position that he will save anything he might have to say until he is aware of the specific charge against him and the evidence which he will have to meet. He should also resist any attempts to persuade him, voluntarily, to attend at the police station where his resistance to questioning might be overcome much more easily.

Why is it, then, that the successful interrogation of mere "suspects" in police stations frequently occurs? The following passage illustrates both the basis upon which such interrogation proceeds and the police motivation for it:

> It is, of course, still the common practice for a suspect to be invited to come to the police station to be questioned. It is doubtful whether many people

know that they have the right to refuse to go and when once there have the right to leave at any time unless they have been charged. Questioning is much more effective in a police station where the suspect feels himself to be at the mercy of the police. In the course of questioning it is not unusual for pressure to be put upon the suspect to be co-operative. If the suspect is poor and uneducated and ignorant of his legal rights, the pressure is likely to be effective. This is the real reason why interrogation either before or after an arrest in a police station is the usual standard method of investigation. It is extremely convenient.[9]

Such interrogation occurs because persons are often unaware that they are entitled to refuse. In effect, there is a mistaken belief that one is required to submit in these circumstances. Of course, if there is sufficient evidence to lay a charge, there is no problem with the police taking the person into custody and, once there, to commence interrogation. (The subject is still legally entitled to refuse to cooperate.)

Thus, where sufficient grounds for an arrest do not exist, the police must obtain "voluntary" attendance in order to conduct the interrogation at the police station. A Report of the Australian Law Reform Commission pointed out that:

> As the police will readily acknowledge, the law is being somewhat less than carefully observed. The concept of "voluntary co-operation" would appear to be very much stretched in the Australian police practice.[10]

The Report also makes reference to the related problems of denying a person in custody access to friends, relatives and counsel, including the frustration of inquiries about the whereabouts of a person in custody and the problems resulting from his transfer from one police station to another. The motivation for such tactics on the part of police is obvious. If legal counsel is permitted, the suspect may learn of his true legal status and cease to "cooperate". Moreover, contact with the "outside world" might reduce the subtle atmosphere of coercion which is conducive to effective interrogation from a police perspective.[11]

The courts most frequently encounter police interrogation practices when, at trial, an earlier out-of-court statement of the accused to a police officer is submitted in evidence against that accused. A long line of case law has reinforced the condition for admissibility of such evidence.

The classic formulation of the rule is that of Lord Sumner in *Ibrahim*

---

9 J. Honsburger, "The Power of Arrest and the Duties and Rights of Citizens and the Police" in [1963] *Lectures L.S.U.C. 1* at 10.

10 *Report No. 2 (An Interim Report): Criminal Investigation* (1975) at 28.

11 Techniques of interrogation which have been used by Canadian police to break down the resistance of suspects have been described and discussed in some detail: see Ratushny, *supra*, note 7, ch. 5 at 191-309.

v. R.,[12] as adopted in subsequent Supreme Court of Canada decisions.[13] The earlier statement of an accused may only be introduced at his trial where the Crown has first established that the statement was made voluntarily. However, "voluntariness" takes on the technical meaning of not having been given by the accused because of "fear of prejudice" or "hope of advantage" held out by a "person in authority". At the stage when the Crown wishes to introduce such a statement, a *voir dire* must be held to inquire into the circumstances of the taking of the statement. The onus is on the Crown to establish "voluntariness". The police are not required to warn the subject that he has no legal obligation to answer, but the absence of a warning may be a factor to consider in determining voluntariness.[14]

The voluntariness rule does not operate significantly as a restraint upon police interrogation techniques. The courts have restricted its application narrowly to the categories of "fear of prejudice" or "hope of advantage". Lying, fraud and trickery on the part of police officers have been held to be irrelevant where they cannot be directly related to either of these phrases. The case law has established that, if the circumstances do not fit these categories, there is no overriding discretion on the part of the trial judge to exclude the statement, no matter how abhorrent the judge might consider those circumstances to be.[15] There are also special and serious problems in relation to the assessment of credibility on the *voir dire*.[16]

The limitations upon the effectiveness of the voluntariness rule are compounded by the general common law rule applicable to the admissibility of evidence, other than the statements of an accused. The general rule is that, if evidence is relevant, it is admissible no matter how objectionable police conduct might have been in obtaining such evidence.[17] The lesson for the interrogator is clear. It is illustrated by the following passage from an interrogation manual which has been used by Canadian police:

---

12 [1914] A.C. 599 (P.C.).

13 *Prosko v. R.* (1922), 63 S.C.R. 226; *Boudreau v. R.*, [1949] S.C.R. 262; *Piché v. R.*, [1971] S.C.R. 23, to name but a few.

14 For a detailed exposition of the application of the rule in Canada, see F. Kaufman, *The Admissibility of Confessions*, 3rd rev. ed. (Toronto: Carswell, 1979) and Ratushny, *supra*, note 7, ch. 3 at 95-150.

15 *R. v. Dinardo* (1981), 61 C.C.C. (2d) 52 (Ont. Co. Ct.), leave to appeal to S.C.C. refused (1981), 39 N.R. 448 (S.C.C.), *per* Borins Co. Ct. J., applying *Rothman v. R.* (1981), 59 C.C.C. (2d) 30 (S.C.C.). But compare the important discussion by Lamer J. in the *Rothman* case.

16 See Ratushny, *supra*, note 7, at 233-243 and 248-252.

17 *R. v. Wray* (1970), 11 C.R.N.S. 235 (S.C.C.).

Certainly *to begin with* in any interrogation we are going to do everything
that is legal and right . . .

But there is a point . . . [at] which the interrogator must make a decision:
does he now leave the interrogation room without the statement or does he
now proceed with other techniques which he knows will not allow the
statement in but may give him information which will lead to the securing
of other evidence which itself may be admissible. I suggest that at this point
that the Marquis of Queensbury Rules go out the window and the interrogator
must open up his bag of tricks and go for the recovery of the weapon or
the stolen property or the names of accomplices or any evidence which may
be presented in court *regardless of the method employed to secure that evidence.*
[emphasis added][18]

The manual advocates a series of interrogation techniques dependent upon
deceit and "brainwashing". Violence is not condoned since, it suggests,
these other methods are quite effective. Nevertheless, the implication is
clear. If the non-violent methods are not successful, they should be carried
further. The author points out that, even if evidence were stolen or located
through hitting the suspect over the head with a baseball bat, it would
still be admissible in court.

The problems raised by police interrogation techniques have surfaced
frequently in Canada and have been recognized in other jurisdictions. The
Morand Commission[19] confirmed a number of complaints of brutality in
the interrogation of suspects including the application of a stapler to the
penis of one suspect and the application of another mechanical device
known as "the claw" to the penis of another. The Report of this Commission
also commented upon the credibility of police officers testifying at its
hearings:

It is with considerable regret that I am bound to report that one of the most
disturbing things which came out in the hearings was the extent to which
I found the evidence of police officers mistaken, shaded, deliberately
misleading, changed to suit the circumstances and sometimes entirely and
deliberately false.[20]

Of course, not all police witnesses before the Commission had committed
perjury. However, a sufficient number did to warrant careful scrutiny of
police evidence.

In 1979, the Manitoba Police Commission conducted an inquiry into
interrogation techniques used by certain officers of the Winnipeg Police
Department. It recommended that the officers concerned be charged with
assault causing bodily harm and also made a number of broader obser-

---

18 Ratushny, *supra*, note 7 at 207 *et seq.*

19 The Royal Commission Into Metropolitan Toronto Police Practices (Morand J. Commissioner, 1976).

20 *Ibid.* at 123.

vations and recommendations with respect to police interrogation procedures. Such inquiries continue to be held in various parts of Canada from time to time but public reaction soon subsides and the problem is forgotten.

All of this is merely to provide a context for considering the *Charter of Rights* provisions by indicating that there are serious problems — both real and potential — in relation to the investigatory stage of our criminal process.[21] One aspect of these problems is the inadequacy of the "voluntariness" rule as a basis for the admissibility of statements of an accused, particularly in relation to the difficulties in assessing credibility and in relation to the companion *Wray* rule[22] rendering other evidence admissible no matter how it has been obtained. However, another aspect relates to the basic integrity of our criminal process. Detailed protections are provided at the trial stage — a specific accusation, the presumption of innocence, the assistance of counsel, a public forum and others. However, all of these can be ignored in the secrecy of the police station if the suspect is ignorant of his right to decline to attend or to answer, or, even if he is aware of that right, if his resistance can be overcome by police interrogation.

(a) Section 10(a)

How then, does the *Charter of Rights* affect this stage of our criminal process? Section 10(a) of the Charter provides:

> Everyone has the right on arrest or detention
> (a) to be informed promptly of the reasons therefor;

The wording is similar to section 2(c)(ii) of the *Canadian Bill of Rights* which speaks of the "right" of "a person who has been arrested or detained . . . to be informed promptly of the reason for his arrest or detention". In his analysis of the *Bill of Rights* provisions, Professor Tarnopolsky described it as "a very straightforward clause which does not alter existing law".[23] This observation is equally applicable to section 10(a) of the Charter.

---

21 Nor are these problems uniquely Canadian. Major public studies of these problems have been published in the United States: The American Law Institute, *A Model Code of Pre-Arraignment Procedure* (1975); Australia: The Australian Law Reform Commission, *Report No. 2 (An Interim Report): Criminal Investigation* (1975); Scotland: The Committee appointed by the Secretary of State for Scotland and the Lord Advocate, *Criminal Procedure in Scotland (Second Report)* (1975); England: The Criminal·Law Revision Committee, *Eleventh Report: Evidence (General)* (1972) and *Report of the Royal Commission on Criminal Procedure* (1981).

22 *Supra*, note 17.

23 *The Canadian Bill of Rights*, 2nd ed. rev. (Toronto: Macmillan, 1975) at 239.

The powers and duties in relation to arrest are defined in the classic common law case of *Christie v. Leachinsky*.[24] Essentially, a police officer must inform the person arrested of the true ground of the arrest and failure to do so may leave the officer liable for false imprisonment. This requirement does not exist if the circumstances are such that the person must know the general nature of the offence which prompted the arrest or if the person makes it impractical to inform him, for example, by attacking the officer or running away. Finally, it is not necessary that technical language be used provided the person "knows in substance" the reason for the arrest. If the arrest is with a warrant, the *Criminal Code* requires the officer "to have it with him, where it is feasible to do so, and to produce it when requested" and also, "where it is feasible to do so [to give notice], of the process or warrant under which he makes the arrest".[25]

The words "on arrest or detention" have been the subject of considerable judicial attention. However, since this has occurred in the context of section 10(b), it is discussed under the next heading.

Section 10(a) has not given rise to serious problems of interpretation. The courts have adopted the "relativity" established by the *Leachinsky* case[26] which relates the nature of the obligation to the particular situation at hand. In *R. v. Eatman*,[27] it was held that the word "promptly" had different meanings in different circumstances. However, where the arrest situation was very passive, the Charter duty had to be fulfilled at the scene. The failure to inform the person of the reasons for arrest could not be cured subsequently by providing the information at the police station. Moreover, the failure to comply with this clear and mandatory Charter requirement is sufficient, in itself, to bring the administration of justice into disrepute.

In *R. v. Kelly*,[28] the Ontario Court of Appeal pointed out the subtle difference between "promptly" in section 10(a) and "without delay" in section 10(b). The latter does not convey the notion of "immediacy". Mr. Justice Martin suggested a logical rationale for drawing such a distinction:

> With respect to para. (*a*), a person is not obliged to submit to an arrest if he does not know the reason for it . . . It is, accordingly, essential that he be informed promptly or immediately of the reasons. On the other hand, the relevant interest protected by para. (*b*) . . . is that of not prejudicing one's

---

24   [1947] A.C. 573 (H.L.).

25   R.S.C. 1970, c. C-34, s. 29 [R.S.C. 1985, c. C-46, s. 29]. Detailed provisions with respect to "Compelling Appearance of Accused" are contained in Part XIV [XVI] of the Code.

26   *Supra*, note 24.

27   (1982), 45 N.B.R. (2d) 163 (Q.B.).

28   (1985), 17 C.C.C. (3d) 419 (Ont. C.A.).

legal position by something said or done without, at least, the benefit of legal advice.[29]

In this case, the accused was screaming and yelling at the time of his arrest and it would have made no sense to inform him of his right to counsel.

(b) Section 10(b)

It already has been suggested that the voluntariness rule has not operated significantly as a restraint upon police interrogation techniques.[30] At one time, the Supreme Court had emphatically laid down the requirement that a proper caution be given to an arrested person as a precondition of admissibility.[31] A few years later, the same court concluded that a caution or warning was not essential. It became only one factor to be considered in addressing the central issue of voluntariness.[32]

The caution or warning in question in these cases did not relate to the right to counsel. Rather it was a caution that the accused was under no obligation to answer. There was no requirement, whatsoever, to advise an individual of any right to consult counsel. Indeed, statements were found to be voluntary even after counsel had been requested and actively denied.[33] The most that could be said was that the denial of counsel *might* be a factor to be weighed against the Crown in assessing voluntariness.[34]

In *R. v. Howard*,[35] the Ontario Court of Appeal clearly disapproved of police conduct in denying counsel:

> After Trudel made it clear that he wanted his lawyer to be present and had called him, Corporal McCurdy should not have continued his examination which made a mockery of Trudel's right to counsel and his right to remain silent.[36]

Nevertheless, the voluntariness rule did not provide a basis for exclusion. Instead, the statement was rejected on the narrow basis that it fell within the residual discretion permitted by the *Wray* case.[37] In other words, the

---

29 *Ibid.* at 424.

30 *Supra*, note 7.

31 *Gach v. R.* (1943), 79 C.C.C. 221 (S.C.C.).

32 *Boudreau v. R.* (1949), 94 C.C.C. 1 (S.C.C.).

33 *Hogan v. R.* (1974), 18 C.C.C. (2d) 65 (S.C.C.); *R. v. Ballegeer*, [1969] 3 C.C.C. 353 (Man. C.A.); *R. v. Letendre*, [1975] 6 W.W.R. 360 (Man. C.A.).

34 *R. v. Materi*, [1977] 2 W.W.R. 728 at 735 (B.C.C.A.), *per* Bull J.A. See also *R. v. Demers* (1970), 13 C.R.N.S. 338 (Que. S.C.), where improper police conduct was held to vitiate their credibility in relation to the issue of voluntariness.

35 (1983), 3 C.C.C. (3d) 399 (Ont. C.A.).

36 *Ibid.*, at 414, *per* Howland C.J.

37 *Supra*, note 17.

evidence was of tenuous probative value in comparison to its potential prejudice to the accused.

The underlying rationale for the voluntariness rule relates to a concern for the reliability of the evidence. The voluntariness rule itself does not require the weighing of probative value. Rather, it imposes a more specific test and an exclusionary consequence because of a fear of *potential* unreliability. There is an obvious implication for police behaviour but that is indirect.[38]

The basic purpose of the rule does not reflect any fundamental value other than the danger of relying upon unreliable evidence. It does prohibit threats and inducements, but only in relation to the admissibility of statements. The identical police conduct, and actual violence, was considered irrelevant to the admissibility of other forms of evidence.[39]

The requirements of section 10(b) of the Charter rest on a different basis. This protection is an attempt to ensure that the suspect or accused has the opportunity to become fully aware of his legal rights. The same value is reflected in section 2(c) of the *Canadian Bill of Rights*. Moreover, the distinguished Ouimet Commission[40] had recommended that the right to counsel be specified in the *Criminal Code* together with a provision requiring that reasonable means be taken to inform the accused of his rights. The failure so to inform the accused or to provide an opportunity to consult counsel after such a request would render any subsequent statement inadmissible.

In *Clarkson v. R.*[41] Madam Justice Wilson articulated the nature of the right to counsel in section 10(b):

> This constitutional provision is clearly unconcerned with the probative value of any evidence obtained by the police but rather, . . . the concern [is] for fair treatment of an accused person.[42]

and later:

> [T]he purpose of the right, as indicated by each of the members of this Court writing in *Therens, supra*, is to ensure that the accused is treated fairly in the criminal process.[43]

---

38 *De Clercq v. R.*, [1966] 2 C.C.C. 190 at 194 (Ont. C.A.) *per* Laskin J.A., aff'd *infra* note 122.

39 *R. v. Wray, supra*, note 17.

40 *Report of the Canadian Committee on Corrections* (Ouimet J. Chairman, 1969).

41 [1986] 1 S.C.R. 383. Estey, Lamer, Le Dain and La Forest JJ. concurred with Wilson J. while Chouinard J. concurred with the narrower reasons of McIntyre J.

42 *Ibid.* at 394.

43 *Ibid.* at 396, referring to *R. v. Therens, infra*, note 47.

Precisely how does the right to counsel relate to the accused being treated fairly in the criminal process?

One approach to this question is to examine the procedural protections which are available to an accused at trial. The accused is given (a) a public trial (b) after a specific accusation including particulars (c) according to specific rules of procedure and evidence and (d) represented by counsel to insure that all of these protections are provided. Moreover, the accused is (e) entitled to know the evidentiary "case to meet"[44] before deciding whether or not to respond. In other words, the accused hears all the Crown witnesses under oath and tested by cross-examination before deciding whether to respond and, if so, in what manner and to what extent.

All of these protections are present in the courtroom. They are absent during interrogation at the police station. Thus, section 10(b) can be seen as an attempt to provide justice in the "gatehouses" as well as in the "mansions" of our criminal justice system.[45] How is a criminal justice system to be described if it jealously guards such protections at the trial stage while "turning a blind eye" to the pre-trial stage? Such a system certainly would be inconsistent. It might be described as lacking in integrity — and perhaps even as being hypocritical!

Another possible approach is to think in terms of placing the accused who is facing police interrogation in the same position as a lawyer. In other words, when faced with the serious potential consequences of the criminal process, all accused persons should be placed in an equal position in law. They should understand exactly what is involved and know the most personally advantageous manner in which to respond. The *Ouimet Report* recognized the "unacceptability of a system of law enforcement based upon keeping people in ignorance of their rights".[46] Once again, fairness comes down to a matter of consistency and integrity within the criminal justice system.

The Supreme Court of Canada has not yet fully explored the underlying rationale for the right to counsel protection in section 10(b). The adoption of the principle of "fairness to an accused" is a useful first step in extricating the courts from the limitations of "probative value". However, it will be necessary to go further and explain what "fairness" entails. There are many pitfalls in attempting to do so and these will be considered at the conclusion of this part, where practical problems of law enforcement are also considered.

---

44 *Dubois v. R.*, [1985] 2 S.C.R. 350 at 366.
45 See generally Y. Kamisar, "Equal Justice in the Gatehouse and Mansions of American Criminal Procedure", in *Criminal Justice in Our Times*, A.D. Howard, ed. (Charlottesville: University Press of Virginia, 1965).
46 *Supra*, note 40 at 144.

The most significant judicial decision to date in relation to the application of the Charter to confessions may well be *R. v. Therens*.[47] That is so in spite of Mr. Justice Lamer's qualification:

> Whether s. 10(b) extends any further, so as to encompass, for example, the principle of *Miranda v. Arizona*, 384 U.S. 436 (1966), and apply to matters such as interrogation and police line-ups, need not be decided in this case and I shall refrain from so doing.[48]

In *Therens*, the court explored the meaning of "detention" under section 10(b). The issue is of crucial importance since it is the mechanism which triggers the operation of the right to counsel. But as soon as the threshold into detention is crossed, the right to counsel and to be informed of that right become operative without delay.

The Supreme Court of Canada had the benefit of the analysis of Mr. Justice Tallis, who wrote for the majority of the Saskatchewan Court of Appeal.[49] In his reasons, Tallis J.A. distinguished the earlier Supreme Court decision on the issue of detention in *Chromiak v. R.*[50] and elaborated upon the manner in which the Charter should be interpreted in this context. He also injected a healthy dose of common sense:

> When you consider the circumstances of this case and in particular the context of the demand that was made to him, it cannot be said that the respondent accused was free to depart as he pleased. To say that he was not detained is simply a fiction which overlooks the plain meaning of words from the viewpoint of an average citizen.[51]

In other words, Mr. Justice Tallis chose to apply the spirit or purpose of the right to counsel rather than merely a strict and narrow interpretation of detention.[52]

In the Supreme Court of Canada, Mr. Justice Le Dain was the only judge to address the meaning of "detention" in section 10(b).[53] He stated that detention encompassed the following situations:

1. " . . . a restraint of liberty other than arrest in which a person may reasonably require the assistance of counsel . . ." or "physical constraint";

---

47 [1985] 1 S.C.R. 613.

48 *Ibid.* at 625.

49 (1983), 5 C.C.C. (3d) 409 (Sask. C.A.), aff'd *supra*, note 47.

50 (1979), 49 C.C.C. (2d) 257 (S.C.C.). See also *Trask v. R.*, [1985] 1 S.C.R. 655 and *Rahn v. R.*, [1985] 1 S.C.R. 659.

51 *Therens, supra*, note 49 at 424.

52 See also the first edition of this text, at 344-345.

53 *Therens, supra*, note 47. Dickson C.J., McIntyre and Lamer JJ. agreed with his reasons, while Estey J. (Beetz, Chouinard and Wilson JJ. concurring) did not adopt those reasons in relation to the meaning of "detention".

2. " ... when a police officer or other agent of the State assumes control over the movement of a person by a demand or direction which may have significant legal consequence and which prevents or impedes access to counsel".

However, he went on to add a third category:

3. The element of psychological compulsion, in the form of a reasonable perception of suspension of freedom of choice, is enough to make the restraint of liberty involuntary. Detention may be effected without the application or threat of application of physical restraint if the person concerned submits or acquiesces in the deprivation of liberty and reasonably believes that the choice to do otherwise does not exist.[54]

In the same vein as the court below, Mr. Justice Le Dain elaborated that it simply was not realistic to look only to "the precise limits of police authority". It was also necessary to consider the dynamics of the relationship between the police officer and the citizen.

This approach could have the salutary effect of extending the protection of section 10(b) to aspects of police interrogation which were not affected by the voluntariness rule. Consider the following situations, for example:

(a) A suspect refuses to accompany an officer voluntarily to the police station but, after further discussion, perceives that he is required to do so, even though there is no express demand or direction on the part of the police officer.

(b) A suspect attends at the police station voluntarily, but subsequently asks to be excused. He is not told that he *must* remain, but the subject is changed and the questioning continues.

(c) A suspect attends at the police station for questioning and repeatedly asks to call his lawyer. The request is repeatedly denied, but there is no attempt to leave and, therefore, no overt indication that the suspect would be prevented from leaving.

(d) A suspect agrees to accompany the police to the station but, before leaving home, tells his wife to call his lawyer to have him meet the husband at the police station. The lawyer subsequently arrives, but the desk sergeant refuses the lawyer access to the interrogation room.

Suppose that in each of these situations, after a few hours of questioning, a statement is obtained. Under the voluntariness rule, the courts would likely hold that there was no evidence of "fear of prejudice" or "hope of advantage". There was no evidence that the police would have

---

54 *Ibid.* at 642.

prevented him from leaving at any time.

On the other hand, the implication of the *Therens* case might be to require a warning as to the right to counsel in each situation together with access to counsel where requested. In contrast with the voluntariness cases, some outward manifestation of coercion on the part of the police officers would not be necessary. The courts could conclude that there was a "reasonable perception of suspension of freedom of choice".

Indeed, the Charter already has been invoked as the basis for an action for damages in a situation similar to the fourth example given above. In *Crossman v. R.*,[55] Mr. Justice Walsh awarded $500 in damages against the R.C.M.P. under section 24(1) of the Charter for a breach of section 10(b).

Of course, the extension of Charter protections is not universally perceived as a net gain for society. As Grant Garneau has recently observed:

> Thus detention short of arrest is the point at which the legal rights of an individual being questioned come into direct conflict with the use of interrogation as a viable investigation procedure. Here the individual has the greatest need to obtain and instruct counsel without delay and enforcement officials have the strongest aversion to the intrusion of counsel.[56]

The author cites examples of police officers deliberately delaying arrest even where grounds existed in order to continue with interrogation unhindered by any need to caution the accused.

A number of recently reported decisions have addressed the question of when general police questioning crosses the threshold of "detention", thereby rendering operative the protection of section 10(b) of the Charter. In *R. v. Esposito*,[57] two police officers attended at the home of a "possible" suspect, were invited in by his mother and then questioned him in his living room. The officer who conducted the questioning testified that he had no grounds upon which to arrest the suspect until an admission was made with respect to certain invoices. At that point, the suspect was arrested and taken into custody. The Ontario Court of Appeal held that the circumstances were not sufficient to constitute a "detention" situation:

> There is no evidence on the record that the appellant actually believed that his freedom was restrained, and in my view, the circumstances would not lead him reasonably to believe that his freedom had been restrained.[58]

---

55 (1984), 12 C.C.C. (3d) 547 (F.C.T.D.).

56 G. Garneau, "The Application of the Charter of Rights to the Interrogation Process" (1986), 35 *U.N.B.L.J.* 35 at 40.

57 (1985), 24 C.C.C. (3d) 88 (Ont. C.A.), leave to appeal to S.C.C. refused (1986), 24 C.C.C. (3d) 88n (S.C.C.). See also *R. v. Reddick* (1987), 77 N.S.R. (2d) 439 (C.A.).

58 *Esposito, ibid.* at 101.

The accused did not testify on the *voir dire*. Nor was the police officer questioned in relation to any direct or indirect compulsion.

The *Esposito* case suggests that the *Therens* decision need not constitute a bar to effective police questioning in reasonable circumstances. However, variations might be introduced which could be problematic. For example, suppose that the questioning had extended well beyond the point at which grounds for arrest were clear. Would an inference of compulsion be drawn more readily? The court pointed out that the police officers only considered Esposito to be a "possible" suspect. Would the situation have been any different if he was the only suspect and, indeed, a decision had been taken to charge him but the officers were merely seeking a confession as "icing on the cake"?

In *R. v. Rodenbush*,[59] the accused married couple sought to enter Canada from the United States. The couple were taken into a room to await a closer examination of their suitcases in another room. The customs inspector who had been carrying on a conversation with the couple was called aside and told by his superintendent that cocaine was found. He was instructed to question the couple and then arrest them. The appellants lied in response to questions about their suitcases, were arrested and only then were informed of their right to counsel.

The British Columbia Court of Appeal held that there was no doubt that when the couple was asked to enter the room in which the interview occurred, they were detained under section 10 of the Charter as interpreted by the Supreme Court in *Therens*.[60] The manner in which the couple was asked to enter the room is not described. However, it would appear to fall within the third category of *Therens* related to "psychological compulsion".

The court proceeded to consider whether the statements should be excluded as a result of the Charter contravention. It was highly critical of the customs superintendent:

> He knew or should be deemed to know that detention and questioning of a person whom he was about to arrest might garner incriminating evidence *before* the *Charter* warning was delivered. This then constituted a flagrant infringement of the appellant's constitutional rights.[61]

The court held that the statements should be excluded pursuant to section 24(2) of the Charter on the basis of "all the circumstances". The instruction to delay the arrest pending interrogation was considered to be a deliberate flouting of the accused's Charter rights.

---

59 (1985), 21 C.C.C. (3d) 423 (B.C.C.A.).
60 *Supra*, note 47.
61 *Supra*, note 59 at 427.

It is far from clear from the *Therens* case that section 10(b) requires that an arrest be carried out as soon as the decision to arrest has been made. The Charter only states that the warning and corresponding access to counsel must occur upon detention or arrest. In *Rodenbush*,[62] there was both a detention and grounds for an arrest. The detention generated the requirement of a warning. The decision to delay the arrest while conducting an interrogation was a strong factor in applying section 24(2).

What, then, would be the situation if there were no detention yet ample grounds and an actual decision to arrest? On a strict reading of *Therens*, *Rodenbush* and section 10 of the Charter, it could be argued that to delay the decision to arrest is inconsequential. Since there has been no detention or actual arrest, section 10 is not operative. The delay in arrest which was criticized in *Rodenbush* was only considered there in relation to section 24(2), but first there must be a Charter breach before that section can come into play.

On the other hand, if *Rodenbush* is interpreted in the same broad spirit as *Therens*, the absence of a formal arrest or of any form of detention should not be conclusive as to the inapplicability of section 10. The Rodenbush couple were arrested for all practical purposes although not strictly so in law. The fundamental question, however, is not whether they were *legally* arrested but whether their circumstances cried out for legal counsel. Just as the subjective perceptions of the suspect might constitute "detention" as in *Therens*, subjective perceptions of the enforcement officer (that is, having decided to arrest) should constitute an "arrest" for the limited purpose of the applicability of section 10 of the Charter. If this interpretation is given to *Rodenbush*, it can be viewed not merely as an application of *Therens*, but also as an important and expansive complement to it.

However, another recent decision of the Ontario Court of Appeal took a much narrower approach to the *Therens* decision. In *R. v. Bazinet*,[63] the issue was essentially the same as that in *Esposito*,[64] although the facts were somewhat different. In both cases, the police officers came to the home of the possible suspect. However, whereas in *Esposito* the questioning occurred in the suspect's living room, in *Bazinet* the suspect volunteered to accompany the officers to the police station. This offer was entirely at the initiative of the suspect in response to a request to ask some questions. After almost two hours of questioning, the accused confessed to the homicide which was under investigation.

The circumstances in *Bazinet* were certainly more coercive than those

---

62 *Supra*, note 59.

63 (1986), 25 C.C.C. (3d) 273 (Ont. C.A.).

64 *Supra*, note 57.

in the *Esposito* case. The questioning occurred in the police station and continued for almost two hours. Bazinet had been awakened by the police and had eaten nothing from that time until after the confession had been obtained. At the start of the interrogation, blood was noticed on Bazinet's clothes and he was asked to give them up for analysis. At a certain point, the nature of the questioning changed with the police confronting the accused with some of the evidence which they had. Nevertheless, no evidence was presented by the accused as to any reasonable psychological detention on his part. In that context, the court might have simply concluded that it did not view the circumstances as leading to such a conclusion.

However, the court chose to go much further by advancing a significant restriction upon the third category of "detention" described by Mr. Justice Le Dain in the *Therens* case.[65] It held, in effect, that "psychological compulsion" could only constitute detention where it occurred in response to a "demand or direction" issued by a police officer. It is submitted that this is an unnecessarily restrictive interpretation of the judgment in question and that the passages quoted earlier are capable of standing by themselves as a separate category. The references to a demand or direction were natural in the context of *Therens*, which involved a demand for a breath sample. However, that narrow factual context should not preclude the application of the broader concept to other situations.

It is disappointing that the court seemed to take greater comfort in the increasingly narrow formulation of "custodial interrogation" in the American Supreme Court than in the expansive approach taken by our own. Moreover, this approach fails to take into account the flexibility available in Canada through the application of section 24(2) of the Charter. Under this provision, even though section 10 may have been violated, the evidence need not be excluded. The great virtue of *Therens* is in recognizing the *reality* of detention even in the absence of its *formality*. Such a realistic approach is particularly needed in relation to police interrogation. Even if the police station interrogation of Bazinet did involve a "detention", whether at the commencement of questioning or at the point of discovering the blood-stained clothing or at the time when the interrogation became confrontational, such a Charter breach need not have resulted in exclusion of the subsequent confession.

More recent decisions of the Ontario Court of Appeal do appear to recognize the broader implications of the *Therens* decision. In *R. v. Soares*,[66] the trial judge had held that the accused had not been arrested or detained when certain statements were given as a result of police questioning. However, on appeal, Mr. Justice Morden concluded that:

---

65 *Supra*, note 47.
66 (1987), 34 C.C.C. (3d) 403 (Ont. C.A.).

[T]he trial judge in coming to his conclusion on whether the appellant was in "detention" applied a test that, although it was in accord with decisions then binding on him, has turned out to be the wrong test. I cannot say on the basis of the record before us that if he had applied the *Therens* test in the Supreme Court of Canada he inevitably would have come to the same conclusion.[67]

A new trial was ordered on the basis that the *Therens* interpretation of section 10(b) could not be applied without certain findings of fact involving the "dynamics of the situation".

Finally, the court has sought to suggest the kinds of factors which should be taken into consideration in determining whether a person, who is subsequently an accused, was detained at the time of questioning at the police station. These are:

1. the precise language of the request to attend at the police station;
2. whether it was indicated that the person could choose to have the interview at home;
3. whether the person expressed a preference as to where it would occur;
4. whether the person attended alone following a request or was escorted by an officer;
5. whether an arrest occurred at the conclusion of the interview;
6. whether the questioning was part of the general investigation of an offence or whether suspicion had focussed on the person as the perpetrator with the object of the questioning to be to obtain incriminating statements;
7. whether the police had reasonable and probable grounds to believe that the person had committed the offence in question;
8. whether the questions were of a general nature to elicit information or whether they were confrontational with respect to guilt; and
9. whether the person had a subjective belief that he was detained.[68]

However, the court indicated that the last factor was not conclusive. The issue was framed in terms of whether there was a reasonable belief of detention on the part of that person. Thus personal factors such as low intelligence, emotional disturbance, youth and lack of sophistication were circumstances to be considered.

What is the practical effect of these decisions with respect to "detention" upon police investigation? The situation might be summarized along the following lines:

1. The police are free to question anyone until: (a) the person reaches

---

67 *Ibid.*, at 425.
68 *R. v. Moran* (1987), 36 C.C.C. (3d) 225 (Ont. C.A.); *R. v. Grafe* (1987), 60 C.R. (3d) 139 (Ont. C.A.).

the point of psychological detention within the *Therens* definition; or (b) police suspicion focusses upon the suspect to the extent that the decision to arrest had been taken and the suspect would not be permitted to leave if he attempted to do so.

2. At either of these points, section 10(b) would become operative, creating the obligation on the part of the police to inform the suspect of the rights guaranteed by that section.

3. While the point of psychological detention might appear to be problematic for the police, in order to establish a Charter violation the accused would have to demonstrate on the *voir dire* that such a situation existed. In addition, the accused would have to establish that it was a reasonable perception in the circumstances. It is this objective element which provides guidance to the police in determining when their obligation under section 10(b) arises. If the police are occasionally tardy but not unreasonably so, the discretion in section 24(2) may still save many statements from exclusion.

4. While the focussing of police suspicion might appear to be problematic for the accused, the police could be required to assert on the *voir dire* that this point had not been reached. As in relation to the perception of the accused, the police would also have to establish the reasonableness of their perception of the status of the accused as a mere suspect or as an accused.

It now has been established that the phrase "without delay" in section 10(b) refers not only to the right to retain and instruct counsel but also to the right to be informed of that right.[69] However, the question as to what is necessary to constitute a satisfactory fulfilment of the obligation to inform and to provide access to counsel is not so easily resolved.

In *R. v. Shields*,[70] Justice Borins indicated that while the accused had been *informed* of his right to counsel, inadequate information had been provided to give effect to that right:

> In the present case, the recitation of his rights to Mr. Shields became meaningless in the absence of providing him with any information as to how he could exercise his rights when it became apparent that he neither had nor knew a lawyer.

He elaborated further:

> Without attempting to establish a precise verbal formula, to give effect to the right created by s. 10(*b*), it should be explained, in easily understood language, to an accused that he has the right to talk to a lawyer before and

---

69 *R. v. Kelly, supra,* note 28. See also text corresponding to note 28, *supra,* related to the interpretation of "without delay".

70 (1983), 10 W.C.B. 120 (Ont. Co. Ct.).

during questioning, that he has a right to a lawyer's advice and presence even if he cannot afford to hire one, that he will be told how to contact a lawyer, if he does not know how to do so and that he has a right to stop answering questions at any time until he has talked to a lawyer. To make certain that he understands his rights and to avoid equivocal and uninformed waivers, the explanation of the rights should, if possible, be written, as should any waiver of them.[71]

This appears to be the broadest formulation to date in the case law.

In *R. v. Nelson*,[72] Mr. Justice Scollin had also suggested that the obligation on the part of the police could extend beyond merely informing the accused of the right under section 10(b):

Real opportunity is what is meant by [this] provision of the Charter, not the incantation of a potted version of the right followed immediately by conduct which pressured a waiver.

He added:

To make the right effective, particularly in the case of an unsophisticated and uneducated accused, he should obviously be asked whether he does wish to retain and instruct counsel. . . . If the answer is that he does . . ., a reasonable opportunity must then, without delay, be given to him to do so.[73]

In rejecting statements which had been taken at the police station, his Lordship stressed the determining factors of the educational and social background of the accused, the apparently deliberate delay in informing the accused as to a significant change in the charge (the victim had died), the failure to make any real inquiry as to the accused's choice and the failure to ensure that a real opportunity was given to the accused to consult counsel if he so wished.

Thus, in both of these cases, the accused were informed of their right to counsel, but something more was required. In *Shields*,[74] the accused responded by stating that he did not have a lawyer and did not know any lawyers. At trial, he testified that he was unaware of any referral service and had never heard of "duty counsel". In such circumstances, it seems reasonable for Justice Borins to have expected the police to go further than reading the "potted version" from their plastic card. The response of the accused to the police and at the *voir dire* indicated a practical barrier to achieving the protection provided by section 10(b). In such circumstances, the police should have elaborated beyond the bare recitation which serves

---

71 *Ibid.*, quoted in *R. v. Anderson* (1984), 10 C.C.C. (3d) 417 at 424-425 (Ont. C.A.).
72 (1982), 3 C.C.C. (3d) 147 (Man. Q.B.).
73 *Ibid.*, at 152-153.
74 *Supra*, note 70.

as an adequate starting point and, in most cases, also as a fulfilment of the police obligation.

Similarly, in *Nelson*,[75] there were special circumstances relating to the social and educational background of the accused. Taken together with the manner in which the accused responded to the police, they created an obligation on the part of the police at least to ask whether the accused did, indeed, wish to consult counsel.

In *R. v. Anderson*,[76] the Ontario Court of Appeal emphasized these special circumstances in interpreting the *Shields* and *Nelson* cases. It was also pointed out that in *Nelson*, there was some defect in the manner in which the accused was informed of the right in the first place. In *Anderson* itself, no special circumstances were found to exist which would impose any greater obligation on the police than merely to inform the accused of the right to counsel. Nothing in the testimony of the accused suggested any impairment, lack of understanding or inadequacy which would inhibit the retention of counsel. On the contrary, the accused testified that he had retained counsel in the past and had been informed frequently of the right to remain silent.

The court specifically rejected any obligation on the part of the police, as suggested by Mr. Justice Borins in *Shields*, to inform an accused *how* a lawyer might be contacted or as to the availability of legal aid. This was seen to impose too high an obligation on the police. The *Anderson* decision has been criticized for taking too rigid an approach to the issue of police obligation by insisting upon a prior request from the accused. Mr. Stanley Cohen observed:

> [This] may leave the impression that all ancillary aspects of the right to counsel (such as private consultation, silence until counsel attends or is contacted after a request is made, or even legal aid) must be specifically requested without any particular information or advice in regard thereto being supplied by the police. These aspects of the right to counsel have "to be asked for in some way". . . . Not addressed is how one asks for what one does not know about.[77]

This concern is well taken. It would be unfortunate if the interpretation of section 10 of the Charter were to follow the general path of the voluntariness rule by requiring specific violations such as a "threat" or an "inducement".

The purpose of section 10(b) must be to make counsel available to the detainee or, as Mr. Justice Scollin has put it, "the essence of the provision

---

75 *Supra*, note 72.
76 *Supra*, note 71.
77 S.A. Cohen, "The Impact of Charter Decisions on Police Behaviour" (1984), 39 C.R. (3d) 264 at 277.

is opportunity". If that opportunity can be provided simply by informing the detainee that it exists, that is sufficient. If the detainee is passive, reticent, inarticulate and inadequate in social skills and does not respond, it would seem reasonable to expect a police officer to go further and ask whether the person does wish to talk to a lawyer. If the detainee says he will not be calling a lawyer because he cannot afford to hire one, should the Charter protection simply be abandoned? Or should the police be expected to take the further step of explaining the availability of legal aid or duty counsel?

The Ontario Court of Appeal also addressed the detainee's understanding of his Charter rights in *R. v. Baig*,[78] where the court stated:

> [I]n the ordinary case, after the Charter rights under s. 10(*b*) have been read, the suspect will acknowledge that he understands his rights in response to the officer's question.[79]

In this case, the accused made no such acknowledgment and the trial judge held that the police should have asked again whether the accused understood. However, the Court of Appeal adopted its earlier decision in *Anderson* and stressed the failure of the accused to ask for an opportunity to retain or instruct counsel:

> There is . . . no duty on the prosecution to probe into the suspect's degree of understanding or comprehension or to adduce positive evidence in the absence of special circumstances . . . or in the absence of words or conduct from which it could be reasonably inferred that the suspect did not understand his rights.[80]

The accused was sober, displayed no difficulty of hearing, appeared to be intelligent and had a good grasp of the English language. His failure to acknowledge explicitly that he understood his rights did not constitute "special circumstances".

In *McAvena v. R.*[81] the Saskatchewan Court of Appeal took the position that it might not be sufficient to satisfy section 10(b) for the right to counsel to be recited to the accused and for the accused merely to appear to understand. Chief Justice Bayda articulated five attributes to the duty to inform under this provision. The "owner" of the right must be informed:

> (1) in language which accurately describes the owner's right to counsel without delay, (2) in language and means of communication which the owner can understand and appreciate, (3) at a time when he is capable of understanding and appreciating the right to counsel without delay, (4) before he yields up evidence which may be incriminating against him, and (5) in sufficient time

---

78 (1985), 20 C.C.C. (3d) 515 (Ont. C.A.), aff'd [1987] 2 S.C.R. 537.
79 *Ibid.* at 524.
80 *Ibid.* at 524.
81 (1987), 56 C.R. (3d) 303 (Sask. C.A.).

to give the owner an opportunity to obtain and instruct counsel before the obtaining of evidence described in (4).[82]

He described this formulation as being in conformity with the "purposive interpretation" which must be adopted in construing constitutional rights.

What if a detainee does state that he wishes to retain counsel? All questioning must cease until he has been afforded the opportunity of consulting counsel. This was established in *R. v. Manninen*,[83] where the accused responded emphatically: "I ain't saying anything until I see my lawyer. I want to see my lawyer." Nevertheless, questioning continued and the statements obtained were ultimately rejected by the Supreme Court of Canada.

A similar issue had arisen in *R. v. Ferguson*,[84] where the accused was arrested and informed of his rights at 10:05 a.m. At 10:41 a.m., at the police station, he asked to call his lawyer and received full cooperation from the police. He eventually called a friend to obtain a lawyer for him and informed the police that he had nothing to say until he talked to his lawyer. At 1:00 p.m. a conversation with the police took place at which little was said. However, at 2:47 p.m., a further conversation took place, without any further caution being given, in which serious admissions were made.

The Ontario Court of Appeal in *Ferguson* distinguished its own earlier decision in *Manninen*,[85] which had not yet reached the Supreme Court, on the basis that here the accused was not denied counsel but was given every opportunity to speak to his lawyer. The trial judge found that the accused had simply made voluntary replies to routine investigation questions. In the words of the Court of Appeal:

> A suspect who has been made aware of his constitutional rights under the Charter is, of course, free to remain silent but is also free to talk if he thinks that it will serve his purpose to do so.[86]

The court stated that the conduct of the police officers had not been "exemplary or beyond criticism". However, they upheld the trial judge's assessment that section 10(b) had not been infringed.

This result should be compared with the earlier *Howard* case,[87] in which the same court considered further questioning following a phone

---

82 *Ibid.*, at 309.

83 (1987), 58 C.R. (3d) 97 at 100 (S.C.C.).

84 (1985), 20 C.C.C. (3d) 256 (Ont. C.A.).

85 *Supra*, note 83.

86 *Ferguson, supra*, note 84 at 259. See also *R. v. Stone* (1984), 12 W.C.B. 324 (B.C.C.A.).

87 *Supra*, note 35.

call to a lawyer to constitute a mockery of the right to counsel. It must be viewed as somewhat ironical that in the earlier case the court was able to exclude the statements without the assistance of the Charter and even without the assistance of the voluntariness rule. In *Ferguson*, the statement was admitted in related circumstances *in spite of* the Charter.

In *Ferguson*, the accused was questioned after he had asked for counsel and before counsel arrived at the police station. If that is the case, should there be any difference if counsel has been retained?[88] The reality of the situation is, of course, that the police officer, in the isolated setting of the police station, will attempt to wear down the resistance of the prisoner by engaging him in conversation and subtly moving to questioning about the offence.

If this is permitted, we may be led back to the pre-Charter cases such as *R. v. Settee*,[89] where over a period of seven days in custody, the accused was questioned on nine separate occasions, in addition to being subjected to a four-and-one-half-hour car ride. He was questioned both before and after consulting counsel, although after talking to his lawyer he remained silent and questioning was not resumed for a couple of days. In spite of these facts, Chief Justice Culliton was able to say:

> As well, I am satisfied that the questioning was not to induce an admission of guilt, but rather to obtain an explanation in the light of the facts actually discovered during the course of the investigation. Conveying such information to the accused afforded him the opportunity of explaining.[90]

With great respect, it is difficult to appreciate the distinction which the court in the *Ferguson* case sought to draw between its facts and those in the *Manninen* case.[91] The *Manninen* decision should be interpreted as clearly establishing that statements made following a request for counsel are not admissible in the absence of an actual waiver.

Madam Justice Wilson addressed the issue of waiver of the right to counsel in *Clarkson v. R.*[92] Her analysis begins with a reference to her court's earlier condition for the waiver of statutory procedural guarantees. Such a waiver

> ... is dependent upon it being clear and unequivocal that the person is waiving the procedural safeguard and is doing so with full knowledge of the rights

---

88 The answer is "no", according to *R. v. Stone, supra*, note 86.
89 (1975), 29 C.R.N.S. 104 (Sask. C.A.).
90 *Ibid.* at 117-118. *Cf. R. v. McCorkell*, discussed in M.H. Harris, "Notes and Comments Concerning Statements to Police Officers" (1964), 7 C.L.Q. 395 (Ont. C.A.).
91 *Supra*, note 83.
92 *Supra*, note 41.

the procedure was enacted to protect and of the effect the waiver will have on those rights in the process.[93]

In the context of section 10(b), she rejected the suggestion that a waiver should only be concerned with the probative value of the evidence. Other values are at stake:

> While this constitutional guarantee cannot be forced upon an unwilling accused, any voluntary waiver in order to be valid and effective must be premised on a true appreciation of the consequences of giving up the right.[94]

Thus it is not sufficient that the accused merely comprehend his or her words. In addition, the accused must appreciate the *consequences* of giving up that right.

The *Clarkson* case dealt with an accused's drunken assertion that there was "no point" in retaining counsel in the face of a murder charge. Madam Justice Wilson concluded simply that this

> . . . could not possibly have been taken seriously by the police as a true waiver of her constitutional right. . . . Rather, the actions of the police in interrogating the intoxicated appellant seem clearly to have been aimed at extracting a confession which they feared they might not be able to get later when she sobered up and appreciated the need for counsel.[95]

Again, the Supreme Court appears to have captured the reality of the situation rather than merely asking whether there was any specific request for counsel on the part of the accused or any specific misconduct on the part of the police.

The requirement of a "clear and unequivocal" waiver in every situation in which no request for counsel occurs, could form a powerful aspect of the protection embodied in section 10(b). It would, of course, add an entirely new dimension to the obligation of police officers which was discussed earlier.

Just as the *Bazinet* decision[96] interpreted *Therens*[97] very narrowly, *Clarkson* could be interpreted as merely involving "special circumstances". In other words, the intoxicated condition of the accused extended the obligation beyond merely advising the accused of the rights embodied in section 10(b) in skeletal form. However, if the underlying foundation for the decision is emphasized, a broader mandate for the courts may be perceived. To require "a true appreciation of the consequences of giving

---

93 *Korponey v. A.G. Canada* (1982), 65 C.C.C. (2d) 65 at 74 (S.C.C.), quoted at pp. 394-395 of *Clarkson, supra,* note 41.

94 *Clarkson, ibid.* at 396.

95 *Ibid.* at 397.

96 *Supra,* note 63.

97 *Supra,* note 47.

up the right" suggests a very real desire to give effect to the "spirit" as well as to the "form" of the Charter.

What are the practical implications of such an approach for law enforcement? Will it result in "the paralysis of law enforcement"?[98] Will police officers soon become the perceived wrongdoers?[99] Will this be a departure from a Canadian tradition of trust in our police?[100] Emotive comments of this nature seem to appear with increasing frequency in our law reports and they are bound to continue to increase in the months and years to come.

Unfortunately, there is an inherent contradiction in the reliance upon police warnings as the vehicle for attempting to ensure the equal treatment of detainees at the pre-trial stage. Are we not putting the police in an extremely awkward position? As a good investigator, the police officer must strive to obtain a statement. However, in pursuing that goal, he must draw to the attention of the accused an avenue which, if adopted, is almost certain to ensure that a statement is *not* obtained. Can we reasonably expect that warnings are likely to be given in the most effective manner?

Consider the situation from another perspective. If a suspect does obtain legal advice, what is that advice to be in the vast majority of cases? It will be to say absolutely nothing to police. A person who is fully conversant with the law will say absolutely nothing to the police when questioned as a possible suspect. What is the logical conclusion for law reform if the goal is to place everyone in that position? Obviously, it is to render *all* statements to police officers inadmissible. Of course, that is a totally unacceptable alternative from a practical or political point of view. However, it does illustrate the dilemma of a system which relies on confessions as an important element of proof yet purports to offer everyone complete freedom not to engage in pre-trial questioning by the police.

3. THE ROLE OF THE ACCUSED AT THE TRIAL STAGE

A central issue with respect to the application of section 11 of the Charter is the meaning of "charged with an offence". It is only after that condition has been met that the rights embodied in sections 11(a) to 11(i) become operative. Following dozens of lower court decisions, the Supreme Court of Canada addressed the issue in *Wigglesworth v. R.*[101]

Madam Justice Wilson, delivering the majority judgment, established

---

98 *R. v. Altseimer* (1982), 1 C.C.C. (3d) 7 at 13 (Ont. C.A.), *per* Zuber J.A.).

99 *R. v. Duguay* (1985), 18 C.C.C. (2d) 289 at 301 (Ont. C.A.), again *per* Zuber J.A.

100 *R. v. Strachan* (1986), 24 C.C.C. (2d) 205 (B.C.C.A.), *per* Esson J.A.

101 [1987] 2 S.C.R. 541.

two tests for the interpretation of these opening words of section 11. The first requirement is that the offence under consideration be criminal or penal "by nature":

> In my view, if a particular matter is of a public nature, intended to promote public order and welfare within a public sphere of activity, then that matter is the kind of matter which falls within s. 11. It falls within the section because of the kind of matter it is. That is to be distinguished from private, domestic or disciplinary matters which are regulatory, protective or corrective and which are primarily intended to maintain discipline, professional integrity and professional standards or to regulate conduct within a limited sphere of activity.[102]

Nevertheless, even if the offence were not criminal or penal "by nature", it still might fall within the protection of section 11 if it carried a "true penal consequence" as a sanction. Thus a disciplinary offence under the *Royal Canadian Mounted Police Act*[103] was held not to be criminal or penal "by nature" but it was subject to section 11 because a potential penalty of imprisonment for one year constituted a "true penal consequence".

In *Wigglesworth*, the court specifically refrained from discussing the possible application of section 7 of the Charter, which had not been raised by the appellant. However, a recent decision of the same court in another case suggests a potentially vast scope for the application of section 7, quite apart from the "substantive due process" component of that section.

In *Reference re s. 94(2) of Motor Vehicle Act (B.C.)*,[104] Mr. Justice Lamer, delivering the majority judgment, gave a broad interpretation of "the principles of fundamental justice" found in section 7. He concluded that all the legal rights embodied in sections 8 to 14 of the Charter address specific deprivations of the principles of fundamental justice. These sections are merely examples of the manner in which "life, liberty and security of the person" might be violated unless "fundamental justice" were present:

> To put matters in a different way, ss. 7 to 14 could have been fused into one section, with inserted between the words of s. 7 and the rest of those sections the oft-utilized provision in our statutes, "and, without limiting the generality of the foregoing" (s. 7) the following shall be deemed to be in violation of a person's rights under this section.[105]

Thus, each of the provisions of sections 8 to 14 of the Charter, inclusive, must now be interpreted in the context of section 7.

If that is the case, the condition of being charged with an offence

---

102 *Ibid.* at 560.
103 R.S.C. 1970, c. R-9 [now R.S.C. 1985, c. R-10].
104 [1985] 2 S.C.R. 486.
105 *Ibid.* at 502-503. This view was expressed again by Lamer J. in *Mills v. R.*, [1986] 1 S.C.R. 863.

would also be enveloped by the broader condition of "life, liberty and security of the person". Where the latter is threatened, the protections embodied in section 11 would be available by virtue of section 7, even though the tests established by Madam Justice Wilson in the *Wigglesworth* case had not been met. Moreover, under section 7, there need not be an actual denial of life, liberty or security of the person. A potential denial is sufficient to render mandatory the principles of fundamental justice.[106]

The dimension of the decision in the *Section 94(2) Reference* has not even started to be explored. For example, as applied to section 10(b), discussed in the previous section, it could mean that a "detention" may not be necessary to generate the constitutional right to counsel. The principles of fundamental justice might require a right to counsel where there is a potential loss of "liberty" quite apart from any arrest or detention.

(a) Section 11(a)

In the first edition of this book, the importance of the right to a specific accusation was discussed.[107] It is important that the accused know the exact misconduct which is alleged, the scope of the proceedings against him and the identity of the accuser. Some of the pre-Charter cases were discussed and it was concluded that:

> While the right to a specific accusation is extremely important, the Criminal Code contains detailed protections in this respect. It may well be, therefore, that s. 11(*a*) will not have a significant impact upon the criminal process in the immediate future.[108]

This prediction has proven to be accurate. In *R. v. Lucas*,[109] the Nova Scotia Court of Appeal found that section 11(a) enshrines the rights contained in section 510 [581] of the *Criminal Code*. There have been no decisions of major significance in relation to section 11(a) of the Charter.

(b) Section 11(c)

Another well-recognized protection for an accused at his criminal trial is his right not to testify as a witness at that trial. Section 11(c) of the Charter provides:

> Any person charged with an offence has the right

. . .

---

106 *Singh v. Min. of Employment & Immigration*, [1985] 1 S.C.R. 177.
107 See pp. 351-354.
108 At 354.
109 (1983), 150 D.L.R. (3d) 118 (N.S.C.A.).

(c) not to be compelled to be a witness in proceedings against that person in respect of the offence;

Prior to the Charter, there was no express provision making the accused non-compellable as a witness at his trial. The *Canada Evidence Act*[110] contains no such provision. Rather, the non-compellability arises by incorporation of the position of an accused at common law. At common law, the accused was neither competent nor compellable as a witness. The *Canada Evidence Act* has modified the common law position by making the accused competent to testify in his own defence,[111] but has not changed his status of being non-compellable by the Crown. Thus, while it may sound contradictory, it properly can be said that the non-compellability of an accused was *specifically* adopted in Canada by the *implied* incorporation of a common law principle.[112]

An important feature of the approach which was taken to make the accused competent was that, if he decided to take the stand on his own behalf, he could also be required to testify against himself. No attempt was made in the Act to protect him against cross-examination which might incriminate him at the trial at which he testified. Thus, an accused who testifies is treated much like any other witness:

> When a person on trial claims the right to give evidence on his own behalf, he comes under the ordinary rule as to cross-examination in criminal cases. He may be asked all questions pertinent to the issue, and cannot refuse to answer those which may implicate him . . . [H]e may be convicted out of his own mouth. He cannot be compelled to testify, but when he offers and gives his evidence he has to take the consequences.[113]

Another consequence is that he is subject to cross-examination as to previous convictions on the issue of credibility.[114]

What does it mean to say that an accused cannot be compelled to testify? What form of "compulsion" are we talking about? No one has seriously suggested that a witness should be forced to testify through the infliction of torture. Where an ordinary witness refuses to testify, the usual

---

110 R.S.C. 1970, c. E-10 [R.S.C. 1985, c. C-5].

111 *Ibid.*, s. 4(1).

112 See generally, "Is There a Right Against Self-Incrimination in Canada?" *supra*, note 3 at 28 *et seq.*

113 *R. v. Connors* (1893), 5 C.C.C. 70 at 72 (Qué. C.A.), *per* Wurtele J. See also *R. v. Whittaker* (1924), 42 C.C.C. 162 at 167-168 (Alta. S.C.), *per* Walsh J.; *Maxwell v. D.P.P.* (1934), 24 Cr. App. R. 152 (H.L.); *R. v. Gauthier* (1975), 33 C.R.N.S. 46 (S.C.C.).

114 *R. v. D'Aoust* (1902), 5 C.C.C. 407 (Ont. C.A.); *R. v. Mulvihill* (1914), 22 C.C.C. 354 (B.C.C.A.); *R. v. Cippola* (1928), 49 C.C.C. 129 (Ont. C.A.); *R. v. Dalton* (1935), 64 C.C.C. 140 (N.S.C.A.); *R. v. Miller* (1940), 74 C.C.C. 270 (B.C.C.A.). The Charter has had no impact on this consequence: *R. v. Corbett* (1984), 43 C.R. (3d) 193 (B.C.C.A.); *R. v. Kulba* (1986), 27 C.C.C. (3d) 349 (Man. C.A.).

sanction is to adjourn and remand the witness in custody[115] or to punish the witness for contempt of court.[116] A further sanction might be imposed where the witness is an accused. In these circumstances, the failure to testify might be taken into account in assessing his guilt with respect to the charge he is facing.

In Canada, the non-compellability of an accused at his trial renders him immune from the sanctions normally faced by a witness who refuses to testify. Does it also protect an accused from adverse inferences being drawn against him as a result of his failure to testify? Section 4(5) [4(6)] of the *Canada Evidence Act* suggests that such a protection was intended. It provides:

> The failure of the person charged, or of the wife or husband of such person, to testify, shall not be made the subject of comment by the judge or by counsel for the prosecution.

However, far from infusing this provision with a vitality to enhance the protection which it appears to give to an accused, the courts have treated it in a very narrow fashion.

The courts have read into section 4(5) [4(6)] the limitation that it applies only to jury trials.[117] Thus, comment is freely permitted at a trial before a judge alone. The word "comment" has also been interpreted narrowly so that indirect references to the accused's failure to testify have been permitted.[118] Even where the comment has been found to fall within section 4(5) [4(6)], appellate courts have been quick to apply section 613(1)(b)(iii) [686(1)(b)(iii)] of the *Criminal Code* to overlook the transgression on the basis that it constituted "no substantial wrong or miscarriage of justice".[119] Moreover, our courts have stated that, while an accused may refuse to testify and while direct comment may not be made to the jury on this refusal, the jury is perfectly entitled to weigh the accused's failure to testify against him, in assessing the evidence. In other words, the trier of fact may take this factor into account as giving extra weight to any evidence which the Crown has adduced.[120] It might also be considered by an appellate court in determining whether or not section 613(1)(b)(iii)

---

115 *Criminal Code*, s. 472 [545].

116 *Ibid.* s. 8 [9].

117 *R. v. Binder* (1948), 6 C.R. 83 (Ont. C.A.); *Pratte v. Maher* (1963), 43 C.R. 214 (Qué. C.A.); *R. v. Bouchard*, [1970] 5 C.C.C. 95 (N.B.C.A.).

118 *Wright v. R.*, [1945] S.C.R. 319, *R. v. Dawley* (1946), 89 C.C.C. 134 (B.C.C.A.); *McConnell v. R.*, [1968] S.C.R. 802; *Avon v. R.*, [1971] S.C.R. 650. *Cf. Bigaouette v. R.*, [1927] S.C.R. 112, applied in *R. v. Groulx* (1953), 16 C.R. 145 (Ont. C.A.).

119 *McConnell v. R.*, *supra*, note 118; *Avon v. R.*, *supra*, note 118.

120 *Corbett v. R.* (1973), 25 C.R.N.S. 296 (S.C.C.); *R. v. Vezeau* (1975), 34 C.R.N.S. 309 (S.C.C.). *Cf. R. v. Chambers* (1980), 54 C.C.C. (2d) 569 (Man. C.A.).

[686(1)(b)(iii)] of the *Criminal Code* should apply.[121]

The narrow approach of the courts to the non-compellability "protection" is demonstrable in other situations as well. For example, in *De Clercq v. R.*,[122] the Supreme Court of Canada permitted the accused, testifying at a *voir dire* on the admissibility of his confession, to be asked if the confession was true, even though the sole issue on the *voir dire* is that of voluntariness. Mr. Justice Hall pointed out that the very purpose of the *voir dire* was to allow an accused to testify on the issue of voluntariness without requiring him to testify on the issue of guilt:

> If an accused cannot testify on the *voir dire* without being liable to be asked questions bearing directly on his guilt or innocence, he is put in a situation where he cannot do so without in effect being deprived from the benefit of the rule against compulsory self-incrimination.[123]

This, however, was a dissenting view. The majority, through some unexplained process of reasoning,[124] concluded that the question as to the truth of the confession was relevant to the issue of credibility. They were certainly not in the least inhibited by any transcending concept of the non-compellability of the accused.

The *Canadian Bill of Rights* provision with respect to self-incrimination states that no law shall be construed or applied so as to:

> 2.(d) authorize a court, tribunal, commission, board or other authority to compel a person to give evidence if he is denied counsel, protection against self-incrimination or other constitutional safeguards.

Section 2(d) obviously embodies the privilege of a witness which is contained in section 5(2) of the *Canada Evidence Act* (and section 13 of the Charter). In *Curr v. R.*,[125] Mr. Justice Laskin stated, in *obiter*, that section 2(d) also "means, in the case of an accused person, that he cannot be

---

121 *Caccamo v. R.* (1975), 29 C.R.N.S. 78 (S.C.C.). See also *Ambrose v. R.*; *Hutchison v. R.*, [1977] 2 S.C.R. 717; *Corbett v. R.*, *supra*, note 120. *R. v. Vezeau, ibid.*; *Avon v. R.*, *supra* note 155.

122 [1968] S.C.R. 902.

123 *Ibid.* at 923. Pigeon J., dissenting, also referred to "the rule against compulsory self-incrimination".

124 See E. Ratushny, "Unravelling Confessions" (1971), 13 *C.L.Q. 453* at 470 *et seq.* Ironically, the Privy Council recently rejected the English Court of Appeal decision which had been relied upon by the majority in *De Clercq*. Instead, it adopted a Saskatchewan decision which had been ignored by the Supreme Court of Canada: *Wong Kam-Ming v. R.*, [1980] A.C. 247 (P.C.). The Alberta Court of Appeal has held that it was bound to follow *De Clercq* rather than *Wong Kam-Ming*: *R. v. Sawchyn* (1981), 60 C.C.C. (2d) 200 (Alta. C.A.), leave to appeal refused (1981), 33 A.R. 198 (Alta. C.A.). See also *R. v. Tarrant* (1980), 55 C.C.C. (2d) 425 (Ont. Co. Ct.).

125 (1972), 18 C.R.N.S. 281 (S.C.C.).

made a compellable witness".[126] It is submitted that, on the wording of the provision, such an interpretation is, at best, questionable.[127]

Section 11(c) of the Charter, therefore, clearly establishes for the first time in Canada the concept of the non-compellability of an accused at his trial as a fundamental right. This status could well cause our courts to reassess the narrow scope which has been given to the non-compellability rule in the past,[128] for example, in relation to section 4(5) [4(6)] of the *Canada Evidence Act.* However, these issues have not yet been addressed in the reported cases.

Rather, the interpretation of section 11(c) by the courts has been limited largely to confirming that it has not altered the previous state of the law. This provision has been interpreted to confer only testimonial protection that is, to apply only to oral or testimonial proof and not to physical or bodily proof. Thus it has no application to fingerprints,[129] footprints,[130] compulsory breath tests[131] or the production of documents.[132] Nor does it apply to statements made prior to trial in response to police questioning[133] or even to statements given under compulsion of provincial motor vehicle accident legislation.[134]

In assessing the testimonial protection which the Charter provides to an accused, it is necessary to consider section 11(c) in the context of section 13. The latter provision has been drafted narrowly to permit incriminating testimony to continue to be compelled at proceedings other than the accused's actual criminal trial. The problem has been documented extensively[135] and that discussion will not be repeated here. The basic problem is that many of the protections provided by the criminal process may be subverted by calling the suspect or accused as a witness at some

---

126 *Ibid.* at 300.

127 See Ratushny, *supra*, note 7 at 90.

128 *Cf.* the decision in *Re Uszinska and France* (1980), 52 C.C.C. (2d) 39 at 42 (Ont. H.C.), where Robins J., then of the Ontario High Court, refused an order to enforce letters rogatory on the basis that to do so "would be in conflict with basic notions of justice in Canada" by infringing the accused's "absolute right in law to refuse to enter the witness-box".

129 *Re Jamieson and R.* (1982), 70 C.C.C. (2d) 430 (Qué. S.C.),

130 *R. v. Nielsen* (1984), 16 C.C.C. (3d) 39 (Man. C.A.), leave to appeal to S.C.C. refused (1985), 31 Man. R. (2d) 240 (S.C.C.); *R. v. Wadden* (1986), 71 N.S.R. (2d) 253 (C.A.).

131 *R. v. Altseimer, supra*, note 98; *Gaff v. R.* (1984), 15 C.C.C. (3d) 126 (Sask. C.A.), leave to appeal to S.C.C. refused (1984), 15 C.C.C. (3d) 126n (S.C.C.).

132 *Amway Corp. v. R.* (1986), 34 D.L.R. (4th) 190 (F.C.C.A.), leave to appeal to S.C.C. granted (1987), 81 N.R. 318n (*sub nom. Canada v. Amway Corp.*) (S.C.C.).

133 *R. v. Esposito, supra*, note 57, discussed *supra* under section 10(b).

134 *R. v. Sydholm* (1983), 22 M.V.R. 37 (B.C. Co. Ct.), leave to appeal to B.C.C.A. refused (May 9, 1983) (B.C.C.A.).

135 See Ratushny, *supra*, note 7 at 78-87 and 347-404.

other proceeding prior to his criminal trial.

It is true that such a witness may prevent his testimony from being introduced at any subsequent criminal trial. However, the damage may be done in other ways. The earlier hearing might be used as a "fishing expedition" to subject the witness to extensive questioning with a view to uncovering possible criminal conduct. The questioning might also be used to investigate a particular offence. For example, the accused might be required to reveal possible defences, the names of potential defence witnesses and other evidence. Moreover, the publicity generated by the hearing may seriously prejudice the likelihood of a fair trial.

The problem is that the initial hearing is likely to have none of the protections guaranteed by the criminal process. There will be no specific accusation, no presumption of innocence, no protections against prejudicial publicity, no rules of evidence and so on. It is submitted that there is a serious crisis of integrity in a criminal process whose detailed protections may so easily be ignored. Nor are these merely theoretical problems.

In the case of *R. v. Johansen*,[136] the father of a deceased child was called to testify at the inquest. Although no charges had been laid, the facts pointed to child battery. The Alberta Court of Appeal concluded that it was likely that the father would be charged with an offence relating to the death of the child. Nevertheless, the suspect was compellable under the Alberta legislation.

This investigative technique was sanctioned by the Supreme Court of Canada in the case of *Faber v. R.*[137] The earlier decision of the court, in *Batary v. A.G. Saskatchewan*,[138] has been restricted in scope to rendering such a witness non-compellable only where the witness has already been charged with an offence involving the death in question. Moreover, *Batary* has also been restricted to coroner's inquests, so that even a person who has been charged may be called at other proceedings such as public inquiries.[139]

Until recently, it was a frequent practice in the province of Quebec to use the coroner's inquest in place of the preliminary inquiry where a death was involved. The criminal charge was postponed, the inquest was held and the suspect was either examined or imprisoned for a year for contempt. Moreover, the Quebec Police Commission Inquiry into Orga-

---

136 [1976] 2 W.W.R. 113 (Alta. C.A.).
137 (1975), 32 C.R.N.S. 3 (S.C.C.).
138 [1965] S.C.R. 465.
139 *R. v. Qué. Mun. Comm.; Ex Parte Longpré*, [1970] 4 C.C.C. 133 (Qué. C.A.). See also *Royal American Shows Inc. v. Laycraft*, [1978] 2 W.W.R. 169 (Alta. S.C.) and *Orysiuk v. R.* (1977), 37 C.C.C. (2d) 445 (Alta. C.A.).

nized Crime[140] recently operated as a regular part of the machinery of criminal justice in that province. The result is that the rights of an accused, in practice, may vary drastically from province to province.

In the first edition of this book, it was submitted that, while section 13 of the *Charter* provides little prospect for dealing with this problem, section 11(c) might hold greater promise. Since this is the first clear articulation of the non-compellability of the accused in Canadian law, it would be open to the courts at some stage to hold that the non-compellability provision in section 11(c) is so undermined by compellability at other hearings that "person charged with an offence" should be interpreted as including a "person likely to be charged" and that "proceedings against that person" should be interpreted as including any proceedings which would prejudice his status as a potential accused in another forum. In other words, an opportunity now exists to give a broad interpretation to section 11(c) and, thereby, to achieve the opposite result to the Supreme Court decisions in *Faber* and *Di Iorio*.[141]

This issue has not yet been addressed by the Supreme Court of Canada. However, the decisions of the lower courts have rejected such an expansive interpretation of section 11(c). In this area, as well, the cases have simply confirmed the previous state of the law.

In *Re Michaud and Min. of Justice (N.B.)*,[142] the accused was charged with the murder of his wife but discharged at the preliminary inquiry. The Minister of Justice subsequently directed that a coroner's inquest be convened and the former accused was served a summons to attend and testify. The court held that even if the witness were to be considered to be a "person charged with an offence", section 11(c) offered no protection. He was not being compelled to testify "in *proceedings* against that person *in respect of the offence*". Since the courts had repeatedly held in the past that there was no *lis*, no accused and no charge, the argument that the inquest was being used as a mechanism for criminal investigation was rejected.

A number of cases have held that a person charged with a criminal offence still may be obliged to testify on discovery or at a civil trial.[143] Section 11(c) has not had the effect of nullifying the reasoning in the pre-

---

140 The compellability of suspects by this body has also met the legal sanction of the Supreme Court of Canada: *Di Iorio v. Montreal Jail Warden, supra*, note 4.

141 *Supra*, notes 137 and 4, respectively.

142 (1982), 3 C.C.C. (3d) 325 (N.B.Q.B.).

143 *Tricontinental Investments Co. v. Guarantee Co. of North America* (1982), 39 O.R. (2d) 614 (Ont. H.C.); *Caisse Populaire Laurier d'Ottawa Ltée v. Guertin; Caisse Populaire Laurier d'Ottawa Ltée v. Simard* (1983), 43 O.R. (2d) 91 (Ont. H.C.), varied (1984), 46 O.R. (2d) 422 (Div. Ct.); *Saccomanno v. Swanson* (1987), 34 D.L.R. (4th) 462 (Alta. Q.B.).

Charter decision of *Stickney v. Trusz.*[144] Similarly, the courts have held that a person alleged to be a party to the same offence as the accused, but who is not being tried with the accused, is a compellable witness for the Crown at the trial of the accused.[145]

Unless the Supreme Court of Canada should choose to depart significantly from these authorities, this serious gap in the protection of individual rights under the Charter will continue to exist. It is likely that that is exactly what the drafters of the Charter intended. Section 13 is drafted narrowly to reflect merely the kind of protection formerly available under section 5(2) of the *Canada Evidence Act.* The wording of section 11(c) would have to be "stretched" to support its application to a witness who is not actually on trial at the proceeding in question.

However, that no longer may be necessary in order to address the problem. It was pointed out at the beginning of this discussion of section 11, that the restrictions imposed by the wording of this provision may be released in appropriate cases by resort to section 7. There may not exist a more clear and compelling case for the application of the Lamer *dicta* in the *Reference re Section 94(2)* case[146] than to bring consistency and integrity to the self-incrimination provision contained in section 11(c) and section 13 of the Charter. Indeed, in *Dubois v. R.,*[147] Mr. Justice Lamer, writing for the majority of the Supreme Court of Canada, specifically adopted the following passage from the first edition of this chapter:

> In many ways, it is the principle of a "case to meet" which is the real underlying protection which the "non-compellability" rule seeks to promote. The important protection is not that the accused need not testify, but that the Crown must prove its case before there can be an expectation that he will respond, whether by testifying himself, or by calling other evidence. However, even where a "case to meet" has been presented, the burden of proof remains upon the Crown to the end.[148]

---

144 (1973), 16 C.C.C. (2d) 25 (Ont. H.C.), aff'd 17 C.C.C. (2d) 478 (Ont. Div. Ct.), aff'd 17 C.C.C. (2d) 480 (Ont. C.A.), leave to appeal to S.C.C. refused 28 C.R.N.S. 127n (Ont. C.A.).

145 *Re. Crooks and R.* (1982), 2 C.C.C. (3d) 57 (Ont. H.C.), aff'd (1982), 2 C.C.C. (3d) at 64 (Ont. C.A.); *R. v. Walters* (1982), 2 C.C.C. (3d) 512 (B.C.C.A.); *R. v. Bleich* (1983), 7 C.C.C. (3d) 176 (Man. Q.B.); *Re Welton and R.* (1986), 29 C.C.C. (3d) 226 (Ont. H.C.). See also *Re Amorelli and R.* (1983), 6 C.C.C. (3d) 93 (Que. S.C.) with respect to *Criminal Code* ss. 180, 185.

146 *Supra*, note 104.

147 *Supra*, note 44.

148 The quoted passage is at pp. 358-359 of the first edition. The decisions to date on the inter-relationship of section 7 and the concept of self-incrimination have not addressed the "case to meet" principle. See *R.L. Crain Inc. v. Couture* (1984), 10 C.C.C. (3d) 119 (Sask. Q.B.); *Re Gaw and Yeomans* (1984), 14 C.C.C. (3d) 134 (F.C.T.D.), rev'd (1985), 22 C.C.C. (3d) 311 (*sub nom. Yeomans v. Gaw*) (F.C.C.A.); *Haywood Securities v. Inter-Tech Resource Group Inc.* (1985), 24 D.L.R. (4th) 724 (B.C.C.A.), leave

He concluded that the concept of a "case to meet" is common to sections 11(c), 11(d) and 13. The *Dubois* decision is discussed in the final part of this chapter dealing with section 13.

The precise scope of a unified right against self-incrimination will have to be fashioned carefully. However, at a minimum it should permit a potential witness to refuse to provide testimony which would be personally incriminating in the absence of a specific and binding grant of immunity from prosecution in relation to the subject-matter of such testimony.

(c) Section 11(d)

The starting point for considering the nature of the "presumption of innocence" embodied in section 11(d) is now the Supreme Court of Canada decision in *R. v. Oakes*.[149] Chief Justice Dickson spoke in the following glowing terms:

> The presumption of innocence protects the fundamental liberty and human dignity of any and every person accused by the State of criminal conduct. An individual charged with a criminal offence faces grave social and personal consequences, including potential loss of physical liberty, subjection to social stigma and ostracism from the community, as well as other social, psychological and economic harms. In light of the gravity of these consequences, the presumption of innocence is crucial. It ensures that until the State proves an accused's guilt beyond all reasonable doubt, he or she is innocent. This is essential in a society committed to fairness and social justice. The presumption of innocence confirms our faith in humankind; it reflects our belief that individuals are decent and law-abiding members of the community until proven otherwise.[150]

He concluded that the presumption of innocence contains three basic components:

1. the burden of proof is upon the Crown;
2. the standard of proof is beyond a reasonable doubt; and
3. the method of proof is according to "fairness" or due process.

The *Oakes* case involved a challenge to section 8 of the *Narcotic*

---

to appeal to S.C.C. granted (1986), 68 N.R. 319n (*Sub nom. Brunnhuber v. Haywood Securities Inc.*) (S.C.C.); *Thompson Newspapers Ltd. v. Director of Investigation & Research (Can.)* (1986), 25 C.C.C. (3d) 233 (Ont. H.C.), appeal dismissed (1986), 30 C.C.C. (3d) 145 (Ont. C.A.); leave to appeal to S.C.C. granted (1987), 61 O.R. 605n (S.C.C.); *Seaway Trust Co. v. Kilderkin Investments Ltd.* (1986), 29 D.L.R. (4th) 456 (Ont. H.C.).

149 [1986] 1 S.C.R. 103.

150 *Ibid.*, at 119-120. Dickson C.J.C. delivered the majority judgment (Chouinard, Lamer, Wilson and Le Dain JJ. concurring). Estey J. (McIntyre J. concurring) preferred, in part, the reasons of Martin J.A. in the court below (Ont. C.A.).

Control Act.[151] The effect of this section is that the Crown must first prove possession of a narcotic beyond a reasonable doubt. After such a finding, the accused has the legal burden of proving on a balance of probabilities that the possession of the narcotic was not for the purpose of trafficking. Chief Justice Dickson characterized this provision as a "basic fact presumption" which involves the drawing of a conclusion upon proof of a different fact. It was also a "mandatory" presumption since the trier of fact did not have a discretion to draw a conclusion other than the specified presumption. Finally, while the presumption was "rebuttable", the legal burden of proof was placed upon the accused on the standard of a balance of probabilities. Such a provision is generally described as a "reverse onus clause".

Chief Justice Dickson then canvassed the authorities on reverse onus clauses in Canada, the United States and under the *European Convention.* He refused to be bound by the earlier decisions under the *Canadian Bill of Rights,* which was described as "fundamentally different from the Charter". The lower court decisions under the Charter were described as having "solidly accorded a high degree of protection to the presumption of innocence". Any infringements of section 11(d) were only permissible when they could be justified under section 1. He concluded that:

> In general one must, I think, conclude that a provision which requires an accused to disprove on a balance of probabilities the existence of a presumed fact, which is an important element of the offence in question, violates the presumption of innocence in s. 11(*d*). If an accused bears the burden of disproving on a balance of probabilities an essential element of an offence, it would be possible for a conviction to occur despite the existence of a reasonable doubt. This would arise if the accused adduced sufficient evidence to raise a reasonable doubt as to his or her innocence but did not convince the jury on a balance of probabilities that the presumed fact was untrue.[152]

As a result, section 8 of the *Narcotic Control Act* was a clear violation of section 11(d) of the Charter and could only be upheld if it could be found to be a reasonable limit meeting the conditions of section 1.

The analysis which followed provides a comprehensive formula for the application of section 1 of the Charter. (Since this provision is the subject of another chapter, it will not be discussed here.) Chief Justice Dickson concluded that the objective of protecting society from the extremely serious problem of trafficking was a sufficiently important objective to warrant overriding a Charter right in certain cases. However, section 8 of the *Narcotic Control Act* did not survive scrutiny of the means

---

151 R.S.C. 1970, c. N-1 [now R.S.C. 1985, c. N-1].
152 *Oakes, supra,* note 149 at 132-133.

chosen by Parliament to achieve its objective. There was no rational connection between the possession of even a small quantity of narcotics and the inference of trafficking. Therefore, section 8 could not survive, and it was not necessary to consider the further requirements of minimal intrusion to achieve the goal of proportionality between the effects of the provision and the basic objective.

While the *Oakes* decision provides a solid foundation for the application of section 11(d), concerns have been expressed that it could be narrowly confined to situations in which the legal burden on the accused relates to an important element of the offence:

> Consider, for example, how easily Parliament might avoid s. 11(*d*). Instead of reversing the onus of proof on an element of the offence, the element might be deleted from the definition of the crime. On its face, the provision would have nothing to do with the burden of proof.[153]

This concern is well-founded. If the Charter can be displaced merely by the mechanics of legislative drafting, it will soon lose its integrity.

Nor is there much doubt that our politicians will sanction such an approach when it suits their objectives. Consider, for example, the provisions of Bill C-54 in relation to pornography.[154] The Bill made dealing in pornography an offence and defined both dealing and pornography in extremely broad terms. In what was described in the marginal notes as "Defences", it then provided that "the court shall find the accused not guilty if the accused establishes, on a balance of probabilities, that the matter or communication in question has artistic merit". Presumably, the government argument is that this is not a "reverse onus" clause but rather a "defence" which is not encompassed by section 11(d).

Any hopes that our Supreme Court will tolerate such a subterfuge should be demolished by the court's bold and principled decision in *Vaillancourt v. R.*[155] Mr. Justice Lamer, speaking for the majority on this issue, expanded upon the meaning of "elements of the offence" in the context of section 11(d):

> This means that, before an accused can be convicted of an offence, the trier of fact must be satisfied beyond reasonable doubt of all of the essential elements of the offence. These essential elements include not only those set out by the legislature in the provision creating the offence but also those required by s. 7 of the *Charter* . . .

---

153 T.A. Cromwell & A.W. MacKay, "Oakes in the Supreme Court: a Cautious Initiative Unimpeded by Old Ghosts" (1986), 50 C.R. (3d) 34 at 39.

154 *An Act to amend the Criminal Code and other Acts in consequence thereof* (received only first reading by the dissolution of parliament).

155 [1987] 2 S.C.R. 636.

> Sections 7 and 11(*d*) will also be infringed where the statutory definition of the offence does not include an element which is required under s. 7.[156]

He went on to point out that the essence of the interpretation of section 11(d) in *Oakes* was to preclude an accused being convicted despite the existence of a reasonable doubt on an essential element of the offence. Therefore, it makes little difference whether that results from the existence of a reverse onus provision or from the elimination of the need to prove an essential element.

Mr. Justice Lamer also described another scenario:

> Finally, the legislature, rather than simply eliminating any need to prove the essential element, may substitute proof of a different element. In my view, this will be constitutionally valid only if upon proof beyond reasonable doubt of the substituted element it would be unreasonable for the trier of fact not to be satisfied beyond reasonable doubt of the existence of the essential element. If the trier of fact may have a reasonable doubt as to the essential element notwithstanding proof beyond a reasonable doubt of the substituted element, then the substitution infringes ss. 7 and 11(*d*).[157]

In *Vaillancourt*, the court held that section 213(d) of the *Criminal Code* violated the Charter in permitting a conviction for murder in the absence of proof beyond a reasonable doubt of at least objective foreseeability.

It is submitted that our courts should bring the same incisive analysis to the application of section 11(d) to other areas. The result should not vary because the legislative form can be characterized as an "excuse" or a "justification" or a "defence". In other words, it may be necessary frequently to go beyond the definition of the offence in the statute in question to ascertain "all of the essential elements" of that offence.

It should not be surprising that sections 7 and 11(d) converged to achieve the result in *Vaillancourt*. Indeed, in *Oakes*, Chief Justice Dickson stated that:

> Although protected expressly in s. 11(*d*) of the *Charter*, the presumption of innocence is referable and integral to the general protection of life, liberty and security of the person contained in s. 7 of the *Charter*.[158]

Moreover, at the end of the previous section, reference was made to the first edition of this chapter and Mr. Justice Lamer's conclusion in *Dubois*[159] that the concept of a "case to meet" is common to sections 11(c), 11(d)

---

156 *Ibid.* at 654-655, *per* Lamer J. (Dickson C.J. and Wilson J. concurring). Beetz J. (Le Dain J. concurring) gave separate reasons agreeing with Lamer J. as to the violation of s. 11(d). La Forest J. concurred in the result but without reference to s. 11(d). McIntyre J. dissented.

157 *Ibid.* at 656.

158 *Supra*, note 149 at 119.

159 *Supra*, note 44.

and 13 which are some examples of the protections established by section 7.

The application of the standard of proof beyond a reasonable doubt is particularly important with respect to certain kinds of evidence. For example, there are frequently great dangers in relying upon eyewitness identification. There is a similar danger with respect to circumstantial evidence. Therefore, the burden on the Crown is so great that "[e]ven a high degree of probability does not constitute proof beyond a reasonable doubt".[160] The consequences of an adjudication of guilt are so serious that a very high standard is required in every case.

The concept of a "case to meet" is more closely related to the following policy basis:

> There is a strong policy in favour of government's leaving people alone, and there is a complementary strong policy which demands that any contest between government and governed be a "fair" one. It follows that the government should not disturb the peace of an individual by way of compulsory appearances and compulsory disclosures which may lead to his conviction unless sufficient evidence exists to establish probable cause. Obviously, if the individual's peace is to be preserved, the government must obtain its *prima facie* case from sources other than the individual.[161]

Can this policy be extended to the pre-trial or investigative stage? In the *Marcoux* case,[162] Mr. Justice Dickson stated that, ordinarily, evidence of a refusal to enter into an identification line-up would not be admissible since such evidence might "impinge on the presumption of innocence and the jury may gain the impression that there is a duty on the accused to prove he is innocent".[163] What is the precise basis, implied in this *obiter dicta*, for the ordinary exclusion of such evidence? The emphasis is upon the potential prejudicial effect upon the jurors at trial. It may not be possible for them to apply the standard of proof beyond a reasonable doubt if the suggestion is made that the accused should have cooperated with the police.

Of course, the reason why an individual need not enter a police line-up is the same as the reason why one need not provide a statement to the police. The principle of the rule of law insists that there is no proscription or obligation except to the extent that it is specifically defined in law.[164]

---

160 *R. v. Rabey* (1977), 17 O.R. (2d) 1 at 26 (C.A.), *per* Martin J.A., delivering the judgment of the court (Dubin and MacKinnon JJ.A.). See also *R. v. Blunden* (1976), 30 C.C.C. (2d) 122 (Ont. C.A.).

161 *Wigmore on Evidence*, McNaughton rev. (Boston: Little, Brown, 1961) at 2251.

162 *Marcoux v. R.*, *supra*, note 4.

163 *Ibid.* at 219.

164 See also *R. v. Burns*, [1965] 4 C.C.C. 298 (Ont. H.C.); *R. v. Shaw*, [1965] 1 C.C.C. 130 (B.C.C.A.); *R. v. Sweeney (No. 2)* (1977), 35 C.C.C. (2d) 245 (Ont. C.A.); *R. v. Eden*, [1970] 3 C.C.C. 280 (Ont. C.A.); *R. v. Itwaru* (1969), 10 C.R.N.S. 184 (N.S.C.A.).

In these circumstances, to introduce at trial evidence of an earlier refusal to cooperate with the police could affect the presumption of innocence, even though there had been no requirement to cooperate.

4. THE POSITION OF A WITNESS AT OTHER HEARINGS

At common law, a witness was entitled to refuse to answer particular questions where the answer would tend to incriminate the witness or expose the witness to a penalty or forfeiture. This common law privilege is still operative in England today. However, in Canada, it was replaced by the more limited privilege contained in section 5(2) of the *Canada Evidence Act*. Under this provision, a witness cannot refuse to give incriminating testimony, but such testimony can be excluded from subsequent proceedings such as a trial of the witness as an accused.

The potential abuses which could stem from this state of the law were addressed earlier, in relation to section 11(c).[165] Essentially, the problem would have been best resolved by providing an immunity in section 13 similar to that which existed at common law. However, the narrow manner in which the section has been drafted suggests that the only avenue for pursuing a possible solution is likely to be section 11(c).

(a) Section 13

Section 13 of the *Canadian Charter of Rights and Freedoms* provides:

> 13. A witness who testifies in any proceeding has the right not to have any incriminating evidence so given used to incriminate that witness in any other proceedings, except in a prosecution for perjury or for the giving of contradictory evidence.

The case of *Dubois v. R.*[166] is the key decision in interpreting this section. The appellant had given evidence at his trial for murder and was convicted. He was unrepresented and did not claim the protection of section 5(2) of the *Canada Evidence Act*. The Alberta Court of Appeal ordered a new trial, where the Crown sought to introduce as part of its case the evidence which the accused had given at the first trial.

Mr. Justice Lamer, again delivering the majority decision,[167] clearly resolved a number of uncertainties in relation to the interpretation of section 13. He concluded that the section 13 protection is operative, not when

---

165 *Supra*, notes 44 *et seq.*

166 *Supra*, note 44. See also *R. v. Mannion*, [1986] 2 S.C.R. 272, extending the application of *Dubois* to the introduction of earlier testimony on cross-examination.

167 *Ibid.* Dickson C.J., Estey, Chouinard, Wilson and Le Dain JJ. concurring, McIntyre J. dissenting.

a witness gives testimony, but on the future occasion when it is sought to use that testimony to incriminate its author. The protection applies whether the initial testimony had been given voluntarily or under compulsion, and no objection is necessary along the lines of the requirement in section 5(2) of the *Canada Evidence Act*.

He also rejected the suggestion of a requirement that the testimony be incriminating not only in the subsequent proceedings but also in the forum in which it was given initially. He considered such a literal interpretation to defeat the nature and purpose of the section and to lead to an absurdity. Nor will the courts enter into an assessment, at the subsequent proceeding, of whether the evidence is actually "incriminating". If it is sought to be introduced by the Crown, section 13 will operate to render it inadmissible.

However, the central issue in the *Dubois* case was the meaning of the words "any other proceedings". Does a new trial on the same charge with respect to the same incident fall within this phrase? Mr. Justice McIntyre, in dissent, concluded that a new trial could not be considered as another proceeding. One commentator was in strong agreement:

> His conclusion, shared by virtually all of the courts below who considered the problem, was that a new trial was part of the same proceeding as the initial trial . . . [T]he cases which hold that, on a new trial ordered by a Court of Appeal, it is not necessary to prefer a new indictment, to arraign the accused, or to take a plea from the accused support McIntyre J.'s conclusion.[168]

The author concluded with the following:

> It is hoped that *Dubois* will represent an anomaly rather than the seminal case in the interpretation of s. 11(c) of the Charter.[169]

In my view, there is no doubt that *Dubois* is, indeed, a seminal case.

The fundamental importance of the Lamer analysis in *Dubois* is to cut through the specific case law in relation to the procedure to be followed at a new trial. It is also to ignore the rhetoric which abounds in relation to the phrase "self-incrimination" or the "Fifth Amendment" in the United States. Instead, the Lamer judgment reflects a search for the underlying, functional principle which had to prevail if the Charter were to be applied with consistency and integrity.

The underlying principle which was isolated, articulated and applied for the first time in the Supreme Court of Canada is the concept of a "case to meet". This means that before an accused need respond there must be a specific offence established by law, a specific accusation in

---

168 D.H. Doherty, "Annotation" (1986), 48 C.R. (3d) 194 at 196.
169 *Ibid.* at 197.

relation to that offence *and* a specific body of evidence in support of that accusation. It is this specific body of evidence or "case to meet" to which the accused must respond. At the subsequent trial in *Dubois*, the Crown might present the same evidence differently or, indeed, different evidence.

The evidence of the accused at the first trial was in response to the "case to meet" which was presented by the Crown at that first trial. If the first trial was improper and a new trial is ordered, the Crown has a new obligation to present its case. It is only when that has been done that the accused need decide whether to respond and, if so, the most effective manner to do so. If the accused decides to testify and lies on the stand at the new trial, that is a separate offence for which another charge can be brought.

The importance of this concept of the "case to meet" has been discussed in relation to section 11(c).[170] It also has been expressed in the following manner:

> Thus, our criminal process knows no continuing inquiry whereby the accused may be called before a judicial officer from time to time and asked questions, perhaps based on the testimony of witnesses who have been questioned in the absence of the accused. There is no gradual building up of a *dossier* in this manner. The accused need only respond once. The Crown must present its evidence at an open trial. The accused is entitled to test and to attack it. If it does not reach a certain standard, then and only then is the accused required to respond or to stand convicted.[171]

The underlying importance of this concept was recognized by Mr. Justice Lamer when he described it as being "common" to sections 11(c), 11(d) and 13.

5. CONCLUSION

The conclusion of the first edition of this chapter was as follows:

> There are few certainties about the manner in which our courts are likely to interpret the Charter. With respect to the role of the accused, there are major gaps in the Charter's coverage of pre-trial interrogation and in the compellability of witnesses at hearings other than criminal trials. At the same time, there is considerable scope for creativity in developing consistent principles which can ensure the integrity of our criminal process.[172]

In less than five years, the impact of the Supreme Court decisions in this

---

170 *Supra*, at 29 *et seq.*

171 First edition of this book, at p. 359.

172 *Ibid.* at 365-366.

area has been dramatic. The decisions in *Therens,*[173] *Clarkson,*[174] the *Section 94(2) Reference,*[175] *Oakes,*[176] *Dubois*[177] and *Vaillancourt*[178] form a creative and consistent collection of authorities which will contribute greatly to ensuring the integrity of the Charter in its application to the role of the accused in the criminal process.

---

173 *Supra,* note 47.
174 *Supra,* note 41.
175 *Supra,* note 104.
176 *Supra,* note 149.
177 *Supra,* note 44.
178 *Supra,* note 155.

13

Certain Guarantees of Criminal Procedure*
(Sections 11(b), (f), (h), 12 and 14)

*André Morel***

1. The Right To Be Tried Within a Reasonable Time (s. 11(b))
2. The Right to Trial By Jury
3. The Right to the Assistance of an Interpreter
4. The Right Not To Be Tried or Punished Again for the Same Offence
5. Protection Against Cruel and Unusual Treatment or Punishment

1. THE RIGHT TO BE TRIED WITHIN A REASONABLE TIME (S. 11(b))

The right of any person charged with an offence to be tried within a reasonable time, while not found in the *Canadian Bill of Rights* or in

---

* Translated from the French.

** The author wishes to express his gratitude to Me Jean Leclair, former student of law at the Faculty of Law, University of Montréal, for his indispensable work as research assistant.

any other federal legislation,[1] is not new. Some commentators have traced its origin as far back as the *Magna Carta* at the same time acknowledging that there existed at that time no effective remedy to ensure that the King respected his promise not to delay or defer the administration of justice.[2] Even when the common law writ of *habeas corpus* began to be used towards the end of the 16th century to secure the liberty of persons illegally detained by the Crown, it was of little effect in practice, as shown by Holdsworth in his *History of English Law*.[3] In fact, it was the existence of the many defects in this writ that led finally to the passing of the *Habeas Corpus Act*[4] in 1679. Since that time, English courts have routinely emphasized that this Act was intended not only to allow a court to review quickly the legality of an accused person's detention, but also to ensure a speedy trial for prisoners accused of treason or felony.[5]

Canadian cases prior to the *Canadian Charter of Rights and Freedoms*, though not numerous,[6] affirmed that the right to be tried within a reasonable time was acknowledged here, as in England, even if the remedies provided were not always entirely satisfactory or perfectly guaranteed.[7] Thus, while section 11(b) of the Charter is the first Canadian legislative text to formulate this right directly,[8] it is not a text which creates a new right. Moreover the section draws on a provision of the *International Covenant on Civil and Political Rights*, which asserts the equal right of any person accused of a criminal offence "to be tried without undue delay".[9] The novelty consists not only in the legislative affirmation of the right in section 11(b) nor in the constitutional character it now enjoys, but lies principally in the fact that under section 24(1) of the Charter any violation of the right

---

1 Bill C-19 *Criminal Law Amendment Act, 1984*, 2nd Sess., 32 Parl., 1983-84 (1st reading) s. 130, proposed to incorporate into the *Criminal Code* a number of provisions to regulate the matter of a "trial within a reasonable time".

2 *Rahey v. R.*, [1987] 1 S.C.R. 588 at 634 (La Forest J.).

3 W. Holdsworth, *A History of English Law*, vol. IX, (London: Sweet & Maxwell, 1966) at 108-125.

4 *An Act for the better securing the Liberty of the Subject*, 1679 (U.K.), 31 Car. II, c. 2.

5 See the decisions cited by R.J. Sharpe in "Notes and Comments, R. v. Chapman and Currie" (1971-72), 14 *C.L.Q.* 399 at 401.

6 *R. v. Cameron* (1897), 1 C.C.C. 169 (Qué. Q.B.); *R. v. Dean* (1913), 21 C.C.C. 310 (B.C.S.C.); *R. v. Thompson (No. 1)* (1946), 86 C.C.C. 193 (Ont. H.C.); *R. v. Chapman* (1971), 2 C.C.C. (2d) 237 (Ont. Dist. Ct.); *R. v. Koski*, [1972] 1 W.W.R. 398 (B.C.S.C.).

7 As argued by Sharpe, *supra*, note 5 at 407-408.

8 By amendment in 1982 (S.Q. 1982, c. 61, s. 11), proclaimed October 1, 1983, *the Charter of human rights and freedoms*, R.S.Q., c. C-12, provides also, at s. 32.1, that: "Every accused person has a right to be tried within a reasonable time."

9 Art. 14, para. 3(c). See also art. 9(3) of this *Covenant*, as well as arts. 5(3) and 6(1) of the *Convention on the Protection of Human Rights and Fundamental Freedoms*.

will henceforth be sanctioned by an appropriate remedy, something which was not the case before.

It is interesting as well as relevant to note that the Sixth Amendment to the United States Constitution had already constitutionalized this common law right, by declaring at the end of the eighteenth century that: "In all criminal prosecutions, the accused shall enjoy the right to a speedy and public trial." American courts have consistently interpreted the requirement of a "speedy trial" as meaning "a trial within a reasonable time". Given the similar meaning of the American and Canadian texts, albeit expressed with slightly different wording, commentators and courts in this country were quick to seek guidance in the long American experience. In this regard, the Supreme Court of Canada has very rightly warned our courts against an excessive reliance on American concepts and precedents. In the words of Mr. Justice La Forest, these precedents can be useful, but Canadian courts "should be wary of drawing too ready a parallel between constitutions born to different countries in different ages and in very different circumstances".[10]

American case law has nevertheless been quite influential, as we shall see in analyzing the various issues relating to the right to be tried within a reasonable time. These include (a) the identification of interests which this right is intended to protect, (b) the determination of the beneficiaries of the right and the relevant delay, (c) the various factors to be considered in determining whether the delay is unreasonable, and (d) the appropriate remedy for violation of the right.

(a) Protected Interests

Section 11(b) of the Charter does not affirm an intrinsic right, one that is inherent in the human person such as the right to life, liberty and security of the person, the right to be treated equally or the right to enjoy certain fundamental freedoms. It does not command recognition in and of itself or because of its inherent value; rather, its recognition is justified through its relation to other values. This is true of all the rights set out in sections 8 to 14 of the Charter. Because the right set out in section 11(b) is a means to an end rather than an end in itself, it is important to identify the objectives it is designed to serve. For this reason, the purposive interpretation is all the more relevant and decisive.

It is clear that the right to be tried within a reasonable time, as set out in section 11(b) of the Charter, has a life of its own and is not limited

---

10 *Rahey v. R.*, *supra*, note 2 at 639. Even if all the judges were not as explicit regarding this question as La Forest J., their reasons for judgment reveal nonetheless the same kind of reservations respecting American case law on the right to a speedy trial.

to only those situations formerly covered by the *Habeas Corpus Act*. This Act was intended, it is true, to guarantee individual freedom. To a great extent, it was intended to put a stop to the kind of abuse that was still prevalent in seventeenth century England which resulted in the lengthy detention of a prisoner without ever bringing him before a court to stand trial. Such abuse is not likely to occur today, for an accused person who is incarcerated can be released on bail in the event that he is not promptly brought to trial.

Even though the right to be tried within a reasonable time is no longer limited to the few situations in which the writ of *habeas corpus* was available, it nevertheless remains fundamentally a means by which the physical liberty of an accused person is protected by preventing an unduly prolonged incarceration prior to trial. But it is important to note that a person's freedom of movement is also restrained while he is released on bail and that section 11(b) is equally designed to restrict the duration of such violations.[11]

The concern to prevent the prolonged detention of persons who have not been convicted and who have not had the chance to defend themselves goes to the heart of section 11(b), for as Mr. Justice Lamer has said: "Such persons are, in effect, purging a sentence before they have ever been found guilty."[12]

Nonetheless, the protection of an accused person's physical liberty is not the only interest underlying the right to be tried within a reasonable time. Even before the coming into force of the Charter, the criminal justice system had begun to acknowledge the psychological, social and monetary repercussions that a person charged with a criminal offence must inevitably experience. These consequences are unnecessarily exacerbated if the person is unable to obtain a quick settlement of his case and, eventually, the removal of all suspicion against him as a result of his acquittal.[13] There was thus recognition that the right to be tried within a reasonable time seeks also to limit these prejudicial consequences of being charged with an offence.

It should not then be surprising to find that the courts have recognized a direct link between section 11(b) and the right to security of the person protected by section 7 of the Charter. Under section 11(b), the security

---

11 *Mills v. R.*, [1986] 1 S.C.R. 863 at 918-919 (Lamer J.); *Rahey v. R.*, *supra*, note 2 at 642 (La Forest J).

12 *Mills v. R.*, *ibid.*, note 11 at 927.

13 Thus, in *R. v. Chapman*, *supra*, note 6 at 241, Mr. Justice Vannini emphasized the consequences for Currie's family and professional life. Similarly, in *R. v. Koski*, *supra*, note 6 at 400, Mr. Justice Munroe declared, in speaking of the accused: "He has been subjected during the past 13 months to embarrassment, expense, and a continuing state of anxiety."

of the accused's person is protected by minimizing in time the adverse consequences of a criminal charge. According to Mr. Justice Lamer, such consequences are varied and include "stigmatization of the accused, loss of privacy, stress and anxiety resulting from a multitude of factors, including possible disruption of family, social life and work, legal costs, uncertainty as to the outcome and sanction".[14]

In addition to protecting the accused against violations of his liberty and security, section 11(b) also protects his interest in having a fair trial, for excessive delay in beginning the trial prejudices the ability of the accused to mount a full and complete defence. An unreasonable lapse of time may effectively deprive an accused of access to certain evidence, as a result of the disappearance of important witnesses for example, or reduce the effectiveness of his defence due to the fading memories of witnesses regarding relevant events.

It should be noted that this issue has been the subject of vigorous debate among members of the Supreme Court of Canada. Both Lamer J. and Dickson C.J.C. take the view that undermining the ability of an accused person to defend himself is not related to the right to be tried within a reasonable time, but rather to the right to a fair trial which is expressly guaranteed by section 11(d) of the Charter. Thus, if the right to a fair trial is not one of the interests which section 11(b) was meant to protect, interference with the ability of an accused to defend himself fairly arising from a delay would not be a factor to consider in determining whether his right to trial within a reasonable time has been violated. In this respect, the structural features of the Canadian Charter would be fundamentally different from those of the *American Bill of Rights*.[15]

However, the majority of Supreme Court judges do not share this view. In their opinion, the rights set out in the several paragraphs of section 11 are not mutually exclusive and it is possible for there to be a degree of overlap between two distinct provisions.[16] Mr. Justice La Forest, in his decision in the *Rahey* case, even shows that this method of analyzing the right to be tried within a reasonable time is compatible with its historical roots in English law.[17]

In summary, in affirming that the object of section 11(b) is to protect the right of an accused to a fair trial as well as his liberty and security interests, Canadian courts find themselves in fundamental agreement with the position adopted by the Supreme Court of the United States in *Barker*

---

14 *Mills v. R.*, *supra*, note 11 at 920.

15 *Ibid.* at 921-923; *Rahey v. R.*, *supra*, note 2 at 606-608.

16 *Mills v. R.*, *supra*, note 11 at 968-969 (Wilson J.); *Rahey v. R.*, *supra*, note 2 at 643-644 (La Forest J.), at 622 (Wilson J.), at 617 (Le Dain).

17 *Rahey v. R.*, *ibid.* at 645.

v. Wingo[18] in 1972. The American court there held that the right to a speedy trial has three objectives:

> (i) to prevent oppressive pretrial incarceration; (ii) to minimize anxiety and concern of the accused; and (iii) to limit the possibility that the defense will be impaired.[19]

(b) The Beneficiaries of the Right and the Calculation of the Time Frame

Like all rights set out in section 11 of the Charter, the right to be tried within a reasonable time is only available to a "person charged with an offence" ("*inculpé*" in the French version). Although the interpretation of these words gave rise to conflicting opinions for a certain period of time, such differences now appear for the most part to have been resolved. Indeed, it now seems well established that the words "person charged with an offence" or "*inculpé*" may not be defined differently depending on the right in question, but must rather receive "a constant meaning throughout, one that harmonizes with the various paragraphs of the section".[20] This is why a person subject to extradition procedures is not a person charged with an offence within the meaning of section 11.[21]

Moreover, the scope of section 11 is itself limited, according to the Supreme Court, to "persons prosecuted by the State for public offences involving punitive sanctions, i.e., criminal, quasi-criminal and regulatory offences" or to persons charged with offences which are not of a penal nature *per se* but which "involve the imposition of true penal consequences".[22]

Clearly, then, the benefit of section 11(b) is accorded to all persons charged with an offence under the *Criminal Code* or under any statute of a penal or quasi-criminal nature.[23] A person is "charged" as soon as he becomes the subject of a summons, warrant or appearance notice issued pursuant to applicable federal or provincial legislation.

It is also quite clear that a person serving a sentence of imprisonment

---

18 407 U.S. 514 (1972).

19 *Ibid.*, at 532.

20 *Canada v. Schmidt*, [1987] 1 S.C.R. 500 at 519; and *Lyons v. R.*, [1987] 2 S.C.R. 309 at 353.

21 *Canada v. Schmidt, ibid.*; *Argentina (Republic) v. Mellino*, [1987] 1 S.C.R. 536; *United States v. Allard*, [1987] 1 S.C.R. 564.

22 *Wigglesworth v. R.*, [1987] 2 S.C.R. 541 at 554, 561.

23 It is thus right and proper that the benefit of section 11(b) was refused to a person who had filed a complaint with a human rights commission: *Re Kodellas and Sask. Human Rights Comm.* (1987), 34 D.L.R. (4th) 30 (Sask. Q.B.), motion to extend deadline to appeal [1987] 3 W.W.R. 558 (Sask. C.A.).

is not thereby deprived of the right to be tried in a reasonable time, if he is also charged with an offence other than that for which he has been incarcerated.[24] However, it is doubtful that a person serving time in a prison or penitentiary could invoke section 11(b) if he were accused of a disciplinary offence.[25]

Disciplinary offences are generally excluded from the scope of section 11 because they "are primarily intended to maintain discipline, professional integrity and professional standards or to regulate conduct within a limited private sphere of activity".[26] Nevertheless, a person who is accused of a disciplinary offence could rely on section 7 of the Charter for protection against excessive delay. Section 7 guarantees respect for the principles of fundamental justice, a standard that is somewhat less demanding than that set out in section 11(b).[27]

Determining what class of persons is entitled to invoke the right set out in section 11(b) is a distinct question from that of determining what period of time should be taken into account in deciding whether a trial has been held within a reasonable time. However, this distinction has not always been clearly appreciated.[28] While the first issue is common to all the rights set out in section 11, the second is unique to the right guaranteed in paragraph (b). Thus, one should not necessarily conclude that the laying of charges serves to define both the beneficiaries of the right and the start of the time period which must be considered to determine whether an accused person has been tried within a reasonable time. The latter question can be adequately answered, in my view, only by taking into account the various interests which section 11(b) of the Charter was meant to protect.

If the sole object of section 11(b) were to protect the accused person's liberty and security, as Mr. Justice Lamer maintained with the concurrence of Chief Justice Dickson, it would be logical to conclude that the relevant time in determining whether a delay has been reasonable does not begin until "the start of the impairment of the accused's interests in the liberty and security of the person." This key moment would be defined *not in*

---

24 *R. v. Cardinal* (1985), 21 C.C.C. (3d) 254 (Alta. C.A.), leave to appeal to S.C.C. refused (1987), 51 Alta. L.R. (2d) xii (note) (S.C.C.) *R. v. Musitano* (1986), 24 C.C.C. (3d) 65 (Ont. C.A.), leave to appeal to S.C.C. refused (1987), 62 O.R. (2d) ix (note) (S.C.C.).

25 *Contra: Re Russell and Radley* (1984), 11 C.C.C. (3d) 289 (F.C.T.D.).

26 *Wigglesworth v. R.*, *supra*, note 22 at 560.

27 *Canada v. Schmidt*, *supra*, note 20 at 520-522; *Argentina v. Mellino*, *supra*, note 21 at 548-551; *U.S. v. Allard*, *supra*, note 21 at 572; *Wigglesworth v. R.*, *supra*, note 22 at 558.

28 See *R. v. Belcourt* (1982), 69 C.C.C. (2d) 286 (B.C.S.C.); *R. v. Boron* (1983), 36 C.R. (3d) 329 (Ont. H.C.); *Re R. and Carter* (1983), 9 C.C.C. (3d) 173 (B.C.S.C.), aff'd (1984), 11 C.C.C. (3d) 284 (B.C.C.A.), leave to appeal to S.C.C. granted (1984), 8 D.L.R. (4th) 156b (S.C.C.); *R. v. Lefort* (1984), 12 C.C.C. (3d) 332 (Qué. S.P.).

terms of the technical laying of the charge against the accused, but rather in terms of the act which effectively deprives him of his liberty or security of his person, namely, the *service* of a summons, the *execution* of a warrant, the arrest without warrant or the issuance of an appearance notice. On this approach, any delay occurring prior to such an act would not be relevant, for until such an act takes place "the individual will not normally be subject to restraint nor will he or she stand accused before the community of committing a crime".[29]

As noted above, however, the majority of Supreme Court judges take the view that the right guaranteed by section 11(b) of the Charter is also meant to ensure the fairness of the trial and in particular the capacity of the accused to present a complete defence. It thus becomes relevant to inquire as well whether the delay experienced by an accused has had the effect of diminishing or undermining this capacity. It is obvious that cases could arise where the time lapse occurring before the service of a summons or the execution of a warrant could cause or contribute to the inability of an accused to present a full defence. Such would certainly be the case if an inordinate length of time elapsed between the issuance and the service of a summons or the issuance and the execution of a warrant, assuming of course that the accused was not fleeing or hiding from the authorities and the delay was the result of negligence on the part of the police.[30] In any event, it is quite clear that the person against whom an information is laid becomes "charged" as soon as the justice who receives the information issues either a summons or a warrant for arrest.

The lapse of time between the moment the authorities become aware of the commission of an offence and the actual laying of charges against the accused could also be considered relevant, in my view, in determining whether a violation of section 11(b) has occurred. Where suspects are in fact known to the police but without reasonable cause the police are unduly slow in laying charges against those whom they suspect, the latter's right to a fair trial is arguably jeopardized, and this we have seen is one of the legitimate interests protected by section 11(b). One can imagine, for example, facts analogous to those in *Rourke v. R.*[31] where the police delayed for almost 17 months before laying charges against the accused, even though they were aware of the alleged offences shortly after their commission and had knowledge of the movements of the accused. In that case, the effect of the long delay was to deprive the accused of the possibility

---

29 *Mills v. R., supra*, note 11 at 944-946.
30 *R. v. Cardinal, supra*, note 24; *Re Gray and R.* (1983), 70 C.C.C. (2d) 62 (Sask. Q.B.); *Re Primeau and R.* (1982), 1 C.C.C. (3d) 207 (Sask. Q.B.); *R. v. Jensen* (1983), 7 C.R.R. 185 (Alta. Q.B.); *R. v. Chiasson* (1985), 20 C.R.R. 23 (Ont. Dist. Ct.).
31 [1978] 1 S.C.R. 1021.

of calling two witnesses in his defence at the time of the trial.

In order for an accused to be able to claim in such circumstances that his right to be tried in a reasonable time has been violated, it would be necessary to ackowledge that the lapse of time prior to the laying of charges is relevant where it was abnormally long and unjustified and has caused a real prejudice to his defence.[32] Of course, section 11(b) does not guarantee the right to a fair trial, but rather the right to be protected against unreasonably long delays on the ground that such delays have the effect of infringing the accused's liberty and the security of his person beyond what is normal or necessary, as well as denying his right to a fair trial. Even though, prior to the laying of charges against a person, neither his liberty nor security of person is at risk, the fairness of his trial may nonetheless be compromised by an unreasonable delay that occurs before no less than after the laying of charges. Thus, one could conclude, without distorting or changing the purpose of section 11(b), that the right protected by this paragraph is violated where there is excessive and undue delay in laying charges against a person and this inherently unreasonable delay has the effect of depriving the person of his right to present a full defence to the charges. Could such a person not claim, *from the moment charges are laid against him*, the benefit of section 11(b)?

This interpretation is not the one that has generally prevailed to date. On the contrary, our courts have tended toward the view that the relevant time period begins to run from the moment the charges are laid. In support of this position, they have relied mainly on the wording of section 11(b), and, occasionally, on the conclusions found in American case law[33] and the authority of the *Rourke* decision.[34] At most, in certain cases the courts have been willing to concede that a delay prior to the laying of charges could be relevant if it tended to exacerbate the prejudice suffered by the accused as a result of the delay occurring after the laying of charges.[35]

The Supreme Court of Canada as well appears to have adopted this

---

32 *R. v. H.W. Corkum Construction Co.* (1983), 5 C.C.C. (3d) 575 (N.S.C.A.), leave to appeal to S.C.C. refused (1983), 60 N.S.R. (2d) 270n (S.C.C.); *R. v. Biggar* (1982), 1 C.C.C. (3d) 23 (Man. Prov. Ct.); *R. v. Schatkowsky* (1985), 15 C.R.R. 129 (Man. Prov. Ct.); *Perreault v. R.* (1985), 19 C.R.R. 101 (Ont. Dist. Ct.).

33 *United States v. Marion*, 404 U.S. 307 (1971).

34 *R. v. Antoine* (1983), 5 C.C.C. (3d) 97 (Ont. C.A.); *R. v. Young* (1984), 10 C.R.R. 307 (Ont. C.A.); *R. v. Kalanj* (1986), 26 C.C.C. (3d) 136 (B.C.C.A.); *R. v. Belcourt, supra,* note 28; *R. v. Forsberg* (1982), 2 C.R.R. 60 (B.C. Prov. Ct.); *R. v. Lefort, supra,* note 28.

35 *R. v. Devji* (1985), 19 C.C.C. (3d) 310 (B.C.C.A.); *R. v. Kalanj, supra,* note 34; *Re R. and Morrison* (1984), 13 C.C.C. (3d) 386 (Ont. H.C.), aff'd (1984), 14 C.C.C. (3d) 320 (Ont. C.A.), leave to appeal to S.C.C. refused (1985), 58 N.R. 338 (S.C.C.); *R. v. Atwood* (1983), 7 C.R.R. 191 (N.S.T.D.). See also the opinion of Madam Justice Wilson in *Carter v. R., infra,* note 36 at 987.

position particularly in *Carter v. R.*[36] The court there affirmed that only the time elapsing after the laying of charges should be considered in determining whether an accused has been tried within a reasonable time. However, the court justified this position on the grounds that the fair trial interest is not one of the interests which section 11(b) is designed to protect and that a person's liberty and security are not endangered until charges are laid. As noted above, this restrictive analysis of the right set out in section 11(b) is no longer shared by the majority of the court.

If, notwithstanding the above, one maintains the view that the relevant time begins to run only with the laying of charges, an accused who claims that his right to a fair trial has been breached by unreasonable delay prior to the laying of charges should invoke other sections of the Charter, namely section 11(d), which specifically guarantees a fair trial, or section 7, which protects against violations of the principles of fundamental justice.[37]

The courts have acknowledged that there are some situations where the relevant time begins to run before the person is charged with the offence for which he must be tried. This occurs, for example, if the charges originally laid against an accused are withdrawn and a decision is then made to lay different charges relating to the same facts.[38] It also occurs where the accused has been discharged following a preliminary inquiry but an indictment is issued pursuant to section 507[577] of the *Criminal Code.*[39] In these circumstances, the right to be tried within a reasonable time operates from the moment the first charges are laid against the accused.

Generally, a person who complains of not having been tried within a reasonable time will claim that an excessive delay occurred between the time when charges were laid and the beginning of trial. However, as the Supreme Court of Canada has had occasion to point out, the right to be tried within a reasonable time is not extinguished once the trial begins within a reasonable time after the laying of charges. The right remains operative at least until judgment has been rendered, for the abnormal prolongation of the trial itself can violate the interests which section 11(b) is designed to protect, namely, the security of the accused's person and the fairness of his trial.[40] This interpretation is supported by the French version of section 11(b) which speaks of a right "*d' être jugé* dans un délai raisonnable". Mr. Justice La Forest analyzed this wording in the following manner:

---

36 [1986] 1 S.C.R. 981.

37 *Ibid.*, at 986. *R. v. Young, supra,* note 34.

38 *Mills v. R., supra,* note 11, p. 946-947; *Carter v. R., supra,* note 36, p. 985.

39 R.S.C. 1970, c. C-34 [R.S.C. 1985, c. C-46]. See *Re Garton and Whelan* (1984), 14 C.C.C. (3d) 449 (Ont. H.C.).

40 *Rahey v. R., supra,* note 2 at 610-611 (Lamer J.) and at 632-633 (La Forest J.).

While "*jugé*" can mean "tried" as well as "judged", it does not mean "tried" in the sense of "brought to trial", which would be more properly expressed as "*subir son procès*". Rather, it means "tried" in the sense of "adjudicated" and thus clearly encompasses the conduct of a judge in rendering a decision.[41]

It is worth noting that the same arguments could be made in cases where it takes an excessive amount of time to dispose of an appeal from the judgment at trial. However, this question was not resolved by the court, for it did not arise on the facts of the case.[42]

(c) Relevant Factors

It is universally admitted that what constitutes a reasonable time cannot be determined *a priori* and in the abstract. The reasonable or unreasonable nature of a delay depends on the circumstances of each individual case. It is useful, nevertheless, to attempt to identify the principal factors which the courts should take into account in determining whether in a given case a violation of section 11(b) has occurred. The majority of Canadian courts[43] have adopted the approach of the United States Supreme Court as set out in *Barker v. Wingo*.[44] This has led to general acceptance of a test involving the weighing of the following four factors: (i) the length of the delay, (ii) the reason for the delay, (iii) the claim of the right by the accused, and (iv) the prejudice suffered by the accused.

In *Rahey v. R.*,[45] the Supreme Court of Canada expressed a certain disapproval of the unqualified adoption of the American approach, although the level of disapproval varied among the several judges who participated in the decision. It is not easy at this point to discern any consensus on the relevant factors.

There appears to be agreement that in determining whether a delay in unreasonable, the court must take into account the time requirements inherent in the nature of a particular case (for example, the number of witnesses to be called, the relative complexity of the facts to be proved,

---

41 *Ibid.*, at 632.

42 *Ibid.*, at 611 and 633.

43 See, *e.g.*, *R. v. Antoine, supra*, note 34; *R. v. Beason* (1984), 7 C.C.C. (3d) 20 (Ont. C.A.); *Re R. and Thompson* (1983), 8 C.C.C. (3d) 127 (B.C.C.A.); *R. v. Heaslip* (1983), 9 C.C.C. (3d) 480 (Ont. C.A.); *R. v. Donald* (1984), 9 C.C.C. (3d) 574 (B.C.C.A.); *R. v. Deloli* (1985), 20 C.C.C. (3d) 153 (Man. C.A.); *R. v. Devji, supra*, note 35.

44 *Supra*, note 18 at 530.

45 *Supra*, note 2 at 604-610 (Lamer J.), at 616-617 (Le Dain J.), at 622-625 (Wilson J.), and at 636-642 (La Forest J.).

etc.).[46] On the other hand, a shortage of institutional resources will not excuse delay where such resources have not been allocated in a reasonable manner, having regard to real needs.[47]

Moreover, the Supreme Court of Canada appears to have rejected the view that "in not invoking his right, it would be difficult for the defendant to prove that he had not been brought to trial quickly".[48] In the opinion of the court, the relevant factor here is quite rightly whether the defendant ultimately waived his right to complain of the delay. On this point, Mr. Justice Lamer offers some important clarifications. First, "delay which is requested, caused by, or consented to, by the accused should normally be excluded from consideration when assessing the reasonableness of the overall period of delay". Second, a waiver should not be inferred from silence, but should be unequivocal and informed, except where the accused himself has caused the delay. Finally, the waiver does not affect the right itself but merely excludes such time as is waived from the calculation of reasonable time.[49]

Finally, the very fact of being charged with an offence inevitably causes some prejudice to the accused. It must be recognized that the purpose of section 11(b) is to ensure that the accused does not suffer abnormal prejudice as a result of unreasonable delay. Thus, one of the factors which must be considered is whether the accused has suffered unusual prejudice. Of course, interference with a person's liberty can be objectively established while interference with his security of person can be presumed. The severity of the interference increases with the length of the delay. Since section 11(b) also protects the right to make a full and complete defence, one must also recognize, as the Supreme Court of Canada has done, that where a delay interferes with the right of an accused to a fair trial, this prejudice

---

46 *Re Kott and R.* (1983), 7 C.C.C. (3d) 317 (Que. C.A.); *R. v. Sayer* (1987), 34 C.C.C. (3d) 176 (Sask. C.A.); *Re Balderstone and R.* (1982), 2 C.C.C. (3d) 37 at 55 (Man. Q.B.), upheld for other reasons (1983), 8 C.C.C. (3d) 532 (Man. C.A.), leave to appeal to S.C.C. refused (1983), 8 C.C.C. (3d) 532n (S.C.C.); *R. v. Dahlem* (1983), 29 Sask. R. 108 (Q.B.).

47 *R. v. Heaslip, supra*, note 43; *R. v. Misra* (1986), 32 C.C.C. (3d) 97 (Sask. C.A.), reversed *infra*, note 217; *R. v. Sayer, supra*, note 46; *R. v. Coughland* (1987), 2 W.C.B. (2d) 249 (N.B.C.A.); *Christie v. R.* (1985), 20 C.R.R. 358 (P.E.I.S.C.); *R. v. Grandma Lee's Inc.* (1986), 24 C.R.R. 153 (Ont. Dist. Ct.). *Contra: Re Coghlin and R.* (1982), 70 C.C.C. (2d) 455 (Ont. H.C.); *Re Jack and R.* (1982), 1 C.C.C. (3d) 193 (Nfld. T.D.).

48 *Barker v. Wingo, supra*, note 18 at 532. However, Canadian courts have often taken this factor into account: see *R. v. Antoine, supra*, note 34; *R. v. Deloli, supra*, note 43.

49 *Mills v. R., supra*, note 11 at 927-931; *Rahey v. R., supra*, note 2 at 612-613. See also *R. v. Heaslip, supra*, note 43; and *R. v. Sayer, supra*, note 46.

is an important factor which must be taken into account.[50] It is not, however, an essential factor. If, in a given case, this factor were not present, the court might nonetheless conclude after weighing the other relevant factors that the right of an accused to be tried within a reasonable time had been violated.[51]

(d) Remedies

Where a person's rights under the Charter have been violated, a court may, pursuant to section 24(1) of the Charter, grant "such remedy as the court considers appropriate and just in the circumstances". This section has always been viewed as conferring on a court a very large discretionary power. The choice of the appropriate remedy, however, is necessarily constrained to a greater or lesser degree by the nature of the right which has been violated.

As I have argued elsewhere,[52] the right to be tried within a reasonable time enshrined in section 11(b) of the Charter belongs to a category of rights that of necessity calls for a compensatory remedy because it is impossible once the right has been violated to come up with a remedy that could effectively erase the effects of the violation. In such cases, nothing can be done to eliminate the prejudice which has been caused or to allow the victim the opportunity to exercise the right of which he has unjustly been deprived. This is due to the fact that section 11(b) includes a temporal element, such that violations of the right consist precisely in the failure to have acted within the time allowed. A subsequent action can therefore never repair the initial failure.

For this reason, I do not share the opinion of those who maintain that an appropriate remedy for failure to bring the accused to trial within a reasonable time could often be an order to accelerate the pace of the procedures.[53] As emphasized by Mr. Justice Lamer, to find that section 11(b) has been violated and "to allow a trial to proceed after such a finding

---

50 *Rahey v. R.*, *supra*, note 2 at 617 (Le Dain J.), at 622-623 (Wilson J.) at 645-647 (La Forest J.) See also *Re Coghlin and R.*, *supra*, note 47; *Re Garton and Whelan*, *supra*, note 39.

51 *Rahey v. R.*, *supra*, note 2 at 617 (Le Dain J.), and at 646 (La Forest J.). For similar reasoning, see *R. v. Beason*, *supra*, note 43; *R. v Deloli*, *supra*, note 43; *Contra: R. v. McGrath* (1985), 19 C.R.R. 222 (Nfld. C.A.); *R. v. Chartrand* (1983), 5 C.R.R. 88 (Man. Co. Ct.).

52 A. Morel, "Le droit d'obtenir réparation en cas de violation de droits constitutionnels", in *La Charte canadienne des droits et libertés: Concepts et impacts*, (Montréal: Editions Thémis, 1985) p. 253 at 258-260.

53 *Mills v. R.*, *supra*, note 11 at 974 (La Forest J.); *Rahey v. R.*, *supra*, note 2 at 648 (La Forest J.); *R. v. Kissick* (1983), 25 Sask. R. 8 (Q.B.).

would be to participate in a further violation of the *Charter*".[54] Of course, where it is established that further delay would give rise to a violation of an accused person's right, it is open to a court to take preventive measures. In so acting, however, the court would not be applying section 24(1), for on these facts the accused person's right has not yet been violated.[55]

It follows that a violation of the right to be tried within a reasonable time necessarily entails the consequence that the proceedings in question must be stopped, for the accused person can no longer be tried within a reasonable time and therefore must not be tried. A stay of proceedings is therefore the only solution, albeit a radical one.[56] With some reluctance, American courts have reached the same conclusion, even though it means releasing without trial an accused person who may be guilty.[57] One must admit that such a result may cause the courts to hesitate before finding a violation of section 11(b). Perhaps only flagrant cases will move them to find a breach. The danger is, of course, that the radical nature of the remedy may have the effect of eroding the right itself.[58]

2. THE RIGHT TO TRIAL BY JURY (S. 11(f))

As is well known, the right to trial by jury in criminal matters is not found in the *Canadian Bill of Rights*. Given the importance accorded the jury and its traditional role in the common law as a guarantor of individual freedoms, this omission is surprising. Quite properly, the framers of the Charter took care to include the right to trial by jury among those guaranteed by section 11 to "any person charged with an offence". Like the *American Bill of Rights*, though expressed in less general terms than one finds in the Sixth Amendment,[59] section 11(f) of the Charter provides:

> Any person charged with an offence has the right
>
> . . .
>
> except in the case of an offence under military law tried before a military

---

54 *Mills v. R.*, *supra*, note 11 at 947.

55 *R. v. Beason*, *supra*, note 43.

56 *Mills v. R.*, *supra*, note 11 at 947-948; *Rahey v. R.*, *supra*, note 2 at 614-615, 617, 621. It should be noted, moreover, that the Supreme Court of Canada in the *Mills* decision ruled that a provincial court judge hearing a preliminary inquiry is not a court of competent jurisdiction within the meaning of section 24 of the Charter; it is thus the trial judge, as a general rule, who has the jurisdiction to determine if section 11(b) has been violated.

57 *Barker v. Wingo*, *supra*, note 18 at 522.

58 *Rahey v. R.*, *supra*, note 2 at 618 and 637-638.

59 "In all criminal prosecutions, the accused shall enjoy the right to a speedy and public trial, by an impartial jury."

tribunal, to the benefit of trial by jury where the maximum punishment for the offence is imprisonment for five years or a more severe punishment.

This provision of the Charter combines a statement of principle with a specific exception.

(a) The Principle

The principle as formulated in section 11(f) would appear at first sight to raise few serious problems of interpretation. Nevertheless, it has been the subject to date of a number of cases which warrant examination.

(i) *The Criminal Code*

It should be noted, first of all, that the general provisions of the *Criminal Code* which establish in what cases an accused must or may be tried by jury are not in conflict with the basic principle set out in section 11(f). On the one hand, section 427 [469] of the *Criminal Code* indicates which indictable offences are within the exclusive jurisdiction of a court composed of a judge and jury as provided in section 429 [471]. Section 483 [553], on the other hand, enumerates offences which come within the absolute jurisdiction of a provincial court judge. The withdrawal of such offences from the competence of a judge sitting with a jury could possibly be inconsistent with the requirements of section 11(f) of the Charter. However, none of these offences is punishable by a maximum sentence of five years' imprisonment or more. In fact, for this category of criminal offences, the most frequent maximum sentence is imprisonment for two years. With respect to all other offences in the *Criminal Code*, excepting those that are punishable by summary conviction, the choice of procedure rests with the accused, who may opt for trial by jury or trial before a provincial court judge or a judge sitting without a jury.[60] The constitutional guarantee is thus honoured by these provisions as well.

A. *Section 498 [568].* It is of course true that, under section 498 [568] of the *Criminal Code*, the Attorney General may require an accused who is charged with an offence punishable by more than five years' imprisonment to submit to trial by jury, even where the accused has elected a different mode of trial under sections 464 [536] or 491 [561]. In such circumstances, the accused is deprived of the right to choose which he would have enjoyed were it not for the intervention of the Attorney General. In my view, however, this provision is no more a violation of the right

---

60 *Criminal Code*, ss. 464 [536], 488 [558] and 491 [561].

protected by section 11(f) of the Charter than is the right of choice itself, in cases where the accused prefers to be tried by a provincial court judge or a judge without a jury.

Not everyone shares this view. According to Peter Hogg,[61] for example, by enshrining in section 11(f) the right to the "benefit" of trial by jury, the framers of the Charter meant to guarantee the accused the right to waive this benefit at will. On this approach, neither the Crown nor the court could deprive an accused, without his consent, of the implicit right to be tried without a jury, if that be his choice. While this interpretation is generous, it presents a number of difficulties.

In the first place, it implies a reading of section 11(f) that very nearly sets the provision on its head. What is guaranteed is no longer the right to insist on the benefit of trial by jury but rather the right to choose to be tried without a jury. More seriously, this interpretation is based on the assumption that trial by jury not only is advantageous to the accused — something we could not deny without ignoring its historical development — but also that the advantage of trial by jury exists *exclusively* for the benefit of the accused. It thus rules out the possibility that it may also be used to better serve the interests of justice. Only by granting this assumption can one accept the view that an accused can never be required, against his will, to submit to a trial by jury.[62] Since this assumption cannot be granted in my view, it follows that there is no constitutional infirmity in a provision like section 498 [568] of the *Criminal Code*, which enables the Attorney General in some circumstances to override the choice of an accused to be tried without a jury.

As I understand it, to guarantee the right to the benefit of a trial by jury is an implicit recognition that this form of trial is advantageous to an accused and that accordingly he must not be deprived of this advantage by law. Moreover, where an offence is punishable by five years' imprisonment or more, the law must necessarily secure for the benefit of the accused the possibility of being tried by a court composed of a judge and jury. In such cases the law may offer an accused the choice to be tried in some other fashion, but it cannot deprive him of the right to a trial by jury. Only the accused himself can waive this right.

B. *Section 430 [473].* For the reasons canvassed above, I would submit that section 11(f) of the Charter does not preclude Parliament from

---

61 P.W. Hogg, *Canada Act 1982 Annotated* (Toronto: Carswell, 1982) at 42. For a similar view, see also M. Manning, *Rights, Freedoms and the Courts: A Practical Analysis of the Constitutional Act, 1982* (Toronto: Emond-Montgomery, 1983) at 416.

62 *R. v. Briltz*, Sask. Q.B., January 10, 1983, unreported, cited in *R. v. Turpin* (1985), 18 C.R.R. 323 (Ont. H.C.), rev'd (1987), 30 C.R.R. 193 (Ont. C.A.).

requiring that certain serious indictable offences be tried by a court composed of a judge and jury, as was the case before the coming into force of the 1985 amendments to the *Criminal Code*. Although the new section 430 [473] of the Code reduces the exclusive jurisdiction of a judge sitting with a jury, this change was not introduced on the understanding that the Charter guarantees an accused the right to opt for trial without a jury. Rather, the concern was that, by conferring on accused persons in Alberta a privilege that was not available elsewhere in Canada,[63] the previous version of section 430 [473] was inconsistent with the right to equality guaranteed by section 15 of the Charter.

The new version of section 430 [473] permits all persons charged with an offence listed in section 427 [469] to be tried by a judge of a superior court of criminal jurisdiction without a jury. For the new procedure to apply, however, not only must the accused prefer this option, but the Attorney General must consent as well. The law here once again recognizes that the interest of the accused is not the only interest at stake. In so doing it does not, in my view, run counter to the constitutional guarantee. The purpose of section 11(f) is to ensure that a person accused of a serious offence is not deprived of the benefit of a trial by jury without his consent. This does not mean that the accused's consent is the only one required for an election for a trial without a jury.

C. *Waiver by the accused.* It so happens, however, that the *Criminal Code* confers the right to make this choice on the accused alone. If he elects to be tried without a jury under section 464 [536] or if he makes a new election to the same effect under section 491 [561], his decision does indeed amount to a valid waiver of the right to trial by jury. Moreover, unless the law itself provides for the revocation of his decision, he cannot invoke section 11(f) of the *Charter* to claim he has the right to set aside his waiver and require a trial by jury. Similarly, if an appeal court orders a new trial following an appeal from acquittal, the accused is precluded from electing to be tried before a jury where he has waived such a right at the time of his first trial. This does not constitute a violation of his rights under section 11(f) of the *Charter*.[64]

D. *Hybrid offences.* Nor is the Charter breached, one may readily conclude, by *Criminal Code* provisions which provide in the case of certain offences for a penalty of five years' imprisonment or more if the Crown proceeds by way of indictment or a lesser penalty if the Crown proceeds

---

63 *R. v. Turpin, ibid., R. v. Martin* (1987), 27 C.R.R. 193 (Ont. H.C.).
64 *Re Attorney General Canada and Switzer* (1985), 22 C.R.R. 27 (B.C.S.C.).

by way of summary conviction. The right of an accused to the benefit of trial by jury depends upon the penalty attached to the offence with which he is actually charged,[65] not the penalty to which he would have been subject had the Crown charged him with an indictable offence. It seems reasonable to argue — in contrast to a more literal interpretation of the wording of section 11(f) which does not take account of the purpose behind the guarantee — that the right to trial by jury is only guaranteed where the accused is actually exposed, by virtue of the offence charged, to a maximum penalty of at least five years' imprisonment.[66]

E. *Dangerous offenders.*   Given that rights guaranteed by the Charter "must be interpreted in light of the interests [they were] meant to protect",[67] there is good reason to suppose that, where an application is made to have an accused declared a dangerous offender under Part XXI [XXIV] of the *Criminal Code*, the accused may require this application to be heard and determined by a court composed of a judge and jury. If this is so, section 689(2) [754(2)] of the *Criminal Code*, which prohibits the presence of a jury in these circumstances, violates section 11(f) of the Charter. Under section 688 [753] of the Code, once a judge determines that an accused is a dangerous offender, he may sentence the accused, "in lieu of any other sentence" that might be imposed for the offence of which he is guilty, to a different penalty that is more severe than five years' imprisonment.

In *Lyons v. R.*,[68] however, the Supreme Court of Canada ruled that the proceedings to have an accused declared a dangerous offender were not equivalent to accusing him of having committed an offence, but were merely part of the sentencing process. A person subject to such proceedings was therefore not charged with an offence. Moreover, the words "person charged with an offence" which are used at the beginning of section 11 of the Charter must have "a constant meaning that harmonizes with the various paragraphs of the section".[69] According to the majority of the court, where an application is made to have an offender declared dangerous, the offender could not invoke the rights set out in section 11(d) and (e). It follows that he cannot require the application to be heard in the presence

---

65 The English version of section 11(f) is not as explicit in this regard as the French version.

66 *Darbishire v. R.* (1983), 83 D.T.C. 5164 (Ont. Co. Ct.), aff'd (1984), 11 W.C.B. 5 (Ont. C.A.). It is also clear that a person charged with several offences, all of which fall within the exclusive jurisdiction of a provincial court judge, could not claim the right to trial by jury by arguing that he is subject to more than five years' imprisonment.

67 *R. v. Big M. Drug Mart Ltd.*, [1985] 1 S.C.R. 295 at 344.

68 *Supra*, note 20 at 349-353 (La Forest J.); see the dissenting judgment of Mr. Justice Lamer at 372-379.

69 *Ibid.* at 353. Mr. Justice La Forest here repeats the interpretation he gave in *Canada v. Schmidt*, *supra*, note 20 at 519.

of a jury, even if he were liable to be sentenced to detention for an indeterminate period as punishment for the offence of which he has been found guilty.

F. *Section 526.1 [598]*. Section 526.1 [598] of the *Criminal Code* creates a difficult problem for which courts to date have offered divergent solutions. Pursuant to this provision, an accused who chooses a trial by jury but fails to appear on the date set for the trial, or who is absent during the trial, loses his right to be tried by jury, unless he can provide a legitimate excuse to justify his absence. In such cases, the accused is "deemed to have elected" to be tried without a jury.

According to the Ontario Court of Appeal in *R. v. Bryant*,[70] the right to trial by jury continues to exist as long as the accused has not voluntarily chosen to be tried otherwise. The law cannot deprive a person of a constitutional right simply by creating a presumption of waiver, particularly in a context where the waiver must be voluntary and made with full knowledge of its consequences before it is considered valid.

A contrary view was adopted by the British Columbia Court of Appeal, which held that if an accused intends to exercise his right to a trial by jury, it is not enough to simply choose this form of trial; he must continue to exercise the right by being present at his trial. Should he voluntarily decide not to appear, in the absence of a legitimate excuse to justify his absence, he is no longer exercising the right and the law rightly presumes that he has validly waived it. Section 526.1 [598] of the *Criminal Code* does nothing more than fix the proceedings by which such an accused will be tried.[71]

The disagreement between these two Courts of Appeal goes beyond this initial question, however, and extends to the proper application of the reasonable limits clause of section 1 of the Charter. Insofar as the Ontario Court of Appeal is concerned, the purpose of section 526.1 [598] is to prevent the abuse that could occur as a consequence of the system of pretrial release of the accused.[72] While the court agreed that such a purpose is legitimate, in its view the Crown had failed to demonstrate that depriving the absconding accused of the right to trial by jury was necessary in order

---

70 (1984), 15 D.L.R. (4th) 66 (Ont. C.A.).

71 *R. v. McNabb* (1987), 55 C.R. (3d) 369 (B.C.C.A.), leave to appeal to S.C.C. granted (1987), 59 C.R. (3d) xxxiv (note) (S.C.C.). Similarly, *R. v. Crate* (1984), 1 D.L.R. (4th) 149 (Alta. C.A.); *R. v. Allan* (1982), 2 C.R.R. 46 (Alta. Q.B.); *R. v. Gladue* (1982), 2 C.C.C. (3d) 175 (B.C.S.C.); *R. v. Ramirez* (1982), 9 W.C.B. 107 (Alta. Q.B.); and *R. v. Gosselin*, J.E. 85-533 (Qué. S.C.).

72 See the *Bail Reform Act*, R.S.C. 1970, c. 2 (2nd Supp.), which amended the *Criminal Code*.

to achieve that purpose.[73] The British Columbia Court of Appeal, on the other hand, felt that Parliament was attempting to preserve public confidence in the criminal justice system against those who would seek to abuse it. In its view, the means chosen by Parliament to achieve this purpose were reasonable and not at all excessive.[74]

G. *Contempt of court.* On various occasions the courts have been called upon to decide whether persons accused of contempt of court may rely on section 11(f) of the Charter to require a trial before a jury. While the response has uniformly been negative, there has been little uniformity in the reasons for judgment offered by the courts.

In the *Laurendeau* case,[75] the court ruled that a person who is cited for contempt of court is not "charged with an offence" within the meaning of section 11(f) of the Charter, since contempt of court is not an offence but is rather "the exercise of a power essential to the administration of justice" [translation].[76] These conclusions were firmly rejected by the Ontario Court of Appeal in the *Cohn* decision.[77] Speaking of contempt in the face of the court, Mr. Justice Goodman wrote that "it has the characteristics of a criminal offence" and that "a person cited for contempt is charged with an offence within the meaning of section 11". More recently, the Supreme Court of Canada clearly recognized in the *Vermette* case,[78] although the Charter was not in issue in the case, that "criminal contempt, as preserved by s. 8 of the [*Criminal*] *Code*, is an offence".

In denying the right to trial by jury in the *Cohn* case,[79] the Ontario Court of Appeal reasoned that contempt of court is an offence which in fact is no longer punishable by five years' imprisonment or more, for over the course of the past several decades the penalty for contempt has never exceeded two years' imprisonment. As Jean-Claude Hébert has shown,

---

73 *R. v. Bryant, supra,* note 70 at 73-84.

74 *R. v. McNabb, supra,* note 71 at 377-378.

75 *P.G. du Québec v. Laurendeau* (1983), 33 C.R. (3d) 40 (Qué. S.C.), aff'd [1983] C.A. 223 (Qué. C.A.), leave to appeal to S.C.C. refused (1983), 4 D.L.R. (4th) 702n (S.C.C.).

76 *Ibid.* at 42. The same conclusion was reached in *R. v. Berheim,* (April 12, 1983) No. 700-01-2337-825 (Que. S.C.) *per* Bergeron J. This was referred to and criticized by J.-C. Hébert, "L 'incidence de la Charte canadienne sur l'outrage au tribunal" (1984), 18 *R.J.T.* 183 at 208-210.

77 *R. v. Cohn* (1984), 15 C.C.C. (3d) 150 at 160 (Ont. C.A.); applied in *R. v. Doz* (1985), 19 C.C.C. (3d) 434 (Alta. C.A.), rev'd [1987] 2 S.C.R. 463. For a similar view, see L. Smith, "Charter Equality Rights: Some General Issues and Specific Applications in British Columbia to Elections, Juries and Illegitimacy" (1984), 18 *U.B.C.L. Rev.* 351 at 386-387.

78 *R. v. Vermette,* [1987] 1 S.C.R. 577 at 586, and comments on this decision by J.-C. Hébert, "L 'outrage au tribunal et le procès par jury" (1987), 47 *R. du B.* 537.

79 *Supra,* note 77 at 169-170.

this reasoning is dubious in that it focusses not on the maximum penalty attached to an offence, but on the actual sentence imposed.[80] The maximum penalty set for an offence is a measurable indication of the seriousness of the crime. It is for this reason that the framers of the Charter chose it as the criterion for determining when an accused can require a trial by jury. Moreover, it appears that the Supreme Court of Canada has clearly indicated with respect to other Charter provisions that the manner in which a law is applied in practice is not a relevant consideration in deciding whether the law is consistent with a constitutional norm.[81]

One could doubtless show that where a prosecutor chooses to proceed by way of summary conviction because it is necessary to act quickly in order to protect the integrity of the court, denial of the right to trial by jury is justifiable under the test set out in section 1 of the Charter.[82] However, now that the court has decided in the *Vermette* case that "procedure by indictment for the punishment of contempt *ex facie* . . . is preserved by s. 8 of the [*Criminal*] *Code* and remains available,"[83] it will be more difficult to use summary procedures in the case of contempt *ex facie*.[84]

It follows that in order to deny that the right to trial by jury is available in cases of contempt *ex facie*, one of the following propositions must be established: either at common law, as it presently stands, contempt of court is not an offence that is punishable by imprisonment of five years or more; or the guarantee of section 11(f) of the Charter, given its wording, does not apply to offences like contempt that do not carry a maximum penalty

---

80 Hébert, *supra*, note 76 at 211.

81 In *Valente v. R.*, [1985] 2 S.C.R. 673, with respect to the judiciary independence guaranteed in paragraph 11(d) of the Charter, the court found (at 702) that " . . . while tradition reinforced by public opinion may operate as a restraint upon the exercise of power in a manner that interferes with judicial independence, it cannot supply essential conditions of independence for which specific provision of law is necessary."

Similarly, in *R. v. Smith*, [1987] 1 S.C.R. 1045, where it was decided that the minimum sentence of seven years' imprisonment imposed by section 5(2) of the *Narcotic Control Act*, R.S.C. 1970, c. N-1 [now R.S.C. 1985, c. N-1] violated s. 12 of the Charter, Mr. Justice Lamer found that the impugned section could not be saved by arguing that the Crown had the discretionary power not to lay charges for importation where that might violate the Charter, but rather the power to lay charges for a less serious offence (at 1078).

82 *Re Layne and R.* (1984), 14 C.C.C. (3d) 149 (B.C.S.C.). This reasoning would appear more compatible with the Charter than that found in the *Cohn* decision, *supra*, note 77, at 176, to the effect that, where a judge imposes a sentence of five years' imprisonment, it is the sentence, rather than the mode of proceedings, which would be illegal.

83 *R. v. Vermette, supra*, note 78, p. 583.

84 Hébert, *supra*, note 78 at 539-540.

set by the law, but rather are punishable by an unlimited period of imprisonment.

(ii) *Other Federal Laws*

Under section 27(2) [34(2)] of the *Interpretation Act*,[85] the procedure for trying offences created by the federal statutes other than the *Criminal Code* is governed by the procedural provisions of the Code. It follows that in all cases where a statute creates an indictable offence, the accused enjoys the right to elect and may benefit from a trial by jury if that is his choice.

A. *Competition Act.*   The new *Competition Act*,[86] which replaced the former *Combines Investigation Act*[87] and amended several of its provisions, creates various offences that are punishable by imprisonment for five years and which are defined as indictable offences.[88] Section 46 [73], it is true, provides that the Attorney General of Canada may in all such cases commence prosecution in the Trial Division of the Federal Court, where trial takes place without a jury, rather than in a superior court of criminal jurisdiction. However, where the prosecution concerns an individual, the Attorney General can make this choice only if the individual in question consents. Where consent is given, the individual effectively waives his right to the benefit of a trial by jury.

Where the accused is a corporation, on the other hand, section 44(3) [67(3)] provides that the prosecution must always take place without a jury. The validity of this provision has been challenged under section 11(f) of the Charter. One sees in the judicial response to these challenges the clash between a literal and a purposive interpretation of this constitutional guarantee.[89] If one focusses on the actual wording of section 11(f), it is true that the right to benefit from a trial by jury is a function of the seriousness of the offence of which a person is accused, rather than the likelihood of that accused being deprived of his liberty for a long period of time. On this basis, one could argue that by expressly choosing this criterion the framers of the Charter guaranteed corporations accused of

---

85 R.S.C. 1970, c. I-23 [R.S.C. 1985, c. I-21].

86 R.S.C. 1970, c. C-23 [R.S.C. 1985, c. C-34], am. 1986, c. 26, Pt. II [R.S.C. 1985, c. 19 (2nd Supp.), Pt. II].

87 R.S.C. 1970, c. C-23 am. 1974-75-76, c. 76 [R.S.C. 1985, c. C-34].

88 Such are s. 32 [45], 32.2 [47], 32.3 [48], 36 [52], 36.1 [53], 36.3 [55], 36.4 [56], 37.2 [59], 38 [61] and 46.1 [74].

89 See and contrast the opinions of Nemetz J. and Anderson J. with the dissenting opinion of Seaton J. in *PPG Industries Can. Ltd. v. A.G. Canada* (1983), 3 C.C.C. (3d) 97 (B.C.C.A.); *R. v. Bogardus, Wilson Ltd.* (1982), 2 C.C.R. 110 (B.C. Prov. Ct.).

serious offences the right to a trial by jury. Moreover, the words "any person" or *"tout inculpé"* at the beginning of section 11 are broad enough to include corporations, even though it is obvious that they would be unable to benefit from certain of the rights included in the section, such as those set out in paragraphs (c) and (e).

There are difficulties with this, however. For one thing, as we have just seen, this interpretation presupposes that the word "person" need not be assigned a uniform meaning that is compatible with each paragraph of section 11. This is contrary to the view adopted by the Supreme Court of Canada,[90] which leads logically to the conclusion that only individuals can claim the benefit of the constitutional guarantees set out in section 11 of the Charter. Moreover, the court's position on this question is compatible with a purposive analysis of section 11(f).[91] The framers of the Charter chose to guarantee the right to trial by jury only in the case of certain serious offences which are defined by reference to a single criterion, namely the maximum term of imprisonment. Of course, a large fine is also indicative of the serious nature of an offence. The absence of any reference to fines suggests that the purpose of the provision was to protect the liberty of the person, as enshrined in section 7, and it would be contrary to "the principles of fundamental justice" to expose a person to the possibility of losing his liberty for a prolonged period without securing for him the right to be tried by a jury of his peers.[92] If one accepts this line of reasoning, which in my view is more persuasive than the former, there is no reason to extend to corporations the right to benefit from trial by jury, regardless of the level of fine to which a corporation might be subject.

B. *Young Offenders Act.* There is no point in dwelling on the provisions of the former *Juvenile Delinquents Act*,[93] now repealed, which allowed a child to be confined to an industrial school or correctional home for more than five years following a trial without a jury before a youth court judge. These provisions were unsuccessfully challenged. In the view of the courts, a juvenile prosecuted under this statute could not claim the right guaranteed by section 11(f).[94]

---

90 *Canada v. Schmidt, supra,* note 20 at 519. This interpretation was adopted in *Lyons v. R., supra,* note 20 at 353.

91 *R. v. Big M Drug Mart Ltd., supra,* note 67 at 334.

92 This interpretation appears to conform with the opinion of Mr. Justice Lamer in *Reference re s. 94(2) of the Motor Vehicle Act (B.C.)*, [1985] 2 S.C.R. 486.

93 R.S.C. 1970, c. J-3.

94 *R. v. S.B.* (1983), 3 C.C.C. (3d) 390 (B.C.C.A.); and *R. v. D.T.* (1983), 37 C.R. (3d) 29 (Ont. H.C.); leave to appeal to C.A. refused (1984), 39 C.R. 95 (Ont. C.A.).

Section 52 of the new *Young Offenders Act*[95] has also been challenged on the grounds that it effectively deprives young offenders less than 18-years-old of the right to trial by jury, regardless of the seriousness of the offence with which they are charged. Relying on section 20 of the Act, the Ontario Court of Appeal quite rightly concluded that this section is not inconsistent with section 11(f) of the Charter. Under section 20, a young offender found guilty of an offence set out in the *Criminal Code* or any other federal statute can be deprived of his liberty for a period of no longer than two years and in certain cases not more than three, irrespective of the penalty which could be imposed on an adult found guilty of the same offence. Thus, the young offender cannot claim to be charged with an offence for which the punishment provided would entitle him to the benefit of a trial by jury.[96]

(iii) *The Make-up and Operation of Juries*

Lastly, a number of questions arise regarding the validity of statutes which might modify the make-up of criminal juries, change the rule of unanimity or reduce the number of jurors (as section 561 [632] of the *Criminal Code* does for the Yukon and the Northwest Territories).[97] In the United States, laws of a similar nature have been challenged, with uneven success, on the basis of the "due process" guarantee in the Fourteenth Amendment or the right to an impartial jury in the Sixth Amendment.[98] Since the formulation of these constitutional protections differs from the analogous Charter provisions, one must use care in relying on American decisions in the Canadian context.[99] Nevertheless, the validity of future laws attempting to change the make-up or manner of operation of juries is far from assured. The issue will turn on the nature and importance of the proposed change.

On the one hand, it would be difficult to maintain that section 11(f) of the Charter has effectively constitutionalized the jury system as it existed in 1982. On the other, it is clear that any changes in the statutory provisions governing juries will have to conform to guarantees in the Charter, particularly sections 7 and 15. One can easily imagine situations where

---

95 S.C. 1980-81-82-83, c. 110 [R.S.C. 1985, c. Y-1].

96 *R. v. R.L.* (1986), 26 C.C.C. (3d) 417 (Ont. C.A.).

97 This section provides that a jury will be composed of six persons. See *R. v. Smith* (1983), 33 C.R. (3d) 83 (N.W.T.S.C.); *R. v. Punch* (1985), 22 C.C.C. (3d) 289 (N.W.T.S.C.) and *R. v. Fatt* (1986), 24 C.R.R. 259 (N.W.T.S.C.).

98 The American case law is particularly referred to by Hogg, *supra*, note 61 at 43, and by Manning, *supra*, note 61 at 43.

99 L. Friedland, "Criminal Justice and the Charter" (1983), 13 *Man. L.J.* 549 at 567.

legislation would be contrary to either the principles of fundamental justice or the principle of equality before the law.[100]

(iv) *More Severe Punishment*

Canadian law provides for punishment mainly by fine or by imprisonment. Thus, interpretation of the words "or a more severe punishment" poses no difficulty. However, we may ask what would happen if a form of corporal punishment, such as the lash, abolished in 1972,[101] were reinstated: could punishment of less than five years' imprisonment accompanied by the lash be considered as punishment more severe than five years' imprisonment? At first glance, it appears difficult to compare the severity of two punishments which are different in nature. Nevertheless, it would seem that punishment which causes physical injury is, by its very nature, more severe than simple deprivation of liberty. We know that punishment by the lash was considered to be an aggravation of punishment when combined with imprisonment and that, historically, the gradual abolition of corporal punishment known to the English criminal law was the result of a humanistic movement and that, by replacing corporal punishment with imprisonment, it was felt that the severity of traditional punishment was being reduced.[102] Therefore, there would be reason to believe that, should Parliament reinstate corporal punishment offences, those accused of such offences would be entitled to trial by jury.

Fines, regardless of amount,[103] are in our opinion less severe than imprisonment. Here again, although we are comparing punishments which differ in nature, it appears that fines must be considered less severe than a denial of freedom, as they only affect an individual's property. This view, although it may seem subjective, is upheld by the traditional common law protection accorded to personal freedom and by the fact that in the eyes of the law and for those who must apply it, imprisonment is always considered a more severe punishment than a fine.

(b) The Exception

Of all federal legislation, there is one well-known Act which denies the accused the benefit of trial by jury, even though the offence of which

---

100 Smith, *supra*, note 77 at 387-397.

101 *Criminal Law Amendment Act, 1972*, S.C. 1972, c. 13, ss. 10, 59, 70.

102 A. Morel, "Les crimes et les peines: évolution des mentalités au Québec au XIXe siècle" (1978), 8 *R.D.U.S.* 392.

103 In this regard, ss. 32(1) [46(1)] [am. 1986, c. 26, s. 30(1)] and 33 [49] [re-en. 1986, c. 26, s. 34] of the *Competition Act* provide for fines of $10,000,000 and $5,000,000, respectively.

he is accused is punishable by five years' imprisonment or a more severe punishment. The *National Defence Act*[104] provides that members of the armed forces accused of "service offences" (as defined in section 2) may be judged and punished by a court martial. The procedure before this court differs in many respects from the procedure before regular criminal courts, notably by deprivation of the right to trial by jury. It would seem, therefore, that the purpose of section 11(f) of the Charter in its first part is to make sure that a person charged under the *National Defence Act* will not have the right to the benefit of trial by jury. By reason of this exception, the deprivation of the right for the military personnel charged before a court martial would not be inconsistent with the Charter.

Nonetheless, as obvious as this conclusion may appear at first glance, it is perhaps not well founded in every respect. There is enough of a significant distinction between the French and English versions of section 11(f) to merit further study:

> (f) Except in the case of an offence under military law tried before a military tribunal

> f) *sauf s'il s'agit d'une infraction relevant de la justice militaire*

While it is true that the French text is sufficiently general to include any offences within the jurisdiction of a military tribunal, this is less clearly the case in the English text. The French text is concerned with offences defined only in relation to the nature of the tribunal before which it may be tried — a military tribunal as opposed to an ordinary criminal court. In the English text, the offence is further qualified by the type of law which defines the offence — military law as opposed to civilian law. Is this a significant difference?

The difference would not be significant if the only offences within the jurisdiction of courts martial were specifically military offences or civilian offences related to military life and military discipline. However, this is not the case. Section 2 of the *National Defence Act* defines "service offence" (consequently within the jurisdiction of military tribunals) as:

> an offence under this Act, the *Criminal Code* or any other Act of Parliament, committed by a person while subject to the Code of Service Discipline.

As Mr. Justice McIntyre of the Supreme Court of Canada remarked in *MacKay v. R.*: "If we are to apply the definition of service offence literally, then all prosecutions of servicemen for any offences under any penal statute of Canada could be conducted in military courts."[105] However, section 11(f) of the Charter does not use the words "service offence" or "*infraction*

---

104 R.S.C. 1970, c. N-4 and amendments [R.S.C. 1985, c. N-5].
105 [1980] 2 S.C.R. 370, at 408.

militaire", the technical expressions adopted in the *National Defence Act*. Furthermore, in the English text, it is not simply a matter of "an offence tried before a military tribunal", which would have tended to confirm the interpretation that the exception applied to all offences so long as proceedings were conducted before a military tribunal. Section 11(f) should have been so written, if its intent was that the forum (military tribunal) before which the case was tried should be the only element used to determine the scope of the exception.

By referring instead to "an offence under military law tried before a military tribunal", the text adds a qualification which could be construed as restrictive. It is definitely not restrictive if the expression "military law" designates all that is to be found in the *National Defence Act* and if "an offence under military law" is equivalent to "service offence" in the meaning of that statute. This is by no means certain.

In *MacKay v. R.*,[106] the three justices of the Supreme Court who gave opinions agreed to a clear distinction between military law and what they called "ordinary civil law". Mr. Justice Ritchie, spoke of "two legal systems" and quoted with approval Mr. Justice Cattanach, who said in *MacKay v. Rippon*:

> The military law, which stands side by side with the general law of the land, is equally part of the law of the land but it is limited to members of the armed services and other persons who are subject to that law.[107]

Similarly, Chief Justice Laskin and Mr. Justice McIntyre spoke of "offences against the ordinary law",[108] of "ordinary civil law" or "general civil law",[109] contrasting these notions with that of "military law". Mr. Justice McIntyre also noted that we have inherited legal traditions which long ago led English and European societies to develop "a separate body of law which has become known as military law".[110]

The clear distinction between military law as a "separate body of law" and ordinary law has a historical basis. Suffice it to recall that as late as the end of the eighteenth century, the respective jurisdiction of civil courts and military tribunals was defined by Lord Loughborough in *Grant v. Gould*[111] in the following terms:

---

106 *Ibid.* at 392.
107 [1978] 1 F.C. 233, at 238 (T.D.).
108 *MacKay v. R., supra*, note 105, at 380.
109 *Ibid.* at 402.
110 *Ibid.*
111 (1792), 126 E.R. 434 at 450, referred to by M. L. Friedland, *Double Jeopardy* (Oxford: Clarendon Press, 1969), at 438.

> In this country, all the delinquencies of soldiers are not triable, as in most countries in Europe, by martial law; but where they are ordinary offences against the civil peace, they are tried by the common law courts.

It was not until 1879, in England, that legislation recognized the competence of military tribunals to judge a serviceman accused of an offence against ordinary criminal law.[112]

There is, therefore, some reason to ask whether the words "an offence under military law" found in the English version of section 11(f) of the Charter must receive the same definition as the expression "service offence" in the *National Defence Act*. There is reason to doubt this.

One must not lose sight of the fact that we are in the presence of an exception to a provision which, in other respects, guarantees any accused the right to the benefit of trial by jury. This provision is itself part of a Charter whose first section "guarantees the rights and freedoms set out in it". It is sufficient to say that the exception must receive a restrictive interpretation and that it is proper to ascribe to the expression "an offence under military law" the strict meaning of these words,[113] which is the result of a secular historical tradition. This was the interpretation of the Supreme Court of the United States in *O'Callaghan v. Parker*,[114] where it was decided that a serviceman, accused of a criminal offence unrelated to military discipline, could not be deprived of the right to trial by jury. The remarks of Mr. Justice Douglas on behalf of the court deserve to be repeated here: '[H]istory teaches that expansion of military discipline beyond its proper domain carries with it a threat to liberty."

One will recall that Mr. Justice McIntyre in the *MacKay* case adopted a view similar to that of American courts when he said:

> The principle which should be maintained is that the rights of the serviceman at civil law should be affected as little as possible considering the requirements of military discipline and the efficiency of the service.[115]

In applying this principle to the facts in *MacKay*, he concluded:

> I would therefore hold that the provisions of the *National Defence Act*, in so far as they confer jurisdiction upon courts martial to try servicemen in Canada for offences which are offences under the penal statutes of Canada

---

112 Friedland, *ibid.* at 335-353.
113 See *Black's Law Dictionary*, 5th ed. (St-Paul, Minn.: West Publishing Co., 1979), V. "Military Offences" and "Military Law"; *Jowitt's Dictionary of English Law*, 2nd ed. by J. Burke (London: Sweet & Maxwell, 1977), "Military Law"; and R.S. Vasan, ed., *The Canadian Law Dictionary* (Toronto: Law & Business Publications (Canada) Inc., 1980), V."Military Law".
114 395 U.S. 258 at 265 (1969). See also *Relford v. Commandant of U.S. Disciplinary Barracks*, 401 U.S. 355 (1971).
115 *Supra*, note 105 at 408.

for which civilians might also be tried, and where the commission and nature of such offences have no necessary connection with the service, in the sense that their commission does not tend to affect the standards of efficiency and discipline of the service, are inoperative as being contrary to the *Canadian Bill of Rights* in that they create inequality before the law for the serviceman involved.[116]

On the basis of Mr. Justice McIntyre's opinion, the Court Martial Appeal Court quite rightly refused to give the words "an offence under military law" as extended a meaning as the definition of "service offence" set out in section 2 of the *National Defence Act*. Since the coming into force of the Charter, the Court Martial Appeal Court has held on several occasions that the exception set out in section 11(f) should apply only to cases where the alleged offence has a real nexus with military discipline. Where the offence is not genuinely connected to the morale, discipline or efficiency of the armed forces, the member of the armed forces retains his right to the benefit of a trial by jury before a court of general criminal jurisdiction.[117] The courts should be slow to conclude in any given case that there is a real nexus between the criminal offence in question and military discipline. Evidence of such military nexus should be required before concluding that a member of the armed forces is not entitled to the constitutional guarantee of trial by jury.[118]

3. THE RIGHT TO THE ASSISTANCE OF AN INTERPRETER (S. 14)

Section 14 of the *Canadian Charter of Rights and Freedoms* guarantees the right to an interpreter in the following terms:

A party or witness in any proceedings who does not understand or speak the language in which the proceedings are conducted or who is deaf has the right to the assistance of an interpreter.

This section of the Charter repeats in substance the provisions of section 2(g) of the *Canadian Bill of Rights*,[119] but differs somewhat in its

---

116 *Ibid.* at 411.

117 *R. v. MacDonald* (1983), 6 C.C.C. (3d) 551 (Ct. Martial App. Ct.); *R. v. Catudal* (1985), 18 C.C.C. (3d) 189 (Ct. Martial App. Ct.); *R. v. MacEchern* (1985), 24 C.C.C. (3d) 439 (Ct. Martial App. Ct.); and *R v. Sullivan* (1986), 27 C.R.R. 1 (Ct. Martial App. Ct.), leave to appeal to S.C.C. refused (1986), 27 C.R.R. 1n (S.C.C.).

118 D.J. Corry, "Military Law under the *Charter*" (1986), 24 *Osgoode Hall L.J.* 67 at 100-103.

119 This section provides that: "[N]o law of Canada shall be construed or applied so as to . . . (g) deprive a person of the right to the assistance of an interpreter in any proceedings in which he is involved or in which he is a party or a witness, before a court, commission, board or other tribunal, if he does not understand or speak the language in which such proceedings are conducted."

actual wording and content.[120] The differences between the two texts cannot be ignored. As Mr. Justice Le Dain pointed out in connection with the right to the assistance of counsel contained in section 10 of the Charter, differences in wording and context, along with the constitutional nature of the document itself, properly influence the interpretation and application of Charter provisions.[121] However, even though the case law decided under section 2(g) of the *Bill of Rights* is no longer necessarily conclusive, one should not conclude that it has no relevance at all.[122]

(a) Substantive and Textual Differences

The one significant difference in content between section 14 of the Charter and the corresponding section of the *Bill of Rights* is the inclusion in section 14 of deaf persons. This formally extends to the deaf the same right to the assistance of an interpreter as previously enjoyed by persons unable to understand or speak the language of the proceedings. This new reference to the right of the deaf, however, reflects what the courts already do in practice. Although there appear to be no reported Canadian cases on the right of the deaf to the assistance of an interpreter, the English case *R. v. Lee Kun*,[123] decided by the Court of Criminal Appeal in 1915, has been followed in Canada[124] as well as in England.[125] In delivering the judgment of the court in that case, Lord Reading held that the assistance of an interpreter was an appropriate recourse in cases where an accused was deaf or mute, for such a person could understand and make himself understood only through the use of writing or signs.[126] The wording of

---

120 Note also that the Canadian provisions differ from the terms of art. 14(3)(f) of the *International Covenant on Civil and Political Rights*, which applies only to the accused in criminal proceedings, but which, on the other hand, provides for the right free of charge. On this point the *Canadian Charter* is silent. See also *infra*, note 177.

121 *R. v. Therens*, [1985] 1 S.C.R. 613 at 638-640.

122 See *R. v. Oakes*, [1986] 1 S.C.R. 103 at 124 (Dickson C.J.C.) regarding decisions rendered under the *Bill of Rights* which deal with the presumption of innocence.

123 [1916] 1 K.B. 337 (C.C.A.).

124 The relevant passage of this decision is really a long *obiter dictum* of the court, but it is regularly cited by Canadian courts in dealing with the right to the assistance of an interpreter or to trial in one's own language particularly in criminal cases. See, *e.g.*, *R. v. Prince*, [1946] D.L.R. 659 at 666 (B.C.C.A.); *R. v. Randall* (1963), 38 D.L.R. (2d) 624 at 628 (N.B.C.A.); *R. v. Murphy; Ex parte Belisle and Moreau* (1968), 69 D.L.R. (2d) 530 at 536 (N.B.C.A.); *R. v. Watts; Ex parte Poulin* (1968), 69 D.L.R. (2d) 526 at 529 (B.C.S.C.), aff'd (1969), 1 D.L.R. (3d) 239 (B.C.C.A.).

125 Archbold, *Pleading, Evidence and Practice in Criminal Cases*, 39th ed. by S. Mitchell (London: Sweet & Maxwell, 1976) para. 347 at pp. 135-136.

126 *R. v. Lee Kun, supra*, note 123 at 342. It is worth noting, by way of comparison, that Quebec's *Code of Civil Procedure*, R.S.Q. c. C-25, provides in art. 296 that "A person

section 14 of the Charter does not exclude the possibility of using writing to communicate with a party or a witness who is deaf. Nevertheless, it does appear to grant him the right, if he so chooses and where he is able to understand sign language, to insist on the assistance of an interpreter.

Section 14 makes no specific mention of a party or witness who is simply mute. This is a regrettable oversight on the part of the drafters. Such persons, it appears, are outside the scope of section 14, unless it can be argued that they come within the words "[those who] do not speak the language in which the proceedings are conducted". However, this interpretation is unlikely, given the wording of section 14, which stresses the inability to speak the particular language of a trial rather than the inability to speak because of a physical disability.[127] If the words "[those who] do not understand . . . the language in which the proceedings are conducted" had been intended to include the deaf, there would have been no reason to mention them specifically. On the other hand, it is certainly possible to argue that, while a deaf person suffers from an inability to hear the language of the proceedings, he does not necessarily suffer from an inability to understand that language. The specific inclusion of the deaf could have been judged necessary in light of this possible distinction. In the case of mute persons, by way of contrast, one could say they are included in the class of persons, who do not speak the language of the proceedings, for in fact they are unable to use any spoken language at all.[128] Such an interpretation would avoid depriving the party or witness who is mute of the benefit of this constitutional provision.[129]

Although there are numerous differences in wording between section 14 of the Charter and section 2(g) of the *Bill of Rights*, not all are of equal importance. The most noteworthy difference consists in transforming the negative formulation found in the *Bill of Rights* — "no law of Canada shall be construed or applied so as to . . . deprive a person of the right

---

afflicted with an infirmity which renders him unable to speak, or to hear and speak, may take the oath or solemnly affirm and testify, either by writing under his hand, or by signs with the aid of an interpreter."

127 In this respect, s. 14 of the Charter differs from section 6 of the *Canada Evidence Act*, R.S.C. 1970, c. E-10 [R.S.C. 1985, c. C-15], which provides: "A witness who is unable to speak may give his evidence in any other manner in which he can make it intelligible."

128 It must be noted that this interpretation is difficult to reconcile with the wording of s. 14 in its French version, which refers to a party or a witness "*qui ne peuvent suivre les procédures*". Since a person who is mute only is perfectly able to "*suivre les procédures*", he would not be covered by s. 14. However, if he testifies through sign language rather than a written text, the assistance of an interpreter would be necessary for him to be understood. The English version ("a party or witness in any proceedings") does not raise the same problem of interpretation.

129 For a contrary position, see J. Fortin, *Preuve pénale* (Montréal: Editions Thémis, 1984) No. 252, at 186.

to the assistance of an interpreter" — into a positive formulation: "A party or witness . . . has the right to the assistance of an interpreter". This new wording is more clearly declarative of a right, quite apart from the fact that the right in question, formerly recognized only by statute or the common law, is now raised to the level of a constitutional norm. The effect is both to confirm and to reinforce the traditional attitude of the courts, which have consistently viewed the right to the assistance of an interpreter as imposing a duty on the judge to provide this assistance to any person who cannot understand and follow the proceedings of a trial in which he is involved and to any person who cannot testify in the language of the trial.

(b) The Purpose of the Right

It is now well established that in interpreting a Charter provision it is important to take into account its aim or purpose, for the rights and freedoms guaranteed by the Charter must be interpreted "in light of the interests [they were] meant to protect".[130] As emphasized by Mr. Justice Beetz, the right to an interpreter set out in section 14 of the Charter is related directly to the right to a fair hearing, which is itself "a fundamental right deeply and firmly embedded in the very fabric of the Canadian legal system".[131] Of course, the right to an interpreter is "but an aspect of the right to a fair hearing".[132] Certain other aspects are protected by the series of provisions, including most notably section 7, which the Charter groups together under the heading *Legal Rights*. What section 14 seeks to protect is the right of the parties "to be heard and understood by a court and the right to understand what is going on in court".[133] It is by reference to this purpose that the true scope of the provision which guarantees the right to the assistance of an interpreter must be determined.

(c) Areas of Application

The right to the assistance of an interpreter has been invoked and

---

130 *R. v. Big M Drug Mart Ltd.*, *supra*, note 67 at 344. See also *Hunter v. Southam Inc.*, [1984] 2 S.C.R. 145 at 156-157; *R. v. Therens*, *supra*, note 121 at 641; *Reference s. 94(2) of the Motor Vehicle Act B.C.*, *supra*, note 92 at 499-500; and *R. v. Oakes*, *supra*, note 122 at 119.

131 *MacDonald v. Montreal (City)*, [1986] 1 S.C.R. 460 at 499-500.

132 *MacDonald, ibid.*

133 *Société des Acadiens du Nouveau-Brunswick Inc. v. Assn. of Parents for Fairness in Education*, [1986] 1 S.C.R. 549 at 577.

applied most frequently in the context of criminal and penal proceedings.[134] Moreover, the case law has traditionally associated the right to the assistance of an interpreter with the right or the obligation of an accused to be present at his trial. Thus, the Supreme Court of Canada in *Attorney General of Ontario v. Reale*,[135] ruled that an accused, though physically present at his trial, was not present within the meaning of section 577(1) [now 650(1)] of the *Criminal Code* if he was unable to understand the language of the proceedings. This reasoning is similar to what one finds in the earlier case of *R. v. Lee Kun*: "The reason why the accused should be present at the trial is that he may hear the case made against him and have the opportunity, having heard it, of answering it."[136] The right of an accused to be informed of the evidence against him, as well as his right to make a full and complete defence, are essential components of the right to a fair trial.[137] This right cannot be ensured without the assistance of an interpreter in cases where the accused does not understand the language in which all or part of the proceedings are conducted, or where he is disabled by deafness.

However, it is clear that section 14 of the Charter was not drafted so as to limit the right to the assistance of an interpreter to accused persons, as would have been the case had this right been included in section 11, which sets out the rights of persons charged with an offence. The relationship between the right to the assistance of an interpreter and the right to be present at one's trial in order to defend oneself clearly demonstrates that it is the right to be heard which is being protected. Thus, the right to the assistance of an interpreter extends to all cases where the right to be heard, either expressly or indirectly (by virtue of the right to be present), is provided for by law, as well as to all cases where the rules of natural justice require that the party be heard.[138] This indeed is precisely how Canadian courts have understood this right in the past. In *Unterreiner v. R.*,[139] it was held that the absence of a competent interpreter could amount to a denial of natural justice serious enough to order a new trial.

---

134 However, the *Criminal Code* nowhere speaks of an interpreter except in the Schedule to Part XXIV [XXVII] which is alluded to in s. 772(1) [840]. It establishes, among other things, the "Fees and allowances that may be allowed to interpreters".

135 [1975] 2 S.C.R. 624.

136 *Supra*, note 123 at 341.

137 *MacDonald v. Montreal, supra*, note 131 at 499.

138 This passage in the first edition of this work (Tarnopolsky & Beaudoin, *The Canadian Charter of Rights and Freedoms, Commentary* (Toronto: Carswell, 1982) at 380), was referred to with approval by Madam Justice Wilson in the *Société des Acadiens du Nouveau-Brunswick Inc.* case, *supra*, note 133 at 622, but without identifying the source.

139 (1980), 51 C.C.C. (2d) 373 at 380 (Ont. Co. Ct.).

Outside the domain of criminal law and provincial penal law, immigration hearings constitute one of the areas in which the right to the assistance of an interpreter is routinely invoked.[140] The former *Immigration Inquiries Regulations*,[141] it is true, expressly provided for this right and the regulations currently in force have clear provisions to the same effect.[142] This makes it all the more significant that the courts have considered the right to the assistance of an interpreter to flow implicitly from what was previously section 26(1) of the *Immigration Act*[143] (now section 29(1) of the *Immigration Act 1976*), [144] which states that:

> An inquiry by an adjudicator shall be held in the presence of the person with respect to whom the inquiry is to be held wherever practicable.

In *Weber v. Minister of Manpower & Immigration*, Mr. Justice Urie of the Federal Court of Appeal wrote as follows:

> The case at bar is, of course, not a criminal one but is a proceeding administrative in nature which must be decided on a quasi-judicial basis. The requirements of section 2(g) [*Canadian Bill of Rights*] would appear to embrace it and since the rights of an individual are certainly at issue, the reasoning in the *Reale* case [*infra*, note 153] would appear applicable in an inquiry of this nature.[145]

He then added:

> That this view is correct is reinforced by observing that section 26(1) of the *Immigration Act* [R.S.C. 1970, c. I-2] requires that a special inquiry be held in the presence of the person concerned wherever practicable, just as an accused in a criminal trial must be present.[146]

In the context of civil proceedings as well, the right to the assistance of an interpreter is meant to ensure to both plaintiff and defendant an effective exercise of their right to a "complete and fair hearing" of the case, as was recognized by the Québec Superior Court in *Labrie v. Les Machineries Kraft du Québec Inc.*[147] In this case, the services of an interpreter

---

140 *Leiba v. Min. of Manpower & Immigration*, [1972] S.C.R. 660; *Weber v. Min. of Manpower & Immigration*, [1977] 1 F.C. 750 (C.A.); C.J. Wydrzynski, *Canadian Immigration Law and Procedure* (Aurora: Canada Law Book, 1983) at 476.

141 C.R.C. 1978, c. 939 r. 4; repealed by SOR/80-833.

142 *Immigration Regulations, 1978*, SOR/78-172, rr. 27, 28.

143 R.S.C. 1970, c. I-2 [repealed 1976-77, c. 52, s. 128(1)].

144 S.C. 1976-77, c. 52.

145 *Supra*, note 140 at 754.

146 *Ibid.*

147 [1984] C.S. 263 at 275. Similarly, in *The Law of Evidence in Civil Cases* (Toronto: Butterworths, 1974) at 477-478, John Sopinka and Sidney N. Lederman point out that the primary consideration of a judge when deciding whether to allow the use of an

were required not for the benefit of the court, but for the benefit of the plaintiff, who had the "right to understand" testimony given in English by a witness for the defendant. In consequence, the court found as follows:

> Counsel for the plaintiff was duty-bound to ask the question in French so that the plaintiff could understand. The interpreter was necessary to translate the question into English for the witness, who had a right to understand the question before replying. [. . .] His response, given in English, then had to be translated in order to respect the right of the plaintiff. The role of the interpreter was thus essential at every stage. [translation] [148]

As this case well illustrates, the right guaranteed by section 14 of the Charter is distinct from the language rights that are entrenched elsewhere in the Constitution. In the clear words of the Supreme Court of Canada, "both types of rights are conceptually different".[149] Language rights, that is, the right to use either French or English, enjoyed by persons before the courts of Quebec or New Brunswick and before courts established by Parliament, "are those of litigants, counsel, witnesses, judges and other judicial officers who actually speak, *not those of parties or others who are spoken to*".[150] By contrast, the right to the assistance of an interpreter is a mechanism to ensure that the parties "understand what is happening in the courtroom" and that they themselves and their witnesses are understood by the court.[151] This rationale is applicable regardless of the type of litigation, the language spoken by the parties or the tribunal hearing the case.

(d) Scope of the Right

Although section 14 of the Charter does not specify the exact scope of the right conferred on parties or witnesses to the assistance of an interpreter, any more than section 2(g) of the *Bill of Rights* does, this follows logically from the purpose for which the right is guaranteed.

With respect to witnesses, as Chief Justice McNair has explained in *R. v. Randall*,[152] the role of an interpreter "is to make intelligible to the tribunal the testimony of a witness who is unable to express himself in a language familiar to the Judge and jury" and to ensure that this testimony

---

interpreter in a civil trial is "that the witness, especially where he is a party, should be permitted to put before the court his evidence as fully and accurately and as fairly and effectively as all the circumstances permit".

148 *Labrie, ibid.*
149 *MacDonald v. Montreal, supra,* note 133 at 500. See also the judgment in *Société des Acadiens du Nouveau-Brunswick, supra,* note 133 at 574, 577.
150 *MacDonald v. Montreal, supra,* note 133 at 483 (emphasis added).
151 *Ibid.* at 499; *Société des Acadiens du Nouveau-Brunswick, supra,* note 131 at 577.
152 *Supra,* note 124 at 628.

will not be lost due to the failure to translate the questions put to the witness and his answers. This explains why a witness is not entitled to have the entire proceedings translated for his benefit, but only the portion of the proceedings that is relevant to his own testimony. The cases are unanimous on this point.

With respect to an accused or a party to a proceeding, the position is different. A party must have the benefit of interpretation throughout the proceedings.[153] This follows from the basic principle on which his right to the assistance of an interpreter is founded. Any person who is a party to proceedings, whether as accused, as plaintiff or defendant, or as the subject of an inquiry, has the right to a fair and impartial trial or hearing and this in turn entails the right to understand all that is said by the witnesses, by counsel and by the judge, arbiter or member of the board of inquiry.[154] It also entails the right to defend himself or to be heard and the right to instruct counsel accordingly.[155]

This explains why the courts, even prior to the Charter, insisted that any party to proceedings, regardless of their character, must be in a position to follow each and every stage of the proceedings. The language in which the guarantee of section 14 is drafted certainly confirms this approach. It follows that the plaintiff or defendant in a civil action can require the assistance of an interpreter not only during the course of the trial itself, but also during preliminary procedures such as the examination for discovery.[156] Similarly, a person charged with an offence has the right to an interpreter at every stage of the proceedings, including the arraignment

---

153 In *R. v. Reale* (1974), 13 C.C.C. (2d) 345 at 349, (Ont. C.A.), aff'd [1975] 2 S.C.R. 624, the Ontario Court of Appeal declared: "In our opinion, the right not to be deprived of the assistance of an interpreter when the circumstances require such assistance extends to every essential part of the proceedings." See also Sopinka & Lederman, *supra*, note 147 at 479.

154 Rule 28(b) of the *Immigration Regulations, 1978, supra*, note 142, requires that "the adjudicator presiding at the inquiry shall administer an oath to the interpreter whereby the interpreter swears to translate accurately to the best of his ability all the questions asked, answers given and statements made at the inquiry." See also *Turkiewicz v. R.* (1979), 10 C.R. (3d) 352 at 362 (Ont. C.A.).

155 *R. v. Berger* (1975), 27 C.C.C. (2d) 357 at 375 (B.C.C.A.); leave to appeal to S.C.C. refused 27 C.C.C. (2d) 357n (S.C.C.); *R. v. Tsang* (1985), 27 C.C.C. (3d) 365 at 370 (B.C.C.A.); *Labrie c. Les Machineries Kraft, supra*, note 147 at p. 275.

156 *Ferncraft Leather Inc. v. Roll*, 1979, (Que. C.A.), reported in J. Deschênes, *Ainsi parlèrent les tribunaux: Conflits linguistiques au Canada, 1968-1980* (Montréal : Wilson & Lafleur, 1980), Vol. I, at 483. However, this case was decided on the basis of art. 305 of *Quebec's Code of Civil Procedure*.

for purposes of entering a plea,[157] the preliminary inquiry,[158] all *voir dire*,[159] the instructions to the jury[160] and the hearing on sentencing.[161]

On the other hand, section 14 of the Charter does not apply to the pre-judicial phase of criminal or penal process, for properly speaking there are no "parties" at this stage. However, section 10(a) of the Charter indirectly grants to an arrested or detained person, who is not a "party" to a proceeding, the right to the services of an interpreter where necessary. At least this would seem to be the effect of "the right on arrest or detention to be informed promptly of the reasons therefor", found in section 10(a). One could hardly claim to have discharged a duty to inform where the information is not communicated in a language understood by the person arrested or detained.[162]

Given its underlying purpose, the right to the assistance of an interpreter is of fundamental importance. This suggests that any attempt to replace the services of an interpreter with a substitute, such as providing a resume of the testimony given by a particular witness or providing the parties afterwards with a translation of any parts they did not understand, will not be adequate for the purposes of section 14.[163] Nor will it be acceptable to deny the right to an interpreter on the grounds that the relevant testimony is neither long nor complex,[164] or that the use of an interpreter will slow down the proceedings or cause some other inconvenience, such as reducing the effectiveness of a cross-examination.[165] In

---

157 *MacDonald v. Montreal, supra,* note 131 at 498; *R. v. Karas* (1961), 131 C.C.C. 414 (B.C.C.A.). For a contrary decision, see *Gondariz v. R.,* [1972] C.A. 807 (Que. C.A.); see, however, the dissenting opinion of Deschênes J. at 809-814.

158 *Blentzas v. R.,* N.S.C.A., September 19, 1983, unreported, reported in R.H. McLeod *et al.* (eds), *The Canadian Charter of Rights: The Prosecution and Defence of Criminal and Other Statutory Offences* (Toronto: Carswell, 1983), para. 22.4.

159 *R. v. Petrovic* (1984), 13 C.C.C. (3d) 416 (Ont. C.A.).

160 *A.G. Ontario v. Reale, supra,* note 135.

161 The Supreme Court of Canada ruled in *R. v. Gardiner,* [1982] 2 S.C.R. 368 at 414, that: "Sentencing is the critical stage of the criminal justice system." The court also determined, in *Lowry v. R.,* [1974] S.C.R. 195, that an accused has a right to be heard at this stage of the proceedings. See also *Schofield v. R.* (1976), 36 C.R.N.S. 135 (N.B.C.A.).

162 See, by way of analogy, *R. v. Tanguay* (1984), 27 M.V.R. 1 (Ont. Co. Ct.), which deals with the duty under s. 10(b) of the Charter to inform the person arrested in a language he understands.

163 *Weber v. Min. of Manpower & Immigration, supra,* note 140 at 753; *R. v. Petrovic, supra,* note 159 at 422.

164 This rationale was given by the Quebec Court of Appeal in *Sadjade v. R.* (1982), 67 C.C.C. (2d) 189 at 191, but its decision was overruled by the Supreme Court of Canada which ordered a new trial; *infra,* note 190.

165 The contrary opinion expressed by Sopinka & Lederman, *supra,* note 147 at 479, is not, in my view, well-founded.

Attorney General of Ontario v. Reale,[166] for example, the Supreme Court of Canada quite properly ordered a new trial on the grounds that the presiding judge violated section 2(g) of the *Bill of Rights* when, upon giving his charge to the jury, he dismissed the interpreter whose services the accused had enjoyed from the beginning of the trial. While recognizing that the presiding judge might have been justified in fearing that the activity of the interpreter would distract the jury, the court ruled that he should have found some other means to ensure their undivided attention.

(e) Invoking the Right

Determining whether a person has sufficient knowledge of a language to enable him to follow the proceedings inevitably involves the exercise of judicial discretion.[167] One must admit that the manner in which this discretion has been exercised by some judges in the past is open to strong criticism.[168] Now that there is a constitutional guarantee, however, despite the absence of express criteria, the courts are likely to recognize the right of anyone who asks to require the services of an interpreter. Of course, attempts to exercise this right that are clearly made in bad faith should still be rejected.[169] However, as the Ontario Court of Appeal has indicated, "it would require cogent and compelling evidence for a trial judge to conclude that the request for an interpreter is not made in good faith, but for an oblique motive".[170]

Although there exists no general duty requiring a judge to inform witnesses or parties to an action of their right to the assistance of an interpreter, such assistance should be provided, even where no specific request has been made, as soon as it appears to the court that such assistance would be useful.[171] Failure to provide an interpreter in these circumstances would, in effect, amount to a denial of justice, with all that that entails.

---

166 *Supra*, note 135.
167 *Ferncraft Leather Inc. v. Roll*, *supra*, note 156; *Malartic Hygrade Gold Mines (Qué.) Ltd. v. Québec (Prov.)*, [1983] C.S. 953 at p. 958 (Qué. S.C.).
168 In *Sadowski v. R.*, [1963] B.R. 677 (Qué. C.A.), the presiding judge rejected the statement of the accused that he understood neither French or English, basing his judgment on the belief that the accused, after several years of residence in Canada, would surely have had occasion to learn the basics of one or the other of the country's official languages. The Quebec Court of Appeal dismissed the accused's appeal even though he had not been represented by counsel at his trial. In *Gondariz v. R.*, *supra*, note 157, the Court of Appeal dismissed the appeal of an accused who understood neither French nor English, and against whom a plea of guilty had been entered to charges which had been read to her in French only. See also the *Sadjade* case, *supra*, note 164.
169 *R. v. Kent* (1986), 27 C.C.C. (3d) 405 (Man. C.A.).
170 *R. v. Petrovic*, *supra*, note 159 at 423. See also *R. v. Tsang*, *supra*, note 155 at 371.
171 *R. v. Tsang*, *supra*, note 155 at 371-372.

It is also inadvisable for a court to embark upon an inquiry into the level of competence of a party or witness to speak or understand the language of the proceedings, unless the request for a interpreter appears frivolous.[172] How is one to determine the critical level of linguistic competence below which a person who speaks with difficulty or understands imperfectly loses the right guaranteed in section 14 of the Charter? In this regard, there is much wisdom in the comments of Mr. Justice Lacourcière in the *Petrovic* case,[173] suggesting that even though a person is able to use and understand a language sufficiently to meet the needs of everyday life, he may nevertheless be unable to follow proceedings in which he is involved without the assistance of an interpreter where the outcome of the proceedings will affect him in a serious way. This may be so even in cases where the liberty of the person is not at risk.

It is reasonable to suppose that the right to the assistance of an interpreter impliedly includes the right of a party or witness to insist that the interpreter is competent[174] and impartial. Otherwise, the exercise of the right would be compromised and the purpose for which it was granted would be defeated. It is the responsibility of the judge to ensure that the interpreter chosen possesses the qualities of competence and impartiality.[175] As the judge in *Unterreiner v. R.*[176] points out, this is a question

---

172 *R. v. Petrovic, supra,* note 159 at 423; *R. v. Tsang, supra,* note 155 at 371. In *Roy v. Hackett* (1985), 9 O.A.C. 273 at 278 (Ont. Div. Ct.), rev'd (1987), 62 O.R. (2d) 365 (C.A.), one finds the following statement: "It is obvious that only the witness or party is able to determine if he can follow the proceedings in the language being used. It therefore follows that the witness or party, who states that he is unable to follow the proceedings without the assistance of an interpreter, has an absolute right to one." [translation] See also *Serrurier v. Ottawa (City)* (1983), 42 O.R. (2d) 321 (C.A.). Unless there are specific circumstances which lead one to believe that a request is not made in good faith, but rather for ulterior motives, I do not share the view of Sopinka & Lederman, *supra,* note 147 at 478, that a judge can allow an examination and cross-examination to take place in order to determine whether a witness has sufficient aptitude in the language of the proceedings.

173 *Supra,* note 159 at 423: "A person may be able to communicate in a language for general purposes while not possessing sufficient comprehension or fluency to face a trial with its ominous consequences without the assistance of a qualified interpreter. Even if that person speaks broken English or French and understands simple communications, the right constitutionally protected by s. 14 of the Charter is not removed."

174 Wydrzynski, *supra,* note 140 at 476-478. In *Leiba v. Manpower & Immigration, supra,* note 140, the appellant who spoke Romanian, Yiddish and Hebrew was assisted by an interpreter who spoke only English and German.

175 In *Unterreiner v. R..*, *supra,* note 139, the court affirmed that it would have been necessary to hold an inquiry on the competence of the interpreter before swearing him in.

176 *Supra,* note 139 at 379: "There is precious little caselaw authority on the question of the credentials of and procedures for the swearing in of an interpreter in a trial or related proceeding."

that has scarcely been addressed by the courts.[177] Nevertheless, some things are clear. It is clear that neither the judge nor counsel for one of the parties may assume the role of interpreter, regardless of his linguistic abilities or his capacity to act impartially.[178] Similarly, a witness cannot be allowed to translate his own testimony for the benefit of one of the parties.[179] One would also want to challenge the impartiality of an interpreter who was related to one of the parties, by way of family or other interest.[180]

(f) Waiver of the Right

There is no simple or obvious answer to the question whether a person can waive the right guaranteed by section 14 of the Charter. One must bear in mind the point made by the Supreme Court of Canada that this right is an aspect of the right to a fair hearing.[181] It is moreover one of the elements constituting the "principles of fundamental justice" enshrined in section 7 of the Charter.[182] One will also bear in mind what Madam Justice Wilson had to say, speaking for the majority in *Clarkson v. R.*,[183] on the waiver of the right to legal counsel found in section 10(b) of the

---

177 The question of the costs involved in using an interpreter is also something the courts have rarely had the opportunity to address. In *Labrie c. Les Machineries Kraft du Québec Inc.*, *supra*, note 147 at 275, the court held that "[i]n the absence of any specific legislation or government directive declaring that the costs are to be met by the public purse" [translation], the costs of the interpreter follow the outcome of the case and are not necessarily borne by the party requiring the assistance. It is noteworthy that in Quebec the provincial *Charter of human rights and freedoms*, s. 36, provides that the assistance of an interpreter must be provided *free of charge* to all accused persons who do not understand the language used at the hearing or who suffer from deafness. Likewise, r. 28(a) of the *Immigration Regulations, 1978*, *supra*, note 142, provides that the services of an interpreter "must be provided at no cost". Although s. 14 of the Charter does not expressly guarantee the services of an interpreter free of charge, a number of commentators argue that the government should bear the costs of interpretation, either as a general rule in all cases or in certain defined circumstances only. In this regard, see Hogg, *supra*, note 61 at 49; Manning, *supra*, note 61 at 458; and D.C. McDonald, *Legal Rights in the Canadian Charter of Rights and Freedoms: A Manual of Issues and Sources* (Toronto: Carswell, 1982) at 125-126. One could argue that the constitutional guarantee entails that the costs should be borne by the government, for a person might be influenced to waive his right to an interpreter on account of the costs involved. This would effectively undermine the right guaranteed by the Charter.

178 In this regard, see the views of Mr. Justice Kaufman in *Sadjade v. R.*, *supra*, note 164 at 191 (C.A.); and *Turkiewicz v. R.*, *supra*, note 154 at 362.

179 R. v. Petrovic, *supra*, note 159 at 422-423.

180 *Unterreiner v. R. supra*, note 139 at 380: Sopinka & Lederman, *supra*, note 147 at 480.

181 *MacDonald v. Montreal*, *supra*, note 131; see text accompanying note 132.

182 *Reference re s. 94(2) of the Motor Vehicle Act (B.C.)*, *supra*, note 92 at 502-503.

183 [1986] 1 S.C.R. 383 at 394-396.

Charter. She points out that, in the *Korponey* case,[184] the Supreme Court of Canada established that the waiver of a procedural right is valid only where it is "clear and unequivocal that the person is waiving the procedural safeguard and is doing so with full knowledge of the rights the procedure was enacted to protect and of the effect the waiver will have on those rights in the process".[185]

In principle, then, it is possible for a party to proceedings to waive his constitutional right to the assistance of an interpreter, provided the waiver is voluntary and unequivocal. However, it is doubtful that a person unrepresented by counsel could validly waive his right,[186] especially in penal proceedings where the absence of an interpreter would effectively deprive the accused of his right to make a full and complete defence and could amount, in effect, to his not really being present at his trial.[187] Although the same considerations are not present in the case of a civil trial, before accepting the waiver of a person who is not represented by counsel, the court should ensure that the decision to waive was taken with full knowledge of the consequences.[188]

(g) Sanctions for Violating the Right

In the absence of a valid waiver, any denial of the right to the assistance of an interpreter occurring in the course of any proceedings whatever should give rise to a remedy as provided in section 24(1) of the Charter. In most cases, the only appropriate and just remedy will be to quash the verdict or judgment of the trial judge and to order a new trial or hearing. Ordinarily this will be the only way to ensure that the party whose right has been violated receives a fair hearing. This applies to all types of proceedings, including civil[189] and criminal trials,[190] administrative inquiries[191] and hearings before arbitration boards.[192] The remedy is the same, moreover, whether the right to an interpreter has been totally or only partially violated. Of course, if the violation of which an accused complained occurred solely in the course of his hearing on sentencing, it would obviously be inappropriate to quash the verdict itself. In such circumstances the appellate

---

184 *Korponey v. A.G. Canada*, [1982] 1 S.C.R. 41.

185 *Ibid.* at 49.

186 C.-A. Sheppard, "Droit à l'interprète" (1964), 24 *R. du B.* 148.

187 Fortin, *supra*, note 129, No. 253, at 186, questions that an accused can waive his right to an interpreter, even in cases where he is represented by counsel.

188 *Clarkson v. R.*, *supra*, note 183 at 396.

189 *Serrurier v. Ottawa*, *supra*, note 172.

190 *A.G. Ontario v. Reale*, *supra*, note 135; *Sadjade v. R.* [1983] 2 S.C.R. 361.

191 *Leiba v. Min. of Manpower & Immigration*, *supra*, note 140.

192 *Roy v. Hackett*, *supra*, note 172.

court would simply quash the sentence and order a new hearing on sentencing, unless in the circumstances it was able to substitute its own sentence for that imposed below.[193]

4. THE RIGHT NOT TO BE TRIED OR PUNISHED AGAIN FOR THE SAME OFFENCE (S. 11(h))

Section 11(h) of the *Canadian Charter of Rights and Freedoms* provides:

> 11. Any person charged with an offence has the right
>
> . . .
>
> (h) if finally acquitted of the offence, not to be tried for it again and, if finally found guilty and punished for the offence, not to be tried or punished for it again.

This provision guarantees any person charged with an offence who has previously been acquitted or found guilty of the same offence the right not to be tried again.[194] This is known as the double jeopardy rule, which is often expressed by the maxim *nemo debet bis puniri pro uno delicto* or by the expression *non bis in idem*.[195] The antiquity of the rule at common law as in other legal systems, if not that of its observance, need no longer be demonstrated.[196] It has been said that "[n]o other procedural doctrine is more fundamental or all pervasive".[197] Mr. Justice Rand of the Supreme Court of Canada is also often quoted:

> At the foundation of criminal law lies the cardinal principle that no man shall be placed in jeopardy twice for the same matter.[198]

However, despite the fundamental nature of the rule and despite its consecration in the Fifth Amendment of the *American Bill of Rights*,[199] section 2 of the *Canadian Bill of Rights* makes no mention of it. At most we might argue that it is implicitly referred to in section 2(d): "other constitutional safeguards";[200] however, the case law does not offer any

---

193   *R. v. Petrovic, supra,* note 159 at 428.

194   The same guarantee is found in par. 7 of art. 14 of the *International Covenant on Civil and Political Rights*: "No one shall be liable to be tried or punished again for an offence for which he has already been finally convicted or acquitted in accordance with the law and penal procedure of each country."

195   M.L. Friedland, *Double Jeopardy* (Oxford: Clarendon Press, 1969) at 6, 15.

196   *Ibid.* at 5-16.

197   *Ibid.* at 3.

198   *Cullen v. R.,* [1949] S.C.R. 658 at 668.

199   "[N]or shall any person be subject for the same offence to be twice put in jeopardy of life or limb".

200   Considering the nature of the other guarantees found in para. (d), the English version lends itself better to such an interpretation than the French.

examples of such an application.

In its traditional form, the rule against double jeopardy allows a person accused of an offence of which he has been acquitted or found guilty not to be in peril of being found guilty a second time. In procedural terms these special pleas are known as *autrefois acquit* or *autrefois convict*. However, contemporary legal understanding of the concept of double jeopardy covers a number of hypotheses or situations wider and more diverse than the case of an individual accused again of the same offence. The concept is no longer limited to its narrow traditional framework, nor is it raised only by a plea of *autrefois acquit* or *convict*. For a quarter of a century, courts in England and in Canada have given a broad interpretation to the concept and have recognized the application of special defences such as *issue estoppel* and the rule against multiple convictions.[201] Thus, one cannot appreciate the scope of the guarantee set out in section 11(h) without reference to the relatively recent development of the concept of double jeopardy in common law.

Before proceeding, however, one should note that the constitutional protection against double jeopardy applies to both provincial and federal penal law as well as the criminal law *per se*, and that nothing in the wording of section 11(h) limits its application either to offences punishable by indictment or to summary conviction offences.

It long remained uncertain whether the provisions of the *Criminal Code* restrict availability of the special pleas of *autrefois* to indictable offences. The Supreme Court of Canada has clearly laid to rest this uncertainty in *R. v. Riddle*,[202] where it held that a person accused of a summary conviction offence still benefits, at common law, from the special pleas of *autrefois acquit* and *autrefois convict*, in the absence of clear statutory provisions to the contrary. In this regard, section 11(h) of the Charter confirms the state of Canadian criminal law and gives it a written constitutional basis. Henceforth, any statutory provision which would deprive a person accused of a summary conviction offence of the right guaranteed in section 11(h) would be of no force or effect as provided in section 52(1) of the *Constitution Act, 1982*.

However, what exactly is the right guaranteed by section 11(h) of the Charter to persons charged with an offence? The language used by the

---

201 *Kienapple v. R.*, [1975] 1 S.C.R. 729; *Gushue v. R.*, [1980] 1 S.C.R. 798. With respect to these developments, reference should be made to: P. Béliveau & D. Labrèche, "L'élargissement du concept de 'double jeopardy' en droit pénal canadien: de *bis puniri* à *bis vexari*" (1977), 37 *R. du B.* 589; H. Leonoff & D. Deutscher, "The Plea and Related Matters", in V.M Del Buono (ed.), *Criminal Procedure in Canada* (Toronto: Butterworths, 1982) at 229, 246 *et seq.*; R.E. Salhany *Canadian Criminal Procedure*, 4th ed. (Aurora: Canada Law Book, 1984) at 248-253.

202 [1980] 1 S.C.R. 380.

drafter in formulating this provision appears to strictly limit the character and scope of the right.

Section 11(h) clearly envisages two situations. The first is that of a person who has in the past been definitively acquitted of an offence and who is subsequently charged with the same offence. Under section 11(h) of the Charter, he has the right to resist being tried for this offence once again. The second situation is that of a person who has in the past been definitively declared guilty of and punished for an offence and who is subsequently charged with the same offence again. Section 11(h) ensures that he will not be tried or punished a second time for that same offence.

The wording of section 11(h) is such that an accused is guaranteed recourse to this special plea only where two conditions are met:

(1) The offences must be identical, involving identical charges and an identical cause (in other words, the identical offences must relate to the same object in the same criminal transaction); and
(2) The previous trial must have concluded with a verdict of acquittal or with a verdict of guilt followed by sentencing.

These conditions are narrower and more onerous than those by which Canadian criminal law admits recourse to the pleas of *autrefois acquit* or *autrefois convict*.

(a) Identity of Offences

Section 11(h) speaks specifically of the right of the person charged with an offence for which he has been finally acquitted or for which he has been finally found guilty and punished, "not to be tried *for it* again". It thus appears to guarantee recourse to the *autrefois* pleas only in cases where subsequent proceedings deal with exactly the same offence as that for which the accused has been acquitted or punished. It appears that this formulation does not readily lend itself to the more flexible concept of the identity of offences with which we are familiar or the criteria recognized by statute or the common law to determine whether two offences are identical for this purpose. The rules on point in the *Criminal Code* itself go far beyond what the language of section 11(h) appears to contemplate and so offer a wider protection for an accused than the constitutional guarantee.

Such a protection is section 537(2)(a) [609(2)(a)] of the *Criminal Code* which specifically provides that the applicability of the pleas of *autrefois acquit* or *autrefois convict* must be judged by the "in peril test".[203] Nor does the guarantee include the rules by which the *Criminal Code* has

---

203 Friedland, *supra*, note 195 at 101-109.

broadened the requirement of identity of charges: section 537(1)(a) [609(1)(a)] of the *Criminal Code* allows pleas of *autrefois* where the offence of which a person is accused is a lesser offence included in the one for which the accused has already answered. Section 538(1) [610(1)] of the Code bars a subsequent indictment when the offence differs only with regard to aggravating circumstances. Nor are the special provisions of the *Criminal Code* in matters of homicide (section 538(2), (3) and (4) [610 (2), (3) and (4)]) covered by section 11(h) of the Charter.

If any or all of the above rules are not encompassed by this section, one could nevertheless argue that they form part of the principles of fundamental justice enshrined in section 7 of the Charter, at least in cases where a person's right to life, liberty or security of the person is in question.[204]

Given the wording of section 11(h), it is clear that an accused cannot rely on it where he is charged with two different offences. As the court affirmed in *R. v. Krug*,[205] this provision of the Charter applies only "if the offences involved are identical in that they contain the same elements and constitute one and the same offence arising out of the same set of circumstances". This explains why section 11(h) is not violated when a person who has been convicted of attempted murder, for example, is charged with and convicted of using a fire arm during the commission of the same criminal offence,[206] or when a person is convicted of both refusing to provide a sample of his breath and driving while his abilities were impaired.[207]

The requirement of strict identity of offences clearly set out in section 11(h) of the Charter has the effect of removing from the reach of this provision the defences of *issue estoppel* and *res judicata*.[208] In both cases, these defences are applicable only where a person has been charged with different offences. However, as the courts have pointed out on a number of occasions, these defences very likely form part of the principles of

---

204 By way of analogy see the comment of Mr. Justice La Forest in *Canada v. Schmidt*, *supra*, note 20 at 520-529.

205 (1982), 7 C.C.C. (3d) 324 at 331-332 (Ont. Dist. Ct.), aff'd (1983), 7 C.C.C. (3d) 337 (Ont. C.A.), rev'd in part [1985] 2 S.C.R. 255.

206 *R. v. Travers* (1985), 14 C.C.C. (3d) 34 (N.S.C.A.); *R. v. Morin* (1983), 24 Sask. R. 57 (Q.B.).

207 *R. v. Dacey* (1983), 61 N.S.R. (2d) 255 (C.A.).

208 *R. v. Krug*, *supra*, note 205; *R. v. Travers*, *supra*, note 206. *Contra: R. v. Morgentaler* (1985), 22 C.C.C. (3d) 353 (Ont. C.A.), rev'd [1988] 1 S.C.R. 30. M.L. Friedland, "Criminal Justice and the Charter", (1983), 12 *Man. L.J.* 549 at 568; P.W. Hogg, *Constitutional Law of Canada*, 2nd ed. (Toronto: Carswell, 1985), at 777.

fundamental justice protected by section 7 of the Charter.[209]

Finally, one must note the important judgment of the Supreme Court of Canada in *Wigglesworth v. R.*,[210] where a Royal Canadian Mounted Police officer, found guilty of a disciplinary offence, invoked section 11(h) of the Charter to challenge *Criminal Code* charges laid against him which were based on the same facts. The judgment of the court in this case restricts, in principle, the rights set out in section 11 to "persons prosecuted by the State for public offences involving punitive sanctions, i.e., criminal, quasi-criminal and regulatory offences".[211] However, in exceptional circumstances, a person accused of a disciplinary offence may benefit from the rights guaranteed by section 11 if the offence were to "involve the imposition of true penal consequences". This was the case in *Wigglesworth*. Nevertheless, the majority of the court, following *R. v. Prince*,[212] held that disciplinary offences are separate and distinct from criminal offences for the purposes of applying the double jeopardy rule set out in section 11(h) of the Charter. In the result, Wigglesworth had not been judged and punished twice for the same offence.[213]

(b) Previous Acquittal or Conviction

Only a person who has already been finally acquitted, or finally convicted and punished, for an offence can benefit from the rule prohibiting double jeopardy. This is explicitly stated in section 11(h) of the Charter and it has been confirmed many times by the courts which have refused to apply this constitutional provision where proceedings commenced against an accused have for some reason been interrupted before an acquittal or conviction, or the acquittal or conviction has not yet become final due to an appeal.

This explains why an accused who is discharged following a preliminary inquiry may not invoke section 11(h) to prevent a new prosecution for the same offence being commenced against him. His discharge does

---

209 *R. v. Travers, supra*, note 206 at 55-56 (dissenting opinion of Jones J.A.); *R. v. Morgentaler, supra*, note 208; *R. v. Leskiw* (1986), 26 C.C.C. (3d) 166 (Ont. Dist. Ct.); *R. v. T.R. (No. 2)* (1984), 11 C.C.C. (3d) 49 (Alta. Q.B.). See the comment of Madam Justice Wilson regarding "the possibility that constitutionally guaranteed procedural protections may be available in a particular case under s. 7 of the Charter even though s. 11 is not available": *Wigglesworth v. R., supra*, note 22 at 562.

210 *Supra*, note 22.

211 *Ibid.* at 554.

212 [1986] 2 S.C.R. 480.

213 See also *Trumbley v. Metropolian Toronto Police*, [1987] 2 S.C.R. 577, and *Trimm v. Durham Regional Police*, [1987] 2 S.C.R. 582.

not amount to a judgment of acquittal.[214] (He may, however, have grounds to claim an abuse of process.) The result is the same where new charges are laid after Crown counsel has directed that proceedings be stayed because of an error in the indictment.[215] The position is different, of course, where the court itself orders that the proceedings be stayed permanently, for such a decision amounts to an acquittal.[216]

Section 11(h) does not prevent the holding of a new trial where the jury is released because it cannot agree on a verdict[217] or where the Attorney General successfully appeals from a verdict of acquittal. In neither of these two cases is there a final conviction or acquittal. Moreover, section 11(h) probably does not invalidate provisions in the *Criminal Code* which enable the Attorney General, in certain cases, to appeal from a judgment or verdict of acquittal,[218] although the arguments to the contrary are not lacking in merit.[219]

Finally, it should be stressed that a person against whom extradition proceedings are taken cannot invoke section 11(h) to prevent his extradition to a foreign state by arguing that he has already been acquitted or found guilty in the foreign state of the offence of which he is accused. The Supreme Court has rightfully determined that the Charter does not apply to criminal procedures in the country requesting the extradition, that the extradition hearing is not a trial and that the person subject to such a hearing is not being tried in Canada.[220] It is before the court in the foreign state that a person would have to argue his objection to being tried again.

(c) Punishment

The right not to be punished again for an offence for which one has already been found guilty and punished has generated considerable litigation. Frequently, the commission of a penal or criminal offence not only results in the imposition of the penalty attached to that offence, but is also accompanied by other consequences of a punitive nature. In such

---

214 *Re Michaud and Min. of Justice (N.B.)* 1982), 3 C.C.C. (3d) 325 (N.B.Q.B.); *Re Lamberti and Didkowski and R.* (1983), 26 Sask. R. 213 (Q.B.); *Re Oshaweetok and R.* (1985), 16 C.C.C. (3d) 392 (N.W.T.S.C.).

215 *Re Burrows and R.* (1983), 6 C.C.C. (3d) 54 (Man. C.A.), leave to appeal to S.C.C. refused (1983), 150 D.L.R. (3d) 317n (S.C.C.). See also *R. v. Leskiw, supra*, note 209; *R. v. Timmons* (1985), 69 N.S.R. (2d) 133 (T.D.).

216 *R. v. Jewitt*, [1985] 2 S.C.R. 128.

217 *R. v. Misra* (1985), 44 C.R. (3d) 179 (Sask. Q.B.).

218 *R. v. Morgentaler, supra*, note 208; *R. v. Century 21 Ramos Realty Inc.* (1987), 32 C.C.C. (3d) 353 (Ont. C.A.), leave to appeal to S.C.C. refused (1987), 38 C.C.C. (3d) vi (note) (S.C.C.). Friedland, *supra*, note 208 at 569.

219 Manning, *supra*, note 61 at 425-426..

220 *Canada v. Schmidt, supra*, note 20.

cases, it is arguable that the person has been punished more than once for the same offence.

Often a person found guilty of a criminal offence will also, as a consequence of his conviction, experience sanctions of a civil or administrative nature,[221] such as the loss or suspension of a licence, the forfeiture of certain property,[222] dismissal from a police force of which he is a member,[223] refusal of his application for citizenship[224] or even an order of deportation.[225] Sometimes the administrative sanction is imposed even prior to the conviction in criminal proceedings.[226] In all such cases, the courts have held, albeit for different reasons, that the imposition of civil or administrative sanctions provides no grounds for invoking the protection against double punishment contained in section 11(h).

The courts have also rejected attempts by persons subject to probation orders to invoke section 11(h) to avoid being tried both for the commission of a criminal offence and for failure to comply with the probation order.[227]

Finally, attempts have also been made to question the validity of *Criminal Code* provisions which provide for a greater sentence where the accused is a second offender. The argument that such provisions effectively impose new punishment for the first offence has not succeeded.[228] The same result would be reached respecting the provisions of Part XXI [XXIV] of the *Criminal Code*, which allow the courts to declare someone a dangerous offender and to impose a sentence of imprisonment for an indeterminate period taking into account his previous convictions.

It is well known that the *National Defence Act*[229] included provisions which, in certain circumstances, deprived a member of the armed forces of the plea of *autrefois convict*. Contrary to ordinary criminal law principles,

---

221 *R. v. Huber* (1985), 36 M.V.R. 10 (Ont. C.A.) leave to appeal to S.C.C. refused (1985), 36 M.V.R. xxxviii (note) (S.C.C.); *Johnston v. Superintendent of Motor Vehicles* (1987), 27 C.R.R. 206 (B.C.S.C.). See also *Hardy v. Manitoba Public Insurance Corp.* (1984), 28 M.V.R. 101 (Man. Co. Ct.).

222 *Re R. and Green* (1983), 5 C.C.C. (3d) 95 (Ont. H.C.); *R. v. Sewid* (1986), 1 W.C.B. (2d) 319 (B.C. Co. Ct.).

223 *MacDonald v. Marriott* (1984), 7 D.L.R. (4th) 697 (B.C.S.C.).

224 *Re Citizenship Act and re Noailles*, [1985] 1 F.C. 852 (T.D.).

225 *Re Gittens and R.* (1982), 68 C.C.C. (2d) 438 (F.C.T.D.).

226 *Re Eagle Disposal Systems Ltd. and Min. of Environment* (1983), 9 C.C.C. (3d) 500 (Ont. H.C.) aff'd (1984), 47 O.R. (2d) 332 (C.A.); *R. v. Ferraro* (1983), 10 W.C.B. 204 (Ont. Prov. Ct.); *Layers v. Min. of Finance* (1985), 16 C.R.R. 17 (B.C.S.C.).

227 *R. v. Daniels* (1985), 44 C.R. (3d) 184 (Sask. Q.B.). See also with respect to probation orders: *R. v. Linklater* (1983), 9 C.C.C. (3d) 217 (Y.T.C.A.); *R. v. Elendiuk* (1986), 27 C.C.C (3d) 94 (Alta. C.A.); and with respect to mandatory supervision under the *Parole Act: R. v. De Baie* (1983), 6 C.R.R. 204 (N.S.C.A.); and *R. v. Belliveau; Belliveau v. Warden of Dorchester Penitentiary* (1984), 55 N.B.R. (2d) 82 (C.A.).

228 *R. v. Bourne* (1983), 21 M.V.R. 216 (B.C.S.C.).

229 *Supra*, note 104.

the Act allowed a civil court to retry a member of the armed forces for an offence for which he had already been found guilty and punished by a service tribunal. This excessively harsh rule, long devoid of any justification, has been severely criticized by Friedland in particular.[230] I have also tried to demonstrate the conflict between this rule and section 11(h). Moreover, it would be mistaken in my view to think that section 1 of the Charter could be used to attempt to justify such a serious limitation of one of the fundamental principles of criminal law.[231]

Fortunately, this situation was recently corrected by the *Statute Law (Canadian Charter of Rights and Freedoms), Amendment Act* which repealed sections 56 [66] 61 [71] and 129 [151] and replaced them with new provisions.[232] These sections clearly state that a person subject to the *Code of Service Discipline,* who has been acquitted or found guilty and punished by a service tribunal or by a civil court, cannot be tried again for the same offence or for "any other substantially similar offence arising out of the facts that gave rise to the offence". In the result, any conflict with section 11(h) has been effectively cured.

5. PROTECTION AGAINST CRUEL AND UNUSUAL TREATMENT OR PUNISHMENT (S. 12)

In affirming that "[e]veryone has the right not to be subjected to any cruel and unusual treatment or punishment", section 12 of the Charter gives constitutional recognition to a right which already was set out in section 2(b) of the *Canadian Bill of Rights.*[233] Although the wording of the two texts is different, there is little evidence that these differences (like the one which is evident between the French and English versions of section 12 itself[234]) have been used to justify giving a new interpretation to the constitutional guarantee. The courts have generally taken the view that there is no reason not to follow decisions based on the *Bill of Rights.* Indeed, it is arguable that section 12 of the Charter has retained the overt aspects of section 2(b) which served to justify a strict interpretation of the provision:

---

230 *Supra*, note 195 at 350-351.
231 A. Morel, "Certain Guarantees of Criminal Procedure", Chapter 12 of the first edition of this work, *supra*, note 138 at 386-389.
232 S.C. 1985, c. 26, ss. 50, 51, 52 [R.S.C. 1985, c. 31 (1st Supp.), ss. 45, 46, 47]. The provision of Part III (ss. 48-65 [42-57]) concerning the *National Defence Act* came into force on October 2, 1986: SI/86-192.
233 "[N]o law of Canada shall be construed or applied so as to ... (b) impose or authorize the imposition of cruel and unusual treatment or punishment".
234 The English version of section 12 puts more emphasis on the infliction of the punishment than the French which states: *"Chacun a droit à la protection contre tous traitements ou peines cruels et inusités."*

first, the retention of the adjective "unusual" to describe the prohibited treatment or punishment and, second, the use of the expression "cruel *and* unusual" instead of "cruel *or* unusual".[235] As a result, arguments in favour of changing past attitudes[236] can be based on little more than the bare fact that this norm has now been entrenched in the Constitution and that there now exists a "new constitutional mandate for judicial review".[237] It may be of some use to recall the main points of the case law which predates the Charter.

Section 2(b) of the *Bill of Rights* has been invoked before the courts on many occasions since 1960 and its scope appears to be well established.[238] In particular, a review of the leading cases based on the *Bill of Rights* clearly shows that the punishment or treatment had to be both cruel *and* unusual before there was a violation of the provision. The courts have consistently held that the clear language of section 2(b) required a conjunctive reading: thus, punishment was declared valid even though it is cruel so long as it is not also unusual.

This reading was recognized by the Manitoba Court of Appeal as early as 1965. The court refused to rule inoperative section 136 of the *Criminal Code*[239] which, until modified in 1972,[240] permitted a sentence of whipping for an individual found guilty of rape. Without deciding on the cruelty of the punishment, Mr. Justice Schultz remarked that corporal punishment was in use in society and that furthermore the whip was a punishment which was a part of our legal system well before 1960.[241] Other courts later came to the same conclusion when the validity of other provisions of the *Criminal Code* were disputed, namely, sections 660 and 661 of the Code (now sections 688 [753] and 689 [754]), allowing the

---

235 It must be underlined that the text of the Charter does not conform in this regard with art. 7 of the *International Covenant on Civil and Political Rights* which states that: "No one shall be subjected to torture or to cruel, inhuman or degrading treatment or punishment."

236 *R. v. Therens, supra,* note 121 at 639 (Le Dain J.).

237 *R. v. Smith, supra,* note 81 at 1069.

238 K. Lippel, "In the Light of the Recent Supreme Court Judgment: *Regina v. Miller & Cockriell*" (1977), 12 *R.J.T.* 355; S. Berger, "The Application of the Cruel and Unusual Punishment Clause under the *Canadian Bill of Rights*" (1978), 24 *McGill L.J.* 161; J.S. Leon, "Cruel and Unusual Punishment: Sociological Jurisprudence and the Canadian Bill of Rights" (1978), 36 *U.T.Fac.L. Rev.* 222; W.S. Tarnopolsky, "Just Desserts or Cruel and Unusual Treatment or Punishment? Where Do We Look for Guidance" (1978), 10 *Ottawa L. Rev.* 1; M. Jackson, "Cruel and Unusual Treatment or Punishment?" (1982), *U.B.C. L. Rev.* (Charter ed.) 189.

239 Replaced by s. 144, subsequently repealed S.C. 1980-81-82, c. 125, s. 6.

240 *Criminal Law Amendment Act, 1972, supra,* note 101, s. 70.

241 *R. v. Dick* [1965] 1 C.C.C. 171 (Man. C.A.).

court to impose indeterminate detention on an accused declared a habitual criminal and today termed a dangerous offender, and[242] sections 523 and 526 of the Code (now sections 542 [614] and 546 [618]) authorizing detention of an accused who is insane until the pleasure of the lieutenant governor is known.[243] In 1976, the Ontario Court of Appeal adopted similar reasoning and reversed the decision of a trial judge that he was not bound by the provisions of section 5(2) of the *Narcotic Control Act*,[244] providing for a minimum sentence of 7 years' imprisonment for a person found guilty of the offence of importing narcotics. Under the circumstances of the case, the punishment appeared both cruel and unusual because it was disproportionate.[245] Arnup J.A. felt that, on the contrary, the minimum sentence of imprisonment prescribed by the Act could not be qualified as cruel where Parliament was clearly of the view that such a sentence was necessary in order that it have the desired dissuasive effect.[246]

Finally, in *Miller v. R.*,[247] the Supreme Court of Canada had to determine the validity of the death penalty in the context of section 2(b) of the *Canadian Bill of Rights*. The court unanimously decided that the provisions of the *Criminal Code* which prescribed the death penalty for persons found guilty of the murder of a police officer or prison guard,[248] were not in breach of the *Bill of Rights*. Mr. Justice Ritchie emphasized that the adjectives "cruel and unusual" must be "read conjunctively" and that "having regard to the fact that the death penalty for murder had been a part of the law of England from time immemorial and that, at the time when this murder was committed and the trial was held, it had been a feature of the criminal law of Canada since Confederation, it cannot be said to have been 'unusual' punishment in the ordinary accepted meaning of that word".[249]

But Chief Justice Laskin, supported by Spence J. and Dickson J., did not agree with this reasoning. He proposed another approach according to which the two terms are "interacting expressions colouring each other, so to speak, and hence to be considered together as a compendious expression of a norm."[250] He felt that the criterion to apply was "whether

---

242 *R. v. Buckler*, [1970] 2 O.R. 614 (Prov. Ct.); and *R. v. Roestad*, [1972] 1 O.R. 814 (Co. Ct.), application for leave to appeal refused 19 C.R.N.S. 235n (Ont. C.A.).

243 *Ex parte Kleinys* (1965), 49 D.L.R. (2d) 225 (B.C.S.C.).

244 R.S.C. 1970, c. N-1 [now R.S.C. 1985, c. N-1].

245 *R. v. Shand* (1976), 64 D.L.R. (3d) 626 (Ont. Co. Ct.), rev'd *infra*, note 246.

246 *R. v. Shand* (1977), 70 D.L.R. (3d) 395 (Ont. C.A.).

247 [1977] 2 S.C.R. 680.

248 These were ss. 214 and 218 of the 1970 *Criminal Code*.

249 *Miller v. R.*, *supra*, note 247 at 706.

250 *Ibid.* at 690.

the punishment prescribed is so excessive as to outrage standards of decency".[251]

As has been the case regarding other provisions in the Charter, some courts have relied on the minority judgment of Chief Justice Laskin to justify their departure from the narrow interpretation prevalent under the *Bill of Rights* and to give a broader scope to the constitutional guarantee.[252] Moreover, it is this approach that the Supreme Court of Canada recently adopted in its judgment in *R. v. Smith*.[253] The court here ends the debate as to whether the expression "cruel and unusual" is disjunctive or conjunctive by adopting the interpretation of Laskin C.J., according to which these words are the "compendious expression of a norm". There is thus a violation of the right set out in section 12 of the Charter if the punishment or treatment "is so excessive as to outrage standards of decency".[254]

In order to determine the scope of this constitutional provision, Mr. Justice McIntyre, in the same decision, provided an historical analysis which is extremely illuminating and to my mind conclusive.

It is well known that the English *Bill of Rights* of 1688-89 first prohibited the imposition of "cruel and unusual punishment" in an effort to end the resort to arbitrary and barbarous punishments for an unduly repressive purpose, as practised under the reign of the Stuarts. Not surprisingly, the same prohibition was written into the Eighth Amendment to the *American Constitution* in 1791. However, if the sole effect of section 12 of the *Canadian Charter* were to control the *nature* of punishments inflicted and to prevent Parliament or the courts from inventing inhuman punishments, one would have to agree with Mr. Justice McIntyre that this constitutional provision would be nearly obsolete, for the danger of such punishments being inflicted today is, to say the least, remote. Furthermore, the concept of cruel and unusual punishment has evolved in the course of the twentieth century so as to include punishment which, because of its extreme severity or excessive duration, appears to be *disproportionate* given the seriousness of the offence and other relevant circumstances. Finally, both the *Canadian Bill of Rights* and subsequently the Charter broadened the original prohibition of cruel and unusual punishment to "treatment" as well. This would include in particular the *conditions*

---

251 *Ibid.* at 688.
252 *R. v. Tobac* (1985), 20 C.C.C. (3d) 49 (N.W.T.C.A.); *Re Gittens and R.*, *supra*, note 225; *Re Mitchell and R.* (1983), 6 C.C.C. (3d) 193 (Ont. H.C.); *Re Moore and R.* (1984), 10 C.C.C. (3d) 306 (Ont. H.C.); *R. v. Morrison* (1983), 10 W.C.B. 171 (Ont. Co. Ct.).
253 *Supra*, note 81.
254 *Ibid.* at 1072 (Lamer J.) and 1088-1089 (McIntyre J.).

governing the application of punishment or the conditions under which sentences are served.[255]

Punishment or treatment can therefore be cruel and unusual because of its very nature or because it is disproportionate. The same is true, in my view, of arbitrary punishment or treatment. Lastly, one will have to examine the question of how the reasonable limits provision of section 1 of the Charter may apply to section 12.

(a) Punishment or Treatment which is Cruel and Unusual by its Very Nature

The original prohibition on the use of cruel and unusual punishment was meant to suppress the practice of condemning individuals to punishment which was essentially cruel by its very nature and to which it was not usual to have recourse. The suppression of the more barbarous of the punishments practised by previous generations does not take away the original import of this prohibition, even if today that is no longer its only significance. Moreover, the conception of what is a fundamentally cruel punishment is relative and changes depending on the level of progress achieved by society. History teaches us as much. One need only think of the atrocious means used to carry out a sentence of capital punishment for high treason, accepted in England until 1814 and in Canada until 1868.[256] Clearly, what constitutes cruel punishment *per se* can only be determined by reference to the moral standards of a society, and such standards evolve, often rapidly.

Our judgment of the quality or nature of punishment or treatment is determined in large measure by our appreciation of what human dignity entails and the degree to which it should be respected. Cruel and unusual punishment or treatment is, first and foremost, punishment or treatment which is *per se* so excessive as to outrage standards of decency. As Chief Justice Laskin observed: "This is not a precise formula for section 2(b), but I doubt whether a more precise one can be found."[257]

There are, in my view, punishments and treatments which inherently, by their very nature or because of the way they are applied, violate section 12 of the Charter. It would seem to follow that, if certain punishments or treatments are *always* incompatible with human dignity, one does not have to inquire, as did Mr. Justice Lamer in the *Smith* case, whether the

---

255 *Ibid.* at 1086-1087.

256 54 Geo III, s. 146 and 33-34 Vict., c. 23, s. 31 (England); and 1867-68, 31 Vict., c. 69, s.4 (Canada). See W. Vondenvelden, *The Trial of David McLane for High Treason* (Québec: 1797).

257 *Miller v. R., supra*, note 247 at 688.

effect of the sentence "is grossly disproportionate to what would have been appropriate", for, having said that, he must then observe that "the effect of the sentence ... includes its nature"[258] — an observation that is somewhat surprising. The effect of the punishment is not a relevant criterion here.

While the analysis just referred to seems inappropriate and open to challenge in my view, the basic position adopted by Lamer J. and McIntyre J. is sound: corporal punishments such as the lash, which was abolished only 15 years ago, are by their very nature incompatible with contemporary standards of respect for the human person. The same can be said of surgical interventions such as lobotomy or castration if they were imposed on certain categories of criminals.[259] If that is so, one will no doubt wonder all the more how the death penalty, assuming it were to be re-established by Parliament, could escape the same censure. The death penalty nonetheless is still a punishment under current military law for certain serious military offences.[260] If such punishment, like all forms of corporal punishment, is by its very nature inconsistent with human dignity, it is difficult to see how it could be justified by showing that it is not inordinately disproportionate to the seriousness of certain crimes.

It is obvious, however, that certain kinds of treatment, rather than punishment, will more frequently lend themselves to challenge on the ground that by their very nature or quality they are contrary to the norm enshrined in section 12 of the Charter. The living conditions (either normal or exceptional) of incarcerated offenders provide a number of examples. Here is a world where the "civilizing influence"[261] of the twentieth century has not yet fully penetrated. Without passing judgment on future cases which might come before the courts, Mr. Justice McIntyre does mention a number of situations where the type of treatment to which prisoners are subjected could possibly be challenged:

> the frequency and conditions of searches within prisons,[262] dietary restrictions as a disciplinary measure, ... denial of contact with those outside the prison, and imprisonment at locations far distant from home, family and friends, a condition amounting to virtual exile which is particularly relevant to women since there is only one federal penitentiary for women in Canada.[263]

---

258 *R. v. Smith, supra,* note 81 at 1073.

259 *Ibid.* at 1074, 1087. See the *Sexual Sterilization Act,* S.A. 1928, c. 37 (later R.S.A. 1970, c. 341, repealed 1972, c. 87); and the *Sexual Sterilization Act,* S.B.C. 1933, c. 59 (found also in R.S.B.C. 1960, c. 353, repealed 1973, c. 79).

260 *National Defence Act, supra,* note 104, ss. 63-66 [73-76], 68-70 [78-80], 95 [105].

261 The expression is borrowed from Mr. Justice McIntyre in *Smith, supra,* note 81 at 1086.

262 *Weatherall v. A.G. Canada* (1987), 59 C.R. (3d) 247 (F.C.T.D.), rev'd in part (*sub nom. Weatherall v. Canada*) (1988), 65 C.R. (3d) 27 (F.C.A.).

263 *R. v. Smith, supra,* note 81 at 1087. By way of illustration, see *Collin v. Kaplan* (1982), 1 C.C.C. (3d) 309 (F.C.T.D.); *Re Maltby and A.G. Sask.* (1982), 2 C.C.C. (3d) 153

One will also have to look closely at the effect of section 12 on regulations which authorize the segregation of prisoners in solitary confinement, including the conditions under which such confinement is administered. This type of punishment or treatment could be cruel and unusual not only because it is excessive in specific circumstances, but also because of its intrinsic nature. It will be remembered that the Federal Court in *McCann v. R.*[264] found that the methods used to impose solitary confinement on prisoners at New Westminster, British Columbia, were cruel and unusual within the meaning of the *Bill of Rights*. As for the court's conclusion that the solitary confinement of certain prisoners was a necessary measure to ensure order and discipline, this is not necessarily determinative of the question today under the new constitutional provision.

Finally, there is little doubt that an order of deportation is not, in and of itself, a cruel and unusual punishment or treatment. However, to the extent that Cabinet decisions are subject to Charter scrutiny and the executive branch of government is bound by the provisions of the Charter,[265] there is reason to believe that the execution of a deportation order in some circumstances could contravene section 12 of the Charter. This could occur if the person subject to deportation has serious reasons to fear that he will become a victim of persecution in the country to which he is being deported.[266]

(b) Punishment or Treatment which is Disproportionate

Punishment or treatment which is not in itself cruel and unusual can nevertheless become so if it is excessive. In the *Smith* decision,[267] the Supreme Court of Canada ruled unanimously that excessive punishment or treatment can violate the guarantee set out in section 12 of the Charter. But whereas, for Mr. Justice McIntyre, the punishment must be "so excessive as to outrage standards of decency", Mr. Justice Lamer took the view that the test to apply is the less demanding one of "gross disproportionality". In the view of McIntyre J., the punishment provided in law or imposed

---

(Sask. Q.B.), aff'd (1984), 13 C.C.C. (3d) 308 (Sask. C.A.) *Re Soenen and Thomas* (1983), 8 C.C.C. (3d) 224 (Alta. Q.B.); *R. v. Hudye* (1983), 7 C.R.R. 363 (Sask. Prov. Ct.); *Piché v. Solicitor-General Canada* (1984), 17 C.C.C. (3d) 1 (F.C.T.D.); *Weatherall v. A.G. Canada, supra,* note 262. P. Russell, "Cruel and Unusual Treatment or Punishment: The Use of Section 12 in Prison Litigation" (1985), 43 *U.T. Fac. L. Rev.* 185. Reference should also be made to the views of A. Manson, "Fresh Approaches to Defining Cruel and Unusual Treatment or Punishment" (1983), 35 C.R. (3d) 262.

264 [1976] 1 F.C. 570 (C.A.). See also *R. v. Bruce* (1977), 36 C.C.C. (2d) 158 (B.C.S.C.).

265 *Operation Dismantle Inc. v. R.,* [1985] 1 S.C.R. 441 at 455; *Canada v. Schmidt, supra,* note 20 at 518, 521-522.

266 *Contra: Re Gittens and R., supra,* note 225; *Re Vincent and Min. of Employment & Immigration* (1983), 148 D.L.R. (3d) 385 (F.C.A.).

267 *Supra,* note 81.

by a court could be inappropriate without necessarily violating the constitutional prohibition. Mr. Justice Lamer appears to place the threshold lower by requiring only that the effect of the punishment not be grossly disproportionate to what would have been appropriate.[268]

Everyone will agree that punishment can be excessive or disproportionate because of its severity or its duration as measured against the seriousness of the offence and the objective sought. Thus, to use some of the examples offered by Lamer J., a sentence of 20 years' imprisonment for a first offence against property, or one of three months that had to be served in solitary confinement, would clearly be unconstitutional.[269]

Because the test of proportionality is essentially relative, it follows that the mandatory minimal prison terms prescribed for certain offences are not in themselves cruel and unusual. In the majority of cases where the legislator has established such sentences, neither their length nor their severity can be considered excessive, still less, grossly disproportionate, whether the offences in question relate to the use of fire arms (section 83 [85] of the *Criminal Code*) or to serious infractions of provincial highway codes.[270]

The same cannot be said of the minimum penalty of seven years' imprisonment provided for by section 5(2) of the *Narcotic Control Act*. Although this provision was challenged under the *Bill of Rights*, it was upheld on the grounds that the punishment was not so excessive as to be unreasonable, having regard to the concern of Parliament to deter the importation of narcotics into the country.[271] However, a majority of judges of the Supreme Court of Canada have found this provision to be contrary to section 12 of the Charter and declared it invalid.[272] The court so ruled because the offence of importing, as defined under the Act, gave rise inevitably to a sentence of imprisonment which was extremely severe, even where the quantity of narcotic being imported was minimal and without regard to the varying degrees of danger of the narcotic or the purpose of importing. For all these reasons, the court found that the punishment of imprisonment was grossly disproportionate. In other words, the punishment is excessive because the offence is defined in such a general and global fashion that it subjects "small offenders" to an undue punishment. The court did not minimize the importance of the fight against importation

---

268 *R. v. Smith, supra,* note 81 at 1090 (McIntyre J.) and 1072 (Lamer J.).
269 *Ibid.* at 1073.
270 *R. v. Krug, supra,* note 205 at 324, 337; *R. v. Konechny* (1983), 10 C.C.C. (3d) 233 (B.C.C.A.); leave to appeal to S.C.C. refused (1984), 25 M.V.R. 132n (S.C.C.); *R. v. Slaney* (1985), 56 Nfld. & P.E.I.R. 1 (Nfld. C.A.); *R. v. Ross* (1985), 32 M.V.R. 261 (B.C.S.C.).
271 *R. v. Shand, supra,* note 246.
272 *R. v. Smith, supra,* note 81.

and trafficking in narcotics, but found that this objective did not justify a sentence so severe as that imposed by the Act where the offence committed was not above a certain level of seriousness.

Applying the criteria established in the *Smith* decision,[273] the Supreme Court of Canada also held in *Lyons v. R.*[274] that a sentence of detention for an indeterminate period of time imposed on those found to be dangerous offenders did not violate section 12 of the Charter. To arrive at this conclusion, the court considered whether the effects of this sentence were grossly disproportionate. The court was sensitive to the fact that the effects of such a sentence are worse than those experienced by a person condemned to a long sentence but for a known number of years. Were it not for the existence of the procedures for parole to which dangerous offenders are subject by virtue of section 695.1 [761] of the *Criminal Code*, the court was apparently prepared to conclude that a sentence of indeterminate detention constitutes cruel punishment. In the view of the court, parole procedures guarantee that the detention of each offender will be limited to whatever is necessary in each particular case, it being understood that section 12 does not require sentences to be "perfectly suited to accommodate the moral nuances of every crime and every offender".[275]

The same arguments were used in *R. v. Milne*[276] to reject the claim that section 12 of the Charter rendered invalid a sentence of indeterminate detention imposed in 1980 on a person found to be dangerous offender, after he had been found guilty of gross indecency. These arguments were relied on despite the fact that the offence of gross indecency is no longer a "serious personal injury offence" and can no longer give rise to a possible sentence of indeterminate detention. It is arguable that the court here has failed to address the essential issue of the grossly disproportionate character of the punishment imposed under a law which constitutes the basis of the continued detention of the offender. Only Mr. Justice Estey, in his dissenting opinion, approached the issue from this point of view.

One must also question whether section 669(a) [742(a)] of the *Criminal Code* is compatible with the guarantee set out in section 12 of the Charter. This provision, read in conjunction with section 674 [747], establishes a rule by which a person sentenced to life imprisonment for high treason or first degree murder is not eligible for parole before 25 years have been served. The minimal sentence of 25 years' imprisonment was passed by Parliament in 1976 as a replacement for capital punishment,

---

273 *Ibid.*
274 *Supra,* note 20. The issue had already been reviewed in *R. v. Langevin* (1984), 11 C.C.C. (3d) 336 (Ont. C.A.); and in *Re Moore and R.* (1984), 10 C.C.C. (3d) 306 (Ont. H.C.).
275 *Lyons v. R., supra,* note 20 at 345.
276 [1987] 2 S.C.R. 512.

which was abolished at the same time. When one considers the anguish and moral suffering caused by this punishment and its impact on the physical and mental health of prisoners, one is certainly moved to ask whether the effects of this sentence are not grossly disproportionate to the desired goal.[277] If the issue were to be determined solely on the basis of sections 669 [742] and 674 [747] of the Code, one could doubtless conclude that such a punishment "is so excessive as to outrage standards of decency". However, given the approach adopted by the Supreme Court in the *Lyons* case[278] to determine the constitutionality of a sentence of indeterminate detention, the courts here are likely to take into account provisions in section 672 [745] of the *Criminal Code* which provide that, after serving 15 years of his sentence, a prisoner may ask for a reduction in his number of years of imprisonment without eligibility for parole.

Finally, it is important to note that where the issue is not the validity of a statutory provision, as in the cases examined above, but involves a sentence imposed by a judge, section 12 of the Charter may be invoked in my view to challenge any sentence that infringes the constitutional guarantee. The position of the offender here is no different from that of an accused who claims that his right under section 11(e) of the Charter has been violated by reason of unreasonable bail conditions attached to his interim release. In both types of cases, section 24(1) of the Charter offers a remedy.

One must recognize however that section 12 does not enshrine in the Constitution a requirement that each sentence imposed must be appropriate to the particular situation of each offender and take into consideration all relevant circumstances and factors. If a judge imposes a sentence which is alleged to be inappropriate, it may be varied by way of an appeal against sentence, not by way of a challenge based on the Charter.

Section 12 does, however, establish a threshold beyond which a sentence is constitutionally invalid, whether the sentence be determined by a statute or imposed by a judge exercising his discretion. Thus, the constitutional norm will be infringed only if the sentence imposed in a given case is inappropriate to the point of being grossly disproportionate or excessive so as to outrage standards of decency.

---

277 S. Cohen & L. Taylor, *Psychological Survival, The Experience of Long-Term Imprisonment,* (Harmondsworth: Penguin Books, 1972, and N.Y.: Pantheon Books, 1972) (their study concerns prisoners in the Durham Prison in England); T.J. Flanagan, "Lifers and Long-Termers: Doing Big Time", in R. Johnson & H. Toch (eds), *The Pains of Imprisonment* (Beverly Hills: Sage Publications, 1982) at 115; International Centre of Comparative Criminology, *Long-Term Imprisonment: An International Seminar,* organized under the direction of Rizkalla, with the assistance of R. Lévey and R. Zauberman (Montreal: October 1977)

278 *Supra*, note 20.

(c) Arbitrary Punishment or Treatment

In the United States, the arbitrary character of a punishment has been identified by the courts as one of the criteria which can help determine whether the punishment is cruel and unusual within the meaning of the Eighth Amendment to the Constitution. Chief Justice Laskin, in *Miller v. R.*,[279] also recognized the relevance of this criterion for the purposes of interpreting section 2(b) of the *Bill of Rights*, although he felt that in the case before him "questions of discretionary, arbitrary or capricious application of the death penalty" did not arise.

However, in the *Smith* case, Mr. Justice Lamer took the view that there was no reason to adopt here the test developed by American courts, primarily on account of the presence in the Canadian Charter of provisions guaranteeing liberty, such as sections 7 and 9.[280] Mr. Justice McIntyre, on the other hand, held that a punishment is cruel and unusual if it is "arbitrarily imposed in the sense that it is not applied on a rational basis in accordance with ascertained or ascertainable standards".[281] A law which imposed a punishment proportionate to the offence committed could nonetheless be arbitrary and violate section 12 if it imposed a punishment "for reasons or in accordance with criteria which are not rationally connected with the objects of the legislation". This would be the case, in his view, if a law prescribed a procedure for determining sentence which was essentially unpredictable, so that offenders in similar circumstances could be punished in unequal ways.[282]

It was a law of this type that was declared invalid by the Supreme Court of the United States in *Furman v. Georgia*,[283] essentially because it gave an uncontrolled discretionary power to a jury to pronounce sentence and to impose, as it saw fit, either a term of imprisonment or the death penalty. In the eyes of the court, such a situation could give rise to sentences which were arbitrary and discriminatory.

Although Canadian criminal law contains no provisions comparable to those challenged in *Furman v. Georgia*, and although there exists elsewhere in the Charter a guarantee of equality before the law, these are not in my view sufficient reasons for concluding that section 12 of

---

279 *Supra*, note 247 at 690.

280 *R. v. Smith*, *supra*, note 81 at 1074-1076.

281 *Ibid.* at 1098.

282 *Ibid.* at 1103-1106. Mr. Justice Le Dain declared himself in agreement with Mr. Justice McIntyre's approach to the application of the criterion of arbitrariness (at 1111); Madam Justice Wilson asserted that the arbitrary nature of the punishment is quite fundamental (at 1109-1110). Mr. Justice La Forest preferred not to state a view on what significance arbitrariness should have in the interpretation of s. 12 (at 1113).

283 408 U.S. 238 (1972).

the Charter offers no protection against sentences which are imposed in an arbitrary or discriminatory fashion, without regard "to standards or principles which are rationally connected to the purposes of the legislation".[284]

(d) Reasonable Limits Under Section One

Although section 1 of the Charter states quite clearly that all rights guaranteed therein may be restricted by law within certain limits set out in the said section, the relationship between sections 1 and 12 raises a number of conceptual difficulties.

No one doubts that the fundamental freedoms, for example, even though they are expressed in absolute terms, can be limited by laws which respect the criteria established in section 1. Similarly, where the rights set out in the Charter are qualified by terms such as reasonable or unreasonable, it is still possible to conceive of statutory limitations which are justifiable in terms of the importance of the legislative objective being pursued. One feels somewhat uncomfortable, however, when it comes to applying the first of the criteria established by the Supreme Court for the application of section 1 to the right guaranteed by section 12 of the Charter. Under this criterion, one must inquire whether the objective which the measure is designed to serve is "of sufficient importance to warrant overriding" the right of every person not to be subjected to cruel and unusual treatment or punishment. To pose this question is implicitly to recognize that the state has the right in some circumstances to inflict punishment or treatment on some members of society that is so excessive that it is degrading to human dignity. Is it conceivable that punishment or treatment capable of being described in such terms could be justifiable in a free and democratic society?

For this reason I share the view of Mr. Justices McIntyre and Le Dain, who state that a punishment or treatment found to be cruel and unusual could not be justified under section 1 of the Charter: "[I]n s. 12, the *Charter* has created an absolute right."[285] This is so because the right enshrined in section 12 is founded on a fundamental and inviolable principle, the dignity of the human person. Recognition of this principle "is the foundation of freedom, justice and peace in the world".[286]

---

284 *R. v. Smith, supra,* note 81 at 1104 (McIntyre).
285 *Ibid.* at 1085 (McIntyre J.) and 1111 (Le Dain J.).
286 Preamble to the *Universal Declaration of Human Rights* of 1948.

14

The Equality Rights*

William Black and Lynn Smith

1. Introduction
2. The Meaning of Equality
3. Institutional Considerations
4. The Constitutional Context
5. Possible Tests for Inequality in the Context of Judicial Review of Laws Under Section 15
6. Remedies
7. Conclusion

1. INTRODUCTION

The equality provisions of the *Canadian Charter of Rights and Freedoms* represent a new era in Canadian constitutional law. Yet those provisions have numerous and venerable antecedents. The history is far too extensive to allow even the most cursory summary here, but the few

---

* We wish to thank the following for their assistance in the research and preparation of this chapter: Janet Kee, Patrick Madaisky and Ron Parks, We gratefully acknowledge funding assistance from the British Columbia Ministry of the Attorney General.
Note: see Addendum to Chapter 14, p. 648.

examples which follow may give scme sense of the rich history on which the Charter builds.

(a) Historical Sources

As our predecessor in this work noted, the notion of equality as a moral and social ideal can be traced at least as far back as Aristotle.[1] What we now call the principle of formal equality is directly traceable to Aristotle.[2] The concept of equality can also be traced to biblical sources,[3] though Christian doctrine and practice has not always reflected those sources.

In the middle ages, the equality ideal was kept alive by theologians such as St. Augustine, but was virtually inverted in the Augustinian view that all men are equally mired in sin though divine grace may intervene to elevate some.[4] It was not until the seventeenth century that the ideal of social and political equality gained currency through the works of philosophers such as Locke and Rousseau.[5] While these two philosophers did not entirely agree on the nature of the concept of equality, both believed that equality and the autonomy of the individual derived from the natural order. These philosophical ideas were incorporated into the French *Declaration of the Rights of Man and of the Citizen*. The American *Declaration of Independence* also referred to the principle of equality, though it was almost another century before slavery was abolished and the principle was incorporated into the United States Constitution.[6]

More recently, the events of World War II prompted new initiatives to incorporate the principle of equality into both domestic and international

---

1. See W. Tarnopolsky, "The Equality Rights", in Chapter 13 of the first edition of this work, W. Tarnopolsky & G. Beaudoin, eds., *The Canadian Charter of Rights and Freedoms: Commentary* (Toronto: Carswell, 1982) 395 at 398.

2 "Equality consists of treating equals equally and unequals unequally": see P.G. Polyviou, *The Equal Protection of the Laws* (London: Duckworth, 1980) at 7; Aristotle, *Ethics*, Book III.

3 Galatians 3:26-29.

4 S.I. Benn, "Equality, Moral and Social" in P. Edward, ed., *The Encyclopedia of Philosophy* (London: Collier & MacMillan, 1967) Vol. 3, p. 38 at 39.

5 J. Locke, *Second Treatise on Civil Government* (Oxford: Blackwell, 1956), ch. 2; J.-J. Rousseau, *Origin of Inequality* (Chicago: Encyclopedia Brittanica, 1952); J.-J. Rousseau, *On the Social Contract* (New York: St. Martins Press, 1978) at 143-144.

6 In both France and the United States, political theories were influenced strongly by the concept of liberty as well as equality, and over time the tension between these principles became apparent. Indeed, the concept of liberty was sometimes interpreted as precluding any law that would intrude into the private sphere for the purpose of re-distributing economic wealth. See L. Tremblay, "Section 7 of the Charter: Substantive Due Process?" (1984), 18 *U.B.C. L. Rev.* 201 at 213-223.

law. The *Charter of the United Nations* pledged to promote "universal respect for, and observance of, human rights and fundamental freedoms for all without distinction as to race, sex, language, or religion".[7] This pledge was translated into a series of documents, the first of which was the *Universal Declaration of Human Rights*. Later United Nations documents elaborated on the themes of the *Universal Declaration*. Some afford a mechanism by which complaints can be adjudicated and provide an important source of jurisprudence. The most notable of these documents are the *International Covenant on Civil and Political Rights*[8] and the *International Covenant on Economic, Cultural and Social Rights*,[9] both of which Canada ratified in 1976. The latter Covenant seems in many respects to reflect concepts of distributive justice going well beyond formal equality.[10]

The decades following World War II saw important developments at the regional and national levels. The *European Declaration of Human Rights* came into effect in 1953 and was eventually ratified by more than 20 nations, including the United Kingdom.[11] A number of Commonwealth countries incorporated equality guarantees into their constitutions when they achieved independence.[12]

7　L.M. Goodrich, *The United Nations* (1960), at 349 *et seq.*; see also ch. XI, "The Protection of Human Rights", at 242.

8　Adopted December 16, 1966; in force in Canada August 19, 1976; G.A. Res. 220 (XXI), 21 U.N. GAOR, supp. (No. 16), 52, U.N. Doc. A/6316 (1966).

9　Adopted December 16, 1966, in force in Canada August 19, 1976; G.A. Res. 220 (XXI), 21 U.N. GAOR, supp. (No. 16), 49, U.N. Doc. A/6316.

10　As well as the international instruments discussed in this paper, there are numerous others which address specific types of discrimination. These include: *International Convention on the Elimination of All Forms of Racial Discrimination*, adopted December 21, 1965, in force for Canada November 13, 1970, 660 U.N.T.S. 195; *Convention on the Elimination of all Forms of Discrimination Against Women*, adopted December 18, 1979, in force for Canada January 10, 1982, U.N. Doc. A/RES/34/180; *Declaration on the Elimination of All Forms of Intolerance and of Discrimination Based on Religion or Belief*, proclaimed by the General Assembly November 25, 1981, G.A. Res. 36/55, U.N. Doc. A/RES/55; *Convention Concerning Equal Remuneration* (I.L.O.) No. 100, 165 U.N.T.S. 303, ratified by Canada November 1973; *Convention Concerning Discrimination in Respect of Employment and Occupation* (I.L.O.) No. 111, 362 U.N.T.S., ratified by Canada November 26, 1965. For a compilation of provisions in international instruments concerning equality rights see A.F. Bayefsky & M. Eberts, eds., *Equality Rights and the Canadian Charter of Rights and Freedoms* (Toronto: Carswell, 1985), App. III.

11　See art. 14 of the *European Convention on Human Rights and Fundamental Freedoms*, signed November 4, 1950, entered into force September 3, 1953, 213 U.N.T.S. 222. Article 14 does not incorporate an independent equality right, but rather provides that the other enumerated rights shall be secured without discrimination. See also the *American Convention on Human Rights* (22/11/1969).

12　See *e.g.*, *Constitution of India*, Part III ("Fundamental Freedoms"), ss. 12-35 (in force January 26, 1950).

During this same period, the equality provisions in the Fourteenth Amendment to the United States Constitution were given new force by the courts. They provide that no state shall "deny to any person within its jurisdiction the equal protection of the laws . . .". For decades, these provisions were interpreted in a manner that provided little protection to racial minorities and almost no protection to anyone else. But, beginning with *Brown v. Board of Education*[13] in 1954, the courts reinterpreted them so as to prohibit racial segregation and, later, to provide meaningful protection to other minorities and to women.

Within Canada, a number of initiatives to protect equality and non-discrimination rights took place during the post-World War II period, though they did not always fulfill the aspirations of their supporters. Limited antidiscrimination statutes were later consolidated into comprehensive statutes protecting against discrimination in areas such as public services, housing and employment.[14] They remain important today, in part because they afford protection in areas not covered by the Charter and in part because they have generated a body of jurisprudence that may assist in interpreting Charter equality rights.

The *Canadian Bill of Rights*,[15] the immediate precursor of the Charter in the federal sphere of jurisdiction, has not been even a qualified success in protecting equality rights. Section 1(b) of the *Bill of Rights* provides for "the right of the individual to equality before the law and the protection of the law". While the *Drybones* case gave hope that this protection would be effective,[16] its scope was narrowed in a series of decisions that, with noteworthy exceptions,[17] were more remarkable for their conservatism than for the cogency of their reasoning.[18] It is clear that the wording of section 15 is designed to reverse many of these decisions[19] and little purpose would be served by reviewing them in detail, despite the fact that the *Canadian Bill of Rights* remains in effect.

---

13 347 U.S. 483 (1954). See L. Tribe, *American Constitutional Law* (Mineola, N.Y.: Foundation Press, 1978) at 1000-1002, 1019-1025.

14 See W.S. Tarnopolsky & W.F. Pentney, *Discrimination and the Law, Including Equality Rights Under the Charter* 2d ed. (Toronto: De Boo, 1985), ch. II, for the history of these provisions.

15 S.C. 1960, c. 44, reprinted in R.S.C. 1970, App. III [R.S.C. 1985, App. III].

16 *R. v. Drybones*, [1970] S.C.R. 282.

17 See *e.g.*, the decision of McIntyre J. in *MacKay v. R.*, [1980] 2 S.C.R. 370.

18 For a discussion of the court's approach to the *Bill of Rights* during this period, see W.S. Tarnopolsky, "A New Bill of Rights in Light of the Interpretation of the Present One by the Supreme Court of Canada", in [1978] *L.S.U.C. Special Lectures* 161 at 166-191.

19 See A. Bayefsky, "Defining Equality Rights", in Bayefsky & Eberts, *supra*, note 10 at 5-25, 47-49; K.H. Fogarty, *Equality Rights and Their Limitations in the Charter* (Toronto: Carswell, 1987) at 89-134.

The fact that the Charter provides broader equality rights is due in great measure to the many submissions made by equality-seeking individuals and groups to the Special Joint Committee of Parliament that considered the wording of the Charter. More than any other part of the Canadian Constitution, the Charter, particularly in its equality sections, reflects the contributions of ordinary citizens.[20]

(b) Framework of Analysis

At this stage of constitutional development, one cannot rely on case authority to answer many of the questions that section 15 raises. Therefore, before attempting to outline a test for judicial application of section 15, it seems essential to examine the principles underlying the equality sections. That is the subject of Part 2 of this chapter. Part 3 examines the factors that must be considered in translating this meaning into a process of judicial review. Part 4 places section 15 in its constitutional context, and Part 5 assesses the options for translating principles discussed earlier into a test that would allow judicial review of challenged laws and conduct.

Our organization reflects the fact that the Charter is addressed not just to the judiciary but to all branches of government. The fact that the *Constitution Act, 1982* gives the judiciary new powers of enforcement in no way derogates from the obligation of the legislative and executive branches to implement the Constitution, including the equality rights it sets out. Therefore, it seems a mistake to assume that the meaning of the Charter must be restricted on the ground that some broader interpretation would not be fully amenable to judicial enforcement.[21] We also believe, however, that judicial review of the equality sections will be shaped in good part by the institutional characteristics of the courts and by views about the proper relation between the judiciary and other branches of government. Therefore, we examine the full meaning of the equality provisions in Part 2 and reserve discussion about judicial review to Parts 3 and 5.

---

20 Special Joint Committee of the Senate and House of Commons on the Constitution of Canada appointed to report on the October 6, 1980 resolution. The Committee sat during the period from November 7, 1980 to February 9, 1981 and received submissions from over 1200 groups and individuals. See Issue 57 of the *Minutes of Proceedings and Evidence* for the Committee's Report to Parliament submitted on February 13, 1981. For examples of submissions on amendments to equality rights provisions, see *Minutes* 28-11-1980 15:9; 20-11-1980 9:124; 9-12-1980 22:55; 20-11-1980 9:58; 20-11-1980 9:127; 20-11-1980 9:138; 14-11-1980 5A:4; 9-12-1980 22:56-59.1.

21 In an as yet unpublished paper, Brian Slattery develops a "Coordinate Theory" of the Charter, which describes in much greater depth an approach similar to that sketched here.

2. THE MEANING OF EQUALITY

The Supreme Court of Canada has adopted a purposive approach to interpretation of the Charter.[22] The interpretive task is not an easy one. The problem is not to find purposes that will suffice, but to choose among plausible options.[23]

(a) The Notion of Formal Equality and Its Limitations

It has been suggested that the formal principle of equality — that people who are alike should be treated alike and people who are unalike should be treated unalike — is a tautology that provides no assistance to a decision-maker. Peter Weston argues that the principle becomes useful only if one adopts rules for determining whether two persons are alike and whether their treatment is alike, for no two persons are identical and their treatment may or may not be found to differ depending upon the criteria of comparison.[24] For example, a law providing those over a certain age with a pension may or may not be seen as violating the principle of equality, depending on whether one considers that different ages make people unalike (perhaps on the ground that past service to society makes older people more deserving) and whether the potential application of the rule to everyone is seen as like treatment. Weston says that discussion in terms of "equality" hides the true nature of the analysis. It is the sub-rules establishing what counts as a difference that form the true basis of the rights afforded.

This insight provides important but limited assistance in interpreting section 15. We think it shows that the formal principle of equality does not alone suffice, and that one should consciously select the bases of comparison, but not that our constitutional equality rights are empty. Rather, the content of those rights must be derived in part from sources outside the formal principle of equality. Our history suggests that some criteria are consistent with our societal values and others are not. The wording of section 15 (for example, the list of enumerated grounds) and evidence of the function its enactors intended provides further guidance, as do other

---

22 See *Hunter v Southam Inc.*, [1984] 2 S.C.R. 145 at 157.

23 For useful discussions of competing theories of equality rights, see D. Baker, "The Changing Norms of Equality in the Supreme Court of Canada" (1987), 9 *Supreme Court L.Rev.* 497; Bayefsky, *supra*, note 19; A. Brudner, "What are Reasonable Limits to Equality Rights?" (1986), 64 *Can. Bar Rev.* 469; D. Harris, "Equality, Equality Rights and Discrimination under the Canadian Charter of Rights and Freedoms" (1987), 21 *U.B.C. L. Rev.* 389; J. Vickers, "Equality Theories and Their Results: Equality Seeking in a Cold Climate", in L. Smith *et al.*, eds., *Righting the Balance: Canada's New Equality Rights* (Saskatoon: Canadian Human Rights Reporter, 1986) 3.

24 P. Weston, "The Empty Idea of Equality" (1982), 95 *Harv. L. Rev.* 537 at 544-548.

parts of the Constitution and of our legal system.[25]

These sources do not all point in the same direction, however, and Weston's analysis serves to remind us that the substantive meaning of equality is not a matter of logic, but of moral and political choice.[26] It also reminds us that the appropriate choices may vary from era to era and from society to society, and that it is highly unlikely that a theory developed at another time and place will be entirely suited to Canadian conditions today. We can learn from others but must develop our own paradigm.[27]

(b) Bases of Comparison

An element of comparison is central to any equality theory. But what should be compared with what? There is a wide variety of possibilities, and the choice will depend on what objectives are found to underlie the Charter equality rights. We review here some of the more prominent options.

(i) *Deciding Whether People are Alike — Who to Compare with Whom?*

An equality claimant often alleges that others who are like the claimant are treated more favourably. Thus, some other person or group is selected to serve as a reference. Clearly, the choice of who is to be compared with whom will strongly influence the final determination. Since no two people are exactly alike, one must decide what criteria of comparison are relevant.

Sometimes the choice is fairly obvious. For example, if a law punishes only a certain group of people for specified conduct, the reference group will almost certainly be comprised of all who are not members of the group and who engage in the same conduct.[28] In other circumstances, however, the choice may be less clear. For example, a law or policy may prescribe a range of treatment for different people, and one would have

---

25 See, *e.g.*, K. Greenawalt, "How Empty Is the Idea of Equality" (1983), 83 *Columb. L. Rev.* 1167; K. Karst, "Why Equality Matters" (1983), 17 *Ga. L. Rev.* 245; L. Smith, "A New Paradigm for Equality Rights", in *Righting the Balance, supra*, note 23 at 260-262 (hereinafter Smith, 'Paradigm').

26 We use "political" here in its broader sense. The scope of options may be unusually broad, with respect to equality rights. But the nature of the decision-making process is not fundamentally different from decisions that courts make in other contexts. See P. Hogg, *Constitutional Law of Canada*, 2nd ed. (Toronto: Carswell, 1985) at 98-99, 323-324.

27 For a more detailed discussion of these matters, see Smith, "Paradigm", *supra*, note 25 at 353-363.

28 See, *e.g.*, *R. v. Drybones, supra*, note 16.

to decide whether the standard of reference should be the person treated most favourably, the person afforded average treatment, or some other individual or set of individuals.[29]

Another important question is whether the comparison should be at the level of individuals or groups. At one end of the spectrum, an individual might allege that he or she had been singled out for some detriment for reasons having nothing to do with any group characteristic. For example, a person might complain of being stopped by the police when the officer has simply decided to stop every second violator. Alternatively, the reason for the choice might be a characteristic such as race or sex, and a group component would have entered into the picture which might well have a significance going beyond that of arbitrary individual treatment.[30]

A comparison of groups might also be made in a second sense. One might take account of the disproportionate impact of a rule on a group, even though the provision does not affect every member of the group and bears only a statistical correlation with group membership. For example, a requirement that job applicants be over a specified height and weight will affect both women and men, but will exclude a disproportionate number of women.

Sometimes the choice between an individual and a group perspective can be crucial. If one adopts a purely individual approach, statistical correlation of disadvantage with group membership may be overlooked entirely.[31] The issue can also be important at the stage of devising a remedy.

---

29 In *Re Blainey and Ont. Hockey Assn.* (1986), 26 D.L.R. (4th) 728 (Ont. C.A.), leave to appeal to S.C.C. refused (1986), 58 O.R. (2d) 274 (headnote) (S.C.C.), the court dealt with an exemption in the Ontario *Human Rights Code, 1981,* S.O. 1981, c. 53, denying protection from sex discrimination with regard to participation in athletic programs. In finding a violation of equality, the court (at 741) compared those who might be excluded on the basis of grounds such as race or religion with those excluded on the ground of sex. Having adopted this comparison, it was an obvious conclusion that equal benefit of the law had been denied. We think the decision was the right one. (We also agree with the court's conclusion that the exclusion had an adverse effect on female athletes.) However, it is worth noting that the result could have been different if the court had adopted some other reference group for comparison; *e.g.*, persons excluded from athletic programs on the basis of sexual orientation, since they too would have been afforded no protection under the statute at that time.

30 In practice, use of a group characteristic is likely at some point to affect others sharing the characteristic, and thus a prohibition of discrimination on the basis of the characteristic reflects concern for the group as well as for the individual immediately affected.

31 Using our previous example, a short person excluded from employment could complain on the basis of height discrimination itself. But if height discrimination were not a protected ground, there would be protection only if the person could show that he or

For example, if members of a racial minority have been excluded from a fire department, an individualistic approach might provide a remedy only to those individuals who had attempted to join and were wrongly excluded, whereas a group-oriented approach might fashion a remedy that eliminates the statistical disparity in representation, whether or not those who are awarded the jobs had previously been rejected.[32]

(ii) *Deciding Whether Treatment is Alike — What to Compare with What?*

In addition to determining who should serve as a reference for purposes of comparison, the formal principle of equality requires one to determine whether the treatment of the two should or should not be deemed to be alike. Again, it is necessary to decide what criteria are to count in measuring similarity of treatment.

A. *Comparisons in Terms of Consequences.* Many formulations of equality compare the consequences of a rule or practice for some people with the consequences for others.[33] However, any rule or practice will have many consequences, some more remote than others, and an important question is what consequences to take into account. The choice of what consequences to consider can dramatically affect the function served by an equality provision.

Where the equality challenge is to a rule, the most immediate consequence is that specified in the rule itself. For example, if a rule requires that one applicant for a government-training program pass a written examination and that another applicant pass an oral examination, the immediate consequence is to treat people differently in terms of the testing procedure.[34] From this perspective, perfect equality would be achieved if the rule specified exactly the same procedure for every applicant.

---

he was a member of a protected group (*e.g.*, a woman or member of an ethnic minority) and that the group was disproportionately affected by the limitation.

Regarding the importance of the choice between an individualistic and a communitarian approach, see A.W. MacKay, "Judging and Equality: For Whom Does the Charter Toll", in C. Boyle *et al.* eds., *Charterwatch — Reflections on Equality* (hereinafter "*Charterwatch*") (Toronto: Carswell, 1986) 35 at 38.

32 See *Firefighters v. Stotts*, 81 L.Ed.2d 483 U.S.S.C. (1984).

33 The term "consequences" is intentionally somewhat vague, but we use it to refer to results that are tangible (*e.g.*, access to a structure) or measurable in terms of a commonly used scale (*e.g.*, economic consequences) and distinguish it from mental processes, either leading to or resulting from the conduct and more broadly based and conceptual measures such as subordination.

34 It is not always easy to determine what is the most immediate consequence or whether it creates a distinction as compared with others. For example, a selection by lot could

It might be useful instead to compare whether a selection process for applicants for a training program affords everyone an equal opportunity to demonstrate the ability to succeed in the program. Using that criterion, written and oral tests might or might not provide an equal chance to demonstrate ability. Moreover, the use of a single test for all applicants might constitute unlike treatment, using that criterion. For example, if some applicants had a severe sight impairment, a written test often would not afford them equal opportunity to demonstrate ability. Indeed, if the measure is the opportunity to demonstrate ability, different procedures for different applicants may be a necessary condition to achievement of equality. Phrased in the language of the formal principle of equality, the example illustrates the point that it is as important to treat those who are unalike differently as it is to treat like persons in a like manner. The Supreme Court of Canada seems to have had such a situation in mind when it said that equality may be seen as requiring differential treatment of individuals.[35]

One might examine still more remote consequences, such as who is finally selected for the program. In terms of that consequence, it would seldom make sense to seek equality for each individual, for that would mean everyone would be selected or rejected. However the goal of an equal selection rate for different groups may make good sense. In practice, measures of equality that compare more remote consequences usually will focus on groups rather than individuals.

Sometimes the term "identical treatment" is used to refer to a measure in terms of the face of a rule or its most immediate consequences, and terms like "equality of opportunity" and "equality of results" to refer to more remote consequences.[36] These terms are useful in emphasizing that there are different possible criteria of comparison. However, they may be construed as implying that only a few discrete options are available. We have used somewhat different terminology because we think that the possibilities cover a spectrum of options.

---

be seen as contingently treating everyone equally or as ultimately treating those selected differently. Our point here is that more remote consequences are excluded from consideration.

35 *R. v. Big M Drug Mart Ltd.*, [1985] 1 S.C.R. 295 at 347.

36 See, *e.g.* Bayefsky, *supra*, note 19 at 12-25, discussing equality of opportunity and of results. The term "identical treatment" is particularly troublesome, for it implies that "treatment" is necessarily measured in the most immediate terms. Yet if, for example, English were the only language allowed in a proceeding, it is far from clear that the process should be said to have treated an English speaker identically with a person who speaks only French.

The previous examples suggest that uniformity on the face of a rule or in terms of its most immediate consequences is not always a safe touchstone in identifying inequality. Sometimes equality in terms of immediate consequences has a symbolic function that should not be ignored, as any parent handing out cookies knows. Also, it is frequently easier to measure immediate consequences than more remote ones. But in many areas of life it is not clear what point there would be in insisting on an identical process, knowing that the consequences will be quite different for some than for others. Instead, it often makes sense to ask whether the purposes of a process have been achieved in equal measure for all participants.

The failure to take account of this point has magnified the debate about affirmative action programs designed to assist members of disadvantaged groups. Often opponents of affirmative action argue that other applicants whose opportunities are temporarily reduced are being denied equality to cure a social ill. That formulation is misleading. If a selection process tests different individuals by different means (oral and written tests in our earlier example) so as to afford each an equal chance to demonstrate his or her abilities, we have shifted our criteria of comparison but have not abandoned the principle of equality. The same can be said if we adopt a selection process designed to ensure that different groups will be proportionally represented among those selected. It is legitimate to question who should be compared and what criteria should be used to measure their similarity of treatment. But those arguing for "identical treatment" (in terms of immediate consequences and ignoring other consequences) of individuals do not have a claim to the principle of equality that is superior to that of those arguing for a focus on longer-term consequences for groups.

B. *Other Grounds of Comparison.* To this point, our examples have dealt with comparisons between the consequences of applying a particular rule, such as the rule that applicants must pass a specified test. Moreover, it has been assumed that those consequences are fairly tangible and can be traced to a particular decision or activity. However, equality could be measured by criteria of quite a different nature. The following examples illustrate the variety of comparisons that can be made.

(1) Removal of conditions of subordination or disadvantage. Commentators have proposed conceptions of equality that attempt to deal with the unique condition of women and certain minorities. Many of the factors

giving rise to disadvantage to women have no counterpart affecting men. Comparing the consequences of similar decisions does not produce equality when there are no similar situations to use by way of comparison. For example, it makes no sense to ask whether pregnancy of men and of women is treated in the same manner, and it is far from clear what affects men that would count as an event similar to pregnancy. The differences between men and women have been elaborated upon to a great extent in most cultures, and male dominance has meant that the cultural consequences of male-female differences have almost always operated to the disadvantage of women. Catherine MacKinnon proposes that equality be viewed in terms of dominance and subordination and argues that equality requires governmental action to eliminate those factors that contribute to the subordination of women, as well as to eradicate the consequences of a history of subordination.[37] Others have made similar arguments concerning race discrimination, which would have particular relevance to the aboriginal peoples of Canada.[38]

It is worth noting that these approaches retain an element of comparison. But the comparison concerns the relative social, political and economic status of women as compared with men, or of racial minorities as compared with the dominant racial group, rather than the consequences of a particular law or even of the legal system as a whole. The goal would be that the legal system eliminate societal sources of subordination as well as that it not itself be a cause of such subordination.

(2) Creation of conditions for self-fulfillment.   Equality might also be defined in terms of self-fulfillment. The premise is that all humans should have the equal opportunity to develop their potential and to participate in society, even though that goal may require that different people be treated differently and though the forms of fulfillment may vary from individual to individual.[39] The approach incorporates a presumption in favour of inclusion and participation in societal activities, and any exclusion would require special justification.[40] Though the way a decision

---

37 C.A. MacKinnon, "Making Sex Equality Real", in *Righting the Balance, supra*, note 23 at 37-42. See also N.C. Sheppard, "Equality, Ideology and Oppression: Women and the Canadian Charter of Rights and Freedoms", in *Charterwatch, supra*, note 31 at 195.

38 O. Fiss, "Groups and the Equal Protection Clause", in M. Cohen *et al.*, eds., *Equality and Preferential Treatment* (1977) generally and at 124-147.

39 See J. Bankier, "Equality, Affirmative Action, and the Charter: Reconciling Inconsistent Sections" (1985), 1 *Can. J. Women & Law* 134 at 136-137; K. Nielsen, "Radically Egalitarian Justice", paper presented to "Legal Theory Meets Legal Practice" Conference, University of Ottawa, May 1987, generally and at 3-6.

40 We are indebted to Marcia Rioux for calling our attention to this framework.

treats people and the consequences of the decision constitute useful evidence, the comparison ultimately is between the degree to which different individuals and groups develop their full potential. Like the measure in terms of subordination, this concept would provide meaningful equality protection to groups that face unique conditions and obstacles. For example, such an approach might be useful in considering the application of equality rights to people with mental disabilities.

(3) Equal concern and respect. Instead of comparing the consequences of a rule or the status of a group, one might focus on the decision-making process itself. Ronald Dworkin has proposed a meaning of equality in terms of whether that process affords equal concern and respect for all those who will be affected. He describes this as the right to treatment as an equal as contrasted with the right to equal treatment, which is the right to equal distribution of an opportunity, resource or burden. Dworkin states that the right to treatment as an equal is the more fundamental of the two rights.[41]

A comparison in terms of concern and respect highlights the need on occasion to treat people differently in terms of immediate consequences in order to achieve equality of results or of condition, and Dworkin uses the concept in his defence of affirmative action programs. The concept is also valuable in emphasizing the relationship between the principle of equality and the broader concept of human dignity. It may not, however, cover all claims that might come within a Canadian paradigm of equality. For example, a selection process might be thought to reflect equal concern and respect even though it has the unforeseen consequence of excluding a particular group. Also, it is not easily translated into a workable legal test, since criteria like concern and respect are even harder to measure, and thus to compare, than are more tangible consequences of a rule.

(c) Choosing a Canadian Paradigm

We have suggested that section 15 must incorporate substantive content to supplement the formal principle of equality. We must try to deduce a Canadian paradigm that reflects our objectives in incorporating equality rights into the Constitution and also the unique characteristics of Canadian society and the Canadian legal system.[42]

---

41 R. Dworkin, *Taking Rights Seriously* (Cambridge: Harvard U. Press, 1977) at 227. The measure of equal concern and respect was applied in *Re Blainey and Ontario Hockey Association*, *supra*, note 29 at 744; see also *Mahe v. R.*, [1987] 6 W.W.R. 331 at 363 (Alta. C.A.).

42 We believe that a Canadian paradigm of equality rights must take account of historical trends in Canada, such as socialist and conservative influences, as well as of liberalistic

The most obvious source of assistance in this task is the wording of section 15 itself. In particular, we believe a purposive approach must assume that the section incorporates a concept of equality that protects against the more common types of discrimination associated with each of the enumerated grounds. A second source is the legislative history of the section. While the intent of the drafters is not determinative, surely it is relevant.[43] Reading section 15 in its constitutional context provides further assistance.[44] International instruments also play a role, particularly those to which Canada is a signatory.[45] Finally, we believe important assistance is provided by Canadian human rights statutes. Of course, the fact that the Charter is a constitutional document distinguishes it from these statutes. But the wording of section 15 is broader than that of most human rights statutes,[46] and it seems appropriate to adopt the working assumption that the conception of equality reflected in section 15 is no

---

values. But the nature of a paradigm involves a choice of what facts are to be explained, and a given set of facts may be explained equally well by more than one paradigm. Thus, the adoption of a paradigm involves an element of choice. See generally Smith, "Paradigm", *supra*, note 25.

43 There is a lively debate as to whether ultimately the intent of the framers controls constitutional meaning: see J. Ely, *Democracy and Distrust* (Cambridge, Harvard U. Press, 1980) at 1-41; compare *Hunter v. Southam Inc. supra*, note 22 at 155. The fact that a recent nominee to the U.S. Supreme Court, Robert Bork, believes that the Constitution is tied strictly to its original intent caused great controversy about his nomination, for it leads Justice Bork to conclude, *e.g.*, that the U.S. equality provisions do not protect against sex discrimination. See "Judge Bork: Restraint vs. Activism", *New York Times*, September 13, 1987, p. 1, col. 1.

44 Compare *Reference re Bill 30, An Act To Amend the Education Act (Ont.)*, [1987] 1 S.C.R. 1148.

45 See A. Bayefsky, "The Principle of Equality or Non-Discrimination in International Law: Implications for Equality Rights in the Charter", in *Righting the Balance, supra*, note 23 at 117. While we believe it is appropriate to assume that the meaning of equality adopted in s. 15 is consistent with our international obligations, the need for a Canadian paradigm signals caution in applying international standards in too literal a way. Because international instruments and jurisprudence must accommodate different political and social systems and afford a "margin of appreciation" (see *Sunday Times v. U.K.* (1979), 2 E.H.R.R. 245 at para. 58), they may be more valuable in determining the minimum content of s. 15 than in determining the full ambit of that section.

46 We do not think that the wording of s. 15(1) forces one to conclude that the word "discrimination" limits the preceding portions of the section. But some cases have so interpreted it; see *Re Andrews and Law Society of B.C.* (1986), 27 D.L.R. (4th) 600 (B.C.C.A.). In any event, it would seem that the word should be given an interpretation no narrower than that it receives when it is used in human rights legislation.

less broad than that underlying the statutes.[47]

(i) *The Larger Objects of Equality Rights*

The Supreme Court of Canada has counselled us to adopt "a broad, purposive analysis, which interprets specific provisions of a constitutional document in the light of its larger objects".[48] We claim no unique insight in embarking on this difficult task, and a national consensus on some issues may not exist.[49] Nevertheless, further analysis requires us to venture some hypotheses about these elusive matters.

A. *Reduction of Conditions of Disadvantage.* Our conclusion is that a primary purpose of the equality rights provisions is to eliminate or reduce conditions of disadvantage. Different groups are disadvantaged in different ways. For example, religious minorities may endure social exclusion and animosity though relatively affluent, while people who are blind may endure severe economic disadvantage but seldom outright hatred. But these different forms of disadvantage have the common feature that they are persistent, have a significant effect and are often exacerbated by governmental activity and policy.

This object is most obviously reflected in section 15(2), which specifically refers to "the amelioration of conditions of *disadvantaged* individuals or groups". But we think the reduction of conditions of disadvantage is an object of the section as a whole. Section 15(1) lists among the enumerated grounds physical and mental disability (not condition), and it makes sense to assume that the other listed grounds serve a similar function, though stated in neutral terms.[50] Also, section 15 should be read in the context of other sections that are undoubtedly designed to protect minority interests. In particular, section 27 seems clearly aimed

---

47 With regard to the relevancy of human rights jurisprudence as applied to the Constitution, we note that human rights statutes have achieved a status approaching that of a constitutional instrument. See *Winnipeg School Div. No. 1 v. Craton*, [1985] 2 S.C.R. 150 at 156.

48 *Hunter v. Southam, supra*, note 22 at 156; See also *R. v. Oakes*, [1986] 1 S.C.R. 103 at 135-136.

49 See M. Gold, "A Principled Approach to Equality Rights: A Preliminary Inquiry" (1982), 4 *Supreme Ct. L. Rev.* 131 at 155-156.

50 See *Equality for All: Report of the Parliamentary Committee on Equality Rights* (1985) at 105. Though we disagree with Ely in other respects, we agree that judicial review is hardest to justify when asserted on behalf of persons who generally receive their fair share from the political process, though they may have been caused disadvantage by the particular rule or decision under challenge.

at protecting the interests of cultural minorities, sections 25 and 35 protect the rights of aboriginal peoples and section 23 protects minority language education rights. The history of section 28 shows that the section was included to overcome the historical disadvantages affecting women.[51] More generally, our recent history reflects a growing awareness of the problems caused by disadvantage, and increasing willingness to legislatively remedy disadvantage.[52] That trend, together with the legislative history of section 15 itself,[53] supports the view that the section was designed primarily to eliminate such disadvantage.

We do not mean to suggest that section 15 affords no protection to those who are relatively advantaged. But we believe that the section would fail to achieve its larger objects if it were not interpreted in a manner that deals effectively with persistent disadvantage.

B. *Conditions of Subordination.* We also have concluded that the meaning of equality incorporated into section 15 must take into account the dynamics of social subordination. In particular, we cannot ignore the fact that a pervasive feature of our society has been, and to a great extent is, to assign a different and more limiting role to women than to men. That tendency is often exacerbated by our legal system. The cultural subordination of native people creates pervasive harm that is similar in many respects.[54] We think that when section 15 is read in the context of section 28 and of sections 25 and 35, it is reasonable to conclude that a part of its object is to remedy such conditions of subordination.

It has been argued that the legal system must be radically transformed to achieve such a goal.[55] There is an element of truth to this assertion, but it does not follow that the goal is not among the "larger objects" of section 15. It is relevant to note again that section 15 is addressed to all branches of government and to remind ourselves that constitutions reflect

---

51 See K. de Jong, "Sexual Equality: Interpreting Section 28", in Bayefsky & Eberts, *supra*, note 10, p. 493 at 494-512, for an extensive discussion of the history leading to s. 28. The section is discussed in greater detail in Part 4, *infra*.

52 See Tarnopolsky & Pentney, *supra*, note 14, chs. I, II; *Equality Now: Report of the Special Committee on Visible Minorities in Canadian Society* (1984); *Obstacles: Report of the Special Committee on the Disabled and the Handicapped* (1981).

53 See *Equality for All, supra*, note 50 at 105.

54 See S. Sharzer, "Native People: Some Issues", in R. Abella, *Research Studies of the Commission on Equality in Employment* (Ottawa: 1985) at 549 (hereinafter "Abella, *Research Studies*").

55 A. Scales, "The Emergence of Feminist Jurisprudence: An Essay" (1986), 95 *Yale L. J.* 1373 especially at 1393-1394.

our deeper aspirations as well as immediately achievable objectives. Thus, the fact that subordination cannot be eradicated entirely by the legal system, much less by judicial review alone, does not refute the conclusion that section 15 takes account of conditions of subordination.

C. *Protecting Groups as well as Individuals.* Related to the previous two points is the conclusion that a central objective of section 15 is to remedy inequality between groups as well as between individuals. In this respect, the Canadian paradigm may depart from the more individualistic American outlook.[56] Persistent disadvantage is often associated with certain groups.[57] In addition, the list of enumerated grounds in section 15 requires a comparison in terms of group characteristics. In our opinion, the section also is intended to reflect a group perspective in the broader sense of concern for the welfare of groups as a whole.

This conclusion is supported by the reference to the "amelioration of conditions of disadvantage of individuals or *groups*" in section 15(2). It seems to us highly unlikely that this policy concern so obviously shaped section 15(2) but was ignored in framing section 15(1).[58] The conclusion is consistent with the approach taken by the Parliamentary Committee on Equality Rights in recommending measures to implement section 15.[59] Such an objective is hardly anomalous, for other constitutional rights — notably those dealing with language rights, multicultural rights, aboriginal and treaty rights and denominational schools — all reflect goals that extend beyond the individual.

(ii) *Translating Underlying Objectives into a Meaning of Equality*

What meaning of equality fulfills these objectives? It is too early, if

---

56 Compare P. Brest, "The Supreme Court 1975 Term — Foreword: In Defence of the Antidiscrimination Principle" (1976), 90 *Harv. L. Rev.* 1 at 49-50. Regarding the effects of persistent social disadvantage of a group, see *e.g.*, M. Weinfeld, "The Social Costs of Discrimination", in Abella, *Research Studies, supra*, note 54 at 387.

57 See, *e.g.*, R. Abella, *Equality in Employment: A Royal Commission Report* ("The Abella Report") (1984), ch. 2.

58 Note that s. 15(2) does not create an independent right; it only authorizes programs to ameliorate conditions of disadvantage if the government so chooses. If the objective in entrenching equality rights was to change the status of disadvantaged groups, a test that measures such disadvantage accurately is essential and must have been incorporated into s. 15(1). If the intent was to entrench a conception of equality strictly in terms of individual interest, it is unclear why s. 15(2) would be included at all. At best the two subsections would represent an unprincipled compromise.

59 *Equality for All, supra*, note 50 at 5, 105.

it is possible at all, to attempt a comprehensive definition. But we think the following are features of the Canadian paradigm:

A. *The section takes account of group as well as individual interests.* This point was discussed in connection with the underlying objectives of the section and need not be discussed further here.

B. *The section takes account of more remote results as well as the terms of a rule and its immediate consequences.* This conclusion is consistent with the prevailing interpretation of the word "discrimination" in human rights statutes.[60] It also reflects the fact that a more limited meaning would exclude from consideration a large portion of the disadvantage affecting many of the enumerated groups.

It is not always easy to determine how far beyond the level of immediate consequences it is appropriate to look. Different subject matter may call for consideration of a different range of consequences.[61] Sometimes, equality at the level of immediate consequences will be the only goal. But in other cases, the objectives underlying section 15 will require consideration of more remote results, and the section will fail to achieve those objectives if the field of view is limited to immediate consequences.

C. *The section takes account of both intended and unintended consequences.* If the primary purpose of section 15 is to reduce the disparity between persistently disadvantaged groups and others, it seems clear that this goal will be severely compromised if unintended effects are left out of consideration, as the Supreme Court of Canada has recognized.[62]

It has been contended that institutional limitations make it impossible for the judiciary to deal adequately with the problem of unintended effects. Though we disagree, the point is a significant one and is discussed in Part 3. Even if the contention were correct, however, it should not affect the underlying meaning of equality incorporated into section 15 and addressed to the legislature and executive as well as the judiciary. Unintended effects should be considered in the appropriate governmental forum once they

---

60 *Ont. Human Rights Comm. v. Simpsons-Sears Ltd.*, [1985] 2 S.C.R. 536; *Canadian Odeon Theatres Ltd. v. Sask. Human Rights Comm.*, [1985] W.W.R. 717 (Sask. C.A.).

61 Marc Gold has suggested that Canadian views represent an uneasy compromise between different and perhaps irreconcilable conceptions of equality, and it may be impossible to make generalizations about the form and degree of equality that s. 15 protects: *supra*, note 49 at 155-156. As a result, different facts may call for consideration of a different range of consequences.

62 *Ont. Human Rights Comm. v. Simpsons-Sears Ltd.*, *supra*, note 60.

become apparent.[63] Moreover, the possibility that a rule or activity will have unintended effects on disadvantaged groups should be considered at the policy formation stage.

D. *The section takes into account detriment related to unique characteristics of protected groups.* The inclusion of sex discrimination as an enumerated ground is instructive in this regard. Men and women each have unique physical capacities that form part of the definition of the class, and equality of results cannot be achieved if disadvantage relating to such capacities is ignored. In particular, it makes little sense to us to interpret section 15 as affording equality to women only to the extent that they forego the unique child-bearing capacity that is essential to continuance of society.[64] Moreover, as we have noted, the present status of women in society and in our legal system is strongly affected by the dynamics of legal and social subordination.

A meaning of equality that takes account of such subordination must look beyond the effects of a particular law or activity to the broader effects of our legal and social system. It must also incorporate more sophisticated techniques in choosing the appropriate comparative measure. The concept of equal concern and respect points in a promising direction in conjunction with appropriate measures of consequences.

E. *The section incorporates a duty of reasonable accommodation.* This point is related to the previous one. The duty of accommodation takes account of the fact that different people may have to adopt different means to achieve a given result and that differences in treatment at the level of immediate consequences may thus promote greater equality in terms of those results. The duty to accommodate differences has been incorporated into human rights statutes, and we see no reason that would justify excluding it from section 15.[65]

---

63 It is impossible, of course, to take action to deal with unintended adverse effects until they become apparent. If a course of conduct is continued after they become apparent, there is a good argument for treating the consequences as intended. But it is also possible that the assessment will take account only of the intent at the time that a law or policy is adopted. Compare *R. v. Big M Drug Mart, supra,* note 35 at 335.

64 For an extensive discussion of the arguments concerning the need to take such differences into account, see M. Eberts, "Sex-Based Discrimination and the Charter", in Bayefsky & Eberts, *supra,* note 10, p. 183 at 191-193, 218-229.

65 See *Ont. Human Rights Comm. v. Simpsons-Sears Ltd., supra,* note 60, which interpreted the *Ontario Human Rights Code* as incorporating the principle of reasonable accom-

Accommodation is essential if section 15 is to afford a significant measure of equality to people with disabilities. These people must live in a world built for people with average capacity to move, to hear and so forth. We have steps because the average person can climb them but cannot leap tall buildings with a single bound. Not surprisingly, people with a particular physical or mental condition that is not average may find that they cannot operate to full capacity in a world designed for others and that the world sometimes presents them with insurmountable barriers. It must be assumed that the protection afforded by section 15 is not as meaningless as the opportunity to attempt to climb stairs in a wheelchair.

3. INSTITUTIONAL CONSIDERATIONS

Because the Charter is addressed to all branches of government, Part 2 discussed the underlying objectives of section 15 without taking account of institutional constraints on the judiciary. We consider those constraints here, since it seems almost certain that they will help shape the nature of judicial review of section 15.

(a) Reconciling Judicial Review and Democracy

Perhaps the most fundamental argument for limiting judicial review is that it conflicts with the principle of representative democracy which is at the heart of our governmental system. In terms of section 15, the argument is that it is better to entrust the protection of equality to legislators than to judges, who are neither elected nor representative of the population in terms of race, gender, age or socio-economic status. After all, democracy is itself an egalitarian concept.

Critics argue further that judicial review forces the courts into a role that is fundamentally at odds with the judicial process because equality issues cannot be reduced to legal rules, and judges are forced to make policy decisions in the same way as legislators do. Not only does this mean that the two institutions perform the same role, but it interferes with the ability of the courts to perform their traditional adjudicative function in other spheres, it is said.[66]

---

modation. In *Bhinder v. C.N.R.*, [1985] 2 S.C.R. 561, the Supreme Court of Canada refused to hold that a similar doctrine was incorporated into the *Canadian Human Rights Act*, S.C. 1976-77, c. 33. But a comparison of the two judgments suggests that the court treated the duty to accommodate as the norm, but found that the duty was excluded by the particular wording of the federal Act.

66 For a comprehensive discussion of the legitimacy issue, see P. Monahan, "Judicial Review and Democracy: A Theory of Judicial Review" (1987), 21 *U.B.C. L. Rev.* 87.

Various attempts have been made to meet these criticisms. One answer is that the Constitution was itself created by our elected representatives and derives its legitimacy from the (indirectly expressed) consent of the electors.[67] The weakness of this justification is that its logic requires strict adherence to the intent of the framers of the Charter. Thus, it seems inconsistent with the view of the Supreme Court of Canada that constitutional rights must "be capable of growth and development over time to meet new social, political and historical realities often unimagined by its framers".[68] A more practical problem is that it will be frequently impossible to determine what the framers thought about the issue at hand, and the general language of the section will be capable of bearing all the proffered interpretations.[69]

A second defence of judicial review is that there are underlying principles of our system of government that provide guidance to the courts and allow an escape from *ad hoc* decision-making. Proponents of this approach do not always agree on the source of these principles.[70] But they all try to identify sources that are not tied strictly to the intent of the framers. If the principles are themselves incorporated in our legal system, arguably

---

67 See B. Strayer, "Constitutional Interpretation Based on Consent: Whose Consent and Measured When?" paper delivered to "Legal Theory Meets Legal Practice" Conference, University of Ottawa, May 1987. Mr. Justice Strayer suggests that the relevant distinction is between the long-term and short-term will of the electorate and that judicial review "is really the vindication of long-term socio-political goals stated in the Constitution as against the transitory will of passing majorities expressed in legislation". See also *Reference re S. 94(2) of the Motor Vehicle Act (B.C.)*, [1985] 2 S.C.R. 486 at 497; R. Berger, "Some Reflections on Interpretivism" (1986), 55 *Geo. Wash L. Rev.* 1.

Patrick Monahan has noted that the intent underlying the Charter was largely that of bureaucrats who are no more democratically elected than judges: *supra*, note 66 at 116. In addition, Ely notes that the drafters may have intended to incorporate ongoing development of rights and that tying interpretation to their personal views about a provision may miss their point: *supra*, note 43 at 13; Monahan, *supra*, note 66 at 118. This argument is even more persuasive in Canada, where judicial review was incorporated into the document expressly, than in the United States, where it was developed afterwards by the courts: *Marbury v. Madison*, 5 U.S. (1 Cranch) 137 (1803).

68 *Hunter v. Southam Inc.*, *supra*, note 22 at 155.

69 In light of the variety of bodies that participated in enacting the Charter, legislative history about a particular part of the process should be used with some caution. We also note the common law truism that many issues become clear only in the context of applying a rule to specific facts. The enactment of s. 15 has brought into focus issues that attracted little attention during the debates leading up to the enactment of s. 15. In hindsight, much of the analysis at that time (including our own) seems to be of a preliminary nature, and it would be unfortunate if the interpretation of s. 15 did not take account of the insights that have been gained since the enactment of the section.

70 See, *e.g.*, Dworkin, *supra*, note 41 at 184-205; M. Perry, *The Constitution, the Courts and Human Rights: An Inquiry into the Legitimacy of Constitutional Policymaking by the Judiciary* (New Haven: Yale University Press, 1982).

they provide points of constancy while at the same time allowing the adaptation of the Constitution to meet new conditions and needs.

We think that guidance can frequently be derived from such sources. Reference to the general constitutional framework, to the nature of our legal system and to areas of consensus about moral values can at least narrow the parameters of uncertainty. But these sources of guidance will sometimes fail, and this defence suggests that the process of judicial review should take account of the availability of such guidance.

Another reconciliation of judicial review with democratic principles has been suggested by John Hart Ely in the United States and Patrick Monahan in Canada.[71] They contend that judicial intervention is not justified simply because the political process has reached the "wrong" answer; to do so would subvert democratic decision-making. But it is justified when there is reason to believe that the democratic process itself is systematically malfunctioning. As applied to equality, the theory suggests that the legislative process will generally function properly, in part because those who are in the minority on one issue will usually be in the majority on another. But some minorities endure ongoing antipathy or condescension. Those factors can cause their interests to be systematically ignored or undervalued, especially when coupled with under-representation in the legislative process.[72]

This approach is convincing as far as it goes, but it is too limited in our opinion.[73] We doubt that even a perfectly functioning democracy will consistently afford equal concern and respect for the interests of all groups. The legislative process may fail to take fair account of the interests of a group for reasons other than antipathy, condescension or the proportional under-representation of the group. The mere fact of minority status may skew the legislative assessment of an interest. Legislators are elected by majority vote, and it often pays politically to undervalue the interests of a minority even though that minority is popular and is proportionally represented in the process. Also, legislative time is limited and many matters do not attract any legislative attention at all. Problems affecting only a minority are especially susceptible to that risk. This fault would be of little concern if, in the long run, the interests of each individual

71   Ely, *supra*, note 43, chs. 5, 6; Monahan, *supra*, note 66. Points of disagreement between Ely and Monahan are noted below.

72   Ely, *supra*, note 43 at 102-103, 135-179; Monahan, *supra*, note 66 at 146-151. Ely and Monahan differ somewhat in the elaboration of this theory, particularly with regard to the question whether unintended effects should be reviewed by the courts. Compare Ely, *ibid.* at 152-154, with Monahan, *ibid.* at 146-151.

73   For other criticisms of Ely, see B. Hoffmaster, "Theories of Judicial Review", paper delivered to "Legal Theory Meets Legal Practice", Conference, University of Ottawa, May 1987, at 18-23, 31.

were equally served. But some groups, often because of persistently unique conditions and needs, will consistently receive less than their share out of the process, in our opinion.

These phenomena are not always confined to minorities. In particular, lack of equal concern and respect for the interests of women is caused by the substantial under-representation of women in most legislative bodies and by unique physical attributes, traditional social roles and historical exclusion from the political process. Perhaps in some utopian future, women will be proportionally represented in all governmental decision-making bodies and the effects of a history of undervaluing women's interests will have been eradicated. But we are far from those goals, and it seems to us highly unrealistic to count on our present political system to treat men and women with equal care and concern.

In addition, the theories of Ely and Monahan seem not to take account of potential sources of inequality other than the legislation, such as the conduct of civil servants, administrative agencies and a variety of other unelected governmental bodies. The argument in terms of fidelity to the democratic process is much less persuasive as applied to bodies that are no more representative than the courts themselves.[74] Moreover, such conduct often involves a discrete event affecting only a particular individual or a small group of individuals — exactly the kind of conduct that the courts are used to dealing with and that the legislature seldom considers.

Our conclusion is that it would be a mistake to limit judicial review to matters that affect equal participation in the democratic process. In our opinion, that means of resolving the tension between judicial review and democracy misconceives the sources of inequality and would make it impossible for the equality rights provisions to fulfill their underlying purposes. But other ways must be found to mediate this tension, and we propose alternatives in (c) "Limiting Factors — The Options", below.

(b) Other Institutional Constraints

The efficacy of judicial review has been attacked on more practical grounds. It is argued that the litigative process is designed to resolve individual disputes and that the courts are dependent on the litigants both to frame the issues and to choose what material will be presented. As a result, the process is said to be an inappropriate one for considering

---

74 See Strayer, *supra*, note 67 at 3. While the legislature may have ultimate control over executive conduct, that control is often tenuous, especially with regard to everyday activity.

broad questions of policy of the kind that section 15 sometimes presents.[75] These concerns tend to point toward a cautious approach to judicial review that defers to the legislature on policy issues because of its allegedly superior process.

We think that these concerns have some validity but are often overstated. Frequently, critics compare a "warts and all" assessment of the judiciary against a portrayal of an ideal legislative process.[76] Not surprisingly, the latter almost always looks superior. In addition, some weaknesses in the judicial process can be overcome by new techniques, such as more open discussion of underlying purposes and greater access to evidence about social and economic consequences. But even with such modifications, the adjudicative process will be inferior to legislative or administrative processes for making certain kinds of policy determinations. For example, it would be almost impossible for a court to assess the cumulative effect of a range of laws on a particular group; instead the focus is almost always on a particular law or practice. We believe that such limitations must be taken into account in developing a test for judicial review based on section 15.

We do not, however, think that judicial review of social and economic legislation is precluded, as is sometimes proposed, or that section 15 incorporates a special test for dealing with such legislation. We agree with Robin Elliot that such a result would deny protection with respect to many of the interests that prompted the enactment of section 15. It also would withdraw protection with respect to matters the courts are fully competent to evaluate along with ones that may cause more difficulty. The application of a differential test would require the courts to determine when it applied and when it did not, and that delineation could cause as much difficulty as it would avoid.[77]

Andrew Petter raises two other concerns. One is that the expense of litigation is a barrier that will screen out a disproportionate number of challenges by members of disadvantaged groups. Not only will the groups who most need assistance be denied it, but the interpretation of the Charter will unconsciously be molded in a way that favours the interests of the advantaged groups who most often come before the courts. His second

---

75 D. Smiley, "The Case Against the Canadian Charter of Human Rights" (1969), 2 *Can. J. Pol. Sci.* 277 at 282-285; P. Weiler, "Of Judges and Rights, or Should Canada Have a Constitutional Bill of Rights" (1981), 60 *Dal Rev.* 205 at 223-226.

76 See, *e.g.*, D. Schmeiser, "The Entrenchment of a Bill of Rights" (1981), 19 *Alta. L. Rev.* 375 at 378-382.

77 R. Elliot, *Judicial Review of Social and Economic Legislation under Section 15 of the Charter*, as yet unpublished paper delivered at the Stanford Lectures, August, 1986; *contra: Reference re Ss.32 & 34 of Workers Compensation Act* (Nfld.) (1987), 67 Nfld. & P.E.I.R. 16 (Nfld. C.A.).

concern is that judges are drawn from a narrow social and economic spectrum and reflect the conservative values of the legal system in which they were schooled.[78] We share both concerns. They demonstrate the need to make resources available so that disadvantaged groups have access to the courts.[79] They also support the goal of making the judiciary more representative.[80] They have also influenced our analysis of the application of section 15. However, we are more optimistic than Petter that means can be found to reduce the effect of these factors so that judicial review remains a legitimate and effective, if imperfect, means of protecting equality interests.

(c) Limiting Factors — The Options

We are convinced that unless some account is taken of the institutional constraints on the courts, judicial review will unduly intrude on the other branches of government and at the same time impose an unacceptable burden on the courts. There are several plausible ways to accommodate these constraints. We review four alternatives here:

1. limiting the grounds of distinction that will be considered;
2. adopting different levels of scrutiny for different grounds of discrimination;
3. excluding consideration of unintended effects on a group; and
4. deferring routinely to legislative and executive decisions.

We prefer the first and consider the second a plausible option. The last two would, in our opinion, seriously undermine the ability of the courts to remedy claims properly within their sphere. We discuss each in turn.[81]

---

78 A. Petter, "The Politics of the Charter" (1986), 8 *Supreme Ct. L. Rev.* 473 at 486-488.

79 A program has been established to provide such assistance to those challenging conduct within federal jurisdiction. Petter's concerns will be exacerbated if assistance is not provided with regard to provincial challenges. Legal aid provides some assistance but is often confined to criminal cases. We should note that Petter views such assistance as misplaced in light of other limitations on the effectiveness of the Charter: *ibid.* at 482-483.

80 It seems realistic to set as at least a long-term goal that the judiciary include proportional representation of women and of racial, religious and ethnic groups. It is highly unlikely that it will ever attain proportional representation of all parts of the economic scale, and equal representation based on grounds such as age and mental disability is neither a sensible nor an attainable goal.

81 Our suggestion that judicial application might not implement the full meaning of equality that we outlined raises a question: if a law or practice conflicts with the larger meaning of equality, how could a court refuse to strike it down? We think that the answer lies in the fact that the courts are not the only legitimate expositors of constitutional meaning and that others may sometimes be in a better position to evaluate certain kinds of issues.

(i) *Limitation of Grounds which may be used to invoke Section 15*

By its terms, section 15 applies "without discrimination and, *in particular*, without discrimination based on *race, national or ethnic origin, colour, religion, sex, age or mental or physical disability*" [emphasis added]. The cases[82] and commentaries[83] reflect a clear consensus that the list of grounds is not exhaustive, and both named ("enumerated") and unnamed ("unenumerated") grounds may give rise to equality claims.[84] That conclusion is supported by the legislative history of the section.[85]

The opinion to date is mixed, however, as to whether the grounds of distinction covered are completely open-ended. The Saskatchewan Court of Appeal held that the principle of *ejusdem generis* does not apply and that a distinction may be covered though it does not form a part of

---

Where a court is in a position to say that the Constitution has been violated, it must refuse to recognize the offending law or practice law. But where the court is not in a position to make an authoritative determination about constitutionality, it may refuse to intervene. This explanation is easily harmonized with judicial deference with regard to some matters. We also think it may in some circumstances justify a blanket refusal to make certain types of determinations on the ground that, because of the nature of the issue, a court would never be in a position to say with the requisite certainty that its assessment was more accurate than that of the body responsible for the challenged provision.

Brian Slattery has discussed the respective responsibilities of the different branches of government and has reached similar conclusions: *supra*, note 21. He suggests that the degree of judicial responsibility in any particular circumstance will turn on a number of factors, including relative institutional competence regarding the issue at hand. Thus, the logic of the theory does not require a stance of uniform judicial deference. Laurence Tribe explains the American "political questions" doctrine on similar grounds: *supra*, note 13 at 79. This explanation seems to us not to be precluded by the majority decision in *Operation Dismantle v. R.*, [1985] 1 S.C.R. 441 especially at 459, though it is somewhat more difficult to reconcile with the concurring decision of Wilson J.

82 See *e.g.*, *Re Andrews and Law Society of B.C.*, *supra*, note 46 at 608-609; *R. v. Hamilton* (1986), 17 O.A.C. 241 at 257 (Ont. C.A.), leave to appeal to S.C.C. refused (1987), 22 O.A.C. 240n (S.C.C.); *McBeth v. Governors of Dalhousie College & Univ.* (1986), 26 D.L.R. (4th) 321 (N.S.C.A.); *Zutphen Brothers Construction Ltd. v. Dywidag Systems International (Can.) Ltd.* (1987), 35 D.L.R. (4th) 433 (N.S.C.A.), leave to appeal to S.C.C. granted (1987), 80 N.S.R. (2d) 270n (S.C.C.); but *cf. Jardine v. Jardine* (1986), 26 D.L.R. (4th) 634 (N.B.Q.B.).

83 See *e.g.*, Bayefsky, *supra*, note 45 at 117; Gold, *supra*, note 49 at 153; A. McLellan, "Marital Status and Equality Rights", in Bayefsky & Eberts, *supra*, note 10, p. 411 at 414-415.

84 That interpretation is consistent with the interpretation given to s. 1(b) of the *Canadian Bill of Rights*, though no such claim was ever successful. See, *e.g.*, *R. v. Burnshine*, [1975] 1 S.C.R. 693; *MacKay v. R.*, *supra*, note 17; compare *Bliss v. A.G. Canada*, [1979] 1 S.C.R. 183.

85 See Fogarty, *supra*, note 19 at 110-111.

any genus common to the enumerated grounds.[86] Similiar reasoning was adopted by the Supreme Court of British Columbia.[87] Additional cases, though less explicit, have considered grounds that could not plausibly come within any limited list of distinctions.[88] In contrast, other cases have held that the list of proscribed grounds is not unlimited and that some distinctions fall outside section 15.[89]

There has been some discussion of the matter by commentators. Robin Elliot has argued that the list should be open-ended, citing the difficulty of drawing lines between what would be covered and what would not, the fact that section 15 would otherwise be narrower than the *Canadian Bill of Rights* and the view that section 15 requires that every individual be treated with equal concern and respect.[90] Anne Bayefsky suggests that international judicial authority also supports this result.[91] On the other hand, Marc Gold argues that the section is limited to grounds sharing at least some of the characteristics of the enumerated grounds.[92]

We recognize the force of Elliot's argument for interpreting section 15 so as to cover any ground of distinction whatsoever. Arbitrary treatment and irrational exclusion are reprehensible, no matter what the basis. Nevertheless, we have concluded that an extended but limited list of grounds is the best of problematic alternatives for taking account of the institutional constraints on the courts.[93]

---

86 *Reference re French Language Rights of Accused in Sask. Criminal Proceedings*, [1987] 5 W.W.R. 577 (Sask. C.A.).

87 *Wilson v. Medical Services Comm. of B.C.* (1987), 9 B.C.L.R. (2d) 350 (B.C.S.C.), rev'd (August 5, 1988) No. CA007160, CA007198 (B.C.C.A.) (*obiter dictum*); see also *Streng v. Winchester (Township)* (1986), 25 C.R.R. 357 (Ont. H.C.).

88 See, *e.g.*, *Zutphen Brothers Construction Ltd. v. Dywidag Systems International Can. Ltd.*, *supra*, note 82; *Streng v. Winchester*, *supra*, note 87 (procedural advantages accorded governmental entity in litigation); *R. v. D.*, [1985] 6 W.W.R. 79 (Sask. Q.B.) (date of offence); *Fraser v. A.G. Nova Scotia* (1986), 74 N.S.R. (2d) 91 (T.D.) (public as compared with private employees); *McBeth v. Governors of Dalhousie College & Univ.*, *supra*, note 82 (represented and unrepresented litigants); *R. v. R.* (1986), 28 C.C.C. (3d) 188 (Ont. H.C.) (accused as compared to complainant re publication of identity).

89 *Koch v. Koch* (1985), 23 D.L.R. (4th) 609 (Sask. Q.B.) (residency requirements); *Re Election Act (B.C.)*; *Scott v. A.G. British Columbia* (1986), 3 B.C.L.R. (2d) 376 (S.C.) (registered and unregistered voters); *McDonnell v. Fédération des Franco-Colombiens* (1987), 31 D.L.R. (4th) 296 (B.C.C.A.) (excluding official language as a ground because covered by other Charter sections).

90 Elliot, *supra*, note 77.

91 Bayefsky, *supra*, note 45 at 134.

92 M. Gold, "Equality: What Does It Mean?", in Canadian Institute for Professional Development, *Equality Rights and Employment: Preparing for Fundamental Change — East* (Toronto, 1986) A-1 at A-23-27.

93 In previous articles, the present authors have suggested the contrary: see W. Black, "A Walk Through the Charter", in *Righting the Balance*, *supra*, note 23 p. 47 at 57;

This interpretation seems to us the option most consistent with what in our view is a primary purpose of section 15 — the alleviation of inequality for persistently disadvantaged groups. If that purpose could be fully achieved while protecting against every other sort of irrational or arbitrary distinction as well, any limitation would be unwarranted. But we think that the courts will find some way to take account of institutional constraints and that an unlimited list of grounds will result in other restrictions on the section that could seriously degrade the protection afforded to disadvantaged groups.[94]

An unlimited list of grounds tends to weaken the arguments in favour of judicial review, and weakened justification is likely to be transformed into weakened protection in the long run. If there is no reason to believe that a particular claimant's interests generally are undervalued in the legislative process, one justification for judicial review disappears. If those adversely affected by a decision have nothing in common but that fact, it is unlikely that those individuals will be persistently disadvantaged by the legal system. More fundamentally, when the ground of distinction has nothing to do with human characteristics or identity (manufacturers of different products, for example), we doubt our societal values require that the two groups be given equal advantages, even presumptively.[95]

Another relevant consideration is the burden on the courts that an unrestricted list would impose. Obviously, the case load will be affected by the number of reviewable distinctions, and the most problematic grounds are likely to consume an undue proportion of judicial time. The burden could quickly become unmanageable if courts had to consider unintended effects on any individual or collection of individuals. Yet, exclusion of unintended effects from challenge would greatly weaken the protection afforded disadvantaged groups. In addition, the interpretation of section 15 is likely to be influenced by the interests of the litigants most often

---

Smith, "Paradigm", *supra*, note 25 at 255. While these statements dealt primarily with the conclusion that the enumerated list is not exhaustive, we concede that they provide no hint of some further limitation.

94 We note also that if the arbitrary treatment concerns a fundamental right, it will often come within another section of the Charter, *e.g.*, the protection against arbitrary detention in s. 9 or the guarantee of a fair hearing in s. 11.

95 *Cf. Re Aluminum Co. of Can. and Ontario* (1986), 55 O.R. (2d) 522 (Div. Ct.), leave to appeal to Ont. C.A. refused (1986), 19 Admin. L.R. xliii (note) (Ont. C.A.), which concerned different treatment of aluminum steel cans in a law concerning returnable containers. Where the favoured and disfavoured entities are as similar as two can-makers, there is an intuitive feeling that they should be treated equally. However, that feeling depends upon a narrow definition of equality. For example, there would be little emotional or legal force to an argument that an increase in electricity rates causes unconstitutional inequality to aluminum makers or that bottle makers must have accommodation because the container is breakable.

before the courts. If unrestricted grounds are coupled with disproportionate litigation resources, the interpretation of section 15 may come to reflect the interests of the powerful rather than the disadvantaged.[96]

The wording of section 15 provides support for placing limits on the reviewable distinctions. The inclusion of an enumerated but not exhaustive list of grounds suggests that section 15 does not purport to guarantee overall fairness in the world. Yet, if section 15 were to apply to any distinction whatsoever, it would come close to doing just that.[97] Also relevant is the reference in section 15(2) to "the amelioration of conditions of disadvantaged individuals or groups" including those disadvantaged on the enumerated grounds. If section 15 is to be read as incorporating a coherent set of purposes, we think this language should be read as indicating that the focus of the section as a whole is to remedy disadvantage for named groups and those akin to them.

It is not easy to predict exactly how the courts would narrow section 15 if forced to consider any distinction. One possibility is that they would adopt for all grounds a very limited definition of what constitutes equality, perhaps by imposing a requirement of intent or refusing to require reasonable accommodation. A second possibility is that the standards used in applying section 15 would become incoherent, in part because different claims would have so little similarity with one another, and the result would be *ad hoc* assessments providing only sporadic protection to anyone.

A third possibility is that courts would adopt different levels of scrutiny for different grounds of distinction. We discuss this possibility further in the next section. In our opinion, this option is clearly superior to those just mentioned. But it would require courts to delineate between grounds and thus undermines one of the arguments for an unrestricted list. Also, American experience suggests that the test applicable to grounds unlike those enumerated might become so lax as to provide almost no protection and thus not to be worth the resulting complications.[98]

---

96 Petter, *supra*, note 78.

97 Also, where an otherwise dissimilar collection of individuals complains that they are caused disadvantage by a particular rule, there is a considerable chance that the rule under challenge was a trade-off for other benefits. The court would face the difficult task of evaluating the net effect of a set of laws (*e.g.*, the net effect of taxation on two individuals) or would limit examination to one side of the legislative equation. In contrast, where groups are persistently disadvantaged, the assumption that a particular detriment is offset by other benefits is unwarranted.

98 See the extensive discussion and criticism of the use of levels of scrutiny in *McKinney v. Univ. of Guelph Bd. of Governors*, (1987), 63 O.R. (2d) 1 (C.A.), leave to appeal to S.C.C. granted April 21, 1988 (S.C.C.) For discussion of the American tests, see R. Schwemm, "From *Washington* to *Arlington Heights* and beyond: Discriminatory Purpose in Equal Protection Litigation", [1977] *U. Ill. Law Forum* 961 at 962-963;

It will not always be easy to decide what grounds of distinction are covered. However, the problem is no less manageable, in our opinion, than are the other alternatives for taking account of institutional constraints. In developing the principles for inclusion and exclusion, courts have a rich body of resources to draw upon, including international instruments to which Canada is a signatory, experience under other constitutional guarantees or conventions, and Canadian human rights legislation.

An overall thread which runs through the list in section 15 is that the grounds characterize groups who have suffered historical powerlessness in our society, leading to exclusion from full participation. The powerlessness manifests itself in different ways and in different degrees, as do the ways in which full participation has been restricted. However, it remains a common feature of the enumerated grounds against which other distinctions might be assessed.

In addition, we think the list in section 15 reflects other features common to most of the enumerated grounds. These other features include relative permanency, a history of animosity or bias, lack of control over the characteristic and importance of the characteristic to the personal sense of worth and identity. Not all characteristics on the list are permanent, but most are. Not all have given rise to animosity, but several have.

It might be objected that some of these features are not common to every enumerated ground and thus do not help define a genus. We disagree with that proposition. As linguistic philosophy has pointed out, we can use the word "game" quite sensibly, despite the fact that it may refer to activities as disparate as playing hopscotch and mailing an envelope with a chess move in it. To use another metaphor, a rope is an entity though it is made up of a number of interwoven strands, none of which stretches from one end to the other.

Age is a characteristic which fits with some difficulty into all of the common features of the list which may be discerned. Though beyond our control, we progress through its stages, and while young persons are excluded from political power, older people are not. In our view, however, the inclusion of "age" does not mean that the list should be read as if open-ended. Rather, it suggests that the equality cases involving age should be considered in the light of the reasons for which age must have been included on the list.[99]

L. Simon, "Racially Prejudiced Governmental Actions: A Motivation Theory of the Constitutional Ban Against Racial Discrimination" (1978), 15 *San Diego L. Rev.* 1041 at 1113-1114.

99 Thus, we think that the interests of those at either end of the age spectrum deserve the greatest consideration. See *Stoffman v. Vancouver General Hospital*, [1988] 2 W.W.R.

It would be unduly speculative to suggest exactly what grounds would be included in an extended but limited list. The Parliamentary Committee on Equality Rights concluded that sexual orientation and marital and family status are included.[100] Political belief might be included on the basis that it not only is important to the lives of many individuals but also to our governmental system, and would reinforce other Charter rights such as freedom of expression and association and the right to vote. Citizenship is problematic.[101] It is not permanent and is within the eventual control of a person. Unless we abandon the concept of citizenship entirely, it is clearly relevant to some legitimate governmental purposes such as participation in the elections. On the other hand, the exclusion of non-citizens from the political process favours inclusion here, as does some degree of historical bias and the frequent correlation between citizenship and the enumerated grounds of national and ethnic origin.

We have doubts as to whether geography should be an included ground, though we concede it has in a number of instances received favourable treatment in the courts.[102] For many individuals, residence or location is far from permanent, and it seldom plays a major role in self-identity; it has not traditionally given a rise to pejorative governmental treatment, at least domestically.[103] Moreover, our Constitution reflects a careful balancing of geographical interests, and we doubt that section 15 was intended to make important changes in that matrix.[104]

---

708 (B.C.C.A.), leave to appeal to S.C.C. granted [1988] 4 W.W.R. lxxi (note) (S.C.C.), which struck down a regulation that terminated doctors' admitting privileges to the hospital at age 65. *Connell v. Univ. of B.C.; Harrison v. Univ. of B.C.*, [1988] 2 W.W.R. 688 (B.C.C.A.), leave to appeal to S.C.C. granted [1988] 4 W.W.R. lxxii (note) (S.C.C.), struck down a provision in the British Columbia *Human Rights Act*, S.B.C. 1984, c. 22, limiting protection against age discrimination to those between the ages of 45 and 65. *McKinney v. Univ. of Guelph Bd. of Governors*, supra, note 98, upheld a provision of the *Ontario Human Rights Code* limiting protection against age discrimination to those under the age of 65, but the decision is narrow, and the court concluded only that the limitation could be justified with respect to the particular employment at issue in the case.

100 *Equality For All*, supra, note 50 at 25-34; see also P. Girard, "Sexual Orientation as Human Rights Issue in Canada 1969-1985", in *Charterwatch*, supra, note 31 at 267.

101 See generally *Re Andrews and Law Society of B.C.*, supra, note 46.

102 See e.g., *R. v. Bailey* (1985), 17 C.R.R. 1 (Y.T.S.C.); *R. v. Hamilton*, supra, note 82; *R. v. McPherson* (1986), 47 Alta. L.R.(2d) 64 (Alta. Q.B.); *R. v. Y.D.* (1985), 22 C.C.C. (3d) 464 (N.B.Q.B.).

103 Where geography coincides with other factors such as race or language, we think those factors should be considered directly and that laws which use geography as a surrogate for such grounds should be treated as if they specified the ground explicitly.

104 The cases that have struck down laws on the basis of geographical inequality have all concerned a federal law that did not apply uniformly throughout the country and thus do not directly challenge our federal system. Even so, the ubiquity of economic

In the event that section 15 is not limited solely to enumerated and analogous grounds, we believe there are better options than extending judicial review to any distinction in any circumstance. One is to allow judicial review with regard to any distinction when the claim involves a fundamental interest otherwise protected in the Charter. The option is similar to the "fundamental rights/fundamental interests" strand of protection in the United States.[105] A second and similar option would be to extend such protection whenever access to the courts is affected, whether or not another Charter right is involved, on the ground that such access is fundamental to our legal system. One or the other of these options would cover a number of Charter cases in which an equality argument was accepted, but which otherwise would fall outside the test we describe.[106]

(ii) *Levels of Scrutiny*

Alternatively, the test might incorporate differential standards of review for different grounds of discrimination, producing something akin to the levels of scrutiny incorporated into the United States "equal protection clause."[107] As applied by the American courts, that approach applies a very strict (some would say unattainable) test for the validity of racial distinctions. An intermediate test applies to sex discrimination and certain other grounds, and a very lax "minimum scrutiny" test extends to any other distinction whatsoever.

A Canadian version would almost certainly divide up the grounds differently. The American division has been strongly influenced by the legacy of slavery in that country and has origins in an era when inequality for women was accepted as the norm. Thus, it is unnecessary to review

---

provisions applying only to certain parts of the country belies a consensus in favour of complete geographic uniformity. See, *e.g.*, *Canada - Nova Scotia Oil and Gas Agreement Act*, S.C. 1984, c. 29.

105 See Tribe, *supra*, note 13 at 1002-1011.

106 Examples include *Zutphen Brothers Construction Ltd. v. Dywidag Systems International Ltd. supra*, note 82, which concerned a suit against the Crown, and *McBeth v. Governors of Dalhousie College & Univ.*, *supra*, note 82 which concerned costs to a litigant who represented herself and thus concerned access to the judicial system though it did not involve any other Charter right. Compare *MacKay v. R.*, *supra*, note 17. One might conceivably also include uniform geographical application of the federal criminal law, arguing that the severity of the intrusion distinguishes it from other laws and governmental activity. See *Reference re French Language Rights of Accused in Sask. Criminal Proceedings*, *supra*, note 86. Such recognition would explain cases such as *R. v. Hamilton*, *supra*, note 82; *Tremblay v. R.*, (1985), 20 C.C.C. (3d) 454 (Sask. Q.B.); *Paquette v. R.* (1986), 26 C.C.C. (3d) 289 (Alta. Q.B.), rev'd (1988), 38 C.C.C. (3d) 353 (Alta. C.A.), leave to appeal to S.C.C. refused 41 C.C.C. (3d) vi (note) (S.C.C.).

107 For a general discussion of levels of scrutiny, see Tarnopolsky, *supra*, note 1 at 403-407.

the American standards in detail.[108] But a similar framework could be devised that took account of Canadian patterns of inequality and of the wording of section 15. For example, a different level of scrutiny might apply to the grounds enumerated in section 15 or to some subset of those grounds.[109]

In our view, this option would accommodate to some extent the institutional constraints on the courts. It could afford strong protection to at least some grounds of discrimination, and relatively strong protection to all of the enumerated grounds (and perhaps to others related to them), while allowing leeway in evaluating other more problematic distinctions. Like the limitation of grounds option, it provides an explanation for the inclusion of the enumerated list. Nevertheless, we think that the adoption of levels of scrutiny is inferior to the limitation of protected grounds as a means of accounting for institutional constraints.

In the United States, delineating levels of scrutiny has proved to be a difficult task. Perhaps as a result of that fact, the courts have often used a formalistic approach that conceals whatever principles underlie the determination. The task would be even more difficult in Canada, where neither our history nor the wording of section 15 allows one ground to serve as a paradigm in the way that race does in the United States. That fact would make a principled approach to choices even less likely here. Also, if each ground is associated with a particular level of scrutiny, there is little room for flexibility to take account of other factors, such as whether or not the exclusion was intentional.[110]

(iii) *Unintended Effects*

Another possible limitation would be to consider only intentional

---

108 Therefore, our brief summary has ignored many nuances concerning the American levels of scrutiny approach. For example, it is possible that the test incorporates a spectrum of intermediate standards rather than a single standard of intermediate scrutiny. For a fuller description of the approach, see Tarnopolsky, *ibid.*

109 Tarnopolsky, *ibid.* at 422. More recent comments of Mr. Justice Tarnopolsky suggest that he may be in the process of re-evaluating this approach; comments at a Conference on the *Canadian Charter of Rights and Freedoms*, University of Ottawa, February 1985. In *McKinney v. Univ. of Guelph Bd. of Governors, supra,* note 98, the Court extensively reviews the Americal level of scrutiny approach and rejects it.

110 In the United States, this lack of flexibility has caused the courts to refuse to recognize unintended adverse effects for the purposes of the "equal protection clause" even though they are recognized for the purposes of antidiscrimination statutes and other constitutional rights such as freedom of religion. See W. Black, "Intent or Effects: Section 15 of the Charter of Rights and Freedoms", in J.M. Weiler & R.M. Elliot, eds., *Litigating the Values of a Nation: The Canadian Charter of Rights and Freedoms* (Toronto: Carswell, 1985) p. 120 at 141-143.

distinctions and to ignore unintended effects on a group. As we noted in Part 2, such a limitation would prevent the courts from affording meaningful protection in a range of circumstances that frequently cause disadvantage related to grounds enumerated in section 15. It is undeniable, however, that the consideration of unintended effects imposes an additional burden on the judiciary.

The cases decided to date regarding section 15 are inconclusive, in part because most of them have considered distinctions that were explicit and obviously intended.[111] However, Canadian case law in related areas points in the direction of taking unintended effects into account for the purposes of section 15.

In the *Simpsons-Sears* case,[112] the Supreme Court of Canada held that the *Ontario Human Rights Code* prohibits conduct that has an unintended adverse effect on a group, as well as intentional discrimination. It seems clear that such protection is now the statutory norm in Canada.

The Supreme Court of Canada has also held that other sections of the Charter protect against unintended intrusion on the guaranteed rights and freedoms. Most notably, Chief Justice Dickson stated in the *Big M Drug Mart* case that one must examine the effects as well as the purpose of a statute in determining whether there has been a violation of freedom

---

111 In *Horbas v. Min. of Employment & Immigration (Can.)* (1985), 22 D.L.R. (4th) 600 (F.C.T.D.), the court rejected on the facts the contention that the immigration rules concerning entry of spouses had an unintended adverse impact on persons of certain religions or national or ethnic origins. *Wilson v. Medical Services Comm. of B.C.*, *supra*, note 87, rejected the contention that provisions concerning participation by doctors in the medical services plan had an adverse impact on women and younger doctors, but the court also stated that both purpose and effect were relevant in applying s. 15. In *R. v. Punch* (1985), 48 C.R. (3d) 374 at 385 (N.W.T.S.C.), the court held that the provision of the *Criminal Code* specifying that juries in the Northwest Territories are to be composed of six rather than 12 members violates s. 15. The court relied in part on the conclusion that smaller juries create an unintended risk of disproportionately excluding women and members of ethnic groups. But the force of the case is undermined by the failure to cite evidence supporting that conclusion and by the statement that "discrimination" in s. 15 involves stigma or an unwarranted stereotype. It seems, at the very least, more difficult to find such consequences if the effect on the group was not contemplated by the decision-maker.

Other cases contain *obiter dicta* that effects as well as purpose are relevant: see, *e.g.*, *Reference re French Language Rights of Accused in Sask. Criminal Proceedings*, *supra*, note 86; *Re Andrews and Law Society of B.C.*, *supra*, note 46 at 609. But they are countered by cases that have defined equality in ways that seem to preclude consideration of unintended effects: see, *e.g.*, *Re B.C. & Yukon Building & Construction Trades Council and A.G. British Columbia* (1986), 22 D.L.R. (4th) 540 at 549 (B.C.S.C.).

112 *Ont. Human Rights Comm. v. Simpsons-Sears Ltd.*, *supra*, note 60. While the case was pending, the Ontario *Human Rights Code, 1981*, S.O. 1981, c. 53. was amended to make clear that unintended effects came within the protection. See also *C.N.R. v. Canada (Human Rights Comm.)*, [1987] 1 S.C.R. 1114 at 1136-1137.

of religion.[113] The concurring judgment of Wilson J. went even further in suggesting that the primary focus in applying the Charter is an examination of effects rather than purpose.[114] In *Edwards Books*, the court again took account of unintended effects though it upheld the legislation.[115] Because section 2(b) and section 15 of the Charter have the common function of protecting religious groups against unwarranted intrusion on their interests, it would be somewhat anomalous if one section covered unintended effects while the other did not. The result would be broader protection against religious discrimination than against discrimination on any other ground.

American jurisprudence provides reasons for uncertainty, however. Like the Canadian courts, the United States Supreme Court has interpreted freedom of religion in a manner that protects against unintended intrusions on the right.[116] Statutory protection against discrimination has also been interpreted as covering unintended adverse impact.[117] Yet, the United States Supreme Court has stated that unintended impact on a racial group or on women will not be treated as race or sex discrimination for the purposes of the "equal protection clause" of the United States Constitution.[118]

Two justifications might be given for excluding unintended effects.[119] The first assumes that the legislative process only goes awry if influenced by some pejorative judgment about a group. Unintended effects thus provide no indication that the group has been treated unfairly, and there is no reason for judicial intervention. We do not agree. As we noted, we think the legislative process may undervalue the interests of persistently disadvantaged groups for reasons other than condescension or animosity. The causes of such undervaluation include the under-representation of a group in the decision-making body and the tendency to overlook the concerns of minorities.

The second line of argument is that the courts are incapable of assessing such unintended effects, however unfair they may be. Cases such as *Simpson-Sears* and *Big M Drug Mart* are distinguished on the ground

---

113 *R. v. Big M Drug Mart Ltd.*, *supra*, note 35 at 331.

114 *Ibid.* at 359.

115 *Edwards Books & Art Ltd. v. R.*, [1986] 2 S.C.R. 713.

116 See, *e.g.*, *Sherbert v. Verner*, 374 U.S. 398 (1963); *Wisconsin v. Yoder*, 406 U.S. 205 (1972).

117 *Griggs v. Duke Power Co.*, 401 U.S. 424 (1971).

118 *Washington v. Davis*, 426 U.S. 229 (1976); *Village of Arlington Heights v. Metro Housing Dev. Corp.*, 429 U.S. 252 (1977); *Personnel Administrator of Mass. v. Feeney*, 442 U.S. 256 (1979); see also *Castenda v. Partida.*, 430 U.S. 482 (1977). Since the United States minimum scrutiny test covers all distinctions, there would frequently still be a modicum of protection. For example, the law considered in *Feeney* makes an explicit distinction between veterans and non-veterans that would be subject to minimum scrutiny, but the claimant was not afforded the higher level of scrutiny that applies to sex discrimination.

119 For a more extensive discussion of the issue of intent, see Black, *supra*, note 110.

that section 15 covers a much wider area and thus presents greater difficulties. That argument deserves to be taken into account, but we do not think it justifies placing unintended effects outside the scope of protection.[120]

While unintended effects may sometimes raise complex and unfamiliar issues, on other occasions the issues raised will be straightforward ones that the courts have considered in other contexts. If experience in applying section 15 shows that we need restrictions on judicial review of unintended effects, controls can be developed that are sensitive to the particular sources of difficulty that arise. For example, courts might give greater deference to legislative or executive determinations about some complex economic effects (the effects of a particular form of taxation on minorities, perhaps) than they would with regard to other unintended effects (for example, the effect of a height and weight requirement on employment opportunities for women). It is even possible that some substantive areas might be excluded from judicial review because experience demonstrated the inability of the judiciary to evaluate them competently. However, the complete exclusion of protection against unintended effects would seem to be far too unsophisticated an instrument to deal with the many variables that deserve consideration.

In addition, any difficulties in incorporating protection against unintended impact must be discounted by the difficulty that would arise in drawing the line between intentional and unintentional conduct. The existing authorities reveal considerable confusion on this point. Some equate "intent" with malice toward a disadvantaged group, or at least a pejorative judgment about the group,[121] while other cases treat conduct

---

120 See *Ont. Human Rights Comm. v. Simpsons-Sears Ltd.*, *supra*, note 60; *R. v. Big M Drug Mart Ltd.*, *supra*, note 35. The concept of unintended adverse impact on a group requires some reconsideration of the "principle of universal application" described in *MacKay v. R.*, *supra*, note 17, in interpreting the *Canadian Bill of Rights*. If a law has a disproportionate adverse effect on a protected group, "universal application" should not save it. On the other hand, unless one limits the grounds of distinction that will be reviewed, it does not make sense even presumptively to require that every law affect every individual in exactly the same way.

121 Compare *Re B.C. & Yukon Building & Construction Trades Council and A.G. British Columbia*, *supra*, note 111 at 549 (suggesting that singling out alone is not enough if it is not for the purpose of treating persons differently simply because they are members of a class). Other statements are more ambiguous but carry a similar connotation: *Shewchuk v. Ricard* (1986), 28 D.L.R. (4th) 429 at 435 (B.C.C.A.) (*per* Nemetz C.J.B.C. concurring) leave to appeal to S.C.C. refused [1987] 2 W.W.R. lxx (note) (S.C.C.). ("The distinctions in the act [providing a benefit for mothers but not fathers] are not for the purpose of discriminating against males").

as discriminatory in the absence of evidence of malice.[122] The problem is particularly difficult since the decision under challenge is often one of a collective body such as a legislature which may have no single motivation or objective.

We have suggested that section 15 be interpreted as limiting judicial review to the enumerated grounds and other grounds analogous to them. If the possible grounds of challenge under section 15 were completely open-ended, we would have greater concern about the ability of the judiciary to deal with unintended effects. Almost any law has an adverse impact on some collection of people — sales taxes disproportionately hurt big consumers, traffic laws penalize drivers, and so forth. Thus, the potential challenges would be almost limitless if unintended impact on any collection of individuals were to give rise to a claim.[123]

Our conclusion is that excluding unintended effects from consideration in reviewing section 15 would seriously compromise the purposes underlying section 15 and that institutional considerations can be met by means that are more consistent with those purposes.[124] If judicial review were extended to an unlimited list of grounds, however, there would be a strong argument for considering unintended effects only with respect to enumerated grounds and those related to them.

(iv) *Routine Deference*

Last, and in our opinion least in all senses, is the option of a single, comprehensive standard incorporating great deference to legislative and executive decisions and providing watered-down protection in an infinitude

---

122 See, *e.g.*, *Ont. Human Rights Comm. v. Etobicoke*, [1982] 1 S.C.R. 202. In *C.N.R. v. Canada (Human Rights Comm.)*, *supra*, note 112, the court cited a continuing confusion of the notions of "intent" and "malice". See also W. Black, "From Intent to Effect: New Standards in Human Rights" (1980), 1 C.H.R.R. c/1; Ontario Ministry of the Attorney General, *Sources for the Interpretation of Equality Rights under the Charter: a Background Paper*, January 1985, at 243-245. For this reason, it is sometimes difficult to determine whether seemingly consistent statements about the necessity of consent in fact hide a difference of opinion. Compare *Re Ont. Human Rights Comm. and Simpsons-Sears Ltd.*, *supra*, note 60, with *South West Africa Cases (Second Phase)*, 1966, dissenting opinion of Tanaka J., in I. Brownlie, *Basic Documents on Human Rights*, 2d ed. (1981), at 441.

123 Also, if the collectivity disproportionately affected would not be considered an identifiable group for any purpose other than the terms of the law or policy under challenge, it may be sensible to presume that the detriment caused by that law is counterbalanced by other benefits afforded by the legal system. That presumption would be inapt as applied to members of a persistently disadvantaged and identifiable group.

124 Other sources of protection are inadequate. Human rights legislation covers a limited range of activity, is subject to repeal, and may be subject to the explicit terms of other legislation.

of cases. The result would be a replication of the experience under the *Canadian Bill of Rights*, which would provide very little protection to disadvantaged groups (or anyone else).[125] It also has similarities to the American "minimum scrutiny" test, except that it would apply to all grounds of discrimination.[126]

In our opinion, this solution cannot be justified. It is inconsistent with the purposes underlying section 15, primarily because it would do very little to assist disadvantaged groups. It also takes only the crudest account of the institutional limitations of the judiciary since it would preclude probing review even with respect to issues that the courts are fully competent to evaluate.[127] The legislative history of section 15 provides clear evidence of an intent to overturn the extreme deference of the courts in applying the equality provisions of the *Canadian Bill of Rights*.[128] In addition, the list of enumerated grounds in section 15 seems to have been designed in part to depart from the American test of minimum scrutiny, which also incorporates such deference. Deference with regard to section 15 would be anomalous, for cases interpreting other Charter rights have rejected a stance of uniform deference.[129] While the application of section 15 cannot ignore institutional constraints, the response should be in terms of more carefully refined limits.

4. THE CONSTITUTIONAL CONTEXT

Section 15(1) is at the centre of a number of Charter provisions, all of which relate to equality, and consideration of an equality challenge will often require consideration of two or more of these provisions. Therefore, before outlining a procedure for considering equality challenges, it is useful to review briefly the sections that may come into play.

(a) Section 15(1)

It is clearly impossible to give any capsule summary of the meaning of section 15(1). Our purpose here is merely to call attention to its structural

---

125 Though the result would be the same, the reasoning would not be identical. For a review of the reasoning under the *Bill of Rights*, see Tarnopolsky, *supra*, note 1 at 406-422, and Tarnopolsky, *supra*, note 18 at 166-191.

126 For a description of minimum scrutiny, see Tribe, *supra*, note 13 at 994-1000.

127 *E.g.*, Charter challenges to administrative conduct: see *e.g.*, *Headley v. Public Service Comm. Appeal Bd.* (1987), 35 D.L.R. (4th) 568 (F.C.A.), amended (1987), 75 N.R. 319 (F.C.A.); compare *Singh v. Min. of Employment & Immigration*, [1985] 1 S.C.R. 177.

128 See Bayefsky, *supra*, note 19 at 11-25; Tarnopolsky, *supra*, note 1 at 421-422.

129 See, *e.g.*, *Hunter v. Southam Inc.*, *supra*, note 22; *R. v. Big M Drug Mart*, *supra*, note 35; *R. v. Oakes*, [1986] 1 S.C.R. 103.

quirks. Our predecessor in this work suggested that section 15(1) "has taken the form of a camel that a committee charged with designing a horse achieves".[130] There is even disagreement about how many rights are included. One school of thought suggests that there are four separate guarantees of equality (equality before the law, under the law, equal protection of the law and equal benefit of the law).[131] Others have suggested the possibility that the first portion ("equal before and under the law") sets out the spheres of activity which the section covers, and that the following part of the subsection defines the rights.[132]

Though the wording is inelegant, there seems to be consensus that it has clarified some important matters, which seem to be accepted almost without question in the cases:

1. Section 15 applies to the substantive content of the law as well as to the manner in which laws are administered.[133] Thus, the section would apply both to a law containing a discriminatory provision[134] and to inequality in the implementation of an otherwise unobjectionable law.[135]
2. The section applies regardless of the nature of the substantive provisions contained in the law. In particular, it applies to laws affording benefits (unemployment insurance, for example) as well as to laws that prohibit or regulate.[136]

Beyond those points, there is considerable disagreement about the function of the various parts of section 15(1). For example, some commentators have suggested that inclusion of the words "equal protection" may have been intended to incorporate American jurisprudence, since

---

130 Tarnopolsky, *supra*, note 1 at 396. Much of the inelegance seems to have resulted from attempts to circumvent limits the courts had placed on the equality section of the *Canadian Bill of Rights*.

131 See, *e.g.*, Eberts, *supra*, note 64 at 206.

132 See R. Elliot, "Interpreting the Charter — Use of the Earlier Versions as an Aid" (1982), *U.B.C. L. Rev.* (Charter ed.) 11 at 17; K. Lysyk, "Definition and Enforcement of Charter Equality Rights", in *Righting the Balance, supra*, note 23, p. 215 at 216-218. Mr. Justice Lysyk notes that this question may not be of great significance if the latter two formulations are interpreted broadly, and it is noteworthy that the interrelationship between the different formulations has not attracted much judicial attention.

133 See, *e.g.*, Bayefsky, *supra*, note 19, 1, at 3-4, 12.

134 See, *e.g.*, *Re Andrews and Law Society of B.C.*, *supra*, note 46. For a discussion of the relationship between equality and law enforcement activities, see C. Boyle & S. Noonan, "Prostitution and Pornography: Beyond Formal Equality," in *Charterwatch, supra*, note 31, p. 225 at 240-244.

135 See, *e.g.*, *Headley v. Public Service Comm. Appeal Bd.*, *supra*, note 127, where the challenge failed but the section was applied; compare *Reference re French Language Rights of Accused in Sask. Criminal Proceedings, supra*, note 86.

136 Gold, *supra*, note 49 at 135-136; Tarnopolsky, *supra*, note 1 at 421.

the same words appear in the United States Constitution, while others have suggested otherwise.[137] There is also debate about the function of the words "equal benefit". Some commentators suggest that it was intended only to ensure that a group cannot be unjustifiably excluded from a law providing a benefit.[138] Others suggest that it affects more fundamentally the meaning of equality incorporated in the section.[139] The last part of the section ("without discrimination . . .") has proved to be a source of major disagreement. Some commentators have stated that it is the first portion of the section that is primary and that the "without discrimination" language serves primarily as a grammatical bridge to the list of enumerated grounds.[140] In contrast, some cases and commentators have placed more emphasis on the "without discrimination" clause, to the point that what precedes it becomes little more than a preamble.[141]

(b) Section 15(2)

It seems to be generally agreed that the purpose of section 15(2) is to ensure that section 15 does not preclude affirmative action programs.[142] There has been a great debate in the United States as to whether the "equal protection clause" in the American Constitution precludes such pro-grams.[143] Section 15(2) seems to have been designed to avoid similar controversy in Canada.

The subsection has been read by some as an exception to the provisions of section 15(1).[144] Others have suggested that section 15 should be read as a whole and that section 15(2) helps to define the meaning of the equality rights set out in section 15(1).[145] We generally agree with the latter view.

---

137 Compare Bayefsky, *supra*, note 19 at 13, with Gold, *supra*, note 49 at 139-145.

138 Tarnopolsky, *supra*, note 1 at 421; see *Bliss v. A.G. Canada, supra*, note 84.

139 See Bayefsky, *supra*, note 19 at 21.

140 *Ibid.* at 26-27.

141 See *Re Andrews and Law Society of B.C., supra*, note 46. The issue is discussed more fully below in Part 5.

142 See *Rebic v. Collver* (1986), 28 C.C.C. (3d) 154 at 166 (B.C.C.A.) (*per* Macfarlane J.A., concurring); Fogarty, *supra*, note 19 at 113-114.

143 For a review of this history, see Tarnopolsky, *supra*, note 1 at 423-430; M. Cornish, "Affirmative Action and S. 15(2) of the Charter", in Canadian Institute for Professional Development, *Equality Rights and Employment: Preparing for Fundamental Change - East* (Toronto, 1986) C-1-29.

144 See *Weatherall v. A.G. Canada*, [1988] 1 F.C. 369 (T.D.), rev'd in part (1988), 65 C.R. (3d) 27 (F.C.A.); *Shewchuk v. Ricard supra*, note 121 at 447. See also P. Blache, "Affirmative Action: To Equality Through Inequalities", in *Litigating the Values of a Nation, supra*, note 110 p. 165 at 179.

145 A. Bayefsky, "The Orientation of Section 15 of the Canadian Charter of Rights and Freedoms" in *Litigating the Values of a Nation, supra*, note 110, p. 105 at 111-112;

If section 15(1) does not itself provide for the amelioration of conditions of disadvantaged individuals and groups, the two subsections would seem to reflect views of equality that are fundamentally at odds with one another. That is not to say that subsection (2) has no operative effect. On occasion, different equality interests will come into conflict, and section 15(2) provides a guide as to how to resolve those conflicts.[146]

It seems clear that section 28 does not preclude affirmative action programs pursuant to section 15(2) that apply to members of one sex.[147] Such a result would be inconsistent not only with the purposes of section 15, taken as a whole, but it would fail to account for the reference in subsection (2) to programs for persons disadvantaged due to sex.[148] The more plausible interpretation is that section 28 refers to the section as a whole rather than to section 15(1) in isolation.,

What kinds of provisions meet the criteria set out in section 15(2)? Affirmative action programs can take a variety of forms which reflect different conceptions of equality.[149] Some are much broader than others. It is too early to define precisely what kinds of programs will be found consistent with section 15(2). But a unanimous Supreme Court of Canada decision applying the *Canadian Human Rights Act* supports a liberal interpretation of permissible affirmative action.[150] While section 15 was not at issue, we think it embodies a similar approach to affirmative action. On the other hand, the *Apsit* case[151] reflects a narrower approach. It suggests that there must be a causal relationship between the plan and the cause of the disadvantage.

There is some potential for affirmative action plans to conflict with the right to equal benefit of the law. Affirmative action plans are necessarily limited to certain specified groups.[152] As a result, they will inevitably exclude some people who have suffered comparable disadvantage, and those people may claim a denial of equal benefit of the law. Therefore,

---

W. Tarnopolsky, "The Equality Rights in the Canadian Charter of Rights and Freedoms" (1983), 61 *Can. Bar Rev.* 242 at 257.

146 Such situations are discussed in Part 5, *infra*.

147 See *Weatherall v. A.G. Canada, supra,* note 144 at 436-437.

148 See Eberts, *supra,* note 64, at 216-217; Tarnopolsky, *supra,* note 1 at 436-437.

149 See Blache, *supra,* note 144 at 176-178.

150 See *C.N.R. v. Canada (Human Rights Comm.), supra,* note 112.

151 *Apsit. v. Man. Human Rights Comm.* (1985), 22 C.R.R. 134 (Man. Q.B.), additional reasons at [1988] 1 W.W.R. 277 (Man. Q.B.), rev'd in part (December 7, 1988) Doc. No. 63188 (Man. C.A.). It is inappropriate for us to comment extensively, since one of us (Black) was a witness in the case.

152 It would almost never be administratively possible to measure the disadvantage suffered by each individual applicant to, *e.g.,* an educational program. Moreover, a requirement that every program include every individual who is disadvantaged in a way comparable to that of members of the groups included in the program would be to refuse to take

section 15 will sometimes require consideration of competing equality interests.

In considering such conflicts, we think the appropriate guide is that a provision which adversely affects others must contribute significantly to the achievement of the goals of an affirmative action program.[153] In addition, we derive guidance from the fact that section 15(2) specifies that the program should have as its *object* the amelioration of conditions of disadvantaged groups. This wording suggests that a law or program is not saved by section 15(2) if the benefit to a disadvantaged group is an accidental side-effect rather than the purpose of the provision. We also think that a program would be suspect if the criteria for inclusion in the program were inconsistent with the goal of ameliorating disadvantage — if the most severely disadvantaged members of a group were excluded, for example.[154]

(c) Section 28

Section 28 of the Charter reads:

---

account of the added harm that is caused when the disadvantage is to an identifiable group, as compared with individual disadvantage. The latter point is discussed in Part 2, *supra*.

153 See *Shewchuk v. Ricard, supra,* note 121, where a particular statute allowed unwed mothers but not fathers to sue for child maintenance. In a concurring judgment, Chief Justice Nemetz upheld the legislation as an affirmative action program for women. We disagree with this reasoning since the only benefit for women that derives from the exclusion of men would be that a tiny proportion of women whose children were in the custody of the unwed father would be exempt from paying maintenance. Certainly such a result does almost nothing to rectify any significant source of disadvantage to women. The argument would, of course, be otherwise if the attack had been on the *inclusion* of women.

154 See *Harrison v. Univ. of B.C.; Connell v. Univ. of B.C.,* [1986] 6 W.W.R. 7 (B.C.S.C.), additional reasons at [1987] 2 W.W.R. 378 (B.C.S.C.), where the court found that a provision in the British Columbia *Human Rights Act* limiting the prohibition of age discrimination in employment to those between the ages of 45 and 65 would come within s. 15(2). It seems clear that those over 65 are even more clearly disadvantaged with respect to employment than are those within the specified ages. On appeal, the limitation on protected ages was struck down: *Connell v. Univ. of B.C., supra,* note 99.

An issue arises if a scheme taken as a whole provides a net benefit to a disadvantaged group, but a member of the group challenges a particular part of the scheme that, taken in isolation, causes detriment. *E.g.,* the *Young Offenders Act,* S.C. 1980-81-82-83, c. 110 [R.S.C. 1985, c. Y-1], generally operates to the benefit of young people, but deprives them of specific benefits such as the possibility of an intermittent sentence: see *R. v. G.* (June 16, 1986) C.A. No. V000261 (B.C.C.A.). We have no universal solution to this problem, but think it is relevant whether or not the particular provision causing disadvantage is integral to the scheme.

Notwithstanding anything in this Charter, the rights and freedoms referred to in it are guaranteed equally to male and female persons.

There have been few cases or commentaries centred on section 28.[155] As the former Professor Tarnopolsky has pointed out, because of its history section 28 must be seen as squarely directed toward overcoming the majority decisions of the Supreme Court of Canada which narrowly construed the "equality before the law" clause in section 1(b) of the *Canadian Bill of Rights,* rendering it a dead letter so far as protection against sex discrimination was concerned.[156] As well, section 28 was designed to ensure that the American experience, in which sex discrimination was afforded a lower standard of protection than race discrimination, would not be replicated.

In only a handful of cases have courts applied section 28, and what very little discussion there has been at the appellate level reveals different approaches to section 28. In both *Shewchuk v. Ricard*[157] and *Reference Re Family Benefits Act (N.S.), S.5,*[158] the issue was whether social legislation which provided benefits for women should be struck down because it failed to provide benefits for men.[159] In both, it was argued that section 28 requires any sex discrimination to be seen as a *prima facie* infringement of section 15. The British Columbia Court of Appeal in *Shewchuk* declined to interpret section 28 as affecting the standard by which the legitimacy of the

---

155 See de Jong, *supra*, note 51 at 493; Eberts, *supra*, note 64 at 211; D. Gibson, *The Law of the Charter: General Principles* (Toronto: Carswell, 1986) at 69; Tarnopolsky, *supra*, note 1 at 436; Gold, *supra*, note 49. The cases are discussed briefly below.

156 Tarnopolsky, *supra*, note 1 at 436. de Jong, *supra*, note 51 at 494-512 has reviewed the history of the struggle between politicians and representatives of women's groups which led to the final wording of s. 28. de Jong summarizes her view of the process which led to s. 28 as follows (at 512): "The history of section 28 indicates that Canadian politicians were reluctant to enforce or promote the principle of sexual equality without an explicit directive to do so. Public support for the women's lobby, along with the strength of the lobby itself, provided the necessary political directive, which section 28 now embodies. This solution and the manner in which it was achieved now represent a clear instruction to the courts to enforce the principle of sexual equality as part of the Supreme Law of Canada." See also C. Hosek, "Women and the Constitutional Process," in K. Banting & R. Simeon, eds., *And No One Cheered: Federalism, Democracy and the Constitution Act* (Toronto: Methuen, (1983) and P. Kome, *The Taking of 28: Women Challenge The Constitution* (1983).

157 *Supra*, note 121.

158 (1986), 75 N.S.R. (2d) 338 (C.A.).

159 In *Shewchuk*, *supra*, note 121, it was the *Child Paternity and Support Act*, R.S.BC. 1979, c. 49, which permitted women who were mothers of children born out of wedlock to apply for declarations of paternity and consequential financial support from the fathers. In *Reference re Family Benefits Act, supra*, note 158, it was legislation which permitted single mothers to receive welfare benefits only available to single fathers if they were disabled.

legislation would be tested.[160] In contrast, the Nova Scotia Court of Appeal in the *Family Benefits Act* case, found that section 28 makes legislative classifications based on sex *prima facie* discriminatory.[161]

In a few cases dealing with *Criminal Code* provisions contemplating only female victims and only male perpetrators of sexual offences, the courts have been influenced by section 28 in concluding that section 15 prohibits such legislation.[162] In some cases dealing with family law issues, such as consent to adoption by natural fathers, section 28 has come into play.[163] As well, in one appellate case dealing with a challenge to the *Criminal Code* prohibition against obscenity, Mr. Justice Anderson, in concurring reasons, invoked section 28 in the context of a discussion about the effect of pornography on the degradation of women, and the threat such an effect poses to the achievement of true equality between the sexes.[164]

The lack of authoritative cases is likely to continue for an appreciable period of time, since section 28 by its very nature will not provide the main linchpin for Charter challenges. However, the presence of section 28 in the Charter may have a pervasive effect on the way in which sex equality claims are viewed. In our view, it would be unfortunate if that effect proved to be a prescription for identical treatment of men and women in all cases, even where identical treatment worsens or perpetuates disadvantage.

Although a literal interpretation of section 28 may lead one to the conclusion that it does no more than reiterate what follows from the language of the Charter (the expressions "everyone", "every citizen", "any person", "every individual" and "any member of the public" are clearly referable to both men and women),[165] it can hardly be said that section 28 accomplishes nothing. Historically, there have been many instances in which courts indeed took the position that such general language did not

---

160 *Supra*, note 121.

161 *Supra*, note 158 at 354.

162 See, *e.g.*, *R. v. Howell* (1986), 57 Nfld. & P.E.I.R. 198 at 203 (Nfld. Dist. Ct.) *R. v. D.I.L.* (1985), 46 C.R. (3d) 172 at 176 (Ont. Dist. Ct.), rev'd (1986), 51 C.R. (3d) 296 (Ont. C.A.). See also *R. v. Punch*, *supra*, note 111 at 392, where the issue was the constitutional validity of the provision for six-person juries in the Northwest Territories, but s. 28 was referred to in the context of arguments about the necessity for juries to be representative of the population.

163 *N.M. v. B.C. Superintendent of Family & Child Services*, [1987] 3 W.W.R. 176 (B.C.S.C.), where the court said (at 187): "If marital status is a protected ground for women, then it must also be for men."

164 *R. v. Red Hot Video Ltd.* (1985), 18 C.C.C. (3d) 1 at 23 (B.C.C.A.), leave to appeal to S.C.C. refused (1985), 46 C.R. (3d) XXV (note) (S.C.C.).

165 E.A. Driedger makes this point in "The Canadian Charter of Rights and Freedoms" (1982), 14 *Ottawa L. Rev.* 373.

apply to women, and section 28, if all that it does is install a one-way ratchet against backsliding on this issue, has accomplished something.[166] As de Jong points out,[167] even a literal interpretation of section 28 should lead to the conclusion that both men and women are legal persons, rather than the perhaps different conclusion that the rights and freedoms in the Charter are guaranteed to male persons and to female persons. In other words, section 28 should properly be seen as making a statement about the elevation of women to full legal personhood. If so, consequential change in the concept of "legal personhood" is necessary to ensure that women do fully have that status. On this substantive basis, section 28 could have enormous consequences.[168]

In addition, we think that the following can be said about section 28:

1. The rights and freedoms in the Charter are guaranteed to both male and female persons, and are guaranteed *equally* to male and female persons. This should mean, for example, that whatever "liberty" and "security of the person" mean in section 7 of the Charter, different physical capacities do not justify a lower standard in considering intrusions affecting only women.[169]
2. de Jong argues that section 28 means that sex discrimination can never be justified under section 1.[170] Others have argued to the contrary.[171] Precluding section 1 review would likely lead to differential standards of review.[172] We have discussed above the problems we perceive with

---

166 The history of women's entry into the legal profession shows many such cases, See L. Smith, M. Stephenson & G. Quijano, "The Legal Profession and Women: Finding Articles in British Columbia" (1973), 8 *U.B.C. L. Rev.* 137. Of course, *Edwards v. A.G. Canada*, [1930] A.C. 124 (P.C.) provides a paradigm example.

167 *Supra*, note 51 at 517.

168 For a discussion of how such a substantive interpretation would fit in with a theory of equality centering on the subordination of women to men, see MacKinnon, *supra*, note 37 at 37.

169 This could have important consequences if, for example, attempts were made to force a woman to undergo medical treatment recommended for the sake of a foetus which she is carrying. For commentary on this and related issues, see S. Rogers, "Fetal Rights and Maternal Rights: Is There a Conflict?" (1986), 1 *Can. Jo. Women & Law* 156; J. Gallagher, "Prenatal Invasions & Interventions: What's Wrong with Fetal Rights" (1987), 10 *Harvard Women's Law Jo.* 9. For a Canadian case in which such issues have arisen, see *Re R.* (1987), 9 R.F.L. (3d) 415 (B.C. Prov. Ct.).

170 de Jong, *supra*, note 51 at 525; see also A. Tremblay, "Le principe d'égalité et les clauses anti-discriminatoires" (1984), 18 *R.J.T.* 329 at 341.

171 Eberts, *supra*, note 64 at 216; Gibson, *supra*, note 155 at 69. *Reference Re Family Benefits Act (N.S.), S. 5, supra,* note 158, the court went on to consider s. 1 after concluding that sex discrimination would constitute a *prima facie* violation.

172 Although not necessarily.

differential standards of review. More importantly, we fear that if resort to section 1 is precluded, this might correspondingly impair the courts' ability to deal appropriately with claims brought by men attacking legislation which benefits women. For these reasons, while we agree that section 28 makes it clear that sex discrimination is to be taken seriously, we do not think the use of section 1 is blocked.

3. Section 28 guarantees that the multicultural interests recognized in section 27 are themselves afforded equally to men and women and ensures that section 27 does not justify inequality based on sex with respect to other rights.

4. We agree with de Jong that section 28 forms a substantive part of each right and freedom referred to in the Charter.[173]

5. The use of the term "notwithstanding" in section 28 and its legislative history strongly support the conclusion that section 33 will not be available to protect legislation which violates the guarantees of sex equality.[174]

6. As we have noted, section 28 does not preclude the existence of affirmative action programs for the benefit of women.

7. As we note in Part 5, section 28 does not preclude section 15 from taking account of the historical and ongoing disadvantage of women as compared with men.[175]

(d) Other Charter Sections Relevant to Equality

Several other sections of the Charter are relevant to section 15 either because they embody special qualifications to that section or because they assist in its interpretation. Section 25 specifies that Charter rights "shall not be construed so as to abrogate or derogate from any aboriginal treaty or other rights or freedoms that pertain to the aboriginal peoples of Canada . . .". This section must be read together with section 35 which entrenches such rights. Thus, it seems clear that a land claims settlement could not be challenged on the ground that it provides benefits only to aboriginal peoples.[176] However, section 35(4) provides that the rights afforded by the section shall apply equally to men and women.[177] Section 29 preserves

---

173 de Jong, *supra*, note 51 at 520.

174 See de Jong, *ibid*, and Gibson, *supra*, note 155 at 128-129, 69-70.

175 See *infra*, in text relating to note 304.

176 While it seems clear that s. 25 immunizes such a provision on grounds of alleged race discrimination, it is much more controversial whether it would apply if such a settlement contained terms that discriminate on some other ground such as sex. For a discussion of this issue, see D. Sanders, ch. 17 "Pre-existing Rights: The Aboriginal Peoples of Canada", *infra*.

177 Compare *A.G. Canada v. Lavell*, [1974] S.C.R. 1349.

other constitutional rights in respect of denominational, separate or dissentient schools.[178]

Section 27, which specifies that the Charter be interpreted in a manner consistent with the preservation and enhancement of the multicultural heritage of Canadians, provides valuable assistance in interpreting section 15. Because the goals of section 27 so obviously require special measures to preserve multicultural heritage against the forces of assimilation, the section supports a conception of equality that allows for differential treatment in order to achieve equality of more remote results. The section also supports the provision that section 15 is not a purely individualistic provision and that it provides for equality from a group perspective.[179]

5. POSSIBLE TESTS FOR INEQUALITY IN THE CONTEXT OF JUDICIAL REVIEW OF LAWS UNDER SECTION 15

We have suggested a paradigm of equality underlying section 15, and described some institutional constraints upon the process of judicial review, arguing from these premises to a particular framework of analysis for equality claims. We will now address more specifically the question of what test or tests might be used by the courts in adjudicating challenges to legislation or practices under section 15. We will review some of the tests which have emerged in the case law to date. We will then propose a test which would fit within the framework of analysis we have developed. At the outset, we will discuss some preliminary issues about the application of the Charter.

(a) Scope of Application of the Charter

Two ways in which the scope of the application of section 15 is liable to be limited are by restricting the class of parties who may be called upon to answer for alleged violations of equality rights (referred to here as "defendants"), and by restricting the class of parties who may be permitted to assert equality rights (referred to here as "plaintiffs"[180]).

---

178 *Reference re Bill 30, An Act to amend the Education Act (Ont.), supra,* note 44, which discussed the preservation of these rights even apart from s. 29.

179 See Tarnopolsky, *supra* note 1 at 437-439.

180 We recognize that in some cases the mode of proceeding will make this terminology inaccurate and also that Charter claims can arise in contexts in which the "defendant" to the Charter claim is the plaintiff in the style of cause, and the "plaintiff" is the defendant in the style of cause.

(i) *Limitation on "Defendants"*

Against whom are the section 15 equality rights enforceable? The issue of the application of the Charter is addressed elsewhere in this volume, so we will restrict our comments to a few particular issues relating to section 15. The Supreme Court of Canada, in *Retail, Wholesale & Department Store Union, Local 580 v. Dolphin Delivery Ltd.*,[181] has held that by virtue of section 32, the Charter applies only to legislatures and governments, and to (presumably) all legislative, executive and administrative activities of government. Despite the argument that section 52(1) of the *Constitution Act* entails application of the Charter to the common law as a whole, the court held that the Charter applies only to that portion of the common law relating to government.[182] Thus it extends to non-governmental actors only in those areas in which the legislature has spoken.[183] Most importantly in the context of a discussion about equality rights, the court in *Dolphin Delivery* approved the Ontario Court of Appeal decision in *Re Blainey and Ontario Hockey Association*,[184] and said that the case illustrates the kind of connection with government which must exist before the Charter will be applicable.[185] In the *Blainey* case, the provision of the *Ontario Human Rights Code* exempting amateur athletics from the prohibition against discrimination on the basis of sex was challenged, and held to be unconstitutional.[186] The issue of the application of the Charter was argued on several bases, including governmental funding as providing a nexus sufficient to attract the application of the Charter. However, the court held that the Charter applied, not because of the relationship of the government to the activity regulated, but because

---

181 (1986), 33 D.L.R. (4th) 174 (S.C.C.).

182 This argument turns on section 52(1)'s statement that the Charter is the "Supreme law of Canada". For an example of a common law rule affecting private parties which was challenged under the Charter, see *Power v. Moss* (1986), 38 C.C.CL.T. 31 (Nfld. S.C.T.D.), where the court held that the rule permitting husbands but not wives to sue for damages for loss of consortium contravened section 15(1). It seems that this case would now have to be decided differently.

183 *Dolphin Delivery, supra*, note 181 at 194. Thus, the court held there was no basis for asserting a right to freedom of expression in opposition to an application to restrain secondary picketing based upon the common law torts of conspiracy in restraint of trade and inducing breach of contract, because the action was between two private litigants.

184 *Supra*, note 29.

185 *Dolphin Delivery, supra*, note 181 at 196.

186 Although the legislation permitted not only boys' teams to exclude girls, but also girls' teams to exclude boys, the court said that the record indicated that the exclusion of girls was the prevalent problem and held that the legislation had the purpose and effect of discriminating against females within the meaning of s. 15(1).

of the fact that the permission to discriminate had been embodied in legislation. In *Dolphin Delivery*, the court said:

> In the *Blainey* case, a lawsuit between private parties, the Charter was applied because one of the parties acted on the authority of a statute, i.e., s. 19(2) of the Ontario *Human Rights Code, 1981*, which infringed the Charter rights of another. *Blainey* then affords an illustration of the manner in which Charter rights of private individuals may be enforced and protected by the courts, that is, by measuring legislation — government action — against the Charter.[187]

There are important implications about section 15 in *Dolphin Delivery* and *Blainey*. First, it seems that the Charter may only apply when the government has chosen a legislative drafting style which sets out a general prohibition against discrimination along with specified exclusions from coverage, rather than a style which lists specific prohibitions but remains silent about matters not covered, thus leaving the common law permission to discriminate in effect.

Second, where the drafting style permits, it seems that the effect of the Charter on human rights legislation will be greater than might have been predicted. Governments may infringe equality rights not only through creating discrimination, but also through permitting it, even when the permission amounts to no more than a preservation of the common law position.[188]

---

187 *Supra*, note 181 at 197.

188 In other words, in the *Blainey* case, *supra*, note 29, no one compelled any amateur athletic organizations to be single-sex; they were permitted to be so. That the effect of this was to disadvantage females was accepted by the court. The part the government played was to leave untouched the common law position that private social organizations may determine their own membership. A similar issue arose in the mandatory retirement cases in Ontario and British Columbia. In *McKinney v. Univ. of Guelph Bd. of Governors*, *supra*, note 98, the majority held that while the Charter does not apply to the respondent universities directly, s. 15(1) of the Charter is infringed by s. 9(a) of the *Ontario Human Rights Code*. That provision excepts from the employment discrimination prohibition in the Code, discrimination based on age where the age in question is less than 18 or more than 64 years. The majority went on to hold that, with respect to university professors, the infringement is justified under s. 1 of the Charter. In *Connell v. Univ. of B.C.*, *supra*, note 99, and in *Stoffman v. Vancouver General Hospital*, *supra*, note 99, the British Columbia Court of Appeal reached a similar conclusion that s. 15(1) of the Charter is infringed by the exclusion of persons aged under 45 and over 65 from the protection against age discrimination in employment under the British Columbia *Human Rights Act*, but disagreed that s. 1 justified the infringement. On the subject of the powers of a legislature in the human rights field, the court said (at 698, in the *Connell* decision): "The trial judge had expressed concern that legislatures might be required to legislate to the full extent of s. 15 or vacate the field. In our respectful opinion that does not follow. We are of the view that the legislature could partially

The relationship between sections 52 and 15 of the Charter is an issue which has not yet been discussed by the Supreme Court, but about which *Dolphin Delivery* gives rise to some inferences. Both sections use the term "law": section 52 in stating the supremacy of the Charter in Canadian law, and section 15 in guaranteeing equality rights — they are rights to be equal before and under, and with respect to equal protection and benefit of, *the law*. If "law" is used in the same sense in sections 15 and 52, section 15 contains a replication of similar limits on application.[189]

Intuitively, it seems that the Charter should apply in areas in which judges have created inequalities and embodied them in common law rules,[190] just as much as in areas where legislatures have done so. As well, the particular line drawn by the Supreme Court in *Dolphin Delivery* seems very difficult to apply, and creates significant anomalies.[191] The court left an opening for dealing with these problems when it said, toward the end of the majority reasons in *Dolphin Delivery*, that "the judiciary ought to apply and develop the principles of the common law in a manner consistent with the fundamental values enshrined in the Constitution",[192] whether or not the Charter actually applies. Thus, the Charter could have a significant indirect effect on non-governmental activity, assuming that the equality rights are seen as part of the fundamental values enshrined in the Constitution.

Although we think, with respect, that the Supreme Court of Canada will have to re-evaluate *Dolphin Delivery* in order to deal with some of these problems, it is indisputable that there will be areas which the Charter equality rights do not reach.[193] Thus, the test we outline below includes

---

occupy the field provided that the legislation did not offend the Charter. In partially occupying the field, the government must not treat one group differently than another if to do so would be unreasonable or unfair." It would seem to follow that s. 15 will impose a fairly high measure of uniformity on human rights legislation across the country.

189   For a discussion of the meaning of "law" in ss. 52, 15 and 1, see *Douglas/Kwantlen Faculty Ass. v. Douglas College*, [1988] 2 W.W.R. 718 (B.C.C.A.), leave to appeal to S.C.C. granted [1988] 4 W.W.R. lxxii (note) (S.C.C.).

190   Such as the one at issue in *Power v Moss, supra,* note 182.

191   Between the government and private litigants; between different governmental activities classified as "public" or "private"; between provinces which have adopted different legislative drafting styles; between Quebec, with the *Civil Code* governing many areas which are under the common law in the rest of the country, and the common law provinces. For a comment on *Dolphin Delivery* and some of these problems, see B. Slattery, "The Charter's Relevance to Private Litigation: Does *Dolphin* Deliver" (1987), 32 *McGill L.J.* 905.

192   *Supra,* note 181 at 198.

193   There is not space to begin to develop a theory as to when this should be, but we think that such a theory should be formulated with a view to the purposes of the Charter. If the purposes of the Charter include both the maximization of liberty for individuals

a question relating to the identity of the defendant and the application of the Charter to the dispute.

(ii) *Limitation on "Plaintiffs"*

Who may invoke equality rights? The chief (perhaps only) limitation would be to disallow corporate persons from the use of the section.

We begin with the observation that corporations[194] are artificial creatures of statute, created for specific legal purposes (in particular, limited liability). Corporations have no sex, race, religion, or any of the other characteristics named in section 15, with the possible exception of national origin. They are legal devices and not living creatures.[195] The ideal of equality has always been associated with the inherent dignity and worth of human beings as, simply, human beings. In principle, therefore, it is counter-intuitive to include corporations in the class of beings which are inherently equal.

With specific reference to section 15, it must be asked whether the inclusion of corporations would serve the purposes of section 15 or hinder them. Assuming that the purposes of section 15 are connected with the elimination of the comparative disadvantages of the members of disadvantaged groups, and of those groups akin to them, inclusion of corporations would clearly not serve those purposes. Alternatively, even if we assume a broader purpose for section 15, encompassing not only elimination of comparative disadvantage for members of disadvantaged groups, but also prohibition of unfairness or arbitrariness in a more general way,

---

and the alleviation of disparities between disadvantaged groups and their advantaged counterparts, then the theory of application of the Charter should not proceed from the premise that only governments can violate fundamental rights, nor from the premise that a certain "zone of privacy" must always be preserved (see J. Whyte "Is the Private Sector Affected by the Charter?" in *Righting the Balance, supra,* note 23). Rather, the theory of application of the Charter should also take into account the feminist point that the division of our legal, social and economic systems into "public" and "private" spheres reflects the patriarchal origins of those systems more than it reflects logical analysis: See, *e.g.*, H. Lessard, "The Idea of the 'Private': A Discussion of State Action Doctrine and Separate Sphere Ideology', in *Charterwatch, supra,* note 31 at 107; K. O'Donovan, *Sexual Divisions in Law* (London, Eng.: Weidenfeld & Nicholson, 1985). The relegation of women's entitlements, relationships and domestic work into the "private" sphere has the effect of making much of women's lives legally invisible. Yet it is in the "private" sphere that much of the inequality that affects women occurs: *e.g.*, the non-inclusion of domestic work in assessing damages for personal injuries and in assessing maintenance and custody awards, and the physical or mental domestic abuse which has been said to affect one of eight Canadian women: see L. MacLeod, *Wife Battering in Canada: The Vicious Circle* (1980).

194 Including societies and other corporate entities.

195 Although we are used to thinking of corporations as living organisms in certain contexts, we should not mistake this metaphor for reality.

inclusion of corporations would not further those purposes, which would still be centrally focussed on human beings. Unfair or arbitrary treatment of humans has a significance which does not apply to legal devices.

The English version of the Charter guarantees equality to "every individual". This phrase replaced the expression "everyone" found in earlier versions,[196] and was accompanied by an explanatory note saying that the change was made "to make it clear that this right would apply to natural persons only".[197]

The equally authoritative French version reads:

> La loi ne fait acception de personne et s'applique également à tous, et tous ont droit à la même protection . . .

It should also be noted, however, that section 24(1) gives "*toute personne*" the right to apply for a remedy under the Charter.[198]

In the English version, "individual" is a more specific term than others used in the Charter (such as "anyone", "everyone", "any person") and, as Peter Hogg argues, its use probably excludes a corporation.[199] Its ordinary and natural meaning connotes a human being. The same is not the case with respect to the French version's use of "*personne*" and "*tous*",[200] but neither does the French version expressly include corporate

---

196 "Every individual" first appeared in the third version which was tabled in the House of Commons on February 13, 1981.

197 See Elliot, *supra*, note 132 at 38.

198 Arguably, s. 24 is neutral on this issue, since it uses "personne" in the French version, but specifies "toute personne, victime de violation ou de négation des droits ou libertés qui lui sont garantis par la présente charte . . .", and in the English version says "Anyone whose rights or freedoms, as guaranteed by this Charter, have been infringed or denied . . .". In the light of the fact that the English version of s. 24 does not use the term "individual" but instead says "anyone", it is plausible that "personne" was used in different senses in different sections of the Charter. The differences in the English versions can assist in distinguishing them. Although normally one would construe a word the same way throughout an instrument, this is not a "rigid canon of construction": *Halsbury's Laws of England*, 3d ed., Vol. 36, p. 396, para. 595; *Martin v. Lowry*, [1926] 1 K.B. 550 at 561 (C.A.). Thus, while "personne" in s. 24 allows for corporate persons to seek remedies for Charter violations, "personne" in s. 15 may allow only for human persons to assert equality claims.

199 Hogg, *supra*, note 26 at 798.

200 "Personne" is a word with numerous possible and ordinary meanings. It is defined in Jeraute's *Vocabulaire Francais-Anglais et Anglais-Francais de Termes et Locutions Juridiques* as "person, individual/(Jur.) person, being, body". For a discussion of this point, see *Ass. des Détaillants en Alimentation du Québec v. Ferme Carnaval Inc.*, [1986] R.J.Q. 2513 (Que. S.C.), where the court said at 2533: "L'expression 'ne fait acception de personne' est indéfinie et ne précise pas le type de personne qui peut-être visée. Le pronom 'tous' est également indéfini."

entities.[201] In *R. v. Big M Drug Mart Ltd.*,[202] Chief Justice Dickson said: "Section 24(1) sets out a remedy for individuals (whether real persons or artificial ones such as corporations) whose rights under the *Charter* have been infringed." While this could be taken as saying something about the meaning of "individual" in section 15, we think it more likely not to have been so intended.

In summary, the wording of the English version tends to support exclusion of corporations; the French version tends toward neutrality or inclusion; the legislative history (which is relevant although not determinative[203]) strongly indicates exclusion. Eric Gertner[204] argues that this is a case in which the more "liberal" version should be chosen. In the light of the history and the purpose of section 15, we think any presumption in favour of that choice is rebutted.

The courts to date have been close to unanimity in finding that section 15 does not apply to corporations.[205] However, they have not always shut the door firmly against corporate claims. For example, in the *Smith Kline* case, [206] the trial court found that although the corporate plaintiff had

---

201 It may be significant however, that the French version uses "individu" in s. 15(2).

202 *Supra*, note 35, at 313.

203 See *Reference re S. 94(2) Motor Vehicle Act (B.C.)*, *supra*, note 67.

204 "Are Corporations Entitled to Equality?: Some Preliminary Thoughts' (1986), 19 C.R.R. 288. See also T.M. Wakeling & G.D. Chipeur, "An Analysis of Section 15 of the Charter After the First Two Years or How Section 15 Has Survived the Terrible Twos" (1987), 25 *Alta. L. Rev.* 407 at 431-434.

205 The Court of Appeal for British Columbia put it succinctly in *Milk Bd. v. Clearview Dairy Farm Inc.* (1987), 12 B.C.L.R. (2d) 116 at 125; leave to appeal to S.C.C. refused [1987] 4 W.W.R. lxvi (note) (S.C.C.): "I agree with Toy, J. that no s. 15(1) right is infringed. I do not agree with him that a corporation is within s. 15(1): first, because a corporation is not an individual; and secondly, because a corporation has no race, national or ethnic origin, colour, religion, sex, age, mental or physical disability, nor any other comparable quality." See also *Parkdale Hotel Ltd. v. A.G. Canada* (1986), 27 D.L.R. (4th) 19 (F.C.T.D.); *Re Weinstein and Min. of Education (B.C.)* (1985), 20 D.L.R. (4th) 609 (B.C.S.C.); *Homemade Winecrafts (Canada) Ltd. v. A.G. British Columbia* (1986), 26 D.L.R. (4th) 468 (B.C.S.C.); *Mund v. Municipal Corp. of Medicine Hat* (1985), 67 A.R. 11 (Q.B.); *Re Aluminum Co. of Can. and Ontario*, *supra*, note 95; *Assn. des Détaillants en Alimentation du Québec v. Ferme Carnaval Inc.*, *supra*, note 200. For an exceptional case holding that corporate plaintiff had standing to challenge a provision of the *Surface Rights Act* on the basis of s. 15(1), see *Cabre Exploration Ltd. v. Arndt*, [1986] 4 W.W.R. 261 (Alta. Q.B.), aff'd [1988] 5 W.W.R. 289 (Alta. C.A.).

206 *Smith, Kline & French Laboratories Ltd. v. A.G. Canada* (1986), 24 D.L.R. (4th) 321 (F.C.T.D.), aff'd (1986), 34 D.L.R. (4th) 584 (F.C.A.), leave to appeal refused (1987), 27 C.R.R. 286n (S.C.C.). The Federal Court of Appeal commented (at 588, note 1): "Any possible problems resulting from the attempt by corporate plaintiffs to assert rights which can only be enjoyed by individuals are resolved by the trial judge's finding, not put in issue on appeal, that the individual plaintiffs possessed the necessary standing to assert the claims in their own behalf."

no claim under section 15(1), the individual plaintiffs, who were inventors of medicines and employees of the corporate plaintiff, did have a claim despite the fact that they had assigned the patents to their employer.[207]

A corporation's claim that legislation which affects it adversely infringes the Charter thereby, must be distinguished from a corporation's argument based upon unconstitutionality arising from the terms or effect of legislation on others who are human beings. We cannot review the issues of standing which are relevant here, but point out that in cases such as *R. v. Big M Drug Mart Ltd.*,[208] the courts have found that "any accused, whether corporate or individual, may defend a criminal charge by arguing that the law under which the charge is brought is constitutionally invalid." In *Zutphen Brothers Construction Ltd. v. Dywidag Systems International Canada Ltd.*[209] the Nova Scotia Court of Appeal extended this principle into the civil context and said that a corporation could challenge the jurisdictional provisions of the *Federal Court Act*[210] (conferring exclusive jurisdiction on the Federal Court to hear claims against the federal Crown) on the basis that those provisions violate an individual's right to equality before and under the law.[211]

---

207 They were found to have a sufficient interest in that the value of their services, past and future, was affected by the impugned legislation. On the other hand, a similar move in the *Milk Board* case, *supra*, note 205 at 246, by the trial judge seems to have been disapproved by the Court of Appeal. The trial judge had said that, if it were necessary, he would lift the corporate veil or permit an amendment to the pleadings to join as parties the principals of the corporation asserting equality rights if he had found that discrimination had occurred.

208 *Supra*, note 35 at 313. See also *Edwards Books & Art Ltd. v. R.*, *supra*, note 115.

209 *Supra*, note 82 at 447.

210 R.S.C. 1970, c. 10 (2nd. Supp.) [now R.S.C. 1985, c. F-7]. A remedy was granted to the corporation in this case, consisting of an order permitting the joinder of Her Majesty the Queen in right of Canada as a third party in an action, on the basis of s. 15 of the Charter. This remedy entailed, it seems, striking down the legislative provision and finding that the common law rule (which prohibits a subject from suing the Crown at all) to be unconstitutional. This is perhaps an application of the rule in *Dolphin Delivery*, *supra*, note 181, that the common law relating to the government is subject to the Charter.

211 We note that the *Zutphen Brothers* case, *supra*, note 82, is one which could not succeed under our theory of s. 15, since neither a named ground nor one akin to it was invoked. However, assuming that s. 15 grounds do exist, in a case where a rule of civil procedure is unconstitutional because of s. 15, any person affected by that rule should be able to point out its unconstitutionality. For example, suppose that a rule of procedure required an in person appearance to defend against an action, with no possible exceptions for differently abled persons. Presumably, anyone could rely upon the unconstitutionality of that rule to resist its application in a particular case, even one unrelated to physical abilities. This is different from saying that any person has standing to challenge any law — the rules for standing developed by the Supreme Court of Canada in the triology of cases are determinative of that issue: *Thorson v. A.G. Canada* (1974), 43 D.L.R. (3d) 1 (S.C.C.); *McNeil v. N.S. Bd. of Censors* (1975), 55 D.L.R. (3d) 632 (S.C.C.); *Min. of Justice (Can.) v. Borowski* (1982), 130 D.L.R. (3d) 588 (S.C.C.).

In summary, whether or not corporations are permitted to initiate actions invoking section 15 in their own names, there seems little doubt that corporations will figure in section 15 litigation. However, not only because of the institutional constraints which militate restricting access to section 15, but also because of the legislative history, wording and principles underlying section 15, we think that it is only inequalities affecting human beings which are contemplated by the section and that "individual" should be read in the manner thus far adopted by the courts.

(b) Tests Discernible in Early Judicial Decisions

Writing at a time when there have been no Supreme Court of Canada decisions on section 15, it would be a mistake to address the case law to date in great detail. However, some of the trends which have appeared can be described and discussed relatively briefly, in an attempt to describe some possible tests rather than in an attempt to analyze the cases in an exhaustive way.

There are indications that the analysis in some of the decisions is inspired by a concern to limit the number of cases which may be litigated under section 15, and the number of occasions upon which government is called upon to justify the way in which it has drawn legislative distinctions. This is a thoroughly understandable concern. It becomes acute if it is assumed that any ground at all may be used to invoke section 15, and that the *Oakes* principles[212] for section 1 assessment are to apply to

---

212 *R. v. Oakes, supra*, note 48. In that case, the Supreme Court of Canada said that the following framework of analysis should be applied in assessing the reasonableness of limitations on *Charter* rights (at 138-140):

"To establish that a limit is reasonable and demonstrably justified in a free and democratic society, two central criteria must be satisfied. First, the objective, which the measures responsible for a limit on a Charter right or freedom are designed to serve, must be 'of sufficient importance to warrant overriding a constitutionally protected right or freedom': *R. v. Big M Drug Mart Ltd., supra,* [note 35] at p. 352. The standard must be high in order to ensure that objectives which are trivial or discordant with the principles integral to a free and democratic society do not gain s. 1 protection. It is necessary, at a minimum, that an objective relate to concerns which are pressing and substantial in a free and democratic society before it can be characterized as sufficiently important.

Second, once a sufficiently significant objective is recognized, then the party invoking s. 1 must show that the means chosen are reasonable and demonstrably justified. This involves 'a form of proportionality test': *R. v. Big M Drug Mart Ltd., supra,* [note 35] at p. 352. Although the nature of the proportionality test will vary depending on the circumstances, in each case courts will be required to balance the interests of society with those of individuals and groups. There are, in my view, three important components of a proportionality test. First, the measures adopted must be carefully designed to achieve the objective in question. They must not be arbitrary, unfair or based on irrational

distinctions of all types. In a substantial majority of the cases which have reached the appellate level, the grounds asserted have not been enumerated in section 15;[213] in most of those, the grounds are not clearly akin to the enumerated ones.[214] The concern may be keenly felt in those cases if there is a perception that the primary purpose of section 15 — the alleviation of disadvantage of particular disadvantaged groups and of groups similar to them — is getting lost.[215]

---

considerations. In short, they must be rationally connected to the objective. Second, the means, even if rationally connected to the objective in this first sense, should impair 'as little as possible' the right or freedom in question: *R. v. Big M Drug Mart Ltd., supra*, [note 35] at p. 352. Third, there must be a proportionality between the *effects* of the measures which are responsible for limiting the *Charter* right or freedom, and the objective which has been identified as of 'sufficient importance'.

With respect to the third component, it is clear that the general effect of any measure impugned under s. 1 will be the infringement of a right or freedom guaranteed by the *Charter*; this is the reason why resort to s. 1 is necessary. The inquiry into effects must, however, go further. A wide range of rights and freedoms are guaranteed by the *Charter*, and an almost infinite number of factual situations may arise in respect of these. Some limits on rights and freedoms protected by the *Charter* will be more serious than others in terms of the nature of the right or freedom violated, the extent of the violation and the degree to which the measures which impose the limit trench upon the integral principles of a free and democratic society. Even if an objective is of sufficient importance, and the first two elements of the proportionality test are satisfied, it is still possible that, because of the severity of the deleterious effects of a measure on individuals or groups, the measure will not be justified by the purposes it is intended to serve. The more severe the deleterious effects of a measure, the more important the objective must be if the measure is to be reasonable and demonstrably justified in a free and democratic society."

213 Examples of cases raising claims based at least in part on unenumerated grounds are *Re Andrews and Law Society of B.C., supra*, note 46: *Re McDonald and R.* (1985), 21 C.C.C. (3d) 330 (Ont. C.A.); *Smith, Kline & French Laboratories v. A.G. Canada, supra*, note 206; *Headley v. Public Service Comm. Appeal Bd., supra*, note 127; *McBeth v. Governors of Dalhousie College & Univ., supra*, note 82; *R. v. Hamilton, supra*, note 82; *Zutphen Bros. Construction Ltd. v. Dywidag Systems International (Can.) Ltd., supra*, note 209; *R. v. Century 21 Ramos Realty Inc.* (1987), 19 O.A.C. 25 (C.A.), leave to appeal to S.C.C. refused (1987), 22 O.A.C. 319n (S.C.C.); *R. v. Frohman; R. v. M.C.O.* (1987), 19 O.A.C. 180 (C.A.); *R. v. Ertel* (1987), 20 O.A.C. 257 leave to appeal to S.C.C. refused (1987), 24 O.A.C. 320n (S.C.C.); *R. v. Turpin* (1987), 22 O.A.C. 261 (C.A.); *Mahé v. R.*, August 26, 1987 (Alta. C.A.); *Reference re Ss. 32 & 34 of the Workers' Compensation Act (Nfld.), supra*, note 77; *Reference re French Language Rights of Accused in Sask. Criminal Proceedings, supra*, note 86.

214 In our collection of appellate cases to approximately January 10, 1988, there are 49 involving non-enumerated grounds and 20 involving enumerated grounds. We have not counted nine cases (such as *Andrews*) in which this classification is unclear.

215 See *e.g.*, the statement in *R. v. Century 21 Ramos Realty Inc., supra*, note 213 at 38, that the equality provisions are intended to eliminate, not perpetuate, stereotypes about groups of people; the statement in *Rebic v. Collver, supra*, note 142 at 164, about the

One of the most important issues in the section 15 cases has concerned the balancing process in which the necessity for legislation may be weighed against its effect on an individual. Should such balancing occur when deciding whether there has been an infringement of section 15, or when determining whether an infringement is a "reasonable limit" within the meaning of section 1? There has been a substantial amount of academic commentary on this subject.[216] There has also been some discussion in the case law.[217] To a great extent, in both the cases and the academic commentary, the issue is connected with the meaning given to the term "discrimination" in section 15(1). Those who argue for a balancing process under section 15(1) say that "discrimination" should be read in a sense which recognizes its pejorative connotation, and which screens out cases where no real harm is done to the person complaining or where the distinction is warranted in all of the circumstances. On the other hand, those who argue for a balancing process under section 1 say that section 15 should be read as a positive guarantee of equality and not primarily as an antidiscrimination provision, and that "discrimination" should be read in the sense of "distinction" or "harmful distinction" so that the question whether a distinction is warranted in all of the circumstances is considered under section 1.[218] Naturally, there are intermediate positions between these two.[219] As will be seen in the discussion below, the opinions of the appellate courts have differed on this issue.

In our opinion, it is more appropriate for any balancing process to take place under section 1, for the reasons given in our discussion below of the *Andrews* case.[220] We think that the restriction of the grounds in

---

difficulties faced by equality-seeking groups (*per* MacFarlane J.A.); the discussion in *Re Andrews and Law Society of B.C.*, *supra*, note 46 at 606, about the dangers of trivializing the s. 15 rights.

216 For two articles taking different points of view, see Smith, "Paradigm", *supra*, note 25 at 376-379, and Harris, *supra*, note 23.

217 See, *e.g.*, *Re Andrews and Law Society of B.C.*, *supra*, note 46 at 608-609; *Smith, Kline & French Laboratories Ltd. v. A.G. Canada*, *supra*, note 206 at 593; *Reference re S. 32 & 34 of the Workers' Compensation Act (Nfld.)*, *supra*, note 77 at 42-43; *Reference re French Language Rights of Accused in Sask. Criminal Proceedings*, *supra*, note 86.

218 While it may be possible to read s. 15 such that "without discrimination" modifies only "every individual is equal before and under the law" rather than "has the right to the equal protection and equal benefit of the law", it seems more likely that "without discrimination" will be seen as modifying all four parts of the equality guarantee.

219 *E.g.*, Harris, *supra*, note 23.

220 *Re Andrews and Law Society of B.C.*, *supra*, note 46. The reasons include the advantages in using the kind of rigorous checklist developed in *R. v. Oakes*, *supra*, note 48, quoted in note 212, *supra*, for focussing the judicial mind on the interests at stake and on the

the manner we have suggested makes this approach workable even with the high standard governments must meet under *Oakes.* It may be, however, that the courts in the end determine that these reasons are outweighed by others,[221] and that in order to determine whether there has been an infringement of a section 15 right, they must look at issues of reasonableness and proportionality within section 15. Even so, courts will still have to decide what factors are taken into account in assessing reasonableness and proportionality. It is the content of the assessment which will be significant, whether it takes place under section 15 or section 1.[222]

The approaches which we discuss in the following sections are not all of those which have been developed by the courts, and often are not completely distinct analytically from one another. However, they represent the more prominent formulations to date.

(i) The "Similarly Situated" Test

As we have discussed, the precept that likes must be treated alike and unalikes must be treated unalike is basic to equality theory. Courts have incorporated a question about whether "similarly situated" people are being treated similarly into their analysis of equality claims. (In fact, in one context the question has been used to eliminate a whole class of cases: those in which an individual is seeking to compare herself or himself with the Crown.)[223] In an early decision, *Re McDonald and R.*, the Ontario Court of Appeal said:

> It can reasonably be said, in broad terms, that the purpose of s. 15 is to require "that those who are similarly situated be treated similarly": Tussman and

---

argued necessity to infringe constitutional rights; bringing the analysis out into the open; placing the onus on the government to justify departures from the principle of the universal application of the law; and consistency with the analysis developed under other parts of the Charter.

221 An important factor may be the concern that the *Oakes* test is too rigorous if every distinction or every harmful distinction is to amount to a violation of s. 15(1).

222 An interesting contrast is provided by the mandatory retirement cases. The British Columbia Court of Appeal, which has decided to assess reasonableness under s. 15, struck down the *Human Rights Act* section permitting mandatory retirement: *Connell v. Univ. of B.C., supra,* note 99; *Stoffman v. Vancouver General Hospital, supra,* note 99. On the other hand, the Ontario Court of Appeal, which has said the assessment of reasonableness is for s. 1, determined that mandatory retirement is a reasonable limitation (at least for university professors): *McKinney v. Univ. of Guelph Bd. of Governors, supra,* note 98.

223 In *R. v. Stoddart* (1987), 20 O.A.C. 365, the Ontario Court of Appeal held that s. 15 only applies where there is discrimination between individuals, and the Crown is not an "individual". Even if so, the Court said, the Crown and an accused are not similarly situated.

tenBroek, "The Equal Protection of the Laws", 37 Cal. L. Rev. 341 (1948), at p. 344.[224]

In the *McDonald* case, a young man wished to be tried in youth court rather than in an ordinary court of criminal jurisdiction. He would have been entitled to be tried in youth court if the allegation had been either that he committed an offence after April, 1985, or that the offence had been committed and the trial held in any of four provinces other than Ontario. Applying its test to this case, the court decided that the accused was not similarly situated to others who had been charged with committing offences at an earlier time, but did seem to conclude that he was similarly situated to others who had allegedly committed offences at the same time as him but in other parts of Canada. Nevertheless, the court concluded the legislation constituted a reasonable limit under section 1.

The British Columbia Court of Appeal applied similar reasoning in *Rebic v. Collver*.[225] In the *Rebic* case, the issue was the constitutionality of section 542(2) [now 614(2)] of the *Criminal Code*, which provides that a person accused of an indictable offence who is found to be insane at the time the offence was committed, shall be acquitted but kept in strict custody at the pleasure of the Lieutenant Governor of the province. The argument was that a person acquitted by reason of insanity is similarly situated to other persons who have been acquitted though they committed the *actus reus* of the crime.[226] However, those sane acquittees are allowed to go free. MacFarlane J.A. found that section 15 was infringed for that reason, but that the legislation was saved by section 1. The majority[227] found that the relevant comparison was not between sane and insane acquittees who had committed the act, but between persons acquitted because they had not committed the act and those acquitted because, although they had committed the act, they were insane at the time. Using that comparison, the insane acquittees were not similarly situated to other acquitted persons and section 15 was not infringed.[228]

The *McDonald* and *Rebic* cases show the weaknesses of the "similarly situated" test *simpliciter*. In *McDonald*, no explanation is given why young offenders are similarly situated despite geography, but not despite the date

---

224 *Supra*, note 213 at 349.
225 *Supra*, note 142.
226 *E.g.*, because of a successful defence of duress or automatism.
227 *Per* Esson J.A.
228 The majority of the court did not deal with the argument about other persons found to have committed the act charged who were set free — *e.g.*, those who succeeded in a defence of automatism. The minority reasons refer to this point. However, it was important to the majority that the impugned provisions formed part of a scheme under which insane persons were granted special treatment in recognition of their special condition.

of the alleged offence.[229] In *Rebic*, the two sets of reasons show different choices as to the appropriate comparisons, but no principled explanation for the choices. When the choice made determines the outcome, as it does for the majority in *Rebic*, with little review of the issues contemplated by the *Oakes* test, we are left with a result but no great assistance in deriving principles to apply in the next case.

In later cases, the Ontario Court of Appeal has elaborated on the meaning of "similarly situated", saying that equality is an "essentially relational concept" and that "[t]he concern for equality is that those who are similarly situated *with respect to the purpose of the law* be treated similarly. . . ".[230]

In *R. v. Century 21 Ramos Realty Inc.*[231] the court said:

> It is usually possible to find differences between classes of persons and, on the basis of these differences, conclude that the persons are not similarly situated. However, what are perceived to be significant "differences" between persons or classes of persons could be the result of stereotypes based on existing inequalities which the equality provisions of the *Charter* are designed to eliminate, not perpetuate. The effects of past discrimination between classes of persons can result in these classes in fact not being similarly situated. Certain differences, such as the biological ones between the sexes, result in there being no actual comparable class, as with respect to reproductive issues. While some of these situations may well require differential treatment in the interests of equality, it is important that some differences between the classes of persons not operate to prevent a valid s. 15 equality analysis by concluding that classes are not similarly situated. Rather, the determination of whether persons are similarly situated must also consider the relevance of the differences and, thus, the question ought to be whether the differences among those being treated differently by the legislation in question are relevant for the purposes of that legislation.[232]

This addition can improve the "similarly situated" test by giving some guidance as to the relevant criteria for assessing similarity and difference: they are to be found in the purposes of the legislation in question.[233]

---

229 There seems to be a connection with the fact that the case involves criminal law in a country with a federal criminal system. Inconsistencies in the criminal process have proved successful bases for equality claims in several cases: *R. v. Hamilton, supra*, note 82; *R. v. Bailey, supra*, note 102; *R. v. Frohman, supra*, note 213; *R. v. Y.D., supra*, note 102; *R. v. Punch, supra*, note 111.

230 *R. v. R.L.* (1986), 26 C.C.C. (3d) 417 at 424-425 (Ont. C.A.) (emphasis added).

231 *Supra*, note 213 at 38.

232 The court goes on to apply the *Andrews* "reasonable and fair" test, "for the purposes of this case" (at 42).

233 In effect, this also seems to have been the analysis undertaken in the *Rebic* case, *supra*, note 142, although it was not expressed in terms of legislative purpose. J. Tussman and J. tenBroek "The Equal Protections of the Laws" (1948), 37 *Cal. L. Rev.* 341 cited in *Re McDonald and R., supra*, note 213, framed their test in relation to the law's purposes in light of this problem.

However, there are still many important questions. First, how is legislative purpose chosen? There is often a wide range of possible purposes, and the choice often determines the outcome of the test. Second, does an improper purpose suffice to find a distinction to be based upon a "difference" and therefore acceptable? Occasionally, legislatures enact provisions aimed at disadvantaging particular groups or at "helping" them in ways which they themselves find unhelpful. It would drastically curtail the effect of section 15 to permit legislation to pass review so long as the distinction it makes accurately carries out its purposes, whatever those purposes may be.[234] Third, with respect to areas where there are indissoluble differences between groups of people (such as gender differences), the "similarly situated" test permits outcomes which we think are inconsistent with the purpose of section 15. It could, for example, permit the conclusion that pregnant women are differently situated from other workers with respect to the purpose of a particular statute governing disability benefits, and therefore that they may be denied those benefits. On the other hand, it could also permit the conclusion that pregnant women are similarly situated with other workers under a statute governing hours of work and holidays and therefore it is inappropriate to permit a maternity leave program.

Taking these problems into account, the "similarly situated" test appears at best to be incomplete. The decision about what "counts" as similar or different (sometimes the term "criteria of relevance" is used to refer to this concept[235]) is what really matters. The test provides inadequate guidance as to how the criteria of relevance should be selected.

Although the "similarly situated" test is incomplete, and unduly limiting if taken as determinative, the assurance of rational consistency which this test provides can form a useful part of a test for equality under the Charter. As the Ontario Court of Appeal says in *R. v. Century 21 Ramos Realty Inc.*, "the determination of whether two or more particular classes of persons are in fact similarly situated becomes the analytical point of departure in any s. 15 analysis."[236] We emphasize, however, that this point of departure should not be the final destination.

---

234 This problem did not arise in *R. v. Century 21 Ramos Realty Inc.*, *supra*, note 213, the facts of which related to prosecutorial discretion to proceed by way of indictment or summary conviction.

235 See Bayefsky, *supra*, note 19 at 3.

236 *Supra*, note 213 at 38.

(ii) *The "Reasonable and Fair" Test*

This test was enunciated by the British Columbia Court of Appeal in *Re Andrews and Law Society of British Columbia*[237] as follows:

> My response to the first question is that the question to be answered under s. 15 should be whether the impugned distinction is reasonable or fair, having regard to the purposes and aims and its effect on persons adversely affected. I include the word "fair" as well as "reasonable" to emphasize that the test is not one of pure rationality but one connoting the treatment of persons in ways which are not unduly prejudicial to them. The test must be objective and the discrimination must be proved on a balance of probabilities: *R. v. Oakes* (applying this test to s. 1). The ultimate question is whether a fair-minded person, weighing the purposes of legislation against its effects on the individuals adversely affected and giving due weight to the right of the legislature to pass laws for the good of all, would conclude that the legislative means adopted are unreasonable or unfair.[238]

In the *Andrews* case, the issue was the constitutionality of section 42 of the *Barristers and Solicitors Act* of British Columbia, which requires Canadian citizenship of those who wish to practise law in the province. The Court of Appeal held it to be an infringement of section 15, not saved by section 1, and therefore unconstitutional.[239]

The *Andrews* test incorporates the "similarly situated" test while extending it somewhat.[240] The issue is not to be only whether similarly situated persons are treated similarly in the light of the purposes of the legislation, but also whether the treatment is "reasonable" and "fair" having regard to the purposes and aims of the legislation and its effects. The test enunciated in *Andrews* leaves little room for the application of section 1.[241]

---

237 *Supra*, note 46.

238 *Ibid.* at 609.

239 Subsequently, in the mandatory retirement cases, *supra*, note 99, the British Columbia Court of Appeal applied the *Andrews* test and concluded that mandatory retirement constitutes age discrimination which infringes s. 15 and is not saved by s. 1. *Andrews* has been followed in numerous other British Columbia cases, as well as in the Newfoundland Court of Appeal: *Reference re Ss. 32 & 34 Workers Compensation Act (Nfld.)*, *supra*, note 77.

240 The court says that the essential meaning of the constitutional requirement of equal protection and equal benefit is that persons who are "similarly situated be similarly treated" and, conversely, that persons who are "differently situated be differently treated", citing Tussman and tenBroek, *supra*, note 233, and *Re Weinstein and Min. of Education (B.C.)*, *supra*, note 205 at 622.

241 The court said in *Re Andrews and Law Society of B.C.*, *supra*, note 46 at 610: "It follows that s. 1 will function so as to permit legislation which is discriminatory to be upheld, provided the necessary conditions are met. It may well be that generally discrimination

The court gives four reasons for its decision to reject a two-stage approach significantly involving section 1 as well as section 15.[242]

1. It cannot have been the intention of Parliament to call every legislative distinction between people an infringement of section 15 — that would be to trivialize the fundamental rights guaranteed by the Charter.
2. The words "without discrimination" must be given some content.
3. It cannot have been the intention of Parliament that the government be required to demonstrably justify under section 1 all laws which draw distinctions between people — otherwise "such universally accepted and manifestly desirable legal distinctions as those prohibiting children or drunk persons from driving motor vehicles" would be required to run the gauntlet of section 1.
4. To define "discrimination" as synonymous with "distinction" will be to "elevate section 15 to the position of subsuming the other rights and freedoms defined by the Charter".

We think that the first, third and fourth reasons all reflect the concern we have discussed, about an overbroad effect of section 15, and proceed on the assumption that the grounds upon which section 15 may be invoked are as extensive as the ways in which human beings or activities may be classified. This is supported by the court's use of the example of "prohibiting drunk persons from driving motor vehicles", as one which could require justification under section 1. The concern about an overbroad effect is a real one. Such an effect would be apt indeed to lead to the trivializing of Charter rights and overburdening of government lawyers. For that reason we have argued for a limitation of the grounds upon which section 15 may be invoked, to those which are named or akin to those named.

A related concern expressed by the court is that the government should not have to justify the most obvious cases of necessary legislation, even

---

cannot be justified in a free and democratic society. But it is not true that it can never be justified. Circumstances may arise where discriminatory measures can be justified. For example, in times of war, the internment of enemy aliens might be argued to be justifiable under s. 1, notwithstanding the fact that this is discriminatory and would not be tolerated in peace time. Viewed thus, s. 1 plays a vital role in the determination of the validity of legislation impugned on the basis of s. 15. The role, while essential, is limited; most cases may not disclose circumstances which can be argued to justify discriminatory legislation. This, in my view, is as it should be. The procedures and tests set out in *R. v. Oakes* for determination of the issues raised by s. 1 are more suitable for the determination of whether an established right can be limited on the ground of overriding circumstances than to the determination of the initial question of whether the legislation in question violates a right at all."

242 *Ibid.* at 606.

where the legislation involves one of the named grounds. An example used by the court is prohibiting children from driving. With respect, we think this is not a legitimate reason for eschewing a two-stage approach. If the necessity for a provision is so obvious, it will pass section 1. If it cannot pass section 1, given that it involves a group whose disadvantage has been recognized in section 15, it should be held unconstitutional. The manner in which section 1 was applied by Dickson C.J.C. in the *Edwards Books* case[243] shows how it can operate in a context very similar to that of equality rights, and allow legislation to pass muster where a good and serious attempt has been made to accommodate diverse interests. Further, as other courts have subsequently concluded,[244] to follow the *Andrews* approach is to render section 1 irrelevant in equality rights litigation. This is inconsistent with the Supreme Court's view of section 1 expressed in *Oakes*[245] and has the potential to lead to inordinate difficulties in the proof of equality claims.[246]

That leaves the court's second reason, stemming from a concern to give some meaning to the term "discrimination". Again, we suggest this concern is better met through limiting the list of grounds which can be used to invoke section 15. We suggest it should be limited to grounds related to groups which have been the subject of "discrimination" in the sense of unfair, prejudicial treatment. Discrimination leads to inclusion within section 15 protection expressly or by analogy. Thus, if section 15(1) is limited as we suggest and only takes account of distinctions affecting members of disadvantaged groups, not only "discrimination" but also the last portion of section 15(1) is thereby given meaning.

With reference to the content of the test, the court in *Andrews* invokes fairness as well as reasonableness as touchstones for the validity of legislation although it does not elaborate on what counts as "fair" or "reasonable". The court explains that it wishes to go beyond a mere rationality test and prevent treatment of persons which is "unduly prejudicial" to them. However, there is no discussion as to what will count as unduly prejudicial. Without guidance, the content of these terms will be poured in according to the particular views of the judge deciding the

---

243 *Supra*, note 115.
244 *McKinney v. Univ. of Guelph Bd. of Governors, supra*, note 98; *Reference re French Language Rights of Accused in Sask. Criminal Proceedings, supra*, note 86; *Smith, Kline & French Laboratories Ltd. v. A.G. Canada, supra*, note 206 at 593; *Reference re Family Benefits Act (N.S.), S. 5, supra*, note 159 at 351.
245 *Supra*, note 48.
246 See *McKinney v. Univ. of Guelph Bd. of Governors, supra*, note 98.

case, and will vary accordingly.[247] Certainly, it is possible that a great deal could be read into the term "fair"; as easily , it could mean no more than that there is an absence of evidence of actual undue prejudice toward the group affected.

It must be noted as well that the balancing process described is problematic. A fair-minded person is to place on one side of the scale the purposes of the legislation and the right of the legislature to pass laws for the good of all, and on the other side of the scale, the effects of the legislation on individuals adversely affected, and from that to determine whether the means adopted by the legislature are unreasonable or unfair. There is some contrast between these concepts and the relative clarity and specificity of the process used in *Oakes*.[248] For example, we note the omission of an express reference to "least drastic means"[249] or to an explicit requirement of proportionality.[250]

(iii) *Tests Oriented Towards Grounds*

There have been indications in a few cases that the contents of the list of grounds in section 15 have had an important role in the formulation of the test for violations of equality rights. In *Smith Kline & French Laboratories Ltd. v. Attorney General of Canada*, [251] the plaintiffs sought a declaration that the compulsory licensing provisions of section 41(4) of the *Patent Act* are unconstitutional on several bases, including section 15 of the Charter. Strayer J., at trial, refused the declaration, employing a test for violation of equality rights which would view a distinction based upon one of the enumerated grounds as *prima facie* in breach of section

---

247 It is not necessary to go far back in history to find examples of cases in which it seemed to particular adjudicators eminently fair and reasonable to treat particular groups differently and disadvantageously: see, *e.g.*, the series of cases in Canada, England and the United States in which women were denied entry to the legal profession because of their sex despite legislation which could have permitted them: A. Sachs & J. Wilson, *Sexism and the Law* (1978). See also *supra*, note 166.

248 *Supra*, note 48.

249 To some extent, the *Andrews* discussion of the "fit" between legislative ends and means suggests a least drastic means component, but this is not at all clear. Compare the reasons of Dickson C.J.C. in *Oakes*, supra, note 48, and in *Edwards Books*, *supra*, note 115.

250 The language in *Oakes*, is set out *supra*, at note 212. There is no corresponding discussion about proportionality in *Andrews*, although possibly the words "reasonable and fair" could encompass it. This leaves open the possibility that, so long as a measure creating a distinction seems "reasonable and fair" in the light of the legislative purpose, it matters not what proportion exists between the effect on the individual and the necessity for the measure.

251 *Supra*, note 206.

15(1), but a distinction on other grounds as breaching the section only if it failed to pass a rationality test as in *MacKay v. R.*[252] On appeal, the decision was affirmed in result, but for different reasons. Hugessen J. said that a short answer to the section 15 argument is that the section is irrelevant to "discrimination" resulting directly from a "voluntarily assumed package of rights and obligations",[253] such as those of an inventor who chooses to patent an invention. However, assuming that inventors of pharmaceutical products are, as a matter of fact though not of law, obliged to patent their processes, and therefore do not fall within the above exclusion, the court held that section 15(1) still was not violated. It applied as the basic test the "similarly situated" test, but instead of relying upon the purpose of the legislation as the touchstone for relevance, the court said that there is no single criterion that will serve to delimit the permissible grounds for categorization, and that even some categories based on one of the enumerated grounds will not need justification under section 1. The suggested criteria for determining whether a categorization is permissible may be drawn from the text of section 15,[254] from other rights, liberties and freedoms enshrined in the Charter,[255] and from the underlying values

---

252 *Supra*, note 17 (per McIntyre J). The *MacKay* test of McIntyre J. has played a prominent role in a number of decisions under section 15 of the Charter, notably *R. v. Hamilton, supra*, note 82; *Rebic v. Collver, supra*, note 142, as well as the Federal Court of Appeal decisions. That test is summarized by McIntyre J. as follows (at 407): " . . . as a minimum it would be necessary to inquire whether any inequality has been created for a valid federal constitutional objective, whether it has been created rationally in the sense that it is not arbitrary or capricious and not based upon any ulterior motive or motives offensive to the provisions of the *Canadian Bill of Rights*, and whether it is a necessary departure from the general principle of universal application of the law for the attainment of some necessary and desirable social objective. Inequalities created for such purposes may well be acceptable under the *Canadian Bill of Rights*". The test in *MacKay*, although it may go further than American minimal scrutiny, is nonetheless a species of rationality test. The feature which distinguishes it from the *Canadian Bill of Rights* jurisprudence which preceded it is that it spells out the factors which must be taken into account and states a presumption in favour of laws of general application.

253 Examples given *supra*, note 206, at 589 (34 D.L.R.) include becoming a judge and suffering the restrictions imposed by s. 36 of the *Judges Act*, obtaining a licence to fish for trout and being restricted from fishing for salmon, and purchasing a lot with particular zoning and being restricted to that kind of construction.

254 Thus, the court says, one should look to whether or not there is "discrimination" in the pejorative sense of the word and as to whether the categories are based on enumerated grounds or ones analogous to them, thus concentrating upon the personal characteristics of the claimants. Questions of prejudice are the focus and it may be recognized that for some people equality has a different meaning than for others.

255 The court says that some categories may affect independently recognized rights or freedoms, *e.g.*, freedom of religion. On the other hand, categories whose main impact is on property or economic rights may be less subject to scrutiny.

inherent in the Canadian free and democratic society.[256]

The Court discussed the "reasonable and fair" test enunciated in *Andrews*, but said that that test is impossible to reconcile with the Supreme Court of Canada decision in *R. v. Oakes*[257] in that it seems to leave no room for the application of section 1. Applying its test to the case before it, the court held that there was no violation of equality rights since:

> [T]he categories created . . . bear no remote relation to those enumerated in s. 15 and carry within them no suggestion of discrimination, prejudice or stereotype. The interests in which plaintiffs claim to have suffered are purely economic and commercial in nature; no question of liberty, freedom or human rights is involved. Finally, the text of ss 41(4) is a direct and specific expression of parliamentary will; as pointed out by the trial judge, it was adopted after the existing state of the law had been reviewed by at least three commissions and a parliamentary committee; there could hardly be a more deliberate expression of the views of a free and democratic society.[258]

The court added that the plaintiffs would have failed on the reasonable and fair test or any other test which has been suggested; to succeed, they would have to persuade a court that:

> Section 15 guarantees absolute equality to every individual in every conceivable circumstance and that every possible distinction that can result in one receiving a benefit or incurring a disadvantage which is not enjoyed or suffered by all can only be justified, if at all, under section 1[259]

---

256 Thus, the court says, an appropriate degree of judicial deference and restraint is indicated where a legislature has clearly and consciously made a deliberate choice. The degree lessens the further the alleged inequalities are removed from the expression of legislative will, either by delegation or indirection. Even in cases where the legislative will is clear and direct, room will remain for judicial intervention to prevent the tyranny of the majority.

257 *Supra*, note 48.

258 *Supra*, note 206, at 593 (34 D.L.R.).

259 *Ibid.* at 594. A later Federal Court of Appeal case, *Headley v. Public Service Comm. Appeal Bd.*, *supra*, note 127, involved an applicant for a position with the Canada Employment and Immigration Commission who did not have proficiency in one of the languages required for the position. She argued that two incumbents in the position had not had to meet the same requirements when they were hired or at present. MacGuigan J. (Pratte and Urie JJ. concurred in the result only) expressed agreement with the view that s. 15 does include "internal limits" and said that (at 577):

> "I find the internal limit "discrimination" to be required in all cases, but in some cases, *viz* those based on the enumerated grounds, the drafters have already made the fundamental determination that pejorative distinctions based on those grounds constitute discrimination, whereas in other cases the complainant has to prove that discrimination results. In all cases, however, the discrimination has to be more than trivial. In result, then, though not in concept, this analysis resembles the distinction drawn by American courts between strict scrutiny and minimal scrutiny. In Canada I believe the distinction is not made on the authority of the courts but on that of the Constitution itself.

Thus we see that the Federal Court of Appeal has attempted to discern the meaning of section 15 taking into account the listed grounds and the implications which they have for the meaning of equality. While we think that the particular test used by the Federal Court has problems,[260] we think that the reference to the grounds points in a promising direction.

Other courts have, in various ways, found assistance in interpreting section 15 through examining the contents of the listed grounds. In *Mahé v. R.*, the Alberta Court of Appeal said:

> I say that the key to s. 15 is the *kind* of distinction made, not the mere fact of distinction . . . Certainly the list of offending acts offered in s. 15 have in common that Canadian society accepts that, as a criteria for distinction, they *prima facie* offer no rational basis for distinction *and* have historically been examples of invidious discrimination. It may well be that any additions to the list must meet the same test. I would not lightly add new categories. (I accept, however, that a distinction that has no rational basis and is capricious and arbitrary might also, just for that reason, offend s. 15.)[261]

In Andrews,[262] the British Columbia Court of Appeal took the listed grounds into account: it looked at them to determine whether citizenship could be asserted as an invalid basis for distinction. (This suggests a "threshold test" which, in the context of *Andrews*, is different from what we are proposing in arguing for a limited list of grounds. The major difference is that we argue for a limitation on grounds in order to allow for serious review of unintended effects on members of disadvantaged groups.)

. . . the fact that the drafters spelled out as grounds the principal natural and unalterable facts about human beings — race, national or ethnic origin, colour, religion (admittedly, not wholly a natural and unalterable fact), and sex — can only mean, I believe, that non-trivial pejorative distinctions based on such categories are intended to be justified by governments under s. 1 rather than to be proved as infringements by complainants under s. 15. In sum, some grounds of distinction are so presumptively pejorative that they are deemed to be inherently discriminatory."

Since the appellant did not have the benefit of proceeding under an enumerated ground, MacGuigan J. said that she failed to establish an infringement of s. 15, whether the criterion of establishing *prima facie* discrimination was the lack of a rational basis for the action, or whether it was the *MacKay* test (the latter being expressed as preferable). The other two members of the court preferred to decide the case on the basis that the applicant was not similarly situated with those who had been hired prior to her.

260 It does not appear to permit any non-enumerated grounds to receive careful scrutiny, and there is a reference to the plaintiffs' interests as "purely economic and commercial in nature; no question of liberty, freedom or human rights is involved" (*supra*, note 206, at 593 (34 D.L.R.)), which may be taken as support for the proposition that "social/economic" legislation should be exempted from Charter review.

261 *Supra*, note 41 at 52. Emphasis in original.

262 *Supra*, note 46 at 610.

As well, in the *Reference re Family Benefits Act (N.S.), S. 5* case,[263] the Nova Scotia Court of Appeal, because of section 28, concluded that "legislative classifications based on sex" would be *prima facie* discriminatory. However, there have been clear statements from a number of courts that the list of grounds will not play an important role in the interpretation of section 15. The Saskatchewan Court of Appeal[264] rejected an argument that section 15(1) should be read as comprehending only discrimination on the enumerated grounds and on grounds *ejusdem generis* with them, saying that the listing in section 15(1) is clearly not exhaustive and the *ejusdem generis* construction is inappropriate in the context of a constitutional document which should be given a generous rather than a legalistic interpretation.[265] The court added:

> This is not to say that the listing of certain grounds and not others is wholly immaterial — the basis upon which a distinction rests may well bear upon whether, and the ease with which, that distinction may be justified, another matter altogether — but in our opinion ss. 15(1) is not to be construed in the narrow fashion contended for.[266]

The Ontario Court of Appeal has reached a similar conclusion about the non-exhaustiveness of the list of grounds in section 15.[267] However, it has left the question open whether there might be different requirements for establishing a *prima facie* case depending upon whether the ground of discrimination alleged is enumerated.[268]

(iv) *Tests Focussing neither on other Elements*

While declining to impose any limitations through the listed grounds,

---

263 *Supra*, note 158 at 354.
264 *Reference re French Language Rights of Accused* in *Sask. Criminal Proceedings, supra*, note 86.
265 *Ibid.*
266 *Ibid.*
267 *R. v. Century 21 Ramos Realty Inc., supra*, note 213. *R. v. Ertel, supra*, note 213; *R. v. Turpin, supra*, note 213.
268 *McKinney v. Univ. of Guelph Bd. of Governors, supra*, note 98. The court did, in this decision, reject the argument that there should be differing standards of scrutiny for various enumerated grounds, with a lower standard of scrutiny for age. However, it said: "The application of standards of review under s. 1 to legislation which *prima facie* infringes equality rights under s. 15 is primarily an evidentiary and forensic problem. Each case is different and it is to be expected that the justification of discriminatory legislation will be more difficult in some cases than in others. This does not mean that different standards of proof apply to different categories of cases. It means, simply, that meeting the onus of establishing s. 1 limitations of s. 15 rights requires careful factual analysis in every case."

the Saskatchewan Court of Appeal[269] and the Ontario Court of Appeal[270] have used tests for the violation of section 15 which incorporate the "similarly situated" test referred to above, but expand upon it, in the context of determining whether one of the forms of equality mandated by section 15 has been denied. The Ontario court has said that there should be a three-step analysis:

1. Identify the class or classes or persons who are said to be treated differently.
2. Determine whether those classes are "similarly situated" in the light of the purposes of the legislation.
3. Determine whether there is "discrimination" in the sense of prejudicial or adverse treatment.[271]

Despite earlier doubt,[272] the court rejected the *Andrews* "reasonable and fair" test in *McKinney* saying:

> *Ertel* and *Turpin* demonstrate the difficulty of articulating the pejorative sense of the word "discrimination". In these cases and others, various descriptions have been applied to legislation which may discriminate against individuals under s. 15(1), including "invidious", "unfair", "irrational", "adverse", and "prejudicial". These decisions, nevertheless, make it clear that this court has not accepted the *Andrews* view that the party impugning legislation must also prove that it is "unreasonable".
>
> In the present case there can be no doubt that s. 9(a) has a prejudicial and adverse impact on university staff over the age of 65 in comparison with others under that age. Because of these easily observable prejudicial effects, the section discriminates against staff over the age of 65 and denies the equal treatment to which they are entitled under s. 15(1). The finding that s. 9(a) discriminates contrary to s. 15(1) is readily distinguishable from the question whether it can be justified as a reasonable limit on s. 15(1) rights under s. 1.
>
> Reasonableness, then, is a matter to be determined within the context of s. 1, where the rights of the person challenging the legislation can be balanced against the interests of other people and the societal values which the legislation may be claimed to assert or uphold. With respect, we are of the

---

269 *Reference re French Language Rights of Accused in Sask. Criminal Proceedings, supra,* note 86.

270 *McKinney v. Univ. of Guelph Bd. of Governors, supra,* note 98; *R. v. Ertel, supra,* note 213; *R. v. Turpin, supra,* note 213.

271 *R. v. Ertel, supra,* note 213 at 272.

272 See *R. v. Century 21 Ramos Realty Inc., supra,* note 213 at 42; *R. v. Ertel, supra,* note 213 at 272. In those cases the court indicated some adherence to the view in *Andrews* that discrimination must be read in the "pejorative" sense and that there must be a review as to fairness or reasonableness in the determination whether there is a violation of s. 15.

view that to require proof of unreasonableness for a finding of discrimination under s. 15(1) distorts the operation of the *Charter.* The burden of proof which properly falls on the upholder of the distinction under s. 1 is shifted to the challenger. If in a given case the requirement is not met, real discrimination could be defined out of existence and the open discussion of competing rights and values, which s. 1 requires, would be forestalled.[273]

In a case challenging the Saskatchewan government's failure to proclaim Part XIV.1 of the *Criminal Code* permitting an accused to have his trial conducted in French, the Saskatchewan Court of Appeal reached a similar conclusion about the relationship between sections 15 and 1, and disagreed with the *Andrews* test. It said that one of the important aspects of section 15 is its enunciation of positive equality rights rather than negative non-discrimination rights. It concluded that section 15 involves two distinct "plains of definition",[274] the first concerning the concepts of equality and the second, the term "discrimination". The first was not extensively discussed, beyond a reference to the "similarly situated" test. The definition of "discrimination" adopted by the court was derived from three international human rights treaties adopted by Canada:[275]

> Picking up on the definition common to those treaties, and assuming the whole of the section is modified by the phrase "without discrimination", we construe the term to mean any distinction, exclusion, restriction, or preference whose purpose or effect is to nullify or impair the enjoyment of the forms of equality enshrined in the section.[276]

To conclude this review of the approaches to section 15, we refer to this statement in *Reference re An Act To Amend the Education Act (Ont.)*[277] by the Ontario Court of Appeal:

> In our view, s. 15(1) read as a whole constitutes a compendious expression of a positive right to equality both in the substance and the administration of the law. It is an all-encompassing right governing all legislative action. Like the ideals of "equal justice" and "equal access to the law," the right to equal protection and equal benefit of the law now enshrined in the Charter rests on the moral and ethical principle fundamental to a truly free and

---

273 *Supra*, note 98 at 40.

274 *Reference re French Language Rights of Accused in Sask. Criminal Proceedings, supra*, note 86.

275 *International Convention on the Elimination of All Forms of Racial Discrimination, supra*, note 10; *Convention on the Elimination of All Forms of Discrimination Against Women, supra*, note 10; the *Convention Concerning Discrimination in Respect of Employment and Occupation, supra*, note 10.

276 *Reference re French Language Rights of Accused in Sask. Criminal Proceedings, supra*, note 86.

277 (1986), 25 D.L.R. (4th) 1 (Ont. C.A.), aff'd *supra*, note 44.

democratic society that all persons should be treated by the law on a footing of equality with equal concern and equal respect.[278]

Although such statements of general principle are far from the articulation of a "test" for deciding cases, they provide, in our view, real guidance in beginning such articulation.

(c) Elements of a Test for Applying Section 15

(i) *Introductory Comments to the Test*

A test for whether or not equality rights are violated by a legislative provision or governmental practice should take account of both the paradigm of equality underlying section 15, and the institutional constraints on judicial review.

On the premise that section 15 of the Charter should be given a purposive interpretation, as discussed above in Part 2, "The Meaning of Equality", we suggest the following elements should form part of the test applied in judicial review of legislation. The test we set out here may not be the definitive answer to all problems in this area, but it is an example of where the considerations which we have discussed could lead courts in deciding equality claims.

We have been influenced in our development of this test by the overall experience of equality claims under the Charter as well as by the decisions in section 15 cases to date.

As of December 31, 1987, we have collected a total of 205 superior court cases in which section 15 arguments have been seriously considered.[279] Of those cases, 151 found that there was no violation of section 15(1). In the 54 cases in which a violation was found, 12 involved sex discrimination,[280] four were based on age, one each on race and disability, 18 on geographical disparities, and 16 on other unenumerated grounds.

We have been influenced as well by the reasoning in the cases decided to date. In *Re Andrews and Law Society of B.C.*,[281] there is the "reasonable and fair" formulation, which we think can form part of the test, and which builds on the basic notion that similarly situated persons should be treated

---

278 *Ibid.* at 42.

279 We have eliminated cases in which the Charter was ruled not to apply, for example, as well as those in which Charter arguments were raised but not discussed by the court.

280 Eight were claims for the benefit of men, four for women. Of the six cases in which the violation was found not to be saved by section 15(2) or section 1, three were for the benefit of men, and three for women.

281 *Supra*, note 46 at 609.

similarly, emphasized in many of the cases (such as *McDonald*,[282] *Blainey*,[283] and *Reference re Education Act*[284]). As well, from *Andrews*, we can learn the importance of giving a meaning to the term "discrimination".

The *Century 21 Ramos Realty* case,[285] in its criticism of the "similarly situated" test, shows a concern for carrying out the purposes of the Charter, which the court states would be unfulfilled by a test permitting distinctions disadvantaging women simply because based on biological reality. A related point is made in *Reference re Family Benefits Act (N.S.), s. 5*,[286] in which the impact of section 28 on the interpretation of section 15 sex equality rights is discussed. In the Federal Court of Appeal and Alberta Court of Appeal cases, we see a focus on the enumerated grounds as setting the scope of section 15, and a discussion of the overall context in which limitations on equality rights should be assessed. As well, in the Newfoundland Court of Appeal cases (*Reference re Ss. 32 & 34 of Workers' Compensation Act (Nfld.)*[287] and *A.G. Newfoundland & Labrador Housing Corporation v. Williams*[288]), we see the concern that the equality provisions in the Charter should not stand in the way of legitimate governmental activity.

In several cases (see MacFarlane J.A.'s reasons in *Shewchuk*,[289] as well as the reasons of the Saskatchewan Court of Appeal in *Reference re French Language Rights*[290] and of the Ontario Court of Appeal in *McKinney*[291]), there is a discussion of the appropriate place for the onus in assessing limitations on section 15 rights, and of the relationship between sections 15 and 1. There are references (for example, in *Rebic*[292]) to the lack of resources in disadvantaged groups to meet that onus. Finally, in the Supreme Court of Canada cases interpreting section 1(b) of the *Canadian Bill of Rights*,[293] there is a basic notion of equality before the law which continues to form part of the guarantees under section 15 of the Charter and which provides some (limited) assistance in interpreting

---

282 *Supra*, note 213 at 349.

283 *Supra*, note 29 at 744.

284 *Supra*, note 277 at 42 (dissent by Howlands C.J.O. and Roberts J.A.).

285 *Supra*, note 213 at 38.

286 *Supra*, note 158 at 354.

287 *Supra*, note 77.

288 (1987), 62 Nfld. & P.E.I.R. 269 at 277-278 (Nfld. C.A.).

289 *Supra*, note 121 at 341-342.

290 *Supra*, note 86.

291 *Supra*, note 98.

292 *Supra*, note 142 at 376.

293 *R. v. Drybones*, *supra*, note 16; *A.G. Canada v. Lavell*, *supra*, note 177; *Mackay v. R.*, *supra*, note 17.

it.[294] The combination of this principle with the important principles safeguarding the rights of criminally accused persons and seeking uniformity of criminal law in a national system, has led to a large number of section 15 equality cases in which distinctions in the criminal law system have been challenged.[295]

We assume in our discussion of a possible test that the greater part of the balancing process between competing interests or between the necessities of society and rights of individuals should take place within the framework of section 1 of the Charter, rather than within section 15. However, a test functionally similar to ours could be developed in the context of the approach taken in the *Andrews* decision,[296] whereby the balancing process takes place during the assessment of whether or not there has been a violation of section 15 equality rights. We are describing only the "section 1 balancing" model due to constraints of time and space, but a "section 15 balancing" model can fairly readily be extrapolated from it.

We have frequently used the terms "legislation" and "provision" in this discussion. This does not presume that only acts of the legislature are subject to section 15 review. On the contrary, we think there are many acts of the executive branch[297] (and many aspects of the common law[298]) which could lead to section 15 violations. We are using the terminology of "legislation" and "provision" only as a form of shorthand.

One further introductory note to the test: basically, it contemplates that section 15 applies only to enumerated grounds and those akin to them. However, we see the arguments to the contrary and recognize that there would be several important cases in which the courts have granted section

---

294 By referring to the Diceyan notion of "equality before the law" adopted in the Supreme Court of Canada cases, we are not expressing the view that those decisions were correct in their understanding of the meaning of equality under the *Canadian Bill of Rights*, let alone under the Charter. We think, however, that the guarantee of "equality before the law" at least includes protection against differential treatment in the administration of the legal system, and that this is such a fundamental guarantee (that we are all subject to the same laws administered by the ordinary courts of the land) that it may apply in a broader way (*i.e.*, on any ground) than the other guarantees in s. 15.

295 In our data base of superior court cases, 42 percent have arisen in the context of the criminal law.

296 *Supra*, note 46.

297 See *Reference re French Language Rights of Accused in Sask. Criminal Proceedings, supra*, note 86, as an example of such an executive act. *R. v. Hamilton, supra*, note 82, provides another illustration.

298 Such as in *Power v. Moss, supra*, note 182.

15 review which would be excluded under our test.[299] Should the courts accept those arguments and conclude that such cases warrant review, we have suggested some alternative ways in which such review might be accomplished without detracting from the focus on disadvantaged groups which we consider to be required by section 15.

(ii) *Steps of Analysis*

The steps of analysis which we discuss next illustrate one way in which the principles we have discussed could be implemented. We have included a chart (see page 647) to make it clear how the analysis flows from one step to the next.

1. *Application of the Charter.* Does the Charter apply to the litigants and the activity in question? (If the answer is "no", the inquiry ends here.)
2. *Restriction of grounds to which section 15 applies.* In its terms or any of its consequences, does the impugned provision affect differentially a group of human beings defined by one of the characteristics named in section 15 or by a characteristic akin to those? (If the answer to this question is "no", section 15 is not applicable.)
3. *Detrimental effect on a disadvantaged group relative to its counterpart.* If the answer to question 2 is "yes", and the provision does affect differentially a group of human beings defined by one of the characteristics named in section 15 or by a characteristic akin to them, the next question is whether the provision incorporating the distinction has the purpose or effect of increasing the disadvantage of a disadvantaged group relative to that of its counterpart? In other words, does it function so as to magnify inequality in terms of the consequences it is appropriate to take account of in the circumstances?[300] (If the answer to this question is "yes", there is a *prima facie* violation of section 15(1). If it is "no", one moves to step 4, which sets out an alternative set of criteria.)
4. *Reasonable relationship to a legitimate purpose and fairness in the circumstances.* If the answer to question 3 is "no", two further questions should be asked: (a) Is the purpose of the law legitimate? (b) Is the differential effect created in the impugned provision reasonably related to the purpose of the law, and is it fair? (If the answer to all parts

---

299 *E.g., R. v. Hamilton, supra,* note 82; *McBeth v. Governors of Dalhousie College & Univ., supra,* note 82; *Zutphen Brothers Construction Ltd. v. Dywidag Systems International (Can.) Ltd., supra,* note 82. Even cases such as *Re Andrews and Law Society of B.C., supra,* note 46, and *Reference re French Language Rights of Accused in Sask. Criminal Proceedings, supra,* note 86, would be excluded if they were viewed as based on grounds neither enumerated nor akin to those in s. 15.

300 See Part 2, *supra,* for a fuller discussion of what is meant by this concept.

is "yes", there is no violation. If the answer to any part is "no", there is a *prima facie* violation of section 15(1).)

5. *Affirmative action program.* If there is a violation of section 15(1), determined either at the stage of step 3 or step 4, then it must be determined whether the provision falls within the meaning of section 15(2). (If the provision does fall within the meaning of section 15(2), then the inquiry ends. If it does not, then there must be an assessment under section 1.)

6. *Reasonable limits prescribed by law and demonstrably justified in a free and democratic society.* Having found a *prima facie* violation of section 15(1) which is not "saved" by section 15(2), the court must determine whether the provision in question constitutes a reasonable limitation on the equality rights under section 15, prescribed by law and demonstrably justified in a free and democratic society. The review at this stage would be conducted according to the principles set out in the *Oakes* case.[301] (If the provision is found to be a reasonable limitation, the inquiry ends. If not, it proceeds to questions of remedy.)

We will now review and elaborate upon these suggested elements in a test for equality violations.

A. *Application of the Charter.* The questions addressed here would be those discussed above in this Part under "Scope of Application of the Charter": does the Charter apply to the defendant or respondent named, at the instigation of the person alleging a violation?

B. *Restriction of Grounds to Which Section 15 Applies.* This is the most important way in which this proposed test attempts to deal with institutional constraints. Not only would a restriction of grounds substantially reduce the judicial workload, judging from the cases which have come forward to date,[302] but it also would eliminate some of the most vexing cases — ones which, we suggest, are vexing only because they are so dissonant with the true purpose of the section and at the same time upon one literal reading seem to be covered by it.[303]

The statement of the test which we have proposed, therefore, would screen out at a threshold stage cases in which the alleged inequality arose from considerations outside the scope of the named grounds or those akin

---

301 *Supra*, note 48.

302 See the statistics, *supra*, note 280 and note 295.

303 *E.g.*, the *Aluminum Co. of Canada* case, *supra*, note 95 and *Century 21 Ramos Realty Inc.*, *supra*, note 213.

to them. For the reasons we have discussed above in Part 3, we think that this is the most efficacious way to take account of the appropriate limits of judicial review, and that the determination of whether a ground is excluded or included could be assisted by a reference not only to the purpose of section 15, but also to international instruments, human rights legislation, and jurisprudence under them. At the conclusion of this Part, we refer to some alternative steps which could be added should it be desired to extend protection to all distinctions involving fundamental rights or interests, or to extend protection in some other ways.

C. *Detrimental Effect on a Disadvantaged Group Relative to its Counterpart.* This step distinguishes between claims brought by members of persistently disadvantaged groups and claims brought by members of the advantaged counterpart groups, for example, between claims brought by women as opposed to men, or racial minorities as opposed to majorities. It provides that where a provision operates to increase the disadvantage of the disadvantaged subset, there is a *prima facie* violation of section 15(1). This does not preclude other claims, since step 4 of our proposed test affords protection to both the advantaged and disadvantaged subsets of the named and akin groups. The result is that the distinction between advantaged and disadvantaged becomes relevant to the process of analysis, not to the existence of protection.

The reason for making this distinction in the analysis is our view that a primary purpose of section 15 is to overcome inequalities; this purpose cannot be fulfilled if the section is available to strike down provisions because they fail to increase the advantage of already-advantaged groups. There would be little need for an equality guarantee if in fact everyone had the same relative disadvantages. To the extent that the objective of section 15 is equality of condition for different groups, a law that improves the condition of a disadvantaged group simply does not create inequality even though its immediate consequences disfavour the advantaged group. The latter group is no more denied protection than the healthy are denied hospital services.

We think that the wording of section 15(1) supports this approach; why else, for example, would "disability" be used rather than a neutral term, like "condition"? Either all of the named grounds are read in the way we suggest (consistent with "disability") or that one ground is anomalous. We suggest section 15 should be read so as to fulfill its purpose and in the process to avoid anomaly. As well, this view of the meaning of "equality" is supported by the wording of section 15(2), which specifically protects programs designed to change the balance between advantaged and disadvantaged counterparts of groups.

De Jong has argued[304] that section 28 operates on section 15(1) to ensure that "the quality of protection of section 15 rights is equal for male and female persons" and that therefore there must be identical standards of review whether claims of sex discrimination are raised by men or women. We do not think, however, that the test we propose is inconsistent with section 28, although we agree that section 28 operates on section 15. What section 15 guarantees are "equality rights". We have concluded that those rights take into account a meaning of equality going beyond a guarantee of identical treatment and that the purpose of section 15 is the alleviation of persistent disadvantage. The disadvantage of women is a historical fact. Therefore, we think that it is consistent with the statement in section 28 that the equality rights (as all others in the Charter) are "guaranteed equally to men and women", to frame a test that deals with this historical disadvantage.

Below we discuss some alternative steps which could be added to the analysis, one of which would permit assessment of some claims by advantaged subsets on the same basis as their disadvantaged counterparts (for example, claims brought by men where the men in question are, according to the evidence, in a situation of concrete disadvantage). This also would be consistent with section 28.

We will deal with three elements of this question separately: (1) the determination of "disadvantage"; (2) "appropriate consequences to take into account"; (3) "magnify disadvantage".

(1) The determination of "disadvantage". The applicant, having shown that the distinction relates to one of the named or akin grounds, must also show membership in the disadvantaged subset of the category in question if this step of analysis is to apply. We think that it is clear from the wording of section 15(2) that the framers of the Charter contemplated that courts would be able to determine whether or not individuals[305] or groups are disadvantaged. The task would be no different under section 15(1), though that is not to say it will always be easy.

Often, the decision about whether a person is a member of a disadvantaged group will be straightforward. For example, in Canada at this time, there is abundant evidence to show that black people form part

---

304 *Supra,* note 51 at 527.

305 We think that, in context, the reference to "disadvantaged individuals" must be seen as a reference to disadvantage through possession of a characteristic which is referred to in the enumerated or akin grounds. If the alternative view were taken, that "disadvantaged individuals or groups" could refer to any individual or group disadvantaged in a particular situation, in isolation from the context of section 15(2), then the reference to "affirmative action programs" in the heading would not make sense.

of a disadvantaged group with respect to employment, representation in public institutions, economic position, and so on.[306] Under the named ground of "sex" there are the two well-known subsets. There is abundant evidence to show that it is women, although in a majority in numbers, who are the disadvantaged group.[307]

However, it is not always perfectly clear which subset of a group is disadvantaged in particular contexts. For example, are native people disadvantaged in terms of social benefits, given that they are immune from certain forms of taxation?

One possible way of dealing with such questions would be to say that the group to which the applicant belongs must be shown to be disadvantaged with respect to the type of interest at stake. A weakness in this answer would be that disadvantage in life does not come in discrete packages; nor does advantage. To address the example in the preceding paragraph, while native people are immune from certain forms of taxation, that immunity could be seen as part of a historic compromise relating to lands, and unrelated to claims for social benefits. If that larger picture is taken into account, it is difficult to see how non-natives could be seen as disadvantaged for the purpose of challenges under section 15 to the benefits afforded to natives.

Even under this approach, the "interest" would have to refer to more than the effect of the particular provision under challenge. For example, if a law restricted the employment opportunities of men in women's prisons, the question would be who is disadvantaged in *employment*, not who is disadvantaged in employment in women's prisons.

A second way of dealing with this problem would be to say that a group is either generally disadvantaged or advantaged at a particular time, and the court should not be concerned about whether there has been disadvantage in the particular interest to which the claim relates. This approach would serve better for dealing with inequalities affecting women, and perhaps native people and some racial or ethnic minorities, where the inequalities derive from a social system in which differences in life expectations and in dignity and respect are deeply embedded and pervasive.

---

306 See, *e.g.*, the *Abella Report*, *supra*, note 57; B. Billingsley & L. Muszynski, *No Discrimination Here?*, Social Planing Council of Metropolitan Toronto and Urban Alliance on Race Relations, May 1985.

307 The characteristics of the relationship between men and women which lead to the conclusion that women are the disadvantaged group include pervasive unequal pay, unequal ownership of property, victimization through rape, domestic battery, sexual abuse as children, systematic sexual harassment, and so on. See C.A. MacKinnon, *Feminism Unmodified: Discourses on Life and Law* (1987) at 23-25, 40-41, 169-170, 277-279. See also the *Abella Report*, *supra*, note 57, and works on particular areas such as MacLeod. *supra*, note 193.

To take the opposite approach in such cases could lead to the erosion of the position of such disadvantaged groups in those areas in which they have achieved some security of expectation, while leaving untouched those areas in which they are systematically disadvantaged in ways which it is difficult for the law to touch directly.[308]

However, these arguments do not seem to us to apply particularly well to other cases, such as groups defined by age or by religious affiliation. In such areas as those, there is much to be said for a more contextual assessment of disadvantage.

We doubt that the decision of how to assess disadvantage can be reduced to a rule; instead the appropriate measure will depend on factors such as the ground of disadvantage alleged, the forms of disadvantage associated with that ground and the nature of the provision under challenge. Those factors would have to be assessed in light of the objective of remedying persistent disadvantage which we think underlies section 15. Because of the difficulties in this area and the fact that institutional constraints may prevent the courts from examining all the factors that ideally would be taken into account, we tend to the view that most assessments of disadvantage should be categorical rather than contextual.

(2) "Appropriate consequences to take into account". We have discussed above in Part 2, our view that a crucial issue in equality decision-making is determining the appropriate consequences to take into account in making comparisons. In some (perhaps many) cases, this determination would be relatively straightforward. For example, with the internment of the Japanese in World War II, there would likely be little dispute about the appropriate level of consequences.[309] Similarly, consider a provincial Public Service Commission policy requiring a valid driver's licence for all civil service positions, whether or not driving is regularly required in a position, and a complaint by a visually-impaired person that such a policy affects her in her eligibility for positions for which she is otherwise qualified. Probably there would be agreement that the appropriate level of consequences would be equal opportunity to be considered for work for which the ability to drive was not essential.[310] In other cases, the determination

---

308 Particularly if the Charter is taken to apply only to legislation and direct governmental activity, leaving common law rules immune from review. See the discussion at note 193, *supra*.

309 The appropriate level of consequences would be the treatment of Japanese Canadians as opposed to all other Canadians.

310 Certainly there would be room for some disagreement on the fine points: should the appropriate level of consequences be equal opportunity to be considered for all positions in which driving is not essential? important? a substantial part? a significant part? any part? The point is, however, that the starting place would likely be uncontroversial.

of this issue would not be particularly straightforward, and the types of considerations we have discussed above would come into play. However, there is no doubt that such issues arise on any view of equality.[311] We think they are more likely to be resolved satisfactorily if they are openly recognized and assessed.

(3) "Magnify disadvantage". Once it has been determined that a group is disadvantaged and once an appropriate level of consequences has been identified, the next question is whether the particular provision serves to magnify the disadvantage of the group in terms of those consequences. In many cases, this will be a relatively simple matter. In some others, it will be more difficult. This question is at least an implicit part of every equality test.[312] Again, we think it is desirable to make this stage of analysis explicit.

D. *Reasonable Relationship to a Legitimate Legislative Objective and Fairness in the Circumstances.* This step is meant to embody the essence of the "reasonable and fair" test,[313] with the addition of the explicit questioning of purpose. It permits a court to find a violation of section 15(1) where legislation affects differentially a group of persons defined on one of the bases named in section 15 or akin to them (even where the claim is not brought by a member of the disadvantaged subset of the group) and where the legislation seems arbitrary or clearly over- or under-inclusive. In such cases, it should have to be justified, whether under section 1 or otherwise.

It is here that the courts could deal with cases where an advantaged group of people is singled out for treatment worse than that of its counterpart.[314] Where that treatment serves the purpose of narrowing the

---

311 Even purely juridical equality: there, the pre-determination has been made that the appropriate level of consequences is identity of treatment under the law.

312 Under some views, it arises in the form of a decision about whether someone is "similarly situated" to someone else. Under the *Andrews* test (*supra*, text corresponding to notes 237-250) it would occur either at the "similarly situated" stage or at the stage of assessing whether there was discrimination in the sense of treatment or results which were unfair or unreasonable in all of the circumstances. In order to get to the "unfair or unreasonable" test in *Andrews*, it must first be determined that there is differential treatment or results which are prejudicial.

313 See *Re Andrews and Law Society of B.C.*, *supra*, note 46. It should be noted that this test is not dissimilar to the one enunciated by McIntyre J. in *MacKay v. R.*, *supra*, note 17.

314 We say "singled out" because it may be inappropriate in most cases to look at a more remote level of consequences. Possibly, this might occur when it is a disadvantaged subset of an advantaged group (*e.g.*, physically disabled men, which is affected at a more remote level of consequences.

gap between the advantaged and disadvantaged counterparts of the group to an extent which is more than *de minimis*, then the provision would pass the test and the inquiry would end.[315] If not, the result would be inconsistent with step 3.[316]

On the other hand, where there is no such connection with a legitimate purpose, the provision will be irreconcilable with section 15. However, in Part 7 "Remedies", below, we will suggest that if courts consider themselves institutionally incapable of reading legislation so as to remedy under-inclusiveness through providing benefits to excluded groups, they should, in some cases, equally refuse to strike the legislation down.

E. *Affirmative Action Program.* There are two possible reasons that section 15(2) would come into play: (a) the legislation is found, at step 3, to magnify inequality for a disadvantaged group; or (b) the legislation is found, at step 4, to affect people differentially on one or more of the bases named in section 15 or akin to them, and not to be reasonable and fair in the light of its legislative purpose.

It is the first situation that calls for comment. How could legislation which has been determined to magnify inequality for a disadvantaged group nevertheless ameliorate the conditions of a disadvantaged group? Ordinarily, such legislation could not, and section 15(2) would not apply. However, it is not inconceivable that a provision is detrimental to the relative position of one disadvantaged group and is at the same time part of a program to ameliorate the conditions of another disadvantaged group. For example, an affirmative action program for one racial minority could have a detrimental effect on the relative position of another racial minority.[317]

In many cases under our proposed test, the issue will not reach the stage of section 15(2). For example, provisions allowing for women who

---

315 Again, perhaps with the exception of a case where there is an inordinate effect on disadvantaged individuals within the advantaged subset.

316 Moreover, there would be a reasonable relationship with a legitimate purpose and it must be "fair" under s. 15 to take steps to overcome disadvantage. The United States Supreme Court case of *Mississippi University for Women v. Hogan*, 73 L. Ed. 2d 1090 (1981) illustrates another possible situation in which this kind of dispute could arise. We would think that the preservation of single-sex institutions for women, where women wish it, would usually be seen as a legitimate purpose given the distance which is still to be bridged before women have achieved social and economic equality, and that it would be fair, in the interests of lessening inequality, to permit such institutions to stand despite challenges under section 15(1). Such an issue is presently being litigated in Canada: see *Tomen v. Federation of Women Teachers Ass. of Ont.* (1987), 61 O.R. (2d) 489 (H.C.).

317 The *Edwards Books* case, *supra*, note 115, provides an illustration. The *Retail Businesses Act* provided a partial accommodation for Saturday Sabbath observers, but none for those whose holy day is any other day than Saturday or Sunday.

are bearing children to take time off from employment and return to their jobs, or to receive benefits during that period, would not reach section 15(2).[318] However, a program to provide for the admission to job-training programs of persons with particular physical disabilities but not others, or persons of certain minority racial groups but not others, could reach section 15(2) and be saved by it. Thus, section 15(2) would serve two purposes: it would clarify the meaning of equality in section 15(1), and it would allow for governments to address inequality programs one at a time if necessary, in a world with limited resources.

F. *Reasonable Limits Prescribed by Law and Demonstrably Justified in a Free and Democratic Society.* The role for section 1 is to evaluate, according to the *Oakes* principles,[319] whether the legislation, although infringing the equality rights of a disadvantaged group, is nevertheless demonstrably justifiable in a free and democratic society. The analysis would reach section 1 if the legislation were found to violate section 15(1) either at step 3 or step 4, and not to be exempted by section 15(2). If the balancing takes place under section 1 rather than section 15, a larger number of cases would reach section 1. If the balancing is largely done under section 15, although it is not likely that legislation would frequently pass the section 1 test, having failed at the earlier stages, it is possible. For example, a governmental program which is held to have the unintended effect of magnifying inequality for a particular religious group (perhaps a business holidays Act) could nevertheless be found to be reasonable and demonstrably justified in a free and democratic society.

Cases involving claims by ten-year-old applicants for drivers' licences or cardiac patients who wish to be pilots on government-owned airlines would be considered under section 1 according to the model we are proposing. It is tempting to say that the government should not have to spend the time to justify such obviously reasonable provisions as those which set age limits on driving or medical conditions for the employment of airline pilots but, in our view, that temptation should be resisted. If the provisions are so obviously reasonable, then they will quickly pass section 1 review. If they do not pass section 1 review, then they are not obviously reasonable. And whether the review of such claims takes place under section 15 or section 1, such claims can still be brought if people see fit to do so. We do not see why there would be any discernible difference in the expenditure of resources to meet them, one way or the other. And

318 Such provisions should not reach s. 15(2) because they would not be found to increase inequality for a disadvantaged group under step 3, and they would be found to be pursuant to a legitimate purpose and to be reasonable under step 4.

319 *Supra*, note 48.

the placing of an expectation upon government to justify distinctions which work to the disadvantage of groups defined according to the named or akin grounds, seems to us not only justifiable and consistent with the purpose of section 15, but required by the framework of the Charter as a whole.

(iii) *Alternatives*

Although we are suggesting only one, we have identified at least four ways in which protection could be expanded beyond that afforded to disadvantaged groups under our proposed test. By and large, these methods are not mutually exclusive, although adoption of all might push the limits of the institutional constraints which we have discussed. Our discussion of these methods attempts to evaluate them against the objectives we have discussed — implementing the purpose of section 15, which we consider to be the alleviation of disadvantage of disadvantaged groups, giving effect to the wording of section 15, and permitting the use of section 15 to remedy arbitrary treatment in some range of circumstances consistent with the Canadian understanding of a free and democratic society.

The four possible ways we have identified are:

1. The option actually incorporated in step 4 above, whereby there is rationality review of any legislation which has a deleterious purpose or effect with respect to members of any named or akin classification.

2. Allow protection for certain members of advantaged groups, where those members are factually disadvantaged in a way related to that categorization (for example, impecunious men with single parent responsibilities who are denied benefits afforded to women in comparable circumstances). Such a claim would be assessed using the same standard of review afforded to the disadvantaged groups.

3. Allow claims brought by anyone who is differentially affected in interests which are determined to be "fundamental" in that they are otherwise protected under the Charter or are central to our understanding of a free and democratic society,[320] where the claimant is able to satisfy the court, on a balance of probabilities, that the impugned provision treats them differentially, has no reasonable relationship to a legitimate legislative purpose and is unfair in the circumstances. There would be no need to show membership in a disadvantaged group or even that the detriment is related to a named or akin ground.

4. Allow protection for persons who are not affected in a way related

---

320 Along the lines of the American "fundamental rights/fundamental interests" strand of equal protection. See Tribe, *supra*, note 13.

to categorization on the basis of disadvantaged or akin groups, but who are treated differentially in their access to the legal system in ways which might be described as violations of "equality before the law" in an expanded sense, that is, in ways which are not reasonably related to legitimate governmental objectives and are unfair in the circumstances.[321]

The second possible way of expanding the scope of section 15 is an alternative to the one we have chosen for dealing with claims based upon enumerated or akin grounds, but not brought by members of generally disadvantaged groups. We think that it has some merit. The distinction between it and the way we have chosen is that we allow for all claims by members of the advantaged subset, but afford them a lesser standard of review; it allows for a limited number of claims by members of the advantaged subset (only when certain members of the subset can prove disadvantage in a particular context) but affords such claims the same standard of review as that provided for the disadvantaged groups (a rigorous standard). We prefer our approach because:

(a) the exercise of determining whether members of a normally advantaged group are disadvantaged in a particular context raises all of the problems of determining disadvantage which we have discussed, but in heightened form;

(b) of the standard of review that is contemplated, the risk of coming to the point of striking down legislation that actually benefits a disadvantaged group seems higher, particularly if remedies for under-inclusive provisions are limited to striking them down;

(c) in principle, there is something to be said for a reading of section 15 which permits *any* distinction drawn upon the lines of a named or enumerated categorization to be brought to the attention of the courts. While there might be other ways to deal with "separate but equal" problems, certainly one of the most straightforward is to say that any distinction is to some degree questionable. That is what the first way we have suggested permits — a questioning of distinctions drawn upon, for example, racial, religious, or sexual lines, just because of that fact. Nevertheless, where such distinctions work to the benefit of a disadvantaged group, they should be preserved. Our test attempts to do that by permitting legislation which has a reasonable relationship to a legitimate purpose (such as remedying inequality) to stand.

---

321 Alternatives 2 and 4 were suggested to us by Mary Eberts and were argued by the Women's Legal Education and Action Fund in its intervention in the *Andrews* argument in the Supreme Court of Canada.

As for the third and fourth alternatives, these would deal in different ways with claims relating to inequalities affecting individuals in important ways, but not in ways related to their possession of particular characteristics of the sort section 15 specifies. We have not incorporated the third one into our test, in part because most of the fundamental interests which would likely be recognized are already guaranteed in other parts of the Charter and it is unclear how much is added by guaranteeing such interests "equally". We think it is usually preferable in such cases that the inequality be considered as a factor affecting the legitimacy of the intrusion on the other right, rather than as a separate claim.

The fourth alternative would deal with cases in which the complaint is of unequal access to the legal system or uneven treatment in the criminal justice system.[322] Such claims seem resonant with the notion of "equality before the law" discussed by Dicey and recognized in the cases under section 1(b) of the *Canadian Bill of Rights*,[323] although they would not necessarily have succeeded under that rubric. Equality with respect to the administration and process of the law may constitute a fundamental interest not necessarily recognized under other parts of the Charter yet so significant as to warrant protection. That may be a message from the courts in the cases under section 15 to date.

In the end, however, we think it unnecessary in giving effect to section 15 to adopt any of these alternatives except the first. There are risks in making section 15 available for claims not based upon named or akin categorizations — not the least of which is that the resources of the persons and groups who will attempt to bring such claims may be so much greater than those of members of the disadvantaged groups that the meaning of the section will become skewed as a result of the amount of litigation focussed on the "fundamental interests" or "process claims" issues. We think that most claims which seem central to fulfilling the purpose of the Charter could succeed under other provisions, such as section 7 and the other "legal rights" sections.

6. REMEDIES

We are not discussing remedies under section 15 in any detail because there is a chapter on enforcement of Charter rights elsewhere in this volume. However, there is one particularly acute problem in the area of enforcement of equality rights which should be emphasized. That is the

---

322 Such as *R. v. Hamilton, supra,* note 82; *McBeth v. Governors of Dalhousie College & Univ., supra,* note 82; *Reference re French Language Rights of Accused in Sask. Criminal Proceedings, supra,* note 86.

323 Such as *MacKay v. R., supra,* note 17.

potential that legislative provisions which benefit a group, or part of a group, will be struck down because they are under-inclusive, but will not be replaced by suitably expanded provisions.[324] Particularly in the area of sex discrimination, there is a concern that legislative provisions designed in some specific ways to alleviate the disadvantage of women, yet not falling within the meaning of section 15(2), will be mowed down by an absolutist definition of sex equality or even by an application of our step 4 (where the provisions are rationally indefensible), leaving women worse off than they were before and men no better off.

By way of example, in *Shewchuk v. Ricard,*[325] the issue was the failure to provide for men, equally with women, the right to apply for maintenance for children born out of wedlock under the *Child Paternity and Support Act* of British Columbia. The argument was raised by a man who was resisting an application by the mother for a declaration of paternity and an order for the payment of maintenance for a child. He argued that the Act under which he had been summonsed was unconstitutional under section 15.

The purpose of the legislation as a whole was undoubtedly legitimate — to provide a means for mothers of children born out of wedlock to seek declarations of paternity and orders for the payment of maintenance for the children. It was difficult, however, to see what purpose was served by the challenged feature of the legislation, namely the exclusion of men. There could be no serious argument that scarce resources dictated the exclusion of men in order to provide for more needy women, given the very small number of men who would ever be in a position to apply. Nor could the purpose have been to further the best interests of children, since the effect of excluding men was to reduce the number of possible sources of maintenance for the out of wedlock children. Further, the legislation did not constitute an affirmative action program within the meaning of section 15(2).[326] However, there was no specific provision explicitly excluding men which could have been struck down: the problem was that the wording of the statute referred to "mothers", not "parents". The most

---

324 For two cases in which this problem materialized, see *Reference re Family Benefits Act (N.S.), S. 5, supra,* note 159, and *Shewchuk v. Ricard, supra,* note 121.

325 *Ibid.*

326 Although Nemetz C.J.B.C. held that it was an affirmative action program (at 329), he was in the minority and we think, with respect, that he was wrong in his reading of s. 15(2). We think that s. 15(2) is designed to permit programs which are specifically designed to overcome comparative disadvantages in particular areas. Here, the provision of a remedy for women and not for men who find themselves with custody of out of wedlock children did not meet that description since any minimal improvement in the position of women resulting from excluding men from the program was surely an unintended side-effect of the legislation, rather than its purpose.

desirable result would have been to read the legislation so ast to provide benefits to both parents. Although the United States Supreme Court has recognized the availability of the remedy of "extension" in similar circumstances,[327] Canadian courts have, to date, refrained from adopting this approach.[328] Further, Supreme Court of Canada statements leave some doubt that that court will be prepared to expand its range of remedies far beyond declarations of invalidity.[329]

In our view, the extension remedy makes sense in a case such as *Shewchuk*, where probably more violence is done to the wishes of the legislature through striking down legislation than through declaring that it will apply to persons not contemplated at the time of its passage. To deny the possibility of such a remedy is to make a great deal turn on the happenstance of legislative drafting styles. For example, in *N.M. v. B.C. Superintendent of Family & Child Services*,[330] the issue was the constitutionality of section 8(1)(b) of the British Columbia *Adoption Act*, which authorized an adoption order to be made with the consent only of the mother and not of the father where the mother and father had never been married and the child not previously adopted. Because the wording of the section permitted it,[331] the court was able to strike down the portion which allowed the mother alone to consent to adoption (holding it unconstitutional under section 15 on the grounds of marital and sex discrimination), but leave the rest of the provision intact. With a different drafting style, the court would have been forced to either strike down the

---

327 See *Orr v. Orr*, 440 U.S. 268; *Orr v. Orr*, So. 2d 895; *Welsh v. U.S.*, 298 U.S. 333 (1970). See also R. Ginsburg, "Some Thoughts on Judicial Authority to Remedy Unconstitutional Legislation" (1979), 28 *Cleveland State L. Rev.* 301; D. Beers, "Extension Versus Invalidation of Under-inclusive Statutes: A Remedial Alternative" (1975), 12 *Columbia J.L. & Soc. Prob.* 115; D. Mossop, "Extension: A Constitutional Cure for Underinclusiveness" (1987), 45 *The Advocate* 707.

328 See also *Reference re Family Benefits Act (N.S.), S. 5, supra*, note 159.

329 *Hunter v. Southam, supra*, note 22 with reference to "reading down". However, the Ontario Court of Appeal, in *R. v. Hamilton, supra*, note 82, arguably did something far beyond that: the proclamation of legislation in Ontario despite the deliberate act of the federal and provincial governments in failing to proclaim it. See also the Saskatchewan *Reference re French Language Rights of Accused in Sask. Criminal Proceedings, supra*, note 86.

330 *Supra*, note 163.

331 R.S.B.C. 1979, c. 4, s. 8(1): "Subject to the provisions of subsection (8), no adoption order may be made without the written consent to adoption of . . . (b) the parents or surviving parent of the child, provided that, if the child is illegitimate at the time the mother's consent was signed and has not previously been adopted, only the mother's consent is required, and, notwithstanding anything contained in the *Legitimacy Act*, no further consent shall be required by reason of the legitimation of the child."

legislation permitting adoptions or let it stand despite any unconstitutionality.[332]

In *Shewchuk*, the British Columbia Court of Appeal refused to consider the remedy of "extension".[333] It proceeded on the basis that the only alternatives available to it were striking down the legislation or letting it stand.[334] Both of those alternatives are unpalatable (tolerating unjustifiable exclusion of needy single fathers for no reason, or providing "equality with a vengeance" by depriving disadvantaged women of statutory protection). If those are the alternatives, we reluctantly conclude that the purpose of the section is better served by letting the legislation stand, although extension seems a far more efficacious alternative.[335] This would be on the basis that the court is recognizing an institutional constraint upon its own capacities, and denying a remedy where the remedy sought would create more inequality than it cures.

---

332 We do not necessarily think that the result in the *N.M.* case would have been the same under our test, since there are arguably some sound reasons connected with the alleviation of women's inequality which could support treating natural mothers and fathers differently. These could include the importance of permitting adoptions to proceed expeditiously when the mother wishes them to, given the overwhelming number of cases in which the mother of an out-of-wedlock child has sole responsibility for its upbringing. Another consideration would be the possibility that women would be compelled to say who the fathers of their children are, raising a privacy issue.

333 Although it was argued by counsel for the intervenor public interest groups.

334 *Shewchuk v. Ricard, supra,* note 121. Proceeding in two stages, it said that the legislation did violate s. 15(1), but that it was saved by s. 1. Following *Oakes,* it concluded that the principal objective for the Act as a whole was to permit the identification of fathers of illegitimate children, and a basis for "shifting the financial responsibility for the child from the public to the private domain" (at 342). Fathers could prove maternity and seek maintenance under the *Family Relations Act,* so that "the law, in the broad sense, does not preclude the father from establishing maternity". The means chosen to achieve the important public objective of permitting the identification of fathers of illegitimate children were consistent with the *Oakes* proportionality test, the court said, since they were not arbitrary, irrational or unfair, they interfered as little as possible with the right of the father to have a remedy, and there were no severe deleterious effects in the case before the court. In our respectful view, the error in this reasoning is in the assessment of purpose as if the challenge was to the legislation as a whole rather than to the fact that it excluded men. While the legislation as a whole undoubtedly had an important and legitimate purpose, the exclusion of men did nothing (or so little as to be *de minimis*) to further that purpose.

335 The Nova Scotia Court of Appeal decision in *Reference re Family Benefits Act (N.S.), S. 5, supra,* note 158, is another case in point. Extension would likely have been the appropriate remedy in that case, on the basis that the denial of benefits to single needy fathers was unnecessary to the government's ability to provide benefits to single needy mothers.

7. CONCLUSION

The test that we have proposed would have the effect of permitting cases raised by members of disadvantaged groups to reach the stage of requiring justification more readily than other cases. It would also have the effect of precluding some cases altogether. For the reasons we have discussed, we think these results are more consistent with the purpose of section 15 and the institutional constraints governing judicial review than any other scheme of which we have become aware, and that the framework we propose is at least as workable as others which have been developed. Any framework will have areas of difficulty; we think that ours is not unique in that respect. What we have tried to do, however, is suggest a method of analysis which will direct inquiry into the issues which seem crucial to fulfilling the purposes of the section, and which will permit openness in dealing with the complex policy considerations which arise.

FLOW CHART FOR EQUALITY RIGHTS TEST

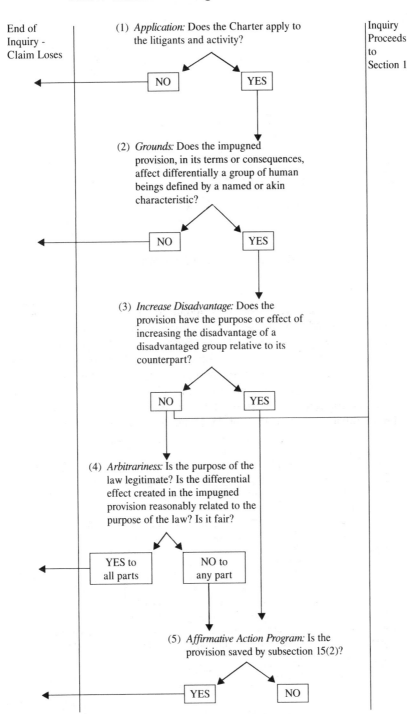

End of
Inquiry -
Claim Loses

Inquiry
Proceeds
to
Section 1

(1) *Application:* Does the Charter apply to
the litigants and activity?

NO   YES

(2) *Grounds:* Does the impugned
provision, in its terms or consequences,
affect differentially a group of human
beings defined by a named or akin
characteristic?

NO   YES

(3) *Increase Disadvantage:* Does the
provision have the purpose or effect of
increasing the disadvantage of a
disadvantaged group relative to its
counterpart?

NO   YES

(4) *Arbitrariness:* Is the purpose of the
law legitimate? Is the differential
effect created in the impugned
provision reasonably related to the
purpose of the law? Is it fair?

YES to
all parts

NO to
any part

(5) *Affirmative Action Program:* Is the
provision saved by subsection 15(2)?

YES   NO

Addendum to Chapter 14:
The Equality Rights

William Black and Lynn Smith

This addendum provides a brief update to Chapter 14 in light of the Supreme Court of Canada decision in *Andrews v. Law Society of B.C.*[1] (February 2, 1989) agreeing with the disposition of the case below but adopting different reasoning.[2] The summary and discussion that follow are intended only to flag some of the more important aspects of the decision and some areas in which it touches upon the subject-matter of this chapter.

The court rejected the "similarly situated" test,[3] saying that for there to be an infringement of section 15(1) there must be discrimination in a sense similar to that developed in human rights legislation:

> I would say then that discrimination may be described as a distinction, whether intentional or not but based on grounds relating to personal characteristics of the individual or group, which has the effect of imposing burdens,

---

1 (1985), 66 B.C.L.R. 363 (S.C.) (Taylor J.), overturned on appeal (1986), 2 B.C.L.R. (2d) 305 (C.A.). The Court of Appeal decision is discussed in chapter 14 at p. 618, text accompanying notes 237-250. The Supreme Court's decision in *Andrews* was its first on the meaning of s. 15(1) and its relationship with s. 1.

2 The court dismissed the appeal, holding that s. 42 of the *Barristers and Solicitors Act*, R.S.B.C. 1979, c. 26, which required that members of the Bar be Canadian citizens, infringed s. 15(1) of the Charter and was not justified under s. 1 (*per* Wilson J., Dickson C.J. and L'Heureux-Dubé J. concurring.) McIntyre and Lamer JJ. dissented on the issue of justification under s. 1, and would have upheld the legislation. LaForest J. wrote separate reasons concurring with the dismissal of the appeal. LeDain J. heard the appeal but took no part in the decision.

3 Discussed in chapter 14 at p. 614, text accompanying notes 223-236.

obligations, or disadvantages on such individual or group not imposed upon others, or which withholds or limits access to opportunities; benefits, and advantages available to other members of society. Distinctions based on personal characteristics attributed to an individual solely on the basis of association with a group will rarely escape the charge of discrimination, while those based on an individual's merits and capacities will rarely be so classed.[4]

Rejected as well was the "reasonable and fair" test used in the Court of Appeal decision. The court held that that test avoided the error of finding all distinctions to be violations of section 15(1), but failed to leave any significant role for section 1. Instead, the "enumerated and analogous grounds" approach[5] was at least provisionally approved. That approach requires that the "analysis of discrimination . . . must take place within the context of the enumerated grounds and those analogous to them."[6] Thus, at the section 15(1) stage there is to be an assessment whether the alleged ground of discrimination is enumerated or analogous, whether the person complaining is not receiving equal treatment before and under the law or the law has a differential impact on that person in its protection or benefit, and whether the legislative impact of the law is discriminatory.[7] At the section 1 stage, there is to be review of possible justifications for the law based on reasonableness.[8]

To what extent does the Supreme Court of Canada decision in *Andrews* contradict or confirm the approach to section 15 discussed in Chapter 14? We think the following can be said:

---

4 McIntyre J. at 19. All members of the court express agreement, at least in a general way, with McIntyre J.'s analysis of equality and discrimination: Wilson J. at 2; LaForest J. at 2.

5 Illustrated in the reasons of Hugessen J.A. in *Smith, Kline & French Laboratories v. Canada (Attorney General)*, discussed in chapter 14 at p. 621, notes 251-260. See also the discussion of possible tests stemming from such an approach.

6 McIntyre J. at 25.

7 McIntyre J. at 26-27.

8 At this juncture, the members of the court differ both as to the justifiability of the citizenship requirements and as to the nature of the review under s. 1. The plurality of three (*per* Wilson J.) indicates that the *Oakes* analytical framework is to be used, saying (at p. 5): "Given that s. 15 is designed to protect those groups who suffer social, political and legal disadvantage in our society, the burden resting on government to justify the type of discrimination against such groups is appropriately an onerous one." Wilson J. concludes that the proferred justifications for the citizenship requirement do not pass the *Oakes* tests. On the other hand, McIntyre J. (at p. 29) holds that the *Oakes* requirement that there be "pressing and substantial" concerns creates too stringent a standard and would "frequently deny the community-at-large the benefits associated with sound social and economic legislation". On the basis that the legislative choice to impose a citizenship requirement was reasonable, McIntyre and Lamer JJ. would find it justified under s. 1. La Forest J., in separate concurring reasons, agrees with McIntyre J.'s approach to s. 1 but concludes that the legislation fails to pass even that less stringent test.

1. The analytical framework is on the whole consistent with the approach discussed in this chapter. However, the court leaves many issues open for future decisions.
2. The approach to equality will be different from that taken by the Supreme Court under the *Canadian Bill of Rights.*[9]
3. In general, principles applied under human rights legislation are equally applicable in considering questions of discrimination under section 15(1).[10]
4. Narrow, formalistic versions of the "similarly situated" test are rejected as being unhelpful and resulting in no meaningful protection against discrimination.[11]
5. The purpose of section 15 is connected with the promotion of a society in which all are secure in the knowledge that they are recognized at law as human beings equally deserving of concern, respect and consideration.[12]
6. The enumerated grounds reflect the most common and probably the most destructive forms of discrimination and as such should receive particular attention.[13] However, the enumerated grounds are not exclusive and other possible grounds may arise. It may be necessary for alleged violations of section 15 to be based upon enumerated or analogous grounds, but the existence or nature of any limit on the grounds covered by section 15 is an issue specifically left open.[14]
7. Section 15 gives the right to equality not only with respect to express differentiation but also with respect to the unintended effects of facially neutral provisions.[15]
8. There is no suggestion in the reasons of Wilson J. that legislation in the social or economic realm should have any particular immunity from judicial review. La Forest J. suggests a limited role for the courts in reviewing legislation in that area,[16] as does McIntyre J., in the context of applying section 1.[17]

---

9 McIntyre J. at 14-15 and 10-12.
10 McIntyre J. at 19.
11 McIntyre J. at 9-12.
12 McIntyre J. at 15.
13 McIntyre J. at 19.
14 Wilson J. at 4. La Forest J.'s reasons also leave open the possibility of claims not based upon enumerated or analogous grounds, at least where there is differentiation between individuals or groups that is grossly unfair and devoid of any rational relationship to a legitimate state purpose (at 4).
15 See the definition of discrimination quoted above in this Addendum, from McIntyre J. at 19.
16 La Forest J. at 4.
17 *Supra*, note 8.

9. Section 1 has an important role to play and the onus is on the defenders of the legislation or other provision to establish that it is justifiable.[18]
10. The decision does not rule out a differential test for disadvantaged groups and provides some indirect support for that approach.[19]
11 Although the meaning of "discrimination" rather than the meaning of "equality" is emphasized, the court gives the two concepts a meaning consistent with the notion of equality discussed in Chapter 14, encompassing the notion that it can be as serious a denial of equality to treat people identically when that is inappropriate as it is to treat people differently when that is inappropriate.[20]

---

18 With, however, the differential approaches to s. 1 discussed at note 8, *supra*.
19 See Wilson J. at 3, where she says that the determination about whether a group is analogous to those specified in s. 15 "is not to be made only in the context of the law which is subject to challenge but rather in the context of the place of the group in the entire social, political and legal fabric of our society. While legislatures must inevitably draw distinctions among the governed, such distinctions should not bring about or reinforce the disadvantage of certain groups and individuals by denying them the rights freely accorded to others."
20 McIntyre J. at 8-9, 12-13, 15-16.

15

Language Rights*

(*Sections 16-22*)

André Tremblay and Michel Bastarache**

1. INTRODUCTION

This study deals with sections 16-22 of the *Canadian Charter of Rights and Freedoms*,[1] which are grouped under the heading "Official Languages of Canada". The object of the study is to consider the meaning and scope of these provisions and to determine the ways in which they affect

---

  * Translated from French.
 ** With the collaboration of Me Carole Tremblay.
  1 Part I of the *Constitution Act, 1982* [en. by the *Canada Act, 1982* (U.K.), 1982, c. 11, Sched. B.].

constitutional law. Since their proclamation on April 17, 1982, they have been considered in a number of legal decisions. We will take into account the developments in the intervening six years in order to determine the content and types of rights that may be claimed by citizens and the corresponding duties of the federal authorities.[2]

It is useful to start this examination of the sections devoted to "Official Languages of Canada" with an initial review of the constitutional context into which they were inserted in 1982, having regard in particular to the division of legislative authority and to existing language rights.

The authority to legislate on matters relating to language was not provided for explicitly in 1867. This authority was incidental or ancillary to the matters assigned to each of the two levels of government. Thus, the federal Parliament and the provincial legislatures may legislate on language to the extent to which it relates to one or another of the categories of matters within their respective legislative competence. Legislative competence concerning language, therefore, is essentially a matter of concurrence. As expressed by the Supreme Court of Canada in *Jones* v. *A.G. New Brunswick*,[3] the federal and provincial governments can each separately "add to the range of privileged or obligatory use of English and French in institutions or activities" falling within their respective control.

Nevertheless, in the exercise of this legislative competence regarding language, the federal Parliament and, in varying degrees, the provincial legislatures, must respect a number of guarantees or constitutional rights which are not subject to alteration. Among the language guarantees which existed in 1982 and which continue to have effect, we find section 133 of the *Constitution Act, 1867*,[4] which applies federally and in Quebec.[5]

---

2 The section of this chapter which was devoted to section 23 of the Charter in the original version has been deleted from this version. Section 23 merits separate treatment because of the many and sometimes complex issues it raises and the importance of the guarantees it provides.

3 [1975] 2 S.C.R. 182 at 195.

4 Section 133 reads as follows: "Either the English or the French Language may be used by any Person in the Debates of the Houses of the Parliament of Canada and of the Houses of the Legislature of Quebec; and both those Languages shall be used in the respective Records and Journals of those Houses; and either of those Languages may be used by any Person or in any Pleading or Process in or issuing from any Court of Canada established under this Act, and in or from all of any of the Courts of Quebec. The Acts of the Parliament of Canada and of the Legislature of Quebec shall be printed and published in both those Languages."

5 Provisions which are in all respects analogous to those of s. 133 apply to Manitoba. They are contained in s. 23 of the *Manitoba Act, 1870*, reprinted in R.S.C. 1970, App. II, No. 8 [R.S.C. 1985, No. 8], whose binding effects have been recently confirmed

This section contains genuine constitutional guarantees of a linguistic nature; but, as was emphasized by Mr. Justice Beetz in *MacDonald v. City of Montreal*,[6] they are minimal and limited:

> Section 133 has not introduced a comprehensive scheme or system of official bilingualism, even potentially, but a limited form of compulsory bilingualism at the legislative level, combined with an even more limited form of optional unilingualism at the option of the speaker in Parliamentary debates and at the option of the speaker, writer or issuer in judicial proceedings or processes.
>
> . . .
>
> This incomplete but precise scheme is a constitutional minimum which resulted from a historical compromise arrived at by the founding people who agreed upon the terms of the federal union.

This limited form of language guarantees extends to the debates and documents pertaining to proceedings of the federal Parliament and the National Assembly of Québec. They also include the language of legislation of Parliament and the National Assembly of Québec,[7] as well as the language of the federal and Québec courts. The constitutional guarantees are rather modest but rigid. On the one hand, at the federal level, section 133 is constitutionally entrenched by section 21 of the *Constitution Act, 1982*; on the other hand, as to its application to Québec, this section may only be modified through the procedure provided for by section 43 of the *Act*.

---

by the Supreme Court in *Reference re Manitoba Language Rights*, [1985] 1 S.C.R. 721. This was followed by the order in *Re Manitoba Language Rights*, [1985] 2 S.C.R. 347. Moreover, certain language guarantees could flow from s. 110 of the *Northwest Territories Act*, R.S.C. 1886, c. 50 [re-en. 1891, c. 22, s. 18], and apply to Alberta and Saskatchewan through the effect of s. 16 of their respective constitutive statutes (*Alberta Act*, 1905, c. 3, reprinted in R.S.C. 1970, App. II, No. 19 [R.S.C. 1985, No. 20]; Saskatchewan Act, 1905, c. 42, reprinted in R.S.C. 1970, App. II, No. 20 [R.S.C. 1985, No. 21]). This issue has been determined by the Supreme Court of Canada in *R. v. Mercure*, [1988] 1 S.C.R. 243, on appeal from (1986), 24 D.L.R. (4th) 193 (Sask. C.A.). The language rights guaranteed by s. 110 are part of the internal constitution of Saskatchewan and Alberta, but not of the Constitution of Canada, and may thus be unilaterally amended by those provinces, under s. 45 of the *Constitution Act, 1982*.

6 [1986] 1 S.C.R. 460 at 496 (*per* Beetz J. for the majority).

7 Québec legislation subject to s. 133 includes statutes adopted by the National Assembly of Québec and legislative measures emanating from the provincial government, comprising regulations adopted by the government, a minister or a group of ministers, as well as regulations of the administration and quasi-public bodies which, before entering into force, require the approval of the government, a minister or a group of ministers. It includes as well the rules of practice of the courts and quasi-judicial tribunals. Nevertheless, the bylaws of municipal bodies and school boards are not included: *A.G. Québec v. Blaikie*, [1981] 1 S.C.R. 312. Section 23 of the *Manitoba Act, 1870* is to the same effect: see *Reference re Manitoba Language Rights, supra*, note 5.

The federal Parliament as well as the National Assembly of Québec can go beyond the minimal requirements of section 133 and legislate in relation to the status and use of French, English or another language in the institutions, undertakings and matters falling within their respective legislative competence. The legislative assembly of Manitoba can similarly add to the guarantees of section 23 of its constitutive Act. Since 1982, the federal Parliament and the legislative assembly of New Brunswick can also legislatively extend the language rights conferred by sections 16 to 22 of the Charter.

Such an incidental or ancillary power[8] to legislate on language matters actually means that Parliament can legislate in relation to the language of work and communication in the postal service, in federal Crown corporations, in inter-provincial communications and in banks, as well as other areas. The provinces can legislate in relation to the language used in schools, universities, municipal corporations, business and other institutions or undertakings falling within their legislative competence.

Parliament and the legislatures may act freely as regards language matters, as long as they do not derogate from the constitutional guarantees. This is what the *Jones* decision[9] established. Since the *Charter of Rights and Freedoms* came into force, the same constitutional principle applies: Parliament and the legislature of New Brunswick, which are covered by sections 16 to 22 of the Charter, may not diminish the rights guaranteed by these sections; but they, as well as the legislatures of the other provinces, may go beyond these sections and legislate in relation to languages in those matters falling within their jurisdiction.[10] One of the characteristics of the Charter, then, is constitutional continuity.

The first indication of this continuity is that the sections under consideration are doubly entrenched: first, by section 33 of the Charter, and second, by section 41 of the *Constitution Act, 1982*. Section 33 indicates that it will be impossible for Parliament and the legislature of New Brunswick to derogate from sections 16 to 22 by means of statutes which expressly declare that they apply notwithstanding the Charter.

Section 41(c) provides that the use of French or English is a question which, for constitutional amendment purposes, requires that resolutions be made by the Senate, the House of Commons and the legislative assembly

---

8 G.A. Beaudoin, ed., *Essais sur la Constitution* (Ottawa: l'Université d'Ottawa, 1979) at 191. See also A.L.C. de Mestral & W. Fraiberg, "Language Guarantees and the Power to Amend the Canadian Constitution" (1966-67), 12 *McGill L.J.* 502 at 505-506.

9 *Supra*, note 3.

10 As we will see further on, s. 16(3) of the Charter enshrines this constitutional principle which was established in the *Jones* decision, *supra*, note 3.

of each province.[11] We could say that the language provisions of the Charter are truly fundamental and are at the highest level of the constitutional hierarchy. They even come ahead, in this area, of the great fundamental freedoms set out in section 2 of the Charter, freedom of conscience and religion, of thought, belief, opinion and expression, of the press, of peaceful assembly and freedom of association, all of which become less "fundamental" than language rights.[12]

Constitutional continuity is also evident in the content of certain provisions which reproduce section 133 of the *Constitution Act, 1867*[13] or which maintain in force the rights, privileges or obligations existing under the terms of some other Canadian constitutional provision.[14]

If the Charter only perpetuates what already exists concerning language matters, it would not be of much interest. However, such is not the case, as it introduces certain innovations upon which we will subsequently dwell more fully. More specifically, we will analyze the fundamental principle of linguistic equality (section 16(1)) and the constitutional goal of advancing the equality of status or use of French and English (section 16(3)). We will then examine the other provisions that are written into the constitutional continuum previously mentioned, paying particular attention to the new section 20(1) guarantees.[15]

2. THE FUNDAMENTAL PRINCIPLE OF LINGUISTIC EQUALITY

Section 16(1) of the Charter sets out:

---

11 Amendment of the provisions of ss. 16-22 applicable only to New Brunswick requires resolutions of the Senate, the House of Commons and the legislative assembly of that province, as is provided for in s. 43 of the *Constitution Act, 1982*.

12 Nevertheless, we will see that at the level of judicial interpretation, the linguistic guarantees must, according to the Supreme Court, be treated with more caution than is the case with the fundamental rights.

13 This is the case with ss. 17(1), 18(1) and 19(1) of the Charter which, as we will see further on, reproduce those aspects of s. 133 applicable at the federal level.

14 See s. 21 of the Charter.

15 The provisions of ss. 16-22 of the Charter have been discussed by several authors: *inter alia*, B.B. Pelletier, "Les pouvoirs de légiférer en matière de langue après la 'Loi constitutionnelle de 1982" (1984), 25 *C. de D.* 227-297; J.E. Magnet, "The Charter's Official Languages Provisions: The Implications of Entrenched Bilingualism" [1982] 4 *Supreme Ct. L.R.* 163-193; A. Tremblay, "L'interprétation des dispositions constitutionnelles relatives aux droits linguistiques", in *La Charte canadienne des droits et libertés, ses débuts, ses problèmes, son avenir*, Institut Canadien d'Administration de la Justice (Cowansville: Yvon Blais, 1984) at 217-228; M. Bastarache, (ed), *Les droits linguistiques au Canada*, chs. 2, 3, 4, 8, (Cowansville: Yvon Blais, 1986) at 72-273, 521-547; P. Foucher, *L'interprétation des droits linguistiques constitutionnels par la Cour suprême du Canada* (1987), 19 Ottawa L.R. 381-411.

English and French are the official languages of Canada and have equality of status and equal rights and privileges as to their use in all institutions of the Parliament and government of Canada.

(a) Statutory Antecedents of the Principle: Section 2 of the *Official Languages Act*

It may be useful to mention that section 16(1) is relatively new, in constitutional terms, and that it first appeared in the Resolution which was tabled in the House of Commons on October 6, 1980. In fact, its equivalent cannot be found in any constitutional proposal made by any level of government since the Victoria Charter, 1971. The proposals which come closest to the wording of section 16(1) are the following:

Section 10 of the Victoria Charter:

English and French are the official languages of Canada having the status and protection set forth in this Part.

Section 14 of the Federal Draft Resolution of January 19, 1977:

English and French are the official languages of Canada having the status and protection set forth in this Part, but no provision in this Part shall derogate from any right, privilege, or obligation existing under any other provision of the constitution.

Section 13 of Bill C-60 (1978):

The English and French languages are the official languages of Canada for all purposes declared by the Parliament of Canada or the legislature of any province, acting within the legislative authority of each respectively.

The main feature of these passages is that, in the first two cases, the meaning of the concept "official languages of Canada" was specified by limiting it to what the other provisions expressly ensured in terms of rank and guarantees. In the third case, the definition and designation of French and English as the official languages of Canada could be the subject of legislation by Parliament and by provincial legislatures acting "within the legislative authority of each respectively". This would not have resulted in a very stringent constitutional duty, notwithstanding the other rights and guarantees provided by Bill C-60.

In fact, section 2 of the *Official Languages Act*[16] really provided the inspiration for section 16(1). Section 2 reads as follows:

The English and French languages are the official languages of Canada for all purposes of the Parliament and Government of Canada, and possess and

---

16 R.S.C. 1970, c. O-2 [R.S.C. 1985, c. O-3].

enjoy equality of status and equal rights and privileges as to their use in all the institutions of the Parliament and Government of Canada.

Although section 16(1) does not include the words "for all purposes of the Parliament and Government of Canada", it seems to us that the section should read as if these words had indeed been included. In other words, French and English are the official languages of Canada at the federal level and only as regards those matters falling into classes of federal subjects; the only exception to the rule concerns New Brunswick. The English version of section 16(1), which does not contain a semi-colon after Canada, as well as section 16(2), concerning New Brunswick, seem to us to be especially clear on this particular point.

In contrast with the French version of the *Official Languages Act*, the French version of section 16(1) of the Charter omits the comma after "status", the pronoun "*elles*" found after "Canada" is replaced by the pronoun "*ils*", and the noun "*emploi*" is replaced by "*usage*". These minor changes deserve to be mentioned, but no more. It can be fairly stated that section 16(1) raises the wording of section 2 of the *Official Languages Act* to the rank of a constitutional norm of the first order.

(b) The Scope of Section 16(1) of the Charter: a Declaration Which Prevails over all other Federal Legislation

Obviously, lawyers and courts will be very tempted to make reference to the interpretation given to section 2 of the *Official Languages Act* to define the scope of section 16(1). What they will undoubtedly argue is that the legislative authorities which passed section 16(1) were no doubt aware of the interpretation given to section 2, as they virtually copied it in section 16(1); they will also undoubtedly say that a Parliament, even when adopting a constitution, is not presumed to derogate from existing law beyond the words used, especially when the new constitutional norm uses the language of the ordinary laws.

This argument, even though enticing, may turn out to be unconvincing. First, the legislative context of the statutory provision may be very different and, second, the interpretation of a constitutional text calls for a particular approach and for the application of particular principles because of its status in the hierarchy of norms, especially when it concerns provisions contained in a charter of rights.[17] The very serious consequences which could result from the interpretation of a constitutional norm will in certain cases cause the courts to proceed with a certain amount of restraint, as

---

17 The Supreme Court clearly emphasized the distinction between the guarantees provided by legislation, in that case the *Canadian Bill of Rights*, and those enshrined in the Constitution, to conclude that the meaning and scope of the former are not determinative

they demonstrated as the ultimate interpreters of the *Constitution Act, 1867*. In other circumstances, in particular with respect to the Charter, the courts will adopt an approach that is generally broader, more liberal and evolutionary.[18]

Whatever the situation, the courts will not be able to disregard the cases concerning section 2 of the *Official Languages Act*, but they will not regard them as decisive — first, for the reasons we have just given, and second, on the ground that these cases are not conclusive. It is in this light that we will discuss the cases on section 2, and study the various questions that section 16(1) raises. Let us note that from the beginning to the present time, this section has been commented upon only in an incidental manner by the courts, and that there has not been a definitive ruling as to its meaning and scope. We will be returning to this subject.

(i) *The "Official" Character of English and French*

In our opinion, to assert that "French and English are the official languages of Canada" invites speculative questions, and it would be unwise to delve into them. In considering this phrase alone, we could conclude that, henceforth, federal public authorities have the duty to make their bilingualism apparent or to appear bilingual in their external dealings. It would be unwise to try to derive any more meaning from the first phrase of section 16(1), and especially to read it separately from the second proposition contained in the same section. Moreover, the English version of this section shows that the two propositions in the section are connected, and that the second one serves to specify the statement of principle conveyed by the first.[19]

In *Bureau métropolitain des écoles protestantes de Montréal* v. *Ministre*

---

of the meaning and scope of the latter: see *R.* v. *Big M Drug Mart Ltd.*, [1985] 1 S.C.R. 295 at 341-344 (Dickson C.J. in particular specified that it is necessary to rely on distinct principles of constitutional interpretation applicable to the supreme law of Canada).

18 We will see that the Supreme Court made an exception to this approach as concerns language guarantees in the Charter. For examples of the preferential approach to the area of rights and freedoms, see *Hunter* v. *Southam Inc.*, [1984] 2 S.C.R. 145; *R.* v. *Big M Drug Mart Ltd.*, *supra*, note 17.

19 To date, only Wilson J. has ruled on the first proposition of s. 16(1). In *Société des Acadiens du Nouveau-Brunswick Inc.* v. *Assn. of Parents for Fairness in Education*, [1986] 1 S.C.R. 549 at 619, in a dissenting opinion, she read "the opening statement [that] 'English and French are the official languages of Canada' as declaratory and the balance of the section as identifying the main consequence in the federal context of the official status which has been declared, namely that the two languages have equality of status and have the same rights and privileges as to their use in all institutions of the Parliament and government of Canada".

de l'Education du Québec,[20] Chief Justice Deschênes of the Superior Court considered the very vague statement "French is the official language of Québec", and concluded:

> The section reads:
> "1. French is the official language of Québec."
> As paradoxical as this statement may seem, this section, considered alone, has little concrete meaning. The Canadian constitution does not, in fact, define the concept of "official language", and the substance of this concept is not to be discovered or provided in encyclopedia definitions. Professor Bonenfant is correct in stating that:
> "Following the proclaiming that a language is official, laws must be enacted which attach specific legal effects to the consequences of this proclamation. The official character of a language can, as we have seen, be strengthened or weakened according to frequency of use, but specific laws recognizing the use of the language, or allowing for the legal effects of its use in a variety of areas, are nonetheless needed".[21] [Translation]

Mr. Justice Pratte of the Appeal Division of the Federal Court, affirmed in *Association des gens de l'air du Québec* v. *Lang*:[22]

> To say that French and English are official languages is simply to state that these two languages are those which are normally used in communications between the government and its citizens.

It can also be said that the official character of a language, when it is so declared in a fundamental text, is not subject to the legislative authority of Parliament or legislative bodies covered by the declaration, subject of course to constitutional amendment, and it at the very least guarantees citizens the right to deal with the government or governments concerned in the official language of their choice.

(ii) *Equality of Status and Equal Rights and Privileges of French and English as to their Use in all Institutions of the Parliament and Government of Canada*

Section 16(1) recognizes that the official languages themselves enjoy an equality of status, and equal rights and privileges as to their use; this section is not formally directed to either French or English speakers. In other words, this section is not expressly directed to people or citizens, unlike other Charter sections which identify those who are entitled to rights:

---

20 [1976] 1 C.S. 430 at 452 (Qué. S.C.).
21 Quoting J.C. Bonenfant, "La compétence constitutionnelle et juridique pour instituer une langue ou des langues officielles au Québec", in *Rapport de la Commission d'enquête sur la situation de la langue française et sur les droits linguistiques au Québec*, livre II (Québec: éditeur officiel du Québec, 1972) at 289.
22 [1978] 2 F.C. 371 at 376 (C.A.).

"everyone", "every citizen", "any person charged with an offence", "a party", "a witness", "anyone", "any member of the public".

This form of legislation raises certain problems. First, who will be qualified to complain about possible contraventions of section 16(1)? Individuals who are most affected? Taxpayers and citizens unaffected by the section? Groups that are affected? The different levels of government? Does this section set forth collective or individual rights?

These initial questions are most certainly relevant, but they are not as central as others which concern the actual scope of section 16(1) and its legal value as the basis of judicial remedies. In other words, let us begin by asking ourselves whether this section has any concrete or autonomous significance and if it creates a remedy. Later, we will deal very briefly with the question of *locus standi*.

The current state of Canadian law does not allow us to determine precisely the object of the declaration of equality of status, rights and privileges as to their use at the federal level. *A priori*, there are two hypotheses. The declaration can be considered as purely platonic or abstract, like a preamble which sets forth a goal or a general rule whose scope would be determined by sections 17-22. The aim of the declaration would not be to establish complete or absolute bilingualism, but only the level or forms of bilingualism specified in the subsequent sections. According to the second hypothesis, section 16(1) would be seen as containing the fundamental and autonomous principle of language policy at the federal level, or what can be called the cornerstone or pivot of all language provisions at the federal level. Section 16(1) would have the effect of restricting the powers of the federal government, which would have the constitutional duty to ensure equality of status and the equal rights and privileges of French and English. It would also have the effect of leading to extensive judicial review of the constitutionality of the federal laws and rules which would be contrary to the principle of equality. This interpretation has already been adopted for section 2 of the federal *Official Languages Act* by Chief Justice Deschênes in *Joyal* v. *Air Canada*:[23]

> Section 2 of chapter O-2 actually goes further than section 1 of Bill C-22, and the explanation for this is undoubtedly that there is a radical difference between the situation each Act is aimed at resolving. Parliament could not stop at a statement of principle concerning the official status of English and French in Canada; the tangible results had to be foreseen immediately and this status had to be at once firmly rooted in the Canadian reality. From this follows the concrete conclusion of the principle: "they (the two official languages) possess and enjoy equality of status and equal rights and privileges as to their use in all institutions of the Parliament and government of Canada".
>
> This provision for equality in chapter O-2, which is absent from Bill

---

23 [1976] 2 C.S. 1211 at 1215-1216.

C-22 in accordance with the basic postulate of the Bill, established the principle of official languages in our country and gives it a basis in fact.

Section 2 of chapter O-2 therefore contains much more than the simple ethereal principle to which the defence would like to restrict it.

It is also significant that in using in the *Thorson* case (*Thorson v. A.G. Canada*, [1975] 1 S.C.R. 138, 151) the same language as was used by Air Canada, the Supreme Court of Canada reached, in 1974, the exact opposite conclusion then the one Air Canada submitted to the Court in support of this particular aspect of its brief:

> It (the *Official Languages Act*) is both declaratory and directory in respect of the use of English by the federal authorities and agencies . . . etc. [trans]".

[Translation]

This point of view, eminently respectable and held by a very distinguished jurist, could have been adopted by the Supreme Court, had the latter tended to be liberal and reformist concerning official language matters. But history tells us that our courts have not been very active in this area. The remarks of Chief Justice Deschênes were made concerning an ordinary Act of Parliament and they were not enthusiastically adopted in subsequent decisions.

In the *Gens de l'air du Québec* case,[24] the Federal Court used language suggesting that the scope of section 2 of the *Official Languages Act* should be defined by the other provisions of the Act. Mr. Justice Marceau of the Federal Court commented:

> The only question which the Court would face in the argument put forward here is whether the Order impugned is void because it is contrary to the provisions of the *Official Languages Act*, and this question itself is divided into two parts, one of whether the alleged contradiction in fact exists, and the other of whether such a contradiction, assuming that it exists, compels the Court to find the Order void. . . . It is clear that section 2 is what the mise-en-cause Commissioner of Official Languages, Mr. Spicer, has many times called the "cornerstone" of the Act in his reports (in particular, see the second *Annual Report*, 1971-72, p. 17). It is clear that it is more than the expression of wishful thinking or a platonic or inconsequential declaration of principle. In it, Parliament has clearly expressed its will, which permits the conclusion that counsel for the plaintiffs adopted from the reasons of the Chief Justice of the Superior Court . . . to the effect that "this provision of equality . . . established the principle of official languages of our country, and gives it a basis in fact".
>
> However, on the practical level of the legal rights and duties flowing from it, I do not see how section 2 can be isolated from the whole of the Act. In my opinion, it is a "declaration of status", which could not be formulated in stronger terms, but which remains introductory. Parliament sets out the conclusions to be drawn from it in the following sections where, in section

---

24 *Assn. des gens de l'air du Québec Inc.* v. *Lang*, [1977] 2 F.C. 22 (T.D.), aff'd *supra*, note 22.

9 *et seq.* in particular, it defines the "duties" which it imposes on departments and agencies of the Government of Canada, to give effect to its "declaration of status". Section 9 sets out the general rule in this regard.

[The Honourable Judge cited s. 9 of the Act which deals with among other things the duty imposed on departments and agencies of the Government of Canada, judicial, quasi-judicial or administrative bodies, or Crown corporations to ensure "to the extent that it is feasible to do so, that members of the public in locations other than those referred to in that subsection, where there is a significant demand therefor by such persons, can obtain available services from and can communicate with it in both official languages"].

"To the extent that it is feasible for it to do so": in my opinion, these are the basic terms to be considered. Parliament did not claim to introduce complete bilingualism in practice immediately, because obviously the facts in the context of which it was legislating did not permit it to do so. The status has been declared and the irrevocable goal defined, the duty to take steps to reach the goal is imposed, but the speed of progress toward the goal (everywhere but at a head or central office, since the bilingual districts had not been established) is measured in terms of feasibility. Here we see the origin of the idea of the "Commissioner of Official Languages" which section 19 *et seq.* develop and put into operation.[25]

The Federal Court of Appeal did not give section 2 of the *Official Languages Act* a constraining or inevitable effect, either. Mr. Justice Pratte, in the appeal of the *Gens de l'air* case, observed:

In my view the impugned Order does not contradict the first part of section 2 of the *Official Languages Act* because, as I have already said, a language may be an official language in a country even though, for safety reasons, its use is prohibited in certain exceptional circumstances.

In any case, it is not on the first part of section 2 that counsel for the appellants based his arguments, but on the second part, which states that the two languages are equal. In this connection it should be noted that the equality proclaimed by section 2 cannot be an absolute equality, since this would imply, among other things, that the two languages were used with equal frequency. The equality referred to is, as I understand it, a relative equality requiring only that in identical circumstances the two languages receive the same treatment. If, as some people maintain, it was more dangerous to use French than English for air communications in Canada and Quebec, it seems to me that the use of French for this type of communication could be prohibited without contradicting the principle of equality enshrined in section 2. The fact that it was more dangerous to speak French in the air than English would be a circumstance that would justify treating the two languages differently.[26]

Mr. Justice Le Dain, whose opinion was shared by Mr. Justice Hyde, also authorized the government, for safety reasons, to derogate from the *Official Languages Act* under legislation concerning aeronautics, even if he did see much more than a pious wish in the section:

---

25 *Ibid.* at 33-35.

26 *Assn. des gens de l'air du Québec Inc.* v. *Lang, supra,* note 22 at 376-377.

As I read section 2 it is more than a mere statement of principle or the expression of a general objective or ideal. That it is in relation to the *Official Languages Act* as a whole — the expression of the essential spirit of the Act to which reference is made in other provisions — but it is also the affirmation of the official status of the two languages and the legal right to use French, as well as English, in the institutions of the federal government. Other sections of the Act, such as sections 9 and 10, are concerned with what must be done by way of implementation to make this an effective right and practical reality. What is chiefly involved is the provision of sufficient bilingual personnel in the public service to ensure that, in the words of section 9, "[m]embers of the public can obtain available services from and can communicate with it in both official languages". There are other provisions in the Act which impose specific duties on institutions of the Government of Canada to give effect to the official status of the two languages but section 2 would appear to be the only provision from which one may derive a right to use French, as well as English, as a language of work as well as a language of service in the federal government. As such, it is in my respectful opinion more than a merely introductory provision, but rather the legal foundation of the right to use French, as well as English, in the public service of Canada, whether as a member of the service or a member of the public who has dealings with it. Of course, the practical implementation required to make that an effective right is another thing.[27]

These judicial statements, while pertinent and important, cannot all be true at the same time. If we must rely on the reasoning of those judges favouring a minimal interpretation of section 2 of the *Official Languages Act*, and who consider it more of an introductory proposal (as is the case for Justices Marceau and Pratte, and to a lesser degree for Justices Le Dain and Hyde), we should say that sections 17 to 22 convey the entire content of the fundamental principle set out in section 16(1). This could lead to nonsense to the extent that these sections do not deal with the right to use French or English as the language of work in institutions of the Parliament and government of Canada. Sections 17 to 22 refer to:

Section 17(1): the right to use both official languages in any debates and other proceedings of Parliament.

Section 18(1): the printing and publication of the documents of Parliament in both official languages.

Section 19(1): the right to use either French or English in any process in any court established by Parliament.

Section 20(1): the right of any citizen to communicate with any federal institution in either official language.

Section 21: the language rights which exist or are continued by virtue

---

27 *Ibid.* at 379-380.

of any other provision of the Constitution of Canada. These other provisions do not concern the language of work in the federal government.

Section 22:   language rights other than those for French and English. This section is not relevant.

In sum, section 16(1) is more than an introductory provision: it should guarantee at the very least a fundamental right and autonomous use (language of work) of both official languages in federal institutions. Even in resorting to the methodology used by the judges of the Federal Court, it is difficult to say that sections 17 to 22 would actually neutralize what is clearly a right concerning the language of work, as set out in section 16(1).

Other reasons lead us to recognize a real constitutional standard, one that is autonomous and independent, in section 16(1). First, the limitations and restrictions included in the *Official Languages Act*, which the Federal Court used to limit the scope of section 2, are not included in the Charter. In order to abrogate or derogate from the language rights recognized in sections 16 to 22, it will be necessary to proceed in accordance with section 1 of the Charter. Therefore, while it was formerly possible to derogate from the *Official Languages Act* by means of special legislation, now all federal laws restricting any right set out in sections 16 to 22 should be based on section 1 of the Charter.[28] Next, historical documentation, accepted today as extrinsic evidence, can at the very least demonstrate the exceptionally important place language rights occupy in the process of constitutional revision. It can be assumed that those who conceived the *Constitution Act, 1982*, wanted to constitutionalize something other than mere insignificance.

For these reasons, the courts should give section 16(1) a specific legal scope, separate from the other sections of the Charter. The Commissioner of Official Languages has continually expressed the same opinion.[29]

But there are indications that the highest court in the country would not be of this opinion. In fact, in three recent decisions[30] bearing on

---

28 A federal Act that would restrict one of the guarantees contained in ss. 17(1), 18(1) or 19(1) of the Charter could not be saved through the application of s. 1 since it would at the very same time be contrary to s. 133 of the *Constitution Act, 1867*. No restriction is permitted with respect to this latter section.

29 See the various annual reports by the Commissioner of Official Languages, especially the *1976 Report* (at 15-16) and the *1978 Report* (at 10).

30 These are *MacDonald* v. *Montreal (City)*, *supra*, note 6; *Bilodeau* v. *A.G. Manitoba*, [1986] 1 S.C.R. 449; *Société des Acadiens* v. *Assn. of Parents*, *supra*, note 19. In the *Mercure* case, *supra*, note 5, the Supreme Court refused to come back on the interpretation adopted in these three cases.

language rights, the Supreme Court specified the approach that it intends to take in the interpretation of the guarantees relating to language under the Charter. After an initial preference for a broad interpretation in giving language rights greater protection,[31] the court, by a majority, has recently adopted an attitude of strict judicial restraint, deferring to the legislative power and the political process considered responsible for the effective and concrete advancement of the equality of status and use of the two official languages. As Mr. Justice Beetz puts it: "the courts should pause before they decide to act as instruments of change with respect to language rights [. . . they] should approach them with more restraint than they would in construing legal rights."[32]

Paradoxically, section 16 served to support the reasoning behind this restrictive attitude towards the interpretation of language rights. The fact that section 16(1) establishes that, in Canada, the two official languages have equal status would seem to favour a generous and active implementation of language rights by the courts, an interpretation which would contribute to the actual achievement of this goal of equality.[33]

In the *Société des Acadiens* case, the majority of the Supreme Court seems rather to have considered that the equality stated in section 16(1) had not been achieved and that, because of this, it would constitute more a political goal or an ideal. Thus, section 16, the introductory section of the part entitled "Official Languages of Canada",[34] contains, according to Mr. Justice Beetz,

> a principle of advancement or progress in the equality of status or use of the two official languages. I find it highly significant however that this principle of advancement is linked with the legislative process referred to in s. 16(3), which is a codification of the rule in *Jones v. Attorney General of New Brunswick*, [1975] 2 S.C.R. 182. The legislative process, unlike the judicial one, is a political process and hence particularly suited to the advancement of rights founded on political compromise.

. . .

---

31 This approach was generally maintained in *Jones* v. *A.G. New Brunswick, supra,* note 3; *A.G. Quebec* v. *Blaikie, supra,* note 7; *Reference re Manitoba Language Rights, supra,* note 5, notably at 744.

32 *Société des Acadiens* v. *Assn. of Parents, supra,* note 19 at 578. For a comment on this case, see R. Bilodeau, "L'analyse critique de l'affaire *Société des Acadiens du Nouveau Brunswick* et l'avenir précaire du bilinguisme judiciaire au Canada" (1986), 32 *McGill L.J.* 232-243.

33 In *Société des Acadiens, ibid.* at 565, only Dickson C.J.C. seemed ready to recognize the *present* right to equality of status and privileges for the official languages and to give effect to this in the interpretation of s. 19(2), which was an issue in this case.

34 *Ibid.* at 578.

> In my opinion, s. 16 of the *Charter* confirms the rule that the courts should exercise restraint in their interpretation of language rights provisions.[35]

To intervene too actively in the linguistic evolution of Canada and to impose certain constitutional duties with a view to the advancement towards equality of the two languages, would, in the opinion of Mr. Justice Beetz, be to risk checking the eventual adherence of certain provinces to the guarantees of sections 16 to 22:

> It is public knowledge that some provinces other than New Brunswick — and apart from Quebec and Manitoba — were expected ultimately to opt into the constitutional scheme prescribed by ss. 16 to 22 of the *Charter*, and a flexible form of constitutional amendment was provided [s. 43] to achieve such an advancement of language rights. But again, this is a form of advancement brought about through a political process, not a judicial one.
>
> If however the provinces were told that the scheme provided by ss. 16 to 22 of the *Charter* was inherently dynamic and progressive, apart from legislation and constitutional amendment, and that the speed of progress of the scheme was to be controlled mainly by the courts, they would have no means to know with relative precision what it was that they were opting into. This would certainly increase their hesitation in so doing and would run contrary to the principle of advancement contained in s. 16(3).[36]

Some may find this type of argument disconcerting, especially insofar as it appears in the interpretation of a constitutional text (the Charter), whose content, by its very nature, is essentially evolutionary and bound to change over the course of the years. Does not the drafting of the provisions of the Charter in terms necessarily vague, extensive and open-ended rightly call for an active role on the part of the courts in order to define and put them into effect according to the development of our free and democratic society? Does the somewhat more political character of language questions in Canada justify an attenuation of the fundamental nature of the constitutional guarantees conferred in this area? Sections 16 to 22 of the Charter, moreover, do not escape the commonly accepted principle that the framers gave the courts the mandate to ensure the compatibility of legislative and executive measures with the guarantees contained in the Canadian Charter. They also provided that remedies might be granted in cases of a violation of these guarantees.

It is true that the *Société des Acadiens* case did not explicitly and

---

35 *Ibid.* at 579, 580. Wilson J. in her dissent would have been prepared to recognize in s. 16 an actual scope and to give effect to the principle of development which flows from this provision. According to her reasoning, in each case it would be a matter for the court to determine what stage had been reached in the evolution towards bilingualism and whether the challenged conduct could be considered as consonant with this stage of evolution (at 619).

36 *Ibid.* at 579-580.

definitively settle the questions relating to the meaning and actual scope of section 16(1). The main issue dealt with in that case related to section 19 and the right of a litigant to use the official language of his choice before the courts established by the province of New Brunswick.[37] The Supreme Court thus did not directly rule on the scope of section 16(1), but rather raised it to establish the reach of the rights conferred by section 19.

Nevertheless, the principles set out in the majority judgment which state that the progression towards the equality of languages rests, above all, on the legislative process or constitutional amendment rather than on the courts, and the principle of obligatory judicial restraint which flows from this premise, lead one to predict a somewhat feeble judicial involvement in the context of section 16(1).

Would the court be willing to discover an independent and mandatory right to use either official language in federal institutions as a language of work? Or will it only be a matter of a right connected to a process of advancement which relates exclusively to the legislative domain? In this latter case, the enshrinement of the principle of the equality of the official languages could well remain a dead letter. Insofar as being a constitutional right without a judicial sanction, this equality would thus depend upon political pressures and legislative action to experience any development.

In any case, neither the issue of the declaratory or mandatory character of section 16(1) nor that of determining if that provision might be the basis for certain judicial remedies having been decided in a definitive fashion, a brief examination is in order.

If, for instance, the court concluded that there was an independent right to use the two official languages as the language of work, it could at the very least, in a declaratory action, observe that federal legislation is inconsistent with section 16(1) and, under section 52 of the *Constitution Act, 1982*, declare the inconsistent legislation to be of no force or effect. But equality is not necessarily the outcome of a judgment of this sort. Equality can only be achieved through injunction or other appropriate remedies.

The chief difficulty lies in determining whether the enforcement provided under section 24 of the Charter can also be used to obtain redress in the case of a violation of section 16(1). Inasmuch as section 16(1) asserts the right to use either official language as a language of work in all the institutions of the Parliament and government of Canada, it seems to us that anyone to whom this right has been denied may, under section 24

---

37 It was a matter of determining if the right included the right to be heard and understood no matter what official language was selected by the litigant.

of the Charter, apply to the proper court to obtain a remedy. Who would have standing to take such an action? This question is dealt with in the chapter written by Professor D. Gibson.[38] Individuals employed by the federal government or by federal institutions whose rights are directly infringed may institute proceedings. But what about those groups systematically put at a disadvantage? We believe that the wording of section 24 could possibly restrict remedies to individuals whose rights have been infringed. In short, section 16(1) could be regarded as setting forth only individual rights — this in view of the implementation mechanisms provided under section 24.

The courts would still exercise their discretion to classify section 16(1) as a mandatory or directory provision. We agree with the following comment made by Chief Justice Deschênes in the *Joyal* case:

> The court cannot come to this conclusion; it cannot renounce its responsibilities; it cannot refuse to consider on its own merit a remedy which falls within its jurisdiction, in the absence of a clear indication of the will of Parliament. [Translation][39]

Let us briefly recall that a directory provision does not provide for any sanction of the unconstitutionality of contravening statutes, but in the case of a mandatory provision, recourse is available to specific remedies (injunction and damages) to sanction contravention.[40]

W.F. Craies made this distinction very clear in his classic exposition of statutory construction. He pointed out that the courts presume that statutes providing no specific remedies do not rule out common law remedies:

> When a statute creates a duty, one of the first questions for judicial consideration is what is the sanction for its breach, or the mode for compelling the performance of the duty? This question usually resolves itself into the enquiry whether the Act is mandatory or directory, *i.e.* absolute or discretionary. If it is directory, the courts cannot interfere to compel performance or punish breach of duty, and disobedience to the Act does not entail any invalidity. If the Act is mandatory, disobedience entails legal consequences, which may take the shape of public or private remedy obtainable in a court of justice, or the avoidance of some contract, instrument, or document without the intervention of any court . . . . Where, in a statute creating a duty, no special remedy is prescribed for compelling performance of the duty or punishing its neglect, the courts will, as a general rule, presume that the

---

38 See chapter 19, "Enforcement of the Canadian Charter of Rights and Freedoms", *infra.*

39 *Joyal* v. *Air Canada, supra,* note 23 at 1220.

40 See R.W. Kerr, "Blaikie and Forest: The Declaratory Action as a Remedy Against Unconstitutional Legislation" (1980), 26 *McGill L.J.* 97; J.E. Magnet "Validity of Manitoba Laws after Forest: What is to be done?" (1979-80), 10 *Man. L.J.* 241.

appropriate common law remedy by indictment, mandamus, or action was intended to apply.[41]

In *Bilodeau* v. *A.G. Manitoba*,[42] Chief Justice Freedman of the Manitoba Court of Appeal made the distinction, suggesting that a failure to comply with even mandatory provisions does not necessarily result in nullities. This was contrary to the decision in the Quebec case of *Société Asbestos Ltée* v. *Société nationale de l'amiante*.[43]

The Supreme Court settled the debate in ruling on the issue of the mandatory or directory character of section 133 of the *Constitution Act, 1867*, and section 23 of the *Manitoba Act, 1870*. In *Reference re Manitoba Language Rights*,[44] the court affirmed the mandatory character of the constitutional guarantees provided by these sections[45] and the duty of the courts to protect the language rights flowing from them. Any law inconsistent with these rights, therefore, becomes invalid. In the *Joyal* case,[46] the analysis of the statute led Mr. Justice Deschênes to conclude that the plaintiff had an enforceable right. However, all judges do not examine statutes in the same manner and not all of them are inclined to find legal obligations in generally worded enactments. The zeal some judges show in defending and implementing common law remedies does not stop others from showing moderation where certain problems are likely to fall within the political domain.

That was what the Supreme Court led us to understand in the *Société des Acadiens* case[47] and it could very well be that section 16 will only be given a declaratory scope and that it will be necessary to rely on Parliament for its implementation. It is possible, then — to use the words of Chief Justice Deschênes — that this new constitutional standard, which imposes obligations in a federal area of jurisdiction, may "go unheeded when a violation occurs and should be regarded as a platonic assertion of good intention without sanction".[48]

---

41 W.F. Craies, *On Statute Law*, 7th ed. by S.G.G. Edgar (London: Sweet & Maxwell, 1971) at 229-230.

42 [1981] 5 W.W.R. 393 (Man. C.A.), aff'd *supra*, note 30.

43 [1979] C.A. 342 (Qué. C.A.). See also *P.G. Québec* v. *Collier*, [1983] C.S. 366 (Qué. S.C.), aff'd [1985] C.A. 589 (Qué. C.A.), leave to appeal to S.C.C. granted (1986), 65 N.R. 160n (*sub nom. A.G. Québec* v. *Collier*) (S.C.C.).

44 *Supra*, note 5.

45 *Ibid.*, at 742-743. The result was the same in the *Mercure* case, *supra*, note 5.

46 *Joyal* v. *Air Canada*, *supra*, note 23 at 1217; this hypothesis is dismissed by the Chief Justice.

47 *Supra*, note 19.

48 *Joyal* v. *Air Canada*, *supra*, note 23 at 1217: this hypothesis is dismissed by the Chief Justice.

(c) The Implementation of Linguistic Equality

As we saw above, section 16(1) essentially guarantees the equality of status and the equal rights of the two official languages as to their use in all institutions of the Parliament and government of Canada. Section 16(1) therefore concerns the language of work. The language of communication is dealt with under section 20.

The federal sectors affected by section 16(1) are all the institutions of the Parliament and government of Canada, that is, the public organizations of the federal government. To be more specific, section 16(1) applies unquestionably to the departments, branches and agencies of the government; it also applies to judicial[49] and quasi-judicial bodies and to Crown corporations created by an Act of Parliament. In the *Joyal* case,[50] all the intervenors, the Attorney General of Canada included, unanimously agreed to recognize Air Canada as a federal institution.

The Armed Forces, the Royal Canadian Mounted Police and Canada Post, among others, should also be regarded as federal institutions. But would Bell Canada, banks, federal companies or C.P. Rail be subject to this section? These constitute, strictly speaking, federal institutions, as they are legal entities instituted by federal authorities and falling under federal jurisdiction, although not all in the same way. It is difficult to imagine section 16(1) applying to banks or federally incorporated companies doing business only in Alberta or British Columbia. In our opinion, the scope of this section would include only public institutions of the federal government — those which are created, controlled and financed by the federal government. Therefore, federal institutions operating in and financed by the private sector, even if they are controlled by the federal government, are not within the scope of section 16(1).

Section 16(1) does not create a duty for the bureaucrats or employees of the institutions subject to this section to become bilingual. This change is not mandatory under the section, just as all citizens who deal with the federal authorities are not required to become bilingual. Under section 16(1), federal authorities are required to ensure that equality as to the use of both official languages be respected by the staff of all federal institutions. We feel that federal authorities should, in practical terms,

---

49　See the opinion of Dickson C.J. in *Société des Acadiens, supra,* note 19, according to which the expression "an institution of the Parliament or Government of Canada" includes the courts and the judiciary (at 565). See however, *Re St-Jean and R.,* September 26, 1986 (Y.T. S.C.), in which Mr. Justice Meyer held that the expression did not include the Assembly or government of the Yukon; this decision is under appeal.

50　*Supra,* note 23.

enable their employees to work mostly in the language of their choice.[51] This section in fact protects the unilingualism of the majority of federal employees because, as we will see, the right provided under section 20 to communicate in either official language with all institutions only refers to institutional bilingualism. This is a requirement which can easily be met by employing a few bilingual persons in federal institutions serving the public.

Proceedings to enforce section 16(1) may be restricted to suing for a declaratory judgment or they may embrace remedies as such novel affirmative action. Obviously, the administrative remedy which already exists under the terms of the *Official Languages Act* (the complaint to the Commissioner of Official Languages), continues to exist, because the Charter in no way affects this Act. Courts will no doubt raise few difficulties over entertaining actions for declaratory judgment.[52] Common law remedies can be exercised where an interpretation of section 24 of the Charter permits such remedy, or where this section is held to be mandatory legislation.

One question which will inevitably be raised, if the courts hold section 16(1) to be mandatory, is what will be the extent of the means of redress likely to be ordered? Could the courts follow the American example in situations of linguistic inequality resulting from systemic discrimination, in order to eliminate obstacles to actual linguistic equality?[53] Could they, for example, order federal institutions to start integrating a certain contingent of Francophones according to a program of integration? Could they even order that money be provided for the historically disadvantaged minority?

To the extent that the provisions of the Charter create rights to claim public services in both official languages, it is clear that their implementation will not be possible unless the courts accept a more active role. Any right must give rise to a remedy[54] and the courts are invested with

---

51 Moreover, this is the opinion expressed by the Commissioner of Official Languages respecting s. 2 of the *Official Languages Act*: see the *1970-71 Report*, by K. Spicer, at 5; see also M. Yalden's *1977 Report*, at 14. Basing ourselves on the latter report, we feel that it can be said that s. 16(1) would not exempt all federal employees to work "at times" in their second language. But if, in reality, it is mainly Francophones who must work "at times" in English, there is not equality under s. 16(1), especially if, "at times" means all the time.

52 This procedure can also be used in Québec law: see *Bureau métropolitain des écoles protestantes de Montréal* v. *Ministre de l'Éducation du Québec, supra*, note 20.

53 See, *e.g., U.S.* v. *Ironworkers, Local 86*, 443 F. 2d 544 (1971); *cert.* denied 404 U.S. 984 (1971). Also see *United Steelworkers of America* v. *Weber*, 443 U.S. 193 (1979).

54 See *Ashby* v. *White* (1703), 92 E.R. 126 at 136; *Re Lévesque* v. *A.G. Canada* (1985), 25 D.L.R. (4th) 184 (F.C. T.D.).

the necessary authority to sanction breaches of constitutional duties.[55] They even have the duty to act in this sense.[56] Of course, mandatory injunctions in constitutional matters are novel; they are nevertheless not unknown in our system:

> There are many situations however in which the courts do undertake an ongoing role in the regulation and management of litigants' affairs. In family law, custody and access orders are subject to ongoing review . . . . In the commercial area, orders appointing receivers directly involve the court in the management of the most complex business arrangements. Similarly, the jurisdiction to protect infants and the mentally incompetent often involves repeated applications to the court for direction, as does the more familiar jurisdiction concerning the administration of estates and trusts.[57]

In constitutional matters, certain interesting precedents have been recently created. In the *Lévesque* case,[58] a *mandamus* was ordered to give effect to a prisoner's right to vote, while in *Marchand* v. *Simcoe County Board of Education*,[59] an injunction was ordered against a school board which was contravening the rights provided for in section 23 of the Charter. In *Crossman* v. *R.*,[60] a person denied his right to consult counsel was awarded $500 damages to be paid by the Crown. These developments respond to the appeals of experts who consider that the courts should embark upon this road:

> It can hardly be doubted that often injunctions, will be "appropriate and just in the circumstances" . . . . While one might expect Canadian judges to be less adventurous than their American brethren, there can be little doubt that injunctions, both in negative and mandatory form, will play an important role in the implementation of the rights guaranteed by the *Charter.*[61]

3. THE CONSTITUTIONAL PURPOSE OF ADVANCING THE EQUALITY OF STATUS OR USE OF FRENCH AND ENGLISH

Section 16(3) of the Charter sets forth:

---

55 *Swann* v. *Charlotte-Mecklenburg Board of Education*, 402 U.S. 1 at 15 (U.S. S.C., 1971).

56 *Reference re Manitoba Language Rights, supra*, note 5 at 744-746, 753.

57 R.J. Sharpe, *Injunctions and Specific Performance* (Toronto: Canada Law Book, 1983) at 23.

58 *Supra*, note 54.

59 (1986), 55 O.R. (2d) 638 (H.C.), additional reasons at (1986), 12 C.P.C. (2d) 140 (Ont. H.C.).

60 (1984), 12 C.C.C. (3d) 547 (F.C. T.D.).

61 Sharpe, *supra*, note 57 at 120. See also D. Gibson, *The Law of the Charter: General Principles* (Toronto: Carswell, 1986) at 198 *et seq.*; and the chapter of the present work dealing with implementation.

Nothing in this Charter limits the authority of Parliament or a legislature
to advance the equality of status or use of English and French.

This provision enshrines the principle found in *Jones v. A.G. New Brunswick*.[62] From this perspective, it confirms the power of the federal
Parliament and the legislature of New Brunswick to add by legislation
to the linguistic guarantees that they must adhere to in the context of
sections 16 to 22. It also gives to Québec the power to add to what is
provided for in section 133 of the *Constitution Act, 1867*, and for Manitoba
to go beyond the requirements of section 23 of the *Manitoba Act, 1870*.
The legislatures of the remaining provinces may also, independently of
the constitutional guarantees to which they are not subject, legislate to
improve the status of the official languages. But the sole object of section
16(3) should not be to confirm the existing principles. It also specifies
that the other provisions of the Charter do not limit any authority to adopt
laws which promote the development of the equality of status or use of
both official languages. What was actually desired with this provision was
to assure that the power to provide a privileged status for French and English
in a statute could not be challenged by virtue of the rights forbidding
discrimination contained in section 15 of the Charter. Section 16(3) could
thus prevent the measures designed to promote equal access to both official
languages from being struck down.

This issue is presently being examined in cases bearing on the right
to trial in the language of choice provided for by Part XIV.1 [XVII] of
the *Criminal Code*. Under these provisions, a person accused of an offence
has the right to a trial in the official language of his or her choice. Though
enacted by the federal Parliament, they enter into effect in a province only
upon a proclamation to that effect.[63] In those provinces which have not
yet issued such proclamation, the accused may not claim the right conferred
by the federal legislation. This disparity in the application of Part XIV.1
[XVII] of the *Criminal Code* has been challenged on the ground that it
would amount to discriminatory treatment. It thus would be contrary to
section 15 of the Charter as depriving those accused of the equal application
of the law. What was sought was an order allowing the choice of language,
even in the absence of the Code provisions. In this context, the question
asked was whether section 16(3) of the Charter could be an obstacle to
the application of section 15 if that Part XIV.1 [XVII] of the *Criminal
Code* would have been adopted with a view to favouring the equality of

---

62 *Supra*, note 3; as was recognized by the Supreme Court in *Société des Acadiens, supra*,
note 19, at 579.

63 This method of implementing Part XIV.1 [XVII] of the *Criminal Code*, R.S.C. 1970,
c. C-34 [R.S.C. 1985, c. C-46], is provided for by s. 6 of the *Criminal Law Amendment
Act*, S.C. 1977-78, c. 36.

status and use of the official languages.[64]

This question has not yet been definitively settled. Nevertheless, in view of the circumstances within which it has been examined, one can ask if section 16(3) might be properly raised to resist the application of section 15. In fact it is not so much the favourable treatment accorded to both official languages which is denounced as discriminatory, but rather the fact that this favourable treatment does not equally benefit all accused, irrespective of the location of their trial. Additionally, section 15 is not raised in order to limit the power of Parliament to advance the development towards equality of both official languages, but rather to oblige the exercise of this power in order to benefit all accused in criminal matters.

4. THE CONSTITUTIONAL GUARANTEE OF THE CONTINUATION OF EXISTING LANGUAGE RIGHTS, OR GUARANTEE OF "LIMITED CONCERN"

The third main feature of the section on language in the Charter is the continuation of guarantees that exist by virtue of any constitutional provisions. Section 133 of the *Constitution Act, 1867*, remains in force in Québec[65] as well as section 23 of the *Manitoba Act, 1870*. Federal and provincial legislative powers, which incidentally empower Parliament or the legislatures to legislate on language matters, are in no way affected. Section 21 of the Charter provides as follows:

> Nothing in sections 16 to 20 abrogates or derogates from any right, privilege or obligation with respect to the English and French languages, or either of them, that exists or is continued by virtue of any other provisions of the Constitution of Canada.

It is clear that this provision does not entrench language rights that

---

64 On this question, see, *inter alia, R.* v. *Paré* (1986), 31 C.C.C. (3d) 260 (B.C. S.C.); *Ringuette* v. *A.G.* (1987), 63 Nfld. & P.E.I.R. 126 (Nfld. C.A.), leave to appeal to S.C.C. refused (1987), 65 Nfld. & P.E.I.R. 270n (S.C.C.), where it was concluded that s. 16(3) excluded reliance on s. 15; *Paquette* v. *R.*, [1986] 3 W.W.R. 232 (Alta. Q.B.), rev'd [1988] 2 W.W.R. 44 (Alta. C.A.), leave to appeal to S.C.C. refused (1988), 60 Alta. L.R. (2d) lv, (note) (S.C.C.); *Tremblay* v. *R.* (1985), 20 C.C.C. (3d) 454 (Sask. Q.B.); *Reference re French Language Rights of Accused in Sask. Criminal Proceedings*, [1987] 5 W.W.R. 577 (Sask. C.A.), which held the opposite. If it was finally decided that s. 16(3) was not applicable in the circumstances, the issue would remain open to determine whether the federal legislation infringes s. 15. The Supreme Court of Canada declined to hear the appeal in *Ringuette* as well as the first form of the appeal in *Paquette*. The decision in *Reference re French Language Rights* was appealed, but only on the issue of the rights flowing from s. 110 of the *Northwest Territories Act*.

65 Note that the part of s. 133 applicable in the federal context remains in force pursuant to s. 21 of the Charter. One of the problems raised by the continuity of the application of s. 133 was mentioned in the text corresponding to note 28, *supra*.

exist by virtue of ordinary enactments, such as those recognized by the federal *Official Languages Act* or the *Canadian Bill of Rights* (the right to an interpreter provided under section 2(g) of the Bill). These rights will coexist with those set out in the Charter. The Charter deals with the content of section 133 of the *Constitution Act, 1867* for the purposes of the federal government and, for the benefit of the public, ensures the equality of French and English as languages of service or communication between citizens and federal institutions. It is important to examine this more closely.

Insofar as the Charter reproduces section 133 of the *Constitution Act, 1867* for federal purposes, it is of limited interest to us. Section 133 is well known, and has been the subject of many studies and judgments specifying its scope. Furthermore, it does not seem that sections 17, 18 and 19, the sections that reproduce section 133, merit closer examination.[66] By way of introduction, let us recall a passage in *Jones v. A.G. New Brunswick*, in which the Supreme Court gave an accurate description of the rights proclaimed in section 133:

> The words of s. 133 themselves point out its limited concern with language rights; and it is, in my view, correctly described as giving a constitutionally based right to any person to use English or French in legislative debates in the federal and Quebec Houses and in any pleading or process in or issuing from any federally established Court or any Court of Quebec, and as imposing an obligation of the use of English and French in the records and journals of the federal and Quebec legislative Houses and in the printing and publication of federal and Quebec legislation.[67]

The Supreme Court has recently ruled on the subject of the language of pleadings and process before the courts. We will examine these new developments in the section devoted to section 19 of the Charter.

(a) Debates and Other Proceedings of Parliament

Section 17(1) of the Charter sets forth:

Everyone has the right to use English or French in any debates and other proceedings of Parliament.

On the other hand, section 133 stipulates:

---

66 The majority decision in *Société des Acadiens, supra,* note 19, clearly established the continuity of s. 133 of the *Constitution Act, 1867,* and ss. 17-19 of the Charter. According to the court, the language of ss. 17, 18 and 19 was clearly and deliberately taken from the English version of s. 133 and, as a consequence, the same interpretation applies. See the reasons of Beetz J. at 573-575.

67 *Jones* v. *A.G. New Brunswick, supra,* note 3 at 193.

Either the English or the French Language may be used by any Person in the Debates of the Houses of the Parliament of Canada.[68]

Members of Parliament will therefore have the additional constitutionally based right of using French and English in the proceedings of Parliament. They do not have the corresponding right to be understood,[69] which means that there is no constitutional requirement to provide simultaneous interpretation of the debates. We do not believe that these words alter parliamentary practices, since Members of Parliament had, before 1982, the right to use French or English in the proceedings of parliamentary commissions or committees with which section 17(1) is apparently concerned.

(b) Parliamentary Statutes and Records: The Increase in Bilingualism or Equality of the Two Languages

Section 18(1) of the Charter provides that:

The statutes, records and journals of Parliament shall be printed and published in English and French and both language versions are equally authoritative.

The corresponding part of section 133 provides:

and both those Languages shall be used in the respective Records and Journals of those Houses. . . . The Acts of Parliament of Canada . . . shall be printed and published in both those Languages.[70]

Once again, this section reproduces section 133 of the *Constitution Act, 1867*, in specifying that no one version of the statutes, records and journals shall prevail. Therefore, this pronouncement will not permit the federal legislator to order that, where the English and French versions are incompatible, one version shall prevail over the other. In *Bureau métropolitain des écoles protestantes de Montréal* v. *Ministre de l'Éducation du Québec*,[71] Chief Justice Deschênes of the Quebec Superior Court suggested that a rule providing that, where the two versions differed, the

---

68 Section 23 of the *Manitoba Act, 1870*, which corresponds to s. 133, contains an official French version which reads: "L'usage de la langue française ou de la langue anglaise sera facultatif dans les débats des Chambres de la législature."

69 *Société des Acadiens* v. *Assn. of Parents, supra*, note 19, at 574.

70 To the same effect, s. 23 of the *Manitoba Act, 1870*, provides that: "and both those languages shall be used in the Respective Records and Journals of those Houses. . . . The Acts of the Legislature shall be printed and published in both those languages." For an historical analysis of language guarantees applicable to parliamentary documents, see J.E. Magnet, "Canada's System of Official Bilingualism: Constitutional Guarantees for the Legislative Process" (1986), 18 *Ottawa L. Rev.* 227-267.

71 *Supra*, note 20 at 453-454.

French version would prevail, could be a valid "ultimate rule of interpretation".[72] In view of the wording of section 18, this opinion is no longer tenable insofar as being applicable to the federal level.

In the same case, the Chief Justice declared that the obligation to use simultaneously both languages exists, not only as regards printing and advertising, but also respecting the adoption and sanctioning of laws. This opinion was reiterated by him in *Blaikie* v. *P.G. Québec*,[73] and the Supreme Court of Canada confirmed it on appeal. The court observed:

> Sections 8 and 9 of the *Charter of the French Language*, reproduced above, are not easy to reconcile with s. 133 which not only provides but requires that official status be given to both French and English in respect of the printing and publication of the Statutes of the Legislature of Quebec. It was urged before this Court that there was no requirement of enactment in both languages, as contrasted with printing and publishing. However, if full weight is given to every word of s. 133 it becomes apparent that this requirement is implicit. What is required to be printed and published in both languages is described as "Acts" and texts do not become "Acts" without enactment. Statutes can only be known by being printed and published in connection with their enactment so that Bills be transformed into Acts. Moreover, it would be strange to have a requirement as in s. 133, that both English and French "shall be used in the . . . Records and Journals" of the Houses . . . of the Quebec Legislature and not to have this requirement extend to the enactment of legislation.[74]

In accordance with the second judgment handed down by the Supreme Court in this same case,[75] it must be specified that section 18(1) will also apply to regulations passed by the federal government, by a minister or a group of ministers, by the federal administration or federal public institutions, which are subject to the approval of the government, a minister or a group of federal ministers. Section 18(1) will also apply to the rules of practice adopted by federal courts or quasi-judicial bodies established by the federal Parliament.

Finally, let us mention that the scope of the terms, "laws, records and journals" of Parliament will eventually be determined by the Supreme Court. Thus, in *A.G. Quebec* v. *Collier*,[76] it was a matter of determining whether certain sessional documents tabled in the National Assembly of Quebec for the purpose of developing the content of two Bills were covered by section 133. The issue would arise also with respect to the reported

---

72 *Ibid.*

73 [1978] C.S. 37 at 44-48 (Qué. S.C.), aff'd [1978] C.A. 351 (Qué. C.A.), aff'd *infra*, note 74.

74 *A.G. Québec* v. *Blaikie*; *A.G. Québec* v. *Laurier*, [1979] 2 S.C.R. 1016 at 1022.

75 *A.G. Québec* v. *Blaikie*, [1981] 1 S.C.R. 312.

76 [1985] C.A. 559 (Qué. C.A.), leave to appeal to S.C.C. granted December 16, 1985 (S.C.C.).

debates (Hansard). In *Waite* v. *Manitoba (Min. of Highways & Transportation)*,[77] the court distinguished between the linguistic requirements relating to the enactment of statutes and those relating to the maintenance of the records and journals in order to conclude that the failure to respect the former gave rise to invalidity in every case, whereas invalidity did not necessarily flow from a failure to respect the latter.

(c) Proceedings in Courts Established by Parliament

Section 19(1) reads as follows:

Either English or French may be used by any person in, or in any pleading in or process issuing from, any court established by Parliament.

Here again, the formulation of section 133 of the *Constitution Act, 1867*, provides:

and either of those Languages may be used by any Person or in any Pleading or Process in or issuing from any Court of Canada established under this Act.[78]

In the *Blaikie* case,[79] section 133 was broadly interpreted as including administrative tribunals carrying out judicial or quasi-judicial duties:

The reference in s. 133 to "any of the Courts of Quebec" ought to be considered broadly as including not only so-called s. 96 Courts but also Courts established by the Province and administered by provincially appointed Judges. It is not a long distance from this latter class of tribunal to those which exercise judicial power, although they are not courts in the traditional sense. If they are statutory agencies which are adjudicative, applying legal principles to the assertion of claims under their constituent legislation, rather than settling issues on grounds of expediency or administrative policy, they are judicial bodies, however, some of their procedures may differ not only from those of Courts but also those of other adjudicative bodies . . . They [both Privy Council decisions] nonetheless lend support to what is to us the proper approach to an entrenchment provision, that is, to make it effective through the range of institutions which exercise judicial power, be they called courts or adjudicative agencies. In our opinion, therefore, the guarantee and require-ments of s. 133 extend to both.
    It follows that the guarantee in s. 133 of the use of either French or English "by any person or in any pleading or process in or issuing from . . . all or any of the Courts of Quebec" applies to both ordinary Courts and

---

77 (1985), 25 D.L.R. (4th) 696 (Man. Q.B.), aff'd (1987), 47 Man. R. (2d) 247 (C.A.).
78 The official French version of s. 23 of the *Manitoba Act, 1870*, is to the same effect: "et dans toute plaidoirie ou pièce de procédure . . . par devant tous les tribunaux ou émanant des tribunaux de la province, il pourra étre également fait usage, à faculté, de l'une ou l'autre de ces langues."
79 *Supra*, note 74.

other adjudicative tribunals. Hence, not only is the option to use either language given to any person involved in proceedings before the Courts of Quebec or its other adjudicative tribunals (and this covers both written and oral submissions) but documents emanating from such bodies or issued in their name or under their authority may be in either language, and this option extends to the issuing and publication of judgments or other orders.[80]

These remarks are perfectly applicable to the interpretation of section 19(1) of the Charter. Several recent decisions have defined the scope of the linguistic guarantees in the judicial field. In two majority decisions,[81] the Supreme Court ruled on the interpretation to be given to section 133 of the *Constitution Act, 1867*, and section 23 of the *Manitoba Act, 1870*, in relation to the language of documents and process issuing from the courts of Quebec and Manitoba. The reasons given in respect of these two sections would appear to apply equally to section 19 of the Charter.[82] According to the court, the right to employ French or English in pleadings in vesting into the author or drafter of these documents; no corresponding linguistic guarantee applies to the person receiving the documents or the reader of these documents. As a consequence, there is no obligation for the judge or the court to issue a summons or any other document in the two official languages or in the language of the recipient. The author or drafter of the documents of a court, like a participant in Parlimentary debates, has the right to write in the official language of his or her choice.

In the *Société des Acadiens* case,[83] the Supreme Court had to settle the issue of the linguistic rights of the party speaking orally before the courts. The reasons given by the court bear on section 19(2) of the Charter; they would also apply in the same way to section 19(1) as well as to section 133 for Québec and section 23 for Manitoba. According to the majority decision, the right conferred to a party to employ English or French before the courts does not imply the right to be heard and understood by the tribunal independently of the language used. This right to be heard and understood would relate rather to the right to a fair hearing, guaranteed by the common law. Mr. Justice Beetz put this point as follows:

> It is my view the rights guaranteed by s. 19(2) of the *Charter* are of the same nature and scope as those guaranteed by s. 133 of the *Constitution Act, 1867* with respect to the courts of Canada and the courts of Quebec. . . . These language rights are the same as those guaranteed by s. 17 of the *Charter* with respect to parliamentary debates. They vest in the speaker or in the

---

80 *Ibid.* at 1028, 1030.
81 *MacDonald* v. *Montreal (City)*, *supra*, note 6; *Bilodeau* v. *A.G. Manitoba*, *supra*, note 30.
82 As indicated by Beetz J. in *Société des Acadiens, supra*, note 19, at 571-572, 573; Dickson CJ.C. expressing his dissent on this point, at 561, 562.
83 *Ibid.*

writer or issuer of court processes and give the speaker or the writer the constitutionally protected power to speak or to write in the official language of his choice. And there is no language guarantee, either under s. 133 of the *Constitution Act, 1867,* or s. 19 of the *Charter,* any more than under s. 17 of the *Charter,* that the speaker will be heard or understood, or that he has the right to be heard or understood in the language of his choice.[84]

Further on in his reasons, Mr. Justice Beetz added and concluded:

> The common law right of the parties to be heard and understood by a court and the right to understand what is going on in court is not a language right but an aspect of the right to a fair hearing. It is a broader and more universal right than language rights. . . . It belongs to the category of rights which in the *Charter* are designated as legal rights.

> . . .

> I have no difficulty in holding that the principles of natural justice as well as s. 13(1) of the *Official Languages of New Brunswick Act* "entitle a party pleading in a court of New Brunswick to be heard by a court, the member or members of which are capable of understanding the proceedings, the evidence and the arguments, written and oral, regardless of the official language used by the parties."
> But in my respectful opinion, no such entitlement can be derived from s. 19(2) of the *Charter.*[85]

In the judicial field, we see that the constitutional guarantees in linguistic matters remain minimal and that the courts, following the rules of interpretation prescribed by the Supreme Court in this area and in the three recently rendered decisions, will likely not intervene so as to improve, add to or modify the political compromise reached by the framers. The Supreme Court has clearly signalled that it belongs to the legislative authority and to the political domain to improve the linguistic guarantees in the direction of a real equality of status and usage of both official languages, including their use before the courts. Thus, absent a constitutional protection, legislation will be required before an accused or a party can fully exercise (that is, beyond what is required under the principles of natural justice) the right to be fully understood by the court no matter what official language is used. More importantly, legislation will also be required for the right to obtain a trial in the official language of choice throughout Canada.[86]

---

84 *Ibid.* at 574-575.

85 *Ibid.* at 577, 580.

86 As we have seen previously, the federal Parliament added certain provisions to the *Criminal Code* in order to permit the right to a trial in the official language of choice everywhere in Canada (Part XIV.1 [XVII]). Nevertheless, these provisions are not in effect in all the provinces. See the *Criminal Law Amendment Act,* S.C. 1977-78, c. 36, s. 6.

(d) The Right to Communicate in French and English with the Head Offices of Federal Institutions

Section 20(1) sets forth:

> Any member of the public in Canada has the right to communicate with, and to receive available services from, any head or central office of an institution of the Parliament or government of Canada in English or French, and has the same right with respect to any other office of any such institution where
> (a) there is a significant demand for communications with and services from that office in such language; or
> (b) due to the nature of the office, it is reasonable that communications with and services from that office be available in both English and French.

Obviously, the model for this section was section 9 of the *Official Languages Act*. Section 20(1) deals with the language of service or communication between citizens and federal institutions. This section imposes an obligation on federal institutions to be able to communicate in both official languages, but this same obligation is not imposed on citizens. As the public has a constitutionally-based right to be served in either French or English by federal institutions, these institutions will have a corresponding duty to hire a sufficient number of employees who are capable of communicating and rendering services in both official languages.

Let us note the difference between sections 17 and 19 of the Charter, which provide the right to use French or English in the debates and proceedings of Parliament, *in* matters before the courts and, *in* all acts of procedure, and section 20, which confers the right to use both official languages *to communicate with* federal institutions. This difference in drafting has been noted in the majority decision in the *Société des Acadiens* case[87] to justify a more limited scope of the guarantees of sections 17 and 19. According to the Supreme Court, the right *to communicate* in one or the other language presupposes the right to be heard and understood in these languages. Thus, the user must have the possibility of being understood directly by his interlocutor.[88] Moreover, section 20 recognizes the right to use the two languages *to receive* services granted by the federal institutions.

This does not mean that federal institutions must become fully bilingual. We believe that, so long as central federal institutions and other offices of these institutions subject to section 20 have the necessary employees and documents to dispense services of equal quality to the public in both official languages, the constitutional obligation will have been

---

87 *Supra*, note 19.
88 *Ibid.* at 575.

satisfied.[89] Services offered by these institutions should, therefore, be available in both languages.

Administrators will have to ensure that their personnel are recruited and employed according to constitutional norms. The head or central office of federal institutions will have to take special care, because in their case the principle of equality of the two languages as languages of service is obligatory and will have to be respected. As for the other offices of these institutions, they will have to conform to the same principle of equality of French and English as languages of service, where there is a large demand, or if the use of French and English is justified by the activities of the office. If the office meets either one of these criteria (the court must ultimately come to a decision on this matter), it is generally bound by the same linguistic obligations as central federal institutions.

(e) Rights and Privileges of Other Languages

Section 22 affirms:

Nothing in sections 16 to 20 abrogates or derogates from any legal or customary right or privilege acquired or enjoyed either before or after the coming into force of this Charter with respect to any language that is not English or French.

In those regions of Canada where, by law or custom, government services are provided in a language other than French or English, the Charter has not changed anything. The Charter does not guarantee, of course, that these services will be provided indefinitely in a language other than French or English.

5. CONCLUSION

As we have seen, the linguistic regime provided for in sections 16 to 22 of the Charter fits into a constitutional continuum, at least at the Federal level. But what is new is that this regime expressly translates the evolving character of language guarantees in Canada: the principle of equality of both official languages as to status and usage finds itself enshrined and must be achieved concretely and effectively. For that, effective implementation measures are necessary and certain practices will

---

89 The nature of the obligation flowing from s. 20 has not been settled by the courts. In her dissenting judgment in *Société des Acadiens, supra,* note 19, Wilson J. is nevertheless of the opinion (at 619), that the government is obliged to provide the best possible services, taking into account the development of bilingualism in Canada, and not services of equal quality. This result comes from the application of the principle of policy found in s. 16(1) in the interpretation of s. 20(1).

have to be abandoned or replaced. It must be admitted that equality has not yet been achieved. However, equality is not a static thing which, once established, would be established forever; it must be verified in achievements and evolve in accordance with needs and circumstances.

The provisions of the Charter represent a step in the right direction to the extent that they will produce effects. On this subject, the Supreme Court seems to have signified that the judicial mandate is to be very restrained. According to the court, courts should not intervene to control the rhythm of the evolution of the linguistic regime established by the Charter. Thus, it falls to the legislative process and, if needed, the framers to bring about and maintain the equality of status and use of the official languages. In this way, the instruments of linguistic changes have been clearly lodged in the political arena. It will be necessary to rely on the legislators to fully exercise their power, if not their duty, to implement and advance these constitutional guarantees.

16

Education Rights of Provincial Official Language Minorities*
(*Section 23*)

Michel Bastarache

1. Introduction
2. Categories of Protected Persons.
3. Guaranteed Rights.
4. Limits of Guaranteed Rights.
5. Remedies.
6. Conclusion.

1. INTRODUCTION

In its first decision on the application of section 23 of the *Canadian Charter of Rights and Freedoms*,[1] the Supreme Court of Canada described the guarantees provided in that section as follows:

---

* Translated from French.
1 Section 23 provides:
    (1) Citizens of Canada

Section 23 of the *Charter* is not, like other provisions in that constitutional document, of the kind generally found in such charters and declarations of fundamental rights. It is not a codification of essential, pre-existing and more or less universal rights that are being confirmed and perhaps clarified, extended or amended, and which, most importantly, are being given a new primacy and inviolability by their entrenchment in the supreme law of the land. The special provisions of s. 23 of the *Charter* make it a unique set of constitutional provisions, quite peculiar to Canada.[2]

This statement appears to place section 23 rights in the same category as those language rights which the Supreme Court said, in *MacDonald v. City of Montreal*,[3] resulted from a political compromise. However,

"it is not open to the courts, under the guise of interpretation, to improve upon, supplement or amend this historical constitutional compromise."[4]

Are we to conclude from this statement that section 23 will be interpreted restrictively? It would appear not, since the Supreme Court itself has stated that, in certain cases, it can breathe life into a political compromise.[5] That view also appears consistent with the opinion expressed earlier by the court concerning the remedial purpose of section 23:

This set of constitutional provisions was not enacted by the framers in a vacuum. When it was adopted, the framers knew, and clearly had in mind

---

    (a) whose first language learned and still understood is that of the English or French linguistic minority population of the province in which they reside, or

    (b) who have received their primary school instruction in Canada in English or French and reside in a province where the language in which they received that instruction is the language of the English or French linguistic minority population of the province,

    have the right to have their children receive primary and secondary school instruction in that language in that province.

    (2) Citizens of Canada of whom any child has received or is receiving primary or secondary school instruction in English or French in Canada, have the right to have all their children receive primary and secondary instruction in the same language.

    (3) The right of citizens of Canada under subsections (1) and (2) to have their children receive primary and secondary school instruction in the language of the English or French linguistic minority population of a province.

    (a) applies wherever in the province the number of children of citizens who have such a right is sufficient to warrant the provision to them out of public funds of minority language instruction; and

    (b) includes, where the number of those children so warrants, the right to have them receive that instruction in minority language educational facilities provided out of public funds.

2 *A.G. Quebec v. Que. Assn. of Protestant School Bds.*, [1984] 2 S.C.R. 66 at 79.

3 [1986] 1 S.C.R. 460.

4 *Ibid.* at 496.

5 *Reference re Bill 30, An Act to Amend the Education Act*, [1987] 1 S.C.R. 1148 at 1176.

the regimes governing the Anglophone and Francophone linguistic minorities in various provinces in Canada so far as the language of instruction was concerned. They also had in mind the history of those regimes, both earlier ones . . . as well as more recent ones . . . . Rightly or wrongly, — and it is not for the courts to decide, — the framers of the Constitution manifestly regarded as inadequate some — and perhaps all — of the regimes in force at the time the *Charter* was enacted, and their intention was to remedy the perceived defects of these regimes by uniform corrective measures, namely those contained in s. 23 of the *Charter*, which were at the same time given the status of a constitutional guarantee.[6]

Although the Ontario Court of Appeal clearly found that section 23 must be interpreted in broad and liberal fashion because it enacts new rights,[7] the Alberta Court of Appeal chose a two-step rule of interpretion:

> I conclude that the two ideas reflected in s. 23 are to offer strong rights to the s. 23 group to prevent assimilation and foster the growth of both official languages everywhere in Canada and, at the same time, interfere as little as possible with provincial legislative jurisdiction over educational institutions.[8]

The Court of Appeal of Prince Edward Island recognized the remedial purpose of section 23 and the necessity of interpreting that provision so as to guarantee the section's full benefit to those persons protected by it, but also acknowledged that it should act prudently, since section 23 rights are the result of a political compromise.[9]

If the purpose of section 23, interpreted historically,[10] is to protect provincial linguistic minorities from assimilation, as the Royal Commission on Bilingualism and Biculturalism suggested in 1968,[11] that section must be seen as granting a real collective right. It is true that that right exists from the moment a person contemplated by section 23 claims it. It is also clear, though, that it can be exercised only where there exist a minimum

---

6 *A.G. Québec v. Qué. Assn. of Protestant School Bds.*, *supra*, note 2 at 79.

7 *Reference re Education Act (Ont.) and Minority Language Rights* (1984), 10 D.L.R. (4th) 491 at 507, 518 (Ont. C.A.).

8 *Mahé v. Alberta*, [1987] 6 W.W.R. 331 at 351 (Alta. C.A.), leave to appeal to S.C.C. granted [1988] 2 W.W.R. lxvi (note) (S.C.C.), followed in *Comm. des écoles fransaskoises v. Saskatchewan*, [1988] 3 W.W.R. 354 (Sask. Q.B.).

9 *Reference re School Act of P.E.I.* (1988), 49 D.L.R. (4th) 499 (P.E.I. C.A.).

10 *Reference re Education Act (Ont.) and Minority Language Rights*, *supra*, note 7 at 530–531.

11 *Report of the Royal Commission on Bilingualism and Biculturalism*, Book II, Education (Ottawa: Queen's Printer, 1967–69) at 8.

number of beneficiaries.[12] These considerations will make it very difficult for the courts to decide whether the provinces are meeting the requirements of section 23 and whether the standards used to determine whether numbers are sufficient are constitutionally valid.

2. CATEGORIES OF PROTECTED PERSONS

The beneficiaries of section 23 rights fall into three immutable categories:[13]

(1) Canadian citizens whose first language learned and still understood is that of the English or French linguistic minority population of the province, except in Quebec where this provision is not in effect;

(2) Canadian citizens who received their primary school instruction in Canada in the language of the provincial linguistic minority population; and

(3) Citizens of Canada who have at least one child who has received or is receiving primary or secondary school instruction in Canada in the language of the official language minority of the province.

The education rights provided under section 23 are conferred on eligible parents. From a liberal interpretation of the *Constitution Act*, then, it may be concluded that every person who holds parental authority is contemplated by that section. It is obvious, however, that many children who qualify for instruction in the minority language are incapable of expressing themselves in that language. This situation poses a major problem with respect to admissions to minority educational facilities. In *Commission des écoles fransaskoises v. Saskatchewan*,[14] the Court of Queen's Bench of Saskatchewan examined one aspect of this problem: whether the minority facility should be reserved exclusively for children of persons protected by section 23. The court resolved this difficulty by drawing a distinction between the right to instruction and the right to a facility. In the first instance, the court found that section 23 "permits designated programs to be offered in physical facilities shared with schools where English is the language of instruction", whereas, in the second, it ruled

---

12 On this point, see P. Carignan, "De la notion de droit collectif et de son application en matière scolaire au Québec" (1984), 18 *R.J.T.* 1 at 100; P. Foucher, "Language Rights and Education", in M. Bastarache, ed., *Language Rights in Canada* (Montreal: Yvon Blais, 1986) at 272.

13 *A.G. Québec v. Qué. Assn. of Protestant School Bds.*, *supra*, note 2 at 84, in which the court decided that a province may not restrict the eligibility of protected persons by invoking section 1 of the Charter, since such a restriction would be equivalent to a negation of that right for the persons who would be affected.

14 *Supra*, note 8.

that the minority, which is responsible for managing its facility, may restrict access to the institution to children protected by section 23.[15] In Prince Edward Island, the court resolved this matter indirectly, saying that the province must guarantee "equality of opportunity and equality of education",[16] emphasizing that instruction in French where French is the first language is distinct from all other types of instruction, including French immersion.[17] The Supreme Court of Nova Scotia also found that section 23 contains a duty to provide "a separate facility" to those persons enjoying the rights guaranteed by this section.[18]

All of this, however, does not answer the question whether the children of the linguistic minority of the province must be made to suffer from the presence of children incapable of communicating in their language. In our view, reasonable limits may be imposed on the rights of those who may prejudicially affect the other children. Those limits would consist in placing children incapable of following the regular program in remedial classes or schools.[19] The purpose of these classes should be to bring the children enrolled in them up to an adequate level of linguistic competence to enable them to return to regular classes as soon as possible.

3. GUARANTEED RIGHTS

Given the remedial purpose of section 23,[20] the courts have concluded that the nature of guaranteed rights must be determined on the basis of the need to enable the linguistic minority to remain viable. The right to instruction has consequently been defined as guaranteeing access to a program designed to suit the needs of the minority and reflecting its values and culture.[21] This means that immersion programs do not in any way

---

15 *Ibid.* The same approach is adopted in *Reference re Education Act (Ont.) and Minority Language Rights, supra,* note 7; see *Education Act,* R.S.O. 1980, c. 129; see also *Education Act,* 1986, S.O. 1986, c. 29, ss. 273, 277(m)(1)3.

16 *Reference re School Act of P.E.I., supra,* note 9.

17 *Ibid.*

18 *Lavoie v. A.G. Nova Scotia* (1988), 47 D.L.R. (4th) 586 (N.S. T.D.).

19 On a similar question, see the opinion of Richard C.J. in *Société des Acadiens du Nouveau-Brunswick Inc. v. Minority Language School Bd. No. 50* (1983), 48 N.B.R. (2d) 361 (Q.B.), additional reasons at (1983), 50 N.B.R. (2d) 41 (Q.B.).

20 See *Report of the Royal Commission on Bilingualism and Biculturalism,* Book II, *supra,* note 11 at 8-9.

21 *Reference re Education Act (Ont.) and Minority Language Rights, supra,* note 7 at 529; *Mahé v. Alberta* (1985), 22 D.L.R. (4th) 24 (Alta. Q.B.), aff'd *supra,* note 8; *Marchand v. Simcoe County Bd. of Education* (1986), 29 D.L.R. (4th) 596 at 618 (Ont. H.C.), additional reasons at (1986), 12 C.P.C. (2d) 140 (Ont. H.C.); *Comm. des écoles fransaskoises v. Saskatchewan, supra,* note 8; *Reference re School Act of P.E.I., supra,* note 9.

form a constitutionally valid alternative to instruction in the first language. That was the conclusion of the Court of Queen's Bench of New Brunswick which, in handling a similar problem, found as follows:

> From the evidence presented at trial, as well as from the whole of the expert testimony it appears . . . that the grouping of Francophone and Anglophone pupils under the same roof and in the same system, leads to linguistic interference, to the weakening of the first and second languages and, consequently, to assimilation.[22]

Although it is clear at first glance that a distinction must be drawn between access to a program and access to the minority school or facility, the Alberta Court of Appeal confused the two and found that both rights follow from section 23(1)(a). From the premises that the words "instruction" and "facility" are "institutionally neutral" and unclear, and that the province has unlimited discretion to choose the mode of instruction,[23] the court reasoned that the Charter guaranteed "effective language instruction" and that "the application of the right . . . [will] be case-specific, and will turn on evidence of what is and is not effective as an instructional tool".[24] This approach was not taken in Ontario, Saskatchewan, Prince Edward Island or Nova Scotia. The Alberta Court of Appeal nevertheless did not deny the importance of the minority school. Judge Kerans wrote:

> I accept the argument of the appellants that the most effective guarantee to prevent assimilation is a facility under the exclusive control of that group. Any diminution in that power inevitably dilutes the uniqueness of the school and opens it to the influence of an insensitive if not hostile majority.[25]

In fact, the right to facilities was specifically recognized by the Ontario Court of Appeal, which agreed that facilities "must reflect the minority culture and . . . appertain to the minority".[26] This conclusion is in fact consistent with those of education experts, who have determined through exhaustive studies that schools not reserved for members of the minority alone are centres of assimilation.[27] The Court of Queen's Bench of Saskatchewan and the Prince Edward Island Court of Appeal shared this view.[28]

---

22 *Société des Acadiens du Nouveau-Brunswick Inc. v. Minority Language School Bd. No. 50*, *supra*, note 19 at 390-391. See a similar decision in *Whittington v. Bd. of School Trustees of School District No. 63*, June 22, 1987 (B.C. S.C.), and *Reference re School Act of P.E.I.*, *supra*, note 9.

23 *Mahé v. Alberta*, *supra*, note 8 at 350-351.

24 *Ibid.* at 353.

25 *Ibid.* at 354.

26 *Reference re Education Act (Ont.) and Minority Language Rights*, *supra*, note 7 at 528-529.

27 *Education and the Needs of Franco-Ontarians*, 1985, Vol. 1; *Franco-Ontarian Elementary and Secondary Education*, Working Paper No. 22.

28 *Comm. des écoles fransaskoises v. Saskatchewan*, *supra*, note 8; *Reference re School Act of P.E.I.*, *supra*, note 9.

The courts have also recognized that the right of representatives of the minority to manage minority educational facilities is implicit in section 23. This conclusion apparently surprised the provinces, because the proceedings of the Joint Committee of the Senate and House of Commons clearly show that this management right was specifically rejected by members of Parliament in 1981.[29] It was nevertheless clear to the judges who examined the history of educational rights that a minimum of control was needed to make the guarantees provided under section 23 effective.

The Ontario Court of Appeal found that the idea that facilities belong to the minority is explicit in the French version of the Charter and that section 23(3)(b) must be considered as guaranteeing more than simply physical facilities.[30] It also provides a management right that is broad enough to correct the injustices of the past and to ensure that the facilities of the minority reflect its culture. First, that right should include guaranteed representation at the institutional level. Second:

> those representatives should be given exclusive authority to make decisions pertaining to the provision of minority language instruction and facilities within their jurisdiction, including the expenditure of the funds provided for such instruction and facilities, and the appointment and direction of those responsible for the administration of such instruction and facilities.[31]

The court determined that there was a field of exclusive but limited authority, leaving broad discretionary power to the province to establish by law a school system that meets the particular needs of the linguistic minority of the province.

The Court of Queen's Bench of Alberta adopted the same reasoning[32] and specified the nature of the management power. The Alberta Court of Appeal, however, took another route. Judge Kerans found as follows:

> In my view, s. 23(3)(*b*) guarantees to s. 23 students, where numbers warrant, an educational system (with all its complexity and cost) that not only offers the same quality of education as other systems but is run by the minority language group or its representatives.[33]

Although this interpretation appears liberal, it in fact means that the management right will be recognized only in provinces where the minority is very large.

---

29 See P. Foucher, "Les droits scolaires des Acadiens et la Charte" (1984), 33 *U.N.B.L.T.* 97 at 114; Joint Committee on the Constitution, 1st Sess., 32nd Parl. 38:108, 38:111, 48:113.

30 *Reference re Education Act (Ont.) and Minority Language Rights, supra*, note 7 at 525, 527.

31 *Ibid.* at 533.

32 *Mahé v. Alberta, supra*, note 21 at 57.

33 *Mahé v. Alberta, supra*, note 8 at 354.

In Saskatchewan, the court adopted a simpler solution:

[W]here the number of eligible children is sufficient to warrant the provision of a separate facility, then the system of parents' advisory councils does not meet the requirements of the Charter because the legislative scheme fails to recognize, in that event, the right of the minority group to manage and control.[34]

In Prince Edward Island, the constitutional question raised concerned the minority's right to take part in the development and provision of the French program. The court found this approach more reasonable than that involving exclusive management because it called upon the language groups to co-operate.[35] It rejected the idea of an autonomous system, but stated that the system prescribed by the *School Act* must in no instance leave the minority at the mercy of the majority.[36]

In concrete terms, it is reasonable to assume that the management right is essential to the maintenance of a valid educational program for the linguistic minority of the province. In our view, it is obvious that that right must include the power to appoint and exercise control over teachers, to make admissions decisions, to decide on the location of the schools, to control the setting of school district boundaries and to control the budget for the minority's programs and facilities. These powers appear to be the only ones that meet the requirement described by Mr. Justice Sirois in *Marchand v. Simcoe County Board of Education*: to provide "the right to a full and complete education, not a limited, partial or truncated one which necessarily would be an inferior education, a second class one."[37]

The background to section 23 is very interesting in this regard.[38] In 1969, in the White Paper entitled *The Constitution and the People of Canada*, the government suggested that there be freedom of choice in educational matters. This suggestion was re-stated in the report of the Special Joint Committee of the Senate and House of Commons in 1972. In 1977-78, however, the provincial premiers turned their attention exclusively to the protection of the education rights of linguistic minorities. In 1978, those rights were recognized in Bill C-60 as belonging to parents, who were categorized on the basis of their mother tongue. Two categories of beneficiaries were then adopted in the first version of the constitutional resolution of 1981, the first being defined on the basis of mother tongue, the second on the family unit. A somewhat different version of the present text was subsequently proposed on February 13, 1981. Thus, the way in

---

34 *Comm. des écoles fransaskoises v. Saskatchewan, supra,* note 8 at 367.

35 *Reference re School Act of P.E.I., supra,* note 9.

36 *Ibid.*

37 *Supra,* note 21 at 618.

38 See Foucher, *supra,* note 12 at 274-277.

which the section has evolved reflects a clear intent to protect the minorities first and foremost by guaranteeing them the essential means to maintain their culture.[39]

The educational and cultural services provided under section 23 must also be equivalent to those provided to the majority. In 1984, the Ontario Court of Appeal found that the principle of equality is inherent in section 23.[40] The High Court of Ontario applied the same principle, adding that section 15 of the Charter may serve to reinforce the principle of equality present in section 23.[41]

The Saskatchewan Court of Appeal saw no need to refer to section 15,[42] whereas the Court of Appeal of Prince Edward Island summarized its position in the following terms:

> Those opportunities available to the majority linguistic group are the criteria by which must be judged equivalent opportunities available to the minority linguistic group. This does not mean that all of the amenities which may be available to the majority group, where that group exists in large numbers, must all be made available to the minority group, where it exists in its own separate educational facility, having only a minimum number of pupils.
>
> What it does mean is that where there exists a comparable equivalency of numbers in separate educational facilities, there should exist a comparable equivalency of amenities and opportunities, regardless of the linguistic group involved.[43]

In Alberta, the debate over section 15 generated a number of surprising statements. Judge Kerans wrote: "the majority and the minority being . . . not similarly situated, [they] can be treated differently. Otherwise, majority rule is unconstitutional".[44] He then stated that section 23 was an exception to section 15 and that it presupposed that the province might implement minority education rights in a special way.[45] Rejecting the notion that the Alberta school system was somehow "English",[46] the judge then refused to recognize that Alberta francophones could demand, in the name of equality, the right to a school system organized along the same lines as the public system of Alberta.[47]

In our view, section 23 on its own requires that equivalent services be provided to the minority. We nevertheless believe that an education

---

39 E. Apps, "Minority Language Education Rights" (1985), 43 *U.T. Fac. L. Rev.* 44 at 61.

40 *Reference re Education (Ont.) and Minority Language Rights, supra,* note 7 at 533.

41 *Marchand v. Simcoe County Bd. of Education, supra,* note 21 at 616.

42 *Comm. des écoles fransaskoises v. Saskatchewan, supra,* note 8.

43 *Reference re School Act of P.E.I., supra,* note 9.

44 *Mahé v. Alberta, supra,* note 8 at 362.

45 *Ibid.* at 365.

46 *Ibid.* at 366.

47 *Ibid.* at 367.

Act that fails to provide a system of instruction in the language of the minority and does not establish the conditions in which children will be grouped together or the criteria for the establishment of facilities to serve them will create systemic discrimination against the minority and will thereby conflict with section 15 of the Charter.

4. LIMITS OF GUARANTEED RIGHTS

Given the dual nature of the rights provided under section 23, which are both individual and collective, some sort of numerical condition must clearly be set for their implementation. There exist two numbers tests. On this point, the Ontario Court of Appeal expressed the following view:

> Further, one might also draw attention to the fact that both paras. 3(a) and 3(b) refer to the "numbers warrant" test. The repetition in para 3(d), even though in slightly different terms, would not be necessary unless the facilities there referred to are different from those included in the providing of instruction. It would appear, further, that a different numbers test would apply. Logically a larger number would be required for para 3(b) than for para 3(a). No one questions that para 3(b) at least means "minority language education facilities", separate from majority language education facilities, where numbers warrant.[48]

The reasoning of the Ontario Court of Appeal was adopted without change in Saskatchewan and Prince Edward Island.[49] Two tests were also instituted in Alberta, but the second was used to justify the right to a "school system" rather than to a school and will therefore be more demanding.[50]

Two more difficult questions arise concerning the application of these tests: what criteria will be used to determine whether numbers warrant, and is it possible for a province to set a single number that will apply in all cases?

Section 23 contains no indicator that would provide an easy answer to these questions. The Minister of Justice at the time the Charter was adopted merely said that "reasonableness" should prevail.[51] The Ontario Court of Appeal espoused his view when it found that it was probably not reasonable to impose a fixed number in a province such as Ontario. It added, however, that if a number had to be set, it should be established by the legislature because the latter:

> is uniquely qualified to demonstrate and provide the substantiation for the

---

48 *Reference re Education Act (Ont.) and Minority Language Rights, supra,* note 7 at 527.
49 *Comm. des écoles fransaskoises v. Saskatchewan, supra,* note 8.
50 *Mahé v. Alberta, supra,* note 8 at 354–355.
51 Joint Committee on the Constitution, *supra,* note 29, 38:37.

fixed number as being the appropriate one for the various districts of the province.[52]

The Prince Edward Island Court of Appeal was not convinced that it would be reasonable to apply a fixed number throughout the province.[53] It found, however, that such a number, if necessary, should be set by the Lieutenant-Governor in Council or the legislature.[54] To the Courts of Appeal of Prince Edward Island[55] and Ontario,[56] it was clear that the power to fix the number could not be delegated to local authorities.

Where no number is set by legislative or regulatory means, how can it be determined whether numbers warrant? What criteria should apply? Under what conditions must the counting be carried out?

The Court of Appeal of Prince Edward Island formally rejected the idea that local school boards should be given discretionary power to decide how students should be grouped for the purposes of section 23. In its view, provincial directives are needed to protect the minorities, which must not be forced to appeal to the courts any time they wish.[57] This idea was similar to that expressed earlier by the Ontario Court of Appeal.[58]

The Court of Queen's Bench of Alberta nevertheless chose to list the factors that must guide the government in exercising its powers:

> One of the criteria could be a consideration of cost.
>
> . . . .
>
> Other factors which should be considered in deciding ". . . where numbers warrant" are:
>
> — the distance a student must travel and the time he or she must spend in transit to reach the educational facility;
>
> — the age of the children involved;
>
> — the possibility of providing residence accommodation for eligible students; and
>
> — the impact such arrangements would have on the social and other development of the children.[59]

This passage gave rise to a major debate concerning the first criterion,

---

52 *Reference re Education Act (Ont.) and Minority Language Rights, supra,* note 7 at 521.
53 *Reference re School Act of P.E.I., supra,* note 9.
54 *Ibid.*
55 *Ibid.*
56 *Reference re Education Act (Ont.) and Minority Language Rights, supra,* note 7 at 521.
57 *Reference re School Act of P.E.I., supra,* note 9.
58 *Reference re Education Act (Ont.) and Minority Language Rights, supra,* note 7 at 520–522.
59 *Mahé v. Alberta, supra,* note 21 at 46, 47.

that of cost. Can this factor be considered relevant to the issue when the wording of section 23 provides that, where the number of children is sufficient, instruction or facilities, as the case may be, must be provided out of public funds? Would it not be reasonable to apply the precedent set in *McLeod v. Salmon Arm School Trustees*[60] in which it was found that a shortage of funds was no reason to justify a refusal to provide service where there exists a duty to provide that service? On this point, the Alberta Court of Appeal ruled as follows:

> Numbers command consideration of what teaching arrangements are (a) necessary in terms of a successful program and (b) reasonable in terms of a corresponding cost. Numbers, in my view, are relevant only as the criterion for reasonable cost.[61]

According to Judge Kerans, the numbers criterion may be explained as follows:

> Obviously . . . the reason for the limit is not to burden a province with substantial extra cost. As at trial here, per pupil cost comparisons inevitably will be made.[62]

The Court of Appeal of Prince Edward Island also found that costs were a factor to be considered:

> Evidentiary factors relating to the cost, travelling distance, size of the area are only some of the matters that would have to be considered.[63]

In its view, no final list may be compiled. However, the minority must be afforded equality of opportunity, due consideration being given to local situations. This would also appear to be the position of the Court of Queen's Bench of Saskatchewan[64] and of the Supreme Court of Nova Scotia.[65]

The question is a difficult one, and section 23 of course offers neither the means to resolve it nor any unusual solutions. It does, however, prescribe a regime that may be applied to a minority and which necessarily involves the creation of classes, schools and even small school boards in which per pupil costs will be higher than in the majority system. If section 23 is remedial in nature, it is illogical to reverse its provisions so as to state that numbers will be sufficient where costs are justified. In our view, where ordinary school transportation arrangements make it possible to bring together a sufficient number of students to justify, in educational terms,

---

60 [1952] 2 D.L.R. 562 at 563 (B.C. C.A.).

61 *Mahé v. Alberta, supra,* note 8 at 358.

62 *Ibid.* at 359.

63 *Reference re School Act of P.E.I., supra,* note 9.

64 *Comm. des écoles fransaskoises v. Saskatchewan, supra,* note 8.

65 *Lavoie v. A.G. Nova Scotia, supra,* note 18.

the creation of a class or school, the duty to pay the related costs must be imposed without consideration of the fact that those costs may be higher than in the case of children belonging to the linguistic majority.

The accessory question that arises is of course to determine the geographical area over which the duty to bring together the necessary number of pupils should extend. The Ontario Court of Appeal found that the question whether numbers are sufficient cannot be determined by calculating the number of eligible children within the present boundaries of the school boards.[66] According to the court, those boundaries are not immutable; they exist for administrative purposes and may not constitute an obstacle to the exercise of a constitutional right. The Court of Queen's Bench of Saskatchewan expressed the same opinion,[67] although it emphasized that a province is not required to change boundaries to facilitate the bringing together of sufficient numbers of eligible children, since other means may be employed to achieve that objective. The Court of Appeal of Prince Edward Island reached the same conclusion, but emphasized the fact that the words "wherever in the province" used in section 23 do not mean that the province is required to permit the assembly in one place of all pupils residing in the province.[68]

Another major problem arises in deciding whether there are a sufficient number of children for the purposes of section 23. That problem is to determine whether one must take into account the number of eligible pupils, within the meaning of section 23, or the number of pupils for whom an application has been submitted or the number of pupils actually enrolled.

In 1982, Professor Magnet wrote:

> If the numbers test in section 23 were only to entrench the status quo, a request by fifteen to twenty-five qualified parents should trigger the right to French instruction. However, viewed as a remedial provision, section 23 must be deemed to change something. This suggests that the right to minority language instruction arises with lesser numbers. On this view, it would appear that the right to minority language instruction will accrue under section 23 if requests are received from twelve, ten, eight or even five qualified parents. This view of section 23 links the numbers test to experienced demand. The problem is that demand is easily suppressed. If it is clear to the local population that the government resists providing minority language education, many parents will not ask. Many more will not ask unless the service is advertised or otherwise known to be available. Courts should scrupulously avoid accepting evidence that demand is insufficient unless minority language

---

66 *Reference re Education Act (Ont.) and Minority Language Rights, supra,* note 7 at 522.
67 *Comm. des écoles fransaskoises v. Saskatchewan, supra,* note 8; see also *Mahé v. Alberta, supra,* note 21 at 43.
68 *Reference re School Act of P.E.I., supra,* note 9.

education is actively offered. Until that happens, experienced demand cannot be considered as a true reflection of demand for constitutional purposes.[69]

This question was carefully reviewed in Prince Edward Island, where the Court of Appeal rejected the idea that demographic data could be used to justify the establishment of classes or schools.[70] In the court's view, however, the number of requests made would constitute valid data only in cases where the population had been well informed of its rights and where services had been actively offered.[71] This approach was in fact adopted by Mr. Justice Hallett, of the Supreme Court of Nova Scotia, who rejected the results of the survey as a measurement of sufficient demand,[72] but ordered the school board to which a request had been submitted to advertise a French program, indicating an appropriate location, and to enrol students.[73]

In the *Marchand* case,[74] Mr. Justice Sirois of Supreme Court of Ontario adopted a different approach. Based on the number of students who met the requirements of section 23 and who were enrolled in primary schools, the petitioners had established that there were potentially more than 700 students for the French-language secondary school where actual enrolment was only 220. Taking into account various factors and expert testimony, the judge ordered that a facility accommodating 400 students be built.[75]

In Alberta, the results obtained by the plaintiffs in *Mahé v. Alberta*[76] were much less satisfactory. The latter established at trial that 2,948 parents were qualified under section 23, but that only 242 children were in fact enrolled in Edmonton's only French-language school, the *École Maurice Lavallée*, which provided instruction from grades 1 to 6 inclusive.[77] In the lower court decision, Mr. Justice Purvis had concluded that the numbers were sufficient to justify both the right to instruction and the right to a facility,[78] but Judge Kerans of the Court of Appeal overturned that decision:

> Because I take an entirely different view of the nature of the right under s. 23(3)(b), it follows that I must reconsider the finding of the learned trial judge. The question, at base, is whether 242 pupils warrant the installation,

---

69 J.E. Magnet, "Minority Language Education Rights" (1982), 4 *Supreme Ct. L. Rev.* 195 at 206.

70 *Reference re School Act of P.E.I., supra,* note 9.

71 *Ibid.*

72 *Lavoie v. A.G. Nova Scotia, supra,* note 18.

73 *Ibid.*

74 *Marchand v. Simcoe County Bd. of Education, supra,* note 21.

75 *Ibid.* at 612.

76 *Supra,* note 21.

77 *Ibid.* at 21, 30.

78 *Ibid.* at 50.

in the Edmonton area, of a totally separate, minority language controlled school system in the region.[79]

In our view, the Alberta Court of Appeal improperly applied the section 23 test by granting that current enrolment in a program that is incomplete — given the evidence establishing unsatisfactory transportation conditions and confusion between the French-language and French immersion programs — should be used to determine whether there were a satisfactory number of children. This approach in fact makes it possible to use negation of the first right to justify negation of the second.

Section 29 of the *Charter of Rights and Freedoms*, which preserves constitutionally recognized rights to denominational schools,[80] also constitutes a certain limit to the application of section 23 since it prevents the latter from being implemented in such a way as to infringe denominational rights. In practice, this means that, although the guarantees of section 23 are applicable to the denominational sector,[81] changes to the organization of that sector are possible only if they do not adversely affect the exercise of guaranteed denominational rights.[82] In Quebec, an attempted reorganization has already been aborted.[83] In Ontario, the government has agreed to establish a French-language school board comprising a Catholic sector and a public sector in the Ottawa-Carleton region in 1988. This project will likely give rise to legal action which will make it possible to clarify the relation between sections 23 and 29 of the Charter.

In concluding this section, we wish to discuss briefly the matter of the application of section 1 of the Charter with respect to educational rights. As mentioned above, the Supreme Court of Canada has refused to allow section 1 to limit or modify the categories of beneficiaries described in section 23.[84] That section has nevertheless been invoked for other purposes. The government of Alberta did so to justify a regulation imposing instruction in English during 20 percent of classroom time in French-language classes. In the absence of any evidence, Judge Kerans granted that this was a "self-evidently reasonable limit under s. 1, if indeed it is a limit".[85] According to the judge, section 23 does not prescribe Hugh MacLennan's "two solitudes".

The government of Prince Edward Island invoked section 1 to justify

---

79 *Mahé v. Alberta, supra*, note 8 at 359.

80 These rights are recognized in Quebec, Ontario, Saskatchewan, Alberta, the Yukon Territory and the Northwest Territories.

81 *Reference re Education Act (Ont.) and Minority Language Rights, supra*, note 7 at 544-545.

82 *Mahé v. Alberta, supra*, note 8 at 357.

83 *Comm. des écoles catholiques de Montréal v. P.G. Québec*, J.E. 85-643.

84 See *supra*, note 13 and related text.

85 *Mahé v. Alberta, supra*, note 8 at 361.

the delegation of powers to the school boards to determine whether 25 students could reasonably be assembled for the purposes of instruction in French. Citing *R. v. Oakes*,[86] the court rejected the argument advanced by the Attorney General because the latter had not demonstrated the need for such a restriction of guaranteed rights.[87] It added that the restriction imposed by regulation was the result of an administrative decision, something that was also inconsistent with the requirements of section 1.

A similar question was put to the Court of Queen's Bench of Saskatchewan, where the province argued that its regulations, which set conditions for the establishment of French-language classes in addition to that concerning sufficient numbers, were justified under section 1. The court answered this argument in the following terms:

> It is still an open question whether this section applies to the rights guaranteed by section 23 and, if it does, whether section 23 rights can be limited to the point of denying them.
> I am of the view that, in any event, the constitutional deficiencies which I have identified cannot pass the two-stage inquiry defined by the Supreme Court in *R. v Oakes.*.[88]

In light of the above decisions, it is clear that the courts will offer the greatest resistance to any limits that would prevent the application of section 23 in certain specific cases. This view appears reasonable, given the fact that section 23 already contains its own limits. When section 1 is invoked to influence the terms and conditions of the right's application, the courts, following the example of the Alberta Court of Appeal, will probably be much more receptive. It is unfortunate, however, that the courts of Alberta have accepted such limits as being self-evident. This is a very dangerous situation in that it is the majority that decides what must be done in the interests of the minority. Should it develop any further, a policy of assimilation could be seen as justified for the sake of social peace.

5. REMEDIES

Section 52(1) of the *Charter of Rights and Freedoms* will of course be invoked to encourage the court to conclude that incompatible sections of any provincial Act are unconstitutional.[89] However, section 24 of the Charter opens the door to other remedies: injunction, *mandamus*, damages, among others. These remedies are also necessary because education rights are also social rights, rights which require positive action on the govern-

---

86 [1986] 1 S.C.R. 103.

87 *Reference re School Act of P.E.I.*, *supra*, note 9.

88 *Comm. des écoles fransaskoises v. Saskatchewan*, *supra*, note 8.

89 See, *e.g.*, *Comm. des écoles fransaskoises v. Saskatchewan*, *supra*, note 8.

ment's part for their implementation.

A legal vacuum would be created if incompatible provisions in provincial legislation were to be declared unconstitutional. Where a province has not legislated to implement section 23 and its legislation does not directly conflict with the provisions of the Charter, a ruling that the provincial provisions are unconstitutional would be small compensation. It is in these cases that the problem of the province's obligation to legislate arises.

In *Reference re Education Act of Ontario and Minority Language Rights*,[90] the Ontario Court of Appeal found as follows:

> The Legislature has exclusive power to make laws in relation to education and to establish a system for the management thereof that it deems suitable to conditions in the province. S. 23 limits this power in respect to minority language education. The rights conferred by this section . . . impose a duty on the provincial legislature to provide for educational facilities which, viewed objectively, can be said to be or to appertain to the linguistic minority in that they can be regarded as part and parcel of the minority's social and cultural fabric.

This finding was apparently not enough to persuade the Alberta Court of Appeal. Although convinced that the *School Act* did not provide an acceptable mechanism for the implementation of section 23, the court found that the Act was not unconstitutional "because it does not purport to be in compliance with s. 23 and is therefore supplementary to (and not contradictory of) any *Charter* rights".[91] Judge Kerans added: "I suppose it is conceivable that Alberta could comply with its constitutional obligation without enactment."[92] Although it seems reasonable to suggest that there exists a duty to legislate when refusal to do so will result in the negation of the rights of the persons protected by section 23, the court refused to state that there was any constitutional obligation in this regard.[93]

The Court of Appeal of Prince Edward Island followed the decision of the British Columbia Court of Appeal in *Re Hoogbruin and A.G. British Columbia*[94] and concluded that the legislature indeed had a duty to introduce a mechanism for the implementation of section 23.[95] It also refused to attach any importance to the fact that the *School Act* was passed before 1982, and agreed that the provincial Act conflicted with the *Constitution Act* in those respects where both were not perfectly compatible with one another:

---

90 *Supra*, note 7 at 547.
91 *Mahé v. Alberta, supra*, note 8 at 361.
92 *Ibid.* at 361.
93 *Ibid.* at 362.
94 [1986] 2 W.W.R. 700 at 721 (B.C. C.A.).
95 *Reference re School Act of P.E.I., supra*, note 9.

A person reading a particular piece of legislation has the right to assume that it is valid. There is no justification for provincial legislation conforming to one specific right given in the *Charter* and not conforming to other specific rights in the *Charter*. Simply put, the *School Act* cannot be in conflict with a specific right expressly given in the *Charter*. It is incumbent upon the legislature to enact a proper legislative framework which will reflect the rights given by s. 23.[96]

This approach is the only one compatible with the duty of the courts described in *Hunter v. Southam Inc.*,[97] in which the Supreme Court of Canada refused to read down an Act with a view to invalidating it. Incompatibility may in fact be indirect in many cases. Refusal to apply section 52 or section 24 in those cases will create an inequality in the application of the Act among the beneficiaries of section 23. Systemic discrimination exists if members of the minority group are placed at a real disadvantage with respect to access to educational services equivalent to those provided to the linguistic majority.[98]

It is also clear that the absence of mechanisms for the implementation of section 23 perpetuates the institutional barriers that form the subject of court action taken by the beneficiaries of section 23. If such mechanisms are not introduced, the electoral system will fail in representing the linguistic minority, the boundaries of school districts will be drawn so as not to bring together sufficient numbers of protected pupils, and the discretionary powers of local authorities will subject the rights of the minority to the will of the representatives of the linguistic majority.

The power of the courts to force school boards to provide specific services is unassailable. It is also necessary. Professor Sharpe makes the point as follows:

> In dealing with minority language education rights and equality rights in particular, the courts will be asked to mandate affirmative measures. This will require the provision of certain services and facilities and the positive repair of past wrongs . . . . Orders of this kind do involve the courts in a continuing relationship with the concerned parties and institutions.[99]

Although some courts have proved highly obstinate,[100] others have agreed to issue injunctions and to maintain their jurisdiction for as long

---

96   *Ibid.*
97   [1984] 2 S.C.R. 145.
98   See *Marchand v. Simcoe County Bd. of Education, supra,* note 21 at 618.
99   R.J. Sharpe, *Injunctions and Specific Performance* (Toronto: Canada Law Book, 1983) at 485; see also Magnet, *supra,* note 69 at 216.
100   *Mahé v. Alberta, supra,* note 8 at 269; *Comm. des écoles fransaskoises v. Saskatchewan, supra,* note 8.

as is needed to ensure their decisions are executed.[101] This approach is very promising. As Professor Gibson has written:

> As the importance of injunctive relief increases in particular situations, the reluctance of courts to undertake supervisory responsibility decreases. Few legal matters are as important as compliance by governmental authorities with constitutionally entrenched safeguards.[102]

6. CONCLUSION

The implementation of section 23 is a major challenge for the government of Canada. Unfortunately, the Canadian provinces have thus far refused to take action to correct the inadequacies of their school systems. Since 1982, Ontario has been the only province to legislate in this regard, while New Brunswick is the only one whose legislation was perfectly compatible with the requirements of section 23 at that date.[103]

In light of the difficulty the linguistic minorities of the provinces are experiencing in securing the establishment of French-language classes and schools, and indeed the right to manage their own facilities, it appears clear that recourse to the courts will still be needed to give momentum to the reform movement heralded by the *Canadian Charter of Rights and Freedoms* ten years ago.

---

101 *Marchand v. Simcoe County Bd. of Education, supra,* note 21 at 619; *Lavoie v. A.G. Nova Scotia, supra,* note 18.

102 D. Gibson, "Enforcement of the Canadian Charter of Rights and Freedoms", Chapter 19, *infra,* at 781.

103 P. Foucher, *Conditional Language Rights of Official Language Minorities in Canada* (Ottawa: Canadian Law Information Council, 1985).

17

Pre-Existing Rights:
The Aboriginal Peoples of Canada
(*Sections 25 and 35*)

Douglas Sanders

1. General overview
2. The Indian, Inuit and Metis peoples
3. Special rights and equality
4. Section 35: Existing Aboriginal and treaty rights
5. Treaties and the treaty process
6. International law developments
7. Conclusions.

1. GENERAL OVERVIEW

In 1984, the Supreme Court of Canada ruled in *Guerin v. R.*[1] that the Musqueam Indian band have legal rights to their reserve lands. The ruling should have been obvious. It meant that Indians have rights to lands designated for their use by government and on which their homes and community buildings stand. Yet federal lawyers argued throughout the case

---

1 [1984] 2 S.C.R. 335.

that Indians had no legal rights to reserve lands.

In *Guerin*, the Supreme Court ruled that Indian rights to reserves were rights surviving from the pre-contact Indian legal order. The rights did not originate in the *Indian Act*[2] or any other British or Canadian enactment. The idea that some pre-contact Indian rights survive in Canadian law is recognized in the *Constitution Act, 1982*. But until recently it was commonly assumed that Indians had been roaming hunters without political institutions or a legal order. While such views are now discredited, *Guerin* is the first decision of the Supreme Court of Canada to recognize Indian rights based on the pre-contact Indian legal order and not on British or Canadian actions. In this, *Guerin* represents a major change in judicial premises.

In 1886, in the *St. Catharines Milling* case,[3] Chancellor Boyd, a respected Ontario trial judge, ruled that Indians were to be treated "justly and graciously", but had no legal rights to their traditional lands. They had no "fixed abodes" and were "heathens and barbarians". In issue were Indian territorial rights which had been recognized by Great Britain in the Royal Proclamation of 1763 and by the government of Canada in the negotiation of Treaty Three in 1871. Alexander Morris, the federal treaty commissioner and Lieutenant Governor of the Northwest Territories, testified at trial. The ruling meant his treaty negotiations were mere show — "delusive mockery" in the words of a different judge.[4] Yet Chancellor Boyd's judgment was widely praised. The praise assumed the judgment was scholarly, when it was not. It failed to note that Boyd's reasoning was rejected on appeal (though the outcome remained the same). And the praise was unconcerned with the fact that Boyd rejected any Indian legal rights. The judgment cannot be described as an example of legal positivism, for it rejected legal rights recognized in the Proclamation and the Treaty.

The *St. Catharines Milling* case was decided by the Judicial Committee of the Privy Council in 1888.[5] The Judicial Committee held that Indians had rights to their traditional territories, but said those rights "could only be ascribed" to the Royal Proclamation of 1763. But the Proclamation had recognized Indian territorial rights as pre-existing. The Proclamation confirmed the process of signing treaties with Indian tribes, a pattern dating back to at least 1609. The treaties dealt with pre-existing rights. This misreading of the Proclamation was no accident. Between 1763 and 1888, the natural

---

2 R.S.C. 1970, c. I-6 [R.S.C. 1985, c. I-5].

3 *St. Catharines Milling Co. v. R.* (1885), 10 O.R. 196 at 206 (Ch. Div.), aff'd 13 O.A.R. 148 (C.A.), aff'd 13 S.C.R. 577, aff'd *infra*, note 5. See D. Sanders, "The Nishga Case" (1978), 36 *The Advocate* 121; D. Smith, "*Aboriginal Rights A Century Ago*", *The Beaver* (January 1987) Vol. 67, No. 1, p. 4.

4 Gynne J., in *Ontario Mining v. Seybold* (1902), 32 S.C.R. 1 at 19; aff'd [1903] A.C. 73 (P.C.).

5 (1888), 14 A.C. 46 (P.C.).

rights ideas of the treaty tradition had given way to legal positivism. Under positivism, legal rights come from the State. Therefore, the Proclamation was reinterpreted by the Judicial Committee as a grant, under which the state gave rights to Indians.

At the end of the nineteenth century, the prevailing positivist philosophy meant that the choice for the courts was between no Indian rights or granted Indian rights. Within that restrictive framework, the Judicial Committee came down on the side of the Indians. But what was given with one hand (granted rights) was partly taken away by the other. The rights were less than a fee simple title. They were a "personal and usufructuary right, dependent upon the goodwill of the sovereign" (words which have never been given clear meaning). And Indian territorial rights were non-transferable. Decisions after *St. Catharines* were less positive. In *R. v. Syliboy*,[6] a lower court ruled that treaties had no legal meaning or force, a decision referred to by the federal government as authoritative for decades. In *Point v. Dibblee*,[7] a lower court ruled that the government was not bound by the *Indian Act* and could give away reserve lands.

The first sign of changing attitudes came in a hunting rights case in Alberta in 1932.[8] Indian rights in the area had been recognized in the documents transferring Rupert's Land to Canada, in Treaty Seven and in the Indian hunting rights provisions in the *Constitution Act, 1930*.[9] Wesley, an Indian, was charged with killing a deer for food in violation of provincial game laws. Because of the clear provisions of the *Constitution Act, 1930*, any judge should have acquitted Wesley. Instead the trial judge treated the provincial game law as superior to the Constitution. This legally absurd ruling was overturned by the Alberta appeal court. Mr. Justice McGillivray took the opportunity to review at length the recognition of Indian rights in the Articles of Capitulation of Montreal, the Royal Proclamation of 1763, the transfer of Rupert's Land, the negotiations and terms of Treaty Seven and the *Constitution Act, 1930*. The decision stressed the history of recognition of Indian rights in Canadian law and a wish to uphold the honour of the Crown in its dealings with the Indian tribes. McGillivray showed some passion for the issue, using multiple arguments in favour of Indian hunting rights.

---

6 [1929] 1 D.L.R. 307 (N.S. Co. Ct.). The decision was specifically criticized by Dickson C.J., in *R. v. Simon*, [1985] 2 S.C.R. 387 at 399.

7 [1934] O.R. 142 (S.C.).

8 *R. v. Wesley*, [1932] 4 D.L.R. 774 (Alta. C.A.); the decision is discussed in D. Sanders, "The Queen's Promises", in L.A. Knafla, *Law and Justice in a New Land* (Toronto: Carswell, 1986) 100.

9 1930 (U.K.), C. 26, reprinted in R.S.C. 1970, App. II, c. 25 [R.S.C. 1985, App. II, c. 26].

A second decision in the 1930s enforced treaty rights.[10] Treaty Six promised a "medicine chest" at the home of the Indian agent. Indian Affairs spent money on health services and medicines for members of the Mistawasis band in Saskatchewan and deducted the cost from the band's own funds which were held by the federal government. Chief Dreaver sued for an accounting. The Exchequer Court ruled that the "medicine chest" promise obligated the government to supply medicines at no cost to the band. The decision represented both a liberal interpretation of treaty terms and judicial enforcement of treaty promises. The decision never made the law reports, suggesting it was an oddity, of no future interest to judges and lawyers.

There were curious developments in the Northwest Territories in the 1950s and 1960s, then the edge of the known world for most Canadians. The Northwest Territories had very traditional Indian and Inuit populations with high dependence on hunting, fishing and trapping. The territorial judge was a Prairie populist, Jack Sissons, formerly a Conservative member of Parliament and a vocal critic of the "bright boys" who he said tried to run the North from their ivory towers in Ottawa.[11] He made rulings adapting criminal law to the harsh realities of northern Inuit life and upholding hunting rights and traditional family law. But only his innovation on Inuit customary adoptions has endured. In the *Katie* case in 1961, Sissons recognized Inuit customary adoptions as legally valid, without benefit of precedent or legal theory:

> The Eskimos, and particularly those in outlying settlements and distant camps, are clinging to their culture and way of life which they have found to be good. These people are in process of cultural change and have a right to retain whatever they like of their culture until they are prepared of their own free will to accept a new culture. In particular, although there may be some strange features in Eskimo adoption custom which the experts cannot understand or appreciate, it is good and has stood the test of many centuries and these people should not be forced to abandon it and it should be recognized by the Court.[12]

Sissons systematically registered Inuit customary adoptions during the various circuits of the court. After initial resistance, this new system was accepted by the child welfare authorities in the Northwest Territories. In the end it was a pleasing success story. The legality of customary adoptions

---

10 *Dreaver v. R.*, April 10, 1935, Angers J. (Ex. Ct.).

11 See his autobiography, J. Sissons, *Judge of the Far North* (Toronto: McClelland & Stewart, 1968).

12 *Re Katie* (1961), 32 D.L.R. (2d) 686 at 687 (N.W.T. Terr. Ct.). Other cases dealing with customary adoptions are *Re Beaulieu* (1969), 3 D.L.R. (3d) 479 (N.W.T. Terr. Ct.); *Re Wah-Shee* (1975), 57 D.L.R. (3d) 743 (N.W.T. S.C.); *Re Tagornak* (1984), 1 C.N.L.R. 185 (N.W.T. S.C.); *Michell v. Dennis*, [1984] 2 W.W.R. 499 (B.C. S.C.).

was challenged in the *Deborah* case,[13] the first time natural parents sought to reverse a customary adoption. Mr. Justice William Morrow, Sisson's successor, knew this case would be appealed and was anxious to protect the judicial innovation. His judgment gave statistics on the number of recognition orders that had been made since the *Katie* case,[14] to make sure the appeal court realized that Inuit customary adoptions were now a well-established part of the legal system in the Northwest Territories.

The Court of Appeal upheld the recognition system, simply noting that custom had always been regarded as a source of law in the British common law tradition. This was both true and completely novel. The early common law had developed in England by incorporating custom, but no Canadian court had ever based a decision on custom found in the new world.[15] What were the implications of the ruling? Could property rights be based on custom? When land claims began to be argued in the courts, the arguments relied on the historical recognition of Indian territorial rights by British and Canadian authorities. Alternative approaches, such as reliance on custom or on theories of colonial acquisition, were not invoked.

While the customary adoption cases were never appealed to the Supreme Court of Canada, Sisson's decisions on Indian and Inuit hunting rights were appealed and overturned by the Supreme Court over and over again. The major case has a folkloric character. Michael Sikyea, an Indian on welfare and recovering from tuberculosis, shot a duck for food while hunting muskrats. Treaty Eight promised hunting and fishing rights. Sikyea was charged under the federal *Migratory Birds Convention Act*.[16] Sissons wrote:

> It is notorious that a few years ago a government official spoke to one of the local Indian chiefs and pointed out that shooting ducks in the spring was contrary to the Migratory Birds Convention. The chief asked what was this convention and was told it was a treaty between Canada and the United States. He then queried, "Did the Indians sign the treaty?" The reply was, "No." "Then" the chief declared, "We shoot the ducks."
>
> The Indians have their constitutional rights and their own treaty preserving their ancient hunting rights.
>
> The old chief was on sound ground. There is or should be as much or

---

13 *Re Deborah* (1972), 5 W.W.R. 203 (N.W.T. C.A.).

14 *Supra*, note 12.

15 There had been earlier recognition of customary marriages both judicially and in the practices of the Department of Indian Affairs, but that had lapsed before the Northwest Territories cases and played no role in them. The recognition had not been based on the recognition of custom in English law. See D. Sanders, "Family Law and Native People" (Law Reform Commission of Canada, 1975) unpublished background paper.

16 R.S.C. 1952, c. 179 [now R.S.C. 1970, c. M-12 (R.S.C. 1985, c. M-7)].

more sanctity to a treaty between Canada and its Indians as to a treaty between Canada and the United States.[17]

Sissons was not clear on the legal character of the Indian hunting rights or the treaty. He described the hunting rights as "vested" and "ancient". He seemed to give the treaty legal force by the Royal Proclamation of 1763, which, he said, applied in the Northwest Territories. He acquitted Sikyea by narrowly construing the *Migratory Birds Convention Act* and finding a number of technical problems with the Crown's case, including a failure to prove that the duck in question was a wild duck.

Sissons was overturned on appeal.[18] Mr. Justice Johnson spoke of an Indian "right" to hunt, though his judgment is unclear on its legal character. He ruled that the Royal Proclamation did not apply in the Northwest Territories and found the *Migratory Birds Convention Act* in clear conflict with any Indian hunting "right". He expressed regret that the Queen's promises had not been honoured and that the government had apparently acted absent-mindedly:

> How are we to explain this apparent breach of faith on the part of the government, for I cannot think it can be described in any other terms? This cannot be described as a minor or insignificant curtailment of these treaty rights, for game birds have always been a most plentiful, a most reliable and a readily obtainable food in large areas of Canada. I cannot believe that the government of Canada realized that in implementing the Convention they were at the same time breaching the treaties that they had made with the Indians. It is much more likely that these obligations under the treaties were overlooked — a case of the left hand having forgotten what the right hand had done.[19]

The decision of the Supreme Court of Canada is now embarrassing.[20] Mr. Justice Hall spent two pages discussing whether it had been adequately proven that the duck was wild, not tame, and dismissed the other issues in two sentences, simply agreeing with the judgment of Mr. Justice Johnson. The Supreme Court decision provoked a satire called "*R. v. Ojibway*",[21]

---

17 *R. v. Sikyea* (1962), 40 W.W.R. 494 at 496 (N.W.T. Terr. Ct.), rev'd *infra*, note 18.

18 *R. v. Sikyea* (1964), 46 W.W.R. 65 (N.W.T. C.A.), aff'd *infra* note 20.

19 *Ibid.* at 74. Johnson did not deal with s. 88 of the *Indian Act* (then s. 87) and it was, therefore, not dealt with explicitly in the Supreme Court of Canada judgment, which simply adopted Johnson's reasoning on most points. The section was argued before the Supreme Court of Canada. The omission in the judgments is odd, for s. 88 was used by the Ontario Court of Appeal in *A.G. Canada v. George* (1964), 45 D.L.R. (2d) 705 (Ont. C.A.), aff'd *infra*, note 22. to uphold Indian hunting rights against the *Migratory Birds Convention Act.* When *George* came before the Supreme Court of Canada, the majority took *Sikyea* as rejecting a s. 88 argument. Cartwright C.J. dissented on the point, suggesting it had not been properly considered by the court in *Sikyea.*

20 [1964] S.C.R. 642.

21 (1965-66), 8 *C.L.Q.* 137.

where an accused was convicted under the *Small Birds Act* for shooting a horse covered with feathers in Queen's Park. Most readers did not realize the satire mocked the Supreme Court decision in *Sikyea*.

The *Sikyea* decision and its progeny established that Indian hunting and fishing rights could be taken away by general federal legislation.[22] There was no need for Parliament to demonstrate an intention to end Indian rights. It did not matter whether the hunting was protected by treaty, took place on a reserve or occurred in one of the three Prairie provinces (and therefore under the provisions of the *Constitution Act, 1930*). Indian hunting rights were upheld against provincial laws but only on reserves or where the rights were enforceable under the *Constitution Act, 1930*, or under section 88 of the *Indian Act*.[23] Indians had rights only if they flowed from the division of powers, the Constitution or legislation.

In British Columbia, the hunting and fishing rights cases of the 1960s were attempts to reopen the aboriginal title issue. There are no treaties for most of British Columbia, and Indians have asserted territorial rights from the early days of colonial settlement. The dispute has a long history, with federal plans for a reference to the Supreme Court of Canada early in the century, and hearings by a Special Joint Committee of the Senate and House of Commons in 1927. After the Second World War, Canada planned to establish an Indian claims commission, modelled on one in the United States. Even though the idea was supported by both the Liberal and Conservative parties in the 1960s, no commission was ever established.

The British Columbia aboriginal title issue was argued in *R. v. White*[24] in the context of hunting rights. The Indians were covered by one of fourteen small treaties on Vancouver Island. The provincial lawyers argued that the document was not a treaty, merely a private transaction with the Hudson's Bay Company. Tom Berger for the Indians argued aboriginal rights, viewing the treaty promise as simply a confirmation of the aboriginal right to hunt. The county court judge agreed and one judge of the British Columbia Court of Appeal gave a long judgment upholding Indian aboriginal rights. The Supreme Court of Canada in one short paragraph held the treaty enforceable against provincial law by section 88 of the *Indian Act*.[25]

The *White* case had the effect of reviving the aboriginal rights issue

---

22 *R. v. George*, [1966] S.C.R. 267; *Daniels v. White*, [1968] S.C.R. 517; *R. v. Derriksan* (1976), 71 D.L.R. (3d) 159 (S.C.C.); *R. v. Jack*, [1980] 1 S.C.R. 294.

23 *R. v. White* (1965), 52 D.L.R. (2d) 481 (S.C.C.); *R. v. Moosehunter*, [1981] 1 S.C.R. 282; *Dick v. R.*, [1985] 2 S.C.R. 309.

24 *Supra*, note 23.

25 Judgment of Norris J.A. in the B.C. Court of Appeal (1964), 52 W.W.R. 193, aff'd *supra*, note 23. The decision in *Dick v. R., supra*, note 23, makes it clear that s. 88 of the *Indian Act* (then s. 87) was operative.

in Canada. In the same period, aboriginal and treaty rights issues were being reborn in litigation in various parts of the world. Arthur Laing, the Minister of Indian Affairs, expressed some willingness to discuss the aboriginal title issue, but only if the various tribes in British Columbia united in one negotiating team. Given the very unusual tribal diversity in British Columbia, this was an unrealistic demand. When attempts to form a province-wide organization failed, the Nishga tribe initiated their own court action seeking a declaration of continuing ownership of their traditional territories. Frank Calder, the head of the Nishga Tribal Council, was the first Indian member of a provincial legislature. He hired fellow New Democratic Party member Tom Berger to handle the case.

Litigation was a risky strategy, and other Indian leaders did not support the Nishga initiative. The Supreme Court of Canada had consistently ruled against Indian and Inuit rights, with the single exception of Berger's *White* case, which was based, in the end, on a provision of the *Indian Act*. Yet what was there to lose? None of the politicians recognized aboriginal rights. In June 1969, the federal government presented a White Paper on Indian policy: the claims commission idea was abandoned, aboriginal title claims were rejected and both the treaties and Indian special status were to be phased out. The White Paper mobilized Indian opposition. The reformist new government of Pierre Elliot Trudeau was embarrassed by the unexpected Indian opposition and began funding Indian political organizations. A system of provincial and federal organizations representing Indians, Inuit and Metis rapidly came into existence.[26]

Aboriginal title issues converged in the mid 1970s, mainly in response to energy projects in the North. Quebec announced the huge James Bay hydroelectric project. The federal government sponsored plans for the Mackenzie valley natural gas pipeline, touted as the costliest private project in history. With these and other projects on the public agenda, the Supreme Court of Canada gave judgment in the *Calder* case in January 1973.[27] The court split evenly on the question of the survival of Nishga aboriginal title. Mr. Justice Hall, who nine years earlier had dismissed Sikyea's treaty right to hunt, devoted his last months on the court to writing a judgment supporting the Nishga. Like Mr. Justice Sissons, he was a tory Prairie populist. Until the last minute, Hall thought he had a majority. But Mr. Justice Pigeon ruled solely on a procedural question. There was no majority on the aboriginal title issue. Hall thought it was the James Bay controversy that led Pigeon to limit his decision.

Calder significantly altered the framework for arguing aboriginal

---

26 S.M. Weaver, *Making Canadian Indian Policy : The Hidden Agenda* (Toronto: Univ. of Toronto Press, 1980).

27 *Calder v. British Columbia*, [1973] S.C.R. 313.

rights. By the *St. Catharines Milling* case,[28] there were no Indian legal rights unless they were recognized by some British or Canadian action. The issue for British Columbia had become trapped in the historical-legal question whether the Royal Proclamation of 1763 applied west of the Rocky mountains. Indian rights could not exist in British Columbia, the analysis went, if the area was *terra incognita* in 1763, that is land not known to the British. The fact the land was known to and controlled by the tribes was irrelevant. The issue was British law, not Indian realities. Berger tried to transform the framework of analysis by arguing that the British common law recognized the doctrine of Indian aboriginal title to land. He found evidence of common law recognition in the treaty tradition, the Royal Proclamation of 1763 and in early nineteenth century decisions of the United States Supreme Court.[29] He argued a general tradition of British recognition of Indian rights, which meant that specific recognition of Indian rights in British Columbia was not required. Berger relied on the United States judicial decisions of the early nineteenth century. The cases from the late nineteenth century and most of the twentieth century supported the other side.

Mr. Justice Judson, in the most quoted passage from the case, stated:

> Although I think that it is clear that Indian title in British Columbia cannot owe its origin to the Proclamation of 1763, the fact is that when the settlers came, the Indians were there, organized in societies and occupying the land as their forefathers had done for centuries. That is what Indian title means and it does not help one in the solution of this problem to call it a "personal or usufructuary right". What they are asserting in this action is that they have a right to continue to live on their lands as their forefathers had lived and that this right has never been lawfully extinguished. There can be no question that this right was "dependent on the goodwill of the Sovereign".[30]

This was the most radical pronouncement in the judgment. It grounded Indian rights on Indian organization and occupation, without regard to general or specific recognition in British or Canadian law. But while Judson started from Indian occupation and control, he did not in fact rule that historic Indian control of territories meant they had legal rights to those territories in British and Canadian law. He slid by the question. Whether or not they had rights, he upheld the general land legislation enacted in British Columbia before 1871.

Mr. Justice Hall was concerned with bringing aboriginal title within positivist assumptions. He argued that the Royal Proclamation of 1763

---

28 *Supra*, note 3.
29 The Marshall judgments are discussed in Burke, "The Cherokee Cases: A Study in Law, Politics and Morality" (1968-69), 21 *Stanford L. Rev.* 500.
30 *Calder, supra*, note 27 at 328.

applied to British Columbia. With some fervour, he argued three other positivist ways of upholding Nishga title. The Royal Proclamation came to apply to British Columbia after 1763, because like the *Magna Carta*, it "followed the flag". In any case, it was simply confirmatory of the common law, which recognized aboriginal title. In any case, uniform practice bound Canada to treat Indians in British Columbia like the Indians in the Prairies. Hall, like Sissons and McGillivray before him, gave multiple reasons for upholding Indian rights. He then argued that those property rights could only be taken away by explicit legislative acts. The pre-confederation land legislation did not meet that requirement.

It remains an anomaly that Mr. Justice Judson, who rejected Nishga rights, accepted that those rights would arise from Nishga realities, while Mr. Justice Hall, who upheld Nishga rights, asserted them as based on British and Canadian law.

There were other anomalies. Mr. Justice Judson ruled against Nishga aboriginal title, but went on to cite United States cases to the effect that aboriginal title could be taken without compensation. Mr. Justice Hall ruled in favour of Nishga title, but went on to assert that a taking would require compensation. This indicated that both judges saw the case as about a settlement, not about an assertion of title. But the legal formulation of the issue could not acknowledge that the Nishga were seeking a negotiated settlement.

In one passage, Hall seemed concerned with the integrity of British colonialism:

> In respect to this Proclamation, it can be said that when other exploring nations were showing a ruthless disregard of native rights, England adopted a remarkably enlightened attitude towards the Indians of North America.[31]

Hall was vindicating English colonialism, seeing British Columbia as an anomaly. The honour of the Crown was still in issue.

What did the *Calder* decision mean? Berger argued that both Judson and Hall had recognized Indian title to land, differing only on how that title could be taken away.[32] Eight months later, the Quebec Superior Court ordered the halt to the James Bay hydroelectric project on the basis of unextinguished Indian and Inuit title, but in the context of recognition of Indian rights in the *Quebec Boundaries Extension Act* of 1912. Quebec

---

31 *Ibid.* at 395. The honour of the Crown also features in the dissenting judgment of Cartwright C.J., in *R. v. George*, *supra*, note 22, and in *R. v. Taylor* (1981), 34 O.R. (2d) 360 (C.A.).

32 *Northern Frontier, Northern Homeland* (Report of the Mackenzie Valley Pipeline Inquiry) (Supply & Services Canada, 1977) at 165; the same analysis of the *Calder* decision occurs in *Living Treaties; Lasting Agreements* (Report of the Task Force to Review Comprehensive Claims Policy) (Department of Indian Affairs, December 1985) at 7, 44.

officials said the injunction cost them one million dollars a day. The Court of Appeal hastily lifted the injunction, pending a full hearing. The dispute was resolved by a negotiated settlement.[33] The Northwest Territories Supreme Court found a claim to aboriginal rights registrable in their land titles system. The ruling was overturned on points of statutory interpretation.[34] The Federal Court upheld Inuit aboriginal rights in the Northwest Territories, while restricting them to hunting rights.[35] Aboriginal rights claims were now serious legal issues, though the initial set of decisions was inconclusive.

Prime Minister Trudeau, a former law professor, read the judgments in the *Calder* case[36] and was said to have been more impressed by Hall's reasoning than Judson's. It was politically opportune for his minority government to shift policy on aboriginal rights claims, for both opposition parties said they supported the Indians. In August 1973, the government announced a policy of negotiating settlements of aboriginal title claims in major non-treaty areas of the country. The focus was on British Columbia, northern Quebec and the Northern Territories. Southern Quebec and the Maritimes were excluded from the policy.[37]

In the spring of 1974, the federal government appointed Tom Berger, now a judge, to conduct an inquiry on the proposed Mackenzie Valley pipeline. Berger held community hearings in every Indian village, and skillfully organized national media coverage. The inquiry gave Indian claims their highest profile in modern Canadian history. In 1977, his report was published, with dozens of photographs and a lucid, readable text.[38] No inquiry report had ever been so well presented. It became a best seller. It supported Indian claims and killed the pipeline.

The pressures for frontier development eased as the world economy went into recession. The period produced the James Bay and Northern Quebec Agreement of 1975, the Northeastern Quebec Agreement of 1978 (a supplementary agreement to the James Bay settlement) and the agreement with the Inuvialuit of the Western Arctic in 1984. Agreements

---

33 Diamond, "Aboriginal Rights: The James Bay Experience", in M. Boldt *et al.*, eds., *The Quest for Justice: Aboriginal Peoples and Aboriginal Rights* (Toronto: Univ. of Toronto Press, 1985) 265.

34 *Re Paulette*, [1973] 6 W.W.R. 97 (N.W.T. S.C.), rev'd on other grounds [1976] 2 W.W.R. 193 (N.W.T. C.A.), aff'd (*sub nom. Paulette v. R.*), [1977] 2 S.C.R. 628.

35 *Baker Lake v. Min. of Indian Affairs & Northern Development* (1979), 107 D.L.R. (3d) 513 (F.C.T.D.).

36 *Supra*, note 27.

37 See *In All Fairness: A Native Claims Policy* (Supply and Services Canada, 1981); *Living Treaties: Lasting Agreements* (Report of the Task Force to Review Comprehensive Claims Policy, Department of Indian Affairs) (December 1985); *Comprehensive Land Claims Policy* (Supply & Services Canada, 1987).

38 *Supra*, note 32.

in principle to settle Indian land claims in the Yukon and Northwest Territories were signed in 1988, and negotions continue on the final terms. Some significant settlements of "specific claims" have occurred in various parts of the country. But many issues flowing from the litigation and the government policy statements of the mid-1970s have not been dealt with.

In 1978, Prime Minister Trudeau reopened discussions on the Constitution. The National Indian Brotherhood sought inclusion in the constitutional reform process and Indians became major players in the constitutional fights.[39] The 1982 Constitutional amendments include three Indian rights sections. Section 35 recognizes and affirms existing aboriginal and treaty rights. Section 25 protects the rights of the aboriginal peoples from the egalitarian provisions of the Charter. Section 37 promised one (extended to four) First Minister's Conferences on aboriginal rights. The Conference of 1983 agreed to amendments confirming that land claims agreements were "treaties" within sections 35 and 25 and requiring a First Minister's Conference with aboriginal representation preceding any amendment to constitutional provisions mentioning aboriginal peoples.

Indian assertions of a right to self-government clearly emerged in the North around the time of the Berger inquiry. Berger's report supported those assertions. Indians developed new terminology, talking of "Indian government" and Indian "First Nations". In 1983, a special parliamentary committee urged constitutional recognition of the right of Indian First Nations to self-government.[40] Non-Indian politicians adopted the new terminology. The First Ministers Conferences of 1984, 1985 and 1987 focussed on self-government. No federal or provincial politician directly opposed the concept but, in the end, there was no agreement on a constitutional amendment recognizing the right.

As the constitutional conferences were being played out, the courts re-emerged as the major forum. In 1983, 1984 and 1985, the Supreme Court of Canada rendered judgments dealing with the *Indian Act*, reserve lands and treaties.

In *Nowegijick v. R.*,[41] the Supreme Court of Canada dealt with the interpretation of the *Indian Act*. In issue was a tax exemption section originally drafted before Canada had income taxation. Longstanding federal policy treated the section as exempting income earned on a reserve. While Nowegijick had earned his income off the reserve, he lived on reserve and worked for a band-owned company whose office was on the reserve.

---

39 D. Sanders, "The Indian Lobby", in K. Banting & R. Simeon, *And No One Cheered: Federalism, Democracy and The Constitution Act* (Toronto: Methuen, 1983) 301.

40 *Report of the Special Committee on Indian Self-Government*, Chairman K. Penner (Supply & Services Canada, 1983).

41 [1983] 1 S.C.R. 29.

Indians were seeking to broaden the interpretation of the *Indian Act* section. The Federal Court of Appeal gutted the section, ruling that it granted no exemption from income taxation. The Supreme Court of Canada upheld the Indian position. Chief Justice Dickson stated:

> It is legal lore that, to be valid, exemptions to tax laws should be clearly expressed. It seems to me, however, that treaties and statutes relating to Indians should be liberally construed and doubtful expressions resolved in favour of the Indians . . . . In *Jones v. Meehan*, 175 U.S. 1 (1899), it was held that Indian treaties "must . . . be construed, not according to the technical meaning of [their] words . . . but in the sense in which they would naturally be understood by the Indians".[42]

This was the first Canadian case to state a special doctrine of interpretation of statutes and treaties in cases involving Indian rights. It was a clear departure from the *Sikyea* line of cases,[43] where any general federal legislation could take away Indian hunting and fishing rights. It was also inconsistent with the argument accepted by Judson in *Calder*[44] that general pre-Confederation land legislation had ended any Indian territorial rights in British Columbia.

In 1984, the Supreme Court of Canada decided the *Guerin* case.[45] The Musqueam Band had sued the federal government for damages for the mismanagement of surrendered reserve lands. The federal lawyers argued that there could be no federal trust responsibility because (a) the property involved did not belong to the Indian band but to the government, and (b) any trust was a political trust (or a "higher" trust), and unenforceable in the courts. The Supreme Court of Canada held that Indians had a legal interest in reserve lands, described as a "historic reality", a "a pre-existing legal right" and as arising out of "a longstanding connection" with the land. The Indian right was not created by the Royal Proclamation or by the *Indian Act*. In the course of his judgment, Chief Justice Dickson stated:

> In *Calder v. Attorney General of British Columbia* . . . this Court recognized aboriginal title as a legal right derived from the Indians' historic occupation and possession of their tribal lands. With Judson and Hall JJ. writing the principal judgments, the Court split three-three on the major issue of whether the Nishga Indians' aboriginal title to their ancient tribal territory had been extinguished by general land enactments in British Columbia. The Court also split on the issue of whether the Royal Proclamation of 1763 was applicable to Indian lands in that province. Judson and Hall JJ. were in agreement, however, that aboriginal title existed in Canada (at least where it had not been extinguished by appropriate legislative action) independently of the Royal

---

42 *Ibid.* at 36.
43 *Supra*, notes 17, 18, 20.
44 *Supra*, note 27.
45 *Supra*, note 1.

Proclamation. Judson J. stated expressly that the Proclamation was not the "exclusive" source of Indian title. . . . Hall J. said . . . that "aboriginal title does not depend on treaty, executive order or legislative enactment".[46]

Dickson noted that the ruling in *Calder* "went beyond" *St. Catharines Milling*.[47] And Dickson went beyond *Calder*. In *Calder*, Judson never said that aboriginal title was legally recognized and Hall grounded aboriginal title in the common law and the Royal Proclamation of 1763. Now, 11 years later, Dickson reinterpreted *Calder* as (a) upholding a legal Indian title to traditional lands on the basis of pre-existing occupation and (b) as dividing on whether the title was extinguished by general land legislation. The ruling on Indian title was an essential part of the decision in *Guerin*. It was the basis for Dickson's conclusion that the Musqueam band had legal rights to their reserve lands. While the outcome was hardly startling, the court was giving recognition to pre-existing rights, as such, for the first time in its history. And it was clearly signalling the seriousness with which it regarded aboriginal title claims.

The next year, the Supreme Court of Canada gave judgment in a treaty hunting rights case.[48] In issue were hunting rights under a 1752 treaty, the same treaty held to be meaningless in the 1929 *Syliboy* decision.[49] *Syliboy* was reargued. The Crown argued that the document was not a treaty, it had been terminated by subsequent hostilities, it did not promise hunting rights (only allowing the pre-existing "liberty" to hunt to continue) and off-reserve hunting rights had been extinguished by widespread non-Indian settlement. The Supreme Court repeated themes from *Nowegijick*[50] and *Guerin*. Treaties were to be interpreted in favour of Indian rights. The treaty confirmed a pre-existing right to hunt. As in *White*[51] twenty years earlier, the treaty promise was upheld against provincial law. The *Sikyea*[52] line of cases, which allowed casual termination of Indian rights by federal law, were cited and distinguished, without any indication of disapproval.

The Nova Scotia Court of Appeal said the treaty was terminated by

---

46 *Ibid.* at 376-377.

47 *Supra*, note 3.

48 *R. v. Simon, supra*, note 6. Other pro-treaty decisions are *R. v. Taylor, supra*, note 31; *R. v. Bartleman* (1984), 12 D.L.R. (4th) 73 (B.C. C.A.); *Sioui v. A.G. Quebec*, [1987] 4 C.N.L.R. 118 (Que. C.A.) leave to appeal to S.C.C. granted (1988), 87 N.R. 80n (S.C.C.)). In *Horse v. R.*, [1988] 1 S.C.R. 187, the court was invited to hold that treaty hunting rights co-existed with private property rights of farmers. Mr. Justice Estey repeated the favourable interpretation statements from *Nowegijick, supra*, note 41, and *Simon*, but rejected the Indian argument.

49 *Supra*, note 6.

50 *Supra*, note 41.

51 *Supra*, note 23.

52 *Supra*, notes 17, 18, 20.

subsequent hostilities, taking that as a rule of international law. In the Supreme Court of Canada, all counsel took the position that the treaties were not international law documents, while arguing, in the alternative, that international law rules supported their particular position on the termination or non-termination of the treaty. Chief Justice Dickson rejected the idea that the Treaty had been terminated by subsequent hostilities. He stated: "An Indian treaty is unique; it is an agreement *sui generis* which is neither created nor terminated according to the rules of international law."[53] The description of an Indian treaty as *sui generis* had been suggested by counsel for Simon to counter the argument of termination by subsequent hostilities. The rejection of the rules of international law, while stated generally, was in that context. None of the counsel had cited or argued any of the international law cases or writings on the status of tribes or of treaties with tribes.

In 1985, two Indian rights arguments were rejected by the Supreme Court of Canada. In both cases, provincial hunting laws were applied to Indians in non-treaty areas, following the earlier decision in *Kruger v. R.*[54] The court was unwilling to create exceptions.

In *Dick v. R.*,[55] the court made it fairly clear that provincial hunting laws only applied in non-treaty situations as a result of the wording of section 88 of the *Indian Act*. Without section 88, provincial hunting laws would not apply to Indians because such laws affected Indians as Indians and were, for that reason, beyond provincial legislative competence. The decision upheld broad federal jurisdiction over Indian rights. It was a straightforward interpretation of section 88 of the *Indian Act*, and, perhaps, it demonstrated the Supreme Court's unease about reversing one of its previous decisions. While the court has changed direction on Indian issues, it has not, to date, reversed a previous ruling.

The second 1985 decision, *Jack v. R.*,[56] is difficult to explain. Evidence established a religious purpose for the hunting. The fresh deer meat was to be burned to satisfy the spirit of an ancestor, believed to be present in the area. Acts to placate spirits of the dead are generally unfamiliar to North Americans, but are widespread in other parts of the world, particularly among tribal peoples. The case arose before the 1982 constitutional amendments protecting freedom of conscience and religion. The Supreme Court was invited to carve out a religious exception to the

---

53 *R. v. Simon, supra*, note 6 at 404.

54 (1977), 75 D.L.R. (3d) 434 (S.C.C.).

55 *Supra*, note 23.

56 *Jack v. R.*, [1985] 2 S.C.R. 332; A. Hayward, "R. v. Jack and Charlie and the Constitution Act, 1982: Religious Freedom and Aboriginal Rights in Canada" (1984), 10 *Queen's L.J.* 165.

provincial hunting law. But the court seemed unconvinced that a valid religious activity was involved and upheld a conviction.

British Columbia has been the source of much of the recent litigation. At the end of 1986, the British Columbia Court of Appeal ruled in *Sparrow v. R.*[57] that Indians had an existing aboriginal right to harvest salmon for food. The federal government had argued that a hundred years of the *Fisheries Act* and regulations had supplanted any aboriginal rights that might have existed. The Court of Appeal found the long history of special provisions for Indian food fishing to be a confirmation or recognition of an aboriginal right, which was now protected by section 35 of the *Constitution Act, 1982.* Another holding of pre-existing aboriginal rights have occured at the Québec provincial court level in *Eastmain Band v. Gilpin.* In question was a curfew for children under 16, something the Band was specifically authorized to enact. Rather than hold that the Band Council, like other municipal level government, only had powers specifically given it, the court upheld the bylaw as within Cree residual sovereignty. Cree legislative rights were not confined to specifically delegated powers.[57a]

In 1984 and 1985, there were highly publicized Indian protests in British Columbia over logging and fishing. A trial judge granted an injunction to prevent the Indian occupation of Meares Island, ruling solidly against Indian aboriginal title claims. But just as he was finishing writing his judgment, Chief Justice Dickson's judgment in *Guerin*[58] was released. The judge refused to believe that Dickson meant what he said about aboriginal title. The issue went to the Court of Appeal where injunctions were granted against both the Indians and the logging company pending a resolution of the aboriginal title issue. By the end of 1988, interim injunctions prevented logging or other activities in four areas of British Columbia on the basis of aboriginal title claims.[59] In May 1987, the trial began in the British Columbia Supreme Court on a major aboriginal title case, brought by the Gitksan Wet'suset'en Tribal Council. The Indians now argued for land and jurisdiction as well as invoke international law.

With this overview in mind, we can examine certain specific issues and developments.

---

57 [1987] 2 W.W.R. 577 (B.C. C.A.), leave to appeal to S.C.C. granted [1987] 4 W.W.R. lxvii (note) (S.C.C.).

57a [1987] 3 C.N.L.R. 54.

58 *Supra*, note 1.

59 *MacMillan Bloedel v. Mullin*, [1985] 3 W.W.R. 577 (B.C.C.A.); *Hunt v. Halcan* (1987), 34 D.L.R. (4th) 504 (B.C.S.C.); but see *A.G. Ontario v. Bear Island Foundation* (1984), 15 D.L.R. (4th) 321 (Ont. H.C.).

2. THE INDIAN, INUIT AND METIS PEOPLES

The *Constitution Act, 1867,* refers to "Indians". The *Constitution Act, 1982* refers to "the Aboriginal Peoples of Canada", defined as including the "Indian, Inuit and Metis Peoples of Canada". Questions have been raised about this shift in terminology, most often about the Metis.

The paradigm of aboriginal policy in North America is

(a) a treaty with an Indian collectivity,
(b) an Indian reserve,
(c) an Indian band or tribal council,
(d) federal Indian legislation concerned with the reserve system, and
(e) a federal Indian department concerned with the on-reserve population.

There are two variant aboriginal populations in North America, the Inuit and the Aleut. Both are located in Arctic or sub-Arctic areas where neither Canada nor the United States had extended their historic aboriginal policies. The different treatment was not between Inuit and Aleut on the one hand and Indians on the other, for traditional policies had not been extended to any aboriginal group in the North. The Inuit and Aleut have been held to be in the same legal category as Indians. The Supreme Court of Canada ruled that Eskimos were "Indians" for constitutional purposes in a 1939 reference case.[60] Eskimos and Aleut were included with Indians in the *Alaska Native Claims Settlement Act* of 1972.[61] Inuit and Indians obtained parallel land claims settlements in the James Bay and Northern Québec Agreement of 1975. Land claims proposals in the Northwest Territories involve the idea of separate Inuit and Indian regional governments, Nunavut and Denendah. Indian reserves made sense in the context of fertile lands and agricultural settlement. They made no sense in the North. In the last twenty years a distinctive policy paradigm has emerged for the North, with regional aboriginal governments in Greenland, Northern Québec, and the North Slope in Alaska.

In summary, Aleut, Inuit and Indians are in the same constitutional category in the United States and Canada, but the policy paradigm of Indian policy developed in the South does not work in the North. A new policy paradigm of regional aboriginal governments in the North has emerged, but is not yet uniformly in place. The established examples are in areas of almost exclusive aboriginal population. They do not give guidance for areas like Northern Scandinavia and Yukon where there are substantial non-indigenous populations.

---

60 *Re Eskimos,* [1939] 2 D.L.R. 417 (S.C.C.).

61 For an analysis of the Alaska settlement and its current problems see T.R. Berger, *Village Journey: The Report of the Alaska Native Review Commission* (Hill & Wang, 1986).

The Metis are a unique Canadian population. From 1670 to 1870, the vast Prairie region of Canada was a fur trade empire managed by great trading companies. By 1870, a distinct mixed blood "Metis" population had emerged from unions of fur traders and Indians, typically French men and Cree women. The Hudson's Bay Company post at Red River was the regional centre and the focal point of the Metis "New Nation". The Metis defended their autonomy against the Selkirk settlers and against the Hudson's Bay Company. In 1869-1870, they resisted incorporation of the region into Canada without special recognition of Metis rights. Riel wanted a Metis controlled province and provincial control of Crown lands. The federal government agreed to create the new province of Manitoba, but retained the Crown lands. The *Manitoba Act, 1870*[62] established a system of homestead-style land grants for Metis, justified on a stated recognition of a "half-breed" share in "Indian title". The federal government promoted rapid European settlement in Manitoba and the Prairie West, resulting in a dispersal of most Metis west and north. Speculation in Metis land grants was encouraged by the government and profited leading settler families.[63]

The Metis history is distinctive, creating problems in any re-assertion of Metis rights. Metis political agitation in the 1930s led to the establishment of some Metis reserves in Saskatchewan and Alberta. The Alberta "settlements" have survived and are governed by provincial legislation, a local variant of the basic aboriginal policy paradigm.[64] Current litigation seeks to reopen the legal questions around the land grants system formulated in 1870 in the *Manitoba Act.*[65]

While Inuit are "Indians" and mixed-blood Indians are "Indians", there has been no formal resolution of the legal question of whether "Metis" are "Indians" for the purposes of federal legislative jurisdiction over "Indians, and Lands reserved for the Indians". In the First Ministers Conferences on aboriginal rights, held between 1983 and 1987, there were discussions on the issue. The federal government stated their view that Metis were under provincial jurisdiction. Alberta, the only province with a system of Metis reserves, agreed. The Native Council of Canada had always argued in favour of federal jurisdiction. But the Native Council had ceased to represent most Metis and the new Metis National Council

---

62 1870, c. 3, reprinted in R.S.C. 1970, App. II, No. 8 [R.S.C. 1985, App. II, No. 8].

63 See D. Sanders, "Metis Claims in Western Canada", in H.W. Daniels, *The Forgotten People: Metis and Non-status Indian Land Claims* (Ottawa: Native Council of Canada, 1979).

64 See J. Sawchuk et al., *Metis Land Rights in Alberta: A Political History* (Metis Assn. of Alberta, 1981), c. 6.

65 See *Dumont v. A.G. Canada* (1987), 48 Man. R. (2d) 4 (Q.B.), rev'd (1988), 52 Man. R. (2d) 291 (C.A.); D.N. Sprague, "Government Lawlessness in the Administration of Manitoba Land Claims, 1870-1887" (1980), 10 *Man. L.J.* 415.

contained elements satisfied with provincial jurisdiction. The idea of a reference to the Supreme Court of Canada on the question was discussed, but not pursued.[66]

If the federal government enacted legislation dealing with Metis, the courts would most likely uphold the legislation as within federal jurisdiction over "Indians". But the federal government, which has spent money on Metis for two decades, shows no interest in Metis legislation. Without federal legislation, Metis are effectively no different from non-aboriginal Canadians. By default, they and other "non-status Indians" are within provincial legislative jurisdiction.[67]

3. SPECIAL RIGHTS AND EQUALITY

Section 91(24) of the *Constitution Act, 1867*, assumed the continuation of special legislation for Indians and Indian lands. No norm of equality was established in Canadian law until the *Canadian Bill of Rights* of 1960. The Supreme Court of Canada applied the *Bill of Rights* in the famous *Drybones* case of 1969 to invalidate a minor provision of the *Indian Act* prohibiting public drunkenness by Indians.[68] But the real fight over special Indian legislation and equality norms came in *A.G. Canada v. Lavell*.[69] The *Indian Act* discriminated on the basis of sex in defining who was an Indian for the purposes of reserve residency and federal Indian programs. Reflecting the nineteenth century British and Canadian norms, the *Indian Act* made the male the head of the nuclear family, with the wife and children taking his status. Unlike the public drunkenness provision challenged in *Drybones*, the sections in question in *Lavell* were a central part of the scheme of the *Indian Act*. The Supreme Court of Canada deferred to the mandate

---

66 See D. Sanders, "An Uncertain Path: The Aboriginal Constitutional Conferences", in J.M. Weiler & R.M. Elliot, eds., *Litigating the Values of a Nation: The Canadian Charter of Rights and Freedoms* (Toronto: Carswell, 1986), p. 62 particularly at 67–69. The position of the Metis National Council on federal jurisdiction was debated at an annual convention in 1986, with Saskatchewan Metis pressing for an assertion of federal jurisdiction, but Alberta Metis opposing: "Government Jurisdiction a Hot Topic", *Windspeaker* (Edmonton: October 3, 1986), p. 5.

67 There is an anomaly that provincial legislation dealing with kinship (*Natural Parents v. Superintendent of Child Welfare*, [1976] 2 S.C.R. 751) and with hunting rights (*Dick v. R.*, *supra*, note 23) seem to have been held to deal with "Indians as Indians" and therefore cannot apply to Indians without federal incorporation by reference through s. 88 of the *Indian Act*. Yet Metis, non-status Indians and Inuit, who could be brought within federal legislative jurisdiction over Indians, have no exemption from such provincial laws. The outcome is sensible, but the legal theory is not yet in place.

68 *R. v. Drybones*, [1970] S.C.R. 282.

69 [1974] S.C.R. 1349.

for special Indian legislation in the *Constitution Act, 1867*, allowing the sexual discrimination to stand.

The Supreme Court judgment did not end the controversy and the sexual discrimination in the *Indian Act* became the leading equality issue in the country. The issue was taken to the United Nations Human Rights Committee under the provisions of the *International Covenant on Civil and Political Rights*. The Committee avoided the sexual discrimination question, ruling that the complainant had been denied her right as a member of a cultural minority to associate with other members of her cultural group.[70] Internationally, the decision is seen as the major success of the individual complaint procedure under the Optional Protocol to the *International Covenant on Civil and Political Rights*.

In the debates on the *Charter of Rights and Freedoms*, two examples of the need for the Charter were used: the wartime relocation of Japanese-Canadians and the sexual discrimination in the *Indian Act*. Yet each of the various drafts of the new constitutional provisions had some kind of saving clause, protecting Indian special rights from other provisions of the Charter. The final wording, found in section 25, gives sweeping protection to Indian special status:

> The guarantee in this Charter of certain rights and freedoms shall not be construed so as to abrogate or derogate from any aboriginal treaty or other rights or freedoms that pertain to the aboriginal peoples of Canada including
>
> (a) any rights or freedoms that have been recognized by the Royal Proclamation of October 7, 1763; and
> (b) any rights or freedoms that now exist by way of land claims agreements or may be so acquired.

The fact that this logically protected the *Indian Act* membership system from scrutiny under the Charter seemed not to be noticed. When women fought to have section 28 included in the Charter as an overriding norm of sexual equality, they were not concerned with section 25 but with the legislative override provision in section 33. It was only later that debate occurred over the possibility that section 25 protected the *Indian Act* membership system and was not affected by section 28.

The *Lavell* issue was resolved legislatively in 1985.[71] The reform allowed women who had lost status by marriage to regain status, but otherwise transferred the power over band membership rules to the bands. Some urged that the legislation should limit band powers by specifically prohibiting sexual discrimination or by stating that the *Charter of Rights and Freedoms* applied. In the end, there was a deliberate decision not to

---

70 *Lovelace v. Canada*, [1983] *Can. Hum. Rts. Y.B.*, 305.
71 *An Act to Amend the Indian Act*, S.C. 1985, c. 27.

include such provisions. The women's Legal Education and Action Fund decided not to challenge the 1985 *Indian Act* amendments, though they clearly perpetuated some of the effects of the earlier sexual discrimination. The only court challenge to date has come from a group of bands in Alberta, arguing that complete band control of membership is an unextinguished aboriginal and treaty right.[72] Any conflict between Indian special status and equality has been decisively resolved in favour of special status. *Indian Act* liquor provisions seem the solitary exception.

This pattern of judicial deference to the constitutional mandate for special treatment of Indians has been confirmed in a 1987 ruling of the Supreme Court of Canada upholding provincial funding of Roman Catholic secondary schools in Ontario. The constitutional recognition of a role for denominational schools was analogized by Mr. Justice Estey with the special legislative mandate on Indians. Both, he said, allow legislation which is selective, preferential, discriminatory or distinctive.[73]

The other side of this coin is the proposition that the Canadian Constitution recognizes both individual rights and group rights. The *Charter of Rights and Freedoms* is primarily about individual rights, but has provisions for collective rights of aboriginal peoples and francophones. This follows the Canadian tradition of general provisions on individual human rights and specific provisions for named minorities. While the Charter drew on the provisions of the *International Covenant on Civil and Political Rights*, it did not copy the general minority rights provisions, Article 27:

> In those States in which ethnic, religious or linguistic minorities exist, persons belonging to such minorities shall not be denied the right, in community with the other members of their group, to enjoy their own culture, to profess and practise their own religion, or to use their own language.

Section 27 of the Charter is much more modest, establishing an interpretive norm around the concept of multiculturalism:

> This Charter shall be interpreted in a manner consistent with the preservation and enhancement of the multicultural heritage of Canadians.

Neither aboriginal peoples nor Québécois see multiculturalism as particularly relevant to their aspirations, though both benefit from the more general recognition of collective or group rights in our time.[74]

---

72 *Twinn v. R.*, [1987] 2 F.C. 450 (T.D.).

73 *Reference re Bill 30, An Act to Amend the Education Act (Ont.)*, [1987] 1 S.C.R. 1148. Another recent equality decision involving Indians is *R. v. Rocher* (1984), 14 D.L.R. (4th) 210 (N.W.T. C.A.).

74 See, *e.g.*, *Edwards Books & Art Ltd. v. R.*, [1986] 2 S.C.R. 713 at 781, 808.

4. SECTION 35: EXISTING ABORIGINAL AND TREATY RIGHTS

Section 35 provides:

> 35(1) The existing aboriginal and treaty rights of the aboriginal peoples of Canada are hereby recognized and affirmed.
> (2) In this Act, "aboriginal peoples of Canada" includes the Indian, Inuit and Metis peoples of Canada.
> (3) For greater certainty, in subsection (1) "treaty rights" includes rights that now exist by way of land claims agreements or may be so acquired.
> (4) Notwithstanding any other provision of this Act, the aboriginal and treaty rights referred to in subsection (1) are guaranteed equally to male and female persons.

The original version of this section was agreed to in corridor bargaining between federal politicians and aboriginal leaders in January 1981.[75] It was dropped in the closed First Ministers Meeting the following November. It was restored after public protests, with the addition of the word "existing" in subsection (1). Premier Lougheed of Alberta, the only Premier to admit opposition to section 35, insisted on the new word. He was concerned with assertions that "treaty and aboriginal rights" had a more ample content than had been generally assumed, including rights to self-government. On a more practical level, the wording change covered his reversal of position, when the other opposing Premiers had publicly abandoned him. Lougheed later, disingenuously, suggested that adding the word "existing" had strengthened the recognition of rights in section 35. It seems clear that the added word is meaningless. The original wording was never designed to revive treaty or aboriginal rights which had been legally terminated before 1982. And the additional word would not have the effect of freezing our understanding of the content of "treaty and aboriginal rights". The federal Minister of Justice was correct when he asserted in 1981 that the word "existing" only made explicit what had always been implicit in the section.

The consequences of section 35 are in relation to (a) the legal enforceability of the rights and (b) how such rights can be taken away.

Treaties were never accorded a clear legal status in Canadian law.[76] The courts enforced treaty promises involving the payment of moneys, either annuity payments or moneys for medicines, on the basis of contract law. That basis would not work for other treaty promises when they came into conflict with legislation, such as federal and provincial hunting laws.

---

75 D. Sanders, "The Indian Lobby", *supra*, note 39 at 301.

76 For a review of authorities, see D. Sanders, *"Prior Claims: Aboriginal People in the Constitution of Canada"*, in M. Beck & I. Bernier, *Canada and the New Constitution: The Unfinished Agenda* (Montreal: Institute for Research in Public Policy, 1983) Vol. 1, 227 at 244.

In *Sikyea*,[77] treaty hunting rights were argued against the federal *Migratory Birds Convention Act*. While the decisions in *Sikyea* do not make the point clearly, the Indian hunting right, taken on its own, could not be sustained on any established positivist basis. It was not enforceable on the basis of contract law. The right had not been given legal force by section 88 of the *Indian Act*. The *Constitution Act, 1930*, did not apply. The case involved a naked treaty hunting right, unassisted by legislative or constitutional provisions, asserted against federal legislation. Did the treaty have legal force? Sissons at trial gave one of his classic shotgun judgments, invoking everything from the Royal Proclamation of 1763 to the *Canadian Bill of Rights* of 1960. He said nothing coherent on the legal status of the treaty.[78] On appeal, Mr. Justice Johnson said the Indian right to hunt had "always been recognized". He said the right had its "origin" in the Royal Proclamation of 1763. Since the Proclamation, he said, did not apply to the Northwest Territories, the right to hunt was rooted in the fact that "the Government of Canada has treated all Indians across Canada, including those living on lands claimed by the Hudson Bay Company, as having an interest in the lands that required a treaty to effect its surrender".[79] This led to treaty rights, for the Indian interest in land was the foundation of the treaty. Johnson's reasoning was a blatant conversion of policy into law, an analysis lifted directly from McGillivray in *Wesley*[80] and later repeated by Hall in *Calder*.[81] Johnson went on to make a somewhat more defensible argument about the legal status of the treaty promise:

> Discussing the nature of the rights which the Indians obtained under the treaties, Lord Watson, speaking for the judicial committee . . . said . . .:
>
> > "Their Lordships have had no difficulty in coming to the conclusion that, under the treaties, the Indians obtained no right to their annuities, whether original or augmented, beyond a promise and agreement, which was nothing more than a personal obligation by its governor, as representing the old province, that the latter should pay the annuities as and when they became due; . . ."
>
> While this refers only to the annuities payable under the treaties, it is difficult to see that the other covenants in the treaties, including the one we are here concerned with, can stand on any higher footing. It is always to be kept in mind that the Indians surrendered their rights in the territory in exchange for these promises. This "promise and agreement", like any other, can of course, be breached, and there is no law of which I am aware that

---

77 *Supra*, notes 17, 18, 20.
78 *Sikyea, supra*, note 17.
79 *Sikyea, supra*, note 18 at 67.
80 *Supra*, note 8.
81 *Supra*, note 27.

would prevent Parliament by legislation, properly within sec. 91 of the *B.N.A. Act, 1867,* ch. 3, from doing so.[82]

The treaty hunting right promises were on no "higher footing" than the promises of annuities. This meant that the hunting rights promises had no legal character, for contract law would not make the promise enforceable against legislation. Rather than drawing that conclusion, Johnson went on as if there was a legal basis for treaty hunting rights and found that their survival was inconsistent with the *Migratory Birds Convention Act,* because the Act and regulations clearly addressed the issue of special rights for Indians and Inuit.

But the conclusion is inescapable that there was no legal basis for the enforcement of the particular treaty rights in the *Sikyea* case. The treaty hunting rights had no legal status with or without the conflict with the *Migratory Birds Convention Act.* Johnson did not want to come to that conclusion, but an objective reading of his judgment requires it.

What happened to such non legal treaty promises when section 35 came into force? The treaty promises had not been legally extinguished in the past, for they had never legally existed. If "existing aboriginal and treaty rights" in section 35 only referred to treaty rights which had a legal existence, then the section only applied to the money payments which were enforceable by contract law. Otherwise the courts were enforcing the *Indian Act* or the Constitution and not the treaties as such. We are driven to the conclusion that section 35, for the first time, gave legal enforceability to these previously unenforceable treaty promises. This conclusion can only be avoided if the courts now hold that Indian treaties, as such, are legally enforceable in Canadian law, apart from section 35. Such a ruling does not seem on the horizon. Even the upholding of aboriginal title in *Guerin*[83] does not give a legal basis for enforcing treaty promises dealing with hunting rights. Dickson's description of Indian treaties in *Simon*[84] as *sui generis* does not give a basis for their enforcement, as such, outside the limited parameters of contract law. A holding that the treaties are international law treaties would not help. It would not give them domestic enforceability.

Section 35 is the only logical basis for now holding that treaties, as such, are legally enforceable in Canadian law. *Sikyea* should now be reargued. In the 1960s, the issue in *Sikyea* was nonlegal treaty rights on the one hand and a federal statute on the other. Now the issue is constitutionally enforceable treaty rights on the one hand and a federal statute on the other. Section 35 could be held to have given legal existence

---

82 *Supra,* note 18 at 69.
83 *Supra,* note 1.
84 *Supra,* note 6.

to treaty rights which had only paper existence before 1982. Now those rights can prevail over federal statutes.

Of course it can be said that this is an argument for reversing the *Sikyea* group of cases when section 35 was not intended, in itself, to expand rights existing in 1982. First, it is not clear from the drafting history that section 35 was intended to have no effect on the substantive *status quo*. The drafting process for this section was thoroughly political. The government representatives thought they were innovating. No clear legal analysis of what the section meant was presented by any of the parties during its peculiar evolution, for aboriginal issues had been taken off the immediate constitutional review agenda in June 1980 and politicians were not being briefed in the area. Second, the *Sikyea* line of cases is now inconsistent with the norms of interpretation articulated by the Supreme Court of Canada in *Nowegijick*[85] and *Simon*. To reverse *Sikyea* would be to bring earlier judicial decisions into line with current decisions and redress the clearest example of government breach of treaty promises. Some provinces raised the anomaly in constitutional discussions that provincial law had to comply with treaty promises (by section 88 of the *Indian Act*) but the federal government, with primarily responsibility for Indian policy, was free to breach the treaties. That anomaly would end. Third, the argument presented here does reflect accurately the changing perception of treaties in Canadian law. Section 35 did make a change in the legal status of treaties, no matter how section 35 and the status of treaties may be rationalized or reinterpreted by politicians or judges in the future.

What of aboriginal rights? Before 1982, aboriginal rights, as such, had never been accorded a clear legal status in Canadian law.[86] As with treaty rights, some pattern of explicit recognition of aboriginal rights developed in the British and Canadian legal systems, notably with the Royal Proclamation of 1763, the documents transferring the Hudson's Bay Company territories and the Northwestern Territories to Canada and in the *Manitoba Act* of 1870. No legal basis for aboriginal rights developed independently of those acts of recognition until *Guerin*.[87] As with treaties, section 35 was dealing with aboriginal rights which did not clearly have a legal basis of their own in Canada in 1982. Was section 35 giving legal character to "rights" which had previously had none, apart from legislative or constitutional confirmation?

By 1982, the legal debate on aboriginal rights was shifting from whether such rights existed in law to whether they had been terminated.

---

85 *Supra*, note 41.
86 For a review of authorities see Sanders, "Prior Claims", *supra*, note 76 at 241.
87 *Supra*, note 1.

That shift was launched in *Calder*,[88] but it was only with the Supreme Court of Canada's restatement of the *Calder* decision in *Guerin* that the issue has been clearly reformulated in these new terms. With that reformulation, the problem of the legal character of aboriginal rights has been ended judicially, and section 35 is not to be seen as shifting aboriginal rights from a nonlegal into a legal category. With aboriginal rights recognized as legal rights, the issue is whether particular aboriginal rights survive or have been legally ended or diminished.

Acquisition theory, that is, the legal principles involved in the acquisition of colonies, can be used either to establish that some aboriginal rights survive the acquisition of the area as a colony or be used to limit or deny the survival of aboriginal rights. Litigation in Australia has been preoccupied with using acquisition theory to establish some aboriginal rights. Now that Canadian law accepts the survival of aboriginal rights, acquisition theory could be used in this country to establish limitations on those rights. Canadian law currently has no acquisition theory, as such, that could explain which aboriginal rights survive and which do not. The only acquisition theory apparently around in Canadian law is "occupation and settlement", which would deny the survival of any aboriginal rights and therefore is in conflict with both *Guerin* and section 35.

The logical analytical framework, consistent with *Guerin*, is for the courts to begin with the proposition that Indians and Inuit had a full range of territorial, legal and political rights. European colonial powers first took control over Indian foreign relations by effectively asserting suzerainty over the tribes and blocking their relations with other European powers. Incrementally other rights were assumed by the European colonial power and Indian autonomy was further reduced. This historical approach abandons two alternative theories that are both now indefensible. The first is that the Indian tribes had no legal order. The second is that "discovery" or the planting of a flag or some blind imperial enactment aimed at the new world had the effect of completely ending Indian rights on a particular date.

Logically there should be no single rule for the extinguishment of aboriginal rights. There should be different rules for the taking of different aboriginal rights. The taking of Indian external sovereignty in what is now Canada was not accomplished by conquest, consent or explicit legislative act. What was explicit was the creation of British and Canadian sovereignty, which necessarily reduced Indian and Inuit sovereignty. There is no reason why the implicit taking of Indian external sovereignty should mean that internal self-government or territorial rights should be able to be taken in the same way. These are the questions that need to be canvassed in

---

88 *Supra*, note 27.

the current aboriginal title cases.

This discussion has concerned the effect of section 35 on the legal enforceability of aboriginal and treaty rights. Section 35 has a second consequence. Once it is found that there are currently existing aboriginal or treaty rights, those rights are recognized and affirmed with the consequence that they cannot be altered other than by consent or constitutional amendment.

The first cases invoking section 35 were challenges to the *Sikyea* group of cases. The courts held that section 35 had no effect on those rulings, without exploring the analysis suggested here. The Supreme Court of Canada has yet to consider this issue.[89]

5. TREATIES AND THE TREATY PROCESS

The constitutional recognition of aboriginal and treaty rights means that such rights can only be altered or terminated by consent or by constitutional amendment. Consent is an available means of dealing with these rights because they are of a different nature than the individual legal rights or even the collective language rights found in the *Charter of Rights and Freedoms*. Aboriginal and treaty rights are a mix of public law and private law rights. Historically they have always been able to be dealt with by consent. This is recognized in the treaty tradition, in the Royal Proclamation of 1763 and in other constitutional documents including the constitutional amendments of 1982 and 1983. By equating "land claims agreements" with treaties, the constitutional amendments of 1982 and 1983 explicitly recognize the continuing amenability of aboriginal and treaty rights to consensual modification or clarification. This is not a change in Canadian practice. The treaty process has never been terminated in Canada. It has not been ended by legislation, constitutional provision, express policy or longstanding practice. While many assume that treaties are a phenomenon of the nineteenth century, the federal government continued to sign new treaties into the 1920s and signed adhesions to existing treaties at least as late as 1956. The James Bay Agreement of 1975 and other major aboriginal title settlements in 1978 and 1984 are now unmistakably "treaties" as a result of the constitutional provisions of 1982 and 1983.

Because the treaty process was still in existence in 1982, the

---

89 *See R. v. Eninew* (1984), 12 C.C.C. (3d) 365 (Sask. C.A.); *R. v. Hare*, [1985] 3 C.N.L.R. 139 (Ont. C.A.). In *R. v. Flett*, [1987] 5 W.W.R. 115 (Man. Prov. Ct.), Martin Prov. Ct. J. ruled that the 1982 amendments reversed the *Sikyea* decision, relying on a misreading of the British Columbia Court of Appeal decision in *Sparrow, supra,* note 57. It is assumed the decision will be appealed.

constitutional amendments of that year contained within them a special process for constitutional change for aboriginal peoples. The category of treaty rights in sections 25 and 35 was not frozen as of 1982. Section 35 would apply to treaty rights in existence from time to time. New treaties might terminate older treaty rights. New treaties could deal with treaty or aboriginal rights and create new treaty rights. A settlement of aboriginal title claims in British Columbia would produce a "treaty" within sections 25 and 35, whether the document was so labelled or not. A distinctive aspect of this continuing treaty and constitutional process is its involvement of the federal government and aboriginal people, without a need to include provincial governments. It is a bilateral process, as opposed to the multilateral process of the First Ministers Conferences on aboriginal rights.

The federal government has not publicly commented on the continuing treaty process for two reasons. They did not want to antagonize the provinces during the period of aboriginal constitutional conferences. As well, they had no immediate intention to institute a bilateral process with aboriginal groups beyond the land claims processes already in place (though the innovation of the *Sechelt Self-Government Act* of 1986 was a result of negotiation and Indian consent).[90]

6. INTERNATIONAL LAW DEVELOPMENTS

Treaty and aboriginal rights are recognized and affirmed by section 35 of the *Constitution Act, 1982*. This, together with recent judicial decisions, has given treaty and aboriginal rights, as such, a clear legal status in domestic Canadian law. Indians will continue to assert an international law status to the treaties. Domestic legal status for the treaties is, of course, not incompatible with their being instruments under international law. While Chief Justice Dickson rejected any international law status for the treaties, he did not do so on the basis of section 35. Nor did he invoke any international law authorities on the status of treaties with indigenous populations. The relevant material was not argued before them. It is not clear that any such material was argued before him.

Treaty-making began in the early seventeenth century in New England as a response to organized Indian tribes, with effective control over populations and territories. The competition between colonial powers encouraged the formalization of the treaty process, but treaty-making continued after inter-European competition ended. In the United States, treaties with Indians were given the force of domestic legislation by the same constitutional process used for treaties with European nations. The United States Supreme Court described the tribes as "domestic, dependent

---

90 *Sechelt Indian Band Self-Government Act*, S.C. 1986, c. 27.

nations" and said that the principle of United States Indian law derived from international law. Later Indians rights were held to be subject to United States legislative power. Treaty-making was ended by Congressional decree in 1871, with rights under prior treaties being specifically preserved.[91]

International law accepted colonialism as valid and gave no force to treaties with indigenous peoples. Native tribes were outside the exclusive club of nation states. Today, colonialism is a violation of international law and certain non-state peoples are recognized as having the right of self-determination. The International Court of Justice's ruling on the Western Sahara in 1975 destroyed most of the theories which had justified the European takeover of populated lands. We are left without an international law justification for the British acquisition of Canada, other than the consent of the tribes expressed in treaties or in other forms of acquiescence.

There have been two major innovations in international law in the period since the Second World War. The first is the ending of colonialism and the second is the construction of an international law on human rights. An international concern with indigenous peoples began in the 1950s and 1960s with reports of genocide in the jungle interior of South America. The concern with indigenous peoples arose within the United Nations in the context of a major study on racial discrimination. The special *rapporteur* suggested a separate study on indigenous people, recognizing that they faced distinctive problems. In 1971, the United Nations Sub-Commission on Prevention of Discrimination and Protection of Minorities launched a study on "The problem of discrimination against indigenous populations", nominally headed by a representative from Ecuador, but handled completely by a staff member from Guatemala. The report was completed in 1983, but was only published in a regular way in 1987, and only in part. Even before the report was completed, the Sub-Commission moved on one of the recommendations, a continuing committee to study the issues and draft standards for state treatment of indigenous populations. The Working Group on Indigenous Populations held its first session in 1982. It meets for five days in Geneva immediately before the annual summer sitting of the Sub-Commission. In 1985, it began drafting standards for inclusion in a declaration, eventually to be enacted by the General Assembly. Canada has expressed support for the Working Group and has contributed to a voluntary fund to pay the costs for indigenous representatives who would not otherwise be able to make the trip to Geneva. Each session involves aboriginal leaders from Canada and representatives of

---

91 B.F. Strickland & C.F. Wilkinson, eds., *Felix S. Cohen's Handbook of Federal Indian Law*, (Michie-Bobbs-Merrill, 1982); D. Sanders, *"Aboriginal Self-Government in the United States"*, Background Paper No. 5, *Aboriginal Peoples and Constitutional Reform*, (Institute of Intergovernmental Relations, Queen's Univ. 1985).

the Canadian government. Both the initial chairman and the present chairwoman have visited Canada, spoken at conference and met with indigenous leaders. Madame Erica-Irene Daes, the present chairwoman, was seated as an observer at the First Ministers Conference on aboriginal rights in Ottawa in March 1987.[92]

Canada appeared supportive of the United Nations iniative on indigenous peoples, but by the 1987 session of the Working Group that support seemed to have disappeared. The Canadian presentation to the 1987 session sought to deflect concern from indigenous peoples in Canada in two ways. Canada insisted thta any standards must be "universal" in character, though no one had ever suggested non-universal standards. It was reasonably clear that Canada wanted attention to be paid to indigenous populations in Eastern Europe and perhaps other parts of the world, something that would lessen attention to North America. As well, Canada suggested priority be given to indigenous populations that faced the most serious problems. Again this would shift attention away from Canada. When the Working Group decided in 1987 to proceed with a study on treaties between indigenous peoples and States, Canada objected, arguing that this breached the principle of "universality". Their objections did not prevail. The Canadian member of the Sub-Commission abstained in the vote which authorized the study, lessening the appearance of expert independence he had established in earlier sessions. The issue went to the U.N. Human Rights Commission. Canada proposed a resolution only authorizing consultations on the idea of a study. The final resolution authorized the preparation of an outline for a study on the "potential utility of treaties". Any study is to be "forward looking". It should not dredge up past sins (and perhaps not even look at past treaties). Canada took the occasion to state its view that Canadian Indian treaties were not international law treaties.[93]

When Canada signed both the *International Covenant on Civil and Political Rights* and its Optional Protocol, we opened the possibility for individuals to challenge Canada's compliance with the Covenant by submitting a "communication" to the United Nations Human Rights Committee. As noted earlier, the *Lovelace* case from Canada stands as the major success, internationally, of this individual complaints procedure. There are currently two other complaints before the Human Rights

---

92 D. Sanders, "The Re-Emergence of Indigenous Questions in International Law", [1983] *Can. Hum. Rts. Y.B.* 3; Smith, "Canadian Talks on Native Rights under Scrutiny by U.N. Body", *Toronto Star* (March 25, 1987) p. A-1.

93 Natives, Ottawa clash on UN study, *Globe and Mail*, February 27, 1988, p. A-3; Ottawa denies treaties exist, natives claim, *Vancouver Sun*, February 27, 1988, p. A-8; A question of treaties (editorial), *Globe and Mail*, March 9, 1988, p. A-6; Ottawa derailed UN rights study, Crees say, *Globe and Mail*, March 10, 1988, p. A-8.

Committee that are being pursued. The first is the assertion by the Mic Mac tribe that Canada has denied the tribe its right of self-determination, as provided in Article One of the Covenant. A second complaint on self-determination rights has been brought by the Lubicon Lake Indian Band in Northern Alberta, but focussing on the denial of their rights to lands and natural resources. Canada has argued that the individual complaints procedure is not available on claims to self-determination. It has also denied that Indian collectivities are "peoples" with a right to "self-determination."

Canada's international reputation on indigenous questions has been good. The failures and frustrations are clear to us at home, but other countries are impressed by the seriousness with which aboriginal issues are treated in Canada today. But recent Canadian behaviour at the United Nations detracts from this reputation.

7. CONCLUSIONS

In the *Simon* decision, Chief Justice Dickson rejected the reasoning of Mr. Justice Patterson in the 1929 *Syliboy* case.[94] He commented:

> It should be noted that the language used by Patterson J., illustrated in this passage, reflects the biases and prejudices of another era in our history. Such language is no longer acceptable in Canadian law and indeed is inconsistent with a growing sensitivity to native rights in Canada.[95]

This is a remarkably straightforward use of intellectual history in a judgment. The statement is obviously true. There has been a major shift in attitudes to native people and that shift is reflected in government policy and in the rulings of the courts. This evolution has occurred not simply in Canada but in other parts of the Americas and the world. In general, the Canadian legal system in 1945 recognized no rights of Indians, Inuit or Metis which were not granted by constitutional or legislative provisions. Treaties had no definable legal status. Now, with the judicial and constitutional changes, treaty and aboriginal rights have a legal basis in the Canadian Constitution, but their essential validity derives from the pre-contact aboriginal legal order.

This is only part of the story. The shift in political and judicial attitudes has created contradictions that have yet to be resolved. The *Sikyea* group of cases[96] are now in conflict with more recent judicial decisions. The 1973 federal policy on aboriginal title claims has produced only three settlements. The lack of progress on land claims in British Columbia has

---

94 *Supra*, note 6.
95 *Simon, supra*, note 6 at 399.
96 *Supra*, notes 17, 18, 20.

led to public demonstrations and litigation. Some "specific claims" issues, such as treaty land entitlement in Saskatchewan, seem stalled. The general acceptance of the concept of Indian self-government has led to more talk and writing than action.[97] The first concrete result has been special self-government legislation for a single, well-organized Indian band in British Columbia.[98] No general approach of self-government is in place. And, of course, there are still major social and economic problems in native communities. We are in a much more positive period, but old problems are not resolved quickly.

---

97 About a dozen studies have been published by the project on Aboriginal Peoples and Constitutional Reform, Institute of Intergovernmental Relations, Queen's University, mostly on self-government.

98 *Sechelt Indian Band Self-Government Act, supra,* note 90.

18

Multiculturalism and Collective Rights: Approaches to Section 27*

Joseph Eliot Magnet

Section 27 of the *Canadian Charter of Rights and Freedoms* stipulates:

> This Charter shall be interpreted in a manner consistent with the preservation and enhancement of the multicultural heritage of Canadians.

---

* My thoughts on this subject began to coalesce as a result of a stimulating conference sponsored by the Canadian Human Rights Foundation in 1986. The conference proceedings, including my own preliminary sketch of this topic ("Interpreting Multiculturalism"), are published in *Multiculturism and the Charter, infra*, note 1). In further pursuit of this fascinating subject, I have had to revise my ideas on several key points.

1. SECTION 27 AND CONSTITUTIONAL INTERPRETATION

Section 27 is on its face an interpretational rule. As such, it is but one member of a family of such interpretational provisions in the *Constitution Act, 1982*. Sections 21, 22 and 29 provide that nothing in certain Charter provisions "abrogates or derogates" from other specified rights. Sections 25, 26 and 37.1(4) stipulate that certain Charter guarantees "shall not be construed" to prejudice certain pre-existing rights. Section 31 states that the Charter does not "extend" the legislative powers of any authority.

Apart from section 27, these provisions are defensive in nature. They enjoin the courts, in the discharge of their high responsibility to expound the Charter, not to disturb the sensitive national compromises upon which the Canadian Confederation is constructed.

Section 27 differs from these provisions in that, while partially defensive in terms ("preservation . . . of the multicultural heritage of Canadians"), it is not so limited. The provision is also dynamic, requiring those responsible for applying the Charter to contribute to the "enhancement" of Canadian multiculturalism. Equally, preservation of Canada's multicultural heritage may require a more aggressive posture than mere passivity.

Because of its uniqueness in constitutional law generally,[1] section 27 bristles with difficulties of application. In terms, it portends a substantive

---

1   There is apparently no equivalent in constitutional law to s. 27 of the Charter: see M.R. Hudson, "Multiculturalism, Government Policy and Constitutional Enshrinement — A Comparative Study", Canadian Human Rights Foundation, in *Multiculturalism and the Charter: A Canadian Legal Perspective* (Toronto: Carswell, 1987) at 59. However, the Constitution of the Republic of Nicaragua, arts. 89-91, has similar concepts although cast in an autonomy framework. Those articles read:

   89. The Communities of the Atlantic Coast are indivisible parts of the Nicaraguan people, enjoy the same rights and have the same obligations as all Nicaraguans.

   The Communities of the Atlantic Coast have the right to preserve and develop their cultural identities within the framework of national unity, to be granted their own forms of social organization, and to administer their local affairs according to their traditions.

   The state recognizes communal forms of land ownership of the Communities of the Atlantic Coast. Equally it recognizes their enjoyment, use and benefit of the waters and forests of their communal lands.

   90. The Communities of the Atlantic Coast have the right to the free expression and preservation of their languages, art and culture. The development of their culture and their values enrich the national culture. The state shall create special programs to enhance the exercise of these rights.

   91. The state is obligated to enact laws promoting and assuring that no Nicaraguan shall be the object of discrimination for reasons of language, culture or origin.

meaning — to the extent, at least, that it orients the crucially important *Charter of Rights and Freedoms* in Canada's politico-juridical structure. Difficulties of application have given rise to widely differing expectations as to the significance of Canada's constitutional commitment to the multiculturalism principle. The compendious phrase "the multicultural heritage of Canadians" has become a political "mirror on the wall", inviting those reflecting in it to see the most flattering view of their own ideas.

2. SHOULD SECTION 27 BE TAKEN SERIOUSLY?

One commentator has gone so far as to reject altogether any substantive scope for the application of section 27. Professor Peter Hogg took the view that there is little point in searching for serious constitutional purposes or a potent legal meaning in the phrase "the multicultural heritage of Canadians". Professor Hogg considered that "s. 27 may prove to be more of a rhetorical flourish than an operative provision".[2]

Professor Hogg's abrupt dismissal of section 27 may be buttressed by recent criticism of multiculturalism policy. Howard Brotz observed that multiculturalism policy cannot be evaluated unless one understands "the real meaning of the term culture underneath all the rhetorical ambiguities of current usage".[3] Brotz pointed out that the word "culture" is an eighteenth century German invention which signifies "way of life" — an "organic whole, rooted in the soil, rooted in the authentic life of a people seen as a community bound together by pervasive traditions and moral ties which altogether transcended the pettiness of self-interest". When culture is understood in this sense, Brotz denied that Canada possesses "any [cultural] diversity at all. Canadians of all ethnic groups, as in the United States, stand for exactly the same thing which is a bourgeois way of life". Brotz condemned the emphasis on ethnic plurality as trivial — "'multiculturalism' turns out to be a choice of pizzas, wonton soup and kosher style pastrami sandwiches to which one can add ethnic radio programs".[4] Moreover, Brotz argued, the banal formula "pluralism and equality" confuses understanding of the Quebec question, which is a real political question raising problems of allegiance. This is the only ethno-political problem in Canada. Brotz emphasized that the Quebec question is not a cultural issue, but a language issue.

---

2 P.W. Hogg, *Constitutional Law of Canada; Canada Act, 1982 Annotated* (Toronto: Carswell 1982) at 72. In the same vein, Michael Hudson characterized s. 27 as "a barrier to discrimination that may be redundant in light of s. 15, or a collective right which may be too vague to benefit any group": *supra*, note 1 at 26.

3 H. Brotz, "Multiculturalism in Canada: A Model" (1980), 6 *Can. Pub. Pol.* 41 at 41–42.

4 *Ibid.* at 44.

Notwithstanding Professor Hogg's blunt rejection of section 27 as possessing constitutional substance, it appears unlikely that it will be read out of the Constitution. Section 27 was the result of intensive lobbying by Canada's ethno-cultural communities for greater respect and a larger share of the power available in Canada's political system. To date, courts have been responsive to these concerns, and have relied on section 27 to shape the meanings of fundamental freedoms and language rights in a way that contradicts Professor Hogg's abrupt dismissal. The courts are seriously groping for ways to pour content into section 27. Multiculturalism is a principle which has suffused the energies radiated by all segments of Canada's governmental structure.

3. DOMESTIC SOURCES

Although multiculturalism has enjoyed longstanding importance in Canadian political debate, its acknowledged standing has not been accompanied by clear agreement about the content of the multiculturalism principle. This is particularly evident from examination of the documentary sources ultimately finding expression in section 27. The sources of section 27 are especially important because constitutional interpretation in Canada pays scrupulous regard to background policies, statutes and statements in searching for the objects and purposes informing specific constitutional texts.[5]

The constitutional record with respect to enshrinement of section 27 is sparse. Despite its brevity, the documentary background illustrates the wide variety of meanings different actors would impart to the multiculturalism concept.

From the 1940s, Canadian governments became increasingly sensitive to the problems experienced by the numerous waves of immigrants to Canadian shores. According to the 1961 census, persons of ethnic origins other than British or French accounted for 26 percent of the Canadian population. Numerous conferences and advisory bodies sought to comprehend the problem as one of good citizenship "pertaining to national unity".[6]

A significant change in orientation occurred with the work of the

---

5 See *Hunter v. Southam Inc.*, [1984] 2 S.C.R. 145; *R. v. Therens* (1985), 59 N.R. 122 (S.C.C.); *A.G. Canada v. C.N. Transport Ltd.* (1984), 49 N.R. 241 (S.C.C.) (*per* Laskin C.J.C.: "I have examined the pre-confederation debates in the then provincial Parliament of Canada [in order to shed light on the meaning of the specific words of s. 92(14) of the *Constitution Act, 1867*]"); *R. v. Videoflicks* (1984), 5 O.A.C. 1 24-25 (Ont. C.A.), rev'd in part [1986] 2 S.C.R. 713 (*sub nom. Edwards Books & Art Ltd. v. R.*) (examination of the constitutional record of s. 27 in order to elucidate its meaning).

6 Canada, *Multiculturalism and the Government of Canada* (Ottawa: 1984) at 7.

Royal Commission on Bilingualism and Biculturalism in the 1960s. The Commission, and the government, were lobbied by representatives of Canada's ethno-cultural communities for greater recognition of their contribution to Canada. The Commission responded dramatically. In Volume IV of its *Report*, the Commission noted that "the presence in Canada of many people whose language and culture are distinctive by reason of their birth or ancestry represents an inestimable enrichment that Canadians can not afford to lose". The Commission noted that "a number of cultural groups in Canada [possess] a clear sense of identity. They want, without in any way undermining national unity, to maintain their own linguistic and cultural heritage".[7] The Commission wholeheartedly endorsed maintenance of a strong sense of original cultures, as something that affects people and nations deeply. The Commission went so far as to modify its own terms of reference,[8] eliminating the concept of "biculturalism" in favour of a "multicultural" policy.

The Commission recommended preservation of cultural heritage by strengthening prohibitions on discrimination, by promoting other cultures and languages through broadcasting and educational institutions, and by funding agencies whose objectives are to promote distinctive cultural identity in Canada.

The Commission's work forms the cornerstone of modern multiculturalism policy in Canada. The Commission's recommendations were implemented by the Government of Canada in its much-heralded multiculturalism policy of 1971. This policy, announced in the House of Commons, embraced four initiatives:

> (1) resources permitting . . . to assist all Canadian cultural groups that had demonstrated a desire and effort to continue to develop a capacity to grow and contribute to Canada, and a clear need for assistance;

> (2) to assist members of all cultural groups to overcome cultural barriers to full participation in Canadian society;

> (3) to promote creative encounters and interchange among all Canadian cultural groups in the interest of national unity; and

> (4) to continue assistance to immigrants to acquire at least one of Canada's official languages in order to become full participants in Canadian society.[9]

---

7 Canada, *Report of the Royal Commission on Bilingualism and Biculturalism* (Ottawa: 1969) Vol. IV, pp. 8-14.

8 "To recommend what steps should be taken to develop a Canadian confederation on the basis of an equal partnership between the two founding races, taking into account the contribution made by the other ethnic groups": *ibid.* at 3.

9 Canada, *House of Commons Debates* (October 8, 1971) (statement of Prime Minister Pierre E. Trudeau).

What is striking about these four themes is their great diversity, ranging as they do among policy orientations of non-discrimination, promotion of cultural autonomy, mutual understanding, and modes of adaptation and assimilation. While it is possible to see contradictions between the four themes (for example, promotion of cultural autonomy and assimilation), it is more likely that the 1971 statement is a vestigial policy, very much in the process of formation.

The Prime Minister's 1971 speech oriented multiculturalism policy around two poles which have had long-term significance. "A policy of multiculturalism", stated the Prime Minister, first "should help to break down discriminatory attitudes and cultural jealousy". The Prime Minister's second point was that multiculturalism policy was guided by the belief "that adherence to one's ethnic group is influenced . . . by the group's (collective will to exist)".[10] These two themes — freedom from discrimination and group survival — are important elements of the constitutional background which ultimately led to entrenchment of section 27.

There is no reference to the multiculturalism principle in the *Victoria Charter*, although the *Molgat-MacGuigan Report* of 1972 recommended that:

> The preamble to the Constitution should formally recognize that Canada is a multicultural country.[11]

In June 1978, the federal government introduced Bill C-60 in order to encourage public discussion of proposed changes to the Constitution. Part I of Bill C-60 contained a Statement of Aims of the Canadian Federation, one of which reads:

> To ensure throughout Canada equal respect for the many origins, creeds and cultures . . . that help shape its society.

In the Draft Constitution of October, 1980, the Statement of Aims was omitted. There was no other reference in that text to the multicultural principle. In response to this omission, representatives of the ethno-cultural communities appeared before the Hayes-Joyal Committee and made strenuous submissions. "I refuse to be made a second class citizen", stated Mr. Jan Federowicz of the Canadian Polish Congress.[12] The Congress elaborated in its brief:

> A document which singles out the so-called "founding races" for special

---

10 *Ibid.*

11 Canada, Parliament, *Report of the Joint Committee of the Senate and House of Commons on the Constitution of Canada* (Ottawa: Queen's Printer, 1972) recommendation 27.

12 *Proceedings of the Special Joint Committee of the Senate and House of Commons on the Constitution of Canada* (October 20, 1980) 9:105.

mention and special privilege will become increasingly objectionable and irrelevant, not to say racist.[13]

Almost one quarter of the more than 100 witnesses before the Hayes-Joyal Committee made submissions on the multicultural issue embracing such themes as non-discrimination, equality, cultural autonomy, cultural perpetuation, pluralism, heritage language rights and educational autonomy.

The government responded. On January 12, 1981, the Minister of Justice introduced before the Committee a suggested amendment which was identical to the current text of section 27. In proposing this amendment, the Minister referred in general terms to the extensive submissions made by the ethno-cultural communities, leaving the impression that the proposed amendment was in direct response.[14]

This review of the constitutional background to section 27 reveals a wide spectrum of opinion — a stunning array of diversity — as to the content of the multicultural principle.[15] There is nothing in the government's previous policies, legislation, statements, or in any other documentary sources that alleviates the ambiguity permeating the text of section 27. The multiple-meaning aura radiated by section 27 is important. It allows a court or other interpreting body latitude to apply the multiculturalism principle to a wide range of situations in imaginative, polymorphous and multitudinous ways. Given the embryonic development of the multiculturalism principle in current governmental policy, and always on the assumption that the courts will strain seriously to actualize the multicultural ideal in practice, the array of opportunities for interpretation offers hope to multiculturalism's supporters — and a challenge to authorities applying the Charter.

4. INTERNATIONAL SOURCES

The model for section 27 of the Charter was Article 27 of the 1966 *International Covenant on Civil and Political Rights*, which provides as follows:

In those States in which ethnic, religious or linguistic minorities exist, persons belonging to such minorities shall not be denied the right, in community with

---

13 Canadian Polish Congress, *Brief on Constitutional Reform* (1980).

14 See generally Hudson, *supra*, note 1, who carefully reviewed the constitutional background in fine detail.

15 "The conclusion seems to be that there was no clear consensus on the meaning of the term [multiculturalism] during the critical years 1980-1982 when the Charter was being drafted": *ibid.* at 26.

the other members of their group, to enjoy their own culture, to profess and practice their own religion, or to use their own language.

This provision, unique among international law instruments,[16] was ratified by Canada in 1976. The importance of the Covenant as a source of interpretation for the Charter has been widely recognized by both the courts and commentators.[17] The language of the two documents is similar in many instances. Draft versions of the Charter expressly referred to the Covenant in explanatory notes.[18] This importance makes the meaning which has been ascribed to Article 27 highly relevant to interpretation of the Charter's section 27, and thus requires examination of the jurisprudence, legislative history and critical commentary relating to the Article.

Article 27 developed from the *International Protection of Minorities System*. This was a scheme of multilateral treaties and declarations established in the post-World War I period and supervised by the League of Nations.[19] The provisions pertaining to the various minorities were substantially similar, securing in essence

for certain elements incorporated in a State, the population of which differs from them in race, language or religion, the possibility of living peaceably alongside that population and co-operating amicably with it, while at the same time preserving the characteristics which distinguish them from the majority, and satisfying the ensuing special needs.[20]

Although the System was never specifically abolished, it did not survive the chaotic upheavals of World War Two.

---

16 An attempt was made in 1961 to introduce a similar provision into the *European Convention on Human Rights*, but it was never adopted. See W. McKean, *Equality and Discrimination under International Law* (Oxford: Clarendon, 1983) at 212-214.

17 Article 27 itself was referred to in *R. v Videoflicks Ltd.*, *supra*, note 5 at 25. Regarding the use of international instruments in Charter interpretation generally, see Cohen & Bayefsky "The Canadian Charter of Rights and Freedoms and Public International Law" (1983), 61 Can. Bar Rev. 265; *R. v. Videoflicks*, *supra*, note 5 at 20 (O.A.C.); *R. v. Big M Drug Mart Ltd.* (1984), 5 D.L.R. (4th) 121 at 149 (Alta. C.A.), aff'd *infra*, note 39; *R. v. Konechny* (1983), 6 D.L.R. (4th) 350 at 359 (B.C.C.A.) leave to appeal to S.C.C. refused (1984), 25 M.V.R. 132n (S.C.C.); *R.W.D.S.U., Local 544 v. Saskatchewan* (1985), 39 Sask. R. 193 at 218-19 (C.A.), rev'd (1987), 56 Sask. R. 277 (S.C.C.). The Supreme Court of Canada cited the Covenant and other instruments as evidence of the widespread acceptance of a specific right in *R. v. Oakes*, [1986] 1 S.C.R. 103, without discussion of the justifications for use of such instruments.

18 R. Elliot, "Interpreting the Charter: Use of Earlier Version as an Aid", [1982] *U.B.C.L. Rev.* (Charter ed.) 11.

19 The system did not apply universally, but rather to a number of smaller powers and newly-created states "within a continuous stretch of territory spreading all the way from the Baltic Sea to the Persian Gulf". *See* Y. Dinstein, "Collective Human Rights of Peoples and Minorities" (1976), 25 *Int'l & Comp. L.Q.* 102 at 114.

20 *Minority Schools in Albania*, [1935] *P.C.I.J. Reports* (AB/64) 17.

During the formative years of the United Nations, the emphasis on human rights shifted to prohibition of discrimination against individuals.[21] This is the focus of the *Universal Declaration of Human Rights* of 1948, which does not specifically guarantee the rights of ethnic, religious or linguistic minorities. However, concern for the plight of minorities soon led to detailed consideration of their position by United Nations bodies. A thorough study was undertaken by the Sub-Commission on Prevention of Discrimination and Protection of Minorities, third session, in 1950. A proposed resolution of this body, after going through various drafting stages,[22] was ultimately adopted as Article 27 of the Covenant by the General Assembly at its twenty-first session in 1966.

Through the drafting stages of Article 27, a number of points were made regarding its scope of application and the nature of the obligations which it imposed. First, although the provision has a collective aspect ("in community with other members of their group"), it was primarily designed to benefit individuals. At one point the representative from India specifically noted that the article did not apply to "minorities considered as groups".[23] Second, Article 27 provides protection only to "separate or distinct groups, well-defined and long-established on the territory of the state".[24] It does not protect subsequently-created immigrant minorities. To establish this point, the Latin American nations insisted on the addition of the words "in those States in which ethnic, religious or linguistic minorities *exist*". Third, there was some question as to whether Article 27 was to apply to autochthonous groups. Australia, for example, insisted that its aborigines "had no separate competing culture of their own, for as a group they had only reached the level of food gatherers."[25] Fourth, Article 27 was intended primarily to prevent state interference with minority culture, religion and

---

21 Some may have been wary of extending special protection to subnational groups in the light of wartime experiences with "fifth columns" and Hitler's invasions launched on the pretext of rescuing German-speaking minorities. This is the view expressed by J.N. Saxena, in "International Protection of Minorities and Individual Human Rights" (1983), 23 *Ind. J. Int'l L.* 38 at 44.

22 The resolution was amended after discussion by the Commission on Human Rights, ninth session, 1953. At this stage Art. 27 emerged in its final form. Further consideration by the Third Committee of the General Assembly, sixteenth session, 1961-62, yielded no changes. For a detailed account of the legislative history of Art. 27, see F. Capotorti, "Study on the Rights of Persons belonging to Ethnic, Religious and Linguistic Minorities" (1979), U.N. Doc. E/CN.4/Sub.2/384/Rev.1 at 31-34.

23 Third Committee of the General Assembly, 1961; U.N. Doc. A/C.3/SR.1103 at 215, para. 39.

24 Annotations on the Draft International Covenants on Human Rights (summarizing the work of the Commission on Human Rights, ninth session), 1955, U.N. Doc. A/2929 at 63, para. 184.

25 Commission on Human Rights, ninth session, 1953, U.N. Doc. E/CN.4/SR.369 at 11.

language, and not to impose on states the burden of implementing specific programs to protect these elements: "It was generally agreed that the text . . . would not, for example, place States and Governments under the obligation of providing special schools for persons belonging to linguistic minorities."[26]

Thus the transition from the territorially limited yet substantively robust guarantees of the *International Protection of Minorities System* to the broad statements of principle in Article 27 of the Covenant was not without difficulties. Nevertheless, subsequent interpretation of Article 27 has left behind many of the restrictive and paternalistic attitudes evident in the *travaux préparatoires*. In *Lovelace v. Canada*,[27] the only case to date decided under Article 27, the Human Rights Committee upheld the complaint of an Indian woman who had lost her right to live on a reserve on marriage to a non-Indian, by operation of section 12(1)(b) of the *Indian Act*.[28] The Committee stated:

> The right to live on a reserve is not as such guaranteed by article 27 of the Covenant. Moreover, the *Indian Act* does not interfere directly with the functions which are expressly mentioned in that article. However, in the opinion of the Committee the right of Sandra Lovelace to access to her native culture and language "in community with the other members" of her group, has in fact been, and continues to be interfered with, because there is no place outside of the Tobique Reserve where such a community exists.[29]

Though the language of the opinion is cautious, the result contrasts strikingly with the comments cited above. The Committee had no hesitation in applying Article 27 to protect native culture and language. Furthermore, the Committee underlined the crucial role which the institution (in this case, the reserve) plays in providing the individual with access to the culture of the group. This marks a return to the spirit of the *International Protection of Minorities System* in which the centrality of institutions is recognized in the form of provisions granting autonomy and an equitable share of state funds to certain specified minorities for religious, charitable and scholastic matters.[30]

---

26 Capotorti, *supra*, note 22 at 36.

27 [1983] Can. Hum. Rts. Y.B. 305 (U.N. Hum. Rts. Ctee.).

28 R.S.C. 1970, c. I-6 [R.S.C. 1985, c. I-5].

29 *Lovelace, supra*, note 27 at 312.

30 *E.g.*, Art. 9 of the Treaty with Poland provided that minorities would be granted an equitable share in the enjoyment of the sums which may be provided out of public funds for educational, religious or charitable purposes. Art. 10 established a mechanism whereby committees appointed by the Jewish communities would distribute this proportionate share to Jewish schools. Art. 2 of the Treaty with Romania accorded local autonomy in regard to scholastic and religious matters to the "communities of the Czecklers and Saxons". See Capotorti, *supra*, note 22, at 19, footnote 21.

In a study prepared for the United Nations Sub-Committee on Prevention of Discrimination and Protection of Minorities, Professor Capotorti calls into question the distinction made between "well-established" and immigrant minorities:

> In view of the general nature of the rules for the protection of human rights adopted within the framework of the United Nations, it is . . . inadmissible that a distinction could be made between "old" and "new" minorities. It is certainly not the function of article 27 to encourage the formation of new minorities; where a minority exists, however, the article is applicable to it, regardless of the date of its formation.[31]

Professor Capotorti expressed the view that Article 27 goes beyond prohibiting states from interfering with private exercise of the rights guaranteed therein. In addition, he thought, Article 27 created affirmative obligations on states:

> There is reason to question whether the implementation of article 27 of the Covenant does not, in fact, call for active intervention by the State. At the cultural level, in particular, it is generally agreed that, because of the enormous human and financial resources which would be needed for a full cultural development, the right granted to members of minority groups to enjoy their own culture would lose much of its meaning if no assistance from the government concerned was forthcoming.[32]

Professor Capotorti recommended that a Declaration or Convention be enacted to clarify and define the state obligations under Article 27.

In view of this recommendation, the Commission on Human Rights established a working group to consider the problem. The starting point for the group was a draft declaration submitted by Yugoslavia, which provides, *inter alia*:

> Art. 3. For the purpose of realizing conditions of full equality and complete development of minorities as collectivities and of their individual members, *it is essential to take measures* which will enable them freely to express their characteristics, to develop their culture, education, language, traditions and customs and to participate on an equitable basis in the cultural, social, economic and political life of the country in which they live.[33]

While this broad statement of positive obligation has not been adopted, preliminary agreement has been reached on the following draft article:

> 1. [Persons belonging to] [national or] ethnic, linguistic and religious minorities (hereinafter referred to as minorities) have the right to respect for, *and*

---

31 *Ibid.* at 35.

32 *Ibid.* at 36. For similar views, see Saxena, *supra*, note 21 at 49; L.B. Sohn, "The Rights of Minorities", in *The International Bill of Rights*, L. Henkin, ed. (New York: Columbia Univeristy Press, 1981) 270 at 282.

33 U.N. Doc. E/CN. 4/L.1367/Rev.1 (1978).

the promotion of, their ethnic, cultural, linguistic and religious identity without any discrimination.[34]

These materials indicate the modern tendency towards a clear, if not universal, recognition that states must do more for minorities under Article 27 than merely refrain from interfering with them.

To summarize the salient features of the foregoing examination of the background to Article 27, the following points may be made:

1. The inspiration for Article 27 was drawn from the International Protection of Minorities System. This System covered only a limited territory, and was directed at least in part at the protection of certain specific groups, but it was substantively robust in offering to these groups some control of their own institutions, and other measures tailored to their special needs.

2. In securing the universal agreement necessary to gain inclusion of Article 27 in a generally applicable guarantee of civil and political rights, certain problems arose as to the scope of application and the nature of the obligations imposed on states by Article 27. These problems are evident in the *travaux préparatoires,* and are to some extent reflected in the qualified language of Article 27.

3. Subsequent interpretation of Article 27, in the *Lovelace* case, the Capotorti report, the Working Committee of the Human Rights Commission and academic commentary, has moved a considerable distance from the restrictive and paternalistic attitudes of the *travaux préparatoires.*

4. Specifically, this more recent interpretation would not confine the application of Article 27 to historically well-established minorities, and would treat Article 27 as imposing affirmative obligations on states.

What assistance can be derived towards interpreting Canada's section 27 from this examination of its international precursor? On a textual comparison alone, these international materials should delineate the minimum content of section 27. The Charter provision avoids many of the possible weaknesses of Article 27 of the Covenant. Section 27 is not limited to either groups or individuals, but is directed to the preservation and enhancement of the multicultural heritage of all Canadians. It is not phrased in the negative. It was included in the Charter at the behest of more recent immigrant groups, so there can be no question that they fall

---

34 U.N. Doc. E/CN.4/1985/WG.5/L.2, January 18, 1985 (emphasis added). Even in this form, there is reluctance on the part of some participants to accept that affirmative state measures are mandated. See U.N. Doc. E/CN.4/1986/43 (March 10, 1986) at 5-6.

outside its application. Section 27 suffers in the comparison to Article 27 of the Covenant only in that it is not free-standing, but must be applied as an interpretational tenet. Once implicated by a claim under another Charter right or freedom, section 27's scope and strength of application should exceed the structural limits of its international counterpart.

Beyond a textual comparison of the two provisions, it would seem likely that trends under the Charter's section 27 will follow those established under Article 27 of the Covenant, towards ever greater recognition of the dictates of the special needs of cultural minorities. As the obligations under the Covenant provision become more sharply defined (perhaps by means of a Declaration or Convention), and the jurisprudence of the Human Rights Committee fleshes out these definitions, Canadian courts and policy makers will inherit valuable precedents. Enlightened application of the multiculturalism principle in Canada may also provide a model for the international bodies charged with interpreting the Covenant, allowing the two provisions to develop in symbiosis.

5. JURISPRUDENCE

If application of the multiculturalism principle in Canadian courts had the potential to furnish a developed doctrinal model to other nations and international bodies, this potential has not been realized thus far. At this early stage of Charter litigation no coherent doctrine has yet matured around section 27. Canadian courts contradict each other in their attempts to interpret the Charter so as to preserve and enhance multiculturalism.

The most detailed exposition of section 27 to date comes from Tarnopolsky J.A., in *R. v. Videoflicks*.[35] His Lordship traced the history of the section, including its connection with Article 27 of the *International Covenant on Civil and Political Rights*, and reached the following result:

> [M]y conclusion that a law infringes freedom of religion, if it makes more difficult and more costly to practise one's religion, is supported by the fact that such a law does not help to preserve and certainly does not serve to enhance or promote that part of one's culture which is religiously based.[36]

This case upheld convictions of four businesses for remaining open on a Sunday contrary to the *Retail Business Holidays Act*, but allowed a fifth appeal brought by Saturday-observing Jews.

The differences of judicial opinion regarding section 27 are well illustrated by the varied approaches taken to the Sunday closing problem. It seems to be agreed that the section informs the meaning of freedom

---

35 *Supra*, note 5.
36 *Ibid.* at 25 (O.A.C.).

of religion, since "there can be no doubt but that religion is one of the main constituent parts of the culture of most societies".[37] There is no similar consensus on the effect of the section. According to one view, it directs that "a measure of equal treatment be dispensed when interpreting any problem involving the *Charter* and a problem involving multicultural considerations". However, this focus on equality conflicts with constitutionally-entrenched preferred status for certain groups, so "it may be that full equality is neither possible nor desirable".[38] This perspective emphasizes the status of cultural minorities relative to the majority.

A similar but bolder view is taken by Dickson C.J.C. in two cases which reached the Supreme Court: *R. v. Big M Drug Mart Ltd.*[39] and *Edwards Books and Art Ltd. v. R.* (the latter being the appeal from *Videoflicks*).[40] In the first case, the court invalidated a federal statute which imposed Sunday as a day of rest for avowedly religious reasons.[41] The Chief Justice maintained that "to accept that Parliament retains the right to compel universal observance of the day of rest preferred by one religion is not consistent with the preservation and enhancement of the multicultural heritage of Canadians".[42] He elaborated as follows:

> [A]s I read the *Charter*, it mandates that the legislative preservation of a Sunday day of rest should be secular, the diversity of belief and non-belief, the diverse socio-cultural backgrounds of Canadians make it constitutionally incompetent for the federal Parliament to provide legislative preference for any one religion at the expense of those of another religious persuasion.[43]

In *Edwards Books*, the Supreme Court considered just such a "secular" preservation of Sunday as a day of rest. The Chief Justice referred to section 27 as supporting a meaning of freedom of religion, comprising protection both from direct and indirect coercion. Any more restrictive interpretation would be "inconsistent with the Court's obligation under s. 27".[44] The court found the *Retail Business Holidays Act* infringed on freedom of religion in that it gave an economic advantage to Sunday observers as compared to observers of other days such as the Sabbath. The Chief Justice upheld the statute as a "reasonable limit" on freedom of religion under section 1 of the Charter. This ruling was motivated by an exemption in the Act

---

37 *R. v. W.H. Smith*, [1983] 5 W.W.R. 235 at 258 (Alta. Prov. Ct.), *per* Jones Prov. Ct. J.
38 *Ibid.*
39 [1985] 1 S.C.R. 295.
40 *Supra*, note 5.
41 *Lord's Day Act*, R.S.C. 1970, c. L-13, s. 4.
42 *R. v. Big M Drug Mart Ltd.*, *supra*, note 39 at 337-338.
43 *Ibid.* at 351.
44 *Edwards Books & Art Ltd. v. R.*, *supra*, note 5 at 758 (S.C.R.), *per* Dickson C.J.C.

which allows stores of less than a certain size to stay open on Sunday if closed the previous Sunday.

Madam Justice Wilson in the same case used section 27 in a strikingly different way. Her Ladyship declined to uphold the statute under section 1. She reasoned that the exemption allows some but not all of the members of Sunday-observing minorities to do business on Sundays. This effectively introduces "an invidious distinction into the group and sever[s] the religious and cultural tie that binds them together".[45] Therefore, section 27 expressly precluded the court from interpreting section 1 as relevant to the statutory scheme.

Mr. Justice La Forest took yet another view of section 27. His Lordship concentrated on the provision's effect with respect to the position of cultural minorities *vis-à-vis* each other, rather than relative to the dominant majority. Moslems, he noted, are also a sizable group in Canadian society. They observe neither Saturday nor Sunday as a day of rest. Thus, "it is not at first sight easy to see why an exemption is not constitutionally required for Moslems, if it is required for Jews and other Saturday observers. The provision of the *Charter*, s. 27, favouring multiculturalism would reinforce this way of looking at things."[46]

The cases on minority education rights delineate two views on the effect of section 27 which are almost diametrically opposed. In *Reference re Education Act of Ontario and Minority Language Rights*,[47] the Ontario Court of Appeal treated the section as a constitutional imperative:

> In the light of s. 27, s. 23(3)(*b*) should be interpreted to mean that minority language children must receive their instruction in facilities in which the educational environment will be that of the linguistic minority. Only then can the facilities reasonably be said to reflect the minority culture and appertain to the minority.

However, on the issue of full funding for Catholic schools under consideration in *Reference re an Act to Amend the Education Act (Ont.)*,[48] the minority judgment of the same court came close to suggesting that section 27 effectively prevents a government from conferring a benefit on one cultural group without making it available to all:

> As matters presently stand, no government policy has yet been formulated which takes into account the reality that denominational schools other than

---

45 *Ibid.* at 804 (S.C.R.) *per* Wilson J.

46 *Ibid.* at 804 (S.C.R.) *per* La Forest J.

47 (1984), 10 D.L.R. (4th) 491 at 529 (Ont. C.A.). S. 27 was also referred to, but not discussed, in a similar setting in *Mahe v. Alberta* (1985), 64 A.R. 35 at 40 (Q.B.), aff'd (1987), 80 A.R. 161 (C.A.), leave to appeal to S.C.C. granted (1988), 85 A.R. 80 (S.C.C.).

48 (1986), 53 O.R. (2d) 513 at 562 (C.A.), *per* Howland C.J.O. and Robins J.A., aff'd [1987] S.C.R. 1148.

Roman Catholic exist in Ontario or which seeks to accommodate the Charter rights of supporters of those schools or promote the proclaimed objective of s. 27 to preserve and enhance the multicultural heritage of Canadians.

The right to representation of an accused's ethnic group in a jury has been suggested as a corollary of section 27, with mixed success. In *R. v. Kent*,[49] the Manitoba Court of Appeal rejected the notion that an Indian accused had the right to a jury composed exclusively or proportionately of persons of his race. The court held that section 27 supported the Crown's position that every qualified person is entitled to be called for jury duty. Here, as in the 1986 *Reference re An Act to Amend the Education Act*, section 27 was used to bar preferential treatment for any one group. However, in *R. v. Punch*,[50] section 27 was invoked to strike down the provisions in the *Criminal Code*[51] permitting the use of six-person juries in the Northwest Territories. The reason offered was that a 12-person jury would be more likely to reflect accurately the multicultural composition of the Northwest Territories' population.

An inventive, though unusual, application of section 27 is found in *R. v. Keegstra*.[52] The court considered whether *Criminal Code* proscription against hate propaganda, offensive to freedom of expression, could be justified under section 1. Owing to evidentiary problems, material on similar laws in other "free and democratic societies" and similar international instruments was not available for the court's consideration (though some British material was admitted under a provision of the *Canada Evidence Act*). Faced with limited resources on which to base a comparison the trial judge cited section 27 as supporting the inherent reasonableness of the limits on freedom of expression which the *Criminal Code* proscription imposed.

From the above cases, it may be observed that the multiculturalism principle enshrined in section 27 is applicable to a wide variety of situations, and can suggest a correspondingly wide range of results. Even on similar issues, section 27 encourages approaches fundamentally opposed to each other. The broad sweep of the text, combined with the paucity of accumulated doctrine, have made section 27 a flexible but unpredictable tool in the hands of the judiciary.

6. NEED FOR MEDIATING PRINCIPLES

Orthodox methods of constitutional interpretation offer little assis-

---

49 (1986), 40 Man. R. (2d) 160 at 175 (C.A.).
50 [1986] 1 W.W.R. 592 at 609–610 (N.W.T. S.C.).
51 R.S.C. 1970, c. C1-134 [R.S.C. 1985, c. C-46].
52 (1984), 19 C.C.C. (3d) 254 at 277 (Alta. Q.B.).

tance in approaching section 27 of the Charter. The reason is, as we have seen, that concentration on the text of section 27 reveals no coherent principle which courts can apply. There is no readily apparent meaning to be gleaned from the words of the text — no intelligible or agreed upon content for the multiculturalism principle. Nor does investigation of the constitutional sources behind section 27 yield much in the way of a coherent multiculturalism principle which courts can apply. Instead, one discovers a vast heterogeneity of meanings or ideologies, not one of which is so sufficiently developed that it can form a principled approach to section 27. These difficulties are compounded by the fact that section 27 is not a free-standing provision — it is only an interpretational guide. In terms, section 27 is meant to orient judicial appreciation of Canada's entire Charter-based system. In other words, interpretation of section 27 is beset by the difficulty that section 27 is itself an interpretational principle.

Because of textual and doctrinal ambiguity, coherent application of section 27 requires development of "mediating principles" — precepts which render useful and intelligible the words of the text. The concept of a "mediating principle" was developed by Professor Owen Fiss in relation to the equal protection clause in this way:

> [Mediating principles] "stand between" the courts and the Constitution — to give meaning and content to an ideal embodied in the text. These principles are offered as a paraphrase of the particular textual provision, but in truth the relationship is much more fundamental. They give the provision its only meaning as a guide for decision.
> The words [of the equal protection clause] do not state an intelligible rule of decision. In that sense the text has no meaning. . . . This ambiguity has created the need for a mediating principle, and the one chosen by courts and commentators is the antidiscrimination principle.[53]

Obviously the choice of a mediating principle dictates the juridical content of the constitutional provision in question. It was the stifling narrowness of the antidiscrimination principle that impelled Professor Fiss to analyze the interpretational process in this way, and to argue for the appropriateness of additional wider mediating principles relevant to constitutional norms of equality.

It is my thesis that choice, development and enrichment of mediating principles is the key to unlocking the mysteries of section 27. In what follows, I wish to outline various alternative principles capable of making section 27 intelligible. The alternatives are not mutually exclusive, nor do they exhaust the potential meanings of section 27. But they do capture the predominant urges of the multiculturalism idea.

---

53 O.M. Fiss, "Groups and the Equal Protection Clause" (1976), 5 *Phil. & Pub. Affs.* 107 at 107-108.

Before listing a menu of mediating principles appropriate to section 27, it would be wise to inquire into the minimum conditions which such ideas must satisfy in order to be acceptable as juridically useful precepts. There are three such conditions. First, a coherent mediating principle must be capable of reconciling or balancing the interests of majority and minority groups. Majoritarian systems allow the majority wide latitude to dictate the core values which motivate socio-economic development. These will often conflict with the needs of minority groups which desire to develop in their own distinctive ways. An acceptable multiculturalism principle must be capable of moderating the power of the majority to interfere with the self-perceived interests of minorities, without unduly compromising the legitimate interest of the majority to govern according to the democratic principle. Second, while any multiculturalism principle necessarily implies high regard for the autonomy and diversity of minorities, the limit is reached when excessive centrifugal pressure on the political system imperils national unity. Third, a multiculturalism principle must be analytically and intellectually intelligible to a high degree. As a working tool, it must be amenable of easy application by the practising bar, bench and other actors in Canada's politico-juridical system.

7. MEDIATING PRINCIPLES

(a) Antidiscrimination

While a strong antidiscrimination principle flows from the Charter's equality guarantees at section 15, this leaves something to be desired from the perspective of ethno-cultural communities. Section 15 provides equality and antidiscrimination guarantees to "every *individual* [La loi ... s'applique également *à tous*]". On a strict interpretation, section 15 does not apply to groups. However, it is not a particularly long stretch to reach that interpretation from the text of section 15. The application of section 27 to the antidiscrimination principle in section 15 assists courts in taking that step. With respect to other Charter guarantees, section 27 itself contains an antidiscrimination principle, applicable to groups, at least insofar as a group *qua* group claims protection of Charter rights.

Any juridical system which is oriented around preservation and enhancement of ethnicity must pay scrupulous regard to the antidiscrimination principle. Discrimination is the principal pain associated with maintenance of distinctive cultural traits. If the cost of maintaining cultural boundaries is too high, assimilation becomes increasingly attractive to individual members of ethno-cultural minorities. Assimilation is the opposite of "preservation and enhancement". For this reason, the antidiscrimination precept is an obvious and important principle mediating exposition of section 27.

Ethno-cultural minorities must interact with other groups in Canada's political system. Ethnic minorities pursue political agendas necessary to their maintenance and development. If discrimination significantly inhibits the minority's access to the political system, or impedes its ability to interact with dominant groups, the minority's ability to develop is impaired. For this second reason, a strong antidiscrimination principle inhabits any juridical system meaning to maintain and enhance distinctive cultural groups in Canada.

The limits of the antidiscrimination principle in service of group preservation and enhancement are striking. Antidiscrimination measures focus on individuals. They are designed to correct instances of individual prejudice. The antidiscrimination precept is awkward in coming to terms with group inequality in the sense of compelling remedial measures. The reason is that affirmative action necessarily inflates the power of disadvantaged minorities at the expense of other groups, thereby increasing jealousy and resentment. Affirmative action frequently benefits those in the targeted minority who are least in need of assistance. This contributes to the low status of the more disadvantaged members of the target minority.[54]

The antidiscrimination principle emanates from ideals of equality, not multiculturalism. To some extent, a concentrated focus on advantages that one group obtains *vis-à-vis* other groups is counterproductive to enhancement and development of the distinctive cultural pluralism which inspires section 27. The equality perspective gives rise to unprofitable but compelling arguments that it is illegitimate to confer benefits on one group, without simultaneously making such benefits available to all others.[55] The practical effect of this limit is to retard progress for all groups.

(b) Symbolic Ethnicity

One critical aspect of section 27, requiring the interposition of mediating principles, is the concept of "cultural heritage". Curial habits of mind invite an excursus through the dictionaries in search of definitions.

---

54 "[A]ffirmative action does injustice to low-income women, to low-status men, and to mothers who work at home. Affirmative action also ignores the dilemma of negative fertility and its implications for pension fundability and the ability of society to care for the aged": C. Winn, "*Affirmative Action for Women: More Than a Case of Simple Justice*" (1985), 28 *Can. Pub. Admin.* 24.

55 *Reference re an Act to Amend the Education Act, (Ont.), supra,* note 48. The argument was unsuccessful with the majority of three, but formed the principal basis of the opinion delivered by Howland C.J.O. and Robins J.A.

The exercise is unlikely to prove profitable. The social sciences have struggled arduously with the intricately related phenomenon of ethnicity, and made impressive strides. The social science materials may be recast as mediating principles useful in expounding section 27.

Social psychology is particularly relevant. Social psychologists have demonstrated that the individual self is incomplete without integration into a social group. The thesis maintains that formation of an individual self is not possible without experiencing that self from the perspective of other members of the social group into which the individual has integrated. "The individual experiences himself as such, not directly, but only indirectly from the particularist standpoints of other individual members from the same social group, or from the generalized standpoint of the social group as a whole to which he belongs."[56]

The ethnic individual completes a significant aspect of personality — forms a self — by voluntary identification with an ethnic group. This process is here termed "symbolic ethnicity". Symbolic ethnicity is a psychological idea which conceives of "cultural heritage" as a voluntary identification of the self with the traditions and history of a particular group. The link completes the ethnic individual's identity in the sense that it allows that individual to form a self — to experience his being from the attitudes and reflexes of his ethnic community.

Attacks on cultural heritage are thus attacks on the individual selfs of the ethnic group's members. This is how they are experienced, notwithstanding that the ethnic individual's tie to his community is voluntary. Practices which restrict autonomy of ethnic communities to develop in their own distinctive way, or to manifest freely their community experiences in daily rituals, institutions and social interaction with others, choke the self-development of individual members of ethnic communities.

As a mediating principle, symbolic ethnicity concentrates the attention of courts on these aspects of personality in expounding associated Charter rights. At the minimum, courts applying section 27 through the mediation of "symbolic ethnicity" would have to pay scrupulous regard to the need for the group to develop the essential attributes of its personality, and to express these in ways that can be internalized by individuals. Courts equally would have to concentrate their attention on the individual's need for access to the group and its activities.

How might these considerations become practically important? While one might not have thought of the Wednesday night folk dance as an activity loaded with constitutional significance, the "symbolic ethnicity" principle

---

56 G.H. Mead, *Mind, Self and Society* (Chicago: Univ. of Chicago Press, 1962) at 138. See also G.H. Mead, *On Social Psychology* (Chicago: Univ. of Chicago Press, 1964) at 19, 33 *et seq.*

may require revision of this view. Voluntary cultural activities, such as film festivals, folk events, religious occasions, provisions of educational opportunities including language instruction and the like implicate constitutional guarantees for section 2 fundamental freedoms — religion, expression, assembly and association. They also touch on equality values through the allocation of governmental facilities such as school gymnasia, parks and the expenditure of funds. In considering governmental obstruction of, or disinclination to facilitate, these and related activities, courts would have to assume an aroused sense of respect for the importance of symbolic ethnicity as a critical inspiration behind Canada's constitutional commitment to the multiculturalism principle.

Symbolic ethnicity, like the antidiscrimination principle, has limits. Symbolic ethnicity emphasizes social psychological attitudes rather than institutional structures. It is thus in the service of "a collection of individuals who use ethnic characteristics when it suits their psychological needs," not "a mosaic of internally integrated ethnic groups".[57] By allowing those who make and interpret policy to sense that their multiculturalism obligations end with the provision of space and money to ethnic organizations, the symbolic ethnicity principle diverts attention from the more difficult questions of allocation of power between groups in Canada's political system.

(c) Structural Ethnicity

(i) *Definition*

A second principle drawn from the social sciences goes far beyond the dictates of symbolic ethnicity as applied to section 27. I will call the second mediating principle "structural ethnicity". "Structural ethnicity" refers to the capacity of a collectivity to perpetuate itself, control leakage, resist assimilation and propagate its beliefs and practices. This form of ethnicity is not a matter of voluntary individual choice. Rather, it requires the creation, by the group or government, of an institutional infrastructure which can nurture the well-being of the group and maintain the group's sense of self-justification. Structural ethnicity is significantly more difficult to "preserve and enhance" than symbolic ethnicity because the autonomy and power required to support, operate and expand the minority's institutional structure brings the minority into direct conflict with other groups.

---

57 L. Roberts & R. Clifton, "Exploring the Ideology of Canadian Multiculturalism" (1982), 8 *Can. Pub. Pol.* 88 at 89-90.

(ii) *Content*

What would be embraced by an adequate institutional infrastructure designed for group preservation? At a minimum, the following would be included:

1. mechanisms through which the group can interact with other groups, particularly the dominant or governing groups in the society (political structures);
2. economic structures to dampen the assimilating pressures exerted by the mainstream economy;
3. mechanisms for propagation and transmission of the group's beliefs (ethnic schools, religious institutions and ethnic associations);
4. mechanisms of group definition, *i.e.*, legal right to define membership by including or excluding individuals (a power of excommunication or exclusion exercised by *e.g.* a priesthood or band council);
5. defensive mechanisms able to restrict the group's members from exposure to alternative norms, values and practices (e.g. governing structures and social norms in Hutterite agricultural communities).

(iii) *Examples and Application*

Some examples might serve to illustrate the diversity of forms in which the institutional infrastructure may be manifested. Guaranteed representation in legislative bodies for aboriginal communities, reformulation of territorial boundaries to create ethnic majorities, or funding for political lobbies such as the *Fédération des Francophones hors-Québec* are accepted political structures which enhance the multicultural heritage of present-day Canadians as appreciated from the perspective of structural ethnicity. Economic initiatives justified by the multicultural principle could include creation of agencies such as the Metis Development Corporation, the abandonment of tax room by government in favour of aboriginal self-governing entities, or the establishment in Western Canada of a major French-language research university.[58] These economic initiatives are crucial if Metis communities are to resist fragmentation by the need to find employment in economically active areas, if aboriginal communities are to utilize self-government as a means of self-preservation or if Western francophones are to resist the assimilating pressure exerted by the virtually exclusive use of English as the language of work.

Application of the structural ethnicity principle in education is crucial. It impacts significantly on the extant demands of ethnic, religious and linguistic minorities for greater segregation of and control over educational

---

58 See J.E. Magnet, *The Future of Official Language Minorities* (1986) 27 *C. de D.* 189-201.

facilities, resources and governing structures. The principle would assist linguistic minorities, official or otherwise, to achieve homogenous, self-governing educational structures organized on linguistic lines, or at least some facsimile thereof. It would strengthen the claims of religious minorities to control their schools, and to imbue the atmosphere therein with religious flavour. These tendencies of the structural ethnicity principle as applied to education further the multicultural ideal by aggressively transmitting culture from one generation to the next. The process is intensified by restricting children in the cultural group from access to alien norms during their crucial formative years.

The structural ethnicity principle also has important ramifications in the context of competing claims concerning group definition. The principle mandates that the group have significant power to define its boundaries, and thus to establish and apply criteria for including or excluding members.[59] This power will on occasion collide with constitutional norms of free association, due process and equality which underline society's high interest in limiting this power to responsible uses. Society's interest takes on added relevance where, as mandated by the structural ethnicity principle, government devolves power and resources on the group. In that event, access to group membership becomes a means to enjoyment of government-derived benefits, a phenomenon which commands an aroused sense of respect for constitutional guarantees of individual rights.

Some would maintain that where government benefits are implicated, government ought to retain complete control over the conditions of entitlement. This traditional, paternalistic view is not tenable in light of recent judicial and legislative developments.

By *An Act to Amend the Indian Act* (the *"Reinstatement Act"*),[60] an Indian band is given power to "assume control of its own membership" (section 10(1)) on condition that it establish membership rules in writing and respect the right of existing and reinstated band members to be registered in the band. Membership in the band includes tangible benefits: the right to live on a reservation, to share in band revenues and profits and to claim a portion of band property upon leaving. The power to control membership is a departure from the former system of registration with the Department of Indian and Northern Affairs. The Act has been challenged by six Alberta Indians on their own behalf, and on behalf of their bands. The plaintiffs assert a constitutionally guaranteed aboriginal right to determine membership which, they submit, is infringed by controls imposed under the Act. Plaintiffs also claim interference with their Charter-

---

59 This problem is discussed in greater detail *infra* under Part 9: Problems of Cultural Autonomy.

60 S.C. 1985, c. 27 [R.S.C 1985, c. 32 (1st Supp.)].

protected association rights with respect to reinstatement of certain Indians excluded under the former *Indian Act*. A motion to strike the claim for disclosing no reasonable cause of action was dismissed.[61] A "structural ethnicity" application of section 27 would impact significantly on the approach the court takes to interpretation of association guarantees when the case eventually comes on for trial. From this perspective, section 27 would add weight to the plaintiffs' claim that their association rights should take precedence over the government's concern to guarantee fairness to individuals affected by the unrestricted power to control membership asserted by the plaintiffs.

In *Caldwell v. Stuart*,[62] the Supreme Court of Canada considered the complaint of a Roman Catholic teacher who was not rehired by a Catholic school because she married a divorced man in a civil ceremony, contrary to Church dogma. The complaint underscored conflict between the teacher's individual right to freedom of religion, and the Church's historic power to define the standards necessary to insure a Catholic atmosphere in the school. In dismissing the teacher's complaint, the court emphasized "the special nature and objectives of the school" and found "the acceptance and observance of the Church's rules regarding marriage . . . reasonably necessary to assure the achievement of the objects of the school".[63] These results were reached notwithstanding that the school enjoyed government benefits and subsidies. Although this case was not litigated under the Charter, it should be clear that a structural ethnicity approach to section 27 would strengthen the controversial conclusion arrived at by the Supreme Court.

The tragic sense — shared suffering — solidifies ethnic communities. Groups that endure oppression, that share long common histories of persecution, acquire tremendous motivation to coalesce in a defensive posture as a bulwark against external challenge. A key formative feature of the social psychology of Canadian Hutterites is the bitter experience of persecution dating back to their origins in 1528. Regarded as heretics, Hutterites fled before successive orthodoxies, settling in Canada between 1918 and 1922. Oppression continued in their adopted Canadian homeland. The *Land Sales Prohibition Act, 1942* (Alberta) regarded Hutterites as enemy aliens, and prohibited all transfer of land to them.

Hutterites live communally under a clearly defined, highly autocratic authority structure. There is no privately held property, nor does any devolve upon individuals when they leave the community. Socialization of children is rigorously controlled, as is exposure to outsiders and outside

---

61 *Twinn v. R.*, [1987] 2 F.C. 450 (T.D.) (Strayer J.).
62 [1984] 2 S.C.R. 603.
63 *Ibid.* at 625.

norms. A religiously inspired austerity ethic forbids "worldly" pleasures such as radio, television, dancing, jewelry and higher education.[64] Final authority in all spiritual and temporal colony matters rests with a "senior preacher" whose lifetime position is partly elective and partly selected by "divine guidance". Women are excluded from all decision-making bodies, and denied the vote for senior preacher and other governing offices.

The characteristic ethnic feature of Hutterites is a governing structure that fosters dependency of individuals on the group, in the sense that individual Hutterites are unprepared for movement to or participation in the larger society. The community assumes much legal power normally exercised by state organs, particularly with respect to education, voting rights and property. To some extent maintenance of this structure requires *prima facie* infringement of constitutional norms manifest in the Charter.

This last observation brings the structural ethnicity principle sharply into focus. When judges and politicians undertake the delicate task of testing conflicting Charter values against practices essential to Hutterite ethnic persistence, the principle will moderate the force of Charter precepts based on individual rights. From this point of view, the structural ethnicity principle inherent in section 27 will temper Charter norms by underlining the crucial role defensive structuring plays in preservation of certain groups.[65]

It will thus be seen that, to the extent the structural ethnicity principle inheres in section 27, a dramatic impact on Canada's Charter system results. While some might recoil from imbedding the multiculturalism idea this deep in Canadian political culture, it is only fair to point out that the idea is not novel as an inspiration for Canada's political system. The creation of the Quebec provincial government and legislature, and the vesting in them of the substantial powers flowing from section 92(13) of the *Constitution Act, 1867*, is the best example of devolving political power on one ethnic group in order to ensure the security of that group and enhance its capacity to perpetuate itself and develop in its own particular way. This constitutional structure is paralleled at the federal level by dual central institutions comprising, for example, substantial Quebec representation in the House of Commons, Senate and Supreme Court of Canada. Such examples are in accordance with an important principle of successful

---

64 See generally Boldt, "Maintaining Ethnic Boundaries: The Case of the Hutterites" in R.N. Bienvenue & J.E. Goldstein, *Ethnicity and Ethnic Relations in Canada*, 2nd ed. (Toronto: Butterworths, 1985) at 91.

65 This kind of balancing between individual and group rights protected under various human rights codes has an established precedent in statutory exceptions to the discrimination prohibition. For example, s. 20 of the *Charter of Human Rights and Freedoms*, R.S.Q. 1977, c. C-12, deems non-discriminatory distinctions, exclusions or preferences oriented around "the well-being of an ethnic group".

federalism — that, generally speaking, "federal systems have been most successful where the provincial units have reflected, or have been reorganized to reflect, as far as possible, the most fundamental regional interests within the society.[66] In this sense, Canada belongs to a family of pluralistic nations where political power is divided along ethno-cultural lines.

Although federalism is an important reconciler of ethnic tension in Canada, the drawing of provincial boundaries created new minorities: English and French Catholics in Ontario, anglophone Protestants in Quebec, francophones in the provinces with anglophone majorities. Canada's Constitution makers responded to the insecurities of these groups by constitutional mechanisms fully compatible with the urges underlying the structural ethnicity principle. Canadian minorities are protected by collective rights and institutional autonomy with respect to language, religious education, governmental services and representation in the provincial legislatures; and the federal government has been placed in a protector's role with respect to the institutions by which linguistic and religious minorities preserve and enhance their distinctiveness.

The conflicts which are managed by these constitutional processes will continue to be worked out in the post-Charter world. An aroused sense of respect for the structural ethnicity principle should caution Canadian courts to take special care in tampering with the delicate national compromises respecting minorities on which Canada's political structure is erected. These fragile fault lines are newly vulnerable in light of the individualistic urges flowing from the Charter.

The structural ethnicity principle would tend to "preserve" the integrity of these sensitive national understandings. It would also "enhance" their management in the sense that it invites courts to be inventive in finding new dimensions of autonomy and power for minorities where old constitutional machinery is antiquated. Nor is the structural ethnicity principle limited to historic rivalries. Section 27 fell into place at the insistence of the "third force" — the immigrant minorities. It must be taken to extend to the claims for greater power welling up from ethnic minorities unprotected by historic constitutional provisions.

Obviously, the absurd case is a claim that the structural ethnicity principle goes so far as to guarantee to every sub-national group its own provincial government. Nor can the principle increase the powers of those provincial governments, like Quebec, predominantly under the control of one ethnic group. Section 31 of the Charter explicitly precludes a Charter interpretation which extends the legislative powers of any body or authority. However, the structural ethnicity principle may nevertheless encourage

---

66 R.L. Watts, *Multicultural Societies and Federalism* (Ottawa: Queen's Printer, 1970) (Studies of the Royal Commission on Bilingualism and Biculturalism, No. 8) at 86.

creation of quasi-autonomous administrative structures less independent than semi-sovereign provincial entities endowed with legislative power. The creation of quasi-autonomous administrative structures under the control of particular groups is a powerful means of ensuring that these groups have the capacity to maintain themselves and to develop according to their particular perception of their own special requirements.

We have already taken a preliminary look at how international law norms and especially the *International System for the Protection of Minorities* pay high regard to administrative autonomy as an important means of guaranteeing the security and collective well-being of minority groups. The *Versailles Treaty* with Poland, 1919, served as a model for the post-World War One treaties containing protections for minorities. The *Versailles Treaty* guaranteed to Polish nationals belonging to racial, religious or linguistic minorities the right, at their own expense, to establish, manage and control charitable, religious and social institutions, schools and other educational establishments. Within these institutions, the minorities were guaranteed the right to use their own language and freely exercise their religious precepts. Where the minority was especially concentrated, it was granted special, additional rights with respect to language.[67]

In the *Minority Schools in Albania* case,[68] the Permanent Court of International Justice explained the central thrust of the *International System for the Protection of Minorities*:

> The idea underlying the treaties for the protection of minorities is to secure for certain elements incorporated in a State, the population of which differs from them in race, language or religion, the possibility of living peaceably alongside that population and co-operating amicably with it, while at the same time *preserving the characteristics which distinguish them from the majority, and satisfying the ensuing special needs*; [emphasis added]

The court continued:

> In order to attain this object, two things are regarded as particularly necessary, and have formed the subject of provisions in these treaties.
>
> The first is to ensure that nationals belonging to racial, religious or linguistic minorities shall be placed in every respect on a footing of perfect equality with the other nationals of the state.
>
> The second is *to ensure for the minority elements suitable means for the preservation of their racial peculiarities, their traditions and their national characteristics.*
>
> *The two requirements are indeed closely interlocked, for there would be no true equality between a majority and a minority if the latter were deprived*

---

67 See Dinstein, *supra*, note 19 at 115.

68 (1934), Series A-B, Fasc. no. 63, Judgments, Orders and Advisory Opinions of the Permanent Court of International Justice, p. 17.

of its own institutions, and were consequently compelled to renounce that which constitutes the very essence of its being a minority; [emphasis added].

The *Albania* case makes clear that administrative autonomy with respect to institutions (like schools) of central importance in preservation and maintenance of minorities, is an obligation imposed by the international law system. It is this system, and this associated obligation, which was codified in Article 27 of the *International Covenant on Civil and Political Rights* which itself was the precursor of section 27 of the *Canadian Charter of Rights*. Accordingly, administrative autonomy over institutions essential to group maintenance *and enhancement* ought to prompt an aroused sense of respect on the part of those charged with interpreting the Charter.

Administrative autonomy could take many forms. The federal or provincial legislatures could devolve power upon locally elected assemblies that remain subordinate to the senior government. This distinguishes the system from federalism, where the powers of regional units are co-ordinate to the centre, and may not be unilaterally rescinded. The regionalism principle characterizes the Italian Constitution, which, because of communal problems, divides the jurisdiction into five autonomous regions. The regions enjoy extensive powers including financial autonomy backed by taxing powers and a guaranteed share of national taxes, control over police, roads, transport, agriculture and industry. The regions are governed by a regional council and an executive *giunta* with a president. Between 1922 and 1972, the United Kingdom Parliament devolved power upon the ethnically distinct community in Northern Ireland, with similar extensive powers.[69] Another form of administrative autonomy is decentralization of the national administration by creation of regional offices staffed by national officers, but with power to implement distinct regional policies. The Scottish Office in Edinburgh, for example, has regional administrative powers in relation to education, police, justice, health, agriculture and fisheries.

Within existing Canadian governmental structures, the principle of administrative autonomy may be effectuated by a realignment of the boundaries of local government units. Local government units could be organized on the basis of ethnically distinct populations. Units so constituted could be granted enhanced powers.

A final example of administrative autonomy is the creation of community development authorities. Various aspects of the community support system could be devolved on these groups. Canada already has some experience with such institutions in both the public and private

---

69 See generally C. Palley, "The Role of Law in Relation to Minority Groups", in Alcock, Taylor & Welton, *The Future of Cultural Minorities* (London: MacMillan, 1979), 120 at 143 *et seq.*, who makes, and elaborates on these points.

domains, with community groups being given responsibility and funding to administer colleges, libraries, museums, social welfare systems and the like. This model admits of more flexible implementation in cases where ethnically distinct groups lack territorial concentration.

In implementing such structures, a sterile notion of symmetry between groups, or an unsophisticated concept of equality, may not be the most appropriate criteria. Historical and demographic considerations, as well as the wishes of the groups involved, may make the claims of some communities to such structures stronger than others. Thus it is easy to see how the structural ethnicity principle can be pressed into service to buttress the claims of aboriginal communities in the North to self-government by focussing the attention of policy makers on ethnically distinct local or regional government entities. It would be more difficult to countenance a claim to administrative autonomy by members of a group who have demonstrated little historical cohesiveness, and, as an organized entity, show no desire for the responsibilities of self-administration.

8. THE MULTICULTURALISM PRINCIPLE AND COLLECTIVE RIGHTS

All charters of rights are inspired by a profound sense of individual liberty, which derives from the eighteenth century philosophers, and which found archetypal expression in the *American Bill of Rights* in 1791. The overriding function of a Charter of Rights "is to provide . . . for the unremitting protection of individual rights and liberties."[70] Constitutions provide a framework for the legitimate exercise of governmental power.[71] Charters of Rights create within that framework a private area of human space in which conscience reigns supreme as the motivator of human action. Within the protected domain, government cannot use majoritarian preferences to obstruct the operation of individual conscience as the motivator of human action. As the Supreme Court of Canada explained the purpose of Charter-protected fundamental freedoms in *R. v. Big M. Drug Mart Ltd.*: "[An] emphasis on individual conscience and individual judgment . . . lies at the heart of our democratic tradition."[72]

Such a forceful statement of protection of the individual is a welcome and necessary addition to Canada's constitutional system. Yet integration of a Charter jurisprudence into Canada's governmental structure requires sensitivity to the special nature of Canada's constitutional traditions. The unique genius of Canadian constitutionalism is rooted in the principle of

---

70 *Hunter v. Southam Inc., supra,* note 5 at 155.
71 *Ibid.*
72 *Supra,* note 39 at 346.

bi-nationality and cultural pluralism. Canada's federal system proceeds directly from the requirements of a bi-national state.[73] Canada's fundamental commitment to cultural pluralism is entrenched deep into its constitutional structure by the creation of special autonomous status for aboriginal communities; self-governing institutions for denominational education; distinct protection in the machinery of government for linguistic minorities; and protection of the linguistic integrity of certain minority language electoral districts.[74] This tradition was extended and reinforced by proclamation of the *Canadian Charter of Rights* in 1982, one third of the provisions of which pertain to the collective rights of semi-autonomous groups.[75] One cannot, therefore, speak seriously about Canadian multiculturalism without considering the unique role played by collective rights of autonomous communities within the Canadian federation.[76]

Notwithstanding the long tradition of collective rights as a distinctive mark of Canadian constitutional development, one cannot help but notice that the administration of collective rights in Canadian courts has been unsatisfactory. So far from preserving and enhancing the security of Canadian minorities, situations in which Canadian minorities sought protection through collective rights mechanisms engendered bitter hostility and perilous conflict. There are virtually no collective rights cases which the minorities won.[77] Even in the very few cases in which claims brought under collective rights provisions succeeded, the minorities usually failed

---

73 "[B]ut . . . we found that such a [legislative union] was impracticable. In the first place, it would not meet the assent of the people of Lower Canada, because they felt that in their peculiar position — being in a minority, with a different language, nationality, and religion from the majority . . . their institutions and their laws might be assailed . . . . So that those who were, like myself, in favour of a Legislative Union, were obliged to modify their views and accept the project of a Federal Union as the only scheme practicable": speech of Sir John A. MacDonald on the motion to adopt the Quebec Resolutions, as reprinted in H.E. Egerton & W.L. Grant, *Canadian Constitutional Development* (Toronto: Musson Book, 1907) at 362-363.

74 See generally J.E. Magnet, "Collective Rights, Cultural Autonomy and the Canadian State" (1986), 32 *McGill L.J.* 170 at 172-173, and notes therein cited.

75 *Canadian Charter of Rights and Freedoms*, ss. 16-23, 25, 27, 29; *Constitution Act, 1982*, Parts II, IV and IV.1.

76 The position and problems of collective rights in Canadian constitutional law are canvassed in Magnet, *supra*, note 74.

77 *Winnipeg v. Barrett*, [1892] A.C. 445 (P.C.); *Ottawa Roman Catholic Separate School Trustees v. Mackell*, [1917] A.C. 62 (P.C.); *Tiny Roman Catholic Separate School Trustees v. R.*, [1928] A.C. 363 (P.C.); *Robin v. Collège de St-Boniface* (1986), 15 D.L.R. (4th) 198 (Man. C.A.), leave to appeal to S.C.C. refused (1986), 21 C.R.R. 384n (S.C.C.); *MacDonald v. Montreal (City)*, [1986] 1 S.C.R. 460; *Société des Acadiens du Nouveau-Brunswick Inc. v. Assn. of Parents for Fairness in Education*, [1986] 1 S.C.R. 549.

to achieve their objectives.[78] This dismal record must give pause to those who would propose collective rights machinery as a principal reconciler of ethnic tension in the Canadian mosaic.

The collective rights theory is that constitutional texts should guarantee protection to minorities respecting crucial institutions or participation in the machinery of government. The problem with the theory is that the constitutional texts are extremely general. The collective rights theory thus relies on the courts for elaboration and ultimate application, usually during periods of high conflict. As has been frequently noted, the judiciary is drawn predominantly from majority groups, and reflects their attitudes. Collective rights litigation has often occurred during times of local hysteria directed at minority groups — the Manitoba school crisis, Regulation 17, the Manitoba language rights crisis. Judges are not immune from this hysteria. The generality of constitutional texts has proven insufficient to prevent judges from being swept along by temporary social pathology. The courts are placed in a difficult position. Constitutional texts are inadequate to divert the judiciary's attention from an all too understandable desire to keep peace in the Canadian family, usually by sacrificing minority rights to preservation of the *status quo*.

One might reply to this observation that the collective rights theory is correct, but that the composition of the judiciary needs changing. Apart from the obvious time that this would require, the reply neglects institutional limits of the courts, and the appointment process. It is difficult to see how any government would appoint persons who have shown tendencies antithetical to the will of the majority, even if willing to appoint some members of minority groups. Even where minority judges have sympathy for the difficult circumstances in which minorities sometimes find themselves, their influence is limited, particularly in courts of appeal or of last resort, whose multi-member representation is dominated by the majority.

Collective rights litigation is adversarial. It pits minority groups against an easily incensed majority, often in a bitter struggle for minority survival. In order to fight the battle, minority groups have to retain lawyers, usually from the majority's elite. Government often pays for the minority's legal representation and uses the opportunity to influence or distort the minority's objectives or principles.[78a] Minorities must contest the struggle before the

---

78 *Brophy v. A.G. Manitoba*, [1895] A.C. 202 (P.C.); *Pellant v. Hebert* (1981), 12 R.G.D. 242; *Bertrand v. Dussault* (January 30, 1909), reported in *Re Forest and Registrar of Manitoba Court of Appeal* (1977), 77 D.L.R. (3d) 445 (Man. C.A.); *A.G. Manitoba v. Forest*, [1979] 2 S.C.R. 1032; *Reference re Manitoba Language Rights*, [1985] 1 S.C.R. 721.

78a See section 18 application filed in Federal Court, Trial Division, on February 6, 1989, T-250-89, *Allan Singer* v. *Canadian Council on Social Development and Secretary of State for Canada*.

judiciary. It is an alienating and frightening experience. The experience leaves bitter, divisions between warring factions within the minority group. These problems have appeared over and over again, and would appear to be structural.[79]

In view of Canada's hundred-plus years of sorry experience with collective rights, one cannot help but search further for alternate mechanisms to safeguard the security of minority groups. It would be best if constitutional structures required as little alteration as possible to implement suggested measures, lest one risk advocating change in the utopic tense.

The chief value of Canada's collective rights tradition is the recognition that minorities require a degree of institutional autonomy to counterbalance the forces of assimilation, and to check the majority's excesses during overheated periods. Canada's tradition has been to create institutional autonomy with greater or lesser degrees of self-government. The problems with the design of Canadian collective rights provisions appear to result from inadequate mechanisms for the protection of minority institutions. I have already alluded to the problem of too ready reliance on the courts for the first line of defence against majority aggression. Canada's collective rights system has further defects. Minority institutions are insufficiently autonomous. They are too highly integrated with majority institutions in overarching structures of the higher levels of government. For example, decisions on funding, language of instruction, and curriculum content for minorities language schools are made initially by the Ministry of Education. Ministry structures are not decentralized, and do not reflect the theory of minority autonomy. Thus, linguistic minorities, if aggrieved by Ministry decisions on these matters, are on the defensive, able only to submit to the vagaries of the court process under constitutionally protected collective rights. This process usually disappoints them.

It would be better if the self-governing institutions were more truly autonomous, and their borders made more impermeable to majority interference. This would require decentralization or multiplication of functions in overarching government structures. If this were done, the

---

79 I am speaking from experience as legal counsel for several minority groups during the language difficulties of the 1980s. Time and again I watched the strains described in the text eat away at the minority groups internal cohesiveness, leaving them exhausted, fearful, insular and resentful. The Franco-Manitoban community was wracked by bitter internal divisions after the *Manitoba Language Rights Reference, ibid.* So too with the Acadian community of Cape Breton during and after the fight for an Acadian school. My strong impression is that this crippling of the minority community is a structural feature of collective rights litigation. Having failed to gain its objectives *vis-à-vis* the majority, factions within the community are all too easily tempted to turn their guns on each other.

minority could more easily avoid the courts while still enjoying the institutional autonomy indicated by the collective rights theory. The minority's community resources would be developed as the group became more self-reliant and more responsible for exercising authority over its own affairs. Enhancement of institutional autonomy would be a potent means to secure for minority communities the security which the proponents of collective rights intend, but which rarely is delivered under the current collective rights system.

Institutional autonomy is constitutionally mandated for several Canadian minorities. Section 27 could be usefully applied to support claims for promotion of self-governing structures both within and outside these specific guarantees. Policy makers could take a cue from section 27 to build minority self-government into ever higher levels of senior bureaucracies. If rigorously applied, section 27 may require State withdrawal from areas of institutional monopoly, such as, for example, police services on aboriginal reserves, or taxing powers for ethnic, linguistic or denominational schools. Through its impact on Charter jurisprudence and government policy, section 27, especially as mediated by the structural ethnicity principle, could orient Canada's constitutional system towards a model of institutional autonomy as a means of preserving and enhancing cultural identity.

Minority institutions are usually established outside of crisis periods. In times of ethnic peace they do not directly threaten the majority, and, apart from small scale jealousy, do not usually engage its ire. To the extent that courts review claims of interference with minority institutions during relatively peaceful periods, many of the difficulties adverted to above do not arise. Courts should be scrupulous to use these opportunities to build greater institutional autonomy into these structures through section 27, just as should policy architects in the executive branch when the institutions are created. If sufficiently autonomous, a constitutionally protected network of institutions could provide minorities with effective means of self-protection without the attendant disadvantages of collective rights litigation.

A further problem with the collective rights idiom entrenched in Canada's Constitution is the courts' failure to develop relevant interpretational tenets for judicial administration. Charters of rights act negatively. Traditionally, they impose limits on governments, inhibiting them from impinging on rights and freedoms deemed fundamental. By contrast, collective rights usually act positively. Collective rights require government to undertake certain affirmative obligations — translate and publish laws in two languages, establish minority language educational structures, appropriate moneys for denominational education. Courts steeped in the individual rights tradition familiar to Charter theorists are poorly equipped with constitutional doctrine to administer collective rights provisions effectively.

Section 27 could fill the interpretational lacunae surrounding Canada's system of collective rights. The language of section 27 — "preservation and *enhancement*" — is conducive to establishment of doctrines presupposing an affirmatively acting constitutional law, at least with respect to cultural groups. As previously noted, this is the current direction of section 27's international law precursor, Article 27 of the *International Covenant on Civil and Political Rights*.

9. PROBLEMS OF CULTURAL AUTONOMY

(a) Minimum Standards

The Charter is inspired by an ideal of individual dignity and development. A strong belief in the capacity of individuals to develop and find fulfilment has committed Canada constitutionally to protecting the freedom of individuals to form and hold ideas, to receive and consider the ideas of others, to express beliefs, to act on them, to assemble and associate together to practise or advocate beliefs of all kinds, and to be free of prejudicial distinctions based on belief.

The Charter also guarantees obverse freedoms: the right to reject beliefs or orthodoxies of all kinds, to refuse to express or consider an idea, to decline to act on any belief or to assemble or associate in furtherance of it, to reject orthodox practices, and to be free of prejudicial discrimination because of refusal to conform to orthodoxy.[80] The Charter expresses the axiomatic belief of Canadians that an inquiring mind, the capacity to communicate in new ways with others, to grow, to develop through exposure to new ideas, practices and associations are important ingredients in obtaining fulfilment.

The mechanism by which the Charter implements the philosophy of individual fulfilment is by imposing restraints on the exercise of governmental authority. These restraints are couched in terms of minimum standards of respect for individual autonomy. Even in pursuit of admittedly desirable social and economic policy goals for the community at large, governmental bodies may not unduly restrict thought or its expression or advocacy. Nor, more generally, may government truncate the operation of individual conscience as a primary motivator of personal conduct. The Charter ensures that individuals will be treated by government with

---

80 *R. v. Big M Drug Mart Ltd.*, *supra*, note 39 at 336; *National Bank of Canada v. R.C.U.*, [1984] 1 S.C.R. 269 at 295.

minimum standards of decency, consistent with the great eighteenth century ideals of personal liberty.

The Charter equally articulates Canadians' constitutional commitment to finding fulfilment in another way — through participation in groups. Group participation fosters identity, belonging and a sense of community. In Canada, group identification is strong, sufficiently robust to have emanated in enhanced collective rights in the constitutional reform process in 1982, and in an interpretational article that casts an ethnic glow over all guarantees, individual and collective, found in Canada's pre-eminent statement of human rights.

Finding fulfilment through group identification is markedly different than the processes of growth consequent on individual exploration and experimentation. Individual growth involves trying the new, and accepting or rejecting it. Commitment to community involves celebrating tradition, participating in ritual, allegiance to old beliefs and values, subject at most to slow evolution. Ideals of individual liberty and personal fulfilment are fostered through the system of individual rights entrenched in the Charter. Ideals of fulfilment through group identification are enhanced through the system of institutional autonomy for certain minorities, as fortified by the Charter's group rights provisions. A difficult problem occurs when government devolves limited forms of self-governing power on groups, in that the individual and group rights systems come into conflict.

In exercising its regulatory powers, government must observe minimum standards of respect for individual autonomy. Presumably, when government devolves certain of these powers on groups, these groups must equally observe minimum standards of respect for personal liberty. However, if groups must respect and encourage the same high standards of individual autonomy as government, their very basis for existence may be compromised. It is difficult to see how a denominational school, the *raison d'être* of which is inculcating a set of religious tenets through example, can survive promotion of free thinking in key staff members. This is why the courts allow denominational schools to dispense with the services of teachers who seriously depart from denominational standards: "within the denominational school religious instruction, influence and example form an important part of the educational process".[81] Again, it would be difficult to see how Hutterite communities could survive rigid application of the "one person, one vote" precept flowing from the democratic and equality guarantees of the Charter. Yet unyielding application of the individual rights sections of the Charter would dictate such results insofar as general governmental functions are devolved on the

---

81 *Re Essex County Roman Catholic School Bd. and Porter* (1978), 21 O.R. (2d) 255 at 257 (C.A.); *Caldwell v. Stuart, supra*, note 62.

communities.[82]

At the same time as the Canadian constitutional system recognizes a special need of Canadian minorities for group autonomy, commitment to a Charter-based system requires that groups exercising general governmental functions respect fundamental norms of due process, personal liberty and equality. Thus, the systems of individual and group rights in the Charter come squarely into conflict. There is no readily apparent doctrine to regulate this considerable difficulty.

In Charter cases, minimum standards of respect for individual autonomy must be specified with precision in analysis under section 1, the omnibus limitations clause. Section 27 could provide a springboard to regulating the conflict between individual and group rights in two ways. Section 27 could be applied directly to the specific Charter right under which a claim is made in order to inform the definition of that right. Alternatively, section 27 could be applied to section 1 in particular cases.

If section 27 were applied to section 1, it could alter the minimum standards of respect for personal liberty universally applicable to government, in favour of the special needs of semi-autonomous groups to preserve their special characteristics. As applied to section 1, section 27 may well come to mean that groups exercising semi-autonomous power may be less respectful of individual rights than government proper, if this is necessary to preserve the essential features of the groups' identity, and inseverable incidents of its status and necessary powers. This will be a doctrine that will have to take shape on a case-by-case basis. Although it is hard to see why self-governing aboriginal communities exercising policing powers on reserves should require the ability to conduct unreasonable searches in derogation of section 8, it is easier to see why denominational schools should be able to intrude on the section 2 guarantee of freedom from enforced conformity to religious practice for its teaching staff.[83] This is the lesson of the *Caldwell* case.[84]

The idea that Charter precepts of individual autonomy may suffer diminution at the hands of partially self-governing minorities enjoying collective rights should not shock. The idea is already woven deeply into the design of the Charter. In 1982 and 1983, the Constitution makers exempted historic collective rights from the Charter's discipline. Sections 21, 22, 25, 29, 35(4) and 37.1(4) preserve the original collective rights of linguistic minorities, aboriginal peoples and denominational schools

---

82 *Avery v. Midland County*, 390 U.S. 474 (1968); *Hadley v. Junior College District*, 25 L. Ed. (2d) 45 (1970).

83 *R. v. Big M Drug Mart, supra*, note 39 at 336-337.

84 *Supra*, note 62.

from dilution by individual rights claimed under the Charter.[85] It is therefore neither novel nor shocking to suggest that section 27 be applied to limit individual rights when found to be in competition with the special requirements of semi-autonomous cultural groups. The Charter's exclusionary provisions just referred to operate by exempting certain historic guarantees from the Charter. Under the structural ethnicity thesis offered here, section 27 would blunt, but not negate, the Charter's force. The exclusionary provisions apply only to certain historic constitutional guarantees. Section 27 would extend beyond these guarantees to regulate any conflict between Charter claims to personal liberty and collective entitlements to autonomy.

Section 27 is a flexible instrument capable of lowering minimum standards flowing from the individual rights sections of the Charter. As such, it would supplement the protection offered historic groups in covering matters falling outside traditional constitutional entitlements. For those semi-autonomous groups not protected by historic constitutional guarantees, section 27 would offer the sole, though not insubstantial, constitutional shield. Under the structural ethnicity theory, section 27 would dilute the Charter's individual rights only with respect to structures and processes essential to group preservation and enhancement.

Section 27 is a better vehicle than the exclusionary theory. The exclusionary thesis is too unsubtle in assuming that semi-autonomous groups require wholesale power to override Charter values in order to protect themselves. Section 27, by contrast, simultaneously recognizes two

---

85 A question has been raised as to the scope of the exemption granted by s. 29. In *Reference re An Act to Amend the Education Act (Ont.), supra,* note 48, the majority considered that the exemption extended not only to rights guaranteed by the Constitution (*i.e.,* rights existing at Confederation), but also to "rights and privileges granted by laws enacted under the authority of the Constitution". The majority limited this principle as follows: "Laws and the Constitution . . . are excluded from application to separate schools only to the extent they derogate from such schools as Catholic (or in Quebec, Protestant) institutions. It is this essential Catholic nature which is preserved and protected by s. 93 of the *Constitution Act, 1867* and s. 29 of the Charter" (at 576). The minority held that "[s]ection 29 is specifically made applicable only to the *constitutionally guaranteed* rights . . . of separate schools. It serves to preserve those rights by ensuring that they are immune from Charter attack notwithstanding that they may contravene the Charter. . . . We reject the notion that every future piece of legislation enacted by the province under s. 93 which confers rights or privileges on Roman Catholic separate schools is placed by s. 29 beyond the purview of the Charter. . . . To be protected by s. 29 the rights and privileges must be *constitutionally guaranteed.* . . . A guarantee does not attach to rights or privileges conferred by an ordinary provincial statute" at 546, 549-550). While the Supreme Court is now considering this conflict, it is important to note that both majority and dissent agree that, at the minimum, s. 29 protects the core of collective rights guaranteed by the Constitution in 1867 from attack based upon the individual rights sections of the Charter.

key modes of Canadian constitutionalism. Section 27 pays high regard to the semi-autonomous status of certain groups. At the same time, section 27 allows individual rights in the Charter to operate as a safeguard against oppression by self-governing majorities in the group intent on crushing Charter-protected values without demonstrable need. The advantage of section 27 is that it permits a balancing of individual and collective values.

(b) Inclusion and Exclusion

Defining the boundaries of cultural groups raises difficult problems. This is especially so where the group enjoys or seeks government-derived powers or benefits. A high regard for group autonomy suggests investment of substantial powers of self-definition in groups. However, where the group enjoys powers or distributes entitlements derived from government, government has interests in ensuring that the group use its power of self-definition reasonably — that the group not exclude certain individuals for irrational or abusive purposes. Equally, where government devolves power upon groups (for example, taxing powers delegated to denominational school boards), government has an interest in overseeing that the power of self-definition not be used oppressively to extend the group's boundaries to include objecting individuals.

Some writers would accord certain communities plenary power of self-definition. Professor Cobo is of opinion that indigenous populations must be allowed unrestricted power to decide who is or is not indigenous — a virtual unlimited authority to include or exclude members of the community.[86] Even with respect to aboriginal communities, it is hard to see how the government has no interest in definition of the group. Government provides moneys to the communities based on numbers; the communities' interest in exaggerating the numbers are directly opposed to the government's monetary interest in minimizing them. For this reason, estimates of the number of aboriginal people in Canada vary widely. Also, different representative bodies have interests in defining the communities

---

86 J.R.M. Cobo, *Study of the Problem of Discrimination Against Indigenous Populations* (Report to the Sub-Commission on the Prevention of Discrimination and Protection of Minorities) U.N. Doc. No. E/CN.4/Sub. 2/1986/7 and addendums 1-4. I am grateful to L.M. Kelleher for drawing the relevance of this document to my attention.

in antagonistic ways.[87] Dispute over who is Metis — the historic Red River population and descendants, or any person with mixed Indian blood — produced a deep division in the Native Council of Canada, and the formation of a rival association, the Metis National Council. Government has an interest to ensure that it is negotiating with and funding legitimate, representative bodies, a concern that orbits around definition of the community. Finally, as noted by L.M. Kelleher, only the Federal Government ment possesses external sovereignty, and is recognized as the entity which can and must answer to international tribunals in respect of the treatment of minority populations. Groups, even aboriginal communities, cannot answer themselves, because they are not states. Government thus has an interest to ensure that international human rights norms to which it is bound are observed by semi-self-governing communities, including an interest to oversee that criteria of inclusion and exclusion do not violate Canada's international human rights obligations. Canada will have to answer to the international community for any violations.[88]

Notwithstanding government's interest, the power of self-definition is crucial to the security of cultural groups. This consideration obviously justifies *prima facie* self-definitional power for cultural minorities. The group's security interest is buttressed by constitutional guarantees for freedom of association. State interference with self-definition may offend the right of each member in the group, or of the group as an entity, to associate only with those of their or its choosing. Associational freedoms come into relevance if the state excludes members which the group wants to accept. So too, the right not to associate[89] inhibits government from including members against their or the group's will.

Prima facie power of self-definition may be safely assumed. The

---

87 Some interesting disputes have arisen over the representative legitimacy of aboriginal groups. Under ss. 37 and 37.1 of the *Constitution Act, 1982*, a First Ministers' Conference must be convened, with an agenda item respecting matters directly affecting aboriginal peoples, "and the Prime Minister of Canada shall invite representatives of those peoples to participate in the discussions on those matters". Disputes have arisen about which aboriginal representative groups should be invited by the Prime Minister. One such dispute was litigated: *Prairie Treaty Nations Alliance v. Mulroney*, March 29, 1985 (Ont. H.C.) reproduced in J.E. Magnet, *Constitutional Law of Canada* (2nd ed.) 1985 Vol. II, at 1592. P.T.N.A. requested the court to require the Prime Minister to invite them to the conference because, in their submission, there was no appropriate representative of the aboriginal peoples whom P.T.N.A. represented at the conference.

88 L.M. Kelleher, *Non-Discrimination Concepts in Aboriginal Law* (paper presented at the 1987 meeting of the Canadian Association of Law Teachers).

89 *Lavigne v. O.P.S.E.U.* (1986), 29 D.L.R. (4th) 321 at 368 (Ont. H.C.), *per* White J.: "[A] right to freedom of association which did not include a right not to associate would not really ensure 'freedom'". Rev'd on other grounds (1988), 41 D.L.R. (4th) 86 (Ont. H.C.).

significant questions relate to the limits on this power. How far may government interfere? How far may groups forcibly include objecting members? How far are groups free to exclude or excommunicate on the basis of criteria which the group itself determines? Section 27 may afford a solution to this problem by acting on the interpretation of associational guarantees in section 2(d), and permissible limits to them under section 1. A group's associational freedom to self define, even without assistance from section 27, should be of sufficient strength to resist government interference to the point at least where the group's security, its status and essential capacities, are threatened. Section 27 should reduce the power of government to interfere even further. Section 27 mandates government to preserve and enhance Canada's multicultural heritage. A structural ethnicity approach to section 27, as acting on section 2(d) or on section 1, would augment the group's institutional autonomy and power to evolve in its own distinctive way. Freedom to self define, to control membership, is at the core of this autonomy. Section 27 should carry the associational freedom to self define beyond threats to the group's security and survival to embrace the group's capacity to evolve in its own particular manner.

The language of section 27, especially as mediated by the structural ethnicity principle, suggests positive obligations on government to assist groups to define their boundaries. Government undoubtedly has a margin of appreciation to decide how best to discharge this obligation. So long as it is acting responsibly in pursuit of ways to discharge its obligation, government ought to be free of court control. But if government does nothing to enhance a group's desire to identify its members or otherwise to assist groups to draw their boundaries, courts ought to give careful consideration to complaints seeking affirmatively acting remedies. In this event, there is every reason for courts to apply sections 2(d) and 27 together so as to require government to divulge membership lists in its possession, to require government to enumerate certain groups either specially or through the census, or to provide moneys in support of an advertising campaign designed to persuade individuals to self-identify.

Although associational guarantees impose a restraint on government devolving power on groups to include members forcibly, a few precedents already exist. The use of public government structures to implement aboriginal self-government implies forcible inclusion of certain non-aboriginal persons in the jurisdiction of the governing aboriginal group. These persons are subjected to coercive powers of taxation and regulation by the governing aboriginal community. The thesis on which this is done is to preserve and enhance the cultural survival of the aboriginal group, and in recognition of the fact that forcible inclusion of others may be necessary to achieve this purpose. Labour unions are given compulsory powers to check off dues from all employees of a particular employer, whether or not such employees are members of the union. The theses on which this is done are to prevent "free riding" — inhibition of free riders taking the benefits of collective bargaining without having to shoulder the burdens; and also to recognize that unions should exist, and can only exist if adequately financed.

Canada's constitutional commitment to freedom of association implies the right not to associate. Even aboriginal law recognizes the right of aboriginal persons to drop out of the group and assimilate.[90] One of the four stated goals of the multiculturalism policy as explained by Prime Minister Trudeau in the House of Commons was that the barriers to assimilation be removed for those who want to assimilate. The general principle, thus, would appear to be that groups have little power of forcible inclusion. Nevertheless, the examples just cited suggest an exception: that is, section 27 supports an obligation on government to devolve powers of forcible inclusion on quasi-autonomous groups to the extent that such powers are essential to the group's security or survival.

Powers of exclusion for the group are easier to justify. Associational guarantees buttress the right of group members not to associate with others, even with those who self-identify as group members. This right would be moderated to some extent when the group is in possession of governmentally derived powers or benefits, for reasons previously discussed. The general principle, thus, would appear to be that group boundaries are defined by self-identification subject to the right of the group to reject members infringing the group's membership criteria. Government would possess a reserve power to check irresponsible uses of group exclusionary practices or powers in cases where membership in the group entitles individuals to significant governmental powers or benefits.

10. CONCLUSION

Section 27 must be implemented through the development and application of "mediating principles". Three mediating principles are developed here: non-discrimination, symbolic ethnicity and structural ethnicity. All are relevant; all should be utilized by those responsible to interpret the Charter.

Structural ethnicity is particularly challenging as an axis around which interpretation of the Charter will have to orbit. Structural ethnicity implies creation, maintenance and enhancement of an institutional infrastructure through which cultural communities can preserve and enhance their

---

90 F. Cohen, *Handbook of Federal Indian Law* (Charlottesville, Va.: Michie Co., 1982) at 22, citing *United States v. Crook*, 25 F. Cas. 695 (C.C.D. Neb., 1879).

communal lives. It implies a degree of autonomy for the communities in controlling this infrastructure. This would extend Canada's collective rights machinery which has created limited autonomy for certain historical minorities.

The collective rights system has been marked by tragic disappointments throughout Canadian constitutional history. It fails regularly to deliver on the promises made to minorities at Confederation. The problem is structural: too-ready reliance on litigation brought about by insufficient autonomy for minorities at the higher levels of government. Section 27 should attune courts and policy architects to these problems. Section 27 should require more sensitive attention to the problem of autonomy in preserving and enhancing the security of cultural communities.

Collective rights, and the autonomy they imply, conflict with the individual rights sections of the Charter. Section 27 can regulate this conflict by raising or lowering the minimum standards of respect for personal liberty self-governing entities must observe. Section 27 moderates the discipline of the Charter where assertion of individual rights threatens the survival of cultural communities. In this way, section 27 can orient Charter development towards the special demands of binationality and cultural pluralism which characterize Canada's very special constitutional tradition.

19

Enforcement of the Canadian Charter of Rights and Freedoms*

(*Section 24*)

Dale Gibson and Scott Gibson

1. INTRODUCTION

Words are not enough. An astute English judge observed, almost three

---

* The material for this chapter was prepared in 1987. For additional thoughts by one of the co-authors, see D. Gibson, "Non-destructive Charter Responses to Legislative Inequalities," Alta. L.R., forthcoming.

centuries ago, that "it is a vain thing to imagine a right without a remedy."[1] The world's most resounding constitutional declaration of civil liberties would not confer legally meaningful protection unless accompanied by an effective mechanism for enforcement. The *Canadian Charter of Rights and Freedoms* includes certain enforcement provisions. This chapter examines those provisions and attempts to assess their effect and adequacy.

There are three remedial or enforcement measures expressly provided. Section 24 contains two of these — the right to seek an appropriate remedy from the courts:

> 24.(1) Anyone whose rights or freedoms, as guaranteed by this Charter, have been infringed or denied may apply to a court of competent jurisdiction to obtain such remedy as the court considers appropriate and just in the circumstances.

and the right to have certain evidence excluded from court proceedings if obtained in contravention of the Charter:

> 24.(2) Where, in proceedings under subsection (1), a court concludes that evidence was obtained in a manner that infringed or denied any rights or freedoms guaranteed by this Charter, the evidence shall be excluded if it is established that, having regard to all the circumstances, the admission of it in the proceedings would bring the administration of justice into disrepute.

Additional protection is contained in section 52(1) of the *Constitution Act, 1982* which, although not strictly a part of the Charter, is applicable to its provisions:

> 52.(1) The Constitution of Canada is the supreme law of Canada, and any law that is inconsistent with the provisions of the Constitution is, to the extent of the inconsistency, of no force or effect.

Because section 52 is the subject of a separate study,[2] this commentary will deal primarily with the remedies contained in section 24 of the Charter. It will be necessary, however, to make some observations about section 52 and other remedial powers that go beyond section 24.

---

1 *Per* Holt C.J. in *Ashby v. White* (1703), 2 Ld. Raym. 938 at 953, 92 E.R. 126. For a useful examination of various remedial and procedural aspects of Charter litigation, see R.J. Sharpe, ed., *Charter Litigation* (Toronto: Butterworths, 1987).

2 On s. 52, see R. Tassé, Chapter 3, "Application of the Canadian Charter of Rights and Freedoms," *supra*. See also D. Gibson, *The Law of the Charter: General Principles*, (Toronto: Carswell, 1986) at 184 *et seq.*, and D. Gibson, "Section 15 in the Courts: An Impression of Year One" in K.E. Mahoney & S.L. Martin, eds., *Equality and Judicial Neutrality* (Toronto: Carswell, 1987).

2. GENERAL ENFORCEMENT — SECTION 24(1)

(a) Other Countries

Not every constitution that guarantees rights and freedoms contains express enforcement provisions. The Constitution of the United States is silent on the question of enforcement, for example, but the courts of that country have not allowed this silence to prevent granting appropriate remedies for violations of constitutionally entrenched rights.

Many constitutions do include explicit remedial provisions of the type contained in section 24(1) of the Canadian Charter. Among these are the constitutions of India, Nigeria, West Germany and a considerable number of smaller countries.[3] Although there does not appear to be much jurisprudence interpreting and applying these various remedial guarantees, the Indian experience has been somewhat instructive, and will be referred to occasionally below.

---

3 The Constitution of India (1949) provides as follows:

Right to Constitutional Remedies

32. Remedies for enforcement of rights conferred by this part. — (1) The right to move the Supreme Court by appropriate proceedings for the enforcement of the rights conferred in this Part is guaranteed.

(2) The Supreme Court shall have power to issue directions or orders or writs, including writs in the nature of *habeas corpus, mandamus*, prohibition, *quo warranto* and *certiorari*, whichever may be appropriate, for the enforcement of any of the rights conferred by this Part.

(3) Without prejudice to the powers conferred on the Supreme Court by clauses (1) and (2), Parliament may by law empower any other court to exercise within the local limits of its jurisdiction all or any of the powers exercisable by the Supreme Court under clause (2).

(4) The right guaranteed by this article shall not be suspended except as otherwise provided for by this Constitution.

226. Power of High Courts to issue certain writs. — (1) Notwithstanding anything in Article 32, every High Court shall have power, throughout the territories in relation to which it exercises jurisdiction, to issue to any person or authority, including in appropriate cases, any Government, within those territories directions, orders or writs, including writs in the nature of *habeas corpus*, mandamus, prohibition, *quo warranto* and *certiorari*, or any of them, for the enforcement of any of the rights conferred by Part III and for any other purpose.

(2) The power conferred by clause (1) to issue directions, orders or writs to any Government, authority or person may also be exercised by any High Court exercising jurisdiction in relation to the territories within which the cause of action, wholly or in part, arises for the exercise of such power, notwithstanding that the seat of such Government or authority or the residence of such person is not within those territories.

(b) History of Section 24(1)

The forerunner of section 24(1) was an enforcement provision proposed by the Government of Canada in Bill C-60, introduced in Parliament in June 1978, but never passed:

> 24. Where no other remedy is available or provided for by law, any individual may, in accordance with the applicable procedure of any court in Canada of competent jurisdiction, request the court to define or enforce any of the individual rights and freedoms declared by this Charter, as they extend or apply to him or her, by means of a declaration of the court or by means of an injunction or similar relief, accordingly as the circumstances require.

This first attempt to give legal teeth to the proposed Charter, while widely applauded in principle, was criticized by some for not going far enough.[4] The restriction of available remedies to declarations, injunctions and "similar relief" was thought by critics to be especially unfortunate; the addition of such relief as damages and the exclusion of evidence obtained in violation of the Charter was urged. The Government of Canada took heed of this advice in a tentative proposal for rewording the section

---

(3) Where any party against whom an interim order, whether by way of injunction or stay or in any other manner, is made on, or in any proceedings relating to, a petition under clause (1), without —

(a) furnishing to such party copies of such petition and all documents in support of the plea for such interim order; and

(b) giving such party an opportunity of being heard, makes an application to the High Court for the vacation of such order and furnishes a copy of such application to the party in whose favour such order has been made or the counsel of such party, the High Court shall dispose of the application within a period of two weeks from the date on which it is received or from the date on which the copy of such application is so furnished, whichever is later, or where the High Court is closed on the last day of that period, before the expiry of the next day afterwards on which the High Court is open; and if the application is not so disposed of, the interim order shall, on the expiry of that period, or, as the case may be, the expiry of the said next day, stand vacated.

(4) The power conferred on a High Court by this article shall not be in derogation of the power conferred on the Supreme Court by clause (2) of Article 32.

There are also enforcement provisions in the Constitutions of Nigeria (1963), s. 42; Papua New Guinea (1975), s. 57; The Bahamas (1963), s. 28; Barbados (1966), s. 24; Fiji (1970), s. 17; Republic of Gambia (1970), s. 28; Republic of Ghana (1979), s. 35; Dominica (1978), s. 18; Botswana (1966), s. 16; TuValu (1968), s. 17; St. Lucia (1978), s. 16; Saint-Vincent (1979), s. 16; Sierra Leone (1978), s. 18; Solomon Islands, s. 18; Zimbabwe (1979), s. 24; Mauritius (1977), s. 17; Republic of Malta (1964), s. 47; Kenya (1969), s. 84; Grenada (1963), s. 16; Kiribati (1979), s. 17; Jamaica (1962), s. 25; Federal Republic of Germany (1949), art. 19; Western Samoa (1960), s. 4; Vanuatu (New Hebrides) (1980), s. 6.

4 See, *e.g.*, D. Gibson, "Charter or Chimera: A Comment on the Proposed Canadian Charter of Rights and Freedoms" (1979), 9 *Man. L.J.* 363 at 384-385.

which it advanced at the Federal-Provincial Conference of First Ministers on the Constitution in February 1979:

> Where no other effective recourse or remedy exists, courts are empowered to grant such relief or remedy for a violation of Charter rights as may be deemed appropriate and just in the circumstances.[5]

The informal intergovernmental discussions that took place during the summer of 1980 resulted in the qualification or abandonment of several important features of the Charter, as previously drafted, in the apparent hope of achieving a "lowest common denominator" type of consensus. The enforcement provision was one of the victims. Federal representatives had first proposed a slightly modified version of their 1979 suggestion:

> Where no other effective recourse or remedy is available or provided for by law, anyone whose rights or freedoms as declared by this Charter have been infringed or denied to his or her detriment has the right to apply to a court of competent jurisdiction to obtain such relief or remedy as the court deems appropriate and just in the circumstances.[6]

However, when it appeared that no such provision would be acceptable to the governments of certain provinces, this approach to enforcement was abandoned altogether. The Resolution introduced in Parliament by Prime Minister Trudeau in October 1980 contained no express enforcement provision other than a statement, similar to the present section 52(1), that laws inconsistent with the Charter would be void.[7]

This omission drew strong criticism during the hearings of the Special Joint Committee of the Senate and House of Commons that studied the Resolution from December 1980 to February 1981.[8] It was not surprising, therefore, that when the Report of the Committee proposed, with the government's approval, a number of amendments to the Resolution, reinstatement of the enforcement clause was among them.[9]

The version finally adopted incorporated at least two improvements

---

5 Federal-Provincial Conference of First Ministers on the Constitution, *Federal Draft Proposals Discussed by First Ministers*, Document No. 800-010/037 (Ottawa, February 5-6, 1979).

6 Continuing Committee of Ministers on the Constitution, *Discussion Draft: Rights & Freedoms Within the Canadian Federation*, Document No. 830-81/027 (Ottawa, July 4, 1980) s. 19. This document is often referred to as the "*Summer Draft*" or "*July Draft.*"

7 House of Commons, *Proposed Resolution for a Joint Address to Her Majesty the Queen Respecting the Constitution of Canada* (October 10, 1980).

8 See, *e.g.*, the evidence of Professor Walter Tarnopolsky on behalf of the Canadian Civil Liberties Association in *Minutes of Proceedings & Evidence of the Special Joint Committee of the Senate & House of Commons on the Constitution of Canada*, No. 7 (November 18, 1980) at 15 *et seq.* The Committee's Minutes and Proceedings will be referred to hereinafter as "*Committee Proceedings.*"

9 *Committee Proceedings No. 57 — Report to Parliament* (February 13, 1981) at 15.

over all previous drafts. The use of such terms as "individual" and "his or her" in earlier versions in reference to those who could invoke the section had seemed to imply that corporations would not qualify for its protection. This difficulty, which was mentioned during the hearings,[10] appears to have been the reason for using the more inclusive term "anyone" ("toute personne" in the French text) in the final version. Another potential problem lay in the requirement of earlier drafts that the provision apply only where "no other remedy is available or provided by law." It could have been applied to deny relief whenever *any* remedy — even a distinctly inferior one — was possible. Elimination of those words in the final draft should ensure that the relief available under section 24(1) is independent of any other possible remedies, although the availability of other suitable forms of relief is, of course, one of the "circumstances" a court may take into account in deciding whether it would be "appropriate and just" to award a remedy under section 24(1).

However, the new draft did not succeed in removing all ambiguities and problems. The rest of this section will attempt to identify some of the remaining problems, examine the courts' solutions to those problems which have been adjudicated, and suggest approaches to the solution of those which have yet to be adjudicated.

(c) Standing to Sue[11]

Who may seek relief for Charter violations? There are two categories: those whose own interests are distinctly affected by the alleged violation; and those who act in support of a public interest that is so affected. Different considerations apply to each category.

(i) *Private Interest*

Those whose private interests are involved have an undoubted right to standing. Section 24(1) makes that clear:

> Anyone whose rights or freedoms, as guaranteed by this Charter, have been infringed or denied may apply to a court of competent jurisdiction to obtain such remedy as the court considers appropriate and just in the circumstances.

This is no discretionary matter — the court must entertain the application

---

10 Evidence of Business Council on National Issues, *Committee Proceedings* No. 33 (January 7, 1981) at 135.

11 See B.L. Strayer, *The Canadian Constitution and the Courts: The Function and Scope of Judicial Review*, 3rd ed. (Toronto: Butterworths, 1983) at 133 *et seq*. This section is extracted from Gibson, *The Law of the Charter, supra*, note 2, at 264 *et seq*. For a discussion of the related question of standing to intervene, see Gibson, *ibid.*, at 271 *et seq*.

of anyone who falls within this category. This conclusion may appear academic in light of the undoubted fact that any *relief* sought under section 24(1) is in the court's discretion anyway. It is not entirely academic, however, because the *right of audience* is in itself a very important safeguard in any country where freedom of the press prevails. If journalists can observe and publicize a citizen's contention that he or she has been deprived of rights or freedoms guaranteed by the Charter, the result may be public pressure for a political solution to the problem. The public spotlight may also force a reluctant court to take a plaintiff's complaints more seriously in a trial on the merits than it would in a preliminary determination of standing.

To qualify for this right of standing, persons must be themselves affected by the allegedly unconstitutional law or action. Section 24(1) applies only to "anyone whose rights or freedoms . . . have been infringed or denied," and not to those who seek to champion the rights of others.

Standing based on private interest has been recognized in a wide range of circumstances. Where a newspaper reporter was denied access to a trial, the newspaper had standing to challenge the ruling,[12] and a reporter similarly had standing to challenge an order banning the publication of evidence presented at a preliminary hearing.[13] A lawyer was accorded standing to attack the constitutionality of procedural rules permitting costs to be assessed against solicitors.[14] The interest must be substantial, however; a grandmother was held not to have standing, on the basis of her freedom of association with her grandchild, to question the constitutional validity of a statute under which an order of wardship was made concerning the child.[15]

Persons accused of offences would appear to have standing to challenge the constitutionality of the laws under which they are prosecuted or the procedures or investigative practices upon which the prosecution is based. So far as the law creating the offence is concerned, this was firmly established by the Supreme Court of Canada in *R. v. Big M Drug Mart Ltd.*[16] The accused in that case was a corporation alleged to have

---

12 *Re Southam Inc. and R.* (1982), 141 D.L.R. (3d) 341 (Ont. H.C.), aff'd on other grounds 146 D.L.R. (3d) 408 (Ont. C.A.).

13 *R. v. Harrison* (1984), 14 C.C.C. (3d) 549 (Que. S.P.).

14 *Danson v. A.G. Ontario* (1985), 20 D.L.R. (4th) 288 (Ont. H.C.), aff'd (1986), 27 D.L.R. (4th) 758 (Div. Ct.), rev'd (1987), 41 D.L.R. (4th) 129 (Ont. C.A.).

15 *P.M.W. v. Director of Child Welfare* (1985), 40 Alta. L.R. (2d) 31 (Q.B.). There was a possibility that she might be granted "public interest" standing, but the court declined to do so because there was another method — appeal — by which the issue could be determined.

16 [1985] 1 S.C.R. 295.

violated provisions of the *Lord's Day Act*.[17] It defended on the ground that the Act violated freedom of conscience and religion under section 2 of the Charter. The Crown contended that, since a corporation cannot hold religious or any other beliefs, the accused's rights had not been infringed or denied, and it accordingly had no standing under section 24(1). The court, in allowing the defence and striking down the Act, held that accused persons always possess standing, *apart from section 24(1)*, to question the constitutionality of the laws under which they are charged:

> Section 24(1) sets out a remedy for individuals (whether real persons or artificial ones such as corporations) whose rights under the *Charter* have been infringed. It is not, however, the only recourse in the face of unconstitutional legislation. Where, as here, the challenge is based on the unconstitutionality of the legislation, recourse to s. 24 is unnecessary and the particular effect on the challenging party is irrelevant.
>
> Section 52 sets out the fundamental principle of constitutional law that the Constitution is supreme. The undoubted corollary to be drawn from this principle is that no one can be convicted of an offence under an unconstitutional law. The respondent did not come to court voluntarily as an interested citizen asking for a prerogative declaration that a statute is unconstitutional
> . . . .
>
> Any accused, whether corporate or individual, may defend a criminal charge by arguing that the law under which the charge is brought is constitutionally invalid. Big M is urging that the law under which it has been charged is inconsistent with s. 2(*a*) of the *Charter* and by reason of s. 52 of the *Constitution Act, 1982*, it is of no force or effect.
>
> Whether a corporation can enjoy or exercise freedom of religion is therefore irrelevant. The respondent is arguing that the legislation is constitutionally invalid because it impairs freedom of religion — if the law impairs freedom of religion it does not matter whether the company can possess religious belief. An accused atheist would be equally entitled to resist a charge under the Act.[18]

While the *Big M* case is strictly authority only for constitutional attacks on the laws themselves based on section 52(1) of the *Constitution Act, 1982*, its underlying rationale can be extended as well to Charter challenges by accused persons to questionable investigative or prosecutorial practices. Section 52(1) probably applies to more than laws. In any event, the *Big M* decision seems to suggest that, entirely apart from section 52(1), the fact that one is being criminally prosecuted creates standing in itself. As the court pointed out, accused persons do not "come to court voluntarily." They are brought there, contrary to their wishes, by authority of law. Surely they have standing, with respect to all matters relevant to the prosecution, for that reason alone. It would be difficult to imagine a more legitimate

---

17 R.S.C. 1970, c. L-13.
18 *Big M Drug Mart, supra*, note 16, at 313-314 (*per* Dickson J.).

or substantial private interest than the need to defend oneself from criminal prosecution.

There have been a few decisions that appear to cast doubt on that proposition. In *R. v. Taylor*[19] and *R. v. Rowbotham*,[20] for example, accused persons were denied standing to challenge the admissibility of evidence obtained by allegedly unconstitutional searches of premises belonging to and occupied by other persons. And in *R. v. Johnstone*,[21] an accused was denied the right to question the constitutionality of age limits imposed on the selection of jurors under the *Nova Scotia Juries Act*.[22] These decisions are based on very narrow views of the scope of the particular Charter rights in question: that it is only the person who or whose property is being searched who is protected against unreasonable search and seizure, and that the right to equality in the choice of jurors is a right of the jurors rather than of the accused. Those views are highly debatable. More important to the present discussion, however, is the fact that these are not properly questions of standing at all; they are substantive questions of scope that every accused person should have the standing to raise in his or her defence.

In what circumstances can the private interests of one person be protected by Charter litigation brought under section 24(1) on behalf of that person by someone else? This would certainly seem to be possible where someone acts as trustee, committee, guardian *ad litem* or next friend to a person who is under some disability.

It was also possible, prior to the advent of the Charter, in the case of *habeas corpus* applications. If only the imprisoned person had the status to challenge the validity of a detention, the right of *habeas corpus* could be nullified by simply preventing the prisoner from gaining the court's attention. In recognition of this special difficulty of imprisoned persons, the courts have permitted outsiders to apply for *habeas corpus* on behalf of prisoners, even where there is neither authority to do so from the prisoner nor any special relationship between the applicant and the prisoner.[23] This right undoubtedly persists after the Charter is in force, since section 26 stipulates that existing rights are not eroded by the Charter. It is even possible that the right has now been constitutionally entrenched, and thus removed from the reach of legislative alteration, if the guarantee of *habeas corpus* in section 10(*c*) of the Charter can be construed to incorporate

---

19 (1983), 8 C.R.R. 29 (B.C. S.C.).

20 (1984), 11 C.R.R. 302 (Ont. H.C.).

21 (1985), 68 N.S.R. (2d) 302 (N.S. T.D.).

22 S.N.S. 1969, c. 12.

23 D.A.C. Harvey, *The Law of Habeas Corpus in Canada* (Toronto: Butterworths, 1974) at 76, citing *Ex Parte Thaw* (1913), 22 C.C.C. 1 (Que. S.C.): *Re Thaw; Boudreau v. Thaw* (1913), 22 C.C.C. 3 (Que. S.C.).

by reference all associated procedural safeguards.[24] The equivalent provision of the Constitution of India has been held, by exception to the normal requirement of personal interest, to guarantee *habeas corpus* applications by strangers.[25]

Could this right of strangers to apply for relief on behalf of others be extended to other remedies? One writer has pointed out that strangers have been accorded standing, as of right, to apply for writs of prohibition, although it appears to be treated as a discretionary question where *certiorari* is concerned, and strangers do not seem to have been granted even discretionary status to apply for injunction or *mandamus.*[26] This state of inconsistency would seem to call for judicial or legislative reform. Perhaps what is needed is recognition of a principle analogous to "agency of necessity," whereby strangers might apply on behalf of others in circumstances where the persons whose rights are involved cannot be reasonably expected to act on their own behalf.

The right to challenge Charter violations that are impending, but have not yet occurred, is sometimes doubted, but it seems undeniable. To the extent that the inherent jurisdiction of a superior court is involved (for example, to grant an order of prohibition), the right to seek relief against apprehended violations has always existed, and, as discussed later, even the restricted language of section 24(1) probably supports relief for impending violations.

What burden of proof lies on a person whose standing to sue is questioned? In *Piercey v. General Bakeries Ltd.,*[27] it was held sufficient to show a *prima facie* case that the right asserted existed, and had been infringed or denied. This would seem to be a logical extension of the general rule that a person need only show an arguable case on a preliminary motion to strike pleadings.

(ii) *Public Interest*

Until 1974, private parties were seldom if ever recognized as having standing to defend purely public interests in Canadian courts, unless they did so with the consent and in the name of the Attorney General. It was thought to be the law that a person could not otherwise challenge the

---

24 Such an interpretation is facilitated by the use of the passive voice: "Every one has the right on arrest or detention . . . to have the validity of the detention determined by way of *habeas corpus.*" The French text, "de faire contrôler," is compatible with such an interpretation.

25 D.D. Basu, *Commentary on the Constitution of India*, 5th Ed. (Calcutta: Sarkar & Sons, 1965) Vol. 2, at 280.

26 Strayer, *supra*, note 11, at 151 *et seq.*

27 (1986), 31 D.L.R. (4th) 373 (Nfld. T.D.).

constitutionality of a statute or a governmental action if he or she was not privately affected by the law or action in a more significant manner than other citizens who were subject to it. The classic example of that restrictive approach was the case of *Saumur v. A.G. Quebec*,[28] in which the Supreme Court of Canada denied standing to attack a law prohibiting the distribution of Jehovah's Witnesses' literature because the applicant had not yet been prosecuted for violating the law.

The law concerning standing in constitutional matters has been dramatically modified, however, by more recent decisions of the Supreme Court of Canada: *Thorson v. A.G. Canada*,[29] *Nova Scotia Board of Censors v. McNeil*,[30] and *Minister of Justice of Canada v. Borowski*.[31]

The *Thorson* case[32] concerned the right of an ordinary taxpayer to seek a declaration concerning the constitutional validity of the federal *Official Languages Act*.[33] The court held, by a six to three majority, that the question of standing is a discretionary matter within the control of the court at first instance. Among the various factors that should be taken into account by a court when deciding whether to exercise this discretion, the "justiciability" of the question in issue was stated to be "central," and the court indicated that there is never any doubt as to the justiciability of genuine constitutional disputes:

> The question of the constitutionality of legislation has in this country always been a justiciable question.[34]

Other factors to be considered were the availability of other appropriate remedies,[35] and whether the statute in question is "regulatory" or "declaratory" (since it is more likely that persons affected would have more opportunities to challenge regulatory Acts than declaratory Acts).[36] The question whether tax revenues are involved was stated not to be vital:

> It is not the alleged waste of public funds alone that will support standing but rather the right of the citizenry to constitutional behaviour by Parliament.[37]

---

28 [1964] S.C.R. 252. Although that decision applies strictly to the law of Quebec, a similar approach has been taken by courts in the common law provinces. See, *e.g.*, *Cowan v. C.B.C.* (1966), 56 D.L.R. (2d) 578 (Ont. C.A.).

29 [1975] 1 S.C.R. 138.

30 [1976] 2 S.C.R. 265.

31 [1981] 2 S.C.R. 575.

32 *Supra*, note 29.

33 R.S.C. 1970, c. O-2 [R.S.C. 1985, c. O-3].

34 *Thorson, supra*, note 29, at 151.

35 *Ibid.*, at 147.

36 *Ibid.*, at 147.

37 *Ibid.*, at 163.

The court concluded that the discretion to grant standing should have been exercised in the plaintiff's favour.

In the *McNeil* case,[38] the recognition of standing by members of the public was extended further, and some explanation of the majority reasons in *Thorson* was provided. The case concerned an attempt by a Nova Scotia journalist to have a provincial film censorship statute declared unconstitutional. This statute differed from the Act considered in the *Thorson* case in that it was "regulatory" as well as "declaratory": it restricted the activities of film exhibitors and subjected them to penalties for breach of its provisions. The plaintiff was not connected with the film business; he had no greater interest in the legislation than any other member of the public. His claim for standing to challenge the constitutionality of the Act was resisted by the provincial Attorney General on the ground that this statute, unlike that involved in the *Thorson* case, was regulatory in nature. The court was unanimous in granting standing to the plaintiff. Although it did not altogether abandon the distinction between regulatory and declaratory statutes, the court held that since the Act's declaratory function, *vis-à-vis* members of the general public, was one of its "central aspects,"[39] members of the public could challenge its constitutionality.

This discretionary right to standing was broadened even further by the *Borowski* decision.[40] Borowski, a long-time opponent of abortion, sought a judicial declaration that the provisions of the *Criminal Code*[41] permitting therapeutic abortions in certain circumstances were invalidated by the guarantee of "the right of the individual to life" contained in section 1(*a*) of the *Canadian Bill of Rights*. He had previously been unsuccessful in challenging the provisions in question by other means. The Supreme Court of Canada held, by a majority of seven to two, that Borowski should be granted standing. This represented an extension of the *Thorson/McNeil* principles in three respects. First, the court was unanimous in holding that no distinction should be drawn for this purpose between constitutional challenges based on the *British North America Act* [*Constitution Act, 1867*], as in the previous cases, and those based, as in *Borowski*, solely on the *Canadian Bill of Rights*. Second, standing was granted even though the legislation was not "declaratory," but merely "exculpatory."[42] Third, and most important, Borowski was permitted to sue even though the legislation was *totally inapplicable to him*: he was not even affected as a member

---

38 *Supra*, note 30.
39 *Ibid.*, at 271.
40 *Supra*, note 31 at 587 (majority) and 575 (dissent).
41 R.S.C. 1970, c. C-34 [R.S.C. 1985, c. C-46].
42 *Supra*, note 31 at 596.

of the general public,[43] as McNeil had been by the censorship statute.

Mr. Justice Martland, on behalf of the majority, summed up the effect of these three decisions as follows:

> [T]o establish status as a plaintiff in a suit seeking a declaration that legislation is invalid, if there is a serious issue as to its invalidity, a person need only to show that he is affected by it directly or that he has a genuine interest as a citizen in the validity of the legislation and that there is no other reasonable and effective manner in which the issue may be brought before the Court.[44]

The position immediately prior to the enactment of the Charter therefore appears to have been that standing to seek a declaration that a law or practice is unconstitutional is always within the discretionary power of a court to grant, and that the discretion ought to be exercised in favour of citizens who raise legitimate constitutional issues, so long as the aspects of the impugned law which affect the general public are significant and there are no other appropriate legal remedies readily available. Whether this discretionary status to sue could also be accorded where remedies other than a declaration of invalidity were sought is not certain, but this would appear to be so for at least injunction and *certiorari*.[45]

This discretionary standing on the part of individuals and corporations to challenge, in the public interest, the constitutional validity of laws or governmental practices continues to be available, over and above any standing as of right that section 24(1) of the Charter may bestow. In the *Big M Drug Mart* decision,[46] Dickson C.J. commented, on behalf of a majority of the Supreme Court of Canada, that if the respondent "had been engaged in . . . 'public interest litigation'," and "had come to court . . . as an interested citizen asking for a prerogative declaration," rather than as the accused in a criminal prosecution:

> [I]t would have had to fulfill the status requirements laid down by this Court in the trilogy of "standing" cases.[47]

That test has been followed in a number of lower court decisions granting standing to various public interest litigants.[48]

Although most public interest litigation for declaratory relief on constitutional grounds seeks to challenge the validity of *laws*, the standing to request such relief under section 52(1) of the *Constitution Act, 1982*

---

43 *Ibid.*, at 578.

44 *Ibid.*, at 598.

45 See Strayer, *supra*, note 11, at 151 *et seq.*

46 *Supra*, note 16.

47 *Ibid.*, at 313.

48 *National Citizens' Coalition v. A.G. Canada* (1984), 11 D.L.R. (4th) 481 (Alta. Q.B.); *Re Scott and A.G. British Columbia* (1986), 29 D.L.R. (4th) 544 (B.C. S.C.).

appears also to include challenges to unconstitutional *conduct*.

There is a suggestion to the contrary in the concurring reasons of Wilson J. in *Operation Dismantle Inc. v. R.*[49] In that case, the plaintiffs were questioning the constitutionality of a federal cabinet decision to allow United States authorities to test cruise missiles in Canada. While discussing their standing to sue, Madam Justice Wilson commented, after noting that the challenge appeared to be based on section 52(1), that "that provision is directed to 'laws' which are inconsistent with the provisions of the Constitution."[50]

It is submitted that the *dictum* attributes too limited a scope to the subsection. It will be noted that the subsection consists of two clauses, connected by the word "and." The second clause addresses laws that are inconsistent with the Constitution, but the opening clause is much broader. It decrees, without qualification, that "the Constitution of Canada is the supreme law of Canada." Because the principle of rule of law subjects everyone, including government officials, to the law, this part of section 52(1) seems clearly to require that governmental actions comply with the Constitution, whether or not these actions take the form of laws. This interpretation appeared to be adopted by Dickson C.J. in his majority reasons for judgment in the same case. He suggested that section 52(1) may apply to "all acts taken pursuant to powers granted by the law."[51]

(d) Impending Infringements

Probably the most serious weakness in the draftsmanship of section 24(1) is that by restricting its protection to "anyone whose rights or freedoms, as guaranteed by this Charter, *have been* infringed or denied,"[52] it could be construed as excluding judicial consideration of impending infringements which have not yet come into force or have not yet been applied to the complainant.

Several different types of possible impending infringements come to mind. One type is illustrated by the previously mentioned case of *Saumur v. A.G. Québec*,[53] in which the Supreme Court of Canada denied a member of the Jehovah's Witnesses sect the right to challenge the constitutional validity of a law prohibiting the distribution of certain sect literature. The court held that, unless he actually broke the law in question, was prosecuted

---

49 [1985] 1 S.C.R. 441.

50 *Ibid.*, at 483.

51 *Ibid.*, at 459.

52 Emphasis added.

53 *Supra*, note 28. Although that decision applies strictly to the law of Quebec, a similar approach has been taken by courts in the common law provinces. See, *e.g.*, *Cowan v. C.B.C.*, *supra*, note 28.

and raised the constitutional issue in defence, the plaintiff would lack standing to seek judicial relief. Another type of impending violation might arise from a law empowering authorities to infringe rights or freedoms in some arbitrary fashion, such as by randomly searching homes in the hope of finding evidence of illegal activity, if the law had not yet been employed against the plaintiff. A third would be a situation where police or other authorities plan to take measures like those in the previous example, but without lawful authority, and have not yet acted. Finally, a legislative body — municipal, provincial or federal — might simply be debating the desirability of passing a law that some believe would violate the Charter.

It was in contemplation of situations like these that the Constitution of Nigeria, and several others that have borrowed their phraseology from Nigeria, was drafted to include anticipated as well as past and present infringements:

> 42.(1) Any person who alleges that any of the provisions of this Chapter has been, is being, or *likely to be* contravened in any State in relation to him may apply to a High Court in that State for redress.[54]

The absence of the future tense in the equivalent Canadian provision might be interpreted to prevent its application to impending infringements. This restrictive interpretation is not the only possibility, however.

The drafting history of section 24(1) would seem to indicate that impending violations were intended to be included. The first version, in *Bill C-60* of 1978, involved no temporal limitation. In fact, the only two remedies provided for in that version — declaration and injunction — were both capable of applying to apprehended future violations. When the forerunner of the present version was first suggested in 1979 (again with no temporal restrictions), it was generally regarded as an expansion of the earlier draft, intended to meet criticisms that the earlier draft did not provide a sufficiently broad range of remedies. The French text does not employ the past tense expressly: "Toute personne, victime de violation ou de négation des droits ou libertés . . . ." There is nothing in the evidence heard by the 1980-81 Special Joint Committee of the Senate and the House of Commons that would indicate any suggestion that the ambit of the enforcement section should be limited if reinstated in the Resolution. It appears therefore, that the temporal restriction in the English text was the result of a drafting accident rather than of an advertent policy.

While the orthodox approach to statutory interpretation would deny courts the right to consult this historical material as direct evidence of the meaning of section 24(1), it permits it to be examined as general

---

54 Constitution of Nigeria (1963) (emphasis added).

background information to indicate the "mischief" that was sought to be suppressed by the provision.[55] There is no evidence that the mischief addressed by section 24(1) — infringements and denials of Charter rights — excluded inchoate violations. The evidence is all to the contrary.

Viewed against this background, section 24(1) can properly be construed as applying to impending as well as to past infringements. Such an interpretation would do little violence to the language used in the section, because in most inchoate situations the threat of a future violation of rights has *immediate* restrictive consequences on the activities of the plaintiff. Consider the choice faced by Mr. Saumur, for example: either to cease the distribution of literature about his religion or run the risk of prosecution. His response — to cease distribution — constituted a serious and *immediate* restriction on his religious freedom.

Similarly, in the hypothetical situation of proposed random police searches of houses, with or without legislative sanction, it can be argued that the threat would likely cause cautious persons to take immediate protective steps, such as by removing or destroying innocent but embarrassing material from their houses or perhaps pulling up their roots and moving to a freer province or country. Or they might simply suffer mental anguish, worrying about the possibility of a police raid. These would be *present* violations of the rights of those who so responded — intrusions into their private lives that they should not have to put up with. Even in the case of a mere legislative debate about whether to pass legislation that might violate the Charter, citizens' rights can be said to be immediately affected by worry, as well as by the cost and inconvenience of any anticipatory protective measures they might feel compelled to take. It is not suggested that courts would have the power to prohibit such debates; only that a citizen who wishes to have a court's opinion about the constitutionality of a measure currently under debate should be entitled to have it.

In other words, in most foreseeable situations of apprehended but unexecuted Charter violations, there is likely to be sufficient immediate impact on the conduct or peace of mind of Canadians that section 24(1) can properly be construed as applicable.

Moreover, Charter cases involving challenges to the constitutionality of *laws* do not require the remedial authority of section 24(1); such challenges are based on section 52(1), and are therefore not affected by any possible difficulties with the wording of section 24(1).[56]

Early judicial decisions on the question tend to uphold that conclusion.

---

55 *Schneider v. R.* (1980), 103 D.L.R. (3d) 29 (B.C. S.C.), rev'd (1981), 111 D.L.R. (3d) 632 (B.C. C.A.), aff'd (1982) 139 D.L.R. (3d) 417 (S.C.C.).

56 This distinction was noted in *R. v. King* (1983), 3 C.R.D. 725.100-06 (Ont. Co. Ct.).

In *Re Kravets and Minister of Employment & Immigration*,[57] Strayer J. of the Federal Court of Canada held that an order of prohibition was available to an applicant in an immigration matter for the purpose of preserving the *status quo* until Charter rights could be adjudicated. Appropriate redress was found to be available before as well as after any infringement. In *National Citizens' Coalition Inc. v. A.G. Canada*,[58] Medhurst J. of the Alberta Court of Queen's Bench stated:

> I do not believe that the wording in s. 24(1) in the past tense would exclude actions that are based on impending breaches. A present violation would include those situations where the action is so reasonably foreseeable in the near future that concern is therefore present at this time.[59]

While the latter case involved a situation of public rather than private interest, there is no evidence that the quoted comment was intended to be restricted to those situations.

Comments by members of the Supreme Court of Canada in *Operation Dismantle Inc. v. R.*,[60] while perhaps not conclusive, tend to support this approach. Dickson C.J., for the majority, stated: "A person . . . cannot be held liable under the law for an action unless that action causes the deprivation, *or threat of deprivation*, of legal rights."[61] And although he held that the statement of claim disclosed no cause of action in that case because of the impossibility of proving a causal link between the actions complained of and such an actual or threatened deprivation of rights, he added: "I am not suggesting that remedial action by the courts will be inappropriate where future harm is alleged."[62] Wilson J., while differing with the majority about some aspects of the decision, seemed to agree on this point, referring to the plaintiff's need to "establish at least a threat of violation."[63]

It seems safe to conclude, therefore, that impending Charter contra-

---

57 [1985] 1 F.C. 434 (T.D.). See also *Que. Assn. of Protestant School Bds. v. A.G. Quebec (No. 2)*, [1982] C.S. 673 at 685 (Que. S.C.), aff'd [1983] C.A. 77 (Que. C.A.), aff'd [1984] 2 S.C.R. 66; *R.L. Crain Inc. v. Couture* (1983), 6 D.L.R. (4th) 478 at 516-518 (Sask. Q.B.); *R. v. Sophonow (No. 2)* (1983), 150 D.L.R. (3d) 590 at 599 (Man. C.A.), leave to appeal to S.C.C. granted (1984), 11 C.R.R. 183n (S.C.C.); *R. v. T.R.(No. 1)* (1984), 7 D.L.R. (4th) 205 (Alta. Q.B.); *Re Walton and A.G. Canada* (1984), 13 D.L.R. (4th) 379 (N.W.T. S.C.). But see *Re N. and D.* (1985), 49 O.R. (2d) 490 (Fam Ct.), where, oddly, a compulsory blood test in a paternity dispute was held to involve only an "impending" intrusion on the subject's rights; and *R. v. King, supra*, note 56.

58 *Supra*, note 48.

59 *Ibid.*, at 485.

60 *Supra*, note 49.

61 *Ibid.*, at 456 (emphasis added).

62 *Ibid.*, at 456.

63 *Ibid.*, at 486.

ventions can be the subject of judicial relief, probably under section 24(1), but at least under the courts' inherent remedial powers. The mere *allegation* of an impending violation is not enough to justify judicial intervention, however; the threat must be proved by a preponderance of probability. As Mr. Justice Dickson put it: "[T]he courts will not take remedial action where the occurrence of future harm is not probable."[64]

(e) "Court of Competent Jurisdiction"

Before a court can grant a Charter remedy, it must be established that it has jurisdiction to do so. As one judge put it: "I have sympathy for the applicants . . . . But sympathy cannot clothe me with jurisdiction."[65]

Rather than specifying a particular tribunal to enforce the provisions of the Charter, section 24(1) directs complainants to apply for relief to "a court of competent jurisdiction." The term "court of competent jurisdiction" has long been employed in legislation to refer to courts that possess jurisdiction independent of that legislation itself. Collins M.R. offered the following interpretation in a 1907 decision of the English Court of Appeal:

> [I]t is said that the use of the words "a Court of competent jurisdiction" implies that there is a special provision made for recovery before a particular Court, and therefore to the exclusion of every other Court . . . . [T]he expression . . . seems to me to be only a compendious expression covering every possible Court which by enactment is made competent to entertain a claim.[66]

A similar interpretation has been adopted by virtually all Canadian courts called upon to apply section 24(1). The Ontario Court of Appeal, for example, has said:

> The weight of authority is that s. 24(1) does not create courts of competent jurisdiction, but merely vests additional powers in courts which are already found to be competent independently of the Charter.[67]

Consensus as to this general principle has not avoided some uncertainty as to its application. Doubtful matters include the meaning of "court," the parameters of competence under section 24(1), section 52(1) and "inherent jurisdiction," and the distinction between the competence of the court and the appropriateness of the remedy.

---

64 *Ibid.*, at 458.
65 *Per* Collier J., in *Re Vergis and Canada Lab. Rel. Bd.* (1982), 142 D.L.R. (3d) 747 at 750 (F.T.D.).
66 *R. v. Garrett*, [1907] 1 K.B. 881 at 885-886 (C.A.).
67 *R. v. Morgentaler* (1984), 14 D.L.R. (4th) 184 at 190 (Ont. C.A.) (*per* Brooke J.A.). See also remarks of Wilson J. in the *Singh* case, *infra*, note 74.

(i) *"Court"*

Although the English text speaks of a "court" of competent juris-diction, the French version uses the term "tribunal," which is broad enough to include quasi-judicial administrative bodies as well as courts.[68] One writer has suggested that the narrower construction should prevail, limiting the scope of the section to courts of record,[69] but other writers contend that administrative tribunals are included,[70] and there is also judicial authority to that effect.[71]

Even if that view did not prevail and the section were held to be restricted to full-fledged courts, it should be borne in mind that a number of specialized tribunals, such as the Immigration Appeal Board,[72] have a status of courts.

It is possible that the Charter could also be enforced in certain circumstances by arbiters other than "courts" and "tribunals." Suppose, for example, that an arbitration were held in a dispute between the Government of Canada and one of its employees as to whether the employee should be dismissed for openly supporting a particular political party. Since the Constitution of Canada, which includes the Charter, is declared by section 52(1) to be the "supreme law of Canada," and since arbitrators are normally required to function in accordance with law, it would seem that the arbitrator would be obliged to take account of all relevant parts of the Charter.

(ii) *Competence Under Section 24(1)*

Not every court, tribunal or other arbiter would have jurisdiction over every Charter violation, of course. It would always be necessary to establish that the situation is within the jurisdiction of the body approached. At least

---

68 A. Gautron, "French/English Discrepancies in the Canadian Charter of Rights and Freedoms" (1982), 12 *Man. L.J.* 220 at 229-230.

69 E.G. Ewaschuk, "The Charter: An Overview and Remedies" (1982), 26 C.R. (3d) 54 at 69.

70 G.J. Smith & J.G. Richards, "Applying the Charter," in G.J. Smith, ed., *Charter of Rights and Administrative Law, 1983-84* (Law Society of Upper Canada Bar Admission Course Materials) (Toronto: Carswell, 1983); M. Manning, *Rights, Freedoms and the Courts: A Practical Analysis of the Constitution Act, 1982* (Toronto: Emond-Montgomery, 1982), at 470.

71 *Re Nash and R* (1982), 70 C.C.C. (2d) 490 (Nfld. Prov. Ct.): *Re Moore and R.* (May 12, 1986) (B.C. S.C.).

72 *Immigration Act, 1976*, S.C. 1976-77, c. 52, s. 65(1) [R.S.C. 1985, c. I-2, s. 63(1)]; *Law v. Solicitor Gen. of Canada* (1983), 144 D.L.R. (3d) 549 (F.C.T.D.), rev'd in part (1984), 11 D.L.R. (4th) 608 (F.C.A.). The status of boards that are merely stated to have "all the powers of a court of record," such as the Manitoba Public Utilities Board (*Public Utilities Board Act*, C.C.S.M., c. P280, s. 10), is doubtful.

three types of jurisdictional competence are possible, relating to (a) the subject matter, (b) the parties and (c) the remedy, and the Supreme Court of Canada seems to have held that each of these jurisdictional requirements must be satisfied in order to seek a remedy under section 24(1).[73]

Competence as to *subject matter* presents few problems. Consider the position of a court of exclusively criminal jurisdiction, such as the provincial court of one of the provinces. If a person, prosecuted in such a court for breach of some statute, defended on the ground that the statute offended the "equality before the law" provisions of the Charter, the court would certainly be empowered to give effect to the defence. But if the discriminatory statute involved instead the unequal distribution of some benefit, such as rent subsidies or unemployment insurance, the person discriminated against could obtain no assistance from a criminal court, and would have to seek his or her remedy from a court of general civil jurisdiction.

The plaintiff must, in other words, always establish that the subject with respect to which the alleged Charter violation took place is within the competence of the court, tribunal or arbiter approached. Madam Justice Wilson, speaking for half of a six-judge panel of the Supreme Court of Canada in *Singh v. Minister of Employment & Immigration*, confirmed this interpretation:

> Section 24(1) of the *Charter* provides remedial powers to "a court of competent jurisdiction." As I understand this phrase, it premises the existence of jurisdiction from a source external to the *Charter* itself.[74]

Therefore, she held, the court could not consider alleged Charter violations by a body not subject to the jurisdiction of the court appealed from in the particular proceedings.

An application to the Trial Division of the Federal Court of Canada to quash on Charter grounds an indeterminate sentence imposed on the plaintiff by a provincial court judge under the "dangerous offender" provisions of the *Criminal Code* was struck out because such matters are entirely outside the jurisdiction of the Federal Court.[75] A request by defence counsel in a criminal trial before a jury to address the jury on the question whether the trial had been unreasonably delayed contrary to section 11(*b*) of the Charter was refused because questions of law are entirely beyond the competence of juries.[76] A review and alteration by one provincial court judge of bail orders made by another provincial court judge was held to be invalid because reviewing previous bail orders is not one of the functions

---

73 *R. v. Mills*, [1986] 1 S.C.R. 863.
74 [1985] 1 S.C.R. 177 at 222.
75 *R. v. Jackson* (1984), 5 C.R.D., 425.20-09 (F.C.T.D.).
76 *R. v. Robinson* (1984), 36 Sask. R. 310 (Q.B.).

bestowed on such judges.[77] The Trial Division of the Federal Court has no jurisdiction to review or stay the execution of orders made by the Canada Labour Relations Board, though an appeal may lie to the Federal Court of Appeal.[78] Courts of Appeal and their individual members have been held not to have the jurisdiction to deal with Charter claims at first instance because their competence is purely appellate.[79]

It should be remembered, however, that jurisdictional questions are not necessarily "either/or" matters. Jurisdictional spheres often overlap, especially where constitutional issues are involved. The Supreme Court of Canada has confirmed, for example, that both the Federal Court of Canada and the provincial superior courts are competent to entertain challenges to the constitutionality of federal legislation,[80] and this has been held to apply to challenges based on the Charter.[81]

Competence as to the *parties* involved in the dispute is also necessary. This requirement is not likely to raise frequent problems, since most courts have jurisdiction over most persons and legal entities engaged in activities within the area served by the court.

However, the *Federal Court Act*[82] purports to create some important exceptions to this general rule by stipulating, in sections 17 and 18, that certain claims against the Crown in the right of Canada, and actions seeking injunctions, prerogative remedies or declaratory relief against "any federal board, commission of other tribunal" are within the "exclusive" jurisdiction of the Federal Court of Canada. While it is beyond the scope of this book to examine the ambit of those exceptions, or the doubts that have been raised as to their constitutional validity,[83] it should be noted that considerable high-level adjudication will be required before one can state unequivocally which courts are competent to rule on alleged Charter violations by agencies of the government of Canada.

Competence as to *remedy* is also required, although that is not to say that courts are necessarily limited to those remedies which were exercised prior to the Charter. Some courts lack the normal jurisdiction to award certain forms of relief, such as injunctions or damages over specified sums,[84] and victims of Charter violations should accordingly

---

77 *Re R. and Brooks* (1982), 143 D.L.R. (3d) 482 (Ont. H.C.).

78 *Re Vergis and Canada Lab. Rel. Bd.*, *supra*, note 65.

79 *ACL Can. Inc. v. Hunter* (1983), 3 D.L.R. (4th) 336 (Qué. C.A.) (*per* Nichols J.A. in Chambers); *R. v. Crate* (1983), 1 D.L.R. (4th) 149 (Alta. C.A.).

80 *A.G. Canada v. Law Society of B.C.*; *Jabour v. Law Society of B.C.*, [1982] 2 S.C.R. 307.

81 *Lavers v. Min. of Finance* (1985), 18 D.L.R. (4th) 477 (B.C. S.C.).

82 R.S.C. 1970, c. 10 (2nd Supp.) [R.S.C. 1985, c. F-7].

83 See *James Richardson & Sons Ltd. v. M.N.R.* (1980), 117 D.L.R. (3d) 557 (Man. Q.B.).

84 *E.g.*, *Continental Bank of Can. v. Rizzo* (1985), 50 C.P.C. 56 (Ont. Dist. Ct.).

choose their tribunals with an eye to the remedies available therefrom, as well as the types of disputes and categories of parties they are empowered to entertain. It has been held, for example, that a provincial court judge presiding at a preliminary inquiry under the *Criminal Code* is not a court of competent jurisdiction for the purposes of an application for relief under section 24(1), as the provincial court judges' remedial powers are restricted to committal and discharge.[85] A county court judge entertaining an appeal from a conviction and suspension of driver's licence under highway traffic legislation has been held to have no power to award damages after overturning the conviction.[86]

It is grammatically possible to interpret the section as not including remedies within the meaning of "competent jurisdiction." It will be noted that the subsection deals *separately* with the questions of "competent jurisdiction" and "remedy." After directing complainants to a court of competent jurisdiction, the section then empowers the court to provide "such remedy as the court considers appropriate and just in the circumstances." Although this could be construed to refer only to remedies within the court's normal competence, it would have been easy for the drafters of the section to say so expressly; they did not. It is therefore open to the courts to find that the term "court of competent jurisdiction" refers only to jurisdiction over subject matter and parties, every court having been given unlimited discretionary competence over remedies by the concluding words of the section. If this approach were accepted, it would be applicable to statutory courts, whose normal powers, unlike those of courts of "inherent jurisdiction," are restricted to those bestowed on them by statute, the Charter being a "statute" for that purpose.[87]

Professor Hogg once stated a preference for this broader interpretation,[88] pointing out that section 24(1) provides a remedy for alleged denials of constitutional rights. If the remedy for constitutional violations were subject to legislative control, constitutional rights would be no stronger, in realistic terms, than the remedies the legislators were willing to permit. Since one of the primary purposes of the Charter is to ensure that legislators respect the rights it enshrines, an interpretation of section

---

85 *R. v. Mills, supra,* note 73.

86 *R. v. Tso Tung Quan* (1984), 9 C.R.R. 375 (B.C. Co. Ct.).

87 *Re Johnson and Ontario* (1985), 16 D.L.R. (4th) 441 (Ont. H.C.).

88 P.W. Hogg, *Constitutional Law of Canada,* 2nd ed. (Toronto: Carswell, 1985) at 696. See also J.C. Levy, "The Invocation of Remedies Under the Charter of Rights and Freedoms: Some Procedural Considerations" (1983), 13 Man. L.J. 523. In *R. v. Erickson* (1984), 13 C.C.C. (3d) 269 at 275 (B.C. C.A.), Esson J.A. said: "Next there is the question as to the extent of the power of the court under s. 24(1) to grant remedies which are not otherwise authorized by law. It is clear that the *Charter* confers some such powers."

24(1) that left enforcement of the Charter ultimately in the hands of the legislators undoubtedly puts that purpose at risk.

The Supreme Court of Canada seems to have rejected that interpretation in *R. v. Mills*.[89] Both the majority and minority judges in that case appear to have stated, in *obiter dicta*, that extra-Charter competence is required as to remedy, as well as to subject-matter and parties. Read closely, the reasons for judgment of Mr. Justice McIntyre, for the majority, could be interpreted as leaving open the possibility that remedial jurisdiction could be based on section 24(1) itself. It is doubtful that such an interpretation was intended, however.

Nevertheless, his Lordship did urge the courts, acting within their jurisdictional limits, to "devise, as the circumstances arise, imaginative remedies to serve the needs of individual cases."[90] This probably means that, while some remedial competence outside the Charter is required, the Supreme Court will be sympathetic to expansive interpretations and novel applications of those existing powers.

It should not be forgotten that the remedial powers of most courts are already extensive — especially in the case of courts of inherent jurisdiction. It has been observed that the inherent jurisdiction of superior courts in procedural matters "may be invoked in an apparently inexhaustible variety of circumstances, and may be exercised in different ways."[91]

(iii) *Appropriateness*

The relief authorized by section 24(1) must be "appropriate and just in the circumstances." Many of the remedies that courts have denied on the ground that they are not competent to grant them would probably have been denied as "inappropriate" even if the court had regarded itself as competent.

Existing legal procedures have established an orderly and well-understood division of labour among the various participants in the adjudicative process. These procedures are generally regarded, for the most part, as the fairest and most efficient methods of conducting litigation. It would make little sense in most cases to abandon or disrupt the system just because Charter rights are involved. In *Re Anson and R.*,[92] MacFarlane J.A. of the British Columbia Court of Appeal stated, in support of a refusal

---

89 *Supra*, note 73.

90 *Ibid.*, at 955.

91 I.H. Jacob, "The Inherent Jurisdiction of the Court" (1970), 23 *Curr. Legal Probs.* 23; approved in *Canada Labour Congress v. Bhindi* (1985), 17 D.L.R. (4th) 193 at 203 (B.C. C.A.). And see *Danson v. A.G. Ontario, supra*, note 14.

92 (1983), 146 D.L.R. (3d) 661 (B.C. C.A.).

by a Supreme Court judge to prohibit a lower court judge, on Charter grounds, from proceedings with a trial:

> [E]ach level of the judiciary should be free to perform its proper function, and . . . counsel should not be encouraged to seek solutions to legal questions prematurely at the supervisory or appellate level. . . . [T]here will be cases where it may be appropriate to grant prerogative relief. Such cases should be few and far between, but it is best to leave the decision in those cases to the fair and proper exercise of the discretion of the judge.[93]

In *Re Blackwoods Beverages Ltd. and R.*,[94] Monnin C.J.M., of the Manitoba Court of Appeal, commented:

> [T]he Charter was not intended to disturb what is and was a well-organized legal system, nor to cause its paralysis. The Charter is the supreme law of the country, it must be applied and given the most liberal and free interpretation but it must do so within the existing trial system. . . . [T]he ordinary trial procedure of information, preliminary hearing, committal, trial and appeals at various levels of appellate jurisdiction must not be disturbed. On the contrary, that hierarchy must be respected for the proper, efficient and speedy administration of justice. Otherwise we will have nothing but a series of jumping jack-in-the-box effects, of up and down from trial level to appellate level with no specific and exact procedure to follow.

For these reasons, courts have usually refused to follow extraordinary procedures in Charter cases. Pre-trial hearings to suppress evidence obtained by unconstitutional means have been rejected.[95] Motions to stay criminal proceedings on Charter grounds have been held to be more appropriate for consideration by the trial court than by an appellate court.[96] Courts of appeal have often declined to entertain appeals from interlocutory rulings on Charter issues until the trial stage has been completed.[97]

It must be stressed, however, that many, if not most, of these rulings are discretionary decisions as to what is "appropriate and just in the circumstances"; they are not the inexorable consequences of immutable jurisdictional principles. It has already been pointed out that there is considerable jurisdictional overlap among judicial and quasi-judicial bodies. Many of the conventionally respected boundaries are matters of convenience rather than of competence.

When the courts are requested to draw upon the discretionary reservoir

---

93 *Ibid.*, at 672-673.

94 (1984), 15 D.L.R. (4th) 231 at 237 (Man. C.A.), leave to appeal to S.C.C. refused (1985), 15 D.L.R. (4th) 231n (S.C.C.).

95 *Ibid.*; *Re R. and Siegel* (1982), 142 D.L.R. (3d) 426 (Ont. H.C.).

96 *Re Krakowski and R.* (1983), 146 D.L.R. (3d) 760 (Ont. C.A.).

97 *Re Laurendeau and R.* (1983), 4 D.L.R. (4th) 702 (Que. C.A.), leave to appeal to S.C.C. refused (1983), 4 D.L.R. (4th) 702n; *R. v. Morgentaler* (1984), 14 D.L.R. (4th) 184 (Ont. C.A.); *R. v. Ritter* (1984), 7 D.L.R. (4th) 623 (B.C. C.A.).

of extraordinary remedial powers that they may have under either section 24(1) or their inherent authority, they should do so sparingly and with due regard for normal procedural considerations. But they must be prepared to use those powers where, because of unusual circumstances, it would be "appropriate and just" to do so. The passage quoted above from the *Anson* case[98] acknowledged this, and Matas J.A. who dissented in the *Blackwoods* case, observed:

> The superior courts have generally ruled against interference with the orderly trial process, whether in the granting of prerogative relief or the granting of relief requested on the basis of the inherent jurisdiction of the court, or under s. 24(1) of the Charter. But exceptions to the rule may be made in exceptional cases.[99]

(iv) *Competence under Section 52(1) and Inherent Jurisdiction*

Limitations in the remedial powers granted by section 24 of the Charter are not necessarily fatal to claims excluded by the limits, because section 24 is not the sole source of relief for Charter violations.

In countries like the United States, which have constitutional guarantees of rights and freedoms but no express enforcement machinery, the guarantees have been enforced through ordinary processes of judicial review. This was also the case in Canada prior to the adoption of the *Constitution Act, 1982,* as is illustrated by the ruling of the Supreme Court of Canada giving legal effect to language guarantees contained in section 133 of the *Constitution Act, 1867* and section 23 of the *Manitoba Act.*[100]

Any argument that the narrower powers of section 24 have replaced for Charter purposes the pre-Charter power of the courts to enforce constitutional rights without an express mandate is rebutted by section 26, which stipulates that the Charter is not to be so construed as to deny pre-existing rights.

On the contrary, section 52(1) of the *Constitution Act, 1982* now provides an explicit recognition of the principle upon which pre-Charter judicial enforcement of constitutional rights was based — that unconstitutional laws are invalid:

> The Constitution of Canada is the supreme law of Canada, and any law that is inconsistent with the provisions of the Constitution is, to the extent of the inconsistency, of no force or effect.

The Supreme Court of Canada has indicated that section 52(1)

---

98 *Supra*, note 92.

99 *Blackwoods, supra,* note 94, at 244.

100 *A.G. Manitoba v. Forest,* [1979] 2 S.C.R. 1032; *A.G. Qué. v. Blaikie; A.G. Quebec v. Laurier,* [1979] 2 S.C.R. 1016.

involves a remedy for Charter violations that is independent of section 24(1). In *R. v. Big M Drug Mart Ltd.*,[101] Mr. Justice Dickson, speaking for a majority of the court, stated:

> Section 24(1) sets out a remedy for individuals . . . whose rights under the *Charter* have been infringed. It is not, however, the only recourse in the face of unconstitutional legislation. Where, as here, the challenge is based on the unconstitutionality of the legislation, recourse to s. 24 is unnecessary
>
> . . . .
>
> Section 52 sets out the fundamental principle of constitutional law that the Constitution is supreme.

He went on to explain that persons prosecuted under unconstitutional laws may always raise section 52 as a defence, and that interested citizens may also rely on it to attack unconstitutional laws in "public interest litigation" if they can establish standing under the *Thorson/McNeil/Borowski* principles.

It should also be remembered that superior courts possess inherent jurisdiction that could be relied upon in situations that are found to be beyond judicial reach even under section 52(1). This possibility will be examined more fully later.

(f) Types of Remedies Available[102]

Section 24(1), which empowers "a court of competent jurisdiction" to award "such remedy as the court considers appropriate and just in the circumstances" to anyone whose Charter rights or freedoms "have been infringed or denied," is the most broad-ranging of the Charter's remedial provisions. The variety of remedies available under this provision is restricted by only three factors:

(a) the extent of court's normal remedial armaments (which in the case of superior courts is virtually unlimited);
(b) the need for the remedy to be "appropriate and just"; and
(c) the breadth of judicial imagination.

(i) Positive and Negative Remedies

Courts are more familiar with "shalt nots" than with "shalts." They have traditionally been readier to award negative, prohibitory types of remedy than positive, mandatory ones. Although the Charter is expressed in terms of positive rights and freedoms rather than of duties and

---

101 *Supra*, note 16, at 313.
102 Based on extracts from Gibson, *The Law of the Charter, supra*, note 2, at 192 *et seq.*

responsibilities, the remedies sought by persons alleging violation of their Charter rights are most often of a negative type: striking down a law or a governmental action that offends the Charter, rejecting evidence obtained in violation of the Charter or acquitting an accused who was denied Charter rights.

In some circumstances, however, the most appropriate remedy may involve positive action by the defendant to restore the plaintiff's Charter rights, or to compensate for their deprivation. The payment of monetary damages to compensate for lost income might, for example, be the most suitable remedy for discrimination in employment. More elaborate forms of positive relief might sometimes also be called for: an order to provide employment or a denied service to a victim of discrimination, or perhaps an order to carry out an affirmative action program for the benefit of historically disadvantaged groups. In these situations the courts' customary unease with positive remedies could pose problems.

The problems can be overcome, however. They are not primarily legal in nature. Under section 24(1), the courts have all the legal authority they require to award positive relief whenever appropriate. Their normal remedial arsenal includes a wide range of positive measures, from monetary damages to mandatory injunctions and writs of *mandamus*. The major obstacles to the granting of positive remedies are not procedural. They are rooted, rather, partly in judicial attitudes and partly in the ambiguous phrasing of some of the rights guaranteed by the Charter.

The attitudinal problem is largely a thing of the past. Canadian courts used to exhibit extreme deference toward the elected arms of government. They regarded it as less intrusive to tell the government that it could not pass a particular law or pursue a specific line of action than to tell it what law should be enacted or what line of action should be taken. They also showed considerable reluctance to order conduct which would require detailed or long-lasting judicial supervision. The Charter has now given judges a constitutional mandate to do what they were previously reluctant to do, however, and the first few years of Charter litigation have clearly demonstrated that judges are taking this responsibility seriously. Due deference is still paid to democratic decision-making, but where political decisions contravene constitutional rights, the courts are no longer reluctant to award appropriate remedies.

The other major obstacle to positive relief is that the Charter is sometimes unclear about whether it is bestowing a substantive right to positive assistance in certain circumstances. Several of the Charter's substantive rights would mean little if the courts were unable or unwilling to enforce them by positive remedies. These include the right to vote (section 3), the right to an interpreter in court (section 14), the right to certain public services in either French or English (section 20), and the right to minority language instruction and educational facilities (section 23). In those cases, there can be little doubt that positive relief was intended.

Other rights are expressed in language that could be construed as calling for only negative remedies. The availability of positive relief in those cases depends upon the substantive nature of the rights in question.

(ii) *Acquittal and Staying or Quashing Proceedings*

The Charter is invoked most frequently in criminal proceedings and, when the Charter claim is successful in such cases, it sometimes results in dismissal of the prosecution. It would be rare for an acquittal, in the strict sense, to be appropriate (except where the exclusion of evidence under section 24(2) left the Crown with insufficient evidence to support a conviction), since most Charter rights involve either procedural safeguards or the constitutional validity of the law creating the prohibition, rather than the question whether the accused did or did not do what he or she was charged with. What a court may do, however, when a Charter defence succeeds in a criminal case, is to quash the indictment or information or stay the prosecution.[103]

This does not mean that every Charter infringement by police or prosecuting authorities should result in a dismissal of the prosecution.[104] Only where the violation has prejudiced the accused's defence and cannot be satisfactorily remedied in any other way is dismissal an "appropriate and just" remedy.

Some courts and writers have argued for too narrow an application of the dismissal remedy, however. In *R. v. Blackstock*,[105] for example, Judge Lee of the Saskatchewan Provincial Court seemed to equate it with the exclusion of evidence under section 24(2) of the Charter, contending that one of the factors to be considered in deciding whether to stay proceedings is whether the Charter infringement "would either cause the further prosecution of the offence to appear to be scandalous to the public or cause the administration of justice to appear in an unfavourable light."[106] This view disregards the clear wording of section 24, which explicitly restricts the evidentiary remedy to circumstances where the administration of justice would be jeopardized, and conspicuously avoids any such restriction in the case of other remedies.

---

103 *E.g., R. v. Heaslip* (1983), 9 C.C.C. (3d) 480 (Ont. C.A.).

104 *R. v. Erickson, supra*, note 88; *R. v. Williams* (1984), 12 W.C.B. 37 (B.C. Co. Ct.).

105 (1983), 29 C.R. (3d) 249 (Sask. Prov. Ct.), aff'd (1983), 32 C.R. (3d) 91 (Sask. Q.B.). Other criteria, such as whether the criminal charge "is of a minor nature" are even more questionable.

106 *Ibid.*, at 255 (Prov. Ct.).

Under section 605(1)(*a*) [676(1)(*a*)] of the *Criminal Code*, appeals by the Crown lie only from acquittals, and because of the technical distinctions between acquittal, quashing of the indictment or information and staying of proceedings, considerable confusion prevailed at one time as to whether the Crown could appeal a trial court's decision to quash or stay. That confusion was cleared up by the Supreme Court of Canada in *R. v. Jewitt*,[107] a case in which narcotics proceedings against the accused were stayed by the trial judge on the ground that the Crown had been guilty of an abuse of process. The Crown's attempt to appeal the decision was resisted on the ground that a stay did not amount to an acquittal. The Supreme Court of Canada ruled (after confirming that proceedings can be stayed for abuse of process, although "only in the clearest of cases"[108] that both an order to quash and an order to stay are "tantamount to a judgment or verdict of acquittal" where

> (a) the decision to stay was not based on procedural considerations, but rather on questions of law: and (b) the decision was a final decision, that is to say, a judgment rendered on a question of law after the accused was placed in jeopardy.[109]

Chief Justice Dickson, who wrote the court's reasons, stressed that "substance and not form should govern":

> Whatever the words used, the judge intended to make a final order disposing of the charge against the respondent. If the order of the Court effectively brings the proceedings to a final conclusion in favour of an accused then I am of opinion that, irrespective of the terminology used, it is tantamount to a judgment or verdict of acquittal and therefore appealable by the Crown.[110]

The decision affects more than appealability, of course. It also means that decisions to stay or quash on Charter grounds will support a defence of *autrefois acquit.*[111]

Refusal by a trial judge to quash or stay on Charter grounds has been held to be unappealable on an interlocutory basis, though it can be reviewed as part of a regular appeal from conviction.[112] Whether this is a discretionary matter, or the result of a lack of jurisdiction, is open to doubt. It is possible, however, that a review of the refusal could be obtained by prerogative order. That possibility will be discussed in the next section.

---

107 [1985] 2 S.C.R. 128.

108 *Ibid.*, at 137.

109 *Ibid.*, at 145.

110 *Ibid.*, at 148.

111 *Ibid.*, at 148.

112 *R. v. Ritter, supra,* note 97; *R. v. Morgentaler, supra,* note 97.

(iii) *Prerogative Remedies*[113]

The power of the courts to review the actions of lower courts, administrative tribunals, public officers and others by means of the discretionary prerogative remedies of *certiorari*, prohibition, *mandamus*, *quo warranto* and *habeas corpus* is a vital part of the remedial arsenal available for Charter infringements.

With the exception of *habeas corpus*, which is governed by somewhat different principles and will be discussed separately, these remedies apply primarily, if not exclusively, to jurisdictional error by public authorities.[114] Decisions made outside an authority's jurisdiction may be set aside by *certiorari* or prevented in advance by prohibition. The authority for a decision or a proposed decision may be questioned by *quo warranto*. Refusal to exercise jurisdiction may be countered by an order of *mandamus*. While these remedies do not permit the superior court to examine the merits of decisions made within jurisdiction or to order jurisdiction to be exercised in any particular way, a rather generous view is taken of what constitutes "jurisdictional" error. Acting on the authority of laws that contravene the Charter, ignoring responsibilities under the Charter, or behaving in a manner that violates the Charter all qualify as jurisdictional error, reviewable by prerogative remedy. As MacFarlane J.A. of the British Columbia Court of Appeal said, approving an order of *mandamus* requiring a provincial court judge to proceed with a preliminary hearing after staying proceedings on Charter grounds:

> I agree that the review tribunal ought not, if the judge had evidence before him on which he could rest his conclusion, to substitute its opinion on that evidence for the opinion held by the judge having jurisdiction to try the issue. But if it is clear that the judge has not applied proper legal criteria in reaching his conclusion on a preliminary objection, and that such conclusion could not have been reached if all the proper factors had been considered then I think it is open to the reviewing tribunal to set aside the order made, and compel the judge to proceed with the hearing on the merits.[115]

Although it was once thought that *certiorari* and prohibition are

---

113 See D.P. Jones & A.S. de Villars, *Principles of Administrative Law* (Toronto: Carswell, 1985) at 357 *et seq.*; P.J. Connelly, "Relief Under the Charter and the Prerogative Remedies" (1983), 26 *C.L.Q.* 35.

114 It was suggested in *Re Pagan* (1984), 5 C.R.D. 750.40-01 (B.C. S.C.) that, in addition to jurisdictional error, prerogative review is applicable to challenge decisions made under unconstitutional laws. While this is true, it is really just another type of jurisdictional question.

115 *R. v. Thompson* (1983), 3 D.L.R. (4th) 642 at 656 (B.C. C.A.). See also *Potma v. R.* (1983), 144 D.L.R. (3d) 620 at 631 (Ont. C.A.), leave to appeal to S.C.C. refused 144 D.L.R. (3d) 620n (S.C.C.) where Robins J.A. said that "the issue of fundamental fairness of process . . . like denial of natural justice, goes to the question of jurisdiction."

available only in the case of judicial or quasi-judicial decisions, and not in the case of purely "administrative" or "ministerial" decisions, this view no longer prevails.[116] All jurisdictional errors by public authorities, whether or not they have a judicial quality, are potentially reviewable by prerogative order.

This does not necessarily mean that they will be reviewed, however. Prerogative relief is discretionary; doubly so, in fact, because, in addition to the general discretion bestowed by the "appropriate and just" provision of section 24(1), the prerogative remedies are inherently discretionary — available only where, in the court's opinion, exceptional circumstances justify their use. While "exceptional circumstances" are, by definition, undefinable, they are most often found to exist where there is no regular avenue for review or, where there is, that avenue is less satisfactory than prerogative review for some reason. Before the Supreme Court of Canada confirmed the ability of the Crown to appeal from orders of trial judges quashing indictments or staying prosecutions,[117] prerogative review seemed suitable.[118] But this is no longer the case. Where a normal appeal channel exists and there are no extraordinary reasons for not employing it, superior courts will decline to exercise their prerogative supervisory powers.[119] As Chief Justice Howland stated, for the Ontario Court of Appeal, assuming that a superior court has the power to grant prerogative relief,

> it had a discretion to refuse to exercise such jurisdiction where the provincial court in turn had jurisdiction, and the right could be enforced in that court. If the Supreme Court has inherent jurisdiction, it should only be assumed where a Supreme Court Judge in the exercise of his discretion considered that the special circumstances of a particular case merit it. This is the same approach which should be taken by the Supreme Court in deciding whether to grant prerogative relief. Counsel should be discouraged from seeking to enforce rights under the Charter, such as the right to a trial within a reasonable time, prematurely in the Supreme Court.[120]

Habeas corpus, a prerogative means of challenging unlawful detention,[121] differs from the other prerogative remedies in several respects. It is not restricted to situations of jurisdictional error, and it is available against private as well as public detainers. Moreover, it is explicitly guaranteed

---

116 Jones & de Villars, *supra*, note 113, at 362-63.
117 *R. v. Jewitt, supra*, note 107.
118 *R. v. Thompson, supra*, note 115; *Re R. and Beason* (1983), 1 D.L.R. (4th) 218 (Ont. C.A.).
119 *R. v. Kendall; R. v. McCaffery* (1983), 144 D.L.R. (3d) 185 (Alta. C.A.); *R. v. Anson, supra*, note 92; *Re Bank of N.S. and R.* (1983), 150 D.L.R. (3d) 762 (Sask. C.A.).
120 *Re Krakowski and R., supra*, note 96, at 762-763.
121 See D.A.C. Harvey, *The Law of Habeas Corpus in Canada* (Toronto: Butterworths, 1974).

by the Charter in a separate section (section 10(*c*)) that is not subject to the "appropriate and just" qualification of section 24(1):

> 10. Everyone has the right on arrest or detention
>
> . . .
>
> (c) to have the validity of the detention determined by way of *habeas corpus* and to be released if the detention is not lawful.

The manner in which *habeas corpus* is referred to in section 10 raises a strong possibility that the court has no discretion to refuse. The discretion incorporated in section 24(1) is clearly absent, and although *habeas corpus* has traditionally shared the discretionary character of all prerogative remedies,[122] its unqualified description in section 10 as a "right," accompanied by the right "to be released if the detention is not lawful," suggests that that characteristic may have been constitutionally removed.[123]

A number of other questions have arisen concerning the *habeas corpus* remedy under section 10. Does it permit challenging the *form* of custody, as opposed to the fact of custody? The Supreme Court of Canada has held that it does, although without specific reference to section 10 of the Charter.[124] Does the fact that the section refers to *both* the "validity" of the detention and to whether it is "lawful" mean that even lawful custody can be challenged on other grounds of "validity," such as reasonableness or humanity? A majority of the Alberta Court of Appeal has held that *habeas corpus* is available to review the reasonableness of custody as well as its lawfulness.[125] Does the right to *habeas corpus* include a right to *certiorari* in aid? Although a pre-Charter decision of the Supreme Court of Canada casts some doubt on the matter,[126] it is now settled that a right to *certiorari* in aid exists.[127]

Whatever further effects the entrenchment of *habeas corpus* in the Charter may have, some things seem clear. Being constitutionally entrenched, the right to *habeas corpus* cannot be denied by statutory privative clauses, unless, of course, they are authorized by a section 33 opt-out or are held to constitute a reasonable limit under section 1.[128] And in circumstances where a person is detained under a decision from

---

122 *Ibid.*, at 13.
123 It was treated as discretionary in *Reference re Mental Health Act* (1984), 5 D.L.R. (4th) 577 (P.E.I. C.A.).
124 *Cardinal v. Director of Kent Institutions*, [1985] 2 S.C.R. 643; *R. v. Miller* [1985] 2 S.C.R. 613.
125 *Hicks v. R.* (1982), 129 D.L.R. (3d) 146 (Alta. C.A.).
126 *Mitchell v. R.* (1976), 61 D.L.R. (3d) 77 (S.C.C.).
127 *Cardinal, supra,* note 124; *Miller, supra,* note 124.
128 *Jack v. R.* (1982), 1 C.C.C. (3d) 193 (Nfld. T.D.).

which no appeal lies, *habeas corpus* appears to provide a means of reviewing the decision.[129]

(iv) *Declarations of Rights*

Another form of relief, of particular importance where other remedies are unavailable, is a judicial declaration as to the parties' respective rights and obligations. This remedy existed before the Charter came into force,[130] and section 26 of the Charter ensures that it remains available.

To the extent that the declaration sought concerns the constitutionality of laws, the right to seek it is independent of section 24(1). In *R. v. Big M Drug Mart Ltd.*,[131] Dickson C.J. stated: "Where, as here, the challenge is based on the unconstitutionality of the legislation, recourse to s. 24 is unnecessary." This means that the "appropriate and just" requirement of that section is not applicable. Whether it also means that the courts' pre-Charter discretion to refuse a declaration where it is desirable to do so is not clear, but an argument can be made to the effect that section 52 establishes an absolute constitutional requirement, in respect of which anyone with standing to sue[132] is entitled to a declaration.

Declaratory relief is not restricted to the constitutionality of laws. Declarations can also be made concerning the interpretation of laws, the legality of official behaviour, the rights of the applicant and even, it seems, the meaning of nonlegal constitutional conventions.[133] Where such declarations involve Charter rights or freedoms, they would appear to fall within the scope of section 24(1), but even if they do not, they would seem to be discretionary in character.

The discretionary, flexible and non-formal nature of the remedy was stressed in a judgment written for the Supreme Court of Canada by Mr. Justice Dickson in *Solosky v. R.*:

> Declaratory relief is a remedy neither constrained by form nor bounded by substantive content, which avails persons sharing a legal relationship, in respect of which a "real issue" concerning the relative interests of each has been raised and falls to be determined.

. . .

---

129 *Re Meier and R.* (1983), 150 D.L.R. (3d) 132 (B.C. S.C.), aff'd (1983), 3 D.L.R. (4th) 567 (B.C. C.A.), leave to appeal to S.C.C. refused 3 D.L.R. (4th) 567n (S.C.C.); *R. v. Cameron* (1982), 3 C.C.C. (3d) 496 (Alta. C.A.).

130 *E.g., A.G. Manitoba v. Forest, supra*, note 100.

131 *Supra*, note 16, at 313.

132 *Reference re Resolution to Amend the Constitution*, [1981] 1 S.C.R. 753. This may be restricted to reference cases.

133 See discussion of Wilson J. in *Operation Dismantle Inc. v. R., supra*, note 49, at 509 *et seq.*

The first factor is directed to the "reality of the dispute." It is clear that a declaration will not normally be granted when the dispute is over and has become academic, or where the dispute has yet to arise and may not arise. ... [H]owever, one must distinguish, on the one hand, between a declaration that concerns "future" rights and "hypothetical" rights, and, on the other hand, a declaration that may be "immediately available" when it determines the rights of the parties at the time of the decision together with the necessary implications and consequences of these rights, known as "future rights."

. . .

Once one accepts that the dispute is real and that the granting of judgment is discretionary, then the only further issue is whether the declaration is capable of having any practical effect in resolving the issues in the case.[134]

The term "practical effect" in the concluding sentence of this quotation must not be misunderstood. It does not refer to a concrete legal remedy. The beauty of declarations of right is that they can be made in situations where the law does not provide for a more specific remedy. The "practical effect" referred to may in some cases be the fact that the moral or political force of the declaration itself often leads to appropriate voluntary redress. Mr. Justice Dickson made this clear in *Kelso v. R.*,[135] in which an employee of the federal government sought a declaration that he had been transferred to another position illegally. The Crown contended that a declaration would have no "practical effect," because the Public Service Commission possessed the sole legal power to make appointments. Mr. Justice Dickson commented:

It is quite correct to state that the Court cannot actually appoint Mr. Kelso to the Public Service. The administrative act of appointment must be performed by the Commission. But the Court is entitled to "declare" the respective rights of the appellant and the respondent.

The Public Service Commission is not above the law of the land. If it breaches a contract, or acts contrary to statute, the courts are entitled to so declare.[136]

Caution should also be used when applying Mr. Justice Dickson's comment in *Solosky* that "a declaration will not normally be granted when the dispute is over and has become academic."[137] Stress should be placed on "normally." Some Charter issues are of such general significance that they ought to be the subject of a judicial declaration even after the dispute has become moot so far as the immediate parties are concerned. In *Howard*

---

134 [1980] 1 S.C.R. 821 at 830, 832, 833.
135 [1981] 1 S.C.R. 199.
136 *Ibid.*, at 210.
137 *Solosky, supra,* note 134 at 832.

v. Stony Mountain Institution[138] for example, the Federal Court of Appeal issued a declaratory judgment concerning the right of prisoners in federal penitentiaries to be represented by counsel at disciplinary hearings, even though the prisoner in question had already served the sentence imposed by the challenged proceeding.

(v) *Injunctions*

The equitable remedy of injunction — both prohibitory and mandatory — has a large role to play in Charter litigation whenever it is sought to prevent or require certain acts being done in circumstances where prerogative relief is not appropriate.

Although permanent injunctions would be suitable for the enforcement of some Charter rights,[139] the type of injunction usually sought is an interlocutory order, intended to preserve the *status quo* until the parties' respective rights and obligations under the Charter can be fully determined.[140]

Being an equitable remedy, injunction relief is inherently discretionary, quite apart from the "appropriate and just" requirement of section 24(1). This means that the court always takes account of the "balance of convenience" when deciding whether to award an injunction. In a constitutional setting, an additional factor must be weighed in the balance beyond the interests of the litigants. The interest of the public at large in maintaining the protection and advantages of impugned legislation, pending a final determination of its validity, must be taken into account.

In *A.G. Manitoba v. Metropolitan Stores Ltds.*,[141] the respondent employer sought an interlocutory injunction restraining the Manitoba Labour Board from imposing a first contract pending a determination of the validity of the "first contract" provisions of the Board's enabling legislation. The Supreme Court of Canada refused to reverse the motions court judge's decision denying the injunction on the basis that the public interest in the continued operation of the legislation outweighed the admittedly irreparable harm potentially suffered by the employer.

In the case of interlocutory injunctions,[142] where the goal is to freeze the situation until a final judgment can be rendered, an injunction will normally be granted only to prevent "irreparable harm" occurring in the

---

138 (1985), 19 D.L.R. (4th) 502 (Fed. C.A.), appeal quashed [1987] 2 S.C.R. 687.

139 A permanent injunction was sought, unsuccessfully, in *Operation Dismantle, supra*, note 49.

140 *E.g., Black v. Law Society of Alta.* (1983), 5 C.R.R. 305 (Alta. Q.B.), rev'd 8 D.L.R. (4th) 347 (Alta. C.A.).

141 [1987] 1 S.C.R. 110 (S.C.C.).

142 See *American Cyanamid Co. v. Ethicon Ltd.*, [1975] 1 All E.R. 504 (H.L.).

interim. Harm will not usually be regarded as "irreparable" if it is such that an award of damages after the event would be considered adequate compensation.

An example of an interim injunction being granted to prevent irreparable harm is *Rio Hotel Ltd. v. Liquor Licensing Bd. (N.B.)*,[143] where the applicant hotel, which had admittedly violated the conditions of its liquor permit relating to the presence of nude dancers on the premises, challenged the validity of those conditions on the basis of the Charter as well as sections 91 and 92 of the *Constitution Act, 1867*. It had lost in the New Brunswick Court of Appeal and was threatened with the cancellation of its permit, when the Supreme Court of Canada granted the applicant leave to appeal as well as a stay of proceedings before the Liquor Licensing Board, pending the determination of its appeal. The stay was granted subject to compliance with an expedited schedule for filing materials and for hearing the appeal.

Even when not prepared to issue a formal injunction, a court may restrict the parties' interim behaviour in other ways. In *Southam v. Hunter*,[144] Cavanagh J. of the Alberta Court of Queen's Bench indicated that he had instructed officials wishing to carry out a disputed search that, if they attempted to do so pending determination of an application for an interlocutory injunction (which he subsequently refused), they would be guilty of contempt.

Interim injunctions have been denied in several Charter cases on the ground that irreparable harm would not be suffered.[145] In *Gould v. A.G. Canada*,[146] a prisoner in a federal penitentiary challenged, under section 3 of the Charter, the statute prohibiting prisoners voting in federal elections. Because a pending election would occur before the merits of the claim could be determined, the trial judge issued an interlocutory mandatory injunction to prison authorities requiring them to allow the prisoner to vote. The Federal Court of Appeal set aside this injunction, stating that the effect of the order would be that the prisoner

> without having had his action tried, is entitled to act and be treated as though he had already won . . . The proper purpose of an interlocutory injunction is to preserve or restore the *status quo*, not to give the plaintiff his remedy, until trial.[147]

---

143 [1987] 2 S.C.R. 59 (S.C.C.).

144 (1982), 136 D.L.R. (3d) 133 at 144 (Alta. Q.B.), aff'd 147 D.L.R. (3d) 420 (Alta. C.A.), aff'd [1984] 2 S.C.R. 145 (S.C.C.).

145 *Southam Inc. v. Hunter, ibid.*; *Morgentaler v. Ackroyd* (1983), 150 D.L.R. (3d) 59 (Ont. H.C.); *Marchand v. Simcoe County Bd. of Education* (1984), 10 C.R.R. 169 (Ont. H.C.).

146 [1984] 2 S.C.R. 124 (S.C.C.).

147 *A.G. Canada v. Gould* [1984] 1 F.C. 1133 at 1140 (C.A.), aff'd *supra*, note 146.

The Supreme Court of Canada agreed.

In the United States, injunctive relief has been employed extensively in civil rights litigation. Courts have been willing to issue injunctions ordering the carrying out of such complicated operations as desegregating school systems and restructuring state electoral boundaries.[148] In the past, British and Commonwealth courts have not been quite so adventurous in their use of injunctions. There is reason to believe, however, that Canadian courts are free to use injunctions as creatively as their American counterparts if they see fit to do so. The American decisions are based, after all, on the same fundamental principles of English law that apply in the common law provinces of Canada. Moreover, there are indications that British, Canadian and Commonwealth courts have been taking a somewhat more liberal approach to the granting of injunctions recently. Given the unique nature and extraordinary importance of the rights and freedoms guaranteed by the Charter, there is strong justification for an extension of that trend where Charter violations are involved.

The most effective way to demonstrate the validity of the foregoing thesis may be to examine briefly two alleged obstacles to the use of "civil rights injunctions" in Canada. They are (1) the reluctance of courts to make orders requiring continuous detailed supervision; and (2) the Crown's historic immunity from injunctive relief. Neither is necessarily fatal to the granting of "civil rights injunctions" in appropriate cases.

British and Commonwealth courts have tended in the past to decline to make orders, particularly specific performance orders and mandatory injunctions, where they have perceived difficulty maintaining continuous future supervision over their observance.[149] Even if this were an invariable rule, it would not stand in the way of injunctive relief in many civil rights situations. Simple prohibitory injunctions seldom involve undue supervisory difficulties, for example,[150] and many of the Charter's provisions can be enforced in that manner. Interlocutory injunctions are similarly free from problems of continuing supervision. Even short-term mandatory injunctions can provide significant enforcement of civil liberties, as witness a British decision ordering the British Broadcasting Corporation to broadcast a certain television program by a political party during an election campaign.[151]

In any event, the courts' reluctance to undertake long-term supervision

---

148 See O.M. Fiss, *The Civil Rights Injunction* (Bloomington: Indiana U. Press, 1978).

149 *Powell Duffryn Steam Coal Co. v. Taff Vale Railway Co.* (1874), 9 Ch. App. 331 at 334 (*per* James L.J.); *Ryan v. Mutual Tontine Westminster Chambers Assn.*, [1893] 1 Ch. 116 (C.A.).

150 I.C.F. Spry, *The Principles of Equitable Remedies*, 2nd ed. (London: Sweet & Maxwell, 1980) at 485.

151 *Evans v. B.B.C.*, *The Times*, February 26, 1974 (C.A.).

has never been an absolute rule. It has always been less evident in injunction cases than where specific performance was sought,[152] and even in the latter cases it has been less common recently than in the past. The 1981 edition of the classic British text, *Modern Equity*, by Hanbury and Maudsley,[153] is instructive:

> Recent decisions indicate a relaxation of the principle.[154] The real question is whether there is a sufficient definition of what has to be done in order to comply with the order of the court.[155] In *Beswick v. Beswick*[156] specific performance was ordered of a contract to make a regular payment to the plaintiff for life. In *Sky Petroleum Ltd. v. V.I.P. Petroleum Ltd.*[157]an interlocutory injunction, which was regarded as tantamount to specific performance, was granted to enforce the defendant's obligation to supply petrol regularly to the plaintiff. And, in the analogous sphere of mandatory injunctions, the requirement of supervision has not been regarded as an insurmountable obstacle.[158]

It is all a matter of discretion. Equitable remedies are always discretionary, and the tendency to deny orders requiring detailed supervision has involved nothing more than a disinclination by courts to make orders which, as a practical matter, would be difficult to enforce. But, as an Australian authority on equitable remedies points out, it is a question of degree: as the importance of injunctive relief increases in particular situations, the reluctance of courts to undertake supervisory responsibility decreases.[159] Few legal matters are as important as compliance by governmental authorities with constitutionally entrenched safeguards. It may well be, moreover, that American experience, which has shown continuing judicial supervision to be less difficult than previously supposed, will persuade Canadian courts that innovative uses of injunctions to protect against serious Charter violations are as feasible, in appropriate circumstances, as the protection is important.

---

152 Even where specific performance is involved, there has long been greater willingness to undertake supervision in the case of building contracts: E.H.T. Snell, *Principles of Equity*, 27th ed. by R. Megarry & P.V. Baker (London: Sweet & Maxwell, 1973) at 580-581; F.H. Lawson, *Remedies of English Law* (Harmondsworth: Penguin Books, 1972) at 249.

153 H.G. Hanbury & R. H. Maudsley, *Modern Equity*, 11th ed. (London: Stevens, 1981) at 54.

154 See G. Treitel, *The Law of Contract*, 5th ed. (London: Stevens, 1979) at 760-761.

155 *Tito v. Waddell (No. 2)*, [1977] Ch. 106 at 322 (*per* Megarry V.C.).

156 [1968] A.C. 58 (H.L.).

157 [1974] 1 W.L.R. 576 (Ch. D.). And see C.H. Giles & Co. v. Morris, [1972] 1 W.L.R. 307 (Ch. D.).

158 *Redland Bricks Ltd. v. Morris*, [1970] A.C. 652 (H.L.); *Gravesham Borough Council v. British Railway Bd.*, [1978] Ch. 379; *Shiloh Spinners Ltd. v. Harding*, [1973] A.C. 691 at 724 (H.L.).

159 Spry, *supra*, note 150, at 484.

In *Black v. Law Society of Alta.*,[160] McDonald J. stated:

I consider that it is a case in which the Court should assume an active supervisory role to ensure that the case reaches trial swiftly. . . .

. . .

I shall be available to counsel to further the object of expediting the trial of this action.

While this was only an interlocutory injunction, and the "supervisory" duties were admittedly simple and familiar, the statement could constitute a straw in the wind.

The other principle that might be thought to present a serious impediment to the extensive use of injunctions to enforce the Charter is the Crown's historic immunity, as the fount of equity, from equitable remedies — an immunity that extended as well to officers and agents of the Crown acting with Crown authority.[161] Although Crown liability is now governed by statute in most jurisdictions, this principle has been preserved in Canada, at both federal and provincial levels, either by express provision or by implication.[162] If such immunity were applicable to enforcement of the Charter, it would not pose an absolute obstacle to civil rights injunctions, since it would not cover claims against police officers, administrative authorities or municipal officials, unless acting in a Crown capacity or with Crown authority. It could, nevertheless, rule out the possibility of injunctive remedies in many situations where such relief would be appropriate.

A strong case can be made, however, for the proposition that the

---

160 *Supra*, note 140, at 318.

161 P.W. Hogg, *Liability of the Crown in Australia, New Zealand and the United Kingdom* (1971) at 22 *et seq.*; B.L. Strayer, "Injunctions Against Crown Officers" (1964), 42 *Can. Bar Rev.* 1; J.J. Tokar, "Injunctive Relief Against the Crown" (1985), 15 *Man. L.J.* 97. In *Carlic v. R.* (1967), 65 D.L.R. (2d) 633, the Manitoba Court of Appeal issued an interim injunction against the Crown, among other defendants. This was criticized by the Judicial Committee of the Privy Council in *Jaundoo v. A.G. Guyana*, [1971] A.C. 972 (P.C.).

162 Alberta: *Proceedings Against the Crown Act*, R.S.A. 1980, c. P-18, s. 17(1), (2); British Columbia: *Crown Proceedings Act*, R.S.B.C. 1979, c. 86, s. 11 (2); Manitoba: *Proceedings Against the Crown Act*, C.C.S.M., c. P140, s. 17; New Brunswick: *Proceedings Against the Crown Act*, R.S.N.B. 1973, c. P-18, s. 14(2); Newfoundland: *Proceedings Against the Crown Act*, S.N. 1973, c. 59, s. 17; Nova Scotia: *Proceedings Against the Crown Act*, R.S.N.S. 1967, c. 239, s. 15(2); Ontario: *Proceedings Against the Crown Act*, R.S.O. 1980, c. 393, s. 18; Prince Edward Island: *Crown Proceedings Act*, R.S.P.E.I. 1974, c. C-31, s. 15(2); Quebec: *Code of Civil Procedure*, R.S.Q. 1977, arts. 94.2, 100; Saskatchewan: *Proceedings Against the Crown Act*, R.S.S. 1978, c. P-27, s. 17(2); Canada: no express legislative prohibition, but see *Grand Council of Crees (Que.) v. R.* (1981), 124 D.L.R. (3d) 574 (F.C.A.), leave to appeal to S.C.C. refused 41 N.R. 354.

Crown's immunity to injunctions is not applicable where Charter violations are involved. The Charter is a constitutional document, superior in status to all ordinary laws, and the courts have held, in other contexts, that a government cannot clothe itself with immunity from judicial scrutiny of the constitutionality of its actions. This is so whether the ostensible immunity is based on legislation that refers directly to constitutional challenges,[163] or on more general procedural rules.[164]

In *Lévesque v. A.G. Canada,*[165] Rouleau J. of the Federal Court Trial Division found that:

> If the *Canadian Charter of Rights and Freedoms*, which is part of the Constitution of Canada, is the supreme law of the country, it applies to everyone, including the Crown or a Minister acting in his capacity as a representative of the Crown. Accordingly, *a fortiori* the Crown or one of its representatives cannot take refuge in any kind of declinatory exception or rule of immunity derived from the common law so as to avoid giving effect to the Charter.

It is also possible to advance an even more fundamental argument: that the guarantee of equality before the law embedded in section 15 of the Charter renders the Crown's special legal immunity unconstitutional. While there is as yet too little jurisprudence on section 15 to support a confident opinion, it seems likely that an equality rights attack on Crown immunity would succeed unless it could be upheld as a reasonable limit under section 1. The answer to that question might vary according to the type of Crown immunity involved. In the case of immunity from injunctions, the policy arguments favouring immunity do not seem strong.[166]

Even if these arguments are mistaken, and the Crown's immunity from injunctive relief extends to Charter violations, there can be no doubt about the Crown's susceptibility to declaratory judgments,[167] and in most circumstances a judicial declaration that a governmental agency had acted unconstitutionally would, for practical purposes, be as helpful to the wronged individual as an injunction.

It may therefore be concluded that there are no insurmountable obstacles to the development of innovative enforcement measures along the lines of American injunctive remedies.

---

163 *Amax Potash Ltd. v. Saskatchewan*, [1977] 2 S.C.R. 576 (S.C.C.).
164 *B.C. Power Corp. v. B.C. Elec. Co.*, [1962] S.C.R. 642 (S.C.C.).
165 (1985), 25 D.L.R. (4th) 184 at 191-192 (F.C.T.D.).
166 See Tokar, *supra*, note 161, at 98-100.
167 See Hogg, *supra*, note 161, and the legislation listed, *supra*, note 162.

(vi) *Damages*[168]

The right to be compensated by monetary damages for the violation of one's constitutional rights was rarely recognized in pre-Charter days, but it was not entirely unheard-of. Damages were occasionally awarded for constitutional violations that happened also to constitute private law wrongs.[169] And in *Canada v. Prince Edward Island*,[170] the Federal Court of Canada acknowledged a right to be financially redressed for deprivation of a right that was purely constitutional in nature. In that case, the government of Prince Edward Island sued the government of Canada for compensation for being deprived of a constitutionally guaranteed ferry service, and the court held that the province was entitled to a declaration that it was entitled to damages. Chief Justice Jackett stated:

> [W]hen there is a statutory right to have something done with no express sanction for breach, there is, *prima facie*, an implied right to be compensated for a breach of such right.[171]

While the court stressed that this was a right of the province as a collectivity rather than of individual citizens, Charter rights present a different situation, being, for the most part, individual rather than collective rights. Courts have already held on several occasions that the sweeping remedial powers of section 24(1) permit damages to be awarded to the victims of Charter infringements. Illegal imprisonment of an accused person for "contempt" in seeking an adjournment to obtain counsel was stated by a judge of the Alberta Court of Queen's Bench to be a possibly appropriate situation for compensation.[172] He pointed out that the French text refers to "réparation." The Federal Court of Canada, Trial Division, ordered the Crown to pay compensation for the illegal seizure and destruction of a person's property,[173] and for an unconstitutional transfer of a prison inmate from a medium security institution to a maximum security institution.[174] Although the Federal Court of Appeal subsequently denied damages to the subject of an unconstitutional search and seizure

---

168 See M.L. Pilkington, "Damages as a Remedy for Infringment of the Canadian Charter of Rights and Freedoms" (1984), 62 *Can. Bar Rev.* 517.

169 *E.g.*, *Roncarelli v. Duplessis*, [1959] S.C.R. 121; *Gershman v. Man. Vegetable Producers' Marketing Bd.*, [1976] 4 W.W.R. 406 (Man. C.A.); *Chaput v. Romain*, [1955] S.C.R. 834.

170 (1977), 83 D.L.R. (3d) 492 (F.C.A.).

171 *Ibid.*, at 512.

172 *R. v. Germain* (1984), 53 A.R. 264 (Q.B.).

173 *Bertram S. Miller Ltd. v. R.* (1985), 18 D.L.R. (4th) 600 (F.C.T.D.) rev'd [1986] 3 F.C. 291 (C.A.), leave to appeal to S.C.C. refused (1986), 75 N.R. 158n (S.C.C.).

174 *Collin v. Lussier* (1983), 6 C.R.R. 89 (F.T.D.), rev'd on other grounds [1985] F.C. 124 (C.A.).

in *Vespoli v. R.*,[175] it was because the court could find "no solid evidence that the appellants really suffered damage as a consequence of the illegal seizures."

It may not always be necessary to establish actual damage, however. In *Crossman v. R.*,[176] the Federal Court of Canada, Trial Division, awarded $500 *punitive* damages to a person who was denied the right to counsel in flagrant circumstances, even though the individual suffered no resulting harm, having failed to make any statements during the time he was without counsel, and having eventually pleaded guilty anyway.

There are, as yet, many unanswered questions in this realm. Are the cases correct that say there can be liability to pay damages based solely on a constitutional obligation, where there would be no private law wrong apart from the Constitution? Upon whom does liability fall: the Crown alone, or also the individual Crown officers involved?[177] Is the *Crossman* case correct in imposing liability for punitive damages where no actual loss occurred? A good deal of litigation will be required before the exact shape and significance of this heretofore rare remedy is known.[178]

(vii) *Other Remedies*

Section 24(1) places no restrictions on the types of remedies that a court with jurisdiction may treat as appropriate and just, and the courts have exhibited great imagination and pragmatism in exercising this broad-ranging authority.

Timing of proceedings.   In many situations, the Charter infringement can be satisfactorily redressed by adjustments in the timing of proceedings. It may be sufficient remedy for past delay to require that trial proceed immediately.[179] A temporary stay of proceedings may be ordered to permit a preliminary Charter argument to be considered.[180] Where the only prejudice to the accused of unreasonable delay is the disappearance of an important defence witness, the court may order an adjournment to

---

175 (1984), 84 D.T.C. 6489 (F.C.A.).

176 (1984), 9 D.L.R. (4th) 588 (F.C.T.D.).

177 It was suggested in *R. v. Germain, supra,* note 172, and in *Vespoli v. R., supra,* note 175, that the individuals are not liable if they acted in good faith.

178 For a discussion of similar questions under the Constitution of Trinidad and Tobago, see *Maharaj v. A.G. Trinidad & Tobago,* [1978] 2 All. E.R. 670 (P.C.).

179 *R. v. Montgomery* (1982), 8 W.C.B. 158 (Qué. S.C.).

180 *R.L. Crain Inc. v. Couture* (1982), 15 A.C.W.S. (2d) 370 (Sask. Q.B.). There was a logical problem in applying s. 24(1) here, because the argument concerned whether the court was one of "competent jurisdiction" under that section. Presumably, the stay was based on the court's inherent powers.

permit the defence and the Crown to search for the witness, and decide later, if the witness cannot be found, whether the charge should be dismissed.[181]

Regulation of proceedings. Other forms of regulation of proceedings may also be necessary to remedy or avoid Charter violations. "Gag orders" prohibiting the publication of evidence or the identity of witnesses may occasionally be regarded as appropriate, for example, although the requirements of "public hearing" under section 11(*d*) and "freedom of the press and other media" under section 2(*b*) seriously limit the circumstances in which this would be so.[182]

Quashing of search warrants and other orders. The quashing of search warrants[183] and other orders[184] of subordinate authorities is a common form of relief.

Return of the goods. Where items have been seized in an unconstitutional manner, the court may order the return of the goods.[185] Like all remedial powers under section 24(1), however, this power is discretionary, and it has been held that the discretion may properly be exercised by delaying the return until a lawful warrant can be obtained, in cases where the items may be required for the purpose of prosecution. In *Dobney Foundry Ltd. v. A.G. Canada,*[186] Esson J.A. of the British Columbia Court of Appeal ruled, in chambers, that because "public interest in the effective detection and proof of crime and the prompt apprehension and conviction of offenders is [not] to be ignored," it was reasonable to delay the return of illegally seized documents, even though the Crown, having not yet examined them, could not state categorically that they would be required for prosecution. It is submitted that this approach could encourage illegal search and seizure practices. While the court does appear to have a discretion in the matter under section 24(1), and it is true that other swift methods of regaining possession of illegally detained goods (such as replevin) are also discretionary, it is submitted that a too generous exercise of the discretion in favour of the Crown would impair unduly the right

---

181 *R. v. Spina* (1983), 10 W.C.B. 8 (Ont. Dist. Ct.).

182 See *R. v. Harrison, supra,* note 13.

183 *E.g., Re Chapman and R.* (1984), 9 D.L.R. (4th) 244 (Ont. C.A.).

184 *Re Mason and R* (1983), 43 O.R. (2d) 321 (Ont. H.C.).

185 *Re Chapman and R., supra,* note 183; *Dobney Foundry Ltd. v. A.G. Canada,* [1985] 3 W.W.R. 626 (B.C. C.A.); *Lewis v. M.N.R.* (1984), 15 D.L.R. (4th) 310 (F.C.T.D.).

186 *Ibid.,* at 634.

under section 8 of the Charter to be secure from unreasonable searches and seizures.

Appointment of counsel.   Is the appointment of counsel one of the remedies a court may order under section 24(1)? It has been held that a provincial court judge conducting a preliminary hearing does not have the jurisdiction to make such an appointment.[187] The rationale for this decision — that section 24(1) restricts courts to the remedies over which they have jurisdiction independent of the Charter — was examined above.[188] Even if correct, it leaves open the possibility that a superior court judge would have the power to appoint counsel. Alberta Provincial Court Judge Litsky has held that, even if he has no power to appoint counsel, he has the authority to "direct" such appointment, and to adjourn the trial pending the appointment.[189]

Passing sentence.   Where a Charter violation has occurred which does not affect the cogency of the case against an accused, the court may convict, but should take the violation into account when passing sentence.[190] In *R. v. Dewael*,[191] an Ontario county court judge employed section 24(1) to avoid imposing a mandatory jail sentence because the accused, who had pleaded guilty, was ill, and medical evidence indicated that a mandatory jail sentence would "no doubt end in her death." In those circumstances, it was held that the statutory requirement of imprisonment would be "cruel and unusual," contrary to section 12 of the Charter.

Costs.   In some circumstances, the appropriate remedy for denial of a Charter right may be an award of costs. *Re Marshall and R.*[192] is an example. The accused was kept in custody a little longer than lawfully authorized, apparently so he could be turned over to police from another jurisdiction. The accused sought release from custody of the second police

---

187 *Re Legal Services Society and Brahan* (1983), 148 D.L.R. (3d) 692 (B.C. S.C.). See also *R. v. Lyons (No. 2)* (1982), 141 D.L.R. (3d) 376 (B.C. C.A.), where it was held that a judge of the Court of Appeal has no such power with respect to a case pending before the Supreme Court of Canada.

188 See text related to notes 269 *et seq., infra.*

189 *R. v. Powell* (1984), 51 A.R. 191 (Prov. Ct.), application for judicial review refused 36 Alta. L.R. (2d) lxi (Q.B.). His holding that he would have no power to stay proceedings if counsel were not appointed seems questionable.

190 *R. v. Sybrandy* (1983), 9 W.C.B. 328 (Ont. Prov. Ct.); *R. v. Elliott* (1984), 57 A.R. 49 (Prov. Ct.); *R. v. Petrovic* (1984), 10 D.L.R. (4th) 697 (Ont. C.A.).

191 (1984), 12 C.R.R. 117 (Ont. Co. Ct.), *per* Clements Co. Ct. J.

192 (1984), 13 C.C.C. (3d) 73 (Ont. H.C.).

force and, although the court refused to grant such relief,[193] it ordered the Crown to pay the costs of the application on a solicitor-and-client basis. It has been held, however, that the jurisdiction of provincial courts to award costs is quite limited.[194] Even when the power exists, it is discretionary, of course, and a court may decline to exercise it.[195]

3. EXCLUSION OF EVIDENCE: SECTION 24(2)[196]

The problem of what to do about evidence that has been obtained illegally, but is probative of a matter under litigation, has long vexed legal authorities and has been solved differently in different jurisdictions.

The traditional English approach generally followed in Canada has been to accept and rely on the tainted evidence (in most circumstances), and to leave the punishment of any illegality involved to separate proceedings. In the United States and certain other jurisdictions,[197] a very different rule has been developed: evidence obtained by unconstitutional means is inadmissible, no matter how reliable or cogent it may be to the issues in dispute.[198]

The approach adopted in section 24(2) of the Charter appears to be a middle position, somewhere between the English and American rules. Evidence obtained in contravention of the Charter must be excluded if, in the circumstances, its admission "would bring the administration of justice into disrepute."

(a) Application

The application of section 24(2) involves numerous considerations that cannot be explored in depth in the present context,[199] but should be kept in mind by anyone seeking to invoke the guarantee:

— Unlike the remedies under section 24(1), the exclusion of evidence is not discretionary. Courts *"shall"* exclude evidence obtained in

---

193 It appears that the accused was free by the time the reserved judgment was delivered in any event.

194 *R. v. Halpert* (1984), 15 C.C.C. (3d) 292 (Ont. Co. Ct.); *R. v. 421375 Ont. Ltd.* (1984), 5 C.R.D. 525.100-02 (Ont. Co. Ct.).

195 *Re Canadiana Recreational Products Ltd. and R.* (1987), 17 C.C.C. (3d) 473 (Ont. H.C.).

196 See Gibson, *The Law of the Charter, supra*, note 2, at 219 *et seq.*

197 The Scottish position is much less receptive to the admissibility of illegally obtained evidence than the common law. See, *e.g.*, Walker & Walker, *Law of Evidence in Scotland*, 1964 at 2.

198 See *Mapp v. Ohio*, 367 U.S. 643 (1961); S.R. Schlesinger, *Exclusionary Injustice: The Problem of Illegally Obtained Evidence* (1977).

199 Examined more fully in Gibson, *supra*, note 2.

violation of the Charter if its admission would bring the administration of justice into disrepute.

— Section 24(2) is the *sole* evidentiary remedy; section 24(1) has been construed not to permit exclusion of evidence.[200]

— "Administration of justice" certainly includes all aspects of the *criminal justice system*, from police to courts. In the writer's opinion, it also includes the *civil and administrative adjudicative processes*, though views are divided about the latter category.[201]

— Although the English version of section 24(1) refers to what "would" bring justice into disrepute, it is widely agreed, in light of the French text, that evidence should be excluded if it *could* have that effect.[202]

— It is disrepute in the eyes of the *general public*, not of a restricted legal audience, that counts.[203]

— So far, the courts have relied exclusively on argument and *judicial notice* to determine the likely impact on public opinion of the admission of unconstitutional evidence. Whether other aids, such as *public opinion polls*, are also available is a matter of dispute.[204]

— Whether those who invoke the section must establish a *causal link* between the Charter violation and the obtaining of the evidence is not yet certain, but it is generally assumed that they must. There is some support, however, for the view that they need not prove more than a significant possibility of causation.[205]

(b) Elements of Disrepute

What factors are to be taken into account in deciding whether the administration of justice would or would not tend to be brought into disrepute by the admission of particular kinds of evidence? Courts are directed by section 24(2) to have regard to "all the circumstances," but no further elaboration or guidance is offered by the Charter. Obviously, therefore, no list of factors to be considered could ever be exhaustive.

Both the Ouimet Committee and the Law Reform Commission of Canada had recommended against this vague approach. They supported

---

200 *R. v. Therens*, [1985] 1 S.C.R. 613.
201 See Gibson, *supra*, note 2, at 231 *et seq.*
202 *Ibid.*, at 234-235.
203 *Ibid.*, at 235.
204 *Ibid.*, at 236 *et seq.*
205 *Ibid.*, at 247 *et seq.*

the principle of a wide judicial power to exclude illegal or unconstitutional evidence, but they suggested that it should be accompanied by a listing of factors to be taken into account in exercising that power:

> In order to reduce the inherent difficulties in the exercise of any legal discretionary power and to a certain extent to avoid the danger of too great a disparity between the legal decisions, the legislators should indicate the criteria that should be applied in the exercise of discretion and set out guidelines for general use of such powers.[206]

The McDonald Commission was of the same opinion.[207]

Although the approach recommended by these reports was not adopted in either the Charter or section 178.16(2) [189(2)] of the *Criminal Code*, the courts have been developing their own lists of factors to guide themselves when attempting to determine whether particular investigative abuses would bring the administration of justice into disrepute. While these lists can never be exhaustive, they serve much the same purpose as the legislated lists suggested by the pre-Charter reports, and include most of the same factors.

It may be instructive to begin with the criteria considered by Justices Estey and Lamer in the *Rothman* case.[208] It will be recalled that this was a pre-Charter case, and that only those two judges (along with Chief Justice Laskin, who concurred in the Estey judgment) considered the reputation of the administration of justice to be relevant. The case was a prosecution for trafficking in *cannabis* resin, and the disputed evidence had been obtained by planting a police officer, posing as a prisoner, in the accused's cell. The majority of the Supreme Court of Canada admitted the evidence without considering the question of discrediting the administration of justice.

Of the three judges who did regard that question as germane, two dissented concerning the admissibility of the evidence, and the other concurred in the result reached by the majority. The dissenters, Justice Estey and Chief Justice Laskin, were of the view that the police conduct would bring the administration of justice into disrepute. Their only stated criterion for reaching that conclusion was that the conduct involved a "determined subversion" of the accused's rights.[209]

The third judge, Mr. Justice Lamer, held that acceptance of the

---

206 Law Reform Commission of Canada, *The Exclusion of Illegally Obtained Evidence* (Study paper) (1974) at 28.

207 Commission of Inquiry Concerning Certain Activities of the Royal Canadian Mounted Police, Second Report, *Freedom and Security Under the Law*, Vol. 2 (Ottawa: August 1981) at 1046-1047.

208 *Rothman v. R.*, [1981] 1 S.C.R. 640.

209 *Ibid.*

evidence would not bring the administration of justice into disrepute. He offered a much fuller explanation of the factors that influenced his decision. Evidence should not be rejected, he said, merely because it is produced by "conduct on the part of the authorities a given judge might consider somewhat unfortunate, distasteful or inappropriate."[210] Then, after stating that the conduct must be so shocking as to justify the judiciary dissociating themselves from it, he continued:

> The judge, in determining whether under the circumstances the use of the statement in the proceedings would bring the administration of justice into disrepute, should consider all of the circumstances of the proceedings, the manner in which the statement was obtained, the degree to which there was a breach of social values, the seriousness of the charge, the effect the exclusion would have on the result of the proceedings. It must also be borne in mind that the investigation of crime and the detection of criminals is not a game to be governed by the Marquess of Queensbury rules. The authorities, in dealing with shrewd and often sophisticated criminals, must sometimes of necessity resort to tricks or other forms of deceit and should not through the rule be hampered in their work. *What should be repressed vigorously is conduct on their part that shocks the community.* That a police officer pretend to be a lock-up chaplain and hear a suspect's confession is conduct that shocks the community; so is pretending to be the duty legal-aid lawyer eliciting in that way incriminating statements from suspects or accused; injecting Pentothal into a diabetic suspect pretending it is his daily shot of insulin and using his statement in evidence would also shock the community; but generally speaking, pretending to be a hard drug addict to break a drug ring would not shock the community; nor would, as in this case, pretending to be a truck driver to secure the conviction of a trafficker; in fact, what would shock the community would be preventing the police from resorting to such a trick.[211]

It is important to bear in mind that these remarks, made in a pre-Charter case by a judge whose interpretation differed from that of the other two judges who considered the question, are of limited authority in a Charter context. Nevertheless, Justice Lamer's approach was considered in many of the early decisions under section 24(2), and his emphasis on that which "shocks the public" was widely followed.

The paraphrase has not been universally approved, however. Chief Justice Howland of Ontario noted, for example:

> If the evidence is obtained in such a manner as to shock the Canadian community as a whole, it would no doubt be inadmissible as bringing the administration of justice into disrepute. There may, however, be instances where the administration of justice is brought into disrepute within s. 24(2) without necessarily shocking the Canadian community as a whole. In my opinion, it is preferable to consider every case on its merits as to whether

---

210 *Ibid.*, at 696.
211 *Ibid.*, at 697 (emphasis added).

it satisfies the requirements of s. 24(2) of the Charter and not to substitute a "community shock" or any other test for the plain words of the statute.[212]

In *R. v. Therens*,[213] Mr. Justice Le Dain, after noting that many courts have adopted the "community shock" test, expressed agreement with Ontario Chief Justice Howland: "[W]e should not substitute for the words of s. 24(2) another expression of the standard." Mr. Justice McIntyre concurred in the entire Le Dain judgment, but the rest of the Supreme Court of Canada judges were silent on this question.

As to the factors to be considered when deciding what would shock the public or otherwise bring the administration of justice into disrepute, those referred to by Justices Lamer and Estey in the *Rothman* case[214] have all been taken into account in Charter decisions, along with several other factors they did not mention. Although they are numerous, and can never be listed exhaustively, the relevant factors can be grouped into three main categories:

(a) those that concern the seriousness of the Charter violation;
(b) those that concern the necessity of obtaining the evidence in question by the method employed; and
(c) other considerations.

Of these three categories, the first two seem to be much more significant than the third. Public opinion is shocked by learning of egregious abuses of suspects' rights during investigations by police or other authorities; it is equally shocked by reports of criminals going free because of "legal technicalities." Courts called upon to make admissibility rulings under section 24(2) of the Charter must accordingly balance these two competing considerations. Justice Le Dain referred to the balancing exercise in these terms in the *Therens* case:[215]

> [T]he two principal considerations in the balancing which must be undertaken are the relative seriousness of the constitutional violation and the relative seriousness of the criminal charge.

It is submitted that this formulation misdescribes the second category somewhat. There is much more to be considered in favour of admitting unconstitutional evidence than the seriousness of the charge, and that factor, as we will see, is of limited usefulness. Mr. Justice Anderson, of the British Columbia Court of Appeal, has described the basic equation more fully:

---

212 *R. v. Simmons* (1984), 45 O.R. (2d) 609 at 634 (C.A.).
213 *Supra*, note 200, at 651.
214 *Supra*, note 208.
215 *Supra*, note 200, at 652.

> A balance must be struck between the need for firm and effective law enforcement and the right of the citizen to be as free as reasonably possible from illegal and unreasonable conduct on the part of the police.[216]

Each of these categories will be considered separately.

(i) *Seriousness of Charter Violation*

The element to which the Law Reform Commission, in its pre-Charter Study Paper, proposed giving first priority was the seriousness of the violation of rights involved: "[T]he more serious the illegality, the more the court should be strict in not admitting it as evidence."[217] The *Report on Evidence* referred to this element as "the extent to which human dignity and social values were breached in obtaining the evidence."[218] The McDonald Commission made much of this consideration as well, dealing separately with three different aspects of it:

(a) the extent to which human dignity and social values were breached in obtaining the evidence;

(b) whether any harm was inflicted on the accused or others;

(c) the seriousness of any breach of the law in obtaining the evidence as compared with the seriousness of the offence with which the accused is charged.[219]

The Law Reform Commission Study Paper stressed in this regard that it is not sufficient merely to distinguish breaches of *procedural* requirements from violations of *substantive* requirements. Some procedural infringements can have very serious consequences, while some substantive infractions may not have significant ramifications.[220]

The early decisions under section 24(2) of the Charter have given great weight to factors relating to the seriousness of the Charter breach. There seems to be wide agreement with the observation of the Alberta Court of Appeal that "where the illegality . . . is due to a minor technicality, it would trivialize the *Charter* to exclude the evidence on the ground of that technicality."[221] On the other hand, serious Charter breaches are not

---

216 *R. v. Cohen* (1983), 5 C.C.C. (3d) 156 (B.C. C.A.). While Anderson J.A. dissented in that case, the quoted observation reflects the approach taken by most courts.

217 Study Paper, *supra*, note 206, at 28.

218 Law Reform Commission of Canada, *Report on Evidence* (1977), proposed Evidence Code, s. 15(2).

219 *Supra*, note 207, at 1046-1047.

220 Study Paper, *supra*, note 206, at 28.

221 *R. v. Heisler* (1984), 11 C.R.R. 334 (Alta. C.A.).

tolerated without very strong justification, and even a series of small infractions have been held to add up to a serious violation:

> It may well be that no one of those errors individually would suffice to bring the matter within s. 24(2), but here we have such a concatenation of errors, trivial or otherwise, and apparent disregard or indifference to the niceties and the normal rules of procedure in matters of this kind, that the community would be shocked by the acceptance of evidence obtained in this fashion, and to permit it to be admitted would tend to bring the administration of justice into disrepute.[222]

The importance of the right involved, as an abstract principle, is not the key; denial of the same right (for example, the right to counsel) in two different situations could have minor consequences in one case and disastrous ones in the other. The essential consideration must be the seriousness of the *detriment* resulting to the accused from the violation in question. It has been held, for example, that the duty of the police under section 10 of the Charter to advise accused persons of their right to counsel requires "even greater care" in the case of juveniles than with respect to adults, and that failure to carry out the duty should lead more readily to the exclusion of evidence in the former case than in the latter.[223]

Another illustration can be found in the courts' greater tendency to exclude evidence obtained from unreasonable searches and seizures contrary to section 8 of the Charter where the suspect's home was violated than where other premises were involved. Whereas "from time immemorial the inviolability of a person's home has been held up and defended as one of the most cherished values,"[224] other premises are less important: "[A] warehouse is less sacrosanct than a home."[225]

Seriousness of impact is sometimes related to the fairness of the investigative methods employed, since methods which violate "human dignity and social values," to use the words of the McDonald Report,[226] are likely to be regarded by the public as more serious or "shocking" than more forthright Charter contraventions. Trickery always smacks of unfairness, but some forms may be thought to be more so than others. In his *dictum* in the *Rothman* case,[227] for example, Mr. Justice Lamer expressed the view that the public would be shocked by the acceptance of evidence obtained by a police officer posing as the suspect's priest or lawyer, but not as a fellow prisoner.

---

222 *R. v. Thompson* (1983), 2 C.R.D. 850.50-06 (B.C. Co. Ct.).
223 *Re A.D.*, [1983] W.C.D. 108 (B.C. Prov. Ct.).
224 *R. v. Carriere* (1983), 32 C.R. (3d) 117 (Ont. Prov. Ct.).
225 *R. v. Tomaselli* (1984), 4 C.R.D. 850.60-19 (Ont. Gen. Sess.). See also *R. v. Penner*, [1984] W.C.D. 157 (B.C. Co. Ct.).
226 *Supra*, note 207, at 1046-1047.
227 *Supra*, note 208.

The Supreme Court of Canada, in *R. v. Therens*,[228] its first decision under section 24(2), gave prominence to "flagrancy" as a test of the seriousness of Charter violations for this purpose. In rejecting evidence obtained from a breath sample taken from the accused without informing him of his right to counsel, the majority said:

> Here the police authority has *flagrantly* violated a *Charter* right . . . Such an *overt* violation . . . must . . . result in the rejection of the evidence thereby obtained.[229]

Even the two dissenting judges, who would have admitted the evidence, agreed that in determining the seriousness of the violation one should consider "whether it was deliberate, wilful or flagrant."[230]

Since flagrancy, in its primary meaning, has to do with conspicuousness, and the term was used by the majority in tandem with "overt," one might wonder whether a surreptitious or covert Charter violation by authorities would be permitted to produce admissible evidence. However, since that conclusion would be nonsensical, the court must have meant by "flagrant" that which is conspicuous for its wrongfulness and would produce public controversy if exposed in a courtroom. It is not clear whether the dissenters, by associating "flagrant" with "deliberate," intended to indicate synonymity in this context, but their words do serve as a reminder that deliberateness can be a test of the seriousness of a Charter contravention. It will be considered more fully later.[231]

The consequences of the Charter violation for the legal system may in some cases be an even more important factor in determining disrepute than its impact on the individual. In *R. v. Caron*,[232] the disputed evidence was obtained on the strength of a search warrant issued after a police officer had misrepresented the purpose of the search to the issuing magistrate. Judge Bernstein of the Ontario District Court excluded the evidence, saying that the act of an informant in deliberately withholding evidence from a judicial officer "so as to prevent that officer from deciding an issue which only he had the authority to decide" would shock the community, or the right thinking members of it.[233]

Another case that ought to have had the same result, but for a questionable ruling as to causation, was *R. v. Clarke*,[234] in which the police,

---

228 *Supra*, note 200.
229 *Ibid.*, at 621 (*per* Estey J.) (emphasis added).
230 *Ibid.*, at 652 (*per* Le Dain J.).
231 See text associated with note 254, *infra*.
232 (1982), 31 C.R. (3d) 255 (Ont. Dist. Ct.). See also *R. v. Sarnia Home Entertainment Library Ltd.* (1984), 11 C.R.R. 106 (Ont. Prov. Ct.).
233 *Caron, ibid.*, at 260.
234 (1985), 19 C.C.C. (3d) 106 (Alta. C.A.).

in order to plant an informer in the accused's cell and protect the deception from discovery, arranged to have the informer appear before a provincial court judge on a trumped-up charge and be remanded in custody. According to the Court of Appeal, the judge "presumably was ignorant of the charade before him." While the general public might not always frown upon obtaining confessions by trickery, the deception of judges by police is something else altogether. Few factors would have a greater detrimental impact on public esteem for the administration of justice than the knowledge that evidence obtained by compromising the integrity of the legal system itself may be admissible.

The gravity of the offence with which the accused is charged undoubtedly affects the seriousness of the impact of a Charter violation. A violation that produces evidence upon which someone is convicted of murder obviously will have much more serious consequences for the individual than an identical violation that merely results in a conviction for careless driving. It is doubtful, however, that this factor should be taken into account, because, by the same token, the more serious the offence, the greater is the justification to obtain a conviction. Probably these two factors are of equal weight, and should be allowed to cancel each other out.[235]

(ii) *Necessity*

The Ouimet Committee suggested that consideration should be given to

> whether there existed a situation of urgency in order to prevent the destruction or loss of evidence, or other circumstances which in the particular case justified the action taken.[236]

Both the Study Paper[237] and the *Report on Evidence*[238] of the Law Reform Commission adopted this element, and the Report referred separately to the "importance of the evidence" as well. The McDonald Commission also called for "urgency" to be considered.[239] The courts have taken this advice, and have frequently held that it would not shock the public to admit unconstitutionally obtained evidence in circumstances where investigators had no reasonable alternative to proceeding as they did to secure

---

235 See text associated with notes 242 and 243, *infra*.
236 *Report on Committee on Corrections* (1969).
237 *Supra*, note 206.
238 *Supra*, note 218, proposed Evidence Code, s. 15(2).
239 *Supra*, note 207, at 1047.

evidence necessary to prove a charge.[240] In some situations the public might be shocked if they did *not* do so.

Several factors are involved here. One is that the evidence is important enough to the outcome of the case in question to justify using unconstitutional means. Another is that the means employed were the only ones (or the least offensive ones) available in the circumstances to obtain the evidence. A third is reliability; it would be difficult to justify as "necessary" evidence that is merely suggestive in nature or is of dubious reliability.[241]

A fourth factor, to which several courts have given attention, is the importance of the case itself, the theory being that the more serious the alleged offence, the more justifiable is the unconstitutional conduct by the authorities.[242] However, as explained above, this factor has just the opposite effect when considered in relation to "seriousness of the Charter violation" on the other side of the scale: the more serious the charge, the more serious the consequences of denying the accused his or her constitutional rights.[243] It would seem advisable, therefore, to remove this factor from both sides of the balance.

It should not be concluded from the above discussion that evidence obtained by Charter violations should be admitted whenever there is no other way to obtain evidence necessary to support a conviction. While this is an important element, it must always be weighed against the harm to the citizen's rights. The attitude that criminals must be convicted at all costs has in it, as Mr. Justice Laskin stated in the *Hogan* case, "too much of the philosophy of the end justifying the means."[244] Section 24(2) does permit ends to justify means in some circumstances, but only where, *on balance*, the importance of obtaining the evidence by the particular means employed is found by the court to be greater than the importance of protecting the constitutional rights of the subject.

(iii) *Other Considerations*

Having taken account, on the one hand, of the seriousness of a Charter violation in terms of its impact on both the individual and the legal system, and, on the other, of the importance to effective law enforcement of admitting the resulting tainted evidence, a court would seem to have all

---

240 *E.g.*, *R. v. Noble* (1984), 14 D.L.R. (4th) 216 (Ont. C.A.); *R. v. Maitland* (1984), 4 C.R.D. 850.60-15 (N.W.T. S.C.); *R. v. Zlomanchuk* (1984), 30 Man. R. (2d) 283 (Q.B.).
241 This was referred to as a relevant factor, among many others, in *R. v. Dixon* (1984), 4 C.R.D. 425.60-01 (B.C. S.C.).
242 *E.g.*, *R. v. Stevens* (1983), 1 D.L.R. (4th) 465 (N.S. C.A.); *R. v. Hamill* (1984), 13 D.L.R. (4th) 275 (B.C. C.A.); *dictum* of Le Dain J., in *R. v. Therens, supra*, note 200.
243 See text associated with note 235, *supra*.
244 *Hogan v. R.*, [1975] 2 S.C.R. 574.

the information it could plausibly require to decide whether public opinion would be shocked by the admission of the evidence. Public opinion is not always rooted in plausibility, however, and courts have sometimes taken heed of certain other factors in their rulings under section 24(2). The most common of these additional factors are the two somewhat related criteria of deterrence and wilfulness.

Deterrence of unconstitutional behaviour by police seems to be the basic rationale for the American rule that evidence obtained as a result of an unconstitutional search or seizure should automatically be excluded.[245] However, it is clear from the history of the enactment of section 24(2)[246] that the American rule of total exclusion was not desired by those who fashioned the Charter, and that the unique Canadian solution embodied in section 24(2) was clearly intended to permit the admissibility of evidence resulting from some forms of unconstitutional police behaviour. Only those forms of unconstitutionally obtained evidence whose admission would bring the administration of justice into disrepute can be excluded. Since *any* exclusion would have a deterrent effect on police, the question of deterrence should be of no assistance in deciding *what* to exclude.

Deterrence does have a legitimate role to play in police disciplinary and training programs,[247] and even in certain other Charter proceedings. If, for example, the victim of an unreasonable search or seizure claimed punitive damages against the perpetrators, the deterrent effect of such an award might well be an influential factor in the court's decision.[248] But the decision to admit or to exclude evidence under section 24(2) is supposed to be based on the effect the decision would have on the attitudes of the *public*, not of the police.

Some courts have overlooked this fact, and have paid heed to deterrence in making decisions under section 24(2). Judge Dureault of the Manitoba County Court, for example, has said:

> [O]ne sure way of having the police conform to the law is for the courts to exclude in proceedings initiated by the police any evidence obtained in a manner which constitutes a breach of *Charter* rights. That . . . ought to be the clear message to all law-enforcement agencies of the land.[249]

Most courts seem to disregard deterrence, however. As Judge Salhany of

---

245 "The rule's prime purpose is to deter future unlawful police conduct": *per* Powell J., in *U.S. v. Calandra*, 414 U.S. 338 at 347 (1974).

246 See Gibson, *The Law of the Charter, supra*, note 2, at 222 *et seq.*

247 The McDonald Commission Report laid stress on the usefulness of training and internal discipline as an alternative to the exclusion of evidence: *supra*, note 207, at 1046.

248 See text associated with note 168, *supra*.

249 *Unrau v. R.* (1983), 24 Man. R. (2d) 5 at 8 (Co. Ct.). See also *Jackie v. R.* (1983), 26 Sask. R. 294 (Q.B.); *R. v. Dixon, supra*, note 241.

the Ontario County Court has stated: "It is not the function of the court to exclude evidence in order to discipline the police."[250]

It is possible to interpret the Supreme Court of Canada's decision in *R. v. Therens*[251] as supporting the relevance of deterrence under section 24(2). In rejecting breathalyzer evidence obtained without informing the accused of his right to counsel, Mr. Justice Estey stated, for a majority of the court:

> To do otherwise than reject this evidence . . . would be to invite police officers to disregard *Charter* rights of the citizens and to do so with an assurance of impunity.[252]

It would appear from an examination of the entire judgment, however, that Mr. Justice Estey did not treat this as the *reason* for excluding the evidence. The reason for doing so was that the violation was so "flagrant" and "overt" as to bring the administration of justice into disrepute. The fact that exclusion would discourage similar future abuses by the police was simply a *consequence* of carrying out the Charter's edict under section 24(2).

While they generally regard deterrence as irrelevant, many courts nevertheless place considerable importance on the investigator's state of mind: on whether the Charter violation was advertent, wilful or malicious. This may seem inconsistent. If section 24(2) is not intended to serve a deterrent or disciplinary purpose, and relates only to the state of mind of the *public*, why should the courts concern themselves at all with what went on in the investigator's mind?[253] Should that not be a matter for disciplinary action only?

The pre-Charter reports that urged the adoption of a provision like section 24(2) seemed to see no inconsistency.[254] Of the three criteria proposed by the Ouimet Committee, priority was given to the question whether the breach of rights is deliberate. Inadvertent error by investigators should be treated less seriously than deliberate violations, it suggested, since it is the latter which "may reduce respect for the entire criminal

---

250 *R. v. Dickson* (1984), 4 C.R.D. 850.60-01 (Ont. Co. Ct.). See also *R. v. Cameron* (1983), 7 C.R.R. 370 (B.C. S.C.), rev'd (1984) 16 C.C.C. (3d) 240 (B.C. C.A.); *R. v. Rowbotham, supra*, note 20.

251 *Supra*, note 200.

252 *Ibid.*, at 622.

253 Y.M. Morissette, "The Exclusion of Evidence Under the Canadian Charter of Rights and Freedoms: What to Do and What Not to Do" (1984), 29 *McGill L.J.* 521 at 554, refers to recent American cases illustrating the link between deterrence and police wilfulness: "The efficacy of exclusion as a deterrent is proportional to the flagrancy of the police misconduct."

254 Nor did the author in earlier writings on this topic.

process."[255] The Law Reform Commission Study Paper also placed great weight on this factor, although it was not listed first.[256] The Study Paper pointed out that bad faith on the part of law enforcement officers would be especially telling, if it could be established, but that in view of the difficulty normally involved in proving a person's intentions, it might be more useful simply to distinguish "deliberate" from "innocent" (presumably inadvertent) infractions. The Law Reform Commission *Report on Evidence* summarized this factor as "wilfulness."[257] The courts have not seemed to notice any inconsistency either, and have been more willing to take account of "wilfulness," "deliberateness" and their absence, than to reject any consideration of deterrence.[258]

The key question is whether the public would be shocked, and it seems to be universally conceded that the public would be more shocked by the admission of evidence obtained through a deliberate Charter violation than through an accidental one. In *R. v. Caron*,[259] the case where the police officer obtained a search warrant by misrepresenting to the magistrate the true object of the search, the judge who rejected the resulting evidence laid stress, in doing so, on the deliberateness of the police conduct. Mr. Justice Le Dain, in the *Therens* case,[260] described the Charter violations that justify the exclusion of evidence as "deliberate, wilful or flagrant." As Justice Le Dain pointed out, deliberateness is simply one factor to be taken into account when determining the relative seriousness of the Charter violation. Small, inadvertent Charter contraventions, on the other hand, have been held not to call for the exclusion of evidence,[261] although they may do so if the total impact of several such errors in a single case is significant.[262]

It would be wrong, however, to assume, as some courts appear to,[263] that the *absence* of wilfulness necessarily supports the admissibility of evidence. The public may well be shocked by Charter violations that are intentional, though not "wilful," and even by mere carelessness, if it results in a serious contravention of an individual's Charter rights. The McDonald

---

255 Ouimet Report, *supra*, note 236, at 74.

256 *Supra*, note 206, at 28.

257 S. 15(2) of the proposed Evidence Code, *supra*, note 218, referred to "whether . . . inflicted wilfully or not."

258 Trainor J. was consistent in *R. v. Dixon*, *supra*, note 241, in taking account of *both* wilfulness and deterrence.

259 *Supra*, note 232.

260 *Supra*, note 200.

261 *E.g.*, *R. v. Hynds* (1982), 70 C.C.C. (2d) 186 (Alta. Q.B.); *R. v. Lapointe* (1983), 4 C.R.D. 850.50-05 (Ont. Co. Ct.).

262 *R. v. Thompson*, *supra*, note 222.

263 *R. v. Tontarelli* (1982), 8 W.C.B. 259 (Ont. Co. Ct.); *R. v. Zlomanchuk*, *supra*, note 240; *R. v. Chapin* (1983), 2 D.L.R. (4th) 538 (Ont. C.A.).

Royal Commission, which accepted wilfulness as an important factor, pointed out that:

> [I]f only the wilfulness of the violation were to be considered, this would place a premium on the ignorance of the officer. Therefore, to ensure that police forces are motivated to train and educate officers adequately, *the court should be required to consider whether the officer's ignorance was inexcusable.* This would, we hope, have the effect, in the case of inadvertent error, of requiring the judge to determine whether adequate police training procedures were undertaken.[264]

In short, while a guilty state of mind on the part of an investigator would be likely to shock the public, the absence of such guilt is no guarantee against shock.

Other factors are occasionally proposed for consideration, but few seem appropriate. Mr. Justice McDonald's book, *Legal Rights in the Canadian Charter of Rights and Freedoms,*[265] suggests that "the extent to which a victim of a violation of a right guaranteed by the Charter has another remedy" may influence a decision under section 24(2). It is difficult to understand, on principle, why this should be so. If the purpose of section 24(2) is to preserve respect for the legal system in the minds of members of the general public, reliance by a court on evidence obtained by means that shock the public would undermine that purpose whether or not the person convicted on the evidence had a right to damages or some other ancillary remedy.

Another factor of dubious relevance is the accused's honesty or cooperativeness in dealing with investigators. In *R. v. Sabourin,*[266] a Manitoba County Court judge held that an accused, who was denied the right to counsel upon detention on an impaired driving charge, was not entitled to a remedy under section 24(2) because he had attempted to hide the fact that he had been driving by switching places with his passenger and lying about it in court:

> Since the appellant has been dishonest before the court, the court finds itself obliged to refuse the appellant the remedy he is claiming and which, under other circumstances, should be granted to him.[267]

This rationale for admitting the evidence, which the Court of Appeal chose not to discuss when affirming the decision on other grounds, is open to serious doubt. If it were accepted that an accused's behaviour toward the

---

264 *Supra,* note 207, at 1046 (emphasis added).
265 D.C. McDonald, *Legal Rights in the Canadian Charter of Rights and Freedoms* (Toronto: Carswell, 1982) at 153.
266 (1983), 25 Man. R. (2d) 258 (Man. Co. Ct.), aff'd on other grounds 13 C.C.C. (3d) 68 (Man. C.A.).
267 *Ibid.,* at 266 (Co. Ct.).

police and the court is a basis for denying the protection of section 24(2), that provision would be effectively reduced in status to a discretionary remedy, and those who "stand on their rights" might find that by doing so they place the rights in jeopardy. Just as evidence should not be rejected merely to deter police wrongdoing, so it should not be admitted merely to punish the accused's wrongdoing or lack of cooperation.[268]

4. INHERENT POWERS OF SUPERIOR COURTS

The inherent remedial power of superior courts with respect to matters within their jurisdiction[269] is limited only by express legal proscription. Mr. Justice Beck of the Alberta Supreme Court once described "the development of remedial methods of giving effect to substantive law and the rights and obligations arising therefrom" as "a power . . . inherent in the court."[270] Relying on English authority to the effect that "every superior court is the master of its own practice," he continued:

> I think that, without any statutory rules of practice, the court can, should a case arise . . . award such remedies, though they be new, as may appear to be necessary to work out justice between the parties.[271]

An aspect of this inherent power is the judicial enforcement of constitutional rights in countries like the United States, which have a constitutional *Bills of Rights*, but no express enforcement machinery. The willingness of Canadian courts to perform a similar function without any explicit remedial authority can be seen in recent rulings of the Supreme Court of Canada on the language guarantees contained in section 133 of the *Constitution Act, 1867* and section 23 of the *Manitoba Act*.[272]

The *Manitoba Language Reference*,[273] in particular, demonstrated remedial inventiveness of the highest order. It will be recalled that the Supreme Court of Canada declared all unilingual statutes passed in Manitoba during a 95-year period to be invalid, but endowed them with

---

268 *R. v. Heisler* (1983), 7 C.R.R. 1; rev'd 11 C.C.C. (3d) 475 (Alta. C.A.).

269 Jacob, *supra*, note 91; See *Canada Labour Congress v. Bhindi, supra*, note 91 at 203; *Danson v. A.G. Ontario, supra*, note 14.

270 *Williams v. United Mine Workers of America, Local 1562* (1919), 45 D.L.R. 150 at 177 (Alta. C.A.). The innovation involved was to permit an action to be maintained against an unincorporated trade union. The substantive decision of the Alberta Court was reversed by the Supreme Court of Canada: 59 S.C.R. 240; but the procedural question was not conclusively resolved.

271 *Ibid.*, at 178, *per* Beck J. quoting from his article: "The Development of the Law" (1916), 36 C.L.T. 373 at 382. The English authority cited was *Scales v. Cheese* (1844), 12 M. & W. 685, 152 E.R. 1374.

272 *A.G. Manitoba v. Forest, supra*, note 100; *A.G. Québec v. Blaikie, supra*, note 100.

273 *Reference re Manitoba Language Rights*, [1985] 1 S.C.R. 721.

temporary validity during a judicially determinable minimum compliance period in order to avoid legal chaos. The court found the authority to grant such temporary relief in no more explicit a source than the principle of the "the rule of law," upon which the Constitution is based. Similar remedial powers, innovative if necessary, can be expected to be exercised by courts faced with significant infringements of constitutional rights in the future if the explicit remedial provisions of section 24(1) and (2) and section 52(1) should prove to be inadequate.

It could be argued, to the contrary, that because section 24 and section 52(1) provide certain explicit remedies for the breach of Charter rights, any other remedies that might otherwise have been available are impliedly denied: *expressio unius est exclusio alterius.* However, such an interpretation would, so far as section 24 is concerned, offend section 26 of the Charter:

> The guarantee in this Charter of certain rights and freedoms shall not be construed as denying the existence of any other rights or freedoms that exist in Canada.[274]

It would be possible, of course, to read section 26 as referring only to *substantive* rights and freedoms, and not to the remedial rights conferred by section 24, but it is highly unlikely that any court would be persuaded to adopt so narrow a view. Although section 52(1), not being a part of the Charter in the strict sense, may not be subject to section 26,[275] it was enacted at the same time as part of the same endeavour to strengthen the constitutional rights of Canadians, and it is almost certain to be construed, like the Charter, as an expression or expansion of existing rights rather than as a limitation of them. There was no suggestion in the *Manitoba Language Reference* that section 52(1) hampered in any way the court's power to grant temporary validity to statutes that, on the basis of that section, were of "no force or effect."

It appears, therefore, that neither section 24 nor section 52(1) restrict the courts' historic intrinsic authority to provide suitable remedies for violations of legal wrongs.

5. ENFORCEMENT STATUTES

It should not be forgotten, either, that it is within the power of the Parliament of Canada and of the provincial legislatures, legislating within

---

274 S. 25 similarly provides that the Charter should not be read as limiting aboriginal rights.

275 In one sense, s. 52(1) *is* part of the Charter. It applies to all Charter rights and freedoms, and provides an important means of enforcing them. Earlier Charter drafts included a provision like s. 52(1), and it was moved to its present location only because it was recognized that the principle it expresses has a broader application than to the Charter alone.

their respective jurisdictions, to expand the remedies available for Charter infractions. The United States Congress has enacted enforcement provisions for constitutional rights,[276] and similar measures are possible for Canada. The *Evidence Acts*, federal and provincial, for example, could be amended to provide for a more (but not less) extensive exclusion of unconstitutionally obtained evidence than that which is called for by section 24(2) of the Charter.

---

276 *E.g., Voting Rights Act,* 1965, 42 U.S.C.A., ss. 1973 *et seq.; Civil Rights Act,* 1964, 42 U.S.C.A. ss. 2000 *et seq.;* and see L. Tribe, *American Constitutional Law* (Mineola, N.Y.: Foundation Press, 1978) at 224 *et seq.*

Bibliography*

Compiled by Iva Caccia, Librarian, Human Rights Research and Education Centre, University of Ottawa

GENERAL CONSIDERATIONS

Abella, R., "Public Policy and Canada's Judges: The Impact of the Charter of Rights and Freedoms" (1986), 20 L. Soc. Gaz. 217.

Association canadienne-française pour l'avancement des sciences — Section des sciences juridiques, *La charte canadienne des droits et libertés et les droits collectifs et sociaux* (Quebec, 1983).

Association du Barreau canadien — Québec, *L'adhésion du Québec à l'Accord du Lac Meech. Actes du Colloque tenu à Montréal le 14 novembre 1987* (Montreal, 1988).

Axworthy, T. S., "Colliding Visions: The Debate Over the Charter of Rights and Freedoms 1980-81" in J. M. Weiler & R. M. Elliot, eds., *Litigating the Values of a Nation: The Canadian Charter of Rights and Freedoms* (Toronto: Carswell, 1986) 13.

Baker, C. E., "Non-Canadian Constitutional Experience Relevant to the Fundamental Freedoms Provisions of the Charter: Some United States Experience and Points of View" (1983), 13 Man. L.J. 609.

Bala, N. & Cruickshank, D., "Children and the Charter of Rights" in B. Landau, ed., *Children's Rights in the Practice of Family Law* (Toronto: Carswell, 1986) 28.

Banks, M. A., "Constitutional Law — Citing Canada's Constitution — Problems and Proposed Solutions" (1983), 61 Can. Bar Rev. 499.

Banting, K. G., *The Welfare State and Canadian Federalism*, 2d ed. (Kingston & Montreal: McGill-Queen's University Press, 1987).

Banting, K. G. & Simeon, R., eds., *And No One Cheered: Federalism; Democracy & the Constitution Act* (Toronto: Methuen, 1983).

Barreau du Québec. Formation permanente, Année Judiciaire 1982-83, *La charte canadienne des droits et libertés. Cours données en collaboration avec l'Association du Barreau canadien à Montréal et à Québec les 11 et 18 juin, 1982* (Montreal, 1983).

Barreau du Québec. Formation permanente, Année Judiciaire 1983-84, *L'interaction des chartes canadienne et québécoise des droits et libertés. Cours données à Québec et à Montréal, les 28 et 30 novembre 1983* (Montreal, 1984).

Barry, L. D., "Law, Policy and Statutory Interpretation Under a Constitutionally Entrenched Canadian Charter of Rights and Freedoms" (1982), 60 Can. Bar Rev. 237.

---

* This bibliography includes material available by August 1988.

Baudouin, J.-L., "Qu'en est-il du droit civil?" in G.-A. Beaudoin, éd., *Vos clients et la Charte — Liberté et égalité* (Cowansville, Que.: Yvon Blais, 1988) 27.

Beaudoin, G.-A., "La charte canadienne des droits et libertés — Influence américaine, influence européenne" (1985), 1 Etudes Maritainiennes 59.

Beaudoin, G.-A., ed., *Charter Cases 1986-87: Proceedings of the October 1986 Colloquium of the Canadian Bar Association in Montreal / Causes invoquant la Charte 1986-87: Actes de la Conférences de l'Association du Barreau candien tenue à Montréal en octobre 1986* (Cowansville, Que.: Yvon Blais, 1987).

Beaudoin, G.-A., "Comparaison entre la Charte canadienne des droits et libertés et le Bill of Rights américain" in Canadian Institute for Advanced Legal Studies, *Cambridge Lectures 1983* (Toronto: Butterworths, 1983) 52.

Beaudoin, G.-A., "Considérations sur l'influence de la religion en droit public au Canada" (1984), 15 R.G.D. 589.

Beaudoin, G.-A., "Etude de différents secteurs de la Charte" in Barreau du Québec, Formation permanente, *La charte canadienne des droits et libertés* (Montreal: 1983) 1.

Beaudoin, G.-A., "General Overview: The First Twenty-Five Rulings of the Supreme Court" in G.-A. Beaudoin, ed., *Charter Cases 1986-87* (Cowansville, Que.: Yvon Blais, 1987) 41.

Beaudoin, G.-A., *Le partage des pouvoirs*, 3rd ed. (Ottawa: Editions de l'Université d'Ottawa, 1983).

Beaudoin, G.-A., ed., *The Supreme Court of Canada: Proceedings of the October 1985 Conference / La Cour suprème du Canada: Actes de la Conférence d'octobre 1985* (Cowansville, Que.: Yvon Blais, 1986).

Beaudoin, G.-A., *Your Clients and the Charter - Liberty and Equality: Proceedings of the October 1987 Colloquium of the Canadian Bar Association in Montreal / Vos clients et la Charte — Liberté et éqalité: Actes de la Conférence de l'Association du Barreau canadien tenue à Montréal en octobre 1987* (Cowansville, Que.: Yvon Blais, 1988).

Beaupre, M., *Interpreting Bilingual Legislation*, 2nd ed. (Toronto: Carswell, 1986).

Beaupre, R. M., "Vers l'interprétation d'une Constitution bilingue" (1984), 25 C. de D. 939.

Beck, S. M. & Bernier, I., eds., *Canada and the New Constitution: The Unfinished Agenda* (Montreal: Institute for Research on Public Policy, 1983).

Beckton, C. F. & MacKay, A. W., eds., *The Courts and the Charter* (Toronto: University of Toronto Press, 1985).

Bender, P., "The Bill of Rights and the Limits of the Criminal Sanction" in A. W. MacKay et al., eds., *The Canadian Charter of Rights: Law Practice Revolutionized* (Halifax: Faculty of Law, Dalhousie University, 1982) 169.

Berger, T. R., "The Charter and Canadian Identity" (1985), 23 U.W.O.L. Rev. 1.

Bilson, R. E., "A Worker's Charter: What Do We Mean by Rights?" (1985), 11 Can. Pub. Policy 749.

Bisson, A.-F., "La Charte québécoise des droits et libertés de la personne et le dogme de l'interprétation spécifique des textes constitutionnels" (1986), 17 R.D.U.S. 19.

Black, W. W., "Charter of Rights — Application to Pre-Enactment Events", [1982] U.B.C.L. Rev. (Charter ed.) 59.

Black, W. W., "A Walk Through the Charter" in L. Smith et al., eds., *Righting the Balance: Canada's New Equality Rights* (Toronto: Canadian Human Rights Reporter, 1986) 47.

Blair, D. G., "The Charter and the Judges: A View from the Bench" (1983), 13 Man. L.J. 445.

Blair, D. G., "Do Too Many Rights Make Wrong?" (1983), 7 L. Soc. Gaz. 156.

Brun, H., "The Canadian Charter of Rights and Freedoms as an Instrument of Social Development" in C. F. Beckton & A. W. Mackay, eds., *The Courts and the Charter* (Toronto: The University of Toronto Press, 1985) 1.

Brun, H., *Chartes des droits de la personne. Legislation, jurisprudence et doctrine*, 2è éd. (Montréal: Wilson & Lafleur, 1988).

Brunelle, C., "La primauté du droit: la situation des immigrants et des réfugiés en droit canadien au regard des Chartes et des textes internationaux" (1987), 28 C. de D. 585.

Cairns, A. C., "The Canadian Constitutional Experiment" (1984), 9 Dalhousie L.J. 87.

Canadian Bar Association - Ontario, Continuing Legal Education, *A Practical View of the Charter for Solicitors and Barristers, Toronto, June 10, 1986* (Toronto: 1986).

Canadian Institute for Professional Development, *The Charter and the Corporation: New Vistas for Corporate Rights — October 1985* (Toronto, 1986).

Canadian Institute for the Administration of Justice, *The Canadian Charter of Rights and Freedoms: Initial Experience, Emerging Issues, Future Challenges* (Cowansville, Que.: Yvon Blais, 1983).

Castel, J. G. "The Canadian Charter of Rights and Freedoms" (1983), 61 Can. Bar Rev. 1.

Chrétien, J., "The Negotiation of the Charter: The Federal Government Perspective" in J. M. Weiler & R. M. Elliot, eds., *Litigating the Values of a Nation: A Canadian Charter of Rights and Freedoms* (Toronto: Carswell, 1986) 3.

Claydon, J., "Comparative and International Sources for Interpreting the Charter: A Selective Annotated Bibliographic Guide" in Canadian Bar Association — Ontario, Continuing Legal Education, ed., *A Practical View of the Charter for Solicitors and Barristers* (Toronto, 1986) 3.

Claydon, J., "International Human Rights Law and the Interpretation of the Canadian Charter of Rights and Freedoms" (1982), 4 Sup. Ct. L. Rev. 287.

Cohen, M., "Towards a Paradigm of Theory and Practice: The Canadian Charter of Rights and Freedoms — International Law Influences and Interactions", [1986] Can. Hum. Rts. Y.B. 47.

Cohen, M. & Bayefsky, A. F., "The Canadian Charter of Rights and Freedoms and Public International Law" (1983), 61 Can. Bar Rev. 265.

Colvin, E., "Constitutional Jurisprudence in the Supreme Court of Canada" (1982), 4 Sup. Ct. L. Rev. 3.

Continuing Legal Education Society of British Columbia, *The Canadian Charter of Rights and Freedoms* (Vancouver: 1982).

Continuing Legal Education Society of British Columbia, *Charter of Rights — 1987* (Vancouver: 1987).

De Mestral, A. et al., ed., *The Limitation of Human Rights in Comparative Constitutional Law / La limitation des droits de l'homme en droit constitutionnel comparé* (Cowansville, Que.: Yvon Blais, 1986).

Deschênes, J., "Le rôle du droit comparé dans l'évolution récente des droits de la personne au Canada" in A. de Mestral et al., eds., *La limitation des droits de l'homme en droit constitutionnel comparé* (Cowansville, Que.: Yvon Blais, 1986) 581.

Le Devoir, *Le Québec et le Lac Meech* (Montreal: Guérin, 1987).

Driedger, E. A., "The Canadian Charter of Rights and Freedoms" (1982), 14 Ottawa L. Rev. 366.

Edwards, J.L.J., "The Charter, Government and the Machinery of Justice" (1987), 36 U.N.B.L.J. 41.

Elliot, R., "Interpreting the Charter — Use of the Earlier Versions as an Aid", [1982] U.B.C.L. Rev. (Charter ed.) 11.

Fairley, H. S., "Developments in Constitutional Law: The 1984-85 Term" (1986), 8 Sup. Ct. L. Rev. 53.

Fichaud, J., "Analysis of the Charter and its Application to Labour Law" (1984), 8 Dalhousie L.J. 402.

Finch, L. S. G., "View from the Bench: More Questions Than Answers" in Continuing Legal Education Society of British Columbia, ed., *Charter of Rights — 1987* (Vancouver: 1987) 1.1.01.

Finkelstein, N., *Laskin's Canadian Constitutional Law*, 5th ed. (Toronto: Carswell, 1986).

Finkelstein, N., "Laskin's Four Classes of Liberty" (1987), 66 Can. Bar Rev. 227.

Finkelstein, N., "The Relevance of Pre-Charter Case Law for Post-Charter Adjudication" (1982), 4 Sup. Ct. L. Rev. 267.

Finkelstein, N. & Rogers, B. MacL., eds., *Charter Issues in Civil Cases* (Toronto: Carswell, 1988).

Fitzgerald, P., "Canadian Rights and Freedoms — First Class or Charter?" (1983), 13 Man. L.J. 176.

Gagné, J., "La primauté du droit et la Charte canadienne des droits et libertés" (1987), 1 R.J.E.L. 45.

Gautron, A., "French/English Discrepancies in the Canadian Charter of Rights and Freedoms" (1982), 12 Man. L.J. 220.

Gibbins, R. et al., "Canadian Federalism, the Charter of Rights and the 1984 Election" (1985), 15 Publius 155.

Gibson, D., "Charter of Chimera? A Comment on the Proposed Canadian Charter of Rights and Freedoms" (1978-79), 9 Man. L.J. 363.

Gibson, D., "Interpretation of the Canadian Charter of Rights and Freedoms: Some General Considerations" in W. S. Tarnopolsky & G.-A. Beaudoin, eds., *The Canadian Charter of Rights and Freedoms: Commentary* (Toronto: Carswell, 1982) 25.

Gibson, D., "Judges as Legislators: Not Whether but How" (1987), 25 Alta L. Rev. 249.

Gibson, D., *The Law of the Charter: General Principles* (Toronto: Carswell, 1986).

Gibson, D., "Tort Law and the Charter of Rights" (1986-87), 16 Man. L.J. 213.

Gold, M., "The Rhetoric of Constitutional Argumentation" (1985), 35 U.T.L.J. 154.

Goldie, D. M. M., "The Supreme Court of Canada and the Common Law — A Future Consideration" in G.-A. Beaudoin, ed., *The Supreme Court of Canada* (Cowansville, Que.: Yvon Blais, 1985) 115.

Goreham, R. A., "Canadian Charter of Rights and Freedoms — Criminal Procedure — Retrospective Effect" (1983), 61 Can. Bar Rev. 413.

Grafstein, L., "Look Back in Anger: The 1987 Constitutional Accord. Report of the Special Joint Committee of the Senate and the House of Commons" (1988), 46 U.T. Fac. L. Rev. 226.

Green, L.C., "The Canadian Charter of Rights and International Law" (1982), 26 Can. Y.B. Int'l L. 3.

Hagan J., "Can Social Sciences Save Us? The Problems and Prospects of Social Science Evidence in Constitutional Litigation" in R. J. Sharpe, ed., *Charter Litigation* (Toronto: Butterworths, 1987) 327.

Hayward, M. A., "International Law and the Interpretation of the Canadian Charter of Rights and Freedoms: Uses and Justifications" (1985), 23 U.W.O.L. Rev. 9.

Heard, A. D., "Military Law and the Charter of Rights" (1988), 11 Dalhousie L.J. 514.

Hogg, P. W., *Canada Act 1982 Annotated* (Toronto: Carswell 1982).

Hogg, P. W., "The Charter of Rights and Social and Economic Reform" in Canadian Institute for Advanced Legal Studies, ed., *Cambridge Lectures, 1983* (Toronto: Butterworths, 1985) 45.

Hogg, P. W., "A Comparison of the Canadian Charter of Rights and Freedoms with the Canadian Bill of Rights" in W. S. Tarnopolsky & G.-A. Beaudoin, ed., *The Canadian Charter of Rights and Freedoms: Commentary* (Toronto: Carswell, 1982) 1.

Hogg, P. W., *Constitutional Law of Canada*, 2nd ed. (Toronto: Carswell, 1985).

Hogg, P. W., "Legislative History in Constitutional Cases" in R. J. Sharpe, ed., *Charter Litigation* (Toronto: Butterworths, 1987) 131.

Hogg, P. W., *Meech Lake Constitutional Accord Annotated* (Toronto: Carswell, 1987).

Hovius, B., "The Legacy of the Supreme Court of Canada's Approach to the Canadian Bill of Rights: Prospects for the Charter" (1982), 28 McGill L.J. 31.

Humphrey, J., "The Canadian Charter of Rights and Freedoms and International Law" (1986), 50 Sask. L. Rev. 13.

Huppé, L., "Une bien petite Charte" (1987), 47 R. du B. 813.

Huppé, L., "La renonciation de l'individu aux droits et libertés qui lui garantit la Charte canadienne des droits et libertés" (1986), 46 R. du B. 684.

Hutchinson, A. C., "Charter Litigation and Social Change: Legal Battles and Social Wars" in R. J. Sharpe, ed., *Charter Litigation* (Toronto: Butterworths, 1987) 357.

Jacobs, F.G., "Non-Canadian Constitutional Experience Relevant to the Fundamental Freedoms Provisions of the Charter: The European Convention on Human Rights" (1983), 13 Man. L.J. 599.

Kaufman, F., "The Canadian Charter: A Time for Bold Spirits, not Timorous Souls" (1986), 31 McGill L.J. 456.

Knopff, R. & Morton, F.L., "Nation-Building and the Canadian Charter of Rights and Freedoms" in A. Cairns & C. Williams, eds., *Constitutionalism, Citizenship and Society in Canada* (Toronto: University of Toronto Press, 1985) 133.

La Forest, G. V., "The Canadian Charter of Rights and Freedoms: An Overview" (1983), 61 Can. Bar Rev. 19.

Laberge, H., *Réflexions sur l'opportunité de prévoir dans un document constitutionnel la protection des droits de la personne et des droits linguistiques* (Quebec: Conseil de la langue française, 1981).

Langlois, R., "La Charte et les règles d'interprétation constitutionnelle" in G.-A. Beaudoin, ed., *Causes invoquant la Charte 1986-87* (Cowansville, Que.: Yvon Blais, 1987) 385.

Laskin, J. B., "Corporations and the Charter: The Door Opens Wider" (1985), 2 Bus. & L. 78.

Law Society of Upper Canada. Continuing Legal Education, *The Charter: The Civil Context* (Toronto: 1983).

Lederman, W. R., "The Power of the Judges and the New Canadian Charter of Rights and Freedoms", [1982] U.B.C.L. Rev. (Charter ed.) 1.

Lyon, N., "The Charter as a Mandate for the New Ways of Thinking About Law" (1984), 9 Queen's L.J. 241.

MacDonald, D.C., "L'impact de la doctrine et de la jurisprudence de la Convention européenne des droits de l'homme sur l'interprétation de la Charte canadienne des droits et libertés" in D. Turp & G.-A. Beaudoin, ed., *Perspectives canadiennes et européennes des droits de la personne* (Cowansville, Que., Yvon Blais, 1986) 91.

MacDonald, R. A., "Postscript and Prelude — The Jurisprudence of the Charter: Eight Theses" (1982), 4 Sup. Ct. L. Rev. 321.

MacKay, A. W., "The Canadian Charter of Rights and Freedoms: A Springboard to Students' Rights" (1984), 4 Windsor Y.B. Access Just. 174.

MacKay, A. W., "Interpreting the Charter of Rights: Law, Politics and Poetry" in G.-A. Beaudoin, ed., *Charter Cases 1986-87* (Cowansville, Que.: Yvon Blais, 1987) 347.

MacKay, A. W., "Judicial Process in the Supreme Court of Canada: The Patriation Reference and Its Implication for the Charter of Rights" (1983), 21 Osgoode Hall L.J. 55.

MacKay, A. W. & Bauman, R. W., "The Supreme Court of Canada: Reform Implications for an Emerging National Institution" in C. F. Beckton & A. W. MacKay, eds., *The Courts and the Charter* (Toronto: University of Toronto Press, 1985) 37.

MacKay, A. W. et al., eds., *The Canadian Charter of Rights: Law Practice Revolutionalized* (Halifax: Faculty of Law, Dalhousie University, 1982).

Magnet, J. E., *Constitutional Law of Canada*, 3rd ed. (Toronto: Carswell, 1987).

Manley-Casimir, M. E. & Sussel, T. A., *Courts in the Classroom: Education and the Charter of Rights and Freedoms* (Calgary: Detselig, 1983).

Manning, M., *Rights, Freedoms and the Courts: A Practical Analysis of the Constitution Act, 1982* (Toronto: Emond-Montgomery, 1982).

Matas, D., "The Working of the Charter" (1986), 16 Man. L.J. 111.

Matkin, J. G., "The Negotiation of the Charter of Rights: The Provincial Perspective" in J. M. Weiler & R. M. Elliot, ed., *Litigating the Values of a Nation: The Canadian Charter of Rights and Freedoms* (Toronto: Carswell, 1986) 27.

McConnell, W. H., "Recent Developments in Canadian Law: Constitutional Law" (1986), 18 Ottawa L. Rev. 721.

McEvoy, J. P., "The Charter As a Bilingual Instrument" (1986), 64 Can. Bar Rev. 155.

McGinn, F., "The Canadian Charter of Rights and Freedom: Its Impact on Law Enforcement" (1982), 31 U.N.B.L.J. 177.

McKercher, W. R., ed., *The U.S. Bill of Rights and the Canadian Charter of Rights and Freedoms* (Toronto: Ontario Economic Council, 1983).

McLeod, R. M. et al., *The Canadian Charter of Rights: The Prosecution and Defence of Criminal and Other Statutory Offences* (Toronto: Carswell, 1983-1987).

McMahon, M., "The Canadian Charter of Rights and Freedoms: A Study in the Creation and Use of Legal Authority" (1984), 6 Can. Crim. Forum 131.

McMurtry, R. R., "The Search for a Constitutional Accord — A Personal Memoir" (1983), 8 Queen's L.J. 28.

McWhinney, E., *Canada and the Constitution 1979-1982: Patriation and the Charter of Rights* (Toronto: University of Toronto Press, 1982).

McWhinney, E., "The Canadian Charter of Rights and Freedoms: the Lessons of Comparative Jurisprudence" (1983), 61 Can. Bar Rev. 55.

Mendes, E. P., "Interpreting the Canadian Charter of Rights and Freedoms:

Applying International and European Jurisprudence on the Law and Practice of Fundamental Rights" (1982), 20 Alta. L. Rev. 383.

Monahan, P. J., "A Critic's Guide to the Charter" in R. J. Sharpe, ed., *Charter Litigation* (Toronto: Butterworths, 1987) 383.

Monahan, P. J., "Judicial Review and Democracy" (1987), 21 U.B.C.L. Rev. 85.

Monahan, P. J., *Politics and the Constitution: the Charter, Federalism and the Supreme Court of Canada* (Toronto: Carswell, 1987).

Morel, A., "La coexistence des chartes canadienne et québécoise: problèmes d'interaction" (1986), 17 R.D.U.S. 49.

Morgan, B. G., "Proof of Facts in Charter Litigation" in R. J. Sharpe, ed., *Charter Litigation* (Toronto: Butterworths, 1987) 159.

Morton, F. L., "Group Rights Versus Individual Rights in the Charter: The Special Cases of Natives and the Quebecois" in N. Nevitte & A. Kornberg, ed., *Minorities and the Canadian State* (Oakville, Ont.: Mosaic Press, 1985) 71.

Morton, F. L., "The Political Impact of the Canadian Charter of Rights and Freedoms" (1987), 20 Can. J. Pol. Sci. 31.

Morton, F. L. & Pal, L. A., "The Impact of the Charter of Rights on Public Administration" (1985), 28 Can. Pub. Admin. 221.

Morton, F. L. & Withey, M. J., "Charting the Charter, 1982 — 1985: A Statistical Analysis", [1987] Can. Hum. Rts. Y.B. 65.

Mossop, D. W., "'Charteritis' and Other Legal Diseases" (1985), 43 Advocate 201.

Moull, W. D., "Business Law Implication of the Canadian Charter of Rights and Freedoms" (1984), 8 C.B.L.J. 449.

O'Grady, J., "A Trip Through Charter Land" (1983), 31 Chitty's L. J. 1.

Penner, R., "Constraints on the Political Will" (1984), 4 Windsor Y.B. Access Just. 355.

Pépin, G., "L'administration publique et le principe de l'égalité" (1984), 44 R. du B. 137.

Perras, D. W., "The Canadian Charter of Rights and Freedoms: Some Questions Raised" (1983), 47 Sask. L. Rev. 165.

Petter, A., "Immaculate Deception: The Charter's Hidden Agenda" (1987), 45 Advocate 857.

Petter, A., "The Politics of the Charter: Lessons From the Early Charter Decisions of the Supreme Court of Canada" (1986), 8 Sup. Ct. L. Rev. 473.

Pigeon, L.-P., "L'efficacité des décisions de justice en droit public interne (constitutionnel)" (1985), 26 C. de D. 995.

Pratt, A., "The Charter and How to Approach It: A Guide for the Civil Practitioner" (1983), 4 Advocates' Q. 425.

Pratte, S., "La primauté du droit. L'origine du principe et son évolution dans le contexte de la Charte canadienne des droits et libertés" (1986), 27 C. de D. 685.

Ratushny, E., "The Need for a Common Perception of Human Rights in a World of Diversity: A Canadian Perspective" (1987), 28 C. de D. 487.

Rémillard, G., "Les règles d'interprétation de la Charte canadienne des droits et libertés" in G.-A. Beaudoin, éd., *La Cour suprême du Canada* (Cowansville, Que.: Yvon Blais, 1986) 265.

Rémillard, G., "Les règles d'interprétation relatives à la Charte canadienne des droits et libertés et à la Charte des droits et libertés de la personne du Québec" in D. Turp & G.-A. Beaudoin, eds., *Perspectives canadiennes et européennes des droits de la personne* (Cowansville, Que.: Yvon Blais, 1986) 205.

Richards, J. G. & Smith, G. J., "Applying the Charter" (1983), 4 Advocates' Q. 129.

Roman, A., "The Charter of Rights: Renewing the Social Contract?" (1983), 8 Queen's L.J. 188.

Roman, A., "The Possible Impact of the Canadian Charter of Rights and Freedoms on Administrative Law" (1985), 26 C. de D. 339.

Romanow, R., "And Justice for Whom?" (1986), 16 Man. L.J. 102.

Romanow, R., "Making Canada's Constitution: Reflections of a Participant" in A. W. MacKay et al., eds., *The Canadian Charter of Rights: Law Practice Revolutionized* (Halifax: Faculty of Law, Dalhousie University, 1982) 105.

Romanow, R., "'Reworking the Miracle': The Constitutional Accord 1981" (1983), 8 Queen's L.J. 74.

Romanow, R. et al., *Canada . . . Notwithstanding: The Making of the Constitution 1976-1982* (Toronto: Carswell, 1984).

Russell, P. H., "The Effect of a Charter of Rights on the Policy-Making Role of Canadian Courts" (1982), 25 Can. Pub. Admin. 1.

Russell, P. H., "The Political Purposes of the Canadian Charter of Rights and Freedoms" (1983), 61 Can. Bar Rev. 30.

Ryan, H. R. S., "The Impact of the Canadian Charter of Rights and Freedoms on the Canadian Correctional System", [1983] Can. Hum. Rts. Y.B. 99.

Salhany, R. E., *The Origin of Rights* (Toronto: Carswell, 1985).

Samek, R., "Law and Convention: A Peep Behind the Patriation Case" in A. W. MacKay et al., eds., *The Canadian Charter of Rights: Law Practice Revolutionized* (Halifax: Faculty of Law, Dalhousie University, 1982) 29.

Samek, R., "Untrenching Fundamental Rights" (1982), 4 McGill L.J. 755.

Schmeiser, D. & Wood, R. J., "Student Rights Under the Charter" (1985), 49 Sask. L. Rev. 49.

Schwartz, B., *Fathoming Meech Lake* (Winnipeg: Legal Research Institute of the University of Manitoba, 1987).

Scott, I. G., "The Role of the Attorney General and the Charter of Rights" in G.-A. Beaudoin, ed., *Charter Cases 1986-87* (Cowansville, Que.: Yvon Blais, 1987) 129.

Sharpe, R. J., ed., *Charter Litigation* (Toronto: Butterworths, 1987).

Sharpe, R. J., "Judicial Development of Principles in Applying the Charter" in

N. Finkelstein & B. M. Rogers, ed., *Charter Issues in Civil Cases* (Toronto: Carswell, 1988) 3.

Shumiatcher, M., "Chaff from the Charter's Threshing Floor" (1983), 13 Man. L.J. 437.

Smiley, D., "A Dangerous Deed: the Constitution Act, 1982" in K. Banting & R. Simeon, eds., *And No One Cheered: Federalism, Democracy & the Constitution Act* (Toronto: Methuen, 1983) 74.

Smith, G. J., ed. (Law Society of Upper Canada Bar Admission Course Materials), *Charter of Rights and administrative law, 1983-1984* (Toronto: Carswell, 1983).

Sopinka, J., "The Charter: A View from the Bar" in G.-A. Beaudoin, ed., *Charter Cases 1986-87* (Cowansville, Que.: Yvon Blais, 1987) 403.

Stone, D. & Walpole, F. K., "The Canadian Constitution Act and the Constitution of the United States: A Comparative Analysis" (1983), 2 Can.-Amer. L.J. 1.

Swinton, K., "What Do the Courts Want From the Social Sciences?" in R. J. Sharpe, ed., *Charter Litigation* (Toronto: Butterworths, 1987) 187.

Tarnopolsky, W. S., "A Comparison Between the Canadian Charter of Rights and Freedoms and the International Covenant on Civil and Political Rights" (1983), 8 Queen's L.J. 211.

Tarnopolsky, W. S., "The Constitution and Human Rights" in K. Banting & R. Simeon, eds., *And No One Cheered: Federalism, Democracy & the Constitution Act* (Toronto: Methuen, 1983) 261.

Tarnopolsky, W. S., "The New Canadian Charter of Rights and Freedoms as Compared and Contrasted with the American Bill of Rights" (1983), 5 Hum. Rts. Q. 227.

Tarnopolsky, W. S., "Sources communes et parenté de la Convention européenne et des instruments canadiens des droits de la personne" in D. Turp & G.-A. Beaudoin, ed., *Perspectives canadiennes et européennes des droits de la personne* (Cowansville, Qué., Yvon Blais, 1986) 61.

Tarnopolsky, W. S. & Beaudoin, G.-A., ed., *The Canadian Charter of Rights and Freedoms: Commentary* (Toronto: Carswell, 1982).

Taylor, M. R., "The Status of Individual Rights and Freedoms Under the Constitution Act, 1981" (1982), 40 Advocate 119.

Tremblay, G., "La Charte canadienne des droits et libertés et quelques leçons tirées de la Convention européenne des droits de l'homme" (1982), 23 C. de D. 795.

Turp, D., "Le recours au droit international aux fins de l'interprétation de la Charte canadienne des droits et libertés: un bilan jurisprudentiel" (1984), 18 R.J.T. 353.

Turp, D. & Beaudoin, G.-A., ed., *Perspectives canadiennes et européennes des droits de la personne: Actes des journées strasbourgeoises de l'Institut canadien d'études juridiques supérieures 1984* (Cowansville, Que.: Yvon Blais, 1986).

Weiler, J. & Elliot, R. M., ed., *Litigating the Values of a Nation: the Canadian Charter of Rights and Freedoms* (Toronto: Carswell, 1986).

Weiler, P. C. "The Evolution of the Charter; A View From the Outside" in J. M. Weiler & R. M. Elliot, ed., *Litigating the Values of a Nation: the Canadian Charter of Rights and Freedoms* (Toronto: Carswell, 1986) 49.

Weiler, P. C., "Rights and Judges in a Democracy: A New Canadian Version" (1984-85), 18 U. Mich. J.L. Ref. 51.

Williams, C., "The Changing Nature of Citizen Rights" in A. Cairns & C. Williams, eds., *Constitutionalism, Citizenship and Society in Canada* (Toronto: University of Toronto Press, 1985) 99.

Woehrling, J., "Le rôle du droit comparé dans la jurisprudence des droits de la personne — rapport canadien" in A. De Mestral et al., ed., *La limitation des droits de l'homme en droit constitutionnel comparé* (Cowansville, Que.: Yvon Blais, 1986) 449.

Zellick, G., "The European Convention on Human Rights: Its Significance for Charter Litigation" in R. J. Sharpe, ed., *Charter Litigation* (Toronto: Butterworths, 1987) 97.

PREAMBLE

Gagné, J., "La primauté du droit et la Charte canadienne des droits et libertés" (1987), 1 R.J.E.L. 45.

Polka, B., "The Supremacy of God and the Rule of Law in the Canadian Charter of Rights and Freedoms: A Theological-political Analysis" (1987), 32 McGill L.J. 854.

SECTION 1: REASONABLE LIMITS

Abella, R. S., "Limitations on the Right to Equality Before the Law" in A. de Mestral et al., eds., *The Limitation of Human Rights in Comparative Constitutional Law* (Cowansville, Que: Yvon Blais, 1986) 223.

Anisman, P., "Application of the Charter: A Structural Approach," in P. Anisman & A. M. Linden, eds., *The Media, the Courts and the Charter* (Toronto: Carswell, 1986) 1 at 21.

Arbess, D. J., "Limitations on Legislative Override Under the Canadian Charter of Rights and Freedoms: A Matter of Balancing Values" (1983), 21 Osgoode Hall L.J. 115.

Aubert, J.-F., "Limitations des droits de l'homme: le rôle respectif du législateur et des tribunaux" in A. de Mestral et al., eds., *La limitation des droits de l'homme en droit constitutionnel comparé* (Cowansville, Que.: Yvon Blais, 1986) 185.

Beaudoin, G.-A., "Les clauses dérogatoires et limitatives des instruments canadiens des droits de la personne" in D. Turp & G.-A. Beaudoin, éds., *Perspectives canadiennes et européennes des droits de la personne* (Cowansville, Que.: Yvon Blais, 1986) 139.

Beckton, C. F., "Section 27 and Section 15 of the Charter" in Canadian Human Rights Foundation, ed., *Multiculturalism and the Charter: A Legal Perspective* (Toronto: Carswell, 1987) 1.

Bender, P. A., "Justifications for Limiting Constitutionally Guaranteed Rights and

Freedoms: Some Remarks About the Proper Role of Section One of the Canadian Charter" (1983), 13 Man. L.J. 669.

Binette, A., "La mise en oeuvre judiciaire de l'article 1 de la Charte canadienne et le droit de la preuve", [1986] C. de D. 939.

Braun, S., "Should Commercial Speech Be Accorded Prima Facie Constitutional Recognition Under the Canadian Charter of Rights and Freedoms" (1986), 18 Ottawa L. Rev. 37.

Brun, H., "Quelques notes sur les articles 1, 2, 7 et 15 de la Charte canadienne des droits et libertés" (1982), 23 C. de D. 781.

Canadian Bar Association, *A Blueprint for Implementation of Constitutional Equality Rights: Submission to the Parliamentary Special Committee on Equality Rights* (Ottawa: 1985) 53.

Carnerie, F., "Euthanasia and Self-Determination: Is There a Charter Right to Die in Canada?" (1987), 32 McGill L.J. 299 at 330.

Christian, T. J., "The Limitation of Liberty: A Consideration of Section 1 of the Charter of Rights and Freedoms", [1982] U.B.C.L. Rev. (Charter ed.) 105.

Christian, T. J., "The Limited Operation of the Limitations Clause" (1987), 25 Alta. L. Rev. 264.

Conklin, W. E., "Interpreting and Applying the Limitations Clause: An Analysis of Section 1" (1982), 4 Sup. Ct. L. Rev. 75.

Corry, D. J., "Military Law Under the Charter" (1986), 24 Osgoode Hall L.J. 67.

Cotler, I., "Freedom of Expression" in A. de Mestral, ed., *The Limitation of Human Rights in Comparative Constitutional Law* (Cowansville, Que.: Yvon Blais, 1986) 353.

Creighton, G. D., "Edwards Books and Section 1: Cutting Down Oakes?" (1987), 55 C.R. (3d) 309.

Cromwell, T. A. & MacKay, A. W., "Oakes in the Supreme Court: A Cautious Initiative Unimpeded by Old Ghosts" (1986), 50 C.R. (3d) 34.

De Mestral, A. et al., eds., *The Limitation of Human Rights in Comparative Constitutional Law* (Cowansville, Que.: Yvon Blais, 1986).

Doherty, D. H., "The Charter and Reforming the Law of Evidence" (1987), 58 C.R. (3d) 314.

Elliot, R., "Freedom of Expression and Pornography: The Need for a Structured Approach to Charter Analysis" in J. M. Weiler & R. M. Elliot, eds., *Litigating the Values of a Nation: The Canadian Charter of Rights and Freedoms* (Toronto: Carswell, 1986) 308.

Etherington, B., "Constitutional Law — Charter of Rights and Freedoms, Section 2(b) and 1 — Application of the Charter to the Common Law in Private Litigation — Freedom of Expression — Picketing in Labour Disputes — Retail, Wholesale and Dept. Store Union, Local 580 v. Dolphin Delivery Ltd." (1987), 66 Can. Bar Rev. 818.

Falconer, J., "The ALERT Demand and the Right to Counsel: The Problem with Talbourdet" (1986), 28 Crim. L.Q. 390.

Finkelstein, N., "A Question of Emphasis: The State's Burden in Federal Republic of Germany v. Rauca" (1982), 30 C.R. (3d) 430.

Finkelstein, N., "Section 1: The Standard for Assessing Restrictive Government Actions and the Charter's Code of Procedure and Evidence" (1983), 9 Queen's L.J. 143.

Finkelstein, N., "Sections 1 and 15 of the Canadian Charter of Rights and Freedoms and the Relevance of the U.S. Experience" (1985), 6 Advocate 188.

Finkelstein, N., "Section 15, Section 1, and the Relevance of the U.S. Experience" in Law Society of Upper Canada, Continuing Education Department, ed., *Equality: Section 15 and Charter Procedures* (Toronto, 1985) ch. B.

Fogarty, K. H., *Equality Rights and Their Limitations in the Charter* (Toronto: Carswell, 1987).

Gagnon, J. D., "Les effets de la Charte canadienne des droits et libertés sur le droit du travail" (1984), 18 R.J.T. 131.

Gibson, D., *The Law of the Charter: General Principles* (Toronto: Carswell, 1986) 133.

Gibson, D., "Reasonable Limits Under the Canadian Charter of Rights and Freedoms" (1985), 15 Man. L.J. 27.

Goldie, D. M. M., "Section 1 of the Canadian Charter of Rights and Freedoms," in Legal Education Society of British Columbia, ed., *Charter of Rights — 1987* (Vancouver: 1987) 11.1.01.

Grant, I. & MacKay, A. W., "Constructive Murder and the Charter: In Search of Principle" (1987), 25 Alta. L. Rev. 129 at 150.

Greschner, D., "Two Approaches for Section One of the Charter" (1985), 49 Sask. L. Rev. 336.

Hogg, P. W., "Section One of the Canadian Charter of Rights and Freedoms" in A. de Mestral et al., eds., *The Limitation of Human Rights in Comparative Constitutional Law* (Cowansville, Que.: Yvon Blais, 1986) 3.

Hovius, B., "The Limitation Clauses of the European Convention on Human Rights: A Guide for the Application of Section 1 of the Charter?" (1985), 17 Ottawa L. Rev. 213.

Ivankovich, I. F., "Prolonging the Sunday Closing Imbroglio: Regina v. Videoflicks Ltd." (1986), 24 Alta. L. Rev. 334.

Klinck, D. R., "The Quest for Meaning in Charter Adjudication: Comment on R. v. Therens" (1985), 31 McGill L.J. 104 at 114.

Lahey, K. A., "The Charter and Pornography: Toward a Restricted Theory of Constitutionally Protected Expression" in J. M. Weiler & R. M. Elliot, eds., *Litigating the Values of a Nation: The Canadian Charter of Rights and Freedoms* (Toronto: Carswell, 1986) 265.

Langlois, R., "Les clauses limitatives des chartes canadienne et québécoise des droits et libertés et le fardeau de la preuve" in D. Turp & G.-A. Beaudoin, eds., *Perspectives canadiennes et européennes des droits de la personne* (Cowansville, Que.: Yvon Blais, 1984) 159.

Langlois, R., "La preuve dans les affaires mettant en cause la Charte canadienne des droits et libertés" (1985), 45 R. du B. 617.

Low, M., "The Canadian Charter of Rights and Freedoms and the Role of the Courts: An Initial Survey" (1984), 18 U.B.C.L. Rev. 69.

MacDonald, M., "Obscenity, Censorship and Freedom of Expression: Does the Charter Protect Pornography?" (1985), 43 U.T. Fac. L. Rev. 130 at 139.

MacKay, A. W., "Constitutional Interpretation. Legislative History. Interpreting the Charter of Rights: Law, Politics and Poetry" in G.-A. Beaudoin, ed., *Charter Cases 1986-87* (Cowansville, Qué.: Yvon Blais, 1986) 34.

MacKay, A. W. & Cromwell, T. A., "Oakes: A Bold Initiative Impeded by Old Ghosts" (1983), 32 C.R. (3d) 221.

Mallory, J. R., "Beyond 'Manner and Form': Reading Between the Lines in Operation Dismantle Inc. v. R." (1986), 31 McGill L.J. 480.

Manning, M., "Proof of Facts in Constitutional Cases" in G.-A. Beaudoin, ed., *Charter Cases 1986-87* (Cowansville, Que.: Yvon Blais, 1987) 271.

Marx, H., "Entrenchment, Limitations and Non-Obstante (ss. 1, 33 and 52)" in W.S. Tarnopolsky & G.-A. Beaudoin, eds., *The Canadian Charter of Rights and Freedoms: Commentary* (Toronto: Carswell, 1982) 61.

Monahan, P., "Judicial Review and Democracy: A Theory of Judicial Review" (1987), 21 U.B.C.L. Rev. 87 at 106.

Monahan, P., *Politics and the Constitution: The Charter, Federalism and the Supreme Court of Canada* (Toronto: Carswell, 1987).

Morel, A., "La clause limitative de l'article 1 de la Charte canadienne des droits et libertés: une assurance contre le gouvernement des juges" (1983), 61 R. du B. 81.

Morgan, B. G., "Evidentiary Issues Affecting Section 1 and Section 15 Claims" in Law Society of Upper Canada, Continuing Education Department, ed., *Equality: Section 15 and Charter Procedures* (Toronto: 1985) ch. J.

Ontario Attorney General, *Sources for the Interpretation of Equality Rights Under the Charter: A Background Paper* (Toronto: 1985) 109.

Penner, R., "Constraints on the Political Will" (1984), 4 Windsor Y.B. Access Just. 355.

Pratt, A., "The Charter and How to Approach It: A Guide for the Civil Practitioner" (1983), 4 Advocates' Q. 423.

Proulx, D., "La Loi 101, la clause-Québec et la Charte canadienne devant la Cour suprême: un cas d'espèce?" (1985), 16 R.G.D. 167.

Rand, C. L., "Is the Capital Gain Exemption Unconstitutional?" (1987), 9 Can. Community L.J. 49.

Regel, A. R, "Hate Propaganda: A Reason to Limit Freedom of Speech" (1985), 49 Sask. L. Rev. 303.

Reilly, J. W., "Annotation: R. v. Squires" (1986), 50 C.R. (3d) 321.

Rémillard, G., "Les conditions d'application de la Charte canadienne des droits et libertés" in Barreau du Québec, Formation permanente, ed., *L'interaction des chartes canadienne et québécoise des droits et libertés* (Montreal: 1984) 1.

Rémilliard, G., "La charte canadienne des droits et libertés: les conditions d'application de la Charte" in Barreau du Québec, Formation permamente, ed., *La charte canadienne des droits et libertés* (Montreal: 1983) 55.

Ross, J. M., "Limitations on Human Rights in International Law: Their Relevance to the Canadian Charter of Rights and Freedoms" (1984), 6 Hum. Rts. Q. 180.

Ryan, H. R. S., "The Impact of the Canadian Charter of Rights and Freedoms on the Canadian Correctional System", [1983] Can. Hum. Rts. Y.B. 99 at 118.

Segal, M. D., "The Impact of R. v. Therens on Various Forms of State Constraint" (1986), 38 M.V.R. 71.

Sharpe, R. J., "Commercial Expression and the Charter" (1987), 37 U. T. Fac. L. Rev. 229 at 255.

Slattery, B., "Canadian Charter of Rights and Freedoms — Override Clauses Under Section 33 — Whether Subject to Judicial Review Under Section 1" (1983), 61 Can. Bar Rev. 391.

Smith, L., "Charter Equality Rights: Some General Issues and Specific Applications in British Columbia to Elections, Juries and Illegitimacy" (1984), 18 U.B.C.L. Rev. 351 at 363.

Stuart, D., "Annotation: R. v. Killen" (1986), 49 C.R. (3d) 242.

Stuart, D., "Oakes is Not Enough" (1985), 43 C.R. (3d) 315.

Stuart, D. & Manson, A., "Ref Re Section 94(2) of Motor Vehicle Act, R.S.B.C. 1979 c. 288" (1986), 48 C.R. (3d) 295.

Tarnopolsky, W. S., "Limitations on Equality Rights" in A. de Mestral et al., eds., *The Limitation of Human Rights in Comparative Constitutional Law* (Cowansville, Que.: Yvon Blais, 1986) 325.

Weiler, J. M., "The Regulation of Strikes and Picketing Under the Charter" in J. M. Weiler & R. M. Elliot, eds., *Litigating the Values of a Nation: The Canadian Charter of Rights and Freedoms* (Toronto: Carswell, 1986) 211 at 235.

White, J. D., "Annotation: Reference Re Section 94(2) of Motor Vehicle Act, R.S.B.C." (1986), 48 C.R. (3d) 291.

Whitley, S. J., "The Manitoba Language Reference: Judicial Consideration of 'Language Charged with Meaning'" (1986), 15 Man. L.J. 295.

Woehrling, J., "Le rôle du droit comparé dans la jurisprudence des droits de la personne — rapport canadien" in A. de Mestral et al., eds., *La limitation des droits de l'homme en droit constitutionnel comparé* (Cowansville, Que.: Yvon Blais, 1986) 449.

Wright, K. E., "Do You Mind If I Join You? — The Constitutional Validity of Section 520(1) of the Criminal Code" (1986), 28 C. L.Q. 491.

SECTION 2: FUNDAMENTAL FREEDOMS
Section 2(a): Freedom of conscience and religion

Bale, G., "Constitutional Values in Conflict: Full Funding for Ontario's Catholic High Schools" (1986), 18 Ottawa L. Rev. 533.

Beaudoin, G.-A., "La protection constitutionnelle des minorités" (1986), 27 C. de D. 31.

Beaudoin, G.-A., "Le multiculturalisme et les droits confessionnels et linguistiques: une vue succincte" in Canadian Human Rights Foundation, ed., *Multiculturalism and the Charter: A Legal Perspective* (Toronto: Carswell, 1987) 15.

Black, W. W., "Religion and the Right of Equality" in A. F. Bayefsky & M. Eberts, eds., *Equality Rights and the Canadian Charter of Rights and Freedoms* (Toronto: Carswell, 1985) 131.

Brun, H., "Un aspect crucial mais délicat des libertés de conscience et de religion des articles 2 et 3 des Chartes canadienne et québécoise: l'objection de conscience" (1987), 28 C. de D. 185.

Cotler, I., "Freedom of Assembly, Association, Conscience and Religion (s.2(a), (c) and (d))" in W. S. Tarnopolsky & G.-A. Beaudoin, eds., *The Canadian Charter of Rights and Freedoms: Commentary* (Toronto: Carswell 1982) 123.

Cotler, I., "Freedom of Conscience and Religion" in G.-A. Beaudoin, ed., *Your Clients and the Charter — Liberty and Equality* (Cowansville, Que.: Yvon Blais, 1988) 101.

Creighton, G. D., "Edwards Books and Section 1: Cutting Down Oakes?" (1987), 55 C.R. (3d) 309.

Fairley, H. S., "Developments in Constitutional Law: The 1984-85 Term" (1986), 8 Sup. Ct. L. Rev. 53.

Fairweather, G., "The Rights of Religious Minorities" (1986), 27 C. de D. 89.

Ginn, D., "Indian Hunting Rights: Dick v. R., Jack and Charlie v. R. and Simon v. R." (1986), 31 McGill L.J. 527.

Hayward, A., "R. v. Jack and Charlie and the Constitution Act, 1982: Religious Freedom and Aboriginal Rights in Canada" (1984), 10 Queen's L.J. 165.

Hébert, J.-C., "Troubler la paix ou les libertés fondamentales" (1985), 19 R.J.T. 227.

Ivankovich, I. F., "Prolonging the Sunday Closing Imbroglio: Regina v. Videoflicks Ltd." (1986) 24 Alta L. Rev. 334.

Lyon, N., "The Teleological Mandate of the Fundamental Freedoms Guarantee: What to do with Vague but Meaningful Generalities" (1982), 4 Sup. Ct. L. Rev. 57.

Macklem, P., "Freedom of Conscience and Religion in Canada" (1984), 42 U.T. Fac. L. Rev. 51.

Ouellette, M., "La Charte canadienne et certains problèmes de bioéthique" (1984), 18 R.J.T. 271.

Patenaude, P., "L'objection éthique et la Charte canadienne des droits et libertés" in Association canadienne-française pour l'avancement des sciences, éd., *La*

Charte canadienne des droits et libertés et les droits collectifs et sociaux (Quebec: 1983) 126.

Petter, A., "Not 'Never on a Sunday': R. v. Videoflicks Ltd. et al." (1985), 49 Sask. L. Rev. 96.

Rozefort, W., "Are Corporations Entitled to Freedom of Religion Under the Canadian Charter of Rights and Freedoms?" (1986), 15 Man. L. J. 199.

Salhany, R. E., *The Origin of Rights* (Toronto: Carswell, 1985) 11.

Westeringh, W., "The Scope of Freedom of Conscience and Religion Contained in Section 2(a) of the Canadian Charter of Rights and Freedoms" in British Columbia Continuing Legal Education Society, ed., *Charter of Rights — 1987* (Vancouver: 1987) 7.1.01.

Zylberberg, J., "Le droit étatique des minorités religieuses" (1986), 27 C. de D. 57.

Section 2(b): Freedom of Thought, Belief, Opinion and Expression, Including Freedom of the Press

aa., "The Zundel Appeal: A Criminal Reports Forum" (1987), 56 C.R. (3d) 77.

Adam, G. S., "The Charter and the Role of the Media: A Journalist's Perspective" in P. Anisman & A. M. Linden, eds., *The Media, the Courts and the Charter* (Toronto: Carswell, 1986) 39.

Anisman, P. & Linden, A. M., eds., *The Media, the Courts and the Charter* (Toronto: Carswell, 1986).

Arbour, L., "The Politics of Pornography: Towards an Expansive Theory of Constitutionally Protected Expression" in J. M. Weiler & R. M. Elliot, eds., *Litigating the Values of a Nation: the Canadian Charter of Rights and Freedoms* (Toronto: Carswell, 1986) 294.

Archambault, J.-D., "La liberté d'expression des avocats garantie par les Chartes: récents développements judiciaires" (1985), 45 R. du B. 329.

Atkey, R. "Corporate Political Activity" (1985), 23 U.W.O.L. Rev. 129.

Bakan, J., "Pornography, Law and Moral Theory" (1985), 17 Ottawa L. Rev. 1.

Barron, J. A. "Public Access to the Media Under the Charter: An American Appraisal" in P. Anisman & A. M. Linden, eds., *The Media, the Courts and the Charter* (Toronto: Carswell, 1986) 177.

Baum, D. J. "Public Inquiries, Access and Publication: Lessons from Grange" in P. Anisman & A. M. Linden, eds., *The Media, the Courts and the Charter* (Toronto: Carswell, 1986) 405.

Beckton, C., "Freedom of Expression — Access to the Courts" (1983), 61 Can. Bar Rev. 101.

Beckton, C., "Freedom of Expression (s. 2(b))" in W. S. Tarnopolsky & G.-A. Beaudoin, eds., *The Canadian Charter of Rights and Freedoms: Commentary* (Toronto: Carswell, 1982) 75.

Beckton, C., "Freedom of Expression in Canada — How Free?" (1983), 13 Man. L.J. 583.

Beckton, C., "Freedom of the Press in Canada: Prior Restraints" in P. Anisman & A. M. Linden, eds., *The Media, the Courts and the Charter* (Toronto: Carswell, 1986) 119.

Beckton, C., "Obscenity and Censorship Re-Examined Under the Charter of Rights" (1983), 13 Man. L.J. 351.

Bessner, R., "The Constitutionality of the Group Libel Offences in the Canadian Criminal Code" (1988), 17 Man. L.J. 183.

Binette, A., "La liberté d'expression commerciale" (1987), 28 C. de D. 341.

Borovoy, A. A., "Freedom of Expression: Some Recurring Impediments" in R. S. Abella & M. L. Rothman, eds., *Justice Beyond Orwell* (Montreal: Yvon Blais, 1985) 125.

Boyd, N., "Censorship and Obscenity: Jurisdiction and the Boundaries of Free Expression" (1985), 23 Osgoode Hall L.J. 37.

Braun, S., "Freedom of Expression v. Obscenity Censorship: The Developing Canadian Jurisprudence" (1986), 50 Sask. L. Rev. 39.

Braun, S., "Should Commercial Speech Be Accorded Prima Facie Constitutional Recognition Under the Canadian Charter of Rights and Freedoms" (1986), 18 Ottawa L. Rev. 37.

Braun, S., "Social and Racial Tolerance and Freedom of Expression in a Democratic Society: Friends or Foes? Regina v. Zundel" (1988), 11 Dalhousie L.J. 471.

Cameron, J., "Comment: The Constitutional Domestication of Our Courts — Openness and Publicity in Judicial Proceedings Under the Charter" in P. Anisman & A. M. Linden, eds., *The Media, the Courts and the Charter* (Toronto: Carswell, 1986) 331.

Canada, Law Reform Commission of Canada, *Hate Propaganda* (Ottawa: 1986).

Canada, Law Reform Commission of Canada, *Public and Media Access to the Criminal Process* (Ottawa: 1987).

Cotler, I., "Freedom of Expression" in A. de Mestral et al., eds., *The Limitation of Human Rights in Comparative Constitutional Law* (Cowansville, Que.: Yvon Blais, 1986) 353.

Cotler, I., "Hate Literature" in R. S. Abella & M. L. Rothman, eds., *Justice Beyond Orwell* (Montreal: Yvon Blais, 1985) 117.

Doody, M. R., "Freedom of the Press, the Canadian Charter of Rights and Freedoms and a New Category of Qualified Privilege" (1983), 61 Can. Bar Rev. 124.

Duplé, N., "Les libertés d'opinion et d'expression: nature et limites" (1987), 21 R.J.T. 541.

Elliot, R., "Freedom of Expression and Pornography: The Need for a Structured Approach to Charter Analysis" in J. M. Weiler & R. M. Elliot, eds., *Litigating the Values of a Nation: the Canadian Charter of Rights and Freedoms* (Toronto: Carswell, 1986) 308.

Esson, W. A. "The Judiciary and Freedom of Expression" (1985), 23 U.W.O. L. Rev. 159.

Etherington, B., "Constitutional Law — Charter of Rights and Freedoms, Section

2(b) and 1 — Application of the Charter to the Common Law in Private Litigation — Freedom of Expression — Picketing in Labour Disputes — Retail, Wholesale and Dept. Store Union, Local 580 v. Dolphin Delivery Ltd." (1987), 66 Can. Bar Rev. 818.

Fichaud, J., "Analysis of the Charter and Its Application to Labour Law" (1984), 8 Dalhousie L.J. 402 at 416.

Finkelstein, M., "The Charter and the Control of Content in Broadcast" in N. Finkelstein & B. McL. Rogers, eds., *Charter Issues in Civil Cases* (Toronto: Carswell, 1988) 213.

Finkelstein, M., "Commercial Expression" in N. Finkelstein & B. McL. Rogers, eds., *Charter Issues in Civil Cases* (Toronto: Carswell, 1988) 199.

Finkelstein, N., "Section 1: The Standard for Assessing Restrictive Government Actions and the Charter's Code of Procedure and Evidence" (1983), 9 Queen's L. J. 143.

Gagnon, J.-D., "L'arrêt Dolphin Delivery: la porte est-elle ouverte ou fermée?" (1987), 32 R.D. McGill 924.

Gagnon, J.-D., "Les effets de la Charte canadienne des droits et libertés sur le droit du travail" (1984), 18 R.J.T. 131.

Giles, J., "S. 2(b) — Freedom of Expression" in Continuing Legal Education Society of British Columbia, ed., *Charter of Rights — 1987* (Vancouver: 1987) 2.1.01.

Glasbeek, H.J., "Comment: Entrenchment of Freedom of Speech for the Press-fettering of Freedom of Speech of the People" in P. Anisman & A. M. Linden, eds., *The Media, the Courts and the Charter* (Toronto: Carswell, 1986) 100.

Grant, A., "Criminal Investigation" in P. Anisman & A. M. Linden, eds., *The Media, the Courts and the Charter* (Toronto: Carswell, 1986) 267.

Greenspan, E. L., "Comment: Another Argument Against Television in the Courtroom" in P. Anisman & A. J. Linden, eds., *The Media, the Courts and the Charter* (Toronto: Carswell, 1986) 497.

Harrison, M., "Information, Privacy and the Press" in R. S. Abella & M. L. Rothman, eds., *Justice Beyond Orwell* (Montreal: Yvon Blais, 1985) 189.

Hébert, J.-C., "L'incidence de la Charte canadienne sur l'outrage au tribunal" (1984), 18 R.J.T. 183.

Henry, D. J., "Electronic Public Access to Court: A Proposal for Its Implementation Today" in P. Anisman & A. M. Linden, eds., *The Media, the Courts and the Charter* (Toronto: Carswell, 1986) 441.

Herrndorf, P., "The Media and the Legal System" in R. S. Abella & M. L. Rothman, eds., *Justice Beyond Orwell* (Montreal: Yvon Blais, 1985) 436.

Hughes, P., "Tensions in Canadian Society: The Fraser Committee Report" (1986), 6 Windsor Y.B Access Just. 282.

Hunter, L. A. W., "Comment on Competition Law and the Media" in P. Anisman & A. M. Linden, eds., *The Media, the Courts and the Charter* (Toronto: Carswell, 1986) 285.

Jefferson, J. E., "Loosing the Gag: Free Press and Fair Trial" (1985), 43 U.T. Fac. L. Rev. 100.

Kushner, H., "Election Polls, Freedom of Speech and the Constitution" (1983), 15 Ottawa L. Rev. 515.

Lahey, K. A., "The Charter and Pornography: Toward a Restricted Theory of Constitutionally Protected Expression" in J. M. Weiler & R. M. Elliot, eds., *Litigating the Values of a Nation: the Canadian Charter of Rights and Freedoms* (Toronto: Carswell, 1986) 265.

Latour, S., "La publicité des procès: règle ou exception?" (1985), 19 R.J.T. 107.

Lederman, S. N. *et al.*, "Confidentiality of News Sources" in P. Anisman & A. M. Linden, eds., *The Media, the Courts and the Charter* (Toronto: Carswell, 1986) 227.

Legge, L. L., "Freedom of Expression of Lawyers: The Rules of Professional Conduct" (1985), 23 U.W.O. L. Rev. 165.

Lepofsky, M. D., "Constitutional Right to Attend and Speak About Criminal Court Proceedings — An Emerging Liberty" (1982), 30 C.R. (3d) 87.

Lepofksy, M. D., *Open Justice: The Constitutional Right to Attend and Speak About Criminal Proceedings* (Toronto: Butterworths, 1985).

Lepofsky, M. D., "Section 2(b) of the Charter and Media Coverage of Criminal Court Proceedings" (1983), 34 C.R. (3d) 63.

Linden, A. M., "Limitations on Media Coverage of Legal Proceedings: A Critique and Some Proposals for Reform" in P. Anisman & A. M. Linden, eds., *The Media, the Courts and the Charter* (Toronto: Carswell, 1986) 301.

Lipsett, E. H., "Freedom of Expression and Human Rights Legislation: A Critical Analysis of s. 2 of the Manitoba Human Rights Act" (1983), 12 Man. L.J. 285.

Low, D. M., "Les zones de conflit entre les règles du 'contempt of court' et les droits et libertés garantis par la Charte canadienne des droits et libertés" in D. Turp G.-A. Beaudoin, ed., *Perspectives canadiennes et européennes des droits de la personne* (Cowansville, Que., Yvon Blais, 1986) 543.

MacDonald, M., "Obscenity, Censorship, and Freedom of Expression: Does the Charter Protect Pornography?" (1985), 43 U.T. Fac. L. Rev. 130.

MacKay, A. W., "Freedom of Thought, Belief, Opinion and Expression Including Freedom of the Press and Other Media of Communications and Freedom of Peaceful Assembly: Whose Interests are Protected?" in G.-A. Beaudoin, ed., *Your Clients and the Charter — Liberty and Equality* (Cowansville, Que.: Yvon Blais, 1988) 131.

Mahoney, K. E., "Obscenity and Public Policy: Conflicting Values — Conflicting Statutes" (1986), 50 Sask. L. Rev. 75.

Mahoney, K. E., "Obscenity, Morals and the Law: A Feminist Critique" (1985), 17 Ottawa L. Rev. 33.

Mandel, M., "Freedom of Expression and National Security" (1985), 23 U.W.O. L. Rev. 205.

Manning, M., "Comment: The Lawyers' Public Duty" in P. Anisman & A. M. Linden, eds., *The Media, the Courts and the Charter* (Toronto: Carswell, 1986) 346.

Manson, A., "Freedom of the Press and Juries, Prisons and Prisoners" in P. Anisman & A. M. Linden, eds., *The Media, the Courts and the Charter* (Toronto: Carswell, 1986) 355.

Martin, R., "An Open Legal System" (1986), 23 U.W.O. L. Rev. 169.

Mertl, S. & Ward, J., "Keegstra: The Trial, the Issues, the Consequences" (Saskatoon: Western Producer Prairie Books, 1985).

Moon, R., "Walk But Don't Talk: Soliciting and Freedom of Expression" (1987), 54 C.R. (3d) 85.

Noonan, S., "Pornography: Preferring the Feminist Approach of the British Columbia Court of Appeal to That of the Fraser Committee" (1985), 45 C.R. (3d) 61.

Proulx, M., "Le droit de s'exprimer" in R. S. Abella & M. L. Rothman, eds., *Justice Beyond Orwell* (Montreal: Yvon Blais, 1985) 43.

Regel, A.R., "Hate Propaganda: A Reason to Limit Freedom of Speech" (1984-85), 49 Sask. L. Rev. 303.

Reilly, J. W., "Annotation: R. v. Squires" (1986), 50 C.R. (3d) 321.

Rogers, B. McL., "Freedom of the Press Under the Charter" in N. Finkelstein & B. McL. Rogers, eds., *Charter Issues in Civil Cases* (Toronto, Caraswell, 1988) 171.

Russell J. S., "Discrimination on the Basis of Political Convictions or Beliefs" (1985), 45 R. du B. 377.

Ryan, H.R.S., "The Trial of Zundel, Freedom of Expression and the Criminal Law" (1985), 44 C.R. (3d) 334.

Sack, J., "The Impact of the Charter on Public Sector Employees" in Canadian Bar Association — Ontario, Continuing Legal Education, ed., *The Practical View of the Charter for Solicitors and Barristers* (Toronto: 1986).

Salhany, R. E., *The Origin of Rights* (Toronto: Carswell, 1985) 31.

Sharpe, R. J., "The Charter and Commercial Free Speech" in Canadian Institute for Professional Development, ed., *The Charter and the Corporation: New Vistas for Corporate Rights* (Toronto: 1986) G-1.

Sharpe, R. J., "The Charter and Defamation: Will the Courts Protect the Media?" in P. Anisman & A. M. Linden, eds., *The Media, the Courts and the Charter* (Toronto: Carswell, 1986) 149.

Sharpe, R. J., "Commercial Expression and the Charter" (1987), 37 U.T.L.J. 229.

Stringer. L. E., "The Equal Right of Employers to Freedom of Expression Under the Canadian Charter of Rights and Freedoms" in Canadian Institute for Professional Development, ed., *Equality Rights and Employment: Preparing for Fundamental Change* (Toronto: 1985) E-1.

Thibault, F. "L'étrange paradoxe d'une liberté devenue obligatoire: La Loi 101 sur l'usage exclusif du français dans l'Etat du Québec" (1987), R. du Droit Public 149.

Tremblay, A., "La liberté d'expression au Canada: le cheminement vers le marché libre des idées" in D. Turp & G.-A. Beaudoin, éd., *Perspectives canadiennes et européennes des droits de la personne* (Cowansville, Que.: Yvon Blais, 1986) 281.

Trotter, G. T., "Annotation to R. v. Skinner" (1987), 58 C.R. (3d) 138.

Vogt, E., "Dupond Reconsidered: Or the "Search for the Constitution and the Truth of Things Generally" (1982), U.B.C. L. Rev. (Charter ed.) 141.

Webber, J., "The Limits to Judges' Free Speech: A Comment on the Report of the Committee of Investigation Into the Conduct of the Hon. Mr. Justice Berger" (1984), 29 McGill L.J. 369.

Weiler, J. M., "The Regulation of Strikes and Picketing Under the Charter" in J. M. Weiler & R. M. Elliot, eds., *Litigating the Values of a Nation: the Canadian Charter of Rights and Freedoms* (Toronto: Carswell, 1986) 211.

Woehrling, J., "La réglementation linguistique de l'affichage public et la liberté d'expression: P.G. Québec c. Chaussures Brown's Inc." (1987), 32 R.D. McGill 878.

Section 2(c): Freedom of Peaceful Assembly

Cotler, I., "Freedom of Assembly, Association, Conscience and Religion (s. 2(a), (c) and (d))" in W. S. Tarnopolsky & G.-A. Beaudoin, eds., *The Canadian Charter of Rights and Freedoms: Commentary* (Toronto: Carswell, 1982) 123.

Cotler, I., "Freedom of Expression" in A. de Mestral et al, eds., *The Limitation of Human Rights in Comparative Constitutional Law* (Cowansville, Que: Yvon Blais, 1986) 353 at 362.

Fichaud, J., "Analysis of the Charter and Its Application to Labour Law" (1984), 8 Dalhousie L.J. 402 at 416.

Gagnon, J.-D., "Les effets de la Charte canadienne des droits et libertés sur le droit du travail" (1984), 18 R.J.T. 131.

Hébert, J.-C., "Troubler la paix ou les libertés fondamentales" (1985), 19 R.J.T. 227.

MacNeil, M., "Recent Developments in Canadian Law: Labour Law" (1986), 18 Ottawa L. Rev. 83.

Stoykewych, R., "Street Legal: Constitutional Protection of Public Demonstration in Canada" (1985), 43 U.T. Fac. L. Rev. 90.

Vogt, E., "Dupond Reconsidered: Or the "Search for the Constitution and the Truth of Things Generally" (1982), U.B.C. L. Rev. (Charter ed.) 141.

Weiler, J. M., "The Regulation of Strikes and Picketing Under the Charter" in J. M. Weiler & R. M. Elliot, eds., *Litigating the Values of a Nation: the Canadian Charter of Rights and Freedoms* (Toronto: Carswell, 1986) 211.

Section 2(d): Freedom of Association

Adams, G. W., *Canadian Labour Law: A Comprehensive Text* (Aurora: Canada Law Book, 1985).

Baignet, J, "S. 2(d) — Freedom of Association" in Continuing Legal Education Society of British Columbia, ed., *Charter of Rights — 1987* (Vancouver: 1987) 3.1.01.

Beatty, D. M., *Putting the Charter to Work: Designing Constitutional Labour Code* (Kingston: McGill-Queen's University Press, 1987).

Bendel, M., "La liberté d'association dans l'optique de la Charte canadienne des droits et libertés" in D. Turp & G.-A. Beaudoin, eds., *Perspectives canadiennes et européennes des droits de la personne* (Cowansville, Que.: Yvon Blais, 1984) 321.

Bilson, R. E., "A Workers' Charter: What Do We Mean by Rights?" (1985), 11 Can. Pub. Pol'y 749.

Cavalluzzo, P. J. J., "Freedom of Association and the Right to Bargain Collectively" in J. M. Weiler & R. M. Eliot, eds., *Litigating the Values of a Nation: The Canadian Charter of Rights and Freedoms* (Toronto: Carswell, 1986) 189.

Cotler, I., "Freedom of Assembly, Association, Conscience and Religion (s. 2(a), (c) and (d))" in W.S. Tarnopolsky & G. A. Beaudoin, eds., *The Canadian Charter of Rights and Freedoms* (Toronto: Carswell, 1982) 123.

Dorsey, J. E., "Freedom of Association in Employment, Excluded Employees and the Canadian Charter of Rights and Freedoms" (1983), 41 Advocate 233.

Dorsey, J. E., "Freedom of Association in Employment: Excluded Employees and the Canadian Charter of Rights and Freedoms" in C. England, ed., *Essays in Collective Bargaining and Industrial Democracy* (Don Mills, Ont.: CCH Canadian, 1984) 5.

Edwing, K. D., "Freedom of Association in Canada" (1987), 25 Alta L. Rev. 437.

Etherington, B., "Freedom of Association and Compulsory Union Dues: Towards a Purposive Conception of a Freedom to Not Associate" (1987), 19 Ottawa L. Rev. 1.

Fichaud, J., "Analysis of the Charter and its Application to Labour Law" (1984), 8 Dalhousie L. J. 402.

Fichaud, J., "Analysis of the Charter and its Application to Labour Law" in A. W. MacKay et al., eds., *The Canadian Charter of Rights: Law Practice Revolutionized* (Halifax: Faculty of Law, Dalhousie University, 1982) 217.

Finkelstein, N., "The Supreme Court, the Charter and Labour Relations" in N. Finkelstein & B. McL. Rogers, eds., *Charter Issues in Civil Cases* (Toronto: Carswell, 1986) 95.

Gagnon, J.-D., "L'arrêt Dolphin Delivery: la porte est-elle ouverte ou fermée?" (1987), 32 R.D. McGill 924.

Gagnon, J.-D., "Les effets de la Charte canadienne des droits et libertés sur le droit du travail" (1984), 18 R.J.T. 131.

Gall, P. A., "Freedom of Association and Trade Unions: A Double-Edged

Constitutional Sword" in J. M. Weiler & R. M. Elliot, eds., *Litigating the Values of a Nation: The Canadian Charter of Rights and Freedoms* (Toronto: Carswell, 1986) 245.

Golden, A. E., "The Charter, Union Practices and Collective Bargaining" in The Canadian Institute for Professional Development, ed., *Equality Rights and Employment: Preparing for Fundamental Change* (Toronto: 1985) D-1.

Howse, R., "Dolphin Delivery: The Supreme Court and the Public/Private Distinction in Canadian Constitutional Law" (1988), 46 U.T. Fac. L. Rev. 248.

Lapierre, R., "Les libertés syndicales et les chartes de droits" in Association canadienne-française pour l'avancement des sciences, ed., *La Charte canadienne des droits et libertés et les droits collectifs et sociaux: Communications faites le 26 mai 1983 au 2ième Colloque de l'ACFAS à Trois-Rivières* (Quebec: 1983) 137.

MacNeil, M., "Recent Developments in Canadian Law: Labour Law" (1986), 18 Ottawa L. Rev. 83.

Mitchnick, M. G., *Union Security and the Charter* (Toronto: Butterworths, 1987).

Norman, K., "Freedom of Association" in G.-A. Beaudoin, ed., *Your Clients and the Charter — Liberty and Equality* (Cowansville, Que.: Yvon Blais, 1988) 187.

Riggs, C. G., "The Charter of Rights: It's Impact on Collective Bargaining and Employment Law" in The Canadian Institute for Professional Development, ed., *The Charter and the Corporation: New Vistas for Corporate Rights* (Toronto: 1985) F-1.

Sack, J., "The Impact of the Charter on Public Sector Employees" in Canadian Bar Association — Ontario, Continuing Legal Education, ed., *The Practical View of the Charter for Sollicitors and Barristers* (Toronto: 1986).

Saunders, M. E., "S. 2(d) — Freedom of Association" in Continuing Legal Education Society of British Columbia, ed., *Charter of Rights — 1987* (Vancouver, 1987) 3.2.01.

Slattery, B., "The Charter's Relevance to Private Litigation: Does Dolphin Deliver?" (1987), 32 McGill L.J. 905.

Weiler, J. M., "The Regulation of Strikes and Picketing Under the Charter" in J. M. Weiler & R. M. Elliot, eds., *Litigating the Values of a Nation: The Canadian Charter of Rights and Freedoms* (Toronto: Carswell, 1986) 211.

SECTIONS 3-5: DEMOCRATIC RIGHTS

Beaudoin, G.-A., "The Democratic Rights (ss. 3, 4 and 5)" in W. S. Tarnopolsky & G.-A. Beaudoin, eds., *The Canadian Charter of Rights and Freedoms: Commentary* (Toronto: Carswell, 1982) 213.

Beaudoin, G.-A., "Les droits démocratiques" (1983), 61 R. du B. Can. 151.

Edwards, E. R. A., "S. 3, 4, 5 — Democratic Rights" in Continuing Legal Education Society of British Columbia, ed., *Charter of Rights — 1987* (Vancouver: 1987) 6.1.01.

Manson, A., "Annotation: Badger, Carriere and Lukes v. Attorney General of Manitoba" (1986), 51 C.R. (3d) 164.

Robertson, G. B., *Mental Disability and the Law in Canada* (Toronto: Carswell, 1987).

Ryan, H. R. S., "The Impact of the Canadian Charter of Rights and Freedoms on the Canadian Correctional System", [1983] Can. Hum. Rts Y.B. 99 at 104.

Smith, L., "Charter Equality Rights: Some General Issues and Specific Applications in British Columbia to Elections, Juries and Illegitimacy" (1984), 18 U.B.C. L. Rev. 351 at 376.

Staub, J. I., "Mental Incompetency and Civil Rights: Issues Raised by the Justin Clark and Martyn Humm Cases" (1985), 6 Health L. Can. 3.

SECTION 6: MOBILITY RIGHTS

Arkelian, A. J., "Freedom of Movement of Persons Between States and Entitlement to Passports" (1985), 49 Sask. L. Rev. 15.

Arkelian, A. J. "The Right to a Passport in Canadian Law" (1983), Can. Y.B. Int'l L. 284.

Beadry, R. A. J. "Charter Mobility Rights: Five Years Down the Road" in N. Finkelstein & B. McL. Rogers, eds., *Charter Issues in Civil Cases* (Toronto: Carswell, 1988) 151.

Binavince, E. S., "The Impact of the Mobility Rights: The Canadian Economic Union — A Boom or Bust?" in C. F. Beckton et al., eds., *The Canadian Charter of Rights: Law Practice Revolutionized* (Halifax: Faculty of Law, Dalhousie University, 1982) 269.

Binavince, E. S., "The Impact of the Mobility Rights: The Canadian Economic Union — A Boom or a Bust?" (1982), 14 Ottawa L. Rev. 340.

Blache, P., "Les libertés de circultation des personnes sous la Charte canadienne des droits et libertés" in D. Turp & G.-A. Beaudoin, ed., *Perspectives canadiennes et européennes des droits de la personne* (Cowansville, Que.: Yvon Blais, 1984) 373.

Blache, P., "The Mobility Rights (section 6)" in W.S. Tarnopolsky & G.-A. Beaudoin, eds., *The Canadian Charter of Rights and Freedoms: Commentary* (Toronto: Carswell, 1982) 239.

Brown, D. J. M., "Mobility Rights and Right to Life, Liberty and Security of the Person" in Canadian Institute for Professional Development, ed., *The Charter and the Corporation: New Vistas for Corporate Rights* (Toronto: 1985) C-1.

Finkelstein, N., "A Question of Emphasis: The States Burden in Federal Republic of Germany v. Rauca" (1982), 30 C.R. (3d) 430.

Jackman, M., "Interprovincial Mobility Rights Under the Charter" (1985), 43 U.T. Fac. L. Rev. 16.

Jacquier, C., "La liberté de circulation des étudiants au Canada: une liberté garantie et quasi-absolue" (1985), 16 R.G.D. 512.

Laskin, J. B., "Mobility Rights Under the Charter" (1982), 4 Sup. Ct. L. Rev. 89.

Lewis, C. E., "Unlawful Arrest: A Bow to Jurisdiction of the Court, or *Mala Captus Bene Detentus*? Sidney Jaffe: A Case in Point" (1986), 29 C. L.Q. 341.

Matthews Lemieux, V., "Immigration: A Provincial Concern" (1982), 13 Man. L.J. 111.

Moull, W. D., "Business Law Implications of the Canadian Charter of Rights and Freedoms" (1984), 8 Can. Bus. L.J. 449 at 472.

Narvey, K. M., "Trial in Canada of Nazi War Criminals" (1983), 34 C.R. (3d) 126.

Redmond, J. E., "Charter of Rights and Freedoms — Section 6 — Mobility Rights" in British Columbia Continuing Legal Education Society, ed., *Charter of Rights — 1987* (Vancouver: 1987) 10.1.01.

Richards, J. G., "Professional Associations and the Charter" Canadian Bar Association — Ontario, Continuing Legal Education Department, ed., *The Practical View of the Charter for Solicitors and Barristers* (Toronto: 1986).

Ryan, H. R. S., "The Impact of the Canadian Charter of Rights and Freedoms on the Canadian Correctional System" (1983), Can. Hum. Rts Y.B. 99.

Schmeiser, D. A. & Young, K. J., "Mobility Rights in Canada" (1983), 13 Man. L.J. 615.

SECTION 7: FUNDAMENTAL JUSTICE

Bala, N. & Redfearn, J. D., "Family Law and the 'Liberty Interest': Section 7 of the Canadian Charter of Rights and Freedoms" in K. Connelle-Thouez & B. M. Knoppers, eds., *Contemporary Trends in Family Law: A National Perspective* (Toronto: Carswell, 1984) 243.

Bala, N. & Redfearn, J. D., "Family Law and the 'Liberty Interest': Section 7 of the Canadian Charter of Rights and Freedoms" (1983), 15 Ottawa L. Rev. 274.

Beckton, C. F., "The Impact on Women of Entrenchment of Property Rights in the Canadian Charter of Rights and Freedoms" (1985), 9 Dalhousie L.J. 288.

Boyle, C. L. M., *Sexual Assault* (Toronto: Carswell, 1984) 31.

Brandt, G. J., "Canadian Charter of Rights and Freedoms — Right to Property as an Extension of Personal Security — Status of Undeclared Rights" (1983), 61 Can. Bar Rev. 398.

Brown, D. J. M., "Mobility Rights and Right to Life, Liberty and Security of the Person" in Canadian Institute for Professional Development, ed., *The Charter and the Corporation: New Vistas for Corporate Rights* (Toronto: 1985) C-1.

Brun, H., "Quelques notes sur les articles 1, 2, 7 et 15 de la Charte canadienne des droits et libertés" (1982), 23 C. de D. 781.

Cameron, J. "The Motor Vehicle Reference and the Relevance of American Doctrine in Charter Adjudication" in R. J. Sharpe, ed., *Charter Litigation* (Toronto: Butterworths, 1987) 69.

Carnerie, F., "Euthanasia and Self-Determination: Is There a Charter Right to Die in Canada?" (1987), 32 McGill L.J. 299.

Casswell, D. G., "Case Comment: Singh v. Min. of Employment and Immigration" (1986), 24 Alta. L. Rev. 356.

Chapman, B., "Criminal Law Liability and Fundamental Justice: Toward a Theory of Substantive Judicial Review" (1986), 44 U.T. Fac. L. Rev. 153.

Christian, T. J., "Section 7 and Administrative Law (Part I)" (1987), 3 Admin. L.J. 25.

Christian, T. J., "Section 7 of the Charter of Rights and Freedoms: Constraints on State Action" (1984), 22 Alta. L. Rev. 222.

Churgin, M. J., "The Charter of Rights and Freedoms and the Mental Health System: A Comparison of Law as Written and Law as Applied" (1987), 7 Health L. Can. 100.

Colvin, E., "Blood Samples and the Intoxicated Driver in Saskatchewan" (1984), 48 Sask. L. Rev. 359.

Cumming, T., "Fundamental Justice in the Charter" (1986), 11 Queen's L.J. 134.

De Montigny, Y., "La Charte des droits et libertés, la prérogative royale et les "questions politiques" (1984), 44 R. du B. 156.

Doherty, D. H., "The Charter and Reforming the Law of Evidence" (1987), 58 C.R. (3d) 314.

Doherty, D. H., "'Sparing' the Complaint 'Spoils' the Trial" (1984), 40 C.R. (3d) 55.

Duplé, N., "L'article 7 de la Charte canadienne des droits et libertés et les principes de justice fondamentale" (1984), 25 C. de D. 99.

Elliot, R. M., "Section 7" in Continuing Legal Education Society of British Columbia, ed., *The Canadian Charter of Rights and Freedoms* (Vancouver: 1982).

Fairley, H. S., "Developments in Constitutional Law: The 1984-85 Term" (1986), 8 Sup. Ct. L. Rev. 53 at 71.

Fairweather, R. G. L., "Procedural Fairness: A Challenge for the Canadian Human Rights Commission" (1985), 10 Queen's L.J. 430.

Ferguson, G., The Canadian Charter of Rights and Individual Choice of Treatment" (1988), 8 Health L. Can. 63.

Fleming, J., "Hospital Transfers into Nursing Homes: A Potential Charter Remedy for Unwilling Transferees" (1985), 1 J.L. & Social Pol'y 50.

Foy, P. G., "Section 7: Fundamental Legal Rights" in Continuing Legal Education Society of British Columbia, ed., *Charter of Rights — 1987* (Vancouver: 1987) 5.1.01.

Friedland, M. L., "Criminal Justice and the Charter" (1983), 13 Man. L.J. 549.

Garant, P., "L'article 7 de la Charte — toujours énigmatique après 18 mois de jurisprudence" (1983), 13 Man. L.J. 477.

Garant, P., "Fundamental Freedoms and Natural Justice (Section 7)" in W. S. Tarnopolsky & G.-A. Beaudoin, eds., *The Canadian Charter of Rights and Freedoms: Commentary* (Toronto: Carswell, 1982) 257.

Gerhrke, L., "The Charter and Publicly Assisted Housing" (1985), 1 J.L. & Social Pol'y 17.

Gold, A. D., "Charter of Rights — Contempt of Court — R. v. Cohn (September 18, 1984, Ont. C.A.), R. v. Ayres (September 28, 1984, Ont. C.A.)" (1985), 27 C. L.Q. 26.

Gold, A. D., "Charter of Rights — Fundamental Justice — Hearsay Evidence — R. v. Williams, (1985) 18 C.C.C. (3d) 356, Crim. R. (3d) 351, 50 O.R. (2nd) 321 (C.A.)" (1986), 28 C. L.Q. 154.

Gold, A. D., "Charter of Rights — Fundamental Justice — Reference Re Section 94(2) of the Motor Vehicle Act (1983), 4 C.C.C. (3d) 243, 33 Crim. R. (3d) 22, 147 D.L.R. (3d) 539 (B.C.C.A.)" (1983), 26 C. L.Q. 29.

Gordon, R. M., "The Impact of the Canadian Charter of Rights and Freedoms Upon Canadian Mental Health Law: The Dawn of a New Era or Business as Usual?" (1986), 14 Law, Medicine & Health Care 190.

Grant, I., "Dangerous Offenders" (1985), 9 Dalhousie L.J. 347.

Grant, I. & MacKay, A. W., "Constructive Murder and the Charter: In Search of Principle" (1987), 25 Alta L. Rev. 129.

Grey, J. H., "Comment on Singh v. Minister of Employment and Immigration" (1986), 31 McGill L.J. 496.

Grondin, R., "Une doctrine d'abus de procédure revigorée en droit pénal canadien" (1983), 24 C. de D. 673.

Hébert, J.-C., "Le droit disciplinaire et les garanties juridiques fondamentales" (1987), 21 R.J.T. 125.

Hébert, J.-C., "L'incidence de la Charte canadienne sur l'outrage au tribunal" (1984), 18 R.J.T. 183.

Hogg, P. W., "The Meaning of Fundamental Justice" (1986), 18 C.R.R. 70.

Hughes, P., "Tensions in Canadian Society: The Fraser Committee Report" (1986), 6 Windsor Y.B. Access Just. 282.

Jack, D. H., "Suing the Crown and the Application of the Charter" (1986), 7 Advocates' Q. 277.

Janisch, H. N., "Beyond Jurisdiction: Judicial Review and the Charter of Rights" (1983), 43 R. du B. 401.

Jobson, K. & Atkins, A., "Imprisonment in Default and Fundamental Justice" (1986), 28 Crim. L.Q. 251.

Jodouin, A., "La Charte canadienne des droits et libertés et l'élement moral des infractions" (1983), 61 R. du B. 211.

Johnstone, I., "Section 7 of the Charter and Constitutionally Protected Welfare" (1988), 46 U.T. Fac. L. Rev. 1.

Kaiser, H. A., "Involuntary Psychiatry in Nova Scotia: The Review Board Reports (1979-1983) and Recent Proposals for Legislative Change" (1986), 6 Health L. Can. 81.

Keyserlingk, E. W., "Consent to Treatment — The Principles, the Provincial Statutes and the Charter of Rights and Freedoms" (1985), 33 Canada's Mental Health 8.

Kushner, H. L., "The Right to Reasons in Administrative Law" (1986), 24 Alta. L. Rev. 305.

Landau, B., "The Rights of Minors to Consent to Treatment and the Residential Care" in B. Landau, ed., *Children's Rights in the Practice of Family Law* (Toronto: Carswell, 1986) 93.

Lee, T., "Section 7 of the Charter: An Overview" (1985), 43 U.T. Fac. L. Rev. 1.

Lemieux, D. & Savard, E., "Vers une judiciarisation du conseil des ministres?" (1985), 26 C. de D. 361.

Long, L., "The Abortion Issue: An Overview" (1985), 23 Alta L. Rev. 453.

Lowenberger, L., *et al.*, "Welfare: Women, Poverty and the Charter" (1985), 1 J.L. & Social Pol'y 42.

MacDonald, R. A., "Procedural Due Process in Canadian Law: Natural Justice and Fundamental Justice" (1987), 39 U. Fla. L. Rev. 217.

MacKay, A. W., "Fairness After the Charter: A Rose by Any Other Name?" (1985), 10 Queen's L.J. 263.

MacKay, A. W. & Holgate, M., "Fairness in the Allocation of Housing: Legal and Economic Perspectives" (1983), 7 Dalhousie L.J. 383.

MacLauchlan, H. W., "Of Fundamental Justice, Equality and Society's Outcasts: A Comment on R. v. Tremayne and R. v. McLean" (1986), 32 McGill L.J. 213.

Mallory, J. R., "Beyond 'Manner and Form': Reading Between the Lines in Operation Dismantle Inc. v. R." (1986), 31 McGill L.J. 480.

Mandell, C. C., "Annotation: Jamieson v. Comm'r of Corrections" (1986), 51 C.R. (3d) 156.

Manson, A., "Annotation: Krug v. R." (1986), 48 C.R. (3d) 98.

Manson, A., "Annotation: R. v. Swain" (1986), 50 C.R. (3d) 101.

Marshall, T. D. & Callaghan, J., "Whose Values Govern Canada?" (1986), 28 C. L.Q. 291.

Martin, S. L., "Canada's Abortion Law and the Canadian Charter of Rights and Freedoms" (1986), 1 Can. J.W.L. 339.

Martin, S. L., "R. v. Morgentaler et al." (1985), 1 Can. J.W.L. 194.

Mason, A., "Annotation: R. v. LeGallant" (1985), 47 C.R. (3d) 170.

Monahan, P., "Judicial Review and Democracy: A Theory of Judicial Review (Followed by a commentary by Bernard Siegan & Dialogue)" (1987), 21 U.B.C. L.Rev. 87.

Monahan, P., *Politics and the Constitution: The Charter, Federalism and the Supreme Court of Canada* (Toronto: Carswell, 1987).

Mirgan, D. C., "Controlling Prosecutorial Powers — Judicial Review, Abuse of Process and Section 7 of the Charter" (1987), 29 C. L.Q. 15.

Mossman, M. J., "The Charter and the Right to Legal Aid" (1985), 1 J.L. & Social Pol'y 21.

Mullan, D., "Judicial Deference to Administrative Decision-Making in the Age of the Charter" (1985), 50 Sask. L. Rev. 203.

Neudorfer, A., "Cabinet Decisions and Judicial Review" (1985), 1 Admin. L.J. 30.

Neudorfer, A., "Immigration — The Supreme Court Decision vs. Singh" (1986), 2 Admin. L.J. 17.

O'Connor, F., "The Impact of the Canadian Charter of Rights and Freedoms on Parole in Canada" (1985), 10 Queen's L.J. 336.

O'Connor, F. & Pringle Wright, L., "Mirror, Mirror, on the Prison Wall! How Fair Are We? An Analysis of the Common Law Duty to Act Fairly and the Charter Obligation to Comply with Principles of Fundamental Justice" (1984), 26 C. L.Q. 318.

Ouellette, M., "La Charte canadienne et certains problèmes de bioéthique" (1984), 18 R.J.T. 271.

Ouellette, Y., "La Charte canadienne et les tribunaux administratifs" (1984), 18 R.J.T. 295.

Paciocco, D. M. *Charter Principles and Proof in Criminal Cases* (Toronto: Carswell, 1987) 533.

Petraglia, P., "Confidential and Sufficient Information: Procedural Fairness" (1986), 2 Admin. L.J. 46.

Petraglia, P., "Reasonable Apprehension of Bias in Statutory Schemes — The Case of the Canadian Human Rights Act" (1987), 3 Admin. L.J. 7.

Pratte, S., "La primauté du droit. L'origine du principe et son évolution dans le contexte de la Charte canadienne des droits et libertés" (1986), 27 C. de D. 685.

Rankin, M., & Roman, A. J., "Constitutional Law — A New Basis for Screening Constitutional Questions Under the Canadian Charter of Rights and Freedoms — Prejudging the Evidence?: Operation Dismantle Inc. et al. v. The Queen et al." (1987), 66 Can. Bar Rev. 365.

Rivet, M., "Le droit à la vie ou 'l'hominisation' du XXIe siècle: l'éthique et le droit repondent à la science" in D. Turp & G.-A. Beaudoin, eds., *Perspectives canadiennes et européennes des droits de la personne* (Cowansville, Que.: Yvon Blais, 1986) 445.

Shumiatcher, M. C., " 'I Set Before You Life and Death' (Abortion — Borowski and the Constitution)" (1987), 24 U.W.O.L. Rev. 1.

Stevenson, C. P., "A New Perspective on Environmental Rights After the Charter" (1983), 21 Osgoode Hall L.J. 390.

Stuart, D. & Manson, A., "Ref Re Section 94(2) of Motor Vehicle Act, R.S.B.C. 1979 c. 288" (1986), 48 C.R. (3d) 295.

Tremblay, L., "Section 7 of the Charter: Substantive Due Process?" (1984), 18 U.B.C. L. Rev. 201.

Trotter, G. T., "The Absconding Accused and the Charter: "The Show Must Go On!" (1986), 49 C.R. (3d) 391.

Weatherston, R., "Penitentiary Disciplinary Hearings and the Right to Counsel" (1988), 4 Admin. L.J. 8.

Wellsch, T., "The Right of the Civilly Committed Mental Patient to Refuse Treatment" (1984), 48 Sask. L.Rev. 269.

Whitehall, I. G., "Administrative Tribunals and Section 7 of the Charter" in N. Finkelstein & B. McL. Rogers, eds., *Charter Issues in Civil Cases* (Toronto: Carswell, 1988) 257.

Whitley, S., "The Lieutenant-Governor's Advisory Boards of Review for the Supervision of the Mentally Disordered Offender in Canada: A Call for Change" (1985), 7 Int'l J. Law & Psychiatry 385.

Whyte, J. D., "Annotation: Reference Re Section 94(2) of Motor Vehicle Act, R.S.B.C." (1986), 48 C.R. (3d) 291.

Whyte, J. D., "Fundamental Justice: The Scope and Application of Section 7 of the Charter" (1983), 13 Man. L.J. 455.

Woods, S., "Interrogation Law and the Charter: An American Plan for the Renovation" (1985), 43 U.T. Fac. L. Rev. 153.

Woods, V., "Renovating the Gatehouse" (1984), 49 Sask. L. Rev. 239.

Wright, K. E., "Do You Mind If I Join You? — The Constitutional Validity of Section 520(1) of the Criminal Code" (1986), 28 C. L.Q. 491.

Wydrzynski, C. J., *Canadian Immigration Law and Procedure* (Aurora: Canada Law Book, 1983) 472.

Wydrzynski, C. J., "Immigration Law — Determination of Refugee Status — Charter of Rights and Freedoms, Section 7" (1986), 64 Can. Bar Rev. 172.

SECTION 8: SEARCH AND SEIZURE

Angers, L., "A la recherche d'une protection efficace contre les inspections abusives de l'Etat: la Charte québécoise, la Charte canadienne et le Bill of Rights américain" (1986), 27 C. de D. 723.

Auger, B., "Ce qui est abusif au sens de l'article 8 de la Charte canadienne lors de la recherche de preuves" (1986), 27 C. de D. 965.

Braithwaite, B., "The Effect of Section 8 of the Canadian Charter of Rights and Freedoms on Section 10 of the Narcotic Control Act" (1984), 48 Sask. L. Rev. 231.

Breton, M., "Les mandats de perquisition, la Charte canadienne des droits et libertés et la Commission de reforme du droit du Canada" (1984), 1 Cahiers de l'I.Q.A.I. 108.

Brun, H., "Le recouvrement de l'impôt et les droits de la personne" (1983), 24 C. de D. 457.

Chevrette, F., "Les notions de fouilles, perquisitions et saisies abusives: une interprétation littérale ou téléologique?" (1983), 13 Man. L.J. 573.

Chevrette, F., "Protection Upon Arrest or Detention and Against Retroactive Penal Law (ss. 8, 9, 10(c), 11(e), (g) and (i))" in W. S. Tarnopolsky & G.-A. Beaudoin, eds., *The Canadian Charter of Rights and Freedoms: Commentary* (Toronto: Carswell, 1982) 291.

Chisvin, H., "Case Comment: R. v. Dedman" (1985), 34 M.V.R. 165.

Choquette, M., "Les articles 8, 9 et 10 de la Charte canadienne de droits et libertés" (1984), 25 C. de D. 677.

Cohen, S. A., "Roadside Detentions: ALERT Testing and the Right to Counsel" (1986), 51 C.R. (3d) 34.

Colvin, E., "Blood Samples and the Intoxicated Driver in Saskatchewan" (1984), 48 Sask. L. Rev. 359.

Connelly, P. J., "Charter of Rights and Freedoms — Warrantless Search of Business Premises — Whether Under s. 8 — R. v. Rao (1984) 46 O.R. (2d) 80 (C.A.)" (1984), 26 C. L.Q. 410.

Connelly, P. J., "The Fourth Amendment and Section 8 of the Canadian Charter of Rights and Freedoms: What Has Been Done? What Is to Be Done? (1985), 27 C. L.Q. 182.

Corn, G., "Legality of Search and Seizure and Application of Charter of Rights and Freedoms as to Admissibility of Illegally Obtained Evidence" (1985), 1 Can. Curr. Tax J. 75.

Dambrot, M. R., "Section 8 of the Canadian Charter of Rights and Freedoms" (1982), 26 C.R. (3d) 97.

Dawson, D. F., "Unreasonable Search and Seizure: A Comment on the Supreme Court of Canada Judgmment in Hunter v. Southam Inc." (1985), 27 C.L.Q. 450.

Desy, C. & Novek, B. L., "Impact de la Charte canadienne des droits et libertés sur les pouvoirs de perquisition et de saisie en matière fiscale" (1984), 6 R.P.F.S. 125.

Eherke, W. F., "Privacy and the Charter of Rights" (1985), 43 Advocate 53.

Elman, B. P., "Collins v. The Queen: Further Jurisprudence on Section 24(2) of the Charter" (1987), 25 Alta. L. Rev. 477.

Ewaschuk, E. G., "Search and Seizure: Charter Implications" (1982), 28 C.R. (3d) 153.

Falconer, J., "The ALERT Demand and the Right to Counsel: the Problem With Talbourdet" (1986), 28 C.L.Q. 390.

Finkelstein, N., "Constitutional Law — Search and Seizure After Southam" (1985), 63 Can. Bar Rev. 178.

Fontana, J. A., *The Law of Search and Seizure in Canada*, 2nd ed. (Toronto: Butterworths 1984).

Frankel, S. D., "Unreasonable Search or Seizure" in Continuing Legal Education Society of British Columbia, ed., *Charter of Rights — 1987* (Vancouver: 1987) 9.1.01.

Gold, A. D., "Charter of Rights — Right to Counsel — Breathalyzer — R. v. Therens (1985), 18 C.C.C. (3rd) 481, 45 C.R. (3rd) 97, 18 D.L.R. (4th) 655 (S.C.C.)" (1986), 28 C.L.Q. 152.

Gold, A. D., "Charter of Rights — Search and Seizure — Writs of Assistance

— R. v. Noble (1984) 16 C.C.C. (3rd) 146, 42 C.R. (3rd) 209 (Ont. C.A.)" (1986), 28 C.L.Q. 295.

Gold, A. D., "Charter of Rights — Search and Seizure — Review of Warrant — R. v. Komadowski" (1987), 29 C.L.Q. 288.

Gold, A. D., "Search and Seizure — Wiretaps — Consent to Interceptions" (1988), 30 C.L.Q. 25.

Goldstein, E., "Surreptitious Video Surveillance and the Protection of Privacy" (1987), 56 C.R. (3d) 368.

Goodman, W. D., "The Charter and Taxation" in Canadian Institute for Professional Development, ed., *The Charter and the Corporation: New Vistas for Corporate Rights* (Toronto: 1985) E-1.

Hébert, J.-C., "La perquisition d'un dossier médical" (1986), 46 R. du B. 85.

Kosowan, C. A., "A Commentary on the Law of Search and Seizure As Contemplated in Bill C-18 and the Impact of the Charter of Rights on These Provisions" (1986), 10 Prov. Judges J. 20.

Laskin, J. B. "Investigative and Search Powers in the Regulatory Environment: The Impact of the Charter" in N. Finkelstein & B. McL. Rogers, eds., *Charter Issues in Civil Cases* (Toronto: Carswell, 1988) 237.

Luther, G., "Police Power and the Charter of Rights and Freedoms: Creation or Control?" (1987), 51 Sask. L. Rev. 217.

MacCrimmon, M. T., "Developments in the Law of Evidence: The 1984-85 Term" (1986), 8 Sup. Ct. L. Rev. 249 at 290.

MacKay, A. W., "Students As Second Class Citizens Under the Charter" (1987), 54 C.R. (3d) 390.

MacLean, S. C., "Video Surveillance and the Charter of Rights" (1987), 30 C.L.Q. 88.

McCalla, W., *Search and Seizure in Canada* (Aurora, Ont.: Canada Law Book, 1984).

McKinnon, K. R., "The Charter and Its Possible Impact on the Investigatory Powers Under the Income Tax Act" (1983), 8 Queen's L.J. 274.

Murphy, H. L., "The Charter and Search and Seizure" in Canadian Institute for Professional Development, ed., *The Charter and the Corporation: New Vistas for Corporate Rights* (Toronto: 1986) D-1.

Murray, K., "The 'Reasonable Expectation of Privacy Test' and the Scope of Protection Against Unreasonable Search and Seizure Under Section 8 of the Charter of Rights and Freedoms" (1986), 18 Ottawa L. Rev. 25.

O'Donnell, F. C., "The Thin Blue Line: Customs Searches and the Charter of Rights" (1984), 16 Ottawa L. Rev. 467.

Ouellette, Y., "La Charte canadienne et les tribunaux administratifs" (1984), 18 R.J.T. 295.

Potvin, J., *The Effect of the Canadian Charter of Rights and Freedoms on the Income Tax Act* (Ottawa: Canadian Bar Association, 1983).

Reid, A. D. & Young, A. H., "Administrative Search and Seizure Under the Charter" (1985), 10 Queen L. J. 392.

Roman, A. J., "The Possible Impact of the Canadian Charter of Rights and Freedoms on Administrative Law" (1985), 26 C. de D. 339.

Rosenberg, M., "Unreasonable Search and Seizure: Hunter v. Southam Inc." (1985), 19 U.B.C. L. Rev. 271.

Ruby, C., "Charter of Rights — Search & Seizure — Review of Warrant" (1987), 29 C.L.Q. 288.

Salhany, R. E., *The Origin of Rights* (Toronto: Carswell, 1985).

Segal, M. D., "The Impact of R. v. Therens on Various Forms of State Constraint" (1986), 38 M.V.R. 71.

Segal, M. D. & Rosenberg, M., "Bill C-18 Drinking and Driving Amendments" (1986), 35 M.V.R. 21.

Solomon, R., "Drug Enforcement Powers and the Canadian Charter of Rights and Freedoms" (1983), 21 U.W.O. L. Rev. 219.

Thomas, R. B., "Search and Seizure and the Charter. Comment on Kruger Inc. v. M.N.R. (1983) C.T.C. 319 (Fed. T. D.) and New Garden Restaurant and Tavern Ltd. v. M.N.R. (1983) C.T.C. 332 (Ont. H.C.)" (1983), 31 Can. Tax J. 805.

Thomas, R. B., "Search and Seizure and the Charter of Rights" (1984) 32 Can. Tax J. 1117.

Thomas, R. B., "Search and Seizure and the Charter of Rights and Freedoms. Comment on Southam Inc. v. Dir. of Investigation and Research of the Combines Investigation Branch" (1983), 31 Can. Tax J. 676.

Thomson, K. E., "Limiting the Search and Seizure Powers of Combines Investigators: The Southam Decision and its Aftermath" (1985), 10 Can. Bus. L.J. 55.

Ward, R. W., "Search, Seizure and the Canadian Charter of Rights" (1986), 15 Anglo-Am. L. Rev. 37.

Welsh, K., "Breathalyzer, Detention, and the Right to Counsel: R. v. Therens" (1985), 23 Alta. L. Rev. 524.

SECTIONS 9-10: DETAINED/ARRESTED PERSONS' RIGHTS

Bolton, M., "Fallout From R. v. Therens: The B.C.C.A. decision in Rodenbush" (1985), 7 Crim. Lawyers' Assoc. Newsletter 7.

Chevrette, F., "Protection Upon Arrest or Detention and Against Retroactive Penal Law (ss. 8, 9, 10(c), 11(e), (g) and (i))" in W. S. Tarnopolsky & G.-A. Beaudoin, eds., *The Canadian Charter of Rights and Freedoms: Commentary* (Toronto: Carswell, 1982) 291.

Choquette, M., "Les articles 8, 9 et 10 de la Charte canadienne des droits et libertés" (1984), 25 C. de D. 677.

Cohen, S. A., "Controversies in Need of Resolution: Some Threshold Questions Affecting Individual Rights and Police Under the Charter" (1984), 16 Ottawa L. Rev. 97.

Cohen, S. A., "The Impact of Charter Decisions on Police Behaviour" (1984), 39 C.R. (3d) 264.

Coughlan, S., "Police Detention for Questioning: A Proposal" (1985), 28 C.L.Q. 64 & 170.

Edinger, E. R., "Human Rights Tribunals and the R.C.M.P. — Constitutional Principles Confirmed or Confused: Scowby v. Glendinning" (1987), 21 U.B.C.L. Rev. 449.

Frankel, S. D., "Arbitrary Detention or Imprisonment" in Continuing Legal Education Society of British Columbia, ed., *Charter of Rights — 1987* (Vancouver: 1987) 9.2.01.

Gold, A. D., "Charter of Rights — Arbitrary Detention — R. v. Duguay, Murphy and Sevigny (1985), 18 C.C.C. (3rd) 289, 50 O.R. (2nd) 375 (C.A.) MacKinnon ACJO, Martin and Zuber JJ.A." (1985), 28 C.L.Q. 17.

Goreham, R. A., "Canadian Charter of Rights and Freedoms — Criminal Procedure — Retrospective Effect" (1983), 61 Can. Bar Rev. 413.

Grondin, R., "La notion de détention dans la Charte canadienne des droits et libertés" (1985), 16 R.G.D. 665.

Klinck, D. R., "The Quest for Meaning in Charter Adjudication: Comment on R. v. Therens" (1985), 31 McGill L.J. 104.

Luther, G., "Police Power and the Charter of Rights and Freedoms: Creation or Control?" (1987), 51 Sask. L. Rev. 217.

Manson, A., "Annotation: R. v. Swain" (1986), 50 C.R. (3d) 101.

Ratushny, E., "Emerging Issues in Relation to the Legal Rights of a Suspect Under the Canadian Charter of Rights and Freedoms" (1983), 61 Can. Bar Rev. 177.

Salhany, R. E., *The Origin of Rights* (Toronto: Carswell, 1985) 57, 85.

Segal, M. D., "Detention and the Right to Counsel" (1985), 29 M.V.R. 176.

Welsh, K., "Breathalyzer, Detention and the Right to Counsel: R. v. Therens" (1985), 23 Alta. L. Rev. 524.

Woods, S., "Renovating the Gatehouse" (1984), 40 Sask. L.R. 239 at 260.

Ziskrout, J. D., "Arrest and Right to Counsel" in Continuing Legal Education Society British Columbia, ed., *The Canadian Charter of Rights and Freedoms* (Vancouver: 1982).

Ziskrout, J. D., "Section 10 of the Canadian Charter of Rights and Freedoms", [1982] U.B.C. L. Rev. (Charter ed.) 173.

Section 10(b): Right to Counsel

Code, M., "Rights in the Criminal Process as They Affect Regulatory or Quasi-Criminal Proceedings" in N. Finkelstein & B. MacL. Rogers, eds., *Charter Issues in Civil Cases* (Toronto: Carswell, 1988) 279.

Cohen S. A., "Roadside Detentions: ALERT Testing and the Right to Counsel" (1986), 51 C.R. (3d) 34.

Conway, R., "The Right to Counsel and the Admissibility of Evidence" (1985), 28 C.L.Q. 28.

Delisle, R. J., "Annotation to Clarkson v. R." (1986), 50 C.R. (3d) 290.

Duncan, B., "Clarkson: Some Unanswered Questions" (1986), 50 C.R. (3d) 305.

Elman, B. P., "The Right to Counsel Denied: Recent Cases on Section 10(b) of the Charter" (1984), 22 Alta. L. Rev. 501.

Epstein, M. H., "The Guiding Hand of Counsel: The Charter and the Right to Counsel on Appeal" (1988), 30 C.L.Q. 35.

Falconer, J., "The ALERT Demand and the Right to Counsel: the Problem with Talbourdet" (1986), 28 C.L.Q. 390.

Garneau, G. S., "The Application of Charter Rights to the Interrogation Process" (1986), 35 U.N.B.L.J. 35.

Gold, A. D., "Annotation to R. v. Therens" (1986), 28 C.L.Q. 152.

Huppé, L., "La renonciation de l'individu aux droits et libertées que lui garantit la Charte canadienne des droits et libertés" (1986), 46 R. du B. 684.

Jull, K., "Clarkson v. R.: Do We Need a Legal Emergency Department?" (1987), 32 McGill L.J. 359.

Klinck, D. R., "The Quest for Meaning in Charter Adjudication: Comment on R. v. Therens" (1985), 31 McGill L.J. 104.

Libman, R., "On the Road Back to Therens: Case Comment on R. v. Seo" (1986), 38 M.V.R. 199.

Michslyshyn, P. B., "The Charter Right to Counsel: Beyond Miranda" (1987), 25 Alta. L. Rev. 190.

Mossman, M. J., "The Charter and the Right to Legal Aid" (1985) 1 J.L. & Social Pol'y 21.

O'Connor, F., "The Impact of the Canadian Charter of Rights and Freedoms on Parole in Canada" (1985), 10 Queen's L.J. 336.

Paciocco, D. M., *Charter Principles and Proof in Criminal Cases* (Toronto: Carswell, 1987).

Paciocco, D. M., "The Development of Miranda-Like Doctrines Under the Charter" (1987), 19 Ottawa L. Rev. 49.

Peck, R. C., "Section 10(b) of the Canadian Charter of Rights and Freedoms: New Vistas" (1987), 45 Advocates' Q. 31.

Ryan, C. A., "Evidence: s. 10(b) of the Charter: The Right to Retain and Instruct Counsel" in Continuing Legal Education Society of British Columbia, ed., *Charter of Rights — 1987* (Vancouver: 1987) 9.3.01.

Salhany, R.E., *The Origin of Rights* (Toronto: Carswell, 1985).

Segal, M. D., "Detention and the Right to Counsel" (1985), 29 M.V.R. 176.

Segal, M. D., "The Impact of R. v. Therens on Various Forms of State Constraint" (1986), 38 M.V.R. 71.

Stuart, D., "The Charter Right to Counsel: A Status Report" (1987), 58 C.R. (3d) 108.

Weatherston, R., "Penitentiary Disciplinary Hearings and the Right to Counsel" (1988), 4 Admin. L.J. 8.

Welsh, K., "Breathalyzer, Detention, and the Right to Counsel: R. v. Therens" (1985), 23 Alta. L.Rev. 524.

Woods, S., "Interrogation Law and the Charter: an American Plan for the Renovation" (1985), 43 U.T. Fac. L. Rev. 153.

Ziskrout, J. D., "Section 10 of the Canadian Charter of Rights and Freedoms", [1982] 2 U.B.C. L. Rev. (Charter ed.) 173.

SECTION 11: RIGHTS OF THE PERSON CHARGED WITH AN OFFENCE
General Considerations

Bala, N., "The Young Offenders Act: A New Era in Juvenile Justice?" in B. Landau, ed., *Children's Rights in the Practice of Family Law* (Toronto: Carswell, 1986) 238.

Barton, P. G., "Developments in Criminal Procedure: The 1984-85 Term" (1986), 8 Sup. Ct. L. Rev. 195.

Bellemare, D. A., "Quelques réflexions sur le procès du jeune contrevenant" (1984), 44 R. du B. 186.

Braun, S., "Judicial Apprehension of Violation of Legal Rights Under the Canadian Charter of Rights and Freedoms: Towards a Framework of Analysis" (1987), 24 U.W.O.L. Rev. 27.

Breen, T. & Farrell, N., "Production Powers Survive the Charter" (1987), 55 C.R. (3d) 33.

Burns, P. T., "The Canadian Charter of Rights and Freedoms: Rights of Persons Charged" in Continuing Legal Education Society of British Columbia, ed., *The Canadian Charter of Rights and Freedoms* (Vancouver: 1982).

Chevrette, F., "Protection Upon Arrest or Detention and Against Retroactive Penal Law (ss. 8, 9, 10(c), 11(e), (g) and (i)" in W. S. Tarnopolsky & G.-A. Beaudoin, eds., *The Canadian Charter of Rights and Freedoms: Commentary* (Toronto: Carswell, 1982) 291.

Coté-Harper, G., "La Charte canadienne des droits et libertés: Les garanties juridiques et la Charte" in Barreau du Québec, Formation permanente, ed., *La Charte canadienne des droits et libertés* (Montreal: 1982) 93.

Friedland, M. L., "Criminal Justice and the Charter" (1983), 13 Man. L.J. 549.

Friedland, M. L., "Legal Rights Under the Charter" (1982), 24 C.L.Q. 430.

Gertner, E., "The Scope of the Charter: Who is a 'Person Charged With an Offence'" (1984), 5 C.R.R. 129.

Gold, A. D., "The Legal Rights Provisions — A New Vision or Déjà Vu?" (1982), 4 Sup. Ct. L. Rev. 107.

Grondin, R., "Une doctrine d'abus de procédure revigorée en droit pénal canadien" (1983), 24 C. de. D. 673.

Hébert, J.-C., "Le droit disciplinaire et les garanties juridiques fondamentales" (1987), 21 R.J.T. 125.

Hébert, J.-C., "L'incidence de la Charte canadienne sur l'outrage au tribunal" (1984), 18 R.J.T. 183.

Hunter, I. A., "Legal Rights, the Charter and the Ontario Human Rights Code" (1985), 6 Advocates' Q. 160.

Kushner, H. L., "Charter of Rights and Freedoms, Section 11 — Disciplinary Hearings Before Statutory Tribunals" (1984), 62 Can. Bar Rev. 638.

Laprade, B., "Les garanties juridiques et la réparation appropriée en vertu de la Charte canadienne des droits et libertés" in Barreau du Québec, Formation permanente, ed., *L'interaction des chartes canadienne et québecoise des droits et libertés* (Montreal: 1984) 43.

MacKay, A. W., "Fairness After the Charter: A Rose by Any Other Name?" (1985), 10 Queen's L.J. 263.

McDonald, D. C., *Legal Rights in the Canadian Charter of Rights and Freedoms: A Manual of Issues and Sources* (Toronto: Carswell, 1982).

Mitchnick, M. G., "Some Aspects of Practice and Procedure Before the Ontario Labour Relations Board" (1985), 6 Advocate's Q. 201.

Morel, A. "Certain Guarantees of Criminal Procedure (ss. 11(b), (f), (h), 12 and 14)" in W. S. Tarnopolsky & G.-A. Beaudoin, eds., *The Canadian Charter of Rights and Freedoms: Commentary* (Toronto: Carswell, 1982) 367.

Mossman, M. J., "The Charter and the Right to Legal Aid" (1985), 1 J.L. & Social Pol'y 21.

Narvey, K. M, "Trial in Canada of Nazi War Criminals" (1983), 34 C.R. (3d) 126.

O'Connor, F., "The Impact of the Canadian Charter of Rights and Freedoms on Parole in Canada" (1985), 10 Queen's L.J. 336.

Paciocco, D. M., *Charter Principles and Proof in Criminal Cases* (Toronto: Carswell, 1987).

Peck, R. C., "Sections 11, 12 and 13 of the Charter — Recent Cases" in Continuing Legal Education Society of British Columbia, ed., *Charter of Rights — 1987* (Vancouver: 1987) 9.6.01.

Ratushny, E., "The Role of the Accused in the Criminal Process (ss. 10(a) and (b), 11(a), (c), and (d), and 13)" in W. S. Tarnopolsky & G.-A. Beaudoin, eds., *The Canadian Charter of Rights and Freedoms: Commentary* (Toronto: Carswell, 1982) 335.

Varcoe, J. B., "Learning Disabilities and the Court" (1986), 44 Advocate 385.

Whitley, S., "The Lieutenant-Governor's Advisory Boards of Review for the Supervision of the Mentally Disordered Offender in Canada: A Call for Change" (1985), 7 Int'l J. L. & Psychiatry 385.

Section 11(b): Trial Within a Reasonable Time

Doherty, D. H., "Boron: Is Pre-Charge Delay Relevant in Determining Whether s. 11(b) Has Been Infringed?" (1984), 36 C.R. (3d) 338.

Doherty, D. H., "Putting Flesh on the Bones: Judicial Interpretation of Section 11(b) of the Canadian Charter of Rights and Freedoms" in Canadian Bar

Association — Ontario, ed., *Recent Developments in Criminal Law* (Toronto: 1983).

Garton, G., "Re Canadian Charter of Rights and Freedoms, s. 11(b): The Relevance of Pre-Charge Delay in Assessing the Right to Trial Within a Reasonable Time" (1984), 40 Nfld & P.E.I. R. 177.

Gold, A. D., "Charter — Pre-Charge Delay — R. v. Young (June 27, 1984, Ont C.A.)" (1984), 26 C.L.Q. 408.

Johnson, H. R., "Antoine: A Too Cautious Approach to Interpreting Unreasonable Delay" (1983), 34 C.R. (3d) 134.

Manson, A. & Stuart, D., "Annotation: Mills v. R." (1986), 52 C.R. (3d) 5.

Morel, A., "Certain Guarantees of Criminal Procedure (ss. 11(b), (f), (h), 12 and 14)" in W. S. Tarnopolsky & G.-A. Beaudoin, eds., *The Canadian Charter of Rights and Freedoms: Commentary* (Toronto: Carswell, 1982) 367.

Section 11(c): Compellability to Witness

Breen, T. & Farrell, N., "Production Powers Survive the Charter" (1987), 55 C.R. (3d) 33.

Morton, J. C. & Hutchison, S. C., *The Presumption of Innocence* (Toronto: Carswell, 1987).

Paciocco, D. M., *Charter Principles and Proof in Criminal Cases* (Toronto: Carswell, 1987) 479.

Ratushny, E., "The Role of the Accused in the Criminal Process (ss. 10(a) and (b), 11(a), (c), and (d), and 13)" in W. S. Tarnopolsky & G.-A. Beaudoin, eds., *The Canadian Charter of Rights and Freedoms: Commentary* (Toronto: Carswell, 1982) 335.

Whittlen, A., "The Privilege Against Self-Incrimination" (1987), 29 C.L.Q. 66.

Woods, S., "Renovating the Gatehouse" (1985), 49 Sask. L. Rev. 239 at 267.

Section 11(d): Fair Trial

Casswell, D. G., "Case Comment: Singh v. Minister of Employment and Immigration" (1986), 24 Alta. L. Rev. 356.

Connelly, P. J., "Relief Under the Charter and the Prerogative Remedies — Re Krakowski and The Queen (1983), 41 O.R. (2d) 321 (C.A.)" (1983), 26 C.L.Q. 35.

Doherty, D. H., "'Sparing' the Complaint 'Spoils' the Trial" (1984), 40 C.R. (3d) 55.

Gold, A. D., "Charter of Rights — Fundamental Justice — Hearsay Evidence — R. v. Williams (1985), 18 C.C.C. (3rd) 356, 44 C.R. (3rd) 351, 50 O.R. (2nd) 321 (C.A.)" (1986), 28 C.L.Q. 154.

Grey, J. H., "Comment on Singh v. Minister of Employment and Immigration" (1986), 31 McGill L.J. 496.

Manson, A., "Annotation: R. v. Swain" (1986), 50 C.R. (3d) 101.

Mason, A., "Annotation: R. v. LeGallant" (1985), 47 C.R. (3d) 170.

Neudorfer, A., "Immigration — The Supreme Court Decision vs. Singh" (1986), 2 Admin. L.J. 17.

Ratushny, E., "The Role of the Accused in the Criminal Process (ss. 10(a) and (b), 11(a), (c), and (d), and 13)" in W. S. Tarnopolsky & G.-A. Beaudoin, eds., *The Canadian Charter of Rights and Freedoms: Commentary* (Toronto: Carswell, 1982) 335.

Trotter, G. T., "The Absconding Accused and the Charter: 'The Show Must Go On!'" (1986), 49 C.R. (3d) 391.

Wellsch, T., "The Right of the Civilly Committed Mental Patient to Refuse Treatment" (1984), 48 Sask. L. Rev. 269.

Wright, K. E. "Do You Mind if I Join You? — The Constitutional Validity of Section 520(1) of the Criminal Code" (1986), 28 C.L.Q. 491.

Presumption of Innocence

Appelt, A. G., "R. v. Shelley — A New Meaning for the Presumption of Innocence" (1982), 12 Man. L.J. 233.

Cromwell, T. A., "Annotation: R. v. Burge" (1987), 55 C.R. (3d) 131.

Cromwell, T. A. & MacKay, A. W., "Oakes in the Supreme Court: a Cautious Initiative Unimpeded by Old Ghosts" (1986), 50 C.R. (3d) 34.

Doherty, D. H., "The Charter and Reforming the Law of Evidence" (1987), 58 C.R. (3d) 314.

Finley, D., "The Presumption of Innocence and Guilt: Why Carroll Should Prevail Over Oakes" (1984), 39 C.R. (3d) 115.

Gold, A. D., "Charter Defences — House-Breaking Tools — Lawful Excuse — R. v. Holmes (1983), 32 C.R. (3d) 322, 145 D.L.R. (3d) 689 (C.A.)" (1983), 26 C.L.Q. 39.

Gold, A. D., "The Charter of Rights and Its Impact on the Law of Evidence in Criminal Cases" in *Special Lectures of the Law Society of Upper Canada 1984: Law in Transition — Evidence* (Toronto: Richard De Boo, 1984) 87.

Grant, I. & MacKay, A. W., "Constructive Murder and the Charter: In Search of Principle" (1987), 25 Alta. L. Rev. 129.

MacKay, A. W. & Cromwell, T. A., "Oakes: A Bold Initiative Impeded by Old Ghosts" (1983), 32 C.R. (3d) 221.

Morton, J. C. & Hutchison, S. C., *The Presumption of Innocence* (Toronto: Carswell, 1987).

Rosenberg, M., "The Charter: Presumptions and the Duty on the Prosecution to Provide Evidence to the Defence" (1985), 31 M.V.R. 181.

Stuart, D., "Oakes is Not Enough" (1985), 43 C.R. (3d) 315.

Stuart, D., "Presuming Innocence: Why Compromise?" (1983), 32 C.R. (3d) 334.

Public Trial

Anisman, P. & Linden, A. M., eds., *The Media, the Courts and the Charter* (Toronto: Carswell, 1986).

Beckton, C. F., "Freedom of Expression — Access to the Courts" (1983), 61 Can. Bar Rev. 101.

Canada, Law Reform Commission, *Public and Media Access to the Criminal Process* (Ottawa: 1987).

Grant, A., "Criminal Investigation" in P. Anisman & A. M. Linden, eds., *The Media, the Courts and the Charter* (Toronto: Carswell, 1985) 267.

Henry, D. J., "Electronic Public Access to Court: A Proposal for Its Implementation Today" in P. Anisman & A. M. Linden, eds., *The Media, the Courts and the Charter* (Toronto: Carswell, 1985) 441.

Herrndorf, P., "The Media and the Legal System" in R. S. Abella & M. L. Rothman, eds., *Justice Beyond Orwell* (Montreal: Yvon Blais, 1985) 436.

Jefferson, J. E., "Loosing the Gag: Free Press and Fair Trial" (1985), 43 U.T. Fac. L. Rev. 100.

Latour, S., "La publicité des procès: règle ou exception?" (1985) 19 R.J.T. 107.

Lepofsky, D., *Open Justice: The Constitutional Right to Attend and Speak About Criminal Proceedings* (Toronto: Butterworths, 1985).

Lepofsky, M. D., "Constitutional Right to Attend and Speak About Criminal Court Proceedings — An Emerging Liberty" (1982), 30 C.R. (3d) 87.

Lepofsky, M. D., "Section 2(b) of the Charter and Media Coverage of Criminal Court Proceedings" (1983), 34 C.R. (3d) 63.

Linden, A. M., "Limitations on Media Coverage of Legal Proceedings: A Critique and Some Proposals for Reform" in P. Anisman & A. M. Linden, eds., *The Media, the Courts and the Charter* (Toronto: Carswell, 1985) 301.

Low, D. M., "Les zones de conflit entre les règles du 'contempt of court' et droits et libertés garantis par la Charte canadienne des droits et libertés" in D. Turp & G.-A. Beaudoin, eds., *Perspectives canadiennes et européennes des droits de la personne* (Cowansville, Qué.: Yvon Blais, 1986) 543.

MacKay, A. W., "Courts, Cameras and Fair Trials: Confrontation or Collaboration?" (1985), 8 Prov. Judges J. 7.

Manson, A., "Freedom of the Press and Juries, Prisons and Prisoners" in P. Anisman & A. M. Linden, eds., *The Media, the Courts and the Charter* (Toronto: Carswell, 1985) 355.

McDonald, D. C., "Privacy and the Criminal Process" in R. S. Abella & M. L. Rothman, eds., *Justice Beyond Orwell* (Montreal: Yvon Blais, 1985) 193.

Reilly, J. W., "Annotation: R. v. Squires" (1986), 50 C.R. (3d) 321.

Independent Tribunal

Colvin, E., "The Executive and the Independence of the Judiciary" (1987), 51 Sask. L. Rev. 229.

Gold, A. D. "Charter — Court of Competent Jurisdiction" (1986), 28 C.L.Q. 440.

Pépin, G., "L'indépendence judiciaire — l'article 11(d) de la Charte canadienne — une source d'inquiétude particulièrement pour les juges des cours inférieures et une source d'interrogation pour les membres des tribunaux administratifs" (1986), 64 R. du B. Can. 550.

Petraglia, P., "Reasonable Apprehension of Bias in Statutory Schemes — The Case of the Canadian Human Rights Act" (1987), 3 Admin. L.J. 7.

Section 11(e): Bail

Chevrette, F. "Protection Upon Arrest or Detention and Against Retroactive Penal Law (ss. 8, 9, 10(c), 11(e), (g) and (i))" in W. S. Tarnopolsky & G.-A. Beaudoin, eds., *The Canadian Charter of Rights and Freedoms: Commentary* (Toronto: Carswell, 1982) 291.

Del Buono, V., "Bail Under the Canadian Charter of Rights and Freedoms" in V. Del Buono, ed., *Criminal Procedure in Canada* (Toronto: Butterworths, 1982) 169.

Peltomaa, A., "Bail Hearings and the Charter of Rights and Freedoms" (1982), 24 C.L.Q. 427.

Section 11(f): Jury Trial

Bala, N., "Jury Trials for Juveniles? No Charter Right" (1984), 37 C.R. (3d) 30.

Morel, A., "Certain Guarantees of Criminal Procedure (ss. 11(b), (f), (h), 12 and 14)" in W. S. Tarnopolsky & G.-A. Beaudoin, eds., *The Canadian Charter of Rights and Freedoms: Commentary* (Toronto: Carswell, 1982) 367.

Smith, L., "Charter Equality Rights: Some General Issues and Specific Applications in British Columbia to Elections, Juries and Illegitimacy" (1984), 18 U.B.C. L. Rev. 351.

Section 11(h): Double Jeopardy

Hill, J. L., "Knockaert: Double Jeopardy and the Prison Disciplinary System" (1987), 55 C.R. (3d) 189.

Ryan, H. R. S., "The Impact of the Canadian Charter of Rights and Freedoms on the Canadian Correctional System" (1983), Can. Hum. Rts Y.B. 99 at 146.

Section 11(i): Benefit of A Lesser Punishment

Chevrette, F. "Protection Upon Arrest or Detention and Against Retroactive Penal Law (ss. 8, 9, 10(c), 11(e), (g) and (i))" in W. S. Tarnopolsky & G.-A. Beaudoin, eds., *The Canadian Charter of Rights and Freedoms: Commentary* (Toronto: Carswell, 1982) 291.

Opsahl, T. & de Zayas, A., "The Uncertain Scope of Article 15(1) of the International Covenant on Civil and Political Rights" (1983), Can. Hum. Rts Y.B. 237.

Ryan, H. R. S., "The Impact of the Canadian Charter of Rights and Freedoms on the Canadian Correctional System" (1983), Can. Hum. Rts Y.B. 99 at 144.

SECTION 12: CRUEL AND UNUSUAL TREATMENT

Carnerie, F., "Euthanasia and Self-Determination: Is There a Charter Right to Die in Canada?" (1987), 32 McGill L.J. 299.

Gordon, R. M., "The Impact of the Canadian Charter of Rights and Freedoms

Upon Canadian Mental Health Law: The Dawn of a New Era or Business as Usual?" (1986), 14 Law, Medicine and Health Care 190.

Jackson, M., "The Canadian Charter of Rights and Freedoms: Cruel or Unusual Treatment or Punishment?" in Continuing Legal Education Society of British Columbia, ed., *Canadian Charter of Rights and Freedoms* (Vancouver: 1982).

Jackson, M., "Cruel and Unusual Treatment or Punishment?" [1982] U.B.C. L. Rev. (Charter ed.) 189.

Manson, A., "Annotation: R. v. Swain" (1986), 50 C.R. (3d) 101.

Manson, A., "Answering Some Questions About Cruel and Unusual Punishment" (1987), 58 C.R. (3d) 247.

Manson, A., "Fresh Approaches to Defining Cruel and Unusual Treatment or Punishment" (1983), 35 C.R. (3d) 262.

Martin, S. L., "Canada's Abortion Law and the Canadian Charter of Rights and Freedoms" (1986), 1 Can. J.W.L. 339.

Morel, A., "Certain Guarantees of Criminal Procedure (ss. 11(b), (f), (h), 12 and 14)" in W. S. Tarnopolsky & G. A. Beaudoin, eds., *The Canadian Charter of Rights and Freedoms: Commentary* (Toronto: Carswell, 1982) 367.

Ouellette, M., "La Charte canadienne et certains problèmes de bioéthique" (1987), 1 Assurances 90.

Ouellette, M., "La Charte canadienne et certains problèmes de bioéthique" (1984), 18 R.J.T. 271.

Peck, R. C. C., "Sections 11, 12 and 13 of the Charter — Recent Cases" in Continuing Legal Education Society of British Columbia, ed., *Charter of Rights — 1987* (Vancouver: 1987) 9.6.01.

Robertson, G. B., *Mental Disability and the Law in Canada* (Toronto: Carswell, 1987).

Russell, P., "Cruel and Unusual Treatment or Punishment: The Use of Section 12 in Prison Litigation" (1985), 43 U.T. Fac. L. Rev. 185.

Ryan, H. R., "The Impact of the Canadian Charter of Rights and Freedoms on the Canadian Correctional System", [1983] Can. Hum. Rts Y.B. 99 at 149.

Shumiatcher, M. C., "I Set Before You Life and Death" (1987), 24 U.W.O.L. Rev. 1.

Wellsch, T., "The Right of the Civilly Committed Mental Patient to Refuse Treatment" (1984), 48 Sask. L. Rev. 269.

Woods, S., "Renovating the Gatehouse" (1985), 49 Sask. L. Rev. 239.

SECTION 13: SELF-INCRIMINATION

Arbour, L., "Annotation: Dubois v. R." (1986), 48 C.R. (3d) 194.

Doherty, D. H., "Annotation: Dubois v. R. (1986), 48 C.R. (3d) 196.

Hébert, J.-C., "Les aléas du privilège de non-incrimination depuis la Charte" (1984), 44 R. du B. 200.

Hébert, J.-C., "Droit criminel — élargissement de la protection contre l'auto-incrimination?" (1986), 46 R. du B. 574.

Hébert, J.-C., "Le droit disciplinaire et les garanties juridiques fondamentales" (1987), 21 R.J.T. 125.

Maczko, F., "Charter of Rights: Section 13", [1982] U.B.C. L. Rev. (Charter ed.) 213.

Morton, J. C. & Hutchison, S. C., *The Presumption of Innocence* (Toronto: Carswell, 1987).

Paciocco, D. M., *Charter Principles and Proof in Criminal Cases* (Toronto: Carswell, 1987).

Peck, R. C. C., "Sections 11, 12 and 13 of the Charter — Recent Cases" in Continuing Legal Education Society of British Columbia, ed., *Charter of Rights — 1987* (Vancouver: 1987) 9.6.01.

Ratushny, E., "The Role of the Accused in the Criminal Process (ss. 10(a) and (b), 11(a), (c), and (d), and 13)" in W. S. Tarnopolsky & G.A. Beaudoin, eds., *The Canadian Charter of Rights and Freedoms: Commentary* (Toronto: Carswell, 1982) 335.

Salhany, R. E., *The Origin of Rights* (Toronto: Carswell, 1985) 91.

Whittlen, A., "The Privilege Against Self-Incrimination" (1987), 29 C.L.Q. 66.

Woods, S., "Interrogation Law and the Charter: An American Plan for the Renovation" (1985), 43 U.T. Fac. L. Rev. 153.

Wydrzynski, C. J., *Canadian Immigration Law and Procedure* (Aurora: Canada Law Book, 1983).

SECTION 14: RIGHT TO AN INTERPRETER

Abella, R. S., *Access to Legal Services by the Disabled* (Toronto: Queen's Printer for Ontario, 1983) 110.

Algee, A. M., "Les mécanismes de la pratique du droit en langue minoritaire au Canada: une solution pour le Manitoba à partir des experiences des autres provinces" (1986), 15 Man. L.J. 359.

Bilodeau, R., "Le bilinguisme judiciaire et l'Affaire Robin v. College de St-Boniface: traductore, traditore?" (1986), 15 Man. L.J. 333.

Carver, S. & Russell, D., "Interpreting and the Deaf in Legal Settings" (1985), 3:2 Just Cause 6.

Morel, A., "Certain Guarantees of Criminal Procedure (ss. 11(b), (f), (h), 12 and 14)" in W. S. Tarnopolsky & G.-A. Beaudoin, eds., *The Canadian Charter of Rights and Freedoms: Commentary* (Toronto: Carswell, 1982) 367.

Pelletier, B. B., "Les pouvoirs de légiférer en matière de langue après la Loi constitutionnelle de 1982" (1984), 25 C. de D. 227 at 288.

Vlug, H., "The Deaf Young Offender" (1987), 4:4 Just Cause 6.

Warrick, A. & McNaughton, S., "Blissymbol Users in the Courtroom" (1985), 3:2 Just Cause 9.

Wydrzynski, C. J., *Canadian Immigration Law and Procedure* (Aurora, Ont.: Canada Law Book, 1983) 476.

SECTION 15: EQUALITY RIGHTS
General Considerations

Abella, R. S., "The Dynamic Nature of Equality" in K. E. Mahoney & S. L. Martin, eds., *Equality and Judicial Neutrality* (Toronto: Carswell, 1987) 3.

Abella, R. S., "Limitations on the Right to Equality Before the Law" in A. de Mestral et al., eds., *The Limitation of Human Rights in Comparative Constitutional Law* (Cowansville, Que.: Yvon Blais, 1986) 223.

Axworthy, T. S., "Liberalism and Equality" in K. E. Mahoney & S. L. Martin, eds., *Equality and Judicial Neutrality* (Toronto: Carswell, 1987) 43.

Baker, D., "The Changing Norms of Equality in the Supreme Court of Canada" (1987), 9 Sup. Ct. L. Rev. 497.

Baker, J. B., "Fighting City Hall With the Equality Rights Provisions of the Canadian Charter of Rights and Freedoms" (1985), 43 Advocate 69.

Baker, W. G., "'Will Some Be More Equal Than Others?' or 'Whose Charter Is It, Anyway?'" in Continuing Legal Education Society of British Columbia, ed., *Equality Rights* (Vancouver: 1985) 1.1.

Bale, G., "Constitutional Values in Conflict: Full Funding for Ontario's Catholic High Schools" (1986), 18 Ottawa L. Rev. 533.

Bastarache, M., et al., *Language Rights in Canada* (Montreal: Yvon Blais, 1987) 501.

Bayefsky, A. ., "Defining Equality Rights" in A. F. Bayefsky & M. Eberts, eds., *Equality Rights and the Canadian Charter of Rights and Freedoms* (Toronto: Carswell, 1985) 1.

Bayefsky, A. F., "Defining Equality Rights Under the Charter" in K. E. Mahoney & S. L. Martin, eds., *Equality and Judicial Neutrality* (Toronto: Carswell, 1987) 106.

Bafefsky, A. F., "The Orientation of Section 15 of the Canadian Charter of Rights and Freedoms" in J. M. Weiler & R. M. Elliot, eds., *Litigating the Values of a Nation: The Canadian Charter of Rights and Freedoms* (Toronto: Carswell, 1987) 105.

Bayefsky, A. F., "The Principle of Equality or Non-Discrimination in International Law: Implications for Equality Rights in the Charter" in L. Smith et al., eds., *Righting the Balance: Canada's New Equality Rights* (Saskatoon: Canadian Human Rights Reporter, 1985) 117.

Beckton, C. F., "Nonlegal Evidence in Charter Cases: Section 15, a Case Study" in G.-A. Beaudoin, ed., *Charter Cases 1986-87* (Cowansville, Que.: Yvon Blais, 1987) 331.

Beckton, C. F., "Section 15 and Section 1 of the Charter — The Courts Struggle" in G.-A. Beaudoin, ed., *Your Clients and the Charter — Liberty and Equality* (Cowansville, Que.: Yvon Blais, 1988) 273.

Beckton, C. F., "Section 15 of the Charter — Statute Audits and the Search for Equality" (1986), 50 Sask. L. Rev. 111.

Beckton, C. F., "Section 27 and Section 15 of the Charter" in Canadian Human

Rights Foundation, ed., *Multiculturalism and the Charter: A Legal Perspective* (Toronto: Carswell, 1987) 1.

Berlin, M. L. & Metivier, L., "Le droit international humanitaire comme source interprétative de la Charte canadienne des droits et libertés: l'incidence de la Convention européenne des droits de l'homme" (1987), 64 R.D. Int'l & D. comparé 36.

Bissett-Johnson, A. & Bala, N., "Canada: The Charter of Rights Begins to Bite" (1986), 25 J. Fam. L. 29.

Black, W. W., "Intent or Effects: Section 15 of the Charter of Rights and Freedoms" in J. M. Weiler & R. M. Elliot, eds., *Litigating the Values of a Nation: The Canadian Charter of Rights and Freedoms* (Toronto: Carswell, 1986) 120.

Black, W. W. & Smith, L., "Section 15 Equality Rights Under the Charter: Meaning, Institutional Constraints and a Possible Test" in G.-A. Beaudoin, ed., *Your Clients and the Charter — Liberty and Equality* (Cowansville, Que.: Yvon Blais, 1988) 225.

Boyd, N. et al., "Case Law and Drug Convictions: Testing the Rhetoric of Equality Rights" (1987), 29 C.L.Q. 487.

Boyle, C. & Noonan, S., "Prostitution and Pornography: Beyond Formal Equality" (1986), 10 Dalhousie L.J. 225.

Brudner, A., "What are Reasonable Limits to Equality Rights?" (1986), 64 Can. Bar Rev. 469.

Brun, H., "Le recouvrement de l'impôt et les droits de la personne" (1983), 24 C. de D. 457.

Canada, Parliament, House of Commons. Sub-Committee on Equality Rights, *Equality For All: Report* (Ottawa: 1985).

Canadian Bar Association, *A Blueprint for Implementation of Constitutional Equality Rights: Submission to the Parliamentary Special Committee on Equality Rights* (Ottawa: 1985).

Canadian Institute for Professional Development, *Equality Rights and Employment Law: Preparing for Fundamental Change* (Toronto: 1985).

Caron, M., "La Charte québécoise, complément indispensable de la Charte constitutionnelle" in G.-A. Beaudoin, ed., *Vos clients et la Charte — Liberté et égalité* (Cowansville, Que.: Yvon Blais, 1988) 301.

Caron, M., "Le droit à l'égalité dans le Code civil et dans la Charte québécoise des droits et libertés" (1985), 45 R. du B. 345.

Chipeur, G. D., "Section 15 of the Charter Protects People and Corporations — Equally" (1986), 11 Can. Bus. L.J. 304.

Conte, F., "The Constitutionality of Full Public Funding of Roman Catholic Schools in Ontario: Reaping the Harvest Ye Have Sown" (1987), 9 Can. Com. L.J. 64.

De Montigny, Y., "Section 32 and Equality Rights" in A. F. Bayefsky & M. Eberts, eds., *Equality Rights and the Canadian Charter of Rights and Freedoms* (Toronto: Carswell, 1985) 565.

Eberts, M., "The Equality Provisions of the Canadian Charter of Rights and Freedoms" in Canadian Institute for Advanced Legal Studies, ed., *Cambridge Lectures, 1983* (Toronto: Butterworths, 1986) 25.

Eberts, M., "The Equality Provisions of the Canadian Charter of Rights and Freedoms and Government Institutions" in C. F. Beckton & A. W. Mackay, eds., *The Courts and the Charter* (Toronto: University of Toronto Press, 1986) 133.

Eberts, M., "Risks of Equality Litigation" in K. E. Mahoney & S. L. Martin, eds., *Equality and Judicial Neutrality* (Toronto: Carswell, 1987) 89.

Eberts, M., "A Strategy for Equality Litigation Under the Canadian Charter of Rights and Freedoms" in J. M. Weiler & R. M. Elliot, eds., *Litigating the Values of a Nation: The Canadian Charter of Rights and Freedoms* (Toronto: Carswell, 1986) 411.

Eberts, M., "Strategy in Choosing Remedies in Equality Cases: A Response to Dale Gibson" in L. Smith et al., eds., *Righting the Balance: Canada's New Equality Rights* (Saskatoon: Canadian Human Rights Reporter, 1986) 343.

Edwards, E. R. A. "Pleading the Equality Provisions" in Continuing Legal Education Society of British Columbia, ed., *Equality Rights* (Vancouver: 1985) 4.1.

Finkelstein, N., "Section 1: The Standard for Assessing Restrictive Government Actions and the Charter's Code of Procedure and Evidence" (1983), 9 Queen's L.J. 143 at 179.

Finkelstein, N., "Sections 1 and 15 of the Canadian Charter of Rights and Freedoms and the Relevance of the U.S. Experience" (1985), 6 Advocate 188.

Fogarty, K. H., *Equality Rights and Their Limitations in the Charter* (Toronto: Carswell, 1987).

Fournier, F., "Egalité et droits à l'égalité" in L. Smith et al., eds., *Righting the Balance: Canada's New Equality Rights* (Toronto: Canadian Human Rights Reporter, 1986) 25.

Gall, G. L., "Some Miscellaneous Aspects of Section 15 of the Canadian Charter of Rights and Freedoms" (1986), 24 Alta. L. Rev. 462.

Gathercole, R. J., "Funding — Financial & Non-Financial Support for Section 15 Cases" in Continuing Legal Education Society of British Columbia, ed., *Equality Rights* (Vancouver: 1985) 4.2.

Gerhrke, L., "The Charter and Publicly Assisted Housing" (1985), 1 J.L. Social Pol'y 17.

Gertner, E., "Are Corporations Entitled to Equality?: Some Preliminary Thoughts" (1986), 19 C.R.R. 288.

Gibson, D., "Canadian Equality Jurisprudence: Year One" in K. E. Mahoney & S. L. Martin, eds., *Equality and Judicial Neutrality* (Toronto: Carswell, 1987) 128.

Gold, M., "Equality Past and Future: The Relationship Between Section 15 of the Charter and the Equality Provisions in the Canadian Bill of Rights" in Law

Society of Upper Canada. Department of Education, ed., *Equality: Section 15 and Charter Procedures* (Toronto: 1985) ch. A.

Gold, M., "Moral and Political Theories in Equality Rights Adjudication" in J. M. Weiler & R. M. Elliot, eds., *Litigating the Values of a Nation: the Canadian Charter of Rights and Freedoms* (Toronto: Carswell, 1986) 85.

Gold, M., "A Principled Approach to Equality Rights: A Preliminary Inquiry" (1982), 4 Sup. Ct. L. Rev. 131.

Gold, M., "Some Formative Issues in Litigating Equality" in L. Smith et al., eds., *Righting the Balance: Canada's New Equality Rights* (Saskatoon: Canadian Human Rights Reporter, 1986) 243.

Greenawalt, K., "A Neighbour's Reflections on Equality Rights" in L. Smith et al., eds., *Righting the Balance: Canada's New Equality Rights* (Saskatoon: Canadian Human Rights Reporter, 1986) 189.

Harris, D., "Equality, Equality Rights and Discrimination Under the Charter of Rights and Freedoms" (1987), 21 U.B.C. L. Rev. 389.

Hilford, M., "An Examination of Analytical Models for Section 15 of the Canadian Charter of Rights and Freedoms" in Continuing Legal Education Society of British Columbia, ed., *Equality Rights* (Vancouver: 1985) 3.1.

Hughes, P., "Feminist Equality and the Charter: Conflict With Reality?" (1985), 5 Windsor Y.B. Access Just. 39.

Juriansz, R. G., "Equality Rights, Affirmative Action" in N. Finkelstein & B. McL. Rogers, eds., *Charter Issues in Civil Cases* (Toronto: Carswell, 1988) 109.

Juriansz, R. G., "Section 15 and the Human Rights Codes" in G.-A. Beaudoin, ed., *Your Clients and the Charter — Liberty and Equality* (Cowansville, Que.: Yvon Blais, 1988) 321.

Knopff, R., "What Do Constitutional Equality Rights Protect Canadians Against?" (1987), 20 Can. J. Pol. Sci. 265.

Lahey, K. A., "Feminist Theories of (In)Equality" in K. E. Mahoney & S. L. Martin, eds., *Equality and Judicial Neutrality* (Toronto: Carswell, 1987) 71.

Law Society of Upper Canada, Department of Education, *Equality: Section 15 and Charter Procedures* (Toronto: 1985).

Lederman, S. N. & Ristic, A., "The Relationship Between Federal and Provincial Human Rights Legislation and Charter Equality Rights" in L. Smith et al., eds., *Righting the Balance: Canada's New Equality Rights* (Saskatoon: Canadian Human Rights Reporter, 1986) 83.

Lessard, H., "The Idea of the 'Private': A Discussion of State Action Doctrine and Separate Sphere Ideology" (1986), 10 Dalhousie L.J. 107.

Lysyk, K. M., "Definition and Enforcement of Charter Equality Rights" in L. Smith et al., eds., *Righting the Balance: Canada's New Equality Rights* (Saskatoon: Canadian Human Rights Reporter, 1986) 215.

MacKay, A. W., "The Equality Provisions of the Charter and Education: A Structural Analysis" (1986), 11 Can. J. Education 293.

MacKay, A. W., "Judging and Equality: for Whom Does the Charter Toll?" (1986), 10 Dalhousie L.J. 35.

MacLauchlan, H. W., "Of Fundamental Justice, Equality and Society's Outcasts: A Comment on R. v. Tremayne and R. v. McLean" (1986), 32 McGill L.J. 213.

MacPherson, J., "Litigating Equality Rights" in L. Smith et al., eds., *Righting the Balance: Canada's New Equality Rights* (Saskatoon: Canadian Human Rights Reporter, 1986) 231.

Magsino, R. F., "Human Rights, Fair Treatment, and Funding of Private Schools in Canada" (1986), 11 Can. J. Education 245.

McBride, E. J., "Judging and Equality: *quis custodiet ipsos custodes?*" (1986), 10 Dalhousie L.J. 1.

Morgan, B. G., "Evidentiary Issues Affecting Section 1 and Section 15 Claims" in Law Society of Upper Canada, Department of Education, ed., *Equality: Section 15 and Charter Procedures* (Toronto: 1985) ch. J.

Mossop, D., "A Discussion of Systemic Discrimination in a Constitutional Forum" (1986), 44 Advocate 369.

Mossop, D., "Extension: A Constitutional Cure for Underinclusiveness" (1987), 45 Advocates' Q. 707.

Norman, K., "The Charter for the Public Sector and for the Private Sector, Human Rights Codes: A False Dichotomy Leading to the Wrong Result" (1984), 5 C.H.R.R. C/84-5.

Ontario, Attorney General, *Sources for the Interpretation of Equality Rights Under the Charter: A Background Paper* (Toronto: 1985).

Petter, A., "The Charter and Private Action: the Impact of Section 15 on Human Rights Codes" (1984), 5 C.H.R.R. C/84-1.

Proulx, D., "L'inextricable égalité constitutionnelle" in G.-A. Beaudoin, ed., *La cour suprême du Canada* (Cowansville, Qué.: Yvon Blais, 1986) 273.

Rogers, P., "Equality, Efficiency and Judicial Restraint: Towards a Dynamic Constitution" (1986), 10 Dalhousie L.J. 139.

Ross, J., "Levels of Review in American Equal Protection and Under the Charter" (1986), 24 Alta. L. Rev. 441.

Savage, I., "Systemic Discrimination and Section 15 of the Charter" (1986), 50 Sask. L. Rev. 141.

Seale, A. J., "Can the Canada Pension Plan Survive the Charter? Section 15(1) and Sex (In)equality" (1985), 10 Queen's L.J. 441.

Shaw, D. W., "Section 15(1) of the Charter of Rights and Freedoms" in Continuing Legal Education Society of British Columbia, ed., *Charter of Rights — 1987* (Vancouver: 1987) 8.1.01.

Smith, L., "Charter Equality Rights: Some General Issues and Specific Applications in British Columbia to Elections, Juries and Illegitimacy" (1984), 18 U.B.C. L. Rev. 351.

Smith, L., "A New Paradigm for Equality Rights" in L. Smith et al., eds, *Righting the Balance: Canada's New Equality Rights* (Saskatoon: Canadian Human Rights Reporter, 1986) 353.

Smith, L. et al., eds., *Righting the Balance: Canada's New Equality Rights* (Saskatoon: Canadian Human Rights Reporter, 1986).

Tarnopolsky, W. S., "Equality and Discrimination" in R. S. Abella & M. L. Rothman, eds., *Justice Beyond Orwell* (Montreal: Yvon Blais, 1986) 267.

Tarnopolsky, W. S., "The Equality Rights (ss. 15, 27 and 28)" in W. S. Tarnopolsky & G.-A. Beaudoin, eds., *The Canadian Charter of Rights and Freedoms: Commentary* (Toronto: Carswell, 1982) 395.

Tarnopolsky, W. S., "The Equality Rights in the Canadian Charter of Rights and Freedoms" (1983), 61 Can. Bar Rev. 242.

Tarnopolsky, W. S., "Limitations on Equality Rights" in A. de Mestral et al., eds., *The Limitation of Human Rights in Comparative Constitutional Law* (Cowansville, Que.: Yvon Blais, 1986) 325.

Tarnopolsky, W. S. & Pentney, W. F., "Discrimination and the Law, Including Equality Rights Under the Charter", 2nd ed. (1985), (Toronto: Richard De Boo, 1985).

Tremblay, A., "Le principe d'égalité et les clauses anti-discriminatoires" (1986), 18 R.J.T. 329.

Vickers, J. McC., "Equality Theories and Their Results: Equality-Seeking in a Cold Climate" in L. Smith et al., eds., *Righting the Balance: Canada's New Equality Rights* (Saskatoon: Canadian Human Rights Reporter, 1986) 3.

Vickers, J. McC., "Majority Equality Issues of the Eighties" (1983), Can. Hum. Rts Y.B. 47.

Wakeling, T. W., "An Introduction to Section 15(1) of the Charter" (1986), 24 Alta L. Rev. 412.

Whyte, J. D., "The Administration of Criminal Justice and the Provinces" (1984), 38 C.R. (3d) 184.

Whyte, J. D., "Equality or the Federal Principle: Constitutional Values in Conflict" (1987), 54 C.R. (3d) 224.

Whyte, J. D. "Is the Private Sector Affected by the Charter?" in L. Smith et al., eds., *Righting the Balance: Canada's New Equality Rights* (Saskatoon: Canadian Human Rights Reporter, 1986) 145.

Williams, B., "Equality Provisions — Section 15 of the Charter" in Continuing Legal Education Society of British Columbia, ed., *Equality Rights* (Vancouver: 1985) 4.3.

Woehrling, J., "L'article 15(1) de la Charte canadienne des droits et libertés et la langue" (1985) 30 R.D. McGill 266.

Woehrling, J., "Minority Cultural and Linguistic Rights and Equality Rights in the Canadian Charter of Rights and Freedoms" (1985), 31 McGill L.J. 51.

Wydrzynski, C. J., *Canadian Immigration Law and Procedure* (Aurora, Ont.: Canada Law Book, 1983) 467.

Race

Anand, R., "Ethnic Equality" in A. F. Bayefsky & M. Eberts, eds., *Equality Rights and the Canadian Charter of Rights and Freedoms* (Toronto: Carswell, 1985) 81.

Juriansz, R. G., "Issues in Equality Under the Charter on the Grounds of Race, Colour, National or Ethnic Origin, and Religion" in Law Society of Upper Canada, Department of Education, ed., *Equality: Section 15 and Charter Procedures* (Toronto: 1985) ch. F.

Religion

Black, W. W., "Religion and the Right of Equality" in A. F. Bayefsky & M. Eberts, eds., *Equality Rights and the Canadian Charter of Rights and Freedoms* (Toronto: Carswell, 1985) 131.

Juriansz, R. G., "Issues in Equality Under the Charter on the Grounds of Race, Colour, National or Ethnic Origin, and Religion" in Law Society of Upper Canada, Department of Education, ed., *Equality: Section 15 and Charter Procedures* (Toronto: 1985) ch. F.

Macklem, P., "Freedom of Conscience and Religion in Canada" (1984), 42 U.T. Fac. L. Rev. 51.

Sex

Bankier, J. K., "Equality, Affirmative Action, and the Charter: Reconciling 'Inconsistent' Sections" (1985), 1 Can. J.W.L. 134.

Boyle, C. L. M., *Sexual Assault* (Toronto: Carswell, 1984) 31.

Charter of Rights Educational Fund, *Report on the Statute Audit Project: A Preliminary Analysis of Selected Federal and Ontario Laws Based on the Sex Equality Provisions of the Canadian Charter of Rights and Freedoms* (Toronto: 1985).

Corbett, M., "Discrimination in Pension Plans" in Canadian Bar Association — Ontario. Continuing Legal Education, ed., *The Practical View of the Charter for Solicitors and Barristers* (Toronto: 1986).

Creighton, G., "The Charter, the Corporation and Equality Rights" in Canadian Institute for Professional Development, ed., *The Charter and the Corporation: New Vistas for Corporate Rights* (Toronto, 1985) H-1.

De Jong, K. J., "Sexual Equality: Interpreting Section 28" in A. F. Bayefsky & M. Eberts, eds., *Equality Rights and the Canadian Charter of Rights and Freedoms* (Toronto: Carswell, 1985) 493.

Eberts, M., "Sex-Based Discrimination and the Charter" in A. F. Bayefsky & M. Eberts, eds., *Equality Rights and the Canadian Charter of Rights and Freedoms* (Toronto: Carswell, 1985) 183.

Hosek, C., "Equality and Women" in R. S. Abella & M. L. Rothman, eds., *Justice Beyond Orwell* (Montreal: Yvon Blais, 1985) 295.

Jacomy-Millette, A., "Réflexions sur la condition feminine au Canada à l'aube des années 80: égalité ou discrimination?", [1983] Can. Hum. Rts Y.B. 195.

Jones, M. J. B., "Sexual Equality, the Constitution and Indian Status: A Comment on s. 12(1)(b) of the Indian Act" (1984), 4 Windsor Y.B. Access Just. 48.

Kirby, P., "Marrying Out and Loss of Status: The Charter and New Indian Act Legislation" (1985), 1 J. L. Social Pol'y 77.

Lowenberger, L. et al., "Welfare: Women, Poverty and the Charter" (1985), 1 J. L. Social Pol'y 42.

MacKinnon, C. A., "Making Sex Equality Real" in L. Smith et al., eds., *Righting the Balance: Canada's New Equality Rights* (Toronto: Canadian Human Rights Reporter, 1986) 37.

Macklem, T., "Sexual Bias in Custody Disputes: The Tender Years Doctrine: Roebuck v. Roebuck, 45 A.R. 180, 148 D.L.R. (3d) 131 (C.A. 1983)" (1985), 17 Ottawa L. Rev. 171.

MacRae, G. B., "The Effect of Bill 33 on Practice in the Area of Wills, Trusts and Estates" in Continuing Legal Education Society of British Columbia, ed., *Equality Rights* (Vancouver: 1985) 2.3.

Mahoney, K. E., "Day Care and Equality in Canada" (1985), 14 Man. L.J. 305.

Mahoney, K. E. & Martin, S. L., eds., *Equality and Judicial Neutrality* (Toronto: Carswell, 1987).

Martin, S. L., "Canada's Abortion Law and the Canadian Charter of Rights and Freedoms" (1986), 1 Can. J.W.L. 339.

McDonald, M., "Indian Status: Colonialism or Sexism?" (1987), 9 Can. Com. L.J. 23.

Morin, M., "Les stipulations à caractère discriminatoire au sein des régimes de rentes et d'assurance de personnes: dix ans de retard à rattraper" (1986), 46 R. du B. 557.

Morton, F. L. & Pal. L. A., "The Impact of the Charter of Rights on Public Administration" (1985), 28 Can. Pub. Admin. 221.

Pal, L. A. & Morton, F. L., "Bliss v. Attorney General of Canada: From Legal Defeat to Political Victory" (1986), 24 Osgoode Hall L.J. 141.

Rowley, S. W., "Women, Pensions and Equality" (1986), 10 Dalhousie L.J. 283.

Seale, A. J., "Can the Canada Pension Plan Survive the Charter? Section 15(1) and Sex (In)equality" (1985), 10 Queen's L.J. 441.

Sheppard, N. C., "Equality, Ideology and Oppression: Women and the Canadian Charter of Rights and Freedoms" (1986), 10 Dalhousie L.J. 195.

Shrofel, S. M., "Equality Rights and Law Reform in Saskatchewan: An Assessment of the Charter Compliance Process" (1985), 1 Can. J.W.L. 108.

Symes, B., "Equality Theories and Maternity Benefits" in K. E. Mahoney & S. L. Martin, eds., *Equality and Judicial Neutrality* (Toronto: Carswell, 1987) 207.

Age

Atcheson, M. E. & Sullivan, L., "Passage to Retirement: Age Discrimination and the Charter" in A. F. Bayefsky & M. Eberts, eds., *Equality Rights and the Canadian Charter of Rights and Freedoms* (Toronto: Carswell, 1985) 231.

Bala, N. & Cruickshank, D., "Children and the Charter of Rights" in B. Landau, ed., *Children's Rights in the Practice of Family Law* (Toronto: Carswell, 1986) 28.

Brett, N., "Equality Rights and Mandatory Retirement" (1987), 9 Can. Com. L.J. 1.

Flanagan, T., "Policy-Making by Exegesis: The Abolition of 'Mandatory Retirement' in Manitoba" (1985), 11 Can. Pub. Pol'y 40.

Hunter, G. D., "The Concepts of 'Equality' and 'Discrimination Based on Age' Within Section 15(1) of the Charter: A Commentary" in Law Society of Upper Canada, Department of Education, ed., *Equality: Section 15 and Charter Procedures* (Toronto: 1985) ch. D.

Mason, A., "Annotation: R. v. LeGallant" (1985), 47 C.R. (3d) 170.

Morin, M., "Les stipulations à caractère discriminatoire au sein des régimes de rentes et d'assurance de personnes: dix ans de retard à rattraper" (1986), 46 R. du B. 557.

Rand, C. L. "Is the Capital Gain Exemption Unconstitutional?" (1987), 9 Can. Com. L.J. 49.

Reichenfeld, H. F., "Elderly Psychiatric Patients in Institutions — Implications of the Canadian Charter of Rights and Freedoms" (1985), 5 Health L. Can. 83.

Richardson, G., "Condominiums — Prohibitions on Occupation by Children" (1984), 62 Can. Bar Rev. 656.

Stalker, A., "LeGallant: Law Reform and the Charter" (1987), 54 C.R. (3d) 61.

Wilson, J., "Children and Equality Rights" in A. F. Bayefsky & M. Eberts, eds., *Equality Rights and the Canadian Charter of Rights and Freedoms* (Toronto: Carswell, 1985) 293.

Mental or Physical Disability

Baker, D., "Equality Rights of Disabled People" in Law Society of Upper Canada, Department of Education, ed., *Equality: Section 15 and Charter Procedures* (Toronto: 1985) ch. G.

Beatty, H., "Federal-Provincial Fiscal Arrangements: Their Impact on Social Policy and Current Prospects for Reform" (1988), 3 J. L. Social Pol'y 36.

Gordon, R. M., "The Impact of the Canadian Charter of Rights and Freedoms Upon Canadian Mental Health Law: The Dawn of a New Era or Business As Usual?" (1986), 14 Law, Medicine & Health Care 190.

Lepofsky, M. D., "Representing Handicapped Persons' Claims Under the Ontario Human Rights Code and the Canadian Charter of Rights and Freedoms" (1983), 4 Health L. Can. 43.

Lepofsky, M. D. & Bickenbach, J. E., "Equality Rights and the Physically Handicapped" in A. F. Bayefsky & M. Eberts, eds., *Equality Rights and the Canadian Charter of Rights and Freedoms* (Toronto: Carswell, 1985) 323.

Newman, E., "Charter Implications for Procedures Under the Ontario Mental Health Act" (1984), 5 Health L. Can. 60.

Poirier, D. & Goguen, L., "The Canadian Charter of Rights and the Right to Education for Exceptional Children" (1986), 11 Can. J. Education 231.

Ratushny, E., "Implementing Equality Rights: Standards of Reasonable Accommodation With Legislative Force" in L. Smith et al., eds., *Righting the Balance: Canada's New Equality Rights* (Saskatoon: Canadian Human Rights Reporter, 1986) 255.

Reichenfeld, H. F., "Elderly Psychiatric Patients in Institutions — Implications of the Canadian Charter of Rights and Freedoms" (1985), 5 Health L. Can. 83.

Robertson, G. B., *Mental Disability and the Law in Canada* (Toronto: Carswell, 1987).

Staub, J. I., "Mental Incompetency and Civil Rights: Issues Raised by the Justin Clark and Martyn Humm Cases" (1985), 6 Health L. Can. 3.

Thompson, D., "A Consideration of the Mental Capacity Provisions of the Marriage Act in View of the Charter of Rights and Freedoms and Webb v. Webb" (1987), 9 Can. Com. L.J. 101.

Varcoe, J. B. "Learning Disabilities and the Court" (1986), 44 The Advocate 385.

Vickers, D. & Endicott, O., "Mental Disability and Equality Rights" in A. F. Bayefsky & M. Eberts, eds., *Equality Rights and the Canadian Charter of Rights and Freedoms* (Toronto: Carswell, 1985) 381.

Wellsch, T., "The Right of the Civilly Committed Mental Patient to Refuse Treatment" (1984), 48 Sask. L. Rev. 269.

Whitley, S., "The Lieutenant-Governor's Advisory Boards of Review for the Supervision of the Mentally Disordered Offender in Canada: A Call for Change" (1985), 7 Int'l J.L. Psychiatry 385.

Sexual Orientation

Bruner, A., "Sexual Orientation and Equality Rights" (1985), in A. F. Bayefsky & M. Eberts, eds., *Equality Rights and the Canadian Charter of Rights and Freedoms* (Toronto: Carswell, 1985) 457.

Duplé, N., "Homosexualité et droit à l'égalité dans les chartes canadienne et québécoise" (1984), 25 C. de D. 801.

Girard, P., "Sexual Orientation as a Human Rights Issue in Canada 1969-1985" (1986), 10 Dalhousie L.J. 267.

Jefferson, J. E. "Gay Rights and the Charter" (1985), 43 U.T. Fac. L. Rev. 70.

Leopold, M. & King, W., "Compulsory Heterosexuality, Lesbians, and the Law: Case for Constitutional Protection" (1985), 1 Can. J.W.L. 163.

Marital/Family Status

Brun, H., "Le recouvrement de l'impôt et les droits de la personne" (1983), 24 C. de D. 457.

McIntosh, D., "Defining 'Family' — A Comment on the Family Reunification Provisions in the Immigration Act" (1988), 3 J. L. Social Pol'y 104.

McLellan, A. A., "Marital Status and Equality Rights" in A. F. Bayefsky & M.

Eberts, eds., *Equality Rights and the Canadian Charter of Rights and Freedoms* (Toronto: Carswell, 1985) 411.

Morin, M., "Les stipulations à caractère discriminatoire au sein des régimes de rentes et d'assurance de personnes: dix ans de retard à rattraper" (1986), 46 R. du B. 557.

Social Condition

Beatty, H., "Federal-Provincial Fiscal Arrangements: Their Impact on Social Policy and Current Prospects for Reform" (1988), 3 J. L. Social Pol'y 36.

Brun, H., "Le recouvrement de l'impôt et les droits de la personne" (1983), 24 C. de D. 457.

Hathaway, J. C., "Poverty Law and Equality Rights: Preliminary Reflections" (1985), 1 J.L. Social Pol'y 1.

Lowenberger, L. et al., "Welfare: Women, Poverty and the Charter" (1985), 1 J. L. Social Pol'y 42.

MacKay, A. W. & Holgate, M., "Fairness in the Allocation of Housing: Legal and Economic Perspectives" (1983), 7 Dalhousie L.J. 383.

Rand, C. L., "Is the Capital Gain Exemption Unconstitutional?" (1987), 9 Can. Com. L.J. 49.

Section 15(2): Affirmative Action

Bankier, J. K., "Equality, Affirmative Action, and the Charter: Reconciling 'Inconsistent' Sections" (1985), 1 Can. J.W.L. 134.

Bevan, M. J., "Affirmative Action: Section 15(2)" in Law Society of Upper Canada, Department of Education, ed., *Equality: Section 15 and Charter Procedures* (Toronto: 1985) ch. H.

Blache, P., "Affirmative Action: To Equality Through Inequalities?" in J. M. Weiler & R. M. Elliot, eds., *Litigating the Value of a Nation: the Canadian Charter of Rights and Freedoms* (Toronto: Carswell, 1986) 165.

Bosset, P. & Caron, M., "Un nouvel outil de lutte contre la discrimination: les programmes d'accès à l'égalité" (1987), 21 R.J.T. 71.

Cornish, M., "Affirmative Action and s. 15(2) of the Charter" in Canadian Institute for Professional Development, ed., *Equality Rights and Employment: Preparing for Fundamental Change* (Toronto: 1986) C-1.

Gibson, D., "Accentuating the Positive and Eliminating the Negative: Remedies for Inequality Under the Canadian Charter" in L. Smith et al., eds., *Righting the Balance: Canada's New Equality Rights* (Saskatoon: Canadian Human Rights Reporter, 1986) 311.

Juriansz, R. G., "Equality Rights, Affirmative Action" in N. Finkelstein & B. McL. Rogers, eds., *Charter Issues in Civil Cases* (Toronto: Carswell, 1988) 108.

Lepofsky, D., "Equality and Disabled Persons" in R. S. Abella & M. L. Rothman, eds., *Justice Beyond Orwell* (Montreal: Yvon Blais, 1985) 309.

Mahoney, K., "Day Care and Equality in Canada" (1985), 14 Man. L.J. 305 at 310.

Poulantzas, N. M., "Multiculturalism, Affirmative Action Programs Under the Canadian Charter of Rights and Freedoms, and the Protection of Minorities" (1985), 73 Rev. D. Int'l 309.

SECTION 16-23: LANGUAGE RIGHTS
General Considerations

Algee, A. M., "Les mécanismes de la pratique du droit en langue minoritaire au Canada: une solution pour le Manitoba à partir des expériences des autres provinces" (1986), 15 Man. L.J. 359.

Arsenault, P., *L'enchâssement des droits de la minorité canadienne-française dans la Constitution du Canada* (Moncton: l'Université de Moncton, 1982).

Banks, M. A., "Defining 'constitution of the province' — the Crux of the Manitoba Language Controversy" (1986), 31 McGill L.J. 466.

Bastarache, M., "Commentaire sur la décision de la Cour suprême du Canada dans le Renvoi au sujet des droits linguistiques au Manitoba, jugement rendu le 13 juin 1985" (1985), 31 R.D. McGill 93.

Bastarache, M. et al., *Language Rights in Canada* (Montreal: Yvon Blais, 1987).

Beaudoin, G.-A., "Le multiculturalisme et les droits confessionnels et linguistiques: une vue succincte" in Canadian Human Rights Foundation, ed., *Multiculturalism and the Charter: A Legal Perspective* (Toronto: Carswell, 1987) 15.

Bildodeau, R., "La judiciarisation des conflits linguistiques au Canada" (1986), 27 C. de D. 215.

Brandt, G.J., "Parties and Participants in Constitutional litigation: The Minority Language Rights Issue in Quebec and Manitoba" (1986), 35 U.N.B.L.J. 201.

Deschênes, J., *Ainsi parlèrent les tribunaux... Vol II: Conflits linguistiques au Canada, 1968-1985* (Montreal, Wilson & Lafleur, 1985).

Fortier, D'I., "Les droits linguistiques canadiens en évolution" (1986), 27 C. de D. 227.

Foucher, P. & Snow, G., "Le régime juridique des langues dans l'administration publique au Nouveau-Brunswick" (1983), 24 C. de D. 81.

Gibson, D. & Lercher, K., "Reliance on Unconstitutional Laws: The Saving Doctrines and Other Protections" (1986), 15 Man. L.J. 305.

Lacombe, G., "Les droits linguistiques: du rêve à la réalité en Alberta" (1982), 37 Vie Française 23.

Lebel, M., "Les droits linguistiques et la Charte canadienne des droits et libertés" in Association canadienne-française pour l'avancement des sciences — section juridique, ed., *La charte canadienne des droits et libertés et les droits collectifs et sociaux* (Quebec: 1983) 31.

Mackintosh, G. H. A., "Heading Off Bilodeau: Attempting Constitutional Amendment" (1986), 15 Man. L.J. 271.

Magnet, J. E., "The Charter's Official Languages Provisions: The Implications of Entrenched Bilingualism" (1982), 4 Sup. Ct. L. Rev. 163.

Magnet, J. E., "The Future of Official Language Minorities" (1986), 27 C. de D. 189.

Magnet, J. E., "Canada's System of Official Bilingualism: Constitutional Guarantees for the Legislative Process" (1986), 18 Ottawa L. Rev. 227.

Patry, R. M., *La législation linguistique fédérale* (Quebec: Conseil de la langue française du Québec, 1981).

Pelletier, B. B., "Les pouvoirs de légiférer en matière de langue après la 'Loi constitutionnelle de 1982'" (1984), 25 C. de D. 227.

Prujiner, A., "Théorie et réalité de l'égalité juridique des langues au Canada" (1983), 24 C. de D. 11.

Quebec. Conseil de la langue française, *Les droits linguistiques du Québec et le projet fédéral de Charte canadienne des droits et libertés* (Québec: 1981).

Réaume, D., "Language, Rights, Remedies, and the Rule of Law" (1988), 1 Can. J.L. Juris. 35.

Schwartz, B., "The Other Section 23" (1986), 15 Man. L.J. 347.

Sellers, E. A., "Constitutionally Entrenched Linguistic Minority Rights: The Forest and Blaikie Decisions" (1986), 15 Man. L.J. 257.

Thibault, F., "L'étrange paradoxe d'une liberté devenue obligatoire: La loi 101 sur l'usage exclusif du français dans l'État du Québec" (1987), 1 R. du D. Public 149.

Tremblay, A., "L'interprétation des dispositions constitutionnelles relatives aux droits linguistiques" (1983), 13 Man. L.J. 651.

Tremblay, A., "The Language Rights (ss. 16 to 23)" in W.S. Tarnopolsky & G.-A. Beaudoin, eds., *The Canadian Charter of Rights and Freedoms: Commentary* (Toronto: Carswell, 1982) 443.

Whitley, S. J., "The Manitoba Language Reference: Judicial Consideration of 'language charged with meaning'" (1986), 15 Man. L.J. 295.

Woehrling, J., "L'article 15(1) de la Charte canadienne des droits et libertés et la langue" (1985), 30 R.D. McGill 266.

Woehrling, J., "Minority Cultural and Linguistic Rights and Equality Rights in the Canadian Charter of Rights and Freedoms" (1985), 31 McGill L.J. 51.

Section 19: Language of Court Proceedings

Bastarache, M. et al., *Language Rights in Canada* (Montreal: Yvon Blais, 1987) 123.

Bilodeau, R., "Le bilinguisme judiciaire et l'affaire Robin v. Collège de St-Boniface: traductore, traditore?" (1986), 15 Man. L.J. 333.

Bilodeau, R., "Une analyse critique de l'Affaire Société des Acadiens du Nouveau-Brunswick et l'avenir précaire du bilinguisme judiciaire au Canada" (1986), 32 R.D. McGill 232.

Section 23: Minority Language Education Rights

Apps, E., "Minority Language Education Rights" (1985), 43 U.T. Fac. L. Rev. 45.

Beaudoin, G.-A., "La protection constitutionnelle des minorités" (1986), 27 C. de D. 31.

Bilodeau, R., "La langue, l'éducation et les minorités: avant et depuis la Charte canadienne des droits et libertés" (1983), 13 Man. L.J. 371.

Carignan, P., "De la notion de droit collectif et de son application en matière scolaire au Québec" (1984), 18 R.J.T. 1.

Foucher, P., *Constitutional Language Rights of Official Language Minorities in Canada: A Study of the Legislation of the Provinces and Territories Respecting Education Rights of Official Language Minorities and Compliance with Section 23 of the Canadian Charter of Rights and Freedoms* (Ottawa: Canadian Law Information Council, 1985).

Foucher, P., "Les droits scolaires des Acadiens et la Charte" (1984), 33 R. de D.U.N.B. 97.

Gibson, D., "Protection of Minority Rights Under the Canadian Charter of Rights and Freedoms: Can Politicians and Judges Sing Harmony?" (1985), 8 Hamline L.R. 343.

Greschner, D., "Two Approaches for Section One of the Charter" (1985), 49 Sask. L. Rev. 336.

Lebel, M., "Du libre accès à l'accès restreint aux écoles anglaises du Québec" (1983), 24 C. de D. 131.

Magnet, J. E., "Les écoles et la Constitution" (1983), 24 C. de D. 145.

Magnet, J. E., "Minority Language Educational Rights" (1982), 4 Sup. Ct. L. Rev. 195.

Monnin, A., "L'égalité juridique des langues et l'enseignement: les écoles françaises hors-Québec" (1983), 24 C. de D. 157.

Paillé, M., "Conséquences démographiques de la Charte canadienne des droits et libertés sur la clientèle des écoles françaises et anglaises au Québec" in Association canadienne-française pour l'avancement des sciences, ed., *La Charte canadienne des droits et libertés et les droits collectifs et sociaux* (Quebec: 1983) 10.

Proulx, D., "La Loi 101, la clause-Québec et la Charte canadienne devant la Cour suprême: un cas d'espèce?" (1985), 16 R.G.D. 167.

Proulx, D., "La portée de la Charte canadienne des droits et libertés en matière de droits sociaux et collectifs: le cas de l'article 23" in Association canadienne-française pour l'avancement des sciences, ed., *La Charte canadienne des droits et libertés et les droits collectifs et sociaux* (Quebec: 1983) 54.

Proulx, D., "La précarité des droits linguistiques scolaires ou les singulières difficultés de mise en oeuvre de l'article 23 de la Charte canadienne des droits et libertés" (1983), 14 R.G.D. 335.

Roy, M., "La Charte canadienne des droit et libertés: quelques inférences possibles sur les droits scolaires et linguistiques des minorités francophones hors Québec" (1983), 37 Vie française 10.

Schmeiser, D. A, "Multiculturalism in Canadian Education" in Canadian Human

Rights Foundation, ed., *Multiculturalism and The Charter: A Legal Perspective* (Toronto: Carswell, 1987) 167.

Schwartz, B., "The Other Section 23" (1986), 15 Man. L.J. 347.

Tremblay, A., "Droits linguistiques — instruction dans la langue de la minorité" (1983), 61 R. du B. Can. 407.

SECTION 24: ENFORCEMENT
General Considerations

Arvay, J. J., "Practice and Procedure in Charter Cases" (1987), 45 Advocate 493.

Arvay, J. J., "Practice and Procedure in Charter Cases" in British Columbia Continuing Legal Education Society, ed., *Charter of Rights — 1987* (Vancouver: 1987) 4.101.

Baigent, J. & Hoskins, J., "Government Action — Federal and Provincial Governments and Others as Defendants" in Canadian Bar Association, ed., *Preparing and Presenting Charter Cases* (Ottawa: 1986) 1.

Barton, P. G., "Developments in Criminal Procedure: The 1984-85 Term" (1986), 8 Sup. Ct. L. Rev. 195.

Beaudoin, G.-A., "General Overview: The First Twenty-Five Rulings of the Supreme Court" in G.-A. Beaudoin, ed., *Charter Cases 1986-87* (Cowansville, Que.: Yvon Blais, 1987) 41.

Beckton, C. F., "The Future Impact of the Charter of Rights and Freedoms on the Canadian Legal Profession" in A. W. MacKay et al., eds., *The Canadian Charter of Rights: Law Practice Revolutionized* (Halifax: Faculty of Law, Dalhousie University, 1982) 127.

Béliveau, P., "La protection des droits constitutionnels en vertu de l'article 24(1) de la Charte des droits et libertés" (1987), 47 R. du B. 173.

Bilodeau, R., "La judicialisation des conflits linguistiques au Canada" (1986), 27 C. de D. 215.

Binnie, W. I. C., "Standing in Charter Cases" in G.-A. Beaudoin, ed., *Charter Cases 1986-87* (Cowansville, Que.: Yvon Blais, 1987) 77.

Blake, S., "Standing to Litigate Constitutional Rights and Freedoms in Canada and the United States" (1984), 16 Ottawa L. Rev. 66.

Bogart, W. A., "'Appropriate and Just': Section 24 of the Canadian Charter of Rights and Freedoms and the Question of Judicial Legitimacy" (1986), 10 Dalhousie L.J. 81.

Bogart, W. A., "Standing and the Charter: Rights and Identity" in R. J. Sharpe, ed., *Charter Litigation* (Toronto: Butterworths, 1987) 1.

Braun, S., "Judicial Apprehension of Violation of Legal Rights Under the Canadian Charter of Rights and Freedoms: Towards a Framework of Analysis" (1987), 24 U.W.O. L.J. 27.

Bridge, K. A. G., "Judicial Review of Federal Legislation and Administrative Action in the Federal and Provincial Courts: The Law Since Jabour v. Law Society of British Columbia" (1988), 9 Advocates' Q. 77.

Bushnell, S. I., "Leave to Appeal Applications: The 1984-85 Term" (1986), 6 Sup. Ct. L. Rev. 383.

Chevrette, F., "Le fédéralisme gagne-t-il sa cause devant la Cour suprême d'aujourd'hui?" in G.-A. Beaudoin, ed., *La Cour suprême du Canada* (Cowansville, Qué.: Yvon Blais, 1986) 35.

Connelly, P. J., "Relief Under the Charter and the Prerogative Remedies — Re Krakowski and The Queen (1983), 41 O.R. (2d) 321 (C.A.)" (1983), 26 C.L.Q. 35.

Cooper-Stephenson, K., "Past Inequities and Future Promise: Judicial Neutrality in Charter Constitutional Tort Claims" in K. E. Mahoney & S. L. Martin, eds., *Equality and Judicial Neutrality* (Toronto: Carswell, 1987) 226.

Corry, D. J., "Military Law Under the Charter" (1986), 24 Osgoode Hall L. J. 67.

Creighton, G. D., "Re Service Employees International Union, Local 204 and Broadway Manor Nursing Home et al: 'A Court of Competent Jurisdiction,'" (1985), 10 Queen's L.J. 498.

Del Buono, V. M., "The Implications of the Supreme Court's Purpose Interpretation of the Charter" (1986), 48 C.R. (3d) 121.

Doherty, D. H., "What's Done is Done: An Argument in Support of a Purely Prospective Application of the Charter of Rights" (1982), 26 C.R. (3d) 121.

Eberts, M., "Risks of Equality Litigation" in K. E. Mahoney & S. L. Martin, eds., *Equality and Judicial Neutrality* (Toronto: Carswell, 1987) 89.

Eberts, M., "A Strategy for Equality Litigation Under the Canadian Charter of Rights and Freedoms" in J. M. Weiler & R. M. Elliot, eds., *Litigating the Values of a Nation: The Canadian Charter of Rights and Freedoms* (Toronto: Carswell, 1986) 411.

Eberts, M., "Strategy in Choosing Remedies in Equality Cases: A Response to Dale Gibson" in L. Smith et al., eds., *Righting the Balance: Canada's New Equality Rights* (Saskatoon: Canadian Human Rights Reporter, 1986) 343.

Eberts, M., "The Use of Litigation Under the Canadian Charter of Rights and Freedoms as a Strategy for Achieving Change" in N. Nevitte & A. Kornberg, eds., *Minorities and the Canadian State* (Oakville: Mosaic Press, 1985) 53.

Edwards, E. R. A., "Pleading the Equality Provisions" in Continuing Legal Education Society of British Columbia, ed., *Equality Rights* (Vancouver: 1985) 4.1.

Edwards, J. L. J., "The Attorney General and the Charter of Rights" in R. J. Sharpe, ed., *Charter Litigation* (Toronto: Butterworths, 1987) 45.

Fairley, S. H., "Developments in Constitutional Law: The 1984-85 Term" (1986), 8 Sup. Ct. L. Rev. 53.

Fairley, S. H., "Enforcing the Charter: Some Thoughts on An Appropriate and Just Standard for Judicial Review" (1982), 4 Sup. Ct. L. Rev. 217.

Fairweather, R. G. L., "A View from the Commission" in Canadian Bar Association

— Ontario, Continuing Legal Education, ed., *Corporate Counsel: Charter of Rights, Human Rights and the Corporation* (Toronto: 1985).

Finkelstein, N., "The Relevance of Pre-Charter Case Law for Post-Charter Adjudication" (1982), 4 Sup. Ct. L. Rev. 267.

Finkelstein, N., "Section 1: The Standard for Assessing Restrictive Government Actions and the Charter's Code of Procedure and Evidence" (1983), 9 Queen's L.J. 143.

Fleming, J., "Hospital Transfers into Nursing Homes: A Potential Charter Remedy for Unwilling Transferees" (1985), 1 J.L. & Social Pol'y 50.

Fogarty, K. H., *Equality Rights and Their Limitations in the Charter* (Toronto: Carswell, 1987).

Fricot, Y. L. J., "The Challenges of Legislation by Means of the Charter: Evidentiary Issues" (1984), 16 Ottawa L. Rev. 565.

Garton, G. R., "Civil Litigation Under the Charter" in N. Finkelstein & B. McL. Rogers, eds., *Charter Issues in Civil Cases* (Toronto: Carswell, 1988) 73.

Gathercole, R. J., "Funding — Financial & Non-Financial Support for Section 15 Cases" in Continuing Legal Education Society of British Columbia, ed., *Equality Rights* (Vancouver: 1985) 4.2.

Gertner, E., "The Past is Prologue: An Update on the Supreme Court and the Charter" in Canadian Bar Association — Ontario, Continuing Legal Education, ed., *The Practical View of the Charter for Solicitors and Barristers* (Toronto: 1986).

Gibson, D., "Accentuating the Positive and Eliminating the Negative: Remedies for Inequality Under the Canadian Charter" in L. Smith et al., eds., *Righting the Balance: Canada's New Equality Rights* (Saskatoon: Canadian Human Rights Reporter, 1986) 311.

Gibson, D., "Canadian Equality Jurisprudence: Year One" in K. E. Mahoney & S. L. Martin, eds., *Equality and Judicial Neutrality* (Toronto: Carswell, 1987) 128.

Gibson, D., "Enforcement of the Canadian Charter of Rights and Freedoms (section 24)" in W. S. Tarnopolsky & G.-A. Beaudoin, eds., *The Canadian Charter of Rights and Freedoms: Commentary* (Toronto: Carswell, 1982) 489.

Gibson, D., *The Law of the Charter: General Principles* (Toronto: Carswell, 1986).

Gibson, D., "Protection of Minority Rights Under the Canadian Charter of Rights and Freedoms: Can Politicians and Judges Sing Harmony?" (1985), 8 Hamline L. Rev. 343.

Gibson, D., "Protection of Minority Rights Under the Canadian Charter of Rights and Freedoms: Can Politicians and Judges Sing Harmony?" in N. Nevitte & A. Kornberg, eds., *Minorities and the Canadian State* (Oakville: Mosaic Press, 1985) 31.

Gold, A. D., "Charter — Court of Competent Jurisdiction" (1986), 28 C.L.Q. 440.

Gold, M., "Some Formative Issues in Litigating Equality" in L. Smith et al., eds.,

Righting the Balance: Canada's New Equality Rights (Saskatoon: Canadian Human Rights Reporter, 1986) 243.

Grondin, R., "Une doctrine d'abus de procédure revigorée en droit pénal canadien" (1983), 24 C. de D. 673.

Hébert, J.-C., "La Charte canadienne et le contrôle de la discrétion ministerielle du Procureur général en droit criminel" (1986), 46 R. du B. 343.

Hébert, J.-C. "The Court of Appeal and Section 24(1) of the Charter" (1985), 27 C.L.Q. 291.

Hébert, J.-C., "Le recours de l'article 24(1) de la Charte", (1983) R. du B. 951.

Hogg, P. W., "Judicial Review on Federal Grounds: Canada Compared to the United States" in G.-A. Beaudoin, ed., *The Supreme Court of Canada* (Cowansville, Que.: Yvon Blais, 1986) 25.

Hovius, B. & Martin, R., "The Canadian Charter of Rights and Freedoms in the Supreme Court of Canada" (1983), 61 Can. Bar Rev. 354.

Jack, D. H., "Suing the Crown and the Application of the Charter" (1986), 7 Advocates' Q. 277.

Johnston, S., "Supreme Court Charter Decisions, 1984: An Analysis" (1985), 34 U.N.B.L.J. 145.

Jones, D. P., "A Note on the Relationship of Waiver and Estoppel to Jurisdictional Defects in Administrative Law" (1987), 25 Alta. L. Rev. 487.

Kerr, R. W., "The Remedial Power of the Courts After the Manitoba Language Rights Case" (1986), 6 Windsor Y.B. Access Just. 252.

Langlois, R., "La preuve dans les affaires mettant en cause la Charte canadienne des droits et libertés" (1985), 45 R. du B. 617.

Levy, J. C., "The Invocation of Remedies Under the Charter of Rights and Freedoms: Some Procedural Considerations" (1983), 13 Man. L.J. 523.

Low, M., "The Canadian Charter of Rights and Freedoms and the Role of the Courts: An initial Survey" (1984), 18 U.B.C. L. Rev. 69.

Lysyk, K., "Enforcement of Rights and Freedoms Guaranteed by the Charter" (1985), 43 Advocate 165.

Lysyk, K. M., "Definition and Enforcement of Charter Equality Rights" in L. Smith et al., eds., *Righting the Balance: Canada's New Equality Rights* (Saskatoon: Canadian Human Rights Reporter, 1986) 215.

MacDonald, D. C., "L'impact de la doctrine et de la jurisprudence de la Convention européenne des droits de l'homme sur l'interprétation de la Charte canadienne des droits et libertés" in D. Turp & G.-A. Beaudoin, eds., *Perspectives canadiennes et européennes des droits de la personne* (Cowansville, Que.: Yvon Blais, 1984) 91.

MacDonald, R. A., "Postscript and Prelude — The Jurisprudence of the Charter: Eight Theses" (1982), 4 Sup. Ct. L. Rev. 321.

MacKay, A. W., "Fairness After the Charter: A Rose by Any Other Name?" (1985), 10 Queen's L.J. 263.

MacKay, A. W., "Judging and Equality: For Whom Does the Charter Toll?" (1986), 10 Dalhousie L.J. 35.

MacKay, W., "Judicial Process in the Supreme Court of Canada — Past, Present and Future: Its Implications for the New Charter of Rights" in A. W. MacKay et al., eds., *The Canadian Charter of Rights: Law Practice Revolutionized* (Halifax: Faculty of Law, Dalhousie University, 1982) 49.

MacNeil, M., "Recent Developments in Canadian Law: Labour Law" (1986), 18 Ottawa L. Rev. 83.

MacPherson, J., "The Case for Defendant Government in Charter Litigation" in J. M. Weiler & R. M. Elliot, eds., *Litigating the Values of a Nation: The Canadian Charter of Rights and Freedoms* (Toronto: Carswell, 1986) 378.

MacPherson, J., "Litigating Equality Rights" in L. Smith et al., eds., *Righting the Balance: Canada's New Equality Rights* (Saskatoon: Canadian Human Rights Reporter, 1986) 231.

Magnet, J. E., "The Supreme Court of Canada and the Charter of Rights" in G.-A. Beaudoin, ed., *The Supreme Court of Canada* (Cowansville, Que.: Yvon Blais, 1986) 211.

Manning, M., "Evidence — Proof: A Study on Evidence and Particularly on Proof of Non-Legal Data. Proof of Facts in Constitutional Cases" in G.-A. Beaudoin, ed., *Charter Cases* (Cowansville, Qué.: Yvon Blais, 1987) 271.

Manning, M., "The Role of the Supreme Court of Canada Under the Canadian Charter of Rights and Freedoms" in G.-A. Beaudoin, ed., *The Supreme Court of Canada* (Cowansville, Que.: Yvon Blais, 1986) 221.

Manson, A. & Stuart, D., "Annotation: Mills v. R." (1986), 52 C.R. (3d) 5.

McConnell, W. H., "Recent Developments in Canadian Law: Constitutional Law" (1986), 18 Ottawa L. Rev. 721.

McGinn, F., "The Canadian Charter of Rights and Freedoms — Its Impact on Law Enforcement" (1982), 31 U.N.B.L.J. 177.

McLellan, A. A. & Elman, B. P., "The Enforcement of the Canadian Charter of Rights and Freedoms: An Analysis of Section 24" (1984), 21 Alta. L. Rev. 205.

Morel, A., "Le droit d'obtenir réparation en cas de violation de droits constitutionnels" (1984), 18 R.J.T. 253.

Morel, A., "Valorisation de la Charte canadienne par le moyen de la Déclaration: La rhétorique judiciaire trompeuse" in G.-A. Beaudoin, ed., *La Cour suprême du Canada* (Cowansville, Que.: Yvon Blais, 1986) 245.

Morgan, B., "Charter Remedies: The Civil Side After the First Five Years" in N. Finkelstein & B. McL. Rogers, eds., *Charter Issues in Civil Cases* (Toronto: Carswell, 1988) 47.

Morton, F. L., "Charting the Charter — Year One: A Statistical Analysis", [1984-1985] Can. Hum. Rts Y.B. 237.

Morton, F. L., "The Political Impact of the Canadian Charter of Rights and Freedoms" (1987), 20 Can. J. Pol. Sc. 31.

Morton, F. L. & Pal, L. A., "The Impact of the Charter of Rights on Public Administration" (1985), 28 Can. Pub. Admin. 221.

Morton, F. L. & Withey, M. J., "Charting the Charter, 1982 — 1985: A Statistical Analysis", [1987] Can. Hum. Rts Y.B. 65.

Mossop, D. W., "'Charteritis' and Other Legal Diseases" (1985), 43 Advocate 201.

Mullan, D. J. & Roman, A. J., "Minister of Justice of Canada v. Borowski: The Extent of the Citizen's Right to Litigate the Lawfulness of Government Action" (1984), 4 Windsor Y.B. Access Just. 303.

Murphy, M. J., "L'intérêt à poursuivre en vertu du paragraphe 24(1) de la Charte canadienne des droits et libertés" (1986), 35 R.D.U.N.B. 188.

Ouellette, Y., "La Charte canadienne et les tribunaux administratifs" (1984), 18 R.J.T. 295.

Petter, A., "Immaculate Deception: The Charter's Hidden Agenda" in Continuing Legal Education Society of British Columbia, ed., *Charter of Rights — 1987* (Vancouver: 1987) 12.1.01.

Petter, A., "The Politics of the Charter: Lessons from the Early Charter Decisions of the Supreme Court of Canada" (1986), 6 Sup. Ct. L. Rev. 473.

Pilkington, M. L., "Damages as a Remedy for Infringement of the Canadian Charter of Rights and Freedoms" (1984), 62 Can. Bar Rev. 517.

Pilkington, M. L., "Monetary Redress for Charter Infringement" in R. J. Sharpe, ed., *Charter Litigation* (Toronto: Butterworths, 1987) 307.

Pratt, A. "The Supreme Law in the Supreme Court: The First Seven Charter Cases" (1986), 6 Advocates' Q. 409.

Remillard, G., "Les conditions d'application de la Charte canadienne des droits et libertés" in Barreau du Québec. Formation permanente, ed., *L'interaction des Chartes canadienne et québécoise des droits et libertés* (Montreal: 1984) 1.

Richards, J. G. & Smith, G. J., "Applying the Charter" (1983), 4 Advocates' Q. 129.

Roach, K., "Section 24(1) of the Charter: Strategy and Structure" (1986-87), 29 C.L.Q. 222.

Robert, M., "Aperçu de la procédure réglementant l'exercice de la compétence des tribunaux en vertu de la Charte. L'opportunité de procéder par voie d'action ou de requête" in G.-A. Beaudoin, ed., *Causes invoquant la Charte 1986-87* (Cowansville, Que.: Yvon Blais, 1987) 207.

Robinette, J. J., "Remedies for Breach of the Charter of Rights and Freedoms — Relevant Sections" in Canadian Institute for Advanced Legal Studies, ed., *Cambridge Lectures 1983* (Toronto: Butterworths, 1985) 39.

Rogerson, C., "The Judicial Search for Appropriate Remedies Under the Charter: The Examples of Overbreadth and Vagueness" in R. J. Sharpe, ed., *Charter Litigation* (Toronto: Butterworths, 1987) 233.

Roman, A. J., "The Possible Impact of the Canadian Charter of Rights and Freedoms on Administrative Law" (1985), 26 C. de D. 339.

Rosenberg, M., "Examination of Questions Pertaining To: When?" in G.-A. Beaudoin, ed., *Charter Cases 1986-87* (Cowansville, Que: Yvon Blais, 1987) 183.

Russell, P. H., "The First Three Years in Charterland" (1985), 28 Can. Pub. Admin. 367.

Sack, J. et al., "Where to Go and How to Get There: Questions of Forum and Form in Charter Litigation" in G.-A. Beaudoin, ed., *Charter Cases 1986-87* (Cowansville, Que.: Yvon Blais, 1987) 143.

Scott, I. G., "The Role of the Attorney General and the Charter of Rights" (1987), 29 C.L.Q. 187.

Sharpe, R. J., "The Charter of Rights and Freedoms and the Supreme Court of Canada: The First Four Years", 1987 Public Law 48.

Sharpe, R. J., "Choice of Forum" in Law Society of Upper Canada, Department of Education, ed., *Equality: Section 15 and Charter Procedures* (Toronto: 1985) ch. I.

Sharpe, R. J., "Injunctions and the Charter" (1984), 22 Osgoode Hall L.J. 473.

Sharpe, R. J., ed., *Charter Litigation* (Toronto: Butterworths, 1987).

Shumiatcher, M., "Chaff from the Charter's Threshing Floor" (1983), 13 Man. L.J. 437.

Smith, G. J. & Richards, G., "A Colloquy on the Significance of the Charter in Civil Proceedings Against Government" (1986), 2 Admin. L.J. 9.

Sopinka, J., "The Charter: A View from the Bar" in G.-A. Beaudoin, ed., *Charter Cases 1986-87* (Cowansville, Que.: Yvon Blais, 1987) 403.

Spitz, S. L., "Litigation Strategy in Equality Rights: The American Experience" in J. M. Weiler & R. M. Elliot, eds., *Litigating the Values of the Nation: The Canadian Charter of Rights and Freedoms* (Toronto: Carswell, 1986) 385.

Strayer, B. L., *The Canadian Constitution and the Courts: The Function and Scope of Judicial Review*, 3rd ed. (Toronto: Butterworths, 1988).

Swan, K. P., "Intervention and Amicus Curiae Status in Charter Litigation" in G.-A. Beaudoin, ed., *Charter Cases 1986-87* (Cowansville, Que.: Yvon Blais, 1987) 95.

Swan, K. P., "Intervention and Amicus Curiae Status in Charter Litigation" in R. J. Sharpe, ed., *Charter Litigation* (Toronto: Butterworths, 1987) 27.

Turp, D., "Le recours au droit international aux fins de l'interprétation de la Charte canadienne des droits et libertés: un bilan jurisprudentiel" (1984), 18 R.J.T. 353.

Weiler, J., & Elliot, R. M., eds., *Litigating the Values of a Nation: The Canadian Charter of Rights and Freedoms* (Toronto: Carswell, 1986).

Weiler, P. C., "Rights and Judges in a Democracy: A New Canadian Version" (1984), 18 U. Mich. J. L. Ref. 51.

Welch, J., "No Room at the Top: Interest Group Intervenors and Charter Litigation in the Supreme Court of Canada" (1985), 43 U.T. Fac. L. Rev. 204.

Wright, B. & Cavarzan, J., "The Role of the Attorney General in Litigating Charter Claims" in Law Society of Upper Canada, Department of Education, ed., *Equality: Section 15 and Charter Procedures* (Toronto: 1985) ch. L.

Section 24(2): Exclusion of Evidence

Arbour, L., "Annotation: R. v. Manuel" (1986), 50 C.R. (3d) 47.

Brent, A. S., "Illegally Obtained Evidence: An Historical and Comparative Analysis" (1983), 48 Sask. L. Rev. 1.

Chasse, K., "Charter Exclusion — Causation, Nexus and Disrepute" (1986), 21 C.R.R. 227.

Connelly, P. J., "Charter of Rights and Freedoms — Warrantless Search of Business Premises — Whether under s. 8 — R. v. Rao (1984) 46 O.R. (2d) 80 (C.A.)" (1984), 26 C.L.Q. 410.

Conway, R., "The Right to Counsel and the Admissibility of Evidence" (1985), 28 C.L.Q. 28.

Delisle, R. J., "Annotation: Clarkson v. R." (1986), 50 C.R. (3d) 290.

Delisle, R. J., "Collins: An Unjustified Distinction" (1987), 56 C.R. (3d) 216.

Doherty, D. H., "Stevens: Section 24(2) of the Charter on Appeal: Comment on R. v. Stevens" (1983), 35 C.R. (3d) 30.

Duncan, B., "Clarkson: Some Unanswered Questions" (1986), 50 C.R. (3d) 305.

Duncan, B., "The Blind Eye Argument and a Modest Proposal" (1985), 47 C.R. (3d) 16.

Elman, B. P., "Collins v. The Queen: Further Jurisprudence on Section 24(2) of the Charter" (1987), 25 Alta. L. Rev. 477.

Frankel, S. D., "Exclusion of Evidence" in Continuing Legal Education Society of British Columbia, ed., *Charter of Rights — 1987* (Vancouver: 1987) 9.5.01.

Gibson, D., "Determining Disrepute: Opinion Polls and The Canadian Charter of Rights and Freedoms" (1983), 61 Can. Bar Rev. 377.

Gibson, D., *The Law of the Charter: General Principles* (Toronto: Carswell, 1986).

Gibson, D., "Shocking the Public: Early Indications of the Meaning of 'Disrepute' in Section 24(2) of the Charter" (1983), 13 Man. L.J. 495.

Gold, A. D., "Charter of Rights — Arbitrary Detention — R. v. Duguay, Murphy and Sevigny (1985), 178 C.C.C. (3rd) 289, 50 O.R. (2nd) 375 (C.A.) MacKinnon ACJO, Martin and Zuber JJ.A." (1985), 28 C.L.Q. 17.

Gold, A. D., "Charter of Rights — Search and Seizure — Review of Warrant — R. v. Komadowski" (1987), 29 C.L.Q. 288.

Jull, K., "Clarkson v. R.: Do We Need a Legal Emergency Department?" (1987), 32 McGill L.J. 339.

Jull, K., "Exclusion of Evidence and the Beast of Burden" (1988), 30 C.L.Q. 178.

Jull, K., "Remedies for Non-Compliance with Investigative Procedures: A Theoretical Overview" (1985), 17 Ottawa L. Rev. 525.

Klinck, D. R., "The Quest for Meaning in Charter Adjudication: Comment on R. v. Therens" (1985), 31 McGill L.J. 104.

Lachance, C.-A., "L'exclusion de la preuve illégalement obtenue et la Charte" (1984), 62 R. du B. Can. 278.

MacCrimmon, M. T., "Developments in the Law of Evidence: The 1984-85 Term" (1986), 8 Sup. Ct. L. Rev. 249.

Mitchell, G. E., "The Supreme Court of Canada on the Exclusion of Evidence in Criminal Cases Under Section 24 of the Charter" (1988), 30 C.L.Q. 165.

Morissette, Y.-M., "The Exclusion of Evidence Under the Canadian Charter of Rights and Freedoms: What to Do and What Not to Do" (1984), 29 McGill L.J. 521.

O'Donnell, F. C., "The Thin Blue Line: Customs Searches and the Charter of Rights" (1984), 16 Ottawa L. Rev. 467.

Paciocco, D. M., *Charter Principles and Proof in Criminal Cases* (Toronto: Carswell, 1987) 335.

Paciocco, D. M., "The Constitutional Right to Present Defence Evidence in Criminal Cases" (1985), 63 Can. Bar Rev. 519.

Proulx, M., "Redéfinir les rapports de force au procès criminel: L'effet de la règle d'exclusion de l'article 24(2) de la Charte canadienne des droits et libertés" (1986), 20 R.J.T. 109.

Rolls, R. J., "The Use of Evidence in Charter Litigation" in Canadian Bar Association — Ontario. Continuing Legal Education, ed., *The Practical View of the Charter for Solicitors and Barristers* (Toronto: 1986).

Stuart, D., "Annotation: R. v. Strachau" (1986), 49 C.R. (3d) 290.

Welsh, K., "Breathalyzer, Detention, and the Right to Counsel: R. v. Therens" (1985), 23 Alta. L. Rev. 524.

Woods, S., "Interrogation Law and the Charter: An American Plan for the Renovation" (1985), 43 U.T. Fac. L. Rev. 153.

SECTIONS 25 AND 35: ABORIGINAL RIGHTS

Asch, M., *Home and Native Land: Aboriginal Rights and the Canadian Constitution* (Toronto: Methuen, 1984).

Barsch, R. L. & Henderson, J. Y., "Aboriginal Rights, Treaty Rights and Human Rights: Indian Tribes and 'Constitutional Renewal'" (1982), 17 J. Can. Studies 55.

Calder, W., "The Provinces and Indian Self-Government in the Constitutional Forum" in J. A. Long & M. Boldt, eds., *Governments in Conflict? Provinces and Indian Nations in Canada* (Toronto: University of Toronto Press, 1988) 72.

Cardinal, H., "Indian Nations and Constitutional Change" in J. A. Long & M. Boldt, eds., *Governments in Conflict? Provinces and Indian Nations in Canada* (Toronto: University of Toronto Press, 1988) 83.

Emery, G., "Réflexions sur le sens et la portée au Québec des articles 25, 35 et 37 de la Loi constitutionnelle de 1982" (1985), 25 C. de D. 145.

Ginn, D. "Indian Hunting Rights: *Dick v. R.*, *Jack and Charlie v. R.* and *Simon v. R.*" (1986), 31 McGill L.J. 527.

Green, L. C., "Aboriginal Peoples, International Law and the Canadian Charter of Rights and Freedoms" (1983), 61 Can. Bar Rev. 339.

Hawkes, D. C., *Negotiating Aboriginal Self-Government: Developments Surrounding the 1985 First Ministers' Conference* (Kingston: Institute of Intergovernmental Relations, Queen's University, 1987).

Hayward, A., "R. v. Jack and Charlie and the Constitution Act, 1982: Religious Freedom and Aboriginal Rights in Canada" (1984), 10 Queen's L.J. 165.

Little Bear, L.; et al., eds., *Governments in Conflict? Provinces and Indian Nations in Canada* (Toronto: University of Toronto Press, 1988).

Little Bear, L., et al., eds., *Pathways to Self-Determination: Canadian Indians and The Canadian State* (Toronto: University of Toronto Press, 1984).

Lysyk, K.M., "The Rights and Freedoms of the Aboriginal Peoples of Canada (ss. 25, 35 and 37)" in W. S. Tarnopolsky & G.-A. Beaudoin, eds., *The Canadian Charter of Rights and Freedoms: Commentary* (Toronto: Carswell, 1982) 467.

McDonald, M., "Indian Status: Colonialism or Sexism?" (1987), 9 Can. Community L.J. 23.

McMurtry, W. R. & Pratt, A., "Indians and the Fiduciary Concept, Self-Government and the Constitution: Guerin in Perspective" (1986), 3 Can. Native L. Rep. 19.

McNeil, K., "The Constitutional Rights of the Aboriginal Peoples of Canada" (1982), 4 Sup. Ct. L. Rev. 255.

Morgan, E. M, "Self-Government and the Constitution: A Comparative Look at Native Canadian and American Indians" (1984), 12 American Indian L. Rev. 39.

Morse, B. W., & Broves, R. K., "Canada's Forgotten Peoples: Aboriginal Rights of Metis and Non-Status Indians" (1987), 2 Law & Anthropology — Internationales Jahrbuch fur Rechtsanthropologie 139.

Nakatsuru, S., "A Constitutional Right of Indian Self-Government" (1985), 43 U.T. Fac. L. Rev. 72.

Opekokew, D., *The Political and Legal Inequities Among Aboriginal Peoples in Canada* (Kingston: Institute of Intergovernmental Relations, Queen's University, 1987).

O'Reilly, J., "La Loi constitutionnelle de 1982, droit des autochtones" (1984), 25 C. de D. 125.

Pentney, W., *The Aboriginal Rights Provisions in the Constitution Act, 1982* (Saskatoon: University of Saskatchewan Native Law Centre, 1987).

Pentney, W., "The Rights of the Aboriginal Peoples of Canada and the Constitution Act, 1982: Part I: The Interpretive Prism of Section 25" (1988), 22 U.B.C. L. Rev. 21.

Sanders, D., "Article 27 and the Aboriginal Peoples of Canada" in Canadian Human

Rights Foundation, ed., *Multiculturalism and the Charter: A Legal Perspective* (Toronto: Carswell, 1987) 155.

Sanders, D., "The Constitution, the Provinces, and Aboriginal Peoples" in J. A. Long et al., eds., *Governments in Conflict? Provinces and Indian Nations in Canada* (Toronto: University of Toronto Press, 1988) 151.

Sanders, D., "The Indian Lobby" in K. Banting & R. Simeon, eds., *And No One Cheered: Federalism, Democracy & The Constitution Act* (Toronto: Methuen, 1983) 301.

Sanders, D., "Prior Claims" in S. M. Beck & I. Bernier, eds., *Canada and the New Constitution: The Unfinished Agenda* (Montreal: Institute for Research in Public Policy, 1983) 225.

Sanders, D., "The Renewal of Indian Special Status" in A. F. Bayefsky & M. Eberts, eds., *Equality Rights and the Canadian Charter of Rights and Freedoms* (Toronto: Carswell, 1985) 529.

Sanders, D., "The Rights of the Aboriginal Peoples of Canada" (1983), 61 Can. Bar Rev. 314.

Sanders, D., "An Uncertain Path: The Aboriginal Constitutional Conferences" in J. M. Weiler & R. M. Eliot, eds., *Litigating the Values of a Nation: The Canadian Charter of Rights and Freedoms* (Toronto: Carswell, 1986) 62.

Schwartz, B., *First Principles, Second Thoughts: Aboriginal Peoples, Constitutional Reform and Canadian Statecraft* (Montreal: Institute for Research on Public Policy, 1986).

Scott, I. G. & McCabe, J.T.S., "The Role of the Provinces in the Elucidation of Aboriginal Rights in Canada" in J. A. Long et al, eds., *Governments in Conflict? Provinces and Indian Nations in Canada* (Toronto: University of Toronto Press, 1988) 59.

Slattery, B., "The Constitutional Guarantee of Aboriginal and Treaty Rights" (1983), 8 Queen's L.J. 232.

Wildsmith, B. H., *Aboriginal Peoples and Section 25 of the Canadian Charter of Rights and Freedoms* (Saskatoon: University of Saskatchewan Native Law Centre, 1988).

SECTION 26: OTHER RIGHTS

Stevenson, C. P., "A New Perspective on Environmental Rights After the Charter" (1983), 21 Osgoode Hall L.J. 390.

SECTION 27: MULTICULTURALISM

Anand, R., "Ethnic Equality" in A. F. Bayefsky & M. Eberts, eds., *Equality Rights and the Canadian Charter of Rights and Freedoms* (Toronto: Carswell, 1985) 81.

Beaudoin, G.-A., "Le multiculturalisme et les droits confessionnels et linguistiques: une vue succincte" in Canadian Human Rights Foundation, ed., *Multiculturalism and The Charter: A Legal Perspective* (Toronto: Carswell, 1987) 15.

Beaudoin, G.-A., "La protection constitutionnelle des minorités" (1986), 27 C. de D. 31.

Beckton, C. F., "Section 27 and Section 15 of the Charter" in Canadian Human Rights Foundation, ed., *Multiculturalism and The Charter: A Legal Perspective* (Toronto: Carswell, 1987) 1.

Berger, T. R., "The Charter and Canadian Identity" (1985), 23 U.W.O.L. Rev. 1.

Canadian Human Rights Foundation, *Multiculturalism and the Charter: A Legal Perspective* (Toronto: Carswell, 1987).

Gall, G. L., "Multiculturalism and the Fundamental Freedoms: Section 27 and Section 2" in Canadian Human Rights Foundation, ed., *Multiculturalism and the Charter: A Legal Perspective* (Toronto: Carswell, 1987) 29.

Gall, G. L., "Some Miscellaneous Aspects of Section 15 of the Canadian Charter of Rights and Freedoms" (1986), 24 Alta. L. Rev. 462.

Gibson, D., "Protection of Minority Rights Under the Canadian Charter of Rights and Freedoms: Can Politicians and Judges Bring Harmony?" in N. Nevitte & A. Kornberg, eds., *Minorities and the Canadian State* (Oakville: Mosaic Press, 1985) 31.

Hudson, M. R., "Multiculturalism, Government Policy and Constitutional Enshrinement: A Comparative Study" in Canadian Human Rights Foundation, ed., *Multiculturalism and the Charter: A Legal Perspective* (Toronto: Carswell, 1987) 59.

Ivankovich, I. F., "Prolonging the Sunday Closing Imbroglio: Regina v. Videoflicks Ltd." (1986), 24 Alta. L. Rev. 334.

Lebel, M., "Quelques réflexions autour de l'article 27 de la Charte canadienne des droits" in Canadian Human Rights Foundation, ed., *Multiculturalism and the Charter: A Legal Perspective* (Toronto: Carswell, 1987) 139.

Magnet, J. E., "Collective Rights, Cultural Autonomy and the Canadian State" (1986), 32 McGill L.J. 170.

Magnet, J. E., "Interpreting Multiculturalism" in Canadian Human Rights Foundation, ed., *Multiculturalism and the Charter: A Legal Perspective* (Toronto: Carswell, 1987) 145.

Nevitte, N. & Kornberg, A., eds., *Minorities and the Canadian State* (Oakville: Mosaic Press, 1985).

Petter, A., "Not 'Never on a Sunday': R. v. Videoflicks Ltd. et al." (1985), 49 Sask. L. Rev. 96.

Poulantzas, N. M., "Multiculturalism, Affirmative Action Programs Under the Canadian Charter of Rights and Freedoms and the Protection of Minorities" (1985), 73 Rev. de D. Int'l 309.

Sanders, D., "Article 27 and the Aboriginal Peoples of Canada" in Canadian Human Rights Foundation, ed., *Multiculturalism and the Charter: A Legal Perspective* (Toronto: Carswell, 1987) 155.

Schmeiser, D. A., "Multiculturalism in Canadian Education" in Canadian Human Rights Foundation, ed., *Multiculturalism and the Charter: A Legal Perspective* (Toronto: Carswell, 1987) 167.

Tarnopolsky, W. S., "The Effect of Section 27 on the Interpretation of the Charter" in T. Yedlin, ed., *Central and East European Ethnicity in Canada: Adaptation and Preservation* (Edmonton: Central and East European Studies Society of Alberta, 1985) 1.

Tarnopolsky, W. S., "Equality and Discrimination" in R. S. Abella & M. L. Rothman, eds., *Justice Beyond Orwell* (Montreal: Yvon Blais, 1985) 267.

Tarnopolsky, W. S., "The Equality Rights (ss. 15, 27 and 28)" in W. S. Tarnopolsky & G.-A. Beaudoin, eds., *The Canadian Charter of Rights and Freedoms: Commentary* (Toronto: Carswell 1982) 395.

Tarnopolsky, W. S., "The Equality Rights in the Canadian Charter of Rights and Freedoms" (1983), 61 Can. Bar Rev. 242.

Woehrling, J., "La constitution canadienne et la protection des minorités ethniques" (1986), 27 C. de D. 171.

Woehrling, J., "Minority Cultural and Linguistic Rights and Equality Rights in the Canadian Charter of Rights and Freedoms" (1985), 31 McGill L.J. 51.

SECTION 28: SEXUAL EQUALITY
(See Section 15: Sex)
SECTION 29: DENOMINATIONAL SCHOOLS

Bale, G., "Constitutional Values in Conflict: Full Funding for Ontario's Catholic High Schools" (1986), 18 Ottawa L. Rev. 533.

Stainsby, J., "Plus ça change . . . : Education and Equality Rights in the Supreme Court" (1988), 46 U.T. Fac. L. Rev. 259.

SECTION 32: APPLICATION

Baigent, J. & Hoskins, J., "Government Action: Federal and Provincial Governments and Others as Defendants" in G.-A. Beaudoin, ed., *Charter Cases 1986-87* (Cowansville, Que.: Yvon Blais, 1987) 113.

Baker, J. B., "Fighting City Hall with the Equality Rights Provisions of the Canadian Charter of Rights and Freedoms" (1985), 43 Advocate 69.

Belobaba, E. P., "The Charter of Rights and Private Litigation: The Dilemma of Dolphin Delivery" in N. Finkelstein & B. McL. Rogers, eds., *Charter Issues in Civil Cases* (Toronto: Carswell, 1988) 29.

Buckingham, D., "The Canadian Charter of Rights and Freedoms and Private Action Applying the Purposive Approach" (1987), 51 Sask. L. Rev. 105.

Corry, D. J., "Military Law Under the Charter" (1986), 24 Osgoode Hall L.J. 67.

De Montigny, Y., "La Charte des droits et libertés, la prérogative royale et les 'questions politiques'" (1984), 44 R. du B. 156.

De Montigny, Y., "Section 32 and Equality Rights" in A. F. Bayefsky & M. Eberts, eds., *Equality Rights and the Canadian Charter of Rights and Freedoms* (Toronto: Carswell, 1985) 565.

Dussault, R., "Qu'est-ce que le gouvernement et quelle est l'étendue de sa sphère?" in G.-A. Beaudoin, ed., *Vos clients et la Charte — Liberté et égalité* (Cowansville, Que.: Yvon Blais, 1988) 91.

Etherington, B., "Constitutional Law — Charter of Rights and Freedoms, Section 2(b) and 1 — Application of the Charter to the Common Law in Private Litigation — Freedom of Expression — Picketing in Labour Disputes — Retail, Wholesale and Dept. Store Union, Local 580 v. Dolphin Delivery Ltd." (1987), 66 Can. Bar Rev. 818.

Fairweather, R. G. L., "Procedural Fairness: A Challenge for the Canadian Human Rights Commission" (1985), 10 Queen's L. J. 430.

Fichaud, J., "Analysis of the Charter and Its Application to Labour Law" (1984), 8 Dalhousie L. J. 402.

Finkelstein, N. & Rogers, B. McL., eds., *Charter Issues in Civil Cases* (Toronto: Carswell, 1988).

Gagnon, J.-D., "L'arrêt Dolphin Delivery: la porte est-elle ouverte ou fermée?" (1987), 32 R. D. McGill 924.

Gibson, D., "Distinguishing the Governors from the Governed: The Meaning of 'Government' Under Section 32(1) of the Charter" (1983), 13 Man. L. J. 505.

Gibson, D., *The Law of the Charter: General Principles* (Toronto: Carswell, 1986) 85.

Gibson, D., "Protection of Minority Rights under the Canadian Charter of Rights and Freedoms: Can Politicians and Judges Sing Harmony?" (1985), 8 Hamline L. Rev. 343.

Gibson, D., "Tort Law and the Charter of Rights" (1986), 16 Man. L. J. 1.

Gibson, D., "What did Dolphin Deliver?" in G.-A. Beaudoin, ed., *Your Clients and the Charter — Liberty and Equality* (Cowansville, Que.: Yvon Blais, 1988) 75.

Hogg, P., "The Dolphin Delivery Case: The Application of the Charter to Private Action" (1987), 51 Sask. L. Rev. 273.

Hogg, P., "Who Is Bound by the Charter?" in G.-A. Beaudoin, ed., *Your Clients and the Charter — Liberty and Equality* (Cowansville, Que.: Yvon Blais, 1988) 15.

Hough, B., "Equality Provisions in the Charter: Their Meaning and Interrelationships with Federal and Provincial Rights Acts" in A. W. MacKay et al, eds., *The Canadian Charter of Rights: Law Practice Revolutionized* (Halifax: Dalhousie University, 1982) 306.

Howse, R., "Dolphin Delivery: The Supreme Court and The Public/Private Distinction in Canadian Constitutional Law" (1988), 46 U.T. Fac. L. Rev. 248.

Jack, D.H., "Suing the Crown and the Application of the Charter" (1986), 7 Advocates' Q. 277.

Jordan, D. J., "The Charter: Labour and Employment Law" in Continuing Legal Education Society of British Columbia, ed., *Equality Rights* (Vancouver: 1985) 2.2.

Laskin, J. I., "Section 15 of the Charter and Human Rights Legislation" in Law

Society of Upper Canada, Continuing Legal Education Department, eds., *Equality: Section 15 and Charter Procedures* (Toronto: 1985).

Laskin, J. I. & Hughes, P., "The Charter and the Code" in Law Society of Upper Canada, Continuing Legal Education Department, ed., *Human Rights* (Toronto: 1983).

Lederman, S. N. & Ristic, A., "The Relationship Between Federal and Provincial Human Rights Legislation and Charter Equality Rights" in L. Smith et al., eds., *Righting the Balance: Canada's New Equality Rights* (Saskatoon: Canadian Human Rights Reporter, 1986) 83.

Lemieux, D. & Savard, E., "Vers une judiciarisation du conseil des ministres?" (1985), 26 C. de D. 361.

Lessard, H., "The Idea of the "Private": A Discussion of State Action Doctrine and Separate Sphere Ideology" (1986), 10 Dalhousie L. J. 107.

Lewis, C. B., "The Legal Nature of a University and the Student-University Relationship" (1983), 15 Ottawa L. Rev. 249 at 270.

Lluelles, D. & Trudel, P., "L'application de la Charte canadienne des droits et libertés aux rapports de droit privé" (1984), 18 R.J.T. 219.

MacKay, A. W., "The Canadian Charter of Rights and Freedoms: A Springboard to Students' Rights" (1984), 4 Windsor Y.B. Access Just. 174 at 182.

MacKay, A. W., "Students as Second Class Citizens Under the Charter" (1987), 54 C.R. (3d) 390.

MacKay, P., "L'evolution de la souveraineté du Parlement du Canada dans le cadre de la Loi constitutionnelle de 1982: vers une souveraineté multiparlementaire" in Association canadienne-française pour l'avancement des sciences, ed., *La Charte canadienne des droits et libertés et les droits collectifs et sociaux* (Quebec: 1983) 105.

Mallory, J. R., "Beyond 'Manner and Form': Reading Between the Lines in Operation Dismantle Inc. v. R." (1986), 31 McGill L.J. 480.

McLellan, A. A. & Elman, B. P., "To Whom Does the Charter Apply? Some Recent Cases on Section 32" (1986), 24 Alta. L. Rev. 361.

McNairn, C. H. H., "Equality in Public Sector Employment" in Canadian Bar Association — Ontario, Continuing Legal Education Department, ed., *The Practical View of the Charter for Solicitors and Barristers* (Toronto: 1986).

Morel, A., "La coéxistence des chartes canadienne et québécoise: problèmes d'interaction" (1986), 17 R.D.U.S. 49.

Morton, F.␣L. & Pal, L.␣A., "The Impact of the Charter of Rights on Public Administration" (1985), 28 Can. Pub. Admin. 221.

Moull, W. D., "Business Law Implications of the Canadian Charter of Rights and Freedoms" (1984), 8 Can. Bus. L.J. 449.

Neudorfer, A., "Cabinet Decisions and Judicial Review" (1985), 1 Admin. L. J. 30.

Norman, K., "The Charter for the Public Sector and for the Private Sector, Human Rights Codes: A False Dichotomy Leading to the Wrong Result. An Open

Letter to the Hon. J.Gary Lane, Q.C., Minister of Justice and Attorney General" (1984), 5 C.H.R.R. C/84-5.

Otis, G., "The Charter, Private Action and the Supreme Court" (1987), 19 Ottawa L. Rev. 71.

Pepin, G., "The Problem of Section 96 of the Constitution Act, 1867" in C. F. Beckton & A. W. MacKay, eds., *The Courts and the Charter* (Toronto: The University of Toronto Press, 1985) 223.

Petter, A., "The Charter and Private Action: The Impact of Section 15 on Human Rights Codes" (1984), 5 C.H.R.R. C/84-1.

Pilkington, M. L., "Damages as a Remedy for Infringement of the Canadian Charter of Rights and Freedoms" (1984), 62 Can. Bar Rev. 517.

Pratt, A., "The Charter and How to Approach It: A Guide for the Civil Practitioner" (1983), 4 Advocates' Q. 425.

Pratt, A., "The Supreme Law in the Supreme Court: The First Seven Charter Cases" (1986), 6 Advocates' Q. 409.

Pratte, S., "La primauté du droit: L'origine du principe et son évolution dans le contexte de la Charte canadienne des droits et libertés" (1986), 27 C. de D. 685.

Rankin, M. & Roman, A. J., "Constitutional Law — A New Basis for Screening Constitutional Questions Under the Canadian Charter of Rights and Freedoms — Prejudging the Evidence?: Operation Dismantle Inc. et al. v. The Queen et al." (1987), 66 Can. Bar Rev. 365.

Rémilliard, G., "La Charte canadienne des droits et libertés: les conditions d'application de la Charte" in Barreau du Québec, Formation permanente, ed., *La Charte canadienne des droits et libertés* (Montreal, 1983) 55.

Rémillard, G., "Les conditions d'application de la Charte canadienne des droits et libertés" in Barreau du Québec, Formation permanente, ed., *L'interaction des chartes canadienne et québécoise des droits et libertés* (Montreal: 1984) 1.

Richards, J. G., "The Charter and Private and Public Sector Corporations: Scope and Application" in Canadian Institute for Professional Development, ed., *The Charter and the Corporation: New Vistas for Corporate Rights* (Toronto: 1985) A-1.

Richards, J. G., "Professional Associations and the Charter" in Canadian Bar Association — Ontario, Continuing Legal Education Department, ed., *The Practical View of the Charter for Solicitors and Barristers* (Toronto: 1986).

Richards, J. G. & Smith, G. J., "Applying the Charter" (1983), 4 Advocates Q. 129.

Riggs, C. G., "The Charter of Rights: Its Impact on Collective Bargaining and Employment Law" in Canadian Institute for Professional Development, ed., *The Charter and the Corporation: New vistas for Corporate Rights* (Toronto: 1985) F-1.

Roman, A. J., "The Possible Impact of the Canadian Charter of Rights and Freedoms on Administrative Law" (1985), 26 C. de D. 339.

Sack, J., "The Impact of the Charter on Public Sector Employees" in Canadian Bar Association — Ontario, Continuing Legal Education Department, ed., *The Practical View of the Charter for Solicitors and Barristers* (Toronto: 1986).

Slattery, B., "Charter of Rights and Freedoms — Does it Bind Private Persons?" (1985), 63 Can. Bar Rev. 148.

Slattery, B., "The Charter's Relevance to Private Litigation: Does Dolphin Deliver?" (1987), 32 McGill L. J. 905.

Smith, G. J., "The Charter, the Corporation and the Regulatory Process" in Canadian Institute for Professional Development, ed., *The Charter and the Corporation: New Vistas for Corporate Rights* (Toronto: 1985) B-1.

Smith, G. J., ed., *Charter of Rights and Administrative Law* (Toronto: Carswell, 1983).

Smith, G. J. & Richards, J. G., "A Colloquy on the Significance of the Charter in Civil Proceedings Against Government" (1986), 2 Admin. L. J. 9.

Swinton, K., "Application of the Canadian Charter of Rights and Freedoms (ss. 30, 31, 32)" in W. S. Tarnopolsky & G.-A. Beaudoin, eds., *The Canadian Charter of Rights and Freedoms: Commentary* (Toronto: Carswell, 1982) 41.

Tassé, R., "À qui incombe l'obligation de respecter les droits et libertés garantis par la Charte canadienne des droits et libertés?" in G.-A. Beaudoin, ed., *Vos clients et la Charte — Liberté et égalité* (Cowansville, Que.: Yvon Blais, 1988) 35.

Whyte, J. D., "Is the Private Sector Affected by the Charter?" in L. Smith et al., eds., *Righting the Balance: Canada's New Equality Rights* (Saskatoon: Canadian Human Rights Reporter, 1986) 145.

Young, R. E., "The Approving Officer, the Public Interest and Subdivision Appeals" (1985), 43 Advocate 18.

SECTION 33: DEROGATION

aa., "The Charter and S. 33: Holding Politicians Accountable" (1987), 3 Admin. L.J. 21.

Arbess, D. J., "Limitations on Legislative Override Under the Canadian Charter of Rights and Freedoms: A Matter of Balancing Values" (1983), 21 Osgoode Hall L.J. 115.

Bayefsky, A. F., "The Judicial Function Under the Canadian Charter of Rights and Freedoms" (1987), 32 McGill L.J. 791.

Beaudoin, G.-A., "Les clauses dérogatoires et limitatives des instruments canadiens des droits de la personne" in D. Turp & G.-A. Beaudoin, eds., *Perspectives canadiennes et européennes des droits de la personne* (Cowansville, Que.: Yvon Blais, 1984) 139.

Gibson, D., *The Law of the Charter: General Principles* (Toronto: Carswell, 1986).

Gibson, D., "Reasonable Limits Under the Canadian Charter of Rights and Freedoms" (1985), 15 Man. L.J. 27.

Laselva, S. V., "Only in Canada: Reflections on the Charter's Notwithstanding Clause" (1983), 63 Dalhousie Rev. 383.

MacKay, P., "L'évolution de la souveraineté du Parlement du Canada dans le cadre de la Loi constitutionnelle de 1982: vers une souveraineté multiparlementaire" in Association canadienne-française pour l'avancement des sciences, ed., *La Charte canadienne des droits et libertés et les droits collectifs et sociaux* (Quebec, 1983) 105.

Marx, H., "Entrenchment, Limitations and Non-Obstante (ss. 1, 33 and 52)" in W.S. Tarnopolsky & G.-A. Beaudoin, eds., *The Canadian Charter of Rights and Freedoms: Commentary* (Toronto: Carswell, 1982) 61.

Monahan, P., *Politics and the Constitution: The Charter, Federalism and the Supreme Court of Canada* (Toronto: Carswell, 1987).

Rémillard, G., "Les conditions d'application de la Charte canadienne des droits et libertés" in Barreau du Québec. Formation permanente, ed., L'interaction des chartes canadienne et québécoise des droits et libertés (Montreal, 1984) 1 at 39.

Scott, S. A., "Entrenchment by Executive Action: A Partial Solution to 'Legislative Override'" (1982), 4 Sup. Ct. L. Rev. 303.

Slattery, B., "Canadian Charter of Rights and Freedoms — Override Clauses Under Section 33 — Whether Subject to Judicial Review Under Section 1" (1983), 61 Can. Bar Rev. 391.

Weiler, P. C., "The Evolution of the Charter: A View from the Outside" in J. M. Weiler & R. M. Elliot, eds., *Litigating the Values of a Nation: The Canadian Charter of Rights and Freedoms* (Toronto: Carswell, 1986) 49.

SECTIONS 35 AND 37
(See under Section 25)
SECTION 52: CHARTER SUPREMACY

Anand, R., "The Relationship Between Section 15 of the Canadian Charter of Rights and Freedoms and Other Employment Legislation" in The Canadian Institute for Professional Development, ed., *Equality Rights and Employment: Preparing for Fundamental Change* (Toronto: 1985) I-1.

Anderson, J. C., "Effect of Charter of Rights and Freedoms on Provincial School Legislation" in M. E. Manley-Casimir & T. A. Sussel, eds., *Courts in the Classroom: Education and the Charter of Rights and Freedoms* (Calgary: Detselig, 1983).

Barry, L. D., "Law, Policy and Statutory Interpretation Under a Constitutionally Entrenched Canadian Charter of Rights and Freedoms" (1982), 60 Can. Bar Rev. 237.

Bastarache, M., "Commentaire sur la décision de la Cour suprême du Canada dans le Renvoi au sujet des droits linguistiques au Manitoba, jugement rendu le 13 juin 1985" (1986), 31 R.D. McGill 93.

Bayefsky, A. F., "The Judicial Function Under the Canadian Charter of Rights and Freedoms" (1987), 32 McGill L.J. 791.

Bayefsky, A. F., "Parliamentary Sovereignty and Human Rights in Canada — The Promise of the Canadian Charter of Rights and Freedoms" (1983), 31 Political Studies 23.

Beckton, C. F., "Section 15 of the Charter — Statute Audits and the Search for Equality" (1986), 50 Sask. L.R. 111.

Blake, S., "Standing to Litigate Constitutional Rights and Freedoms in Canada and the United States" (1984), 16 Ottawa L. Rev. 66.

Corry, D. J., "Military Law Under the Charter" (1986), 24 Osgoode Hall L.J. 67.

Coté, P.-A., "La préséance de la Charte canadienne des droits et libertés" (1984), 18 R.J.T. 105.

Coulombe, C., "La prépondérance de la Charte des droits et libertés de la personne: son impact sur la législation provinciale" in Barreau du Québec, Formation permanente, ed., *L'interaction des chartes canadienne et québécoise des droits et libertés* (Montreal, 1984) 151.

Eberts, M., "A Strategy for Equality Litigation Under the Canadian Charter of Rights and Freedoms" in J. M. Weiler & R. M. Elliot, eds., *Litigating the Values of a Nation: The Canadian Charter of Rights and Freedoms* (Toronto: Carswell, 1986) 411.

Eberts, M., "The Use of Litigation Under the Canadian Charter of Rights and Freedoms As a Strategy for Achieving Change" in N. Nevitte & A. Kornberg, eds., *Minorities and the Canadian State* (Oakville: Mosaic Press, 1985) 53.

Gibson, D., "Judges as Legislators: Not Whether but How" (1987), 25 Alta. L. Rev. 249.

Gibson, D., *The Law of the Charter: General Principles* (Toronto: Carswell, 1986) 184.

Gibson, D., "So What Can Be Done About It? An Overview of Charter Remedies" in G.-A. Beaudoin, ed., *Charter Cases 1986-87* (Cowansville, Que.: Yvon Blais, 1987) 225.

Gibson, D., "Tort Law and the Charter of Rights" (1986), 16 Man. L.J. 1.

Hogg, P. W., "Supremacy of the Canadian Charter of Rights and Freedoms" (1983), 61 Can. Bar Rev. 69.

Hough, B., "Equality Provisions in the Charter: Their Meaning and Interrelationships with Federal and Provincial Rights Acts" in A. W. MacKay, ed., *Charter of Rights: Law Practice Revolutionized* (Halifax: Faculty of Law, University of Dalhousie, 1982) 306.

Jack, D. H., "Suing the Crown and the Application of the Charter" (1986), 7 Advocates' Q. 277.

Janisch, H. N., "Beyond Jurisdiction: Judicial Review and The Charter of Rights" (1983), 43 R. du B. 401.

Langlois, R., "L'application des règles d'interprétation constitutionnelle" (1987), 28 C. de D. 207.

Laskin, J. I., "Section 15 of the Charter and Human Rights Legislation" in Law Society of Upper Canada, eds., *Equality: Section 15 and Charter Procedures* (Toronto, 1985) ch. C.

Laskin, J. I. & Hughes, P., "The Charter and the Code" in Law Society of Upper

Canada Continuing Legal Education Department, ed., *Human Rights* (Toronto: 1983)

Lederman, S. N. & Ristic, A., "The Relationship Between Federal and Provincial Human Rights Legislation and Charter Equality Rights" in L. Smith et al., eds., *Righting the Balance: Canada's New Equality Rights* (Saskatoon: Canadian Human Rights Reporter, 1986) 83.

Lyon, N., "The Charter as a Mandate for the New Ways of Thinking About Law" (1984), 9 Queen's L.J. 241.

MacDonald, R. A., "Postscript and Prelude — The Jurisprudence of the Charter: Eight Theses" (1982), 4 Sup. Ct. L. Rev. 321.

MacKay, P., "L'évolution de la souveraineté du Parlement du Canada dans le cadre de la Loi constitutionnelle de 1982: vers une souveraineté multiparlementaire" in Association canadienne-française pour l'avancement des sciences, ed., *La Charte canadienne des droits et libertés et les droits collectifs et sociaux* (Quebec: 1983) 105.

Marx, H., "Entrenchment, Limitations and Non-Obstante (ss. 1, 33 and 52)" in W. S. Tarnopolsky & G.-A. Beaudoin, eds., *The Canadian Charter of Rights and Freedoms: Commentary* (Toronto: Carswell, 1982) 61.

Neudorfer, A., "Cabinet Decisions and Judicial Review" (1985), 1 Admin. L.J. 30.

Norman, K., "The Charter for the Public Sector and for the Private Sector, Human Rights Codes: A False Dichotomy Leading to the Wrong Result" (1984), 5 C.H.R.R. C/84-5.

Petter, A., "The Charter and Private Action: The Impact of Section 15 on Human Rights Codes" (1984), 5 C.H.R.R. C/84-1.

Pratte, S., "La primauté du droit. L'origine du principe et son évolution dans le contexte de la Charte canadienne des droits et libertés" (1986), 27 C. de D. 685.

Ratushny, E., "Implementing Equality Rights: Standards of Reasonable Accommodation with Legislative Force" in L. Smith et al., eds., *Righting the Balance: Canada's New Equality Rights* (Saskatoon: Canadian Human Rights Reporter, 1986) 255.

Rémilliard, G., "La Charte canadienne des droits et libertés: les conditions d'application de la Charte" in Barreau du Québec, Formation permanente, ed., *La Charte canadienne des droits et libertés* (Montréal: 1983) 55 at 68.

Rémillard, G., "Les conditions d'application de la Charte canadienne des droits et libertés" in Barreau du Québec, Formation permanente, ed., *L'interaction des chartes canadienne et québécoise des droits et libertés* (Montreal: 1984) 1 at 11.

Richards, J. G., "The Charter and Private and Public Sector Corporations: Scope and Application" in Canadian Institute for Professional Development, ed., *Equality Rights and Employment: Preparing for Fundamental Change* (Toronto: 1985) F-1.

Rogerson, C., "The Judicial Search for Appropriate Remedies Under the Charter:

The Examples of Overbreadth and Vagueness" in R. J. Sharpe ed., *Charter Litigation* (Toronto: Butterworths, 1987) 233.

Shrofel, S. M., "Equality Rights and Law Reform in Saskatchewan: An Assessment of the Charter Compliance Process" (1985), 1 Can. J.W.L. 108.

Strayer, B. L., *The Canadian Constitution and The Courts: The Function and Scope of Judicial Review*, 3d ed. (Toronto: Butterworths, 1988).

Sussel, T. A. & Manley-Casimir, M. E., "The Supreme Court of Canada as a 'National School Board': The Charter and Educational Change" in M. E. Manley-Casimir & T. A. Sussel, eds., *Courts in the Classroom: Education and the Charter of Rights and Freedoms* (Calgary: Detselig, 1983) 213.

Weiler, P. C., "Rights and Judges in a Democracy: A New Canadian Version" (1984-85), 18 U. Mich. J.L. Ref. 51.

Whitley, S. J., "The Manitoba Language Reference: Judicial Consideration of 'Language Charged With Meaning'" (1986), 15 Man. L.J. 295.

Appendix 1

CANADIAN BILL OF RIGHTS
R.S.C. 1985, Appendix III

**An Act for the Recognition and Protection of Human Rights
and Fundamental Freedoms, S.C. 1960, c. 44
As amended by 1985, c. 26, s. 105**

Preamble.

The Parliament of Canada, affirming that the Canadian Nation is
founded upon principles that acknowledge the supremacy of God, the
dignity and worth of the human person and the position of the family
in a society of free men and free institutions;

Affirming also that men and institutions remain free only when
freedom is founded upon respect for moral and spiritual values and the
rule of law;

And being desirous of enshrining these principles and the human rights
and fundamental freedoms derived from them, in a Bill of Rights which
shall reflect the respect of Parliament for its constitutional authority and
which shall ensure the protection of these rights and freedoms in Canada;

therefore, Her Majesty, by and with the advice and consent of the
Senate and House of Commons of Canada, enacts as follows:

PART I

BILL OF RIGHTS

Recognition and declaration of rights and freedoms.

1. It is hereby recognized and declared that in Canada there have
existed and shall continue to exist without discrimination by reason of
race, national origin, colour, religion or sex, the following human rights
and fundamental freedoms, namely,

(*a*) the right of the individual to life, liberty, security of the person
and enjoyment of property, and the right not to be deprived thereof
except by due process of law;

(*b*) the right of the individual to equality before the law and the
protection of the law;

(*c*) freedom of religion;

(*d*) freedom of speech;

(*e*) freedom of assembly and association; and

(*f*) freedom of the press.

Construction of law.

2. Every law of Canada shall, unless it is expressly declared by an Act of the Parliament of Canada that it shall operate notwithstanding the *Canadian Bill of Rights,* be so construed and applied as not to abrogate, abridge or infringe or to authorize the abrogation, abridgment or infringement of any of the rights or freedoms herein recognized and declared, and in particular, no law of Canada shall be construed or applied so as to

(*a*) authorize or effect the arbitrary detention, imprisonment or exile of any person;

(*b*) impose or authorize the imposition of cruel and unusual treatment or punishment;

(*c*) deprive a person who has been arrested or detained

(i) of the right to be informed promptly of the reason for his arrest or detention,

(ii) of the right to retain and instruct counsel without delay, or

(iii) of the remedy by way of *habeas corpus* for the determination of the validity of his detention and for his release if the detention is not lawful;

(*d*) authorize a court, tribunal, commission, board or other authority to compel a person to give evidence if he is denied counsel, protection against self crimination or other constitutional safeguards;

(*e*) deprive a person of the right to a fair hearing in accordance with the principles of fundamental justice for the determination of his rights and obligations;

(*f*) deprive a person charged with a criminal offence of the right to be presumed innocent until proved guilty according to the law in a fair and public hearing by an independent and impartial tribunal, or of the right to reasonable bail without just cause; or

(*g*) deprive a person of the right to the assistance of an interpreter in any proceedings in which he is involved or in which he is a party or a witness, before a court, commission, board or other tribunal, if he does not understand or speak the language in which such proceedings are conducted.

Duties of the Minister of Justice — Exception.

3. (1) Subject to subsection (1), the Minister of Justice shall, in accordance with such regulations as may be prescribed by the Governor in Council, examine every regulation transmitted to the Clerk of the Privy Council for registration pursuant to the *Statutory Instruments Act* and every Bill introduced in or presented to the House of Commons by a Minister of the Crown in order to ascertain whether any of the provisions thereof are inconsistent with the purposes and provisions of this Part and he shall report any such inconsistency to the House of Commons at the first convenient opportunity.

(2) A regulation need not be examined in accordance with subsection (1) if prior to being made it was examined as a proposed regulation in accordance with section 3 of the *Statutory Instruments Act* to ensure that it was not inconsistent with the purposes and provisions of this Part.

Short title.

4. The provisions of this Part shall be known as the *Canadian Bill of Rights.*

PART II

Savings — "Law of Canada" defined — Jurisdiction of Parliament.

5. (1) Nothing in Part I shall be construed to abrogate or abridge any human right or fundamental freedom not enumerated therein that may have existed in Canada at the commencement of this Act.

(2) The expression "law of Canada" in Part I means an Act of the Parliament of Canada enacted before or after the coming into force of this Act, any order, rule or regulation thereunder, and any law in force in Canada or in any part of Canada at the commencement of this Act that is subject to be repealed, abolished or altered by the Parliament of Canada.

(3) The provisions of Part I shall be construed as extending only to matters coming within the legislative authority of the Parliament of Canada.

CONSTITUTION ACT, 1982
R.S.C. 1985, Appendix II, No. 44

Enacted by the Canada Act 1982 (U.K.), c. 11
As amended by the Constitution Amendment Proclamation,
1983, SI/84-102, Schedule, in force June 21, 1984

SCHEDULE B
PART I
CANADIAN CHARTER OF RIGHTS AND FREEDOMS

Whereas Canada is founded upon principles that recognize the supremacy of God and the rule of law:

Guarantee of Rights and Freedoms

Rights and freedoms in Canada.

1. The *Canadian Charter of Rights and Freedoms* guarantees the rights and freedoms set out in it subject only to such reasonable limits prescribed by law as can be demonstrably justified in a free and democratic society.

Fundamental Freedoms

Fundamental freedoms.

2. Everyone has the following fundamental freedoms:
(*a*) freedom of conscience and religion;
(*b*) freedom of thought, belief, opinion and expression, including freedom of the press and other media of communication;
(*c*) freedom of peaceful assembly; and
(*d*) freedom of association.

Democratic Rights

Democratic rights of citizens.

3. Every citizen of Canada has the right to vote in an election of members of the House of Commons or of a legislative assembly and to be qualified for membership therein.

Maximum duration of legislative bodies.

4. (1) No House of Commons and no legislative assembly shall continue for longer than five years from the date fixed for the return of the writs at a general election of its members.

Continuation in special circumstances.

(2) In time of real or apprehended war, invasion or insurrection, a House of Commons may be continued by Parliament and a legislative assembly may be continued by the legislature beyond five years if such continuation is not opposed by the votes of more than one-third of the members of the House of Commons or the legislative assembly, as the case may be.

Annual sitting of legislative bodies.

5. There shall be a sitting of Parliament and of each legislature at least once every twelve months.

Mobility Rights

Mobility of citizens.

6. (1) Every citizen of Canada has the right to enter, remain in and leave Canada.

Right to move and gain livelihood.

(2) Every citizen of Canada and every person who has the status of a permanent resident of Canada has the right
   (*a*) to move to and take up residence in any province; and
   (*b*) to pursue the gaining of a livelihood in any province.

Limitation.

(3) The rights specified in subsection (2) are subject to
   (*a*) any laws or practices of general application in force in a province other than those that discriminate among persons primarily on the basis of province of present or previous residence; and
   (*b*) any laws providing for reasonable residency requirements as a qualification for the receipt of publicly provided social services.

Affirmative action programs.

(4) Subsections (2) and (3) do not preclude any law, program or activity that has as its object the amelioration in a province of conditions of individuals in that province who are socially or economically disad-

vantaged if the rate of employment in that province is below the rate of employment in Canada.

Legal Rights

Life, liberty and security of person.

7. Everyone has the right to life, liberty and security of the person and the right not to be deprived thereof except in accordance with the principles of fundamental justice.

Search or seizure.

8. Everyone has the right to be secure against unreasonable search or seizure.

Detention or imprisonment.

9. Everyone has the right not to be arbitrarily detained or imprisoned.

Arrest or detention.

10. Everyone has the right on arrest or detention
(*a*) to be informed promptly of the reasons therefor;
(*b*) to retain and instruct counsel without delay and to be informed of that right; and
(*c*) to have the validity of the detention determined by way of *habeas corpus* and to be released if the detention is not lawful.

Proceedings in criminal and penal matters.

11. Any person charged with an offence has the right
(*a*) to be informed without unreasonable delay of the specific offence;
(*b*) to be tried within a reasonable time;
(*c*) not to be compelled to be a witness in proceedings against that person in respect of the offence;
(*d*) to be presumed innocent until proven guilty according to law in a fair and public hearing by an independent and impartial tribunal;
(*e*) not to be denied reasonable bail without just cause;
(*f*) except in the case of an offence under military law tried before a military tribunal, to the benefit of trial by jury where the maximum punishment for the offence is imprisonment for five years or a more severe punishment;
(*g*) not to be found guilty on account of any act or omission unless, at the time of the act or omission, it constituted an offence under Canadian or international law or was criminal according to the general

principles of law recognized by the community of nations;

(*h*) if finally acquitted of the offence, not to be tried for it again and, if finally found guilty and punished for the offence, not to be tried or punished for it again; and

(*i*) if found guilty of the offence and if the punishment for the offence has been varied between the time of commission and the time of sentencing, to the benefit of the lesser punishment.

Treatment or punishment.

12. Everyone has the right not to be subjected to any cruel and unusual treatment or punishment.

Self-crimination.

13. A witness who testified in any proceedings has the right not to have any incriminating evidence so given used to incriminate that witness in any other proceedings, except in a prosecution for perjury or for the giving of contradictory evidence.

Interpreter.

14. A party or witness in any proceedings who does not understand or speak the language in which the proceedings are conducted or who is deaf has the right to the assistance of an interpreter.

Equality Rights

Equality before and under law and equal protection and benefit of law.

15. (1) Every individual is equal before and under the law and has the right to the equal protection and equal benefit of the law without discrimination and, in particular, without discrimination based on race, national or ethnic origin, colour, religion, sex, age or mental or physical disability.

Affirmative action programs.

(2) Subsection (1) does not preclude any law, program or activity that has as its object the amelioration of conditions of disadvantaged individuals or groups including those that are disadvantaged because of race, national or ethnic origin, colour, religion, sex, age or mental or physical disability.

Official Languages of Canada

Official languages of Canada.

16. (1) English and French are the official languages of Canada and have equality of status and equal rights and privileges as to their use in all institutions of the Parliament and government of Canada.

Official languages of New Brunswick.

(2) English and French are the official languages of New Brunswick and have equality of status and equal rights and privileges as to their use in all institutions of the legislature and government of New Brunswick.

Advancement of status and use.

(3) Nothing in this Charter limits the authority of Parliament or a legislature to advance the equality of status or use of English and French.

Proceedings of Parliament.

17. (1) Everyone has the right to use English or French in any debates and other proceedings of Parliament.

Proceedings of New Brunswick legislature.

(2) Everyone has the right to use English or French in any debates and other proceedings of the legislature of New Brunswick.

Parliamentary statutes and records.

18. (1) The statutes, records and journals of Parliament shall be printed and published in English and French and both language versions are equally authoritative.

New Brunswick statutes and records.

(2) The statutes, records and journals of the legislature of New Brunswick shall be printed and published in English and French and both language versions are equally authoritative.

Proceedings in courts established by Parliament.

19. (1) Either English or French may be used by any person in, or in any pleading in or process issuing from, any court established by Parliament.

Proceedings in New Brunswick courts.

(2) Either English or French may be used by any person in, or in any pleading in or process issuing from, any court of New Brunswick.

Communications by public with federal institutions.

20. (1) Any member of the public in Canada has the right to communicate with, and to receive available services from, any head or central office of an institution of the Parliament or government of Canada in English or French, and has the same right with respect to any other office of any such institution where

(*a*) there is a significant demand for communications with and services from that office in such language; or

(*b*) due to the nature of the office, it is reasonable that communications with and services from that office be available in both English and French.

Communications by public with New Brunswick institutions.

(2) Any member of the public in New Brunswick has the right to communicate with, and to receive available services from, any office of an institution of the legislature or government of New Brunswick in English or French.

Continuation of existing constitutional provisions.

21. Nothing in sections 16 to 20 abrogates or derogates from any right, privilege or obligation with respect to the English and French languages, or either of them, that exists or is continued by virtue of any other provision of the Constitution of Canada.

Rights and privileges preserved.

22. Nothing in sections 16 to 20 abrogates or derogates from any legal or customary right or privilege acquired or enjoyed either before or after the coming into force of this Charter with respect to any language that is not English or French.

Minority Language Educational Rights

Language of instruction.

23. (1) Citizens of Canada

(*a*) whose first language learned and still understood is that of the English or French linguistic minority population of the province in which they reside, or

(*b*) who have received their primary school instruction in Canada in English or French and reside in a province where the language in which they received that instruction is the language of the English or French linguistic minority population of the province, have the right to have their children receive primary and secondary school instruction in that language in that province.

Continuity of language instruction.

(2) Citizens of Canada of whom any child has received or is receiving primary or secondary school instruction in English or French in Canada, have the right to have all their children receive primary and secondary school instruction in the same language.

Application where numbers warrant.

(3) The right of citizens of Canada under subsections (1) and (2) to have their children receive primary and secondary school instruction in the language of the English or French linguistic minority population of a province

(*a*) applies wherever in the province the number of children of citizens who have such a right is sufficient to warrant the provision to them out of public funds of minority language instruction; and

(*b*) includes, where the number of those children so warrants, the right to have them receive that instruction in minority language educational facilities provided out of public funds.

Enforcement

Enforcement of guaranteed rights and freedoms.

24. (1) Anyone whose rights or freedoms, as guaranteed by this Charter, have been infringed or denied may apply to a court of competent jurisdiction to obtain such remedy as the court considers appropriate and just in the circumstances.

Exclusion of evidence bringing administration of justice into disrepute.

(2) Where, in proceedings under subsection (1), a court concludes that evidence was obtained in a manner that infringed or denied any rights or freedoms guaranteed by this Charter, the evidence shall be excluded if it is established that, having regard to all the circumstances, the admission of it in the proceedings would bring the administration of justice into disrepute.

General

Aboriginal rights and freedoms not affected by Charter.

25. The guarantee in this Charter of certain rights and freedoms shall not be construed so as to abrogate or derogate from any aboriginal treaty or other rights or freedoms that pertain to the aboriginal peoples of Canada including

(*a*) any rights or freedoms that have been recognized by the Royal Proclamation of October 7, 1763; and

(*b*) any rights or freedoms that now exist by way of land claims agreements or may be so acquired.

Other rights and freedoms not affected by Charter.

26. The guarantee in this Charter of certain rights and freedoms shall not be construed as denying the existence of any other rights or freedoms that exist in Canada.

Multicultural heritage.

27. This Charter shall be interpreted in a manner consistent with the preservation and enhancement of the multicultural heritage of Canadians.

Rights guaranteed equally to both sexes.

28. Notwithstanding anything in this Charter, the rights and freedoms referred to in it are guaranteed equally to male and female persons.

Rights respecting certain schools preserved.

29. Nothing in this Charter abrogates or derogates from any rights or privileges guaranteed by or under the Constitution of Canada in respect of denominational, separate or dissentient schools.

Application to territories and territorial authorities.

30. A reference in this Charter to a province or to the legislative assembly or legislature of a province shall be deemed to include a reference to the Yukon Territory and the Northwest Territories, or to the appropriate legislative authority thereof, as the case may be.

Legislative powers not extended.

31. Nothing in this Charter extends the legislative powers of any body or authority.

Application of Charter

Application of Charter.

32. (1) This Charter applies

(*a*) to the Parliament and government of Canada in respect of all matters within the authority of Parliament including all matters relating to the Yukon Territory and Northwest Territories; and (*b*) to the legislature and government of each province in respect of all matters within the authority of the legislature of each province.

Exception.

(2) Notwithstanding subsection (1), section 15 shall not have effect until three years after this section comes into force.

Exception where express declaration.

33. (1) Parliament or the legislature of a province may expressly declare in an Act of Parliament or of the legislature, as the case may be, that the Act or a provision thereof shall operate notwithstanding a provision included in section 2 or sections 7 to 15 of this Charter.

Operation of exception.

(2) An Act or a provision of an Act in respect of which a declaration made under this section is in effect shall have such operation as it would have but for the provision of this Charter referred to in the declaration.

Five year limitation.

(3) A declaration made under subsection (1) shall cease to have effect five years after it comes into force or on such earlier date as may be specified in the declaration.

Re-enactment.

(4) Parliament or a legislature of a province may re-enact a declaration made under subsection (1).

Five year limitation.

(5) Subsection (3) applies in respect of a re-enactment made under subsection (4).

Citation

Citation.

34. This Part may be cited as the *Canadian Charter of Rights and Freedoms.*

Index

[See also the detailed table of contents. Except as mentioned under entries for specific enactments (e.g. Canadian Bill of Rights), concepts are indexed at large as they relate to the Canadian Charter of Rights and Freedoms.]